THE ORIGINAL I CHING ORACLE

Upper Trigram

Lower Trigram		Energy ☰	Space ☷	Shake ☳
Energy	☰	1	11	34
Space	☷	12	2	16
Shake	☳	25	24	51
Gorge	☵	6	7	40
Bound	☶	33	15	62
Root	☴	44	46	32
Radiance	☲	13	36	55
Open	☱	10	19	54

Upper Trigram

Gorge	Bound	Root	Radiance	Open
5	26	9	14	43
8	23	20	35	45
3	27	42	21	17
29	4	59	64	47
39	52	53	56	31
48	18	57	50	28
63	22	37	30	49
60	41	61	38	58

THE ORIGINAL
I CHING
ORACLE

THE PURE AND COMPLETE TEXTS WITH CONCORDANCE

TRANSLATED UNDER THE AUSPICES OF
THE ERANOS FOUNDATION
BY
RUDOLF RITSEMA AND
SHANTENA AUGUSTO SABBADINI

WATKINS

This edition published in the UK in 2005 by
Watkins Publishing, Sixth Floor, Castle House,
75-76 Wells Street, London W1T 3QH

Designed and typeset by Jerry Goldie

Printed by Imago in China

British Library Cataloguing in Publication
data available

ISBN 1 84293 149 0

www.watkinspublishing.com

Contents

Part One

Introduction

I. The Oracle 2
The Book of *Yi* 2
The consultation procedure 12
The language of the *Yi Jing* 18

II. Myth and History 33
The tradition 33
Modern views of the origins of the *Yi* 36
The evolution of the book 41

III. Correlative Thinking 52

Chronological table 61
Notes 62
Index 65

Part Two

The 64 Hexagrams

List of Hexagrams 70
The 64 Hexagrams 74

Part Three

Concordance 679

Bibliography 847

Rudolf Ritsema has been a devoted student of the I Ching since he first encountered it in 1944. He was director of the prestigious Eranos Foundation for thirty years and since his retirement he has published English, Italian and German translations of the I Ching. The present definitive version of the Eranos I Ching is the distillation of his lifelong involvement with the book.

Shantena Augusto Sabbadini trained as a theoretical physicist at the University of Milan and at the University of California. Later he became interested in religion, philosophy and psychology, and in 1991 he joined the Eranos circle and became actively involved in the Eranos conferences as organizer and lecturer.

周易

Zhou Yi

Zhou Yi, "Changes of the Zhou," is the traditional name of this book, a title still used in China. The book originated during the Western Zhou dynasty (1122 to 771 BC) and mythical tradition ascribes its authorship to King Wen, the founder of the Zhou dynasty. During the Han dynasty (206 BC to 220 AD) it was canonized as the first of the "classics," *jing*, the fundamental texts of Chinese culture, and it came to be known also as *Yi Jing*, the "Classic of Change." Under this name, usually better known in its Wade-Giles romanization, I Ching, the book has come to be popularly known in the west.

Part One

Introduction

I | The Oracle

The Book of Yi

The name of the book

The title of this book, I Ching, or *Yi Jing*, as it is written in contemporary Pinyin romanization, can be translated as "Book of Changes" or "Classic of Changes." An older form of the title is *Zhou Yi*, "Changes of the Zhou," from the name of the Zhou dynasty (1122 to 256 BC), under which it came into being. *Jing* simply means "classic": its canonization as a classic took place under the Han dynasty (206 BC to 220 AD), in the framework of the great unification of Chinese culture undertaken by the empire. Since then, the *Yi Jing* has been regarded as the Classic of Classics: for two thousand years it has been to the Chinese the ultimate map of "heaven and earth."

The essential word in the book's name is *yi*, which means, amongst other things, "change." But the *yi* the title of the book points to is not primarily the regular change involved in the cycle of day and night, in the succession of the seasons or in the organic growth of living things. *Yi* refers in the first place to unpredictable change. We find an expressive description of it in another classic, the *Shu Jing*, Book of Documents:

> When in years, months and days the season has no *yi*, the hundred cereals ripen, the administration is enlightened, talented men of the people are distinguished, the house is peaceful and at ease. When in days, months and years the season has *yi*, the hundred cereals do not ripen, the administration is dark and unenlightened, talented men of the people are in petty positions, the house is not at peace.[1]

We have *yi* when things are off track, when chaos irrupts into our life and the usual bearings no longer suffice for orientation. We all know that such times can be very fertile – and extremely painful, disconcerting and full of anxiety. Modern chaos theory pays particular attention to these murky transitions, by which forms transmute into each other. Life itself arises at the boundary between order and chaos: it requires both, it is a daughter of both. On the side of perfect order there is only dead stability, inertia, symmetry, thermodynamic equilibrium. Nothing very interesting can happen there: everything is too predictable, it resembles death more than life. But the side of total disorder is not very interesting either: forms appear and disappear too quickly, there is a total lack of symmetry, everything is too unpredictable. It is on the edge between order and chaos that the subtle dance of life takes place: here the real complexity arises, here forms bend and loop and transmute and evolve.

The *Yi Jing* is the ancient Chinese map of this dance of order and chaos. It is based on two principles, Yin and Yang, that are closely related to the ideas of structure and action, form and energy. Pure Yin is inert structure, dead immobility; pure Yang is chaotic creation and destruction: it is like an arrow, which in its ceaseless forward movement constantly negates the position it had previously reached. But the interplay of Yin and Yang gives birth to the "myriad beings," the endless variety of life and the world. In the *Yi Jing* this dance is encoded in 64 hexagrams, figures composed of six opened or whole lines, diagrams of different combinations of the Yin and Yang principles.

But the book is not originally a philosophical text, although it has been used that way and as such it has attracted a huge amount of philosophical commentary. It was born in the first millennium BC as a divination manual, i.e. as a practical tool to help people ride the waves of change and harness their energy: a tool to deal with *yi*, with critical times. In many ancient cultures these times were seen as intrusions of the divine, of gods and spirits, into human life, and a proper interrogation of these higher powers, engaging them in a dialogue, was considered essential in order to overcome the crisis. An important form of this dialogue are the practices we call divination. The *Yi Jing* was born and continued to be used throughout its long history as one such method of divination, as an oracle.

Synchronicity

Like many other forms of divination, the oracular practice of the *Yi Jing* seeks to discern the outlines of a situation and its development through what in modern scientific terms we call a random procedure. This approach is rather foreign to the contemporary scientific mind, which considers random as essentially equivalent to meaningless. But the assumption of orthodox Western science that there is no meaning to be gleaned from random events was certainly not shared by the ancient Chinese. Their divinatory practices and their whole cosmology were based on a qualitative notion of time, in which all things happening at a given moment in time share some common features, are part of an organic pattern. Nothing therefore is entirely meaningless, and the entry point to understanding the overall pattern can be any detail of the moment, provided we are able to read it. This has been very well described by C.G. Jung in his classic foreword to the translation of the *Yi Jing* by his friend Richard Wilhelm. He writes:

> The Chinese mind, as I see it at work in the I Ching, seems to be exclusively preoccupied with the chance aspect of events. What we call coincidence seems to be the chief concern of this peculiar mind, and what we worship as causality passes almost unnoticed...
>
> The matter of interest seems to be the configuration formed by chance events in the moment of observation, and not at all the hypothetical reasons that seemingly account for the coincidence. While the Western mind carefully sifts, weighs, selects, classifies, isolates, the Chinese picture of the moment encompasses everything down to the minutest nonsensical detail, because all the ingredients make up the observed moment.
>
> Thus it happens that when one throws the three coins, or counts through the forty-nine yarrow stalks, these chance details enter into the picture of the moment of observation and form a part of it – a part that is insignificant to us, yet most meaningful to the Chinese mind...
>
> In other words, whoever invented the I Ching was convinced that the hexagram worked out in a certain moment coincided with the latter in quality no less than in time. To him the hexagram was the exponent of the moment in which it was cast – even more so than the hours of the clock or the divisions of the calendar could be – inasmuch as the hexagram was understood to be an indicator of the essential situation prevailing in the moment of its origin. This assumption involves a certain curious principle that I have termed synchronicity, a concept that formulates a point of view diametrically opposed to that of causality... Synchronicity takes the coincidence of events in space and time as meaning something more than mere chance, namely, a peculiar interdependence of objective events among themselves as well as with the subjective (psychic) state of the observer or observers.[2]

The way in which the oracular use of the *Yi Jing* relates to the configuration of events at any given moment is therefore more akin to the perception of a work of art than to a rational analysis of cause and effect. It is a rich tapestry of meaning, in which all details are subtly connected and somehow necessary – not because of deterministic laws, but because they are part of an organic whole. Of course the Chinese were aware of the existence of causal connections between events, but that aspect was relatively flat and uninteresting to them. On the contrary they were fascinated by and focused their attention on subtler, more complex and less exactly definable connections. The Western notion that comes closest to their approach is Jung's idea of archetypes,[3] and it is no chance that Jung was deeply interested in the *Yi Jing*. He saw the ancient Chinese oracle as

> a formidable psychological system that endeavors to organize the play of archetypes, the "wondrous operations of nature" into a certain pattern, so that a "reading" becomes possible.[4]

The *Yi Jing* can therefore be viewed as a catalog of sixty-four basic archetypal configurations, a road map to the realm Jung called "collective unconscious" and Henry Corbin, in a language less susceptible to reification, "*mundus imaginalis*."[5]

A kaleidoscope of images

Historically the texts of the *Yi Jing* are the result of an accretion process whose beginning can be traced back to shamanic practices of the Shang dynasty (1765 to 1123 BC, see pg.36, *Modern views of the origins of the Yi*). These texts have been described as

> a kaleidoscope of images resulting... from combinations and re-combinations of factual oracular statements. Each one of these images incorporates fragments of ancient statements. In each sentence of the *Yi Jing* we find one, two, three, rarely more, of these combined images, simply juxtaposed, and often strewn with forgotten technical divinatory terms. The whole is without any connection, but exactly like with a kaleidoscope, one is seized, in spite of oneself, by an impression of wonder.[6]

The language of the *Yi Jing* is therefore closer to the language of dreams than to that of philosophical discourse. In spite of the many layers of philosophical interpretation that through the millennia have sought to elucidate them, their vitality lies rather in their proximity to the *mundus imaginalis*. Their constituent images have emerged from shamanic trance, while their organization in terms of the interplay of Yin and Yang through the geometric code of the hexagrams is the result of a long process of classification, systematization and philosophical reflection. Therefore the *Yi Jing* straddles the divide between two radically different frames of mind, between the right and left hemisphere of the brain, metaphorically speaking, or the intuitive and the logical mind, and offers a bridge to move back and forth between the two.

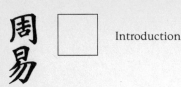

For the oracular use of the *Yi Jing* an understanding of the imaginal nature of its texts is of utmost importance. Because, like dream images, the images of the *Yi Jing* do not have a unique a priori interpretation. Depending on the context, they can be read in many different ways. And the context is given by the consultant's situation and question.

A mirror of the present

It may be useful to state here the approach to the oracular use of the *Yi Jing* that is proposed in this book. The *Yi Jing* has been used and is still used in so many different ways, that it is worthwhile to describe a bit more precisely what the reader can expect from the Eranos *Yi Jing*. The basic philosophy of this approach is an exploration of potential synchronicities. We assume that the random manipulation of the yarrow stalks, or the tossing of the coins, can offer, through the related *Yi Jing* texts and the associative process carried out by the consultant, valid insights about the archetypal energies active in the consultant's situation and psyche and the developmental tendencies contained therein. In this sense we use the *Yi Jing* as a *mirror of the present.*

On the other hand, we do not assume that the *Yi Jing* can foretell the future, because we do not assume that the future is univocally determined. A latent tendency in the present situation may actually develop into an actual consequence: but that is in no way a necessary conclusion, and, what is most important from our human standpoint, the outcome can often be affected by our choices and our actions.

Nor do we assume that the *Yi Jing* offers any imperatives, moral or otherwise. Quite understandably, when we are in a quandary we would very much like to be told what to do, which one is the right choice, and sometimes we approach the *Yi Jing* hoping for that kind of answer. Here again the analogy with dreams may prove a valuable guideline. A *Yi Jing* consultation produces a series of images, which is like a dream connected with a given situation and a given question. Dream images may give us a clear sense of what we want or have to do in a situation, but they never *tell* us what to do. The same applies to the images of the *Yi Jing*. It is crucial to realize that the responsibility for all choices always rests with the consultant herself or himself.

Interrogating the oracle

From the imaginal nature of the *Yi Jing* texts and from the approach to divination outlined above we can derive a few indications about how best to formulate a question to the oracle.

1. Ask only questions that are emotionally significant for you. The emotional charge in your question is the energy that activates the archetypal images in the answer. Only then they can speak to you and cause a rearrangement of your view of the situation. A question asked out of simple curiosity rarely gets a meaningful answer: the psychic energy required for significantly processing the matter is simply not available.

2. Divination is not meant to replace critical reflection and introspection. Interrogating the oracle is useful only after you have deeply examined the situation and yourself and out of this examination you have distilled an appropriate question.

3. Avoid asking the *Yi Jing* what to do, and avoid asking questions that expect yes or no as an answer (e.g., is it right to do this? or will this succeed?). The answer will consist of images, and it will say neither yes nor no: it will be up to you to decide on a yes or a no, based on the resonances that those images call up in you.

4. Avoid alternatives (e.g., should I do this or that?). If the question is formulated as an alternative, it is difficult to decide whether the images contained in your answer refer to "this" or to "that." When you are faced with an alternative, try to make a tentative choice (maybe the choice that is closer to your heart or the one that awakens more energy in you) and "test" it with the *Yi Jing* ("what about doing this?"). The answer will usually indirectly illuminate also the other option. A typical formula we often use at Eranos is "give me an image of... (this situation, this choice, etc.)."

5. Be as specific as possible. Do not be afraid to narrow your question down. The answer to a vast or general question is often difficult to interpret because the images can be read in too many different ways. On the contrary, starting from a concrete and

emotionally significant question, the answer of the oracle frequently expands to include larger issues in the consultant's life (see pg.20, *An example*). In this respect the process of *Yi Jing* divination can be symbolized by an "hourglass shape." In the top half of the hourglass all the complexity and confusion of our existential situation gets narrowed down to a very pointed, specific question. In the lower half, starting from that narrow focus, the oracle's answer opens up to embrace a much larger dimension.

Lines, trigrams, hexagrams

The hexagrams of the *Yi Jing* are based on a binary code whose elementary units are the *opened line*[7] (▬ ▬) and the *whole line* (▬▬▬). The opened line is *supple* and is associated with Yin; the whole line is *solid* and is associated with Yang. Yin and Yang are the fundamental categories of Chinese cosmology, the primary duality arising from the original One:

> Dao begets One.
> One begets two.
> Two begets three.
> And three begets the myriad beings.[8]

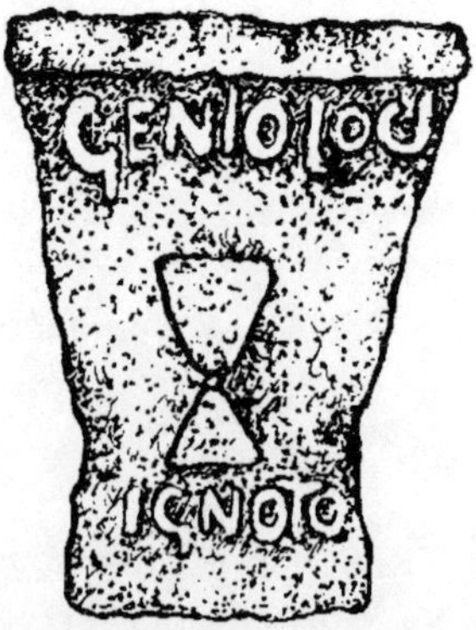

THE STONE SLAB DEDICATED TO THE "UNKNOWN SPIRIT OF THE PLACE" AT ERANOS

Yang is associated with action, initiating, expanding, heaven, fire, sun, bright, dry, hard, male, etc. Yin is associated with form, receptive, contracting, earth, water, moon, dark, moist, soft, female, etc. (see pg.54, *The Yin-Yang cycle*, for a fuller description of this primary duality). All phenomena, the "myriad beings" are generated by the interaction of Yin and Yang.

Just as fundamental as this basic duality in Chinese thought is the idea of change and transformation. The Chinese world view is essentially dynamic and cyclical: all things constantly change, the only permanent reality is change. Thus Yin and Yang are not static categories. They are animated by a cyclical movement which transforms them into each other, just as day turns into night and then into day again, and the seasons follow each other in their yearly round.

The key symbol of this cyclical movement is the *tai ji*:

THE *TAI JI*

When the light quality (Yang) reaches its culmination, it gives birth to the seed of the dark quality (Yin), which at that moment begins to grow. When the dark quality reaches its apex, it develops inside itself the seed of the light quality, which at that moment begins to grow. Noon is when the sun starts setting, midnight is when it starts climbing back towards the horizon. Thus all culmination is necessarily followed by a decrease and all descent by an ascent:

> Being and non-being give birth to each other.
> Difficult and easy complement each other.
> Long and short appear in contrast to each other.
> High and low incline toward each other.[9]
>
> Diminishing, augmenting.
> Increasing: the beginning belonging to decreasing indeed.[10]

In the *Yi Jing*, Yin and Yang are represented by the opened and the whole line. The opened line is Yin, supple, flexible, pliant, tender, adaptable. The whole line is Yang, solid, firm, strong, unyielding, persisting. And just like the two fundamental qualities they represent, the opened and the whole lines are animated by a movement that transforms them into each other. For each type of line we are thus led to consider two possibilities: the line can be "young," i.e. still fully expressing its own nature, or "old," i.e. past its culmination and ready to transform into its opposite. Altogether we have therefore four types of lines:

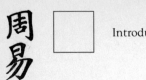

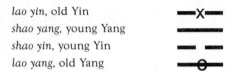

lao yin, old Yin
shao yang, young Yang
shao yin, young Yin
lao yang, old Yang

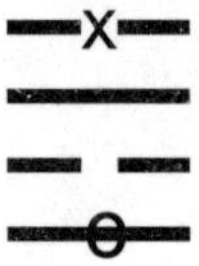

The young lines are stable lines, while the old lines are *transforming*: they are animated by a movement into their opposite and are therefore dealt with in a special way.

Leaving aside for the moment the issue of transformation and focusing merely on the Yin or Yang quality of the lines, we see that they can be combined to form a three-line figure, a *trigram*, in eight possible ways:

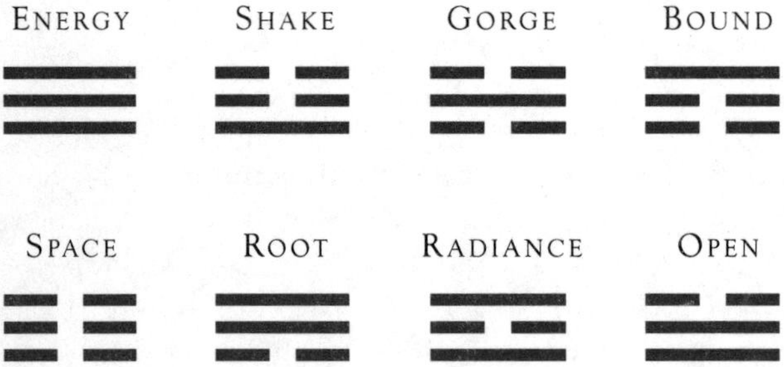

FIGURE 3. THE 8 TRIGRAMS

The 8 trigrams, *ba gua*, have a special significance in Chinese cosmology (see pg.58, *The 8 trigrams and their attributes*), and they are the building blocks of the 64 hexagrams (also called *gua*) of the *Yi Jing*. Each hexagram consists of a lower (or inner) trigram and an upper (or outer) trigram:

Upper Trigram

Lower Trigram	Energy	Space	Shake	Gorge	Bound	Root	Radiance	Open
Energy	1	11	34	5	26	9	14	43
Space	12	2	16	8	23	20	35	45
Shake	25	24	51	3	27	42	21	17
Gorge	6	7	40	29	4	59	64	47
Bound	33	15	62	39	52	53	56	31
Root	44	46	32	48	18	57	50	28
Radiance	13	36	55	63	22	37	30	49
Open	10	19	54	60	41	61	38	58

Hexagram table

The hexagrams are triggers for the inner process that will lead you to your answer. Each corresponds to a basic configuration of archetypal energies. The Chinese saw the 64 hexagrams as an exhaustive catalog of all possible processes between heaven and earth:

> The Book of Changes is vast and great. When one speaks of what is far, it knows no limits. When one speaks of what is near, it is still and right. When one speaks of the space between heaven and earth, it embraces everything.[11]

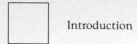

You will use the specific hexagram texts identified by casting the yarrow stalks or tossing the coins as entry points to a deeper intuitive understanding of your situation, as seeds of an associative process to clarify the dynamic forces at work in your psyche.

THE CONSULTATION PROCEDURE

Energy moves in the hexagrams from the bottom up, like sap rising in a tree. The lines in a hexagram are numbered accordingly: the bottom line is the first and the top line the sixth. When you find the lines of your hexagram by counting the yarrow stalks or by tossing the coins, you start from the bottom and sequentially work your way up to the top line. Each toss of the coins or each counting the yarrow stalks gives you one of the four types of line: old Yin, young Yang, young Yin, old Yang.

Before you begin the procedure it is advisable to have your question written down in front of you. Sometimes the exact formulation of the question really makes a difference in the interpretation of the answer.

The coins method

Tossing three coins six times is the simplest and quickest way to form a hexagram. This procedure became popular during the Southern Sung dynasty, in the twelfth to thirteenth century of our era.

Take three coins and decide which side is Yin and which is Yang. The Yin side takes the value 2, the Yang side the value 3. Each toss of the three coins then gives you, upon summing their values, 6, 7, 8 or 9. Write this number down and next to it draw the appropriate type of line according to the following table:

6	old Yin	—x—
7	young Yang	———
8	young Yin	— —
9	old Yang	—o—

Six tosses of the coins identify the six lines of a hexagram (from the bottom up), including their stable or transforming quality.

The yarrow-stalk method

This is the traditional way to form a hexagram. It is quite a bit more involved and slower: it is a form of active meditation, and each step of the procedure has a symbolic significance. A further difference between the two procedures is the fact that the probability of obtaining a transforming Yin or Yang line is symmetric in the coins method and asymmetric in the yarrow-stalk method: in the latter a Yang line transforms three times more often than a Yin line, i.e. a 9 is cast three times more often than a 6. This is traditionally seen as reflecting an intrinsic difference between the two types of line, Yang being more "ready to transform" than Yin.

You need fifty short sticks, traditionally prepared from stalks of yarrow (*Achillea millefolium*), a common plant in all temperate climates. Yarrow stalks are cut during the summer, when the plant is fully developed, and are left to dry for a few months. If you do not have yarrow stalks, any sticks of manageable size, say between three and ten inches long, will do.

The procedure, which will be described explicitly in the following paragraphs, is thus outlined in the *Xi Ci*, the Great Treatise, the fundamental commentary on the cosmological symbolism of the oracular texts:

> The number of the total is fifty. Of these forty-nine are used. They are divided into two portions, to represent the two primal forces. Hereupon one is set apart, to represent the three powers. They are counted through by fours, to represent the four seasons. The remainder is put aside, to represent the intercalary month. There are two intercalary months in five years, therefore the putting aside is repeated, and this gives the whole.[12]

YARROW (ACHILLEA MILLEFOLIUM)

The witness

From the bunch of fifty yarrow stalks take one and put it aside. It will be a silent witness to your whole consultation. It symbolizes the center of the world, the axis of heaven and earth, the one, the unmoving center of all change. The Taoist philosopher Wang Bi (226 to 249) wrote:

Fifty is the number of the great expansion (the number accounting for the transformations of heaven and earth). The fact that only forty-nine [yarrow stalks] are used means that one is not used. Since it is not used, its use is fully realized; since it is not a number [like the others], numbers can accomplish their work. It is the *tai ji* of change...[13]

Forming a line

First step

Divide the remaining forty-nine stalks into two random portions. This opening gesture (which will be repeated three times for each line of the hexagram) is the crucial moment of divination: symbolically it corresponds to opening up to receiving the answer to your question.

Take a stalk from the left portion and put it between the little finger and the ring finger of your left hand. Count the stalks of the right portion by dividing them in groups of four, until you have a remainder of one, two, three or four stalks (if there is an exact number of groups of four stalks, the whole last group is the remainder). Put this remainder between the ring finger and the middle finger of your left hand.

Now count the stalks of the left portion in groups of four in the same way, and put the remainder between the middle finger and the index finger of your left hand.

Set aside the stalks you have between your fingers (if you have done things right, their number will be either five or nine) and collect all groups of four (right and left) in a single bunch again.

Second step

Again divide the bunch into two random portions; again take a stalk from the left portion; and again count the stalks in the right and left portions in groups of four, exactly as before, putting the remainders between the fingers of your left hand. Set aside the stalks you have between your fingers (this time their number will be either four or eight). Keep them separate from those you have set aside before (a convenient way of doing this is laying them across each other): this will remind you that you have just performed the second step of the procedure. Then collect all groups of four (right and left) in a single bunch again.

Third step

Repeat the same sequence of operations a third time: divide in two random portions, take a stalk from the left portion, count the stalks in the right and left portions in groups of four, set aside the remainders (again their number must be either four or eight). This time leave the groups of four spread out in front of you and count them. Their number will be 6, 7, 8 or 9.

Write this number down and next to it draw the appropriate type of line according to the table:

6 old Yin
7 young Yang
8 young Yin
9 old Yang

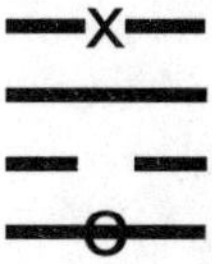

This is the first (i.e., bottom) line of your hexagram.

FORMING A HEXAGRAM

Repeat the same three steps for each of the following lines of your hexagram, building the hexagram from the bottom up.

Primary and potential hexagrams

Whether you have used the coins or the yarrow-stalk method, after six tosses of the coins or after repeating six times the three steps outlined above you will have a complete hexagram. For the sake of concreteness, we will follow through a specific example of consultation.

Let us assume that you have obtained the sequence of numbers:

8, 8, 9, 7, 8, 7.

You will draw the following picture:

7
8
7
9
8
8

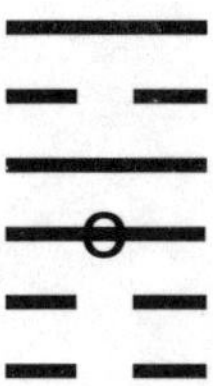

This is your *primary hexagram*, the main key to answering the question you have brought to the oracle. If there are no transforming lines (no sixes or nines), the primary hexagram is the whole answer.

If there are transforming lines (as in the above example), then you need to take their transformation into account also. Beside your primary hexagram you will draw a *secondary* or *potential hexagram* by copying the stable lines (the sevens and eights) unchanged and replacing the transforming lines (the sixes and nines) with their opposite. Thus in the example above:

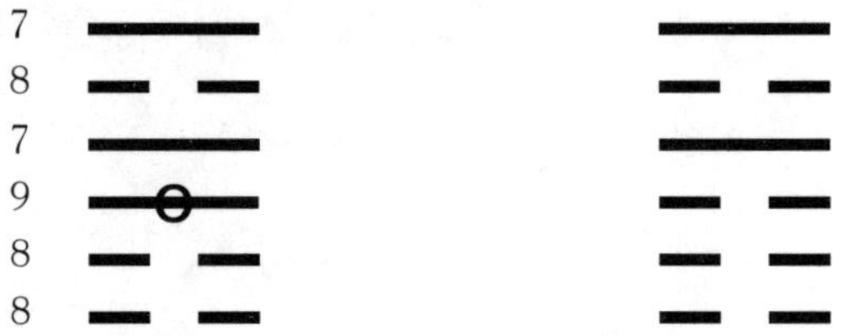

primary hexagram potential hexagram

(Notice that in your potential hexagram the lines are no longer marked as "young" or "old.")

You are now ready to identify your primary and your potential hexagram and to read your answer. The easiest way to identify a hexagram is to look it up in a hexagram table. Find the upper trigram of the hexagram in the top row and the lower trigram in the left column of the table. (Disregard the "young" or "old" quality of the lines: now you only consider their opened or whole quality.) The hexagram and its number are given at the intersection of the corresponding column and row. Thus in the above example the primary hexagram is number 56, Sojourning, and the potential hexagram is number 35, Prospering (See *Hexagram table with example column and rows highlighted*).

Reading your answer

In the Eranos *Yi Jing* the oracular texts are printed in red, while all the added explanatory material is in black. The oracular and the explanatory texts of each hexagram are distributed in various sections, which will be illustrated in detail below (see pg.23, *Sections of a hexagram*).

When in your consultation you have no transforming lines, your answer consists of

- all the texts of your primary hexagram, except the *Transforming Lines* section.

When in your consultation you have transforming lines, your answer consists of:

Lower Trigram \ Upper Trigram	Energy	Space	Shake	Gorge	Bound	Root	Radiance	Open
Energy	1	11	34	5	26	9	14	43
Space	12	2	16	8	23	20	35	45
Shake	25	24	51	3	27	42	21	17
Gorge	6	7	40	29	4	59	64	47
Bound	33	15	62	39	52	53	56	31
Root	44	46	32	48	18	57	50	28
Radiance	13	36	55	63	22	37	30	49
Open	10	19	54	60	41	61	38	58

Hexagram table with example column and rows highlighted

- all the texts of your primary hexagram, except the *Transforming Lines* section;
- in the *Transforming Lines* section only the texts referring to the specific transforming lines you have got;
- the *Image of the Situation* section of your potential hexagram.

Thus, in the example given above, your answer would include:

- all the texts of hexagram 56, except the *Transforming Lines* section;
- the text of *Nine at third*, in the *Transforming Lines* section of hexagram 56;
- the *Image of the Situation* of hexagram 35.

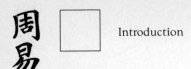

The language of the *Yi Jing* is an imaginal language (see below, *The language of the Yi Jing*). Its words have multiple layers of meaning, which the Eranos *Yi Jing* makes available to the reader through the *Fields of meaning* associated with the oracular texts. While reading your answer, try to hold all these meanings simultaneously and feel free to replace any word in the oracular texts with one of its associated meanings, if that meaning has a particular resonance in you.

There are no rules for interpreting these texts. They do not have an intrinsic meaning, independent from you and from your question. The Chinese commentary tradition suggests that *turning and rolling the words in one's heart* is the key to accessing the "light of the gods." Focus on the words and images that have the strongest impact on you. Remember that the answer does not reside in the words, but arises in the process those words trigger in you. Just as the emotional content of your question is important, so it is important that you let yourself be touched by the answer.

The openness of the oracular texts can be unsettling at first. You may feel overwhelmed by a flood of potential meanings. This wealth of possibilities is an expression of the archetypal nature of the divinatory language. The guiding principle is to listen to the resonances the oracular images arouse in you.

THE LANGUAGE OF THE *YI JING*

Chinese as an imaginal language

The structure of Chinese is very different from that of Western languages. Its grammar is minimal. Its words are signs (ideograms) which evoke images. A single ideogram can function as a verb, a noun or an adjective. By itself an ideogram does not specify a mode, tense or person and it does not distinguish between singular and plural. Furthermore it frequently embraces various related clusters of meanings that slide into each other by a sort of free play of the imagination. In this respect Chinese ideograms are a bit like those iridescent gems that appear of a different color depending on the angle you look at them. Their fluidity of meaning is remarkably similar to the interconnectedness which characterizes archetypal images, as Jung has pointed out.

As an example of the "play of archetypal motifs" in Chinese ideograms let us consider the word "open," *dui*, which is the name of one of the trigrams of the *Yi Jing*.

Open, *DUI*: an open surface, promoting interaction and interpenetration; pleasant, easy, responsive, free, unhindered; opening, passage; the mouth; exchange, barter; straight, direct; meet, gather; place where water accumulates. Ideogram: mouth and vapor, communication through speech.

The ideogram for *dui* is composed of the signs for mouth and vapor, which suggest speech and communication. *Dui* includes the idea of openness, permeability, ease of communication and exchange. Therefore a cluster of meanings extends in the direction of commercial transactions: to barter, to buy, to sell, price, value, equivalent. A market is a meeting place *par excellence*, so *dui* is also to meet, meeting place, gathering; and by extension also a place where water is collected, a marsh, a lake, a pond. The image of this body of water still contains the idea of vapor and of permeability: it is conceived as a wide, flat water surface from which vapors rise, so that there is a permeability, an openness not only horizontally, but vertically as well. And still from the idea of meeting place and gathering, or maybe from the peaceful landscape of the pond, comes another cluster of meanings, which has to do with joy, happiness, satisfaction.

Modern Chinese of course has a number of devices apt to contain this fluidity and make the language more precise. Not so the archaic language of the *Yi Jing*, in which the imaginal fields of single ideograms stand next to each other as islands in an archipelago or as figures in a dream. They are more akin to patterns of a kaleidoscopic image than to building blocks of a logical structure. That is the elusive character of the oracular texts – and the source of their potency as mirrors of psychic reality.

Basic features of the Eranos translation

The Eranos *Yi Jing* attempts to preserve as much as possible of the mirroring potency of the oracular language in English by adopting a translation strategy whose main criteria are outlined below.

Core-words

Each Chinese ideogram is translated consistently by the same English word, which becomes a sort of code identifying the ideogram. This word corresponds as much as possible to a "center" of the field of meanings associated with the ideogram, but is not to be taken as a complete rendering of the ideogram. Rather it is a core-word, a key to enter the semantic field of the ideogram.

Fields of meaning

The semantic field of each ideogram appearing in a given oracular text is described in the *Fields of meaning* immediately following that text. All the associations listed in it resonate together in the Chinese ideogram, and they can be imagined as being simultaneously present in the core-word. They allow the Western reader to access the range of meanings that a Chinese reader immediately perceives in the ideogram. While reading the answer to your question you are free to replace a core-word with any of the words listed in the corresponding *Field of meaning* which evoke a special resonance in you.

Oracular and exegetic texts

Oracular texts are distinguished from appended explanatory texts by their typographical face: they are printed in red, while all else is in black. Furthermore within the oracular texts core-words are printed in boldface. Wherever articles, prepositions and conjunctions have been added to render the text at least minimally legible, these are printed in lightface characters. The lightface words are to be taken only as suggestions: the "naked" Chinese text consists only of the boldface words.

An example

Let us return to the example given above in *Primary and potential hexagrams*. The answer obtained in that consultation was hexagram 56, Sojourning, with the third line transforming. Let us look at how you would read the oracular text of the third line:

NINE AT THIRD

Sojourning: burning one's camp.
Losing one's youthful vassal.
Trial, adversity.

Comments
Sojourning: burning one's camp.
Truly using injury actually.
Using sojourning to **associate below.**
One's righteousness lost indeed.

Fields of meaning

Sojourn, *LÜ*: see *Image of the Situation*. **Burn**, *FEN*: set fire to, destroy, die. **One/one's**, *QI*: see *Preceding Situation*. **Camp**, *CI*: resting place, inn, shed; halt, breathing-spell. Ideogram: two and breath, pausing to breathe.

Lose, *SANG*: be deprived of, forget; destruction, ruin, death; corpse; lament, mourn; funeral. Ideogram: weep and dead. **Youthful**, *TONG*: young person (between eight and fifteen); childish, immature; servant, slave. **Vassal**, *PU*: servant, menial, retainer; helper in heavy work; palace officers, chamberlains; follow, serve, belong to. **Trial**, *ZHEN*: see *Image of the Situation*. **Adversity**, *LI*: danger, hardship, severe; threat or difficulty that must be encountered, rather than avoided; grinding stone; polish, sharpen; a challenge that strengthens and perfects the character; stimulate, excite; cruel demon.

Truly, *YI*: in fact; also; nevertheless. **Use**, *YI*: see *Patterns of Wisdom*. **Injure**, *SHANG*: hurt, wound, damage; grief, distress, mourning; sad at heart, afflicted. **Actually**, *YI*: truly, really, at present. Ideogram: a dart and done, strong intention fully expressed. **Associate**, *YU*: consort with, combine; companions; group, band, company; agree with, comply, help; in favor of. Ideogram: a pair of hands reaching downward meets a pair of hands reaching upward, helpful association. **Below**, *XIA*: anything below, in all senses; lower, inner; lower trigram. **Righteous**, *YI*: proper, just, virtuous, upright; the heart that rules itself; benevolent, loyal, devoted to public good. **Indeed**, YE: see *Hexagrams in Pairs*.

The oracular text is printed in red, and in it each boldface word corresponds to a Chinese ideogram. (In the third line of the *Comments* the particle "to," which is in lightface, does not correspond to a Chinese ideogram: it is only a suggestion, inserted for smoother reading.) Each ideogram is described by its core-word plus the corresponding *Field of meaning*. E.g., for **losing** we find: "**Lose**, *SANG*: be deprived of, forget; destruction, ruin, death; corpse; lament, mourn; funeral. Ideogram: weep and dead." All these nuances of meaning are present in the ideogram rendered in the text by **losing**. When, like here, the graphic image of the ideogram itself adds significantly to its semantic field, this is also described.

In order to avoid cumbersome repetitions, when a word has occurred in one of the previous sections of the same hexagram you are simply referred back to that section for the corresponding *Field of meaning*. E.g., for **sojourning** you are invited to go back to the *Image of the Situation* section, where you find "**Sojourn**, *LÜ*: travel, stay in places other than your home; itinerant troops, temporary residents; visitor, guest, lodger. Ideogram: banner and people around it."

While reading your answer, for each word of the oracular texts read all the associations listed in the corresponding *Field of meaning* and select those that have the strongest resonance in you. E.g., **losing one's youthful vassal** might mean something like "losing someone who is in the position of a subordinate or a helper to you," but also "mourning the death of an immature 'helper' part of yourself." The last reading indeed struck a chord in the case we have taken as an example. That consultation was done by a woman we will call Nora. This is her story:

> At the age of forty-five Nora hasn't left her parents' home yet. She has been a language student at university for fifteen years, and after graduating has been a teacher in a private school near her parents' home. Since her father's death she is taking care of her mother, who is eighty years old. She doesn't like teaching and she didn't feel accepted in the school, but she kept the job for five years because it allowed her to live at home and to assist her mother. Since she left her job at the school, her only occupations are caring for her mother and shopping. She is unhappy with her life and feels that a change is needed, but doesn't know what to do and moreover feels that her choices are limited by the moral obligation to 'serve' her mother.
>
> At first she says that she doesn't have a precise question. She is confused. Maybe she should go back to university for a PhD? Or should she resume teaching? Or should she move into something new? But then what to do with her mother? She goes in all directions at once, she feels lost. The only clear feeling is that she has to decide about her life. The question she would like to ask is: "What orientation should I give to my life?"
>
> That's an example of a question too open for the oracle to give a precise answer. After a long discussion, Nora mentions that actually there is an immediate decision she has to make, but that does not seem important enough to her. She has been offered a job in a trading company where her language skills would be used. But she feels reluctant to give up her ambition for an academic career, and accepting this job would mean putting her mother in an old people's home. She has to answer within four days.
>
> This is a concrete, present matter, which definitely has an emotional impact on Nora, although intellectually she considers it unimportant. What about taking this job? Nora feels a bit disappointed by such a limited question, but finally agrees to ask it. Her answer is hexagram 56, Sojourning, with a transforming line, nine in the third place.
>
> Immediately the answer of the oracle goes to the core of Nora's situation, her being bound to her parental home. The image of Sojourning suggests that it's time to let go of residence in her

mother's house. Moreover it addresses Nora's preoccupation about this job not fulfilling her life dreams by describing it as a "temporary residence." It doesn't need to be a final and irrevocable choice. It is a temporary move in the process of her moving out of her nest.

The texts of the transforming line are even more explicit. They talk about **burning one's camp**: she should burn her bridges behind her. This move implies **losing one's youthful vassal**: giving up her "serving" attitude towards her mother. That in turn involves **truly using injury actually**: painful as it may be, it is necessary to accept the fact of putting her mother in an old people's home. Nora has to cut the umbilical cord connecting her to the mother in order to start living her own adult life. The line texts end with **one's righteousness lost indeed**: Nora must injure not only her mother but also her own sense of righteousness, the image of herself she's identified with, a challenge she has never faced before.

The potential hexagram is 35, Prospering. The corresponding *Field of meaning* is "**Prosper,** *JIN*: grow and flourish as young plants in the sun; increase, progress, permeate, impregnate; attached to. Ideogram: sun and reaching, the daylight world."

The *Image of the Situation* talks about **day-time sun thrice reflected**. It is one of the brightest and sunniest hexagrams in the whole book, suggesting that the proposed course of action can break the deadlock of Nora's life and open up new possibilities.

Sections of a hexagram

The standard reference for all modern versions of the *Yi Jing* is the Palace Edition, published by the Emperor Kang Xi in 1715. In it the *Yi Jing* consists of ten books, known as the Ten Wings, and the references to each hexagram are spread throughout the Ten Wings. For ease of consultation, in contemporary use all the texts relating to the same hexagram are collected under that hexagram's title. The Eranos *Yi Jing* also adopts this much more practical format.

Nevertheless, the texts extracted from various places in the Ten Wings differ widely in origins, style and function. Therefore in each hexagram they are presented in different sections, which are briefly described below.

Under the title of each hexagram you will also find a brief introductory sentence, supplied by the present authors. This sentence is meant only as a suggestion, to give you a first impression of the hexagram when you are not yet familiar with it.

Image of the Situation

This is the fundamental oracular text of each hexagram and its first word is the name of the hexagram itself. Traditionally called *Tuan* (head), this text belongs to the most ancient layer of the *Yi Jing* and together with the main text of the *Transforming Lines* constitutes the First and Second Wing (*Tuan Zhuan*).

If you imagine your answer as a system of concentric circles expanding from a center, the name of your primary hexagram is the center and the *Image of the Situation* of your primary hexagram is the next circle. These two together define the basic archetypal configuration you are dealing with. In a sense, everything else comes on top of this as an amplification or a modification, adds or subtracts emphasis on specific aspects, traces possible lines of development and so on; but the overall frame of reference is defined by the *Image of the Situation* of your primary hexagram.

The next two sections do not include oracular texts, but contain explanatory material related to the structure of the hexagram.

Outer and Inner Trigram

This section analyzes the hexagram in terms of the two trigrams that constitute it. The upper trigram is traditionally associated with the outer aspects of your situation, while the lower trigram reflects the inner (psychic) aspects of your situation. In this respect the transition from the third line (top of the lower trigram) to the fourth line (bottom of the upper trigram) often corresponds to a transition from the inner gestation to the outer manifestation of a certain archetypal image.

The attributes of the two trigrams outlined in this section are drawn from the Eighth Wing, *Shuo Gua*, Discussion of the Trigrams, and their placement in the *Universal Compass* (see pg.53) is based on the correlative system outlined in the *Bo Hu Tong*, Discussions in the White Tiger Hall,[14] the proceedings of the scholarly gathering that consolidated the interpretation of the Confucian classics under the Han in 79 AD.

Counter Hexagram

Beside the upper and lower trigram, two inner or "nuclear" trigrams have attracted the scholars' attention since Han times (206 BC to 220 AD). They consist of the second, third and fourth line and of the third, fourth and fifth line respectively. When these two trigrams are placed one on top of the other, we obtain a *hu gua*, a "twisted hexagram," also called, in modern use, a "nuclear hexagram." The nature of the procedure is such that in a nuclear hexagram the two top lines of the

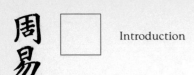

lower trigram are identical to the two bottom lines of the upper trigram: therefore there are only sixteen nuclear hexagrams for the 64 hexagrams. (Furthermore the nuclear hexagrams of number 1 and number 2, composed of all Yang and all Yin lines respectively, coincide with the hexagrams themselves.)

There is no traditional consensus on the interpretation of nuclear hexagrams. In the Eranos *Yi Jing* they are called "counter hexagrams." They correspond to a shift in emphasis – often a shift in the opposite direction compared to that of the primary hexagram, which generally is to be avoided. The "counter hexagram" therefore points to something that is not the case or that should not be done in the given situation.

Preceding Situation

The text of this section is drawn from the Ninth Wing, *Xu Gua*, Sequence of the Hexagrams, which connects the 64 hexagrams in a series, deriving the action of each as a natural consequence of some aspect of the action of the previous one. This section always contains the sentence "To **anterior acquiescence belongs** the **use** of...," followed by the name of the hexagram. This rather awkward formula means that fully availing yourself of the present hexagram requires understanding and accepting its connection with the preceding one. This connection may highlight some aspect of what precedes your situation and your question.

Hexagrams in Pairs

This section, drawn from the Tenth Wing, *Za Gua*, Mixed Hexagrams, draws a comparison between adjacent hexagrams which are structurally related to each other (an odd-numbered one and the following even-numbered one) by emphasizing a specific characteristic of each, sometimes by contrast, sometimes by a more subtle differentiation.

Additional Texts

This section is present in ten hexagrams only. It comes from the *Xi Ci*, Additional Texts,[15] also known as *Da Zhuan*, Great Treatise, which constitutes the Fifth and Sixth Wing and is the largest and most important commentary on the oracular texts. This section relates the action of the hexagram to the realization of *dao*, the exercise of virtue or fulfillment of one's true nature.

Patterns of Wisdom

Together with the *Comments* part of the *Transforming Lines*, the texts of this section constitute the Third and Fourth Wing, *Xiang Zhuan*, Treatise on the Images (or Symbols). They consist of two parts.

The first part identifies the hexagram through the symbols of the two trigrams that compose it (e.g. "**Clouds** and **thunder: sprouting**," or "**Below** the **mountain emerges springwater**. **Enveloping**"). See pg.57, *The 8 trigrams and their attributes* for the symbols of the trigrams.

The second part describes an exemplary behavior, offering as a model a *jun zi*, a "disciple of wisdom," one who strives to manifest *dao* in her or his actions, the "crown prince," or the "earlier kings," sovereigns of a mythical age when humans were in tune with heaven and earth.

Transforming Lines

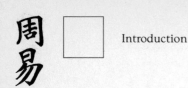

This section contains the oracular texts connected with the individual lines of the hexagram. Each line has a main text and a commentary text. The main text comes from the First and Second Wing, together with the *Image of the Situation*. The commentary text, together with the *Patterns of Wisdom*, comes from the Third and Fourth Wing.

Only the texts corresponding to the transforming lines you have obtained while casting your hexagram (the sixes and nines) belong to your answer. They introduce specific features that complete or alter more or less significantly the general picture given by the *Image of the Situation*. Generally speaking, if the texts of the hexagram as a whole indicate the overall flow of events in the given situation, the single lines can be taken to describe currents and eddies within that "river."

We do not know how oracular responses containing more than one transforming line were traditionally interpreted. Integrating the messages of a number of transforming lines when these are at variance with each other is one of the challenging aspects of *Yi Jing* divination. Sometimes these messages refer to aspects of the situation which develop sequentially in time, and sometimes they describe complementary aspects coexisting in the present.

Image Tradition

This is a commentary text on the *Image of the Situation*, also included in the *Tuan Zhuan*, the First and Second Wing. It amplifies and paraphrases words and sentences of the *Image* and offers a technical analysis of the structure of the hexagram in terms of:

- solid and supple, i.e. relationships between whole and opened lines in the hexagram;
- appropriate or non-appropriate position of individual lines (a whole line is in an appropriate position in an odd-numbered place, an opened line is in an appropriate position in an even-numbered place);
- correspondence or non-correspondence between lines occupying the same position in the upper and the lower trigram, i.e. between the first and fourth, second and fifth, third and sixth line of the hexagram (these are said to be in correspondence if one is whole and the other is opened).

These technical aspects are the foundation of a complex geometry and numerology of the *Yi Jing*. The Eranos *Yi Jing*, focusing on the imaginal content of the oracular texts, does not particularly pursue this line of thought. For this reason the *Image Tradition* has been placed at the end of each hexagram: although adding useful insights, it doesn't fundamentally change the picture defined by the other sections.

Eranos Yi *Jing*	**Wilhelm translation**	**Palace Edition**
Image of the Situation	The Judgment	*Tuan Zhuan* (Wings 1 and 2)
Outer and Inner Trigram	Book II – Discussion of the Trigrams	*Shuo Gua* (Wing 8)
Counter Hexagram	Book II – The Eight Trigrams and Their Application	
Preceding Situation	The Sequence	*Xu Gua* (Wing 9)
Hexagrams in Pairs	Miscellaneous Notes	*Za Gua* (Wing 10)
Additional Texts	Appended Judgments	*Xi Ci* (Wings 5 and 6)
Patterns of Wisdom	The Image	*Xiang Zhuan* (Wings 3 and 4)
Transforming lines – main text	The Lines a)	*Tuan Zhuan* (Wings 1 and 2)
Transforming lines – comments	The Lines b)	*Xiang Zhuan* (Wings 3 and 4)
Image Tradition	Commentary on the Decision	*Tuan Zhuan* (Wings 1 and 2)

SECTIONS OF A HEXAGRAM IN THE ERANOS, WILHELM AND PALACE EDITION OF THE *YI JING*

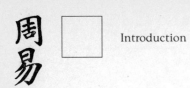

Note to the reader

If you are not yet familiar with the Yi Jing, *the instructions given so far should be amply sufficient to start practicing. Consulting the oracle is the best and easiest way to get acquainted with the book. With practice you will become familiar with the language of the oracular texts and with the unique way in which they speak to you. The rest of this introduction, while not strictly necessary for a divinatory use of the book, is geared to a more in-depth appreciation of the oracular texts and offers useful background information on the history of the book and on the correlative thinking underlying its divinatory use and its philosophy.*

Additional remarks about the Eranos translation

The Eranos *Yi Jing*'s aim is to open up as much as possible of the imaginal richness and flexibility of the oracular texts to a Western user who does not read Chinese. The following remarks are meant to allow the reader to form a clearer picture of the original Chinese texts through the Eranos translation.

Romanization of Chinese ideograms

The romanization of Chinese ideograms in this book follows the Pinyin system, officially adopted by China. In the past a variety of systems have been used in the West, originating considerable confusion. The most widespread of these, and formerly the standard in English-speaking countries, is the *Wade-Giles* system. Wade-Giles in most cases offers a more transparent key to the actual pronunciation of Chinese words, and some terms are much more familiar to the Western reader in their Wade-Giles transcription than in the Pinyin one (two examples are the word *tao* – *dao* in Pinyin – and the title itself of this book, I Ching – *Yi Jing* in Pinyin). But Pinyin is now fast becoming the international standard, and it is definitely worthwhile having a single universal system.

Sources of the Fields of meaning

The associations listed in the *Fields of meaning* are drawn from the classic Chinese dictionary published by the Emperor Kang Xi in 1716 and from a number of valuable Western sources, particularly Wells Williams,[16] Couvreur[17] and the excellent recent dictionary of the Ricci Institute.[18]

The description of the ideograms is based on the *Shuo Wen*, the fundamental Han dictionary published in 121 AD. This traditional way of understanding ideograms does not necessarily fit with modern philological theories about their origins; but it has been kept here because it describes the "aura" surrounding these terms in Chinese literature and poetry.

Composite entries

A basic concept of the Eranos *Yi Jing* is to preserve a one-to-one correspondence between Chinese ideograms and English core-words, so that a core-word unerringly identifies a certain Chinese ideogram. This device allows a Western reader to form as precise an idea as possible of the original Chinese text and makes a concordance to the *Yi Jing* in the English language possible for the first time.

A rigorous application of the above criterion, though, is a very stringent constraint: in some cases a single English word effectively representing the core meaning of a given ideogram simply does not exist. Two further devices have been introduced in order to obviate this.

Hyphen: when two or more English words are needed to render the core meaning of a single Chinese ideogram, they have been joined by a hyphen. Hyphenated words therefore must be read as a single word. Examples: **actualize-dao**, **before-zenith**, **big-toe**, **break-up**, **bushy-tailed**, etc.

Slash: when the core meaning of a Chinese ideogram has two equally important and intimately connected faces which are rendered in English by two distinct words, a slash has been used. Examples: **almost/hint**, **big-toe/thumb**, **day/sun**, etc. In these cases in the text only one aspect of the word will appear, e.g. **sun**, but the entry in the following *Fields of meaning* will list both aspects, e.g. "**Day/sun**, *RI*: the sun and the time of a sun-cycle, a day," reminding us that the words "day" and "sun" are interchangeable and correspond to the same Chinese ideogram.

Special cases

A special case of composite entry is the word **belong/it**, *zhi*, which has two distinct uses in the *Yi Jing*:

> **Belong/it**, *ZHI*: establishes between two terms a connection similar to the Saxon genitive, in which the second term belongs to the first one; at the end of a sentence it refers to something previously mentioned or implied.

The first use of *zhi* is a somewhat emphasized Saxon genitive, in that the Chinese language also has a plain Saxon genitive expressed by simply juxtaposing two

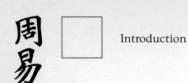

terms (this has been rendered by a lightface "apostrophe s" in the oracular texts). Therefore in the body of a sentence *zhi* has been rendered with **belong** together with a reversal of the order of the two terms it connects. E.g., in

Humbling: the **handle belonging to actualizing-dao indeed.**

the structure of the Chinese sentence is:

humble actualize-dao zhi handle indeed.

The meaning of course is that "humbling is the handle of actualizing-dao."

At the end of a sentence *zhi* has been rendered with **it**. In

Using enveloping the **great: heaviness.**
The **Pattern King uses it.**

it refers to the previously mentioned "heaviness of enveloping the great." (The king mentioned, by the way, is King Wen, the mythical author of the *Yi Jing*, about whom see pg.34, *The Pattern King.*)

Another special case is the general third person pronoun **one/one's**, *qi*, which also means **it/its, he/his, she/her, they/their**. A proper entry for this word in the *Fields of meaning* would be rather cumbersome, as it would list all of the above separated by slashes. In this case we have made an exception to the general rule, adopting in the *Fields of meaning* different listings for the same ideogram, but including a reference to all the other forms. E.g.:

Dragons struggle tending-towards the **countryside.**
Their blood indigo and **yellow.**

They/their, *QI*: general third person pronoun and possessive adjective; also: one/one's, it/its, he/his, she/her.

A **tiger observing: glaring, glaring.**
Its appetites: pursuing, pursuing.

It/its, *QI*: general third person pronoun and possessive adjective; also: one/one's, he/his, she/her, they/their.

Their in the first example and **its** in the second are the same word, *qi*. Notice also that the **it** of **belong/it** is not the same as the **it** of **it/its**.

Idiomatic phrases

Frequently two or more ideograms are used as a unit, they make a short idiomatic phrase which has, in the *Yi Jing*, a specific sense. One such expression, e.g., is **below heaven**, which indicates "the world." In such cases the *Fields of meaning* describe the whole phrase, rather than the single terms. E.g.:

> **Below heaven**, *TIAN XIA*: human world, between heaven and earth.

These idiomatic phrases have their own specific listing in the concordance. E.g., all the occurrences of **below heaven** are listed separately from the occurrences of **below** and those of **heaven** in other contexts (and a reference "see also: **below heaven**" is added to the last two).

Great and small

Some terms are used in the Eranos *Yi Jing* in a special way. The most significant of these are probably the words **great** and **small**. The corresponding *Fields of meaning* are:

> **Great**, *DA*: big, noble, important, very; orient the will toward a self-imposed goal, impose direction; ability to lead or guide one's life; contrasts with small, *XIAO*, flexible adaptation to what crosses one's path.
>
> **Small**, *XIAO*: little, common, unimportant; adapting to what crosses your path; ability to move in harmony with the vicissitudes of life; contrasts with great, *DA*, self-imposed theme or goal.

In the context of the oracular use of the *Yi Jing* these terms more often refer to a way of dealing with situations than to something literally (or even metaphorically) great or small. Accordingly, in the Eranos *Yi Jing* they are generally used in the substantive form the **great** and the **small**. E.g., the expressions usually translated as "great people" (or "the great man") and "small people" are here rendered as the **great** in the **person** and the **small** in the **person**, referring to attitudes the consultant can identify in herself/himself, rather than to "great" or "small" people outside.

The Concordance

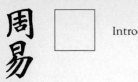

The reader who wishes to acquire an in-depth understanding of the language of the *Yi Jing* is warmly encouraged to make use of the Concordance. Comparing all the contexts in which a given term occurs adds significantly to the understanding of how that term is used in the *Yi Jing*. Noticing in which sections of the hexagrams specific words recur more frequently (or exclusively) offers interesting insights into the language of the various layers of the book. And the possibility of searching for a sentence by simply remembering one or two words is a precious tool for reconstructing past consultations or comparing answers obtained on different occasions.

II | Myth and History

The tradition

The first emperor

The tradition concerning the birth of the *Yi* is intertwined with the myths of origin of Chinese civilization. According to the traditional narrative, the book came into being through the insights of three legendary sages, figures belonging to a liminal space between myth and history. The first author is a fully mythical being, Fu Xi, the first emperor, sometimes represented with a serpent body and a human head. The third one, who is supposed to have carried the work to completion, is a fully historical person, although surrounded by a legendary aura: Confucius, the "master of ten thousand generations." Between them stands the man who is considered the principal author of the book, a figure straddling history and legend: King Wen, the founder of the Zhou dynasty, who ruled China during most of the first millennium BC, the time when the *Yi* actually came into use.

This illustrious genealogy had considerable cultural and political relevance. When the Han dynasty (206 BC to 220 AD) engaged in consolidating the empire by culturally unifying the diverse peoples they were ruling, milestones of the imperial policy were the standardization of writing and the ideological unification of the administration by elevating Confucianism to the rank of official doctrine of the empire. An important step of this program was the canonization of five ancient texts, first and foremost among them the *Yi*, as *jing*, classics, i.e. basic reference works for the whole culture. These books thereby acquired a status comparable to that of religious scriptures: they were commented upon and elaborated by scholars of later generations, but their authority and their sacred origins were never doubted for the next two thousand years.

Contrary to the views of modern scholarship, in the traditional account of the origins of the *Yi* the book developed in a logical progression from trigrams to hexagrams to oracular texts and hermeneutic commentaries. The invention of trigrams is attributed to Fu Xi. The Great Treatise describes this discovery in the following way:

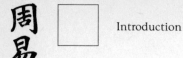

When in early antiquity Bao Xi ruled the world, he looked upward and contemplated the images in heaven; he looked downward and contemplated the forms on earth. He contemplated the patterns on the fur of animals and on the feathers of birds, as well as their adaptation to their habitats. He took as a model, close by, his body, and farther away, things. Thus he invented the eight trigrams in order to enter into connection with the divine light's actualizing-dao and to classify the nature of the myriad beings.[19]

Fu Xi is not here a mythical being with a serpent body, but the first civilizing hero, the one who introduced culture in the natural world. He is called by his appellative of Bao Xi, variously interpreted as Hunter, Tamer of animals and Cook, and a bit later in the same text we are told that

he made knotted cords and used them for nets and baskets in hunting and fishing.

Significantly the invention of the trigrams is connected here with "classifying the nature of the myriad beings." The word "classify," *lei*, has both the connotation of distinguishing and subdividing in rational categories (the beginning of the work of reason) and that of establishing connections and correlations between things on different planes. The 8 trigrams are therefore fundamental cosmological categories embracing the totality of "heaven and earth": as we shall see, they define radii in a *Universal Compass*, a map embracing concepts belonging to entirely different realms, yet mirroring each other through a web of subtle interconnections (see pg.52, *Correlative Thinking*).

The Pattern King

The tradition is somewhat ambiguous about whether Fu Xi discovered just the 8 trigrams or the 64 hexagrams (the old texts often speak interchangeably of the ones and the others, and the same word, *gua*, refers to both). But generally the invention of the hexagrams, as well as the authorship of the basic oracular texts, is attributed to King Wen, the founder of the Zhou dynasty. We find only two brief allusions to the circumstances of such invention in the Great Treatise:

The *Yi* came in use in the period of middle antiquity. Those who composed the *Yi* had great care and sorrow.

> The time at which the *Yi* came to the fore was that in which the house of Yin came to an end and the house of Zhou was rising, that is, the time when King Wen and the tyrant Di Xin were pitted against each other.[20]

"Those who composed the Yi" are King Wen and his son, the Duke of Zhou. Usually the texts of the *Tuan Zhuan* (*Image of the Situation* and main text of the *Transforming Lines* in the Eranos *Yi Jing*) are attributed to the first and the texts of the *Xiang Zhuan* (*Patterns of Wisdom* and *Comments* on the *Transforming Lines* in the Eranos *Yi Jing*) to the second. The "house of Yin" is the Shang dynasty, who ruled over most of China from 1765 BC to 1123 BC.

Si Ma Qian (145 to 86 BC), the first historiographer of the empire, attempts a more detailed account of the genealogy of the Yi in his *Shi Ji*, Records of the Historian:

> The ancients said that Fu Xi, who was simple and sincere, built the eight trigrams of the *Yi*.
>
> When the Count of the West was imprisoned at Youli, he probably developed the eight trigrams into sixty-four hexagrams.
>
> King Wen, imprisoned at Youli, developed the *Zhou Yi*.
>
> At the end of his life, Confucius, who loved the *Yi Jing*, set in order the *Tuan*, the *Xiang*, the *Xi Ci*, the *Shuo Gua* and the *Wen Yen* [the first eight Wings].[21]

King Wen's legend is as follows. The Zhou were originally one of the nomadic tribes roaming the Western border areas of the Shang empire, particularly the Shan Xi, the passes located on the Bronze Road, connecting China with the steppes of Central Asia (the same which became many centuries later the Silk Road). Recruited as military allies, they became vassals of the empire and settled in the plains at the foot of Mount Qi, the "Twin-peaked Mountain." They became sedentary, and their wealth and power gradually increased thanks to the culture of millet, husbandry and commerce with the neighboring empire.

Around the middle of the twelfth century BC the fortunes of the Shang dynasty were declining, while the star of the Zhou was steadily ascending. The Emperor Di Yi, worried about the growing power of his Western neighbors, tried to bind them to his house by giving his three daughters in marriage to the crown prince of the Zhou, Chang, the Shining. Shortly after that, Chang ascended to the throne of the Zhou, and Di Yi was succeeded by his son, Di Xin.

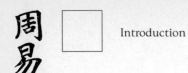

Chang's rule was a model of wisdom, while Di Xin "disobeyed heaven and tortured the beings."[22] The luminous example of his Western neighbor was odious to the tyrant, who had Chang arrested and thrown into a walled cave. In the darkness of this confinement Chang spent seven years meditating on the "great care and sorrow" of the current state of human affairs and on how to bring them back into alignment with "divine actualizing-dao."

He is the one posterity remembers as King Wen: a meaningful name, which defines him as another fundamental civilizing hero. Indeed *wen* means both pattern of wood, stone or animal fur and language, civilization, culture, literature, the written symbol as revelation of the intrinsic nature of things. It is a fitting description of the "classification of the nature of the myriad beings" initiated by Fu Xi through the 8 trigrams and perfected by the "Pattern King" in his dungeon. In his meditations he started with Fu Xi's 8 trigrams and developed the system further by pairing them into hexagrams and appending a text to each hexagram as well as to the individual line. These texts, constituting the *Tuan*, the first two Wings, were later expanded by King Wen's second son, the Duke of Zhou, who added his own commentary (the *Xiang*, Third and Fourth Wing) to elucidate his father's words.

Finally, to Confucius (551 to 479 BC) the tradition attributes the authorship of all the remaining commentaries, particularly of the Great Treatise. Thus the authority of the Classic of Classics is solidly founded and firmly meshed with the ideology of the empire; and the Confucian interpretation, occasionally incorporating insights of other schools, becomes the canonical reading of the *Yi*.

MODERN VIEWS OF THE ORIGINS OF THE *YI*

Bones and tortoise shells

Modern scholarship tells a very different story about the origins of the *Yi*. In this reconstruction the book does not emerge from the philosophical reflections of a few individual sages, but from the divinatory practices of many generations of shamans. The texts did not come at a later date as elucidation of the patterns of lines, but the other way around: divinatory statements came first, and they were later compiled and classified through a symbolic system (or a number of symbolic systems), which eventually evolved into the patterns of lines of the *Yi*.

The first discovery of *jia gu wen*, divinatory inscriptions on tortoise shells and cattle bones, dates from a little over a century ago (1899). It has been described as the most important finding in modern Chinese historiography. These inscriptions are an almost daily record of all kinds of natural and social events of the Shang (1765 to 1123 BC) and early Zhou dynasty. They constitute a vast reservoir of information, which is still far from being completely interpreted and classified. In 1995 Wang Dongliang cited 160,000 pieces identified, from which a repertory of 4,500 words had been compiled, not even half of them deciphered.[23]

The practice which generated these inscriptions was a form of pyromancy – divination by fire. The Shang shamans applied heat through glowing hardwood rods to specific points of animal bones (particularly scapulae of bovines) or tortoise shells, and in a state of trance read the patterns of cracks thus produced as messages from the world of gods and spirits. The resulting oracular statements were often recorded in abbreviated form on the bones or shells themselves, and these physical supports were kept for future reference, eventually constituting real divinatory archives.

As far as the *Yi* is concerned, the essential problem historians are confronted with is how this vast collection of disparate statements regarding specific times and circumstances evolved into a well-organized book, with a universal system of signs and corresponding oracular texts applicable to all situations. A final answer will have to wait for a more thorough understanding of the available material to emerge and maybe also for future discoveries. But the existing evidence is sufficient for tracing at least some hypothetical lines of development.

Léon Vandermeersch has proposed an evolution marked by three stages: cattle-bone divination, tortoise divination and yarrow-stalk divination.

Originally divination may have been an occasional practice accompanying the offering of sacrifices. Cracks spontaneously produced by fire in the bones of sacrificial victims were read as indications of the acceptance or rejection of the offering by gods and spirits, and therefore of success or failure of specific enterprises. Human concern about the future eventually brought about a reversal of the roles of the sacrifice and the ensuing divination: from an accessory quest, the pyromantic interrogation of the victim's bones became the main goal of the process and the sacrifice only a means to that end.

That shift in emphasis brought about the transition from the so-called proto-scapulomancy to scapulomancy proper. It was a shift in meaning and in technique. Pyromantic cracks started being understood as images of transformation processes in a larger context of universal movements; shamans no longer confined themselves to simply reading what the sacrificial fire had left for them to read, but started preparing the bones in specific ways in order to obtain clearer pyromantic patterns. With the emergence of the divinatory purpose as primary, a significant attitude change took place, a shift from an original transcendent religious orientation to an immanent "divinatory rationalism":

> The work of fire happening through the diviner's ember rather than on the priest's altar favors the representation of an immanent dynamism over the representation of a transcendent divine will. Literally as well as metaphorically, divination moves away from the altar.[24]

This shift was further emphasized by the tortoise shell replacing the bovine scapula as the medium *par excellence* of pyromantic divination. This "great progress in divinatory thought," writes Vandermeersch, went hand in hand with "the development of symbolic thought." Indeed in China the tortoise is a powerful cosmological symbol, with its round back representing the heavenly vault; its flat square ventral shell, the earth; and the soft flesh of the animal, the human world between heaven and earth. The adoption of the tortoise shell as support for divination therefore mirrored the intent of viewing the single incidents of individual consultations in the context of a larger cosmological frame: divination no longer revealed the will of the gods, but the subtle laws of transformation of the cosmic dynamism.

It was at this stage that divinatory records started being collected in archives of inscribed tortoise shells. And with this development the oracular formulas started taking on a life of their own, increasingly independent from the circumstances of the original consultation. They gradually assumed a more stereotyped form and were eventually collected in divination manuals, the ultimate example of which is the *Yi*.

The yarrow-stalk oracle

Classic texts talk about yarrow divination and tortoise divination as two parallel techniques, and occasionally discuss how their responses are to be integrated when both are applied to the same query. The archeological evidence is insufficient to definitely decide whether there was filiation of the yarrow technique from the tortoise one. But Vandermeersch claims that there is good reason to think so. One of the arguments in favor of this view is an etymological one: the radical of the ideogram *gua*, "hexagram" or "trigram," is the "reclining T" which is thought to depict a tortoise shell crack. And the same is true for the words *zhan* and *zhen*, both meaning "to divine" and referring to yarrow divination and to tortoise divination without distinction.

According to tradition, the yarrow-stalk consultation procedure was invented by a diviner of the early Zhou dynasty, a historical person about whom we know very little, called Wu Xian, the Conjoining Shaman. His name, once again, is meaningful, since his technique created a bridge between the wild oracular statements of the ancient shamans and the rational philosophy of Yin and Yang. About this invention Vandermeersch writes:

> Ancient Chinese historians did not know that trigrams and hexagrams, as we know them, did not exist under the Shang-Yin; thus they thought that Wu Xian invented a random procedure to select a *gua*. Now we know that *gua* are much more recent, and we understand that what Wu Xian invented was a random procedure for the selection of a [standardized] set of tortoise-shell cracks.[25]

In fact, a common pattern in the bone and tortoise-shell inscriptions are columns of strange signs, vaguely reminiscent of hexagrams (although the number of lines is not necessarily six). The "line" signs belong to only a few types, which have been identified as numbers written in paleographic form. Some numbers, e.g. 1, 5, 6, 7 and 8, recur with particular frequency. We do not know what these numbers refer to, but a plausible guess is that they are codes for specific types of cracks. Indeed actual cracks were also often vertically aligned (we must remember that in mature scapulomancy, shells and bones were prepared so that they would crack at specific points). And these coded crack configurations may well have been associated with standard oracular responses.

Once the tortoise oracle had developed this abstract symbolic form, it was no longer necessary to engage in the cumbersome ritual of pyromancy. Any random procedure to select one of the coded configurations (and the associated divinatory formulas) would do. Very naturally then at this stage the yarrow-stalk procedure came into play as a simplified method to achieve the same results as standardized scapulomancy.

To obtain the *Yi Jing* divination system as we know it, only two more steps were needed:

- the types of lines/cracks are reduced to four, coded by the numbers 6, 7, 8 and 9, and the even or odd character of the number gets connected with the philosophical notions of Yin and Yang;
- the number of lines/cracks is standardized at six.

Quoting Vandermeersch once again:

> We can follow the great developmental phases of Chinese divinatory techniques from Neolithic proto-scapulomancy, based on the crude burning of residual bones of bovine holocausts, to the

Evolution of divinatory techniques in ancient China[26]

Neolithic proto-scapulomancy

- crude burning of unprepared omoplates (left)
- irregular star-shaped cracks on the other side (right)

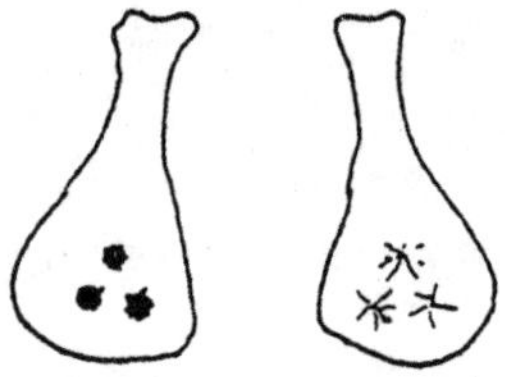

Yin epoch scapulomancy
(14th to 11th century BC)

- use of tortoise ventral plates
- preparation by incision before burning
- standardized 'reclining T' cracks on the other side (right)

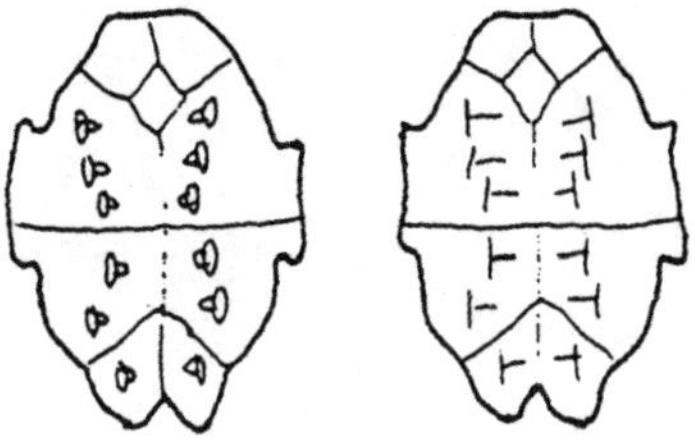

Proto-achilleomancy
(end of Yin – beginning of Zhou epoch, 11th to 10th century BC)

- fragment of tortoise shell with numerical hexagrams; the numbers represent canonical types of cracks, selected by a random procedure

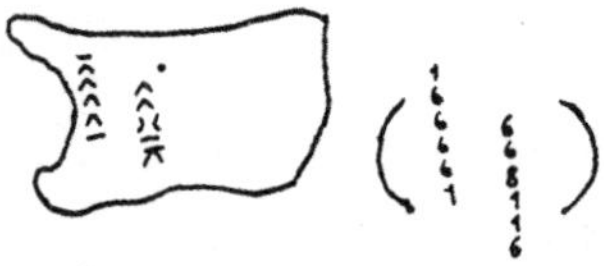

Numerical achilleomancy
(middle of the 1st millennium BC)

- rationalization of the number system used in the numerical hexagrams

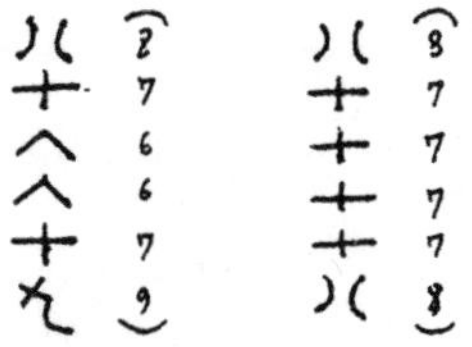

Canonical achilleomancy
(end of the 1st millennium BC)

- algorithmic hexagrams made of odd-valued Yang monograms and even-valued Yin monograms

system of the *Yi Jing*. These phases are: first, the remarkable standardization of scapulomantic diagrams; then, the typological classification of these standardized forms; finally, the algorithmic coding of the system in terms of even and odd numbers. Throughout this process the same logic operates: it is a logic of rationalization of the formal structures of the diagrammatic, numerical or algorithmic configurations produced by divinatory techniques, taken as coded representations of the hidden cosmic connections existent between all phenomena in the universe. As Granet noted so well, Chinese thought works according to a logic of correspondences. The history of divination is an admirable illustration of how this logic works...[27]

THE EVOLUTION OF THE BOOK

The Book of Encompassing Versatility

The *Yi* did not therefore arise as a complete book, but evolved through many centuries. From one of a number of divinatory manuals, it eventually became not only the oracular book *par excellence*, but the Classic of Change, the ultimate reference of Chinese wisdom, revered by all philosophical schools.

Initially, there were archives of inscribed bones and tortoise shells, kept in order to record key events and to evaluate the accuracy of the corresponding predictions. Eventually these pieces were grouped and classified, and their inscriptions formed the material of the first divinatory manuals.

The simpler yarrow consultation method gradually replaced the pyromantic practices, and the recourse to the tortoise shell was reserved for special occasions and very important people. In the *Zhou Li*, Rites of the Zhou, the word *yi* denotes the science of yarrow divination, and three *yi* manuals are mentioned, all based on 8 trigrams and 64 hexagrams, associated with the three mythical/historical dynasties (Xia, 2207 to 1766 BC; Shang, 1765 to 1123 BC; Zhou, 1122 to 256 BC). The last of these is the *Zhou Yi*, whose title can be translated as "Changes of the Zhou," but also as "Encompassing Changes," or "Encompassing Versatility," since the name of the Zhou dynasty means, among other things, "a complete circle, from all sides, universal, encompassing"; and *yi* means, besides "change," "easy, simple, versatile." We have no idea of what that *Zhou Yi* was like, but it is highly probable that it is the ancestor of the *Zhou Yi* that has come down to us.

In 771 BC, the Zhou capital moved East to Luoyang. That date marks the end

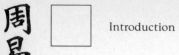

of the Western Zhou and the beginning of the Eastern Zhou dynasty (771 to 256 BC), which saw a progressive weakening of the central power and a general destabilization of the social system. The emperor remained nominally master of the whole country, but in practice rebellious feudatories exerted their power independently of the central government and set up autonomous states warring with each other everywhere. It was a time of great *yi*, of great upheavals and insecurity, in which individuals were often at the mercy of unpredictable changes. The *Huai Nan Zi*, an early Han philosophical treatise, gives an impressive description of the final chaotic phase of the Eastern Zhou, the Warring States period (403 to 256 BC):

> In the later generations, the Seven States set up clan differences. The feudal lords codified their own laws, and each differed in his practices and customs. The Vertical and Horizontal Alliances divided them, raising armies and attacking one another. When they laid siege to cities, they slaughtered mercilessly.... They dug up burial mounds and scattered the bones of the dead. They built more powerful war chariots and higher defense ramparts. They dispensed with the principles of war and were conversant with the road of death, clashed with mighty foes and ravaged without measure. Out of a hundred soldiers who advanced, only one would return....[28]

We can imagine that in these circumstances, in which traditional values were overrun by violence and choice could be a matter of life or death, recourse to the oracle may have often been the only resource. The *Huai Nan Zi* says that at that time "the tortoise had holes bored in its shell until it had no undershell left, and the divining stalks were cast day after day."

Already during the first part of the Eastern Zhou epoch, the Spring and Autumn period (771 to 476 BC), the use of the *Yi* had moved outside the environment of the courts of high-ranking nobility and had reached a much larger class of consultants, principally consisting of the scholars/officials who were the backbone of the Chinese social system. This shift in users changed the scope of yarrow divination, expanding it beyond the limits of state affairs to include private and existential matters. And with this, a change in emphasis and interpretation also took place, in which ethical concerns acquired a much greater weight. The notion of an ideal user of the book started developing: the *jun zi*, the noble, became the "disciple of wisdom," the person who in a consultation does not only seek a personal advantage, but the realization of an intrinsic good, the actualization of *dao* in action.

The following consultation, related in the *Zuo Zhuan*, a history of the Spring and Autumn period, is an interesting testimony of this new ethical concern:

> In 530 BC [the feudatory] Nan-kuai plots a rebellion against his ruler. Consulting the I Ching, he obtains the fifth line statement of hexagram 2, *K'un*, which reads "Yellow skirt, primally auspicious."[29] Greatly encouraged, he shows this to a friend, without mentioning his intentions. The friend replies: "I have studied this. If it is a matter of loyalty and fidelity, then it is possible. If not, it will certainly be defeated... If there is some deficiency [regarding these virtues], although the stalkcasting says 'auspicious', it is not."[30] Thus Nan-kuai's improper purpose renders his whole prognostication invalid. His friend's fundamental assumption is that an act's moral qualities determine its consequences... Only something that is already moral can ever be "auspicious." Here we see how developments in sixth-century moral-cosmological thinking change not only the interpretation of a particular line statement of the *I*, but also the very tasks to which the text could be directed. (Nan-kuai, by the way, disregards this analysis, and within a year he is dead.)[31]

This ethical approach to the *Yi* was particularly emphasized in the Confucian school. As we have mentioned, the tradition attributes to Confucius (551 to 479 BC) all the essential commentaries to the *Yi*. This claim is almost certainly a fabrication of later Confucian scholars. But Confucius may very well have been deeply interested in the *Yi* – since he was very interested in the ancient culture in general and his country of Lu was an important repository of the traditions of the Zhou. Many anecdotes are told about his devotion to the *Yi*. Si Ma Qian, for example, says that Confucius so much perused his copy of the *Yi* that he had to replace the bindings of the bamboo strips three times (books at that time consisted of thin bamboo strips tied together).

The only explicit reference to the *Yi* in the works of Confucius is a quotation of the third line of hexagram 32, Persevering:

> The Master said: "The people of the South have a saying: he who does not persevere cannot be a diviner nor a physician. How well said! He who does not persevere in virtue receives embarrassment and shame." [32] The Master said: "Nevertheless, I do not practice divination."[33]

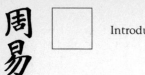

These words possibly hint at what may have been Confucius' real contribution to *Yi* scholarship: a reading of the texts valuing their ethical and educational function over the oracular aspect. This accords with a note contained in the so-called *yi shu*, "lost texts," of the Mawangdui silk manuscript (about this manuscript see pg.47):

> Confucius loved the *Yi* in his old age. At home, he had it on his bedside table; while traveling, he had it in his bag. Zi Gong asked him: "Master, do you also believe in yarrow divination?" Confucius answered: "It is the word of the ancients: I am not interested in its use, I enjoy its texts... I observe the ethical meaning... Between the divining scribes and me, it is the same path, but traveled to different destinations."[34]

If such is indeed the case, then Confucius must have contributed to shape the new approach to the *Yi* which fully emerged a few centuries later, under the Han, when the *Yi* became a book to be read and pondered, rather than consulted; from a manual of divination it turned into a *summa* of the wisdom of the ancients and a general map of the cosmos.

The canonization of the *Yi*

The feudal strife of the Eastern Zhou period came to an end in the last decades of the third century BC, when the Qin dynasty (221 to 207 BC) rose to power and brought the whole country under a single unified administration, building "a centralized state wielding unprecedented power, controlling vast resources and displaying a magnificence which inspired both awe and dread among its subjects."[35]

The rule of the Qin was short-lived, but marked a great turning point in Chinese history. When it collapsed, it left to the Han (206 BC to 220 AD) an important legacy: the idea of empire and the governmental structure to embody it. "For almost four centuries under the Han the implications of this great fact were to work their way out in all aspects of Chinese life... [a process that] in several fundamental respects shaped the intellectual tradition of China until modern times, and not of China only but of Korea and Japan as well."[36]

The Han worked gradually to rebuild the great web of central government that had disintegrated with the fall of the Qin, unifying, organizing and standardizing the vast area and the diverse peoples under their control. A central aspect of this unification was the establishment of a common Chinese cultural identity, which in its general outlines was to last for the next two thousand years.

An important step was the standardization of the written language. Even today in China a variety of local dialects are spoken, in which words have widely different sounds (beside that, the same sound in Chinese corresponds to many different words). People belonging to faraway regions do not necessarily understand each other when they speak. But they do understand each other when they write. The ideographic language creates a bridge between them and allows them to recognize each other as belonging to a common cultural mold.

Confucian thought played a leading part in the Han unification of culture. Parallel with the expanding function of government, there was a broadening of intellectual interest and a growing concern with questions of cosmology and the natural order. It was the conviction of Han philosophers that when the government was in tune with the laws of Heaven prosperity resulted, while strife and famine prevailed if that was not the case. Equally important, in an agricultural society, was the attunement to the concerns of the Earth (irrigation, land usage, flood control and so on); and so the notion of a necessary harmony between Heaven, Earth and Man became a pivotal idea in Chinese thought.

The great Han design of organizing all knowledge into a coherent whole including the natural world and human society was therefore, beside an intellectual pursuit, an important political task. Confucianism, with its emphasis on traditional wisdom and its focus on perfecting human nature through rites, music and literature, was ideally suited to this task. The final product of the Confucian education was the scholar/sage, the learned man endowed with a refined moral sense, whose natural field of action was in government service. During the Han this class of scholarly officials grew to a position of dominance over the entire social system, replacing the feudal aristocracy of former times. Public service was based on a system of competitive examinations which, in times of peace at least, assured the dominant position of the scholars in the bureaucracy.

A central endeavor in this process of cultural unification was the canonization of the books which were to constitute the base of all learning and particularly of the public examination system. To this effect two great gatherings of Confucian scholars were held in the presence of the emperor himself, the last one in 79 AD in a hall of the imperial palace in Luoyang called "the White Tiger Hall." The results were compiled and published in a book called *Bo Hu Tong*, Discussions in the White Tiger Hall, establishing the orthodox interpretation of the five *jing*, the classics, and setting the base of a vast system of correlative thinking (see pg.52, *Correlative Thinking*).

The *Yi Jing*, or Book of Changes, complete with its Ten Wings, was the first of the classics, and was taken as a description of the metaphysical structure of the whole of "heaven and earth." The other four classics were: the *Shu Jing*, Book of Documents, recording the experience and wisdom of the "earlier kings," model for all later rulers; the *Shi Jing*, Book of Songs, repository of a tradition of folk songs and ceremonial hymns; the *Li Ji*, Book of Rites, the ultimate authority in matters of procedure and etiquette; and the *Lü Shi Chun Qiu*, the Spring and Autumn Annals, a collection of moral and political lessons in the guise of historical narrative.

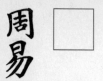

From this time onward the influence of the *Yi Jing* on Chinese culture kept growing. As the first of the classics, it was no longer just a book of divination: it was a tool for structuring thought in all fields, a standard reference for any theory claiming authority. Its influence extended into philosophy, ethics, politics, medicine, esthetics; and, since the openness of its texts allowed many different interpretations, the concise and cryptic oracular core of the book became enveloped in a body of scholarly commentaries.

Philosophical and oracular tradition

The philosophical reflection on the Book of Yi culminated in the vast and elaborate exegetic work of the Neo-Confucian school, during the Sung dynasty (960 to 1279). But meanwhile the divinatory use of the book was never lost. And with it survived an oracular tradition much closer to the shamanic origins of the *Yi*. This approach surfaced in a particularly clear form with the sixteenth-century philosopher Lai Zhi De.

Lai claimed that the Neo-Confucian school, by focusing exclusively on the discursive meaning of the texts and on their implications for "moral principle," had lost sight of the images, which were the true soul of the book. The Book of Yi, said Lai, consists essentially of pre-verbal symbols, its texts are verbalizations of intuitively perceived images. And it can reproduce the natural order of things because it has been generated spontaneously, just like natural phenomena. "The sages," Lai wrote, "did not apply their minds to set it forth."

Therefore these texts, unlike those of the other classics, have no concrete referents. They do not point to any fact or principle, and they cannot be taken as a "definitive outline" of moral action. They acquire a specific meaning only when they answer a specific question, in a concrete life situation.

Lai saw this openness of the *Yi Jing* texts as closely connected with the all-encompassing nature of the oracle. The *Xi Ci* claims that the *Yi* embraces the totality of heaven and earth. But, if each line in the book corresponded to a single occurrence, 384 lines would account for only 384 occurrences. How could then the *Yi*, Lai argued, "be the one and all of heaven and earth"?[37]

The Palace Edition

The oracular and the commentary texts of the Ten Wings were finally collected in a canonical form in the Palace Edition of the *Yi Jing* by the Emperor Kang Xi in 1715. That edition became the standard reference for all later Chinese publications, and is the text on which the present translation is based.

The Mawangdui manuscript

In 1973 silk manuscripts, including a version of the *Yi* and one of the *Lao Zi* were found in a Han tomb dated 168 BC. It was a crucial discovery, affording insights into the evolution of those great works at a date far antecedent anything available up to that point.

The Mawangdui text of the *Yi* differs from the canonical one (the Palace Edition) in a number of interesting ways.

First of all, the graphic representation of the hexagrams is different, having  and  in place of the whole and the opened line. These are variations on the paleographic form of the numbers seven and eight – and at the same time they are remarkably similar to the final form (⚊ and ⚋) of the whole and the opened line. Therefore we can regard the Mawangdui hexagrams as a bridge, a kind of "missing link," between the numeric "proto-hexagrams" recorded on tortoise shells and oracle bones and the canonical hexagrams.

Second, the names of thirty-five out of 64 hexagrams are different, in spite of the fact that overall the oracular texts are remarkably similar to the canonical version.

Third, the order of the hexagrams is different. The Mawangdui order is a systematic sequence obtained by keeping the upper trigram fixed and varying the lower trigram according to a regular rotation. In this way it resembles much more the order of a hexagram table than that of the canonical book. Wang Dongliang[38] interprets this fact as an indication that, at the time of the Mawangdui manuscript, divination was still the prevailing use of the *Yi* and philosophical speculation was not yet the dominant mode. The canonical sequence is "philosophical" in the sense of reflecting a developmental process in which the principles of the cosmos and of the human world are derived from each other according to an internal logic not directly connected with the structure of the signs. The Mawangdui sequence, on the other hand, with its logical arrangement based on the structure of the signs, seems to have the eminently pragmatic purpose of facilitating the search for a given hexagram, i.e. it seems to be tailored to the needs of yarrow-stalk consultation.

Finally, the Mawangdui text consists basically of only two sections, corresponding to the *Tuan* (i.e. the *Image of the Situation* and the main text of the

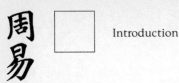

Transforming Lines) and to the *Xi Ci*, the Additional Texts. Therefore the classic organization of the book in Ten Wings must not have been yet in existence at that time. Instead of the remaining eight Wings, the Mawangdui manuscript includes an assortment of commentaries in the form of dialogues between Confucius and his disciples (conventionally called *yi shu*, "lost texts").

The *Yi Jing* comes to the West

The first glimpses of the *Yi Jing* reached the West by way of Jesuit missionaries in the sixteenth and seventeenth centuries. Some of these missionaries had a keen interest in the spirit of the Chinese people they had come to convert, deeply studied their culture and tried to approach them on their philosophical terms, frequently incurring the wrath of the Vatican. One of them, Matteo Ricci, is still remembered in the name of an outstanding contemporary sinological institute.

The early Jesuit missionaries brought to Europe fragments of the Classic of Classics; complete translations came only in the nineteenth century. And it was still a missionary, the German Richard Wilhelm, who finally introduced the *Yi Jing* to the West in a way that won the minds and souls of intellectuals, and eventually also those of a large number of readers and users.

Wilhelm's translation was published in Jena in 1923. It stands out from all previous ones for a radically different attitude toward the *Yi Jing*. Wilhelm regarded it as a book of spiritual guidance of universal value. He wrote in his preface:

> After the Chinese revolution [of 1911], when Tsingtao became the residence of a number of the most eminent scholars of the old school, I met among them my honored teacher Lao Nai-hsüan. I am indebted to him... also because he first opened my mind to the wonders of the Book of Changes.[39]

Wilhelm not only steeped himself in Neo-Confucian philosophy, but took it on as a personal spiritual path; and, having first traveled to the East as a missionary of Western religion, eventually he came back to the West as a missionary of Eastern wisdom. His translation moves from this committed and participatory stance. He endeavored to make the ancient book accessible to the Western mind by translating it as a discursive text in a Neo-Confucian philosophical perspective. His translation is a remarkably readable, poetic and profound text.

Carl Gustav Jung was deeply struck by the "formidable psychological system" the book embodied, and he wrote a foreword for it, which no doubt contributed considerably to its popularity. He also asked Cary F. Baynes, an American student of analytical psychology in Zurich, to undertake an English rendering of Wilhelm's German translation. The English translation took quite some time to complete (meanwhile Richard Wilhelm had died in 1930). When the Wilhelm-Baynes translation was published in the Bollingen Series in 1950, it rapidly caught the attention of a large audience.

Since then the *Yi Jing* has become popular in the West, and numerous translations and commentaries have been published, at all levels of quality and depth (see Bibliography). Many of the works by Westerners are translations of previous translations, quite a few of them of Wilhelm's classic translation.

The *Yi Jing* at Eranos

The present translation originates from the lifelong work of Rudolf Ritsema and from the experiences of the Eranos circle.

Eranos is an East–West research center founded in 1933 in Ascona, Switzerland, by an extraordinarily energetic and intuitive Dutch woman, Olga Froebe-Kapteyn (1881 to 1962).

An important influence on her development was the theologian Rudolf Otto, who saw the religious phenomenon as a universal aspect of the human soul, centered on the sense of an invisible order underlying the apparent randomness of life events. In the early 1920s, at the School of Wisdom of Count Hermann Keyserling in Darmstadt, Germany, Olga met various people who were to have a decisive influence on her life. One of them was Carl Gustav Jung: in his concept of archetypes Olga found a psychological language articulating her religious intuitions. Another crucial encounter was that with Richard Wilhelm, who in 1923 presented his new translation of the *Yi Jing*, shortly before publication, at the School of Wisdom. In the *Yi Jing* Olga saw a natural bridge connecting the transpersonal archetypal dimension with daily life.

Around 1930 she conceived the idea of turning the Ascona house she had received from her father into a center for the spiritual meeting of East and West. The house was wonderfully situated on the shore of Lago Maggiore, combining the mild Mediterranean climate of the lake with the austere beauty of the surrounding Alps; and Ascona had been, since the beginning of the century, a cauldron of innovative cultural, artistic and political movements. In 1932 Olga sought Otto's support for her project. He was too ill at the time to get personally involved, but he suggested the name "Eranos," a Greek word denoting a feast in which each participant brings a contribution, each one gives and receives.

Carl Gustav Jung, on the other hand, was involved in Olga's project from the very beginning and was a crucial formative influence throughout: for the next twenty years he gave a great personal and intellectual contribution to Eranos. He regularly sojourned there every year, and he presented many of his ideas at the "work in progress" stage.

The first Eranos Session, or "Eranos Tagung" (German was the main language spoken at Eranos throughout the first decades), was held in 1933 with the title *Yoga and Meditation in East and West*. From then on the sessions convened every summer in August, and they hosted outstanding intellectual exchanges, involving many of the leading cultural figures of the time.[40]

Initially Olga Froebe would have liked the sessions to have a concrete and experiential character, to be a laboratory for personal and spiritual growth. In this spirit in 1934 she asked Jung to introduce the psychological use of the *Yi Jing* in the Eranos Sessions. But Jung felt that the time was not ripe for such an "unsavory" personal exposure, even within the intimate circle of Eranos. It was much better, he suggested, to focus on the scientific study of archetypal images and of the religious phenomenon in the sense of Rudolf Otto. His view prevailed, and the field of archetypal research provided a vital thread for the Eranos Sessions for over half a century.

Nevertheless Olga Froebe kept nurturing the hope that one day the personal and experiential dimension would be included in the work of Eranos. When she met Rudolf Ritsema in 1948, their common interest in the *Yi Jing* and its use as a tool for self-knowledge created a lasting bond between them.

Rudolf Ritsema (b.1918) first encountered the *Yi Jing* in 1944 through his analyst, Alwina von Keller. Immediately he realized that the book had a central meaning in his life. He borrowed it for a week (the Wilhelm translation was then a rare book, difficult to find in Switzerland during the war years), and, working relentlessly, typed a copy of the whole first volume.

In the following years he devoted himself to the study of the *Yi Jing*. He became interested in the original Chinese text and studied classical Chinese specifically for this purpose. He tried to recover the full range of meaning of each oracular term and, on the basis of his research, started writing commentaries on various passages of the book for the patients of Alwina von Keller and for others.

When in 1948 Rudolf Ritsema came to Eranos, Olga Froebe felt that his way of using the oracle matched the experiential approach she had wished to introduce in the Eranos Sessions. As the friendship between Olga Froebe and the Ritsemas developed, Rudolf and his wife Catherine became progressively more involved in the work of Eranos. From 1956 on, Rudolf and the Basel biologist Adolf Portmann worked together with Olga in the organization of the annual Sessions. In 1961, a year before her death, Olga asked the Ritsemas and Portmann to be her successors and carry on the work of Eranos. In that she was partly motivated by the hope that some day the psychological work with the I Ching would happen at Eranos.

Rudolf Ritsema and Adolf Portmann continued the tradition of the Eranos Sessions devoted to fundamental archetypal research. At the same time Rudolf Ritsema privately carried on his *Yi Jing* research. Around 1970 he grew dissatisfied with writing critical commentaries on the Wilhelm translation, and conceived the idea of an entirely new translation of the *Yi Jing*, a translation in the spirit of the oracular rather than the philosophical tradition, avoiding as much as possible any a priori interpretation, so as to allow the questioner a direct personal contact with the archetypal images.

In 1988 Rudolf Ritsema carried out the transformation of the Eranos Sessions Olga Froebe had wished for fifty-four years before: he brought the *Yi Jing* to the center of the Eranos activities and started the *Eranos Yi Jing Project*. The new sessions, called Eranos Round Table Sessions, were held twice or thrice a year around a large round table. In them all participants asked personal questions of the oracle and the alchemical circle of the people sitting around the table created a resonant body for working on the archetypal images received.

With the collaboration of the American poet Stephen Karcher, Rudolf Ritsema first completed a provisional English translation of the *Yi Jing*, entitled *Chou Yi, The Oracle of Encompassing Versatility*, which was put to the test in the Eranos Round Table Sessions from 1990 to 1992. The work achieved in these sessions led to an improved version of the English translation, published for the general book market in 1994 by Element Books under the title *I Ching, The Classic Chinese Oracle of Change*.

In 1990 the Italian publisher Maurizio Rosenberg participated in the first Eranos Round Table Session and immediately conceived the project of an Italian version of the Eranos *Yi Jing*. In 1991 Shantena Sabbadini started working with Rudolf Ritsema on this project, again translating from the original Chinese, and their translation was published by Red Edizioni, Como, in 1996 with the title Eranos *I Ching, Il libro della versatilità*. Italian Round Table Sessions using the new translation started happening at Eranos beside the English sessions. In 1997 the Swiss linguist Hansjakob Schneider joined Rudolf Ritsema to produce a German translation, which was published in 2000 by O.W. Barth, Munich, under the title *Eranos Yi Jing, Das Buch der Wandlungen*. Finally, Imelda and Pierre Gaudissart, working under the direction of Rudolf Ritsema, produced a French translation, published in 2003 by Encre, Paris, under the title *Le Yi Jing Eranos*.

By the year 2000 the work on the Italian and the German translations, together with the experience of the Eranos Round Table Sessions, had suggested a number of significant improvements on the first English translation published in 1994. That consideration moved the present authors to embark on a new translation, incorporating all the insights developed in a decade of research. That is the book you, reader, have in front of you, a compendium of the *Eranos Yi Jing Project* experience.

The last Eranos Round Table Session was held in November 2002 with the title *Beyond Consolidated Forms: Emergence of Change*.

III | Correlative Thinking

The Universal Compass

The world view embodied in the *Yi Jing* is essentially different from the linear, causal perspective prevalent in our Western thinking. It is based on a system of correlations whose essential features took shape in the Han epoch and were codified by the Discussions in the White Tiger Hall in 79 AD.[41] Everything under heaven can be assigned to a specific phase of a system of interlocked, correlated cycles. The intrinsic dynamics of all phenomena is therefore represented in this system, which is the foundation of all Chinese traditional science. Its logic has been well described by Joseph Needham:

> The key-word in Chinese thought is *Order* and above all *Pattern* (and, if I may whisper it for the first time, *Organism*). The symbolic correlations or correspondences all formed part of one colossal pattern. Things behaved in particular ways not necessarily because of prior actions or impulsions of other things, but because their position in the ever-moving cyclical universe was such that they were endowed with intrinsic natures which made that behavior inevitable for them.... They were thus parts in existential dependence upon the whole world-organism. And they reacted upon one another not so much by mechanical impulsion or causation as by a kind of mysterious resonance.[42]

The words of the *Yi Jing* acquire their full range of meanings when they are understood in this context. The fundamental cycles and their interrelations are displayed in the following diagram, called the *Universal Compass*, which is also reproduced, for ease of consultation, at the back of this book.

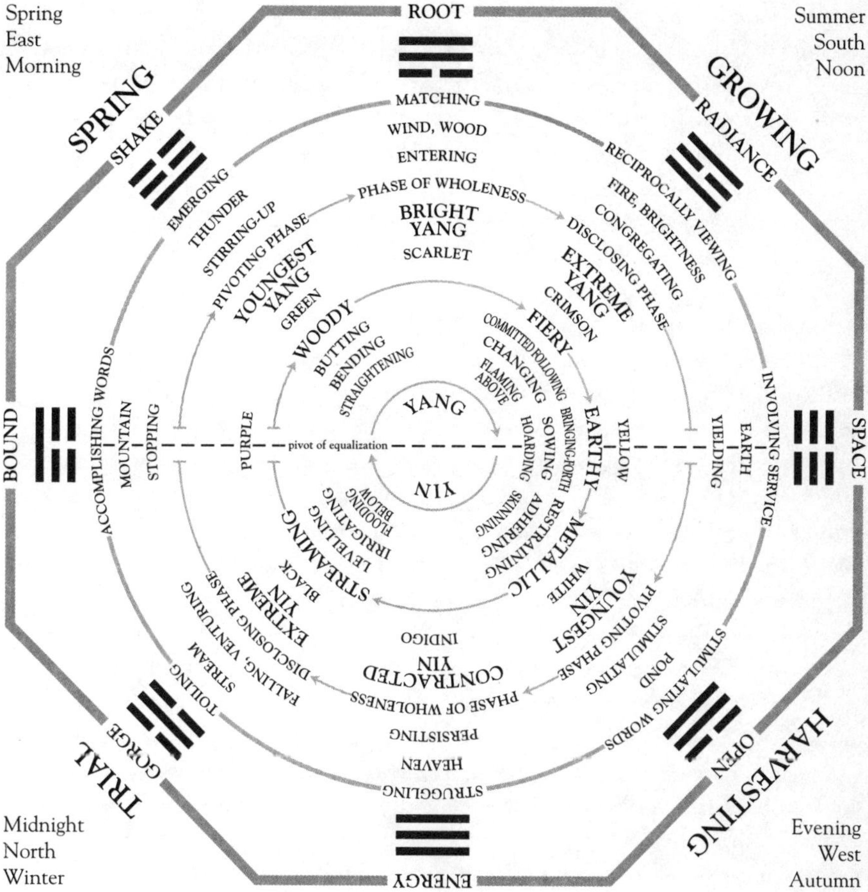

Universal Compass

The cycles represented in the diagram are:

- the cycle of Yin and Yang;
- the yearly and daily solar cycles and the quadrant of the four directions
- the cycle of the 8 trigrams
- the cycle of the five Transformative Moments

The five Transformative Moments (Woody, Fiery, Earthy, Metallic and Streaming) became prominent among various other correlative systems at the beginning of the Han era. While in earlier thought they still retained some characteristics of material substances, in Han cosmology they came to represent moments of all processes in general, phases of the cyclical change of all things on various time-scales. (That is why we avoid the misleading term "elements," which is sometimes used in this context, and we use the adjectival form instead of the nouns "Wood, Fire, Earth, Metal, Water"). The Discussions in the White Tiger Hall developed a vast system of correspondences based on the five Transformative Moments, embracing all kinds of natural and social processes.

An outstanding problem of this system was how to harmonize the base-five cycle of the Transformative Moments with the base-two cycles of Yin and Yang, four seasons, four directions and 8 trigrams. The solution adopted by Han cosmologists consisted in giving the Earthy Moment, as support of all the others, a special location. There are various versions of this special placement: the one adopted in this book is the arrangement described in the *Huai Nan Zi*, which makes the Earthy Moment coincide with the *Pivot of Equalization*, i.e. with the boundary between the Yang and the Yin hemicycles.

The center of the diagram symbolically corresponds to the axis of heaven and earth: it is the axis around which all cycles rotate, the unmoving center of all motions. All processes, actions, qualities and symbols lined up on the same radius are correlated with each other. This correlation is a sort of resonance, similar to that which exists between strings or bells vibrating with the same frequency: even though they may not be in direct contact with each other, when one of them is activated, the others enter into vibration.

Placing the 8 trigrams of the *Yi Jing* in the context of this cosmological system vastly expands their meaning. The locations of the upper (or outer) and of the lower (or inner) trigram of your hexagram in the *Universal Compass* are especially meaningful. Some of their correlations are summarized in the *Outer and Inner Trigram* section of each hexagram. All the resonances that are relevant for your specific question or situation, or that call up a particular emotional response in you, can be included in your answer.

The Yin-Yang cycle

Yin and Yang are the fundamental polarity of this system. As soon as the original unity moves into differentiation the interlocked movement of Yin and Yang arises: the symbol of the One in this differentiating aspect is the *tai ji*, which we have already encountered (pg.9).

These two basic categories of Chinese thinking cannot be adequately translated in Western terms. In order to understand them correctly, we must keep in mind that they represent aspects of processes and not qualities of things. Nothing is intrinsically Yin or Yang.

As a first approximation, we can say that Yang refers to action, and Yin to concrete form in space. For example, when we look at writing as the action of tracing signs on paper, it can be described as Yang; while the signs themselves, the written document produced by this action, can be described as Yin.

Yang is sometimes characterized as "creative," while Yin is characterized as "receptive." But that is not quite correct, because no creation is possible through pure action without ever reaching a consolidated form (and likewise no creation is possible through form without action). All creation is the result of the interpenetration of these two complementary aspects and of their dynamic interplay.

The following list of qualities associated with Yin and Yang can be helpful to get a feeling of how these two basic categories are perceived in Chinese thought:

Yin refers to:	**Yang refers to:**
the shady southern bank of a river	the bright northern bank of a river
the shady northern slope of a mountain	the bright southern slope of a mountain
water	fire
moon	sun
dark	bright
moist	dry
soft	hard
hidden	manifest
static	dynamic
lower	upper
inner	outer
incoming	outgoing
contracting	expanding
inertia	activity
completion	beginning
form	energy
structure	movement
being	doing
waiting	initiating
response	stimulus

The ideogram Yin suggests clouds and shadows of hills.

The ideogram Yang suggests sunrise and a sunlit flag.

YIN AND YANG

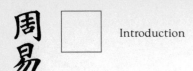

These two complementary aspects of all processes form a cycle, symbolically represented by the *tai ji*. Their alternation is patterned on the cycle of day and night: during the morning hours the light of Yang expands into the darkness of Yin, reaching a peak at noon; then it starts declining, as the darkness of Yin creeps in, and in the evening takes over, enveloping everything in its nightly veil; midnight is at the same time the culmination of Yin and the beginning of the rebirth of Yang. In the *tai ji*, at the point where the dark principle of Yin reaches its maximum expansion we find a light dot, the seed of the rebirth of Yang; and at the point where the light principle of Yang reaches its peak we find a dark dot, the seed of the return of Yin.

Like the daily cycle, the Yin-Yang cycle is articulated in two hemicycles, separated by an axis called the *Pivot of Equalization*, where the two principles balance each other. Each hemicycle starts with a *Pivoting Phase*, the first movement towards the predominance of Yin or Yang; it develops into a *Phase of Wholeness*, in which each principle fully expresses its qualities; and it culminates in a *Disclosing Phase*, in which Yin or Yang reaches an extreme and breaks out of boundaries, thus starting its own decline and restoring the balance of the *Pivot of Equalization*.

The yearly cycle and the four directions

In the *Universal Compass* superposed on the Yin-Yang cycle we find the yearly cycle and the quadrant of the four directions. Four basic divinatory terms in the *Yi Jing* correspond to the seasons of the year. We find them already in the *Image of the Situation* of the first hexagram:

Spring, Growing, Harvesting, Trial.

"Spring" refers to the vernal season, and is associated with East and with sunrise. It represents the beginning, the source, the primal originating power which causes things to emerge from the ground.

"Growing" refers to summer, and is associated with South and with noon. It represents vigorous life, completion, success, the power which brings to maturity what has sprouted in Spring.

"Harvesting" refers to autumn, and is associated with West and with sunset. It represents benefit, nourishment, the power which harvests the fruit that has ripened in Growing, both reaping and gathering.

"Trial" refers to winter, and is associated with North and with midnight. It represents a test, an ordeal, the power which separates what survives the winter from what decays and dies, the lasting from the perishable; it denotes the act of divination itself, which separates valid from worthless, right from wrong.

The five Transformative Moments

The Yin-Yang cycle, the daily and yearly cycles and the quadrant of the four directions interlock with the cycle of the Five Transformative Moments. As we have previously remarked, these categories are not material substances, but moments or phases of all processes, aspects of the dynamic change of things in general.

The Woody Moment, associated with spring, East and sunrise, begins the cycle. It describes organic growth, typically a young sprout breaking through the crust of the earth: its actions are *butting, bending* and *straightening.*

Wood is fuel for fire. Therefore the Fiery Moment follows, associated with summer, South and noon. It describes combustion, glowing and upward motion. The flame remains joined to the wood out of which it arises and gradually changes it into ashes: its actions are *committed following, flaming above* and *changing.*

Ashes, or soil, correspond to the Earthy Moment, associated with the *Pivot of Equalization*, with the transition from Yang to Yin and vice versa. It is the support of all the other Moments. Its actions are *bringing-forth, sowing* and *hoarding.*

The extraction of minerals from the earth brings about the Metallic Moment, associated with autumn, West and sunset. It describes crystallization, concentration, the hard forms of cast metal, the consolidated structures of Yin. Its actions are those of the metallurgic art: *restraining, adhering* and *skinning.*

Melting liquefies solid metallic forms, giving rise to the Streaming Moment, associated with winter, North and midnight. It describes all moving fluids and particularly water. Its actions are *leveling, flooding below* and *irrigating.* By seeping into the soil of the *Pivot of Equalization* this water causes wood to grow, starting a new cycle.

The 8 trigrams and their attributes

Each trigram of the *Yi Jing* has a name, a symbol, a specific action and a position in a family structure:

TRIGRAM NAME	SYMBOL	ACTION	FAMILY ORDER
☰ Energy	Heaven	Persisting	Father
☷ Space	Earth	Yielding	Mother
☳ Shake	Thunder	Stirring-up	Eldest son
☵ Gorge	Stream	Venturing, Falling	Middle son
☶ Bound	Mountain	Stopping	Youngest son
☴ Root	Wood, Wind	Entering	Eldest daughter
☲ Radiance	Fire, Brightness	Congregating	Middle daughter
☱ Open	Pond	Stimulating	Youngest daughter

THE 8 TRIGRAMS AND THEIR ATTRIBUTES

Furthermore the 8 trigrams can be arranged in a cyclical order in two main ways. The older one is called the Sequence of Earlier Heaven or the Primal Arrangement. It is traditionally attributed to Fu Xi and it reflects a cosmic order prior to the human world. In it the trigrams form simple pairs of opposites at the ends of each diameter.

The other cyclical order is called the Sequence of Later Heaven or the Inner World Arrangement. This one is attributed to King Wen and it applies to the human world we inhabit and to its natural cycles.

This rather more intricate arrangement is spelled out in the *Shuo Gua*, the Eighth Wing of the *Yi Jing*, Discussion of the Trigrams, and it is the one that is incorporated in the system of the Universal Compass. The *Shuo Gua* says:

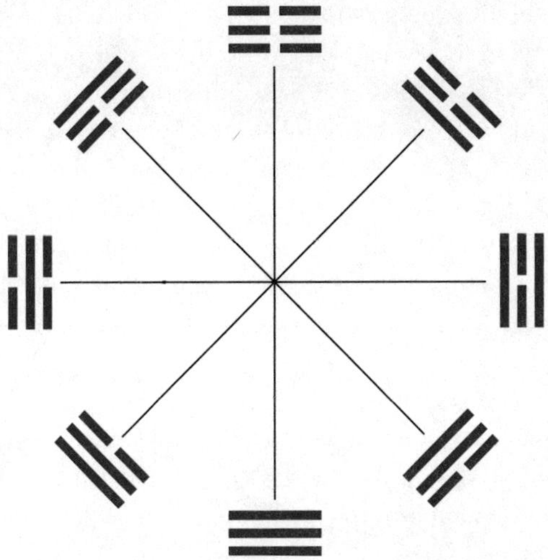

Sequence of Earlier Heaven
(Fu Xi's arrangement)

Sequence of Later Heaven
(King Wen's arrangement)

> The Supreme [manifests] in the Shake by emerging, in the Root by matching, in the Radiance by reciprocally viewing, in Space by involving service, in the Open by stimulating words, in Energy by struggling, in the Gorge by toiling, in the Bound by accomplishing words.[43]

The *Shake* corresponds to the first emergence of Yang: a Yang line enters from below, arousing the energies of the seed sleeping in the earth. It is the time of *emerging*, associated with spring, East, sunrise and the beginning of the Woody Moment.

The *Root* corresponds to the wholeness of Yang and to the full development of the Woody Moment, which brings *matching*, coupling and multiplying.

The *Radiance* corresponds to extreme Yang, associated with summer, South, noon and the Fiery Moment. It is the bright light which allows beings to *view* each other.

Space corresponds to the southwestern pole of the *Pivot of Equalization* and to the Earthy Moment. It is the time of agricultural works and *involving service.*

The *Open* corresponds to the beginning of the Yin hemicycle, to autumn, West, sunset and to the first phase of the Metallic Moment. It is the time of harvest, bringing joyous and *stimulating words.*

Energy corresponds to the wholeness of Yin, where structures have reached their most consolidated form, and a dissolving tendency begins to be felt. It is a time characterized by the *struggle* between these two opposing tendencies.

The *Gorge* corresponds to extreme Yin, to winter, North, midnight and the Streaming Moment. The tendency to dissolution now prevails. The darkness of winter brings trial and *toiling* to a life cycle nearing its end.

The *Bound* corresponds to the northeastern pole of the *Pivot of Equalization* and marks the end of the cycle. At the end of winter life comes to a still point, suspended between death and rebirth. This time is characterized by *accomplishing words*, which articulate what is ending and prepare the beginning of a new cycle.

Chronological Table

2953 to 2838 BC (traditional dates)	Fu Xi (legendary first emperor)
Shang dynasty (1765 to 1123 BC)	Oracular inscriptions on bones and tortoise shells
Western Zhou dynasty (1122 to 771 BC)	King Wen and Duke of Zhou (mythical authors of the *Yi Jing*) Yarrow-stalk oracle
Eastern Zhou dynasty Spring and Autumn period (771 to 476 BC)	*Zhou Yi* Diffusion of the *Yi* among the literati Confucius (551 to 479 BC)
Eastern Zhou dynasty Warring States period (403 to 256 BC)	Confucian commentaries on the *Zhou Yi*
Han dynasty (206 BC to 220 AD)	Mawangdui manuscript (168 BC) Canonization of the *Zhou Yi* Bo Hu Tong, Discussions in the White Tiger Hall (79 AD)
Song dynasty (960 to 1279)	Neo-Confucian commentaries
Ming dynasty (1368 to 1644)	Lai Zhi De's (1525 to 1604) defense of the oracular tradition
Qing dynasty (1644 to 1911)	Jesuit missions in China Kang Xi's (1655 to 1723) Palace Edition First Western translations of the *Yi Jing*
Republic (1912 to 1949)	Wilhelm's German translation (1923) The *Yi Jing* comes to the West as a book of wisdom
Popular Republic (1949–)	Wilhelm-Baynes English translation The *Yi Jing* becomes popular in the West

A BRIEF CHRONOLOGY OF THE *YI JING*

Notes

1 Bernhard Karlgren, *The Book of Documents*, Stockholm, 1950, p. 33, adapted.

2 C. G. Jung, Foreword to *The I Ching, or Book of Changes, Richard Wilhelm Translation*, Bollingen Series XIX, Princeton University Press, 1950

3 See, e.g., C. G. Jung, *The Archetypes and the Collective Unconscious*, CW 9, I, Bollingen Series XX, Princeton University Press, 1959, 1969

4 C. G. Jung, *Mysterium Coniunctionis*, CW 14, 401, Bollingen Series XX, Princeton University Press, 1963, 1970

5 Henry Corbin, "*Mundus imaginalis*, or the Imaginary and the Imaginal", in *Swedenborg and Esoteric Islam*, trans. Leonard Fox, Swedenborg Foundation, West Chester, PA, 1995. See also: Tom Cheetham, *The World Turned Inside Out: Henry Corbin and Islamic Mysticism*, Spring Journal Books, Woodstock, CT, 2003

6 Léon Vandermeersch, "Origine de la divination par l'achillée et forme primitive du Yi Jing," in *Hexagrammes* N° 4, Centre Djohi, Paris, 1988

7 In the Eranos *Yi Jing* the Yin line is called "opened," rather than "open," because "open" is the name of one of the trigrams. The two terms correspond to different Chinese ideograms and have different connotations.

8 *Lao Zi*, chapter 42

9 *Lao Zi*, chapter 2

10 *Yi Jing*, Hexagrams in Pairs 41/42

11 *Xi Ci*, I, 6, Wilhelm-Baynes translation

12 *Xi Ci*, I, 9, Wilhelm-Baynes translation

13 Wang Bi, *Xi Ci Zhu*, I, 8

14 Tjan Tjoe Som, *Po Hu T'ung, The Comprehensive Discussions in the White Tiger Hall*, E.J. Brill, Leiden, 1949 and 1952

15 *Xi Ci*, II, 2 and 7

16 S. Wells Williams, *A Syllabic Dictionary of Chinese Language*, American Presbyterian Mission Press, Shanghai, 1874

17 F. S. Couvreur, S. J., *Dictionnaire classique de la langue chinoise*, troisième édition, Imprimerie de la Mission Catholique, Ho Kien Fou, 1911

[18] Instituts Ricci (Paris-Taipei), *Dictionnaire Ricci de caractères chinois*, Desclée de Brouwer, Paris, 1999

[19] *Xi Ci*, II, 2, Wilhelm-Baynes translation, adapted

[20] *Xi Ci*, II, 7 and 11

[21] Si Ma Qian, *Shi Ji*, chapters 4, 47 and 130

[22] Ban Gu (39-92), *Han Shu*, chapter 30

[23] Wang Dongliang, *Les signes et les mutations*, L'Asiathèque, Paris, 1995, p. 52

[24] Wang Dongliang, op. cit., p. 61–62

[25] Léon Vandermeersch, op. cit., p. 5–24

[26] Léon Vandermeersch, "Origine et évolution de l'achilléomancie chinoise," *Comptes rendus de l'Académie des inscriptions*, novembre-décembre 1990, Boccard, Paris, p. 960

[27] Léon Vandermeersch, op. cit., p. 959–961

[28] *Huai-nan Tzu*, chapter 6, trans. Charles Le Blanc, Hong Kong, 1985, p. 174

[29] In the Eranos translation: "A yellow apron. Spring, significant."

[30] Zuo Zhuan, 12

[31] Kidder Smith Jr., Peter Bol, Joseph Adler, Don Wyatt, *Sung Dynasty Uses of the I Ching*, Princeton University Press, 1990, p. 12–13

[32] In the Eranos translation: "Not persevering in one's actualizing-dao. Maybe to receiving belongs embarrassment. Trial, abashment."

[33] Confucius, *Analects*, *Zi Lu*, XIII, 22

[34] Han Zhongmin, *Boyi shuolüe*, Introduction to the Silk Yi, Beijing, 1992, p. 104–105, quoted in Wang Dongliang, op. cit., p. 92

[35] Wm. Theodore de Bary, Wing-tsit Chan, Burton Watson, *Sources of Chinese Tradition*, Columbia University Press, New York and London, 1960, p. 161

[36] Ibid.

[37] Larry Schultz, *Lai Chih-te (1525–1604) and the Phenomenology of the Classic of Change*, University Microfilms, Ann Arbor, MI, 1982

[38] Wang Dongliang, op. cit., p. 99

[39] Richard Wilhelm, *I Ging, Das Buch der Wandlungen*, Eugen Diederichs, Jena, 1923, p. xlv

40 Among them, besides Jung: Ernst Benz, Jean Brun, Martin Buber, Ernesto Buonaiuti, Joseph Campbell, Henry Corbin, Gilbert Durand, Mircea Eliade, Marie-Louise von Franz, Wolfgang Giegerich, James Hillman, Gerald Holton, Toshihiko Izutsu, Aniela Jaffé, Karl Kerényi, John Layard, Louis Massignon, David Miller, Erich Neumann, Herbert Pietschmann, Manfred Porkert, Adolf Portmann, Ira Progoff, Herbert Read, Shmuel Sambursky, Gershom Scholem, Erwin Schrödinger, Jean Servier, Daisetz Teitaro Suzuki, Paul Tillich, Giuseppe Tucci, Hermann Weyl, Hellmut Wilhelm, Heinrich Zimmer and Victor Zuckerkandl.

For an exhaustive source of the contributions presented at Eranos, see the the *Eranos Jahrbücher/Eranos Yearbooks* (volumes 1-1933 to 13-1945 with articles in German; 14-1946 to 57-1988 with articles in English, French and German; while from 58-1989 onward all articles are in English). The *Eranos Yearbooks* are available from Daimon Verlag, Hauptstrasse 85, CH-8840 Einsiedeln, fax +41 55 4122231, and in the USA from Spring Publishers, 299 E. Quassett Road, Woodstock, CT 06281, USA, fax +1 860 9743195.

41 Tjan Tjoe Som, *Po Hu T'ung, The Comprehensive Discussions in the White Tiger Hall*, E.J. Brill, Leiden, 1949 and 1952

42 Joseph Needham, *Science and Civilization in China*, Vol. 2, Cambridge University Press, 1956, p. 281

43 *Shuo Gua*, 2

Index

A
Achillea millefolium 13
Additional Texts 25, 27, 48
appropriate or non-appropriate position of individual lines 27
archetypal images 6, 18, 50, 51
archetypes 5, 49
axis of heaven and earth 13, 54

B
Baynes, Cary F. 48–9
belong/it 29–30
Bo Hu Tong see Discussions in the White Tiger Hall
boldface and lightface 20, 21
Book of Documents *see Shu Jing*
Book of Encompassing Versatility *see Zhou Yi*
Book of *Yi* 2–12

C
canonization of the *Yi* 2, 33, 45–6, 61
Chang, the Shining 35–6
Chinese ideograms 18–19
classics 2, 24, 33, 45–6, 48
coins method 12
Comments to the Transforming Lines 20, 21, 26, 27, 35
concordance 32
Confucianism 24, 33, 36, 43, 45, 46, 48, 61
Confucius 33, 35, 36, 43–4, 48, 61
consultation procedure 12–18
Corbin, Henry 5
core-words 19, 20, 21, 29
correlative thinking 28, 45, 52–7
correspondence or non-correspondence between lines 27
Counter Hexagram 24–5, 27

D
Da Zhuan see Xi Ci
description of the ideograms 28–9
Di Xin 36
Di Yi 35, 36
"disciple of wisdom" 26, 42
Discussions in the White Tiger Hall (*Bo Hu Tong*) 24, 45, 52, 54, 61
divinatory manuals 38, 41
divinatory rationalism 37–8
Duke of Zhou 35, 36, 61

E
"earlier kings" 26, 45
Eastern Zhou 42, 44, 61
eight trigrams 10, 33–4, 35, 41, 53, 54, 58–60
Eranos 49–51
ethical approach to the *Yi* 42–3
evolution of divinatory techniques 40

F
Fields of meaning 18, 20–1, 21–2, 23, 28–9, 30, 31
formulating a question to the *Yi Jing* 7–8
Froebe-Kapteyn, Olga 49, 50, 51
Fu Xi 33–4, 35, 36, 58, 61

G
great and small 31
Great Treatise *see Xi Ci*
gua 10, 34, 38, 39

H
Han dynasty 2, 24, 28, 33, 42, 44–5, 47, 52, 54, 61
hexagram tables 11, 17
Hexagrams in Pairs 25, 27
Huai Nan Zi 42, 54
hyphen 29

I
Image of the Situation 17, 21, 23, 24, 26, 27, 35, 47, 56
Image Tradition 26–7
introductory sentence of hexagrams 23

J
Jesuits in China 48, 61
jia gu wen 36–7
jun zi 26, 42
Jung, Carl Gustav 4, 5, 18, 48, 49–50

K
Kang Xi 23, 28, 47, 61
Keller, Alwina von 50
King Wen 30, 33, 34–6, 58, 61

L
Lai Zhi De 46, 61
Lao Nai-hsüan 48
Lao Zi 47
Li Ji 46
"lost texts" 44, 48
Lü Shi Chun Qiu 46

M
Mawangdui manuscript 44, 47–8, 61
mirror of the present 6
Mount Qi 35
mundus imaginalis 5

N
Needham, Joseph 52
nuclear hexagram *see* Counter Hexagram

O
old Yang 10, 12, 15
old Yin 10, 12, 15
one/one's 30–1
opened line 8, 9–10, 27, 47
oracular tradition 46, 61
order and chaos 3
order of the hexagrams 47
Otto, Rudolf 49, 50
Outer and Inner Trigram 24, 27, 54

P
Palace Edition of the *Yi Jing* 23, 27, 47, 61
Pattern King *see* King Wen
Patterns of Wisdom 26, 27, 35
Pinyin 2, 28
Pivot of Equalization 54, 56, 57, 60
Portmann, Adolf 50
potential hexagram 16, 23
Preceding Situation 25, 27
primary hexagram 15, 16, 24
pyromancy 37–8

Q
Qin dynasty 44
qualitative notion of time 3–4

R
Ritsema, Rudolf 49, 50–1
romanization of Chinese ideograms 28

S
School of Wisdom 49
sections of a hexagram 23–7
Sequence of Earlier Heaven 58
Sequence of Later Heaven 58
shamans 5, 36, 37, 38–9
Shang dynasty 5, 35, 37, 41, 61
Shi Ji 35
Shi Jing 46
Shu Jing 2, 45
Shuo Gua 24, 27, 35, 58–60
Shuo Wen 28
Si Ma Qian 35, 43
slash 29
Spring and Autumn 42, 43, 46, 61
Spring, Growing, Harvesting, Trial 56
stable lines 10, 16
Sung dynasty 12, 46
synchronicity 3–5

T
tai ji 9, 14, 54, 56
Ten Wings 23, 45, 47, 48
tortoise divination 37, 38, 39, 41, 61
Transformative Moments 53, 54, 57
transforming lines 10, 13, 16–17
Transforming Lines text 17, 24, 26, 27, 35, 47–8
Tuan Zhuan 24, 26, 27, 35, 36, 47
turning and rolling words in one's heart 18

U
Universal Compass 24, 34, 52–4, 56

V
Vandermeersch, Léon 37, 38, 39–41

W
Wade-Giles 28
Wang Bi 13–14
Wang Dongliang 37, 47
Warring States 42, 61
wen 36
Western Zhou 42, 61
whole line 8, 9–10, 27, 47
Wilhelm, Richard 4, 27, 48, 49, 50, 61
Wilhelm-Baynes translation 48–9, 61
Wu Xian 38–9

X
Xi Ci (Great Treatise) 13, 25, 27, 33–4, 34–5, 36, 46, 48

Xiang Zhuan 26, 27, 35, 36
Xu Gua 25, 27

Y
yarrow divination 37, 38–9, 41, 42, 44, 61
yarrow-stalk method 13–15
yi 2–3, 41, 42
Yin and Yang 3, 5, 8–10, 13, 39, 54–5
Yin-Yang cycle 9, 53, 54, 56, 57
young Yang 10, 12, 15
young Yin 10, 12, 15

Z
Za Gua 25, 27
Zhou dynasty 2, 33, 34, 35–6, 37, 38, 41–2, 43, 61
Zhou Li 41
Zhou Yi (Book of Encompassing Versatility) 2, 35, 41–4, 61
Zuo Zhuan 43

Part Two

The 64 Hexagrams

䷀ 01 Energy, *Qian* 74
䷁ 02 Space, *Kun* 84
䷂ 03 Sprouting, *Zhun* 95
䷃ 04 Enveloping, *Meng* 105
䷄ 05 Attending, *Xu* 114
䷅ 06 Arguing, *Song* 124
䷆ 07 The Legions, *Shi* 134
䷇ 08 Grouping, *Bi* 143
䷈ 09 The Small Accumulating, *Xiao Chu* 152
䷉ 10 Treading, *Lü* 161
䷊ 11 Compenetration, *Tai* 171
䷋ 12 Obstruction, *Pi* 181
䷌ 13 Concording People, *Tong Ren* 190
䷍ 14 The Great Possessing, *Da You* 200
䷎ 15 Humbling, *Qian* 209
䷏ 16 Providing, *Yu* 218

䷐ 17 FOLLOWING, *Sui* 228

䷑ 18 DECAY, *Gu* 237

䷒ 19 NEARING, *Lin* 246

䷓ 20 OVERSEEING, *Guan* 255

䷔ 21 GNAWING AND BITING, *Shi He* 264

䷕ 22 ADORNING, *Bi* 273

䷖ 23 STRIPPING, *Bo* 282

䷗ 24 RETURN, *Fu* 290

䷘ 25 WITHOUT ENTANGLEMENT, *Wu Wang* 300

䷙ 26 THE GREAT ACCUMULATING, *Da Chu* 309

䷚ 27 THE JAWS, *Yi* 318

䷛ 28 THE GREAT EXCEEDING, *Da Guo* 327

䷜ 29 THE GORGE, *Kan* 336

䷝ 30 THE RADIANCE, *Li* 345

䷞ 31 CONJUNCTION, *Xian* 354

䷟ 32 PERSEVERING, *Heng* 364

33 Retiring, *Dun* 374

34 The Great's Vigor, *Da Zhuang* 383

35 Prospering, *Jin* 391

36 Brightness Hidden, *Ming Yi* 400

37 Household People, *Jia Ren* 411

38 Polarizing, *Kui* 420

39 Limping, *Jian* 431

40 Unraveling, *Xie* 440

41 Diminishing, *Sun* 450

42 Augmenting, *Yi* 460

43 Parting, *Guai* 471

44 Coupling, *Gou* 481

45 Clustering, *Cui* 490

46 Ascending, *Sheng* 500

47 Confinement, *Kun* 508

48 The Well, *Jing* 519

49 Skinning, *Ge* 528

50 The Vessel, *Ding* 539

51 The Shake, *Zhen* 549

52 The Bound, *Gen* 558

53 Infiltrating, *Jian* 566

54 Converting Maidenhood, *Gui Mei* 576

55 Abounding, *Feng* 585

56 Sojourning, *Lü* 596

57 The Root, *Sun* 605

58 The Open, *Dui* 614

59 Dispersing, *Huan* 622

60 Articulating, *Jie* 631

61 The Center Conforming, *Zhong Fu* 640

62 The Small Exceeding, *Xiao Guo* 649

63 Already Fording, *Ji Ji* 659

64 Not Yet Fording, *Wei Ji* 668

乾

1 ENERGY | *Qian*

The situation described by this hexagram is characterized by the dominance of Yang, the active quality of being which is the base of all creation and destruction, unceasingly driving forward and ever renewing itself. In excess, this force may burn its own creations before they take concrete form. The hexagram Energy is the doubling of the corresponding trigram, and partakes of its attributes.

Image of the Situation

Energy.
Spring, Growing, Harvesting, Trial.

Fields of meaning

Energy/parch, *QIAN/GAN*: unceasing forward movement, dynamic, enduring, untiring; spirit power, manifestation of Yang, that activates all creation and destruction in Space; heaven, sovereign, father. With the pronunciation *GAN*: parch, dry up, burn, exhaust. Ideogram: sprouts or vapors rising from the ground and sunlight, both fecundating moisture and scorching drought. *Symbol*: heaven, *TIAN*; sky, firmament, heavens; the highest realm, situated above the human world, as opposed to the earth, *DI*, located below. Ideogram: great and the one above. *Action*: persist, *JIAN*; tenacious, persevering; strong, robust, dynamic; constant as the motion of heavenly bodies in their orbits. In the family of trigrams *QIAN* is the father. **Spring, Growing, Harvesting, Trial**, *YUAN HENG LI ZHEN*: Spring, Growing, Harvesting and Trial are the four stages of the Time Cycle, the model for all dynamic processes. They indicate that your question is connected to the cycle as a whole rather than a part of it.

Outer and Inner Trigram

In this hexagram the outer and inner aspects of the situation are identical and they are described by the trigram **Energy/parch**, *QIAN/GAN*. Its associations are listed in the corresponding *Field of meaning* above.

Hexagrams in Pairs

Energy: solid.
Space: supple.

Fields of meaning

Energy/parch, *QIAN/GAN*: see *Image of the Situation*. **Solid**, *GANG*: quality of the whole lines; firm, strong, unyielding, persisting. **Space**, *KUN*: surface of the world; support of all existence, manifestation of Yin, where Energy or Yang activates all creation and destruction; all-involving service; earth; moon, wife, mother; rest, receptivity, docile obedience. **Supple**, *ROU*: quality of the opened lines; flexible, pliant, adaptable, tender.

Patterns of Wisdom

Heaven moves persistently.
A **jun zi uses originating strength not** to **pause.**

Fields of meaning

Heaven, *TIAN*: sky, firmament, heavens; the highest realm, situated above the human world, as opposed to the earth, *DI*, located below; Symbol of the trigram Energy, *QIAN*. Ideogram: great and the one above. **Move**, *XING*: move or move something; motivate; emotionally moving; walk, act, do. Ideogram: successive steps. **Persist**, *JIAN*: tenacious, persevering; strong, robust, dynamic; constant as the motion of heavenly bodies in their orbits; Action of the trigram Force, *QIAN*. **Jun zi**: ideal of a person who orders his/her life in accordance with dao rather than willful intention, and uses divination in this spirit. **Use**, *YI*: by means of; owing to; make use of, employ. **Origin**, *ZI*: source, beginning, ground; cause, reason, motive; tracing back to the source; oneself, by oneself; spontaneous, intrinsic. **Strength**, *QIANG*: force, vigor; fortify, invigorate; compel, rely on force; overcome; effort, labor; determined, stubborn. **Not**, *BU*: common term of negation. **Pause**, *XI*: breathe; rest, repose, a breathing-spell; suspended.

Transforming Lines

INITIAL NINE

Immersed dragon, no availing of.

Comments

Immersed dragon, no availing of.
Yang located below indeed.

Fields of meaning
Immerse, *QIAN*: submerge, hide in water; deep, secret, reserved; retire, withdraw. **Dragon**, *LONG*: mythical spirit-being endowed with supreme power, associated with the energy of heaven; can change its shape at will; sleeps under the earth or at the bottom of the waters, wherefrom it emerges in the springtime and rises up to heaven. In the Universal Compass it is associated with the East and with the beginning of the Yang hemicycle. **No**, *WU*: common term of negation. **Avail**, *YONG*: use, employ for a specific purpose; take advantage of; benefit from; capacity. Ideogram: to divine and center, applying divination to central concerns.

Yang, *YANG*: sunny slope of a hill, sunny bank of a river; dynamic and bright aspect of the basic duality (Yin and Yang) manifesting in all phenomena; Yang arouses, transforms and dissolves existing structures; linear thrust, stimulus, drive, focus; quality of a whole line. **Locate**, *ZAI*: be at, be situated at, dwell, reside; in, within; involved with, in the process of. Ideogram: earth and persevere, a place on the earth. **Below**, *XIA*: anything below, in all senses; lower, inner; lower trigram. **Indeed**, *YE*: emphasizes and intensifies the previous statement.

NINE AT SECOND

Viewing a **dragon located** in the **fields**.
Harvesting: **viewing** the **great** in the **person**.

Comments
Viewing a **dragon located** in the **fields**.
Actualizing-dao spreading throughout indeed.

Fields of meaning
View, *JIAN*: vision in all its aspects: seeing, being visible, forming mental images; visit, call on, consult. Ideogram: eye above person, active and receptive sight. **Dragon**, *LONG*: mythical spirit-being endowed with supreme power, associated with the energy of heaven; can change its shape at will; sleeps under the earth or at the bottom of the waters, wherefrom it emerges in the springtime and rises up to heaven. In the Universal Compass it is associated with the East and with the beginning of the Yang hemicycle. **Locate**, *ZAI*: be at, be situated at, dwell, reside; in, within; involved with, in the process of. Ideogram: earth and persevere, a place on the earth. **Field**, *TIAN*: cultivated land, farming land; preferred terrain for hunting, since game in the fields cannot escape the hunt. Ideogram: square divided into four sections, delineating fields. **Harvest**, *LI*: benefit, advantage, profit; realization; sharp, acute, insightful; quality of autumn and West, third stage of the Time Cycle. Ideogram: ripe grain and blade. **Great**, *DA*: big, noble,

important, very; orient the will toward a self-imposed goal, impose direction; ability to lead or guide one's life; contrasts with small, *XIAO*, flexible adaptation to what crosses one's path. **Person/people**, *REN*: humans individually and collectively; an individual; humankind.

Actualize-dao, *DE*: realize dao in action; power, virtue; ability to follow the course traced by the ongoing process of the cosmos. Ideogram: go, straight, and heart. Linked with acquire, *DE*: acquiring that which makes a being become what it is meant to be. **Spread**, *SHI*: expand, diffuse, distribute, arrange, exhibit; add to; aid. Ideogram: flag and indeed, claiming new country. **Throughout**, *PU*: everywhere; universal, general; great, vast. Ideogram: sun and equal, equal to sunlight. **Indeed**, *YE*: emphasizes and intensifies the previous statement.

Nine at Third

A **jun zi completing** the **day: energy parching.**
At **nightfall awe like** in **adversity.**
Without fault.

Comments
Completing the **day: energy parching.**
Reversing: returning to **dao indeed.**

Fields of meaning

Jun zi: see *Patterns of Wisdom*. **Complete**, *ZHONG*: completion of a cycle that begins the next; entire, whole, all. Ideogram: silk cocoons, follow and ice, winter linking one year with the next. **Day/sun**, *RI*: the sun and the time of a sun-cycle, a day. **Energy/parch**, *QIAN/GAN*: see *Image of the Situation*. **Nightfall**, *XI*: day's end, dusk; late; last day of month or year. **Awe**, *TI*: respect, regard, fear; alarmed and cautious, worried; on guard. Ideogram: heart and versatility, the heart expecting change. **Like**, *RUO*: same as, just as; conform, imitate; adverbial suffix indicating similarity. **Adversity**, *LI*: danger, hardship, severe; threat or difficulty that must be encountered, rather than avoided; grinding stone; polish, sharpen; a challenge that strengthens and perfects the character; stimulate, excite; cruel demon. **Without fault**, *WU JIU*: no error or harm in the situation.

Reverse, *FAN*: turn and move in the opposite direction; turn around or upside down (180 degrees); change to the opposite position; contrary. **Return**, *FU*: go back, turn or lead back; recur, reappear, come again; restore, renew, recover; return to an earlier time or place. Ideogram: step and retrace a path. **Dao**, *DAO*: way or path; ongoing process of being and the course it traces for each person or thing; ultimate reality, intrinsic nature; origin. Ideogram: go and head, opening a path.

Indeed, *YE*: emphasizes and intensifies the previous statement.

Nine at Fourth

Maybe capering located at the **abyss.**
Without fault.

Comments
Maybe capering located at the **abyss.**
Advancing: without fault indeed.

Fields of meaning
Maybe, *HUO*: possible but not certain, perhaps. **Caper**, *YUE*: play, frolic, dance and leap for joy, frisk, gambol. Ideogram: foot and feather, light-footed. **Locate**, *ZAI*: be at, be situated at, dwell, reside; in, within; involved with, in the process of. Ideogram: earth and persevere, a place on the earth. **Abyss**, *YUAN*: deep hole or gulf, where backwaters eddy and accumulate; whirlpool, deep water; unfathomable; depth of feelings, deep sincerity. **Without fault**, *WU JIU*: no error or harm in the situation.

Advance, *JIN*: move forward, progress, climb; promote or be promoted; further the development of, augment; offer, introduce. **Indeed**, *YE*: emphasizes and intensifies the previous statement.

Nine at Fifth

Flying dragon located in **heaven.**
Harvesting: viewing the **great** in the **person.**

Comments
Flying dragon located in **heaven.**
The **great** in the **person creative indeed.**

Fields of meaning
Fly, *FEI*: rise in the air, spread one's wings, fly away; let fly; swift. **Dragon**, *LONG*: mythical spirit-being endowed with supreme power, associated with the energy of heaven; can change its shape at will; sleeps under the earth or at the bottom of the waters, wherefrom it emerges in the springtime and rises up to heaven. In the Universal Compass it is associated with the East and with the beginning of the Yang hemicycle. **Locate**, *ZAI*: be at, be situated at, dwell, reside; in, within; involved with, in the process of. Ideogram: earth and persevere, a place on the

earth. **Heaven**, *TIAN*: see *Patterns of Wisdom*. **Harvest**, *LI*: benefit, advantage, profit; realization; sharp, acute, insightful; quality of autumn and West, third stage of the Time Cycle. Ideogram: ripe grain and blade. **View**, *JIAN*: vision in all its aspects: seeing, being visible, forming mental images; visit, call on, consult. Ideogram: eye above person, active and receptive sight. **Great**, *DA*: big, noble, important, very; orient the will toward a self-imposed goal, impose direction; ability to lead or guide one's life; contrasts with small, *XIAO*, flexible adaptation to what crosses one's path. **Person/people**, *REN*: humans individually and collectively; an individual; humankind.

Create, *ZAO*: make, construct, build, form, establish. **Indeed**, *YE*: emphasizes and intensifies the previous statement.

NINE ABOVE

䷀

Overbearing dragon possesses repenting.

Comments

Overbearing dragon possesses repenting.
Overfilling not permitting to **last indeed.**

Fields of meaning

Overbearing, *KANG*: haughty, fierce, overpowering, rigid, unbending; excessive display of force. **Dragon**, *LONG*: mythical spirit-being endowed with supreme power, associated with the energy of heaven; can change its shape at will; sleeps under the earth or at the bottom of the waters, wherefrom it emerges in the springtime and rises up to heaven. In the Universal Compass it is associated with the East and with the beginning of the Yang hemicycle. **Possess**, *YOU*: general term indicating possession; have, own, be endowed with. **Repent**, *HUI*: regret, dissatisfaction with past conduct inducing a change of heart; proceeds from abashment, *LIN*, shame and confusion at having lost the right way.

Overfill, *YING*: fill completely; full, at the point of overflowing; excess, arrogance. Ideogram: vessel and overflow. **Not**, *BU*: common term of negation. **Permit**, *KE*: possible because in harmony with an inherent principle; capable of; approve, authorize. Ideogram: mouth and breath, silent consent. **Last**, *JIU*: endure; long, protracted, permanent, eternal; old, ancient. **Indeed**, *YE*: emphasizes and intensifies the previous statement.

AVAILING OF NINES (ALL LINES TRANSFORMING)

䷀

Viewing a **flock** of **dragons without head.**
Significant.

Comments
Availing of **nines.**
Heavenly actualizing-dao not permitting activating head indeed.

Fields of meaning

View, *JIAN*: vision in all its aspects: seeing, being visible, forming mental images; visit, call on, consult. Ideogram: eye above person, active and receptive sight. **Flock**, *QUN*: herd, group; people of the same kind, friends, equals; crowd, multitude; move in unison, flock together. Ideogram: chief and sheep, flock around a leader. **Dragon**, *LONG*: mythical spirit-being endowed with supreme power, associated with the energy of heaven; can change its shape at will; sleeps under the earth or at the bottom of the waters, wherefrom it emerges in the springtime and rises up to heaven. In the Universal Compass it is associated with the East and with the beginning of the Yang hemicycle. **Without**, *WU*: devoid of; there is not. **Head**, *SHOU*: physical head; leader, sovereign; beginning, origin, model; foremost, superior, upper, front. **Significant**, *JI*: leads to the experience of meaning; favorable, propitious, appropriate. Ideogram: scholar and mouth, wise words of a sage.

Avail, *YONG*: use, employ for a specific purpose; take advantage of; benefit from; capacity. Ideogram: to divine and center, applying divination to central concerns. **Nine**, *JIU*: number nine; transforming whole line; superlative: best, perfect. **Heaven**, *TIAN*: see *Patterns of Wisdom*. **Actualize-dao**, *DE*: realize dao in action; power, virtue; ability to follow the course traced by the ongoing process of the cosmos. Ideogram: go, straight, and heart. Linked with acquire, *DE*: acquiring that which makes a being become what it is meant to be. **Not**, *BU*: common term of negation. **Permit**, *KE*: possible because in harmony with an inherent principle; capable of; approve, authorize. Ideogram: mouth and breath, silent consent. **Activate**, *WEI*: act or cause to act; do, make, manage, make active; be, become; attend to, help; because of. **Indeed**, *YE*: emphasizes and intensifies the previous statement.

Image Tradition

The **great: in-fact energy**'s **Spring.**
The **myriad beings' own beginning.**

Thereupon primordial heaven.
Clouds moving, rain spreading.
The **kinds** of **beings diffuse** in **forms.**

The **great brightening completes** the **beginning.**
In the **six positions** the **season accomplishes.**
The **season rides six dragons used** to **drive** up to **heaven.**

Energy's **dao transforming** and **changing.**
Each correcting innate fate.
Protection: uniting with the **great**'s **harmony.**

Thereupon Harvesting, Trial.
Heads emerging from the **multitude** of **beings.**
The **myriad cities conjoining** to **soothe.**

Fields of meaning

Great, *DA*: big, noble, important, very; orient the will toward a self-imposed goal, impose direction; ability to lead or guide one's life; contrasts with small, *XIAO*, flexible adaptation to what crosses one's path. **In-fact**, *ZAI*: emphatic exclamation; truly, indeed. **Energy/parch**, *QIAN/GAN*: see *Image of the Situation*. **Spring**, *YUAN*: source, origin, head; arise, begin; first generating impulse; great, excellent; quality of springtime and East, first stage of the Time Cycle. **Myriad**, *WAN*: ten thousand; countless, many, everyone. Ideogram: swarm of insects. **Being**, *WU*: creature, thing, any single being; matter, substance, essence; nature of things. **Own**, *ZI*: possession and the things possessed; avail of, depend on; property, riches. **Begin**, *SHI*: commence, start, open; earliest, first; generate. Ideogram: woman and eminent, eminent feminine function of giving birth.

Thereupon, *NAI*: on that ground, then, only then; finally; in spite of that. **Primordial**, *TONG*: original; beginning of a series or lineage; clue, hint; whole, general. **Heaven**, *TIAN*: see *Patterns of Wisdom*. **Clouds**, *YUN*: fog, mist, water vapor; connected with the Streaming Moment. **Move**, *XING*: see *Patterns of Wisdom*. **Rain**, *YU*: rain and all precipitations; sudden shower, fast and furious; abundant dispensation of benefits; associated with the trigram Gorge, *KAN*, and the Streaming Moment. **Spread**, *SHI*: expand, diffuse, distribute, arrange, exhibit; add to; aid. Ideogram: flag and indeed, claiming new country. **Kinds**, *PIN*: species and their essential qualities; sort, class, degree; numerous, innumerable. **Diffuse**, *LIU*: flow out, spread, permeate. **Form**, *XING*: shape, bodily or material appearance; aspect, configuration, circumstance.

Brightness, *MING*: light, radiance, clarity; distinguish, discern, understand; light-giving aspect of fire, of heavenly bodies and of consciousness; brightness and fire are the Symbols of the trigram Radiance, *LI*. **Complete**, *ZHONG*: completion of a cycle that begins the next; entire, whole, all. Ideogram: silk cocoons, follow and ice, winter linking one year with the next. **Six**, *LIU*: number six; transforming opened line; six lines of a hexagram. **Position**, *WEI*: place, location; be at; social standing, rank; position of a line in a hexagram. Ideogram: person standing. **Season**, *SHI*: quality of the time; the right time, opportune, in harmony; planning in accord with the time; season of the year. Ideogram: sun and temple, sacred time. **Accomplish**, *CHENG*: complete, finish, bring about; perfect, full, whole; play one's part, do one's duty; mature. Ideogram: weapon and man, able to bear arms, thus fully developed. **Ride**, *CHENG*: ride an animal or a chariot; have the upper hand, control a stronger power; an opened line above controlling a whole line below. **Dragon**, *LONG*: mythical spirit-being endowed with supreme power, associated with the energy of heaven; can change its shape at will; sleeps under the earth or at the bottom of the waters, wherefrom it emerges in the springtime and rises up to heaven. In the Universal Compass it is associated with the East and with the beginning of the Yang hemicycle. **Use**, *YI*: see *Patterns of Wisdom*. **Drive**, *YU*: drive a cart, ride or tame a horse; govern, rule. With the pronunciation *YA*: go to meet, encounter. **Heaven**, *TIAN*: see *Patterns of Wisdom*.

Dao, *DAO*: way or path; ongoing process of being and the course it traces for each person or thing; ultimate reality, intrinsic nature; origin. Ideogram: go and head, opening a path. **Transform**, *BIAN*: abrupt, radical passage from one state to another; transformation of opened and whole lines into each other in hexagrams; contrasts with change, *HUA*, gradual mutation. **Change**, *HUA*: gradual, continuous change; melt, dissolve; be born, die; influence; contrasts with transform, *BIAN*, sudden mutation. Ideogram: person alive and dead, the life process. **Each**, *GE*: each separate person or thing; particular, distinct; every, all. **Correct**, *ZHENG*: rectify deviation or one-sidedness; proper, straight, exact, regular; constant, rule, model. Ideogram: stop and one, hold to one thing. **Innate**, *XING*: inborn character; spirit, quality, ability; natural, without constraint. Ideogram: heart and produce, spontaneous feeling. **Fate**, *MING*: individual destiny; birth and death as limits of life; issue orders with authority; consult the gods. Ideogram: mouth and order, words with heavenly authority. **Protect**, *BAO*: guard, defend, keep safe; nourish, support. **Unite**, *HE*: join, match, correspond; unison, harmony;

together; close the jaws, shut the mouth. Ideogram: mouths speaking in unison. **Harmony**, *HE*: concord, union; conciliate; at peace, mild; fit, tune, adjust.

Harvest, *LI*: benefit, advantage, profit; realization; sharp, acute, insightful; quality of autumn and West, third stage of the Time Cycle. Ideogram: ripe grain and blade. **Trial**, *ZHEN*: inquiry by divination and its result; righteous, firm; separating wheat from chaff; the kernel, the proven core; quality of winter and North, fourth stage of the Time Cycle. Ideogram: pearl and divination. **Head**, *SHOU*: physical head; leader, sovereign; beginning, origin, model; foremost, superior, upper, front. **Emerge**, *CHU*: come out of, proceed from, spring from, issue forth; appear, be born; bear, generate; leave, flee; Action of the trigram Shake, *ZHEN*. Ideogram: stem with branches and leaves emerging. **Multitude**, *SHU*: crowd, many people; mass, herd; all, the whole. **City**, *GUO*: city, state, country, nation; area of only human constructions; first of the territorial zones: city, suburbs, countryside, forest. **Conjoin**, *XIAN*: come in contact with, join; put together as parts of a previously separated whole; conjunction of celestial bodies; totally, completely; accord, harmony, mutual influence; lit.: broken piece of pottery, the halves of which join to identify partners. **Soothe**, *NING*: calm, pacify; create peace of mind; tranquil, quiet. Ideogram: shelter above heart, dish and breath, physical and spiritual comfort.

坤 ䷁

2 SPACE | *Kun*

The situation described by this hexagram is characterized by the dominance of Yin, the receptive and formative quality of being that allows all things to become what they are, available and nurturing like the surface of the earth supporting all creatures. In excess, this receptivity may become dull, inert immobility. The hexagram Space is the doubling of the corresponding trigram, and partakes of its attributes.

Image of the Situation

> **Space.**
> **Spring, Growing, Harvesting, Trial belonging** to the **female horse.**
> A **jun zi possesses directed going.**
> **Beforehand delusion, afterwards acquiring.**
> A **lord Harvesting.**
> **Western South: acquiring partnering.**
> **Eastern North: losing partnering.**
> **Peaceful Trial, significant.**

Fields of meaning

Space, *KUN*: surface of the world; support of all existence, manifestation of Yin, where Energy or Yang activates all creation and destruction; all-involving service; earth; moon, wife, mother; rest, receptivity, docile obedience. Ideogram: terrestrial globe and stretch out. *Symbol*: earth, *DI*; the earth, ground on which the human world rests; basis of all things, nourishes all things; essential Yin. *Action*: yield, *SHUN*: give way, comply, agree, follow, obey; docile, flexible; bear produce, nourish, provide. In the family of trigrams *KUN* is the mother. **Spring, Growing, Harvesting, Trial**, *YUAN HENG LI ZHEN*: Spring, Growing, Harvesting and Trial are the four stages of the Time Cycle, the model for all dynamic processes. They indicate that your question is connected to the cycle as a whole rather than a part of it. Here this is further qualified by associating Trial, the fourth stage of the Time Cycle, with the qualities belonging to a mare. **Belong/it**, *ZHI*: establishes between two terms a connection similar to the Saxon genitive, in which the second term belongs to the first one; at the end of a sentence it refers to something previously mentioned or implied. **Female**, *PIN*: female animal; female sexual organs, particularly of farm animals; concave, hollow. Ideogram: cattle and ladle, a hollow, reproductive organ. **Horse**, *MA*: symbol of spirited strength in the natural world, earthly counterpart of the dragon; associated with the trigram Energy, *QIAN*, heaven, and high noon. **Jun zi**: ideal of a person who orders his/her life in accordance with dao rather than willful intention, and uses divination in this spirit. **Possessing directed going**, *YOU YOU WANG*: having a goal or purpose, moving in a specific direction. **Before(hand)/earlier**, *XIAN*: anterior, preceding in time; former, past, previous; first, at first. **Delude**, *MI*: bewitch, fascinate, deceive; confused, stupefied, infatuated; blinded by vice. **After(wards)/later**, *HOU*: come after in time, subsequent; put oneself after; behind, back, draw back; the second; attendants, heirs, successors, posterity. **Acquire**, *DE*: obtain the desired object; possession; satisfied, fulfilled; it is permitted; agree with; wish for, desire covetously. Ideogram: go and obstacle, going through obstacles to the goal. **Lord**, *ZHU*: ruler, master, chief, authority; host; domination in the cycle of the Five Transformative Moments. Ideogram: lamp and flame, giving light. **Harvest**, *LI*: benefit, advantage, profit; realization; sharp, acute, insightful; quality of autumn and West, third stage of the Time Cycle. Ideogram: ripe grain and blade. **Western South**, *XI NAN*: corresponds to the neutral Earthy Moment between the Yang and Yin hemicycles; bring forth concrete results, ripe fruits of late summer. **Partner**, *PENG*: companion, friend, peer; join, associate for mutual benefit; commercial venture; two equal or similar things. Ideogram: linked strings of cowrys or coins. **Eastern North**, *DONG BEI*: the Eastern side of North, direction corresponding to the completion of a cycle; border, limit, boundary; mountain; accomplishing words, summing up previous experience; dark, cold winter night. **Lose**, *SANG*: be deprived of, forget; destruction, ruin, death; corpse; lament, mourn; funeral. Ideogram: weep and dead. **Peace**, *AN*: quiet, still, settled, secure, contented; calm, tranquilize, console. Ideogram: woman under a roof, a tranquil home. **Trial**, *ZHEN*: inquiry by divination and its result; righteous, firm; separating wheat from chaff; the kernel, the proven core; quality of winter and North, fourth stage of the Time Cycle. Ideogram: pearl and divination. **Significant**, *JI*: leads to the experience of meaning; favorable, propitious, appropriate. Ideogram: scholar and mouth, wise words of a sage.

Outer and Inner Trigram

In this hexagram the outer and inner aspects of the situation are identical, and they are described by the trigram **Space**, *KUN*. Its associations are listed in the corresponding *Field of meaning* above.

Hexagrams in Pairs

Energy: solid.
Space: supple.

Fields of meaning

Energy/parch, *QIAN/GAN*: unceasing forward movement, dynamic, enduring, untiring; spirit power, manifestation of Yang, that activates all creation and destruction in Space; heaven, sovereign, father. With the pronunciation *GAN*: parch, dry up, burn, exhaust. Ideogram: sprouts or vapors rising from the ground and sunlight, both fecundating moisture and scorching drought. **Solid**, *GANG*: quality of the whole lines; firm, strong, unyielding, persisting. **Space**, *KUN*: see *Image of the Situation*. **Supple**, *ROU*: quality of the opened lines; flexible, pliant, adaptable, tender.

Patterns of Wisdom

Earth's **potency**: **space**.
A **jun zi uses munificent actualizing-dao** to **carry** the **beings**.

Fields of meaning

Earth, *DI*: the earth, ground on which the human world rests; basis of all things, nourishes all things; essential Yin; Symbol of the trigram Space, *KUN*. **Potency**, *SHI*: power, influence, strength; authority, dignity. Ideogram: strength and skill. **Space**, *KUN*: see *Image of the Situation*. **Jun zi**: see *Image of the Situation*. **Use**, *YI*: by means of; owing to; make use of, employ. **Munificent**, *HOU*: liberal, kind, generous; create abundance; thick, large. Ideogram: gift of a superior to an inferior. **Actualize-dao**, *DE*: realize dao in action; power, virtue; ability to follow the course traced by the ongoing process of the cosmos. Ideogram: go, straight, and heart. Linked with acquire, *DE*: acquiring that which makes a being become what it is meant to be. **Carry**, *ZAI*: bear, carry with you; contain, sustain, support; load a ship or cart, cargo; fill in. **Being**, *WU*: creature, thing, any single being; matter, substance, essence; nature of things.

Transforming Lines

INITIAL SIX

Treading frost, hard ice as **culmination**.

Comments
Treading frost, hard ice.
Yin beginning solidification indeed.
Docile involvement in **one's dao**.
Culmination: **hard ice indeed**.

Fields of meaning

Tread, *LÜ*: walk a path or way; step, path, track; footsteps; course of the stars; appropriate action; virtue; salary, means of subsistence. Ideogram: body and repeating steps. **Frost**, *SHUANG*: frozen dew, hoar-frost; severe, frigid. **Hard**, *JIAN*: solid, strong, rigid; harden, fortify, consolidate; resolute, fearless. **Ice**, *BING*: frozen water; icy, freezing; clear, pure. **Culminate**, *ZHI*: bring to the highest degree; arrive at the end or summit; superlative; reaching one's goal.

Yin, *YIN*: shady slope of a hill or bank of a river; consolidating, dark aspect of the basic duality (Yin and Yang) manifesting in all phenomena; Yin creates and conserves structure; spatial extension; build, make things concrete; quality of an opened line. **Begin**, *SHI*: commence, start, open; earliest, first; generate. Ideogram: woman and eminent, eminent feminine function of giving birth. **Solidify**, *NING*: congeal, freeze, curdle, stiffen; coagulate, make solid or firm. **Indeed**, *YE*: emphasizes and intensifies the previous statement. **Docile**, *XÜN*: amiable, mild, yielding, tame; gradual; a docile horse. **Involve**, *ZHI*: devote oneself to; induce, cause, implicate; approach; manifest, express; reach the highest degree of. Ideogram: reach and come up behind. **One/one's**, *QI*: general third person pronoun and possessive adjective; also: it/its, he/his, she/her, they/their. **Dao**, *DAO*: way or path; ongoing process of being and the course it traces for each person or thing; ultimate reality, intrinsic nature; origin. Ideogram: go and head, opening a path.

SIX AT SECOND

Straightening on all **sides**: the **great**.
Not repeating: **without not Harvesting**.

Comments

To **six** at **second belongs stirring-up**.
Straightening used on all **sides indeed**.
Not repeating: **without not Harvesting**.
Earth's **dao shines indeed**.

Fields of meaning

Straighten, *ZHI*: rectify; upright; correct the crooked; proceed directly; sincere, just; blunt, outspoken. **Sides**, *FANG*: cardinal directions; surface of the earth extending to the four cardinal points; everywhere; limits, boundaries. **Great**, *DA*: big, noble, important, very; orient the will toward a self-imposed goal, impose direction; ability to lead or guide one's life; contrasts with small, *XIAO*, flexible adaptation to what crosses one's path. **Not**, *BU*: common term of negation. **Repeat**, *XI*: perform a series of similar acts, practice, rehearse; habit, custom; familiar with, skilled. Ideogram: little bird practicing flight. **Without not Harvesting**, *WU BU LI*: turning point where the balance is swinging from not Harvesting to actually Harvesting.

Six, *LIU*: number six; transforming opened line; six lines of a hexagram. **Two/second**, *ER*: number two; pair, even numbers, binary, duplicate. **Belong/it**, *ZHI*: see *Image of the Situation*. **Stir-up**, *DONG*: excite, influence, move, affect; work, take action; come out of the egg or the bud; Action of the trigram Shake, *ZHEN*. Ideogram: strength and heavy, move weighty things. **Use**, *YI*: see *Patterns of Wisdom*. **Indeed**, *YE*: emphasizes and intensifies the previous statement. **Earth**, *DI*: see *Patterns of Wisdom*. **Dao**, *DAO*: way or path; ongoing process of being and the course it traces for each person or thing; ultimate reality, intrinsic nature; origin. Ideogram: go and head, opening a path. **Shine**, *GUANG*: illuminate, emit light; brilliant, splendid; honor, glory, éclat; distinct from brightness, *MING*, light of heavenly bodies. Ideogram: fire above person.

Six at Third

Containing composition permits Trial.
Maybe adhering to **kingly affairs**.
Without accomplishing, **possessing completion**.

Comments

Containing composition permits Trial.
Using the **season** to **shoot-forth indeed**.
Maybe adhering to **kingly affairs**.
Knowing the **shine** of the **great indeed**.

Fields of meaning

Contain, *HAN*: retain, embody, cherish; withhold, tolerate; contain in the mouth, put a coin in a corpse's mouth. **Composition**, *ZHANG*: a well-composed whole and its structure; beautiful creation; elegant, clear, brilliant; chapter, strophe; distinct from pattern, *WEN*, beauty of intrinsic design. **Permit**, *KE*: possible because in harmony with an inherent principle; capable of; approve, authorize. Ideogram: mouth and breath, silent consent. **Trial**, *ZHEN*: see *Image of the Situation*. **Maybe**, *HUO*: possible but not certain, perhaps. **Adhere**, *CONG*: follow, agree with, comply with, obey; join a doctrine, school, or person; servant, follower. Ideogram: two men walking, one following the other. **King**, *WANG*: sovereign, effective ruler, emperor, seen as connecting heaven and earth; reign, govern. **Affairs**, *SHI*: all kinds of personal activity; matters at hand; business; function, occupation; manage; perform a task; incident, event; case in court. **Without**, *WU*: devoid of; there is not. **Accomplish**, *CHENG*: complete, finish, bring about; perfect, full, whole; play one's part, do one's duty; mature. Ideogram: weapon and man, able to bear arms, thus fully developed. **Possess**, *YOU*: general term indicating possession; have, own, be endowed with. **Complete**, *ZHONG*: completion of a cycle that begins the next; entire, whole, all. Ideogram: silk cocoons, follow and ice, winter linking one year with the next.

Use, *YI*: see *Patterns of Wisdom*. **Season**, *SHI*: quality of the time; the right time, opportune, in harmony; planning in accord with the time; season of the year. Ideogram: sun and temple, sacred time. **Shoot-forth**, *FA*: emit, send out, shoot an arrow; ferment, rise; express, raise one's voice. Ideogram: stance, bow and arrow, shooting from a solid base. **Indeed**, *YE*: emphasizes and intensifies the previous statement. **Know**, *ZHI*: have knowledge of, perceive, experience, remember; know intimately; informed, aware, wise. Ideogram: arrow and mouth, words focused and swift. **Shine**, *GUANG*: illuminate, emit light; brilliant, splendid; honor, glory, éclat; distinct from brightness, *MING*, light of heavenly bodies. Ideogram: fire above person. **Great**, *DA*: big, noble, important, very; orient the will toward a self-imposed goal, impose direction; ability to lead or guide one's life; contrasts with small, *XIAO*, flexible adaptation to what crosses one's path.

Six at Fourth

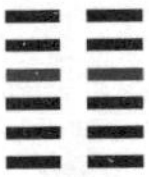

Bundled in the **bag**.
Without fault, without praise.

Comments
Bundled in the **bag, without fault**.
Considering not harmful indeed.

Fields of meaning

Bundle, *GUA*: enclose, envelop, tie up; embrace, include. **Bag**, *NANG*: sack, purse, put in a bag; property, salary. **Without fault**, *WU JIU*: no error or harm in the situation. **Without**, *WU*: devoid of; there is not. **Praise**, *YU*: magnify, eulogize; flatter; fame, reputation. Ideogram: offering words.

Consider, *SHEN*: act carefully, seriously; cautious, attentive, circumspect; still, quiet, sincere. Ideogram: heart and true. **Not**, *BU*: common term of negation. **Harm**, *HAI*: damage, injure, offend; suffer, become ill; obstacle, hindrance; fearful, anxious. **Indeed**, *YE*: emphasizes and intensifies the previous statement.

SIX AT FIFTH

A **yellow apron**. **Spring**, **significant**.

Comments

A **yellow apron**: **Spring**, **significant**.
Pattern located in the **center indeed**.

Fields of meaning

Yellow, *HUANG*: color of the soil in central China, associated with the Earthy Moment leading from the Yang to the Yin hemicycle; emblematic and imperial color of China since the Yellow Emperor (2500 BC). **Apron**, *SHANG*: ceremonial garment; skirt, clothes; curtains of a carriage. Ideogram: garment and manifest, clothing as display. **Spring**, *YUAN*: source, origin, head; arise, begin; first generating impulse; great, excellent; quality of springtime and East, first stage of the Time Cycle. **Significant**, *JI*: see *Image of the Situation*.

Pattern, *WEN*: intrinsic or natural design, pattern of wood, stone or animal fur; ideograms, the symbols of writing as revelation of the intrinsic nature of things; language, civilization, culture; harmonious, beautiful, elegant, polite. **Locate**, *ZAI*: be at, be situated at, dwell, reside; in, within; involved with, in the process of. Ideogram: earth and persevere, a place on the earth. **Center**, *ZHONG*: inner, central; put in the center; middle, stable point enabling you to face inner and outer changes; middle line of a trigram. Ideogram: field divided in two equal parts. **Indeed**, *YE*: emphasizes and intensifies the previous statement.

SIX ABOVE

Dragons struggle tending-towards the **countryside**.
Their blood indigo and **yellow**.

Comments

Dragons struggle tending-towards the **countryside.**

Their dao exhausted indeed.

Fields of meaning

Dragon, *LONG*: mythical spirit-being endowed with supreme power, associated with the energy of heaven; can change its shape at will; sleeps under the earth or at the bottom of the waters, wherefrom it emerges in the springtime and rises up to heaven. In the Universal Compass it is associated with the East and with the beginning of the Yang hemicycle. **Struggle**, *ZHAN*: battle, fight, combat; hostilities; alarmed, terrified. **Tend-towards**, *YU*: move toward without necessarily reaching, in the direction of. **Countryside**, *YE*: cultivated fields and grassland, where nature and human construction interact; third of the territorial zones: city, suburbs, countryside, forest. **They/their**, *QI*: general third person pronoun and possessive adjective; also: one/one's, it/its, he/his, she/her. **Blood**, *XUE*: blood, the Yin fluid that maintains life; money, property. **Indigo**, *XUAN*: color associated with the Metallic Moment; deep blue-black, color of the sky's depths; profound, subtle, deep. **Yellow**, *HUANG*: color of the soil in central China, associated with the Earthy Moment leading from the Yang to the Yin hemicycle; emblematic and imperial color of China since the Yellow Emperor (2500 BC).

Dao, *DAO*: way or path; ongoing process of being and the course it traces for each person or thing; ultimate reality, intrinsic nature; origin. Ideogram: go and head, opening a path. **Exhaust**, *QIONG*: bring to an end; limit, extremity; investigate exhaustively; destitute, indigent; end without a new beginning; distinct from complete, *ZHONG*, end of a cycle that begins the next one. Ideogram: cave and naked person, bent with disease or old age. **Indeed**, *YE*: emphasizes and intensifies the previous statement.

AVAILING OF SIXES (ALL LINES TRANSFORMING)

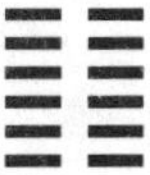

Harvesting perpetual Trial.

Comments

Availing of **sixes**: **perpetual Trial.**

Using the **great** for **completion indeed.**

Fields of meaning

Harvest, *LI*: see *Image of the Situation.* **Perpetual**, *YONG*: continual, everlasting, eternal. Ideogram: flowing water. **Trial**, *ZHEN*: see *Image of the Situation.*

Avail, *YONG*: use, employ for a specific purpose; take advantage of; benefit from; capacity. Ideogram: to divine and center, applying divination to central concerns. **Six**, *LIU*: number six; transforming opened line; six lines of a hexagram. **Use**, *YI*: see *Patterns of Wisdom*. **Great**, *DA*: big, noble, important, very; orient the will toward a self-imposed goal, impose direction; ability to lead or guide one's life; contrasts with small, *XIAO*, flexible adaptation to what crosses one's path. **Complete**, *ZHONG*: completion of a cycle that begins the next; entire, whole, all. Ideogram: silk cocoons, follow and ice, winter linking one year with the next. **Indeed**, *YE*: emphasizes and intensifies the previous statement.

Image Tradition

Culminating in-fact: **space**'s **Spring**.
The **myriad beings' own generation**.
Thereupon yielding receives heaven.
Space: **munificent carrying** the **beings**.

Actualizing-dao unites without delimiting.
Containing generosity: the **shine** of the **great**.
The **kinds** of the **beings conjoining**, **Growing**.
The **female horse**: to the **earth sorted**.
Moving on the **earth without delimiting**.

The **supple yielding**, **Harvesting**, **Trial**.
A **jun zi**: **directed moving**.
Beforehand delusion: **letting-go dao**.
Afterwards yielding: **acquiring constancy**.

Western South: **acquiring partnering**.
Thereupon associating: **sorting movement**.
Eastern North: **losing partnering**.
Thereupon completing possesses reward.

To **peaceful Trial belongs significance**.
Corresponding to the **earth without delimiting**.

Fields of meaning

Culminate, *ZHI*: bring to the highest degree; arrive at the end or summit; superlative; reaching one's goal. **In-fact**, *ZAI*: emphatic exclamation; truly, indeed. **Space**, *KUN*: see *Image of the Situation*. **Spring**, *YUAN*: source, origin, head; arise, begin; first generating impulse; great, excellent; quality of springtime and East, first stage of the Time Cycle. **Myriad**, *WAN*: ten thousand; countless, many, everyone. Ideogram: swarm of insects. **Being**, *WU*: see *Patterns of Wisdom*. **Own**, *ZI*: possession and the things possessed; avail of, depend on; property, riches. **Generate**, *SHENG*: give birth; be born, arise, grow; beget; life, vitality. Ideogram: earth and sprout. **Thereupon**, *NAI*: on that ground, then, only then; finally; in spite of that. **Yield**, *SHUN*: give way, comply, agree, follow, obey; docile, flexible; bear produce, nourish, provide; Action of the trigram Field, *KUN*. **Receive**, *CHENG*: receive gifts or commands from superiors or customers; take in hand; give, offer respectfully; help, support. Ideogram: accepting a seal of office. **Heaven**, *TIAN*: sky, firmament, heavens; the highest realm, situated above the human world, as opposed to the earth, *DI*, located below; Symbol of the trigram Energy, *QIAN*. Ideogram: great and the one above. **Munificent**, *HOU*: see *Patterns of Wisdom*. **Carry**, *ZAI*: see *Patterns of Wisdom*.

Actualize-dao, *DE*: see *Patterns of Wisdom*. **Unite**, *HE*: join, match, correspond; unison, harmony; together; close the jaws, shut the mouth. Ideogram: mouths speaking in unison. **Without**, *WU*: devoid of; there is not. **Delimit**, *JIANG*: define frontiers, boundaries, draw limits. **Contain**, *HAN*: retain, embody, cherish; withhold, tolerate; contain in the mouth, put a coin in a corpse's mouth. **Generous**, *HONG*: liberal, munificent; large, vast, expanded; give or share willingly; develop fully. **Shine**, *GUANG*: illuminate, emit light; brilliant, splendid; honor, glory, éclat; distinct from brightness, *MING*, light of heavenly bodies. Ideogram: fire above person. **Great**, *DA*: big, noble, important, very; orient the will toward a self-imposed goal, impose direction; ability to lead or guide one's life; contrasts with small, *XIAO*, flexible adaptation to what crosses one's path. **Kinds**, *PIN*: species and their essential qualities; sort, class, degree; numerous, innumerable. **Conjoin**, *XIAN*: come in contact with, join; put together as parts of a previously separated whole; conjunction of celestial bodies; totally, completely; accord, harmony, mutual influence; lit.: broken piece of pottery, the halves of which join to identify partners. **Grow**, *HENG*: heavenly influence pervading and nourishing all things; prosper, succeed, expand, develop; effective, favorable; quality of summer and South, second stage of the Time Cycle. With the pronunciation *XIANG*: offer a sacrifice; offer a gift to a superior; accept, enjoy. **Female horse**, *PIN MA*: see *Image of the Situation*. **Earth**, *DI*: see *Patterns of Wisdom*. **Sort**, *LEI*: group according to kind, compare; species, class, genus; resemble; analog, like nature or purpose; norm, model. **Move**, *XING*: move or move something; motivate; emotionally moving; walk, act, do. Ideogram: successive steps.

Supple, *ROU*: see *Hexagrams in Pairs*. **Yield**, *SHUN*: give way, comply, agree, follow, obey; docile, flexible; bear produce, nourish, provide; Action of the trigram Field, *KUN*. **Harvest**, *LI*: see *Image of the Situation*. **Trial**, *ZHEN*: see *Image of the Situation*. **Jun zi**: see *Image of the Situation*. **Direct**, *YOU*: move on or through water; place, residence, focus; that which. Ideogram: pole to sound the depth of water. **Move**, *XING*: move or move something; motivate; emotionally moving; walk, act, do. Ideogram: successive steps. **Beforehand delusion**, *XIAN MI*: see *Image of the Situation*. **Let-go**, *SHI*: lose, let slip; omit, miss, fail; lose control of. Ideogram: drop from the hand. **Dao**, *DAO*: way or path; ongoing process of being and the course it traces for each person or thing; ultimate reality, intrinsic nature; origin. Ideogram: go and head, opening a path. **After(wards)/later**, *HOU*: see *Image of the Situation*. **Acquire**, *DE*: see *Image of the Situation*. **Constancy**, *CHANG*: immutable order; permanent, unchanging, habitual; always; law, rule, custom.

Western South, *XI NAN*: see *Image of the Situation*. **Partner**, *PENG*: see *Image of the Situation*. **Thereupon**, *NÁI*: on that ground, then, only then; finally; in spite of that. **Associate**, *YU*: consort with, combine; companions; group, band, company; agree with, comply, help; in favor of. Ideogram: a pair of hands reaching downward meets a pair of hands reaching upward, helpful association. **Eastern North**, *DONG BEI*: see *Image of the Situation*. **Lose**, *SANG*: see *Image of the Situation*. **Complete**, *ZHONG*: completion of a cycle that begins the next; entire, whole, all. Ideogram: silk cocoons, follow and ice, winter linking one year with the next. **Possess**, *YOU*: general term indicating possession; have, own, be endowed with. **Reward**, *QING*: gift given out of gratitude or benevolence; favor from heaven. Ideogram: heart, follow and deer, the heart expressed through the gift of a deer's skin.

Peaceful Trial, *AN ZHEN*: see *Image of the Situation*. **Belong/it**, *ZHI*: see *Image of the Situation*. **Significant**, *JI*: see *Image of the Situation*. **Correspond**, *YING*: be in agreement or harmony; proper, suitable; resonate together, answer to; relation between the lines (1 and 4, 2 and 5, 3 and 6) when they form the pair opened and whole, supple and solid. Ideogram: heart and obey.

屯

3 SPROUTING | *Zhun* ䷂

The situation described by this hexagram is characterized by the difficulties surrounding a new beginning, like the growth of a tender shoot piercing through hard soil.

Image of the Situation

Sprouting.
Spring, Growing, Harvesting, Trial.
No availing of **possessing directed going.**
Harvesting: installing feudatories.

Fields of meaning

Sprout, *ZHUN*: beginning of growth; collect, assemble, accumulate; difficulty, hardship. Ideogram: sprout piercing hard soil. **Spring, Growing, Harvesting, Trial**, *YUAN HENG LI ZHEN*: Spring, Growing, Harvesting and Trial are the four stages of the Time Cycle, the model for all dynamic processes. They indicate that your question is connected to the cycle as a whole rather than a part of it. **No**, *WU*: common term of negation. **Avail**, *YONG*: use, employ for a specific purpose; take advantage of; benefit from; capacity. Ideogram: to divine and center, applying divination to central concerns. **Possessing directed going**, *YOU YOU WANG*: having a goal or purpose, moving in a specific direction. **Harvest**, *LI*: benefit, advantage, profit; realization; sharp, acute, insightful; quality of autumn and West, third stage of the Time Cycle. Ideogram: ripe grain and blade. **Install**, *JIAN*: set up, establish, erect, nominate; robust, solid; confirm a law or an institution. **Feudatory**, *HOU*: noble entrusted with governing a province; in charge of executive tasks; distinct from prince, *GONG*, representative of the central decisional power at the court.

Outer and Inner Trigram

The upper trigram, **Gorge**, *KAN*, describes the outer aspects of the situation. It has the following associations: precipice, dangerous place; hole, cavity, pit, snare, trap, grave; critical time, test; risky. Ideogram: earth and cavity. *Symbol*: stream, *SHUI*, flowing water; river, tide, flood; fluid, dissolving. Ideogram: rippling water.

Actions: venture and fall. Venture, *XIAN*: face a severe difficulty or obstruction; risk; precipice, cliff, abyss; key point, point of danger. Ideogram: mound and all, everything engaged at one point. Fall, *XIAN*: fall down or into, sink, drop, descend; pit, trap, fault; falling water. In the family of trigrams *KAN* is the middle son.

The lower trigram, **Shake**, *ZHEN*, describes the inner aspects of the situation. It has the following associations: arouse, excite, inspire; awe, alarm, trembling; thunder rising from the depth of the earth; fertilizing intrusion. Ideogram: excite and rain. *Symbol*: thunder, *LEI*, arousing power emerging from the depth of the earth. *Action*: stir-up, *DONG*, excite, influence, move, affect; work, take action; come out of the egg or the bud. Ideogram: strength and heavy, move weighty things. In the family of trigrams *ZHEN* is the eldest son.

Counter Hexagram

The Counter Hexagram of **Sprouting** is hexagram 23, **Stripping**, which switches the emphasis from a beginning growth to stripping away something that is not meant to grow.

Preceding Situation

Possessing heaven and **earth**.
Therefore afterwards the **myriad beings' generation in-truth**.
Overfilling the **interspace belonging** to **heaven** and **earth implies verily** the **myriad beings**.
To **anterior acquiescence belongs** the **use** of **sprouting**.
Sprouting implies overfilling indeed.
Sprouting implies a **beginning belonging** to **beings' generation indeed**.

Fields of meaning

Possess, *YOU*: general term indicating possession; have, own, be endowed with. **Heaven**, *TIAN*: sky, firmament, heavens; the highest realm, situated above the human world, as opposed to the earth, *DI*, located below; Symbol of the trigram Energy, *QIAN*. Ideogram: great and the one above. **Earth**, *DI*: the earth, ground on which the human world rests; basis of all things, nourishes all things; essential Yin; Symbol of the trigram Space, *KUN*. **Therefore**, *RAN*: thus, so it is; truly, certainly. **After(wards)/later**, *HOU*: come after in time, subsequent; put oneself after; behind, back, draw back; the second; attendants, heirs, successors, posterity. **Myriad**, *WAN*: ten thousand; countless, many, everyone. Ideogram: swarm of insects. **Being**, *WU*: creature, thing, any single being; matter, substance, essence;

nature of things. **Generate**, *SHENG*: give birth; be born, arise, grow; beget; life, vitality. Ideogram: earth and sprout. **In-truth**, *YAN*: a final affirmative particle; the preceding statement is complete and correct. **Overfill**, *YING*: fill completely; full, at the point of overflowing; excess, arrogance. Ideogram: vessel and overflow. **Interspace**, *XIAN*: space between, interval; vacant, empty. Ideogram: moonlight coming in through a door ajar. **Belong/it**, *ZHI*: establishes between two terms a connection similar to the Saxon genitive, in which the second term belongs to the first one; at the end of a sentence it refers to something previously mentioned or implied. **Imply**, *ZHE*: further signify; additional meaning. **Very/verily**, *WEI*: the only; in truth; answer; acquiesce; yes. To **anterior acquiescence belongs** the **use** of, *GU SHOU ZHI YI*: understanding and accepting the preceding statement allows the consultant to make proper use of this hexagram. **Use**, *YI*: by means of; owing to; make use of, employ. **Sprout**, *ZHUN*: see *Image of the Situation*. **Indeed**, *YE*: emphasizes and intensifies the previous statement. **Begin**, *SHI*: commence, start, open; earliest, first; generate. Ideogram: woman and eminent, eminent feminine function of giving birth.

Hexagrams in Pairs

> **Sprouting**: **viewing and-also not letting-go one's residing**.
> **Enveloping**: **motley and-also conspicuous**.

Fields of meaning

Sprout, *ZHUN*: see *Image of the Situation*. **View**, *JIAN*: vision in all its aspects: seeing, being visible, forming mental images; visit, call on, consult. Ideogram: eye above person, active and receptive sight. **And-also**, *ER*: joins and contrasts two terms. **Not**, *BU*: common term of negation. **Let-go**, *SHI*: lose, let slip; omit, miss, fail; lose control of. Ideogram: drop from the hand. **One/one's**, *QI*: general third person pronoun and possessive adjective; also: it/its, he/his, she/her, they/their. **Reside**, *JU*: dwell, live in, stay; sit down; fill an office; well-being, rest. Ideogram: body and seat. **Envelop**, *MENG*: cover, pull over, hide, conceal; lid or cover; clouded awareness, dull; ignorance, immaturity; unseen beginnings. Ideogram: plant and covered, hidden growth. **Motley**, *ZA*: mingled, variegated, mixed; disorder. **Conspicuous**, *ZHU*: manifest, obvious, clear; publish.

Patterns of Wisdom

> **Clouds** and **thunder**: **sprouting**.
> A **jun zi uses** the **canons** to **coordinate**.

Fields of meaning
Clouds, *YUN*: fog, mist, water vapor; connected with the Streaming Moment. **Thunder**, *LEI*: thunder; arousing power emerging from the depth of the earth; Symbol of the trigram Shake, *ZHEN*. **Sprout**, *ZHUN*: see *Image of the Situation*. **Jun zi**: ideal of a person who orders his/her life in accordance with dao rather than willful intention, and uses divination in this spirit. **Use**, *YI*: see *Preceding Situation*. **Canons**, *JING*: standards, laws; regular, regulate; the Five Classics. Ideogram: warp threads in a loom. **Coordinate**, *LUN*: twist fibers to make a rope; bind, weave together; adjust, order; lit.: twist silk together into threads.

Lines

INITIAL NINE

A **stone pillar**.
Harvesting: **residing** in **Trial**.
Harvesting: **installing feudatories**.

Comments
Although a **stone pillar**, **purpose moving correctly indeed**.
Using valuing the **below** and the **mean**.
The **great acquires** the **commoners indeed**.

Fields of meaning
Stone, *PAN*: large conspicuous rock, foundation stone; stable, immovable. **Pillar**, *HUAN*: post or tablet marking a grave. **Harvest**, *LI*: see *Image of the Situation*. **Reside**, *JU*: see *Hexagrams in Pairs*. **Trial**, *ZHEN*: inquiry by divination and its result; righteous, firm; separating wheat from chaff; the kernel, the proven core; quality of winter and North, fourth stage of the Time Cycle. Ideogram: pearl and divination. **Installing feudatories**, *JIAN HOU*: see *Image of the Situation*.

Although, *SUI*: even though, supposing that, if, even if. **Purpose**, *ZHI*: focus of mind and heart; intention, will, inclination; continuity in the direction of life. Ideogram: heart and scholar, high inner resolve. **Move**, *XING*: move or move something; motivate; emotionally moving; walk, act, do. Ideogram: successive steps. **Correct**, *ZHENG*: rectify deviation or one-sidedness; proper, straight, exact, regular; constant, rule, model. Ideogram: stop and one, hold to one thing. **Indeed**, *YE*: see *Preceding Situation*. **Use**, *YI*: see *Preceding Situation*. **Value**, *GUI*: regard as valuable, give worth and dignity to; precious, honorable, exalted, illustrious. Ideogram: cowrys (coins) and basket. **Below**, *XIA*: anything below, in all senses; lower, inner; lower trigram. **Mean**, *JIAN*: low, poor, cheap; depreciate, undervalue;

opposite of value, *GUI*. **Great**, *DA*: big, noble, important, very; orient the will toward a self-imposed goal, impose direction; ability to lead or guide one's life; contrasts with small, *XIAO*, flexible adaptation to what crosses one's path. **Acquire**, *DE*: obtain the desired object; possession; satisfied, fulfilled; it is permitted; agree with; wish for, desire covetously. Ideogram: go and obstacle, going through obstacles to the goal. **Commoners**, *MIN*: common people, masses; working class supporting the social hierarchy; undeveloped potential in the individual.

Six at Second

Sprouting thus, hindered thus.
Riding a **horse**, **arraying thus.**
In-no-way illegality, matrimonial alliance.
Woman and **son**'s **Trial**: **not nursing.**
Ten years, thereupon nursing.

Comments
To **six** at **second belongs heaviness.**
Riding a **solid indeed.**
Ten years, thereupon nursing.
Reversing constancy indeed.

Fields of meaning

Sprout, *ZHUN*: see *Image of the Situation*. **Thus**, *RU*: as, in this way; comparable, similar. **Hinder**, *ZHAN*: obstacle, difficulty; advance hesitantly; detour. **Ride**, *CHENG*: ride an animal or a chariot; have the upper hand, control a stronger power; an opened line above controlling a whole line below. **Horse**, *MA*: symbol of spirited strength in the natural world, earthly counterpart of the dragon; associated with the trigram Energy, *QIAN*, heaven, and high noon. **Array**, *BAN*: classify and display; arrange according to rank; assign to a group, as soldiers to their units. Ideogram: knife between two gems, separating values. **In-no-way**, *FEI*: strong negative; not so; bandit, rebel; unjust, immoral. Ideogram: a box filled with opposition. **Illegality**, *KOU*: take by force, violate, invade, sack, break the laws; brutality; enemies, outcasts, bandits. **Matrimonial alliance**, *HUN GOU*: legal institution of marriage; union of two families by marriage. **Woman(hood)**, *NÜ*: woman and what is inherently female. **Son(hood)**, *ZI*: son, male child; heirs, offspring, posterity; living up to the ideal of the ancestors as highest human aspiration; seed, kernel, egg; sage, teacher; nadir, deepest point, midnight, midwinter. **Trial**, *ZHEN*: inquiry by divination and its result; righteous, firm;

separating wheat from chaff; the kernel, the proven core; quality of winter and North, fourth stage of the Time Cycle. Ideogram: pearl and divination. **Not**, *BU*: common term of negation. **Nurse**, *ZI*: care for and protect, act as a mother, love; give birth, raise. Ideogram: child and shelter. **Ten**, *SHI*: number ten; goal and end of reckoning; whole, complete, all; entire, perfected. Ideogram: East–West line crosses North–South line, a grid that contains all. **Year**, *NIAN*: year, annual; harvest; years revolved, years of age. **Thereupon**, *NAI*: on that ground, then, only then; finally; in spite of that.

Six, *LIU*: number six; transforming opened line; six lines of a hexagram. **Two/second**, *ER*: number two; pair, even numbers, binary, duplicate. **Belong/it**, *ZHI*: see *Preceding Situation*. **Heaviness**, *NAN*: difficulty, hardship, distress; arduous, grievous; harass; contrasts with versatility, *YI*, deal lightly with. Ideogram: bird with clipped tail on drying sticky soil. **Solid**, *GANG*: quality of the whole lines; firm, strong, unyielding, persisting. **Indeed**, *YE*: see *Preceding Situation*. **Reverse**, *FAN*: turn and move in the opposite direction; turn around or upside down (180 degrees); change to the opposite position; contrary. **Constancy**, *CHANG*: immutable order; permanent, unchanging, habitual; always; law, rule, custom.

SIX AT THIRD

䷂

Approaching a **stag**: **lacking precaution**.
Thinking of **entering tending-towards** the **forest**'s **center**.
A **jun zi**: **hint not thus stowed** away.
Going, **abashment**.

Comments
Approaching a **stag without precaution**.
Using adhering to **wildfowl indeed**.
A **jun zi stowing it**: **going**, **abashment**, **exhaustion indeed**.

Fields of meaning
Approach, *JI*: come near to, advance toward, reach; nearby; soon, immediately. **Stag**, *LU*: mature male deer with horns. **Lack**, *WU*: strong negative; there is no, without, empty of, absence. **Precaution**, *YU*: provide against, preventive measures; anxious, vigilant, ready; think about, expect; mishap, accident. **Think**, *WEI*: consider, plan; consist in; and, also; just so, precisely. **Enter**, *RU*: penetrate, go into, enter on, encroach on; progress; put into; Action of the trigram Root, *SUN*. **Tend-towards**, *YU*: move toward without necessarily reaching, in the direction of. **Forest**, *LIN*: woods, wilderness; area with no mark of human civilization; fourth of the territorial zones: city, suburbs, countryside, forest. **Center**, *ZHONG*: inner, central;

put in the center; middle, stable point enabling you to face inner and outer changes; middle line of a trigram. Ideogram: field divided in two equal parts. **Jun zi**: see *Patterns of Wisdom*. **Hint/almost**, *JI*: nearly, about to; subtle; barely perceptible first sign. **Not**, *BU*: common term of negation. **Thus**, *RU*: as, in this way; comparable, similar. **Stow**, *ŠHE*: set aside, put away, store, keep; halt, rest in; lodge, hut. **Go**, *WANG*: move away in time or space, depart; become past; dead, gone; contrasts with come, *LAI*, approach in time or space. **Abashment**, *LIN*: see *Preceding Situation*.

Without, *WU*: devoid of; there is not. **Use**, *YI*: see *Preceding Situation*. **Adhere**, *CONG*: follow, agree with, comply with, obey; join a doctrine, school, or person; servant, follower. Ideogram: two men walking, one following the other. **Wildfowl**, *QIN*: birds; four-legged animals; hunt, shoot with an arrow; capture; prisoner. **Indeed**, *YE*: see *Preceding Situation*. **It/belong**, *ZHI*: establishes between two terms a connection similar to the Saxon genitive, in which the second term belongs to the first one; at the end of a sentence it refers to something previously mentioned or implied. **Exhaust**, *QIONG*: bring to an end; limit, extremity; investigate exhaustively; destitute, indigent; end without a new beginning; distinct from complete, *ZHONG*, end of a cycle that begins the next one. Ideogram: cave and naked person, bent with disease or old age.

SIX AT FOURTH

Riding a **horse**, **arraying thus**.
Seeking matrimonial alliance.
Going, **significant**.
Without not Harvesting.

Comments
Seeking and-also going.
Brightness indeed.

Fields of meaning

Ride, *CHENG*: ride an animal or a chariot; have the upper hand, control a stronger power; an opened line above controlling a whole line below. **Horse**, *MA*: symbol of spirited strength in the natural world, earthly counterpart of the dragon; associated with the trigram Energy, *QIAN*, heaven, and high noon. **Array**, *BAN*: classify and display; arrange according to rank; assign to a group, as soldiers to their units. Ideogram: knife between two gems, separating values. **Thus**, *RU*: as, in this way; comparable, similar. **Seek**, *QIU*: search for, aim at, wish for, desire; implore, supplicate; covetous. **Matrimonial alliance**, *HUN GOU*: legal institution of marriage; union of two families by marriage. **Go**, *WANG*: move away in time or space, depart; become past; dead, gone; contrasts with come, *LAI*, approach in time or space. **Significant**, *JI*: leads to the experience of meaning; favorable, propitious, appropriate. Ideogram: scholar and mouth, wise words of a sage. **Without not Harvesting**, *WU BU LI*: turning point where the balance is swinging from not Harvesting to actually Harvesting.

And-also, *ER*: see *Hexagrams in Pairs*. **Brightness**, *MING*: light, radiance, clarity; distinguish, discern, understand; light-giving aspect of fire, of heavenly bodies and of consciousness; brightness and fire are the Symbols of the trigram Radiance, *LI*. **Indeed**, *YE*: see *Preceding Situation*.

Nine at Fifth

Sprouting: **one's juice**.
The **small**: **Trial**, **significant**.
The **great**: **Trial**, **pitfall**.

Comments
Sprouting: **one's juice**.
Spreading, **not-yet shining indeed**.

Fields of meaning
Sprout, *ZHUN*: see *Image of the Situation*. **One/one's**, *QI*: see *Hexagrams in Pairs*. **Juice**, *GAO*: active essence; oil, grease, ointment; fertilizing, rich; genius. **Small**, *XIAO*: little, common, unimportant; adapting to what crosses your path; ability to move in harmony with the vicissitudes of life; contrasts with great, *DA*, self-imposed theme or goal. **Trial**, *ZHEN*: inquiry by divination and its result; righteous, firm; separating wheat from chaff; the kernel, the proven core; quality of winter and North, fourth stage of the Time Cycle. Ideogram: pearl and divination. **Significant**, *JI*: leads to the experience of meaning; favorable, propitious, appropriate. Ideogram: scholar and mouth, wise words of a sage. **Great**, *DA*: big, noble, important, very; orient the will toward a self-imposed goal, impose direction; ability to lead or guide one's life; contrasts with small, *XIAO*, flexible adaptation to what crosses one's path. **Pitfall**, *XIONG*: unfortunate situation, in which the flow of life and spirit is blocked and the experience of meaning is lost; stuck and exposed to danger; inappropriate attitude. Ideogram: person in a pit.

Spread, *SHI*: expand, diffuse, distribute, arrange, exhibit; add to; aid. Ideogram: flag and indeed, claiming new country. **Not-yet**, *WEI*: temporal negative indicating that something is expected to happen but has not yet occurred. **Shine**, *GUANG*: illuminate, emit light; brilliant, splendid; honor, glory, éclat; distinct from brightness, *MING*, light of heavenly bodies. Ideogram: fire above person. **Indeed**, *YE*: see *Preceding Situation*.

Six Above

Riding a **horse, arraying thus.**
Weeping, blood flowing thus.

Comments
Weeping, blood flowing thus.
Is it **permitted long-living indeed?**

Fields of meaning
Ride, *CHENG*: ride an animal or a chariot; have the upper hand, control a stronger power; an opened line above controlling a whole line below. **Horse,** *MA*: symbol of spirited strength in the natural world, earthly counterpart of the dragon; associated with the trigram Energy, *QIAN*, heaven, and high noon. **Array,** *BAN*: classify and display; arrange according to rank; assign to a group, as soldiers to their units. Ideogram: knife between two gems, separating values. **Thus,** *RU*: as, in this way; comparable, similar. **Weep,** *QI*: lament wordlessly; grieved, heartbroken. **Blood,** *XUE*: blood, the Yin fluid that maintains life; money, property. **Flow,** *LIAN*: move like ripples spreading on water; running tears.

Is?, *HE*: ask, inquire; what? which? who? how? why? where? an interrogative particle, often introducing a rhetorical question: is it? is it not? **Permit,** *KE*: possible because in harmony with an inherent principle; capable of; approve, authorize. Ideogram: mouth and breath, silent consent. **Long-living,** *ZHANG*: enduring, lasting, constant; extended, long, large; senior, superior, greater; increase, prosper; respect, elevate. **Indeed,** *YE*: see *Preceding Situation*.

Image Tradition

Sprouting.
Solid and **supple begin** to **mingle and-also** in
heaviness generate.
Stirring-up reaches venturing's **center.**
The **great: Growing, Trial.**

To **thunder** and **rain belongs stirring-up: plenitude**
overfilled.
Heaven creates grasses' duskiness.
Proper installing feudatories and-also not soothing.

Fields of meaning

Sprout, *ZHUN*: see *Image of the Situation*. **Solid**, *GANG*: quality of the whole lines; firm, strong, unyielding, persisting. **Supple**, *ROU*: quality of the opened lines; flexible, pliant, adaptable, tender. **Begin**, *SHI*: see *Preceding Situation*. **Mingle**, *JIAO*: blend with, communicate, join, exchange; trade; copulation; friendship. Ideogram: legs crossed. **And-also**, *ER*: see *Hexagrams in Pairs*. **Heaviness**, *NAN*: difficulty, hardship, distress; arduous, grievous; harass; contrasts with versatility, *YI*, deal lightly with. Ideogram: bird with clipped tail on drying sticky soil. **Generate**, *SHENG*: give birth; be born, arise, grow; beget; life, vitality. Ideogram: earth and sprout. **Stir-up**, *DONG*: excite, influence, move, affect; work, take action; come out of the egg or the bud; Action of the trigram Shake, *ZHEN*. Ideogram: strength and heavy, move weighty things. **Reach**, *HU*: arrive at a goal; move toward and achieve; to, at, in; distinct from tend-towards, *YOU*. **Venture**, *XIAN*: face a severe difficulty or obstruction; risk; precipice, cliff, abyss; key point, point of danger; Action of the trigram Gorge, *KAN*. Ideogram: mound and all, everything engaged at one point. **Center**, *ZHONG*: inner, central; put in the center; middle, stable point enabling you to face inner and outer changes; middle line of a trigram. Ideogram: field divided in two equal parts. **Great**, *DA*: big, noble, important, very; orient the will toward a self-imposed goal, impose direction; ability to lead or guide one's life; contrasts with small, *XIAO*, flexible adaptation to what crosses one's path. **Grow**, *HENG*: heavenly influence pervading and nourishing all things; prosper, succeed, expand, develop; effective, favorable; quality of summer and South, second stage of the Time Cycle. With the pronunciation *XIANG*: offer a sacrifice; offer a gift to a superior; accept, enjoy. **Trial**, *ZHEN*: inquiry by divination and its result; righteous, firm; separating wheat from chaff; the kernel, the proven core; quality of winter and North, fourth stage of the Time Cycle. Ideogram: pearl and divination.

Thunder, *LEI*: see *Patterns of Wisdom*. **Rain**, *YU*: rain and all precipitations; sudden shower, fast and furious; abundant dispensation of benefits; associated with the trigram Gorge, *KAN*, and the Streaming Moment. **Belong/it**, *ZHI*: see *Preceding Situation*. **Plenitude**, *MAN*: fullness; replete, complete, bulging, abundant; proud. **Overfill**, *YING*: see *Preceding Situation*. **Heaven**, *TIAN*: see *Preceding Situation*. **Create**, *ZAO*: make, construct, build, form, establish. **Grass**, *CAO*: all grassy plants and herbs; young, tender plants; rough draft; hastily. **Duskiness**, *MEI*: obscure, indistinct; insufficient light; times of day when it is not fully light. Ideogram: day and not-yet. **Proper**, *YI*: reasonable, fit, right, harmonious; ought, should. **Installing feudatories**, *JIAN HOU*: see *Image of the Situation*. **Not**, *BU*: common term of negation. **Soothe**, *NING*: calm, pacify; create peace of mind; tranquil, quiet. Ideogram: shelter above heart, dish and breath, physical and spiritual comfort.

蒙 ䷃

4 ENVELOPING | *Meng*

The situation described by this hexagram is characterized by something covered because still immature, a young, incompletely formed consciousness, which needs to ripen under the protective veil of envelopment.

Image of the Situation

Enveloping.
Growing.
In-no-way I seek the **youthful enveloping.**
The **youthful enveloping seeks me.**
The **initial oracle-consulting notifies.**
Twice, thrice: obscuring.
Obscuring, by **consequence not notifying.**
Harvesting, Trial.

Fields of meaning

Envelop, *MENG*: cover, pull over, hide, conceal; lid or cover; clouded awareness, dull; ignorance, immaturity; unseen beginnings. Ideogram: plant and covered, hidden growth. **Grow,** *HENG*: heavenly influence pervading and nourishing all things; prosper, succeed, expand, develop; effective, favorable; quality of summer and South, second stage of the Time Cycle. With the pronunciation *XIANG*: offer a sacrifice; offer a gift to a superior; accept, enjoy. **In-no-way,** *FEI*: strong negative; not so; bandit, rebel; unjust, immoral. Ideogram: a box filled with opposition. **I/me/my,** *WO*: first person pronoun; the use of a specific personal pronoun, as opposed to the generic one's, *QI*, indicates an unusually strong emphasis on personal involvement. **Seek,** *QIU*: search for, aim at, wish for, desire; implore, supplicate; covetous. **Youthful,** *TONG*: young person (between eight and fifteen); childish, immature; servant, slave. **Initial,** *CHU*: beginning, incipient, first step or part; bottom line of a hexagram. Ideogram: knife and garment, cutting out the pattern. **Oracle-consulting,** *SHI*: yarrow stalks and their use in divination. **Notify,** *GAO*: proclaim, order, decree; advise, inform; accuse, denounce. Ideogram: mouth and ox head, impressive speech. **Twice, thrice,** *ZAI SAN*: repeatedly. **Obscure,**

DU: confuse, muddle; cloudy, turbid; agitated water; annoy through repetition; disrespectful, corrupted. **Consequence**, *ZE*: reason, cause, result; rule, law, pattern, standard; therefore; very strong connection. **Not**, *BU*: common term of negation. **Harvest**, *LI*: benefit, advantage, profit; realization; sharp, acute, insightful; quality of autumn and West, third stage of the Time Cycle. Ideogram: ripe grain and blade. **Trial**, *ZHEN*: inquiry by divination and its result; righteous, firm; separating wheat from chaff; the kernel, the proven core; quality of winter and North, fourth stage of the Time Cycle. Ideogram: pearl and divination.

Outer and Inner Trigram

The upper trigram, **Bound**, *GEN*, describes the outer aspects of the situation. It has the following associations: limit, frontier; obstacle that prevents from seeing further; stop; still, quiet, motionless; confine, enclose; mountain, sunset, beginning of winter; solid, steady, unshakable; straight, hard, adamant, obstinate. *Symbol*: mountain, *SHAN*, large, immense; limit, boundary. Ideogram: three peaks, a mountain range. *Action*: stop, *ZHI*, bring or come to a standstill, cease, terminate. Ideogram: a foot stops walking. In the family of trigrams *GEN* is the youngest son.

The lower trigram, **Gorge**, *KAN*, describes the inner aspects of the situation. It has the following associations: precipice, dangerous place; hole, cavity, pit, snare, trap, grave; critical time, test; risky. Ideogram: earth and cavity. *Symbol*: stream, *SHUI*, flowing water; river, tide, flood; fluid, dissolving. Ideogram: rippling water. *Actions*: venture and fall. Venture, *XIAN*: face a severe difficulty or obstruction; risk; precipice, cliff, abyss; key point, point of danger. Ideogram: mound and all, everything engaged at one point. Fall, *XIAN*: fall down or into, sink, drop, descend; pit, trap, fault; falling water. In the family of trigrams *KAN* is the middle son.

Counter Hexagram

The Counter Hexagram of **Enveloping** is hexagram 24, **Return**, which switches the emphasis from the orientation to a still hidden future characterizing **Enveloping** to a re-emergence of the past.

Preceding Situation

> **Beings' generation necessarily enveloped.**
> To **anterior acquiescence belongs** the **use** of **enveloping.**
> **Enveloping implies envelopment indeed.**
> To **beings belongs immaturity indeed.**

Fields of meaning

Being, *WU*: creature, thing, any single being; matter, substance, essence; nature of things. **Generate**, *SHENG*: give birth; be born, arise, grow; beget; life, vitality. Ideogram: earth and sprout. **Necessarily**, *BI*: unavoidably, certainly. **Envelop**, *MENG*: see *Image of the Situation*. To **anterior acquiescence belongs** the **use** of, *GU SHOU ZHI YI*: understanding and accepting the preceding statement allows the consultant to make proper use of this hexagram. **Imply**, *ZHE*: further signify; additional meaning. **Indeed**, *YE*: emphasizes and intensifies the previous statement. **Belong/it**, *ZHI*: establishes between two terms a connection similar to the Saxon genitive, in which the second term belongs to the first one; at the end of a sentence it refers to something previously mentioned or implied. **Immature**, *ZHI*: small, tender, young, delicate; undeveloped; conceited, haughty; late grain.

Hexagrams in Pairs

> **Sprouting: viewing and-also not letting-go one's residing.**
> **Enveloping: motley and-also conspicuous.**

Fields of meaning

Sprout, *ZHUN*: beginning of growth; collect, assemble, accumulate; difficulty, hardship. Ideogram: sprout piercing hard soil. **View**, *JIAN*: vision in all its aspects: seeing, being visible, forming mental images; visit, call on, consult. Ideogram: eye above person, active and receptive sight. **And-also**, *ER*: joins and contrasts two terms. **Not**, *BU*: common term of negation. **Let-go**, *SHI*: lose, let slip; omit, miss, fail; lose control of. Ideogram: drop from the hand. **One/one's**, *QI*: general third person pronoun and possessive adjective; also: it/its, he/his, she/her, they/their. **Reside**, *JU*: dwell, live in, stay; sit down; fill an office; well-being, rest. Ideogram: body and seat. **Envelop**, *MENG*: see *Image of the Situation*. **Motley**, *ZA*: mingled, variegated, mixed; disorder. **Conspicuous**, *ZHU*: manifest, obvious, clear; publish.

Patterns of Wisdom

> **Below** the **mountain emerges springwater**.
> **Enveloping**.
> A **jun zi uses** the **fruits** of **movement** to **nurture actualizing-dao**.

Fields of meaning

Below, *XIA*: anything below, in all senses; lower, inner; lower trigram. **Mountain**, *SHAN*: mountain; large, immense; limit, boundary; Symbol of the trigram Bound, *GEN*. Ideogram: three peaks, a mountain range. **Emerge**, *CHU*: come out of, proceed from, spring from, issue forth; appear, be born; bear, generate; leave, flee; Action of the trigram Shake, *ZHEN*. Ideogram: stem with branches and leaves emerging. **Springwater**, *QUAN*: source, spring, fountain, headwaters of a river. Ideogram: water and white, pure water at the source. **Envelop**, *MENG*: see *Image of the Situation*. **Jun zi**: ideal of a person who orders his/her life in accordance with dao rather than willful intention, and uses divination in this spirit. **Use**, *YI*: by means of; owing to; make use of, employ. **Fruit**, *GUO*: tree fruit; fruition, fruit of action; result, effect, product, conclusion; reliable, decisive. Ideogram: tree topped by a round fruit. **Move**, *XING*: move or move something; motivate; emotionally moving; walk, act, do. Ideogram: successive steps. **Nurture**, *YU*: give birth; bring up, rear, raise. **Actualize-dao**, *DE*: realize dao in action; power, virtue; ability to follow the course traced by the ongoing process of the cosmos. Ideogram: go, straight, and heart. Linked with acquire, *DE*: acquiring that which makes a being become what it is meant to be.

Transforming Lines

Initial Six

Shooting-forth enveloping.
Harvesting: availing of **punishing people.**
Availing of **stimulating shackles to fetter.**
Using going: abashment.

Comments
Harvesting: availing of **punishing people.**
Using correcting by **law indeed.**

Fields of meaning

Shoot-forth, *FA*: emit, send out, shoot an arrow; ferment, rise; express, raise one's voice. Ideogram: stance, bow and arrow, shooting from a solid base. **Envelop**, *MENG*: see *Image of the Situation*. **Harvest**, *LI*: see *Image of the Situation*. **Avail**, *YONG*: use, employ for a specific purpose; take advantage of; benefit from; capacity. Ideogram: to divine and center, applying divination to central concerns. **Punish**, *XING*: legal punishment; physical penalty for a severe criminal offense; whip, torture, behead. **People/person**, *REN*: humans individually and collectively; an individual; humankind. **Stimulate**, *SHUO*: rouse to action and good feeling; stir up, urge on; exhort, persuade; say, tell, relate; cheer, delight; joyous, peaceful, restful; Action of the trigram Open, *DUI*. Ideogram: words and exchange. **Shackles**, *GU*: chains used to secure prisoners; restrain freedom; self-restraint. **Fetter**, *ZHI*: tie, manacle; restrain and hinder movement, clog wheels; impede. **Use**, *YI*: see *Patterns of Wisdom*. Go, *WANG*: move away in time or space, depart; become past; dead, gone; contrasts with come, *LAI*, approach in time or space. **Abashment**, *LIN*: distress, shame, regret, humiliation; aware of having lost the right track; leads to repenting, *HUI*, correcting the direction of mind and life.

Correct, *ZHENG*: rectify deviation or one-sidedness; proper, straight, exact, regular; constant, rule, model. Ideogram: stop and one, hold to one thing. **Laws**, *FA*: rules, norms, statutes; model; obey the law. **Indeed**, *YE*: see *Preceding Situation*.

Nine at Second

Enwrapping enveloping, significant.
Letting-in the **wife, significant.**
The **son controls** the **household.**

Comments
The **son controls** the **household.**
Solid and **supple articulated indeed**.

Fields of meaning

Enwrap, *BAO*: envelop, hold, contain; patient, engaged. Ideogram: enfold and self, a fetus in the womb. **Envelop**, *MENG*: see *Image of the Situation*. **Significant**, *JI*: leads to the experience of meaning; favorable, propitious, appropriate. Ideogram: scholar and mouth, wise words of a sage. **Let-in**, *NA*: allow to enter; include, receive, accept, welcome; marry. **Wife**, *FU*: position of married woman as head of the household; distinct from consort, *QI*, which denotes her legal status, and from concubine, *QIE*, secondary wife. Ideogram: woman, hand and broom, household duties. **Son(hood)**, *ZI*: son, male child; heirs, offspring, posterity; living up to the ideal of the ancestors as highest human aspiration; seed, kernel, egg; sage, teacher; nadir, deepest point, midnight, mid-winter. **Control**, *KE*: be in charge; capable of, able to, adequate; check, obstruct, repress. Ideogram: roof beams supporting a house. **Household**, *JIA*: home, house; family; dwell, reside; domestic, within doors; shop, school, doctrine. Ideogram: roof and pig or dog, the most valued domestic animals, living under the same roof with the family.

Solid, *GANG*: quality of the whole lines; firm, strong, unyielding, persisting. **Supple**, *ROU*: quality of the opened lines; flexible, pliant, adaptable, tender. **Articulate**, *JIE*: joint, articulation; a separation which simultaneously establishes the identity of the parts and their connection; express thought through speech; section, chapter, interval; temperance, virtue; rite, ceremony; lit.: nodes of bamboo stalks. **Indeed**, *YE*: see *Preceding Situation*.

SIX AT THIRD

䷃

No availing of **grasping womanhood.**
Viewing a **metallic husband.**
Not possessing body.
Without direction Harvesting.

Comments
No availing of **grasping womanhood.**
Moving, not yielding indeed.

Fields of meaning

No, *WU*: common term of negation. **Avail**, *YONG*: use, employ for a specific purpose; take advantage of; benefit from; capacity. Ideogram: to divine and center, applying divination to central concerns. **Grasp**, *QU*: seize with effort, take and use, appropriate; take as a wife; grasp the meaning, understand. Ideogram: ear and hand, hear and grasp. **Woman(hood)**, *NÜ*: woman and what is inherently female. **View**, *JIAN*: see *Hexagrams in Pairs*. **Metal**, *JIN*: all metals, particularly gold; smelting and casting; perfection, richness; autumn, West, sunset; one of the Five Transformative Moments. **Husband**, *FU*: adult, man, male spouse; scholar, distinguished man; one who can help; manage a household. Ideogram: man with a pin in his hair to show that he is of age. **Not**, *BU*: common term of negation. **Possess**, *YOU*: general term indicating possession; have, own, be endowed with. **Body**, *GONG*: physical being, power and self-expression; oneself; innate quality; distinct from individuality, *SHEN*, which includes the notion of lifespan. **Without direction Harvesting**, *WU YOU LI*: in order to take advantage of the situation, do not impose a direction on events.

Move, *XING*: see *Patterns of Wisdom*. **Yield**, *SHUN*: give way, comply, agree, follow, obey; docile, flexible; bear produce, nourish, provide; Action of the trigram Field, *KUN*. **Indeed**, *YE*: see *Preceding Situation*.

Six at Fourth

Confining enveloping. Abashment.

Comments

To **confining enveloping belongs abashment.**
Solitude distancing substance indeed.

Fields of meaning

Confine, *KUN*: enclose, restrict, limit, oppress; impoverished, distressed, afflicted, exhausted, disheartened, weary. Ideogram: tree in a narrow enclosure. **Envelop**, *MENG*: see *Image of the Situation*. **Abashment**, *LIN*: distress, shame, regret, humiliation; aware of having lost the right track; leads to repenting, *HUI*, correcting the direction of mind and life.

Belong/it, *ZHI*: see *Preceding Situation*. **Solitary**, *DI*: alone, single; isolated, abandoned. **Distance**, *YUAN*: far off, remote; keep at a distance; a long time, far away in time. Ideogram: go and a long way. **Substance**, *SHI*: fullness, richness; essence; real, solid, consistent; results, fruits, possessions; honest, sincere. Ideogram: string of coins under a roof, wealth in the house. **Indeed**, *YE*: see *Preceding Situation*.

Six at Fifth

Youthful enveloping. Significant.

Comments

To a **youthful enveloping belongs significance.**
Yielding uses the **root indeed.**

Fields of meaning

Youthful enveloping, *TONG MENG*: see *Image of the Situation*. **Significant**, *JI*: leads to the experience of meaning; favorable, propitious, appropriate. Ideogram: scholar and mouth, wise words of a sage.

Belong/it, *ZHI*: see *Preceding Situation*. **Yield**, *SHUN*: give way, comply, agree, follow, obey; docile, flexible; bear produce, nourish, provide; Action of the trigram Field, *KUN*. **Use**, *YI*: see *Patterns of Wisdom*. **Root**, *SUN*: base on which things rest, ground, foundation; mild, subtly penetrating; nourishing. **Indeed**, *YE*: see *Preceding Situation*.

NINE ABOVE

Smiting enveloping.
Not Harvesting: activating illegality.
Harvesting: resisting illegality.

Comments
Harvesting: availing of **resisting illegality.**
Above and **below yielding indeed.**

Fields of meaning
Smite, *JI*: hit, beat, attack; hurl against, rush a position; rouse to action. Ideogram: hand and hit, fist punching. Envelop, *MENG*: see *Image of the Situation*. Not, *BU*: common term of negation. Harvest, *LI*: see *Image of the Situation*. Activate, *WEI*: act or cause to act; do, make, manage, make active; be, become; attend to, help; because of. Illegality, *KOU*: take by force, violate, invade, sack, break the laws; brutality; enemies, outcasts, bandits. Resist, *YU*: withstand, oppose; bring to an end; prevent. Ideogram: rule and worship, imposing ethical or religious limits.

Avail, *YONG*: use, employ for a specific purpose; take advantage of; benefit from; capacity. Ideogram: to divine and center, applying divination to central concerns. Above, *SHANG*: anything above in all senses; higher, upper, outer; upper trigram. Below, *XIA*: see *Patterns of Wisdom*. Yield, *SHUN*: give way, comply, agree, follow, obey; docile, flexible; bear produce, nourish, provide; Action of the trigram Field, *KUN*. Indeed, *YE*: see *Preceding Situation*.

Image Tradition

Enveloping. Below the **mountain possesses venturing.**
Venturing and-also stopping. Enveloping.

Enveloping, Growing.
Using Growing to **move.**
The **season's center indeed.**

In-no-way I seek the **youthful enveloping.**
The **youthful enveloping seeks me.**
Purposes in **correspondence indeed.**

The **initial oracle-consulting notifies.**
Using a solid in the **center indeed.**

Twice, thrice: obscuring.
Obscuring, by **consequence not notifying.**
Obscuring enveloping indeed.
Enveloping uses nourishing correctness.
Wise achievement indeed.

Fields of meaning

Envelop, *MENG*: see *Image of the Situation*. Below the mountain, *XIA SHAN*: see *Patterns of Wisdom*. Possess, *YOU*: general term indicating possession; have, own, be endowed with. Venture, *XIAN*: face a severe difficulty or obstruction; risk; precipice, cliff, abyss; key point, point of danger; Action of the trigram Gorge, *KAN*. Ideogram: mound and all, everything engaged at one point. And-also, *ER*: see *Hexagrams in Pairs*. Stop, *ZHI*: bring or come to a standstill, cease, terminate; Action of the trigram Bound, *GEN*. Ideogram: a foot stops walking.

Grow, *HENG*: see *Image of the Situation*. Use, *YI*: see *Patterns of Wisdom*. Move, *XING*: see *Patterns of Wisdom*. Season, *SHI*: quality of the time; the right time, opportune, in harmony; planning in accord with the time; season of the year. Ideogram: sun and temple, sacred time. Center, *ZHONG*: inner, central; put in the center; middle, stable point enabling you to face inner and outer changes; middle line of a trigram. Ideogram: field divided in two equal parts. Indeed, *YE*: see *Preceding Situation*.

In-no-way I seek the youthful enveloping: see *Image of the Situation*. The youthful enveloping seeks me: see *Image of the Situation*. Purpose, *ZHI*: focus of mind and heart; intention, will, inclination; continuity in the direction of life. Ideogram: heart and scholar, high inner resolve. Correspond, *YING*: be in agreement or harmony; proper, suitable; resonate together, answer to; relation between the lines (1 and 4, 2 and 5, 3 and 6) when they form the pair opened and whole, supple and solid. Ideogram: heart and obey.

The initial oracle-consulting notifies: see *Image of the Situation*. Solid, *GANG*: quality of the whole lines; firm, strong, unyielding, persisting. Twice, thrice: obscuring: see *Image of the Situation*. Obscuring, by consequence not notifying: see *Image of the Situation*. Nourish, *YANG*: feed, sustain, support, provide, care for; generate; raise, grow. Correct, *ZHENG*: rectify deviation or one-sidedness; proper, straight, exact, regular; constant, rule, model. Ideogram: stop and one, hold to one thing. Wise, *SHENG*: intuitive universal wisdom; profound understanding; mythical sages of old; holy, sacred, mark of highest distinction. Ideogram: ear and inform, one who knows all from a single sound. Achieve, *GONG*: work done, results, actual accomplishment; praise, worth, merit. Ideogram: workman's square and forearm, combining craft and strength.

需

5 ATTENDING | *Xu*

The situation described by this hexagram is characterized by attending both in the sense of waiting for something to manifest and in that of caring for something that needs attention.

Image of the Situation

> **Attending**.
> **Possessing conformity**.
> **Shining Growing**, **Trial**, **significant**.
> **Harvesting**: **wading** the **great river**.

Fields of meaning

Attend, *XU*: wait, await, wait on; hesitation, delay, doubt; take care of, turn one's mind to; need, require, necessity; obstinate, fixed on. Ideogram: rain and stopped, compelled to wait, or rain and origin, providing what is needed. **Possess**, *YOU*: general term indicating possession; have, own, be endowed with. **Conform**, *FU*: accord between inner and outer; sincere, truthful, verified, reliable; capture; prisoners, spoils. Ideogram: claws over child, a bird brooding on the nest. **Shine**, *GUANG*: illuminate, emit light; brilliant, splendid; honor, glory, éclat; distinct from brightness, *MING*, light of heavenly bodies. Ideogram: fire above person. **Grow**, *HENG*: heavenly influence pervading and nourishing all things; prosper, succeed, expand, develop; effective, favorable; quality of summer and South, second stage of the Time Cycle. With the pronunciation *XIANG*: offer a sacrifice; offer a gift to a superior; accept, enjoy. **Trial**, *ZHEN*: inquiry by divination and its result; righteous, firm; separating wheat from chaff; the kernel, the proven core; quality of winter and North, fourth stage of the Time Cycle. Ideogram: pearl and divination. **Significant**, *JI*: leads to the experience of meaning; favorable, propitious, appropriate. Ideogram: scholar and mouth, wise words of a sage. **Harvest**, *LI*: benefit, advantage, profit; realization; sharp, acute, insightful; quality of autumn and West, third stage of the Time Cycle. Ideogram: ripe grain and blade. **Wading the great river**, *SHE DA CHUAN*: enter the stream of life with a goal or purpose; embark on a significant enterprise.

Outer and Inner Trigram

The upper trigram, **Gorge**, *KAN*, describes the outer aspects of the situation. It has the following associations: precipice, dangerous place; hole, cavity, pit, snare, trap, grave; critical time, test; risky. Ideogram: earth and cavity. *Symbol*: stream, *SHUI*, flowing water; river, tide, flood; fluid, dissolving. Ideogram: rippling water. *Actions*: venture and fall. Venture, *XIAN*: face a severe difficulty or obstruction; risk; precipice, cliff, abyss; key point, point of danger. Ideogram: mound and all, everything engaged at one point. Fall, *XIAN*: fall down or into, sink, drop, descend; pit, trap, fault; falling water. In the family of trigrams *KAN* is the middle son.

The lower trigram, **Energy/parch**, *QIAN/GAN*, describes the inner aspects of the situation. It has the following associations: unceasing forward movement, dynamic, enduring, untiring; spirit power, manifestation of Yang, that activates all creation and destruction in Space; heaven, sovereign, father. With the pronunciation *GAN*: parch, dry up, burn, exhaust. Ideogram: sprouts or vapors rising from the ground and sunlight, both fecundating moisture and scorching drought. *Symbol*: heaven, *TIAN*; sky, firmament, heavens; the highest realm, situated above the human world, as opposed to the earth, *DI*, located below. Ideogram: great and the one above. *Action*: persist, *JIAN*; tenacious, persevering; strong, robust, dynamic; constant as the motion of heavenly bodies in their orbits. In the family of trigrams *QIAN* is the father.

Counter Hexagram

The Counter Hexagram of **Attending** is hexagram 38, **Polarizing**, which switches the emphasis from the caring attitude characterizing **Attending** to a polar opposition.

Preceding Situation

> **Being**'s **immaturity not permitted not nourishing indeed**.
> To **anterior acquiescence belongs** the **use** of **attending**.
> **Attending implies** the **dao belonging** to **drinking** and **taking-in**.

Fields of meaning

Being, *WU*: creature, thing, any single being; matter, substance, essence; nature of things. **Immature**, *ZHI*: small, tender, young, delicate; undeveloped; conceited, haughty; late grain. **Not**, *BU*: common term of negation. **Permit**, *KE*: possible because in harmony with an inherent principle; capable of; approve, authorize. Ideogram: mouth and breath, silent consent. **Nourish**, *YANG*: feed, sustain, support, provide, care for; generate; raise, grow. **Indeed**, *YE*: emphasizes and intensifies the previous statement. To **anterior acquiescence belongs** the **use** of, *GU SHOU ZHI YI*: understanding and accepting the preceding statement allows the consultant to make proper use of this hexagram. **Attend**, *XU*: see *Image of the Situation*. **Imply**, *ZHE*: further signify; additional meaning. **Dao**, *DAO*: way or path; ongoing process of being and the course it traces for each person or thing; ultimate reality, intrinsic nature; origin. Ideogram: go and head, opening a path. **Belong/it**, *ZHI*: establishes between two terms a connection similar to the Saxon genitive, in which the second term belongs to the first one; at the end of a sentence it refers to something previously mentioned or implied. **Drink**, *YIN*: drink, swallow, ingest liquid or food; inhale, suck in. **Take-in**, *SHI*: eat, drink, ingest, absorb, incorporate; food, nourishment.

Hexagrams in Pairs

Attending: **not advancing indeed**.
Arguing: **not connecting indeed**.

Fields of meaning

Attend, *XU*: see *Image of the Situation*. **Not**, *BU*: common term of negation. **Advance**, *JIN*: move forward, progress, climb; promote or be promoted; further the development of, augment; offer, introduce. **Indeed**, *YE*: see *Preceding Situation*. **Argue**, *SONG*: dispute, plead in court, contend before a ruler, demand justice; wrangle, quarrel, litigation. Ideogram: words and public, public disputation. **Connect**, *QIN*: be close, approach, come near; cherish, help, favor; intimate; relatives, kin.

Patterns of Wisdom

Clouds above with-respect-to heaven. **Attending**.
A **jun zi uses drinking** and **taking-in** to **repose delightfully**.

Fields of meaning

Clouds, *YUN*: fog, mist, water vapor; connected with the Streaming Moment. **Above**, *SHANG*: anything above in all senses; higher, upper, outer; upper trigram. **With-respect-to**, *YU*: in relation to, referring to, according to; in, at, until. **Heaven**, *TIAN*: sky, firmament, heavens; the highest realm, situated above the human world, as opposed to the earth, *DI*, located below; Symbol of the trigram Energy, *QIAN*. Ideogram: great and the one above. **Attend**, *XU*: see *Image of the Situation*.

Jun zi: ideal of a person who orders his/her life in accordance with dao rather than willful intention, and uses divination in this spirit. **Use**, *YI*: by means of; owing to; make use of, employ. **Drinking** and **taking-in**, *YIN SHI*: see *Preceding Situation*. **Repose**, *YAN*: rest, leisure, tranquillity; banquet, feast; pleasure, joy. Ideogram: shelter and rest, a wayside inn. **Delight**, *LUO*: take joy or pleasure in; pleasant, relaxed; music as harmony, elegance and pleasure.

Transforming Lines

Initial Nine

Attending tending-towards the **suburbs**.
Harvesting: **availing** of **perseverance**.
Without fault.

Comments
Attending tending-towards the **suburbs**.
Not opposing heaviness in **movement**.
Harvesting: **availing** of **perseverance**, **without fault**.
Not-yet letting-go constancy indeed.

Fields of meaning
Attend, *XU*: see *Image of the Situation*. **Tend-towards**, *YU*: move toward without necessarily reaching, in the direction of. **Suburbs**, *JIAO*: area adjoining a city where human constructions and nature interpenetrate; second of the territorial zones: city, suburbs, countryside, forest. **Harvest**, *LI*: see *Image of the Situation*. **Avail**, *YONG*: use, employ for a specific purpose; take advantage of; benefit from; capacity. Ideogram: to divine and center, applying divination to central concerns. **Persevere**, *HENG*: continue in the same way or spirit; constant, habitual, regular; self-renewing. **Without fault**, *WU JIU*: no error or harm in the situation.

Not, *BU*: common term of negation. **Oppose**, *FAN*: resist; violate, offend, attack; possessed by an evil spirit; criminal. Ideogram: violate and dog, brutal offense. **Heaviness**, *NAN*: difficulty, hardship, distress; arduous, grievous; harass; contrasts with versatility, *YI*, deal lightly with. Ideogram: bird with clipped tail on drying sticky soil. **Move**, *XING*: move or move something; motivate; emotionally moving; walk, act, do. Ideogram: successive steps. **Not-yet**, *WEI*: temporal negative indicating that something is expected to happen but has not yet occurred. **Let-go**, *SHI*: lose, let slip; omit, miss, fail; lose control of. Ideogram: drop from the hand. **Constancy**, *CHANG*: immutable order; permanent, unchanging, habitual; always; law, rule, custom. **Indeed**, *YE*: see *Preceding Situation*.

NINE AT SECOND

Attending tending-towards the **sands**.
The **small possesses words**.
Completing, significant.

Comments
Attending tending-towards the **sands**.
Inundation located in the **center indeed**.
Although the **small possesses words, using completing significant indeed**.

Fields of meaning
Attend, *XU*: see *Image of the Situation*. **Tend-towards**, *YU*: move toward without necessarily reaching, in the direction of. **Sands**, *SHA*: beach, sandbanks, shingle; gravel, pebbles; granulated. Ideogram: water and few, areas laid bare by receding water. **Small**, *XIAO*: little, common, unimportant; adapting to what crosses your path; ability to move in harmony with the vicissitudes of life; contrasts with great, *DA*, self-imposed theme or goal. **Possess**, *YOU*: see *Image of the Situation*. **Word**, *YAN*: spoken word, speech, saying; talk, discuss, address; name, signify. Ideogram: mouth and rising vapor. **Complete**, *ZHONG*: completion of a cycle that begins the next; entire, whole, all. Ideogram: silk cocoons, follow and ice, winter linking one year with the next. **Significant**, *JI*: see *Image of the Situation*.

Inundation, *YAN*: overflowing; propagate, multiply, spread out; abundance, opulence; superfluous. **Locate**, *ZAI*: be at, be situated at, dwell, reside; in, within; involved with, in the process of. Ideogram: earth and persevere, a place on the earth. **Center**, *ZHONG*: inner, central; put in the center; middle, stable point enabling you to face inner and outer changes; middle line of a trigram. Ideogram: field divided in two equal parts. **Indeed**, *YE*: see *Preceding Situation*. **Although**, *SUI*: even though, supposing that, if, even if. **Use**, *YI*: see *Patterns of Wisdom*.

NINE AT THIRD

Attending tending-towards the **bogs**.
Involvement in **illegality culminating**.

Comments
Attending tending-towards the **bogs**.
Calamity located outside indeed.
Originating from **my involvement** in **illegality**.
Respectful consideration, not destroying indeed.

Fields of meaning

Attend, *XU*: see *Image of the Situation*. **Tend-towards**, *YU*: move toward without necessarily reaching, in the direction of. **Bog**, *NI*: wet spongy soil; mire, slush, quicksand; unable to move. **Involve**, *ZHI*: devote oneself to; induce, cause, implicate; approach; manifest, express; reach the highest degree of. Ideogram: reach and come up behind. **Illegality**, *KOU*: take by force, violate, invade, sack, break the laws; brutality; enemies, outcasts, bandits. **Culminate**, *ZHI*: bring to the highest degree; arrive at the end or summit; superlative; reaching one's goal.

Calamity, *ZAI*: disaster from outside; fire, flood, plague, drought, blight, ruin; contrasts with blunder, *SHENG*, indicating personal fault. Ideogram: water and fire, elemental powers. **Locate**, *ZAI*: be at, be situated at, dwell, reside; in, within; involved with, in the process of. Ideogram: earth and persevere, a place on the earth. **Outside**, *WAI*: outer, external; unfamiliar, foreign; ignore, reject; work done outside the home; the upper trigram as indication of the outer aspects of the situation. **Indeed**, *YE*: see *Preceding Situation*. **Origin**, *ZI*: source, beginning, ground; cause, reason, motive; tracing back to the source; oneself, by oneself; spontaneous, intrinsic. **I/me/my**, *WO*: first person pronoun; the use of a specific personal pronoun, as opposed to the generic one's, *QI*, indicates an unusually strong emphasis on personal involvement. **Respect**, *JING*: stand in awe of, honor; reverent, attentive; warn; inner vigilance. Ideogram: teacher's rod taming speech and attitude. **Consider**, *SHEN*: act carefully, seriously; cautious, attentive, circumspect; still, quiet, sincere. Ideogram: heart and true. **Not**, *BU*: common term of negation. **Destroy**, *BAI*: ruin, defeat, failure; violate, subvert, decompose.

SIX AT FOURTH

Attending tending-towards blood.
Emerging originating from the **cave**.

Comments
Attending tending-towards blood.
Yielding uses hearkening indeed.

Fields of meaning

Attend, *XU*: see *Image of the Situation*. **Tend-towards**, *YU*: move toward without necessarily reaching, in the direction of. **Blood**, *XUE*: blood, the Yin fluid that maintains life; money, property. **Emerge**, *CHU*: come out of, proceed from, spring from, issue forth; appear, be born; bear, generate; leave, flee; Action of the trigram Shake, *ZHEN*. Ideogram: stem with branches and leaves emerging. **Origin**, *ZI*: source, beginning, ground; cause, reason, motive; tracing back to the source;

oneself, by oneself; spontaneous, intrinsic. **Cave**, *XUE*: cavern, den, pit; hole used for dwelling; open grave; pierce through.

Yield, *SHUN*: give way, comply, agree, follow, obey; docile, flexible; bear produce, nourish, provide; Action of the trigram Field, *KUN*. **Use**, *YI*: see *Patterns of Wisdom*. **Hearken**, *TING*: listen attentively, obey, accept, acknowledge; examine, judge, decide. Ideogram: ear and actualizing-dao. **Indeed**, *YE*: see *Preceding Situation*.

NINE AT FIFTH

Attending tending-towards taking-in liquor.
Trial, significant.

Comments
Taking-in liquor: **Trial, significant.**
Using the **center**'s **correctness indeed**.

Fields of meaning

Attend, *XU*: see *Image of the Situation*. **Tend-towards**, *YU*: move toward without necessarily reaching, in the direction of. **Take-in**, *SHI*: see *Preceding Situation*. **Liquor**, *JIU*: alcoholic beverages, distilled spirits; spirit which perfects the good and evil in human nature. Ideogram: liquid above fermenting must, separating the spirits. **Trial**, *ZHEN*: see *Image of the Situation*. **Significant**, *JI*: see *Image of the Situation*.

Use, *YI*: see *Patterns of Wisdom*. **Center**, *ZHONG*: inner, central; put in the center; middle, stable point enabling you to face inner and outer changes; middle line of a trigram. Ideogram: field divided in two equal parts. **Correct**, *ZHENG*: rectify deviation or one-sidedness; proper, straight, exact, regular; constant, rule, model. Ideogram: stop and one, hold to one thing. **Indeed**, *YE*: see *Preceding Situation*.

SIX ABOVE

Entering tending-towards the **cave**.
Possessing visitors belonging to **not inviting**: **three people coming**.
To **respecting belongs completion**, **significant**.

Comments

Visitors belonging to **not inviting come**.
To **respecting belongs completion**, **significant**.
Although not an **appropriate position**, **not-yet** the
great letting-go indeed.

Fields of meaning

Enter, *RU*: penetrate, go into, enter on, encroach on; progress; put into; Action of the trigram Root, *SUN*. **Tend-towards**, *YU*: move toward without necessarily reaching, in the direction of. **Cave**, *XUE*: cavern, den, pit; hole used for dwelling; open grave; pierce through. **Possess**, *YOU*: see *Image of the Situation*. **Visitor**, *KE*: guest; stranger, foreign, from afar; squatter; parasite; invader. **Belong/it**, *ZHI*: see *Preceding Situation*. **Not**, *BU*: common term of negation. **Invite**, *SU*: call; urge, exert pressure upon; quick, hurried. **Three/thrice**, *SAN*: number three; third time or place; active phases of a cycle; superlative; beginning of repetition (since one and two are entities in themselves). **People/person**, *REN*: humans individually and collectively; an individual; humankind. **Come**, *LAI*: approach in time or space; move toward, arrive at; future; contrasts with go, *WANG*, move away or become past. **Respect**, *JING*: stand in awe of, honor; reverent, attentive; warn; inner vigilance. Ideogram: teacher's rod taming speech and attitude. **Complete**, *ZHONG*: completion of a cycle that begins the next; entire, whole, all. Ideogram: silk cocoons, follow and ice, winter linking one year with the next. **Significant**, *JI*: see *Image of the Situation*.

Although, *SUI*: even though, supposing that, if, even if. **Appropriate**, *DANG*: suitable, capable, worthy, adequate, competent, equal to; opportune, convenient; whole lines in odd places and opened lines in even places. **Position**, *WEI*: place, location; be at; social standing, rank; position of a line in a hexagram. Ideogram: person standing. **Not-yet**, *WEI*: temporal negative indicating that something is expected to happen but has not yet occurred. **Great**, *DA*: big, noble, important, very; orient the will toward a self-imposed goal, impose direction; ability to lead or guide one's life; contrasts with small, *XIAO*, flexible adaptation to what crosses one's path. **Let-go**, *SHI*: lose, let slip; omit, miss, fail; lose control of. Ideogram: drop from the hand. **Indeed**, *YE*: see *Preceding Situation*.

Image Tradition

Attending. **Hair-growing indeed**.
Venturing located in **precedence indeed**.
Solid persisting and-also not falling.

One's righteousness not confined nor **exhausted actually**.

Attending: **possessing conformity**.
Shining Growing, **Trial**, **significant**.
The **position reaching** the **heavenly position**.
Using the **center**'s **correctness indeed**.

Harvesting: **wading** the **great river**.
Going possesses achievement indeed.

Fields of meaning

Attend, *XU*: see *Image of the Situation*. **Hair-growing**, *XU*: beard, hair; patience symbolized as waiting for hair to grow; hold back, wait for; slow; necessary. **Indeed**, *YE*: see *Preceding Situation*. **Venture**, *XIAN*: face a severe difficulty or obstruction; risk; precipice, cliff, abyss; key point, point of danger; Action of the trigram Gorge, *KAN*. Ideogram: mound and all, everything engaged at one point. **Locate**, *ZAI*: be at, be situated at, dwell, reside; in, within; involved with, in the process of. Ideogram: earth and persevere, a place on the earth. **Precede**, *QIAN*: before, earlier; anterior, former, ancient; ahead, in front. **Solid**, *GANG*: quality of the whole lines; firm, strong, unyielding, persisting. **Persist**, *JIAN*: tenacious, persevering; strong, robust, dynamic; constant as the motion of heavenly bodies in their orbits; Action of the trigram Force, *QIAN*. **And-also**, *ER*: joins and contrasts two terms. **Not**, *BU*: common term of negation. **Fall**, *XIAN*: fall down or into, sink, drop, descend; pit, trap, fault; falling water; Action of the trigram Gorge, *KAN*. **One/one's**, *QI*: general third person pronoun and possessive adjective; also: it/its, he/his, she/her, they/their. **Righteous**, *YI*: proper, just, virtuous, upright; the heart that rules itself; benevolent, loyal, devoted to public good. **Confine**, *KUN*: enclose, restrict, limit, oppress; impoverished, distressed, afflicted, exhausted, disheartened, weary. Ideogram: tree in a narrow enclosure. **Exhaust**, *QIONG*: bring to an end; limit, extremity; investigate exhaustively; destitute, indigent; end without a new beginning; distinct from complete, *ZHONG*, end of a cycle that begins the next one. Ideogram: cave and naked person, bent with disease or old age. **Actually**, *YI*: truly, really, at present. Ideogram: a dart and done, strong intention fully expressed.

Possessing conformity, *YOU FU*: see *Image of the Situation*. **Shining Growing**, **Trial**, **significant**, *GUANG HENG ZHEN JI*: see *Image of the Situation*. **Position**, *WEI*: place, location; be at; social standing, rank; position of a line in a hexagram. Ideogram: person standing. **Reach**, *HU*: arrive at a goal; move toward and achieve; to, at, in; distinct from tend-towards, *YOU*. **Heaven**, *TIAN*: see *Patterns of Wisdom*. **Use**, *YI*: see *Patterns of Wisdom*. **Center**, *ZHONG*: inner, central; put in the center;

middle, stable point enabling you to face inner and outer changes; middle line of a trigram. Ideogram: field divided in two equal parts. **Correct**, *ZHENG*: rectify deviation or one-sidedness; proper, straight, exact, regular; constant, rule, model. Ideogram: stop and one, hold to one thing.

Harvesting: **wading** the **great river**, *LI SHE DA CHUAN*: see *Image of the Situation*. Go, *WANG*: move away in time or space, depart; become past; dead, gone; contrasts with come, *LAI*, approach in time or space. **Achieve**, *GONG*: work done, results, actual accomplishment; praise, worth, merit. Ideogram: workman's square and forearm, combining craft and strength.

訟 ䷅

6 ARGUING | *Song*

The situation described by this hexagram is characterized by being involved in a dispute requiring a bold statement of one's arguments.

Image of the Situation

> **Arguing**.
> **Possessing conformity**.
> **Blocking awe**.
> The **center**, **significant**. **Completing**, **pitfall**.
> **Harvesting**: **viewing** the **great** in the **person**.
> **Not harvesting**: **wading** the **great river**.

Fields of meaning

Argue, *SONG*: dispute, plead in court, contend before a ruler, demand justice; wrangle, quarrel, litigation. Ideogram: words and public, public disputation. **Possess**, *YOU*: general term indicating possession; have, own, be endowed with. **Conform**, *FU*: accord between inner and outer; sincere, truthful, verified, reliable; capture; prisoners, spoils. Ideogram: claws over child, a bird brooding on the nest. **Block**, *ZHI*: obstruct, close, restrain, fill up. **Awe**, *TI*: respect, regard, fear; alarmed and cautious, worried; on guard. Ideogram: heart and versatility, the heart expecting change. **Center**, *ZHONG*: inner, central; put in the center; middle, stable point enabling you to face inner and outer changes; middle line of a trigram. Ideogram: field divided in two equal parts. **Significant**, *JI*: leads to the experience of meaning; favorable, propitious, appropriate. Ideogram: scholar and mouth, wise words of a sage. **Complete**, *ZHONG*: completion of a cycle that begins the next; entire, whole, all. Ideogram: silk cocoons, follow and ice, winter linking one year with the next. **Pitfall**, *XIONG*: unfortunate situation, in which the flow of life and spirit is blocked and the experience of meaning is lost; stuck and exposed to danger; inappropriate attitude. Ideogram: person in a pit. **Harvest**, *LI*: benefit, advantage, profit; realization; sharp, acute, insightful; quality of autumn and West, third stage of the Time Cycle. Ideogram: ripe grain and blade. **View**, *JIAN*: vision in all its aspects: seeing, being visible, forming mental images; visit, call on, consult. Ideogram: eye above person, active and receptive sight.

Great, *DA*: big, noble, important, very; orient the will toward a self-imposed goal, impose direction; ability to lead or guide one's life; contrasts with small, *XIAO*, flexible adaptation to what crosses one's path. **Person/people**, *REN*: humans individually and collectively; an individual; humankind. **Not**, *BU*: common term of negation. **Wading the great river**, *SHE DA CHUAN*: enter the stream of life with a goal or purpose; embark on a significant enterprise.

Outer and Inner Trigram

The upper trigram, **Energy/parch**, *QIAN/GAN*, describes the outer aspects of the situation. It has the following associations: unceasing forward movement, dynamic, enduring, untiring; spirit power, manifestation of Yang, that activates all creation and destruction in Space; heaven, sovereign, father. With the pronunciation *GAN*: parch, dry up, burn, exhaust. Ideogram: sprouts or vapors rising from the ground and sunlight, both fecundating moisture and scorching drought. *Symbol*: heaven, *TIAN*; sky, firmament, heavens; the highest realm, situated above the human world, as opposed to the earth, *DI*, located below. Ideogram: great and the one above. *Action*: persist, *JIAN*; tenacious, persevering; strong, robust, dynamic; constant as the motion of heavenly bodies in their orbits. In the family of trigrams *QIAN* is the father.

The lower trigram, **Gorge**, *KAN*, describes the inner aspects of the situation. It has the following associations: precipice, dangerous place; hole, cavity, pit, snare, trap, grave; critical time, test; risky. Ideogram: earth and cavity. *Symbol*: stream, *SHUI*, flowing water; river, tide, flood; fluid, dissolving. Ideogram: rippling water. *Actions*: venture and fall. Venture, *XIAN*: face a severe difficulty or obstruction; risk; precipice, cliff, abyss; key point, point of danger. Ideogram: mound and all, everything engaged at one point. Fall, *XIAN*: fall down or into, sink, drop, descend; pit, trap, fault; falling water. In the family of trigrams *KAN* is the middle son.

Counter Hexagram

The Counter Hexagram of **Arguing** is hexagram 37, **Household People**, which switches the emphasis from a conflict to the solidarity between members of a household.

Preceding Situation

> **Drinking** and **taking-in necessarily possess arguing**.
> To **anterior acquiescence belongs** the **use** of **arguing**.

Fields of meaning

Drink, *YIN*: drink, swallow, ingest liquid or food; inhale, suck in. **Take-in**, *SHI*:

eat, drink, ingest, absorb, incorporate; food, nourishment. **Necessarily**, *BI*: unavoidably, certainly. **Possess**, *YOU*: see *Image of the Situation*. **Argue**, *SONG*: see *Image of the Situation*. To **anterior acquiescence belongs** the **use** of, *GU SHOU ZHI YI*: understanding and accepting the preceding statement allows the consultant to make proper use of this hexagram.

Hexagrams in Pairs

> **Attending**: **not advancing indeed**.
> **Arguing**: **not connecting indeed**.

Fields of meaning
Attend, *XU*: wait, await, wait on; hesitation, delay, doubt; take care of, turn one's mind to; need, require, necessity; obstinate, fixed on. Ideogram: rain and stopped, compelled to wait, or rain and origin, providing what is needed. **Not**, *BU*: common term of negation. **Advance**, *JIN*: move forward, progress, climb; promote or be promoted; further the development of, augment; offer, introduce. **Argue**, *SONG*: see *Image of the Situation*. **Connect**, *QIN*: be close, approach, come near; cherish, help, favor; intimate; relatives, kin.

Patterns of Wisdom

> **Heaven associated** with **stream**: **contradicting movements**. **Arguing**.
> A **jun zi uses arousing affairs** to **plan beginnings**.

Fields of meaning
Heaven, *TIAN*: sky, firmament, heavens; the highest realm, situated above the human world, as opposed to the earth, *DI*, located below; Symbol of the trigram Energy, *QIAN*. Ideogram: great and the one above. **Associate**, *YU*: consort with, combine; companions; group, band, company; agree with, comply, help; in favor of. Ideogram: a pair of hands reaching downward meets a pair of hands reaching upward, helpful association. **Stream**, *SHUI*: flowing water; river, tide, flood; fluid, dissolving; Symbol of the trigram Gorge, *KAN*. Ideogram: rippling water. **Contradict**, *WEI*: oppose, disregard, disobey; seditious, perverse. **Move**, *XING*: move or move something; motivate; emotionally moving; walk, act, do. Ideogram: successive steps. **Argue**, *SONG*: see *Image of the Situation*. **Jun zi**: ideal of a person who orders his/her life in accordance with dao rather than willful intention, and uses divination in this spirit. **Use**, *YI*: by means of; owing to; make use of, employ. **Arouse**, *ZUO*: stimulate, stir up from inactivity; arise, appear; generate;

begin, invent, make. Ideogram: person and beginning. **Affairs**, *SHI*: all kinds of personal activity; matters at hand; business; function, occupation; manage; perform a task; incident, event; case in court. **Plan**, *MOU*: plot, ponder, deliberate; project, device, stratagem. **Begin**, *SHI*: commence, start, open; earliest, first; generate. Ideogram: woman and eminent, eminent feminine function of giving birth.

Transforming Lines

INITIAL SIX

Not a **perpetual place, affairs**.
The **small possesses words**.
Completing significant.

Comments
Not a **perpetual place, affairs**.
Arguing not permitting long-living indeed.
Although the **small possesses words, one's differentiation brightening indeed**.

Fields of meaning
Not, *BU*: common term of negation. **Perpetual**, *YONG*: continual, everlasting, eternal. Ideogram: flowing water. **Place**, *SUO*: position, location; residence, dwelling; where something belongs or comes from; habitual focus or object. **Affairs**, *SHI*: see *Patterns of Wisdom*. **Small**, *XIAO*: little, common, unimportant; adapting to what crosses your path; ability to move in harmony with the vicissitudes of life; contrasts with great, *DA*, self-imposed theme or goal. **Possess**, *YOU*: see *Image of the Situation*. **Word**, *YAN*: spoken word, speech, saying; talk, discuss, address; name, signify. Ideogram: mouth and rising vapor. **Complete**, *ZHONG*: see *Image of the Situation*. **Significant**, *JI*: see *Image of the Situation*.

Argue, *SONG*: see *Image of the Situation*. **Permit**, *KE*: possible because in harmony with an inherent principle; capable of; approve, authorize. Ideogram: mouth and breath, silent consent. **Long-living**, *ZHANG*: enduring, lasting, constant; extended, long, large; senior, superior, greater; increase, prosper; respect, elevate. **Indeed**, *YE*: see *Hexagrams in Pairs*. **Although**, *SUI*: even though, supposing that, if, even if. **One/one's**, *QI*: general third person pronoun and possessive adjective; also: it/its, he/his, she/her, they/their. **Differentiate**, *BIAN*: argue, dispute, criticize; sophisticated, artful. Ideogram: words and sharp or pungent. **Brightness**, *MING*: light, radiance, clarity; distinguish, discern, understand; light-giving aspect of fire, of heavenly bodies and of consciousness; brightness and fire are the Symbols of the trigram Radiance, *LI*.

NINE AT SECOND

Not controlling arguing.
Converting and-also escaping from **one's capital.**
People, three hundred doors.
Without blunder.

Comments
Not controlling arguing.
Converting, escaping: skulking indeed.
Origin below, arguing above.
Distress culminating reaping indeed.

Fields of meaning

Not, *BU*: common term of negation. **Control**, *KE*: be in charge; capable of, able to, adequate; check, obstruct, repress. Ideogram: roof beams supporting a house. **Argue**, *SONG*: see *Image of the Situation*. **Convert**, *GUI*: accomplish one's destiny; revert to the original place or state; restore, revert; turn into; goal, destination, intention; a girl getting married. Ideogram: arrive and wife, become mistress of a household. **And-also**, *ER*: joins and contrasts two terms. **Escape**, *PU*: flee, run away, turn tail; deserter, fugitive. Ideogram: go and first, precipitous flight. **One/one's**, *QI*: general third person pronoun and possessive adjective; also: it/its, he/his, she/her, they/their. **Capital**, *YI*: populous fortified city, center and symbol of the region it rules. Ideogram: enclosure and official seal. **People/person**, *REN*: humans individually and collectively; an individual; humankind. **Three**, *SAN*: number three; third time or place; active phases of a cycle; superlative; beginning of repetition (since one and two are entities in themselves). **Hundred**, *BO*: numerous, many, all; a whole class or type. **Door**, *HU*: inner door, chamber door; a household; distinct from gate, *MEN*, outer door. **Without**, *WU*: devoid of; there is not. **Blunder**, *SHENG*: mistake due to ignorance or fault; contrasts with calamity, *ZAI*, disaster from without. Ideogram: eye and growth, a film clouding sight.

Skulk, *CUAN*: sneak away and hide; furtive, stealthy; seduce into evil. Ideogram: cave and rat, rat lurking in its hole. **Indeed**, *YE*: see *Hexagrams in Pairs*. **Origin**, *ZI*: source, beginning, ground; cause, reason, motive; tracing back to the source; oneself, by oneself; spontaneous, intrinsic. **Below**, *XIA*: anything below, in all senses; lower, inner; lower trigram. **Above**, *SHANG*: anything above in all senses; higher, upper, outer; upper trigram. **Distress**, *HUAN*: tribulation, grief, affliction, illness. Ideogram: heart and clamor, the heart distressed. **Culminate**, *ZHI*: bring to the highest degree; arrive at the end or summit; superlative; reaching one's goal. **Reap**, *DUO*: harvest, collect, gather, pick. Ideogram: hand and join, taking in both hands.

Six at Third

Taking-in the **ancients' actualizing-dao**.
Trial.
Adversity: **completing**, **significant**.
Maybe adhering to **kingly affairs**.
Without accomplishment.

Comments
Taking-in the **ancients' actualizing-dao**.
Adhering to the **above**, **significant indeed**.

Fields of meaning

Take-in, *SHI*: see *Preceding Situation*. **Ancient**, *JIU*: of old, long before; worn out, spoiled; defunct. **Actualize-dao**, *DE*: realize dao in action; power, virtue; ability to follow the course traced by the ongoing process of the cosmos. Ideogram: go, straight, and heart. Linked with acquire, *DE*: acquiring that which makes a being become what it is meant to be. **Trial**, *ZHEN*: inquiry by divination and its result; righteous, firm; separating wheat from chaff; the kernel, the proven core; quality of winter and North, fourth stage of the Time Cycle. Ideogram: pearl and divination. **Adversity**, *LI*: danger, hardship, severe; threat or difficulty that must be encountered, rather than avoided; grinding stone; polish, sharpen; a challenge that strengthens and perfects the character; stimulate, excite; cruel demon. **Complete**, *ZHONG*: see *Image of the Situation*. **Significant**, *JI*: see *Image of the Situation*. **Maybe**, *HUO*: possible but not certain, perhaps. **Adhere**, *CONG*: follow, agree with, comply with, obey; join a doctrine, school, or person; servant, follower. Ideogram: two men walking, one following the other. **King**, *WANG*: sovereign, effective ruler, emperor, seen as connecting heaven and earth; reign, govern. **Affairs**, *SHI*: see *Patterns of Wisdom*. **Without**, *WU*: devoid of; there is not. **Accomplish**, *CHENG*: complete, finish, bring about; perfect, full, whole; play one's part, do one's duty; mature. Ideogram: weapon and man, able to bear arms, thus fully developed.

Above, *SHANG*: anything above in all senses; higher, upper, outer; upper trigram. **Indeed**, *YE*: see *Hexagrams in Pairs*.

NINE AT FOURTH

Not controlling arguing.
Returning, approaching fate.
Retracting, peaceful Trial.
Significant.

Comments
Returning: approaching fate.
Retracting, peaceful Trial.
Not letting-go indeed.

Fields of meaning

Not, *BU*: common term of negation. Control, *KE*: be in charge; capable of, able to, adequate; check, obstruct, repress. Ideogram: roof beams supporting a house. Argue, *SONG*: see *Image of the Situation*. Return, *FU*: go back, turn or lead back; recur, reappear, come again; restore, renew, recover; return to an earlier time or place. Ideogram: step and retrace a path. Approach, *JI*: come near to, advance toward, reach; nearby; soon, immediately. Fate, *MING*: individual destiny; birth and death as limits of life; issue orders with authority; consult the gods. Ideogram: mouth and order, words with heavenly authority. Retract, *YU*: turn around; change one's attitude; denounce an agreement, repudiate. Peace, *AN*: quiet, still, settled, secure, contented; calm, tranquilize, console. Ideogram: woman under a roof, a tranquil home. Trial, *ZHEN*: inquiry by divination and its result; righteous, firm; separating wheat from chaff; the kernel, the proven core; quality of winter and North, fourth stage of the Time Cycle. Ideogram: pearl and divination. Significant, *JI*: see *Image of the Situation*.

Let-go, *SHI*: lose, let slip; omit, miss, fail; lose control of. Ideogram: drop from the hand. Indeed, *YE*: see *Hexagrams in Pairs*.

NINE AT FIFTH

Arguing. Spring significant.

Comments
Arguing. Spring significant.
Using the **center**'s **correctness indeed.**

Fields of meaning

Argue, *SONG*: see *Image of the Situation*. **Spring**, *YUAN*: source, origin, head; arise, begin; first generating impulse; great, excellent; quality of springtime and East, first stage of the Time Cycle. **Significant**, *JI*: see *Image of the Situation*.

Use, *YI*: see *Patterns of Wisdom*. **Center**, *ZHONG*: see *Image of the Situation*. **Correct**, *ZHENG*: rectify deviation or one-sidedness; proper, straight, exact, regular; constant, rule, model. Ideogram: stop and one, hold to one thing. **Indeed**, *YE*: see *Hexagrams in Pairs*.

NINE ABOVE

Maybe to **bestowing belongs** a **pouched belt**.
Completing dawn thrice depriving of **it**.

Comments
Using arguing acquiesces in **submitting**.
Truly not standing respectfully indeed.

Fields of meaning

Maybe, *HUO*: possible but not certain, perhaps. **Bestow**, *XI*: grant, confer upon; reward, gift; tin, pewter. Ideogram: metal and change. **Belong/it**, *ZHI*: establishes between two terms a connection similar to the Saxon genitive, in which the second term belongs to the first one; at the end of a sentence it refers to something previously mentioned or implied. **Pouched belt**, *PAN DAI*: sash that serves as a purse; money-belt. **Complete**, *ZHONG*: see *Image of the Situation*. **Dawn**, *ZHAO*: early morning, before daybreak. **Three/thrice**, *SAN*: number three; third time or place; active phases of a cycle; superlative; beginning of repetition (since one and two are entities in themselves). **Deprive**, *CHI*: strip of rank, take away a ceremonial garment; lose authority or enthusiasm.

Use, *YI*: see *Patterns of Wisdom*. **Argue**, *SONG*: see *Image of the Situation*. **Acquiesce**, *SHOU*: accept, make peace with, agree to, receive; at rest, satisfied; patient. **Submit**, *FU*: yield, obey, acquiesce; enforce obedience. **Truly**, *YI*: in fact; also; nevertheless. **Not**, *BU*: common term of negation. **Stand**, *ZU*: base, foot, leg; rest on, support; stance; sufficient, capable, worth. Ideogram: foot and calf resting. **Respect**, *JING*: stand in awe of, honor; reverent, attentive; warn; inner vigilance. Ideogram: teacher's rod taming speech and attitude. **Indeed**, *YE*: see *Hexagrams in Pairs*.

Image Tradition

Arguing. Solid above, venture below.
Venturing and-also persisting. Arguing.

Arguing: possessing conformity.
Blocking awe: the **center, significant.**
The **solid comes and-also acquires** the **center indeed.**

Completing, pitfall.
Arguing not permitting accomplishment indeed.

Harvesting: viewing the **great** in the **person.**
Honoring the **center**'s **correctness indeed.**

Not harvesting: wading the **great river.**
Entering tending-towards the **abyss indeed.**

Fields of meaning

Argue, *SONG*: see *Image of the Situation.* **Solid,** *GANG*: quality of the whole lines; firm, strong, unyielding, persisting. **Above,** *SHANG*: anything above in all senses; higher, upper, outer; upper trigram. **Venture,** *XIAN*: face a severe difficulty or obstruction; risk; precipice, cliff, abyss; key point, point of danger; Action of the trigram Gorge, *KAN*. Ideogram: mound and all, everything engaged at one point. **Below,** *XIA*: anything below, in all senses; lower, inner; lower trigram. **And-also,** *ER*: joins and contrasts two terms. **Persist,** *JIAN*: tenacious, persevering; strong, robust, dynamic; constant as the motion of heavenly bodies in their orbits; Action of the trigram Force, *QIAN*.

Possessing conformity, *YOU FU*: see *Image of the Situation.* **Blocking awe,** *ZHI TI*: see *Image of the Situation.* The **center, significant,** *ZHONG JI*: see *Image of the Situation.* **Come,** *LAI*: approach in time or space; move toward, arrive at; future; contrasts with go, *WANG*, move away or become past. **Acquire,** *DE*: obtain the desired object; possession; satisfied, fulfilled; it is permitted; agree with; wish for, desire covetously. Ideogram: go and obstacle, going through obstacles to the goal. **Indeed,** *YE*: see *Hexagrams in Pairs.*

Completing, pitfall, *ZHONG XIONG*: see *Image of the Situation.* **Not,** *BU*: common term of negation. **Permit,** *KE*: possible because in harmony with an inherent principle; capable of; approve, authorize. Ideogram: mouth and breath, silent consent. **Accomplish,** *CHENG*: complete, finish, bring about; perfect, full, whole; play one's part, do one's duty; mature. Ideogram: weapon and man, able to bear arms, thus fully developed.

Harvesting: viewing the **great** in the **person,** *LI JIAN DA REN*: see *Image of the Situation.* **Honor,** *SHANG*: esteem, give high rank to, exalt, celebrate; rise, elevate; put one thing on top of another. **Correct,** *ZHENG*: rectify deviation or one-sidedness; proper, straight, exact, regular; constant, rule, model. Ideogram: stop and one, hold to one thing.

Wading the great river, *SHE DA CHUAN*: see *Image of the Situation.* **Enter,** *RU*: penetrate, go into, enter on, encroach on; progress; put into; Action of the trigram Root, *SUN.* **Tend-towards,** *YU*: move toward without necessarily reaching, in the direction of. **Abyss,** *YUAN*: deep hole or gulf, where backwaters eddy and accumulate; whirlpool, deep water; unfathomable; depth of feelings, deep sincerity.

師

7 THE LEGIONS | *Shi*

The situation described by this hexagram is characterized by the organization of scattered elements into a functional units around a worthy aggregating center, like an army around its commander.

Image of the Situation

> The **legions**.
> **Trial**.
> The **respectable person**, **significant**.
> **Without fault**.

Fields of meaning

Legions, *SHI*: army, troops; leader, general, model, master; organize, make functional; take as a model, imitate, follow. Ideogram: heap and whole, turn confusion into a functional unit. **Trial**, *ZHEN*: inquiry by divination and its result; righteous, firm; separating wheat from chaff; the kernel, the proven core; quality of winter and North, fourth stage of the Time Cycle. Ideogram: pearl and divination. **Respectable**, *ZHANG*: exemplary person, worthy of respect, elder. **Person/people**, *REN*: humans individually and collectively; an individual; humankind. **Significant**, *JI*: leads to the experience of meaning; favorable, propitious, appropriate. Ideogram: scholar and mouth, wise words of a sage. **Without fault**, *WU JIU*: no error or harm in the situation.

Outer and Inner Trigram

The upper trigram, **Space**, *KUN*, describes the outer aspects of the situation. It has the following associations: surface of the world; support of all existence, manifestation of Yin, where Energy or Yang activates all creation and destruction; all-involving service; earth; moon, wife, mother; rest, receptivity, docile obedience. Ideogram: terrestrial globe and stretch out. *Symbol*: earth, *DI*; the earth, ground on which the human world rests; basis of all things, nourishes all things; essential Yin. *Action*: yield, *SHUN*: give way, comply, agree, follow, obey; docile, flexible; bear produce, nourish, provide. In the family of trigrams *KUN* is the mother.

The lower trigram, **Gorge**, *KAN*, describes the inner aspects of the situation.

It has the following associations: precipice, dangerous place; hole, cavity, pit, snare, trap, grave; critical time, test; risky. Ideogram: earth and cavity. *Symbol*: stream, *SHUI*, flowing water; river, tide, flood; fluid, dissolving. Ideogram: rippling water. *Actions*: venture and fall. Venture, *XIAN*: face a severe difficulty or obstruction; risk; precipice, cliff, abyss; key point, point of danger. Ideogram: mound and all, everything engaged at one point. Fall, *XIAN*: fall down or into, sink, drop, descend; pit, trap, fault; falling water. In the family of trigrams *KAN* is the middle son.

Counter Hexagram

The Counter Hexagram of **The Legions** is hexagram 24, **Return**, which switches the emphasis from the forward march of **The Legions** to a re-emergence of the past.

Preceding Situation

> **Arguing necessarily possesses crowds rising-up**.
> To **anterior acquiescence belongs** the **use** of the **legions**.
> The **legions imply crowds indeed**.

Fields of meaning

Argue, *SONG*: dispute, plead in court, contend before a ruler, demand justice; wrangle, quarrel, litigation. Ideogram: words and public, public disputation. **Necessarily**, *BI*: unavoidably, certainly. **Possess**, *YOU*: general term indicating possession; have, own, be endowed with. **Crowds**, *ZHONG*: many people, large group, masses; all, all beings. **Rise-up**, *QI*: stand up, erect; stimulate, excite; undertake, begin, develop. To **anterior acquiescence belongs** the **use** of, *GU SHOU ZHI YI*: understanding and accepting the preceding statement allows the consultant to make proper use of this hexagram. **Legions**, *SHI*: see *Image of the Situation*. **Imply**, *ZHE*: further signify; additional meaning. **Indeed**, *YE*: emphasizes and intensifies the previous statement.

Hexagrams in Pairs

> **Grouping**: **delight**.
> The **legions**: **grief**.

Fields of meaning

Group, *BI*: compare and select, order things and put them in classes; find what you belong with; associate with, unite, join, harmonize; neighbor, near. Ideogram: two men following each other. **Delight**, *LUO*: take joy or pleasure in; pleasant, relaxed; music as harmony, elegance and pleasure. **Legions**, *SHI*: see *Image of the Situation*. **Grieve**, *YOU*: mourn; sorrow, melancholy, anxiety, care, hidden sorrow. Ideogram: heart, head, and limp, heart-sick and anxious.

Patterns of Wisdom

The **earth**'s **center possesses stream**. The **legions**.
A **jun zi uses tolerating** the **commoners** to **accumulate crowds**.

Fields of meaning

Earth, *DI*: the earth, ground on which the human world rests; basis of all things, nourishes all things; essential Yin; Symbol of the trigram Space, *KUN*. **Center**, *ZHONG*: inner, central; put in the center; middle, stable point enabling you to face inner and outer changes; middle line of a trigram. Ideogram: field divided in two equal parts. **Possess**, *YOU*: see *Preceding Situation*. **Stream**, *SHUI*: flowing water; river, tide, flood; fluid, dissolving; Symbol of the trigram Gorge, *KAN*. Ideogram: rippling water. **Legions**, *SHI*: see *Image of the Situation*. **Jun zi**: ideal of a person who orders his/her life in accordance with dao rather than willful intention, and uses divination in this spirit. **Use**, *YI*: by means of; owing to; make use of, employ. **Tolerate**, *RONG*: allow, contain, endure, bear; accept graciously. Ideogram: full stream bed, tolerating and containing. **Commoners**, *MIN*: common people, masses; working class supporting the social hierarchy; undeveloped potential in the individual. **Accumulate**, *CHU*: retain, hoard, gather, herd together; control, restrain; domesticate, tame, train; raise, feed, sustain, bring up. Ideogram: field and black, fertile black soil, accumulated through retaining silt. **Crowds**, *ZHONG*: see *Preceding Situation*.

Transforming Lines

Initial Six

The **legions emerging using ordinance**.
Obstructing virtue: **pitfall**.

Comments
The **legions emerging using ordinance**.
Letting-go the **ordinance**: **pitfall indeed**.

Fields of meaning
Legions, *SHI*: see *Image of the Situation*. **Emerge**, *CHU*: come out of, proceed from, spring from, issue forth; appear, be born; bear, generate; leave, flee; Action of the trigram Shake, *ZHEN*. Ideogram: stem with branches and leaves emerging. **Use**, *YI*: see *Patterns of Wisdom*. **Ordinance**, *LÜ*: law, regulation; discipline, self-mastery. Ideogram: writing and move, codes that govern action. **Obstruct**, *PI*: closed, stopped; bar the way; obstacle; unfortunate, wicked; refuse, disapprove, deny. Ideogram: mouth and not, blocked communication. **Virtue**, *ZANG*: goodness, generosity. **Pitfall**, *XIONG*: unfortunate situation, in which the flow of life and spirit is blocked and the experience of meaning is lost; stuck and exposed to danger; inappropriate attitude. Ideogram: person in a pit.

Let-go, *SHI*: lose, let slip; omit, miss, fail; lose control of. Ideogram: drop from the hand. **Indeed**, *YE*: see *Preceding Situation*.

NINE AT SECOND

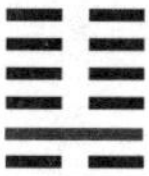

Locating the **legions** in the **center**, **significant**.
Without fault.
The **king thrice bestows fate**.

Comments
Locating the **legions** in the **center**, **significant**.
Receiving heavenly favor indeed.
The **king thrice bestows fate**.
Cherishing the **myriad fiefdoms indeed**.

Fields of meaning
Locate, *ZAI*: be at, be situated at, dwell, reside; in, within; involved with, in the process of. Ideogram: earth and persevere, a place on the earth. **Legions**, *SHI*: see *Image of the Situation*. **Center**, *ZHONG*: see *Patterns of Wisdom*. **Significant**, *JI*: see *Image of the Situation*. **Without fault**, *WU JIU*: see *Image of the Situation*. **King**, *WANG*: sovereign, effective ruler, emperor, seen as connecting heaven and earth; reign, govern. **Three/thrice**, *SAN*: number three; third time or place; active phases of a cycle; superlative; beginning of repetition (since one and two are entities in themselves). **Bestow**, *XI*: grant, confer upon; reward, gift; tin, pewter. Ideogram: metal and change. **Fate**, *MING*: individual destiny; birth and death as limits of life; issue orders with authority; consult the gods. Ideogram: mouth and order, words with heavenly authority.

Receive, *CHENG*: receive gifts or commands from superiors or customers; take in hand; give, offer respectfully; help, support. Ideogram: accepting a seal of office. **Heaven**, *TIAN*: sky, firmament, heavens; the highest realm, situated above the human world, as opposed to the earth, *DI*, located below; Symbol of the trigram Energy, *QIAN*. Ideogram: great and the one above. **Favor**, *CHONG*: receive or confer gifts; obtain grace, win favor; dote on a woman; affection, benevolence towards a subordinate. **Indeed**, *YE*: see *Preceding Situation*. **Cherish**, *HUAI*: carry in the heart or womb; dwell on, think fondly of; cling to; heart, breast. Ideogram: heart and hide, cherish in the heart. **Myriad**, *WAN*: ten thousand; countless, many, everyone. Ideogram: swarm of insects. **Fiefdom**, *BANG*: region governed by a feudatory.

Six at Third

The **legions maybe carting corpses**.
Pitfall.

Comments
The **legions maybe carting corpses**.
The **great without achievement indeed**.

Fields of meaning
Legions, *SHI*: see *Image of the Situation*. **Maybe**, *HUO*: possible but not certain, perhaps. **Cart**, *YU*: a vehicle and its carrying capacity; contain, hold, sustain. **Corpse**, *SHI*: dead human body, effigy, statue; inefficient, useless; impersonate. **Pitfall**, *XIONG*: unfortunate situation, in which the flow of life and spirit is blocked and the experience of meaning is lost; stuck and exposed to danger; inappropriate attitude. Ideogram: person in a pit.

Great, *DA*: big, noble, important, very; orient the will toward a self-imposed goal, impose direction; ability to lead or guide one's life; contrasts with small, *XIAO*, flexible adaptation to what crosses one's path. **Without**, *WU*: devoid of; there is not. **Achieve**, *GONG*: work done, results, actual accomplishment; praise, worth, merit. Ideogram: workman's square and forearm, combining craft and strength. **Indeed**, *YE*: see *Preceding Situation*.

Six at Fourth

The **legions' left camp**.
Without fault.

Comments
The **left camp, without fault.**
Not-yet letting-go constancy indeed.

Fields of meaning
Legions, *SHI*: see *Image of the Situation.* **Left,** *ZUO*: left side, left hand; East; secondary, assistant, inferior; defective, unfavorable. **Camp,** *CI*: resting place, inn, shed; halt, breathing-spell. Ideogram: two and breath, pausing to breathe. **Without fault,** *WU JIU*: see *Image of the Situation.*

Not-yet, *WEI*: temporal negative indicating that something is expected to happen but has not yet occurred. **Let-go,** *SHI*: lose, let slip; omit, miss, fail; lose control of. Ideogram: drop from the hand. **Constancy,** *CHANG*: immutable order; permanent, unchanging, habitual; always; law, rule, custom. **Indeed,** *YE*: see *Preceding Situation.*

Six at Fifth

The **fields possess wildfowl.**
Harvesting: holding-on to **words.**
Without fault.
The **long-living son conducts** the **legions.**
The **junior son carts corpses.**
Trial, pitfall.

Comments
The **long-living son conducts** the **legions.**
Using the **center moving indeed.**
The **junior son carts corpses.**
Commissioning not appropriate indeed.

Fields of meaning
Field, *TIAN*: cultivated land, farming land; preferred terrain for hunting, since game in the fields cannot escape the hunt. Ideogram: square divided into four sections, delineating fields. **Possess,** *YOU*: see *Preceding Situation.* **Wildfowl,** *QIN*: birds; four-legged animals; hunt, shoot with an arrow; capture; prisoner. **Harvest,** *LI*: benefit, advantage, profit; realization; sharp, acute, insightful; quality of autumn and West, third stage of the Time Cycle. Ideogram: ripe grain and blade. **Hold-on,** *ZHI*: lay hold of, seize, take in hand; keep, maintain, look after; manage, control. Ideogram: criminal and seize. **Word,** *YAN*: spoken word, speech, saying; talk, discuss, address; name, signify. Ideogram: mouth and rising vapor. **Without**

fault, *WU JIU*: see *Image of the Situation*. **Long-living**, *ZHANG*: enduring, lasting, constant; extended, long, large; senior, superior, greater; increase, prosper; respect, elevate. **Son(hood)**, *ZI*: son, male child; heirs, offspring, posterity; living up to the ideal of the ancestors as highest human aspiration; seed, kernel, egg; sage, teacher; nadir, deepest point, midnight, mid-winter. **Conduct**, *SHUAI*: lead; leader, chief, commander; follow, follower. **Legions**, *SHI*: see *Image of the Situation*. **Junior**, *DI*: younger relatives who owe respect to their elders. **Cart**, *YU*: a vehicle and its carrying capacity; contain, hold, sustain. **Corpse**, *SHI*: dead human body, effigy, statue; inefficient, useless; impersonate. **Trial**, *ZHEN*: see *Image of the Situation*. **Pitfall**, *XIONG*: unfortunate situation, in which the flow of life and spirit is blocked and the experience of meaning is lost; stuck and exposed to danger; inappropriate attitude. Ideogram: person in a pit.

Use, *YI*: see *Patterns of Wisdom*. **Center**, *ZHONG*: see *Patterns of Wisdom*. **Move**, *XING*: move or move something; motivate; emotionally moving; walk, act, do. Ideogram: successive steps. **Indeed**, *YE*: see *Preceding Situation*. **Commission**, *SHI*: charge somebody with a task; command, order; messenger, agent; obey, follow. Ideogram: person and office. **Not**, *BU*: common term of negation. **Appropriate**, *DANG*: suitable, capable, worthy, adequate, competent, equal to; opportune, convenient; whole lines in odd places and opened lines in even places.

SIX ABOVE

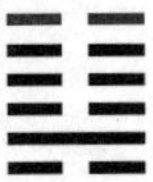

The **great** in the **chief possesses fate**.
Disclosing the **city**, **receiving** a **household**.
The **small** in the **person**, no **availing** of.

Comments

The **great** in the **chief possesses fate**.
Using correct achievement indeed.
The **small** in the **person**, **no availing** of.
Necessarily disarraying the **fiefdoms indeed**.

Fields of meaning

Great, *DA*: big, noble, important, very; orient the will toward a self-imposed goal, impose direction; ability to lead or guide one's life; contrasts with small, *XIAO*, flexible adaptation to what crosses one's path. **Chief**, *JUN*: prince, ruler; lead, direct; wise person. Ideogram: mouth and direct, giving orders. **Possess**, *YOU*: see *Preceding Situation*. **Fate**, *MING*: individual destiny; birth and death as limits of life; issue orders with authority; consult the gods. Ideogram: mouth and order, words with heavenly authority. **Disclose**, *KAI*: open, reveal, unfold, display; enact rites, clear land; final phase of both hemicycles in the Universal Compass. Ideogram: house doors bursting open. **City**, *GUO*: city, state, country, nation; area of only human constructions; first of the territorial zones: city, suburbs, countryside, forest. **Receive**, *CHENG*: receive gifts or commands from superiors or customers; take in hand; give, offer respectfully; help, support. Ideogram: accepting a seal of office. **Household**, *JIA*: home, house; family; dwell, reside; domestic, within doors; shop, school, doctrine. Ideogram: roof and pig or dog, the most valued domestic animals, living under the same roof with the family. **Small**, *XIAO*: little, common, unimportant; adapting to what crosses your path; ability to move in harmony with the vicissitudes of life; contrasts with great, *DA*, self-imposed theme or goal. **Person/people**, *REN*: see *Image of the Situation*. **No**, *WU*: common term of negation. **Avail**, *YONG*: use, employ for a specific purpose; take advantage of; benefit from; capacity. Ideogram: to divine and center, applying divination to central concerns.

Use, *YI*: see *Patterns of Wisdom*. **Correct**, *ZHENG*: rectify deviation or one-sidedness; proper, straight, exact, regular; constant, rule, model. Ideogram: stop and one, hold to one thing. **Achieve**, *GONG*: work done, results, actual accomplishment; praise, worth, merit. Ideogram: workman's square and forearm, combining craft and strength. **Indeed**, *YE*: see *Preceding Situation*. **Necessarily**, *BI*: see *Preceding Situation*. **Disarray**, *LUAN*: throw into disorder, mislay, confuse; out of place; discord, insurrection, anarchy. **Fiefdom**, *BANG*: region governed by a feudatory.

Image Tradition

The **legions**. **Crowds indeed**.
Trial. **Correcting indeed**.
Able to **use crowds** for **correcting**.
Actually permitted using kinghood.
The **solid** in the **center and-also** in **correspondence**.

Moving: **venturing and-also yielding**.
Using the **latter rules below heaven**.
And-also the **commoners adhere** to **it**.
Significant, **furthermore is** it **actually faulty?**

Fields of meaning

Legions, *SHI*: see *Image of the Situation*. **Crowds**, *ZHONG*: see *Preceding Situation*. **Indeed**, *YE*: see *Preceding Situation*. **Trial**, *ZHEN*: see *Image of the Situation*. **Correct**, *ZHENG*: rectify deviation or one-sidedness; proper, straight, exact, regular;

constant, rule, model. Ideogram: stop and one, hold to one thing. **Able/enable**, *NENG*: ability, power, skill, art; competent, talented; duty, function, capacity. Ideogram: an animal with strong hooves and bones, able to carry and defend. **Use**, *YI*: see *Patterns of Wisdom*. **Actually**, *YI*: truly, really, at present. Ideogram: a dart and done, strong intention fully expressed. **Permit**, *KE*: possible because in harmony with an inherent principle; capable of; approve, authorize. Ideogram: mouth and breath, silent consent. **King**, *WANG*: sovereign, effective ruler, emperor, seen as connecting heaven and earth; reign, govern. **Solid**, *GANG*: quality of the whole lines; firm, strong, unyielding, persisting. **Center**, *ZHONG*: see *Patterns of Wisdom*. **And-also**, *ER*: joins and contrasts two terms. **Correspond**, *YING*: be in agreement or harmony; proper, suitable; resonate together, answer to; relation between the lines (1 and 4, 2 and 5, 3 and 6) when they form the pair opened and whole, supple and solid. Ideogram: heart and obey.

Move, *XING*: move or move something; motivate; emotionally moving; walk, act, do. Ideogram: successive steps. **Venture**, *XIAN*: face a severe difficulty or obstruction; risk; precipice, cliff, abyss; key point, point of danger; Action of the trigram Gorge, *KAN*. Ideogram: mound and all, everything engaged at one point. **Yield**, *SHUN*: give way, comply, agree, follow, obey; docile, flexible; bear produce, nourish, provide; Action of the trigram Field, *KUN*. **Latter**, *CI*: this, that, what was last spoken of. **Rule/poison**, *DU*: noxious, malignant, hurtful, destructive; despise, hate; sickness, affliction; govern, direct educate. **Below heaven**, *TIAN XIA*: human world, between heaven and earth. **Commoners**, *MIN*: see *Patterns of Wisdom*. **Adhere**, *CONG*: follow, agree with, comply with, obey; join a doctrine, school, or person; servant, follower. Ideogram: two men walking, one following the other. **It/belong**, *ZHI*: establishes between two terms a connection similar to the Saxon genitive, in which the second term belongs to the first one; at the end of a sentence it refers to something previously mentioned or implied. **Significant**, *JI*: see *Image of the Situation*. **Furthermore**, *YOU*: moreover; in addition to; again. **Is?**, *HE*: ask, inquire; what? which? who? how? why? where? an interrogative particle, often introducing a rhetorical question: is it? is it not? **Actually**, *YI*: truly, really, at present. Ideogram: a dart and done, strong intention fully expressed. **Fault**, *JIU*: unworthy conduct that leads to harm, illness, misfortune; guilt, crime, punishment. Ideogram: person and differ, differ from what you should be.

比

8 GROUPING | *Bi*

The situation described by this hexagram is characterized by sorting and comparing things or people according to their essential nature and grouping what belongs together.

Image of the Situation

Grouping.
Significant.
Retracing the **oracle-consulting**: **Spring, perpetual**
Trial.
Without fault.
Not soothing, on all **sides coming.**
Afterwards husbanding: **pitfall.**

Fields of meaning

Group, *BI*: compare and select, order things and put them in classes; find what you belong with; associate with, unite, join, harmonize; neighbor, near. Ideogram: two men following each other. **Significant**, *JI*: leads to the experience of meaning; favorable, propitious, appropriate. Ideogram: scholar and mouth, wise words of a sage. **Retrace**, *YUAN*: source, origin, beginning; going back to the source; repeat; a second time. Ideogram: pure water at its source. **Oracle-consulting**, *SHI*: yarrow stalks and their use in divination. **Spring**, *YUAN*: source, origin, head; arise, begin; first generating impulse; great, excellent; quality of springtime and East, first stage of the Time Cycle. **Perpetual**, *YONG*: continual, everlasting, eternal. Ideogram: flowing water. **Trial**, *ZHEN*: inquiry by divination and its result; righteous, firm; separating wheat from chaff; the kernel, the proven core; quality of winter and North, fourth stage of the Time Cycle. Ideogram: pearl and divination. **Without fault**, *WU JIU*: no error or harm in the situation. **Not**, *BU*: common term of negation. **Soothe**, *NING*: calm, pacify; create peace of mind; tranquil, quiet. Ideogram: shelter above heart, dish and breath, physical and spiritual comfort. **Sides**, *FANG*: cardinal directions; surface of the earth extending to the four cardinal points; everywhere; limits, boundaries. **Come**, *LAI*: approach in time or space; move toward, arrive at; future; contrasts with go, *WANG*, move away or become past. **After(wards)/later**, *HOU*: come after in time, subsequent; put oneself after; behind, back, draw back; the second; attendants, heirs, successors, posterity. **Husband**, *FU*: adult, man, male spouse; scholar, distinguished man; one who can help; manage a household. Ideogram: man with a pin in his hair to show that he is of age. **Pitfall**, *XIONG*: unfortunate situation, in which the flow of life and spirit is blocked and the experience of meaning is lost; stuck and exposed to danger; inappropriate attitude. Ideogram: person in a pit.

Outer and Inner Trigram

The upper trigram, **Gorge**, *KAN*, describes the outer aspects of the situation. It has the following associations: precipice, dangerous place; hole, cavity, pit, snare, trap, grave; critical time, test; risky. Ideogram: earth and cavity. *Symbol*: stream, *SHUI*, flowing water; river, tide, flood; fluid, dissolving. Ideogram: rippling water. *Actions*: venture and fall. Venture, *XIAN*: face a severe difficulty or obstruction; risk; precipice, cliff, abyss; key point, point of danger. Ideogram: mound and all, everything engaged at one point. Fall, *XIAN*: fall down or into, sink, drop, descend; pit, trap, fault; falling water. In the family of trigrams *KAN* is the middle son.

The lower trigram, **Space**, *KUN*, describes the inner aspects of the situation. It has the following associations: surface of the world; support of all existence, manifestation of Yin, where Energy or Yang activates all creation and destruction; all-involving service; earth; moon, wife, mother; rest, receptivity, docile obedience. Ideogram: terrestrial globe and stretch out. *Symbol*: earth, *DI*; the earth, ground on which the human world rests; basis of all things, nourishes all things; essential Yin. *Action*: yield, *SHUN*: give way, comply, agree, follow, obey; docile, flexible; bear produce, nourish, provide. In the family of trigrams *KUN* is the mother.

Counter Hexagram

The Counter Hexagram of **Grouping** is hexagram 23, **Stripping**, which switches the emphasis from grouping people or things to stripping away something which no longer fits.

Preceding Situation

> **Crowds necessarily possess** a **place** to **group**.
> To **anterior acquiescence belongs** the **use** of **grouping**.
> **Grouping implies groups**.

Fields of meaning

Crowds, *ZHONG*: many people, large group, masses; all, all beings. **Necessarily**,

BI: unavoidably, certainly. **Possess**, *YOU*: general term indicating possession; have, own, be endowed with. **Place**, *SUO*: position, location; residence, dwelling; where something belongs or comes from; habitual focus or object. **Group**, *BI*: see *Image of the Situation*. To **anterior acquiescence belongs** the **use** of, *GU SHOU ZHI YI*: understanding and accepting the preceding statement allows the consultant to make proper use of this hexagram. **Imply**, *ZHE*: further signify; additional meaning.

Hexagrams in Pairs

> **Grouping**: **delight**.
> The **legions**: **grief**.

Fields of meaning

Group, *BI*: see *Image of the Situation*. **Delight**, *LUO*: take joy or pleasure in; pleasant, relaxed; music as harmony, elegance and pleasure. **Legions**, *SHI*: army, troops; leader, general, model, master; organize, make functional; take as a model, imitate, follow. Ideogram: heap and whole, turn confusion into a functional unit. **Grieve**, *YOU*: mourn; sorrow, melancholy, anxiety, care, hidden sorrow. Ideogram: heart, head, and limp, heart-sick and anxious.

Patterns of Wisdom

> The **earth possesses stream above**. **Grouping**.
> The **earlier kings used installing** a **myriad cities** to **connect** the **related feudatories**.

Fields of meaning

Earth, *DI*: the earth, ground on which the human world rests; basis of all things, nourishes all things; essential Yin; Symbol of the trigram Space, *KUN*. **Possess**, *YOU*: see *Preceding Situation*. **Stream**, *SHUI*: flowing water; river, tide, flood; fluid, dissolving; Symbol of the trigram Gorge, *KAN*. Ideogram: rippling water. **Above**, *SHANG*: anything above in all senses; higher, upper, outer; upper trigram. **Group**, *BI*: see *Image of the Situation*. **Earlier Kings**, *XIAN WANG*: ideal rulers of old; the golden age, primal time; mythical sages in harmony with nature. **Use**, *YI*: by means of; owing to; make use of, employ. **Install**, *JIAN*: set up, establish, erect, nominate; robust, solid; confirm a law or an institution. **Myriad**, *WAN*: ten thousand; countless, many, everyone. Ideogram: swarm of insects. **City**, *GUO*: city, state, country, nation; area of only human constructions; first of the territorial zones: city, suburbs, countryside, forest. **Connect**, *QIN*: be close, approach, come near; cherish, help, favor; intimate; relatives, kin. **Relate**, *ZHU*: in regard to; all, every, several. Ideogram: words and imply. **Feudatory**, *HOU*: noble entrusted with governing a province; in charge of executive tasks; distinct from prince, *GONG*, representative of the central decisional power at the court.

Transforming Lines

INITIAL SIX

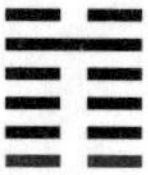

Possessing conformity: **grouping it**.
Without fault.
Possessing conformity: **overfilling** the **jar**.
Completion coming, **possessing more**, **significant**.

Comments
Initial six belonging to **grouping**.
Possessing more, **significant indeed**.

Fields of meaning

Possess, *YOU*: see *Preceding Situation*. **Conform**, *FU*: accord between inner and outer; sincere, truthful, verified, reliable; capture; prisoners, spoils. Ideogram: claws over child, a bird brooding on the nest. **Group**, *BI*: see *Image of the Situation*. **It/belong**, *ZHI*: establishes between two terms a connection similar to the Saxon genitive, in which the second term belongs to the first one; at the end of a sentence it refers to something previously mentioned or implied. **Without fault**, *WU JIU*: see *Image of the Situation*. **Overfill**, *YING*: fill completely; full, at the point of overflowing; excess, arrogance. Ideogram: vessel and overflow. **Jar**, *FOU*: earthenware vessels; wine-jars and drums. Ideogram: jar containing liquor. **Complete**, *ZHONG*: completion of a cycle that begins the next; entire, whole, all. Ideogram: silk cocoons, follow and ice, winter linking one year with the next. **Come**, *LAI*: see *Image of the Situation*. **More**, *TUO*: another, something else; add to. **Significant**, *JI*: see *Image of the Situation*.

Initial, *CHU*: beginning, incipient, first step or part; bottom line of a hexagram. Ideogram: knife and garment, cutting out the pattern. **Six**, *LIU*: number six; transforming opened line; six lines of a hexagram. **Belong/it**, *ZHI*: establishes between two terms a connection similar to the Saxon genitive, in which the second term belongs to the first one; at the end of a sentence it refers to something previously mentioned or implied. **Indeed**, *YE*: emphasizes and intensifies the previous statement.

Six at Second

To **grouping belongs** an **origin inside**.
Trial, **significant**.

Comments

To **grouping belongs** an **origin inside**.
Not the **origin letting-go indeed**.

Fields of meaning

Group, *BI*: see *Image of the Situation*. **Belong/it**, *ZHI*: establishes between two terms a connection similar to the Saxon genitive, in which the second term belongs to the first one; at the end of a sentence it refers to something previously mentioned or implied. **Origin**, *ZI*: source, beginning, ground; cause, reason, motive; tracing back to the source; oneself, by oneself; spontaneous, intrinsic. **Inside**, *NEI*: within, inner, interior; inside of the house and those who work there, particularly women; inside of the body, inner organs; the lower trigram, as opposed to outside, *WAI*, the upper. Ideogram: border and enter. **Trial**, *ZHEN*: see *Image of the Situation*. **Significant**, *JI*: see *Image of the Situation*.

Not, *BU*: common term of negation. **Let-go**, *SHI*: lose, let slip; omit, miss, fail; lose control of. Ideogram: drop from the hand. **Indeed**, *YE*: emphasizes and intensifies the previous statement.

Six at Third

To **grouping belongs in-no-way people**.

Comments

To **grouping belongs in-no-way people**.
Not truly injuring reached.

Fields of meaning

Group, *BI*: see *Image of the Situation*. **Belong/it**, *ZHI*: establishes between two terms a connection similar to the Saxon genitive, in which the second term belongs to the first one; at the end of a sentence it refers to something previously mentioned or implied. **In-no-way**, *FEI*: strong negative; not so; bandit, rebel; unjust, immoral. Ideogram: a box filled with opposition. **People/person**, *REN*: humans individually and collectively; an individual; humankind.

Not, *BU*: common term of negation. **Truly**, *YI*: in fact; also; nevertheless. **Injure**, *SHANG*: hurt, wound, damage; grief, distress, mourning; sad at heart, afflicted. **Reach**, *HU*: arrive at a goal; move toward and achieve; to, at, in; distinct from tend-towards, *YOU*.

SIX AT FOURTH

Outside grouping it.
Trial, significant.

Comments
Outside grouping with-respect-to eminence.
Using adhering to the **above indeed.**

Fields of meaning
Outside, *WAI*: outer, external; unfamiliar, foreign; ignore, reject; work done outside the home; the upper trigram as indication of the outer aspects of the situation. **Group**, *BI*: see *Image of the Situation*. **It/belong**, *ZHI*: establishes between two terms a connection similar to the Saxon genitive, in which the second term belongs to the first one; at the end of a sentence it refers to something previously mentioned or implied. **Trial**, *ZHEN*: see *Image of the Situation*. **Significant**, *JI*: see *Image of the Situation*.

With-respect-to, *YU*: in relation to, referring to, according to; in, at, until. **Eminent**, *XIAN*: worthy, excellent, virtuous; endowed with moral and intellectual power; second only to the wise, *SHENG*. **Use**, *YI*: see *Patterns of Wisdom*. **Adhere**, *CONG*: follow, agree with, comply with, obey; join a doctrine, school, or person; servant, follower. Ideogram: two men walking, one following the other. **Above**, *SHANG*: see *Patterns of Wisdom*. **Indeed**, *YE*: emphasizes and intensifies the previous statement.

NINE AT FIFTH

Manifest grouping.
The **king avails** of **three beaters.**
Letting-go the **preceding wildfowl.**
The **capital**'s **people not admonished.**
Significant.

Comments
To **manifest grouping belongs significance.**
Position correct in the **center indeed.**
Stowing away **revolt, grasping yielding.**

Letting-go the **preceding wildfowl**.
The **capital**'s **people not admonished**.
Above commissioning in the **center indeed**.

Fields of meaning

Manifest, *XIAN*: apparent, conspicuous; illustrious; make clear. **Group**, *BI*: see *Image of the Situation*. **King**, *WANG*: sovereign, effective ruler, emperor, seen as connecting heaven and earth; reign, govern. **Avail**, *YONG*: use, employ for a specific purpose; take advantage of; benefit from; capacity. Ideogram: to divine and center, applying divination to central concerns. **Three/thrice**, *SAN*: number three; third time or place; active phases of a cycle; superlative; beginning of repetition (since one and two are entities in themselves). **Beater**, *CHU*: servant who drives animals toward hunters; order people to their places; drive on, whip up, animate, exhort. **Let-go**, *SHI*: lose, let slip; omit, miss, fail; lose control of. Ideogram: drop from the hand. **Precede**, *QIAN*: before, earlier; anterior, former, ancient; ahead, in front. **Wildfowl**, *QIN*: birds; four-legged animals; hunt, shoot with an arrow; capture; prisoner. **Capital**, *YI*: populous fortified city, center and symbol of the region it rules. Ideogram: enclosure and official seal. **People/person**, *REN*: humans individually and collectively; an individual; humankind. **Not**, *BU*: common term of negation. **Admonish**, *JIE*: warn, scold; precept, order, prohibition. Ideogram: words and warning. **Significant**, *JI*: see *Image of the Situation*.

Belong/it, *ZHI*: establishes between two terms a connection similar to the Saxon genitive, in which the second term belongs to the first one; at the end of a sentence it refers to something previously mentioned or implied. **Position**, *WEI*: place, location; be at; social standing, rank; position of a line in a hexagram. Ideogram: person standing. **Correct**, *ZHENG*: rectify deviation or one-sidedness; proper, straight, exact, regular; constant, rule, model. Ideogram: stop and one, hold to one thing. **Center**, *ZHONG*: inner, central; put in the center; middle, stable point enabling you to face inner and outer changes; middle line of a trigram. Ideogram: field divided in two equal parts. **Indeed**, *YE*: emphasizes and intensifies the previous statement. **Stow**, *SHE*: set aside, put away, store, keep; halt, rest in; lodge, hut. **Revolt**, *NI*: oppose, resist, seek out; contrary, rebellious, refractory. Ideogram: go and rise against, active revolt. **Grasp**, *QU*: seize with effort, take and use, appropriate; take as a wife; grasp the meaning, understand. Ideogram: ear and hand, hear and grasp. **Yield**, *SHUN*: give way, comply, agree, follow, obey; docile, flexible; bear produce, nourish, provide; Action of the trigram Field, *KUN*. **Above**, *SHANG*: see *Patterns of Wisdom*. **Commission**, *SHI*: charge somebody with a task; command, order; messenger, agent; obey, follow. Ideogram: person and office.

SIX ABOVE

To **grouping belongs without** a **head**.
Pitfall.

Comments
To **grouping belongs without** a **head**.
Without a **place** to **complete indeed**.

Fields of meaning

Group, *BI*: see *Image of the Situation*. **Belong/it**, *ZHI*: establishes between two terms a connection similar to the Saxon genitive, in which the second term belongs to the first one; at the end of a sentence it refers to something previously mentioned or implied. **Without**, *WU*: devoid of; there is not. **Head**, *SHOU*: physical head; leader, sovereign; beginning, origin, model; foremost, superior, upper, front. **Pitfall**, *XIONG*: see *Image of the Situation*.

Place, *SUO*: see *Image of the Situation*. **Complete**, *ZHONG*: completion of a cycle that begins the next; entire, whole, all. Ideogram: silk cocoons, follow and ice, winter linking one year with the next. **Indeed**, *YE*: emphasizes and intensifies the previous statement.

Image Tradition

Grouping. **Significant indeed**.
Grouping. **Bracing indeed**.
Below yielding, **adhering indeed**.

Retracing the **oracle-consulting**: **Spring**, **perpetual Trial**.
Without fault.
Using a **solid** in the **center indeed**.

Not soothing, on all **sides coming**.
Above and **below corresponding indeed**.
Afterwards husbanding: **pitfall**.
One's dao exhausted indeed.

Fields of meaning

Group, *BI*: see *Image of the Situation*. **Significant**, *JI*: see *Image of the Situation*. **Indeed**, *YE*: emphasizes and intensifies the previous statement. **Brace/jaw-**

bones, *FU*: braces of a cart; cheeks, maxillary bones; support, consolidate, strengthen, prop up; steady, firm, rigid; help, rescue. **Below**, *XIA*: anything below, in all senses; lower, inner; lower trigram. **Yield**, *SHUN*: give way, comply, agree, follow, obey; docile, flexible; bear produce, nourish, provide; Action of the trigram Field, *KUN*. **Adhere**, *CONG*: follow, agree with, comply with, obey; join a doctrine, school, or person; servant, follower. Ideogram: two men walking, one following the other.

Retracing the **oracle-consulting**: **Spring**, **perpetual Trial**, *YUAN SHI YUAN YONG ZHEN*: see *Image of the Situation*. **Without fault**, *WU JIU*: see *Image of the Situation*. **Use**, *YI*: see *Patterns of Wisdom*. **Solid**, *GANG*: quality of the whole lines; firm, strong, unyielding, persisting. **Center**, *ZHONG*: inner, central; put in the center; middle, stable point enabling you to face inner and outer changes; middle line of a trigram. Ideogram: field divided in two equal parts.

Not soothing, on all **sides coming**, *BU NING FANG LAI*: see *Image of the Situation*. **Above**, *SHANG*: see *Patterns of Wisdom*. **Correspond**, *YING*: be in agreement or harmony; proper, suitable; resonate together, answer to; relation between the lines (1 and 4, 2 and 5, 3 and 6) when they form the pair opened and whole, supple and solid. Ideogram: heart and obey. **Afterwards husbanding**: **pitfall**, *HOU FU XIONG*: see *Image of the Situation*. **One/one's**, *QI*: general third person pronoun and possessive adjective; also: it/its, he/his, she/her, they/their. **Dao**, *DAO*: way or path; ongoing process of being and the course it traces for each person or thing; ultimate reality, intrinsic nature; origin. Ideogram: go and head, opening a path. **Exhaust**, *QIONG*: bring to an end; limit, extremity; investigate exhaustively; destitute, indigent; end without a new beginning; distinct from complete, *ZHONG*, end of a cycle that begins the next one. Ideogram: cave and naked person, bent with disease or old age.

小畜

9 THE SMALL ACCUMULATING
Xiao Chu

The situation described by this hexagram is characterized by the accumulation of a multiplicity of seemingly unrelated events and circumstances, which require a flexible adaptation.

Image of the Situation

The **small accumulating**.
Growing.
Shrouding clouds, **not raining**.
Originating from **my Western suburbs**.

Fields of meaning

Small, *XIAO*: little, common, unimportant; adapting to what crosses your path; ability to move in harmony with the vicissitudes of life; contrasts with great, *DA*, self-imposed theme or goal. **Accumulate**, *CHU*: retain, hoard, gather, herd together; control, restrain; domesticate, tame, train; raise, feed, sustain, bring up. Ideogram: field and black, fertile black soil, accumulated through retaining silt. **Grow**, *HENG*: heavenly influence pervading and nourishing all things; prosper, succeed, expand, develop; effective, favorable; quality of summer and South, second stage of the Time Cycle. With the pronunciation *XIANG*: offer a sacrifice; offer a gift to a superior; accept, enjoy. **Shroud**, *MI*: dense, close together, thick, tight; hidden, secret. **Clouds**, *YUN*: fog, mist, water vapor; connected with the Streaming Moment. **Not**, *BU*: common term of negation. **Rain**, *YU*: rain and all precipitations; sudden shower, fast and furious; abundant dispensation of benefits; associated with the trigram Gorge, *KAN*, and the Streaming Moment. **Origin**, *ZI*: source, beginning, ground; cause, reason, motive; tracing back to the source; oneself, by oneself; spontaneous, intrinsic. **I/me/my**, *WO*: first person pronoun;

the use of a specific personal pronoun, as opposed to the generic one's, *QI*, indicates an unusually strong emphasis on personal involvement. **West**, *XI*: western direction, corresponding to autumn, Harvest, the Metallic Moment and the first phase of the Yin hemicycle of the Universal Compass. **Suburbs**, *JIAO*: area adjoining a city where human constructions and nature interpenetrate; second of the territorial zones: city, suburbs, countryside, forest.

Outer and Inner Trigram

The upper trigram, **Root**, *SUN*, describes the outer aspects of the situation. It has the following associations: base on which things rest, ground, foundation; mild, subtly penetrating; nourishing. *Symbols*: tree/wood and wind. Tree/wood, *MU*: trees and all things woody or wooden; associated with the Wooden Moment. Ideogram: a tree with roots and branches. Wind, *FENG*: wind, breeze, gust; weather and its influence on mood and humor; fashion, usage. *Action*: enter, *RU*, penetrate, go into, enter on, encroach on; progress; put into. In the family of trigrams *SUN* is the eldest daughter.

The lower trigram, **Energy/parch**, *QIAN/GAN*, describes the inner aspects of the situation. It has the following associations: unceasing forward movement, dynamic, enduring, untiring; spirit power, manifestation of Yang, that activates all creation and destruction in Space; heaven, sovereign, father. With the pronunciation *GAN*: parch, dry up, burn, exhaust. Ideogram: sprouts or vapors rising from the ground and sunlight, both fecundating moisture and scorching drought. *Symbol*: heaven, *TIAN*; sky, firmament, heavens; the highest realm, situated above the human world, as opposed to the earth, *DI*, located below. Ideogram: great and the one above. *Action*: persist, *JIAN*; tenacious, persevering; strong, robust, dynamic; constant as the motion of heavenly bodies in their orbits. In the family of trigrams *QIAN* is the father.

Counter Hexagram

The Counter Hexagram of **The Small Accumulating** is hexagram 38, **Polarizing**, which switches the emphasis from flexible adaptation to polar opposition.

Preceding Situation

> **Grouping necessarily possesses** a **place** to **accumulate**.
> To **anterior acquiescence belongs** the **use** of the **small accumulating**.

Fields of meaning

Group, *BI*: compare and select, order things and put them in classes; find what you belong with; associate with, unite, join, harmonize; neighbor, near. Ideogram: two men following each other. **Necessarily**, *BI*: unavoidably, certainly. **Possess**, *YOU*: general term indicating possession; have, own, be endowed with. **Place**, *SUO*: position, location; residence, dwelling; where something belongs or comes from; habitual focus or object. **Accumulate**, *CHU*: see *Image of the Situation*. To **anterior acquiescence belongs** the **use** of, *GU SHOU ZHI YI*: understanding and accepting the preceding statement allows the consultant to make proper use of this hexagram. **Small**, *XIAO*: see *Image of the Situation*.

Hexagrams in Pairs

> The **small accumulating**: **few indeed**.
> **Treading**: **not abiding indeed**.

Fields of meaning

Small accumulating, *XIAO CHU*: see *Image of the Situation*. **Few**, *GUA*: small number; seldom; reduce, diminish; unsupported, solitary. **Indeed**, *YE*: emphasizes and intensifies the previous statement. **Tread**, *LÜ*: walk a path or way; step, path, track; footsteps; course of the stars; appropriate action; virtue; salary, means of subsistence. Ideogram: body and repeating steps. **Not**, *BU*: common term of negation. **Abide**, *CHU*: rest in, dwell; stop oneself; arrive at a place or condition; distinguish, decide; do what is proper. Ideogram: tiger, stop and seat, powerful movement coming to rest.

Patterns of Wisdom

> **Wind moves above heaven**. The **small accumulating**.
> A **jun zi uses highlighting** the **pattern** to **actualize-dao**.

Fields of meaning

Wind, *FENG*: wind, breeze, gust; weather and its influence on mood and humor; fashion, usage; wind and wood are the Symbols of the trigram Root, *SUN*. **Move**, *XING*: move or move something; motivate; emotionally moving; walk, act, do. Ideogram: successive steps. **Above**, *SHANG*: anything above in all senses; higher, upper, outer; upper trigram. **Heaven**, *TIAN*: sky, firmament, heavens; the highest realm, situated above the human world, as opposed to the earth, *DI*, located below; Symbol of the trigram Energy, *QIAN*. Ideogram: great and the one above. **Small accumulating**, *XIAO CHU*: see *Image of the Situation*. **Jun zi**: ideal of a person who orders his/her life in accordance with dao rather than willful intention, and uses divination in this spirit. **Use**, *YI*: by means of; owing to; make use of, employ. **Highlight**, *YI*: praise something worthy; inherent goodness, excellence, beauty, perfect virtue, modesty. **Pattern**, *WEN*: intrinsic or natural design, pattern of wood, stone or animal fur; ideograms, the symbols of writing as revelation of the intrinsic nature of things; language, civilization, culture; harmonious, beautiful, elegant, polite. **Actualize-dao**, *DE*: realize dao in action; power, virtue; ability to follow the course traced by the ongoing process of the cosmos. Ideogram: go, straight, and heart. Linked with acquire, *DE*: acquiring that which makes a being become what it is meant to be.

Transforming Lines

INITIAL NINE

Returning to the **origin**'s **dao**.
Is it **one's fault?**
Significant.

Comments
Returning to the **origin**'s **dao**.
One's righteousness, **significant indeed**.

Fields of meaning

Return, *FU*: go back, turn or lead back; recur, reappear, come again; restore, renew, recover; return to an earlier time or place. Ideogram: step and retrace a path. **Origin**, *ZI*: see *Image of the Situation*. **Dao**, *DAO*: way or path; ongoing process of being and the course it traces for each person or thing; ultimate reality, intrinsic nature; origin. Ideogram: go and head, opening a path. **Is?**, *HE*: ask, inquire; what? which? who? how? why? where? an interrogative particle, often introducing a rhetorical question: is it? is it not? **One/one's**, *QI*: general third person pronoun and possessive adjective; also: it/its, he/his, she/her, they/their. **Fault**, *JIU*: unworthy conduct that leads to harm, illness, misfortune; guilt, crime, punishment. Ideogram: person and differ, differ from what you should be. **Significant**, *JI*: leads to the experience of meaning; favorable, propitious, appropriate. Ideogram: scholar and mouth, wise words of a sage.

Righteous, *YI*: proper, just, virtuous, upright; the heart that rules itself; benevolent, loyal, devoted to public good. **Indeed**, *YE*: see *Hexagrams in Pairs*.

NINE AT SECOND

Hauling-along returning.
Significant.

Comments
Hauling-along returning located in the **center**.
Truly not the **origin letting-go indeed**.

Fields of meaning

Haul-along, *QIAN*: haul or pull, drag behind; pull an animal on a rope. Ideogram: ox and halter. **Return**, *FU*: go back, turn or lead back; recur, reappear, come again; restore, renew, recover; return to an earlier time or place. Ideogram: step and retrace a path. **Significant**, *JI*: leads to the experience of meaning; favorable, propitious, appropriate. Ideogram: scholar and mouth, wise words of a sage.

Locate, *ZAI*: be at, be situated at, dwell, reside; in, within; involved with, in the process of. Ideogram: earth and persevere, a place on the earth. **Center**, *ZHONG*: inner, central; put in the center; middle, stable point enabling you to face inner and outer changes; middle line of a trigram. Ideogram: field divided in two equal parts. **Truly**, *YI*: in fact; also; nevertheless. **Not**, *BU*: common term of negation. **Origin**, *ZI*: see *Image of the Situation*. **Let-go**, *SHI*: lose, let slip; omit, miss, fail; lose control of. Ideogram: drop from the hand. **Indeed**, *YE*: see *Hexagrams in Pairs*.

NINE AT THIRD

Carting: **stimulating** the **spokes**.
Husband and **consort reversing** the **eyes**.

Comments
Husband and **consort reversing** the **eyes**.
Not able to **correct** the **home indeed**.

Fields of meaning

Cart, *YU*: a vehicle and its carrying capacity; contain, hold, sustain. **Stimulate**, *SHUO*: rouse to action and good feeling; stir up, urge on; exhort, persuade; say, tell, relate; cheer, delight; joyous, peaceful, restful; Action of the trigram Open, *DUI*. Ideogram: words and exchange. **Spokes**, *FU*: braces that connect hub and rim of wheel. **Husband**, *FU*: adult, man, male spouse; scholar, distinguished man; one who can help; manage a household. Ideogram: man with a pin in his hair to show that he is of age. **Consort**, *QI*: official partner; legal status of married woman (first wife); distinct from wife, *FU*, which indicates her role as head of the household, and from concubine, *QIE*, secondary wife. **Reverse**, *FAN*: turn and move in the opposite direction; turn around or upside down (180 degrees); change to the opposite position; contrary. **Eye**, *MU*: eye and vision; look, see, glance, observe.

Not, *BU*: common term of negation. **Able/enable**, *NENG*: ability, power, skill, art; competent, talented; duty, function, capacity. Ideogram: an animal with strong hooves and bones, able to carry and defend. **Correct**, *ZHENG*: rectify deviation or one-sidedness; proper, straight, exact, regular; constant, rule, model. Ideogram: stop and one, hold to one thing. **Home**, *SHI*: room, house, dwelling; family; the grave. **Indeed**, *YE*: see *Hexagrams in Pairs*.

Six at Fourth

Possessing conformity.
Blood departing, awe emerging.
Without fault.

Comments
Possessing conformity, awe emerging.
Above uniting purposes indeed.

Fields of meaning

Possess, *YOU*: see *Preceding Situation*. **Conform**, *FU*: accord between inner and outer; sincere, truthful, verified, reliable; capture; prisoners, spoils. Ideogram: claws over child, a bird brooding on the nest. **Blood**, *XUE*: blood, the Yin fluid that maintains life; money, property. **Depart**, *QU*: leave, quit, go; far away, far from; remove, reject, dismiss; lost, gone. **Awe**, *TI*: respect, regard, fear; alarmed and cautious, worried; on guard. Ideogram: heart and versatility, the heart expecting change. **Emerge**, *CHU*: come out of, proceed from, spring from, issue forth; appear, be born; bear, generate; leave, flee; Action of the trigram Shake, *ZHEN*. Ideogram: stem with branches and leaves emerging. **Without fault**, *WU JIU*: no error or harm in the situation.

Above, *SHANG*: see *Patterns of Wisdom*. **Unite**, *HE*: join, match, correspond; unison, harmony; together; close the jaws, shut the mouth. Ideogram: mouths speaking in unison. **Purpose**, *ZHI*: focus of mind and heart; intention, will, inclination; continuity in the direction of life. Ideogram: heart and scholar, high inner resolve. **Indeed**, *YE*: see *Hexagrams in Pairs*.

NINE AT FIFTH

Possessing conformity, binding thus.
Affluence: using one's neighbor.

Comments
Possessing conformity, binding thus.
Not solitary affluence indeed.

Fields of meaning
Possess, *YOU*: see *Preceding Situation.* **Conform,** *FU*: accord between inner and outer; sincere, truthful, verified, reliable; capture; prisoners, spoils. Ideogram: **claws** over child, a bird brooding on the nest. **Bind,** *LÜAN*: tie, connect; **bent,** contracted; interdependent, inseparable. Ideogram: hand and connect. **Thus,** *RU*: as, in this way; comparable, similar. **Affluence,** *FU*: rich, abundant; wealth; **enrich,** provide for; flow toward, accrue. **Use,** *YI*: see *Patterns of Wisdom.* **One/one's,** *QI*: general third person pronoun and possessive adjective; also: it/its, he/his, she/her, they/their. **Neighbor,** *LIN*: person living nearby; extended family; assist, support.

Not, *BU*: common term of negation. **Solitary,** *DI*: alone, single; isolated, abandoned. **Indeed,** *YE*: see *Hexagrams in Pairs.*

NINE ABOVE

Already rain, already abiding.
Honoring actualizing-dao: carrying.
The **wife**'s **Trial: adversity.**
The **moon almost full.**
A **jun zi disciplining, pitfall.**

Comments
Already rain, already abiding.
Actualizing-dao amassing: carrying indeed.
A **jun zi disciplining, pitfall.**
Possessing a **place** to **doubt indeed.**

Fields of meaning
Already, *JI*: completed, done, occurred, finished; past tense; shortly after. **Rain,** *YU*: see *Image of the Situation.* **Abide,** *CHU*: see *Hexagrams in Pairs.* **Honor,** *SHANG*: esteem, give high rank to, exalt, celebrate; rise, elevate; put one thing on top of another. **Actualize-dao,** *DE*: see *Patterns of Wisdom.* **Carry,** *ZAI*: bear, carry with you; contain, sustain, support; load a ship or cart, cargo; fill in. **Wife,** *FU*: position

of married woman as head of the household; distinct from consort, *QI*, which denotes her legal status, and from concubine, *QIE*, secondary wife. Ideogram: woman, hand and broom, household duties. **Trial**, *ZHEN*: inquiry by divination and its result; righteous, firm; separating wheat from chaff; the kernel, the proven core; quality of winter and North, fourth stage of the Time Cycle. Ideogram: pearl and divination. **Adversity**, *LI*: danger, hardship, severe; threat or difficulty that must be encountered, rather than avoided; grinding stone; polish, sharpen; a challenge that strengthens and perfects the character; stimulate, excite; cruel demon. **Moon**, *YUE*: moon and moon-cycle, month; menstruation; Yin. **Almost/hint**, *JI*: nearly, about to; subtle; barely perceptible first sign. **Full**, *WANG*: moon directly facing the sun; 15th day of the lunar month; hopes, expectations, desires. **Jun zi**: see *Patterns of Wisdom*. **Discipline**, *ZHENG*: subjugate vassals, reduce to order; punishing expedition. Ideogram: step and correct, a rectifying move. **Pitfall**, *XIONG*: unfortunate situation, in which the flow of life and spirit is blocked and the experience of meaning is lost; stuck and exposed to danger; inappropriate attitude. Ideogram: person in a pit.

Amass, *JI*: hoard, accumulate, pile up, add up, increase; repeated action, habit; follow, pursue. **Indeed**, *YE*: see *Hexagrams in Pairs*. **Possess**, *YOU*: see *Preceding Situation*. **Place**, *SUO*: see *Preceding Situation*. **Doubt**, *YI*: suspect, distrust, wonder; uncertain, dubious; surmise, conjecture, fear.

Image Tradition

The **small accumulating**.
The **supple acquires** the **position and-also above** and **below correspond** to **it**.
Named: the **small accumulating**.

Persistence and-also root.
The **solid** in the **center and-also** the **purpose moving**.
Thereupon Growing.

Shrouding clouds, **not raining**.
Honoring going indeed.
Originating from **my Western suburbs**.
Spreading, **not-yet moving indeed**.

Fields of meaning

Small accumulating, *XIAO CHU*: see *Image of the Situation*. **Supple**, *ROU*: quality of the opened lines; flexible, pliant, adaptable, tender. **Acquire**, *DE*: obtain the desired object; possession; satisfied, fulfilled; it is permitted; agree with; wish for, desire covetously. Ideogram: go and obstacle, going through obstacles to the goal. **Position**, *WEI*: place, location; be at; social standing, rank; position of a line in a hexagram. Ideogram: person standing. **And-also**, *ER*: joins and contrasts two terms. **Above**, *SHANG*: see *Patterns of Wisdom*. **Below**, *XIA*: anything below, in all senses; lower, inner; lower trigram. **Correspond**, *YING*: be in agreement or harmony; proper, suitable; resonate together, answer to; relation between the lines (1 and 4, 2 and 5, 3 and 6) when they form the pair opened and whole, supple and solid. Ideogram: heart and obey. **It/belong**, *ZHI*: establishes between two terms a connection similar to the Saxon genitive, in which the second term belongs to the first one; at the end of a sentence it refers to something previously mentioned or implied. **Name**, *YUEH*: speak, declare, call. Ideogram: open mouth and tongue.

Persist, *JIAN*: tenacious, persevering; strong, robust, dynamic; constant as the motion of heavenly bodies in their orbits; Action of the trigram Force, *QIAN*. **Root**, *SUN*: base on which things rest, ground, foundation; mild, subtly penetrating; nourishing. **Solid**, *GANG*: quality of the whole lines; firm, strong, unyielding, persisting. **Center**, *ZHONG*: inner, central; put in the center; middle, stable point enabling you to face inner and outer changes; middle line of a trigram. Ideogram: field divided in two equal parts. **Purpose**, *ZHI*: focus of mind and heart; intention, will, inclination; continuity in the direction of life. Ideogram: heart and scholar, high inner resolve. **Move**, *XING*: see *Patterns of Wisdom*. **Thereupon**, *NAI*: on that ground, then, only then; finally; in spite of that. **Grow**, *HENG*: see *Image of the Situation*.

Shrouding clouds, not raining, *MI YUN BU YU*: see *Image of the Situation*. **Honor**, *SHANG*: esteem, give high rank to, exalt, celebrate; rise, elevate; put one thing on top of another. **Go**, *WANG*: move away in time or space, depart; become past; dead, gone; contrasts with come, *LAI*, approach in time or space. **Indeed**, *YE*: see *Hexagrams in Pairs*. **Originating** from **my Western suburbs**, *ZI WO XI JIAO*: see *Image of the Situation*. **Spread**, *SHI*: expand, diffuse, distribute, arrange, exhibit; add to; aid. Ideogram: flag and indeed, claiming new country. **Not-yet**, *WEI*: temporal negative indicating that something is expected to happen but has not yet occurred. **Move**, *XING*: see *Patterns of Wisdom*.

履 ䷉

10 TREADING | *Lü*

The situation described by this hexagram is characterized by making one's own path by treading on dangerous ground, requiring heightened awareness.

Image of the Situation

> **Treading** on a **tiger**'s **tail**.
> **Not snapping** at **people**.
> **Growing**.

Fields of meaning

Tread, *LÜ*: walk a path or way; step, path, track; footsteps; course of the stars; appropriate action; virtue; salary, means of subsistence. Ideogram: body and repeating steps. **Tiger**, *HU*: fierce king of animals; extreme Yang; opposed to and protecting against the demons of extreme Yin on the North–South axis of the Universal Compass. **Tail**, *WEI*: animal's tail; end, last, extreme, remnant. **Not**, *BU*: common term of negation. **Snap**, *DIE*: bite, seize with the teeth. Ideogram: mouth and reach. **People/person**, *REN*: humans individually and collectively; an individual; humankind. **Grow**, *HENG*: heavenly influence pervading and nourishing all things; prosper, succeed, expand, develop; effective, favorable; quality of summer and South, second stage of the Time Cycle. With the pronunciation *XIANG*: offer a sacrifice; offer a gift to a superior; accept, enjoy.

Outer and Inner Trigram

The upper trigram, **Energy/parch**, *QIAN/GAN*, describes the outer aspects of the situation. It has the following associations: unceasing forward movement, dynamic, enduring, untiring; spirit power, manifestation of Yang, that activates all creation and destruction in Space; heaven, sovereign, father. With the pronunciation *GAN*: parch, dry up, burn, exhaust. Ideogram: sprouts or vapors rising from the ground and sunlight, both fecundating moisture and scorching drought. *Symbol*: heaven, *TIAN*; sky, firmament, heavens; the highest realm, situated above the human world, as opposed to the earth, *DI*, located below. Ideogram: great and

the one above. *Action*: persist, *JIAN*; tenacious, persevering; strong, robust, dynamic; constant as the motion of heavenly bodies in their orbits. In the family of trigrams *QIAN* is the father.

The lower trigram, **Open**, *DUI*, describes the inner aspects of the situation. It has the following associations: an open surface, promoting interaction and interpenetration; pleasant, easy, responsive, free, unhindered; opening, passage; the mouth; exchange, barter; straight, direct; meet, gather; place where water accumulates. Ideogram: mouth and vapor, communication through speech. *Symbol*: marsh, *ZE*, open surface of a flat body of water and the vapors rising from it; fertilize, enrich; kindness, favor. *Action*: stimulate, *SHUO*, rouse to action and good feeling; stir up, urge on; exhort, persuade; say, tell, relate; cheer, delight; joyous, peaceful, restful. Ideogram: words and exchange. In the family of trigrams *DUI* is the youngest daughter.

Counter Hexagram

The Counter Hexagram of **Treading** is hexagram 37, **Household People**, which switches the emphasis from treading one's individual path to the sense of community between members of a household.

Preceding Situation

> **Beings accumulate, therefore afterwards possess codes.**
> To **anterior acquiescence belongs** the **use** of **treading**.

Fields of meaning

Being, *WU*: creature, thing, any single being; matter, substance, essence; nature of things. **Accumulate**, *CHU*: retain, hoard, gather, herd together; control, restrain; domesticate, tame, train; raise, feed, sustain, bring up. Ideogram: field and black, fertile black soil, accumulated through retaining silt. **Therefore**, *RAN*: thus, so it is; truly, certainly. **After(wards)/later**, *HOU*: come after in time, subsequent; put oneself after; behind, back, draw back; the second; attendants, heirs, successors, posterity. **Possess**, *YOU*: general term indicating possession; have, own, be endowed with. **Codes**, *LI*: rites, rules, ritual, etiquette; usage, manners; honor, worship. Ideogram: worship and sacrificial vase, handling a sacred vessel. To **anterior acquiescence belongs** the **use** of, *GU SHOU ZHI YI*: understanding and accepting the preceding statement allows the consultant to make proper use of this hexagram. **Tread**, *LÜ*: see *Image of the Situation*.

Hexagrams in Pairs

The **small accumulating**: **few indeed**.
Treading: **not abiding indeed**.

Fields of meaning
Small, *XIAO*: little, common, unimportant; adapting to what crosses your path; ability to move in harmony with the vicissitudes of life; contrasts with great, *DA*, self-imposed theme or goal. **Accumulate**, *CHU*: see *Preceding Situation*. **Few**, *GUA*: small number; seldom; reduce, diminish; unsupported, solitary. **Indeed**, *YE*: emphasizes and intensifies the previous statement. **Tread**, *LÜ*: see *Image of the Situation*. **Not**, *BU*: common term of negation. **Abide**, *CHU*: rest in, dwell; stop oneself; arrive at a place or condition; distinguish, decide; do what is proper. Ideogram: tiger, stop and seat, powerful movement coming to rest.

Additional Texts

Treading: **foundation belonging** to **actualizing-dao indeed**.
Treading: **harmony and-also culmination**.
Treading: **using harmonious movement**.

Fields of meaning
Tread, *LÜ*: see *Image of the Situation*. **Foundation**, *JI*: base of wall or building; ground, root, basis, starting point; establish. **Belong/it**, *ZHI*: establishes between two terms a connection similar to the Saxon genitive, in which the second term belongs to the first one; at the end of a sentence it refers to something previously mentioned or implied. **Actualizing-Dao**, *DAO*: way or path; ongoing process of being and the course it traces for each person or thing; ultimate reality, intrinsic nature; origin. Ideogram: go and head, opening a path. **Indeed**, *YE*: see *Hexagrams in Pairs*. **Harmony**, *HE*: concord, union; conciliate; at peace, mild; fit, tune, adjust. **And-also**, *ER*: joins and contrasts two terms. **Culminate**, *ZHI*: bring to the highest degree; arrive at the end or summit; superlative; reaching one's goal. **Use**, *YI*: by means of; owing to; make use of, employ. **Move**, *XING*: move or move something; motivate; emotionally moving; walk, act, do. Ideogram: successive steps.

Patterns of Wisdom

Heaven above, pond below. Treading.
A **jun zi uses differentiating above** and **below**.
And **rectifying** the **commoners' purpose**.

Fields of meaning
Heaven, *TIAN*: sky, firmament, heavens; the highest realm, situated above the human world, as opposed to the earth, *DI*, located below; Symbol of the trigram Energy, *QIAN*. Ideogram: great and the one above. **Above**, *SHANG*: anything above in all senses; higher, upper, outer; upper trigram. **Pond**, *ZE*: open surface of a flat body of water and the vapors rising from it; fertilize, enrich; kindness, favor; Symbol of the trigram Open, *DUI*. **Below**, *XIA*: anything below, in all senses; lower, inner; lower trigram. **Tread**, *LÜ*: see *Image of the Situation*. **Jun zi**: ideal of a person who orders his/her life in accordance with dao rather than willful intention, and uses divination in this spirit. **Use**, *YI*: see *Additional Texts*. **Differentiate**, *BIAN*: argue, dispute, criticize; sophisticated, artful. Ideogram: words and sharp or pungent. **Rectify**, *DING*: correct, settle, fix; peaceful, tranquil, stable; certain, invariable. **Commoners**, *MIN*: common people, masses; working class supporting the social hierarchy; undeveloped potential in the individual. **Purpose**, *ZHI*: focus of mind and heart; intention, will, inclination; continuity in the direction of life. Ideogram: heart and scholar, high inner resolve.

Transforming Lines

INITIAL NINE

Sheer treading: going.
Without fault.

Comments
To **sheer treading belongs going.**
Solitarily moving desire indeed.

Fields of meaning
Sheer, *SU*: plain, unadorned; original color or state; clean, pure, natural. Ideogram: white silk. **Tread**, *LÜ*: see *Image of the Situation*. **Go**, *WANG*: move away in time or space, depart; become past; dead, gone; contrasts with come, *LAI*, approach in time or space. **Without fault**, *WU JIU*: no error or harm in the situation.

Belong/it, *ZHI*: see *Additional Texts*. **Solitary**, *DI*: alone, single; isolated, abandoned. **Move**, *XING*: see *Additional Texts*. **Desire**, *YUAN*: wish, hope or long for; covet; desired object. **Indeed**, *YE*: see *Hexagrams in Pairs*.

Nine at Second

Treading in **dao**: **smoothing**, **smoothing**.
Shady people: **Trial**, **significant**.

Comments
Shady people: **Trial**, **significant**.
The **center not** the **origin** of **disarray indeed**.

Fields of meaning
Tread, *LÜ*: see *Image of the Situation*. **Dao**, *DAO*: way or path; ongoing process of being and the course it traces for each person or thing; ultimate reality, intrinsic nature; origin. Ideogram: go and head, opening a path. **Smooth**, *TAN*: level, even, flat; extended, vast; tranquil, composed, at ease. **Shady**, *YOU*: retired, solitary, secret, hidden from view; dark, obscure, occult, mysterious; ignorant. Ideogram: small within hill, a cave or grotto. **People/person**, *REN*: see *Image of the Situation*. **Trial**, *ZHEN*: inquiry by divination and its result; righteous, firm; separating wheat from chaff; the kernel, the proven core; quality of winter and North, fourth stage of the Time Cycle. Ideogram: pearl and divination. **Significant**, *JI*: leads to the experience of meaning; favorable, propitious, appropriate. Ideogram: scholar and mouth, wise words of a sage.

Center, *ZHONG*: inner, central; put in the center; middle, stable point enabling you to face inner and outer changes; middle line of a trigram. Ideogram: field divided in two equal parts. **Not**, *BU*: common term of negation. **Origin**, *ZI*: source, beginning, ground; cause, reason, motive; tracing back to the source; oneself, by oneself; spontaneous, intrinsic. **Disarray**, *LUAN*: throw into disorder, mislay, confuse; out of place; discord, insurrection, anarchy. **Indeed**, *YE*: see *Hexagrams in Pairs*.

Six at Third

Squinting enables observing.
Halting enables treading.
Treading on a **tiger**'s **tail**.
Snapping at **people**: **pitfall**.
Martial people activate tending-towards the **great** in the **chief**.

Comments
Squinting enables observing.
Not the **stand** to **use possessing brightness indeed**.
Halting enables treading.
Not the **stand** to **use associating** with **movement indeed**.
To **snapping** at **people belongs** a **pitfall**.
Position not appropriate indeed.
Martial people activate tending-towards the **great** in the **chief**.
Purpose solid indeed.

Fields of meaning
Squint, *MIAO*: look at with one eye; one-eyed; obstructed vision; glance at. **Able/enable**, *NENG*: ability, power, skill, art; competent, talented; duty, function, capacity. Ideogram: an animal with strong hooves and bones, able to carry and defend. **Observe**, *SHI*: see, examine, inspect; consider as; compare, imitate. Ideogram: see and omen, taking what you see into account. **Halt**, *BO*: limp; lame, crippled. **Tread**, *LÜ*: see *Image of the Situation*. **Tiger**, *HU*: see *Image of the Situation*. **Tail**, *WEI*: see *Image of the Situation*. **Snap**, *DIE*: see *Image of the Situation*. **People/person**, *REN*: see *Image of the Situation*. **Pitfall**, *XIONG*: unfortunate situation, in which the flow of life and spirit is blocked and the experience of meaning is lost; stuck and exposed to danger; inappropriate attitude. Ideogram: person in a pit. **Martial**, *WU*: warrior, military, warlike; valiant, powerful; strong, stern; Wu is the name of the son of King Wen, who defeated the last Shang emperor and founded the Zhou dynasty. Ideogram: fight and stop, force deterring aggression. **Activate**, *WEI*: act or cause to act; do, make, manage, make active; be, become; attend to, help; because of. **Tend-towards**, *YU*: move toward without necessarily reaching, in the direction of. **Great**, *DA*: big, noble, important, very; orient the will toward a self-imposed goal, impose direction; ability to lead or guide one's life; contrasts with small, *XIAO*, flexible adaptation to what crosses one's path. **Chief**, *JUN*: prince, ruler; lead, direct; wise person. Ideogram: mouth and direct, giving orders.

Not, *BU*: common term of negation. **Stand**, *ZU*: base, foot, leg; rest on, support; stance; sufficient, capable, worth. Ideogram: foot and calf resting. **Use**, *YI*: see *Additional Texts*. **Possess**, *YOU*: see *Preceding Situation*. **Brightness**, *MING*: light, radiance, clarity; distinguish, discern, understand; light-giving aspect of fire, of heavenly bodies and of consciousness; brightness and fire are the Symbols of the trigram Radiance, *LI*. **Indeed**, *YE*: see *Hexagrams in Pairs*. **Associate**, *YU*: consort with, combine; companions; group, band, company;

agree with, comply, help; in favor of. Ideogram: a pair of hands reaching downward meets a pair of hands reaching upward, helpful association. **Move,** *XING*: see *Additional Texts.* **Belong/it**, *ZHI*: see *Additional Texts.* **Position**, *WEI*: place, location; be at; social standing, rank; position of a line in a hexagram. Ideogram: person standing. **Appropriate**, *DANG*: suitable, capable, worthy, adequate, competent, equal to; opportune, convenient; whole lines in odd places and opened lines in even places. **Purpose**, *ZHI*: see *Patterns of Wisdom.* **Solid**, *GANG*: quality of the whole lines; firm, strong, unyielding, persisting.

Nine at Fourth

Treading on a **tiger**'s **tail**.
Watch-out! **Watch-out**! **Completing significant**.

Comments
Watch-out! **Watch-out**! **Completing significant**.
Purpose moving indeed.

Fields of meaning
Tread, *LÜ*: see *Image of the Situation.* **Tiger**, *HU*: see *Image of the Situation.* **Tail**, *WEI*: see *Image of the Situation.* **Watch-out**, *SU*: warning; inform, relate; accuse; defend or prosecute a case in court. **Complete**, *ZHONG*: completion of a cycle that begins the next; entire, whole, all. Ideogram: silk cocoons, follow and ice, winter linking one year with the next. **Significant**, *JI*: leads to the experience of meaning; favorable, propitious, appropriate. Ideogram: scholar and mouth, wise words of a sage.

Purpose, *ZHI*: see *Patterns of Wisdom.* **Move**, *XING*: see *Additional Texts.* **Indeed**, *YE*: see *Hexagrams in Pairs.*

Nine at Fifth

Parting, **treading**. **Trial**, **adversity**.

Comments
Parting, **treading**: **Trial**, **adversity**.
Position correct and **appropriate indeed**.

Fields of meaning
Part, *GUAI*: separate, fork, cut off, flow in different directions; decide, resolve; prompt, certain, settled. **Tread**, *LÜ*: see *Image of the Situation.* **Trial**, *ZHEN*: inquiry by divination and its result; righteous, firm; separating wheat from chaff; the

kernel, the proven core; quality of winter and North, fourth stage of the Time Cycle. Ideogram: pearl and divination. **Adversity**, *LI*: danger, hardship, severe; threat or difficulty that must be encountered, rather than avoided; grinding stone; polish, sharpen; a challenge that strengthens and perfects the character; stimulate, excite; cruel demon.

Position, *WEI*: place, location; be at; social standing, rank; position of a line in a hexagram. Ideogram: person standing. **Correct**, *ZHENG*: rectify deviation or one-sidedness; proper, straight, exact, regular; constant, rule, model. Ideogram: stop and one, hold to one thing. **Appropriate**, *DANG*: suitable, capable, worthy, adequate, competent, equal to; opportune, convenient; whole lines in odd places and opened lines in even places. **Indeed**, *YE*: see *Hexagrams in Pairs*.

Nine Above

Observing treading: predecessors auspicious.
One's recurring Spring, significant.

Comments
Spring: significance located above.
The **great possesses reward indeed.**

Fields of meaning

Observe, *SHI*: see, examine, inspect; consider as; compare, imitate. Ideogram: see and omen, taking what you see into account. **Tread**, *LÜ*: see *Image of the Situation*. **Predecessor**, *KAO*: deceased father or grandfather; ancestors, the ancients; aged, long-lived; interrogate, test, verify. Ideogram: old and ingenious, wise old man. **Auspicious**, *XIANG*: auspices of good luck and prosperity; sign, omen (good or bad). **One/one's**, *QI*: general third person pronoun and possessive adjective; also: it/its, he/his, she/her, they/their. **Recur**, *XUAN*: return to the same point; turn, pivot, orbit, revolve, spiral. **Spring**, *YUAN*: source, origin, head; arise, begin; first generating impulse; great, excellent; quality of springtime and East, first stage of the Time Cycle. **Significant**, *JI*: leads to the experience of meaning; favorable, propitious, appropriate. Ideogram: scholar and mouth, wise words of a sage.

Locate, *ZAI*: be at, be situated at, dwell, reside; in, within; involved with, in the process of. Ideogram: earth and persevere, a place on the earth. **Above**, *SHANG*: see *Patterns of Wisdom*. **Great**, *DA*: big, noble, important, very; orient the will toward a self-imposed goal, impose direction; ability to lead or guide one's life; contrasts with small, *XIAO*, flexible adaptation to what crosses one's path. **Possess**, *YOU*: see *Preceding Situation*. **Reward**, *QING*: gift given out of gratitude or benevolence; favor from heaven. Ideogram: heart, follow and deer, the heart expressed through the gift of a deer's skin. **Indeed**, *YE*: see *Hexagrams in Pairs.*

Image Tradition

> **Treading**. The **supple treading** on the **solid indeed**.
> **Stimulating and-also corresponding reaches energy**.
> **That uses treading** on a **tiger**'s **tail**.
>
> **Not snapping** at **people**. **Growing**.
> The **solid** in the **center** and **correct**.
> **Treading** on the **supreme position and-also not disheartened**.
> **Shining brightness indeed**.

Fields of meaning

Tread, *LÜ*: see *Image of the Situation.* **Supple**, *ROU*: quality of the opened lines; flexible, pliant, adaptable, tender. **Solid**, *GANG*: quality of the whole lines; firm, strong, unyielding, persisting. **Indeed**, *YE*: see *Hexagrams in Pairs.* **Stimulate**, *SHUO*: rouse to action and good feeling; stir up, urge on; exhort, persuade; say, tell, relate; cheer, delight; joyous, peaceful, restful; Action of the trigram Open, *DUI*. Ideogram: words and exchange. **And-also**, *ER*: see *Additional Texts.* **Correspond**, *YING*: be in agreement or harmony; proper, suitable; resonate together, answer to; relation between the lines (1 and 4, 2 and 5, 3 and 6) when they form the pair opened and whole, supple and solid. Ideogram: heart and obey. **Reach**, *HU*: arrive at a goal; move toward and achieve; to, at, in; distinct from tend-towards, *YOU*. **Energy/parch**, *QIAN/GAN*: unceasing forward movement, dynamic, enduring, untiring; spirit power, manifestation of Yang, that activates all creation and destruction in Space; heaven, sovereign, father. With the pronunciation *GAN*: parch, dry up, burn, exhaust. Ideogram: sprouts or vapors rising from the ground and sunlight, both fecundating moisture and scorching drought. **That**, *SHI*: refers to the preceding statement. **Use**, *YI*: see *Additional Texts.* **Tiger**'s **tail**, *HU WEI*: see *Image of the Situation.*

Not snapping at **people**, *BU DIE REN*: see *Image of the Situation.* **Grow**, *HENG*: see *Image of the Situation.* **Center**, *ZHONG*: inner, central; put in the center; middle, stable point enabling you to face inner and outer changes; middle line of a trigram. Ideogram: field divided in two equal parts. **Correct**, *ZHENG*: rectify deviation or one-sidedness; proper, straight, exact, regular; constant, rule, model. Ideogram: stop and one, hold to one thing. **Supreme**, *DI*: highest, above all on earth; sovereign, lord, emperor. **Position**, *WEI*: place, location; be at; social standing, rank; position of a line in a hexagram. Ideogram: person standing.

Disheartened, *JIU*: chronic disease; sadness, distress; poverty; mourning. **Shine**, *GUANG*: illuminate, emit light; brilliant, splendid; honor, glory, éclat; distinct from brightness, *MING*, light of heavenly bodies. Ideogram: fire above person. **Brightness**, *MING*: light, radiance, clarity; distinguish, discern, understand; light-giving aspect of fire, of heavenly bodies and of consciousness; brightness and fire are the Symbols of the trigram Radiance, *LI*.

泰

11 COMPENETRATION

Tai

The situation described by this hexagram is characterized by an auspicious conjunction of heaven and earth bringing expansion, harmony and peace.

Image of the Situation

> **Compenetration**.
> The **small going**, the **great coming**.
> **Significance Growing**.

Fields of meaning

Compenetrate, *TAI*: communicate, permeate, diffuse; excellent, eminent, supreme; abundant, prosperous; smooth, slippery; extreme, extravagant, prodigal. Ideogram: person in water, connected to the universal medium. **Small**, *XIAO*: little, common, unimportant; adapting to what crosses your path; ability to move in harmony with the vicissitudes of life; contrasts with great, *DA*, self-imposed theme or goal. **Go**, *WANG*: move away in time or space, depart; become past; dead, gone; contrasts with come, *LAI*, approach in time or space. **Great**, *DA*: big, noble, important, very; orient the will toward a self-imposed goal, impose direction; ability to lead or guide one's life; contrasts with small, *XIAO*, flexible adaptation to what crosses one's path. **Come**, *LAI*: approach in time or space; move toward, arrive at; future; contrasts with go, *WANG*, move away or become past. **Significant**, *JI*: leads to the experience of meaning; favorable, propitious, appropriate. Ideogram: scholar and mouth, wise words of a sage. **Grow**, *HENG*: heavenly influence pervading and nourishing all things; prosper, succeed, expand, develop; effective, favorable; quality of summer and South, second stage of the Time Cycle. With the pronunciation *XIANG*: offer a sacrifice; offer a gift to a superior; accept, enjoy.

Outer and Inner Trigram

The upper trigram, **Space**, *KUN*, describes the outer aspects of the situation. It has the following associations: surface of the world; support of all existence, manifestation of Yin, where Energy or Yang activates all creation and destruction; all-involving service; earth; moon, wife, mother; rest, receptivity, docile obedience. Ideogram: terrestrial globe and stretch out. *Symbol*: earth, *DI*; the earth, ground on which the human world rests; basis of all things, nourishes all things; essential Yin. *Action*: yield, *SHUN*: give way, comply, agree, follow, obey; docile, flexible; bear produce, nourish, provide. In the family of trigrams *KUN* is the mother.

The lower trigram, **Energy/parch**, *QIAN/GAN*, describes the inner aspects of the situation. It has the following associations: unceasing forward movement, dynamic, enduring, untiring; spirit power, manifestation of Yang, that activates all creation and destruction in Space; heaven, sovereign, father. With the pronunciation *GAN*: parch, dry up, burn, exhaust. Ideogram: sprouts or vapors rising from the ground and sunlight, both fecundating moisture and scorching drought. *Symbol*: heaven, *TIAN*; sky, firmament, heavens; the highest realm, situated above the human world, as opposed to the earth, *DI*, located below. Ideogram: great and the one above. *Action*: persist, *JIAN*; tenacious, persevering; strong, robust, dynamic; constant as the motion of heavenly bodies in their orbits. In the family of trigrams *QIAN* is the father.

Counter Hexagram

The Counter Hexagram of **Compenetration** is hexagram 54, **Converting Maidenhood**, which switches the emphasis from the expansion characterizing **Compenetration** to simple acceptance of one's allotted destiny.

Preceding Situation

> **Treading and-also compenetrating**.
> **Therefore afterwards peace**.
> To **anterior acquiescence belongs** the **use** of **compenetration**.
> **Compenetration implies interpenetrating indeed**.

Fields of meaning

Tread, *LÜ*: walk a path or way; step, path, track; footsteps; course of the stars; appropriate action; virtue; salary, means of subsistence. Ideogram: body and repeating steps. **And-also**, *ER*: joins and contrasts two terms. **Compenetrate**, *TAI*: see *Image of the Situation*. **Therefore**, *RAN*: thus, so it is; truly, certainly. **After(wards)/later**, *HOU*: come after in time, subsequent; put oneself after; behind, back, draw back; the second; attendants, heirs, successors, posterity. **Peace**, *AN*: quiet, still, settled, secure, contented; calm, tranquilize, console. Ideogram:

woman under a roof, a tranquil home. To **anterior acquiescence belongs** the **use** of, *GU SHOU ZHI YI*: understanding and accepting the preceding statement allows the consultant to make proper use of this hexagram. **Imply**, *ZHE*: further signify; additional meaning. **Interpenetrate**, *TONG*: penetrate freely and reciprocally, permeate, flow through, open a way; see clearly, understand deeply; communicate with; together. **Indeed**, *YE*: emphasizes and intensifies the previous statement.

Hexagrams in Pairs

> **Obstruction** and **compenetration**: **reversing one's sorting indeed**.

Fields of meaning
Obstruct, *PI*: closed, stopped; bar the way; obstacle; unfortunate, wicked; refuse, disapprove, deny. Ideogram: mouth and not, blocked communication. **Compenetrate**, *TAI*: see *Image of the Situation*. **Reverse**, *FAN*: turn and move in the opposite direction; turn around or upside down (180 degrees); change to the opposite position; contrary. **One/one's**, *QI*: general third person pronoun and possessive adjective; also: it/its, he/his, she/her, they/their. **Sort**, *LEI*: group according to kind, compare; species, class, genus; resemble; analog, like nature or purpose; norm, model. **Indeed**, *YE*: see *Preceding Situation*.

Patterns of Wisdom

> **Heaven** and **earth mingling**. **Compenetration**.
> The **crown prince uses property** to **accomplish** the **dao belonging** to **heaven** and **earth**.
> And **braces** the **reciprocity properly belonging** to **heaven** and **earth**.
> And **uses** at **left** and **right** the **commoners**.

Fields of meaning
Heaven, *TIAN*: sky, firmament, heavens; the highest realm, situated above the human world, as opposed to the earth, *DI*, located below; Symbol of the trigram Energy, *QIAN*. Ideogram: great and the one above. **Earth**, *DI*: the earth, ground on which the human world rests; basis of all things, nourishes all things; essential Yin; Symbol of the trigram Space, *KUN*. **Mingle**, *JIAO*: blend with, communicate, join, exchange; trade; copulation; friendship. Ideogram: legs crossed. **Compenetrate**, *TAI*: see *Image of the Situation*. **Crown prince**, *HOU*: sovereign; prince; empress,

mother of an imperial prince. Ideogram: one, mouth and shelter, one with the sovereign's orders. **Use**, *YI*: by means of; owing to; make use of, employ. **Property**, *CAI*: possessions, goods, substance, wealth. Ideogram: pearl and value. **Accomplish**, *CHENG*: complete, finish, bring about; perfect, full, whole; play one's part, do one's duty; mature. Ideogram: weapon and man, able to bear arms, thus fully developed. **Dao**, *DAO*: way or path; ongoing process of being and the course it traces for each person or thing; ultimate reality, intrinsic nature; origin. Ideogram: go and head, opening a path. **Belong/it**, *ZHI*: establishes between two terms a connection similar to the Saxon genitive, in which the second term belongs to the first one; at the end of a sentence it refers to something previously mentioned or implied. **Brace/jawbones**, *FU*: braces of a cart; cheeks, maxillary bones; support, consolidate, strengthen, prop up; steady, firm, rigid; help, rescue. **Reciprocal**, *XIANG*: mutual; assist, encourage, help; bring together, blend with; examine, inspect; by turns. **Proper**, *YI*: reasonable, fit, right, harmonious; ought, should. **Left**, *ZUO*: left side, left hand; East; secondary, assistant, inferior; defective, unfavorable. **Right**, *YOU*: right side, right hand; West, situated at the right of South, which is the reference direction; place of honor. **Commoners**, *MIN*: common people, masses; working class supporting the social hierarchy; undeveloped potential in the individual.

Transforming Lines

INITIAL NINE

Eradicating thatch-grass intertwisted.
Using one's classification.
Disciplining, significant.

Comments
Eradicating thatch-grass: disciplining, significant.
Purpose located outside indeed.

Fields of meaning
Eradicate, *BA*: pull up, root out, extirpate; extricate from difficulties; elevate, promote. **Thatch-grass**, *MAO*: thick grass used for roofs of humble houses. **Intertwist**, *RU*: interlaced, entangled, as roots; forage, straw. **Use**, *YI*: see *Patterns of Wisdom*. **One/one's**, *QI*: see *Hexagrams in Pairs*. **Classification**, *HUI*: class, collection, series; same kind; put or group together. **Discipline**, *ZHENG*: subjugate vassals, reduce to order; punishing expedition. Ideogram: step and correct, a rectifying move. **Significant**, *JI*: see *Image of the Situation*.

Purpose, *ZHI*: focus of mind and heart; intention, will, inclination; continuity

in the direction of life. Ideogram: heart and scholar, high inner resolve. **Locate**, *ZAI*: be at, be situated at, dwell, reside; in, within; involved with, in the process of. Ideogram: earth and persevere, a place on the earth. **Outside**, *WAI*: outer, external; unfamiliar, foreign; ignore, reject; work done outside the home; the upper trigram as indication of the outer aspects of the situation. **Indeed**, *YE*: see *Preceding Situation*.

Nine at Second

Enwrapped in **wasteland**.
Availing of **crossing** the **watercourse**.
Not putting-off abandoning.
Partnering extinguished.
Acquiring honor tending-towards the **center**:
movement.

Comments
Enwrapped in **wasteland**, **acquiring honor tending-towards** the **center**: **movement**.
Using the **shining great indeed**.

Fields of meaning

Enwrap, *BAO*: envelop, hold, contain; patient, engaged. Ideogram: enfold and self, a fetus in the womb. **Wasteland**, *HUANG*: wild, barren, deserted, unproductive land; jungle, moor, heath; reckless, neglectful. **Avail**, *YONG*: use, employ for a specific purpose; take advantage of; benefit from; capacity. Ideogram: to divine and center, applying divination to central concerns. **Cross**, *PING*: cross a dry or frozen river. Ideogram: horse and ice. **Watercourse**, *HE*: river, stream, running water. **Not**, *BU*: common term of negation. **Put-off**, *XIA*: delay; put at a distance; far away, remote in time. **Abandon**, *YI*: leave behind, forget; die; lose through unawareness. Ideogram: go and value, value is gone. **Partner**, *PENG*: companion, friend, peer; join, associate for mutual benefit; commercial venture; two equal or similar things. Ideogram: linked strings of cowrys or coins. **Extinguish**, *WANG*: ruin, destroy; cease, go, die; lost without trace; forget, out of mind; absence, exile. Ideogram: person concealed by a wall, out of sight. **Acquire**, *DE*: obtain the desired object; possession; satisfied, fulfilled; it is permitted; agree with; wish for, desire covetously. Ideogram: go and obstacle, going through obstacles to the goal. **Honor**, *SHANG*: esteem, give high rank to, exalt, celebrate; rise, elevate; put one thing on top of another. **Tend-towards**, *YU*: move toward without necessarily reaching, in the direction of. **Center**, *ZHONG*: inner, central;

put in the center; middle, stable point enabling you to face inner and outer changes; middle line of a trigram. Ideogram: field divided in two equal parts. **Move**, *XING*: move or move something; motivate; emotionally moving; walk, act, do. Ideogram: successive steps.

Use, *YI*: see *Patterns of Wisdom*. **Shine**, *GUANG*: illuminate, emit light; brilliant, splendid; honor, glory, éclat; distinct from brightness, *MING*, light of heavenly bodies. Ideogram: fire above person. **Great**, *DA*: see *Image of the Situation*. **Indeed**, *YE*: see *Preceding Situation*.

NINE AT THIRD

Without evening, not unevening.
Without going, not returning.
Drudgery: Trial, without fault.
No cares: one's conformity.
Tending-towards taking-in possesses blessing.

Comments
Without going, not returning.
Heaven and **earth**'s **border indeed**.

Fields of meaning

Without, *WU*: devoid of; there is not. **Even**, *PING*: level, flatten, equalize; balanced, regular; uniform, peaceful, tranquil; restore quiet, harmonize. **Not**, *BU*: common term of negation. **Uneven**, *BEI*: any difference in level; bank, shore, dam, dike; inclined, tipped over; partial, unjust. **Go**, *WANG*: see *Image of the Situation*. **Return**, *FU*: go back, turn or lead back; recur, reappear, come again; restore, renew, recover; return to an earlier time or place. Ideogram: step and retrace a path. **Drudgery**, *JIAN*: difficult, hard, repetitive work; distressing, sorrowful. Ideogram: perverse and sticky earth, soil difficult to cultivate. **Trial**, *ZHEN*: inquiry by divination and its result; righteous, firm; separating wheat from chaff; the kernel, the proven core; quality of winter and North, fourth stage of the Time Cycle. Ideogram: pearl and divination. **Without fault**, *WU JIU*: no error or harm in the situation. **No**, *WU*: common term of negation. **Care**, *XU*: fear, doubt, concern; heartfelt attachment; relieve, soothe, aid; sympathy, compassion, consolation. Ideogram: heart and blood, the heart's blood affected. **One/one's**, *QI*: see *Hexagrams in Pairs*. **Conform**, *FU*: accord between inner and outer; sincere, truthful, verified, reliable; capture; prisoners, spoils. Ideogram: claws over child, a bird brooding on the nest. **Tend-towards**, *YU*: move toward without necessarily reaching, in the direction of. **Take-in**, *SHI*: eat, drink, ingest, absorb, incorporate; food, nourishment. **Possess**, *YOU*: general term indicating possession; have, own, be endowed with. **Bless**, *FU*: heavenly gifts and favor; happiness, prosperity; spiritual power and goodwill. Ideogram: spirit and plenty.

Heaven, *TIAN*: see *Patterns of Wisdom*. **Earth**, *DI*: see *Patterns of Wisdom*. **Border**, *JI*: boundary, frontier, line that joins and divides; meet, face to face. Ideogram: place and sacrifice, meeting point of the human and the spirit world. **Indeed**, *YE*: see *Preceding Situation*.

Six at Fourth

Fluttering, fluttering.
Not affluence: using one's neighbor.
Not warning: using conformity.

Comments
Fluttering, fluttering, not affluence.
Altogether letting-go the **substance indeed.**
Not warning: using conformity.
In the **center** the **heart**'s **desire indeed.**

Fields of meaning
Flutter, *PIAN*: fly or run about; bustle, fussy. Ideogram: young bird leaving the nest. **Not**, *BU*: common term of negation. **Affluence**, *FU*: rich, abundant; wealth; enrich, provide for; flow toward, accrue. **Use**, *YI*: see *Patterns of Wisdom*. **One/one's**, *QI*: see *Hexagrams in Pairs*. **Neighbor**, *LIN*: person living nearby; extended family; assist, support. **Warn**, *JIE*: alarm, alert, put on guard; caution, inform; guard against, refrain from. Ideogram: spear held in both hands, warning enemies. **Conform**, *FU*: accord between inner and outer; sincere, truthful, verified, reliable; capture; prisoners, spoils. Ideogram: claws over child, a bird brooding on the nest.

Altogether, *JIE*: all, the whole; the same sort, alike; entirely. **Let-go**, *SHI*: lose, let slip; omit, miss, fail; lose control of. Ideogram: drop from the hand. **Substance**, *SHI*: fullness, richness; essence; real, solid, consistent; results, fruits, possessions; honest, sincere. Ideogram: string of coins under a roof, wealth in the house. **Indeed**, *YE*: see *Preceding Situation*. **Center**, *ZHONG*: inner, central; put in the center; middle, stable point enabling you to face inner and outer changes; middle line of a trigram. Ideogram: field divided in two equal parts. **Heart**, *XIN*: the heart as center of being; seat of mind, imagination and affect; moral nature; source of desires, intentions, will. **Desire**, *YUAN*: wish, hope or long for; covet; desired object.

Six at Fifth

Supreme Burgeoning converting maidenhood.
Using satisfaction: Spring, significant.

Comments
Using satisfaction: Spring, significant.
In the **center using** the **movement** of **desire indeed**.

Fields of meaning

Supreme, *DI*: highest, above all on earth; sovereign, lord, emperor. **Burgeon**, *YI*: beginning of growth after seedburst, CHIA; early spring; associated with the Wooden Moment. **Convert**, *GUI*: accomplish one's destiny; revert to the original place or state; restore, revert; turn into; goal, destination, intention; a girl getting married. Ideogram: arrive and wife, become mistress of a household. **Maidenhood**, *MEI*: girl not yet nubile, virgin; younger sister; daughter of a secondary wife. Ideogram: woman and not-yet. **Use**, *YI*: see *Patterns of Wisdom*. **Satisfaction**, *ZHI*: fulfillment, gratification, happiness; take pleasure in, fulfill a need. **Spring**, *YUAN*: source, origin, head; arise, begin; first generating impulse; great, excellent; quality of springtime and East, first stage of the Time Cycle. **Significant**, *JI*: see *Image of the Situation*.

Center, *ZHONG*: inner, central; put in the center; middle, stable point enabling you to face inner and outer changes; middle line of a trigram. Ideogram: field divided in two equal parts. **Move**, *XING*: move or move something; motivate; emotionally moving; walk, act, do. Ideogram: successive steps. **Desire**, *YUAN*: wish, hope or long for; covet; desired object. **Indeed**, *YE*: see *Preceding Situation*.

Six Above

The **bulwark returns tending-towards** the **moat**.
No availing of **legions**.
Originating from the **capital**, **notifying fate**.
Trial, **abashment**.

Comments
The **bulwark returns tending-towards** the **moat**.
One's fate disarrayed indeed.

Fields of meaning

Bulwark, *CHENG*: rampart, city wall; citadel, place walled for defense. **Return**, *FU*: go back, turn or lead back; recur, reappear, come again; restore, renew, recover;

return to an earlier time or place. Ideogram: step and retrace a path. **Tend-towards**, *YU*: move toward without necessarily reaching, in the direction of. **Moat**, *HUANG*: ditch around a city or a fort. **No**, *WU*: common term of negation. **Avail**, *YONG*: use, employ for a specific purpose; take advantage of; benefit from; capacity. Ideogram: to divine and center, applying divination to central concerns. **Legions**, *SHI*: army, troops; leader, general, model, master; organize, make functional; take as a model, imitate, follow. Ideogram: heap and whole, turn confusion into a functional unit. **Origin**, *ZI*: source, beginning, ground; cause, reason, motive; tracing back to the source; oneself, by oneself; spontaneous, intrinsic. **Capital**, *YI*: populous fortified city, center and symbol of the region it rules. Ideogram: enclosure and official seal. **Notify**, *GAO*: proclaim, order, decree; advise, inform; accuse, denounce. Ideogram: mouth and ox head, impressive speech. **Fate**, *MING*: individual destiny; birth and death as limits of life; issue orders with authority; consult the gods. Ideogram: mouth and order, words with heavenly authority. **Trial**, *ZHEN*: inquiry by divination and its result; righteous, firm; separating wheat from chaff; the kernel, the proven core; quality of winter and North, fourth stage of the Time Cycle. Ideogram: pearl and divination. **Abashment**, *LIN*: distress, shame, regret, humiliation; aware of having lost the right track; leads to repenting, *HUI*, correcting the direction of mind and life.

One/one's, *QI*: see *Hexagrams in Pairs*. **Disarray**, *LUAN*: throw into disorder, mislay, confuse; out of place; discord, insurrection, anarchy. **Indeed**, *YE*: see *Preceding Situation*.

Image Tradition

Compenetration.
The **small going**, the **great coming**: **significance Growing**.
By **consequence** of **that heaven** and **earth mingling and-also** the **myriad beings interpenetrating indeed**.
Above and **below mingling and-also their purposes concording indeed**.

Inside Yang and-also outside Yin.
Inside persisting and-also outside yielding.
Inside jun zi and-also outside the **small** in the **person**.
A **jun zi**'s **dao long-living**.
The **small** in the **person**'s **dao dissolving indeed**.

Fields of meaning

Compenetrate, *TAI*: see *Image of the Situation*. The **small going**, the **great coming**, *XIAO WANG DA LAI*: see *Image of the Situation*. **Significance Growing**, *JI HENG*: see *Image of the Situation*. **Consequence**, *ZE*: reason, cause, result; rule, law, pattern, standard; therefore; very strong connection. **That**, *SHI*: refers to the preceding statement. **Heaven** and **earth mingling**, *TIAN DI JIAO*: see *Patterns of Wisdom*. **And-also**, *ER*: see *Preceding Situation*. **Myriad**, *WAN*: ten thousand; countless, many, everyone. Ideogram: swarm of insects. **Being**, *WU*: creature, thing, any single being; matter, substance, essence; nature of things. **Interpenetrate**, *TONG*: see *Preceding Situation*. **Indeed**, *YE*: see *Preceding Situation*. **Above**, *SHANG*: anything above in all senses; higher, upper, outer; upper trigram. **Below**, *XIA*: anything below, in all senses; lower, inner; lower trigram. **They/their**, *QI*: general third person pronoun and possessive adjective; also: one/one's, it/its, he/his, she/her. **Purpose**, *ZHI*: focus of mind and heart; intention, will, inclination; continuity in the direction of life. Ideogram: heart and scholar, high inner resolve. **Concord**, *TONG*: harmonize, unite, equalize, assemble; agree, share in; together, at once, same time and place. Ideogram: cover and mouth, silent understanding and perfect fit.

Inside, *NEI*: within, inner, interior; inside of the house and those who work there, particularly women; inside of the body, inner organs; the lower trigram, as opposed to outside, *WAI*, the upper. Ideogram: border and enter. **Yang**, *YANG*: sunny slope of a hill, sunny bank of a river; dynamic and bright aspect of the basic duality (Yin and Yang) manifesting in all phenomena; Yang arouses, transforms and dissolves existing structures; linear thrust, stimulus, drive, focus; quality of a whole line. **Outside**, *WAI*: outer, external; unfamiliar, foreign; ignore, reject; work done outside the home; the upper trigram as indication of the outer aspects of the situation. **Yin**, *YIN*: shady slope of a hill or bank of a river; consolidating, dark aspect of the basic duality (Yin and Yang) manifesting in all phenomena; Yin creates and conserves structure; spatial extension; build, make things concrete; quality of an opened line. **Persist**, *JIAN*: tenacious, persevering; strong, robust, dynamic; constant as the motion of heavenly bodies in their orbits; Action of the trigram Force, *QIAN*. **Yield**, *SHUN*: give way, comply, agree, follow, obey; docile, flexible; bear produce, nourish, provide; Action of the trigram Field, *KUN*. **Jun zi**: ideal of a person who orders his/her life in accordance with dao rather than willful intention, and uses divination in this spirit. **Small**, *XIAO*: see *Image of the Situation*. **Person/people**, *REN*: humans individually and collectively; an individual; humankind. **Dao**, *DAO*: see *Patterns of Wisdom*. **Long-living**, *ZHANG*: enduring, lasting, constant; extended, long, large; senior, superior, greater; increase, prosper; respect, elevate. **Dissolve**, *XIAO*: liquefy, melt, thaw; diminish, disperse; eliminate, exhaust. Ideogram: water dissolving differences.

否

12 OBSTRUCTION | *Pi* ䷋

The situation described by this hexagram is characterized by a disjunction of heaven and earth temporarily interrupting the flow of life and thwarting communication and development.

Image of the Situation

> To **obstruction belongs in-no-way people**.
> **Not harvesting**: a **jun zi**'s **Trial**.
> The **great going**, the **small coming**.

Fields of meaning

Obstruct, *PI*: closed, stopped; bar the way; obstacle; unfortunate, wicked; refuse, disapprove, deny. Ideogram: mouth and not, blocked communication. **Belong/it**, *ZHI*: establishes between two terms a connection similar to the Saxon genitive, in which the second term belongs to the first one; at the end of a sentence it refers to something previously mentioned or implied. **In-no-way**, *FEI*: strong negative; not so; bandit, rebel; unjust, immoral. Ideogram: a box filled with opposition. **People/person**, *REN*: humans individually and collectively; an individual; humankind. **Not**, *BU*: common term of negation. **Harvest**, *LI*: benefit, advantage, profit; realization; sharp, acute, insightful; quality of autumn and West, third stage of the Time Cycle. Ideogram: ripe grain and blade. **Jun zi**: ideal of a person who orders his/her life in accordance with dao rather than willful intention, and uses divination in this spirit. **Trial**, *ZHEN*: inquiry by divination and its result; righteous, firm; separating wheat from chaff; the kernel, the proven core; quality of winter and North, fourth stage of the Time Cycle. Ideogram: pearl and divination. **Great**, *DA*: big, noble, important, very; orient the will toward a self-imposed goal, impose direction; ability to lead or guide one's life; contrasts with small, *XIAO*, flexible adaptation to what crosses one's path. **Go**, *WANG*: move away in time or space, depart; become past; dead, gone; contrasts with come, *LAI*, approach in time or space. **Small**, *XIAO*: little, common, unimportant; adapting to what crosses your path; ability to move in harmony with the vicissitudes of life; contrasts with great, *DA*, self-imposed theme or goal. **Come**, *LAI*: approach in time or space; move toward, arrive at; future; contrasts with go, *WANG*, move away or become past.

Outer and Inner Trigram

The upper trigram, **Energy/parch**, *QIAN/GAN*, describes the outer aspects of the situation. It has the following associations: unceasing forward movement, dynamic, enduring, untiring; spirit power, manifestation of Yang, that activates all creation and destruction in Space; heaven, sovereign, father. With the pronunciation *GAN*: parch, dry up, burn, exhaust. Ideogram: sprouts or vapors rising from the ground and sunlight, both fecundating moisture and scorching drought. *Symbol*: heaven, *TIAN*; sky, firmament, heavens; the highest realm, situated above the human world, as opposed to the earth, *DI*, located below. Ideogram: great and the one above. *Action*: persist, *JIAN*; tenacious, persevering; strong, robust, dynamic; constant as the motion of heavenly bodies in their orbits. In the family of trigrams *QIAN* is the father.

The lower trigram, **Space**, *KUN*, describes the inner aspects of the situation. It has the following associations: surface of the world; support of all existence, manifestation of Yin, where Energy or Yang activates all creation and destruction; all-involving service; earth; moon, wife, mother; rest, receptivity, docile obedience. Ideogram: terrestrial globe and stretch out. *Symbol*: earth, *DI*; the earth, ground on which the human world rests; basis of all things, nourishes all things; essential Yin. *Action*: yield, *SHUN*: give way, comply, agree, follow, obey; docile, flexible; bear produce, nourish, provide. In the family of trigrams *KUN* is the mother.

Counter Hexagram

The Counter Hexagram of **Obstruction** is hexagram 53, **Infiltrating**, which switches the emphasis from the blockage characterizing **Obstruction** to a progress by gradual and steady penetration.

Preceding Situation

> **Beings not permitted** to **use completing interpenetration**.
> To **anterior acquiescence belongs** the **use** of **obstruction**.

Fields of meaning
Beings not permitted (to **use**), *WU BU KE (YI)*: it is not possible; no one is allowed; it is not in the nature of things. **Complete**, *ZHONG*: completion of a cycle that begins the next; entire, whole, all. Ideogram: silk cocoons, follow and ice, winter linking one year with the next. **Interpenetrate**, *TONG*: penetrate freely and reciprocally, permeate, flow through, open a way; see clearly, understand deeply; communicate with; together. To **anterior acquiescence belongs** the **use** of, *GU SHOU ZHI YI*: understanding and accepting the preceding statement allows the consultant to make proper use of this hexagram. **Obstruct**, *PI*: see *Image of the Situation.*

Hexagrams in Pairs

> **Obstruction** and **compenetration**: **reversing one's sorting indeed**.

Fields of meaning
Obstruct, *PI*: see *Image of the Situation*. **Compenetrate**, *TAI*: communicate, permeate, diffuse; excellent, eminent, supreme; abundant, prosperous; smooth, slippery; extreme, extravagant, prodigal. Ideogram: person in water, connected to the universal medium. **Reverse**, *FAN*: turn and move in the opposite direction; turn around or upside down (180 degrees); change to the opposite position; contrary. **One/one's**, *QI*: general third person pronoun and possessive adjective; also: it/its, he/his, she/her, they/their. **Sort**, *LEI*: group according to kind, compare; species, class, genus; resemble; analog, like nature or purpose; norm, model. **Indeed**, *YE*: emphasizes and intensifies the previous statement.

Patterns of Wisdom

> **Heaven** and **earth not mingling**. **Obstruction**.
> A **jun zi uses parsimonious actualizing-dao** to **expel heaviness**.
> And **not permitting splendor** in **using benefits**.

Fields of meaning
Heaven, *TIAN*: sky, firmament, heavens; the highest realm, situated above the human world, as opposed to the earth, *DI*, located below; Symbol of the trigram Energy, *QIAN*. Ideogram: great and the one above. **Earth**, *DI*: the earth, ground on which the human world rests; basis of all things, nourishes all things; essential Yin; Symbol of the trigram Space, *KUN*. **Not**, *BU*: common term of negation.

Mingle, *JIAO*: blend with, communicate, join, exchange; trade; copulation; friendship. Ideogram: legs crossed. **Obstruct**, *PI*: see *Image of the Situation*. **Jun zi**: see *Image of the Situation*. **Use**, *YI*: by means of; owing to; make use of, employ. **Parsimonious**, *JIAN*: thrifty; moderate, temperate; stingy, scanty. **Actualize-dao**, *DE*: realize dao in action; power, virtue; ability to follow the course traced by the ongoing process of the cosmos. Ideogram: go, straight, and heart. Linked with acquire, *DE*: acquiring that which makes a being become what it is meant to be. **Expel**, *PI*: cast out, repress, exclude, punish; exclusionary laws and their enforcement. Ideogram: punish, authority and mouth, giving order to expel. **Heaviness**, *NAN*: difficulty, hardship, distress; arduous, grievous; harass; contrasts with versatility, *YI*, deal lightly with. Ideogram: bird with clipped tail on drying sticky soil. **Permit**, *KE*: possible because in harmony with an inherent principle; capable of; approve, authorize. Ideogram: mouth and breath, silent consent. **Splendor**, *RONG*: flowering, luxuriant; glory, elegance, honor, beauty; elaborately carved corners of a temple roof. **Benefits**, *LU*: pay, salary, income; have the use of; goods received, revenues; official function.

Transforming Lines

INITIAL SIX

䷋

Eradicating thatch-grass intertwisted.
Using one's classification.
Trial, significant.
Growing.

Comments
Eradicating thatch-grass: Trial, significant.
Purpose located in a **chief indeed.**

Fields of meaning

Eradicate, *BA*: pull up, root out, extirpate; extricate from difficulties; elevate, promote. **Thatch-grass**, *MAO*: thick grass used for roofs of humble houses. **Intertwist**, *RU*: interlaced, entangled, as roots; forage, straw. **Use**, *YI*: see *Patterns of Wisdom*. **One/one's**, *QI*: see *Hexagrams in Pairs*. **Classification**, *HUI*: class, collection, series; same kind; put or group together. **Trial**, *ZHEN*: see *Image of the Situation*. **Significant**, *JI*: leads to the experience of meaning; favorable, propitious, appropriate. Ideogram: scholar and mouth, wise words of a sage. **Grow**, *HENG*: heavenly influence pervading and nourishing all things; prosper, succeed, expand, develop; effective, favorable; quality of summer and South, second stage of the Time Cycle. With the pronunciation *XIANG*: offer a sacrifice; offer a gift to a superior; accept, enjoy.

Purpose, *ZHI*: focus of mind and heart; intention, will, inclination; continuity in the direction of life. Ideogram: heart and scholar, high inner resolve. **Locate**, *ZAI*: be at, be situated at, dwell, reside; in, within; involved with, in the process of. Ideogram: earth and persevere, a place on the earth. **Chief**, *JUN*: prince, ruler; lead, direct; wise person. Ideogram: mouth and direct, giving orders. **Indeed**, *YE*: see *Hexagrams in Pairs.*

Six at Second

Enwrapped in **receiving**.
The **small** in the **person significant**.
The **great** in the **person obstructed**.
Growing.

Comments
The **great** in the **person obstructed**.
Growing.
Not disarraying the **flock indeed**.

Fields of meaning

Enwrap, *BAO*: envelop, hold, contain; patient, engaged. Ideogram: enfold and self, a fetus in the womb. **Receive**, *CHENG*: receive gifts or commands from superiors or customers; take in hand; give, offer respectfully; help, support. Ideogram: accepting a seal of office. **Small**, *XIAO*: see *Image of the Situation.* **Person/people**, *REN*: humans individually and collectively; an individual; humankind. **Significant**, *JI*: leads to the experience of meaning; favorable, propitious, appropriate. Ideogram: scholar and mouth, wise words of a sage. **Great**, *DA*: see *Image of the Situation.* **Obstruct**, *PI*: see *Image of the Situation.* **Grow**, *HENG*: heavenly influence pervading and nourishing all things; prosper, succeed, expand, develop; effective, favorable; quality of summer and South, second stage of the Time Cycle. With the pronunciation *XIANG*: offer a sacrifice; offer a gift to a superior; accept, enjoy.

Not, *BU*: common term of negation. **Disarray**, *LUAN*: throw into disorder, mislay, confuse; out of place; discord, insurrection, anarchy. **Flock**, *QUN*: herd, group; people of the same kind, friends, equals; crowd, multitude; move in unison, flock together. Ideogram: chief and sheep, flock around a leader. **Indeed**, *YE*: see *Hexagrams in Pairs.*

SIX AT THIRD

Enwrapped in **embarrassment**.

Comments
Enwrapped in **embarrassment**.
Position not appropriate indeed.

Fields of meaning

Enwrap, *BAO*: envelop, hold, contain; patient, engaged. Ideogram: enfold and self, a fetus in the womb. **Embarrassment**, *XIU*: shame, confusion; conscious of guilt or fault; shy, blushing; humble offering. Ideogram: sheep, sheepish feeling.

Position, *WEI*: place, location; be at; social standing, rank; position of a line in a hexagram. Ideogram: person standing. **Not**, *BU*: common term of negation. **Appropriate**, *DANG*: suitable, capable, worthy, adequate, competent, equal to; opportune, convenient; whole lines in odd places and opened lines in even places. **Indeed**, *YE*: see *Hexagrams in Pairs*.

NINE AT FOURTH

Possessing fate, without fault.
Cultivating radiant satisfaction.

Comments
Possessing fate, without fault.
Purpose moving indeed.

Fields of meaning

Possess, *YOU*: general term indicating possession; have, own, be endowed with. **Fate**, *MING*: individual destiny; birth and death as limits of life; issue orders with authority; consult the gods. Ideogram: mouth and order, words with heavenly authority. **Without fault**, *WU JIU*: no error or harm in the situation. **Cultivate**, *CHOU*: till fields or gardens; repeat continually, like annual plowing. Ideogram: fields and long life. **Radiance**, *LI*: glowing light, spreading in all directions; the power of consciousness; discriminate, articulate, divide and arrange in order; assemble, attract. Ideogram: bird and weird, magical fire-bird with brilliant plumage. **Satisfaction**, *ZHI*: fulfillment, gratification, happiness; take pleasure in, fulfill a need.

Purpose, *ZHI*: focus of mind and heart; intention, will, inclination; continuity

in the direction of life. Ideogram: heart and scholar, high inner resolve. **Move**, *XING*: move or move something; motivate; emotionally moving; walk, act, do. Ideogram: successive steps. **Indeed**, *YE*: see *Hexagrams in Pairs*.

NINE AT FIFTH

Relaxing the **obstruction**.
The **great** in the **person**, **significant**.
Its extinction, **its extinction**.
Attachment tending-towards a **grove** of **mulberry-trees**.

Comments
To the **great** in the **person belongs significance**.
Position correct and **appropriate indeed**.

Fields of meaning

Relax, *XIU*: rest, stop temporarily; resign, retire; advantage, prosperity. Ideogram: person leaning on a tree. **Obstruct**, *PI*: see *Image of the Situation*. **Great**, *DA*: see *Image of the Situation*. **Person/people**, *REN*: humans individually and collectively; an individual; humankind. **Significant**, *JI*: leads to the experience of meaning; favorable, propitious, appropriate. Ideogram: scholar and mouth, wise words of a sage. **It/its**, *QI*: general third person pronoun and possessive adjective; also: one/one's, he/his, she/her, they/their. **Extinguish**, *WANG*: ruin, destroy; cease, go, die; lost without trace; forget, out of mind; absence, exile. Ideogram: person concealed by a wall, out of sight. **Attach**, *XI*: fasten to, bind, tie; retain, continue; keep in mind; emotional bond. **Tend-towards**, *YU*: move toward without necessarily reaching, in the direction of. **Grove**, *BAO*: luxuriant growth, dense thicket; conceal, screen; sleeping mats; wrapping for food gifts. Ideogram: wrap and bushes. **Mulberry-tree**, *SANG*: the tree on which silkworms live; rural place, tranquillity, retirement.

Belong/it, *ZHI*: see *Image of the Situation*. **Position**, *WEI*: place, location; be at; social standing, rank; position of a line in a hexagram. Ideogram: person standing. **Correct**, *ZHENG*: rectify deviation or one-sidedness; proper, straight, exact, regular; constant, rule, model. Ideogram: stop and one, hold to one thing. **Appropriate**, *DANG*: suitable, capable, worthy, adequate, competent, equal to; opportune, convenient; whole lines in odd places and opened lines in even places. **Indeed**, *YE*: see *Hexagrams in Pairs*.

NINE ABOVE

Subverting the **obstruction**.
Beforehand obstruction, afterwards joy.

Comments
Obstruction completed, by **consequence subverting**.
Is it **permitted long-living indeed?**

Fields of meaning

Subvert, *JING*: overturn, overthrow; leaning, falling; pour out, empty. Ideogram: man, head and ladle, emptying out old ideas. **Obstruct**, *PI*: see *Image of the Situation*. **Before(hand)/earlier**, *XIAN*: anterior, preceding in time; former, past, previous; first, at first. **After(wards)/later**, *HOU*: come after in time, subsequent; put oneself after; behind, back, draw back; the second; attendants, heirs, successors, posterity. **Joy/rejoice**, *XI*: delight, exult; cheerful, merry. Ideogram: joy (music) and mouth, expressing joy.

Complete, *ZHONG*: see *Preceding Situation*. **Consequence**, *ZE*: reason, cause, result; rule, law, pattern, standard; therefore; very strong connection. **Is?**, *HE*: ask, inquire; what? which? who? how? why? where? an interrogative particle, often introducing a rhetorical question: is it? is it not? **Permit**, *KE*: see *Patterns of Wisdom*. **Long-living**, *ZHANG*: enduring, lasting, constant; extended, long, large; senior, superior, greater; increase, prosper; respect, elevate. **Indeed**, *YE*: see *Hexagrams in Pairs*.

Image Tradition

To **obstruction belongs in-no-way people**.
Not harvesting: a **jun zi**'s **Trial**.
The **great going**, the **small coming**.
By **consequence** of **that heaven** and **earth not mingling and-also** the **myriad beings not interpenetrating indeed**.
Above and **below not mingling and-also below heaven without fiefdoms indeed**.

Inside Yin and-also outside Yang.
Inside supple and-also outside solid.
Inside the **small** in the **person and-also outside jun zi**.
The **small** in the **person**'s **dao long-living**.
A **jun zi**'s **dao dissolving indeed**.

Fields of meaning

To **obstruction belongs in-no-way people**, *PI ZHI FEI REN*: see *Image of the Situation*. **Not harvesting**: a **jun zi**'s **Trial**, *BU LI JUN ZI ZHEN*: common term of negation. The **great going**, the **small coming**, *DA WANG XIAO LAI*: see *Image of the Situation*. **Consequence**, *ZE*: reason, cause, result; rule, law, pattern, standard; therefore; very strong connection. **That**, *SHI*: refers to the preceding statement. **Heaven** and **earth not mingling**, *TIAN DI BU JIAO*: see *Patterns of Wisdom*. **And-also**, *ER*: joins and contrasts two terms. **Myriad**, *WAN*: ten thousand; countless, many, everyone. Ideogram: swarm of insects. **Being**, *WU*: creature, thing, any single being; matter, substance, essence; nature of things. **Interpenetrate**, *TONG*: see *Preceding Situation*. **Indeed**, *YE*: see *Hexagrams in Pairs*. **Above**, *SHANG*: anything above in all senses; higher, upper, outer; upper trigram. **Below**, *XIA*: anything below, in all senses; lower, inner; lower trigram. **Below heaven**, *TIAN XIA*: human world, between heaven and earth. **Without**, *WU*: devoid of; there is not. **Fiefdom**, *BANG*: region governed by a feudatory.

Inside, *NEI*: within, inner, interior; inside of the house and those who work there, particularly women; inside of the body, inner organs; the lower trigram, as opposed to outside, *WAI*, the upper. Ideogram: border and enter. **Yin**, *YIN*: shady slope of a hill or bank of a river; consolidating, dark aspect of the basic duality (Yin and Yang) manifesting in all phenomena; Yin creates and conserves structure; spatial extension; build, make things concrete; quality of an opened line. **Outside**, *WAI*: outer, external; unfamiliar, foreign; ignore, reject; work done outside the home; the upper trigram as indication of the outer aspects of the situation. **Yang**, *YANG*: sunny slope of a hill, sunny bank of a river; dynamic and bright aspect of the basic duality (Yin and Yang) manifesting in all phenomena; Yang arouses, transforms and dissolves existing structures; linear thrust, stimulus, drive, focus; quality of a whole line. **Supple**, *ROU*: quality of the opened lines; flexible, pliant, adaptable, tender. **Solid**, *GANG*: quality of the whole lines; firm, strong, unyielding, persisting. **Dao**, *DAO*: way or path; ongoing process of being and the course it traces for each person or thing; ultimate reality, intrinsic nature; origin. Ideogram: go and head, opening a path. **Long-living**, *ZHANG*: enduring, lasting, constant; extended, long, large; senior, superior, greater; increase, prosper; respect, elevate. **Dissolve**, *XIAO*: liquefy, melt, thaw; diminish, disperse; eliminate, exhaust. Ideogram: water dissolving differences.

同人

䷌

13 CONCORDING PEOPLE | *Tong Ren*

The situation described by this hexagram is characterized by cooperation, people united by a common goal.

Image of the Situation

> **Concording people tend-towards** the **countryside.**
> **Growing.**
> **Harvesting: wading** the **great river**.
> **Harvesting**: a **jun zi**'s **Trial**.

Fields of meaning

Concord, *TONG*: harmonize, unite, equalize, assemble; agree, share in; together, at once, same time and place. Ideogram: cover and mouth, silent understanding and perfect fit. **People/person**, *REN*: humans individually and collectively; an individual; humankind. **Tend-towards**, *YU*: move toward without necessarily reaching, in the direction of. **Countryside**, *YE*: cultivated fields and grassland, where nature and human construction interact; third of the territorial zones: city, suburbs, countryside, forest. **Grow**, *HENG*: heavenly influence pervading and nourishing all things; prosper, succeed, expand, develop; effective, favorable; quality of summer and South, second stage of the Time Cycle. With the pronunciation *XIANG*: offer a sacrifice; offer a gift to a superior; accept, enjoy. **Harvest**, *LI*: benefit, advantage, profit; realization; sharp, acute, insightful; quality of autumn and West, third stage of the Time Cycle. Ideogram: ripe grain and blade. **Wading the Great River**, *SHE DA CHUAN*: enter the stream of life with a goal or purpose; embark on a significant enterprise. **Jun zi**: ideal of a person who orders his/her life in accordance with dao rather than willful intention, and uses divination in this spirit. **Trial**, *ZHEN*: inquiry by divination and its result; righteous, firm; separating wheat from chaff; the kernel, the proven core; quality of winter and North, fourth stage of the Time Cycle. Ideogram: pearl and divination.

Outer and Inner Trigram

The upper trigram, **Energy/parch**, *QIAN/GAN*, describes the outer aspects of the situation. It has the following associations: unceasing forward movement, dynamic, enduring, untiring; spirit power, manifestation of Yang, that activates all creation and destruction in Space; heaven, sovereign, father. With the pronunciation *GAN*: parch, dry up, burn, exhaust. Ideogram: sprouts or vapors rising from the ground and sunlight, both fecundating moisture and scorching drought. *Symbol*: heaven, *TIAN*; sky, firmament, heavens; the highest realm, situated above the human world, as opposed to the earth, *DI*, located below. Ideogram: great and the one above. *Action*: persist, *JIAN*; tenacious, persevering; strong, robust, dynamic; constant as the motion of heavenly bodies in their orbits. In the family of trigrams *QIAN* is the father.

The lower trigram, **Radiance**, *LI*, describes the inner aspects of the situation. It has the following associations: glowing light, spreading in all directions; the power of consciousness; discriminate, articulate, divide and arrange in order; assemble, attract. Ideogram: bird and weird, magical fire-bird with brilliant plumage. *Symbols*: fire and brightness. Fire, *HUO*: flame, burn; warming and consuming aspect of burning. Brightness, *MING*: light, radiance, clarity; distinguish, discern, understand; light-giving aspect of fire, of heavenly bodies and of consciousness. *Action*: congregate, *LI*, cling together, adhere to, rely on; couple, pair, herd; beautiful, elegant. Ideogram: deer flocking together. In the family of trigrams *LI* is the middle daughter.

Counter Hexagram

The Counter Hexagram of **Concording People** is hexagram 44, **Coupling**, which switches the emphasis from a meeting based on shared common goals to an encounter driven by powerful instinctual forces, beyond the control of social or personal considerations.

Preceding Situation

> **Beings not permitted** to **use completing obstruction**.
> To **anterior acquiescence belongs** the **use** of
> **concording people**.

Fields of meaning

Beings not permitted (to **use**), *WU BU KE (YI)*: it is not possible; no one is allowed; it is not in the nature of things. **Not**, *BU*: common term of negation. **Complete**, *ZHONG*: completion of a cycle that begins the next; entire, whole, all. Ideogram: silk cocoons, follow and ice, winter linking one year with the next. **Obstruct**, *PI*: closed, stopped; bar the way; obstacle; unfortunate, wicked; refuse, disapprove, deny. Ideogram: mouth and not, blocked communication. To **anterior acquiescence belongs** the **use** of, *GU SHOU ZHI YI*: understanding and accepting the preceding statement allows the consultant to make proper use of this hexagram. **Concording people**, *TONG REN*: see *Image of the Situation*.

Hexagrams in Pairs

> **Great possessing**: **crowds indeed**.
> **Concording people**: **connecting indeed**.

Fields of meaning
Great, *DA*: big, noble, important, very; orient the will toward a self-imposed goal, impose direction; ability to lead or guide one's life; contrasts with small, *XIAO*, flexible adaptation to what crosses one's path. **Possess**, *YOU*: general term indicating possession; have, own, be endowed with. **Crowds**, *ZHONG*: many people, large group, masses; all, ali beings. **Indeed**, *YE*: emphasizes and intensifies the previous statement. **Concording people**, *TONG REN*: see *Image of the Situation*. **Connect**, *QIN*: be close, approach, come near; cherish, help, favor; intimate; relatives, kin.

Patterns of Wisdom

> **Heaven associated** with **fire**. **Concording people**.
> A **jun zi uses sorting** the **clans** to **mark-off** the **beings**.

Fields of meaning
Heaven, *TIAN*: sky, firmament, heavens; the highest realm, situated above the human world, as opposed to the earth, *DI*, located below; Symbol of the trigram Energy, *QIAN*. Ideogram: great and the one above. **Associate**, *YU*: consort with, combine; companions; group, band, company; agree with, comply, help; in favor of. Ideogram: a pair of hands reaching downward meets a pair of hands reaching upward, helpful association. **Fire**, *HUO*: fire, flame, burn; warming and consuming aspect of burning; fire and brightness are the Symbols of the trigram Radiance, *LI*. **Concording people**, *TONG REN*: see *Image of the Situation*. **Jun zi**: see *Image of the Situation*. **Use**, *YI*: by means of; owing to; make use of, employ. **Sort**, *LEI*: group according to kind, compare; species, class, genus; resemble; analog, like nature or purpose; norm, model. **Clan**, *ZU*: extended family with the same ancestor and surname; kin, relatives; tribe, class, kind. Ideogram: flag and spear,

a rallying point. **Mark-off**, *BIAN*: distinguish by dividing; mark off a plot of land; discern, discriminate, differentiate; discuss and dispute; frame which divides a bed from its stand. Ideogram: knife and acrid, sharp division. **Being**, *WU*: creature, thing, any single being; matter, substance, essence; nature of things.

Transforming Lines

Initial nine

Concording people tend-towards the **gate**.
Without fault.

Comments
Emerging from the **gate concording people**.
Furthermore whose fault indeed?

Fields of meaning
Concording people, *TONG REN*: see *Image of the Situation*. **Tend-towards**, *YU*: see *Image of the Situation*. **Gate**, *MEN*: outer door, between courtyard and street; family, sect; a text or master as gate to a school of thought. **Without fault**, *WU JIU*: no error or harm in the situation.

Emerge, *CHU*: come out of, proceed from, spring from, issue forth; appear, be born; bear, generate; leave, flee; Action of the trigram Shake, *ZHEN*. Ideogram: stem with branches and leaves emerging. **Furthermore**, *YOU*: moreover; in addition to; again. **Whose**, *SHUI*: relative and interrogative pronoun, often introducing a rhetorical question; anybody. **Fault**, *JIU*: unworthy conduct that leads to harm, illness, misfortune; guilt, crime, punishment. Ideogram: person and differ, differ from what you should be. **Indeed**, *YE*: see *Hexagrams in Pairs*.

Six at Second

Concording people tend-towards the **ancestors**.
Abashment.

Comments
Concording people tend-towards the **ancestors**.
Abashment: **dao indeed**.

Fields of meaning
Concording people, *TONG REN*: see *Image of the Situation*. **Tend-towards**, *YU*: see *Image of the Situation*. **Ancestry**, *ZONG*: clan, kin, origin; those who bear the

same surname; ancestral hall and tablets; honor, revere. **Abashment**, *LIN*: distress, shame, regret, humiliation; aware of having lost the right track; leads to repenting, *HUI*, correcting the direction of mind and life.

Dao, *DAO*: way or path; ongoing process of being and the course it traces for each person or thing; ultimate reality, intrinsic nature; origin. Ideogram: go and head, opening a path. **Indeed**, *YE*: see *Hexagrams in Pairs*.

NINE AT THIRD

Hiding-away weapons tending-towards the **thickets**.
Ascending one's high mound.
Three year's-time not rising.

Comments
Hiding-away weapons tending-towards the **thickets**.
Antagonistic solid indeed.
Three year's-time not rising.
Peaceful movement indeed.

Fields of meaning

Hide-away, *FU*: hide, conceal; ambush; secret, silent; prostrate, submit. Ideogram: man and crouching dog. **Weapons**, *RONG*: arms; armed people, soldiers; military, violent. Ideogram: spear and armor, offensive and defensive weapons. **Tend-towards**, *YU*: see *Image of the Situation*. **Thicket**, *MANG*: high grass, underbrush, tangled vegetation; rustic, rude, socially inept. **Ascend**, *SHENG*: rise, augment, grow; climb step by step; rise in office; advance through effort; offer a sacrifice; lit.: a measure for fermented liquor, ascension as distillation. **One/one's**, *QI*: general third person pronoun and possessive adjective; also: it/its, he/his, she/her, they/their. **High**, *GAO*: high, elevated, lofty, eminent; honor, respect. Ideogram: high tower. **Mound**, *LING*: grave-mound, barrow; small hill. **Three/thrice**, *SAN*: number three; third time or place; active phases of a cycle; superlative; beginning of repetition (since one and two are entities in themselves). **Year's-time**, *SUI*: duration of a year; beginning of a year. **Not**, *BU*: common term of negation. **Rise**, *XING*: get up, grow, lift; stimulate, promote; enjoy. Ideogram: lift, two hands and unite, lift with both hands.

Antagonistic, *DI*: opposed and equal; competitor, enemy; a contest between equals. **Solid**, *GANG*: quality of the whole lines; firm, strong, unyielding, persisting. **Indeed**, *YE*: see *Hexagrams in Pairs*. **Peace**, *AN*: quiet, still, settled, secure, contented; calm, tranquilize, console. Ideogram: woman under a roof, a tranquil home. **Move**, *XING*: move or move something; motivate; emotionally moving; walk, act, do. Ideogram: successive steps.

Nine at Fourth

Riding one's rampart.
Nowhere controlling aggression.
Significant.

Comments
Riding one's rampart.
Righteousness nowhere controlling indeed.
One's significance.
By **consequence confinement and-also reversal** by **consequence indeed.**

Fields of meaning

Ride, *CHENG*: ride an animal or a chariot; have the upper hand, control a stronger power; an opened line above controlling a whole line below. **One/one's**, *QI*: general third person pronoun and possessive adjective; also: it/its, he/his, she/her, they/their. **Rampart**, *YONG*: defensive wall; bulwark, redoubt. **Nowhere/nothing**, *FU*: strong negative; not a single thing/place; deny, disapprove; impossible, incorrect. **Control**, *KE*: be in charge; capable of, able to, adequate; check, obstruct, repress. Ideogram: roof beams supporting a house. **Aggression**, *GONG*: assault, attack; apply to; criticize; stimulate the vital power; urgent desire. Ideogram: toil and strike. **Significant**, *JI*: leads to the experience of meaning; favorable, propitious, appropriate. Ideogram: scholar and mouth, wise words of a sage.

Righteous, *YI*: proper, just, virtuous, upright; the heart that rules itself; benevolent, loyal, devoted to public good. **Indeed**, *YE*: see *Hexagrams in Pairs*. **Consequence**, *ZE*: reason, cause, result; rule, law, pattern, standard; therefore; very strong connection. **Confine**, *KUN*: enclose, restrict, limit, oppress; impoverished, distressed, afflicted, exhausted, disheartened, weary. Ideogram: tree in a narrow enclosure. **And-also**, *ER*: joins and contrasts two terms. **Reverse**, *FAN*: turn and move in the opposite direction; turn around or upside down (180 degrees); change to the opposite position; contrary.

NINE AT FIFTH

Concording people beforehand cry-out and **sob and-also afterwards laugh**.
Great legions control the **reciprocal meeting**.

Comments
To **concording people belongs** a **before**.
Using the **center**: **straightening indeed**.
Great legions control the **reciprocal meeting**.
Words reciprocally controlling indeed.

Fields of meaning

Concording people, *TONG REN*: see *Image of the Situation*. **Before(hand)/earlier**, *XIAN*: anterior, preceding in time; former, past, previous; first, at first. **Cry-out/outcry**, *HAO*: call out, proclaim; order, command; mark, label, sign; designate, name. **Sob**, *TAO*: cry, weep aloud; wailing children. Ideogram: mouth and omen, ominous sounds. **And-also**, *ER*: joins and contrasts two terms. **After(wards)/later**, *HOU*: come after in time, subsequent; put oneself after; behind, back, draw back; the second; attendants, heirs, successors, posterity. **Laugh**, *XIAO*: manifest joy or mirth; giggle, joke, laugh at, tease; desire; open (of a flower); associated with the Fiery Moment. **Great**, *DA*: see *Hexagrams in Pairs*. **Legions**, *SHI*: army, troops; leader, general, model, master; organize, make functional; take as a model, imitate, follow. Ideogram: heap and whole, turn confusion into a functional unit. **Control**, *KE*: be in charge; capable of, able to, adequate; check, obstruct, repress. Ideogram: roof beams supporting a house. **Reciprocal**, *XIANG*: mutual; assist, encourage, help; bring together, blend with; examine, inspect; by turns. **Meet**, *YU*: come on unexpectedly, encounter; occur, happen; pleasant meeting, lucky coincidence; agree.

Belong/it, *ZHI*: establishes between two terms a connection similar to the Saxon genitive, in which the second term belongs to the first one; at the end of a sentence it refers to something previously mentioned or implied. **Use**, *YI*: see *Patterns of Wisdom*. **Center**, *ZHONG*: inner, central; put in the center; middle, stable point enabling you to face inner and outer changes; middle line of a trigram. Ideogram: field divided in two equal parts. **Straighten**, *ZHI*: rectify; upright; correct the crooked; proceed directly; sincere, just; blunt, outspoken. **Indeed**, *YE*: see *Hexagrams in Pairs*. **Word**, *YAN*: spoken word, speech, saying; talk, discuss, address; name, signify. Ideogram: mouth and rising vapor.

NINE ABOVE

Concording people tend-towards the **suburbs**.
Without repenting.

Comments
Concording people tend-towards the **suburbs**.
Purpose not-yet acquired indeed.

Fields of meaning

Concording people, *TONG REN*: see *Image of the Situation*. **Tend-towards**, *YU*: see *Image of the Situation*. **Suburbs**, *JIAO*: area adjoining a city where human constructions and nature interpenetrate; second of the territorial zones: city, suburbs, countryside, forest. **Without**, *WU*: devoid of; there is not. **Repent**, *HUI*: regret, dissatisfaction with past conduct inducing a change of heart; proceeds from abashment, *LIN*, shame and confusion at having lost the right way.

Purpose, *ZHI*: focus of mind and heart; intention, will, inclination; continuity in the direction of life. Ideogram: heart and scholar, high inner resolve. **Not-yet**, *WEI*: temporal negative indicating that something is expected to happen but has not yet occurred. **Acquire**, *DE*: obtain the desired object; possession; satisfied, fulfilled; it is permitted; agree with; wish for, desire covetously. Ideogram: go and obstacle, going through obstacles to the goal. **Indeed**, *YE*: see *Hexagrams in Pairs*.

Image Tradition

Concording people.
The **supple acquires** the **position**, **acquires** the **center**
and-also the **correspondence reaches energy**.
Named: **concording people**.

Concording people: thus **named**.
Concording people tend-towards the **countryside**.
Growing.
Harvesting: **wading** the **great river**.
Energy moving indeed.

Pattern's **brightness uses persistence**.
The **center correct and-also corresponding**.
A **jun zi correct indeed**.
Verily a **jun zi activating enables interpenetration** of
purposes belonging to **below heaven**.

Fields of meaning

Concording people, *TONG REN*: see *Image of the Situation*. **Supple**, *ROU*: quality of the opened lines; flexible, pliant, adaptable, tender. **Acquire**, *DE*: obtain the desired object; possession; satisfied, fulfilled; it is permitted; agree with; wish for, desire covetously. Ideogram: go and obstacle, going through obstacles to the goal. **Position**, *WEI*: place, location; be at; social standing, rank; position of a line in a hexagram. Ideogram: person standing. **Center**, *ZHONG*: inner, central; put in the center; middle, stable point enabling you to face inner and outer changes; middle line of a trigram. Ideogram: field divided in two equal parts. **And-also**, *ER*: joins and contrasts two terms. **Correspond**, *YING*: be in agreement or harmony; proper, suitable; resonate together, answer to; relation between the lines (1 and 4, 2 and 5, 3 and 6) when they form the pair opened and whole, supple and solid. Ideogram: heart and obey. **Reach**, *HU*: arrive at a goal; move toward and achieve; to, at, in; distinct from tend-towards, *YOU*. **Energy/parch**, *QIAN/GAN*: unceasing forward movement, dynamic, enduring, untiring; spirit power, manifestation of Yang, that activates all creation and destruction in Space; heaven, sovereign, father. With the pronunciation *GAN*: parch, dry up, burn, exhaust. Ideogram: sprouts or vapors rising from the ground and sunlight, both fecundating moisture and scorching drought. **Name**, *YUE*: speak, declare, call. Ideogram: open mouth and tongue.

Tend-towards the **countryside**, *YU YE*: see *Image of the Situation*. **Grow**, *HENG*: see *Image of the Situation*. **Harvesting**: **wading** the **great river**, *LI SHE DA CHUAN*: see *Image of the Situation*. **Move**, *XING*: move or move something; motivate; emotionally moving; walk, act, do. Ideogram: successive steps. **Indeed**, *YE*: see *Hexagrams in Pairs*.

Pattern, *WEN*: intrinsic or natural design, pattern of wood, stone or animal fur; ideograms, the symbols of writing as revelation of the intrinsic nature of things; language, civilization, culture; harmonious, beautiful, elegant, polite. **Brightness**, *MING*: light, radiance, clarity; distinguish, discern, understand; light-giving aspect of fire, of heavenly bodies and of consciousness; brightness and fire are the Symbols of the trigram Radiance, *LI*. **Use**, *YI*: see *Patterns of Wisdom*. **Persist**, *JIAN*: tenacious, persevering; strong, robust, dynamic; constant as the motion of heavenly bodies in their orbits; Action of the trigram Force, *QIAN*. **Correct**, *ZHENG*: rectify deviation or one-sidedness; proper, straight, exact, regular; constant, rule, model. Ideogram: stop and one, hold to one thing. **Jun zi**: see *Image of the Situation*. **Very/verily**, *WEI*: the only; in truth; answer; acquiesce; yes. **Activate**, *WEI*: act or cause to act; do, make, manage, make active; be, become; attend to, help; because of. **Able/enable**, *NENG*: ability, power, skill, art; competent, talented; duty, function, capacity. Ideogram: an animal with strong hooves and bones, able to carry and defend. **Interpenetrate**, *TONG*: penetrate freely and reciprocally, permeate, flow through, open a way; see clearly, understand deeply; communicate with; together. **Purpose**, *ZHI*: focus of mind and heart; intention, will, inclination; continuity in the direction of life. Ideogram: heart and scholar, high inner resolve. **Belong/it**, *ZHI*: establishes between two terms a connection similar to the Saxon genitive, in which the second term belongs to the first one; at the end of a sentence it refers to something previously mentioned or implied. **Below heaven**, *TIAN XIA*: human world, between heaven and earth.

14 THE GREAT POSSESSING | *Da You* 大有 ䷍

The situation described by this hexagram is characterized by a central idea or long-term goal, which acts as an organizing force directing the course of one's life.

Image of the Situation

> The **great possessing**.
> **Spring**, **Growing**.

Fields of meaning

Great, *DA*: big, noble, important, very; orient the will toward a self-imposed goal, impose direction; ability to lead or guide one's life; contrasts with small, *XIAO*, flexible adaptation to what crosses one's path. **Possess**, *YOU*: general term indicating possession; have, own, be endowed with. **Spring**, *YUAN*: source, origin, head; arise, begin; first generating impulse; great, excellent; quality of springtime and East, first stage of the Time Cycle. **Grow**, *HENG*: heavenly influence pervading and nourishing all things; prosper, succeed, expand, develop; effective, favorable; quality of summer and South, second stage of the Time Cycle. With the pronunciation *XIANG*: offer a sacrifice; offer a gift to a superior; accept, enjoy.

Outer and Inner Trigram

The upper trigram, **Radiance**, *LI*, describes the outer aspects of the situation. It has the following associations: glowing light, spreading in all directions; the power of consciousness; discriminate, articulate, divide and arrange in order; assemble, attract. Ideogram: bird and weird, magical fire-bird with brilliant plumage. *Symbols*: fire and brightness. Fire, *HUO*: flame, burn; warming and consuming aspect of burning. Brightness, *MING*: light, radiance, clarity; distinguish, discern, understand; light-giving aspect of fire, of heavenly bodies and of consciousness. *Action*: congregate, *LI*, cling together, adhere to, rely on; couple, pair, herd; beautiful, elegant. Ideogram: deer flocking together. In the family of trigrams *LI* is the middle daughter.

The lower trigram, **Energy/parch**, *QIAN/GAN*, describes the inner aspects of the situation. It has the following associations: unceasing forward movement, dynamic, enduring, untiring; spirit power, manifestation of Yang, that activates all creation and destruction in Space; heaven, sovereign, father. With the pronunciation *GAN*: parch, dry up, burn, exhaust. Ideogram: sprouts or vapors rising from the ground and sunlight, both fecundating moisture and scorching drought. *Symbol*: heaven, *TIAN*; sky, firmament, heavens; the highest realm, situated above the human world, as opposed to the earth, *DI*, located below. Ideogram: great and the one above. *Action*: persist, *JIAN*; tenacious, persevering; strong, robust, dynamic; constant as the motion of heavenly bodies in their orbits. In the family of trigrams *QIAN* is the father.

Counter Hexagram

The Counter Hexagram of **The Great Possessing** is hexagram 43, **Parting**, which switches the emphasis from the sustained tension toward a long-term goal to a sudden breakthrough, like a flooding river overflowing its banks and parting into different streams.

Preceding Situation

> **Associating** with **people concording implies beings necessarily converting in-truth**.
> To **anterior acquiescence belongs** the **use** of the **great possessing**.

Fields of meaning

Associate, *YU*: consort with, combine; companions; group, band, company; agree with, comply, help; in favor of. Ideogram: a pair of hands reaching downward meets a pair of hands reaching upward, helpful association. **People/person**, *REN*: humans individually and collectively; an individual; humankind. **Concord**, *TONG*: harmonize, unite, equalize, assemble; agree, share in; together, at once, same time and place. Ideogram: cover and mouth, silent understanding and perfect fit. **Imply**, *ZHE*: further signify; additional meaning. **Being**, *WU*: creature, thing, any single being; matter, substance, essence; nature of things. **Necessarily**, *BI*: unavoidably, certainly. **Convert**, *GUI*: accomplish one's destiny; revert to the original place or state; restore, revert; turn into; goal, destination, intention; a girl getting married. Ideogram: arrive and wife, become mistress of a household. **In-truth**, *YAN*: a final affirmative particle; the preceding statement is complete and correct. To **anterior acquiescence belongs** the **use** of, *GU SHOU ZHI YI*: understanding and accepting the preceding statement allows the consultant to make proper use of this hexagram. The **great possessing**, *DA YOU*: see *Image of the Situation*.

Hexagrams in Pairs

> The **great possessing**: **crowds indeed**.
> **Concording people**: **connecting indeed**.

Fields of meaning
The **great possessing**, *DA YOU*: see *Image of the Situation*. **Crowds**, *ZHONG*: many people, large group, masses; all, all beings. **Indeed**, *YE*: emphasizes and intensifies the previous statement. **Concord**, *TONG*: see *Preceding Situation*. **People/person**, *REN*: see *Preceding Situation*. **Connect**, *QIN*: be close, approach, come near; cherish, help, favor; intimate; relatives, kin.

Patterns of Wisdom

> **Fire located above heaven**. The **great possessing**.
> A **jun zi uses terminating hatred** to **display improvement**.
> And **yielding** to **heaven** to **relax** into **fate**.

Fields of meaning
Fire, *HUO*: fire, flame, burn; warming and consuming aspect of burning; fire and brightness are the Symbols of the trigram Radiance, *LI*. **Locate**, *ZAI*: be at, be situated at, dwell, reside; in, within; involved with, in the process of. Ideogram: earth and persevere, a place on the earth. **Above**, *SHANG*: anything above in all senses; higher, upper, outer; upper trigram. **Heaven**, *TIAN*: sky, firmament, heavens; the highest realm, situated above the human world, as opposed to the earth, *DI*, located below; Symbol of the trigram Energy, *QIAN*. Ideogram: great and the one above. The **great possessing**, *DA YOU*: see *Image of the Situation*. **Jun zi**: ideal of a person who orders his/her life in accordance with dao rather than willful intention, and uses divination in this spirit. **Use**, *YI*: by means of; owing to; make use of, employ. **Terminate**, *O*: stop, put an end to, bring to a standstill. Ideogram: go and why, no reason to move. **Hate**, *WU*: detest, dread, dislike; averse to, ashamed of; repulsive, vicious, vile, ugly, wicked. Ideogram: twisted bowels and heart. **Display**, *YANG*: spread, extend, scatter, divulge, promote. Ideogram: hand and expand, spreading a message. **Improve**, *SHAN*: make better, reform, perfect; virtuous, wise; mild, docile; clever, skillful. Ideogram: mouth and sheep, gentle speech. **Yield**, *SHUN*: give way, comply, agree, follow, obey; docile,

flexible; bear produce, nourish, provide; Action of the trigram Field, *KUN*. **Relax**, *XIU*: rest, stop temporarily; resign, retire; advantage, prosperity. Ideogram: person leaning on a tree. **Fate**, *MING*: individual destiny; birth and death as limits of life; issue orders with authority; consult the gods. Ideogram: mouth and order, words with heavenly authority.

Transforming Lines

INITIAL NINE

Without mingling with **harm**.
In-no-way faulty.
Drudgery by **consequence without fault**.

Comments
The **great possessing**, **initial nine**.
Without mingling with **harm indeed**.

Fields of meaning
Without, *WU*: devoid of; there is not. **Mingle**, *JIAO*: blend with, communicate, join, exchange; trade; copulation; friendship. Ideogram: legs crossed. **Harm**, *HAI*: damage, injure, offend; suffer, become ill; obstacle, hindrance; fearful, anxious. **In-no-way**, *FEI*: strong negative; not so; bandit, rebel; unjust, immoral. Ideogram: a box filled with opposition. **Fault**, *JIU*: unworthy conduct that leads to harm, illness, misfortune; guilt, crime, punishment. Ideogram: person and differ, differ from what you should be. **Drudgery**, *JIAN*: difficult, hard, repetitive work; distressing, sorrowful. Ideogram: perverse and sticky earth, soil difficult to cultivate. **Consequence**, *ZE*: reason, cause, result; rule, law, pattern, standard; therefore; very strong connection. **Without fault**, *WU JIU*: no error or harm in the situation.

The **great possessing**, *DA YOU*: see *Image of the Situation*. **Initial**, *CHU*: beginning, incipient, first step or part; bottom line of a hexagram. Ideogram: knife and garment, cutting out the pattern. **Nine**, *JIU*: number nine; transforming whole line; superlative: best, perfect. **Indeed**, *YE*: see *Hexagrams in Pairs*.

NINE AT SECOND

The **great chariot used** to **carry**.
Possessing directed going.
Without fault.

Comments

The **great chariot used** to **carry**.
Amassing in the **center**, **not destroying indeed**.

Fields of meaning

Great, *DA*: see *Image of the Situation*. **Chariot**, *CHE*: cart, wheeled traveling vehicle. **Use**, *YI*: see *Patterns of Wisdom*. **Carry**, *ZAI*: bear, carry with you; contain, sustain, support; load a ship or cart, cargo; fill in. **Possessing directed going**, *YOU YOU WANG*: having a goal or purpose, moving in a specific direction. **Without fault**, *WU JIU*: no error or harm in the situation.

Amass, *JI*: hoard, accumulate, pile up, add up, increase; repeated action, habit; follow, pursue. **Center**, *ZHONG*: inner, central; put in the center; middle, stable point enabling you to face inner and outer changes; middle line of a trigram. Ideogram: field divided in two equal parts. **Not**, *BU*: common term of negation. **Destroy**, *BAI*: ruin, defeat, failure; violate, subvert, decompose. **Indeed**, *YE*: see *Hexagrams in Pairs*.

NINE AT THIRD

A **prince avails** of **Growing tending-towards heavenly sonhood**.
The **small** in the **person nowhere controlling**.

Comments

A **prince avails** of **Growing tending-towards heavenly sonhood**.
The **small** in the **person harmful indeed**.

Fields of meaning

Prince, *GONG*: highest title of nobility; noble acting as minister of state in the capital; contrasts with feudatory, *HOU*, governor of a province. **Avail**, *YONG*: use, employ for a specific purpose; take advantage of; benefit from; capacity. Ideogram: to divine and center, applying divination to central concerns. **Grow**, *HENG*: see *Image of the Situation*. **Tend-towards**, *YU*: move toward without necessarily reaching, in the direction of. **Heaven**, *TIAN*: see *Patterns of Wisdom*. **Son(hood)**, *ZI*: son, male child; heirs, offspring, posterity; living up to the ideal of the ancestors as highest human aspiration; seed, kernel, egg; sage, teacher; nadir, deepest point, midnight, mid-winter. **Small**, *XIAO*: little, common, unimportant; adapting to what crosses your path; ability to move in harmony with the vicissitudes of life; contrasts with great, *DA*, self-imposed theme or goal. **Person/people**,

REN: humans individually and collectively; an individual; humankind. **Nowhere/nothing**, *FU*: strong negative; not a single thing/place; deny, disapprove; impossible, incorrect. **Control**, *KE*: be in charge; capable of, able to, adequate; check, obstruct, repress. Ideogram: roof beams supporting a house.

Harm, *HAI*: damage, injure, offend; suffer, become ill; obstacle, hindrance; fearful, anxious. **Indeed**, *YE*: see *Hexagrams in Pairs*.

NINE AT FOURTH

In-no-way one's preponderance.
Without fault.

Comments
In-no-way one's preponderance.
Without fault.
Brightness differentiates clearly indeed.

Fields of meaning
In-no-way, *FEI*: strong negative; not so; bandit, rebel; unjust, immoral. Ideogram: a box filled with opposition. **One/one's**, *QI*: general third person pronoun and possessive adjective; also: it/its, he/his, she/her, they/their. **Preponderance**, *PENG*: forceful, dominant; overbearing, encroaching. Ideogram: drum beats, dominating sound. **Without fault**, *WU JIU*: no error or harm in the situation.

Brightness, *MING*: light, radiance, clarity; distinguish, discern, understand; light-giving aspect of fire, of heavenly bodies and of consciousness; brightness and fire are the Symbols of the trigram Radiance, *LI*. **Differentiate**, *BIAN*: argue, dispute, criticize; sophisticated, artful. Ideogram: words and sharp or pungent. **Clearly**, *ZHE*: brilliant, luminous, shining; perceptive; intuitive knowledge. **Indeed**, *YE*: see *Hexagrams in Pairs*.

SIX AT FIFTH

Your conforming: mingling thus.
Impressing thus. Significant.

Comments
Your conforming: mingling thus.
Trustworthiness uses shooting-forth purpose indeed.
To **impressing thus belongs significance.**
Versatility and-also without preparing indeed.

Fields of meaning

Your/contracted, *JUE*: intensifying possessive pronoun and adjective; concentrate, tense, contract; whooping cough. **Conform**, *FU*: accord between inner and outer; sincere, truthful, verified, reliable; capture; prisoners, spoils. Ideogram: claws over child, a bird brooding on the nest. **Mingle**, *JIAO*: blend with, communicate, join, exchange; trade; copulation; friendship. Ideogram: legs crossed. **Thus**, *RU*: as, in this way; comparable, similar. **Impress**, *WEI*: impose on, intimidate; august, solemn; pomp, majesty. **Significant**, *JI*: leads to the experience of meaning; favorable, propitious, appropriate. Ideogram: scholar and mouth, wise words of a sage.

Trustworthy, *XIN*: truthful, faithful, consistent over time; count on, confide in; examine, verify, prove; loyalty, integrity. Ideogram: person and word, true speech. **Use**, *YI*: see *Patterns of Wisdom*. **Shoot-forth**, *FA*: emit, send out, shoot an arrow; ferment, rise; express, raise one's voice. Ideogram: stance, bow and arrow, shooting from a solid base. **Purpose**, *ZHI*: focus of mind and heart; intention, will, inclination; continuity in the direction of life. Ideogram: heart and scholar, high inner resolve. **Indeed**, *YE*: see *Hexagrams in Pairs*. **Belong/it**, *ZHI*: establishes between two terms a connection similar to the Saxon genitive, in which the second term belongs to the first one; at the end of a sentence it refers to something previously mentioned or implied. **Versatility**, *YI*: sudden and unpredictable change, and the mental mobility and openness required in order to face it; easy, light, simple; occurs in the name of the *Yi Jing*. **And-also**, *ER*: joins and contrasts two terms. **Without**, *WU*: devoid of; there is not. **Prepare**, *BEI*: make ready, provide for; available; complete, sufficient.

NINE ABOVE

The **origin** in **heaven shields it**.
Significant, without not Harvesting.

Comments

The **great possessing**, **above**: **significant**.
The **origin** in **heaven shields indeed**.

Fields of meaning

Origin, *ZI*: source, beginning, ground; cause, reason, motive; tracing back to the source; oneself, by oneself; spontaneous, intrinsic. **Heaven**, *TIAN*: see *Patterns of Wisdom*. **Shield**, *YOU*: heavenly kindness and protection. Ideogram: numinous and right hand, spirit power. **It/belong**, *ZHI*: establishes between two terms a connection similar to the Saxon genitive, in which the second term belongs to the first one; at the end of a sentence it refers to something previously mentioned or implied. **Significant**, *JI*: leads to the experience of meaning; favorable, propitious, appropriate. Ideogram: scholar and mouth, wise words of a sage. **Without not Harvesting**, *WU BU LI*: turning point where the balance is swinging from not Harvesting to actually Harvesting.

The **great possessing**, *DA YOU*: see *Image of the Situation*. **Above**, *SHANG*: see *Patterns of Wisdom*. **Indeed**, *YE*: see *Hexagrams in Pairs*.

Image Tradition

The **great possessing**.
The **supple acquires** the **noble position**: the **great** in the **center**.
And-also above and **below correspond** to **it**.
Named: the **great possessing**.

One's actualizing-dao: **solid persisting and-also pattern brightening**.
The **correspondence reaches heaven and-also** the **season moves**.
That uses Spring, Growing.

Fields of meaning

The **great possessing**, *DA YOU*: see *Image of the Situation*. **Supple**, *ROU*: quality of the opened lines; flexible, pliant, adaptable, tender. **Acquire**, *DE*: obtain the desired object; possession; satisfied, fulfilled; it is permitted; agree with; wish for, desire covetously. Ideogram: go and obstacle, going through obstacles to the goal. **Noble**, *ZUN*: honorable, worthy of respect, eminent. Ideogram: presenting wine to a guest. **Position**, *WEI*: place, location; be at; social standing, rank; position of a line in a hexagram. Ideogram: person standing. **Center**, *ZHONG*: inner, central; put in the center; middle, stable point enabling you to face inner and outer changes; middle line of a trigram. Ideogram: field divided in two equal parts. **And-also**, *ER*: joins and contrasts two terms. **Above**, *SHANG*: see *Patterns of Wisdom*. **Below**, *XIA*: anything below, in all senses; lower, inner; lower trigram. **Correspond**, *YING*: be in agreement or harmony; proper, suitable; resonate together, answer to; relation between the lines (1 and 4, 2 and 5, 3 and 6) when they form the pair opened and whole, supple and solid. Ideogram: heart and obey. **It/belong**, *ZHI*: establishes between two terms a connection similar to the Saxon genitive, in which the second term belongs to the first one; at the end of a sentence it refers to something previously mentioned or implied. **Name**, *YUE*: speak, declare, call. Ideogram: open mouth and tongue.

One/one's, *QI*: general third person pronoun and possessive adjective; also: it/its, he/his, she/her, they/their. **Actualize-dao**, *DE*: realize dao in action; power, virtue; ability to follow the course traced by the ongoing process of the cosmos. Ideogram: go, straight, and heart. Linked with acquire, *DE*: acquiring that which makes a being become what it is meant to be. **Solid**, *GANG*: quality of the whole lines; firm, strong, unyielding, persisting. **Persist**, *JIAN*: tenacious, persevering; strong, robust, dynamic; constant as the motion of heavenly bodies in their orbits; Action of the trigram Force, *QIAN*. **Season**, *SHI*: quality of the time; the right time, opportune, in harmony; planning in accord with the time; season of the year. Ideogram: sun and temple, sacred time. **Move**, *XING*: move or move something; motivate; emotionally moving; walk, act, do. Ideogram: successive steps. **That**, *SHI*: refers to the preceding statement. **Use**, *YI*: see *Patterns of Wisdom*. **Spring Growing**, *YUAN HENG*: see *Image of the Situation*.

謙 ䷎

15 HUMBLING | *Qian*

The situation described by this hexagram is characterized by cutting through pride and arrogance, keeping one's words adherent to one's basic reality.

Image of the Situation

> **Humbling.**
> **Growing.**
> A **jun zi possesses completing.**

Fields of meaning
Humble, *QIAN*: think and speak of oneself in a modest way; respectful, unassuming, retiring, unobtrusive; yielding, compliant, reverent, lowly. Ideogram: words and unite, keeping words close to underlying facts. **Grow**, *HENG*: heavenly influence pervading and nourishing all things; prosper, succeed, expand, develop; effective, favorable; quality of summer and South, second stage of the Time Cycle. With the pronunciation *XIANG*: offer a sacrifice; offer a gift to a superior; accept, enjoy. **Jun zi**: ideal of a person who orders his/her life in accordance with dao rather than willful intention, and uses divination in this spirit. **Possess**, *YOU*: general term indicating possession; have, own, be endowed with. **Complete**, *ZHONG*: completion of a cycle that begins the next; entire, whole, all. Ideogram: silk cocoons, follow and ice, winter linking one year with the next.

Outer and Inner Trigram

The upper trigram, **Space**, *KUN*, describes the outer aspects of the situation. It has the following associations: surface of the world; support of all existence, manifestation of Yin, where Energy or Yang activates all creation and destruction; all-involving service; earth; moon, wife, mother; rest, receptivity, docile obedience. Ideogram: terrestrial globe and stretch out. *Symbol*: earth, *DI*; the earth, ground on which the human world rests; basis of all things, nourishes all things; essential yin. *Action*: yield, *SHUN*: give way, comply, agree, follow, obey; docile, flexible; bear produce, nourish, provide. In the family of trigrams *KUN* is the mother.

The lower trigram, **Bound**, *GEN*, describes the inner aspects of the situation. It has the following associations: limit, frontier; obstacle that prevents from seeing further; stop; still, quiet, motionless; confine, enclose; mountain, sunset, beginning of winter; solid, steady, unshakable; straight, hard, adamant, obstinate. *Symbol*: mountain, *SHAN*, large, immense; limit, boundary. Ideogram: three peaks, a mountain range. *Action*: stop, *ZHI*, bring or come to a standstill, cease, terminate. Ideogram: a foot stops walking. In the family of trigrams *GEN* is the youngest son.ß

Counter Hexagram

The Counter Hexagram of **Humbling** is hexagram 40, **Unraveling**, which switches the emphasis from the simplicity of **Humbling** to a focus on analysis and understanding.

Preceding Situation

> **Possessing** the **great implies**: **not permitted using over-filling**.
> To **anterior acquiescence belongs** the **use** of **humbling**.

Fields of meaning

Possess, *YOU*: see *Image of the Situation*. **Great**, *DA*: big, noble, important, very; orient the will toward a self-imposed goal, impose direction; ability to lead or guide one's life; contrasts with small, *XIAO*, flexible adaptation to what crosses one's path. **Imply**, *ZHE*: further signify; additional meaning. **Not**, *BU*: common term of negation. **Permit**, *KE*: possible because in harmony with an inherent principle; capable of; approve, authorize. Ideogram: mouth and breath, silent consent. **Use**, *YI*: by means of; owing to; make use of, employ. **Overfill**, *YING*: fill completely; full, at the point of overflowing; excess, arrogance. Ideogram: vessel and overflow. To **anterior acquiescence belongs** the **use** of, *GU SHOU ZHI YI*: understanding and accepting the preceding statement allows the consultant to make proper use of this hexagram. **Humble**, *QIAN*: see *Image of the Situation*.

Hexagrams in Pairs

> **Humbling**: **levity**.
> **And-also providing**: **indolence indeed**.

Fields of meaning

Humble, *QIAN*: see *Image of the Situation*. **Levity**, *QING*: light, soft; gentle, easy; alert, agile; frivolous, unimportant, superficial. Ideogram: cart and stream, empty cart floating downstream. **And-also**, *ER*: joins and contrasts two terms. **Provide**, *YU*: prepare for, pre-arrange, think beforehand; ready, satisfied, contented, at ease, relaxed; enthusiasm, joy, pleasure. Ideogram: sonhood and elephant, careful, reverent and strong. **Indolence**, *DAI*: lazy, idle, inattentive, careless; self-indulgent; disdainful, contemptuous. **Indeed**, *YE*: emphasizes and intensifies the previous statement.

Additional Texts

> **Humbling**: the **handle belonging** to **actualizing-dao indeed**.
> **Humbling**: **noble and-also shining**.
> **Humbling**: **using paring** the **codes**.

Fields of meaning

Humble, *QIAN*: see *Image of the Situation*. **Handle**, *BING*: haft; control of, power to. **Belong/it**, *ZHI*: establishes between two terms a connection similar to the Saxon genitive, in which the second term belongs to the first one; at the end of a sentence it refers to something previously mentioned or implied. **Actualize-dao**, *DE*: realize dao in action; power, virtue; ability to follow the course traced by the ongoing process of the cosmos. Ideogram: go, straight, and heart. Linked with acquire, *DE*: acquiring that which makes a being become what it is meant to be. **Indeed**, *YE*: see *Hexagrams in Pairs*. **Noble**, *ZUN*: honorable, worthy of respect, eminent. Ideogram: presenting wine to a guest. **And-also**, *ER*: see *Hexagrams in Pairs*. **Shine**, *GUANG*: illuminate, emit light; brilliant, splendid; honor, glory, éclat; distinct from brightness, *MING*, light of heavenly bodies. Ideogram: fire above person. **Use**, *YI*: see *Preceding Situation*. **Pare**, *ZHI*: cut away, tailor, carve; form, invent; institution, rule; limit, prevent. Ideogram: knife and incomplete. **Codes**, *LI*: rites, rules, ritual, etiquette; usage, manners; honor, worship. Ideogram: worship and sacrificial vase, handling a sacred vessel.

Patterns of Wisdom

> The **earth**'s **center possesses mountain**. **Humbling**.
> A **jun zi uses reducing** the **numerous** to **augment** the **few**.
> And **evaluating** the **beings** to **even spreading**.

Fields of meaning

Earth, *DI*: the earth, ground on which the human world rests; basis of all things, nourishes all things; essential Yin; Symbol of the trigram Space, *KUN*. **Center**, *ZHONG*: inner, central; put in the center; middle, stable point enabling you to face inner and outer changes; middle line of a trigram. Ideogram: field divided in two equal parts. **Possess**, *YOU*: see *Image of the Situation*. **Mountain**, *SHAN*: mountain; large, immense; limit, boundary; Symbol of the trigram Bound, *GEN*. Ideogram: three peaks, a mountain range. **Humble**, *QIAN*: see *Image of the Situation*. **Jun zi**: see *Image of the Situation*. **Use**, *YI*: see *Preceding Situation*. **Reduce**, *POU*: diminish in number; assemble, collect in fewer, larger groups. **Numerous**, *DUO*: great number, many; often. **Augment**, *YI*: increase, advance, promote, enrich, benefit, strengthen; pour in more; superabundant; excessive. Ideogram: water and vessel, pouring in more. **Few**, *GUA*: small number; seldom; reduce, diminish; unsupported, solitary. **Evaluate**, *CHENG*: assess, appraise; weigh, estimate, reckon; designate, name. Ideogram: weigh and grain, attributing value. **Being**, *WU*: creature, thing, any single being; matter, substance, essence; nature of things. **Even**, *PING*: level, flatten, equalize; balanced, regular; uniform, peaceful, tranquil; restore quiet, harmonize. **Spread**, *SHI*: expand, diffuse, distribute, arrange, exhibit; add to; aid. Ideogram: flag and indeed, claiming new country.

Transforming Lines

INITIAL SIX

Humbling, humbling: jun zi.
Availing of **wading** the **great river**.
Significant.

Comments
Humbling, humbling: jun zi.
Lowliness uses originating herding indeed.

Fields of meaning

Humble, *QIAN*: see *Image of the Situation*. **Jun zi**: see *Image of the Situation*. **Avail**, *YONG*: use, employ for a specific purpose; take advantage of; benefit from; capacity. Ideogram: to divine and center, applying divination to central concerns. **Wading the Great River**, *SHE DA CHUAN*: enter the stream of life with a goal or purpose; embark on a significant enterprise. **Significant**, *JI*: leads to the experience of meaning; favorable, propitious, appropriate. Ideogram: scholar and mouth, wise words of a sage.

Lowly, *BEI*: speak and think of oneself humbly; modest, yielding, respectful;

decline, decrease; base, mean, contemptible. **Use**, *YI*: see *Preceding Situation*. **Origin**, *ZI*: source, beginning, ground; cause, reason, motive; tracing back to the source; oneself, by oneself; spontaneous, intrinsic. **Herd**, *MU*: tend cattle; watch over, superintend; ruler, teacher.

Six at Second

The **call** of **humbling**.
Trial, **significant**.

Comments
The **call** of **humbling**.
Trial, **significant**.
In the **center** the **heart acquiring indeed**.

Fields of meaning
Call, *MING*: bird and animal cries, through which they recognize each other; distinctive sound, song, statement. Ideogram: bird and mouth, a distinguishing call. **Humble**, *QIAN*: see *Image of the Situation*. **Trial**, *ZHEN*: inquiry by divination and its result; righteous, firm; separating wheat from chaff; the kernel, the proven core; quality of winter and North, fourth stage of the Time Cycle. Ideogram: pearl and divination. **Significant**, *JI*: leads to the experience of meaning; favorable, propitious, appropriate. Ideogram: scholar and mouth, wise words of a sage.

Center, *ZHONG*: see *Patterns of Wisdom*. **Heart**, *XIN*: the heart as center of being; seat of mind, imagination and affect; moral nature; source of desires, intentions, will. **Acquire**, *DE*: obtain the desired object; possession; satisfied, fulfilled; it is permitted; agree with; wish for, desire covetously. Ideogram: go and obstacle, going through obstacles to the goal. **Indeed**, *YE*: see *Hexagrams in Pairs*.

Nine at Third

The **toil** of **humbling**: **jun zi**.
Possessing completion, **significant**.

Comments
The **toil** of **humbling**: **jun zi**.
The **myriad commoners submit indeed**.

Fields of meaning

Toil, *LAO*: hardship, labor; exert oneself, exhaust oneself; burdened, careworn; worthy actions. Ideogram: strength and fire. **Humble**, *QIAN*: see *Image of the Situation*. **Jun zi**: see *Image of the Situation*. **Possess**, *YOU*: see *Image of the Situation*. **Complete**, *ZHONG*: see *Image of the Situation*. **Significant**, *JI*: leads to the experience of meaning; favorable, propitious, appropriate. Ideogram: scholar and mouth, wise words of a sage.

Myriad, *WAN*: ten thousand; countless, many, everyone. Ideogram: swarm of insects. **Commoners**, *MIN*: common people, masses; working class supporting the social hierarchy; undeveloped potential in the individual. **Submit**, *FU*: yield, obey, acquiesce; enforce obedience. **Indeed**, *YE*: see *Hexagrams in Pairs*.

Six at Fourth

Without not harvesting: **showing humbleness**.

Comments

Without not harvesting: **showing humbleness**.
Not contradicting by **consequence indeed**.

Fields of meaning

Without not Harvesting, *WU BU LI*: turning point where the balance is swinging from not Harvesting to actually Harvesting. **Show**, *HUI*: show, signal, point out. Ideogram: hand and act, giving signals. **Humble**, *QIAN*: see *Image of the Situation*.

Not, *BU*: common term of negation. **Contradict**, *WEI*: oppose, disregard, disobey; seditious, perverse. **Consequence**, *ZE*: reason, cause, result; rule, law, pattern, standard; therefore; very strong connection. **Indeed**, *YE*: see *Hexagrams in Pairs*.

Six at Fifth

Not affluence: **using one's neighbor**.
Harvesting: **availing** of **encroaching** and **subjugating**.
Without not harvesting.

Comments

Harvesting: **availing** of **encroaching** and **subjugating**.
Disciplining, **not submitting indeed**.

Fields of meaning

Not, *BU*: common term of negation. **Affluence**, *FU*: rich, abundant; wealth; enrich, provide for; flow toward, accrue. **Use**, *YI*: see *Preceding Situation*. **One/one's**, *QI*: general third person pronoun and possessive adjective; also: it/its, he/his, she/her, they/their. **Neighbor**, *LIN*: person living nearby; extended family; assist, support. **Harvest**, *LI*: benefit, advantage, profit; realization; sharp, acute, insightful; quality of autumn and West, third stage of the Time Cycle. Ideogram: ripe grain and blade. **Avail**, *YONG*: use, employ for a specific purpose; take advantage of; benefit from; capacity. Ideogram: to divine and center, applying divination to central concerns. **Encroach**, *QIN*: invade, usurp, appropriate; advance stealthily, enter secretly. **Subjugate**, *FA*: hit, cut; submit, make dependent; chastise rebels, subject to rule. Ideogram: man and lance, armed soldiers. **Without not Harvesting**, *WU BU LI*: turning point where the balance is swinging from not Harvesting to actually Harvesting.

Discipline, *ZHENG*: subjugate vassals, reduce to order; punishing expedition. Ideogram: step and correct, a rectifying move. **Submit**, *FU*: yield, obey, acquiesce; enforce obedience. **Indeed**, *YE*: see *Hexagrams in Pairs*.

SIX ABOVE

The **call** of **humbling**.
Harvesting: **availing** of **moving legions**.
Disciplining the **capital city**.

Comments
The **call** of **humbling**.
Purpose not-yet acquired indeed.
Permitted availing of **moving legions**.
Disciplining the **capital city indeed**.

Fields of meaning

Call, *MING*: bird and animal cries, through which they recognize each other; distinctive sound, song, statement. Ideogram: bird and mouth, a distinguishing call. **Humble**, *QIAN*: see *Image of the Situation*. **Harvest**, *LI*: benefit, advantage, profit; realization; sharp, acute, insightful; quality of autumn and West, third stage of the Time Cycle. Ideogram: ripe grain and blade. **Avail**, *YONG*: use, employ for a specific purpose; take advantage of; benefit from; capacity. Ideogram: to divine and center, applying divination to central concerns. **Move**, *XING*: move or move something; motivate; emotionally moving; walk, act, do. Ideogram: successive steps. **Legions**, *SHI*: army, troops; leader, general, model, master; organize, make functional; take as a model, imitate, follow. Ideogram: heap and whole, turn confusion into a functional unit. **Discipline**, *ZHENG*: subjugate vassals, reduce to order; punishing expedition. Ideogram: step and correct, a rectifying move. **Capital**, *YI*: populous fortified city, center and symbol of the region it rules. Ideogram: enclosure and official seal. **City**, *GUO*: city, state, country, nation; area of only human constructions; first of the territorial zones: city, suburbs, countryside, forest.

Purpose, *ZHI*: focus of mind and heart; intention, will, inclination; continuity in the direction of life. Ideogram: heart and scholar, high inner resolve. **Not-yet**, *WEI*: temporal negative indicating that something is expected to happen but has not yet occurred. **Acquire**, *DE*: obtain the desired object; possession; satisfied, fulfilled; it is permitted; agree with; wish for, desire covetously. Ideogram: go and obstacle, going through obstacles to the goal. **Indeed**, *YE*: see *Hexagrams in Pairs*. **Permit**, *KE*: see *Preceding Situation*.

Image Tradition

Humbling, Growing.
Heavenly dao: below fording and-also shining brightness.
Earthly dao: lowly and-also above moving.

Heavenly dao lessens overfilling and-also augments humbling.
Earthly dao transforms overfilling and-also diffuses humbling.
Soul and **spirit harm overfilling and-also bless humbling.**
People's **dao hates overfilling and-also loves humbling.**

Humbling: noble and-also shining.
Lowliness and-also not permitted to **pass-beyond**.
The **completion belonging** to a **jun zi indeed**.

Fields of meaning

Humbling, Growing, *QIAN HENG*: see *Image of the Situation*. **Heaven**, *TIAN*: sky, firmament, heavens; the highest realm, situated above the human world, as opposed to the earth, *DI*, located below; Symbol of the trigram Energy, *QIAN*. Ideogram: great and the one above. **Dao**, *DAO*: way or path; ongoing process of being and the course it traces for each person or thing; ultimate reality, intrinsic nature; origin. Ideogram: go and head, opening a path. **Below**, *XIA*: anything below, in all senses; lower, inner; lower trigram. **Ford**, *JI*: cross a river at a ford or shallow place; embark on a course of action; complete, finish, succeed; help, relieve. Ideogram: water and level, running smooth over a flat bottom. **And-also**, *ER*: see *Hexagrams in Pairs*. **Shine**, *GUANG*: see *Additional Texts*. **Brightness**, *MING*: light, radiance, clarity; distinguish, discern, understand; light-giving aspect of fire, of heavenly bodies and of consciousness; brightness and fire are the Symbols of the trigram Radiance, *LI*. **Earth**, *DI*: see *Patterns of Wisdom*. **Lowly**, *BEI*: speak and think of oneself humbly; modest, yielding, respectful; decline, decrease; base, mean, contemptible. **Above**, *SHANG*: anything above in all senses; higher, upper, outer; upper trigram. **Move**, *XING*: move or move something; motivate; emotionally moving; walk, act, do. Ideogram: successive steps.

Lessen, *KUI*: diminish, injure, wane; lack, defect. **Overfill**, *YING*: see *Preceding Situation*. **Augment**, *YI*: see *Patterns of Wisdom*. **Transform**, *BIAN*: abrupt, radical passage from one state to another; transformation of opened and whole lines into each other in hexagrams; contrasts with change, *HUA*, gradual mutation. **Diffuse**, *LIU*: flow out, spread, permeate. **Soul**, *GUI*: power that creates individual existence; union of volatile-soul, *HUN*, spiritual and intellectual power, and dense-soul, *PO*, bodily strength and movement. *HUN* rises after death, *PO* remains with the body and may communicate with the living. **Spirit**, *SHEN*: spiritual power that confers intensity on heart and mind by acting on the soul, *GUI*; vitality, energy; spirits, ancestors, gods. **Harm**, *HAI*: damage, injure, offend; suffer, become ill; obstacle, hindrance; fearful, anxious. **Bless**, *FU*: heavenly gifts and favor; happiness, prosperity; spiritual power and goodwill. Ideogram: spirit and plenty. **People/person**, *REN*: humans individually and collectively; an individual; humankind. **Hate**, *WU*: detest, dread, dislike; averse to, ashamed of; repulsive, vicious, vile, ugly, wicked. Ideogram: twisted bowels and heart. **Love**, *HAO*: affection; fond of, take pleasure in; fine, graceful.

Noble, *ZUN*: see *Additional Texts*. **Not**, *BU*: common term of negation. **Permit**, *KE*: see *Preceding Situation*. **Pass-beyond**, *YU*: go beyond set time or limits; get over a wall or obstacle. **Complete**, *ZHONG*: see *Image of the Situation*. **Belong/it**, *ZHI*: see *Additional Texts*. **Jun zi**: see *Image of the Situation*. **Indeed**, *YE*: see *Hexagrams in Pairs*.

豫

䷏

16 PROVIDING | *Yu*

The situation described by this hexagram is characterized by providing for oneself and others, preparing for future ease and contentment.

Image of the Situation

> **Providing.**
> **Harvesting: installing feudatories, moving legions.**

Fields of meaning

Provide, *YU*: prepare for, pre-arrange, think beforehand; ready, satisfied, contented, at ease, relaxed; enthusiasm, joy, pleasure. Ideogram: sonhood and elephant, careful, reverent and strong. **Harvest,** *LI*: benefit, advantage, profit; realization; sharp, acute, insightful; quality of autumn and West, third stage of the Time Cycle. Ideogram: ripe grain and blade. **Install,** *JIAN*: set up, establish, erect, nominate; robust, solid; confirm a law or an institution. **Feudatory,** *HOU*: noble entrusted with governing a province; in charge of executive tasks; distinct from prince, *GONG*, representative of the central decisional power at the court. **Move,** *XING*: move or move something; motivate; emotionally moving; walk, act, do. Ideogram: successive steps. **Legions,** *SHI*: army, troops; leader, general, model, master; organize, make functional; take as a model, imitate, follow. Ideogram: heap and whole, turn confusion into a functional unit.

Outer and Inner Trigram

The upper trigram, **Shake,** *ZHEN*, describes the outer aspects of the situation. It has the following associations: arouse, excite, inspire; awe, alarm, trembling; thunder rising from the depth of the earth; fertilizing intrusion. Ideogram: excite and rain. *Symbol*: thunder, *LEI*, arousing power emerging from the depth of the earth. *Action*: stir-up, *DONG*, excite, influence, move, affect; work, take action; come out of the egg or the bud. Ideogram: strength and heavy, move weighty things. In the family of trigrams *ZHEN* is the eldest son.

The lower trigram, **Space,** *KUN*, describes the inner aspects of the situation. It has the following associations: surface of the world; support of all existence, manifestation of Yin, where Energy or Yang activates all creation and destruction; all-involving service; earth; moon, wife, mother; rest, receptivity, docile obedience. Ideogram: terrestrial globe and stretch out. *Symbol*: earth, *DI*; the earth, ground on which the human world rests; basis of all things, nourishes all things; essential Yin. *Action*: yield, *SHUN*: give way, comply, agree, follow, obey; docile, flexible; bear produce, nourish, provide. In the family of trigrams *KUN* is the mother.

Counter Hexagram

The Counter Hexagram of **Providing** is hexagram 39, **Limping**, which switches the emphasis from providing for ease and contentment to progressing among difficulties and obstacles.

Preceding Situation

> **Possessing** the **great and-also enabling humbleness necessarily provides**.
> To **anterior acquiescence belongs** the **use** of **providing**.

Fields of meaning

Possess, *YOU*: general term indicating possession; have, own, be endowed with. **Great**, *DA*: big, noble, important, very; orient the will toward a self-imposed goal, impose direction; ability to lead or guide one's life; contrasts with small, *XIAO*, flexible adaptation to what crosses one's path. **And-also**, *ER*: joins and contrasts two terms. **Able/enable**, *NENG*: ability, power, skill, art; competent, talented; duty, function, capacity. Ideogram: an animal with strong hooves and bones, able to carry and defend. **Humble**, *QIAN*: think and speak of oneself in a modest way; respectful, unassuming, retiring, unobtrusive; yielding, compliant, reverent, lowly. Ideogram: words and unite, keeping words close to underlying facts. **Necessarily**, *BI*: unavoidably, certainly. **Provide**, *YU*: see *Image of the Situation*. To **anterior acquiescence belongs** the **use** of, *GU SHOU ZHI YI*: understanding and accepting the preceding statement allows the consultant to make proper use of this hexagram.

Hexagrams in Pairs

> **Humbling**: **levity**.
> **And-also providing**: **indolence indeed**.

Fields of meaning

Humble, *QIAN*: see *Preceding Situation*. **Levity**, *QING*: light, soft; gentle, easy; alert, agile; frivolous, unimportant, superficial. Ideogram: cart and stream, empty cart floating downstream. **And-also**, *ER*: see *Preceding Situation*. **Provide**, *YU*: see *Image of the Situation*. **Indolence**, *DAI*: lazy, idle, inattentive, careless; self-indulgent; disdainful, contemptuous. **Indeed**, *YE*: emphasizes and intensifies the previous statement.

Additional Texts

> **Redoubling gates**, **smiting clappers**.
> **Used** to **await violent visitors**.
> **Surely grasping relates** to **providing**.

Fields of meaning

Redouble, *CHONG*: repeat, reiterate, add to; weight, heaviness; important, difficult. **Gate**, *MEN*: outer door, between courtyard and street; family, sect; a text or master as gate to a school of thought. **Smite**, *JI*: hit, beat, attack; hurl against, rush a position; rouse to action. Ideogram: hand and hit, fist punching. **Clapper**, *TUO*: board used by watchmen to strike the hours. **Use**, *YI*: by means of; owing to; make use of, employ. **Await**, *DAI*: expect, wait for, prepare to meet (friendly or hostile); provide against. **Violent**, *BAO*: fierce, brutal, cruel; strike hard. **Visitor**, *KE*: guest; stranger, foreign, from afar; squatter; parasite; invader. **Surely**, *GAI*: the preceding statement is undoubtedly true. **Grasp**, *QU*: seize with effort, take and use, appropriate; take as a wife; grasp the meaning, understand. Ideogram: ear and hand, hear and grasp. **Relate**, *ZHU*: in regard to; all, every, several. Ideogram: words and imply. **Provide**, *YU*: see *Image of the Situation*.

Patterns of Wisdom

> **Thunder emerges** from the **earth impetuously**.
> **Providing**.
> The **earlier kings used arousing delight** to **extol actualizing-dao**.
> To **exalting worship belongs** the **supreme above**.
> **Using equaling grandfathers** and **predecessors**.

Fields of meaning

Thunder, *LEI*: thunder; arousing power emerging from the depth of the earth; Symbol of the trigram Shake, *ZHEN*. **Emerge**, *CHU*: come out of, proceed from, spring from, issue forth; appear, be born; bear, generate; leave, flee; Action of the trigram Shake, *ZHEN*. Ideogram: stem with branches and leaves emerging. **Earth**, *DI*: the earth, ground on which the human world rests; basis of all things, nourishes all things; essential Yin; Symbol of the trigram Space, *KUN*. **Impetuous**, *FEN*: sudden energy; lively, spirited, impulsive; excite, arouse. **Provide**, *YU*: see *Image of the Situation*. **Earlier Kings**, *XIAN WANG*: ideal rulers of old; the golden age, primal time; mythical sages in harmony with nature. **Use**, *YI*: see *Additional Texts*. **Arouse**, *ZUO*: stimulate, stir up from inactivity; arise, appear; generate; begin, invent, make. Ideogram: person and beginning. **Delight**, *LUO*: take joy or pleasure in; pleasant, relaxed; music as harmony, elegance and pleasure. **Extol**, *CHONG*: praise, honor, magnify, revere, worship; eminent, lofty. **Actualize-dao**, *DE*: realize dao in action; power, virtue; ability to follow the course traced by the ongoing process of the cosmos. Ideogram: go, straight, and heart. Linked with acquire, *DE*: acquiring that which makes a being become what it is meant to be. **Exalting worsbip**, *YIN JIAN*: superlative of worship; glorify; intensify feelings of praise and awe. **Belong/it**, *ZHI*: establishes between two terms a connection similar to the Saxon genitive, in which the second term belongs to the first one; at the end of a sentence it refers to something previously mentioned or implied. **Supreme**, *DI*: highest, above all on earth; sovereign, lord, emperor. **Above**, *SHANG*: anything above in all senses; higher, upper, outer; upper trigram. **Equal**, *PEI*: on the same level; compete with; accord with; pair; husband or wife; together. **Grandfather**, *ZU*: second ancestor generation; deceased grandfather, honored more than actual father. **Predecessor**, *KAO*: deceased father or grandfather; ancestors, the ancients; aged, long-lived; interrogate, test, verify. Ideogram: old and ingenious, wise old man.

Transforming Lines

INITIAL SIX

The **call** of **providing**.
Pitfall.

Comments
Initial six: the **call** of **providing**.
Purpose exhausted, **pitfall indeed**.

Fields of meaning

Call, *MING*: bird and animal cries, through which they recognize each other; distinctive sound, song, statement. Ideogram: bird and mouth, a distinguishing call. **Provide**, *YU*: see *Image of the Situation*. **Pitfall**, *XIONG*: unfortunate situation, in which the flow of life and spirit is blocked and the experience of meaning is lost; stuck and exposed to danger; inappropriate attitude. Ideogram: person in a pit.

Initial, *CHU*: beginning, incipient, first step or part; bottom line of a hexagram. Ideogram: knife and garment, cutting out the pattern. **Six**, *LIU*: number six; transforming opened line; six lines of a hexagram. **Purpose**, *ZHI*: focus of mind and heart; intention, will, inclination; continuity in the direction of life. Ideogram: heart and scholar, high inner resolve. **Exhaust**, *QIONG*: bring to an end; limit, extremity; investigate exhaustively; destitute, indigent; end without a new beginning; distinct from complete, *ZHONG*, end of a cycle that begins the next one. Ideogram: cave and naked person, bent with disease or old age. **Indeed**, *YE*: see *Hexagrams in Pairs*.

SIX AT SECOND

The **cuirass tends-towards petrification**.
Not completing the **day**.
Trial, **significant**.

Comments
Not completing the **day**, **Trial**, **significant**.
Using the **center**'s **correctness indeed**.

Fields of meaning
Cuirass, *JIE*: armor; tortoise or crab shell; protective covering; border, limit, interval; protection, support; steady, rigid, solid. **Tend-towards**, *YU*: move toward without necessarily reaching, in the direction of. **Petrify**, *SHI*: become stone or stony; rocks, stones; firm, decided; barren, sterile. **Not**, *BU*: common term of negation. **Complete**, *ZHONG*: completion of a cycle that begins the next; entire, whole, all. Ideogram: silk cocoons, follow and ice, winter linking one year with the next. **Day/sun**, *RI*: the sun and the time of a sun-cycle, a day. **Trial**, *ZHEN*: inquiry by divination and its result; righteous, firm; separating wheat from chaff; the kernel, the proven core; quality of winter and North, fourth stage of the Time Cycle. Ideogram: pearl and divination. **Significant**, *JI*: leads to the experience of meaning; favorable, propitious, appropriate. Ideogram: scholar and mouth, wise words of a sage.

Use, *YI*: see *Additional Texts*. **Center**, *ZHONG*: inner, central; put in the center; middle, stable point enabling you to face inner and outer changes; middle line of a trigram. Ideogram: field divided in two equal parts. **Correct**, *ZHENG*: rectify deviation or one-sidedness; proper, straight, exact, regular; constant, rule, model. Ideogram: stop and one, hold to one thing. **Indeed**, *YE*: see *Hexagrams in Pairs*.

Six at Third

Skeptical providing: repenting.
Procrastinating possesses repenting.

Comments
Skeptical providing possesses repenting.
Position not appropriate indeed.

Fields of meaning

Skeptical, *YU*: wonder at, wide-eyed surprise; doubtful; hopeful. Provide, *YU*: see *Image of the Situation*. Repent, *HUI*: regret, dissatisfaction with past conduct inducing a change of heart; proceeds from abashment, *LIN*, shame and confusion at having lost the right way. Procrastinate, *CHI*: delay, retard; leisurely, slow, late. Possess, *YOU*: see *Preceding Situation*.

Position, *WEI*: place, location; be at; social standing, rank; position of a line in a hexagram. Ideogram: person standing. Not, *BU*: common term of negation. Appropriate, *DANG*: suitable, capable, worthy, adequate, competent, equal to; opportune, convenient; whole lines in odd places and opened lines in even places. Indeed, *YE*: see *Hexagrams in Pairs*.

Nine at Fourth

Antecedent providing.
The **great possesses acquiring.**
No doubt.
Partners join-together suddenly.

Comments
Antecedent providing, the **great possesses acquiring.**
Purpose: the **great moving indeed.**

Fields of meaning

Antecedent, *YOU*: come before as origin and cause; through, by, from; depend on; enter by way of. Provide, *YU*: see *Image of the Situation*. Great, *DA*: see *Preceding Situation*. Possess, *YOU*: see *Preceding Situation*. Acquire, *DE*: obtain the desired object; possession; satisfied, fulfilled; it is permitted; agree with; wish for, desire covetously. Ideogram: go and obstacle, going through obstacles to the goal. No, *WU*: common term of negation. Doubt, *YI*: suspect, distrust, wonder; uncertain, dubious; surmise, conjecture, fear. Partner, *PENG*: companion, friend, peer; join, associate for mutual benefit; commercial venture; two equal or similar things. Ideogram: linked strings of cowrys or coins. **Join-together**, *HE*: unite for a purpose. Ideogram: a vase and its lid. **Suddenly**, *ZAN*: quick, prompt, abrupt; collect together. Ideogram: clasp used to gather the hair.

Purpose, *ZHI*: focus of mind and heart; intention, will, inclination; continuity in the direction of life. Ideogram: heart and scholar, high inner resolve. **Move**, *XING*: see *Image of the Situation*. **Indeed**, *YE*: see *Hexagrams in Pairs*.

Six at Fifth

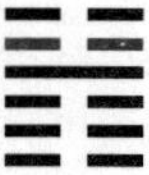

Trial, **affliction**.
Persevering, **not dying**.

Comments
Six at **fifth**: **Trial**, **affliction**.
Riding a **solid indeed**.
Persevering, **not dying**.
The **center not-yet extinguished indeed**.

Fields of meaning
Trial, *ZHEN*: inquiry by divination and its result; righteous, firm; separating wheat from chaff; the kernel, the proven core; quality of winter and North, fourth stage of the Time Cycle. Ideogram: pearl and divination. **Affliction**, *JI*: sickness, disorder, defect, calamity, injury; poison, hate, dislike; cruel, jealous, envious. Ideogram: sickness and dart, a sudden affliction. **Persevere**, *HENG*: continue in the same way or spirit; constant, habitual, regular; self-renewing. **Not**, *BU*: common term of negation. **Die**, *SI*: sudden or untimely death; death penalty; run out of energy; inert, stagnant, fixed.

Six, *LIU*: number six; transforming opened line; six lines of a hexagram. **Five**, *WU*: number five; fivefold articulation of the Universal Compass; the Five Moments and all related qualities: directions, colors, smells, tastes, tones, feelings. **Ride**, *CHENG*: ride an animal or a chariot; have the upper hand, control a stronger power; an opened line above controlling a whole line below. **Solid**, *GANG*: quality of the whole lines; firm, strong, unyielding, persisting. **Indeed**, *YE*: see *Hexagrams in Pairs*. **Center**, *ZHONG*: inner, central; put in the center; middle, stable point enabling you to face inner and outer changes; middle line of a trigram. Ideogram: field divided in two equal parts. **Not-yet**, *WEI*: temporal negative indicating that something is expected to happen but has not yet occurred. **Extinguish**, *WANG*: ruin, destroy; cease, go, die; lost without trace; forget, out of mind; absence, exile. Ideogram: person concealed by a wall, out of sight.

SIX ABOVE

☳☷

Dim providing.
Accomplishment possesses retraction.
Without fault.

Comments
Dim providing located above.
Is it **permitted long-living indeed?**

Fields of meaning

Dim, *MING*: dark, obscure; obtuse, immature; cavern, the underworld. Ideogram: 16th day of the lunar month, when the moon begins to dim. **Provide**, *YU*: see *Image of the Situation*. **Accomplish**, *CHENG*: complete, finish, bring about; perfect, full, whole; play one's part, do one's duty; mature. Ideogram: weapon and man, able to bear arms, thus fully developed. **Possess**, *YOU*: see *Preceding Situation*. **Retract**, *YU*: turn around; change one's attitude; denounce an agreement, repudiate. **Without fault**, *WU JIU*: no error or harm in the situation.

Locate, *ZAI*: be at, be situated at, dwell, reside; in, within; involved with, in the process of. Ideogram: earth and persevere, a place on the earth. **Above**, *SHANG*: see *Patterns of Wisdom*. **Is?**, *HE*: ask, inquire; what? which? who? how? why? where? an interrogative particle, often introducing a rhetorical question: is it? is it not? **Permit**, *KE*: possible because in harmony with an inherent principle; capable of; approve, authorize. Ideogram: mouth and breath, silent consent. **Long-living**, *ZHANG*: enduring, lasting, constant; extended, long, large; senior, superior, greater; increase, prosper; respect, elevate. **Indeed**, *YE*: see *Hexagrams in Pairs*.

Image Tradition

Providing. The **solid corresponding and-also** the **purpose moving**.
Providing uses stirring-up. Providing.

Providing: yielding uses stirring-up.
To **anterior heaven** and **earth** it **thus belongs**.
And-also even-more installing feudatories to **move legions reached**.

Heaven and **earth use yielding** and **stirring-up**.
Anterior sun and **moon not exceeding**.
And-also the **four seasons not straying**.

The **wise person uses yielding** and **stirring-up**.
By **consequence punishing flogging purifies and-also** the **commoners submit**.
The **season belonging** to **providing righteously great actually in-fact**.

Fields of meaning

Provide, *YU*: see *Image of the Situation*. **Solid,** *GANG*: quality of the whole lines; firm, strong, unyielding, persisting. **Correspond,** *YING*: be in agreement or harmony; proper, suitable; resonate together, answer to; relation between the lines (1 and 4, 2 and 5, 3 and 6) when they form the pair opened and whole, supple and solid. Ideogram: heart and obey. **And-also,** *ER*: see *Preceding Situation*. **Purpose,** *ZHI*: focus of mind and heart; intention, will, inclination; continuity in the direction of life. Ideogram: heart and scholar, high inner resolve. **Move,** *XING*: see *Image of the Situation*. **Use,** *YI*: see *Additional Texts*. **Stir-up,** *DONG*: excite, influence, move, affect; work, take action; come out of the egg or the bud; Action of the trigram Shake, *ZHEN*. Ideogram: strength and heavy, move weighty things.

Yield, *SHUN*: give way, comply, agree, follow, obey; docile, flexible; bear produce, nourish, provide; Action of the trigram Field, *KUN*. **Anterior,** *GU*: come before as cause; former, ancient; reason, purpose, intention; grievance, dissatisfaction, sorrow, resulting from previous causes and intentions; situation leading to a divination. **Heaven,** *TIAN*: sky, firmament, heavens; the highest realm, situated above the human world, as opposed to the earth, *DI*, located below; Symbol of the trigram Energy, *QIAN*. Ideogram: great and the one above. **Earth,** *DI*: see *Patterns of Wisdom*. **Thus,** *RU*: as, in this way; comparable, similar. **Belong/it,** *ZHI*: see *Patterns of Wisdom*. **Even-more,** *KUANG*: even more so, all the more. **Installing feudatories** to **move legions,** *JIAN HOU XING SHI*: see *Image of the Situation*. **Reach,** *HU*: arrive at a goal; move toward and achieve; to, at, in; distinct from tend-towards, *YOU*.

Sun/day, *RI*: actual sun and the time of a sun-cycle, a day. **Moon,** *YUE*: moon and moon-cycle, month; menstruation; Yin. **Not,** *BU*: common term of negation. **Exceed,** *GUO*: go beyond, pass by, pass over; surpass, transgress; error, fault, calamity. **Four,** *SI*: number four; number of the cardinal directions and of the seasons; everywhere, on all sides; fourfold articulation of the Universal Compass. **Season,** *SHI*: quality of the time; the right time, opportune, in harmony; planning in accord with the time; season of the year. Ideogram: sun and temple, sacred time. **Not,** *BU*: common term of negation. **Stray,** *TE*: wander, deviate, err; alter; doubt; excess.

Wise, *SHENG*: intuitive universal wisdom; profound understanding; mythical sages of old; holy, sacred, mark of highest distinction. Ideogram: ear and inform, one who knows all from a single sound. **Person/people**, *REN*: humans individually and collectively; an individual; humankind. **Consequence**, *ZE*: reason, cause, result; rule, law, pattern, standard; therefore; very strong connection. **Punish**, *XING*: legal punishment; physical penalty for a severe criminal offense; whip, torture, behead. **Flog**, *FA*: punish with blows, beat, whip; used to find out the truth in judicial proceedings. **Purify**, *QING*: clean a water course; limpid, unsullied; right principles. **Commoners**, *MIN*: common people, masses; working class supporting the social hierarchy; undeveloped potential in the individual. **Submit**, *FU*: yield, obey, acquiesce; enforce obedience. **Righteous**, *YI*: proper, just, virtuous, upright; the heart that rules itself; benevolent, loyal, devoted to public good. **Great**, *DA*: see *Preceding Situation*. **Actually**, *YI*: truly, really, at present. Ideogram: a dart and done, strong intention fully expressed. **In-fact**, *ZAI*: emphatic exclamation; truly, indeed.

隨

17 FOLLOWING | *Sui*

The situation described by this hexagram is characterized by following a person or an example, accepting guidance, taking one's place in a sequence or tradition.

Image of the Situation

> **Following.**
> **Spring, Growing, Harvesting, Trial.**
> **Without fault.**

Fields of meaning

Follow, *SUI*: step behind, come after, move in the same direction; comply with what is ahead; pursue; follow a way or religion; conform to; next, subsequent. Ideogram: go and fall, unavoidable movement. **Spring, Growing, Harvesting, Trial**, *YUAN HENG LI ZHEN*: Spring, Growing, Harvesting and Trial are the four stages of the Time Cycle, the model for all dynamic processes. They indicate that your question is connected to the cycle as a whole rather than a part of it. **Without fault**, *WU JIU*: no error or harm in the situation.

Outer and Inner Trigram

The upper trigram, **Open**, *DUI*, describes the outer aspects of the situation. It has the following associations: an open surface, promoting interaction and interpenetration; pleasant, easy, responsive, free, unhindered; opening, passage; the mouth; exchange, barter; straight, direct; meet, gather; place where water accumulates. Ideogram: mouth and vapor, communication through speech. *Symbol*: marsh, *ZE*, open surface of a flat body of water and the vapors rising from it; fertilize, enrich; kindness, favor. *Action*: stimulate, *SHUO*, rouse to action and good feeling; stir up, urge on; exhort, persuade; say, tell, relate; cheer, delight; joyous, peaceful, restful. Ideogram: words and exchange. In the family of trigrams *DUI* is the youngest daughter.

The lower trigram, **Shake**, *ZHEN*, describes the inner aspects of the situation. It has the following associations: arouse, excite, inspire; awe, alarm, trembling; thunder rising from the depth of the earth; fertilizing intrusion. Ideogram: excite and rain. *Symbol*: thunder, *LEI*, arousing power emerging from the depth of the earth. *Action*: stir-up, *DONG*, excite, influence, move, affect; work, take action; come out of the egg or the bud. Ideogram: strength and heavy, move weighty things. In the family of trigrams *ZHEN* is the eldest son.

Counter Hexagram

The Counter Hexagram of **Following** is hexagram 53, **Infiltrating**, which switches the emphasis from following someone or something to extending one's own influence by gradual and steady penetration.

Preceding Situation

> **Providing necessarily possesses following.**
> To **anterior acquiescence belongs** the **use** of **following**.

Fields of meaning

Provide, *YU*: prepare for, pre-arrange, think beforehand; ready, satisfied, contented, at ease, relaxed; enthusiasm, joy, pleasure. Ideogram: sonhood and elephant, careful, reverent and strong. **Necessarily**, *BI*: unavoidably, certainly. **Possess**, *YOU*: general term indicating possession; have, own, be endowed with. **Follow**, *SUI*: see *Image of the Situation*. To **anterior acquiescence belongs** the **use** of, *GU SHOU ZHI YI*: understanding and accepting the preceding statement allows the consultant to make proper use of this hexagram.

Hexagrams in Pairs

> **Following**: **without anteriority indeed**.
> **Decay**: by **consequence stability indeed**.

Fields of meaning

Follow, *SUI*: see *Image of the Situation*. **Without**, *WU*: devoid of; there is not. **Anterior**, *GU*: come before as cause; former, ancient; reason, purpose, intention; grievance, dissatisfaction, sorrow, resulting from previous causes and intentions; situation leading to a divination. **Indeed**, *YE*: emphasizes and intensifies the previous statement. **Decay**, *GU*: rotting, poisonous; intestinal worms, venomous insects; evil magic; disorder, error; pervert by seduction or flattery; unquiet ghost. Ideogram: dish and worms, putrefaction and poisonous decay. **Consequence**, *ZE*: reason, cause, result; rule, law, pattern, standard; therefore; very strong connection. **Stability**, *CHI*: firmness, solidity; prepare, arrange; careful, respectful.

Patterns of Wisdom

The **pond** in the **center possesses thunder**. **Following**.
A **jun zi uses turning** to **darkness** to **enter** a **reposing pause**.

Fields of meaning

Pond, *ZE*: open surface of a flat body of water and the vapors rising from it; fertilize, enrich; kindness, favor; Symbol of the trigram Open, *DUI*. **Center**, *ZHONG*: inner, central; put in the center; middle, stable point enabling you to face inner and outer changes; middle line of a trigram. Ideogram: field divided in two equal parts. **Possess**, *YOU*: see *Preceding Situation*. **Thunder**, *LEI*: thunder; arousing power emerging from the depth of the earth; Symbol of the trigram Shake, *ZHEN*. **Follow**, *SUI*: see *Image of the Situation*. **Jun zi**: ideal of a person who orders his/her life in accordance with dao rather than willful intention, and uses divination in this spirit. **Use**, *YI*: by means of; owing to; make use of, employ. **Turn**, *XIANG*: direct your mind towards, face. **Darkness**, *HUI*: obscurity, night, mist; make or become dark; last day of the lunar month. **Enter**, *RU*: penetrate, go into, enter on, encroach on; progress; put into; Action of the trigram Root, *SUN*. **Repose**, *YAN*: rest, leisure, tranquillity; banquet, feast; pleasure, joy. Ideogram: shelter and rest, a wayside inn. **Pause**, *XI*: breathe; rest, repose, a breathing-spell; suspended.

Transforming Lines

Initial nine

An **official possesses retraction**.
Trial, **significant**.
Emerging from the **gate**, **mingling possesses achievement**.

Comments
An **official possesses retraction**.
Adhering to **correctness**, **significant indeed**.
Emerging from the **gate**, **mingling possesses achievement**.
Not letting-go indeed.

Fields of meaning

Official, *GUAN*: government official, magistrate, dignitary. **Possess**, *YOU*: see *Preceding Situation*. **Retract**, *YU*: turn around; change one's attitude; denounce an agreement, repudiate. **Trial**, *ZHEN*: inquiry by divination and its result; righteous, firm; separating wheat from chaff; the kernel, the proven core; quality of winter and North, fourth stage of the Time Cycle. Ideogram: pearl and divination. **Significant**, *JI*: leads to the experience of meaning; favorable, propitious, appropriate. Ideogram: scholar and mouth, wise words of a sage. **Emerge**, *CHU*: come out of, proceed from, spring from, issue forth; appear, be born; bear, generate; leave, flee; Action of the trigram Shake, *ZHEN*. Ideogram: stem with branches and leaves emerging. **Gate**, *MEN*: outer door, between courtyard and street; family, sect; a text or master as gate to a school of thought. **Mingle**, *JIAO*: blend with, communicate, join, exchange; trade; copulation; friendship. Ideogram: legs crossed. **Achieve**, *GONG*: work done, results, actual accomplishment; praise, worth, merit. Ideogram: workman's square and forearm, combining craft and strength.

Adhere, *CONG*: follow, agree with, comply with, obey; join a doctrine, school, or person; servant, follower. Ideogram: two men walking, one following the other. **Correct**, *ZHENG*: rectify deviation or one-sidedness; proper, straight, exact, regular; constant, rule, model. Ideogram: stop and one, hold to one thing. **Indeed**, *YE*: see *Hexagrams in Pairs*. **Not**, *BU*: common term of negation. **Let-go**, *SHI*: lose, let slip; omit, miss, fail; lose control of. Ideogram: drop from the hand.

SIX AT SECOND

Tied to the **small son**.
Letting-go the **respectable husband**.

Comments
Tied to the **small son**.
Nowhere joining in **association indeed**.

Fields of meaning

Tie, *XI*: connect, attach, bind; devoted to; relatives. Ideogram: person and connect, ties between humans. **Small**, *XIAO*: little, common, unimportant; adapting to what crosses your path; ability to move in harmony with the vicissitudes of life; contrasts with great, *DA*, self-imposed theme or goal. **Son(hood)**, *ZI*: son, male child; heirs, offspring, posterity; living up to the ideal of the ancestors as highest human aspiration; seed, kernel, egg; sage, teacher; nadir, deepest point, midnight, mid-winter. **Let-go**, *SHI*: lose, let slip; omit, miss, fail; lose control of. Ideogram: drop from the hand. **Respectable**, *ZHANG*: exemplary person, worthy of respect, elder. **Husband**, *FU*: adult, man, male spouse; scholar, distinguished man; one who can help; manage a household. Ideogram: man with a pin in his hair to show that he is of age.

Nowhere/nothing, *FU*: strong negative; not a single thing/place; deny, disapprove; impossible, incorrect. **Join**, *JIAN*: add or bring together, unite; absorb, assimilate; simultaneously, also. Ideogram: hand grasping two grain stalks, two things at once. **Associate**, *YU*: consort with, combine; companions; group, band, company; agree with, comply, help; in favor of. Ideogram: a pair of hands reaching downward meets a pair of hands reaching upward, helpful association. **Indeed**, *YE*: see *Hexagrams in Pairs*.

SIX AT THIRD

䷐

Tied to the **respectable husband**.
Letting-go the **small son**.
Following possesses seeking and **acquiring**.
Harvesting: **residing** in **Trial**.

Comments
Tied to the **respectable husband**.
Purpose: **stowing** away the **below indeed**.

Fields of meaning

Tie, *XI*: connect, attach, bind; devoted to; relatives. Ideogram: person and connect, ties between humans. **Respectable**, *ZHANG*: exemplary person, worthy of respect, elder. **Husband**, *FU*: adult, man, male spouse; scholar, distinguished man; one who can help; manage a household. Ideogram: man with a pin in his hair to show that he is of age. **Let-go**, *SHI*: lose, let slip; omit, miss, fail; lose control of. Ideogram: drop from the hand. **Small**, *XIAO*: little, common, unimportant; adapting to what crosses your path; ability to move in harmony with the vicissitudes of life; contrasts with great, *DA*, self-imposed theme or goal. **Son(hood)**, *ZI*: son, male child; heirs, offspring, posterity; living up to the ideal of the ancestors as highest human aspiration; seed, kernel, egg; sage, teacher; nadir, deepest point, midnight, mid-winter. **Follow**, *SUI*: see *Image of the Situation*. **Possess**, *YOU*: see *Preceding Situation*. **Seek**, *QIU*: search for, aim at, wish for, desire; implore, supplicate; covetous. **Acquire**, *DE*: obtain the desired object; possession; satisfied, fulfilled; it is permitted; agree with; wish for, desire covetously. Ideogram: go and obstacle, going through obstacles to the goal. **Harvest**, *LI*: benefit, advantage, profit; realization; sharp, acute, insightful; quality of autumn and West, third stage of the Time Cycle. Ideogram: ripe grain and blade. **Reside**, *JU*: dwell, live in, stay; sit down; fill an office; well-being, rest. Ideogram: body and seat. **Trial**, *ZHEN*: inquiry by divination and its result; righteous, firm; separating wheat from chaff; the kernel, the proven core; quality of winter and North, fourth stage of the Time Cycle. Ideogram: pearl and divination.

Purpose, *ZHI*: focus of mind and heart; intention, will, inclination; continuity in the direction of life. Ideogram: heart and scholar, high inner resolve. **Stow**, *SHE*: set aside, put away, store, keep; halt, rest in; lodge, hut. **Below**, *XIA*: anything below, in all senses; lower, inner; lower trigram. **Indeed**, *YE*: see *Hexagrams in Pairs*.

Nine at Fourth

Following possesses capture.
Trial, **pitfall**.
Possessing conformity, **locating** in **dao**, **using brightness**.
Is it **faulty**?

Comments
Following possesses capture.
One's righteousness: **pitfall indeed**.
Possessing conformity, **locating** in **dao**.
Brightness achieving indeed.

Fields of meaning

Follow, *SUI*: see *Image of the Situation*. **Possess**, *YOU*: see *Preceding Situation*. **Capture**, *HUO*: obtain, seize, reach; take in a hunt, catch a thief; hit the mark, opportune moment; prisoner, spoils, prey, slave, servant. **Trial**, *ZHEN*: inquiry by divination and its result; righteous, firm; separating wheat from chaff; the kernel, the proven core; quality of winter and North, fourth stage of the Time Cycle. Ideogram: pearl and divination. **Pitfall**, *XIONG*: unfortunate situation, in which the flow of life and spirit is blocked and the experience of meaning is lost; stuck and exposed to danger; inappropriate attitude. Ideogram: person in a pit. **Possess**, *YOU*: see *Preceding Situation*. **Conform**, *FU*: accord between inner and outer; sincere, truthful, verified, reliable; capture; prisoners, spoils. Ideogram: claws over child, a bird brooding on the nest. **Locate**, *ZAI*: be at, be situated at, dwell, reside; in, within; involved with, in the process of. Ideogram: earth and persevere, a place on the earth. **Dao**, *DAO*: way or path; ongoing process of being and the course it traces for each person or thing; ultimate reality, intrinsic nature; origin. Ideogram: go and head, opening a path. **Use**, *YI*: see *Patterns of Wisdom*. **Brightness**, *MING*: light, radiance, clarity; distinguish, discern, understand; light-giving aspect of fire, of heavenly bodies and of consciousness; brightness and fire are the Symbols of the trigram Radiance, *LI*. **Is?**, *HE*: ask, inquire; what? which? who? how? why?

where? an interrogative particle, often introducing a rhetorical question: is it? is it not? Fault, *JIU*: unworthy conduct that leads to harm, illness, misfortune; guilt, crime, punishment. Ideogram: person and differ, differ from what you should be.

One/one's, *QI*: general third person pronoun and possessive adjective; also: it/its, he/his, she/her, they/their. Righteous, *YI*: proper, just, virtuous, upright; the heart that rules itself; benevolent, loyal, devoted to public good. Indeed, *YE*: see *Hexagrams in Pairs*. Achieve, *GONG*: work done, results, actual accomplishment; praise, worth, merit. Ideogram: workman's square and forearm, combining craft and strength.

NINE AT FIFTH

Conformity tends-towards excellence. **Significant**.

Comments

Conformity tends-towards excellence, **significant**.

Position correct in the **center indeed**.

Fields of meaning

Conform, *FU*: accord between inner and outer; sincere, truthful, verified, reliable; capture; prisoners, spoils. Ideogram: claws over child, a bird brooding on the nest. Tend-towards, *YU*: move toward without necessarily reaching, in the direction of. Excellence, *JIA*: superior quality; fine, beautiful, glorious; happy, pleased; rejoice in, praise. Significant, *JI*: leads to the experience of meaning; favorable, propitious, appropriate. Ideogram: scholar and mouth, wise words of a sage.

Position, *WEI*: place, location; be at; social standing, rank; position of a line in a hexagram. Ideogram: person standing. Correct, *ZHENG*: rectify deviation or one-sidedness; proper, straight, exact, regular; constant, rule, model. Ideogram: stop and one, hold to one thing. Center, *ZHONG*: see *Patterns of Wisdom*. Indeed, *YE*: see *Hexagrams in Pairs*.

SIX ABOVE

Grappling ties to **it**.

Thereupon adhering: **holding-fast** to **it**.

The **king avails** of **Growing tending-towards** the **Western mountain**.

Comments
Grappling ties to **it**.
Above exhausted indeed.

Fields of meaning

Grapple, *JU*: grasp and detain; restrain, attach to, hook; stubborn, firm. **Tie**, *XI*: connect, attach, bind; devoted to; relatives. Ideogram: person and connect, ties between humans. **It/belong**, *ZHI*: establishes between two terms a connection similar to the Saxon genitive, in which the second term belongs to the first one; at the end of a sentence it refers to something previously mentioned or implied. **Thereupon**, *NAI*: on that ground, then, only then; finally; in spite of that. **Adhere**, *CONG*: follow, agree with, comply with, obey; join a doctrine, school, or person; servant, follower. Ideogram: two men walking, one following the other. **Hold-fast**, *WEI*: tie, connect, hold together; rope, reins, net. **King**, *WANG*: sovereign, effective ruler, emperor, seen as connecting heaven and earth; reign, govern. **Avail**, *YONG*: use, employ for a specific purpose; take advantage of; benefit from; capacity. Ideogram: to divine and center, applying divination to central concerns. **Grow**, *HENG*: heavenly influence pervading and nourishing all things; prosper, succeed, expand, develop; effective, favorable; quality of summer and South, second stage of the Time Cycle. With the pronunciation *XIANG*: offer a sacrifice; offer a gift to a superior; accept, enjoy. **Tend-towards**, *YU*: move toward without necessarily reaching, in the direction of. **West**, *XI*: western direction, corresponding to autumn, Harvest, the Metallic Moment and the first phase of the Yin hemicycle of the Universal Compass. **Mountain**, *SHAN*: mountain; large, immense; limit, boundary; Symbol of the trigram Bound, *GEN*. Ideogram: three peaks, a mountain range.

Above, *SHANG*: anything above in all senses; higher, upper, outer; upper trigram. **Exhaust**, *QIONG*: bring to an end; limit, extremity; investigate exhaustively; destitute, indigent; end without a new beginning; distinct from complete, *ZHONG*, end of a cycle that begins the next one. Ideogram: cave and naked person, bent with disease or old age. **Indeed**, *YE*: see *Hexagrams in Pairs*.

Image Tradition

Following. The **solid comes and-also below** the **supple**.
Stirring-up and-also stimulating. **Following**.

The **great Growing**, **Trial**, **without fault**.
And-also below heaven following the **season**.

To **following**'s **season belongs** the **righteously great actually in-fact**.

Fields of meaning

Follow, *SUI*: see *Image of the Situation*. **Solid**, *GANG*: quality of the whole lines; firm, strong, unyielding, persisting. **Come**, *LAI*: approach in time or space; move toward, arrive at; future; contrasts with go, *WANG*, move away or become past. **And-also**, *ER*: joins and contrasts two terms. **Below**, *XIA*: anything below, in all senses; lower, inner; lower trigram. **Supple**, *ROU*: quality of the opened lines; flexible, pliant, adaptable, tender. **Stir-up**, *DONG*: excite, influence, move, affect; work, take action; come out of the egg or the bud; Action of the trigram Shake, *ZHEN*. Ideogram: strength and heavy, move weighty things. **Stimulate**, *SHUO*: rouse to action and good feeling; stir up, urge on; exhort, persuade; say, tell, relate; cheer, delight; joyous, peaceful, restful; Action of the trigram Open, *DUI*. Ideogram: words and exchange.

Great, *DA*: big, noble, important, very; orient the will toward a self-imposed goal, impose direction; ability to lead or guide one's life; contrasts with small, *XIAO*, flexible adaptation to what crosses one's path. **Grow**, *HENG*: heavenly influence pervading and nourishing all things; prosper, succeed, expand, develop; effective, favorable; quality of summer and South, second stage of the Time Cycle. With the pronunciation *XIANG*: offer a sacrifice; offer a gift to a superior; accept, enjoy. **Trial**, *ZHEN*: inquiry by divination and its result; righteous, firm; separating wheat from chaff; the kernel, the proven core; quality of winter and North, fourth stage of the Time Cycle. Ideogram: pearl and divination. **Without fault**, *WU JIU*: see *Image of the Situation*. **Below heaven**, *TIAN XIA*: human world, between heaven and earth. **Season**, *SHI*: quality of the time; the right time, opportune, in harmony; planning in accord with the time; season of the year. Ideogram: sun and temple, sacred time. **Belong/it**, *ZHI*: establishes between two terms a connection similar to the Saxon genitive, in which the second term belongs to the first one; at the end of a sentence it refers to something previously mentioned or implied. **Righteous**, *YI*: proper, just, virtuous, upright; the heart that rules itself; benevolent, loyal, devoted to public good. **Actually**, *YI*: truly, really, at present. Ideogram: a dart and done, strong intention fully expressed. **In-fact**, *ZAI*: emphatic exclamation; truly, indeed.

蠱

18 DECAY | *Gu*

The situation described by this hexagram is characterized by the rotting away of something that has become poisonous, a putrefaction that has to run its course in order for a new birth to be possible.

Image of the Situation

> **Decay**.
> **Spring, Growing**.
> **Harvesting**: **wading** the **great river**.
> **Before seedburst three days**.
> **After seedburst three days**.

Fields of meaning

Decay, *GU*: rotting, poisonous; intestinal worms, venomous insects; evil magic; disorder, error; pervert by seduction or flattery; unquiet ghost. Ideogram: dish and worms, putrefaction and poisonous decay. **Spring**, *YUAN*: source, origin, head; arise, begin; first generating impulse; great, excellent; quality of springtime and East, first stage of the Time Cycle. **Grow**, *HENG*: heavenly influence pervading and nourishing all things; prosper, succeed, expand, develop; effective, favorable; quality of summer and South, second stage of the Time Cycle. With the pronunciation *XIANG*: offer a sacrifice; offer a gift to a superior; accept, enjoy. **Harvest**, *LI*: benefit, advantage, profit; realization; sharp, acute, insightful; quality of autumn and West, third stage of the Time Cycle. Ideogram: ripe grain and blade. **Wading the Great River**, *SHE DA CHUAN*: enter the stream of life with a goal or purpose; embark on a significant enterprise. **Before(hand)/earlier**, *XIAN*: anterior, preceding in time; former, past, previous; first, at first. **Seedburst**, *JIA*: seeds bursting forth in spring; first month of springtime; beginning, number one; associated with the Wooden Moment. **Three/thrice**, *SAN*: number three; third time or place; active phases of a cycle; superlative; beginning of repetition (since one and two are entities in themselves). **Day/sun**, *RI*: the sun and the time of a sun-cycle, a day. **After(wards)/later**, *HOU*: come after in time, subsequent; put oneself after; behind, back, draw back; the second; attendants, heirs, successors, posterity.

Outer and Inner Trigram

The upper trigram, **Bound**, *GEN*, describes the outer aspects of the situation. It has the following associations: limit, frontier; obstacle that prevents from seeing further; stop; still, quiet, motionless; confine, enclose; mountain, sunset, beginning of winter; solid, steady, unshakable; straight, hard, adamant, obstinate. *Symbol*: mountain, *SHAN*, large, immense; limit, boundary. Ideogram: three peaks, a mountain range. *Action*: stop, *ZHI*, bring or come to a standstill, cease, terminate. Ideogram: a foot stops walking. In the family of trigrams *GEN* is the youngest son.

The lower trigram, **Root**, *SUN*, describes the inner aspects of the situation. It has the following associations: base on which things rest, ground, foundation; mild, subtly penetrating; nourishing. *Symbols*: tree/wood and wind. Tree/wood, *MU*: trees and all things woody or wooden; associated with the Wooden Moment. Ideogram: a tree with roots and branches. Wind, *FENG*: wind, breeze, gust; weather and its influence on mood and humor; fashion, usage. *Action*: enter, *RU*, penetrate, go into, enter on, encroach on; progress; put into. In the family of trigrams *SUN* is the eldest daughter.

Counter Hexagram

The Counter Hexagram of **Decay** is hexagram 54, **Converting Maidenhood**, which switches the emphasis from the rotting away of something old to the opening onto the future of the marrying maiden.

Preceding Situation

> **Using joy** in **following people implies necessarily possessing affairs**.
> To **anterior acquiescence belongs** the **use** of **decay**.
> **Decay implies affairs indeed**.

Fields of meaning

Use, *YI*: by means of; owing to; make use of, employ. **Joy/rejoice**, *XI*: delight, exult; cheerful, merry. Ideogram: joy (music) and mouth, expressing joy. **Follow**, *SUI*: step behind, come after, move in the same direction; comply with what is ahead; pursue; follow a way or religion; conform to; next, subsequent. Ideogram: go and fall, unavoidable movement. **People/person**, *REN*: humans individually and collectively; an individual; humankind. **Imply**, *ZHE*: further signify; additional meaning. **Necessarily**, *BI*: unavoidably, certainly. **Possess**, *YOU*: general term indicating possession; have, own, be endowed with. **Affairs**, *SHI*: all kinds of personal activity; matters at hand; business; function, occupation; manage; perform a task; incident, event; case in court. To **anterior acquiescence belongs** the **use** of, *GU SHOU ZHI YI*: understanding and accepting the preceding statement allows the consultant to make proper use of this hexagram. **Decay**, *GU*: see *Image of the Situation*. **Indeed**, *YE*: emphasizes and intensifies the previous statement.

Hexagrams in Pairs

Following: **without anteriority indeed**.
Decay: by **consequence stability indeed**.

Fields of meaning
Follow, *SUI*: see *Preceding Situation*. **Without**, *WU*: devoid of; there is not. **Anterior**, *GU*: come before as cause; former, ancient; reason, purpose, intention; grievance, dissatisfaction, sorrow, resulting from previous causes and intentions; situation leading to a divination. **Indeed**, *YE*: see *Preceding Situation*. **Decay**, *GU*: see *Image of the Situation*. **Consequence**, *ZE*: reason, cause, result; rule, law, pattern, standard; therefore; very strong connection. **Stability**, *CHI*: firmness, solidity; prepare, arrange; careful, respectful.

Patterns of Wisdom

The **mountain possesses wind below**. **Decay**.
A **jun zi uses rousing** the **commoners** to **nurture actualizing-dao**.

Fields of meaning
Mountain, *SHAN*: mountain; large, immense; limit, boundary; Symbol of the trigram Bound, *GEN*. Ideogram: three peaks, a mountain range. **Possess**, *YOU*: see *Preceding Situation*. **Wind**, *FENG*: wind, breeze, gust; weather and its influence on mood and humor; fashion, usage; wind and wood are the Symbols of the trigram Root, *SUN*. **Below**, *XIA*: anything below, in all senses; lower, inner; lower trigram. **Decay**, *GU*: see *Image of the Situation*. **Jun zi**: ideal of a person who orders his/her life in accordance with dao rather than willful intention, and uses divination in this spirit. **Use**, *YI*: see *Preceding Situation*. **Rouse**, *ZHEN*: stir up, excite, stimulate; issue forth; put in order. Ideogram: hand and shake, shaking things up. **Commoners**, *MIN*: common people, masses; working class supporting the social hierarchy; undeveloped potential in the individual. **Nurture**, *YU*: give birth; bring up, rear, raise. **Actualize-dao**, *DE*: realize dao in action; power, virtue;

ability to follow the course traced by the ongoing process of the cosmos. Ideogram: go, straight, and heart. Linked with acquire, *DE*: acquiring that which makes a being become what it is meant to be.

Transforming Lines

Initial Six

Managing the **decay belonging** to the **father**.
Possessing sonhood.
Predecessors without fault.
Adversity's **completion**, **significant**.

Comments
Managing the **decay belonging** to the **father**.
Intention received from the **predecessors indeed**.

Fields of meaning

Manage, *GAN*: cope with, deal with; attend to the essential; trunk, stem, spine, skeleton. **Decay**, *GU*: see *Image of the Situation*. **Belong/it**, *ZHI*: establishes between two terms a connection similar to the Saxon genitive, in which the second term belongs to the first one; at the end of a sentence it refers to something previously mentioned or implied. **Father**, *FU*: father, act as a father, paternal, patriarchal; authoritative rule. Ideogram: hand and rod, the. chastising father. **Possess**, *YOU*: see *Preceding Situation*. **Son(hood)**, *ZI*: son, male child; heirs, offspring, posterity; living up to the ideal of the ancestors as highest human aspiration; seed, kernel, egg; sage, teacher; nadir, deepest point, midnight, mid-winter. **Predecessor**, *KAO*: deceased father or grandfather; ancestors, the ancients; aged, long-lived; interrogate, test, verify. Ideogram: old and ingenious, wise old man. **Without fault**, *WU JIU*: no error or harm in the situation. **Adversity**, *LI*: danger, hardship, severe; threat or difficulty that must be encountered, rather than avoided; grinding stone; polish, sharpen; a challenge that strengthens and perfects the character; stimulate, excite; cruel demon. **Complete**, *ZHONG*: completion of a cycle that begins the next; entire, whole, all. Ideogram: silk cocoons, follow and ice, winter linking one year with the next. **Significant**, *JI*: leads to the experience of meaning; favorable, propitious, appropriate. Ideogram: scholar and mouth, wise words of a sage.

Intention, *YI*: thought, idea, opinion; project, expectation; meaning, connotation. Ideogram: heart and sound, the heart behind the words. **Receive**, *CHENG*: receive gifts or commands from superiors or customers; take in hand; give, offer respectfully; help, support. Ideogram: accepting a seal of office. **Indeed**, *YE*: see *Preceding Situation*.

NINE AT SECOND

Managing the **decay belonging** to the **mother**.
Not permitting Trial.

Comments
Managing the **decay belonging** to the **mother**.
Acquiring the **center**: **dao indeed**.

Fields of meaning

Manage, *GAN*: cope with, deal with; attend to the essential; trunk, stem, spine, skeleton. **Decay**, *GU*: see *Image of the Situation*. **Belong/it**, *ZHI*: establishes between two terms a connection similar to the Saxon genitive, in which the second term belongs to the first one; at the end of a sentence it refers to something previously mentioned or implied. **Mother**, *MU*: mother, maternal, feminine; child-bearing and nourishing. Ideogram: two breasts. **Not**, *BU*: common term of negation. **Permit**, *KE*: possible because in harmony with an inherent principle; capable of; approve, authorize. Ideogram: mouth and breath, silent consent. **Trial**, *ZHEN*: inquiry by divination and its result; righteous, firm; separating wheat from chaff; the kernel, the proven core; quality of winter and North, fourth stage of the Time Cycle. Ideogram: pearl and divination.

Acquire, *DE*: obtain the desired object; possession; satisfied, fulfilled; it is permitted; agree with; wish for, desire covetously. Ideogram: go and obstacle, going through obstacles to the goal. **Center**, *ZHONG*: inner, central; put in the center; middle, stable point enabling you to face inner and outer changes; middle line of a trigram. Ideogram: field divided in two equal parts. **Dao**, *DAO*: way or path; ongoing process of being and the course it traces for each person or thing; ultimate reality, intrinsic nature; origin. Ideogram: go and head, opening a path. **Indeed**, *YE*: see *Preceding Situation*.

NINE AT THIRD

Managing the **decay belonging** to the **father**.
The **small possesses repenting**.
Without the **great**, **faulty**.

Comments
Managing the **decay belonging** to the **father**.
Completing without fault indeed.

Fields of meaning

Manage, *GAN*: cope with, deal with; attend to the essential; trunk, stem, spine, skeleton. **Decay**, *GU*: see *Image of the Situation*. **Belong/it**, *ZHI*: establishes between two terms a connection similar to the Saxon genitive, in which the second term belongs to the first one; at the end of a sentence it refers to something previously mentioned or implied. **Father**, *FU*: father, act as a father, paternal, patriarchal; authoritative rule. Ideogram: hand and rod, the chastising father. **Small**, *XIAO*: little, common, unimportant; adapting to what crosses your path; ability to move in harmony with the vicissitudes of life; contrasts with great, *DA*, self-imposed theme or goal. **Possess**, *YOU*: see *Preceding Situation*. **Repent**, *HUI*: regret, dissatisfaction with past conduct inducing a change of heart; proceeds from abashment, *LIN*, shame and confusion at having lost the right way. **Without**, *WU*: see *Hexagrams in Pairs*. **Great**, *DA*: big, noble, important, very; orient the will toward a self-imposed goal, impose direction; ability to lead or guide one's life; contrasts with small, *XIAO*, flexible adaptation to what crosses one's path. **Fault**, *JIU*: unworthy conduct that leads to harm, illness, misfortune; guilt, crime, punishment. Ideogram: person and differ, differ from what you should be.

Complete, *ZHONG*: completion of a cycle that begins the next; entire, whole, all. Ideogram: silk cocoons, follow and ice, winter linking one year with the next. **Without fault**, *WU JIU*: no error or harm in the situation. **Indeed**, *YE*: see *Preceding Situation*.

Six at Fourth

Enriching the **decay belonging** to the **father**.
Going, **viewing abashment**.

Comments

Enriching the **decay belonging** to the **father**.
Going, **not-yet acquiring indeed**.

Fields of meaning

Enrich, *YU*: make richer; material, mental or spiritual wealth; bequeath; generous, abundant. Ideogram: garments, portable riches. **Decay**, *GU*: see *Image of the Situation*. **Belong/it**, *ZHI*: establishes between two terms a connection similar to the Saxon genitive, in which the second term belongs to the first one; at the end of a sentence it refers to something previously mentioned or implied. **Father**, *FU*: father, act as a father, paternal, patriarchal; authoritative rule. Ideogram: hand and rod, the chastising father. **Go**, *WANG*: move away in time or space, depart; become past; dead, gone; contrasts with come, *LAI*, approach in time or space.

View, *JIAN*: vision in all its aspects: seeing, being visible, forming mental images; visit, call on, consult. Ideogram: eye above person, active and receptive sight. **Abashment**, *LIN*: distress, shame, regret, humiliation; aware of having lost the right track; leads to repenting, *HUI*, correcting the direction of mind and life.

Not-yet, *WEI*: temporal negative indicating that something is expected to happen but has not yet occurred. **Acquire**, *DE*: obtain the desired object; possession; satisfied, fulfilled; it is permitted; agree with; wish for, desire covetously. Ideogram: go and obstacle, going through obstacles to the goal. **Indeed**, *YE*: see *Preceding Situation*.

SIX AT FIFTH

Managing the **decay belonging** to the **father**.
Availing of **praise**.

Comments
Managing the **father avails** of **praise**.
Receiving uses actualizing-dao indeed.

Fields of meaning
Manage, *GAN*: cope with, deal with; attend to the essential; trunk, stem, spine, skeleton. **Decay**, *GU*: see *Image of the Situation*. **Belong/it**, *ZHI*: establishes between two terms a connection similar to the Saxon genitive, in which the second term belongs to the first one; at the end of a sentence it refers to something previously mentioned or implied. **Father**, *FU*: father, act as a father, paternal, patriarchal; authoritative rule. Ideogram: hand and rod, the chastising father. **Avail**, *YONG*: use, employ for a specific purpose; take advantage of; benefit from; capacity. Ideogram: to divine and center, applying divination to central concerns. **Praise**, *YU*: magnify, eulogize; flatter; fame, reputation. Ideogram: offering words.

Receive, *CHENG*: receive gifts or commands from superiors or customers; take in hand; give, offer respectfully; help, support. Ideogram: accepting a seal of office. **Use**, *YI*: see *Preceding Situation*. **Actualize-dao**, *DE*: see *Patterns of Wisdom*. **Indeed**, *YE*: see *Preceding Situation*.

NINE ABOVE

Not affairs, a **king**'s **feudatory**.
Honoring highness: **one's affair**.

Comments
Not affairs, a **king**'s **feudatory**.
Purpose permitted by **consequence indeed**.

Fields of meaning

Not, *BU*: common term of negation. **Affairs**, *SHI*: see *Preceding Situation*. **King**, *WANG*: sovereign, effective ruler, emperor, seen as connecting heaven and earth; reign, govern. **Feudatory**, *HOU*: noble entrusted with governing a province; in charge of executive tasks; distinct from prince, *GONG*, representative of the central decisional power at the court. **Honor**, *SHANG*: esteem, give high rank to, exalt, celebrate; rise, elevate; put one thing on top of another. **High**, *GAO*: high, elevated, lofty, eminent; honor, respect. Ideogram: high tower. **One/one's**, *QI*: general third person pronoun and possessive adjective; also: it/its, he/his, she/her, they/their.

Purpose, *ZHI*: focus of mind and heart; intention, will, inclination; continuity in the direction of life. Ideogram: heart and scholar, high inner resolve. **Permit**, *KE*: possible because in harmony with an inherent principle; capable of; approve, authorize. Ideogram: mouth and breath, silent consent. **Consequence**, *ZE*: see *Hexagrams in Pairs*. **Indeed**, *YE*: see *Preceding Situation*.

Image Tradition

Decay. The **solid above and-also** the **supple below**.
Root and-also stopping. **Decay**.

Decay: **Spring**, **Growing**, **and-also below heaven regulated indeed**.

Harvesting: **wading** the **great river**.
Going possesses affairs indeed.

Before seedburst three days.
After seedburst three days.
Completing, by **consequence possessing** a **beginning**.
Heaven moving indeed.

Fields of meaning

Decay, *GU*: see *Image of the Situation*. **Solid**, *GANG*: quality of the whole lines; firm, strong, unyielding, persisting. **Above**, *SHANG*: anything above in all senses; higher, upper, outer; upper trigram. **And-also**, *ER*: joins and contrasts two terms. **Supple**, *ROU*: quality of the opened lines; flexible, pliant, adaptable, tender.

Below, *XIA*: see *Patterns of Wisdom*. **Root**, *SUN*: base on which things rest, ground, foundation; mild, subtly penetrating; nourishing. **Stop**, *ZHI*: bring or come to a standstill, cease, terminate; Action of the trigram Bound, *GEN*. Ideogram: a foot stops walking.

Spring, **Growing**, *YUAN HENG*: see *Image of the Situation*. **Below heaven**, *TIAN XIA*: human world, between heaven and earth. **Regulate**, *ZHI*: govern well, ensure prosperity; arrange, remedy disorder, heal; fit to govern. **Indeed**, *YE*: see *Preceding Situation*.

Harvesting: wading the Great River, *LI SHE DA CHUAN*: see *Image of the Situation*. **Go**, *WANG*: move away in time or space, depart; become past; dead, gone; contrasts with come, *LAI*, approach in time or space. **Possess**, *YOU*: see *Preceding Situation*. **Affairs**, *SHI*: see *Preceding Situation*.

Before seedburst three days, *XIAN JIA SAN RI*: see *Image of the Situation*. **After(wards)/later**, *HOU*: see *Image of the Situation*. **Complete**, *ZHONG*: completion of a cycle that begins the next; entire, whole, all. Ideogram: silk cocoons, follow and ice, winter linking one year with the next. **Consequence**, *ZE*: see *Hexagrams in Pairs*. **Begin**, *SHI*: commence, start, open; earliest, first; generate. Ideogram: woman and eminent, eminent feminine function of giving birth. **Heaven**, *TIAN*: sky, firmament, heavens; the highest realm, situated above the human world, as opposed to the earth, *DI*, located below; Symbol of the trigram Energy, *QIAN*. Ideogram: great and the one above. **Move**, *XING*: move or move something; motivate; emotionally moving; walk, act, do. Ideogram: successive steps.

臨

䷒

19 NEARING | *Lin*

The situation described by this hexagram is characterized by the approach of something higher or greater. This process cannot be rushed, and the gestation must be allowed to run its full course.

Image of the Situation

> **Nearing.**
> **Spring**, **Growing**, **Harvesting**, **Trial**.
> **Culminating tending-towards** the **eighth moon**
> **possesses** a **pitfall**.

Fields of meaning

Near, *LIN*: approach or be approached: behold with care, look on sympathetically; condescend; bless or curse by coming nearer; a superior visits an inferior. **Spring**, **Growing**, **Harvesting**, **Trial**, *YUAN HENG LI ZHEN*: Spring, Growing, Harvesting and Trial are the four stages of the Time Cycle, the model for all dynamic processes. They indicate that your question is connected to the cycle as a whole rather than a part of it. **Culminate**, *ZHI*: bring to the highest degree; arrive at the end or summit; superlative; reaching one's goal. **Tend-towards**, *YU*: move toward without necessarily reaching, in the direction of. **Eight**, *BA*: number eight; number of highly valued essentials: eight trigrams, eight immortals, eight compass points. **Moon**, *YUE*: moon and moon-cycle, month; menstruation; Yin. **Possess**, *YOU*: general term indicating possession; have, own, be endowed with. **Pitfall**, *XIONG*: unfortunate situation, in which the flow of life and spirit is blocked and the experience of meaning is lost; stuck and exposed to danger; inappropriate attitude. Ideogram: person in a pit.

Outer and Inner Trigram

The upper trigram, **Space**, *KUN*, describes the outer aspects of the situation. It has the following associations: surface of the world; support of all existence, manifestation of Yin, where Energy or Yang activates all creation and destruction; all-involving service; earth; moon, wife, mother; rest, receptivity, docile obedience. Ideogram: terrestrial globe and stretch out. *Symbol*: earth, *DI*; the earth, ground on which the human world rests; basis of all things, nourishes all things; essential Yin. *Action*: yield, *SHUN*: give way, comply, agree, follow, obey; docile, flexible; bear produce, nourish, provide. In the family of trigrams *KUN* is the mother.

The lower trigram, **Open**, *DUI*, describes the inner aspects of the situation. It has the following associations: an open surface, promoting interaction and interpenetration; pleasant, easy, responsive, free, unhindered; opening, passage; the mouth; exchange, barter; straight, direct; meet, gather; place where water accumulates. Ideogram: mouth and vapor, communication through speech. *Symbol*: marsh, *ZE*, open surface of a flat body of water and the vapors rising from it; fertilize, enrich; kindness, favor. *Action*: stimulate, *SHUO*, rouse to action and good feeling; stir up, urge on; exhort, persuade; say, tell, relate; cheer, delight; joyous, peaceful, restful. Ideogram: words and exchange. In the family of trigrams *DUI* is the youngest daughter.

Counter Hexagram

The Counter Hexagram of **Nearing** is hexagram 24, **Return**, which switches the emphasis from the approach of something new to a re-emergence of the past.

Preceding Situation

> **Possessing affairs and-also afterwards permitted** the **great**.
> To **anterior acquiescence belongs** the **use** of **nearing**.
> **Nearing implies** the **great indeed**.

Fields of meaning

Possess, *YOU*: see *Image of the Situation*. **Affairs**, *SHI*: all kinds of personal activity; matters at hand; business; function, occupation; manage; perform a task; incident, event; case in court. **And-also**, *ER*: joins and contrasts two terms. **After(wards)/later**, *HOU*: come after in time, subsequent; put oneself after; behind, back, draw back; the second; attendants, heirs, successors, posterity. **Permit**, *KE*: possible because in harmony with an inherent principle; capable of; approve, authorize. Ideogram: mouth and breath, silent consent. **Great**, *DA*: big, noble, important, very; orient the will toward a self-imposed goal, impose direction; ability to lead or guide one's life; contrasts with small, *XIAO*, flexible adaptation to what crosses one's path. To **anterior acquiescence belongs** the **use** of, *GU SHOU ZHI YI*: understanding and accepting the preceding statement allows the consultant to make proper use of this hexagram. **Near**, *LIN*: see *Image of the Situation*. **Imply**, *ZHE*: further signify; additional meaning. **Indeed**, *YE*: emphasizes and intensifies the previous statement.

Hexagrams in Pairs

> To **nearing** and **overseeing belongs righteousness**.
> **Maybe associating**, **maybe seeking**.

Fields of meaning

Near, *LIN*: see *Image of the Situation*. **Oversee**, *GUAN*: contemplate, observe from a distance; look at carefully, gaze at; a high place from where one sees far, monastery, observatory; intelligence, clairvoyance; scry, divine through liquid in a cup. Ideogram: sight and waterbird, aerial view. **Belong/it**, *ZHI*: establishes between two terms a connection similar to the Saxon genitive, in which the second term belongs to the first one; at the end of a sentence it refers to something previously mentioned or implied. **Righteous**, *YI*: proper, just, virtuous, upright; the heart that rules itself; benevolent, loyal, devoted to public good. **Maybe**, *HUO*: possible but not certain, perhaps. **Associate**, *YU*: consort with, combine; companions; group, band, company; agree with, comply, help; in favor of. Ideogram: a pair of hands reaching downward meets a pair of hands reaching upward, helpful association. **Seek**, *QIU*: search for, aim at, wish for, desire; implore, supplicate; covetous.

Patterns of Wisdom

> The **pond possesses earth above**. **Nearing**.
> A **jun zi uses teaching** to **ponder without exhausting**.
> And **tolerating** to **protect** the **commoners without delimiting**.

Fields of meaning

Pond, *ZE*: open surface of a flat body of water and the vapors rising from it; fertilize, enrich; kindness, favor; Symbol of the trigram Open, *DUI*. **Possess**, *YOU*: see *Image of the Situation*. **Earth**, *DI*: the earth, ground on which the human world rests; basis of all things, nourishes all things; essential Yin; Symbol of the trigram Space, *KUN*. **Above**, *SHANG*: anything above in all senses; higher, upper, outer; upper trigram. **Near**, *LIN*: see *Image of the Situation*. **Jun zi**: ideal of a person who orders his/her life in accordance with dao rather than willful intention, and uses divination in this spirit. **Use**, *YI*: by means of; owing to; make use of, employ. **Teach**, *JIAO*: instruct, educate, direct, guide; school, doctrine. **Ponder**, *SI*: reflect, consider, remember; deep thought; desire, wish. Ideogram: heart and field, the heart's concerns. **Without**, *WU*: devoid of; there is not. **Exhaust**, *QIONG*: bring to an end; limit, extremity; investigate exhaustively; destitute, indigent; end without a new beginning; distinct from complete, *ZHONG*, end of a cycle that begins the next one. Ideogram: cave and naked person, bent with disease or old age. **Tolerate**, *RONG*: allow, contain, endure, bear; accept graciously. Ideogram: full stream bed, tolerating and containing. **Protect**, *BAO*: guard, defend, keep safe; nourish, support. **Commoners**, *MIN*: common people, masses; working class supporting the social hierarchy; undeveloped potential in the individual. **Delimit**, *JIANG*: define frontiers, boundaries, draw limits.

Transforming Lines

INITIAL NINE

Conjunction nearing: **Trial, significant**.

Comments

Conjunction nearing: **Trial, significant**.
Purpose moving correctly indeed.

Fields of meaning

Conjoin, *XIAN*: come in contact with, join; put together as parts of a previously separated whole; conjunction of celestial bodies; totally, completely; accord, harmony, mutual influence; lit.: broken piece of pottery, the halves of which join to identify partners. **Near**, *LIN*: see *Image of the Situation*. **Trial**, *ZHEN*: inquiry by divination and its result; righteous, firm; separating wheat from chaff; the kernel, the proven core; quality of winter and North, fourth stage of the Time Cycle. Ideogram: pearl and divination. **Significant**, *JI*: leads to the experience of meaning; favorable, propitious, appropriate. Ideogram: scholar and mouth, wise words of a sage.

Purpose, *ZHI*: focus of mind and heart; intention, will, inclination; continuity in the direction of life. Ideogram: heart and scholar, high inner resolve. **Move**, *XING*: move or move something; motivate; emotionally moving; walk, act, do. Ideogram: successive steps. **Correct**, *ZHENG*: rectify deviation or one-sidedness; proper, straight, exact, regular; constant, rule, model. Ideogram: stop and one, hold to one thing. **Indeed**, *YE*: see *Preceding Situation*.

NINE AT SECOND

Conjunction nearing, significant.
Without not Harvesting.

Comments
Conjunction nearing, significant.
Without not Harvesting.
Not-yet yielding to **fate indeed.**

Fields of meaning
Conjoin, *XIAN*: come in contact with, join; put together as parts of a previously separated whole; conjunction of celestial bodies; totally, completely; accord, harmony, mutual influence; lit.: broken piece of pottery, the halves of which join to identify partners. **Near,** *LIN*: see *Image of the Situation*. **Significant,** *JI*: leads to the experience of meaning; favorable, propitious, appropriate. Ideogram: scholar and mouth, wise words of a sage. **Without not Harvesting,** *WU BU LI*: turning point where the balance is swinging from not Harvesting to actually Harvesting.

Not-yet, *WEI*: temporal negative indicating that something is expected to happen but has not yet occurred. **Yield,** *SHUN*: give way, comply, agree, follow, obey; docile, flexible; bear produce, nourish, provide; Action of the trigram Field, *KUN*. **Fate,** *MING*: individual destiny; birth and death as limits of life; issue orders with authority; consult the gods. Ideogram: mouth and order, words with heavenly authority. **Indeed,** *YE*: see *Preceding Situation*.

SIX AT THIRD

Sweetness nearing.
Without direction Harvesting.
Already grieving over **it.**
Without fault.

Comments
Sweetness nearing.
Position not appropriate indeed.
Already grieving over **it.**
Fault not long-living indeed.

Fields of meaning
Sweet, *GAN*: one of the five tastes: sour, bitter, sweet, acrid and salty; agreeable, pleasant, delightful, refreshing; corresponding to the Earthy Moment. **Near,** *LIN*: see *Image of the Situation*. **Without direction Harvesting,** *WU YOU LI*: in order to take advantage of the situation, do not impose a direction on events. **Already,** *JI*: completed, done, occurred, finished; past tense; shortly after. **Grieve,** *YOU*: mourn; sorrow, melancholy, anxiety, care, hidden sorrow. Ideogram: heart, head,

and limp, heart-sick and anxious. **It/belong**, *ZHI*: establishes between two terms a connection similar to the Saxon genitive, in which the second term belongs to the first one; at the end of a sentence it refers to something previously mentioned or implied. **Without fault**, *WU JIU*: no error or harm in the situation.

Position, *WEI*: place, location; be at; social standing, rank; position of a line in a hexagram. Ideogram: person standing. **Not**, *BU*: common term of negation. **Appropriate**, *DANG*: suitable, capable, worthy, adequate, competent, equal to; opportune, convenient; whole lines in odd places and opened lines in even places. **Indeed**, *YE*: see *Preceding Situation*. **Fault**, *JIU*: unworthy conduct that leads to harm, illness, misfortune; guilt, crime, punishment. Ideogram: person and differ, differ from what you should be. **Long-living**, *ZHANG*: enduring, lasting, constant; extended, long, large; senior, superior, greater; increase, prosper; respect, elevate.

Six at Fourth

Culmination nearing.
Without fault.

Comments
Culmination nearing, without fault.
Position appropriate indeed.

Fields of meaning
Culminate, *ZHI*: see *Image of the Situation*. **Near**, *LIN*: see *Image of the Situation*. **Without fault**, *WU JIU*: no error or harm in the situation.

Position, *WEI*: place, location; be at; social standing, rank; position of a line in a hexagram. Ideogram: person standing. **Appropriate**, *DANG*: suitable, capable, worthy, adequate, competent, equal to; opportune, convenient; whole lines in odd places and opened lines in even places. **Indeed**, *YE*: see *Preceding Situation*.

Six at Fifth

Knowledge nearing.
To the **great** in the **chief belongs propriety**.
Significant.

Comments
To the **great** in the **chief belongs propriety**.
To **moving** the **center belongs designating indeed**.

Fields of meaning

Know, *ZHI*: have knowledge of, perceive, experience, remember; know intimately; informed, aware, wise. Ideogram: arrow and mouth, words focused and swift. **Near**, *LIN*: see *Image of the Situation*. **Great**, *DA*: see *Preceding Situation*. **Chief**, *JUN*: prince, ruler; lead, direct; wise person. Ideogram: mouth and direct, giving orders. **Belong/it**, *ZHI*: see *Hexagrams in Pairs*. **Proper**, *YI*: reasonable, fit, right, harmonious; ought, should. **Significant**, *JI*: leads to the experience of meaning; favorable, propitious, appropriate. Ideogram: scholar and mouth, wise words of a sage.

Move, *XING*: move or move something; motivate; emotionally moving; walk, act, do. Ideogram: successive steps. **Center**, *ZHONG*: inner, central; put in the center; middle, stable point enabling you to face inner and outer changes; middle line of a trigram. Ideogram: field divided in two equal parts. **Designate**, *WEI*: say, express in words, give a name; mean, signify; consider as; talk about. Ideogram: words and belly, describing the essential. **Indeed**, *YE*: see *Preceding Situation*.

SIX ABOVE

Magnanimity nearing.
Significant.
Without fault.

Comments

To **magnanimity nearing belongs significance**.
Purpose located inside indeed.

Fields of meaning

Magnanimous, *DUN*: generous, honest, sincere; important, wealthy; honor, increase; firm, solid. Ideogram: strike and accept, warrior magnanimous in giving and receiving blows. **Near**, *LIN*: see *Image of the Situation*. **Significant**, *JI*: leads to the experience of meaning; favorable, propitious, appropriate. Ideogram: scholar and mouth, wise words of a sage. **Without fault**, *WU JIU*: no error or harm in the situation.

Belong/it, *ZHI*: see *Hexagrams in Pairs*. **Purpose**, *ZHI*: focus of mind and heart; intention, will, inclination; continuity in the direction of life. Ideogram: heart and scholar, high inner resolve. **Locate**, *ZAI*: be at, be situated at, dwell, reside; in, within; involved with, in the process of. Ideogram: earth and persevere, a place on the earth. **Inside**, *NEI*: within, inner, interior; inside of the house and those who work there, particularly women; inside of the body, inner organs; the lower trigram, as opposed to outside, *WAI*, the upper. Ideogram: border and enter. **Indeed**, *YE*: see *Preceding Situation*.

Image Tradition

Nearing.
The **solid drenched and-also long-living**.
Stimulating and-also yielding.
The **solid** in the **center and-also corresponding**.

Great Growing uses correcting.
Dao belonging to **heaven indeed**.

Culminating tending-towards the **eighth moon possesses** a **pitfall**.
Dissolving not lasting indeed.

Fields of meaning

Near, *LIN*: see *Image of the Situation*. **Solid**, *GANG*: quality of the whole lines; firm, strong, unyielding, persisting. **Drench**, *JIN*: soak, penetrate, immerse, steep in; infiltrate gradually; progressive accumulation. **And-also**, *ER*: see *Preceding Situation*. **Long-living**, *ZHANG*: enduring, lasting, constant; extended, long, large; senior, superior, greater; increase, prosper; respect, elevate. **Stimulate**, *SHUO*: rouse to action and good feeling; stir up, urge on; exhort, persuade; say, tell, relate; cheer, delight; joyous, peaceful, restful; Action of the trigram Open, *DUI*. Ideogram: words and exchange. **Yield**, *SHUN*: give way, comply, agree, follow, obey; docile, flexible; bear produce, nourish, provide; Action of the trigram Field, *KUN*. **Center**, *ZHONG*: inner, central; put in the center; middle, stable point enabling you to face inner and outer changes; middle line of a trigram. Ideogram: field divided in two equal parts. **Correspond**, *YING*: be in agreement or harmony; proper, suitable; resonate together, answer to; relation between the lines (1 and 4, 2 and 5, 3 and 6) when they form the pair opened and whole, supple and solid. Ideogram: heart and obey.

Great, *DA*: see *Preceding Situation*. **Grow**, *HENG*: heavenly influence pervading and nourishing all things; prosper, succeed, expand, develop; effective, favorable; quality of summer and South, second stage of the Time Cycle. With the pronunciation *XIANG*: offer a sacrifice; offer a gift to a superior; accept, enjoy. **Use**, *YI*: see *Patterns of Wisdom*. **Correct**, *ZHENG*: rectify deviation or one-sidedness; proper, straight, exact, regular; constant, rule, model. Ideogram: stop and one, hold to one thing. **Dao**, *DAO*: way or path; ongoing process of being and the course it traces for each person or thing; ultimate reality, intrinsic nature; origin. Ideogram: go and head, opening a path. **Belong/it**, *ZHI*: see *Hexagrams in Pairs*. **Heaven**, *TIAN*: sky, firmament, heavens; the highest realm, situated above the human world, as opposed to the earth, *DI*, located below; Symbol of the trigram Energy, *QIAN*. Ideogram: great and the one above. **Indeed**, *YE*: see *Preceding Situation*.

Culminating tending-towards the **eighth moon possesses pitfall**, *ZHI YU BA YUE YOU XIONG*: see *Image of the Situation*. **Dissolve**, *XIAO*: liquefy, melt, thaw; diminish, disperse; eliminate, exhaust. Ideogram: water dissolving differences. **Not**, *BU*: common term of negation. **Last**, *JIU*: endure; long, protracted, permanent, eternal; old, ancient.

觀

䷓

20 OVERSEEING

Guan

The situation described by this hexagram is characterized by contemplating something from a distance, without immediate involvement.

Image of the Situation

> **Overseeing.**
> **Hand-washing and-also not worshipping.**
> **Possessing conformity like** a **presence.**

Fields of meaning

Oversee, *GUAN*: contemplate, observe from a distance; look at carefully, gaze at; a high place from where one sees far, monastery, observatory; intelligence, clairvoyance; scry, divine through liquid in a cup. Ideogram: sight and waterbird, aerial view. **Hand-washing**, *GUAN*: wash the hands before a sacramental act; ablutions, basin. **And-also**, *ER*: joins and contrasts two terms. **Not**, *BU*: common term of negation. **Worship**, *JIAN*: honor the gods and ancestors; offer a sacrifice; recommend, introduce. **Possess**, *YOU*: general term indicating possession; have, own, be endowed with. **Conform**, *FU*: accord between inner and outer; sincere, truthful, verified, reliable; capture; prisoners, spoils. Ideogram: claws over child, a bird brooding on the nest. **Like**, *RUO*: same as, just as; conform, imitate; adverbial suffix indicating similarity. **Presence**, *YONG*: a large head; noble bearing; prestige, dignity; imposing; haughty, conceited.

Outer and Inner Trigram

The upper trigram, **Root**, *SUN*, describes the outer aspects of the situation. It has the following associations: base on which things rest, ground, foundation; mild, subtly penetrating; nourishing. *Symbols*: tree/wood and wind. Tree/wood, *MU*: trees and all things woody or wooden; associated with the Wooden Moment. Ideogram: a tree with roots and branches. Wind, *FENG*: wind, breeze, gust; weather and its influence on mood and humor; fashion, usage. *Action*: enter, *RU*, penetrate, go into, enter on, encroach on; progress; put into. In the family of trigrams *SUN* is the eldest daughter.

The lower trigram, **Space**, *KUN*, describes the inner aspects of the situation. It has the following associations: surface of the world; support of all existence, manifestation of Yin, where Energy or Yang activates all creation and destruction; all-involving service; earth; moon, wife, mother; rest, receptivity, docile obedience. Ideogram: terrestrial globe and stretch out. *Symbol*: earth, *DI*; the earth, ground on which the human world rests; basis of all things, nourishes all things; essential Yin. *Action*: yield, *SHUN*: give way, comply, agree, follow, obey; docile, flexible; bear produce, nourish, provide. In the family of trigrams *KUN* is the mother.

Counter Hexagram

The Counter Hexagram of **Overseeing** is hexagram 23, **Stripping**, which switches the emphasis from contemplating something from a distance to actively getting rid of something that has become obsolete.

Preceding Situation

> The **beings**' **great**, **therefore afterwards permitted overseeing**.
> To **anterior acquiescence belongs** the **use** of **overseeing**.

Fields of meaning

Being, *WU*: creature, thing, any single being; matter, substance, essence; nature of things. **Great**, *DA*: big, noble, important, very; orient the will toward a self-imposed goal, impose direction; ability to lead or guide one's life; contrasts with small, *XIAO*, flexible adaptation to what crosses one's path. **Therefore**, *RAN*: thus, so it is; truly, certainly. **After(wards)/later**, *HOU*: come after in time, subsequent; put oneself after; behind, back, draw back; the second; attendants, heirs, successors, posterity. **Permit**, *KE*: possible because in harmony with an inherent principle; capable of; approve, authorize. Ideogram: mouth and breath, silent consent. **Oversee**, *GUAN*: see *Image of the Situation*. To **anterior acquiescence belongs** the **use** of, *GU SHOU ZHI YI*: understanding and accepting the preceding statement allows the consultant to make proper use of this hexagram.

Hexagrams in Pairs

> To **nearing** and **overseeing belongs righteousness**.
> **Maybe associating**, **maybe seeking**.

Fields of meaning

Near, *LIN*: approach or be approached: behold with care, look on sympathetically; condescend; bless or curse by coming nearer; a superior visits an inferior. **Oversee**, *GUAN*: see *Image of the Situation*. **Belong/it**, *ZHI*: establishes between two terms a connection similar to the Saxon genitive, in which the second term belongs to the first one; at the end of a sentence it refers to something previously mentioned or implied. **Righteous**, *YI*: proper, just, virtuous, upright; the heart that rules itself; benevolent, loyal, devoted to public good. **Maybe**, *HUO*: possible but not certain, perhaps. **Associate**, *YU*: consort with, combine; companions; group, band, company; agree with, comply, help; in favor of. Ideogram: a pair of hands reaching downward meets a pair of hands reaching upward, helpful association. **Seek**, *QIU*: search for, aim at, wish for, desire; implore, supplicate; covetous.

Patterns of Wisdom

> **Wind moves above** the **earth**. **Overseeing**.
> The **earlier kings used inspecting** on all **sides** and
> **overseeing** the **commoners** to **set-up teaching**.

Fields of meaning

Wind, *FENG*: wind, breeze, gust; weather and its influence on mood and humor; fashion, usage; wind and wood are the Symbols of the trigram Root, *SUN*. **Move**, *XING*: move or move something; motivate; emotionally moving; walk, act, do. Ideogram: successive steps. **Above**, *SHANG*: anything above in all senses; higher, upper, outer; upper trigram. **Earth**, *DI*: the earth, ground on which the human world rests; basis of all things, nourishes all things; essential yin; Symbol of the trigram Space, *KUN*. **Oversee**, *GUAN*: see *Image of the Situation*. **Earlier Kings**, *XIAN WANG*: ideal rulers of old; the golden age, primal time; mythical sages in harmony with nature. **Use**, *YI*: by means of; owing to; make use of, employ. **Inspect**, *XING*: examine, inquire, reflect, consider; visit. **Sides**, *FANG*: cardinal directions; surface of the earth extending to the four cardinal points; everywhere; limits, boundaries. **Commoners**, *MIN*: common people, masses; working class supporting the social hierarchy; undeveloped potential in the individual. **Set-up**, *SHE*: establish, institute; arrange, set in order. Ideogram: words and impel, establish with words. **Teach**, *JIAO*: instruct, educate, direct, guide; school, doctrine.

Transforming Lines

INITIAL SIX

Youthful overseeing.
The **small** in the **person**: **without fault.**
A **jun zi**: **abashment.**

Comments
Initial six, **youthful overseeing.**
The **small** in the **person**'s **dao indeed.**

Fields of meaning

Youthful, *TONG*: young person (between eight and fifteen); childish, immature; servant, slave. **Oversee**, *GUAN*: see *Image of the Situation*. **Small**, *XIAO*: little, common, unimportant; adapting to what crosses your path; ability to move in harmony with the vicissitudes of life; contrasts with great, *DA*, self-imposed theme or goal. **Person/people**, *REN*: humans individually and collectively; an individual; humankind. **Without fault**, *WU JIU*: no error or harm in the situation. **Jun zi**: ideal of a person who orders his/her life in accordance with dao rather than willful intention, and uses divination in this spirit. **Abashment**, *LIN*: distress, shame, regret, humiliation; aware of having lost the right track; leads to repenting, *HUI*, correcting the direction of mind and life.

Initial, *CHU*: beginning, incipient, first step or part; bottom line of a hexagram. Ideogram: knife and garment, cutting out the pattern. **Six**, *LIU*: number six; transforming opened line; six lines of a hexagram. **Dao**, *DAO*: way or path; ongoing process of being and the course it traces for each person or thing; ultimate reality, intrinsic nature; origin. Ideogram: go and head, opening a path. **Indeed**, *YE*: emphasizes and intensifies the previous statement.

SIX AT SECOND

Peeping overseeing.
Harvesting: **woman**'s **Trial.**

Comments
Peeping overseeing: **woman**'s **Trial.**
Truly permitting the **demoniac indeed.**

Fields of meaning

Peep, *KUI*: observe from hiding; stealthy, furtive. **Oversee,** *GUAN*: see *Image of the Situation.* **Harvest,** *LI*: benefit, advantage, profit; realization; sharp, acute, insightful; quality of autumn and West, third stage of the Time Cycle. Ideogram: ripe grain and blade. **Woman(hood),** *NÜ*: woman and what is inherently female. **Trial,** *ZHEN*: inquiry by divination and its result; righteous, firm; separating wheat from chaff; the kernel, the proven core; quality of winter and North, fourth stage of the Time Cycle. Ideogram: pearl and divination.

Truly, *YI*: in fact; also; nevertheless. **Permit,** *KE*: see *Preceding Situation.* **Demon,** *CHOU*: malignant genius; horror; ugly, vile, disgraceful, shameful; drunken; detest, hate; strange, ominous; class, group, crowd; similar. Ideogram: fermented liquor and soul. Demon and tiger are opposed on the North–South axis of the Universal Compass; the tiger (Extreme Yang) protects against the demons of Extreme Yin. **Indeed,** *YE*: emphasizes and intensifies the previous statement.

SIX AT THIRD

Overseeing my generation: advancing, withdrawing.

Comments

Overseeing my generation: advancing, withdrawing.
Not-yet letting-go dao indeed.

Fields of meaning

Oversee, *GUAN*: see *Image of the Situation.* **I/me/my,** *WO*: first person pronoun; the use of a specific personal pronoun, as opposed to the generic one's, *QI*, indicates an unusually strong emphasis on personal involvement. **Generate,** *SHENG*: give birth; be born, arise, grow; beget; life, vitality. Ideogram: earth and sprout. **Advance,** *JIN*: move forward, progress, climb; promote or be promoted; further the development of, augment; offer, introduce. **Withdraw,** *TUI*: draw back, retreat, recede; decline, refuse.

Not-yet, *WEI*: temporal negative indicating that something is expected to happen but has not yet occurred. **Let-go,** *SHI*: lose, let slip; omit, miss, fail; lose control of. Ideogram: drop from the hand. **Dao,** *DAO*: way or path; ongoing process of being and the course it traces for each person or thing; ultimate reality, intrinsic nature; origin. Ideogram: go and head, opening a path. **Indeed,** *YE*: emphasizes and intensifies the previous statement.

Six at Fourth

Overseeing the **shine belonging** to the **city**.
Harvesting: **availing** of **hospitality tending-towards** the **king**.

Comments
Overseeing the **shine belonging** to the **city**.
Honoring hospitality indeed.

Fields of meaning

Oversee, *GUAN*: see *Image of the Situation*. **Shine**, *GUANG*: illuminate, emit light; brilliant, splendid; honor, glory, éclat; distinct from brightness, *MING*, light of heavenly bodies. Ideogram: fire above person. **Belong/it**, *ZHI*: see *Hexagrams in Pairs*. **City**, *GUO*: city, state, country, nation; area of only human constructions; first of the territorial zones: city, suburbs, countryside, forest. **Harvest**, *LI*: benefit, advantage, profit; realization; sharp, acute, insightful; quality of autumn and West, third stage of the Time Cycle. Ideogram: ripe grain and blade. **Avail**, *YONG*: use, employ for a specific purpose; take advantage of; benefit from; capacity. Ideogram: to divine and center, applying divination to central concerns. **Hospitality**, *BIN*: both entertain a guest, receive a stranger, and visit someone, enjoy hospitality. **Tend-towards**, *YU*: move toward without necessarily reaching, in the direction of. **King**, *WANG*: sovereign, effective ruler, emperor, seen as connecting heaven and earth; reign, govern.

Honor, *SHANG*: esteem, give high rank to, exalt, celebrate; rise, elevate; put one thing on top of another. **Indeed**, *YE*: emphasizes and intensifies the previous statement.

Nine at Fifth

Overseeing my generation.
A **jun zi**: **without fault**.

Comments
Overseeing my generation.
Overseeing the **commoners indeed**.

Fields of meaning

Oversee, *GUAN*: see *Image of the Situation*. **I/me/my**, *WO*: first person pronoun; the use of a specific personal pronoun, as opposed to the generic one's, *QI*, indicates an unusually strong emphasis on personal involvement. **Generate**,

SHENG: give birth; be born, arise, grow; beget; life, vitality. Ideogram: earth and sprout. **Jun zi**: ideal of a person who orders his/her life in accordance with dao rather than willful intention, and uses divination in this spirit. **Without fault**, *WU JIU*: no error or harm in the situation.

Commoners, *MIN*: see *Patterns of Wisdom*. **Indeed**, *YE*: emphasizes and intensifies the previous statement.

Nine Above

Overseeing one's generation.
A **jun zi**: **without fault**.

Comments
Overseeing one's generation.
Purpose not-yet evened indeed.

Fields of meaning
Oversee, *GUAN*: see *Image of the Situation*. **One/one's**, *QI*: general third person pronoun and possessive adjective; also: it/its, he/his, she/her, they/their. **Generate**, *SHENG*: give birth; be born, arise, grow; beget; life, vitality. Ideogram: earth and sprout. **Jun zi**: ideal of a person who orders his/her life in accordance with dao rather than willful intention, and uses divination in this spirit. **Without fault**, *WU JIU*: no error or harm in the situation.

Purpose, *ZHI*: focus of mind and heart; intention, will, inclination; continuity in the direction of life. Ideogram: heart and scholar, high inner resolve. **Not-yet**, *WEI*: temporal negative indicating that something is expected to happen but has not yet occurred. **Even**, *PING*: level, flatten, equalize; balanced, regular; uniform, peaceful, tranquil; restore quiet, harmonize. **Indeed**, *YE*: emphasizes and intensifies the previous statement.

Image Tradition

The **great**: **overseeing located above**.
Yielding and-also the **root**.
The **center**'s **correctness uses overseeing below heaven**.

Overseeing. **Hand-washing and-also not worshipping**.
Possessing conformity like a **presence**.
Overseeing below and-also changing indeed.

Overseeing the **spirit dao belonging** to **heaven**.
And-also the **four seasons not straying**.
The **wise person uses spirit dao** to **set-up teaching**.
And-also below heaven submits actually.

Fields of meaning

Great, *DA*: see *Preceding Situation*. **Oversee**, *GUAN*: see *Image of the Situation*. **Locate**, *ZAI*: be at, be situated at, dwell, reside; in, within; involved with, in the process of. Ideogram: earth and persevere, a place on the earth. **Above**, *SHANG*: see *Patterns of Wisdom*. **Yield**, *SHUN*: give way, comply, agree, follow, obey; docile, flexible; bear produce, nourish, provide; Action of the trigram Field, *KUN*. **And-also**, *ER*: see *Image of the Situation*. **Root**, *SUN*: base on which things rest, ground, foundation; mild, subtly penetrating; nourishing. **Center**, *ZHONG*: inner, central; put in the center; middle, stable point enabling you to face inner and outer changes; middle line of a trigram. Ideogram: field divided in two equal parts. **Correct**, *ZHENG*: rectify deviation or one-sidedness; proper, straight, exact, regular; constant, rule, model. Ideogram: stop and one, hold to one thing. **Use**, *YI*: see *Patterns of Wisdom*. **Below heaven**, *TIAN XIA*: human world, between heaven and earth.

Hand-washing and-also not worshipping, *GUAN ER BU JIAN*: see *Image of the Situation*. **Possessing conformity like** a **presence**, *YOU FU RUO YONG*: see *Image of the Situation*. **Below**, *XIA*: anything below, in all senses; lower, inner; lower trigram. **Change**, *HUA*: gradual, continuous change; melt, dissolve; be born, die; influence; contrasts with transform, *BIAN*, sudden mutation. Ideogram: person alive and dead, the life process. **Indeed**, *YE*: emphasizes and intensifies the previous statement.

Spirit, *SHEN*: spiritual power that confers intensity on heart and mind by acting on the soul, *GUI*; vitality, energy; spirits, ancestors, gods. **Dao**, *DAO*: way or path; ongoing process of being and the course it traces for each person or thing; ultimate reality, intrinsic nature; origin. Ideogram: go and head, opening a path. **Belong/it**, *ZHI*: see *Hexagrams in Pairs*. **Heaven**, *TIAN*: sky, firmament, heavens; the highest realm, situated above the human world, as opposed to the earth, *DI*, located below; Symbol of the trigram Energy, *QIAN*. Ideogram: great and the one above. **Four**, *SI*: number four; number of the cardinal directions and of the seasons; everywhere, on all sides; fourfold articulation of the Universal Compass. **Season**, *SHI*: quality of the time; the right time, opportune, in harmony; planning in accord with the time; season of the year. Ideogram: sun and temple, sacred time. **Stray**, *TE*: wander, deviate, err; alter; doubt; excess. **Wise**, *SHENG*: intuitive universal wisdom; profound understanding; mythical sages of old; holy, sacred, mark of highest distinction. Ideogram: ear and inform, one who knows all from a single sound. **Person/people**, *REN*: humans individually and collectively; an individual; humankind. **Set-up**, *SHE*: see *Patterns of Wisdom*. **Teach**, *JIAO*: see *Patterns of Wisdom*. **Submit**, *FU*: yield, obey, acquiesce; enforce obedience. **Actually**, *YI*: truly, really, at present. Ideogram: a dart and done, strong intention fully expressed.

21 GNAWING AND BITING | *Shi He*

噬嗑

The situation described by this hexagram is characterized by acting decisively in order to overcome a tenacious obstacle, energetically biting through something one has been gnawing for some time.

Image of the Situation

> **Gnawing** and **biting**.
> **Growing**.
> **Harvesting**: **availing** of **litigating**.

Fields of meaning

Gnaw, *SHI*: chew, bite persistently, bite away; snap at, nibble; reach the essential by removing the unnecessary. Ideogram: mouth and divination, revealing the essential. **Bite**, *HE*: close the jaws, bite through, crush between the teeth; unite, close. Ideogram: mouth and cover. **Grow**, *HENG*: heavenly influence pervading and nourishing all things; prosper, succeed, expand, develop; effective, favorable; quality of summer and South, second stage of the Time Cycle. With the pronunciation *XIANG*: offer a sacrifice; offer a gift to a superior; accept, enjoy. **Harvest**, *LI*: benefit, advantage, profit; realization; sharp, acute, insightful; quality of autumn and West, third stage of the Time Cycle. Ideogram: ripe grain and blade. **Avail**, *YONG*: use, employ for a specific purpose; take advantage of; benefit from; capacity. Ideogram: to divine and center, applying divination to central concerns. **Litigate**, *YU*: legal proceedings, trial, sentence; dispute; take a case to court. Ideogram: two dogs and words, barking arguments at each other.

Outer and Inner Trigram

The upper trigram, **Radiance**, *LI*, describes the outer aspects of the situation. It has the following associations: glowing light, spreading in all directions; the power of consciousness; discriminate, articulate, divide and arrange in order; assemble, attract. Ideogram: bird and weird, magical fire-bird with brilliant plumage. *Symbols*: fire and brightness. Fire, *HUO*: flame, burn; warming and consuming aspect of burning. Brightness, *MING*: light, radiance, clarity; distinguish, discern, understand; light-giving aspect of fire, of heavenly bodies and of consciousness. *Action*: congregate, *LI*, cling together, adhere to, rely on; couple, pair, herd; beautiful, elegant. Ideogram: deer flocking together. In the family of trigrams *LI* is the middle daughter.

The lower trigram, **Shake**, *ZHEN*, describes the inner aspects of the situation. It has the following associations: arouse, excite, inspire; awe, alarm, trembling; thunder rising from the depth of the earth; fertilizing intrusion. Ideogram: excite and rain. *Symbol*: thunder, *LEI*, arousing power emerging from the depth of the earth. *Action*: stir-up, *DONG*, excite, influence, move, affect; work, take action; come out of the egg or the bud. Ideogram: strength and heavy, move weighty things. In the family of trigrams *ZHEN* is the eldest son.

Counter Hexagram

The Counter Hexagram of **Gnawing and Biting** is hexagram 39, **Limping**, which switches the emphasis from decisive action to slow progress among difficulties and obstacles.

Preceding Situation

> **Permitted overseeing and-also afterwards possessing** a **place** to **unite**.
> To **anterior acquiescence belongs** the **use** of **gnawing** and **biting**.
> **Gnawing** and **biting imply uniting indeed**.

Fields of meaning

Permit, *KE*: possible because in harmony with an inherent principle; capable of; approve, authorize. Ideogram: mouth and breath, silent consent. **Oversee**, *GUAN*: contemplate, observe from a distance; look at carefully, gaze at; a high place from where one sees far, monastery, observatory; intelligence, clairvoyance; scry, divine through liquid in a cup. Ideogram: sight and waterbird, aerial view. **And-also**, *ER*: joins and contrasts two terms. **After(wards)/later**, *HOU*: come after in time, subsequent; put oneself after; behind, back, draw back; the second; attendants, heirs, successors, posterity. **Possess**, *YOU*: general term indicating possession; have, own, be endowed with. **Place**, *SUO*: position, location; residence, dwelling; where something belongs or comes from; habitual focus or object. **Unite**, *HE*: join, match, correspond; unison, harmony; together; close the jaws, shut the mouth. Ideogram: mouths speaking in unison. To **anterior acquiescence belongs** the **use** of, *GU SHOU ZHI YI*: understanding and accepting the preceding statement allows the consultant to make proper use of this hexagram. **Gnawing** and **biting**, *SHI HE*: see *Image of the Situation*. **Imply**, *ZHE*: further signify; additional meaning. **Indeed**, *YE*: emphasizes and intensifies the previous statement.

Hexagrams in Pairs

Gnawing and **biting**: **taking-in indeed**.
Adorning: **without complexion indeed**.

Fields of meaning
Gnaw, *SHI*: see *Image of the Situation*. **Bite**, *HE*: see *Image of the Situation*. **Take-in**, *SHI*: eat, drink, ingest, absorb, incorporate; food, nourishment. **Indeed**, *YE*: see *Preceding Situation*. **Adorn**, *BI*: embellish, ornament, deck out, beautify; variegated (flowers); magnificent, elegant, brilliant; also: energetic, passionate, eager, capable of great effort; brave. Ideogram: cowry shells (money) and flowers, linking ornaments and value. **Without**, *WU*: devoid of; there is not. **Complexion**, *SE*: color, hue; physical appearance, expression; beauty.

Patterns of Wisdom

Thunder and **lightning**: **gnawing** and **biting**.
The **earlier kings used brightness** in **flogging** to
enforce the **laws**.

Fields of meaning
Thunder, *LEI*: thunder; arousing power emerging from the depth of the earth; Symbol of the trigram Shake, *ZHEN*. **Lightning**, *DIAN*: lighting flash, electric discharge; sudden clarity; look attentively. **Gnawing** and **biting**, *SHI HE*: see *Image of the Situation*. **Earlier Kings**, *XIAN WANG*: ideal rulers of old; the golden age, primal time; mythical sages in harmony with nature. **Use**, *YI*: by means of; owing to; make use of, employ. **Brightness**, *MING*: light, radiance, clarity; distinguish, discern, understand; light-giving aspect of fire, of heavenly bodies and of consciousness; brightness and fire are the Symbols of the trigram Radiance, *LI*. **Flog**, *FA*: punish with blows, beat, whip; used to find out the truth in judicial proceedings. **Enforce**, *LAI*: compel obedience; imposed by highest authority; arrest, deliver for punishment. **Laws**, *FA*: rules, norms, statutes; model; obey the law.

Transforming Lines

Initial Nine

Shoes locked-up, **submerged feet**.
Without fault.

Comments
Shoes locked-up, **submerged feet**.
Not moving indeed.

Fields of meaning

Shoes, *JU*: footwear, sandals. **Lock-up,** *JIAO*: imprison, lock up the feet; prison, pen. **Submerge**, *MIE*: put out a fire, exterminate; plunge under water, sink, perish. Ideogram: water and destroy. **Foot,** *ZHI*: foot, footprint; foundation, base; walk; stop where the foot rests. **Without fault**, *WU JIU*: no error or harm in the situation.

Not, *BU*: common term of negation. **Move**, *XING*: move or move something; motivate; emotionally moving; walk, act, do. Ideogram: successive steps. **Indeed**, *YE*: see *Preceding Situation*.

Six at Second

Gnawing flesh, **submerging** the **nose**.
Without fault.

Comments
Gnawing flesh, **submerging** the **nose**.
Riding a **solid indeed**.

Fields of meaning

Gnaw, *SHI*: see *Image of the Situation*. **Flesh**, *FU*: skin, muscles and organs as different from bones. **Submerge**, *MIE*: put out a fire, exterminate; plunge under water, sink, perish. Ideogram: water and destroy. **Nose**, *BI*: nose; handle. **Without fault**, *WU JIU*: no error or harm in the situation.

Ride, *CHENG*: ride an animal or a chariot; have the upper hand, control a stronger power; an opened line above controlling a whole line below. **Solid**, *GANG*: quality of the whole lines; firm, strong, unyielding, persisting. **Indeed**, *YE*: see *Preceding Situation*.

SIX AT THIRD

Gnawing seasoned meat.
Meeting poison.
The **small**: **abashment.**
Without fault.

Comments
Meeting poison.
Position not appropriate indeed.

Fields of meaning

Gnaw, *SHI*: see *Image of the Situation*. **Seasoned**, *XI*: dried meat, prepared for a journey. **Meat**, *RU*: flesh of animals; pulp of fruit. **Meet**, *YU*: come on unexpectedly, encounter; occur, happen; pleasant meeting, lucky coincidence; agree. **Poison/rule**, *DU*: noxious, malignant, hurtful, destructive; despise, hate; sickness, affliction; govern, direct educate. **Small**, *XIAO*: little, common, unimportant; adapting to what crosses your path; ability to move in harmony with the vicissitudes of life; contrasts with great, *DA*, self-imposed theme or goal. **Abashment**, *LIN*: distress, shame, regret, humiliation; aware of having lost the right track; leads to repenting, *HUI*, correcting the direction of mind and life. **Without fault**, *WU JIU*: no error or harm in the situation.

Position, *WEI*: place, location; be at; social standing, rank; position of a line in a hexagram. Ideogram: person standing. **Not**, *BU*: common term of negation. **Appropriate**, *DANG*: suitable, capable, worthy, adequate, competent, equal to; opportune, convenient; whole lines in odd places and opened lines in even places. **Indeed**, *YE*: see *Preceding Situation*.

NINE AT FOURTH

Gnawing parched meat-bones.
Acquiring a **metallic arrow.**
Harvesting drudgery, Trial.
Significant.

Comments
Harvesting drudgery, Trial: significant.
Not-yet shining indeed.

Fields of meaning

Gnaw, *SHI*: see *Image of the Situation.* **Parch/energy**, *GAN/QIAN*: dry up, burn, exhaust. With the pronunciation *QIAN*: unceasing forward movement, dynamic, enduring, untiring; spirit power, manifestation of Yang, that activates all creation and destruction in Space; heaven, sovereign, father. Ideogram: sprouts or vapors rising from the ground and sunlight, both fecundating moisture and scorching drought. **Meat-bones**, *ZI*: dried meat with bones; bones left after a meal. **Acquire**, *DE*: obtain the desired object; possession; satisfied, fulfilled; it is permitted; agree with; wish for, desire covetously. Ideogram: go and obstacle, going through obstacles to the goal. **Metal**, *JIN*: all metals, particularly gold; smelting and casting; perfection, richness; autumn, West, sunset; one of the Five Transformative Moments. **Arrow**, *SHI*: arrow, javelin, dart; swift, direct as an arrow. **Harvest**, *LI*: see *Image of the Situation.* **Drudgery**, *JIAN*: difficult, hard, repetitive work; distressing, sorrowful. Ideogram: perverse and sticky earth, soil difficult to cultivate. **Trial**, *ZHEN*: inquiry by divination and its result; righteous, firm; separating wheat from chaff; the kernel, the proven core; quality of winter and North, fourth stage of the Time Cycle. Ideogram: pearl and divination. **Significant**, *JI*: leads to the experience of meaning; favorable, propitious, appropriate. Ideogram: scholar and mouth, wise words of a sage.

Not-yet, *WEI*: temporal negative indicating that something is expected to happen but has not yet occurred. **Shine**, *GUANG*: illuminate, emit light; brilliant, splendid; honor, glory, éclat; distinct from brightness, *MING*, light of heavenly bodies. Ideogram: fire above person. **Indeed**, *YE*: see *Preceding Situation.*

Six at Fifth

Gnawing parched meat.
Acquiring yellow metal.
Trial, adversity.
Without fault.

Comments
Trial, adversity without fault.
Acquiring: appropriate indeed.

Fields of meaning

Gnaw, *SHI*: see *Image of the Situation.* **Parch/energy**, *GAN/QIAN*: dry up, burn, exhaust. With the pronunciation *QIAN*: unceasing forward movement, dynamic, enduring, untiring; spirit power, manifestation of Yang, that activates all creation and destruction in Space; heaven, sovereign, father. Ideogram: sprouts or vapors rising from the ground and sunlight, both fecundating moisture and scorching drought. **Meat**, *RU*: flesh of animals; pulp of fruit. **Acquire**, *DE*: obtain the desired object; possession; satisfied, fulfilled; it is permitted; agree with; wish for, desire covetously. Ideogram: go and obstacle, going through obstacles to the goal. **Yellow**, *HUANG*: color of the soil in central China, associated with the Earthy Moment leading from the Yang to the Yin hemicycle; emblematic and imperial color of China since the Yellow Emperor (2500 BC). **Metal**, *JIN*: all metals, particularly gold; smelting and casting; perfection, richness; autumn, West, sunset; one of the Five Transformative Moments. **Trial**, *ZHEN*: inquiry by divination and its result; righteous, firm; separating wheat from chaff; the kernel, the proven core; quality of winter and North, fourth stage of the Time Cycle. Ideogram: pearl and divination. **Adversity**, *LI*: danger, hardship, severe; threat or difficulty that must be encountered, rather than avoided; grinding stone; polish, sharpen; a challenge that strengthens and perfects the character; stimulate, excite; cruel demon. **Without fault**, *WU JIU*: no error or harm in the situation.

Appropriate, *DANG*: suitable, capable, worthy, adequate, competent, equal to; opportune, convenient; whole lines in odd places and opened lines in even places. **Indeed**, *YE*: see *Preceding Situation*.

Nine Above

Is not **locking-up submerging** the **ears**?
Pitfall.

Comments
Is not **locking-up submerging** the **ears**?
Understanding not bright indeed.

Fields of meaning

Is?, *HE*: ask, inquire; what? which? who? how? why? where? an interrogative particle, often introducing a rhetorical question: is it? is it not? **Lock-up**, *JIAO*: imprison, lock up the feet; prison, pen. **Submerge**, *MIE*: put out a fire, exterminate; plunge under water, sink, perish. Ideogram: water and destroy. **Ear**, *ER*: ear; handle; side. **Pitfall**, *XIONG*: unfortunate situation, in which the flow of life and spirit is blocked and the experience of meaning is lost; stuck and exposed to danger; inappropriate attitude. Ideogram: person in a pit.

Understand, *CONG*: perceive quickly, astute, sharp; discriminate intelligently. Ideogram: ear and quick. **Not**, *BU*: common term of negation. **Brightness**, *MING*: see *Patterns of Wisdom*. **Indeed**, *YE*: see *Preceding Situation*.

Image Tradition

Jaws' center possesses being.
Named: **gnawing** and **biting**.
Gnawing and **biting and-also Growing**.
Solid and **supple apportioned**.

Stirring-up and-also brightening.
Thunder and **lightning uniting and-also composing**.

The **supple acquires** the **center and-also above moves**.
Although not an **appropriate position**, **Harvesting avails** of **litigating indeed**.

Fields of meaning

Jaws, *YI*: mouth, jaws, cheeks, chin; swallow, take in, ingest; feed, nourish, sustain, rear. Ideogram: open jaws. **Center**, *ZHONG*: inner, central; put in the center; middle, stable point enabling you to face inner and outer changes; middle line of a trigram. Ideogram: field divided in two equal parts. **Possess**, *YOU*: see *Preceding Situation*. **Being**, *WU*: creature, thing, any single being; matter, substance, essence; nature of things. **Name**, *YUE*: speak, declare, call. Ideogram: open mouth and tongue. **Gnawing** and **biting**, *SHI HE*: see *Image of the Situation*. **And-also**, *ER*: see *Preceding Situation*. **Grow**, *HENG*: see *Image of the Situation*. **Solid**, *GANG*: quality of the whole lines; firm, strong, unyielding, persisting. **Supple**, *ROU*: quality of the opened lines; flexible, pliant, adaptable, tender. **Apportion**, *FEN*: divide, distribute, distinguish, sort out; part, element.

Stir-up, *DONG*: excite, influence, move, affect; work, take action; come out of the egg or the bud; Action of the trigram Shake, *ZHEN*. Ideogram: strength and heavy, move weighty things. **And-also**, *ER*: see *Preceding Situation*. **Brightness**, *MING*: see *Patterns of Wisdom*. **Thunder**, *LEI*: see *Patterns of Wisdom*. **Lightning**, *DIAN*: see *Patterns of Wisdom*. **Unite**, *HE*: see *Preceding Situation*. **Composition**, *ZHANG*: a well-composed whole and its structure; beautiful creation; elegant, clear, brilliant; chapter, strophe; distinct from pattern, *WEN*, beauty of intrinsic design.

Acquire, *DE*: obtain the desired object; possession; satisfied, fulfilled; it is permitted; agree with; wish for, desire covetously. Ideogram: go and obstacle, going through obstacles to the goal. **Above**, *SHANG*: anything above in all senses; higher, upper, outer; upper trigram. **Move**, *XING*: move or move something; motivate; emotionally moving; walk, act, do. Ideogram: successive steps. **Although**, *SUI*: even though, supposing that, if, even if. **Not**, *BU*: common term of negation.

Appropriate, *DANG*: suitable, capable, worthy, adequate, competent, equal to; opportune, convenient; whole lines in odd places and opened lines in even places. **Position**, *WEI*: place, location; be at; social standing, rank; position of a line in a hexagram. Ideogram: person standing. **Harvesting avails** of **litigating**, *LI YONG YU*: see *Image of the Situation*. **Indeed**, *YE*: see *Preceding Situation*.

賁 ䷕

22 ADORNING | *Bi*

The situation described by this hexagram is characterized by caring for the beauty of outer presentation, enhancing intrinsic value by esthetic sensitivity to details.

Image of the Situation

> **Adorning**,
> **Growing**.
> The **small**.
> **Harvesting**: **possessing directed going**.

Fields of meaning

Adorn, *BI*: embellish, ornament, deck out, beautify; variegated (flowers); magnificent, elegant, brilliant; also: energetic, passionate, eager, capable of great effort; brave. Ideogram: cowry shells (money) and flowers, linking ornaments and value. **Grow**, *HENG*: heavenly influence pervading and nourishing all things; prosper, succeed, expand, develop; effective, favorable; quality of summer and South, second stage of the Time Cycle. With the pronunciation *XIANG*: offer a sacrifice; offer a gift to a superior; accept, enjoy. **Small**, *XIAO*: little, common, unimportant; adapting to what crosses your path; ability to move in harmony with the vicissitudes of life; contrasts with great, *DA*, self-imposed theme or goal. **Harvest**, *LI*: benefit, advantage, profit; realization; sharp, acute, insightful; quality of autumn and West, third stage of the Time Cycle. Ideogram: ripe grain and blade. **Possessing directed going**, *YOU YOU WANG*: having a goal or purpose, moving in a specific direction.

Outer and Inner Trigram

The upper trigram, **Bound**, *GEN*, describes the outer aspects of the situation. It has the following associations: limit, frontier; obstacle that prevents from seeing further; stop; still, quiet, motionless; confine , enclose; mountain, sunset, beginning of winter; solid, steady, unshakable; straight, hard, adamant, obstinate. *Symbol*: mountain, *SHAN*, large, immense; limit, boundary. Ideogram: three peaks, a mountain range. *Action*: stop, *ZHI*, bring or come to a standstill, cease, terminate. Ideogram: a foot stops walking. In the family of trigrams *GEN* is the youngest son.

The lower trigram, **Radiance**, *LI*, describes the inner aspects of the situation. It has the following associations: glowing light, spreading in all directions; the power of consciousness; discriminate, articulate, divide and arrange in order; assemble, attract. Ideogram: bird and weird, magical fire-bird with brilliant plumage. *Symbols*: fire and brightness. Fire, *HUO*: flame, burn; warming and consuming aspect of burning. Brightness, *MING*: light, radiance, clarity; distinguish, discern, understand; light-giving aspect of fire, of heavenly bodies and of consciousness. *Action*: congregate, *LI*, cling together, adhere to, rely on; couple, pair, herd; beautiful, elegant. Ideogram: deer flocking together. In the family of trigrams *LI* is the middle daughter.

Counter Hexagram

The Counter Hexagram of **Adorning** is hexagram 40, **Unraveling**, which switches the emphasis from esthetic appreciation to analysis and understanding.

Preceding Situation

> **Beings not permitted** to **use unconsidered uniting and-also climaxing**.
> To **anterior acquiescence belongs** the **use** of **adorning**.
> **Adorning implies embellishing indeed**.

Fields of meaning

Beings not permitted (to **use**), *WU BU KE (YI)*: it is not possible; no one is allowed; it is not in the nature of things. **Unconsidered**, *GOU*: offhand, impromptu, improvised, careless; improper, illicit. **Unite**, *HE*: join, match, correspond; unison, harmony; together; close the jaws, shut the mouth. Ideogram: mouths speaking in unison. **And-also**, *ER*: joins and contrasts two terms. **Climax**, *YI*: come to a high point and stop; bring to an end, complete; renounce, desist, decline, reject; that is all; already; excessive. To **anterior acquiescence belongs** the **use** of, *GU SHOU ZHI YI*: understanding and accepting the preceding statement allows the consultant to make proper use of this hexagram. **Adorn**, *BI*: see *Image of the Situation*. **Imply**, *ZHE*: further signify; additional meaning. **Embellish**, *SHI*: ornament, paint, brighten, clean; apply cosmetics; patch up the appearance; pretend, make believe. **Indeed**, *YE*: emphasizes and intensifies the previous statement.

Hexagrams in Pairs

Gnawing and **biting**: **taking-in indeed**.
Adorning: **without complexion indeed**.

Fields of meaning
Gnaw, *SHI*: chew, bite persistently, bite away; snap at, nibble; reach the essential by removing the unnecessary. Ideogram: mouth and divination, revealing the essential. **Bite**, *HE*: close the jaws, bite through, crush between the teeth; unite, close. Ideogram: mouth and cover. **Take-in**, *SHI*: eat, drink, ingest, absorb, incorporate; food, nourishment. **Indeed**, *YE*: see *Preceding Situation*. **Adorn**, *BI*: see *Image of the Situation*. **Without**, *WU*: devoid of; there is not. **Complexion**, *SE*: color, hue; physical appearance, expression; beauty.

Patterns of Wisdom

The **mountain possesses fire below**. **Adorning**.
A **jun zi uses brightening** the **multitude** of **standards**
without daring to **sever litigations**.

Fields of meaning
Mountain, *SHAN*: mountain; large, immense; limit, boundary; Symbol of the trigram Bound, *GEN*. Ideogram: three peaks, a mountain range. **Possess**, *YOU*: general term indicating possession; have, own, be endowed with. **Fire**, *HUO*: fire, flame, burn; warming and consuming aspect of burning; fire and brightness are the Symbols of the trigram Radiance, *LI*. **Below**, *XIA*: anything below, in all senses; lower, inner; lower trigram. **Adorn**, *BI*: see *Image of the Situation*. **Jun zi**: ideal of a person who orders his/her life in accordance with dao rather than willful intention, and uses divination in this spirit. **Use**, *YI*: by means of; owing to; make use of, employ. **Brightness**, *MING*: light, radiance, clarity; distinguish, discern, understand; light-giving aspect of fire, of heavenly bodies and of consciousness; brightness and fire are the Symbols of the trigram Radiance, *LI*. **Multitude**, *SHU*: crowd, many people; mass, herd; all, the whole. **Standard**, *ZHENG*: rule, principle; adjust, correct; measure, limit; musical interval. **Without**, *WU*: see *Hexagrams in Pairs*. **Dare**, *GAN*: have the courage to, try, permit oneself; bold, intrepid; rash, offensive. **Sever**, *ZHE*: break off, separate, sunder, cut in two; discriminate, pass judgment on. **Litigate**, *YU*: legal proceedings, trial, sentence; dispute; take a case to court. Ideogram: two dogs and words, barking arguments at each other.

Transforming Lines

INITIAL NINE

Adorning one's feet.
Stowing the **chariot and-also afoot.**

Comments
Stowing the **chariot and-also afoot.**
Righteously nothing to **ride indeed.**

Fields of meaning

Adorn, *BI*: see *Image of the Situation.* **One/one's,** *QI*: general third person pronoun and possessive adjective; also: it/its, he/his, she/her, they/their. **Foot,** *ZHI*: foot, footprint; foundation, base; walk; stop where the foot rests. **Stow,** *SHE*: set aside, put away, store, keep; halt, rest in; lodge, hut. **Chariot,** *CHE*: cart, wheeled traveling vehicle. **And-also,** *ER*: see *Preceding Situation.* **Afoot,** *TU*: travel on foot; footman, foot-soldier; follower, disciple; ruffian, bond-servant; empty, alone.

Righteous, *YI*: proper, just, virtuous, upright; the heart that rules itself; benevolent, loyal, devoted to public good. **Nothing/nowhere,** *FU*: strong negative; not a single thing/place; deny, disapprove; impossible, incorrect. **Ride,** *CHENG*: ride an animal or a chariot; have the upper hand, control a stronger power; an opened line above controlling a whole line below. **Indeed,** *YE*: see *Preceding Situation.*

SIX AT SECOND

Adorning: one's hair-growing.

Comments
Adorning: one's hair-growing.
Associating above, rising indeed.

Fields of meaning

Adorn, *BI*: see *Image of the Situation.* **One/one's,** *QI*: general third person pronoun and possessive adjective; also: it/its, he/his, she/her, they/their. **Hair-growing,** *XU*: beard, hair; patience symbolized as waiting for hair to grow; hold back, wait for; slow; necessary.

Associate, *YU*: consort with, combine; companions; group, band, company; agree with, comply, help; in favor of. Ideogram: a pair of hands reaching downward meets a pair of hands reaching upward, helpful association. **Above,** *SHANG*:

anything above in all senses; higher, upper, outer; upper trigram. **Rise,** *XING*: get up, grow, lift; stimulate, promote; enjoy. Ideogram: lift, two hands and unite, lift with both hands. **Indeed,** *YE*: see *Preceding Situation*.

NINE AT THIRD

Adorned thus, soaked thus.
Perpetual Trial, significant.

Comments
To **perpetual Trial belongs significance.**
To **completing abstention belongs** a **mound indeed.**

Fields of meaning
Adorn, *BI*: see *Image of the Situation*. **Thus,** *RU*: as, in this way; comparable, similar. **Soak,** *RU*: immerse, steep; damp, wet; stain, pollute, blemish; urinate on. **Perpetual,** *YONG*: continual, everlasting, eternal. Ideogram: flowing water. **Trial,** *ZHEN*: inquiry by divination and its result; righteous, firm; separating wheat from chaff; the kernel, the proven core; quality of winter and North, fourth stage of the Time Cycle. Ideogram: pearl and divination. **Significant,** *JI*: leads to the experience of meaning; favorable, propitious, appropriate. Ideogram: scholar and mouth, wise words of a sage.

Belong/it, *ZHI*: establishes between two terms a connection similar to the Saxon genitive, in which the second term belongs to the first one; at the end of a sentence it refers to something previously mentioned or implied. **Complete,** *ZHONG*: completion of a cycle that begins the next; entire, whole, all. Ideogram: silk cocoons, follow and ice, winter linking one year with the next. **Abstain/absolutely-nothing,** *MO*: complete elimination; do not, not any, by no means. **Mound,** *LING*: grave-mound, barrow; small hill. **Indeed,** *YE*: see *Preceding Situation*.

SIX AT FOURTH

Adorned thus, hoary thus.
A **white horse soaring thus.**
In-no-way illegality, matrimonial alliance.

Comments
Six at **fourth.** An **appropriate position** to **doubt indeed.**
In-no-way illegality, matrimonial alliance.
Completing without surpassing indeed.

Fields of meaning

Adorn, *BI*: see *Image of the Situation*. **Thus**, *RU*: as, in this way; comparable, similar. **Hoary**, *BO*: silvery grey hair; old and venerable. **White**, *BO*: color associated with autumn, Harvest and the Metallic Moment; white hair, old age; clear, immaculate, plain, essential; color of death and mourning. **Horse**, *MA*: symbol of spirited strength in the natural world, earthly counterpart of the dragon; associated with the trigram Energy, *QIAN*, heaven, and high noon. **Soar**, *HAN*: fly high; rising sun; firebird with red plumage; white horse; long and hard feather; drawing brush. Ideogram: feathers and dawn. **In-no-way**, *FEI*: strong negative; not so; bandit, rebel; unjust, immoral. Ideogram: a box filled with opposition. **Illegality**, *KOU*: take by force, violate, invade, sack, break the laws; brutality; enemies, outcasts, bandits. **Matrimonial alliance**, *HUN GOU*: legal institution of marriage; union of two families by marriage.

Six, *LIU*: number six; transforming opened line; six lines of a hexagram. **Four**, *SI*: number four; number of the cardinal directions and of the seasons; everywhere, on all sides; fourfold articulation of the Universal Compass. **Appropriate**, *DANG*: suitable, capable, worthy, adequate, competent, equal to; opportune, convenient; whole lines in odd places and opened lines in even places. **Position**, *WEI*: place, location; be at; social standing, rank; position of a line in a hexagram. Ideogram: person standing. **Doubt**, *YI*: suspect, distrust, wonder; uncertain, dubious; surmise, conjecture, fear. **Indeed**, *YE*: see *Preceding Situation*. **Complete**, *ZHONG*: completion of a cycle that begins the next; entire, whole, all. Ideogram: silk cocoons, follow and ice, winter linking one year with the next. **Without**, *WU*: see *Hexagrams in Pairs*. **Surpass**, *YOU*: exceed, transgress; beyond measure, extraordinary; blame.

SIX AT FIFTH

Adorning tends-towards a **hill-top garden**.
A **roll** of **plain-silk**: **petty**, **petty**.
Abashment.
Completing significant.

Comments

To **six** at **fifth belongs significance**.
Possessing joy indeed.

Fields of meaning

Adorn, *BI*: see *Image of the Situation*. **Tend-towards**, *YU*: move toward without necessarily reaching, in the direction of. **Hill-top**, *QIU*: hill with hollow top used for worship and as grave-site; knoll, hillock. **Garden**, *YUAN*: enclosed garden; park, yard; imperial tombs. **Roll**, *SHU*: gather into a bundle, bind together; restrain. **Plain-silk**, *BAI*: unbleached, undyed silk, used as a gift or as a support for writing. **Petty**, *JIAN*: little, small, insignificant. **Abashment**, *LIN*: distress, shame, regret, humiliation; aware of having lost the right track; leads to repenting, *HUI*, correcting the direction of mind and life. **Complete**, *ZHONG*: completion of a cycle that begins the next; entire, whole, all. Ideogram: silk cocoons, follow and ice, winter linking one year with the next. **Significant**, *JI*: leads to the experience of meaning; favorable, propitious, appropriate. Ideogram: scholar and mouth, wise words of a sage.

Six, *LIU*: number six; transforming opened line; six lines of a hexagram. **Five**, *WU*: number five; fivefold articulation of the Universal Compass; the Five Moments and all related qualities: directions, colors, smells, tastes, tones, feelings. **Belong/it**, *ZHI*: establishes between two terms a connection similar to the Saxon genitive, in which the second term belongs to the first one; at the end of a sentence it refers to something previously mentioned or implied. **Possess**, *YOU*: see *Patterns of Wisdom*. **Joy/rejoice**, *XI*: delight, exult; cheerful, merry. Ideogram: joy (music) and mouth, expressing joy. **Indeed**, *YE*: see *Preceding Situation*.

NINE ABOVE

White adorning.
Without fault.

Comments
White adorning, without fault.
Above acquiring purpose indeed.

Fields of meaning

White, *BO*: color associated with autumn, Harvest and the Metallic Moment; white hair, old age; clear, immaculate, plain, essential; color of death and mourning. **Adorn**, *BI*: see *Image of the Situation*. **Without fault**, *WU JIU*: no error or harm in the situation.

Above, *SHANG*: anything above in all senses; higher, upper, outer; upper trigram. **Acquire**, *DE*: obtain the desired object; possession; satisfied, fulfilled; it is permitted; agree with; wish for, desire covetously. Ideogram: go and obstacle, going through obstacles to the goal. **Purpose**, *ZHI*: focus of mind and heart; intention, will, inclination; continuity in the direction of life. Ideogram: heart and scholar, high inner resolve. **Indeed**, *YE*: see *Preceding Situation*.

Image Tradition

Adorning, Growing.
The **supple comes and-also patterns** the **solid**.
Anterior Growing.
Apportioning the **solid above and-also patterning** the **supple**.

The **anterior small**.
Harvesting: **possessing directed going**.
Heavenly pattern indeed.
Pattern's **brightness uses stopping**.
Personal pattern indeed.

Overseeing reaches the **heavenly pattern**.
Using scrutinizing the **seasons' transformation**.
Overseeing reaches the **personal pattern**.
Using changes to **accomplish below heaven**.

Fields of meaning

Adorning, Growing, *BI HENG*: see *Image of the Situation*. **Supple,** *ROU*: quality of the opened lines; flexible, pliant, adaptable, tender. **Come,** *LAI*: approach in time or space; move toward, arrive at; future; contrasts with go, *WANG*, move away or become past. **And-also,** *ER*: see *Preceding Situation*. **Pattern,** *WEN*: intrinsic or natural design, pattern of wood, stone or animal fur; ideograms, the symbols of writing as revelation of the intrinsic nature of things; language, civilization, culture; harmonious, beautiful, elegant, polite. **Solid,** *GANG*: quality of the whole lines; firm, strong, unyielding, persisting. **Anterior,** *GU*: come before as cause; former, ancient; reason, purpose, intention; grievance, dissatisfaction, sorrow, resulting from previous causes and intentions; situation leading to a divination. **Apportion,** *FEN*: divide, distribute, distinguish, sort out; part, element. **Above,** *SHANG*: anything above in all senses; higher, upper, outer; upper trigram.

Small, *XIAO*: see *Image of the Situation*. **Harvesting: possessing directed going,** *LI YOU YOU WANG*: see *Image of the Situation*. **Heaven,** *TIAN*: sky, firmament, heavens; the highest realm, situated above the human world, as opposed to the earth, *DI*, located below; Symbol of the trigram Energy, *QIAN*. Ideogram: great and the one above. **Indeed,** *YE*: see *Preceding Situation*. **Brightness,** *MING*: see *Patterns of Wisdom*. **Use,** *YI*: see *Patterns of Wisdom*. **Stop,** *ZHI*: bring or come to a standstill, cease, terminate; Action of the trigram Bound, *GEN*. Ideogram: a foot stops walking. **Person/people,** *REN*: humans individually and collectively; an individual; humankind.

Oversee, *GUAN*: contemplate, observe from a distance; look at carefully, gaze at; a high place from where one sees far, monastery, observatory; intelligence, clairvoyance; scry, divine through liquid in a cup. Ideogram: sight and waterbird, aerial view. **Reach**, *HU*: arrive at a goal; move toward and achieve; to, at, in; distinct from tend-towards, *YOU*. **Scrutinize**, *CHA*: investigate, observe carefully, get at the truth. Ideogram: sacrifice as central to understanding. **Season**, *SHI*: quality of the time; the right time, opportune, in harmony; planning in accord with the time; season of the year. Ideogram: sun and temple, sacred time. **Transform**, *BIAN*: abrupt, radical passage from one state to another; transformation of opened and whole lines into each other in hexagrams; contrasts with change, *HUA*, gradual mutation. **Change**, *HUA*: gradual, continuous change; melt, dissolve; be born, die; influence; contrasts with transform, *BIAN*, sudden mutation. Ideogram: person alive and dead, the life process. **Accomplish**, *CHENG*: complete, finish, bring about; perfect, full, whole; play one's part, do one's duty; mature. Ideogram: weapon and man, able to bear arms, thus fully developed. **Below heaven**, *TIAN XIA*: human world, between heaven and earth.

剝

䷖

23 STRIPPING | *Bo*

The situation described by this hexagram is characterized by stripping away a worn-out or obsolete form of presentation, cutting away the inessential.

Image of the Situation

> **Stripping.**
> **Not Harvesting: possessing directed going.**

Fields of meaning

Strip, *BO*: flay, peel, skin; remove, uncover; split, slice; reduce to essentials; degrade, decay; slaughter an animal. Ideogram: knife and carve, trenchant action. **Not**, *BU*: common term of negation. **Harvest**, *LI*: benefit, advantage, profit; realization; sharp, acute, insightful; quality of autumn and West, third stage of the Time Cycle. Ideogram: ripe grain and blade. **Possessing directed going**, *YOU YOU WANG*: having a goal or purpose, moving in a specific direction.

Outer and Inner Trigram

The upper trigram, **Bound**, *GEN*, describes the outer aspects of the situation. It has the following associations: limit, frontier; obstacle that prevents from seeing further; stop; still, quiet, motionless; confine, enclose; mountain, sunset, beginning of winter; solid, steady, unshakable; straight, hard, adamant, obstinate. *Symbol*: mountain, *SHAN*, large, immense; limit, boundary. Ideogram: three peaks, a mountain range. *Action*: stop, *ZHI*, bring or come to a standstill, cease, terminate. Ideogram: a foot stops walking. In the family of trigrams *GEN* is the youngest son.

The lower trigram, **Space**, *KUN*, describes the inner aspects of the situation. It has the following associations: surface of the world; support of all existence, manifestation of Yin, where Energy or Yang activates all creation and destruction; all-involving service; earth; moon, wife, mother; rest, receptivity, docile obedience. Ideogram: terrestrial globe and stretch out. *Symbol*: earth, *DI*; the earth, ground on which the human world rests; basis of all things, nourishes all things; essential Yin. *Action*: yield, *SHUN*: give way, comply, agree, follow, obey; docile, flexible; bear produce, nourish, provide. In the family of trigrams *KUN* is the mother.

Counter Hexagram

The Counter Hexagram of **Stripping** is hexagram 2, **Space**, which switches the emphasis from stripping away something that has become obsolete to supporting all things and allowing them to become what they potentially are.

Preceding Situation

Involved in **embellishing**, **therefore afterwards**
Growing, by **consequence used-up actually**.
To **anterior acquiescence belongs** the **use** of **stripping**.
Stripping implies stripped indeed.

Fields of meaning

Involve, *ZHI*: devote oneself to; induce, cause, implicate; approach; manifest, express; reach the highest degree of. Ideogram: reach and come up behind. **Embellish**, *SHI*: ornament, paint, brighten, clean; apply cosmetics; patch up the appearance; pretend, make believe. **Therefore**, *RAN*: thus, so it is; truly, certainly. **After(wards)/later**, *HOU*: come after in time, subsequent; put oneself after; behind, back, draw back; the second; attendants, heirs, successors, posterity. **Grow**, *HENG*: heavenly influence pervading and nourishing all things; prosper, succeed, expand, develop; effective, favorable; quality of summer and South, second stage of the Time Cycle. With the pronunciation *XIANG*: offer a sacrifice; offer a gift to a superior; accept, enjoy. **Consequence**, *ZE*: reason, cause, result; rule, law, pattern, standard; therefore; very strong connection. **Use-up**, *JIN*: exhaust, use all; an empty vessel; extremity, limit. **Actually**, *YI*: truly, really, at present. Ideogram: a dart and done, strong intention fully expressed. To **anterior acquiescence belongs** the **use** of, *GU SHOU ZHI YI*: understanding and accepting the preceding statement allows the consultant to make proper use of this hexagram. **Strip**, *BO*: see *Image of the Situation*. **Imply**, *ZHE*: further signify; additional meaning. **Indeed**, *YE*: emphasizes and intensifies the previous statement.

Hexagrams in Pairs

Stripping: **rotten indeed**.
Return: **reversing indeed**.

Fields of meaning

Strip, *BO*: see *Image of the Situation*. **Rotten**, *LAN*: corrupt, putrid, dirty, worn out; softened, crumbling. **Indeed**, *YE*: see *Preceding Situation*. **Return**, *FU*: go back, turn or lead back; recur, reappear, come again; restore, renew, recover; return to an earlier time or place. Ideogram: step and retrace a path. **Reverse**, *FAN*: turn and move in the opposite direction; turn around or upside down (180 degrees); change to the opposite position; contrary.

Patterns of Wisdom

> **Mountain adjoining with-respect-to earth. Stripping.**
> **Above using munificence, below pacifying** the
> **situation**.

Fields of meaning

Mountain, *SHAN*: mountain; large, immense; limit, boundary; Symbol of the trigram Bound, *GEN*. Ideogram: three peaks, a mountain range. **Adjoin**, *FU*: next to, lean on; join; near, approaching. **With-respect-to**, *YU*: in relation to, referring to, according to; in, at, until. **Earth**, *DI*: the earth, ground on which the human world rests; basis of all things, nourishes all things; essential Yin; Symbol of the trigram Space, *KUN*. **Strip**, *BO*: see *Image of the Situation*. **Above**, *SHANG*: anything above in all senses; higher, upper, outer; upper trigram. **Use**, *YI*: by means of; owing to; make use of, employ. **Munificent**, *HOU*: liberal, kind, generous; create abundance; thick, large. Ideogram: gift of a superior to an inferior. **Below**, *XIA*: anything below, in all senses; lower, inner; lower trigram. **Peace**, *AN*: quiet, still, settled, secure, contented; calm, tranquilize, console. Ideogram: woman under a roof, a tranquil home. **Situation**, *ZHAI*: office, function, place in a hierarchy; dwelling, residence.

Transforming Lines

INITIAL SIX

> **Stripping** the **bed**, **using** the **stand**.
> **Discarding Trial**, **pitfall**.
>
> **Comments**
> **Stripping** the **bed**, **using** the **stand**.
> **Using submerging below indeed**.

Fields of meaning

Strip, *BO*: see *Image of the Situation*. **Bed**, *CHUANG*: sleeping place; couch, sofa, lounge; bench around a well. **Use**, *YI*: see *Patterns of Wisdom*. **Stand**, *ZU*: base, foot, leg; rest on, support; stance; sufficient, capable, worth. Ideogram: foot and calf resting. **Discard**, *MIE*: disregard, ignore; petty, worthless, insignificant, trash. **Trial**,

ZHEN: inquiry by divination and its result; righteous, firm; separating wheat from chaff; the kernel, the proven core; quality of winter and North, fourth stage of the Time Cycle. Ideogram: pearl and divination. **Pitfall**, *XIONG*: unfortunate situation, in which the flow of life and spirit is blocked and the experience of meaning is lost; stuck and exposed to danger; inappropriate attitude. Ideogram: person in a pit.

Submerge, *MIE*: put out a fire, exterminate; plunge under water, sink, perish. Ideogram: water and destroy. **Below**, *XIA*: see *Patterns of Wisdom*. **Indeed**, *YE*: see *Preceding Situation*.

SIX AT SECOND

Stripping the **bed**, **using marking-off**.
Discarding Trial, **pitfall**.

Comments
Stripping the **bed**, **using marking-off**.
Not-yet possessing association indeed.

Fields of meaning

Strip, *BO*: see *Image of the Situation*. **Bed**, *CHUANG*: sleeping place; couch, sofa, lounge; bench around a well. **Use**, *YI*: see *Patterns of Wisdom*. **Mark-off**, *BIAN*: distinguish by dividing; mark off a plot of land; discern, discriminate, differentiate; discuss and dispute; frame which divides a bed from its stand. Ideogram: knife and acrid, sharp division. **Discard**, *MIE*: disregard, ignore; petty, worthless, insignificant, trash. **Trial**, *ZHEN*: inquiry by divination and its result; righteous, firm; separating wheat from chaff; the kernel, the proven core; quality of winter and North, fourth stage of the Time Cycle. Ideogram: pearl and divination. **Pitfall**, *XIONG*: unfortunate situation, in which the flow of life and spirit is blocked and the experience of meaning is lost; stuck and exposed to danger; inappropriate attitude. Ideogram: person in a pit.

Not-yet, *WEI*: temporal negative indicating that something is expected to happen but has not yet occurred. **Possess**, *YOU*: general term indicating possession; have, own, be endowed with. **Associate**, *YU*: consort with, combine; companions; group, band, company; agree with, comply, help; in favor of. Ideogram: a pair of hands reaching downward meets a pair of hands reaching upward, helpful association. **Indeed**, *YE*: see *Preceding Situation*.

SIX AT THIRD

To **stripping belongs without fault**.

Comments
To **stripping belongs without fault**.
Letting-go above and **below indeed**.

Fields of meaning

Strip, *BO*: see *Image of the Situation*. **Belong/it**, *ZHI*: establishes between two terms a connection similar to the Saxon genitive, in which the second term belongs to the first one; at the end of a sentence it refers to something previously mentioned or implied. **Without fault**, *WU JIU*: no error or harm in the situation.

Let-go, *SHI*: lose, let slip; omit, miss, fail; lose control of. Ideogram: drop from the hand. **Above**, *SHANG*: see *Patterns of Wisdom*. **Below**, *XIA*: see *Patterns of Wisdom*. **Indeed**, *YE*: see *Preceding Situation*.

SIX AT FOURTH

Stripping the **bed**, **using** the **flesh**.
Pitfall.

Comments
Stripping the **bed**, **using** the **flesh**.
Slicing close to **calamity indeed**.

Fields of meaning

Strip, *BO*: see *Image of the Situation*. **Bed**, *CHUANG*: sleeping place; couch, sofa, lounge; bench around a well. **Use**, *YI*: see *Patterns of Wisdom*. **Flesh**, *FU*: skin, muscles and organs as different from bones. **Pitfall**, *XIONG*: unfortunate situation, in which the flow of life and spirit is blocked and the experience of meaning is lost; stuck and exposed to danger; inappropriate attitude. Ideogram: person in a pit.

Slice, *QIE*: cut, carve, mince; urge, press; come close, approach, touch; tangent. **Close**, *JIN*: near in time or place, next to; approach; recently, lately; familiar. **Calamity**, *ZAI*: disaster from outside; fire, flood, plague, drought, blight, ruin; contrasts with blunder, *SHENG*, indicating personal fault. Ideogram: water and fire, elemental powers. **Indeed**, *YE*: see *Preceding Situation*.

SIX AT FIFTH

Threading fish.
Using house people's **favor**.
Without not Harvesting.

Comments
Using house people's **favor**.
Completing without surpassing indeed.

Fields of meaning

Thread, *GUAN*: string together; string of a thousand coins; series, sequence. **Fish**, *YU*: all scaly aquatic beings hidden in the water; symbol of abundance; connected with the Streaming Moment. **Use**, *YI*: see *Patterns of Wisdom*. **House**, *GONG*: residence, mansion; surround; fence, walls, roof. **People/person**, *REN*: humans individually and collectively; an individual; humankind. **Favor**, *CHONG*: receive or confer gifts; obtain grace, win favor; dote on a woman; affection, benevolence towards a subordinate. **Without not Harvesting**, *WU BU LI*: turning point where the balance is swinging from not Harvesting to actually Harvesting.

Complete, *ZHONG*: completion of a cycle that begins the next; entire, whole, all. Ideogram: silk cocoons, follow and ice, winter linking one year with the next. **Without**, *WU*: devoid of; there is not. **Surpass**, *YOU*: exceed, transgress; beyond measure, extraordinary; blame. **Indeed**, *YE*: see *Preceding Situation*.

NINE ABOVE

The **ripe fruit not taken-in**.
A **jun zi acquires** a **cart**.
The **small** in the **person strips** the **hut**.

Comments
A **jun zi acquires** a **cart**.
Commoners acquire a **place** to **carry indeed**.
The **small** in the **person strips** the **hut**.
Completing not permitted availing of **indeed**.

Fields of meaning

Ripe, *SHI*: mature, full-grown; great, eminent. **Fruit**, *GUO*: tree fruit; fruition, fruit of action; result, effect, product, conclusion; reliable, decisive. Ideogram: tree topped by a round fruit. **Not**, *BU*: common term of negation. **Take-in**, *SHI*: eat, drink, ingest, absorb, incorporate; food, nourishment. **Jun zi**: ideal of a person who orders his/her life in accordance with dao rather than willful intention, and uses divination in this spirit. **Acquire**, *DE*: obtain the desired object; possession; satisfied, fulfilled; it is permitted; agree with; wish for, desire covetously. Ideogram: go and obstacle, going through obstacles to the goal. **Cart**, *YU*: a vehicle and its carrying capacity; contain, hold, sustain. **Small**, *XIAO*: little, common, unimportant; adapting to what crosses your path; ability to move in harmony with the vicissitudes of life; contrasts with great, *DA*, self-imposed theme or goal. **Person/people**, *REN*: humans individually and collectively; an individual; humankind. **Strip**, *BO*: see *Image of the Situation*. **Hut**, *LU*: thatched hut, cottage, roadside lodge, hovel.

Commoners, *MIN*: common people, masses; working class supporting the social hierarchy; undeveloped potential in the individual. **Place**, *SUO*: position, location; residence, dwelling; where something belongs or comes from; habitual focus or object. **Carry**, *ZAI*: bear, carry with you; contain, sustain, support; load a ship or cart, cargo; fill in. **Indeed**, *YE*: see *Preceding Situation*. **Complete**, *ZHONG*: completion of a cycle that begins the next; entire, whole, all. Ideogram: silk cocoons, follow and ice, winter linking one year with the next. **Permit**, *KE*: possible because in harmony with an inherent principle; capable of; approve, authorize. Ideogram: mouth and breath, silent consent. **Avail**, *YONG*: use, employ for a specific purpose; take advantage of; benefit from; capacity. Ideogram: to divine and center, applying divination to central concerns.

Image Tradition

Stripping. **Stripped indeed**.
The **supple transforms** the **solid indeed**.

Not Harvesting: **possessing directed going**.
The **small** in the **person long-living indeed**.
Yielding and-also stopping it.
Overseeing symbols indeed.

A **jun zi honors** the **dissolving pause** to **overfill emptiness**.
Heaven moves indeed.

Fields of meaning

Strip, *BO*: see *Image of the Situation*. **Indeed**, *YE*: see *Preceding Situation*. **Supple**, *ROU*: quality of the opened lines; flexible, pliant, adaptable, tender. **Transform**,

BIAN: abrupt, radical passage from one state to another; transformation of opened and whole lines into each other in hexagrams; contrasts with change, *HUA*, gradual mutation. **Solid**, *GANG*: quality of the whole lines; firm, strong, unyielding, persisting.

Not Harvesting: possessing directed going, *BU LI YOU YOU WANG*: see *Image of the Situation*. **Small**, *XIAO*: little, common, unimportant; adapting to what crosses your path; ability to move in harmony with the vicissitudes of life; contrasts with great, *DA*, self-imposed theme or goal. **Person/people**, *REN*: humans individually and collectively; an individual; humankind. **Long-living**, *ZHANG*: enduring, lasting, constant; extended, long, large; senior, superior, greater; increase, prosper; respect, elevate. **Yield**, *SHUN*: give way, comply, agree, follow, obey; docile, flexible; bear produce, nourish, provide; Action of the trigram Field, *KUN*. **And-also**, *ER*: joins and contrasts two terms. **Stop**, *ZHI*: bring or come to a standstill, cease, terminate; Action of the trigram Bound, *GEN*. Ideogram: a foot stops walking. **It/belong**, *ZHI*: establishes between two terms a connection similar to the Saxon genitive, in which the second term belongs to the first one; at the end of a sentence it refers to something previously mentioned or implied. **Oversee**, *GUAN*: contemplate, observe from a distance; look at carefully, gaze at; a high place from where one sees far, monastery, observatory; intelligence, clairvoyance; scry, divine through liquid in a cup. Ideogram: sight and waterbird, aerial view. **Symbol**, *XIANG*: image invested with magic connecting visible and invisible; figure, form, shape, likeness; pattern, model; act, play, write. Ideogram: elephant (in ancient times the bones of a dead elephant used to be assembled to look like the living animal).

Jun zi: ideal of a person who orders his/her life in accordance with dao rather than willful intention, and uses divination in this spirit. **Honor**, *SHANG*: esteem, give high rank to, exalt, celebrate; rise, elevate; put one thing on top of another. **Dissolve**, *XIAO*: liquefy, melt, thaw; diminish, disperse; eliminate, exhaust. Ideogram: water dissolving differences. **Pause**, *XI*: breathe; rest, repose, a breathing-spell; suspended. **Overfill**, *YING*: fill completely; full, at the point of overflowing; excess, arrogance. Ideogram: vessel and overflow. **Empty**, *XU*: void; absence of images and concepts; vacant, insubstantial; empty yet fertile space. **Heaven**, *TIAN*: sky, firmament, heavens; the highest realm, situated above the human world, as opposed to the earth, *DI*, located below; Symbol of the trigram Energy, *QIAN*. Ideogram: great and the one above. **Move**, *XING*: move or move something; motivate; emotionally moving; walk, act, do. Ideogram: successive steps.

復

24 RETURN | *Fu*

The situation described by this hexagram is characterized by the re-emergence of something past, returning to a previous time or place or retracing a path in order to correct one's mistakes.

Image of the Situation

Return.
Growing.
Emerging, **entering**, **without affliction**.
Partners come, **without fault**.
Reversing: **returning** to **one's dao**.
The **seventh day comes return**.
Harvesting: **possessing directed going**.

Fields of meaning

Return, *FU*: go back, turn or lead back; recur, reappear, come again; restore, renew, recover; return to an earlier time or place. Ideogram: step and retrace a path. **Grow**, *HENG*: heavenly influence pervading and nourishing all things; prosper, succeed, expand, develop; effective, favorable; quality of summer and South, second stage of the Time Cycle. With the pronunciation *XIANG*: offer a sacrifice; offer a gift to a superior; accept, enjoy. **Emerge**, *CHU*: come out of, proceed from, spring from, issue forth; appear, be born; bear, generate; leave, flee; Action of the trigram Shake, *ZHEN*. Ideogram: stem with branches and leaves emerging. **Enter**, *RU*: penetrate, go into, enter on, encroach on; progress; put into; Action of the trigram Root, *SUN*. **Without**, *WU*: devoid of; there is not. **Affliction**, *JI*: sickness, disorder, defect, calamity, injury; poison, hate, dislike; cruel, jealous, envious. Ideogram: sickness and dart, a sudden affliction. **Partner**, *PENG*: companion, friend, peer; join, associate for mutual benefit; commercial venture; two equal or similar things. Ideogram: linked strings of cowries or coins. **Come**, *LAI*: approach in time or space; move toward, arrive at; future; contrasts with go, *WANG*, move away or become past. **Without fault**, *WU JIU*: no error or harm in the situation. **Reverse**, *FAN*: turn and move in the opposite direction; turn around or upside down (180 degrees); change to the opposite position; contrary. **One/one's**, *QI*: general third person pronoun and possessive adjective; also: it/its, he/his, she/her, they/their. **Dao**, *DAO*: way or path; ongoing process of being and the course it traces for each person or thing; ultimate reality, intrinsic nature; origin. Ideogram: go and head, opening a path. **Seven**, *QI*: number seven; seven planets; seventh day when moon changes from crescent to waxing; the Tangram game analyzes all forms in terms of seven basic shapes. **Day/sun**, *RI*: the sun and the time of a sun-cycle, a day. **Harvest**, *LI*: benefit, advantage, profit; realization; sharp, acute, insightful; quality of autumn and West, third stage of the Time Cycle. Ideogram: ripe grain and blade. **Possessing directed going**, *YOU YOU WANG*: having a goal or purpose, moving in a specific direction.

Outer and Inner Trigram

The upper trigram, **Space**, *KUN*, describes the outer aspects of the situation. It has the following associations: surface of the world; support of all existence, manifestation of Yin, where Energy or Yang activates all creation and destruction; all-involving service; earth; moon, wife, mother; rest, receptivity, docile obedience. Ideogram: terrestrial globe and stretch out. *Symbol*: earth, *DI*; the earth, ground on which the human world rests; basis of all things, nourishes all things; essential Yin. *Action*: yield, *SHUN*: give way, comply, agree, follow, obey; docile, flexible; bear produce, nourish, provide. In the family of trigrams *KUN* is the mother.

The lower trigram, **Shake**, *ZHEN*, describes the inner aspects of the situation. It has the following associations: arouse, excite, inspire; awe, alarm, trembling; thunder rising from the depth of the earth; fertilizing intrusion. Ideogram: excite and rain. *Symbol*: thunder, *LEI*, arousing power emerging from the depth of the earth. *Action*: stir-up, *DONG*, excite, influence, move, affect; work, take action; come out of the egg or the bud. Ideogram: strength and heavy, move weighty things. In the family of trigrams *ZHEN* is the eldest son.

Counter Hexagram

The Counter Hexagram of **Return** is hexagram 2, **Space**, which switches the emphasis from a re-emergence of the past to supporting all things and allowing them to become what they potentially are.

Preceding Situation

> **Beings not permitted** to **use completing using-up**.
> **Stripping exhausted above**, **reversing below**.
> To **anterior acquiescence belongs** the **use** of **return**.

Fields of meaning
Beings not permitted (to **use**), *WU BU KE (YI)*: it is not possible; no one is allowed; it is not in the nature of things. **Complete**, *ZHONG*: completion of a cycle that begins the next; entire, whole, all. Ideogram: silk cocoons, follow and ice, winter linking one year with the next. **Use-up**, *JIN*: exhaust, use all; an empty vessel; extremity, limit. **Strip**, *BO*: flay, peel, skin; remove, uncover; split, slice; reduce to essentials; degrade, decay; slaughter an animal. Ideogram: knife and carve, trenchant action. **Exhaust**, *QIONG*: bring to an end; limit, extremity; investigate exhaustively; destitute, indigent; end without a new beginning; distinct from complete, *ZHONG*, end of a cycle that begins the next one. Ideogram: cave and naked person, bent with disease or old age. **Above**, *SHANG*: anything above in all senses; higher, upper, outer; upper trigram. **Reverse**, *FAN*: see *Image of the Situation*. **Below**, *XIA*: anything below, in all senses; lower, inner; lower trigram. To **anterior acquiescence belongs** the **use** of, *GU SHOU ZHI YI*: understanding and accepting the preceding statement allows the consultant to make proper use of this hexagram. **Return**, *FU*: see *Image of the Situation*.

Hexagrams in Pairs

Stripping: **rotten indeed**.
Return: **reversing indeed**.

Fields of meaning
Strip, *BO*: see *Preceding Situation*. **Rotten**, *LAN*: corrupt, putrid, dirty, worn out; softened, crumbling. **Indeed**, *YE*: emphasizes and intensifies the previous statement. **Return**, *FU*: see *Image of the Situation*. **Reverse**, *FAN*: see *Image of the Situation*.

Additional Texts

Return: the **base belonging** to **actualizing-dao indeed**.
Return: the **small and-also marking-off with-respect-to beings**.
Return: **using** the **origin**'s **knowledge**.

Fields of meaning
Return, *FU*: see *Image of the Situation*. **Base**, *BEN*: root, trunk; origin, cause, foundation. Ideogram: tree with roots in the earth. **Belong/it**, *ZHI*: establishes between two terms a connection similar to the Saxon genitive, in which the second term belongs to the first one; at the end of a sentence it refers to something

previously mentioned or implied. **Actualize-dao**, *DE*: realize dao in action; power, virtue; ability to follow the course traced by the ongoing process of the cosmos. Ideogram: go, straight, and heart. Linked with acquire, *DE*: acquiring that which makes a being become what it is meant to be. **Indeed**, *YE*: see *Hexagrams in Pairs*. **Small**, *XIAO*: little, common, unimportant; adapting to what crosses your path; ability to move in harmony with the vicissitudes of life; contrasts with great, *DA*, self-imposed theme or goal. **And-also**, *ER*: joins and contrasts two terms. **Mark-off**, *BIAN*: distinguish by dividing; mark off a plot of land; discern, discriminate, differentiate; discuss and dispute; frame which divides a bed from its stand. Ideogram: knife and acrid, sharp division. **With-respect-to**, *YU*: in relation to, referring to, according to; in, at, until. **Being**, *WU*: creature, thing, any single being; matter, substance, essence; nature of things. **Use**, *YI*: see *Additional Texts*. **Origin**, *ZI*: source, beginning, ground; cause, reason, motive; tracing back to the source; oneself, by oneself; spontaneous, intrinsic. **Know**, *ZHI*: have knowledge of, perceive, experience, remember; know intimately; informed, aware, wise. Ideogram: arrow and mouth, words focused and swift.

Patterns of Wisdom

> **Thunder located** in the **earth**'s **center**. **Return**.
> The **earlier kings used culminating sun** to **bar** the **passages**.
> **Bargaining sojourners** used culminating sun **not** to **move**.
> The **crown prince** used culminating sun **not** to **inspect** on all **sides**.

Fields of meaning

Thunder, *LEI*: thunder; arousing power emerging from the depth of the earth; Symbol of the trigram Shake, *ZHEN*. **Locate**, *ZAI*: be at, be situated at, dwell, reside; in, within; involved with, in the process of. Ideogram: earth and persevere, a place on the earth. **Earth**, *DI*: the earth, ground on which the human world rests; basis of all things, nourishes all things; essential Yin; Symbol of the trigram Space, *KUN*. **Center**, *ZHONG*: inner, central; put in the center; middle, stable point enabling you to face inner and outer changes; middle line of a trigram. Ideogram: field divided in two equal parts. **Return**, *FU*: see *Image of the Situation*. **Earlier Kings**, *XIAN WANG*: ideal rulers of old; the golden age, primal time; mythical sages in harmony with nature. **Use**, *YI*: see *Additional Texts*. **Culminate**, *ZHI*: bring to the highest degree; arrive at the end or summit; superlative; reaching one's goal. **Sun/day**, *RI*: actual sun and the time of a sun-cycle, a day. **Bar**, *BI*: close a door, stop up a hole; obstruct, exclude, screen. Ideogram: door and hand, closing the door. **Passage**, *GUAN*: market gate, customs house, frontier post; limit, crisis, important point. **Bargain**, *SHANG*: argue over prices; consult, deliberate, do business; traveling merchants; hour before sunrise and sunset. Ideogram: stutter and sentences, repetitive speaking. **Sojourn**, *LÜ*: travel, stay in places other than your home; itinerant troops, temporary residents; visitor, guest, lodger. Ideogram: banner and people around it. **Not**, *BU*: common term of negation. **Move**, *XING*: move or move something; motivate; emotionally moving; walk, act, do. Ideogram: successive steps. **Crown prince**, *HOU*: sovereign; prince; empress, mother of an imperial prince. Ideogram: one, mouth and shelter, one with the sovereign's orders. **Inspect**, *XING*: examine, inquire, reflect, consider; visit. **Sides**, *FANG*: cardinal directions; surface of the earth extending to the four cardinal points; everywhere; limits, boundaries.

Transforming Lines

INITIAL NINE

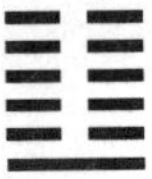

Not distancing return.
Without merely repenting.
Spring, significant.

Comments
To **not distancing belongs return.**
Using adjusting individuality indeed.

Fields of meaning

Not, *BU*: common term of negation. **Distance**, *YUAN*: far off, remote; keep at a distance; a long time, far away in time. Ideogram: go and a long way. **Return**, *FU*: see *Image of the Situation*. **Without**, *WU*: see *Image of the Situation*. **Merely**, *ZHI*: only, just, simply; respect, venerate. **Repent**, *HUI*: regret, dissatisfaction with past conduct inducing a change of heart; proceeds from abashment, *LIN*, shame and confusion at having lost the right way. **Spring**, *YUAN*: source, origin, head; arise, begin; first generating impulse; great, excellent; quality of springtime and East, first stage of the Time Cycle. **Significant**, *JI*: leads to the experience of meaning; favorable, propitious, appropriate. Ideogram: scholar and mouth, wise words of a sage.

Belong/it, *ZHI*: see *Additional Texts*. **Use**, *YI*: see *Additional Texts*. **Adjust**, *XIU*: regulate, repair, clean up, renovate. **Individuality**, *SHEN*: total person: psyche, body and lifespan; character, virtue, duty, pregnancy; distinct from body, *GONG*, physical being. **Indeed**, *YE*: see *Hexagrams in Pairs*.

Six at Second

Relaxing return.
Significant.

Comments
To **relaxing return belongs significance.**
Below using humanity indeed.

Fields of meaning

Relax, *XIU*: rest, stop temporarily; resign, retire; advantage, prosperity. Ideogram: person leaning on a tree. **Return,** *FU*: see *Image of the Situation.* **Significant,** *JI*: leads to the experience of meaning; favorable, propitious, appropriate. Ideogram: scholar and mouth, wise words of a sage.

Belong/it, *ZHI*: see *Additional Texts.* **Below,** *XIA*: see *Preceding Situation.* **Use,** *YI*: see *Additional Texts.* **Humanity,** *REN*: fellow-feeling, regard for others; benevolence, kindness, compassion; fulfill social duties. **Indeed,** *YE*: see *Hexagrams in Pairs.*

Six at Third

Imminent return. Adversity.
Without fault.

Comments
To **imminent return belongs adversity.**
Righteous, without fault indeed.

Fields of meaning

Imminent, *PIN*: on the brink of; pressing, urgent; often, repeatedly. **Return,** *FU*: see *Image of the Situation.* **Adversity,** *LI*: danger, hardship, severe; threat or difficulty that must be encountered, rather than avoided; grinding stone; polish, sharpen; a challenge that strengthens and perfects the character; stimulate, excite; cruel demon. **Without fault,** *WU JIU*: see *Image of the Situation.*

Belong/it, *ZHI*: see *Additional Texts.* **Righteous,** *YI*: proper, just, virtuous, upright; the heart that rules itself; benevolent, loyal, devoted to public good. **Indeed,** *YE*: see *Hexagrams in Pairs.*

SIX AT FOURTH

The **center moving**, **solitary return**.

Comments

The **center moving**, **solitary return**.
Using adhering to **dao indeed**.

Fields of meaning

Center, *ZHONG*: see *Patterns of Wisdom*. Move, *XING*: see *Patterns of Wisdom*. Solitary, *DI*: alone, single; isolated, abandoned. Return, *FU*: see *Image of the Situation*.

Use, *YI*: see *Additional Texts*. Adhere, *CONG*: follow, agree with, comply with, obey; join a doctrine, school, or person; servant, follower. Ideogram: two men walking, one following the other. Dao, *DAO*: see *Image of the Situation*. Indeed, *YE*: see *Hexagrams in Pairs*.

SIX AT FIFTH

Magnanimous return.
Without repenting.

Comments

Magnanimous return, **without repenting**.
The **center uses** the **origin** from the **predecessors indeed**.

Fields of meaning

Magnanimous, *DUN*: generous, honest, sincere; important, wealthy; honor, increase; firm, solid. Ideogram: strike and accept, warrior magnanimous in giving and receiving blows. Return, *FU*: see *Image of the Situation*. Without, *WU*: see *Image of the Situation*. Repent, *HUI*: regret, dissatisfaction with past conduct inducing a change of heart; proceeds from abashment, *LIN*, shame and confusion at having lost the right way.

Center, *ZHONG*: see *Patterns of Wisdom*. Use, *YI*: see *Additional Texts*. Origin, *ZI*: source, beginning, ground; cause, reason, motive; tracing back to the source; oneself, by oneself; spontaneous, intrinsic. Predecessor, *KAO*: deceased father or grandfather; ancestors, the ancients; aged, long-lived; interrogate, test, verify. Ideogram: old and ingenious, wise old man. Indeed, *YE*: see *Hexagrams in Pairs*.

Six Above

Deluding return. Pitfall.
Possessing calamity and **blunder.**
Availing of **moving legions.**
Completing possesses great destruction.
Using one's city's chief: pitfall.
Culminating tending-towards ten years not controlling disciplining.

Comments
To the **deluding return belongs pitfall.**
Reversing the **chief's dao indeed.**

Fields of meaning
Delude, *MI*: bewitch, fascinate, deceive; confused, stupefied, infatuated; blinded by vice. Return, *FU*: see *Image of the Situation*. Pitfall, *XIONG*: unfortunate situation, in which the flow of life and spirit is blocked and the experience of meaning is lost; stuck and exposed to danger; inappropriate attitude. Ideogram: person in a pit. Possess, *YOU*: general term indicating possession; have, own, be endowed with. Calamity, *ZAI*: disaster from outside; fire, flood, plague, drought, blight, ruin; contrasts with blunder, *SHENG*, indicating personal fault. Ideogram: water and fire, elemental powers. Blunder, *SHENG*: mistake due to ignorance or fault; contrasts with calamity, *ZAI*, disaster from without. Ideogram: eye and growth, a film clouding sight. Avail, *YONG*: use, employ for a specific purpose; take advantage of; benefit from; capacity. Ideogram: to divine and center, applying divination to central concerns. Move, *XING*: see *Patterns of Wisdom*. Legions, *SHI*: army, troops; leader, general, model, master; organize, make functional; take as a model, imitate, follow. Ideogram: heap and whole, turn confusion into a functional unit. Complete, *ZHONG*: see *Preceding Situation*. Possess, *YOU*: general term indicating possession; have, own, be endowed with. Great, *DA*: big, noble, important, very; orient the will toward a self-imposed goal, impose direction; ability to lead or guide one's life; contrasts with small, *XIAO*, flexible adaptation to what crosses one's path. Destroy, *BAI*: ruin, defeat, failure; violate, subvert, decompose. Use, *YI*: see *Additional Texts*. One/one's, *QI*: see *Image of the Situation*. City, *GUO*: city, state, country, nation; area of only human constructions; first of the territorial zones: city, suburbs, countryside, forest. Chief, *JUN*: prince, ruler; lead, direct; wise person. Ideogram: mouth and direct, giving orders. Culminate, *ZHI*: see *Patterns of Wisdom*. Tend-towards, *YU*: move toward without necessarily reaching, in the direction of. Ten, *SHI*: number ten; goal and end of reckoning;

whole, complete, all; entire, perfected. Ideogram: East–West line crosses North–South line, a grid that contains all. **Year**, *NIAN*: year, annual; harvest; years revolved, years of age. **Not**, *BU*: common term of negation. **Control**, *KE*: be in charge; capable of, able to, adequate; check, obstruct, repress. Ideogram: roof beams supporting a house. **Discipline**, *ZHENG*: subjugate vassals, reduce to order; punishing expedition. Ideogram: step and correct, a rectifying move.

Belong/it, *ZHI*: see *Additional Texts*. **Reverse**, *FAN*: see *Image of the Situation*. **Dao**, *DAO*: see *Image of the Situation*. **Indeed**, *YE*: see *Hexagrams in Pairs*.

Image Tradition

Return, **Growing**.
Solid reversing.
Stirring-up and-also using yielding movement.
That uses emerging, **entering**, **without affliction**.

Partners come, **without fault**.
Reversing: **returning** to **one's dao**.
The **seventh day comes return**.
Heaven moves indeed.

Harvesting: **possessing directed going**.
The **solid**: **long-living indeed**.
Return to **one's viewing** the **heart belonging** to **heaven** and **earth reached**.

Fields of meaning
Return, Growing, *FU HENG*: see *Image of the Situation*. **Solid**, *GANG*: quality of the whole lines; firm, strong, unyielding, persisting. **Reverse**, *FAN*: see *Image of the Situation*. **Stir-up**, *DONG*: excite, influence, move, affect; work, take action; come out of the egg or the bud; Action of the trigram Shake, *ZHEN*. Ideogram: strength and heavy, move weighty things. **And-also**, *ER*: see *Additional Texts*. **Use**, *YI*: see *Additional Texts*. **Yield**, *SHUN*: give way, comply, agree, follow, obey; docile, flexible; bear produce, nourish, provide; Action of the trigram Field, *KUN*. **Move**, *XING*: see *Patterns of Wisdom*. **That**, *SHI*: refers to the preceding statement. **Emerging, entering, without affliction**, *CHU RU WU JI*: see *Image of the Situation*.

Partners come, without fault, *PENG LAI WU JIU*: see *Image of the Situation*. **Reversing: returning** to **one's dao**, *FAN FU QI DAO*: see *Image of the Situation*. The **seventh day comes return**, *QI RI LAI FU*: see *Image of the Situation*. **Heaven**, *TIAN*: sky, firmament, heavens; the highest realm, situated above the human world, as opposed to the earth, *DI*, located below; Symbol of the trigram Energy, *QIAN*. Ideogram: great and the one above. **Indeed**, *YE*: see *Hexagrams in Pairs*.

Harvesting: possessing directed going, *LI YOU YOU WANG*: see *Image of the Situation*. **Long-living**, *ZHANG*: enduring, lasting, constant; extended, long, large; senior, superior, greater; increase, prosper; respect, elevate. **View**, *JIAN*: vision in all its aspects: seeing, being visible, forming mental images; visit, call on, consult. Ideogram: eye above person, active and receptive sight. **Heart**, *XIN*: the heart as center of being; seat of mind, imagination and affect; moral nature; source of desires, intentions, will. **Belong/it**, *ZHI*: see *Additional Texts*. **Earth**, *DI*: see *Patterns of Wisdom*. **Reach**, *HU*: arrive at a goal; move toward and achieve; to, at, in; distinct from tend-towards, *YOU*.

无妄 ䷘

25 WITHOUT ENTANGLEMENT
Wu Wang

The situation described by this hexagram is characterized by maintaining a sincere and correct attitude, keeping aloof from events which might entangle one in error, confusion or recklessness.

Image of the Situation

> **Without entanglement.**
> **Spring, Growing, Harvesting, Trial.**
> **One's in-no-way correcting possesses blunder.**
> **Not Harvesting: possessing directed going.**

Fields of meaning

Without, *WU*: devoid of; there is not. Entangle, *WANG*: embroil; caught up, involved; disorder, incoherence; foolish, wild, reckless; false, brutish behavior; vain, idle, futile. Spring, Growing, Harvesting, Trial, *YUAN HENG LI ZHEN*: Spring, Growing, Harvesting and Trial are the four stages of the Time Cycle, the model for all dynamic processes. They indicate that your question is connected to the cycle as a whole rather than a part of it. One/one's, *QI*: general third person pronoun and possessive adjective; also: it/its, he/his, she/her, they/their. In-no-way, *FEI*: strong negative; not so; bandit, rebel; unjust, immoral. Ideogram: a box filled with opposition. Correct, *ZHENG*: rectify deviation or one-sidedness; proper, straight, exact, regular; constant, rule, model. Ideogram: stop and one, hold to one thing. Possess, *YOU*: general term indicating possession; have, own, be endowed with. Blunder, *SHENG*: mistake due to ignorance or fault; contrasts with calamity, *ZAI*, disaster from without. Ideogram: eye and growth, a film clouding sight. Not, *BU*: common term of negation. Harvest, *LI*: benefit, advantage, profit; realization; sharp, acute, insightful; quality of autumn and West, third stage of the Time Cycle. Ideogram: ripe grain and blade. Possessing directed going, *YOU YOU WANG*: having a goal or purpose, moving in a specific direction.

Outer and Inner Trigram

The upper trigram, **Energy/parch**, *QIAN/GAN*, describes the outer aspects of the situation. It has the following associations: unceasing forward movement, dynamic, enduring, untiring; spirit power, manifestation of Yang, that activates all creation and destruction in Space; heaven, sovereign, father. With the pronunciation GAN: parch, dry up, burn, exhaust. Ideogram: sprouts or vapors rising from the ground and sunlight, both fecundating moisture and scorching drought. *Symbol*: heaven, *TIAN*; sky, firmament, heavens; the highest realm, situated above the human world, as opposed to the earth, *DI*, located below. Ideogram: great and the one above. *Action*: persist, *JIAN*; tenacious, persevering; strong, robust, dynamic; constant as the motion of heavenly bodies in their orbits. In the family of trigrams *QIAN* is the father.

The lower trigram, **Shake**, *ZHEN*, describes the inner aspects of the situation. It has the following associations: arouse, excite, inspire; awe, alarm, trembling; thunder rising from the depth of the earth; fertilizing intrusion. Ideogram: excite and rain. *Symbol*: thunder, *LEI*, arousing power emerging from the depth of the earth. *Action*: stir-up, *DONG*, excite, influence, move, affect; work, take action; come out of the egg or the bud. Ideogram: strength and heavy, move weighty things. In the family of trigrams *ZHEN* is the eldest son.

Counter Hexagram

The Counter Hexagram of **Without Entanglement** is hexagram 53, **Infiltrating**, which switches the emphasis from abstaining from involvement to extending one's influence by a gradual and steady penetration.

Preceding Situation

> **Returning**, by **consequence not entangled actually**.
> To **anterior acquiescence belongs** the **use** of **without entanglement**.

Fields of meaning

Return, *FU*: go back, turn or lead back; recur, reappear, come again; restore, renew, recover; return to an earlier time or place. Ideogram: step and retrace a path. Consequence, *ZE*: reason, cause, result; rule, law, pattern, standard; therefore; very strong connection. Not, *BU*: common term of negation. Entangle, *WANG*: see *Image of the Situation*. Actually, *YI*: truly, really, at present. Ideogram: a dart and done, strong intention fully expressed. To anterior acquiescence belongs the use of, *GU SHOU ZHI YI*: understanding and accepting the preceding statement allows the consultant to make proper use of this hexagram. **Without**, *WU*: see *Image of the Situation*.

Hexagrams in Pairs

> The **great accumulating**: **season indeed**.
> **Without entanglement**: **calamity indeed**.

Fields of meaning

Great, *DA*: big, noble, important, very; orient the will toward a self-imposed goal, impose direction; ability to lead or guide one's life; contrasts with small, *XIAO*, flexible adaptation to what crosses one's path. **Accumulate**, *CHU*: retain, hoard, gather, herd together; control, restrain; domesticate, tame, train; raise, feed, sustain, bring up. Ideogram: field and black, fertile black soil, accumulated through retaining silt. **Season**, *SHI*: quality of the time; the right time, opportune, in harmony; planning in accord with the time; season of the year. Ideogram: sun and temple, sacred time. **Indeed**, *YE*: emphasizes and intensifies the previous statement. **Without entanglement**, *WU WANG*: see *Image of the Situation*. **Calamity**, *ZAI*: disaster from outside; fire, flood, plague, drought, blight, ruin; contrasts with blunder, *SHENG*, indicating personal fault. Ideogram: water and fire, elemental powers.

Patterns of Wisdom

> **Below heaven thunder moves**. **Beings associate without entanglement**.
> The **earlier kings used** the **luxuriance suiting** the **season** to **nurture** the **myriad beings**.

Fields of meaning

Below, *XIA*: anything below, in all senses; lower, inner; lower trigram. **Heaven**, *TIAN*: sky, firmament, heavens; the highest realm, situated above the human world, as opposed to the earth, *DI*, located below; Symbol of the trigram Energy, *QIAN*. Ideogram: great and the one above. **Thunder**, *LEI*: thunder; arousing power emerging from the depth of the earth; Symbol of the trigram Shake, *ZHEN*. **Move**, *XING*: move or move something; motivate; emotionally moving; walk, act, do. Ideogram: successive steps. **Being**, *WU*: creature, thing, any single being; matter, substance, essence; nature of things. **Associate**, *YU*: consort with, combine; companions; group, band, company; agree with, comply, help; in favor of. Ideogram: a pair of hands reaching downward meets a pair of hands reaching upward, helpful association. **Without entanglement**, *WU WANG*: see *Image of the*

Situation. **Earlier Kings**, *XIAN WANG*: ideal rulers of old; the golden age, primal time; mythical sages in harmony with nature. **Use**, *YI*: by means of; owing to; make use of, employ. **Luxuriance**, *MAO*: thriving, flourishing, exuberant; highly developed, elegant. Ideogram: plants and flourish. **Suit**, *DUI*: correspond to, agree with; consistent; pair; parallel sentences in poetic language. **Season**, *SHI*: see *Hexagrams in Pairs.* **Nurture**, *YU*: give birth; bring up, rear, raise. **Myriad**, *WAN*: ten thousand; countless, many, everyone. Ideogram: swarm of insects.

Transforming Lines

INITIAL NINE

Without entanglement.
Going, significant.

Comments
To **without entanglement belongs going.**
Acquiring purpose indeed.

Fields of meaning
Without entanglement, *WU WANG*: see *Image of the Situation.* **Go**, *WANG*: move away in time or space, depart; become past; dead, gone; contrasts with come, *LAI*, approach in time or space. **Significant**, *JI*: leads to the experience of meaning; favorable, propitious, appropriate. Ideogram: scholar and mouth, wise words of a sage.

Belong/it, *ZHI*: establishes between two terms a connection similar to the Saxon genitive, in which the second term belongs to the first one; at the end of a sentence it refers to something previously mentioned or implied. **Acquire**, *DE*: obtain the desired object; possession; satisfied, fulfilled; it is permitted; agree with; wish for, desire covetously. Ideogram: go and obstacle, going through obstacles to the goal. **Purpose**, *ZHI*: focus of mind and heart; intention, will, inclination; continuity in the direction of life. Ideogram: heart and scholar, high inner resolve. **Indeed**, *YE*: see *Hexagrams in Pairs.*

SIX AT SECOND

Not tilling the **crop. Not clearing** the **plow-land.**
By **consequence, Harvesting: possessing directed going.**

Comments

Not tilling the **crop**. **Not-yet affluence indeed**.

Fields of meaning

Not, *BU*: common term of negation. **Till**, *GENG*: plow, cultivate; labor. **Crop**, *HUO*: grain gathered in autumn; reap, harvest. **Clear**, *ZI*: cultivate wild or overgrown land; reclaim. **Plow-land**, *YU*: newly opened fields, after two or three years plowing. **Consequence**, *ZE*: see *Preceding Situation*. **Harvest**, *LI*: see *Image of the Situation*. **Possessing directed going**, *YOU YOU WANG*: see *Image of the Situation*.

Not-yet, *WEI*: temporal negative indicating that something is expected to happen but has not yet occurred. **Affluence**, *FU*: rich, abundant; wealth; enrich, provide for; flow toward, accrue. **Indeed**, *YE*: see *Hexagrams in Pairs*.

SIX AT THIRD

To **without entanglement belongs calamity**.
Maybe to **attaching belongs cattle**.
To **moving people belongs acquiring**.
To **capital**'s **people belongs calamity**.

Comments

Moving people acquire cattle.
Capital's **people**, **calamity indeed**.

Fields of meaning

Without entanglement, *WU WANG*: see *Image of the Situation*. **Belong/it**, *ZHI*: establishes between two terms a connection similar to the Saxon genitive, in which the second term belongs to the first one; at the end of a sentence it refers to something previously mentioned or implied. **Calamity**, *ZAI*: see *Hexagrams in Pairs*. **Maybe**, *HUO*: possible but not certain, perhaps. **Attach**, *XI*: fasten to, bind, tie; retain, continue; keep in mind; emotional bond. **Cattle**, *NIU*: ox, bull, cow, calf; power and strength of work animals; stubborn. **Move**, *XING*: see *Patterns of Wisdom*. **People/person**, *REN*: humans individually and collectively; an individual; humankind. **Acquire**, *DE*: obtain the desired object; possession; satisfied, fulfilled; it is permitted; agree with; wish for, desire covetously. Ideogram: go and obstacle, going through obstacles to the goal. **Capital**, *YI*: populous fortified city, center and symbol of the region it rules. Ideogram: enclosure and official seal.

Indeed, *YE*: see *Hexagrams in Pairs*.

NINE AT FOURTH

Permitting Trial.
Without fault.

Comments
Permitting Trial, without fault.
Firmly possessing it indeed.

Fields of meaning
Permit, *KE*: possible because in harmony with an inherent principle; capable of; approve, authorize. Ideogram: mouth and breath, silent consent. **Trial**, *ZHEN*: inquiry by divination and its result; righteous, firm; separating wheat from chaff; the kernel, the proven core; quality of winter and North, fourth stage of the Time Cycle. Ideogram: pearl and divination. **Without fault**, *WU JIU*: no error or harm in the situation.

Firm, *GU*: steady, solid, strong, secure; constant, fixed. Ideogram: old and enclosure, long preserved. **Possess**, *YOU*: see *Image of the Situation*. **It/belong**, *ZHI*: establishes between two terms a connection similar to the Saxon genitive, in which the second term belongs to the first one; at the end of a sentence it refers to something previously mentioned or implied. **Indeed**, *YE*: see *Hexagrams in Pairs*.

NINE AT FIFTH

To **without entanglement belongs affliction.**
No simple possesses joy.

Comments
To **without entanglement belong simples.**
Not permitted testing indeed.

Fields of meaning
Without entanglement, *WU WANG*: see *Image of the Situation*. **Belong/it**, *ZHI*: establishes between two terms a connection similar to the Saxon genitive, in which the second term belongs to the first one; at the end of a sentence it refers to something previously mentioned or implied. **Affliction**, *JI*: sickness, disorder, defect, calamity, injury; poison, hate, dislike; cruel, jealous, envious. Ideogram: sickness and dart, a sudden affliction. **No**, *WU*: common term of negation. **Simples**, *YAO*: medicinal herbs, plants used as remedies; herbal healing; medicine; poison. **Possess**, *YOU*: see *Image of the Situation*. **Joy/rejoice**, *XI*: delight, exult;

cheerful, merry. Ideogram: joy (music) and mouth, expressing joy.

Not, *BU*: common term of negation. **Permit**, *KE*: possible because in harmony with an inherent principle; capable of; approve, authorize. Ideogram: mouth and breath, silent consent. **Test**, *SHI*: try, experiment; compare; use, employ. **Indeed**, *YE*: see *Hexagrams in Pairs*.

NINE ABOVE

Without entanglement.
Moving possesses blunder.
Without direction Harvesting.

Comments
To **without entanglement belongs movement**.
To **exhaustion belongs calamity indeed**.

Fields of meaning
Without entanglement, *WÚ WANG*: see *Image of the Situation*. **Move**, *XING*: see *Patterns of Wisdom*. **Possess**, *YOU*: see *Image of the Situation*. **Blunder**, *SHENG*: see *Image of the Situation*. **Without direction Harvesting**, *WU YOU LI*: in order to take advantage of the situation, do not impose a direction on events.

Belong/it, *ZHI*: establishes between two terms a connection similar to the Saxon genitive, in which the second term belongs to the first one; at the end of a sentence it refers to something previously mentioned or implied. **Exhaust**, *QIONG*: bring to an end; limit, extremity; investigate exhaustively; destitute, indigent; end without a new beginning; distinct from complete, *ZHONG*, end of a cycle that begins the next one. Ideogram: cave and naked person, bent with disease or old age. **Calamity**, *ZAI*: see *Hexagrams in Pairs*. **Indeed**, *YE*: see *Hexagrams in Pairs*.

Image Tradition

Without entanglement.
A **solid originating** from the **outside comes**.
And-also activates a **lord with-respect-to** the **inside**.
Stirring-up and-also persisting.

The **solid** in the **center and-also corresponding**.
The **great**'s **Growing uses correcting**.
Fate belonging to **heaven indeed**.

One's in-no-way correcting possesses blunder.
Not Harvesting: possessing directed going.
To **without entanglement belongs going.**
Is it actually?
Heavenly fate not shielding.
Moving actually in-fact.

Fields of meaning

Without entanglement, *WU WANG*: see *Image of the Situation*. **Solid**, *GANG*: quality of the whole lines; firm, strong, unyielding, persisting. **Origin**, *ZI*: source, beginning, ground; cause, reason, motive; tracing back to the source; oneself, by oneself; spontaneous, intrinsic. **Outside**, *WAI*: outer, external; unfamiliar, foreign; ignore, reject; work done outside the home; the upper trigram as indication of the outer aspects of the situation. **Come**, *LAI*: approach in time or space; move toward, arrive at; future; contrasts with go, *WANG*, move away or become past. **And-also**, *ER*: joins and contrasts two terms. **Activate**, *WEI*: act or cause to act; do, make, manage, make active; be, become; attend to, help; because of. **Lord**, *ZHU*: ruler, master, chief, authority; host; domination in the cycle of the Five Transformative Moments. Ideogram: lamp and flame, giving light. **With-respect-to**, *YU*: in relation to, referring to, according to; in, at, until. **Inside**, *NEI*: within, inner, interior; inside of the house and those who work there, particularly women; inside of the body, inner organs; the lower trigram, as opposed to outside, *WAI*, the upper. Ideogram: border and enter. **Stir-up**, *DONG*: excite, influence, move, affect; work, take action; come out of the egg or the bud; Action of the trigram Shake, *ZHEN*. Ideogram: strength and heavy, move weighty things. **Persist**, *JIAN*: tenacious, persevering; strong, robust, dynamic; constant as the motion of heavenly bodies in their orbits; Action of the trigram Force, *QIAN*.

Center, *ZHONG*: inner, central; put in the center; middle, stable point enabling you to face inner and outer changes; middle line of a trigram. Ideogram: field divided in two equal parts. Correspond, *YING*: be in agreement or harmony; proper, suitable; resonate together, answer to; relation between the lines (1 and 4, 2 and 5, 3 and 6) when they form the pair opened and whole, supple and solid. Ideogram: heart and obey. Great, *DA*: see *Hexagrams in Pairs*. Grow, *HENG*: heavenly influence pervading and nourishing all things; prosper, succeed, expand, develop; effective, favorable; quality of summer and South, second stage of the Time Cycle. With the pronunciation *XIANG*: offer a sacrifice; offer a gift to a superior; accept, enjoy. Use, *YI*: see *Patterns of Wisdom*. Correct, *ZHENG*: see *Image of the Situation*. Fate, *MING*: individual destiny; birth and death as limits of life; issue orders with authority; consult the gods. Ideogram: mouth and order, words with heavenly authority. Belong/it, *ZHI*: establishes between two terms a connection similar to the Saxon genitive, in which the second term belongs to the first one; at the end of a sentence it refers to something previously mentioned or implied. **Heaven**, *TIAN*: see *Patterns of Wisdom*. **Indeed**, *YE*: see *Hexagrams in Pairs*.

One's in-no-way correcting possesses blunder, *QI FEI ZHENG YOU SHENG*: see *Image of the Situation*. **Not Harvesting: possessing directed going**, *BU LI YOU YOU WANG*: see *Image of the Situation*. **Go**, *WANG*: move away in time or space, depart; become past; dead, gone; contrasts with come, *LAI*, approach in time or space. **Is?**, *HE*: ask, inquire; what? which? who? how? why? where? an interrogative particle, often introducing a rhetorical question: is it? is it not? **It/belong**, *ZHI*: establishes between two terms a connection similar to the Saxon genitive, in which the second term belongs to the first one; at the end of a sentence it refers to something previously mentioned or implied. **Actually**, *YI*: truly, really, at present. Ideogram: a dart and done, strong intention fully expressed. **Not**, *BU*: common term of negation. **Shield**, *YOU*: heavenly kindness and protection. Ideogram: numinous and right hand, spirit power. **Move**, *XING*: see *Patterns of Wisdom*. **In-fact**, *ZAI*: emphatic exclamation; truly, indeed.

大畜

26 THE GREAT ACCUMULATING *Da Chu*

The situation described by this hexagram is characterized by a central idea or long-term goal, around which a wealth of experiences accumulate.

Image of the Situation

> The **great accumulating**.
> **Harvesting**, **Trial**.
> **Not** in the **household taking-in**. **Significant**.
> **Harvesting**: **wading** the **great river**.

Fields of meaning

Great, *DA*: big, noble, important, very; orient the will toward a self-imposed goal, impose direction; ability to lead or guide one's life; contrasts with small, *XIAO*, flexible adaptation to what crosses one's path. **Accumulate**, *CHU*: retain, hoard, gather, herd together; control, restrain; domesticate, tame, train; raise, feed, sustain, bring up. Ideogram: field and black, fertile black soil, accumulated through retaining silt. **Harvest**, *LI*: benefit, advantage, profit; realization; sharp, acute, insightful; quality of autumn and West, third stage of the Time Cycle. Ideogram: ripe grain and blade. **Trial**, *ZHEN*: inquiry by divination and its result; righteous, firm; separating wheat from chaff; the kernel, the proven core; quality of winter and North, fourth stage of the Time Cycle. Ideogram: pearl and divination. **Not**, *BU*: common term of negation. **Household**, *JIA*: home, house; family; dwell, reside; domestic, within doors; shop, school, doctrine. Ideogram: roof and pig or dog, the most valued domestic animals, living under the same roof with the family. **Take-in**, *SHI*: eat, drink, ingest, absorb, incorporate; food, nourishment. **Significant**, *JI*: leads to the experience of meaning; favorable, propitious, appropriate. Ideogram: scholar and mouth, wise words of a sage. **Wading** the **great river**, *SHE DA CHUAN*: enter the stream of life with a goal or purpose; embark on a significant enterprise.

Outer and Inner Trigram

The upper trigram, **Bound**, *GEN*, describes the outer aspects of the situation. It has the following associations: limit, frontier; obstacle that prevents from seeing further; stop; still, quiet, motionless; confine, enclose; mountain, sunset, beginning of winter; solid, steady, unshakable; straight, hard, adamant, obstinate. *Symbol*: mountain, *SHAN*, large, immense; limit, boundary. Ideogram: three peaks, a mountain range. *Action*: stop, *ZHI*, bring or come to a standstill, cease, terminate. Ideogram: a foot stops walking. In the family of trigrams *GEN* is the youngest son.

The lower trigram, **Energy/parch**, *QIAN/GAN*, describes the inner aspects of the situation. It has the following associations: unceasing forward movement, dynamic, enduring, untiring; spirit power, manifestation of Yang, that activates all creation and destruction in Space; heaven, sovereign, father. With the pronunciation *GAN*: parch, dry up, burn, exhaust. Ideogram: sprouts or vapors rising from the ground and sunlight, both fecundating moisture and scorching drought. *Symbol*: heaven, *TIAN*; sky, firmament, heavens; the highest realm, situated above the human world, as opposed to the earth, *DI*, located below. Ideogram: great and the one above. *Action*: persist, *JIAN*; tenacious, persevering; strong, robust, dynamic; constant as the motion of heavenly bodies in their orbits. In the family of trigrams *QIAN* is the father.

Counter Hexagram

The Counter Hexagram of **The Great Accumulating** is hexagram 54, **Converting Maidenhood**, which switches the emphasis from an accumulation of experiences around a central goal to realizing one's nature by simply accepting one's allotted destiny.

Preceding Situation

> **Possessing without entanglement**, **therefore afterwards permitted accumulating**.
> To **anterior acquiescence belongs** the **use** of the **great accumulating**.

Fields of meaning

Possess, *YOU*: general term indicating possession; have, own, be endowed with. Without, *WU*: devoid of; there is not. Entangle, *WANG*: embroil; caught up, involved; disorder, incoherence; foolish, wild, reckless; false, brutish behavior; vain, idle, futile. Therefore, *RAN*: thus, so it is; truly, certainly. After(wards)/later, *HOU*: come after in time, subsequent; put oneself after;

behind, back, draw back; the second; attendants, heirs, successors, posterity. **Permit**, *KE*: possible because in harmony with an inherent principle; capable of; approve, authorize. Ideogram: mouth and breath, silent consent. **Accumulate**, *CHU*: see *Image of the Situation*. To **anterior acquiescence belongs** the **use** of, *GU SHOU ZHI YI*: understanding and accepting the preceding statement allows the consultant to make proper use of this hexagram. **Great**, *DA*: see *Image of the Situation*.

Hexagrams in Pairs

> The **great accumulating**: **season indeed**.
> **Without entanglement**: **calamity indeed**.

Fields of meaning

The **great accumulating**, *DA CHU*: see *Image of the Situation*. **Season**, *SHI*: quality of the time; the right time, opportune, in harmony; planning in accord with the time; season of the year. Ideogram: sun and temple, sacred time. **Indeed**, *YE*: emphasizes and intensifies the previous statement. **Without**, *WU*: see *Preceding Situation*. **Entangle**, *WANG*: see *Preceding Situation*. **Calamity**, *ZAI*: disaster from outside; fire, flood, plague, drought, blight, ruin; contrasts with blunder, *SHENG*, indicating personal fault. Ideogram: water and fire, elemental powers.

Patterns of Wisdom

> **Heaven located** in the **mountain**'s **center**. The **great accumulating**.
> A **jun zi uses** the **numerous recorded preceding words** to **go** and **move**.
> And **uses accumulating one's actualizing-dao**.

Fields of meaning

Heaven, *TIAN*: sky, firmament, heavens; the highest realm, situated above the human world, as opposed to the earth, *DI*, located below; Symbol of the trigram Energy, *QIAN*. Ideogram: great and the one above. **Locate**, *ZAI*: be at, be situated at, dwell, reside; in, within; involved with, in the process of. Ideogram: earth and persevere, a place on the earth. **Mountain**, *SHAN*: mountain; large, immense; limit, boundary; Symbol of the trigram Bound, *GEN*. Ideogram: three peaks, a mountain range. **Center**, *ZHONG*: inner, central; put in the center; middle, stable point enabling you to face inner and outer changes; middle line of a trigram. Ideogram: field divided in two equal parts. The **great accumulating**, *DA CHU*:

see *Image of the Situation*. **Jun zi**: ideal of a person who orders his/her life in accordance with dao rather than willful intention, and uses divination in this spirit. **Use**, *YI*: by means of; owing to; make use of, employ. **Numerous**, *DUO*: great number, many; often. **Record**, *SHI*: write down, inscribe; learn, memorize, know; annals, monuments. **Precede**, *QIAN*: before, earlier; anterior, former, ancient; ahead, in front. **Word**, *YAN*: spoken word, speech, saying; talk, discuss, address; name, signify. Ideogram: mouth and rising vapor. **Go**, *WANG*: move away in time or space, depart; become past; dead, gone; contrasts with come, *LAI*, approach in time or space. **Move**, *XING*: move or move something; motivate; emotionally moving; walk, act, do. Ideogram: successive steps. **One/one's**, *QI*: general third person pronoun and possessive adjective; also: it/its, he/his, she/her, they/their. **Actualize-dao**, *DE*: realize dao in action; power, virtue; ability to follow the course traced by the ongoing process of the cosmos. Ideogram: go, straight, and heart. Linked with acquire, *DE*: acquiring that which makes a being become what it is meant to be.

Transforming Lines

INITIAL NINE

Possessing adversity.
Harvesting: climaxing.

Comments
Possessing adversity, Harvesting, climaxing.
Not opposing calamity indeed.

Fields of meaning
Possess, *YOU*: see *Preceding Situation*. **Adversity**, *LI*: danger, hardship, severe; threat or difficulty that must be encountered, rather than avoided; grinding stone; polish, sharpen; a challenge that strengthens and perfects the character; stimulate, excite; cruel demon. **Harvest**, *LI*: see *Image of the Situation*. **Climax**, *YI*: come to a high point and stop; bring to an end, complete; renounce, desist, decline, reject; that is all; already; excessive.

Not, *BU*: common term of negation. **Oppose**, *FAN*: resist; violate, offend, attack; possessed by an evil spirit; criminal. Ideogram: violate and dog, brutal offense. **Calamity**, *ZAI*: see *Hexagrams in Pairs*. **Indeed**, *YE*: see *Hexagrams in Pairs*.

NINE AT SECOND

Carting: **stimulating** the **axle-bearing**.

Comments

Carting: **stimulating** the **axle-bearing**.
The **center**, **without surpassing indeed**.

Fields of meaning

Cart, *YU*: a vehicle and its carrying capacity; contain, hold, sustain. **Stimulate**, *SHUO*: rouse to action and good feeling; stir up, urge on; exhort, persuade; say, tell, relate; cheer, delight; joyous, peaceful, restful; Action of the trigram Open, *DUI*. Ideogram: words and exchange. **Axle-bearing**, *FU*: device that fastens the body of a cart to axle and wheels.

Center, *ZHONG*: see *Patterns of Wisdom*. **Without**, *WU*: see *Preceding Situation*. **Surpass**, *YOU*: exceed, transgress; beyond measure, extraordinary; blame. **Indeed**, *YE*: see *Hexagrams in Pairs*.

NINE AT THIRD

A **fine horse**, **pursuing**.
Harvesting drudgery, **Trial**.
Named: **enclosing** the **cart**, **escorting**.
Harvesting: **possessing directed going**.

Comments

Harvesting: **possessing directed going**.
Above uniting purposes indeed.

Fields of meaning

Fine, *LIANG*: excellent, refined, valuable; gentle, considerate, kind; natural. **Horse**, *MA*: symbol of spirited strength in the natural world, earthly counterpart of the dragon; associated with the trigram Energy, *QIAN*, heaven, and high noon. **Pursue**, *ZHU*: chase, follow closely, press hard; expel, drive out. Ideogram: pig (wealth) and go, chasing fortune. **Harvest**, *LI*: see *Image of the Situation*. **Drudgery**, *JIAN*: difficult, hard, repetitive work; distressing, sorrowful. Ideogram: perverse and sticky earth, soil difficult to cultivate. **Trial**, *ZHEN*: see *Image of the Situation*. **Name**, *YUE*: speak, declare, call. Ideogram: open mouth and tongue. **Enclose**, *XIAN*: put inside a fence or barrier; pen, corral; protect; restrain, obstruct; rule, model. **Cart**, *YU*: a vehicle and its carrying capacity; contain, hold, sustain. **Escort**,

WEI: accompany, protect, defend, restrain; guard of honor; military outpost. **Possessing directed going**, *YOU YOU WANG*: having a goal or purpose, moving in a specific direction.

Above, *SHANG*: anything above in all senses; higher, upper, outer; upper trigram. **Unite**, *HE*: join, match, correspond; unison, harmony; together; close the jaws, shut the mouth. Ideogram: mouths speaking in unison. **Purpose**, *ZHI*: focus of mind and heart; intention, will, inclination; continuity in the direction of life. Ideogram: heart and scholar, high inner resolve. **Indeed**, *YE*: see *Hexagrams in Pairs*.

SIX AT FOURTH

To **youthful cattle belongs** a **stable**.
Spring, **significant**.

Comments
Six at **fourth**: **Spring**, **significant**.
Possessing joy indeed.

Fields of meaning
Youthful, *TONG*: young person (between eight and fifteen); childish, immature; servant, slave. **Cattle**, *NIU*: ox, bull, cow, calf; power and strength of work animals; stubborn. **Belong/it**, *ZHI*: establishes between two terms a connection similar to the Saxon genitive, in which the second term belongs to the first one; at the end of a sentence it refers to something previously mentioned or implied. **Stable**, *GU*: shed or pen for cattle and horses. **Spring**, *YUAN*: source, origin, head; arise, begin; first generating impulse; great, excellent; quality of springtime and East, first stage of the Time Cycle. **Significant**, *JI*: see *Image of the Situation*.

Six, *LIU*: number six; transforming opened line; six lines of a hexagram. **Four**, *SI*: number four; number of the cardinal directions and of the seasons; everywhere, on all sides; fourfold articulation of the Universal Compass. **Possess**, *YOU*: see *Preceding Situation*. **Joy/rejoice**, *XI*: delight, exult; cheerful, merry. Ideogram: joy (music) and mouth, expressing joy. **Indeed**, *YE*: see *Hexagrams in Pairs*.

SIX AT FIFTH

To a **gelded pig belong tusks**.
Significant.

Comments
To **six** at **fifth belongs significance**.
Possessing reward indeed.

Fields of meaning

Geld, *FEN*: castrate a male pig; deprive, take out. Pig, *SHI*: all swine, symbol of wealth and good fortune, associated with the Streaming Moment. Belong/it, *ZHI*: establishes between two terms a connection similar to the Saxon genitive, in which the second term belongs to the first one; at the end of a sentence it refers to something previously mentioned or implied. Tusk, *YA*: animal's tooth. Significant, *JI*: see *Image of the Situation*.

Six, *LIU*: number six; transforming opened line; six lines of a hexagram. Five, *WU*: number five; fivefold articulation of the Universal Compass; the Five Moments and all related qualities: directions, colors, smells, tastes, tones, feelings. Possess, *YOU*: see *Preceding Situation*. Reward, *QING*: gift given out of gratitude or benevolence; favor from heaven. Ideogram: heart, follow and deer, the heart expressed through the gift of a deer's skin. Indeed, *YE*: see *Hexagrams in Pairs*.

NINE ABOVE

Is it not the **highway belonging** to **heaven**?
Growing.

Comments
Is it not the **highway belonging** to **heaven**?
Dao: the **great moving indeed**.

Fields of meaning

Is?, *HE*: ask, inquire; what? which? who? how? why? where? an interrogative particle, often introducing a rhetorical question: is it? is it not? Highway, *CHU*: main road, thoroughfare; crossing, intersection. Belong/it, *ZHI*: establishes between two terms a connection similar to the Saxon genitive, in which the second term belongs to the first one; at the end of a sentence it refers to something previously mentioned or implied. Heaven, *TIAN*: see *Patterns of Wisdom*. Grow, *HENG*: heavenly influence pervading and nourishing all things; prosper, succeed, expand, develop; effective, favorable; quality of summer and South, second stage of the Time Cycle. With the pronunciation *XIANG*: offer a sacrifice; offer a gift to a superior; accept, enjoy.

Dao, *DAO*: way or path; ongoing process of being and the course it traces for each person or thing; ultimate reality, intrinsic nature; origin. Ideogram: go and head, opening a path. **Great,** *DA*: see *Image of the Situation*. **Move,** *XING*: see *Patterns of Wisdom*. **Indeed,** *YE*: see *Hexagrams in Pairs*.

Image Tradition

The **great accumulating**.
Solid persisting: **staunch substance**, **resplendent shining**.
The **day renewing one's actualizing-dao**.
The **solid above and-also honoring eminence**.

Able to **stop** and **persist**.
The **great correcting indeed**.

Not in the **household taking-in**, **significant**.
Nourishing eminence indeed.
Harvesting: **wading** the **great river**.
Correspondence reaching heaven indeed.

Fields of meaning
The **great accumulating,** *DA CHU*: see *Image of the Situation*. **Solid,** *GANG*: quality of the whole lines; firm, strong, unyielding, persisting. **Persist,** *JIAN*: tenacious, persevering; strong, robust, dynamic; constant as the motion of heavenly bodies in their orbits; Action of the trigram Force, *QIAN*. **Staunch,** *DU*: firm, solid, reliable; pure, sincere, honest; consolidate, establish. **Substance,** *SHI*: fullness, richness; essence; real, solid, consistent; results, fruits, possessions; honest, sincere. Ideogram: string of coins under a roof, wealth in the house. **Resplendent,** *HUI*: refulgent, splendid, glorious. **Shine,** *GUANG*: illuminate, emit light; brilliant, splendid; honor, glory, éclat; distinct from brightness, *MING*, light of heavenly bodies. Ideogram: fire above person. **Day/sun,** *RI*: the sun and the time of a sun-cycle, a day. **Renew,** *XIN*: new, novel, fresh, recent; restore, improve, correct. **One/one's,** *QI*: see *Patterns of Wisdom*. **Actualize-dao,** *DE*: see *Patterns of Wisdom*. **Above,** *SHANG*: anything above in all senses; higher, upper, outer; upper trigram. **And-also,** *ER*: joins and contrasts two terms. **Honor,** *SHANG*: esteem, give high rank to, exalt, celebrate; rise, elevate; put one thing on top of another. **Eminent,** *XIAN*: worthy, excellent, virtuous; endowed with moral and intellectual power; second only to the wise, *SHENG*.

Able/enable, *NENG*: ability, power, skill, art; competent, talented; duty, function, capacity. Ideogram: an animal with strong hooves and bones, able to carry and defend. **Stop,** *ZHI*: bring or come to a standstill, cease, terminate; Action of the trigram Bound, *GEN*. Ideogram: a foot stops walking. **Correct**, *ZHENG*: rectify deviation or one-sidedness; proper, straight, exact, regular; constant, rule, model. Ideogram: stop and one, hold to one thing. **Indeed**, *YE*: see *Hexagrams in Pairs*.

Not in the **household taking-in**, **significant**, *BU JIA SHI JI*: see *Image of the Situation*. **Nourish**, *YANG*: feed, sustain, support, provide, care for; generate; raise, grow. **Harvesting**: **wading** the **great river**, *LI SHE DA CHUAN*: see *Image of the Situation*. **Correspond**, *YING*: be in agreement or harmony; proper, suitable; resonate together, answer to; relation between the lines (1 and 4, 2 and 5, 3 and 6) when they form the pair opened and whole, supple and solid. Ideogram: heart and obey. **Reach**, *HU*: arrive at a goal; move toward and achieve; to, at, in; distinct from tend-towards, *YOU*. **Heaven**, *TIAN*: see *Patterns of Wisdom*.

頤

䷚

27 THE JAWS | *Yi*

The situation described by this hexagram is characterized by paying attention to how one seeks nourishment and opening to receive it.

Image of the Situation

> The **jaws**.
> **Trial**, **significant**.
> **Overseeing** the **jaws**.
> The **origin** of **seeking mouth**'s **substance**.

Fields of meaning

Jaws, *YI*: mouth, jaws, cheeks, chin; swallow, take in, ingest; feed, nourish, sustain, rear. Ideogram: open jaws. Trial, *ZHEN*: inquiry by divination and its result; righteous, firm; separating wheat from chaff; the kernel, the proven core; quality of winter and North, fourth stage of the Time Cycle. Ideogram: pearl and divination. Significant, *JI*: leads to the experience of meaning; favorable, propitious, appropriate. Ideogram: scholar and mouth, wise words of a sage. Oversee, *GUAN*: contemplate, observe from a distance; look at carefully, gaze at; a high place from where one sees far, monastery, observatory; intelligence, clairvoyance; scry, divine through liquid in a cup. Ideogram: sight and waterbird, aerial view. Origin, *ZI*: source, beginning, ground; cause, reason, motive; tracing back to the source; oneself, by oneself; spontaneous, intrinsic. Seek, *QIU*: search for, aim at, wish for, desire; implore, supplicate; covetous. Mouth, *KOU*: mouth, mouthful; words going out and food coming into the mouth; entrance, hole, passageway. Substance, *SHI*: fullness, richness; essence; real, solid, consistent; results, fruits, possessions; honest, sincere. Ideogram: string of coins under a roof, wealth in the house.

Outer and Inner Trigram

The upper trigram, **Bound**, *GEN*, describes the outer aspects of the situation. It has the following associations: limit, frontier; obstacle that prevents from seeing further; stop; still, quiet, motionless; confine, enclose; mountain, sunset, beginning of winter; solid, steady, unshakable; straight, hard, adamant, obstinate. *Symbol:*

mountain, *SHAN*, large, immense; limit, boundary. Ideogram: three peaks, a mountain range. *Action*: stop, *ZHI*, bring or come to a standstill, cease, terminate. Ideogram: a foot stops walking. In the family of trigrams *GEN* is the youngest son.

The lower trigram, **Shake**, *ZHEN*, describes the inner aspects of the situation. It has the following associations: arouse, excite, inspire; awe, alarm, trembling; thunder rising from the depth of the earth; fertilizing intrusion. Ideogram: excite and rain. *Symbol*: thunder, *LEI*, arousing power emerging from the depth of the earth. *Action*: stir-up, *DONG*, excite, influence, move, affect; work, take action; come out of the egg or the bud. Ideogram: strength and heavy, move weighty things. In the family of trigrams *ZHEN* is the eldest son.

Counter Hexagram

The Counter Hexagram of **The Jaws** is hexagram 2, **Space**, which switches the emphasis from receiving nourishment to nurturing, supporting all things and allowing them to become what they potentially are.

Preceding Situation

> **Beings accumulate**, **therefore afterwards permitted** to **nourish**.
> To **anterior acquiescence belongs** the **use** of the **jaws**.
> The **jaws imply nourishing indeed**.

Fields of meaning

Being, *WU*: creature, thing, any single being; matter, substance, essence; nature of things. Accumulate, *CHU*: retain, hoard, gather, herd together; control, restrain; domesticate, tame, train; raise, feed, sustain, bring up. Ideogram: field and black, fertile black soil, accumulated through retaining silt. Therefore, *RAN*: thus, so it is; truly, certainly. After(wards)/later, *HOU*: come after in time, subsequent; put oneself after; behind, back, draw back; the second; attendants, heirs, successors, posterity. Permit, *KE*: possible because in harmony with an inherent principle; capable of; approve, authorize. Ideogram: mouth and breath, silent consent. Nourish, *YANG*: feed, sustain, support, provide, care for; generate; raise, grow. To anterior acquiescence belongs the use of, *GU SHOU ZHI YI*: understanding and accepting the preceding statement allows the consultant to make proper use of this hexagram. Jaws, *YI*: see *Image of the Situation*. Imply, *ZHE*: further signify; additional meaning. Indeed, *YE*: emphasizes and intensifies the previous statement.

Hexagrams in Pairs

> The **jaws**: **nourishing correctly indeed**.
> The **great exceeding**: **toppling indeed**.

Fields of meaning

Jaws, *YI*: see *Image of the Situation*. **Nourish**, *YANG*: see *Preceding Situation*. **Correct**, *ZHENG*: rectify deviation or one-sidedness; proper, straight, exact, regular; constant, rule, model. Ideogram: stop and one, hold to one thing. **Indeed**, *YE*: see *Preceding Situation*. **Great**, *DA*: big, noble, important, very; orient the will toward a self-imposed goal, impose direction; ability to lead or guide one's life; contrasts with small, *XIAO*, flexible adaptation to what crosses one's path. **Exceed**, *GUO*: go beyond, pass by, pass over; surpass, transgress; error, fault, calamity. **Topple**, *DIAN*: fall over because top-heavy; top, summit.

Patterns of Wisdom

> The **mountain possesses thunder below**. The **jaws**.
> A **jun zi uses considerate words** to **inform**.
> And **articulation** in **drinking** and **taking-in**.

Fields of meaning

Mountain, *SHAN*: mountain; large, immense; limit, boundary; Symbol of the trigram Bound, *GEN*. Ideogram: three peaks, a mountain range. **Possess**, *YOU*: general term indicating possession; have, own, be endowed with. **Thunder**, *LEI*: thunder; arousing power emerging from the depth of the earth; Symbol of the trigram Shake, *ZHEN*. **Below**, *XIA*: anything below, in all senses; lower, inner; lower trigram. **Jaws**, *YI*: see *Image of the Situation*. **Jun zi**: ideal of a person who orders his/her life in accordance with dao rather than willful intention, and uses divination in this spirit. **Use**, *YI*: by means of; owing to; make use of, employ. **Consider**, *SHEN*: act carefully, seriously; cautious, attentive, circumspect; still, quiet, sincere. Ideogram: heart and true. **Word**, *YAN*: spoken word, speech, saying; talk, discuss, address; name, signify. Ideogram: mouth and rising vapor. **Inform**, *YU*: tell; warn; converse, exchange ideas. **Articulate**, *JIE*: joint, articulation; a separation which simultaneously establishes the identity of the parts and their connection; express thought through speech; section, chapter, interval; temperance, virtue; rite, ceremony; lit.: nodes of bamboo stalks. **Drink**, *YIN*: drink, swallow, ingest liquid or food; inhale, suck in. **Take-in**, *SHI*: eat, drink, ingest, absorb, incorporate; food, nourishment.

Transforming Lines

INITIAL NINE

Stowing simply the **magic tortoise**.
Overseeing my pendent jaw.
Pitfall.

Comments
Overseeing my pendent jaw.
Truly not a **stand** for **valuing indeed**.

Fields of meaning
Stow, *SHE*: set aside, put away, store, keep; halt, rest in; lodge, hut. **Simply**, *ER*: just so, only. **Magic**, *LING*: wonderful, subtle; effectiveness, power, intelligence; life force, vital energy; spirit of a being; wizard, diviner. **Tortoise**, *GUI*: turtles; armored animals, shells and shields; long-living; practice divination; image of the macrocosm: heaven, earth and between them the soft flesh of humans. **Oversee**, *GUAN*: see *Image of the Situation*. **I/me/my**, *WO*: first person pronoun; the use of a specific personal pronoun, as opposed to the generic one's, *QI*, indicates an unusually strong emphasis on personal involvement. **Pendent**, *DUO*: hanging; flowering branch, date or grape cluster. **Jaws**, *YI*: see *Image of the Situation*. **Pitfall**, *XIONG*: unfortunate situation, in which the flow of life and spirit is blocked and the experience of meaning is lost; stuck and exposed to danger; inappropriate attitude. Ideogram: person in a pit.

Truly, *YI*: in fact; also; nevertheless. **Not**, *BU*: common term of negation. **Stand**, *ZU*: base, foot, leg; rest on, support; stance; sufficient, capable, worth. Ideogram: foot and calf resting. **Value**, *GUI*: regard as valuable, give worth and dignity to; precious, honorable, exalted, illustrious. Ideogram: cowries (coins) and basket. **Indeed**, *YE*: see *Preceding Situation*.

SIX AT SECOND

Toppling jaws.
Rejecting the **canons**, **tending-towards** the **hill-top**.
The **jaws disciplined**, **pitfall**.

Comments
Six at **second**: **disciplining**, **pitfall**.
Movement letting-go sorting indeed.

Fields of meaning
Topple, *DIAN*: see *Hexagrams in Pairs*. Jaws, *YI*: see *Image of the Situation*. Reject, *FU*: push away, brush off; oppose, contradict, resist; perverse, proud. Ideogram: hand and not, pushing something away. Canons, *JING*: standards, laws; regular, regulate; the Five Classics. Ideogram: warp threads in a loom. Tend-towards, *YU*: move toward without necessarily reaching, in the direction of. Hill-top, *QIU*: hill with hollow top used for worship and as grave-site; knoll, hillock. Discipline, *ZHENG*: subjugate vassals, reduce to order; punishing expedition. Ideogram: step and correct, a rectifying move. Pitfall, *XIONG*: unfortunate situation, in which the flow of life and spirit is blocked and the experience of meaning is lost; stuck and exposed to danger; inappropriate attitude. Ideogram: person in a pit.

Six, *LIU*: number six; transforming opened line; six lines of a hexagram. Two/second, *ER*: number two; pair, even numbers, binary, duplicate. Move, *XING*: move or move something; motivate; emotionally moving; walk, act, do. Ideogram: successive steps. Let-go, *SHI*: lose, let slip; omit, miss, fail; lose control of. Ideogram: drop from the hand. Sort, *LEI*: group according to kind, compare; species, class, genus; resemble; analog, like nature or purpose; norm, model. Indeed, *YE*: see *Preceding Situation*.

SIX AT THIRD

Rejecting the **jaws**. **Trial**, **pitfall**.
Ten years, **no availing** of.
Without direction Harvesting.

Comments
Ten years, **no availing** of.
Dao: the **great rebels indeed**.

Fields of meaning
Reject, *FU*: push away, brush off; oppose, contradict, resist; perverse, proud. Ideogram: hand and not, pushing something away. Jaws, *YI*: see *Image of the Situation*. Trial, *ZHEN*: see *Image of the Situation*. Pitfall, *XIONG*: unfortunate situation, in which the flow of life and spirit is blocked and the experience of meaning is lost; stuck and exposed to danger; inappropriate attitude. Ideogram: person in a pit. Ten, *SHI*: number ten; goal and end of reckoning; whole, complete, all; entire, perfected. Ideogram: East–West line crosses North–South line, a grid that contains all. Year, *NIAN*: year, annual; harvest; years revolved, years of age. No, *WU*: common term of negation. Avail, *YONG*: use, employ for a specific purpose; take advantage of; benefit from; capacity. Ideogram: to divine and center,

applying divination to central concerns. **Without direction Harvesting**, *WU YOU LI*: in order to take advantage of the situation, do not impose a direction on events.

Dao, *DAO*: way or path; ongoing process of being and the course it traces for each person or thing; ultimate reality, intrinsic nature; origin. Ideogram: go and head, opening a path. **Great**, *DA*: see *Hexagrams in Pairs*. **Rebel**, *BEI*: oppose, resist; go against nature or usage; insubordinate; perverse, unreasonable. **Indeed**, *YE*: see *Preceding Situation*.

Six at Fourth

Toppling jaws. Significant.
A **tiger observing: glaring, glaring.**
Its appetites: pursuing, pursuing.
Without fault.

Comments
To **toppling jaws belongs significance.**
Above spreading shine indeed.

Fields of meaning

Topple, *DIAN*: see *Hexagrams in Pairs*. **Jaws**, *YI*: see *Image of the Situation*. **Significant**, *JI*: see *Image of the Situation*. **Tiger**, *HU*: fierce king of animals; extreme Yang; opposed to and protecting against the demons of extreme Yin on the North–South axis of the Universal Compass. **Observe**, *SHI*: see, examine, inspect; consider as; compare, imitate. Ideogram: see and omen, taking what you see into account. **Glare**, *DAN*: stare intensely; obstruct, prevent. Ideogram: look and hesitate, staring without acting. **It/its**, *QI*: general third person pronoun and possessive adjective; also: one/one's, he/his, she/her, they/their. **Appetites**, *YU*: drives, instinctive cravings; wishes, passions, desires, aspirations; long for, seek ardently, covet. **Pursue**, *ZHU*: chase, follow closely, press hard; expel, drive out. Ideogram: pig (wealth) and go, chasing fortune. **Without fault**, *WU JIU*: no error or harm in the situation.

Belong/it, *ZHI*: establishes between two terms a connection similar to the Saxon genitive, in which the second term belongs to the first one; at the end of a sentence it refers to something previously mentioned or implied. **Above**, *SHANG*: anything above in all senses; higher, upper, outer; upper trigram. **Spread**, *SHI*: expand, diffuse, distribute, arrange, exhibit; add to; aid. Ideogram: flag and indeed, claiming new country. **Shine**, *GUANG*: illuminate, emit light; brilliant, splendid; honor, glory, éclat; distinct from brightness, *MING*, light of heavenly bodies. Ideogram: fire above person. **Indeed**, *YE*: see *Preceding Situation*.

SIX AT FIFTH

Rejecting the **canons**.
Residing in **Trial**, **significant**.
Not permitted to **wade** the **great river**.

Comments
To **residing** in **Trial belongs significance**.
Yielding uses adhering to the **above indeed**.

Fields of meaning

Reject, *FU*: push away, brush off; oppose, contradict, resist; perverse, proud. Ideogram: hand and not, pushing something away. **Canons**, *JING*: standards, laws; regular, regulate; the Five Classics. Ideogram: warp threads in a loom. **Reside**, *JU*: dwell, live in, stay; sit down; fill an office; well-being, rest. Ideogram: body and seat. **Trial**, *ZHEN*: see *Image of the Situation*. **Significant**, *JI*: see *Image of the Situation*. **Not**, *BU*: common term of negation. **Permit**, *KE*: see *Preceding Situation*. **Wading the Great River**, *SHE DA CHUAN*: enter the stream of life with a goal or purpose; embark on a significant enterprise.

Belong/it, *ZHI*: establishes between two terms a connection similar to the Saxon genitive, in which the second term belongs to the first one; at the end of a sentence it refers to something previously mentioned or implied. **Yield**, *SHUN*: give way, comply, agree, follow, obey; docile, flexible; bear produce, nourish, provide; Action of the trigram Field, *KUN*. **Use**, *YI*: see *Patterns of Wisdom*. **Adhere**, *CONG*: follow, agree with, comply with, obey; join a doctrine, school, or person; servant, follower. Ideogram: two men walking, one following the other. **Above**, *SHANG*: anything above in all senses; higher, upper, outer; upper trigram. **Indeed**, *YE*: see *Preceding Situation*.

NINE ABOVE

Antecedent jaws.
Adversity, **significant**.
Harvesting: **wading** the **great river**.

Comments
Antecedent jaws, **adversity**, **significant**.
The **great possesses reward indeed**.

Fields of meaning

Antecedent, *YOU*: come before as origin and cause; through, by, from; depend on; enter by way of. **Jaws**, *YI*: see *Image of the Situation*. **Adversity**, *LI*: danger, hardship, severe; threat or difficulty that must be encountered, rather than avoided; grinding stone; polish, sharpen; a challenge that strengthens and perfects the character; stimulate, excite; cruel demon. **Significant**, *JI*: see *Image of the Situation*. **Harvest**, *LI*: benefit, advantage, profit; realization; sharp, acute, insightful; quality of autumn and West, third stage of the Time Cycle. Ideogram: ripe grain and blade. **Wading the Great River**, *SHE DA CHUAN*: enter the stream of life with a goal or purpose; embark on a significant enterprise.

Great, *DA*: see *Hexagrams in Pairs*. **Possess**, *YOU*: see *Patterns of Wisdom*. **Reward**, *QING*: gift given out of gratitude or benevolence; favor from heaven. Ideogram: heart, follow and deer, the heart expressed through the gift of a deer's skin. **Indeed**, *YE*: see *Preceding Situation*.

Image Tradition

The **jaws**. **Trial**, **significant**.
Nourishing correctly, by **consequence significance indeed**.

Overseeing the **jaws**.
Overseeing one's place of **nourishment indeed**.
The **origin** of **seeking mouth**'s **substance**.
Overseeing one's origin: **nourishment indeed**.

Heaven and **earth nourish** the **myriad beings**.
The **wise person nourishes eminence used** to **extend** to the **myriad commoners**.
The **season belonging** to the **jaws great actually in-fact**.

Fields of meaning

Jaws, *YI*: see *Image of the Situation*. **Trial, significant**, *ZHEN JI*: see *Image of the Situation*. **Nourish**, *YANG*: see *Preceding Situation*. **Correct**, *ZHENG*: see *Hexagrams in Pairs*. **Consequence**, *ZE*: reason, cause, result; rule, law, pattern, standard; therefore; very strong connection. **Indeed**, *YE*: see *Preceding Situation*.

Oversee, *GUAN*: see *Image of the Situation*. **One/one's**, *QI*: general third person pronoun and possessive adjective; also: it/its, he/his, she/her, they/their. **Place**, *SUO*: position, location; residence, dwelling; where something belongs or comes from; habitual focus or object. The **origin** of **seeking mouth**'s **substance**, *ZI*

QIU KOU SHI: see *Image of the Situation*.

Heaven, *TIAN*: sky, firmament, heavens; the highest realm, situated above the human world, as opposed to the earth, *DI*, located below; Symbol of the trigram Energy, *QIAN*. Ideogram: great and the one above. **Earth**, *DI*: the earth, ground on which the human world rests; basis of all things, nourishes all things; essential Yin; Symbol of the trigram Space, *KUN*. **Myriad**, *WAN*: ten thousand; countless, many, everyone. Ideogram: swarm of insects. **Being**, *WU*: see *Preceding Situation*. **Wise**, *SHENG*: intuitive universal wisdom; profound understanding; mythical sages of old; holy, sacred, mark of highest distinction. Ideogram: ear and inform, one who knows all from a single sound. **Person/people**, *REN*: humans individually and collectively; an individual; humankind. **Eminent**, *XIAN*: worthy, excellent, virtuous; endowed with moral and intellectual power; second only to the wise, *SHENG*. **Use**, *YI*: see *Patterns of Wisdom*. **Extend**, *JI*: reach to; draw out, prolong; continuous, enduring. **Commoners**, *MIN*: common people, masses; working class supporting the social hierarchy; undeveloped potential in the individual. **Season**, *SHI*: quality of the time; the right time, opportune, in harmony; planning in accord with the time; season of the year. Ideogram: sun and temple, sacred time. **Belong/it**, *ZHI*: establishes between two terms a connection similar to the Saxon genitive, in which the second term belongs to the first one; at the end of a sentence it refers to something previously mentioned or implied. **Great**, *DA*: see *Hexagrams in Pairs*. **Actually**, *YI*: truly, really, at present. Ideogram: a dart and done, strong intention fully expressed. **In-fact**, *ZAI*: emphatic exclamation; truly, indeed.

大過 ䷛

28 THE GREAT EXCEEDING | *Da Guo*

The situation described by this hexagram is characterized by the excessive predominance of a central idea or goal, which may become too heavy to bear.

Image of the Situation

> The **great exceeding**.
> The **ridgepole sagging**.
> **Harvesting**: **possessing directed going**.
> **Growing**.

Fields of meaning

Great, *DA*: big, noble, important, very; orient the will toward a self-imposed goal, impose direction; ability to lead or guide one's life; contrasts with small, *XIAO*, flexible adaptation to what crosses one's path. **Exceed**, *GUO*: go beyond, pass by, pass over; surpass, transgress; error, fault, calamity. **Ridgepole**, *DONG*: highest and key beam in a house; summit, crest. **Sag**, *NAO*: yield, bend, distort, twist; disturbed, confused. **Harvest**, *LI*: benefit, advantage, profit; realization; sharp, acute, insightful; quality of autumn and West, third stage of the Time Cycle. Ideogram: ripe grain and blade. **Possessing directed going**, *YOU YOU WANG*: having a goal or purpose, moving in a specific direction. **Grow**, *HENG*: heavenly influence pervading and nourishing all things; prosper, succeed, expand, develop; effective, favorable; quality of summer and South, second stage of the Time Cycle. With the pronunciation *XIANG*: offer a sacrifice; offer a gift to a superior; accept, enjoy.

Outer and Inner Trigram

The upper trigram, **Open**, *DUI*, describes the outer aspects of the situation. It has the following associations: an open surface, promoting interaction and interpenetration; pleasant, easy, responsive, free, unhindered; opening, passage; the mouth; exchange, barter; straight, direct; meet, gather; place where water accumulates. Ideogram: mouth and vapor, communication through speech. *Symbol*: marsh, *ZE*, open surface of a flat body of water and the vapors rising from it; fertilize, enrich; kindness, favor. *Action*: stimulate, *SHUO*, rouse to action and good feeling; stir up, urge on; exhort, persuade; say, tell, relate; cheer, delight; joyous, peaceful, restful. Ideogram: words and exchange. In the family of trigrams *DUI* is the youngest daughter.

The lower trigram, **Root**, *SUN*, describes the inner aspects of the situation. It has the following associations: base on which things rest, ground, foundation; mild, subtly penetrating; nourishing. *Symbols*: tree/wood and wind. Tree/wood, *MU*: trees and all things woody or wooden; associated with the Wooden Moment. Ideogram: a tree with roots and branches. Wind, *FENG*: wind, breeze, gust; weather and its influence on mood and humor; fashion, usage. *Action*: enter, *RU*, penetrate, go into, enter on, encroach on; progress; put into. In the family of trigrams *SUN* is the eldest daughter.

Counter Hexagram

The Counter Hexagram of **The Great Exceeding** is hexagram 1, **Energy**, which switches the emphasis from the excessive predominance of an overriding concern that cannot be indefinitely sustained to the persistent drive of **Energy**, unceasingly moving forward and ever renewing itself.

Preceding Situation

> **Not nourished**, by **consequence not permitted stirring-up**.
> To **anterior acquiescence belongs** the **use** of the **great exceeding**.

Fields of meaning

Not, *BU*: common term of negation. Nourish, *YANG*: feed, sustain, support, provide, care for; generate; raise, grow. Consequence, *ZE*: reason, cause, result; rule, law, pattern, standard; therefore; very strong connection. Permit, *KE*: possible because in harmony with an inherent principle; capable of; approve, authorize. Ideogram: mouth and breath, silent consent. Stir-up, *DONG*: excite, influence, move, affect; work, take action; come out of the egg or the bud; Action of the trigram Shake, *ZHEN*. Ideogram: strength and heavy, move weighty things. To anterior acquiescence belongs the use of, *GU SHOU ZHI YI*: understanding and accepting the preceding statement allows the consultant to make proper use of this hexagram. The great exceeding, *DA GUO*: see *Image of the Situation*.

Hexagrams in Pairs

The **jaws**: **nourishing correctly indeed**.
The **great exceeding**: **toppling indeed**.

Fields of meaning

Jaws, *YI*: mouth, jaws, cheeks, chin; swallow, take in, ingest; feed, nourish, sustain, rear. Ideogram: open jaws. Nourish, *YANG*: see *Preceding Situation*. Correct, *ZHENG*: rectify deviation or one-sidedness; proper, straight, exact, regular; constant, rule, model. Ideogram: stop and one, hold to one thing. Indeed, *YE*: emphasizes and intensifies the previous statement. The great exceeding, *DA GUO*: see *Image of the Situation*. Topple, *DIAN*: fall over because top-heavy; top, summit.

Patterns of Wisdom

The **pond submerges wood**. The **great exceeding**.
A **jun zi uses solitary establishing not** to **fear**.
And **retiring** from the **age without melancholy**.

Fields of meaning

Pond, *ZE*: open surface of a flat body of water and the vapors rising from it; fertilize, enrich; kindness, favor; Symbol of the trigram Open, *DUI*. Submerge, *MIE*: put out a fire, exterminate; plunge under water, sink, perish. Ideogram: water and destroy. Wood/tree, *MU*: trees and all things woody or wooden; associated with the Wooden Moment; wood and wind are the Symbols of the trigram Ground, *SUN*. Ideogram: a tree with roots and branches. The great exceeding, *DA GUO*: see *Image of the Situation*. Jun zi: ideal of a person who orders his/her life in accordance with dao rather than willful intention, and uses divination in this spirit. Use, *YI*: by means of; owing to; make use of, employ. Solitary, *DI*: alone, single; isolated, abandoned. Establish, *LI*: set up, institute, order, arrange; stand erect; settled principles. Not, *BU*: common term of negation. Fear, *JU*: afraid, apprehensive; stand in awe of; intimidate. Retire, *DUN*: withdraw; run away, flee; conceal yourself, become obscure, invisible; secluded, non-social. Ideogram: walk and swine (wealth through walking away). Age, *SHI*: an age, an epoch, a generation; the world, mankind; time as "in the time of." Without, *WU*: devoid of; there is not. Melancholy, *MEN*: sad, unhappy, chagrined, heavy-hearted. Ideogram: gate and heart, the heart confined or melancholy as gate to the heart.

Transforming Lines

INITIAL SIX

Sacrificing avails of **white thatch-grass.**
Without fault.

Comments
Sacrificing avails of **white thatch-grass.**
The **supple located below indeed.**

Fields of meaning
Sacrifice, *JIE*: straw mat used to hold offerings; make offerings to gods and the dead; depend on, call on, borrow. **Avail,** *YONG*: use, employ for a specific purpose; take advantage of; benefit from; capacity. Ideogram: to divine and center, applying divination to central concerns. **White,** *BO*: color associated with autumn, Harvest and the Metallic Moment; white hair, old age; clear, immaculate, plain, essential; color of death and mourning. **Thatch-grass,** *MAO*: thick grass used for roofs of humble houses. **Without fault,** *WU JIU*: no error or harm in the situation.

Supple, *ROU*: quality of the opened lines; flexible, pliant, adaptable, tender. **Locate,** *ZAI*: be at, be situated at, dwell, reside; in, within; involved with, in the process of. Ideogram: earth and persevere, a place on the earth. **Below,** *XIA*: anything below, in all senses; lower, inner; lower trigram. **Indeed,** *YE*: see *Hexagrams in Pairs*.

NINE AT SECOND

A **withered willow generates** a **sprig.**
A **venerable husband acquires his woman consort.**
Without not Harvesting.

Comments
A **venerable husband** and a **woman consort.**
Exceeding uses reciprocal association indeed.

Fields of meaning
Withered, *KU*: dried up, decayed, rotten; dry wood. Ideogram: tree and old. **Willow,** *YANG*: all fast growing trees: willow, poplar, tamarisk, aspen. Ideogram: tree and versatility. **Generate,** *SHENG*: give birth; be born, arise, grow; beget; life, vitality. Ideogram: earth and sprout. **Sprig,** *TI*: tender new shoot of a tree, twig, new branch. **Venerable,** *LAO*: old, ancient; term of respect due to old age.

Husband, *FU*: adult, man, male spouse; scholar, distinguished man; one who can help; manage a household. Ideogram: man with a pin in his hair to show that he is of age. **Acquire**, *DE*: obtain the desired object; possession; satisfied, fulfilled; it is permitted; agree with; wish for, desire covetously. Ideogram: go and obstacle, going through obstacles to the goal. **He/his**, *QI*: general third person pronoun and possessive adjective; also: one/one's, it/its, she/her, they/their. **Woman(hood)**, *NÜ*: woman and what is inherently female. **Consort**, *QI*: official partner; legal status of married woman (first wife); distinct from wife, *FU*, which indicates her role as head of the household, and from concubine, *QIE*, secondary wife. **Without not Harvesting**, *WU BU LI*: turning point where the balance is swinging from not Harvesting to actually Harvesting.

Exceed, *GUO*: see *Image of the Situation*. **Use**, *YI*: see *Patterns of Wisdom*. **Reciprocal**, *XIANG*: mutual; assist, encourage, help; bring together, blend with; examine, inspect; by turns. **Associate**, *YU*: consort with, combine; companions; group, band, company; agree with, comply, help; in favor of. Ideogram: a pair of hands reaching downward meets a pair of hands reaching upward, helpful association. **Indeed**, *YE*: see *Hexagrams in Pairs*.

NINE AT THIRD

The **ridgepole buckling**. **Pitfall**.

Comments

To the **ridgepole buckling belongs** a **pitfall**.
Not permitted to **use** the **possession** of **bracing indeed**.

Fields of meaning

Ridgepole, *DONG*: see *Image of the Situation*. **Buckle**, *RAO*: bend, twist; distort, wrench out of shape; weak, fragile; flexible. **Pitfall**, *XIONG*: unfortunate situation, in which the flow of life and spirit is blocked and the experience of meaning is lost; stuck and exposed to danger; inappropriate attitude. Ideogram: person in a pit.

Belong/it, *ZHI*: establishes between two terms a connection similar to the Saxon genitive, in which the second term belongs to the first one; at the end of a sentence it refers to something previously mentioned or implied. **Not**, *BU*: common term of negation. **Permit**, *KE*: see *Preceding Situation*. **Use**, *YI*: see *Patterns of Wisdom*. **Possess**, *YOU*: general term indicating possession; have, own, be endowed with. **Brace/jawbones**, *FU*: braces of a cart; cheeks, maxillary bones; support, consolidate, strengthen, prop up; steady, firm, rigid; help, rescue. **Indeed**, *YE*: see *Hexagrams in Pairs*.

NINE AT FOURTH

The **ridgepole crowning**. **Significant**.
Possessing more: **abashment**.

Comments
To the **ridgepole crowning belongs significance**.
Not sagging, **reaching** the **below indeed**.

Fields of meaning
Ridgepole, *DONG*: see *Image of the Situation*. Crown, *LONG*: high, above all others; peak; grandiose, majestic, eminent, venerable. Significant, *JI*: leads to the experience of meaning; favorable, propitious, appropriate. Ideogram: scholar and mouth, wise words of a sage. Possess, *YOU*: general term indicating possession; have, own, be endowed with. More, *TUO*: another, something else; add to. Abashment, *LIN*: distress, shame, regret, humiliation; aware of having lost the right track; leads to repenting, *HUI*, correcting the direction of mind and life.

Belong/it, *ZHI*: establishes between two terms a connection similar to the Saxon genitive, in which the second term belongs to the first one; at the end of a sentence it refers to something previously mentioned or implied. Not, *BU*: common term of negation. Sag, *NAO*: see *Image of the Situation*. Reach, *HU*: arrive at a goal; move toward and achieve; to, at, in; distinct from tend-towards, *YOU*. Below, *XIA*: anything below, in all senses; lower, inner; lower trigram. Indeed, *YE*: see *Hexagrams in Pairs*.

NINE AT FIFTH

A **withered willow generates flowers**.
A **venerable wife acquires her scholarly husband**.
Without fault, **without praise**.

Comments
A **withered willow generates flowers**.
Is it **permitted** to **last indeed**?
A **venerable wife** and a **scholarly husband**.
Truly permitting the **demoniac indeed**.

Fields of meaning
Withered, *KU*: dried up, decayed, rotten; dry wood. Ideogram: tree and old. Willow, *YANG*: all fast growing trees: willow, poplar, tamarisk, aspen. Ideogram: tree and versatility. Generate, *SHENG*: give birth; be born, arise, grow; beget; life,

vitality. Ideogram: earth and sprout. **Flower**, *HUA*: symbol of beauty, elegance, abundance, culture and literature as blooming of the human mind; splendid, noble. **Venerable**, *LAO*: old, ancient; term of respect due to old age. **Wife**, *FU*: position of married woman as head of the household; distinct from consort, *QI*, which denotes her legal status, and from concubine, *QIE*, secondary wife. Ideogram: woman, hand and broom, household duties. **Acquire**, *DE*: obtain the desired object; possession; satisfied, fulfilled; it is permitted; agree with; wish for, desire covetously. Ideogram: go and obstacle, going through obstacles to the goal. **She/her**, *QI*: general third person pronoun and possessive adjective; also: one/one's, it/its, he/his, they/their. **Scholar**, *SHI*: cultured, learned, upright; gentleman, man of distinction, officer. **Husband**, *FU*: adult, man, male spouse; scholar, distinguished man; one who can help; manage a household. Ideogram: man with a pin in his hair to show that he is of age. **Without fault**, *WU JIU*: no error or harm in the situation. **Without**, *WU*: see *Patterns of Wisdom*. **Praise**, *YU*: magnify, eulogize; flatter; fame, reputation. Ideogram: offering words.

Is?, *HE*: ask, inquire; what? which? who? how? why? where? an interrogative particle, often introducing a rhetorical question: is it? is it not? **Permit**, *KE*: see *Preceding Situation*. **Last**, *JIU*: endure; long, protracted, permanent, eternal; old, ancient. **Indeed**, *YE*: see *Hexagrams in Pairs*. **Truly**, *YI*: in fact; also; nevertheless. **Demon**, *CHOU*: malignant genius; horror; ugly, vile, disgraceful, shameful; drunken; detest, hate; strange, ominous; class, group, crowd; similar. Ideogram: fermented liquor and soul. Demon and tiger are opposed on the North–South axis of the Universal Compass; the tiger (Extreme Yang) protects against the demons of Extreme Yin.

SIX ABOVE

Exceeding wading, submerging the **peak. Pitfall.**
Without fault.

Comments

To **exceeding wading belongs** a **pitfall.**
Not permitted fault indeed.

Fields of meaning

Exceed, *GUO*: see *Image of the Situation*. **Wade**, *SHE*: walk in or through a body of water. Ideogram: step and water. **Submerge**, *MIE*: see *Patterns of Wisdom*. **Peak**, *DING*: top of the head, summit, crown; carry on the head; superior. **Pitfall**, *XIONG*: unfortunate situation, in which the flow of life and spirit is blocked and the experience of meaning is lost; stuck and exposed to danger; inappropriate attitude. Ideogram: person in a pit. **Without fault**, *WU JIU*: no error or harm in the situation.

Belong/it, *ZHI*: establishes between two terms a connection similar to the Saxon genitive, in which the second term belongs to the first one; at the end of a sentence it refers to something previously mentioned or implied. **Not**, *BU*: common term of negation. **Permit**, *KE*: see *Preceding Situation*. **Fault**, *JIU*: unworthy conduct that leads to harm, illness, misfortune; guilt, crime, punishment. Ideogram: person and differ, differ from what you should be. **Indeed**, *YE*: see *Hexagrams in Pairs*.

Image Tradition

The **great exceeding**.
The **great implies exceeding indeed**.
The **ridgepole sagging**.
Base and **tip fading indeed**.

The **solid exceeding and-also** in the **center**.
Root and-also stimulating movement.
Harvesting: **possessing directed going**.

Thereupon Growing.
The **season belonging** to the **great exceeding great**
actually in-fact.

Fields of meaning

The **great exceeding**, *DA GUO*: see *Image of the Situation*. **Imply**, *ZHE*: further signify; additional meaning. **Indeed**, *YE*: see *Hexagrams in Pairs*. The **ridgepole sagging**, *DONG NAO*: see *Image of the Situation*. **Base**, *BEN*: root, trunk; origin, cause, foundation. Ideogram: tree with roots in the earth. **Tip**, *MO*: outermost twig, growing end of a branch; last, most distant; secondary, insignificant. **Fade**, *RUO*: lose strength or freshness, wither, wane: fragile, feeble, weak.

Solid, *GANG*: quality of the whole lines; firm, strong, unyielding, persisting. **And-also**, *ER*: joins and contrasts two terms. **Center**, *ZHONG*: inner, central; put in the center; middle, stable point enabling you to face inner and outer changes; middle line of a trigram. Ideogram: field divided in two equal parts. **Root**, *SUN*: base on which things rest, ground, foundation; mild, subtly penetrating; nourishing. **Stimulate**, *SHUO*: rouse to action and good feeling; stir up, urge on; exhort, persuade; say, tell, relate; cheer, delight; joyous, peaceful, restful; Action of the trigram Open, *DUI*. Ideogram: words and exchange. **Move**, *XING*: move or move something; motivate; emotionally moving; walk, act, do. Ideogram: successive steps. **Harvesting: possessing directed going**, *LI YOU YOU WANG*: see *Image of the Situation*.

Thereupon, *NAI*: on that ground, then, only then; finally; in spite of that. **Grow**, *HENG*: see *Image of the Situation*. **Season**, *SHI*: quality of the time; the right time, opportune, in harmony; planning in accord with the time; season of the year. Ideogram: sun and temple, sacred time. **Belong/it**, *ZHI*: establishes between two terms a connection similar to the Saxon genitive, in which the second term belongs to the first one; at the end of a sentence it refers to something previously mentioned or implied. **Great**, *DA*: see *Image of the Situation*. **Actually**, *YI*: truly, really, at present. Ideogram: a dart and done, strong intention fully expressed. **In-fact**, *ZAI*: emphatic exclamation; truly, indeed.

29 THE GORGE 習坎 

Kan

The situation described by this hexagram is characterized by the flow of life being on the brink of a dangerous plunge, which can only be overcome by risking, venturing and falling until a bottom is reached. The hexagram The Gorge is the doubling of the corresponding trigram, and partakes of its attributes.

Image of the Situation

> **Repeated gorge**.
> **Possessing conformity**.
> **Holding-fast** the **heart**, **Growing**.
> **Movement possesses honor**.

Fields of meaning

Repeat, *XI*: perform a series of similar acts, practice, rehearse; habit, custom; familiar with, skilled. Ideogram: little bird practicing flight. Gorge, *KAN*: precipice, dangerous place; hole, cavity, pit, snare, trap, grave; critical time, test; risky. Ideogram: earth and cavity. *Symbol*: stream, *SHUI*, flowing water; river, tide, flood; fluid, dissolving. Ideogram: rippling water. *Actions*: venture and fall. Venture, *XIAN*: face a severe difficulty or obstruction; risk; precipice, cliff, abyss; key point, point of danger. Ideogram: mound and all, everything engaged at one point. Fall, *XIAN*: fall down or into, sink, drop, descend; pit, trap, fault; falling water. In the family of trigrams *KAN* is the middle son. Possess, *YOU*: general term indicating possession; have, own, be endowed with. Conform, *FU*: accord between inner and outer; sincere, truthful, verified, reliable; capture; prisoners, spoils. Ideogram: claws over child, a bird brooding on the nest. Hold-fast, *WEI*: tie, connect, hold together; rope, reins, net. Heart, *XIN*: the heart as center of being; seat of mind, imagination and affect; moral nature; source of desires, intentions, will. Grow, *HENG*: heavenly influence pervading and nourishing all things; prosper, succeed, expand, develop; effective, favorable; quality of summer and South, second stage of the Time Cycle. With the pronunciation *XIANG*: offer a sacrifice; offer a gift to a superior; accept, enjoy. **Move**, *XING*: move or move something; motivate; emotionally moving; walk, act, do. Ideogram: successive steps. **Honor**, *SHANG*: esteem, give high rank to, exalt, celebrate; rise, elevate; put one thing on top of another.

Outer and Inner Trigram

In this hexagram the outer and inner aspects of the situation are identical, and they are described by the trigram **Gorge**. Its associations are listed in the corresponding *Field of meaning* above.

Counter Hexagram

The Counter Hexagram of **The Gorge** is hexagram 27, **The Jaws**, which switches the emphasis from the outer plunge of **The Gorge** to the inward plunge of swallowing.

Preceding Situation

> **Beings not permitted** to **use completing exceeding**.
> To **anterior acquiescence belongs** the **use** of the **gorge**.
> **Gorge implies falling indeed**.

Fields of meaning

Beings not permitted (to **use**), *WU BU KE (YI)*: it is not possible; no one is allowed; it is not in the nature of things. **Complete**, *ZHONG*: completion of a cycle that begins the next; entire, whole, all. Ideogram: silk cocoons, follow and ice, winter linking one year with the next. **Exceed**, *GUO*: go beyond, pass by, pass over; surpass, transgress; error, fault, calamity. To **anterior acquiescence belongs** the **use** of, *GU SHOU ZHI YI*: understanding and accepting the preceding statement allows the consultant to make proper use of this hexagram. **Gorge**, *KAN*: see *Image of the Situation*. **Imply**, *ZHE*: further signify; additional meaning. **Fall**, *XIAN*: fall down or into, sink, drop, descend; pit, trap, fault; falling water; Action of the trigram Gorge, *KAN*. **Indeed**, *YE*: emphasizes and intensifies the previous statement.

Hexagrams in Pairs

> The **radiance above and-also** the **gorge below indeed**.

Fields of meaning

Radiance, *LI*: glowing light, spreading in all directions; the power of consciousness; discriminate, articulate, divide and arrange in order; assemble, attract.

Ideogram: bird and weird, magical fire-bird with brilliant plumage. **Above**, *SHANG*: anything above in all senses; higher, upper, outer; upper trigram. **And-also**, *ER*: joins and contrasts two terms. **Gorge**, *KAN*: see *Image of the Situation*. **Below**, *XIA*: anything below, in all senses; lower, inner; lower trigram. **Indeed**, *YE*: see *Preceding Situation*.

Patterns of Wisdom

Streams reiterated culminate. **Repeated gorge**.
A **jun zi uses constancy** in **actualizing-dao** to **move**.
And **repetition** to **teach affairs**.

Fields of meaning

Stream, *SHUI*: flowing water; river, tide, flood; fluid, dissolving; Symbol of the trigram Gorge, *KAN*. Ideogram: rippling water. **Reiterate**, *JIAN*: repeat, duplicate; recurrent. **Culminate**, *ZHI*: bring to the highest degree; arrive at the end or summit; superlative; reaching one's goal. **Repeat**, *XI*: see *Image of the Situation*. **Gorge**, *KAN*: see *Image of the Situation*. **Jun zi**: ideal of a person who orders his/her life in accordance with dao rather than willful intention, and uses divination in this spirit. **Use**, *YI*: by means of; owing to; make use of, employ. **Constancy**, *CHANG*: immutable order; permanent, unchanging, habitual; always; law, rule, custom. **Actualize-dao**, *DE*: realize dao in action; power, virtue; ability to follow the course traced by the ongoing process of the cosmos. Ideogram: go, straight, and heart. Linked with acquire, *DE*: acquiring that which makes a being become what it is meant to be. **Move**, *XING*: see *Image of the Situation*. **Teach**, *JIAO*: instruct, educate, direct, guide; school, doctrine. **Affairs**, *SHI*: all kinds of personal activity; matters at hand; business; function, occupation; manage; perform a task; incident, event; case in court.

Transforming Lines

INITIAL SIX

Repeated gorge.
Entering tending-towards the **gorge**'s **recess**.
Pitfall.

Comments
Repeated gorge: **entering** the **gorge**.
Letting-go dao: **pitfall indeed**.

Fields of meaning

Repeat, *XI*: see *Image of the Situation.* **Gorge**, *KAN*: see *Image of the Situation.* **Enter**, *RU*: penetrate, go into, enter on, encroach on; progress; put into; Action of the trigram Root, *SUN*. **Tend-towards**, *YU*: move toward without necessarily reaching, in the direction of. **Recess**, *DAN*: pit within a large cave; trap. **Pitfall**, *XIONG*: unfortunate situation, in which the flow of life and spirit is blocked and the experience of meaning is lost; stuck and exposed to danger; inappropriate attitude. Ideogram: person in a pit.

Let-go, *SHI*: lose, let slip; omit, miss, fail; lose control of. Ideogram: drop from the hand. **Dao**, *DAO*: way or path; ongoing process of being and the course it traces for each person or thing; ultimate reality, intrinsic nature; origin. Ideogram: go and head, opening a path. **Indeed**, *YE*: see *Preceding Situation.*

NINE AT SECOND

The **gorge possesses venturing**.
Seeking the **small**: **acquiring**.

Comments
Seeking the **small**: **acquiring**.
Not-yet emerging from the **center indeed**.

Fields of meaning

Gorge, *KAN*: see *Image of the Situation.* **Possess**, *YOU*: see *Image of the Situation.* **Venture**, *XIAN*: face a severe difficulty or obstruction; risk; precipice, cliff, abyss; key point, point of danger; Action of the trigram Gorge, *KAN*. Ideogram: mound and all, everything engaged at one point. **Seek**, *QIU*: search for, aim at, wish for, desire; implore, supplicate; covetous. **Small**, *XIAO*: little, common, unimportant; adapting to what crosses your path; ability to move in harmony with the vicissitudes of life; contrasts with great, *DA*, self-imposed theme or goal. **Acquire**, *DE*: obtain the desired object; possession; satisfied, fulfilled; it is permitted; agree with; wish for, desire covetously. Ideogram: go and obstacle, going through obstacles to the goal.

Not-yet, *WEI*: temporal negative indicating that something is expected to happen but has not yet occurred. **Emerge**, *CHU*: come out of, proceed from, spring from, issue forth; appear, be born; bear, generate; leave, flee; Action of the trigram Shake, *ZHEN*. Ideogram: stem with branches and leaves emerging. **Center**, *ZHONG*: inner, central; put in the center; middle, stable point enabling you to face inner and outer changes; middle line of a trigram. Ideogram: field divided in two equal parts. **Indeed**, *YE*: see *Preceding Situation.*

SIX AT THIRD

To **coming belongs gorge**, **gorge**.
Venturing, **moreover reclining**.
Entering tending-towards the **gorge**'s **recess**.
No availing of.

Comments
To **coming belongs gorge**, **gorge**.
Completing without achieving indeed.

Fields of meaning

Come, *LAI*: approach in time or space; move toward, arrive at; future; contrasts with go, *WANG*, move away or become past. Belong/it, *ZHI*: establishes between two terms a connection similar to the Saxon genitive, in which the second term belongs to the first one; at the end of a sentence it refers to something previously mentioned or implied. Gorge, *KAN*: see *Image of the Situation*. Venture, *XIAN*: face a severe difficulty or obstruction; risk; precipice, cliff, abyss; key point, point of danger; Action of the trigram Gorge, *KAN*. Ideogram: mound and all, everything engaged at one point. Moreover, *QIE*: further, and also. Recline, *ZHEN*: lean back or on; soften, relax; head rest, back support. Enter, *RU*: penetrate, go into, enter on, encroach on; progress; put into; Action of the trigram Root, *SUN*. Tend-towards, *YU*: move toward without necessarily reaching, in the direction of. Recess, *DAN*: pit within a large cave; trap. No, *WU*: common term of negation. Avail, *YONG*: use, employ for a specific purpose; take advantage of; benefit from; capacity. Ideogram: to divine and center, applying divination to central concerns.

Complete, *ZHONG*: see *Preceding Situation*. Without, *WU*: devoid of; there is not. Achieve, *GONG*: work done, results, actual accomplishment; praise, worth, merit. Ideogram: workman's square and forearm, combining craft and strength. Indeed, *YE*: see *Preceding Situation*.

SIX AT FOURTH

A **cup** of **liquor**, a **platter added**.
Availing of a **jar**.
Letting-in bonds originating from the **window**.
Completing, **without fault**.

Comments
A **cup** of **liquor**, a **platter added**.
Solid and **supple**'s **border indeed**.

Fields of meaning

Cup, *ZUN*: quantity a libation vessel contains; wine cup, glass, bottle. Liquor, *JIU*: alcoholic beverages, distilled spirits; spirit which perfects the good and evil in human nature. Ideogram: liquid above fermenting must, separating the spirits. Platter, *GUI*: wood or bamboo plate; bronze vessel for food; sacrificial utensil. Add, *ER*: join to something previous; reiterate, repeat; second, double; assistant. Avail, *YONG*: use, employ for a specific purpose; take advantage of; benefit from; capacity. Ideogram: to divine and center, applying divination to central concerns. Jar, *FOU*: earthenware vessels; wine-jars and drums. Ideogram: jar containing liquor. Let-in, *NA*: allow to enter; include, receive, accept, welcome; marry. Bonds, *YUE*: tie; cords, ropes; contracts, treaties, legal and moral obligations; moderate, restrain; poor. Origin, *ZI*: source, beginning, ground; cause, reason, motive; tracing back to the source; oneself, by oneself; spontaneous, intrinsic. Window, *YOU*: window; open, instruct, enlighten. Complete, *ZHONG*: see *Preceding Situation*. Without fault, *WU JIU*: no error or harm in the situation.

Solid, *GANG*: quality of the whole lines; firm, strong, unyielding, persisting. Supple, *ROU*: quality of the opened lines; flexible, pliant, adaptable, tender. Border, *JI*: boundary, frontier, line that joins and divides; meet, face to face. Ideogram: place and sacrifice, meeting point of the human and the spirit world. Indeed, *YE*: see *Preceding Situation*.

NINE AT FIFTH

The **gorge not overfilled**.
Merely already evened.
Without fault.

Comments

The **gorge not overfilled**.
In the **center not-yet** the **great indeed**.

Fields of meaning

Gorge, *KAN*: see *Image of the Situation*. Not, *BU*: common term of negation. Overfill, *YING*: fill completely; full, at the point of overflowing; excess, arrogance. Ideogram: vessel and overflow. Merely, *ZHI*: only, just, simply; respect, venerate. Already, *JI*: completed, done, occurred, finished; past tense; shortly after. Even, *PING*: level, flatten, equalize; balanced, regular; uniform, peaceful, tranquil; restore quiet, harmonize. Without fault, *WU JIU*: no error or harm in the situation.

Center, *ZHONG*: inner, central; put in the center; middle, stable point enabling you to face inner and outer changes; middle line of a trigram. Ideogram:

field divided in two equal parts. **Not-yet**, *WEI*: temporal negative indicating that something is expected to happen but has not yet occurred. **Great**, *DA*: big, noble, important, very; orient the will toward a self-imposed goal, impose direction; ability to lead or guide one's life; contrasts with small, *XIAO*, flexible adaptation to what crosses one's path. **Indeed**, *YE*: see *Preceding Situation*.

SIX ABOVE

Tied availing of **stranded ropes**.
Dismissing tending-towards dense jujube-trees.
Three year's-time, **not acquiring**.
Pitfall.

Comments
Six above, **letting-go dao**.
Pitfall, **three year's-time indeed**.

Fields of meaning

Tie, *XI*: connect, attach, bind; devoted to; relatives. Ideogram: person and connect, ties between humans. **Avail**, *YONG*: use, employ for a specific purpose; take advantage of; benefit from; capacity. Ideogram: to divine and center, applying divination to central concerns. **Stranded ropes**, *HUI MO*: three-stranded ropes; royal garments; beautiful, honorable. **Dismiss**, *ZHI*: put aside, reject; judge and find wanting. **Tend-towards**, *YU*: move toward without necessarily reaching, in the direction of. **Dense**, *CONG*: close-set, bushy, crowded; a grove. **Jujube-tree**, *JI*: thorny bush or tree; sign of a court of justice or site of official literary examinations; difficulties, pains; firm, correct, strict. **Three/thrice**, *SAN*: number three; third time or place; active phases of a cycle; superlative; beginning of repetition (since one and two are entities in themselves). **Year's-time**, *SUI*: duration of a year; beginning of a year. **Not**, *BU*: common term of negation. **Acquire**, *DE*: obtain the desired object; possession; satisfied, fulfilled; it is permitted; agree with; wish for, desire covetously. Ideogram: go and obstacle, going through obstacles to the goal. **Pitfall**, *XIONG*: unfortunate situation, in which the flow of life and spirit is blocked and the experience of meaning is lost; stuck and exposed to danger; inappropriate attitude. Ideogram: person in a pit.

Six, *LIU*: number six; transforming opened line; six lines of a hexagram. **Above**, *SHANG*: see *Hexagrams in Pairs*. **Let-go**, *SHI*: lose, let slip; omit, miss, fail; lose control of. Ideogram: drop from the hand. **Dao**, *DAO*: way or path; ongoing process of being and the course it traces for each person or thing; ultimate reality, intrinsic nature; origin. Ideogram: go and head, opening a path. **Indeed**, *YE*: see *Preceding Situation*.

Image Tradition

Repeated gorge.
Redoubled venturing indeed.
Stream diffusing and-also not overfilling.
Movement: venturing and-also not letting-go one's trustworthiness.

Holding-fast the **heart, Growing.**
Thereupon using the **solid** in the **center indeed.**
Movement possesses honor. Going possesses achievement indeed.
Heaven's **venture: not permitting ascending indeed.**
Earth's **venture: mountains, rivers, hill-tops, mounds indeed.**

The **King** and the **princes set-up venturing used** to **guard their city.**
The **season belonging** to **venturing avails** of the **great actually in-fact.**

Fields of meaning

Repeated gorge, *XI KAN*: see *Image of the Situation.* **Redouble**, *CHONG*: repeat, reiterate, add to; weight, heaviness; important, difficult. **Venture**, *XIAN*: face a severe difficulty or obstruction; risk; precipice, cliff, abyss; key point, point of danger; Action of the trigram Gorge, *KAN*. Ideogram: mound and all, everything engaged at one point. **Indeed**, *YE*: see *Preceding Situation.* **Stream**, *SHUI*: see *Patterns of Wisdom.* **Diffuse**, *LIU*: flow out, spread, permeate. **And-also**, *ER*: see *Hexagrams in Pairs.* **Not**, *BU*: common term of negation. **Overfill**, *YING*: fill completely; full, at the point of overflowing; excess, arrogance. Ideogram: vessel and overflow. **Move**, *XING*: see *Image of the Situation.* **Let-go**, *SHI*: lose, let slip; omit, miss, fail; lose control of. Ideogram: drop from the hand. **One/one's**, *QI*: general third person pronoun and possessive adjective; also: it/its, he/his, she/her, they/their. **Trustworthy**, *XIN*: truthful, faithful, consistent over time; count on, confide in; examine, verify, prove; loyalty, integrity. Ideogram: person and word, true speech.

Holding-fast the **heart, Growing**, *WEI XIN HENG*: see *Image of the Situation.* **Thereupon**, *NAI*: on that ground, then, only then; finally; in spite of that. **Use**, *YI*: see *Patterns of Wisdom.* **Solid**, *GANG*: quality of the whole lines; firm, strong, unyielding, persisting. **Center**, *ZHONG*: inner, central; put in the center; middle, stable point enabling you to face inner and outer changes; middle line of a trigram. Ideogram: field divided in two equal parts. **Movement possesses honor,** *XING YOU SHANG*: see *Image of the Situation*. Go, *WANG*: move away in time or space, depart; become past; dead, gone; contrasts with come, *LAI*, approach in time or space. **Achieve**, *GONG*: work done, results, actual accomplishment; praise, worth, merit. Ideogram: workman's square and forearm, combining craft and strength. **Heaven**, *TIAN*: sky, firmament, heavens; the highest realm, situated above the human world, as opposed to the earth, *DI*, located below; Symbol of the trigram Energy, *QIAN*. Ideogram: great and the one above. **Permit**, *KE*: possible because in harmony with an inherent principle; capable of; approve, authorize. Ideogram: mouth and breath, silent consent. **Ascend**, *SHENG*: rise, augment, grow; climb step by step; rise in office; advance through effort; offer a sacrifice; lit.: a measure for fermented liquor, ascension as distillation. **Earth**, *DI*: the earth, ground on which the human world rests; basis of all things, nourishes all things; essential Yin; Symbol of the trigram Space, *KUN*. **Mountain**, *SHAN*: mountain; large, immense; limit, boundary; Symbol of the trigram Bound, *GEN*. Ideogram: three peaks, a mountain range. **River**, *CHUAN*: watercourse, large river, stream; flow; continuous, unceasing; associated with the Streaming Moment and the trigram Gorge, *KAN*. **Hill-top**, *QIU*: hill with hollow top used for worship and as grave-site; knoll, hillock. **Mound**, *LING*: grave-mound, barrow; small hill.

King, *WANG*: sovereign, effective ruler, emperor, seen as connecting heaven and earth; reign, govern. **Prince**, *GONG*: highest title of nobility; noble acting as minister of state in the capital; contrasts with feudatory, *HOU*, governor of a province. **Set-up**, *SHE*: establish, institute; arrange, set in order. Ideogram: words and impel, establish with words. **Guard**, *SHOU*: keep in custody; protect, ward off harm, attend to, supervise. **They/their**, *QI*: general third person pronoun and possessive adjective; also: one/one's, it/its, he/his, she/her. **City**, *GUO*: city, state, country, nation; area of only human constructions; first of the territorial zones: city, suburbs, countryside, forest. **Season**, *SHI*: quality of the time; the right time, opportune, in harmony; planning in accord with the time; season of the year. Ideogram: sun and temple, sacred time. **Belong/it**, *ZHI*: establishes between two terms a connection similar to the Saxon genitive, in which the second term belongs to the first one; at the end of a sentence it refers to something previously mentioned or implied. **Avail**, *YONG*: use, employ for a specific purpose; take advantage of; benefit from; capacity. Ideogram: to divine and center, applying divination to central concerns. **Great**, *DA*: big, noble, important, very; orient the will toward a self-imposed goal, impose direction; ability to lead or guide one's life; contrasts with small, *XIAO*, flexible adaptation to what crosses one's path. **Actually**, *YI*: truly, really, at present. Ideogram: a dart and done, strong intention fully expressed. **In-fact**, *ZAI*: emphatic exclamation; truly, indeed.

離

䷝

30 THE RADIANCE
Li

The situation described by this hexagram is characterized by a source of light, warmth and awareness, which gathers people around itself. The hexagram The Radiance is the doubling of the corresponding trigram, and partakes of its attributes.

Image of the Situation

> The **radiance**.
> **Harvesting**, **Trial**.
> **Growing**. **Accumulating female cattle**.
> **Significant**.

Fields of meaning

Radiance, *LI*: glowing light, spreading in all directions; the power of consciousness; discriminate, articulate, divide and arrange in order; assemble, attract. Ideogram: bird and weird, magical fire-bird with brilliant plumage. *Symbols*: fire and brightness. Fire, *HUO*: flame, burn; warming and consuming aspect of burning. Brightness, *MING*: light, radiance, clarity; distinguish, discern, understand; light-giving aspect of fire, of heavenly bodies and of consciousness. *Action*: congregate, *LI*, cling together, adhere to, rely on; couple, pair, herd; beautiful, elegant. Ideogram: deer flocking together. In the family of trigrams *LI* is the middle daughter. **Harvest**, *LI*: benefit, advantage, profit; realization; sharp, acute, insightful; quality of autumn and West, third stage of the Time Cycle. Ideogram: ripe grain and blade. **Trial**, *ZHEN*: inquiry by divination and its result; righteous, firm; separating wheat from chaff; the kernel, the proven core; quality of winter and North, fourth stage of the Time Cycle. Ideogram: pearl and divination. **Grow**, *HENG*: heavenly influence pervading and nourishing all things; prosper, succeed, expand, develop; effective, favorable; quality of summer and South, second stage of the Time Cycle. With the pronunciation *XIANG*: offer a sacrifice; offer a gift to a superior; accept, enjoy. **Accumulate**, *CHU*: retain, hoard, gather, herd together; control, restrain; domesticate, tame, train; raise, feed, sustain, bring up. Ideogram: field and black, fertile black soil, accumulated through retaining silt. **Female**, *PIN*: female animal; female sexual organs, particularly of farm animals; concave, hollow. Ideogram: cattle and ladle, a hollow, reproductive organ. **Cattle**, *NIU*: ox, bull, cow, calf; power and strength of work animals; stubborn. **Significant**, *JI*: leads to the experience of meaning; favorable, propitious, appropriate. Ideogram: scholar and mouth, wise words of a sage.

Outer and Inner Trigram

In this hexagram the outer and inner aspects of the situation are identical, and they are described by the trigram **Radiance**. Its associations are listed in the corresponding *Field of meaning* above.

Counter Hexagram

The Counter Hexagram of **The Radiance** is hexagram 28, **The Great Exceeding**, which switches the emphasis from discriminating consciousness to compulsive pursuit of a central goal.

Preceding Situation

> **Falling necessarily possesses** a **place** to **congregate**.
> To **anterior acquiescence belongs** the **use** of the
> **radiance**.
> **Radiance implies congregating indeed**.

Fields of meaning

Fall, *XIAN*: fall down or into, sink, drop, descend; pit, trap, fault; falling water; Action of the trigram Gorge, *KAN*. **Necessarily**, *BI*: unavoidably, certainly. **Possess**, *YOU*: general term indicating possession; have, own, be endowed with. **Place**, *SUO*: position, location; residence, dwelling; where something belongs or comes from; habitual focus or object. **Congregate**, *LI*: cling together, adhere to, rely on; couple, pair, herd; beautiful, elegant; Action of the trigram Radiance, *LI*. Ideogram: deer flocking together. To **anterior acquiescence belongs** the **use** of, *GU SHOU ZHI YI*: understanding and accepting the preceding statement allows the consultant to make proper use of this hexagram. **Radiance**, *LI*: see *Image of the Situation*. **Imply**, *ZHE*: further signify; additional meaning. **Indeed**, *YE*: emphasizes and intensifies the previous statement.

Hexagrams in Pairs

> The **radiance above and-also** the **gorge below indeed**.

Fields of meaning

Radiance, *LI*: see *Image of the Situation*. **Above**, *SHANG*: anything above in all senses; higher, upper, outer; upper trigram. **And-also**, *ER*: joins and contrasts two terms. **Gorge**, *KAN*: precipice, dangerous place; hole, cavity, pit, snare, trap, grave; critical time, test; risky. Ideogram: earth and cavity. **Below**, *XIA*: anything below, in all senses; lower, inner; lower trigram. **Indeed**, *YE*: see *Preceding Situation*.

Patterns of Wisdom

> **Brightness doubled arouses** the **radiance**.
> The **great** in the **person uses consecutive brightening**
> to **illuminate tending-towards** the **four sides**.

Fields of meaning

Brightness, *MING*: light, radiance, clarity; distinguish, discern, understand; light-giving aspect of fire, of heavenly bodies and of consciousness; brightness and fire are the Symbols of the trigram Radiance, *LI*. **Doubled**, *LIANG*: twice, both; again; dual, a pair. **Arouse**, *ZUO*: stimulate, stir up from inactivity; arise, appear; generate; begin, invent, make. Ideogram: person and beginning. **Radiance**, *LI*: see *Image of the Situation*. **Great**, *DA*: big, noble, important, very; orient the will toward a self-imposed goal, impose direction; ability to lead or guide one's life; contrasts with small, *XIAO*, flexible adaptation to what crosses one's path. **Person/people**, *REN*: humans individually and collectively; an individual; humankind. **Use**, *YI*: by means of; owing to; make use of, employ. **Consecutive**, *JI*: connect, join; continue; line of succession, adoption. Ideogram: continuity of silk thread connecting cocoons. **Illuminate**, *ZHAO*: shine light on, enlighten; care for, supervise. Ideogram: fire and brightness. **Tend-towards**, *YU*: move toward without necessarily reaching, in the direction of. **Four**, *SI*: number four; number of the cardinal directions and of the seasons; everywhere, on all sides; fourfold articulation of the Universal Compass. **Sides**, *FANG*: cardinal directions; surface of the earth extending to the four cardinal points; everywhere; limits, boundaries.

Transforming Lines

INITIAL NINE

Treading, polishing therefore. Respecting it.
Without fault.

Comments

To **treading** and **polishing belongs respect.**
Using expelling fault indeed.

Fields of meaning

Tread, *LÜ*: walk a path or way; step, path, track; footsteps; course of the stars; appropriate action; virtue; salary, means of subsistence. Ideogram: body and repeating steps. Polish, *CUO*: file away imperfections; wash or plate with gold; confused, in disorder, mixed. Ideogram: metal and old, clearing away accumulated disorder. Therefore, *RAN*: thus, so it is; truly, certainly. Respect, *JING*: stand in awe of, honor; reverent, attentive; warn; inner vigilance. Ideogram: teacher's rod taming speech and attitude. It/belong, *ZHI*: establishes between two terms a connection similar to the Saxon genitive, in which the second term belongs to the first one; at the end of a sentence it refers to something previously mentioned or implied. Without fault, *WU JIU*: no error or harm in the situation.

Belong/it, *ZHI*: establishes between two terms a connection similar to the Saxon genitive, in which the second term belongs to the first one; at the end of a sentence it refers to something previously mentioned or implied. Use, *YI*: see *Patterns of Wisdom*. Expel, *PI*: cast out, repress, exclude, punish; exclusionary laws and their enforcement. Ideogram: punish, authority and mouth, giving order to expel. Fault, *JIU*: unworthy conduct that leads to harm, illness, misfortune; guilt, crime, punishment. Ideogram: person and differ, differ from what you should be. Indeed, *YE*: see *Preceding Situation*.

SIX AT SECOND

Yellow radiance. Spring, significant.

Comments

Yellow radiance, Spring, significant.
Acquiring the **center: dao indeed.**

Fields of meaning

Yellow, *HUANG*: color of the soil in central China, associated with the Earthy Moment leading from the Yang to the Yin hemicycle; emblematic and imperial color of China since the Yellow Emperor (2500 BC). Radiance, *LI*: see *Image of the Situation*. Spring, *YUAN*: source, origin, head; arise, begin; first generating impulse; great, excellent; quality of springtime and East, first stage of the Time Cycle. Significant, *JI*: see *Image of the Situation*.

Acquire, *DE*: obtain the desired object; possession; satisfied, fulfilled; it is permitted; agree with; wish for, desire covetously. Ideogram: go and obstacle, going through obstacles to the goal. Center, *ZHONG*: inner, central; put in the center; middle, stable point enabling you to face inner and outer changes; middle line of a trigram. Ideogram: field divided in two equal parts. Dao, *DAO*: way or path; ongoing process of being and the course it traces for each person or thing; ultimate reality, intrinsic nature; origin. Ideogram: go and head, opening a path. Indeed, *YE*: see *Preceding Situation*.

Nine at Third

Radiance belonging to the **sun setting**.
Not drumbeating a **jar and-also singing**.
By **consequence** to the **great** in **old-age belongs lamenting**.
Pitfall.

Comments
Radiance belonging to the **sun setting**.
Is it **permitted** to **last indeed**?

Fields of meaning

Radiance, *LI*: see *Image of the Situation*. Belong/it, *ZHI*: establishes between two terms a connection similar to the Saxon genitive, in which the second term belongs to the first one; at the end of a sentence it refers to something previously mentioned or implied. Sun/day, *RI*: actual sun and the time of a sun-cycle, a day. Set, *ZE*: sunset, afternoon; waning moon; decline. Not, *BU*: common term of negation. Drumbeating, *GU*: beat a skin or earthenware drum; excite, arouse, encourage; joyous, happy. Jar, *FOU*: earthenware vessels; wine-jars and drums. Ideogram: jar containing liquor. And-also, *ER*: see *Hexagrams in Pairs*. Sing, *GE*: chant, sing elegies; associated with the Earthy Moment, turning point from Yang to Yin. Consequence, *ZE*: reason, cause, result; rule, law, pattern, standard; therefore; very strong connection. Great, *DA*: see *Patterns of Wisdom*. Old-age, *DIE*: seventy or older; aged, no longer active. Lament, *JUE*: sigh, express intense regret or sorrow, mourn over; painful recollections. Pitfall, *XIONG*: unfortunate situation, in which the flow of life and spirit is blocked and the experience of meaning is lost; stuck and exposed to danger; inappropriate attitude. Ideogram: person in a pit.

Is?, *HE*: ask, inquire; what? which? who? how? why? where? an interrogative particle, often introducing a rhetorical question: is it? is it not? Permit, *KE*: possible because in harmony with an inherent principle; capable of; approve, authorize. Ideogram: mouth and breath, silent consent. **Last**, *JIU*: endure; long, protracted, permanent, eternal; old, ancient. **Indeed**, *YE*: see *Preceding Situation*.

Nine at Fourth

Assailing thus, its coming thus.
Burning thus. Dying thus. Thrown-out thus.

Comments
Assailing thus, its coming thus.
Without a **place** of **tolerance indeed**.

Fields of meaning

Assail, *TU*: rush against; abrupt attack, suddenly stricken; insolent, offensive. **Thus**, *RU*: as, in this way; comparable, similar. **It/its**, *QI*: general third person pronoun and possessive adjective; also: one/one's, he/his, she/her, they/their. **Come**, *LAI*: approach in time or space; move toward, arrive at; future; contrasts with go, *WANG*, move away or become past. **Burn**, *FEN*: set fire to, destroy, die. **Die**, *SI*: sudden or untimely death; death penalty; run out of energy; inert, stagnant, fixed. **Throw-out**, *QI*: reject, discard, abandon, push aside; renounce, forget.

Without, *WU*: devoid of; there is not. **Place**, *SUO*: see *Preceding Situation*. **Tolerate**, *RONG*: allow, contain, endure, bear; accept graciously. Ideogram: full stream bed, tolerating and containing. **Indeed**, *YE*: see *Preceding Situation*.

Six at Fifth

Emerging tears like gushing.
Sadness like lamenting.
Significant.

Comments
To **six** at **fifth belongs significance**.
Radiance: **king** and **princes indeed**.

Fields of meaning

Emerge, *CHU*: come out of, proceed from, spring from, issue forth; appear, be born; bear, generate; leave, flee; Action of the trigram Shake, *ZHEN*. Ideogram: stem with branches and leaves emerging. **Tears**, *TI*: tears; weep, cry. **Like**, *RUO*: same as, just as; conform, imitate; adverbial suffix indicating similarity. **Gush**,

TUO: water surging in streams; falling tears; heavy rain. **Sad**, *QI*: unhappy, low in spirits, distressed; mourn, sorrow over; commiserate with. **Lament**, *JUE*: sigh, express intense regret or sorrow, mourn over; painful recollections. **Significant**, *JI*: see *Image of the Situation*.

Six, *LIU*: number six; transforming opened line; six lines of a hexagram. **Five**, *WU*: number five; fivefold articulation of the Universal Compass; the Five Moments and all related qualities: directions, colors, smells, tastes, tones, feelings. **Belong/it**, *ZHI*: establishes between two terms a connection similar to the Saxon genitive, in which the second term belongs to the first one; at the end of a sentence it refers to something previously mentioned or implied. **Radiance**, *LI*: see *Image of the Situation*. **King**, *WANG*: sovereign, effective ruler, emperor, seen as connecting heaven and earth; reign, govern. **Prince**, *GONG*: highest title of nobility; noble acting as minister of state in the capital; contrasts with feudatory, *HOU*, governor of a province. **Indeed**, *YE*: see *Preceding Situation*.

NINE ABOVE

The **king avails** of **emerging** to **discipline**.
Possessing excellence.
Severing the **head**. **Capturing in-no-way its demons**.
Without fault.

Comments
The **king avails** of **emerging** to **discipline**.
Using correcting the **fiefdoms indeed**.

Fields of meaning
King, *WANG*: sovereign, effective ruler, emperor, seen as connecting heaven and earth; reign, govern. **Avail**, *YONG*: use, employ for a specific purpose; take advantage of; benefit from; capacity. Ideogram: to divine and center, applying divination to central concerns. **Emerge**, *CHU*: come out of, proceed from, spring from, issue forth; appear, be born; bear, generate; leave, flee; Action of the trigram Shake, *ZHEN*. Ideogram: stem with branches and leaves emerging. **Discipline**, *ZHENG*: subjugate vassals, reduce to order; punishing expedition. Ideogram: step and correct, a rectifying move. **Possess**, *YOU*: see *Preceding Situation*. **Excellence**, *JIA*: superior quality; fine, beautiful, glorious; happy, pleased; rejoice in, praise. **Sever**, *ZHE*: break off, separate, sunder, cut in two; discriminate, pass judgment on. **Head**, *SHOU*: physical head; leader, sovereign; beginning, origin, model; foremost, superior, upper, front. **Capture**, *HUO*: obtain, seize, reach; take in a hunt, catch a thief; hit the mark, opportune moment; prisoner, spoils, prey, slave,

servant. In-no-way, *FEI*: strong negative; not so; bandit, rebel; unjust, immoral. Ideogram: a box filled with opposition. It/its, *QI*: general third person pronoun and possessive adjective; also: one/one's, he/his, she/her, they/their. Demon, *CHOU*: malignant genius; horror; ugly, vile, disgraceful, shameful; drunken; detest, hate; strange, ominous; class, group, crowd; similar. Ideogram: fermented liquor and soul. Demon and tiger are opposed on the North–South axis of the Universal Compass; the tiger (Extreme Yang) protects against the demons of Extreme Yin. Without fault, *WU JIU*: no error or harm in the situation.

Use, *YI*: see *Patterns of Wisdom*. Correct, *ZHENG*: rectify deviation or one-sidedness; proper, straight, exact, regular; constant, rule, model. Ideogram: stop and one, hold to one thing. Fiefdom, *BANG*: region governed by a feudatory. Indeed, *YE*: see *Preceding Situation*.

Image Tradition

Radiance. **Congregating indeed**.
Sun and **moon congregating reach heaven**.
The **hundred grains**, **grasses**, **trees congregating reach** the **earth**.
Redoubled brightness uses congregating to **reach correcting**.
Thereupon changes accomplished below heaven.

The **supple congregating reaches** the **center**'s **correctness**.
Anterior Growing.
That uses accumulating female cattle, **significant indeed**.

Fields of meaning

Radiance, *LI*: see *Image of the Situation*. Congregate, *LI*: see *Preceding Situation*. Indeed, *YE*: see *Preceding Situation*. Sun/day, *RI*: actual sun and the time of a sun-cycle, a day. Moon, *YUE*: moon and moon-cycle, month; menstruation; Yin. Reach, *HU*: arrive at a goal; move toward and achieve; to, at, in; distinct from tend-towards, *YOU*. Heaven, *TIAN*: sky, firmament, heavens; the highest realm, situated above the human world, as opposed to the earth, *DI*, located below; Symbol of the trigram Energy, *QIAN*. Ideogram: great and the one above. Hundred, *BO*: numerous, many, all; a whole class or type. Grains, *GU*: cereal crops, corn; income; substantial, prosperous, bless with plenty. Grass, *CAO*: all grassy plants and herbs; young, tender plants; rough draft; hastily. Tree/wood,

MU: trees and all things woody or wooden; associated with the Wooden Moment; wood and wind are the Symbols of the trigram Ground, *SUN*. Ideogram: a tree with roots and branches. Earth, *DI*: the earth, ground on which the human world rests; basis of all things, nourishes all things; essential Yin; Symbol of the trigram Space, *KUN*. Redouble, *CHONG*: repeat, reiterate, add to; weight, heaviness; important, difficult. Brightness, *MING*: see *Patterns of Wisdom*. Use, *YI*: see *Patterns of Wisdom*. Correct, *ZHENG*: rectify deviation or one-sidedness; proper, straight, exact, regular; constant, rule, model. Ideogram: stop and one, hold to one thing. Thereupon, *NAI*: on that ground, then, only then; finally; in spite of that. Change, *HUA*: gradual, continuous change; melt, dissolve; be born, die; influence; contrasts with transform, *BIAN*, sudden mutation. Ideogram: person alive and dead, the life process. Accomplish, *CHENG*: complete, finish, bring about; perfect, full, whole; play one's part, do one's duty; mature. Ideogram: weapon and man, able to bear arms, thus fully developed. Below heaven, *TIAN XIA*: human world, between heaven and earth.

Supple, *ROU*: quality of the opened lines; flexible, pliant, adaptable, tender. Center, *ZHONG*: inner, central; put in the center; middle, stable point enabling you to face inner and outer changes; middle line of a trigram. Ideogram: field divided in two equal parts. Anterior, *GU*: come before as cause; former, ancient; reason, purpose, intention; grievance, dissatisfaction, sorrow, resulting from previous causes and intentions; situation leading to a divination. Grow, *HENG*: see *Image of the Situation*. That, *SHI*: refers to the preceding statement. Accumulating female cattle, *CHU PIN NIU*: see *Image of the Situation*. Significant, *JI*: see *Image of the Situation*.

咸

31 CONJUNCTION

Xian

The situation described by this hexagram is characterized by the attraction and influence between two complementary parts of a whole.

Image of the Situation

> **Conjunction.**
> **Growing, Harvesting, Trial.**
> **Grasping womanhood, significant.**

Fields of meaning

Conjoin, *XIAN*: come in contact with, join; put together as parts of a previously separated whole; conjunction of celestial bodies; totally, completely; accord, harmony, mutual influence; lit.: broken piece of pottery, the halves of which join to identify partners. **Grow**, *HENG*: heavenly influence pervading and nourishing all things; prosper, succeed, expand, develop; effective, favorable; quality of summer and South, second stage of the Time Cycle. With the pronunciation XIANG: offer a sacrifice; offer a gift to a superior; accept, enjoy. **Harvest**, *LI*: benefit, advantage, profit; realization; sharp, acute, insightful; quality of autumn and West, third stage of the Time Cycle. Ideogram: ripe grain and blade. **Trial**, *ZHEN*: inquiry by divination and its result; righteous, firm; separating wheat from chaff; the kernel, the proven core; quality of winter and North, fourth stage of the Time Cycle. Ideogram: pearl and divination. **Grasp**, *QU*: seize with effort, take and use, appropriate; take as a wife; grasp the meaning, understand. Ideogram: ear and hand, hear and grasp. **Woman(hood)**, *NÜ*: woman and what is inherently female. **Significant**, *JI*: leads to the experience of meaning; favorable, propitious, appropriate. Ideogram: scholar and mouth, wise words of a sage.

Outer and Inner Trigram

The upper trigram, **Open**, *DUI*, describes the outer aspects of the situation. It has the following associations: an open surface, promoting interaction and interpenetration; pleasant, easy, responsive, free, unhindered; opening, passage; the mouth; exchange, barter; straight, direct; meet, gather; place where water accumulates. Ideogram: mouth and vapor, communication through speech. *Symbol*: marsh, *ZE*, open surface of a flat body of water and the vapors rising from it; fertilize, enrich; kindness, favor. *Action*: stimulate, *SHUO*, rouse to action and good feeling; stir up, urge on; exhort, persuade; say, tell, relate; cheer, delight; joyous, peaceful, restful. Ideogram: words and exchange. In the family of trigrams *DUI* is the youngest daughter.

The lower trigram, **Bound**, *GEN*, describes the inner aspects of the situation. It has the following associations: limit, frontier; obstacle that prevents from seeing further; stop; still, quiet, motionless; confine, enclose; mountain, sunset, beginning of winter; solid, steady, unshakable; straight, hard, adamant, obstinate. *Symbol*: mountain, *SHAN*, large, immense; limit, boundary. Ideogram: three peaks, a mountain range. *Action*: stop, *ZHI*, bring or come to a standstill, cease, terminate. Ideogram: a foot stops walking. In the family of trigrams *GEN* is the youngest son.

Counter Hexagram

The Counter Hexagram of **Conjunction** is hexagram 44, **Coupling**, which switches the emphasis from the stable conjunction of two complementary parts of a whole to an energetic but temporary meeting driven by powerful instinctual forces.

Preceding Situation

Possessing heaven and **earth**.
Therefore afterwards possessing the **myriad beings**.
Possessing the **myriad beings**.
Therefore afterwards possessing man and **woman**.
Possessing man and **woman**.
Therefore afterwards possessing husband and **wife**.
Possessing husband and **wife**.
Therefore afterwards possessing father and **son**.
Possessing father and **son**.
Therefore afterwards possessing chief and **servant**.
Possessing chief and **servant**.
Therefore afterwards possessing above and **below**.
Possessing above and **below**.
Therefore afterwards the **codes' righteousness**
possesses a **polishing place**.

Fields of meaning

Possess, *YOU*: general term indicating possession; have, own, be endowed with. **Heaven**, *TIAN*: sky, firmament, heavens; the highest realm, situated above the human world, as opposed to the earth, *DI*, located below; Symbol of the trigram Energy, *QIAN*. Ideogram: great and the one above. **Earth**, *DI*: the earth, ground on which the human world rests; basis of all things, nourishes all things; essential Yin; Symbol of the trigram Space, *KUN*. **Therefore**, *RAN*: thus, so it is; truly, certainly. **After(wards)/later**, *HOU*: come after in time, subsequent; put oneself after; behind, back, draw back; the second; attendants, heirs, successors, posterity. **Myriad**, *WAN*: ten thousand; countless, many, everyone. Ideogram: swarm of insects. **Being**, *WU*: creature, thing, any single being; matter, substance, essence; nature of things. **Man(hood)**, *NAN*: a man; what is inherently male; husband, son. Ideogram: field and strength, men's hard work in the fields. **Woman(hood)**, *NÜ*: see *Image of the Situation*. **Husband**, *FU*: adult, man, male spouse; scholar, distinguished man; one who can help; manage a household. Ideogram: man with a pin in his hair to show that he is of age. **Wife**, *FU*: position of married woman as head of the household; distinct from consort, *QI*, which denotes her legal status, and from concubine, *QIE*, secondary wife. Ideogram: woman, hand and broom, household duties. **Father**, *FU*: father, act as a father, paternal, patriarchal; authoritative rule. Ideogram: hand and rod, the chastising father. **Son(hood)**, *ZI*: son, male child; heirs, offspring, posterity; living up to the ideal of the ancestors as highest human aspiration; seed, kernel, egg; sage, teacher; nadir, deepest point, midnight, mid-winter. **Chief**, *JUN*: prince, ruler; lead, direct; wise person. Ideogram: mouth and direct, giving orders. **Servant**, *CHEN*: attendant, minister, vassal; courtier who can speak to the sovereign; wait on, serve in office. Ideogram: person bowing low. **Above**, *SHANG*: anything above in all senses; higher, upper, outer; upper trigram. **Below**, *XIA*: anything below, in all senses; lower, inner; lower trigram. **Codes**, *LI*: rites, rules, ritual, etiquette; usage, manners; honor, worship. Ideogram: worship and sacrificial vase, handling a sacred vessel. **Righteous**, *YI*: proper, just, virtuous, upright; the heart that rules itself; benevolent, loyal, devoted to public good. **Polish**, *CUO*: file away imperfections; wash or plate with gold; confused, in disorder, mixed. Ideogram: metal and old, clearing away accumulated disorder. **Place**, *SUO*: position, location; residence, dwelling; where something belongs or comes from; habitual focus or object.

Hexagrams in Pairs

Conjunction: inviting indeed.
Persevering: lasting indeed.

Fields of meaning

Conjoin, *XIAN*: see *Image of the Situation*. **Invite**, *SU*: call; urge, exert pressure upon; quick, hurried. **Indeed**, *YE*: emphasizes and intensifies the previous statement. **Persevere**, *HENG*: continue in the same way or spirit; constant, habitual, regular; self-renewing. **Last**, *JIU*: endure; long, protracted, permanent, eternal; old, ancient.

Patterns of Wisdom

The **mountain possesses pond above**. **Conjunction**.
A **jun zi uses emptiness** to **acquiesce** the **people**.

Fields of meaning

Mountain, *SHAN*: mountain; large, immense; limit, boundary; Symbol of the trigram Bound, *GEN*. Ideogram: three peaks, a mountain range. **Possess**, *YOU*: see *Preceding Situation*. **Pond**, *ZE*: open surface of a flat body of water and the vapors rising from it; fertilize, enrich; kindness, favor; Symbol of the trigram Open, *DUI*. **Above**, *SHANG*: see *Preceding Situation*. **Conjoin**, *XIAN*: see *Image of the Situation*. **Jun zi**: ideal of a person who orders his/her life in accordance with dao rather than willful intention, and uses divination in this spirit. **Use**, *YI*: by means of; owing to; make use of, employ. **Empty**, *XU*: void; absence of images and concepts; vacant, insubstantial; empty yet fertile space. **Acquiesce**, *SHOU*: accept, make peace with, agree to, receive; at rest, satisfied; patient. **People/person**, *REN*: humans individually and collectively; an individual; humankind.

Transforming Lines

INITIAL SIX

Conjunction of **one's big-toes**.

Comments
Conjunction of **one's big-toes**.
Purpose located outside indeed.

Fields of meaning

Conjoin, *XIAN*: see *Image of the Situation*. **One/one's**, *QI*: general third person pronoun and possessive adjective; also: it/its, he/his, she/her, they/their. **Big-toe/thumb**, *MU*: in the lower trigram, big-toe; in the upper trigram, thumb; the big-toe enables the foot to walk as the thumb enables the hand to grasp.

Purpose, *ZHI*: focus of mind and heart; intention, will, inclination; continuity

in the direction of life. Ideogram: heart and scholar, high inner resolve. **Locate**, *ZAI*: be at, be situated at, dwell, reside; in, within; involved with, in the process of. Ideogram: earth and persevere, a place on the earth. **Outside**, *WAI*: outer, external; unfamiliar, foreign; ignore, reject; work done outside the home; the upper trigram as indication of the outer aspects of the situation. **Indeed**, *YE*: see *Hexagrams in Pairs*.

Six at Second

Conjunction of **one's calves**.
Pitfall.
Residing, **significant**.

Comments
Although a **pitfall**, **residing significant**.
Yielding not harmful indeed.

Fields of meaning
Conjoin, *XIAN*: see *Image of the Situation*. **One/one's**, *QI*: general third person pronoun and possessive adjective; also: it/its, he/his, she/her, they/their. **Calf**, *FEI*: calf; rely on; prop, rest; sick, weak. **Pitfall**, *XIONG*: unfortunate situation, in which the flow of life and spirit is blocked and the experience of meaning is lost; stuck and exposed to danger; inappropriate attitude. Ideogram: person in a pit. **Reside**, *JU*: dwell, live in, stay; sit down; fill an office; well-being, rest. Ideogram: body and seat. **Significant**, *JI*: see *Image of the Situation*.

Although, *SUI*: even though, supposing that, if, even if. **Yield**, *SHUN*: give way, comply, agree, follow, obey; docile, flexible; bear produce, nourish, provide; Action of the trigram Field, *KUN*. **Not**, *BU*: common term of negation. **Harm**, *HAI*: damage, injure, offend; suffer, become ill; obstacle, hindrance; fearful, anxious. **Indeed**, *YE*: see *Hexagrams in Pairs*.

Nine at Third

Conjunction of **one's thighs**.
Holding-on to **one's following**.
Going, **abashment**.

Comments
Conjunction of **one's thighs**.
Truly not abiding indeed.

Purpose located in **following people**.
A **place** for **holding-on** to the **below indeed**.

Fields of meaning

Conjoin, *XIAN*: see *Image of the Situation*. **One/one's**, *QI*: general third person pronoun and possessive adjective; also: it/its, he/his, she/her, they/their. **Thigh**, *GU*: thigh; strand of a rope; part, section. **Hold-on**, *ZHI*: lay hold of, seize, take in hand; keep, maintain, look after; manage, control. Ideogram: criminal and seize. **Follow**, *SUI*: step behind, come after, move in the same direction; comply with what is ahead; pursue; follow a way or religion; conform to; next, subsequent. Ideogram: go and fall, unavoidable movement. Go, *WANG*: move away in time or space, depart; become past; dead, gone; contrasts with come, *LAI*, approach in time or space. **Abashment**, *LIN*: distress, shame, regret, humiliation; aware of having lost the right track; leads to repenting, *HUI*, correcting the direction of mind and life.

Truly, *YI*: in fact; also; nevertheless. **Not**, *BU*: common term of negation. **Abide**, *CHU*: rest in, dwell; stop oneself; arrive at a place or condition; distinguish, decide; do what is proper. Ideogram: tiger, stop and seat, powerful movement coming to rest. **Indeed**, *YE*: see *Hexagrams in Pairs*. **Purpose**, *ZHI*: focus of mind and heart; intention, will, inclination; continuity in the direction of life. Ideogram: heart and scholar, high inner resolve. **Locate**, *ZAI*: be at, be situated at, dwell, reside; in, within; involved with, in the process of. Ideogram: earth and persevere, a place on the earth. **People/person**, *REN*: see *Patterns of Wisdom*. **Place**, *SUO*: see *Preceding Situation*. **Below**, *XIA*: see *Preceding Situation*.

Nine at Fourth

Trial, **significant**. **Repenting extinguished**.
Wavering, **wavering**: **going**, **coming**.
Partners adhere to **simply pondering**.

Comments
Trial, **significant**. **Repenting extinguished**.
Not-yet influencing harmful indeed.
Wavering, **wavering**: **going**, **coming**.
Not-yet the **shining great indeed**.

Fields of meaning

Trial, *ZHEN*: see *Image of the Situation*. **Significant**, *JI*: see *Image of the Situation*. **Repenting extinguished**, *HUI WANG*: previous errors are corrected, all causes for repenting disappear. **Waver**, *CHONG*: irresolute, hesitating, unsettled; fluctuate, sway to and fro. Go, *WANG*: move away in time or space, depart; become past; dead, gone; contrasts with come, *LAI*, approach in time or space. **Come**, *LAI*: approach in time or space; move toward, arrive at; future; contrasts with go, *WANG*, move away or become past. **Partner**, *PENG*: companion, friend, peer; join, associate for mutual benefit; commercial venture; two equal or similar things. Ideogram: linked strings of cowries or coins. **Adhere**, *CONG*: follow, agree with, comply with, obey; join a doctrine, school, or person; servant, follower. Ideogram: two men walking, one following the other. **Simply**, *ER*: just so, only. **Ponder**, *SI*: reflect, consider, remember; deep thought; desire, wish. Ideogram: heart and field, the heart's concerns.

Not-yet, *WEI*: temporal negative indicating that something is expected to happen but has not yet occurred. **Influence**, *GAN*: excite, act on, touch; affect someone's feelings, move the heart; emotion, feeling. Ideogram: heart and all, pervasive influence. **Harm**, *HAI*: damage, injure, offend; suffer, become ill; obstacle, hindrance; fearful, anxious. **Indeed**, *YE*: see *Hexagrams in Pairs*. **Shine**, *GUANG*: illuminate, emit light; brilliant, splendid; honor, glory, éclat; distinct from brightness, *MING*, light of heavenly bodies. Ideogram: fire above person. **Great**, *DA*: big, noble, important, very; orient the will toward a self-imposed goal, impose direction; ability to lead or guide one's life; contrasts with small, *XIAO*, flexible adaptation to what crosses one's path.

Nine at Fifth

Conjunction of **one's neck**.
Without repenting.

Comments
Conjunction of **one's neck**.
The **purpose**'s **tip indeed**.

Fields of meaning

Conjoin, *XIAN*: see *Image of the Situation*. **One/one's**, *QI*: general third person pronoun and possessive adjective; also: it/its, he/his, she/her, they/their. **Neck**, *MEI*: muscular base of neck, shoulders and arms; source of strength in arms and shoulders; persist. **Without**, *WU*: devoid of; there is not. **Repent**, *HUI*: regret, dissatisfaction with past conduct inducing a change of heart; proceeds from abashment, *LIN*, shame and confusion at having lost the right way.

Purpose, *ZHI*: focus of mind and heart; intention, will, inclination; continuity in the direction of life. Ideogram: heart and scholar, high inner resolve. **Tip**, *MO*:

outermost twig, growing end of a branch; last, most distant; secondary, insignificant. **Indeed**, *YE*: see *Hexagrams in Pairs*.

SIX ABOVE

Conjunction of **one's jawbones**, **cheeks** and **tongue**.

Comments
Conjunction of **one's jawbones**, **cheeks** and **tongue**.
The **spouting mouth stimulating indeed**.

Fields of meaning
Conjoin, *XIAN*: see *Image of the Situation*. **One/one's**, *QI*: general third person pronoun and possessive adjective; also: it/its, he/his, she/her, they/their. **Jawbones/brace**, *FU*: braces of a cart; cheeks, maxillary bones; support, consolidate, strengthen, prop up; steady, firm, rigid; help, rescue. **Cheeks**, *JIA*: cheeks, jaws; speak, articulate. **Tongue**, *SHE*: tongue; clapper in a bell; talkative, wordy.

Spout, *TENG*: spurt, burst forth; open mouth, loud talk. **Mouth**, *KOU*: mouth, mouthful; words going out and food coming into the mouth; entrance, hole, passageway. **Stimulate**, *SHUO*: rouse to action and good feeling; stir up, urge on; exhort, persuade; say, tell, relate; cheer, delight; joyous, peaceful, restful; Action of the trigram Open, *DUI*. Ideogram: words and exchange. **Indeed**, *YE*: see *Hexagrams in Pairs*.

Image Tradition

Conjunction. **Influencing indeed**.
The **supple above and-also** the **solid below**.
The **two agencies' influences correspond using reciprocal association**.

Stopping and-also stimulating.
Manhood below womanhood.
That uses Growing, **Harvesting**, **Trial**.
Grasping womanhood, **significant indeed**.
Heaven and **earth influence and-also** the **myriad beings change** and **generate**.
The **wise person influences people**'s **heart and-also below heaven harmonizes evenness**.

Overseeing one's place to **influence**.
And-also the **motives belonging** to **heaven** and **earth**'s
myriad beings permit viewing actually.

Fields of meaning

Conjoin, *XIAN*: see *Image of the Situation*. **Influence**, *GAN*: excite, act on, touch; affect someone's feelings, move the heart; emotion, feeling. Ideogram: heart and all, pervasive influence. **Indeed**, *YE*: see *Hexagrams in Pairs*. **Supple**, *ROU*: quality of the opened lines; flexible, pliant, adaptable, tender. **Above**, *SHANG*: see *Preceding Situation*. **And-also**, *ER*: joins and contrasts two terms. **Solid**, *GANG*: quality of the whole lines; firm, strong, unyielding, persisting. **Below**, *XIA*: see *Preceding Situation*. **Two/second**, *ER*: number two; pair, even numbers, binary, duplicate. **Agencies**, *QI*: fluid energy, breath, air; configurative power, vital force; interacts with essence, *JING*, to produce things and beings. Ideogram: vapor and rice, heat and moisture producing substance. **Correspond**, *YING*: be in agreement or harmony; proper, suitable; resonate together, answer to; relation between the lines (1 and 4, 2 and 5, 3 and 6) when they form the pair opened and whole, supple and solid. Ideogram: heart and obey. **Use**, *YI*: see *Patterns of Wisdom*. **Reciprocal**, *XIANG*: mutual; assist, encourage, help; bring together, blend with; examine, inspect; by turns. **Associate**, *YU*: consort with, combine; companions; group, band, company; agree with, comply, help; in favor of. Ideogram: a pair of hands reaching downward meets a pair of hands reaching upward, helpful association.

Stop, *ZHI*: bring or come to a standstill, cease, terminate; Action of the trigram Bound, *GEN*. Ideogram: a foot stops walking. **Stimulate**, *SHUO*: rouse to action and good feeling; stir up, urge on; exhort, persuade; say, tell, relate; cheer, delight; joyous, peaceful, restful; Action of the trigram Open, *DUI*. Ideogram: words and exchange. **Man(hood)**, *NAN*: see *Preceding Situation*. **Woman(hood)**, *NÜ*: see *Image of the Situation*. **That**, *SHI*: refers to the preceding statement. **Use**, *YI*: see *Patterns of Wisdom*. **Growing, Harvesting, Trial**, *HENG LI ZHEN*: see *Image of the Situation*. **Grasping womanhood, significant**, *QU NÜ JI*: see *Image of the Situation*. **Heaven**, *TIAN*: see *Preceding Situation*. **Earth**, *DI*: see *Preceding Situation*. **Myriad**, *WAN*: see *Preceding Situation*. **Being**, *WU*: see *Preceding Situation*. **Change**, *HUA*: gradual, continuous change; melt, dissolve; be born, die; influence; contrasts with transform, *BIAN*, sudden mutation. Ideogram: person alive and dead, the life process. **Generate**, *SHENG*: give birth; be born, arise, grow; beget; life, vitality. Ideogram: earth and sprout. **Wise**, *SHENG*: intuitive universal wisdom; profound understanding; mythical sages of old; holy, sacred, mark of highest distinction. Ideogram: ear and inform, one who knows all from a single sound. **People/person**, *REN*: see *Patterns of Wisdom*. **Heart**, *XIN*: the heart as center of being; seat of mind, imagination and affect; moral nature; source of desires, intentions, will. **Below heaven**, *TIAN XIA*: human world, between heaven and earth. **Harmony**, *HE*: concord, union; conciliate; at peace, mild; fit, tune, adjust. **Even**, *PING*: level, flatten, equalize; balanced, regular; uniform, peaceful, tranquil; restore quiet, harmonize.

Oversee, *GUAN*: contemplate, observe from a distance; look at carefully, gaze at; a high place from where one sees far, monastery, observatory; intelligence, clairvoyance; scry, divine through liquid in a cup. Ideogram: sight and waterbird, aerial view. **One/one's**, *QI*: general third person pronoun and possessive adjective; also: it/its, he/his, she/her, they/their. **Place**, *SUO*: see *Preceding Situation*. **Motive**, *QING*: true nature; feelings, desires, passions; sincere, true, real; state of affairs, circumstances. Ideogram: heart and green, germinated in the heart. **Belong/it**, *ZHI*: establishes between two terms a connection similar to the Saxon genitive, in which the second term belongs to the first one; at the end of a sentence it refers to something previously mentioned or implied. **Permit**, *KE*: possible because in harmony with an inherent principle; capable of; approve, authorize. Ideogram: mouth and breath, silent consent. **View**, *JIAN*: vision in all its aspects: seeing, being visible, forming mental images; visit, call on, consult. Ideogram: eye above person, active and receptive sight. **Actually**, *YI*: truly, really, at present. Ideogram: a dart and done, strong intention fully expressed.

恆

32 PERSEVERING

Heng

The situation described by this hexagram is characterized by duration, long-term commitment, steady determination and persistence.

Image of the Situation

> **Persevering**.
> **Growing**.
> **Without fault**.
> **Harvesting**, **Trial**.
> **Harvesting**: **possessing directed going**.

Fields of meaning

Persevere, *HENG*: continue in the same way or spirit; constant, habitual, regular; self-renewing. **Grow**, *HENG*: heavenly influence pervading and nourishing all things; prosper, succeed, expand, develop; effective, favorable; quality of summer and South, second stage of the Time Cycle. With the pronunciation *XIANG*: offer a sacrifice; offer a gift to a superior; accept, enjoy. **Without fault**, *WU JIU*: no error or harm in the situation. **Harvest**, *LI*: benefit, advantage, profit; realization; sharp, acute, insightful; quality of autumn and West, third stage of the Time Cycle. Ideogram: ripe grain and blade. **Trial**, *ZHEN*: inquiry by divination and its result; righteous, firm; separating wheat from chaff; the kernel, the proven core; quality of winter and North, fourth stage of the Time Cycle. Ideogram: pearl and divination. **Possessing directed going**, *YOU YOU WANG*: having a goal or purpose, moving in a specific direction.

Outer and Inner Trigram

The upper trigram, **Shake**, *ZHEN*, describes the outer aspects of the situation. It has the following associations: arouse, excite, inspire; awe, alarm, trembling; thunder rising from the depth of the earth; fertilizing intrusion. Ideogram: excite and rain. *Symbol*: thunder, *LEI*, arousing power emerging from the depth of the earth. *Action*: stir-up, *DONG*, excite, influence, move, affect; work, take action; come out of the egg or the bud. Ideogram: strength and heavy, move weighty things. In the family of trigrams *ZHEN* is the eldest son.

The lower trigram, **Root**, *SUN*, describes the inner aspects of the situation. It has the following associations: base on which things rest, ground, foundation; mild, subtly penetrating; nourishing. *Symbols*: tree/wood and wind. Tree/wood, *MU*: trees and all things woody or wooden; associated with the Wooden Moment. Ideogram: a tree with roots and branches. Wind, *FENG*: wind, breeze, gust; weather and its influence on mood and humor; fashion, usage. *Action*: enter, *RU*, penetrate, go into, enter on, encroach on; progress; put into. In the family of trigrams *SUN* is the eldest daughter.

Counter Hexagram

The Counter Hexagram of **Persevering** is hexagram 43, **Parting**, which switches the emphasis from the sustained devotion to a long-term process of **Persevering** to a sudden breakthrough, like a flooding river overflowing its banks and parting into different streams.

Preceding Situation

> **Dao belonging** to **husband** and **wife**.
> **Not permitted** to **use not lasting indeed**.
> To **anterior acquiescence belongs** the **use** of **persevering**.
> **Persevering implies lasting indeed**.

Fields of meaning

Dao, *DAO*: way or path; ongoing process of being and the course it traces for each person or thing; ultimate reality, intrinsic nature; origin. Ideogram: go and head, opening a path. **Belong/it**, *ZHI*: establishes between two terms a connection similar to the Saxon genitive, in which the second term belongs to the first one; at the end of a sentence it refers to something previously mentioned or implied. **Husband**, *FU*: adult, man, male spouse; scholar, distinguished man; one who can help; manage a household. Ideogram: man with a pin in his hair to show that he is of age. **Wife**, *FU*: position of married woman as head of the household; distinct from consort, *QI*, which denotes her legal status, and from concubine, *QIE*, secondary wife. Ideogram: woman, hand and broom, household duties. **Not**, *BU*: common term of negation. **Permit**, *KE*: possible because in harmony with an inherent principle; capable of; approve, authorize. Ideogram: mouth and breath, silent consent. **Use**, *YI*: by means of; owing to; make use of, employ. **Not**, *BU*:

common term of negation. **Last**, *JIU*: endure; long, protracted, permanent, eternal; old, ancient. **Indeed**, *YE*: emphasizes and intensifies the previous statement. To **anterior acquiescence belongs** the **use** of, *GU SHOU ZHI YI*: understanding and accepting the preceding statement allows the consultant to make proper use of this hexagram. **Persevere**, *HENG*: see *Image of the Situation*. **Imply**, *ZHE*: further signify; additional meaning.

Hexagrams in Pairs

Conjunction: **inviting indeed**.
Persevering: **lasting indeed**.

Fields of meaning

Conjoin, *XIAN*: come in contact with, join; put together as parts of a previously separated whole; conjunction of celestial bodies; totally, completely; accord, harmony, mutual influence; lit.: broken piece of pottery, the halves of which join to identify partners. **Invite**, *SU*: call; urge, exert pressure upon; quick, hurried. **Indeed**, *YE*: see *Preceding Situation*. **Persevere**, *HENG*: see *Image of the Situation*. **Last**, *JIU*: see *Preceding Situation*.

Additional Texts

Persevering: **firmness belonging** to **actualizing-dao indeed**.
Persevering: **motley and-also not restrict**.
Persevering: **using** the **one actualizing-dao**.

Fields of meaning

Persevere, *HENG*: see *Image of the Situation*. **Firm**, *GU*: steady, solid, strong, secure; constant, fixed. Ideogram: old and enclosure, long preserved. **Belong/it**, *ZHI*: see *Preceding Situation*. **Actualize-dao**, *DE*: realize dao in action; power, virtue; ability to follow the course traced by the ongoing process of the cosmos. Ideogram: go, straight, and heart. Linked with acquire, *DE*: acquiring that which makes a being become what it is meant to be. **Indeed**, *YE*: see *Preceding Situation*. **Motley**, *ZA*: mingled, variegated, mixed; disorder. **And-also**, *ER*: joins and contrasts two terms. **Not**, *BU*: common term of negation. **Restrict**, *YA*: repress, oppress, contain, subjugate; narrow, obedient. **Use**, *YI*: see *Preceding Situation*. **One**, *YI*: a single unit; number one; undivided, simple, whole; unique; first.

Patterns of Wisdom

Thunder and **wind**. **Persevering**.
A **jun zi uses establishing**, **not versatility** on all **sides**.

Fields of meaning
Thunder, *LEI*: thunder; arousing power emerging from the depth of the earth; Symbol of the trigram Shake, *ZHEN*. **Wind**, *FENG*: wind, breeze, gust; weather and its influence on mood and humor; fashion, usage; wind and wood are the Symbols of the trigram Root, *SUN*. **Persevere**, *HENG*: see *Image of the Situation*. **Jun zi**: ideal of a person who orders his/her life in accordance with dao rather than willful intention, and uses divination in this spirit. **Use**, *YI*: see *Preceding Situation*. **Establish**, *LI*: set up, institute, order, arrange; stand erect; settled principles. **Not**, *BU*: common term of negation. **Versatility**, *YI*: sudden and unpredictable change, and the mental mobility and openness required in order to face it; easy, light, simple; occurs in the name of the *Yi Jing*. **Sides**, *FANG*: cardinal directions; surface of the earth extending to the four cardinal points; everywhere; limits, boundaries.

Transforming Lines

INITIAL SIX

Diving persevering: **Trial**, **pitfall**.
Without direction Harvesting.

Comments
To **diving persevering belongs pitfall**.
Beginning seeking depth indeed.

Fields of meaning
Dive, *JUN*: deep water; dig; profound, abstruse. **Persevere**, *HENG*: see *Image of the Situation*. **Trial**, *ZHEN*: see *Image of the Situation*. **Pitfall**, *XIONG*: unfortunate situation, in which the flow of life and spirit is blocked and the experience of meaning is lost; stuck and exposed to danger; inappropriate attitude. Ideogram: person in a pit. **Without direction Harvesting**, *WU YOU LI*: in order to take advantage of the situation, do not impose a direction on events.

Belong/it, *ZHI*: see *Preceding Situation*. **Begin**, *SHI*: commence, start, open; earliest, first; generate. Ideogram: woman and eminent, eminent feminine function of giving birth. **Seek**, *QIU*: search for, aim at, wish for, desire; implore, supplicate; covetous. **Depth**, *SHEN*: deep water; profound, abstruse; ardent, strong, intense, inner; sound the depths. **Indeed**, *YE*: see *Preceding Situation*.

NINE AT SECOND

Repenting extinguished.

Comments

Nine at **second**, **repenting extinguished**.
Able to **last** in the **center indeed**.

Fields of meaning

Repenting extinguished, *HUI WANG*: previous errors are corrected, all causes for repenting disappear.

Nine, *JIU*: number nine; transforming whole line; superlative: best, perfect. **Two/second**, *ER*: number two; pair, even numbers, binary, duplicate. **Able/enable**, *NENG*: ability, power, skill, art; competent, talented; duty, function, capacity. Ideogram: an animal with strong hooves and bones, able to carry and defend. **Last**, *JIU*: see *Preceding Situation*. **Center**, *ZHONG*: inner, central; put in the center; middle, stable point enabling you to face inner and outer changes; middle line of a trigram. Ideogram: field divided in two equal parts. **Indeed**, *YE*: see *Preceding Situation*.

NINE AT THIRD

Not persevering in **one's actualizing-dao**.
Maybe to **receiving belongs embarrassment**.
Trial, **abashment**.

Comments

Not persevering in **one's actualizing-dao**.
Without a **place** to **tolerate indeed**.

Fields of meaning

Not, *BU*: common term of negation. **Persevere**, *HENG*: see *Image of the Situation*. **One/one's**, *QI*: general third person pronoun and possessive adjective; also: it/its, he/his, she/her, they/their. **Actualize-dao**, *DE*: see *Additional Texts*. **Maybe**, *HUO*: possible but not certain, perhaps. **Receive**, *CHENG*: receive gifts or commands from superiors or customers; take in hand; give, offer respectfully; help, support. Ideogram: accepting a seal of office. **Belong/it**, *ZHI*: see *Preceding Situation*. **Embarrassment**, *XIU*: shame, confusion; conscious of guilt or fault; shy, blushing; humble offering. Ideogram: sheep, sheepish feeling. **Trial**, *ZHEN*: see *Image of the*

Situation. **Abashment**, *LIN*: distress, shame, regret, humiliation; aware of having lost the right track; leads to repenting, *HUI*, correcting the direction of mind and life.

Without, *WU*: devoid of; there is not. **Place**, *SUO*: position, location; residence, dwelling; where something belongs or comes from; habitual focus or object. **Tolerate**, *RONG*: allow, contain, endure, bear; accept graciously. Ideogram: full stream bed, tolerating and containing. **Indeed**, *YE*: see *Preceding Situation*.

NINE AT FOURTH

The **fields without wildfowl**.

Comments

No lasting whatever in **one's position**.

Peacefully acquiring wildfowl indeed.

Fields of meaning

Field, *TIAN*: cultivated land, farming land; preferred terrain for hunting, since game in the fields cannot escape the hunt. Ideogram: square divided into four sections, delineating fields. **Without**, *WU*: devoid of; there is not. **Wildfowl**, *QIN*: birds; four-legged animals; hunt, shoot with an arrow; capture; prisoner.

No ... whatever, *FEI*: strongest negative; not at all! **Last**, *JIU*: see *Preceding Situation*. **One/one's**, *QI*: general third person pronoun and possessive adjective; also: it/its, he/his, she/her, they/their. **Position**, *WEI*: place, location; be at; social standing, rank; position of a line in a hexagram. Ideogram: person standing. **Peace**, *AN*: quiet, still, settled, secure, contented; calm, tranquilize, console. Ideogram: woman under a roof, a tranquil home. **Acquire**, *DE*: obtain the desired object; possession; satisfied, fulfilled; it is permitted; agree with; wish for, desire covetously. Ideogram: go and obstacle, going through obstacles to the goal. **Indeed**, *YE*: see *Preceding Situation*.

SIX AT FIFTH

Persevering in **one's actualizing-dao**, **Trial**.

The **wife**'s **people**, **significant**.

The **husband** and the **son**, **pitfall**.

Comments

The **wife**'s **people**: **Trial**, **significant**.

Adhering to the **one and-also completing indeed**.

The **husband** and the **son, paring righteously**.
Adhering to the **wife, pitfall indeed**.

Fields of meaning

Persevere, *HENG*: see *Image of the Situation*. **One/one's,** *QI*: general third person pronoun and possessive adjective; also: it/its, he/his, she/her, they/their. **Actualize-dao,** *DE*: see *Additional Texts*. **Trial,** *ZHEN*: see *Image of the Situation*. **Wife,** *FU*: see *Preceding Situation*. **People/person,** *REN*: humans individually and collectively; an individual; humankind. **Significant,** *JI*: leads to the experience of meaning; favorable, propitious, appropriate. Ideogram: scholar and mouth, wise words of a sage. **Husband,** *FU*: see *Preceding Situation*. **Son(hood),** *ZI*: son, male child; heirs, offspring, posterity; living up to the ideal of the ancestors as highest human aspiration; seed, kernel, egg; sage, teacher; nadir, deepest point, midnight, mid-winter. **Pitfall,** *XIONG*: unfortunate situation, in which the flow of life and spirit is blocked and the experience of meaning is lost; stuck and exposed to danger; inappropriate attitude. Ideogram: person in a pit.

Adhere, *CONG*: follow, agree with, comply with, obey; join a doctrine, school, or person; servant, follower. Ideogram: two men walking, one following the other. **One,** *YI*: see *Additional Texts*. **And-also,** *ER*: see *Additional Texts*. **Complete,** *ZHONG*: completion of a cycle that begins the next; entire, whole, all. Ideogram: silk cocoons, follow and ice, winter linking one year with the next. **Indeed,** *YE*: see *Preceding Situation*. **Pare,** *ZHI*: cut away, tailor, carve; form, invent; institution, rule; limit, prevent. Ideogram: knife and incomplete. **Righteous,** *YI*: proper, just, virtuous, upright; the heart that rules itself; benevolent, loyal, devoted to public good.

SIX ABOVE

Rousing persevering, pitfall.

Comments
Rousing persevering located above.
The **great without achievement indeed**.

Fields of meaning

Rouse, *ZHEN*: stir up, excite, stimulate; issue forth; put in order. Ideogram: hand and shake, shaking things up. **Persevere,** *HENG*: see *Image of the Situation*. **Pitfall,** *XIONG*: unfortunate situation, in which the flow of life and spirit is blocked and the experience of meaning is lost; stuck and exposed to danger; inappropriate attitude. Ideogram: person in a pit.

Locate, *ZAI*: be at, be situated at, dwell, reside; in, within; involved with, in the process of. Ideogram: earth and persevere, a place on the earth. **Above**, *SHANG*: anything above in all senses; higher, upper, outer; upper trigram. **Great**, *DA*: big, noble, important, very; orient the will toward a self-imposed goal, impose direction; ability to lead or guide one's life; contrasts with small, *XIAO*, flexible adaptation to what crosses one's path. **Without**, *WU*: devoid of; there is not. **Achieve**, *GONG*: work done, results, actual accomplishment; praise, worth, merit. Ideogram: workman's square and forearm, combining craft and strength. **Indeed**, *YE*: see *Preceding Situation*.

Image Tradition

Persevering. Lasting indeed.
The **solid above and-also** the **supple below**.
Thunder and **wind reciprocally associating**.
Root and-also stirring-up.
Solid and **supple altogether corresponding**.
Persevering.

Persevering Growing, without fault.
Harvesting, Trial.
Lasting with-respect-to one's dao indeed.
Dao belonging to **heaven** and **earth**.
Persevering lasting and-also not climaxing indeed.
Harvesting: **possessing directed going**.
Completing, by **consequence possessing beginning indeed**.

Sun and **moon**: **acquiring heaven and-also enabling lasting** and **illuminating**.
The **four seasons**: **transforming changes and-also enabling lasting** and **accomplishing**.
The **wise person**: **lasting with-respect-to one's dao and-also below heaven changing** and **accomplishing**.

Overseeing one's place to **persevere**.
And-also the **motives belonging** to **heaven** and **earth**'s **myriad beings permit viewing actually**.

Fields of meaning

Persevere, *HENG*: see *Image of the Situation*. **Last**, *JIU*: see *Preceding Situation*. **Indeed**, *YE*: see *Preceding Situation*. **Solid**, *GANG*: quality of the whole lines; firm, strong, unyielding, persisting. **Above**, *SHANG*: anything above in all senses; higher, upper, outer; upper trigram. **And-also**, *ER*: see *Additional Texts*. **Supple**, *ROU*: quality of the opened lines; flexible, pliant, adaptable, tender. **Below**, *XIA*: anything below, in all senses; lower, inner; lower trigram. **Thunder**, *LEI*: see *Patterns of Wisdom*. **Wind**, *FENG*: see *Patterns of Wisdom*. **Reciprocal**, *XIANG*: mutual; assist, encourage, help; bring together, blend with; examine, inspect; by turns. **Associate**, *YU*: consort with, combine; companions; group, band, company; agree with, comply, help; in favor of. Ideogram: a pair of hands reaching downward meets a pair of hands reaching upward, helpful association. **Root**, *SUN*: base on which things rest, ground, foundation; mild, subtly penetrating; nourishing. **Stir-up**, *DONG*: excite, influence, move, affect; work, take action; come out of the egg or the bud; Action of the trigram Shake, *ZHEN*. Ideogram: strength and heavy, move weighty things. **Altogether**, *JIE*: all, the whole; the same sort, alike; entirely. **Correspond**, *YING*: be in agreement or harmony; proper, suitable; resonate together, answer to; relation between the lines (1 and 4, 2 and 5, 3 and 6) when they form the pair opened and whole, supple and solid. Ideogram: heart and obey.

Grow, *HENG*: see *Image of the Situation*. **Without fault**, *WU JIU*: see *Image of the Situation*. **Harvesting, Trial**, *LI ZHEN*: see *Image of the Situation*. **Last**, *JIU*: see *Preceding Situation*. **With-respect-to**, *YU*: in relation to, referring to, according to; in, at, until. **One/one's**, *QI*: general third person pronoun and possessive adjective; also: it/its, he/his, she/her, they/their. **Dao**, *DAO*: see *Preceding Situation*. **Belong/it**, *ZHI*: see *Preceding Situation*. **Heaven**, *TIAN*: sky, firmament, heavens; the highest realm, situated above the human world, as opposed to the earth, *DI*, located below; Symbol of the trigram Energy, *QIAN*. Ideogram: great and the one above. **Earth**, *DI*: the earth, ground on which the human world rests; basis of all things, nourishes all things; essential Yin; Symbol of the trigram Space, *KUN*. **Not**, *BU*: common term of negation. **Climax**, *YI*: come to a high point and stop; bring to an end, complete; renounce, desist, decline, reject; that is all; already; excessive. **Possessing directed going**, *YOU YOU WANG*: see *Image of the Situation*. **Complete**, *ZHONG*: completion of a cycle that begins the next; entire, whole, all. Ideogram: silk cocoons, follow and ice, winter linking one year with the next. **Consequence**, *ZE*: reason, cause, result; rule, law, pattern, standard; therefore; very strong connection. **Possess**, *YOU*: general term indicating possession; have, own, be endowed with. **Begin**, *SHI*: commence, start, open; earliest, first; generate. Ideogram: woman and eminent, eminent feminine function of giving birth.

Sun/day, *RI*: actual sun and the time of a sun-cycle, a day. **Moon**, *YUE*: moon and moon-cycle, month; menstruation; Yin. **Acquire**, *DE*: obtain the desired object; possession; satisfied, fulfilled; it is permitted; agree with; wish for, desire covetously. Ideogram: go and obstacle, going through obstacles to the goal. **Able/enable**, *NENG*: ability, power, skill, art; competent, talented; duty, function, capacity. Ideogram: an animal with strong hooves and bones, able to carry and defend. **Illuminate**, *ZHAO*: shine light on, enlighten; care for, supervise. Ideogram: fire and brightness. **Four**, *SI*: number four; number of the cardinal directions and of the seasons; everywhere, on all sides; fourfold articulation of the Universal Compass. **Season**, *SHI*: quality of the time; the right time, opportune, in harmony; planning in accord with the time; season of the year. Ideogram: sun and temple, sacred time. **Transform**, *BIAN*: abrupt, radical passage from one state to another; transformation of opened and whole lines into each other in hexagrams; contrasts with change, *HUA*, gradual mutation. **Change**, *HUA*: gradual, continuous change; melt, dissolve; be born, die; influence; contrasts with transform, *BIAN*, sudden mutation. Ideogram: person alive and dead, the life process. **Accomplish**, *CHENG*: complete, finish, bring about; perfect, full, whole; play one's part, do one's duty; mature. Ideogram: weapon and man, able to bear arms, thus fully developed. **Wise**, *SHENG*: intuitive universal wisdom; profound understanding; mythical sages of old; holy, sacred, mark of highest distinction. Ideogram: ear and inform, one who knows all from a single sound. **Person/people**, *REN*: humans individually and collectively; an individual; humankind. **Below heaven**, *TIAN XIA*: human world, between heaven and earth.

Oversee, *GUAN*: contemplate, observe from a distance; look at carefully, gaze at; a high place from where one sees far, monastery, observatory; intelligence, clairvoyance; scry, divine through liquid in a cup. Ideogram: sight and waterbird, aerial view. **Place**, *SUO*: position, location; residence, dwelling; where something belongs or comes from; habitual focus or object. **Motive**, *QING*: true nature; feelings, desires, passions; sincere, true, real; state of affairs, circumstances. Ideogram: heart and green, germinated in the heart. **Myriad**, *WAN*: ten thousand; countless, many, everyone. Ideogram: swarm of insects. **Being**, *WU*: creature, thing, any single being; matter, substance, essence; nature of things. **Permit**, *KE*: see *Preceding Situation*. **View**, *JIAN*: vision in all its aspects: seeing, being visible, forming mental images; visit, call on, consult. Ideogram: eye above person, active and receptive sight. **Actually**, *YI*: truly, really, at present. Ideogram: a dart and done, strong intention fully expressed.

遯

33 RETIRING | *Dun*

The situation described by this hexagram is characterized by withdrawing and seclusion, the end of an active involvement.

Image of the Situation

> **Retiring**.
> **Growing**.
> The **small**, **Harvesting**, **Trial**.

Fields of meaning

Retire, *DUN*: withdraw; run away, flee; conceal yourself, become obscure, invisible; secluded, non-social. Ideogram: walk and swine (wealth through walking away). **Grow**, *HENG*: heavenly influence pervading and nourishing all things; prosper, succeed, expand, develop; effective, favorable; quality of summer and South, second stage of the Time Cycle. With the pronunciation *XIANG*: offer a sacrifice; offer a gift to a superior; accept, enjoy. **Small**, *XIAO*: little, common, unimportant; adapting to what crosses your path; ability to move in harmony with the vicissitudes of life; contrasts with great, *DA*, self-imposed theme or goal. **Harvest**, *LI*: benefit, advantage, profit; realization; sharp, acute, insightful; quality of autumn and West, third stage of the Time Cycle. Ideogram: ripe grain and blade. **Trial**, *ZHEN*: inquiry by divination and its result; righteous, firm; separating wheat from chaff; the kernel, the proven core; quality of winter and North, fourth stage of the Time Cycle. Ideogram: pearl and divination.

Outer and Inner Trigram

The upper trigram, **Energy/parch**, *QIAN/GAN*, describes the outer aspects of the situation. It has the following associations: unceasing forward movement, dynamic, enduring, untiring; spirit power, manifestation of Yang, that activates all creation and destruction in Space; heaven, sovereign, father. With the pronunciation *GAN*: parch, dry up, burn, exhaust. Ideogram: sprouts or vapors rising from the ground and sunlight, both fecundating moisture and scorching drought. *Symbol*: heaven, *TIAN*; sky, firmament, heavens; the highest realm, situated above the human world, as opposed to the earth, *DI*, located below. Ideogram: great and

the one above. *Action*: persist, *JIAN*; tenacious, persevering; strong, robust, dynamic; constant as the motion of heavenly bodies in their orbits. In the family of trigrams *QIAN* is the father.

The lower trigram, **Bound**, *GEN*, describes the inner aspects of the situation. It has the following associations: limit, frontier; obstacle that prevents from seeing further; stop; still, quiet, motionless; confine, enclose; mountain, sunset, beginning of winter; solid, steady, unshakable; straight, hard, adamant, obstinate. *Symbol*: mountain, *SHAN*, large, immense; limit, boundary. Ideogram: three peaks, a mountain range. *Action*: stop, *ZHI*, bring or come to a standstill, cease, terminate. Ideogram: a foot stops walking. In the family of trigrams *GEN* is the youngest son.

Counter Hexagram

The Counter Hexagram of **Retiring** is hexagram 44, **Coupling**, which switches the emphasis from the withdrawal characterizing **Retiring** to the powerful impulse to involvement generated by the magnetic attraction of primal Yin and Yang.

Preceding Situation

> **Beings not permitted** to **use lasting residing** in **their place**.
> To **anterior acquiescence belongs** the **use** of **retiring**.
> **Retiring implies withdrawing indeed**.

Fields of meaning

Beings not permitted (to **use**), *WU BU KE (YI)*: it is not possible; no one is allowed; it is not in the nature of things. **Last**, *JIU*: endure; long, protracted, permanent, eternal; old, ancient. **Reside**, *JU*: dwell, live in, stay; sit down; fill an office; well-being, rest. Ideogram: body and seat. **They/their**, *QI*: general third person pronoun and possessive adjective; also: one/one's, it/its, he/his, she/her. **Place**, *SUO*: position, location; residence, dwelling; where something belongs or comes from; habitual focus or object. To **anterior acquiescence belongs** the **use** of, *GU SHOU ZHI YI*: understanding and accepting the preceding statement allows the consultant to make proper use of this hexagram. **Retire**, *DUN*: see *Image of the Situation*. **Imply**, *ZHE*: further signify; additional meaning. **Withdraw**, *TUI*: draw back, retreat, recede; decline, refuse. **Indeed**, *YE*: emphasizes and intensifies the previous statement.

Hexagrams in Pairs

> The **great**'s **vigor**: by **consequence stopping**.
> **Retiring**: by **consequence withdrawing indeed**.

Fields of meaning

Great, *DA*: big, noble, important, very; orient the will toward a self-imposed goal, impose direction; ability to lead or guide one's life; contrasts with small, *XIAO*, flexible adaptation to what crosses one's path. **Vigor**, *ZHUANG*: power, strength; energetic, robust, fully grown, flourishing, abundant; at the peak of age and form; inspirit, animate; damage through unrestrained strength. Ideogram: strength and scholar, intellectual impact. **Consequence**, *ZE*: reason, cause, result; rule, law, pattern, standard; therefore; very strong connection. **Stop**, *ZHI*: bring or come to a standstill, cease, terminate; Action of the trigram Bound, *GEN*. Ideogram: a foot stops walking. **Retire**, *DUN*: see *Image of the Situation*. **Withdraw**, *TUI*: see *Preceding Situation*. **Indeed**, *YE*: see *Preceding Situation*.

Patterns of Wisdom

> **Heaven possesses mountain below**. **Retiring**.
> A **jun zi uses distancing** the **small** in the **person**.
> And **not hating and-also intimidating**.

Fields of meaning

Heaven, *TIAN*: sky, firmament, heavens; the highest realm, situated above the human world, as opposed to the earth, *DI*, located below; Symbol of the trigram Energy, *QIAN*. Ideogram: great and the one above. **Possess**, *YOU*: general term indicating possession; have, own, be endowed with. **Mountain**, *SHAN*: mountain; large, immense; limit, boundary; Symbol of the trigram Bound, *GEN*. Ideogram: three peaks, a mountain range. **Below**, *XIA*: anything below, in all senses; lower, inner; lower trigram. **Retire**, *DUN*: see *Image of the Situation*. **Jun zi**: ideal of a person who orders his/her life in accordance with dao rather than willful intention, and uses divination in this spirit. **Use**, *YI*: by means of; owing to; make use of, employ. **Distance**, *YUAN*: far off, remote; keep at a distance; a long time, far away in time. Ideogram: go and a long way. **Small**, *XIAO*: see *Image of the Situation*. **Person/people**, *REN*: humans individually and collectively; an individual; humankind. **Not**, *BU*: common term of negation. **Hate**, *WU*: detest, dread, dislike; averse to, ashamed of; repulsive, vicious, vile, ugly, wicked. Ideogram: twisted bowels and heart. **And-also**, *ER*: joins and contrasts two terms.

Intimidate, *YAN*: inspire with fear or awe; severe, rigid, strict, austere, demanding; a severe father; tight, a closed door.

Transforming Lines

Initial six

Retiring's **tail**, **adversity**.
No availing of **possessing directed going**.

Comments
To **retiring**'s **tail belongs adversity**.
Not going, **is** it a **calamity indeed?**

Fields of meaning

Retire, *DUN*: see *Image of the Situation*. **Tail**, *WEI*: animal's tail; end, last, extreme, remnant. **Adversity**, *LI*: danger, hardship, severe; threat or difficulty that must be encountered, rather than avoided; grinding stone; polish, sharpen; a challenge that strengthens and perfects the character; stimulate, excite; cruel demon. **No**, *WU*: common term of negation. **Avail**, *YONG*: use, employ for a specific purpose; take advantage of; benefit from; capacity. Ideogram: to divine and center, applying divination to central concerns. **Possessing directed going**, *YOU YOU WANG*: having a goal or purpose, moving in a specific direction.

Belong/it, *ZHI*: establishes between two terms a connection similar to the Saxon genitive, in which the second term belongs to the first one; at the end of a sentence it refers to something previously mentioned or implied. **Not**, *BU*: common term of negation. **Go**, *WANG*: move away in time or space, depart; become past; dead, gone; contrasts with come, *LAI*, approach in time or space. **Is?**, *HE*: ask, inquire; what? which? who? how? why? where? an interrogative particle, often introducing a rhetorical question: is it? is it not? **Calamity**, *ZAI*: disaster from outside; fire, flood, plague, drought, blight, ruin; contrasts with blunder, *SHENG*, indicating personal fault. Ideogram: water and fire, elemental powers. **Indeed**, *YE*: see *Preceding Situation*.

Six at Second

To **holding-on belongs availing** of **skin belonging** to **yellow cattle**.
To **abstaining belongs mastering stimulation**.

Comments
Holding-on avails of **yellow cattle**.
Firm purpose indeed.

Fields of meaning

Hold-on, *ZHI*: lay hold of, seize, take in hand; keep, maintain, look after; manage, control. Ideogram: criminal and seize. **Belong/it**, *ZHI*: establishes between two terms a connection similar to the Saxon genitive, in which the second term belongs to the first one; at the end of a sentence it refers to something previously mentioned or implied. **Avail**, *YONG*: use, employ for a specific purpose; take advantage of; benefit from; capacity. Ideogram: to divine and center, applying divination to central concerns. **Skin**, *GE*: human or animal skin; hide, leather; armor, protection; peel off, remove the covering, skin or hide; change, renew, molt; overthrow, degrade from office. **Yellow**, *HUANG*: color of the soil in central China, associated with the Earthy Moment leading from the Yang to the Yin hemicycle; emblematic and imperial color of China since the Yellow Emperor (2500 BC). **Cattle**, *NIU*: ox, bull, cow, calf; power and strength of work animals; stubborn. **Abstain/absolutely-nothing**, *MO*: complete elimination; do not, not any, by no means. **Master**, *SHENG*: have the upper hand; control, command, win, conquer, check (as in the cycle of the Five Transformative Moments); worthy of, able to. **Stimulate**, *SHUO*: rouse to action and good feeling; stir up, urge on; exhort, persuade; say, tell, relate; cheer, delight; joyous, peaceful, restful; Action of the trigram Open, *DUI*. Ideogram: words and exchange.

Firm, *GU*: steady, solid, strong, secure; constant, fixed. Ideogram: old and enclosure, long preserved. **Purpose**, *ZHI*: focus of mind and heart; intention, will, inclination; continuity in the direction of life. Ideogram: heart and scholar, high inner resolve. **Indeed**, *YE*: see *Preceding Situation*.

NINE AT THIRD

Tied retiring. **Possessing affliction**, **adversity**.
Accumulating servants, **concubines**, **significant**.

Comments
To **tied retiring belongs adversity**.
Possessing affliction, **weariness indeed**.
Accumulating servants, **concubines**, **significant**.
Not permitted the **great** in **affairs indeed**.

Fields of meaning

Tie, *XI*: connect, attach, bind; devoted to; relatives. Ideogram: person and connect, ties between humans. **Retire**, *DUN*: see *Image of the Situation*. **Possess**, *YOU*: see *Patterns of Wisdom*. **Affliction**, *JI*: sickness, disorder, defect, calamity, injury; poison, hate, dislike; cruel, jealous, envious. Ideogram: sickness and dart, a sudden affliction. **Adversity**, *LI*: danger, hardship, severe; threat or difficulty that must be encountered, rather than avoided; grinding stone; polish, sharpen; a challenge that strengthens and perfects the character; stimulate, excite; cruel demon. **Accumulate**, *CHU*: retain, hoard, gather, herd together; control, restrain; domesticate, tame, train; raise, feed, sustain, bring up. Ideogram: field and black, fertile black soil, accumulated through retaining silt. **Servant**, *CHEN*: attendant, minister, vassal; courtier who can speak to the sovereign; wait on, serve in office. Ideogram: person bowing low. **Concubine**, *QIE*: secondary wife taken without ceremony to ensure a male descendant; handmaid. **Significant**, *JI*: leads to the experience of meaning; favorable, propitious, appropriate. Ideogram: scholar and mouth, wise words of a sage.

Belong/it, *ZHI*: establishes between two terms a connection similar to the Saxon genitive, in which the second term belongs to the first one; at the end of a sentence it refers to something previously mentioned or implied. **Weariness**, *BAI*: fatigue; debilitated, exhausted, distressed; weak. **Indeed**, *YE*: see *Preceding Situation*. **Not**, *BU*: common term of negation. **Permit**, *KE*: possible because in harmony with an inherent principle; capable of; approve, authorize. Ideogram: mouth and breath, silent consent. **Great**, *DA*: see *Hexagrams in Pairs*. **Affairs**, *SHI*: all kinds of personal activity; matters at hand; business; function, occupation; manage; perform a task; incident, event; case in court.

NINE AT FOURTH

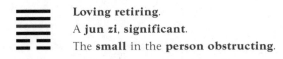

Loving retiring.
A **jun zi**, **significant**.
The **small** in the **person obstructing**.

Comments

A **jun zi lovingly retiring**.
The **small** in the **person obstructing indeed**.

Fields of meaning

Love, *HAO*: affection; fond of, take pleasure in; fine, graceful. **Retire**, *DUN*: see *Image of the Situation*. **Jun zi**: see *Patterns of Wisdom*. **Significant**, *JI*: leads to the experience of meaning; favorable, propitious, appropriate. Ideogram: scholar and mouth, wise words of a sage. **Small**, *XIAO*: see *Image of the Situation*. **Person/people**, *REN*: see *Patterns of Wisdom*. **Obstruct**, *PI*: closed, stopped; bar the way; obstacle; unfortunate, wicked; refuse, disapprove, deny. Ideogram: mouth and not, blocked communication.

Indeed, *YE*: see *Preceding Situation*.

NINE AT FIFTH

Excellent retiring, Trial, significant.

Comments

Excellent retiring, Trial, significant.
Using the **correct purpose indeed**.

Fields of meaning

Excellence, *JIA*: superior quality; fine, beautiful, glorious; happy, pleased; rejoice in, praise. **Retire**, *DUN*: see *Image of the Situation*. **Trial**, *ZHEN*: see *Image of the Situation*. **Significant**, *JI*: leads to the experience of meaning; favorable, propitious, appropriate. Ideogram: scholar and mouth, wise words of a sage.

Use, *YI*: see *Patterns of Wisdom*. **Correct**, *ZHENG*: rectify deviation or one-sidedness; proper, straight, exact, regular; constant, rule, model. Ideogram: stop and one, hold to one thing. **Purpose**, *ZHI*: focus of mind and heart; intention, will, inclination; continuity in the direction of life. Ideogram: heart and scholar, high inner resolve. **Indeed**, *YE*: see *Preceding Situation*.

NINE ABOVE

Rich retiring, without not Harvesting.

Comments

Rich retiring, without not Harvesting.
Without a **place** to **doubt indeed**.

Fields of meaning

Rich, *FEI*: fertile, abundant, fat; manure, fertilizer. **Retire**, *DUN*: see *Image of the Situation*. **Without not Harvesting**, *WU BU LI*: turning point where the balance is swinging from not Harvesting to actually Harvesting.

Without, *WU*: devoid of; there is not. **Place**, *SUO*: see *Preceding Situation*. **Doubt**, *YI*: suspect, distrust, wonder; uncertain, dubious; surmise, conjecture, fear. **Indeed**, *YE*: see *Preceding Situation*.

Image Tradition

Retiring, Growing.
Retiring and-also Growing indeed.
The **solid** in the **appropriate position and-also corresponding.**
Associating with the **season**'s **movement indeed.**

The **small, Harvesting, Trial.**
Drenched and-also long-living.
The **season belonging** to **retiring righteously great actually in-fact.**

Fields of meaning

Retiring, Growing, *DUN HENG*: see *Image of the Situation*. **And-also,** *ER*: see *Patterns of Wisdom*. **Indeed,** *YE*: see *Preceding Situation*. **Solid,** *GANG*: quality of the whole lines; firm, strong, unyielding, persisting. **Appropriate,** *DANG*: suitable, capable, worthy, adequate, competent, equal to; opportune, convenient; whole lines in odd places and opened lines in even places. **Position,** *WEI*: place, location; be at; social standing, rank; position of a line in a hexagram. Ideogram: person standing. **Correspond,** *YING*: be in agreement or harmony; proper, suitable; resonate together, answer to; relation between the lines (1 and 4, 2 and 5, 3 and 6) when they form the pair opened and whole, supple and solid. Ideogram: heart and obey. **Associate,** *YU*: consort with, combine; companions; group, band, company; agree with, comply, help; in favor of. Ideogram: a pair of hands reaching downward meets a pair of hands reaching upward, helpful association. **Season,** *SHI*: quality of the time; the right time, opportune, in harmony; planning in accord with the time; season of the year. Ideogram: sun and temple, sacred time. **Move,** *XING*: move or move something; motivate; emotionally moving; walk, act, do. Ideogram: successive steps.

The **small, Harvesting, Trial,** *XIAO LI ZHEN*: see *Image of the Situation*. **Drench,** *JIN*: soak, penetrate, immerse, steep in; infiltrate gradually; progressive accumulation. **Long-living,** *ZHANG*: enduring, lasting, constant; extended, long, large; senior, superior, greater; increase, prosper; respect, elevate. **Season,** *SHI*: quality of the time; the right time, opportune, in harmony; planning in accord with the time; season of the year. Ideogram: sun and temple, sacred time. **Belong/it,** *ZHI*: establishes between two terms a connection similar to the Saxon genitive, in which the second term belongs to the first one; at the end of a sentence it refers to something previously mentioned or implied. **Righteous,** *YI*:

proper, just, virtuous, upright; the heart that rules itself; benevolent, loyal, devoted to public good. **Great**, *DA*: see *Hexagrams in Pairs*. **Actually**, *YI*: truly, really, at present. Ideogram: a dart and done, strong intention fully expressed. **In-fact**, *ZAI*: emphatic exclamation; truly, indeed.

大壯

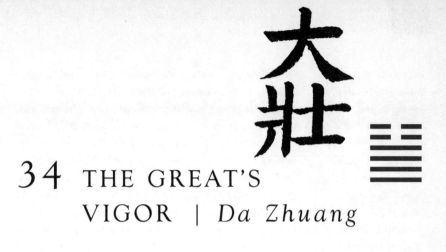

34 THE GREAT'S VIGOR | *Da Zhuang*

The situation described by this hexagram is characterized by the invigorating power of a central idea or long-term goal, which stimulates and spurs to action.

Image of the Situation

> The **great**'s **vigor**.
> **Harvesting**, **Trial**.

Fields of meaning

Great, *DA*: big, noble, important, very; orient the will toward a self-imposed goal, impose direction; ability to lead or guide one's life; contrasts with small, *XIAO*, flexible adaptation to what crosses one's path. Vigor, *ZHUANG*: power, strength; energetic, robust, fully grown, flourishing, abundant; at the peak of age and form; inspirit, animate; damage through unrestrained strength. Ideogram: strength and scholar, intellectual impact. Harvest, *LI*: benefit, advantage, profit; realization; sharp, acute, insightful; quality of autumn and West, third stage of the Time Cycle. Ideogram: ripe grain and blade. Trial, *ZHEN*: inquiry by divination and its result; righteous, firm; separating wheat from chaff; the kernel, the proven core; quality of winter and North, fourth stage of the Time Cycle. Ideogram: pearl and divination.

Outer and Inner Trigram

The upper trigram, **Shake**, *ZHEN*, describes the outer aspects of the situation. It has the following associations: arouse, excite, inspire; awe, alarm, trembling; thunder rising from the depth of the earth; fertilizing intrusion. Ideogram: excite and rain. *Symbol*: thunder, *LEI*, arousing power emerging from the depth of the earth. *Action*: stir-up, *DONG*, excite, influence, move, affect; work, take action; come out of the egg or the bud. Ideogram: strength and heavy, move weighty things. In the family of trigrams *ZHEN* is the eldest son.

The lower trigram, **Energy/parch**, *QIAN/GAN*, describes the inner aspects of the situation. It has the following associations: unceasing forward movement, dynamic, enduring, untiring; spirit power, manifestation of Yang, that activates all creation and destruction in Space; heaven, sovereign, father. With the pronunciation *GAN*: parch, dry up, burn, exhaust. Ideogram: sprouts or vapors rising from the ground and sunlight, both fecundating moisture and scorching drought. *Symbol*: heaven, *TIAN*; sky, firmament, heavens; the highest realm, situated above the human world, as opposed to the earth, *DI*, located below. Ideogram: great and the one above. *Action*: persist, *JIAN*; tenacious, persevering; strong, robust, dynamic; constant as the motion of heavenly bodies in their orbits. In the family of trigrams *QIAN* is the father.

Counter Hexagram

The Counter Hexagram of **The Great's Vigor** is hexagram 43, **Parting**, which switches the emphasis from the concentrated thrust of **The Great's Vigor** to the dispersion of a flooding river parting into different streams.

Preceding Situation

> **Beings not permitted** to **use completing retiring**.
> To **anterior acquiescence belongs** the **use** of the **great**'s **vigor**.

Fields of meaning

Beings not permitted (to **use**), *WU BU KE (YI)*: it is not possible; no one is allowed; it is not in the nature of things. **Complete**, *ZHONG*: completion of a cycle that begins the next; entire, whole, all. Ideogram: silk cocoons, follow and ice, winter linking one year with the next. **Retire**, *DUN*: withdraw; run away, flee; conceal yourself, become obscure, invisible; secluded, non-social. Ideogram: walk and swine (wealth through walking away). To **anterior acquiescence belongs** the **use** of, *GU SHOU ZHI YI*: understanding and accepting the preceding statement allows the consultant to make proper use of this hexagram. The **great**'s **vigor**, *DA ZHUANG*: see *Image of the Situation*.

Hexagrams in Pairs

> The **great**'s **vigor**: by **consequence stopping**.
> **Retiring**: by **consequence withdrawing indeed**.

Fields of meaning

The **great**'s **vigor**, *DA ZHUANG*: see *Image of the Situation*. **Consequence**, *ZE*: reason, cause, result; rule, law, pattern, standard; therefore; very strong connection. **Stop**, *ZHI*: bring or come to a standstill, cease, terminate; Action of the trigram Bound, *GEN*. Ideogram: a foot stops walking. **Retire**, *DUN*: see *Preceding Situation*. **Withdraw**, *TUI*: draw back, retreat, recede; decline, refuse. **Indeed**, *YE*: emphasizes and intensifies the previous statement.

Patterns of Wisdom

> **Thunder located above heaven**. The **great**'s **vigor**.
> A **jun zi uses no codes whatever**, **nowhere treading**.

Fields of meaning

Thunder, *LEI*: thunder; arousing power emerging from the depth of the earth; Symbol of the trigram Shake, *ZHEN*. **Locate**, *ZAI*: be at, be situated at, dwell, reside; in, within; involved with, in the process of. Ideogram: earth and persevere, a place on the earth. **Above**, *SHANG*: anything above in all senses; higher, upper, outer; upper trigram. **Heaven**, *TIAN*: sky, firmament, heavens; the highest realm, situated above the human world, as opposed to the earth, *DI*, located below; Symbol of the trigram Energy, *QIAN*. Ideogram: great and the one above. The **great**'s **vigor**, *DA ZHUANG*: see *Image of the Situation*. **Jun zi**: ideal of a person who orders his/her life in accordance with dao rather than willful intention, and uses divination in this spirit. **Use**, *YI*: by means of; owing to; make use of, employ. **No ... whatever**, *FEI*: strongest negative; not at all! **Codes**, *LI*: rites, rules, ritual, etiquette; usage, manners; honor, worship. Ideogram: worship and sacrificial vase, handling a sacred vessel. **Nowhere/nothing**, *FU*: strong negative; not a single thing/place; deny, disapprove; impossible, incorrect. **Tread**, *LÜ*: walk a path or way; step, path, track; footsteps; course of the stars; appropriate action; virtue; salary, means of subsistence. Ideogram: body and repeating steps.

Transforming Lines

INITIAL NINE

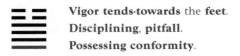

Vigor tends-towards the **feet**.
Disciplining, **pitfall**.
Possessing conformity.

Comments
Vigor tends-towards the **feet**.
One's conformity exhausted indeed.

Fields of meaning

Vigor, *ZHUANG*: see *Image of the Situation*. **Tend-towards**, *YU*: move toward without necessarily reaching, in the direction of. **Foot**, *ZHI*: foot, footprint; foundation, base; walk; stop where the foot rests. **Discipline**, *ZHENG*: subjugate vassals, reduce to order; punishing expedition. Ideogram: step and correct, a rectifying move. **Pitfall**, *XIONG*: unfortunate situation, in which the flow of life and spirit is blocked and the experience of meaning is lost; stuck and exposed to danger; inappropriate attitude. Ideogram: person in a pit. **Possess**, *YOU*: general term indicating possession; have, own, be endowed with. **Conform**, *FU*: accord between inner and outer; sincere, truthful, verified, reliable; capture; prisoners, spoils. Ideogram: claws over child, a bird brooding on the nest.

One/one's, *QI*: general third person pronoun and possessive adjective; also: it/its, he/his, she/her, they/their. **Exhaust**, *QIONG*: bring to an end; limit, extremity; investigate exhaustively; destitute, indigent; end without a new beginning; distinct from complete, *ZHONG*, end of a cycle that begins the next one. Ideogram: cave and naked person, bent with disease or old age. **Indeed**, *YE*: see *Hexagrams in Pairs*.

NINE AT SECOND

Trial, **significant**.

Comments
Nine at **second**: **Trial**, **significant**.
Using the **center indeed**.

Fields of meaning

Trial, *ZHEN*: see *Image of the Situation*. **Significant**, *JI*: leads to the experience of meaning; favorable, propitious, appropriate. Ideogram: scholar and mouth, wise words of a sage.

Nine, *JIU*: number nine; transforming whole line; superlative: best, perfect. **Two/second**, *ER*: number two; pair, even numbers, binary, duplicate. **Use**, *YI*: see *Patterns of Wisdom*. **Center**, *ZHONG*: inner, central; put in the center; middle, stable point enabling you to face inner and outer changes; middle line of a trigram. Ideogram: field divided in two equal parts. **Indeed**, *YE*: see *Hexagrams in Pairs*.

Nine at Third

The **small** in the **person avails** of **vigor**.
A **jun zi avails** of **absence**.
Trial, **adversity**.
The **he-goat butts** a **hedge**.
Ruins its horns.

Comments
The **small** in the **person avails** of **vigor**.
A **jun zi** of **absence indeed**.

Fields of meaning

Small, *XIAO*: little, common, unimportant; adapting to what crosses your path; ability to move in harmony with the vicissitudes of life; contrasts with great, *DA*, self-imposed theme or goal. **Person/people**, *REN*: humans individually and collectively; an individual; humankind. **Avail**, *YONG*: use, employ for a specific purpose; take advantage of; benefit from; capacity. Ideogram: to divine and center, applying divination to central concerns. **Vigor**, *ZHUANG*: see *Image of the Situation*. **Jun zi**: see *Patterns of Wisdom*. **Absence**, *WANG*: emptiness, vacancy; lit.: a net, open spaces between threads; used as a negative. Ideogram: net and lost, empty spaces divide what is kept from what is lost. **Trial**, *ZHEN*: see *Image of the Situation*. **Adversity**, *LI*: danger, hardship, severe; threat or difficulty that must be encountered, rather than avoided; grinding stone; polish, sharpen; a challenge that strengthens and perfects the character; stimulate, excite; cruel demon. **He-goat**, *DI YANG*: ram or buck, particularly a three-year-old male at the peak of strength. **Butt**, *ZHU*: push or strike with the horns; attack, oppose, offend; stir up, excite; associated with the Wooden Moment. **Hedge**, *FAN*: row of bushes, fence, boundary; enclose, protect, fend off. **Ruin**, *LEI*: destroy, break, overturn; debilitated, meager, emaciated; entangled. **It/its**, *QI*: general third person pronoun and possessive adjective; also: one/one's, he/his, she/her, they/their. **Horns**, *JIAO*: physical horns; butt, attack, gore; dispute, test one's strength; headland.

Indeed, *YE*: see *Hexagrams in Pairs*.

Nine at Fourth

Trial, significant.
Repenting extinguished.
The **hedge broken-up**, **not ruined**.
Vigor tends-towards the **great**: to a **cart belong axle-bearings**.

Comments
The **hedge broken-up**, **not ruined**.
Honoring going indeed.

Fields of meaning

Trial, *ZHEN*: see *Image of the Situation*. **Significant**, *JI*: leads to the experience of meaning; favorable, propitious, appropriate. Ideogram: scholar and mouth, wise words of a sage. **Repenting extinguished**, *HUI WANG*: previous errors are corrected, all causes for repenting disappear. **Hedge**, *FAN*: row of bushes, fence, boundary; enclose, protect, fend off. **Break-up**, *JUE*: streams diverging; open a passage for water; break through a dam; separate, break into parts; cut through; decide, pass sentence; absolutely, certainly. Ideogram: water and parting. **Not**, *BU*: common term of negation. **Ruin**, *LEI*: destroy, break, overturn; debilitated, meager, emaciated; entangled. **Vigor**, *ZHUANG*: see *Image of the Situation*. **Tend-towards**, *YU*: move toward without necessarily reaching, in the direction of. **Great**, *DA*: see *Image of the Situation*. **Cart**, *YU*: a vehicle and its carrying capacity; contain, hold, sustain. **Belong/it**, *ZHI*: establishes between two terms a connection similar to the Saxon genitive, in which the second term belongs to the first one; at the end of a sentence it refers to something previously mentioned or implied. **Axle-bearing**, *FU*: device that fastens the body of a cart to axle and wheels.

Honor, *SHANG*: esteem, give high rank to, exalt, celebrate; rise, elevate; put one thing on top of another. **Go**, *WANG*: move away in time or space, depart; become past; dead, gone; contrasts with come, *LAI*, approach in time or space. **Indeed**, *YE*: see *Hexagrams in Pairs*.

SIX AT FIFTH

Losing the **goat**, **tending-towards versatility**.
Without repenting.

Comments
Losing the **goat**, **tending-towards versatility**.
Position not appropriate indeed.

Fields of meaning

Lose, *SANG*: be deprived of, forget; destruction, ruin, death; corpse; lament, mourn; funeral. Ideogram: weep and dead. **Goat**, *YANG*: sheep and goats; associated with stubborn, determined thought and action. **Tend-towards**, *YU*: move toward without necessarily reaching, in the direction of. **Versatility**, *YI*: sudden and unpredictable change, and the mental mobility and openness required in order to face it; easy, light, simple; occurs in the name of the *Yi Jing*.

Without, *WU*: devoid of; there is not. **Repent**, *HUI*: regret, dissatisfaction with past conduct inducing a change of heart; proceeds from abashment, *LIN*, shame and confusion at having lost the right way.

Position, *WEI*: place, location; be at; social standing, rank; position of a line in a hexagram. Ideogram: person standing. **Not**, *BU*: common term of negation. **Appropriate**, *DANG*: suitable, capable, worthy, adequate, competent, equal to; opportune, convenient; whole lines in odd places and opened lines in even places. **Indeed**, *YE*: see *Hexagrams in Pairs*.

SIX ABOVE

The **he-goat butts** a **hedge**.
Not able to **withdraw**, **not able** to **release**.
Without direction Harvesting.
Drudgery, by **consequence significant**.

Comments
Not able to **withdraw**, **not able** to **release**.
Not ruminating indeed.
Drudgery, by **consequence significant**.
Fault not long-living indeed.

Fields of meaning

He-goat, *DI YANG*: ram or buck, particularly a three-year-old male at the peak of strength. **Butt**, *ZHU*: push or strike with the horns; attack, oppose, offend; stir up, excite; associated with the Wooden Moment. **Hedge**, *FAN*: row of bushes, fence, boundary; enclose, protect, fend off. **Not**, *BU*: common term of negation. **Able/enable**, *NENG*: ability, power, skill, art; competent, talented; duty, function, capacity. Ideogram: an animal with strong hooves and bones, able to carry and defend. **Withdraw**, *TUI*: see *Hexagrams in Pairs*. **Release**, *SUI*: let go, free; unhindered; advance, progress; promote, further; reach, succeed; in accord with, conforming to. Ideogram: go and follow one's wishes, unimpeded movement. **Without direction Harvesting**, *WU YOU LI*: in order to take advantage of the situation, do not impose a direction on events. **Drudgery**, *JIAN*: difficult, hard, repetitive work; distressing, sorrowful. Ideogram: perverse and sticky earth, soil difficult to cultivate. **Consequence**, *ZE*: see *Hexagrams in Pairs*. **Significant**, *JI*: leads to the experience of meaning; favorable, propitious, appropriate. Ideogram: scholar and mouth, wise words of a sage.

Ruminate, *XIANG*: ponder and discuss; examine minutely, pay attention to; explain thoroughly. Ideogram: word and sheep, ruminating on words. **Indeed**, *YE*: see *Hexagrams in Pairs*. **Fault**, *JIU*: unworthy conduct that leads to harm, illness, misfortune; guilt, crime, punishment. Ideogram: person and differ, differ from what you should be. **Long-living**, *ZHANG*: enduring, lasting, constant; extended, long, large; senior, superior, greater; increase, prosper; respect, elevate.

Image Tradition

The **great**'s **vigor**.
The **great implies vigor indeed**.
The **solid uses stirring-up**. **Anterior vigor**.

The **great**'s **vigor**. **Harvesting**, **Trial**.
The **great implies correcting indeed**.
The **correct great and-also** the **motives belonging** to **heaven** and **earth permit viewing actually**.

Fields of meaning

The **great**'s **vigor**, *DA ZHUANG*: see *Image of the Situation*. **Vigor**, *ZHUANG*: see *Image of the Situation*. **Imply**, *ZHE*: further signify; additional meaning. **Indeed**, *YE*: see *Hexagrams in Pairs*. **Solid**, *GANG*: quality of the whole lines; firm, strong, unyielding, persisting. **Use**, *YI*: see *Patterns of Wisdom*. **Stir-up**, *DONG*: excite, influence, move, affect; work, take action; come out of the egg or the bud; Action of the trigram Shake, *ZHEN*. Ideogram: strength and heavy, move weighty things. **Anterior**, *GU*: come before as cause; former, ancient; reason, purpose, intention; grievance, dissatisfaction, sorrow, resulting from previous causes and intentions; situation leading to a divination.

Harvesting, **Trial**, *LI ZHEN*: see *Image of the Situation*. **Correct**, *ZHENG*: rectify deviation or one-sidedness; proper, straight, exact, regular; constant, rule, model. Ideogram: stop and one, hold to one thing. **And-also**, *ER*: joins and contrasts two terms. **Motive**, *QING*: true nature; feelings, desires, passions; sincere, true, real; state of affairs, circumstances. Ideogram: heart and green, germinated in the heart. **Belong/it**, *ZHI*: establishes between two terms a connection similar to the Saxon genitive, in which the second term belongs to the first one; at the end of a sentence it refers to something previously mentioned or implied. **Heaven**, *TIAN*: see *Patterns of Wisdom*. **Earth**, *DI*: the earth, ground on which the human world rests; basis of all things, nourishes all things; essential Yin; Symbol of the trigram Space, *KUN*. **Permit**, *KE*: possible because in harmony with an inherent principle; capable of; approve, authorize. Ideogram: mouth and breath, silent consent. **View**, *JIAN*: vision in all its aspects: seeing, being visible, forming mental images; visit, call on, consult. Ideogram: eye above person, active and receptive sight. **Actually**, *YI*: truly, really, at present. Ideogram: a dart and done, strong intention fully expressed.

晉 ䷢

35 PROSPERING | *Jin*

The situation described by this hexagram is characterized by thriving and flourishing like a plant in full sunlight.

Image of the Situation

> **Prospering**.
> A **content feudatory avails** of **bestowing horses** to **enhance** the **multitudes**.
> **Day-time sun thrice reflected**.

Fields of meaning

Prosper, *JIN*: grow and flourish as young plants in the sun; increase, progress, permeate, impregnate; attached to. Ideogram: sun and reaching, the daylight world. Content, *KANG*: peaceful, prosper, at ease; confident strength and poise; joy, delight. Feudatory, *HOU*: noble entrusted with governing a province; in charge of executive tasks; distinct from prince, *GONG*, representative of the central decisional power at the court. Avail, *YONG*: use, employ for a specific purpose; take advantage of; benefit from; capacity. Ideogram: to divine and center, applying divination to central concerns. Bestow, *XI*: grant, confer upon; reward, gift; tin, pewter. Ideogram: metal and change. Horse, *MA*: symbol of spirited strength in the natural world, earthly counterpart of the dragon; associated with the trigram Energy, *QIAN*, heaven, and high noon. Enhance, *FAN*: augment, enhance, increase; thriving, plentiful. Multitude, *SHU*: crowd, many people; mass, herd; all, the whole. Day-time, *ZHOU*: daylight half of the 24-hour cycle. Sun/day, *RI*: actual sun and the time of a sun-cycle, a day. Three/thrice, *SAN*: number three; third time or place; active phases of a cycle; superlative; beginning of repetition (since one and two are entities in themselves). Reflect, *JIE*: receive and pass on; follow in office; inherit; face, respond.

Outer and Inner Trigram

The upper trigram, **Radiance**, *LI*, describes the outer aspects of the situation. It has the following associations: glowing light, spreading in all directions; the power of consciousness; discriminate, articulate, divide and arrange in order; assemble, attract. Ideogram: bird and weird, magical fire-bird with brilliant plumage. *Symbols*: fire and brightness. Fire, *HUO*: flame, burn; warming and consuming aspect of burning. Brightness, *MING*: light, radiance, clarity; distinguish, discern, understand; light-giving aspect of fire, of heavenly bodies and of consciousness. *Action*: congregate, *LI*, cling together, adhere to, rely on; couple, pair, herd; beautiful, elegant. Ideogram: deer flocking together. In the family of trigrams *LI* is the middle daughter.

The lower trigram, **Space**, *KUN*, describes the inner aspects of the situation. It has the following associations: surface of the world; support of all existence, manifestation of Yin, where Energy or Yang activates all creation and destruction; all-involving service; earth; moon, wife, mother; rest, receptivity, docile obedience. Ideogram: terrestrial globe and stretch out. *Symbol*: earth, *DI*; the earth, ground on which the human world rests; basis of all things, nourishes all things; essential Yin. *Action*: yield, *SHUN*: give way, comply, agree, follow, obey; docile, flexible; bear produce, nourish, provide. In the family of trigrams *KUN* is the mother.

Counter Hexagram

The Counter Hexagram of **Prospering** is hexagram 39, **Limping**, which switches the emphasis from thriving to slow progress, hampered by obstacles and difficulties.

Preceding Situation

> **Beings not permitted** to **use completing vigor**.
> To **anterior acquiescence belongs** the **use** of
> **prospering**.
> **Prospering implies advancing indeed**.

Fields of meaning

Beings not permitted (to use), *WU BU KE (YI)*: it is not possible; no one is allowed; it is not in the nature of things. Complete, *ZHONG*: completion of a cycle that begins the next; entire, whole, all. Ideogram: silk cocoons, follow and ice, winter linking one year with the next. Vigor, *ZHUANG*: power, strength; energetic, robust, fully grown, flourishing, abundant; at the peak of age and form; inspirit, animate; damage through unrestrained strength. Ideogram: strength and scholar, intellectual impact. To anterior acquiescence belongs the use of, *GU SHOU ZHI YI*: understanding and accepting the preceding statement allows the consultant to make proper use of this hexagram. Prosper, *JIN*: see *Image of the Situation*. Imply, *ZHE*: further signify; additional meaning. Advance, *JIN*: move forward, progress, climb; promote or be promoted; further the development of, augment; offer, introduce.

Hexagrams in Pairs

> **Prospering: day-time indeed.**
> **Brightness hidden: proscribed indeed.**

Fields of meaning

Prosper, *JIN*: see *Image of the Situation*. Day-time, *ZHOU*: see *Image of the Situation*. Indeed, *YE*: emphasizes and intensifies the previous statement. Brightness, *MING*: light, radiance, clarity; distinguish, discern, understand; light-giving aspect of fire, of heavenly bodies and of consciousness; brightness and fire are the Symbols of the trigram Radiance, *LI*. Hide, *YI*: squat, even, level, equalize; cut, wound, destroy, exterminate; pacified; colorless; distant, remote, barbarian. Proscribe, *ZHU*: exclude, reject by proclamation; denounce, forbid; reprove, seek as a criminal; condemn to death; clear away.

Patterns of Wisdom

> **Brightness emerging above** the **earth. Prospering.**
> A **jun zi uses originating enlightening** to **brighten actualizing-dao.**

Fields of meaning

Brightness, *MING*: see *Hexagrams in Pairs*. Emerge, *CHU*: come out of, proceed from, spring from, issue forth; appear, be born; bear, generate; leave, flee; Action of the trigram Shake, *ZHEN*. Ideogram: stem with branches and leaves emerging. Above, *SHANG*: anything above in all senses; higher, upper, outer; upper trigram. Earth, *DI*: the earth, ground on which the human world rests; basis of all things, nourishes all things; essential Yin; Symbol of the trigram Space, *KUN*. Prosper, *JIN*: see *Image of the Situation*. Jun zi: ideal of a person who orders his/her life in accordance with dao rather than willful intention, and uses divination in this spirit. Use, *YI*: by means of; owing to; make use of, employ. Origin, *ZI*: source, beginning, ground; cause, reason, motive; tracing back to the source; oneself, by oneself; spontaneous, intrinsic. Enlighten, *ZHAO*: cast light on, display, show; instruct, give knowledge; manifest, bright, splendid. Ideogram: sun and call, bring into the light. Actualize-dao, *DE*: realize dao in action; power, virtue; ability to follow the course traced by the ongoing process of the cosmos. Ideogram: go, straight, and heart. Linked with acquire, *DE*: acquiring that which makes a being become what it is meant to be.

Transforming Lines

Initial six

Prospering thus, arresting thus.
Trial, significant.
Absence: conforming.
Enriching, without fault.

Comments
Prospering thus, arresting thus.
Solitary movement: correcting indeed.
Enriching, without fault.
Not-yet acquiescing in **fate indeed.**

Fields of meaning

Prosper, *JIN*: see *Image of the Situation*. Thus, *RU*: as, in this way; comparable, similar. Arrest, *CUI*: stop, drive back, repress; break, destroy, humiliate; force obedience, overpower. Trial, *ZHEN*: inquiry by divination and its result; righteous, firm; separating wheat from chaff; the kernel, the proven core; quality of winter and North, fourth stage of the Time Cycle. Ideogram: pearl and divination. Significant, *JI*: leads to the experience of meaning; favorable, propitious, appropriate. Ideogram: scholar and mouth, wise words of a sage. Absence, *WANG*: emptiness, vacancy; lit.: a net, open spaces between threads; used as a negative. Ideogram: net and lost, empty spaces divide what is kept from what is lost. Conform, *FU*: accord between inner and outer; sincere, truthful, verified, reliable; capture; prisoners, spoils. Ideogram: claws over child, a bird brooding on the nest. Enrich, *YU*: make richer; material, mental or spiritual wealth; bequeath; generous, abundant. Ideogram: garments, portable riches. Without fault, *WU JIU*: no error or harm in the situation.

Solitary, *DI*: alone, single; isolated, abandoned. Move, *XING*: move or move something; motivate; emotionally moving; walk, act, do. Ideogram: successive steps. Correct, *ZHENG*: rectify deviation or one-sidedness; proper, straight, exact, regular; constant, rule, model. Ideogram: stop and one, hold to one thing. Indeed, *YE*: see *Hexagrams in Pairs*. Not-yet, *WEI*: temporal negative indicating that something is expected to happen but has not yet occurred. Acquiesce, *SHOU*: accept, make peace with, agree to, receive; at rest, satisfied; patient. Fate, *MING*: individual destiny; birth and death as limits of life; issue orders with authority; consult the gods. Ideogram: mouth and order, words with heavenly authority.

SIX AT SECOND

Prospering thus, apprehensive thus.
Trial, significant.
Acquiescing in a **compact cuirass**: **blessing**.
Tending-towards one's kingly mother.

Comments
Acquiescing in a **compact cuirass**: **blessing**.
Using the **center**'s **correctness indeed**.

Fields of meaning

Prosper, *JIN*: see *Image of the Situation*. **Thus**, *RU*: as, in this way; comparable, similar. **Apprehensive**, *CHOU*: worried, anxious, anticipating adversity, afraid of what approaches; sadness, melancholy. Ideogram: heart and autumn, dreading the coming winter. **Trial**, *ZHEN*: inquiry by divination and its result; righteous, firm; separating wheat from chaff; the kernel, the proven core; quality of winter and North, fourth stage of the Time Cycle. Ideogram: pearl and divination. **Significant**, *JI*: leads to the experience of meaning; favorable, propitious, appropriate. Ideogram: scholar and mouth, wise words of a sage. **Acquiesce**, *SHOU*: accept, make peace with, agree to, receive; at rest, satisfied; patient. **Compact**, *ZI*: close textured, dense, solid, impenetrable. Ideogram: herb and silk, dense fabric or foliage. **Cuirass**, *JIE*: armor; tortoise or crab shell; protective covering; border, limit, interval; protection, support; steady, rigid, solid. **Bless**, *FU*: heavenly gifts and favor; happiness, prosperity; spiritual power and goodwill. Ideogram: spirit and plenty. **Tend-towards**, *YU*: move toward without necessarily reaching, in the direction of. **One/one's**, *QI*: general third person pronoun and possessive adjective; also: it/its, he/his, she/her, they/their. **King**, *WANG*: sovereign, effective ruler, emperor, seen as connecting heaven and earth; reign, govern. **Mother**, *MU*: mother, maternal, feminine; child-bearing and nourishing. Ideogram: two breasts.

Use, *YI*: see *Patterns of Wisdom*. **Center**, *ZHONG*: inner, central; put in the center; middle, stable point enabling you to face inner and outer changes; middle line of a trigram. Ideogram: field divided in two equal parts. **Correct**, *ZHENG*: rectify deviation or one-sidedness; proper, straight, exact, regular; constant, rule, model. Ideogram: stop and one, hold to one thing. **Indeed**, *YE*: see *Hexagrams in Pairs*.

Six at Third

Crowds: sincerity, repenting extinguished.

Comments

Crowds: to **sincerity belongs purpose.**
Above moving indeed.

Fields of meaning

Crowds, *ZHONG*: many people, large group, masses; all, all beings. **Sincere**, *YUN*: true, honest, loyal; according to the facts; have confidence in, permit, assent. Ideogram: vapor rising, words directed upward. **Repenting extinguished**, *HUI WANG*: previous errors are corrected, all causes for repenting disappear.

Belong/it, *ZHI*: establishes between two terms a connection similar to the Saxon genitive, in which the second term belongs to the first one; at the end of a sentence it refers to something previously mentioned or implied. **Purpose**, *ZHI*: focus of mind and heart; intention, will, inclination; continuity in the direction of life. Ideogram: heart and scholar, high inner resolve. **Above**, *SHANG*: see *Patterns of Wisdom*. **Move**, *XING*: move or move something; motivate; emotionally moving; walk, act, do. Ideogram: successive steps. **Indeed**, *YE*: see *Hexagrams in Pairs*.

Nine at Fourth

Prospering, thus bushy-tailed rodents.
Trial, adversity.

Comments

Bushy-tailed rodents: Trial, adversity.
Position not appropriate indeed.

Fields of meaning

Prosper, *JIN*: see *Image of the Situation*. **Thus**, *RU*: as, in this way; comparable, similar. **Bushy-tailed rodent**, *SHI SHU*: squirrels and other animals who destroy stored grain; mean, thieving people; timid, skulking, mournful, brooding. **Trial**, *ZHEN*: inquiry by divination and its result; righteous, firm; separating wheat from chaff; the kernel, the proven core; quality of winter and North, fourth stage of the Time Cycle. Ideogram: pearl and divination. **Adversity**, *LI*: danger, hardship, severe; threat or difficulty that must be encountered, rather than avoided; grinding stone; polish, sharpen; a challenge that strengthens and perfects the character; stimulate, excite; cruel demon.

Position, *WEI*: place, location; be at; social standing, rank; position of a line in a hexagram. Ideogram: person standing. **Not**, *BU*: common term of negation. **Appropriate**, *DANG*: suitable, capable, worthy, adequate, competent, equal to; opportune, convenient; whole lines in odd places and opened lines in even places. **Indeed**, *YE*: see *Hexagrams in Pairs*.

SIX AT FIFTH

Repenting extinguished.
Letting-go, acquiring: no cares.
Going significant, without not Harvesting.

Comments
Letting-go, acquiring: no cares.
Going possesses reward indeed.

Fields of meaning

Repenting extinguished, *HUI WANG*: previous errors are corrected, all causes for repenting disappear. **Let-go**, *SHI*: lose, let slip; omit, miss, fail; lose control of. Ideogram: drop from the hand. **Acquire**, *DE*: obtain the desired object; possession; satisfied, fulfilled; it is permitted; agree with; wish for, desire covetously. Ideogram: go and obstacle, going through obstacles to the goal. **No**, *WU*: common term of negation. **Care**, *XU*: fear, doubt, concern; heartfelt attachment; relieve, soothe, aid; sympathy, compassion, consolation. Ideogram: heart and blood, the heart's blood affected. **Go**, *WANG*: move away in time or space, depart; become past; dead, gone; contrasts with come, *LAI*, approach in time or space. **Significant**, *JI*: leads to the experience of meaning; favorable, propitious, appropriate. Ideogram: scholar and mouth, wise words of a sage. **Without not Harvesting**, *WU BU LI*: turning point where the balance is swinging from not Harvesting to actually Harvesting.

Possess, *YOU*: general term indicating possession; have, own, be endowed with. **Reward**, *QING*: gift given out of gratitude or benevolence; favor from heaven. Ideogram: heart, follow and deer, the heart expressed through the gift of a deer's skin. **Indeed**, *YE*: see *Hexagrams in Pairs*.

NINE ABOVE

Prospering: one's horns.
Holding-fast avails of **subjugating** the **capital.**
Adversity, significant.
Without fault.
Trial, abashment.

Comments
Holding-fast avails of **subjugating** the **capital.**
Dao not-yet shining indeed.

Fields of meaning

Prosper, *JIN*: see *Image of the Situation*. **One/one's,** *QI*: general third person pronoun and possessive adjective; also: it/its, he/his, she/her, they/their. **Horns,** *JIAO*: physical horns; butt, attack, gore; dispute, test one's strength; headland. **Hold-fast,** *WEI*: tie, connect, hold together; rope, reins, net. **Avail,** *YONG*: see *Image of the Situation*. **Subjugate,** *FA*: hit, cut; submit, make dependent; chastise rebels, subject to rule. Ideogram: man and lance, armed soldiers. **Capital,** *YI*: populous fortified city, center and symbol of the region it rules. Ideogram: enclosure and official seal. **Adversity,** *LI*: danger, hardship, severe; threat or difficulty that must be encountered, rather than avoided; grinding stone; polish, sharpen; a challenge that strengthens and perfects the character; stimulate, excite; cruel demon. **Significant,** *JI*: leads to the experience of meaning; favorable, propitious, appropriate. Ideogram: scholar and mouth, wise words of a sage. **Without fault,** *WU JIU*: no error or harm in the situation. **Trial,** *ZHEN*: inquiry by divination and its result; righteous, firm; separating wheat from chaff; the kernel, the proven core; quality of winter and North, fourth stage of the Time Cycle. Ideogram: pearl and divination. **Abashment,** *LIN*: distress, shame, regret, humiliation; aware of having lost the right track; leads to repenting, *HUI*, correcting the direction of mind and life.

Dao, *DAO*: way or path; ongoing process of being and the course it traces for each person or thing; ultimate reality, intrinsic nature; origin. Ideogram: go and head, opening a path. **Not-yet,** *WEI*: temporal negative indicating that something is expected to happen but has not yet occurred. **Shine,** *GUANG*: illuminate, emit light; brilliant, splendid; honor, glory, éclat; distinct from brightness, *MING*, light of heavenly bodies. Ideogram: fire above person. **Indeed,** *YE*: see *Hexagrams in Pairs*.

Image Tradition

Prospering. Advancing indeed.
Brightness emerging above the **earth.**
Yielding and-also congregating reaching the **great**'s **brightness.**

The **supple advances and-also moves above.**
That uses a **content feudatory availing** of **bestowing horses** to **enhance** the **multitudes.**
Day-time sun thrice reflected indeed.

Fields of meaning

Prosper, *JIN*: see *Image of the Situation.* **Advance,** *JIN*: see *Preceding Situation.* **Indeed,** *YE*: see *Hexagrams in Pairs.* **Brightness,** *MING*: see *Hexagrams in Pairs.* **Emerge,** *CHU*: see *Patterns of Wisdom.* **Above,** *SHANG*: see *Patterns of Wisdom.* **Earth,** *DI*: see *Patterns of Wisdom.* **Yield,** *SHUN*: give way, comply, agree, follow, obey; docile, flexible; bear produce, nourish, provide; Action of the trigram Field, *KUN.* **And-also,** *ER*: joins and contrasts two terms. **Congregate,** *LI*: cling together, adhere to, rely on; couple, pair, herd; beautiful, elegant; Action of the trigram Radiance, *LI.* Ideogram: deer flocking together. **Reach,** *HU*: arrive at a goal; move toward and achieve; to, at, in; distinct from tend-towards, *YOU.* **Great,** *DA*: big, noble, important, very; orient the will toward a self-imposed goal, impose direction; ability to lead or guide one's life; contrasts with small, *XIAO,* flexible adaptation to what crosses one's path.

Supple, *ROU*: quality of the opened lines; flexible, pliant, adaptable, tender. **Move,** *XING*: move or move something; motivate; emotionally moving; walk, act, do. Ideogram: successive steps. **Above,** *SHANG*: see *Patterns of Wisdom.* **That,** *SHI*: refers to the preceding statement. **Use,** *YI*: see *Patterns of Wisdom.* A **content feudatory avails** of **bestowing horses** to **enhance** the **multitudes,** *KANG HOU YONG XI MA FAN SHU*: see *Image of the Situation.* **Day-time sun thrice reflected,** *ZHOU RI SAN JIE*: see *Image of the Situation.*

明夷

36 BRIGHTNESS HIDDEN | *Ming Yi*

This hexagram describes a situation in which the light is wounded or forced to hide, and the work of consciousness can only be carried on underground.

Image of the Situation

> **Brightness hidden.**
> **Harvesting**: **drudgery**, **Trial**.

Fields of meaning

Brightness, *MING*: light, radiance, clarity; distinguish, discern, understand; light-giving aspect of fire, of heavenly bodies and of consciousness; brightness and fire are the Symbols of the trigram Radiance, *LI*. **Hide**, *YI*: squat, even, level, equalize; cut, wound, destroy, exterminate; pacified; colorless; distant, remote, barbarian. **Harvest**, *LI*: benefit, advantage, profit; realization; sharp, acute, insightful; quality of autumn and West, third stage of the Time Cycle. Ideogram: ripe grain and blade. **Drudgery**, *JIAN*: difficult, hard, repetitive work; distressing, sorrowful. Ideogram: perverse and sticky earth, soil difficult to cultivate. **Trial**, *ZHEN*: inquiry by divination and its result; righteous, firm; separating wheat from chaff; the kernel, the proven core; quality of winter and North, fourth stage of the Time Cycle. Ideogram: pearl and divination.

Outer and Inner Trigram

The upper trigram, **Space**, *KUN*, describes the outer aspects of the situation. It has the following associations: surface of the world; support of all existence, manifestation of Yin, where Energy or Yang activates all creation and destruction; all-involving service; earth; moon, wife, mother; rest, receptivity, docile obedience. Ideogram: terrestrial globe and stretch out. *Symbol*: earth, *DI*; the earth, ground on which the human world rests; basis of all things, nourishes all things; essential Yin. *Action*: yield, *SHUN*: give way, comply, agree, follow, obey; docile, flexible; bear produce, nourish, provide. In the family of trigrams *KUN* is the mother.

The lower trigram, **Radiance**, *LI*, describes the inner aspects of the situation. It has the following associations: glowing light, spreading in all directions; the power of consciousness; discriminate, articulate, divide and arrange in order; assemble, attract. Ideogram: bird and weird, magical fire-bird with brilliant plumage. *Symbols*: fire and brightness. Fire, *HUO*: flame, burn; warming and consuming aspect of burning. Brightness, *MING*: light, radiance, clarity; distinguish, discern, understand; light-giving aspect of fire, of heavenly bodies and of consciousness. *Action*: congregate, *LI*, cling together, adhere to, rely on; couple, pair, herd; beautiful, elegant. Ideogram: deer flocking together. In the family of trigrams *LI* is the middle daughter.

Counter Hexagram

The Counter Hexagram of **Brightness Hidden** is hexagram 40, **Unraveling**, which switches the emphasis from hiding the light of consciousness to focusing on analysis and understanding.

Preceding Situation

> **Advancing necessarily possesses** a **place** for **injury**.
> To **anterior acquiescence belongs** the **use** of **brightness hidden**.
> **Hiding implies injury indeed**.

Fields of meaning

Advance, *JIN*: move forward, progress, climb; promote or be promoted; further the development of, augment; offer, introduce. **Necessarily**, *BI*: unavoidably, certainly. **Possess**, *YOU*: general term indicating possession; have, own, be endowed with. **Place**, *SUO*: position, location; residence, dwelling; where something belongs or comes from; habitual focus or object. **Injure**, *SHANG*: hurt, wound, damage; grief, distress, mourning; sad at heart, afflicted. To **anterior acquiescence belongs** the **use** of, *GU SHOU ZHI YI*: understanding and accepting the preceding statement allows the consultant to make proper use of this hexagram. **Brightness hidden**, *MING YI*: see *Image of the Situation*. **Imply**, *ZHE*: further signify; additional meaning. **Indeed**, *YE*: emphasizes and intensifies the previous statement.

Hexagrams in Pairs

Prospering: **day-time indeed**.
Brightness hidden: **proscribed indeed**.

Fields of meaning

Prosper, *JIN*: grow and flourish as young plants in the sun; increase, progress, permeate, impregnate; attached to. Ideogram: sun and reaching, the daylight world. **Day-time**, *ZHOU*: daylight half of the 24-hour cycle. **Indeed**, *YE*: see *Preceding Situation*. **Brightness hidden**, *MING YI*: see *Image of the Situation*. **Proscribe**, *ZHU*: exclude, reject by proclamation; denounce, forbid; reprove, seek as a criminal; condemn to death; clear away.

Patterns of Wisdom

Brightness entering the **earth**'s **center**. **Brightness hidden**.
A **jun zi uses supervising** the **crowds availing** of **darkening and-also brightening**.

Fields of meaning

Brightness, *MING*: see *Image of the Situation*. **Enter**, *RU*: penetrate, go into, enter on, encroach on; progress; put into; Action of the trigram Root, *SUN*. **Earth**, *DI*: the earth, ground on which the human world rests; basis of all things, nourishes all things; essential Yin; Symbol of the trigram Space, *KUN*. **Center**, *ZHONG*: inner, central; put in the center; middle, stable point enabling you to face inner and outer changes; middle line of a trigram. Ideogram: field divided in two equal parts. **Hide**, *YI*: see *Image of the Situation*. **Jun zi**: ideal of a person who orders his/her life in accordance with dao rather than willful intention, and uses divination in this spirit. **Use**, *YI*: by means of; owing to; make use of, employ. **Supervise**, *LI*: oversee, inspect, administer; visit subordinates. **Crowds**, *ZHONG*: many people, large group, masses; all, all beings. **Avail**, *YONG*: use, employ for a specific purpose; take advantage of; benefit from; capacity. Ideogram: to divine and center, applying divination to central concerns. **Darkness**, *HUI*: obscurity, night, mist; make or become dark; last day of the lunar month. **And-also**, *ER*: joins and contrasts two terms.

Transforming Lines

Initial Nine

Brightness hidden tends-towards flying.
Drooping one's wings.
A **jun zi tends-towards moving.**
Three days not taking-in.
Possessing directed going.
A **lordly person possesses words.**

Comments
A **jun zi tends-towards moving.**
Righteously not taking-in indeed.

Fields of meaning

Brightness hidden, *MING YI*: see *Image of the Situation*. Tend-towards, *YU*: move toward without necessarily reaching, in the direction of. Fly, *FEI*: rise in the air, spread one's wings, fly away; let fly; swift. Droop, *CHUI*: hang down, let fall; bow; condescend to inferiors; almost, near; suspended; hand down to posterity. One/one's, *QI*: general third person pronoun and possessive adjective; also: it/its, he/his, she/her, they/their. Wings, *YI*: birds' wings; sails, flanks, side-rooms; shelter and defend. Jun zi: see *Patterns of Wisdom*. Move, *XING*: move or move something; motivate; emotionally moving; walk, act, do. Ideogram: successive steps. Three/thrice, *SAN*: number three; third time or place; active phases of a cycle; superlative; beginning of repetition (since one and two are entities in themselves). Day/sun, *RI*: the sun and the time of a sun-cycle, a day. Not, *BU*: common term of negation. Take-in, *SHI*: eat, drink, ingest, absorb, incorporate; food, nourishment. Possessing directed going, *YOU YOU WANG*: having a goal or purpose, moving in a specific direction. Lord, *ZHU*: ruler, master, chief, authority; host; domination in the cycle of the Five Transformative Moments. Ideogram: lamp and flame, giving light. Person/people, *REN*: humans individually and collectively; an individual; humankind. Possess, *YOU*: see *Preceding Situation*. Word, *YAN*: spoken word, speech, saying; talk, discuss, address; name, signify. Ideogram: mouth and rising vapor.

Righteous, *YI*: proper, just, virtuous, upright; the heart that rules itself; benevolent, loyal, devoted to public good. Indeed, *YE*: see *Preceding Situation*.

SIX AT SECOND

Brightness hidden.
Hiding tending-towards the **left thigh**.
Availing of a **rescuing horse**'s **vigor**, **significant**.

Comments
To **six** at **second belongs significance**.
Yielding used by **consequence indeed**.

Fields of meaning

Brightness hidden, *MING YI*: see *Image of the Situation*. Tend-towards, *YU*: move toward without necessarily reaching, in the direction of. Left, *ZUO*: left side, left hand; East; secondary, assistant, inferior; defective, unfavorable. Thigh, *GU*: thigh; strand of a rope; part, section. Avail, *YONG*: see *Patterns of Wisdom*. Rescue, *ZHENG*: aid, deliver from trouble; pull out, raise up, lift. Ideogram: hand and aid, a helping hand. Horse, *MA*: symbol of spirited strength in the natural world, earthly counterpart of the dragon; associated with the trigram Energy, *QIAN*, heaven, and high noon. Vigor, *ZHUANG*: power, strength; energetic, robust, fully grown, flourishing, abundant; at the peak of age and form; inspirit, animate; damage through unrestrained strength. Ideogram: strength and scholar, intellectual impact. Significant, *JI*: leads to the experience of meaning; favorable, propitious, appropriate. Ideogram: scholar and mouth, wise words of a sage.

Six, *LIU*: number six; transforming opened line; six lines of a hexagram. Two/second, *ER*: number two; pair, even numbers, binary, duplicate. Belong/it, *ZHI*: establishes between two terms a connection similar to the Saxon genitive, in which the second term belongs to the first one; at the end of a sentence it refers to something previously mentioned or implied. Yield, *SHUN*: give way, comply, agree, follow, obey; docile, flexible; bear produce, nourish, provide; Action of the trigram Field, *KUN*. Use, *YI*: see *Patterns of Wisdom*. Consequence, *ZE*: reason, cause, result; rule, law, pattern, standard; therefore; very strong connection. Indeed, *YE*: see *Preceding Situation*.

NINE AT THIRD

Brightness hidden tends-towards the **Southern hounding**.
Acquiring one's great's **head**.
Not permitted affliction, **Trial**.

Comments
To the **Southern hounding belongs purpose**.
Thereupon acquiring the **great indeed**.

Fields of meaning

Brightness hidden, *MING YI*: see *Image of the Situation*. **Tend-towards**, *YU*: move toward without necessarily reaching, in the direction of. **South**, *NAN*: southern direction, corresponds to noon, summer and the Fiery Moment in the Universal Compass; culmination of the Yang hemicycle; reference point of compass; true principles and correct decisions; rulers face South when in their governing function. **Hound**, *SHOU*: hunt with dogs; annual winter hunt; pursue closely, press hard; burn dry fields to drive game; military expedition. **Acquire**, *DE*: obtain the desired object; possession; satisfied, fulfilled; it is permitted; agree with; wish for, desire covetously. Ideogram: go and obstacle, going through obstacles to the goal. **One/one's**, *QI*: general third person pronoun and possessive adjective; also: it/its, he/his, she/her, they/their. **Great**, *DA*: big, noble, important, very; orient the will toward a self-imposed goal, impose direction; ability to lead or guide one's life; contrasts with small, *XIAO*, flexible adaptation to what crosses one's path. **Head**, *SHOU*: physical head; leader, sovereign; beginning, origin, model; foremost, superior, upper, front. **Not**, *BU*: common term of negation. **Permit**, *KE*: possible because in harmony with an inherent principle; capable of; approve, authorize. Ideogram: mouth and breath, silent consent. **Affliction**, *JI*: sickness, disorder, defect, calamity, injury; poison, hate, dislike; cruel, jealous, envious. Ideogram: sickness and dart, a sudden affliction. **Trial**, *ZHEN*: see *Image of the Situation*.

Belong/it, *ZHI*: establishes between two terms a connection similar to the Saxon genitive, in which the second term belongs to the first one; at the end of a sentence it refers to something previously mentioned or implied. **Purpose**, *ZHI*: focus of mind and heart; intention, will, inclination; continuity in the direction of life. Ideogram: heart and scholar, high inner resolve. **Thereupon**, *NAI*: on that ground, then, only then; finally; in spite of that. **Indeed**, *YE*: see *Preceding Situation*.

Six at Fourth

Entering tending-towards the **left** of the **belly**.
Capturing the **heart belonging** to **brightness hidden**.
Tending-towards emerging from the **gate chambers**.

Comments

Entering tending-towards the **left** of the **belly**.

Capturing the **heart**: **intention indeed**.

Fields of meaning

Enter, *RU*: see *Patterns of Wisdom*. Tend-towards, *YU*: move toward without necessarily reaching, in the direction of. Left, *ZUO*: left side, left hand; East; secondary, assistant, inferior; defective, unfavorable. Belly, *FU*: abdomen, receptacle of vital breath; interior; carry on the breast; the left part of the belly is considered to be the seat of emotion. Capture, *HUO*: obtain, seize, reach; take in a hunt, catch a thief; hit the mark, opportune moment; prisoner, spoils, prey, slave, servant. Heart, *XIN*: the heart as center of being; seat of mind, imagination and affect; moral nature; source of desires, intentions, will. Belong/it, *ZHI*: establishes between two terms a connection similar to the Saxon genitive, in which the second term belongs to the first one; at the end of a sentence it refers to something previously mentioned or implied. Brightness hidden, *MING YI*: see *Image of the Situation*. Emerge, *CHU*: come out of, proceed from, spring from, issue forth; appear, be born; bear, generate; leave, flee; Action of the trigram Shake, *ZHEN*. Ideogram: stem with branches and leaves emerging. Gate, *MEN*: outer door, between courtyard and street; family, sect; a text or master as gate to a school of thought. Chambers, *TING*: family rooms; courtyard, hall; domestic. Ideogram: shelter and hall, a secure place.

Intention, *YI*: thought, idea, opinion; project, expectation; meaning, connotation. Ideogram: heart and sound, the heart behind the words. Indeed, *YE*: see *Preceding Situation*.

SIX AT FIFTH

To the **Winnowing Son belongs brightness hidden**.

Harvesting, **Trial**.

Comments

To the **Winnowing Son belongs Trial**.

Brightness not permitted to **pause indeed**.

Fields of meaning

Winnow, *JI*: separate grain from chaff by tossing it in the wind; sieve, winnowing-basket; separate the valuable from the worthless, good from bad. Son(hood), *ZI*: son, male child; heirs, offspring, posterity; living up to the ideal of the ancestors as highest human aspiration; seed, kernel, egg; sage, teacher; nadir, deepest point, midnight, mid-winter. **Winnowing Son**, *JI ZI*, is the name of a brother of the last Shang emperor. Ji Zi shone as a model of moral discrimination in the dark epoch of the decline of the Shang dynasty. **Belong/it**, *ZHI*: establishes between two terms a connection similar to the Saxon genitive, in which the second term belongs to the first one; at the end of a sentence it refers to something previously mentioned or implied. **Brightness hidden**, *MING YI*: see *Image of the Situation*. **Harvest**, *LI*: see *Image of the Situation*. **Trial**, *ZHEN*: see *Image of the Situation*.

Not, *BU*: common term of negation. **Permit**, *KE*: possible because in harmony with an inherent principle; capable of; approve, authorize. Ideogram: mouth and breath, silent consent. **Pause**, *XI*: breathe; rest, repose, a breathing-spell; suspended. **Indeed**, *YE*: see *Preceding Situation*.

SIX ABOVE

Not brightness, darkness.
Initially mounting tending-towards heaven.
Afterwards entering tending-towards earth.

Comments
Initially mounting tending-towards heaven.
Illuminating the **four cities indeed.**
Afterwards entering tending-towards earth.
Letting-go by **consequence indeed.**

Fields of meaning

Not, *BU*: common term of negation. **Brightness**, *MING*: see *Image of the Situation*. **Darkness**, *HUI*: see *Patterns of Wisdom*. **Initial**, *CHU*: beginning, incipient, first step or part; bottom line of a hexagram. Ideogram: knife and garment, cutting out the pattern. **Mount**, *DENG*: ascend, rise; ripen, complete. **Tend-towards**, *YU*: move toward without necessarily reaching, in the direction of. **Heaven**, *TIAN*: sky, firmament, heavens; the highest realm, situated above the human world, as opposed to the earth, *DI*, located below; Symbol of the trigram Energy, *QIAN*. Ideogram: great and the one above. **After(wards)/later**, *HOU*: come after in time, subsequent; put oneself after; behind, back, draw back; the second; attendants, heirs, successors, posterity. **Enter**, *RU*: see *Patterns of Wisdom*. **Earth**, *DI*: see *Patterns of Wisdom*.

Illuminate, *ZHAO*: shine light on, enlighten; care for, supervise. Ideogram: fire and brightness. **Four**, *SI*: number four; number of the cardinal directions and of the seasons; everywhere, on all sides; fourfold articulation of the Universal Compass. **City**, *GUO*: city, state, country, nation; area of only human constructions; first of the territorial zones: city, suburbs, countryside, forest. **Indeed**, *YE*: see *Preceding Situation*. **Let-go**, *SHI*: lose, let slip; omit, miss, fail; lose control of. Ideogram: drop from the hand. **Consequence**, *ZE*: reason, cause, result; rule, law, pattern, standard; therefore; very strong connection.

Image Tradition

> **Brightness entering** the **earth**'s **center**. **Brightness hidden**.
> **Inside pattern bright and-also outside supple yielding**.
>
> **Using enveloping** the **great**: **heaviness**.
> The **Pattern King uses it**.
> **Harvesting**: **drudgery**, **Trial**.
> **Darkening one's brightness indeed**.
>
> **Inside heaviness and-also able** to **correct one's purpose**.
> The **Winnowing Son uses it**.

Fields of meaning

Brightness, *MING*: see *Image of the Situation*. **Enter**, *RU*: see *Patterns of Wisdom*. **Earth**, *DI*: see *Patterns of Wisdom*. **Center**, *ZHONG*: see *Patterns of Wisdom*. **Hide**, *YI*: see *Image of the Situation*. **Inside**, *NEI*: within, inner, interior; inside of the house and those who work there, particularly women; inside of the body, inner organs; the lower trigram, as opposed to outside, *WAI*, the upper. Ideogram: border and enter. **Pattern**, *WEN*: intrinsic or natural design, pattern of wood, stone or animal fur; ideograms, the symbols of writing as revelation of the intrinsic nature of things; language, civilization, culture; harmonious, beautiful, elegant, polite. **And-also**, *ER*: see *Patterns of Wisdom*. **Outside**, *WAI*: outer, external; unfamiliar, foreign; ignore, reject; work done outside the home; the upper trigram as indication of the outer aspects of the situation. **Supple**, *ROU*: quality of the opened lines; flexible, pliant, adaptable, tender. **Yield**, *SHUN*: give way, comply, agree, follow, obey; docile, flexible; bear produce, nourish, provide; Action of the trigram Field, *KUN*.

Use, *YI*: see *Patterns of Wisdom*. **Envelop**, *MENG*: cover, pull over, hide, conceal; lid or cover; clouded awareness, dull; ignorance, immaturity; unseen beginnings. Ideogram: plant and covered, hidden growth. **Great**, *DA*: big, noble, important, very; orient the will toward a self-imposed goal, impose direction; ability to lead or guide one's life; contrasts with small, *XIAO*, flexible adaptation to what crosses one's path. **Heaviness**, *NAN*: difficulty, hardship, distress; arduous, grievous; harass; contrasts with versatility, *YI*, deal lightly with. Ideogram: bird with clipped tail on drying sticky soil. **Pattern**, *WEN*: intrinsic or natural design, pattern of wood, stone or animal fur; ideograms, the symbols of writing as revelation of the intrinsic nature of things; language, civilization, culture; harmonious, beautiful, elegant, polite. **King**, *WANG*: sovereign, effective ruler, emperor, seen as connecting heaven and earth; reign, govern. Pattern King, *WEN WANG*, is the name of the founder of the Zhou dynasty and mythical author of the *Yi Jing*. **It/belong**, *ZHI*: establishes between two terms a connection similar to the Saxon genitive, in which the second term belongs to the first one; at the end of a sentence it refers to something previously mentioned or implied. **Harvesting: drudgery, Trial**, *LI JIAN ZHEN*: see *Image of the Situation*. **Darkness**, *HUI*: see *Patterns of Wisdom*. **One/one's**, *QI*: general third person pronoun and possessive adjective; also: it/its, he/his, she/her, they/their. **Indeed**, *YE*: see *Preceding Situation*.

Able/enable, *NENG*: ability, power, skill, art; competent, talented; duty, function, capacity. Ideogram: an animal with strong hooves and bones, able to carry and defend. **Correct**, *ZHENG*: rectify deviation or one-sidedness; proper, straight, exact, regular; constant, rule, model. Ideogram: stop and one, hold to one thing. **Purpose**, *ZHI*: focus of mind and heart; intention, will, inclination; continuity in the direction of life. Ideogram: heart and scholar, high inner resolve. **Winnow**, *JI*: separate grain from chaff by tossing it in the wind; sieve, winnowing-basket; separate the valuable from the worthless, good from bad. **Son(hood)**, *ZI*: son, male child; heirs, offspring, posterity; living up to the ideal of the ancestors as highest human aspiration; seed, kernel, egg; sage, teacher; nadir, deepest point, midnight, mid-winter. Winnowing Son, *JI ZI*, is the name of a brother of the last Shang emperor. Ji Zi shone as a model of moral discrimination in the dark epoch of the decline of the Shang dynasty.

Some texts of this hexagram refer to the mythical events surrounding the origin of the *Yi Jing*, at the end of the Shang dynasty. It is indeed a time of darkness, which forces intelligence to go underground: but in seclusion and obscurity the seed is sown of a work of light which is to stand the test of time.

Wen Wang, the Pattern King, is the head of the Zhou clan, a Western vassal to the last Shang emperor Di Xin. Wen is a wise and just ruler, one of the ideal models of Chinese civilization. His name is metaphorically meaningful: it refers to the written sign, both as the art of symbolically conveying the natural pattern of manifest reality and as the divinatory art of evoking the still unmanifest pattern of things. It is the base of all culture and civilization. Di Xin, on the other hand, is a corrupt and cruel tyrant. He has Wen locked away in a walled cave for seven years. In his subterranean confinement Wen meditates on the opened and whole lines figures handed down by the mythical emperor sage Fu Xi. By writing oracular texts to elucidate them, he turns them into a tool to orient action at times of darkness and confusion, and lays the base of the book that you, reader, now have in your hands.

Ji Zi, the Winnowing Son, a brother of the emperor Di Xin, remains, amidst the degeneracy and corruption of the court, a model of clarity and discrimination. Imprisoned by his brother, he survives by hiding his light through feigning madness. This allows him in the end to pass on his political wisdom to the next lineage of rulers, when Wu Wang, son of Wen Wang, defeats the tyrant and founds the Zhou dynasty.

家人

37 HOUSEHOLD PEOPLE | *Jia Ren*

The situation described by this hexagram is characterized by the community of a household, people sharing a living space.

Image of the Situation

Household people.
Harvesting: woman's Trial.

Fields of meaning

Household, *JIA*: home, house; family; dwell, reside; domestic, within doors; shop, school, doctrine. Ideogram: roof and pig or dog, the most valued domestic animals, living under the same roof with the family. People/person, *REN*: humans individually and collectively; an individual; humankind. Harvest, *LI*: benefit, advantage, profit; realization; sharp, acute, insightful; quality of autumn and West, third stage of the Time Cycle. Ideogram: ripe grain and blade. Woman(hood), *NÜ*: woman and what is inherently female. Trial, *ZHEN*: inquiry by divination and its result; righteous, firm; separating wheat from chaff; the kernel, the proven core; quality of winter and North, fourth stage of the Time Cycle. Ideogram: pearl and divination.

Outer and Inner Trigram

The upper trigram, **Root**, *SUN*, describes the outer aspects of the situation. It has the following associations: base on which things rest, ground, foundation; mild, subtly penetrating; nourishing. *Symbols*: tree/wood and wind. Tree/wood, *MU*: trees and all things woody or wooden; associated with the Wooden Moment. Ideogram: a tree with roots and branches. Wind, *FENG*: wind, breeze, gust; weather and its influence on mood and humor; fashion, usage. *Action*: enter, *RU*, penetrate, go into, enter on, encroach on; progress; put into. In the family of trigrams *SUN* is the eldest daughter.

The lower trigram, **Radiance**, *LI*, describes the inner aspects of the situation. It has the following associations: glowing light, spreading in all directions; the power of consciousness; discriminate, articulate, divide and arrange in order; assemble, attract. Ideogram: bird and weird, magical fire-bird with brilliant plumage. *Symbols*: fire and brightness. Fire, *HUO*: flame, burn; warming and consuming aspect of burning. Brightness, *MING*: light, radiance, clarity; distinguish, discern, understand; light-giving aspect of fire, of heavenly bodies and of consciousness. *Action*: congregate, *LI*, cling together, adhere to, rely on; couple, pair, herd; beautiful, elegant. Ideogram: deer flocking together. In the family of trigrams *LI* is the middle daughter.

Counter Hexagram

The Counter Hexagram of **Household People** is hexagram 64, **Not Yet Fording**, which switches the emphasis from being presently engaged in a household to being on the brink of a move whose outcome cannot yet be discerned.

Preceding Situation

> **Injury with-respect-to** the **outside implies necessarily reversing with-respect-to** the **household**.
> To **anterior acquiescence belongs** the **use of household people**.

Fields of meaning

Injure, *SHANG*: hurt, wound, damage; grief, distress, mourning; sad at heart, afflicted. With-respect-to, *YU*: in relation to, referring to, according to; in, at, until. Outside, *WAI*: outer, external; unfamiliar, foreign; ignore, reject; work done outside the home; the upper trigram as indication of the outer aspects of the situation. Imply, *ZHE*: further signify; additional meaning. Necessarily, *BI*: unavoidably, certainly. Reverse, *FAN*: turn and move in the opposite direction; turn around or upside down (180 degrees); change to the opposite position; contrary. Household, *JIA*: see *Image of the Situation*. To anterior acquiescence belongs the use of, *GU SHOU ZHI YI*: understanding and accepting the preceding statement allows the consultant to make proper use of this hexagram. People/person, *REN*: see *Image of the Situation*.

Hexagrams in Pairs

> **Polarizing**: **outside indeed**.
> **Household people**: **inside indeed**.

Fields of meaning
Polarize, *KUI*: separate, oppose; contrary, mutually exclusive; distant, absent, remote; conflict, discord, animosity; astronomical or polar opposition. **Outside**, *WAI*: see *Preceding Situation*. **Indeed**, *YE*: emphasizes and intensifies the previous statement. **Household people**, *JIA REN*: see *Image of the Situation*. **Inside**, *NEI*: within, inner, interior; inside of the house and those who work there, particularly women; inside of the body, inner organs; the lower trigram, as opposed to outside, *WAI*, the upper. Ideogram: border and enter.

Patterns of Wisdom

> **Wind originating** from **fire emerging**. **Household people**.
> A **jun zi uses words** to **possess beings and-also movement** to **possess perseverance**.

Fields of meaning
Wind, *FENG*: wind, breeze, gust; weather and its influence on mood and humor; fashion, usage; wind and wood are the Symbols of the trigram Root, *SUN*. **Origin**, *ZI*: source, beginning, ground; cause, reason, motive; tracing back to the source; oneself, by oneself; spontaneous, intrinsic. **Fire**, *HUO*: fire, flame, burn; warming and consuming aspect of burning; fire and brightness are the Symbols of the trigram Radiance, *LI*. **Emerge**, *CHU*: come out of, proceed from, spring from, issue forth; appear, be born; bear, generate; leave, flee; Action of the trigram Shake, *ZHEN*. Ideogram: stem with branches and leaves emerging. **Household people**, *JIA REN*: see *Image of the Situation*. **Jun zi**: ideal of a person who orders his/her life in accordance with dao rather than willful intention, and uses divination in this spirit. **Use**, *YI*: by means of; owing to; make use of, employ. **Word**, *YAN*: spoken word, speech, saying; talk, discuss, address; name, signify. Ideogram: mouth and rising vapor. **Possess**, *YOU*: general term indicating possession; have, own, be endowed with. **Being**, *WU*: creature, thing, any single being; matter, substance, essence; nature of things. **And-also**, *ER*: joins and contrasts two terms. **Move**, *XING*: move or move something; motivate; emotionally moving; walk, act, do. Ideogram: successive steps. **Persevere**, *HENG*: continue in the same way or spirit; constant, habitual, regular; self-renewing.

Transforming Lines

INITIAL NINE

Enclosure: possessing household.
Repenting extinguished.

Comments
Enclosure: possessing household.
Purpose not-yet transformed indeed.

Fields of meaning

Enclose, *XIAN*: put inside a fence or barrier; pen, corral; protect; restrain, obstruct; rule, model. Possess, *YOU*: see *Patterns of Wisdom*. Household, *JIA*: see *Image of the Situation*. Repenting extinguished, *HUI WANG*: previous errors are corrected, all causes for repenting disappear.

Purpose, *ZHI*: focus of mind and heart; intention, will, inclination; continuity in the direction of life. Ideogram: heart and scholar, high inner resolve. Not-yet, *WEI*: temporal negative indicating that something is expected to happen but has not yet occurred. Transform, *BIAN*: abrupt, radical passage from one state to another; transformation of opened and whole lines into each other in hexagrams; contrasts with change, *HUA*, gradual mutation. Indeed, *YE*: see *Hexagrams in Pairs*.

SIX AT SECOND

Without direction releasing.
Located in the **center, feeding.**
Trial, significant.

Comments
To **six** at **second belongs significance.**
Yielding uses the **root indeed.**

Fields of meaning

Without, *WU*: devoid of; there is not. Direct, *YOU*: move on or through water; place, residence, focus; that which. Ideogram: pole to sound the depth of water. Release, *SUI*: let go, free; unhindered; advance, progress; promote, further; reach, succeed; in accord with, conforming to. Ideogram: go and follow one's wishes, unimpeded movement. Locate, *ZAI*: be at, be situated at, dwell, reside; in, within; involved with, in the process of. Ideogram: earth and persevere, a place on the earth. Center, *ZHONG*: inner, central; put in the center; middle, stable point enabling you to face inner and outer changes; middle line of a trigram. Ideogram: field divided in two equal parts. Feed, *KUI*: nourish, prepare and present food; provisions. Trial, *ZHEN*: see *Image of the Situation*. Significant, *JI*: leads to the experience of meaning; favorable, propitious, appropriate. Ideogram: scholar and mouth, wise words of a sage.

Six, *LIU*: number six; transforming opened line; six lines of a hexagram. Two/second, *ER*: number two; pair, even numbers, binary, duplicate. Belong/it, *ZHI*: establishes between two terms a connection similar to the Saxon genitive, in which the second term belongs to the first one; at the end of a sentence it refers to something previously mentioned or implied. Yield, *SHUN*: give way, comply, agree, follow, obey; docile, flexible; bear produce, nourish, provide; Action of the trigram Field, *KUN*. Use, *YI*: see *Patterns of Wisdom*. Root, *SUN*: base on which things rest, ground, foundation; mild, subtly penetrating; nourishing. Indeed, *YE*: see *Hexagrams in Pairs*.

Nine at Third

Household people, **scolding**, **scolding**.
Repenting, **adversity**, **significant**.
The **wife**, the **son**, **giggling**, **giggling**.
Completing, **abashment**.

Comments
Household people, scolding, scolding.
Not-yet letting-go indeed.
The **wife**, the **son**, **giggling**, **giggling**.
Letting-go the **household's articulation indeed**.

Fields of meaning

Household people, *JIA REN*: *Image of the Situation*. Scold, *HE*: rebuke, blame, enforce obedience; severe, stern. Repent, *HUI*: regret, dissatisfaction with past conduct inducing a change of heart; proceeds from abashment, *LIN*, shame and confusion at having lost the right way. Adversity, *LI*: danger, hardship, severe; threat or difficulty that must be encountered, rather than avoided; grinding stone; polish, sharpen; a challenge that strengthens and perfects the character; stimulate, excite; cruel demon. Significant, *JI*: leads to the experience of meaning; favorable, propitious, appropriate. Ideogram: scholar and mouth, wise words of a sage. Wife, *FU*: position of married woman as head of the household; distinct from consort, *QI*, which denotes her legal status, and from concubine, *QIE*, secondary wife.

Ideogram: woman, hand and broom, household duties. **Son(hood)**, *ZI*: son, male child; heirs, offspring, posterity; living up to the ideal of the ancestors as highest human aspiration; seed, kernel, egg; sage, teacher; nadir, deepest point, midnight, mid-winter. **Giggle**, *XI*: laugh or titter uncontrollably; merriment, delight, surprise; foolish. **Complete**, *ZHONG*: completion of a cycle that begins the next; entire, whole, all. Ideogram: silk cocoons, follow and ice, winter linking one year with the next. **Abashment**, *LIN*: distress, shame, regret, humiliation; aware of having lost the right track; leads to repenting, *HUI*, correcting the direction of mind and life.

Not-yet, *WEI*: temporal negative indicating that something is expected to happen but has not yet occurred. **Let-go**, *SHI*: lose, let slip; omit, miss, fail; lose control of. Ideogram: drop from the hand. **Indeed**, *YE*: see *Hexagrams in Pairs*. **Articulate**, *JIE*: joint, articulation; a separation which simultaneously establishes the identity of the parts and their connection; express thought through speech; section, chapter, interval; temperance, virtue; rite, ceremony; lit.: nodes of bamboo stalks.

SIX AT FOURTH

Affluent household: the **great**, **significant**.

Comments

Affluent household: the **great**, **significant**.
Yielding located in the **position indeed**.

Fields of meaning

Affluence, *FU*: rich, abundant; wealth; enrich, provide for; flow toward, accrue. **Household**, *JIA*: see *Image of the Situation*. **Great**, *DA*: big, noble, important, very; orient the will toward a self-imposed goal, impose direction; ability to lead or guide one's life; contrasts with small, *XIAO*, flexible adaptation to what crosses one's path. **Significant**, *JI*: leads to the experience of meaning; favorable, propitious, appropriate. Ideogram: scholar and mouth, wise words of a sage.

Yield, *SHUN*: give way, comply, agree, follow, obey; docile, flexible; bear produce, nourish, provide; Action of the trigram Field, *KUN*. **Locate**, *ZAI*: be at, be situated at, dwell, reside; in, within; involved with, in the process of. Ideogram: earth and persevere, a place on the earth. **Position**, *WEI*: place, location; be at; social standing, rank; position of a line in a hexagram. Ideogram: person standing. **Indeed**, *YE*: see *Hexagrams in Pairs*.

NINE AT FIFTH

The **king imagines possessing** a **household**.
Beings' care, significant.

Comments
The **king imagines possessing** a **household**.
Mingling: reciprocal affection indeed.

Fields of meaning

King, *WANG*: sovereign, effective ruler, emperor, seen as connecting heaven and earth; reign, govern. Imagine, *JIA*: create in the mind; fantasize, suppose; pretend, imitate; fiction, illusion; costume. Ideogram: person and borrow. Possess, *YOU*: see *Patterns of Wisdom*. Household, *JIA*: see *Image of the Situation*. Being, *WU*: see *Patterns of Wisdom*. Care, *XU*: fear, doubt, concern; heartfelt attachment; relieve, soothe, aid; sympathy, compassion, consolation. Ideogram: heart and blood, the heart's blood affected. Significant, *JI*: leads to the experience of meaning; favorable, propitious, appropriate. Ideogram: scholar and mouth, wise words of a sage.

Mingle, *JIAO*: blend with, communicate, join, exchange; trade; copulation; friendship. Ideogram: legs crossed. Reciprocal, *XIANG*: mutual; assist, encourage, help; bring together, blend with; examine, inspect; by turns. Affection, *AI*: love, show affection; benevolent feelings; kindness, regard. Indeed, *YE*: see *Hexagrams in Pairs*.

NINE ABOVE

Possessing conformity, impressing thus.
Completing, significant.

Comments
To **impressing thus belongs significance**.
Reversing designation belonging to **individuality indeed**.

Fields of meaning

Possess, *YOU*: see *Patterns of Wisdom*. Conform, *FU*: accord between inner and outer; sincere, truthful, verified, reliable; capture; prisoners, spoils. Ideogram: claws over child, a bird brooding on the nest. Impress, *WEI*: impose on, intimidate; august, solemn; pomp, majesty. Thus, *RU*: as, in this way; comparable, similar. Complete, *ZHONG*: completion of a cycle that begins the next; entire, whole, all. Ideogram: silk cocoons, follow and ice, winter linking one year with the next. **Significant**, *JI*: leads to the experience of meaning; favorable, propitious, appropriate. Ideogram: scholar and mouth, wise words of a sage.

Belong/it, *ZHI*: establishes between two terms a connection similar to the Saxon genitive, in which the second term belongs to the first one; at the end of a sentence it refers to something previously mentioned or implied. **Reverse**, *FAN*: see *Preceding Situation*. **Designate**, *WEI*: say, express in words, give a name; mean, signify; consider as; talk about. Ideogram: words and belly, describing the essential. **Individuality**, *SHEN*: total person: psyche, body and lifespan; character, virtue, duty, pregnancy; distinct from body, *GONG*, physical being. **Indeed**, *YE*: see *Hexagrams in Pairs*.

Image Tradition

Household people.
The **woman** in the **correct position reaching** the **inside**.
The **man** in the **correct position reaching** the **outside**.
Man and **woman correct**.
The **great belonging** to **heaven** and **earth righteous indeed**.

Household people possess an **intimidating chief in-truth**.
To **father** and **mother belongs designation**.
The **father**, a **father**. The **son**, a **son**.
The **senior**, a **senior**. The **junior**, a **junior**.
The **husband**, a **husband**. The **wife**, a **wife**.
And-also household's **dao correct**.
Correct household and-also below heaven rectified.

Fields of meaning

Household people, *JIA REN*: see *Image of the Situation*. **Woman(hood)**, *NÜ*: see *Image of the Situation*. **Correct**, *ZHENG*: rectify deviation or one-sidedness; proper, straight, exact, regular; constant, rule, model. Ideogram: stop and one, hold to one thing. **Position**, *WEI*: place, location; be at; social standing, rank; position of a line in a hexagram. Ideogram: person standing. **Reach**, *HU*: arrive at a goal; move toward and achieve; to, at, in; distinct from tend-towards, *YOU*. **Inside**, *NEI*: see *Hexagrams in Pairs*. **Man(hood)**, *NAN*: a man; what is inherently male; husband, son. Ideogram: field and strength, men's hard work in the fields.

Outside, *WAI*: see *Preceding Situation*. **Great**, *DA*: big, noble, important, very; orient the will toward a self-imposed goal, impose direction; ability to lead or guide one's life; contrasts with small, *XIAO*, flexible adaptation to what crosses one's path. **Belong/it**, *ZHI*: establishes between two terms a connection similar to the Saxon genitive, in which the second term belongs to the first one; at the end of a sentence it refers to something previously mentioned or implied. **Heaven**, *TIAN*: sky, firmament, heavens; the highest realm, situated above the human world, as opposed to the earth, *DI*, located below; Symbol of the trigram Energy, *QIAN*. Ideogram: great and the one above. **Earth**, *DI*: the earth, ground on which the human world rests; basis of all things, nourishes all things; essential Yin; Symbol of the trigram Space, *KUN*. **Righteous**, *YI*: proper, just, virtuous, upright; the heart that rules itself; benevolent, loyal, devoted to public good. **Indeed**, *YE*: see *Hexagrams in Pairs*.

Possess, *YOU*: see *Patterns of Wisdom*. **Intimidate**, *YAN*: inspire with fear or awe; severe, rigid, strict, austere, demanding; a severe father; tight, a closed door. **Chief**, *JUN*: prince, ruler; lead, direct; wise person. Ideogram: mouth and direct, giving orders. **In-truth**, *YAN*: a final affirmative particle; the preceding statement is complete and correct. **Father**, *FU*: father, act as a father, paternal, patriarchal; authoritative rule. Ideogram: hand and rod, the chastising father. **Mother**, *MU*: mother, maternal, feminine; child-bearing and nourishing. Ideogram: two breasts. **Designate**, *WEI*: say, express in words, give a name; mean, signify; consider as; talk about. Ideogram: words and belly, describing the essential. **Son(hood)**, *ZI*: son, male child; heirs, offspring, posterity; living up to the ideal of the ancestors as highest human aspiration; seed, kernel, egg; sage, teacher; nadir, deepest point, midnight, mid-winter. **Senior**, *XIONG*: elder brother; elder, one to whom respect is due. **Junior**, *DI*: younger relatives who owe respect to their elders. **Husband**, *FU*: adult, man, male spouse; scholar, distinguished man; one who can help; manage a household. Ideogram: man with a pin in his hair to show that he is of age. **Wife**, *FU*: position of married woman as head of the household; distinct from consort, *QI*, which denotes her legal status, and from concubine, *QIE*, secondary wife. Ideogram: woman, hand and broom, household duties. **And-also**, *ER*: see *Patterns of Wisdom*. **Dao**, *DAO*: way or path; ongoing process of being and the course it traces for each person or thing; ultimate reality, intrinsic nature; origin. Ideogram: go and head, opening a path. **Below heaven**, *TIAN XIA*: human world, between heaven and earth. **Rectify**, *DING*: correct, settle, fix; peaceful, tranquil, stable; certain, invariable.

睽

38 POLARIZING | *Kui*

The situation described by this hexagram is characterized by a tension between polar opposites, which needs to be acknowledged and given its proper place.

Image of the Situation

Polarizing.
The **small**'s **affairs**, **significant**.

Fields of meaning
Polarize, *KUI*: separate, oppose; contrary, mutually exclusive; distant, absent, remote; conflict, discord, animosity; astronomical or polar opposition. **Small**, *XIAO*: little, common, unimportant; adapting to what crosses your path; ability to move in harmony with the vicissitudes of life; contrasts with great, *DA*, self-imposed theme or goal. **Affairs**, *SHI*: all kinds of personal activity; matters at hand; business; function, occupation; manage; perform a task; incident, event; case in court. **Significant**, *JI*: leads to the experience of meaning; favorable, propitious, appropriate. Ideogram: scholar and mouth, wise words of a sage.

Outer and Inner Trigram

The upper trigram, **Radiance**, *LI*, describes the outer aspects of the situation. It has the following associations: glowing light, spreading in all directions; the power of consciousness; discriminate, articulate, divide and arrange in order; assemble, attract. Ideogram: bird and weird, magical fire-bird with brilliant plumage. *Symbols*: fire and brightness. Fire, *HUO*: flame, burn; warming and consuming aspect of burning. Brightness, *MING*: light, radiance, clarity; distinguish, discern, understand; light-giving aspect of fire, of heavenly bodies and of consciousness. *Action*: congregate, *LI*, cling together, adhere to, rely on; couple, pair, herd; beautiful, elegant. Ideogram: deer flocking together. In the family of trigrams *LI* is the middle daughter.

The lower trigram, **Open**, *DUI*, describes the inner aspects of the situation. It has the following associations: an open surface, promoting interaction and interpenetration; pleasant, easy, responsive, free, unhindered; opening, passage; the mouth; exchange, barter; straight, direct; meet, gather; place where water accumulates. Ideogram: mouth and vapor, communication through speech. *Symbol*: marsh, *ZE*, open surface of a flat body of water and the vapors rising from it; fertilize, enrich; kindness, favor. *Action*: stimulate, *SHUO*, rouse to action and good feeling; stir up, urge on; exhort, persuade; say, tell, relate; cheer, delight; joyous, peaceful, restful. Ideogram: words and exchange. In the family of trigrams *DUI* is the youngest daughter.

Counter Hexagram

The Counter Hexagram of **Polarizing** is hexagram 63, **Already Fording**, which switches the emphasis from the unresolved tension of **Polarizing** to being engaged in a process which is already on its way to completion.

Preceding Situation

> **Household**'s **dao exhausted**, **necessarily turning-away**.
> To **anterior acquiescence belongs** the **use** of **polarizing**.
> **Polarizing implies turning-away indeed**.

Fields of meaning

Household, *JIA*: home, house; family; dwell, reside; domestic, within doors; shop, school, doctrine. Ideogram: roof and pig or dog, the most valued domestic animals, living under the same roof with the family. **Dao**, *DAO*: way or path; ongoing process of being and the course it traces for each person or thing; ultimate reality, intrinsic nature; origin. Ideogram: go and head, opening a path. **Exhaust**, *QIONG*: bring to an end; limit, extremity; investigate exhaustively; destitute, indigent; end without a new beginning; distinct from complete, *ZHONG*, end of a cycle that begins the next one. Ideogram: cave and naked person, bent with disease or old age. **Necessarily**, *BI*: unavoidably, certainly. **Turn-away**, *GUAI*: turn your back on something and focus on its opposite; contradict, resist; part ways, separate oneself from; cunning, crafty; perverse. To **anterior acquiescence belongs** the **use** of, *GU SHOU ZHI YI*: understanding and accepting the preceding statement allows the consultant to make proper use of this hexagram. **Polarize**, *KUI*: see *Image of the Situation*. **Imply**, *ZHE*: further signify; additional meaning. **Indeed**, *YE*: emphasizes and intensifies the previous statement.

Hexagrams in Pairs

Polarizing: outside indeed.
Household people: inside indeed.

Fields of meaning

Polarize, *KUI*: see *Image of the Situation*. **Outside**, *WAI*: outer, external; unfamiliar, foreign; ignore, reject; work done outside the home; the upper trigram as indication of the outer aspects of the situation. **Indeed**, *YE*: see *Preceding Situation*. **Household**, *JIA*: see *Preceding Situation*. **People/person**, *REN*: humans individually and collectively; an individual; humankind. **Inside**, *NEI*: within, inner, interior; inside of the house and those who work there, particularly women; inside of the body, inner organs; the lower trigram, as opposed to outside, *WAI*, the upper. Ideogram: border and enter.

Patterns of Wisdom

Fire above, pond below. Polarizing.
A **jun zi uses concording and-also dividing.**

Fields of meaning

Fire, *HUO*: fire, flame, burn; warming and consuming aspect of burning; fire and brightness are the Symbols of the trigram Radiance, *LI*. **Above**, *SHANG*: anything above in all senses; higher, upper, outer; upper trigram. **Pond**, *ZE*: open surface of a flat body of water and the vapors rising from it; fertilize, enrich; kindness, favor; Symbol of the trigram Open, *DUI*. **Below**, *XIA*: anything below, in all senses; lower, inner; lower trigram. **Polarize**, *KUI*: see *Image of the Situation*. **Jun zi**: ideal of a person who orders his/her life in accordance with dao rather than willful intention, and uses divination in this spirit. **Use**, *YI*: by means of; owing to; make use of, employ. **Concord**, *TONG*: harmonize, unite, equalize, assemble; agree, share in; together, at once, same time and place. Ideogram: cover and mouth, silent understanding and perfect fit. **And-also**, *ER*: joins and contrasts two terms. **Divide**, *YI*: separate, break apart, sever; oppose; different, foreign, strange, rare.

Transforming Lines

INITIAL NINE

Repenting extinguished.
Losing the **horse, no pursuing: originating** from **returning.**

Viewing hatred in the **person**.
Without fault.

Comments
Viewing hatred in the **person**.
Using expelling fault indeed.

Fields of meaning

Repenting extinguished, *HUI WANG*: previous errors are corrected, all causes for repenting disappear. Lose, *SANG*: be deprived of, forget; destruction, ruin, death; corpse; lament, mourn; funeral. Ideogram: weep and dead. Horse, *MA*: symbol of spirited strength in the natural world, earthly counterpart of the dragon; associated with the trigram Energy, *QIAN*, heaven, and high noon. No, *WU*: common term of negation. Pursue, *ZHU*: chase, follow closely, press hard; expel, drive out. Ideogram: pig (wealth) and go, chasing fortune. Origin, *ZI*: source, beginning, ground; cause, reason, motive; tracing back to the source; oneself, by oneself; spontaneous, intrinsic. Return, *FU*: go back, turn or lead back; recur, reappear, come again; restore, renew, recover; return to an earlier time or place. Ideogram: step and retrace a path. View, *JIAN*: vision in all its aspects: seeing, being visible, forming mental images; visit, call on, consult. Ideogram: eye above person, active and receptive sight. Hate, *WU*: detest, dread, dislike; averse to, ashamed of; repulsive, vicious, vile, ugly, wicked. Ideogram: twisted bowels and heart. Person/people, *REN*: see *Hexagrams in Pairs*. Without fault, *WU JIU*: no error or harm in the situation.

Use, *YI*: see *Patterns of Wisdom*. Expel, *PI*: cast out, repress, exclude, punish; exclusionary laws and their enforcement. Ideogram: punish, authority and mouth, giving order to expel. Fault, *JIU*: unworthy conduct that leads to harm, illness, misfortune; guilt, crime, punishment. Ideogram: person and differ, differ from what you should be. Indeed, *YE*: see *Preceding Situation*.

NINE AT SECOND

Meeting a **lord tending-towards** the **street**.
Without fault.

Comments
Meeting a **lord tending-towards** the **street**.
Not-yet letting-go dao indeed.

Fields of meaning

Meet, *YU*: come on unexpectedly, encounter; occur, happen; pleasant meeting, lucky coincidence; agree. **Lord**, *ZHU*: ruler, master, chief, authority; host; domination in the cycle of the Five Transformative Moments. Ideogram: lamp and flame, giving light. **Tend-towards**, *YU*: move toward without necessarily reaching, in the direction of. **Street**, *XIANG*: public space between dwellings, public square; side-street, alley, lane. Ideogram: place and public. **Without fault**, *WU JIU*: no error or harm in the situation.

Not-yet, *WEI*: temporal negative indicating that something is expected to happen but has not yet occurred. **Let-go**, *SHI*: lose, let slip; omit, miss, fail; lose control of. Ideogram: drop from the hand. **Dao**, *DAO*: see *Preceding Situation*. **Indeed**, *YE*: see *Preceding Situation*.

Six at Third

Viewing the **cart pulled-back**.
One's cattle hampered.
One's person stricken, moreover nose-cut.
Without initially possessing completion.

Comments

Viewing the **cart pulled-back**.
Position not appropriate indeed.
Without initially possessing completion.
Meeting a **solid indeed**.

Fields of meaning

View, *JIAN*: vision in all its aspects: seeing, being visible, forming mental images; visit, call on, consult. Ideogram: eye above person, active and receptive sight. **Cart**, *YU*: a vehicle and its carrying capacity; contain, hold, sustain. **Pull-back**, *YI*: pull or drag something towards you; drag behind; leave traces. **One/one's**, *QI*: general third person pronoun and possessive adjective; also: it/its, he/his, she/her, they/their. **Cattle**, *NIU*: ox, bull, cow, calf; power and strength of work animals; stubborn. **Hamper**, *CHE*: hinder, obstruct, hold or pull back; embarrass. Ideogram: hand and limit. **Person/people**, *REN*: see *Hexagrams in Pairs*. **Stricken**, *YAO*: afflicted by fate; untimely, premature death; bend, break; suffer a wrong. Ideogram: great with a broken point, interrupted growth. **Moreover**, *QIE*: further, and also. **Nose-cutting**, *YI*: punishment through loss of public face or honor; distinct from foot-cutting, *YE*, crippling punishment for serious crime. **Without**, *WU*: devoid of; there is not. **Initial**, *CHU*: beginning, incipient, first step or part;

bottom line of a hexagram. Ideogram: knife and garment, cutting out the pattern. **Possess**, *YOU*: general term indicating possession; have, own, be endowed with. **Complete**, *ZHONG*: completion of a cycle that begins the next; entire, whole, all. Ideogram: silk cocoons, follow and ice, winter linking one year with the next.

Position, *WEI*: place, location; be at; social standing, rank; position of a line in a hexagram. Ideogram: person standing. **Not**, *BU*: common term of negation. **Appropriate**, *DANG*: suitable, capable, worthy, adequate, competent, equal to; opportune, convenient; whole lines in odd places and opened lines in even places. **Indeed**, *YE*: see *Preceding Situation*. **Meet**, *YU*: come on unexpectedly, encounter; occur, happen; pleasant meeting, lucky coincidence; agree. **Solid**, *GANG*: quality of the whole lines; firm, strong, unyielding, persisting.

Nine at Fourth

Polarizing alone.
Meeting Spring, husbanding.
Mingling, conforming.
Adversity, without fault.

Comments
Mingling, conforming, without fault.
Purpose moving indeed.

Fields of meaning

Polarize, *KUI*: see *Image of the Situation*. **Alone**, *GU*: solitary; without a protector; fatherless, orphan-like; unique, exceptional. See also: **Live-alone**. **Meet**, *YU*: come on unexpectedly, encounter; occur, happen; pleasant meeting, lucky coincidence; agree. **Spring**, *YUAN*: source, origin, head; arise, begin; first generating impulse; great, excellent; quality of springtime and East, first stage of the Time Cycle. **Husband**, *FU*: adult, man, male spouse; scholar, distinguished man; one who can help; manage a household. Ideogram: man with a pin in his hair to show that he is of age. **Mingle**, *JIAO*: blend with, communicate, join, exchange; trade; copulation; friendship. Ideogram: legs crossed. **Conform**, *FU*: accord between inner and outer; sincere, truthful, verified, reliable; capture; prisoners, spoils. Ideogram: claws over child, a bird brooding on the nest. **Adversity**, *LI*: danger, hardship, severe; threat or difficulty that must be encountered, rather than avoided; grinding stone; polish, sharpen; a challenge that strengthens and perfects the character; stimulate, excite; cruel demon. **Without fault**, *WU JIU*: no error or harm in the situation.

Purpose, *ZHI*: focus of mind and heart; intention, will, inclination; continuity

in the direction of life. Ideogram: heart and scholar, high inner resolve. Move, *XING*: move or move something; motivate; emotionally moving; walk, act, do. Ideogram: successive steps. Indeed, *YE*: see *Preceding Situation*.

Six at Fifth

Repenting extinguished.
Your ancestor gnawing flesh.
Going, is it **faulty?**

Comments
Your ancestor gnawing flesh.
Going possesses reward indeed.

Fields of meaning
Repenting extinguished, *HUI WANG*: previous errors are corrected, all causes for repenting disappear. Your/contracted, *JUE*: intensifying possessive pronoun and adjective; concentrate, tense, contract; whooping cough. Ancestry, *ZONG*: clan, kin, origin; those who bear the same surname; ancestral hall and tablets; honor, revere. Gnaw, *SHI*: chew, bite persistently, bite away; snap at, nibble; reach the essential by removing the unnecessary. Ideogram: mouth and divination, revealing the essential. Flesh, *FU*: skin, muscles and organs as different from bones. Go, *WANG*: move away in time or space, depart; become past; dead, gone; contrasts with come, *LAI*, approach in time or space. Is?, *HE*: ask, inquire; what? which? who? how? why? where? an interrogative particle, often introducing a rhetorical question: is it? is it not? Fault, *JIU*: unworthy conduct that leads to harm, illness, misfortune; guilt, crime, punishment. Ideogram: person and differ, differ from what you should be.

Possess, *YOU*: general term indicating possession; have, own, be endowed with. Reward, *QING*: gift given out of gratitude or benevolence; favor from heaven. Ideogram: heart, follow and deer, the heart expressed through the gift of a deer's skin. Indeed, *YE*: see *Preceding Situation*.

Nine Above

Polarizing alone.
Viewing a **pig bearing mire.**
Carrying souls: the **one chariot.**
Beforehand to the **bow belongs stretching.**
Afterwards to the **bow belongs stimulating.**

In-no-way illegality, matrimonial alliance.
Going meets rain, by **consequence significant**.

Comments
To **meeting rain belongs significance**.
The **flock**, **doubt extinguished indeed**.

Fields of meaning

Polarize, *KUI*: see *Image of the Situation*. **Alone**, *GU*: solitary; without a protector; fatherless, orphan-like; unique, exceptional. **View**, *JIAN*: vision in all its aspects: seeing, being visible, forming mental images; visit, call on, consult. Ideogram: eye above person, active and receptive sight. **Pig**, *SHI*: all swine, symbol of wealth and good fortune, associated with the Streaming Moment. **Bear**, *FU*: carry on one's back; take on a responsibility; rely on, depend on; burden, duty; mathematical term for minus; defeated; guilty; betray, reject. **Mire**, *TU*: mud, dirt, filth; besmear, blot out. Ideogram: earth and water. **Carry**, *ZAI*: bear, carry with you; contain, sustain, support; load a ship or cart, cargo; fill in. **Soul**, *GUI*: power that creates individual existence; union of volatile-soul, *HUN*, spiritual and intellectual power, and dense-soul, *PO*, bodily strength and movement. *HUN* rises after death, *PO* remains with the body and may communicate with the living. **One**, *YI*: a single unit; number one; undivided, simple, whole; unique; first. **Chariot**, *CHE*: cart, wheeled traveling vehicle. **Before(hand)/earlier**, *XIAN*: anterior, preceding in time; former, past, previous; first, at first. **Bow**, *HU*: wooden bow; curved flag pole; curved, arched. **Belong/it**, *ZHI*: establishes between two terms a connection similar to the Saxon genitive, in which the second term belongs to the first one; at the end of a sentence it refers to something previously mentioned or implied. **Stretch**, *ZHANG*: draw a bow taut; open, extend, spread, display. **After(wards)/later**, *HOU*: come after in time, subsequent; put oneself after; behind, back, draw back; the second; attendants, heirs, successors, posterity. **Stimulate**, *SHUO*: rouse to action and good feeling; stir up, urge on; exhort, persuade; say, tell, relate; cheer, delight; joyous, peaceful, restful; Action of the trigram Open, *DUI*. Ideogram: words and exchange. **In-no-way**, *FEI*: strong negative; not so; bandit, rebel; unjust, immoral. Ideogram: a box filled with opposition. **Illegality**, *KOU*: take by force, violate, invade, sack, break the laws; brutality; enemies, outcasts, bandits. **Matrimonial alliance**, *HUN GOU*: legal institution of marriage; union of two families by marriage. **Go**, *WANG*: move away in time or space, depart; become past; dead, gone; contrasts with come, *LAI*, approach in time or space. **Meet**, *YU*: come on unexpectedly, encounter; occur, happen; pleasant meeting, lucky coincidence; agree. **Rain**, *YU*: rain and all precipitations; sudden shower, fast and furious; abundant dispensation of benefits;

associated with the trigram Gorge, *KAN*, and the Streaming Moment. **Consequence**, *ZE*: reason, cause, result; rule, law, pattern, standard; therefore; very strong connection. **Significant**, *JI*: see *Image of the Situation*.

Flock, *QUN*: herd, group; people of the same kind, friends, equals; crowd, multitude; move in unison, flock together. Ideogram: chief and sheep, flock around a leader. **Doubt**, *YI*: suspect, distrust, wonder; uncertain, dubious; surmise, conjecture, fear. **Extinguish**, *WANG*: ruin, destroy; cease, go, die; lost without trace; forget, out of mind; absence, exile. Ideogram: person concealed by a wall, out of sight. **Indeed**, *YE*: see *Preceding Situation*.

Image Tradition

Polarizing.
Fire stirring-up and-also above.
Pond stirring-up and-also below.

Two women concording: residing.
Their purposes not concording: moving.
Stimulating and-also congregating reaching brightness.

The **supple advances and-also moves above.**
Acquiring the **center and-also correspondence reaching** the **solid.**
That uses the **small**'s **affairs, significant.**

Heaven and **earth: polarizing and-also their affairs concording indeed.**
Man and **woman: polarizing and-also their purposes interpenetrating indeed.**
The **myriad beings: polarizing and-also their affairs sorted indeed.**
The **season belonging** to **polarizing avails** of the **great actually in-fact.**

Fields of meaning

Polarize, *KUI*: see *Image of the Situation*. **Fire**, *HUO*: see *Patterns of Wisdom*. **Stir-up**, *DONG*: excite, influence, move, affect; work, take action; come out of the egg or the bud; Action of the trigram Shake, *ZHEN*. Ideogram: strength and heavy, move weighty things. **And-also**, *ER*: see *Patterns of Wisdom*. **Above**, *SHANG*: see

Patterns of Wisdom. **Pond**, *ZE*: open surface of a flat body of water and the vapors rising from it; fertilize, enrich; kindness, favor; Symbol of the trigram Open, *DUI*. **Below**, *XIA*: see *Patterns of Wisdom*.

Two/second, *ER*: number two; pair, even numbers, binary, duplicate. **Woman(hood)**, *NÜ*: woman and what is inherently female. **Concord**, *TONG*: see *Patterns of Wisdom*. **Reside**, *JU*: dwell, live in, stay; sit down; fill an office; well-being, rest. Ideogram: body and seat. **They/their**, *QI*: general third person pronoun and possessive adjective; also: one/one's, it/its, he/his, she/her. **Purpose**, *ZHI*: focus of mind and heart; intention, will, inclination; continuity in the direction of life. Ideogram: heart and scholar, high inner resolve. **Not**, *BU*: common term of negation. **Move**, *XING*: move or move something; motivate; emotionally moving; walk, act, do. Ideogram: successive steps. **Stimulate**, *SHUO*: rouse to action and good feeling; stir up, urge on; exhort, persuade; say, tell, relate; cheer, delight; joyous, peaceful, restful; Action of the trigram Open, *DUI*. Ideogram: words and exchange. **Congregate**, *LI*: cling together, adhere to, rely on; couple, pair, herd; beautiful, elegant; Action of the trigram Radiance, *LI*. Ideogram: deer flocking together. **Reach**, *HU*: arrive at a goal; move toward and achieve; to, at, in; distinct from tend-towards, *YOU*. **Brightness**, *MING*: light, radiance, clarity; distinguish, discern, understand; light-giving aspect of fire, of heavenly bodies and of consciousness; brightness and fire are the Symbols of the trigram Radiance, *LI*.

Supple, *ROU*: quality of the opened lines; flexible, pliant, adaptable, tender. **Advance**, *JIN*: move forward, progress, climb; promote or be promoted; further the development of, augment; offer, introduce. **Acquire**, *DE*: obtain the desired object; possession; satisfied, fulfilled; it is permitted; agree with; wish for, desire covetously. Ideogram: go and obstacle, going through obstacles to the goal. **Center**, *ZHONG*: inner, central; put in the center; middle, stable point enabling you to face inner and outer changes; middle line of a trigram. Ideogram: field divided in two equal parts. **Correspond**, *YING*: be in agreement or harmony; proper, suitable; resonate together, answer to; relation between the lines (1 and 4, 2 and 5, 3 and 6) when they form the pair opened and whole, supple and solid. Ideogram: heart and obey. **Solid**, *GANG*: quality of the whole lines; firm, strong, unyielding, persisting. **That**, *SHI*: refers to the preceding statement. **Use**, *YI*: see *Patterns of Wisdom*. The **small's affairs, significant**, *XIAO SHI JI*: see *Image of the Situation*.

Heaven, *TIAN*: sky, firmament, heavens; the highest realm, situated above the human world, as opposed to the earth, *DI*, located below; Symbol of the trigram Energy, *QIAN*. Ideogram: great and the one above. **Earth**, *DI*: the earth, ground on which the human world rests; basis of all things, nourishes all things; essential Yin; Symbol of the trigram Space, *KUN*. **Indeed**, *YE*: see *Preceding Situation*. **Season**, *SHI*: quality of the time; the right time, opportune, in harmony; planning in accord with the time; season of the year. Ideogram: sun and temple, sacred time. **Belong/it**, *ZHI*: establishes between two terms a connection similar to the Saxon genitive, in which the second term belongs to the first one; at the end of a sentence it refers to something previously mentioned or implied. **Avail**, *YONG*: use, employ for a specific purpose; take advantage of; benefit from; capacity. Ideogram: to divine and center, applying divination to central concerns. **Great**, *DA*: big, noble, important, very; orient the will toward a self-imposed goal, impose direction; ability to lead or guide one's life; contrasts with small, *XIAO*, flexible adaptation to what crosses one's path. **Actually**, *YI*: truly, really, at present. Ideogram: a dart and done, strong intention fully expressed. **In-fact**, *ZAI*: emphatic exclamation; truly, indeed.

蹇 ䷦

39 LIMPING | *Jian*

This hexagram describes a situation in which progress is hampered by obstacles and difficulties, and it is possible to proceed only haltingly and with heaviness.

Image of the Situation

> **Limping.**
> **Harvesting**: **Western South**.
> **Not Harvesting**: **Eastern North**.
> **Harvesting**: **viewing** the **great** in the **person**.
> **Trial**, **significant**.

Fields of meaning

Limp, *JIAN*: proceed haltingly; lame, weak-legged, afflicted; slow, feeble, weak; unfortunate, difficult. Ideogram: foot and cold, impeded circulation in the feet. **Harvest**, *LI*: benefit, advantage, profit; realization; sharp, acute, insightful; quality of autumn and West, third stage of the Time Cycle. Ideogram: ripe grain and blade. **Western South**, *XI NAN*: corresponds to the neutral Earthy Moment between the Yang and Yin hemicycles; bring forth concrete results, ripe fruits of late summer. **Not**, *BU*: common term of negation. **Eastern North**, *DONG BEI*: the Eastern side of North, direction corresponding to the completion of a cycle; border, limit, boundary; mountain; accomplishing words, summing up previous experience; dark, cold winter night. **View**, *JIAN*: vision in all its aspects: seeing, being visible, forming mental images; visit, call on, consult. Ideogram: eye above person, active and receptive sight. **Great**, *DA*: big, noble, important, very; orient the will toward a self-imposed goal, impose direction; ability to lead or guide one's life; contrasts with small, *XIAO*, flexible adaptation to what crosses one's path. **Person/people**, *REN*: humans individually and collectively; an individual; humankind. **Trial**, *ZHEN*: inquiry by divination and its result; righteous, firm; separating wheat from chaff; the kernel, the proven core; quality of winter and North, fourth stage of the Time Cycle. Ideogram: pearl and divination. **Significant**, *JI*: leads to the experience of meaning; favorable, propitious, appropriate. Ideogram: scholar and mouth, wise words of a sage.

Outer and Inner Trigram

The upper trigram, **Gorge**, *KAN*, describes the outer aspects of the situation. It has the following associations: precipice, dangerous place; hole, cavity, pit, snare, trap, grave; critical time, test; risky. Ideogram: earth and cavity. *Symbol*: stream, *SHUI*, flowing water; river, tide, flood; fluid, dissolving. Ideogram: rippling water. *Actions*: venture and fall. Venture, *XIAN*: face a severe difficulty or obstruction; risk; precipice, cliff, abyss; key point, point of danger. Ideogram: mound and all, everything engaged at one point. Fall, *XIAN*: fall down or into, sink, drop, descend; pit, trap, fault; falling water. In the family of trigrams *KAN* is the middle son.

The lower trigram, **Bound**, *GEN*, describes the inner aspects of the situation. It has the following associations: limit, frontier; obstacle that prevents from seeing further; stop; still, quiet, motionless; confine, enclose; mountain, sunset, beginning of winter; solid, steady, unshakable; straight, hard, adamant, obstinate. *Symbol*: mountain, *SHAN*, large, immense; limit, boundary. Ideogram: three peaks, a mountain range. *Action*: stop, *ZHI*, bring or come to a standstill, cease, terminate. Ideogram: a foot stops walking. In the family of trigrams *GEN* is the youngest son.

Counter Hexagram

The Counter Hexagram of **Limping** is hexagram 64, **Not Yet Fording**, which switches the emphasis from moving forward, even though haltingly and with effort, to being still on the brink of a move whose outcome cannot yet be discerned.

Preceding Situation

Turning-away necessarily possesses heaviness.
To **anterior acquiescence belongs** the **use** of **limping**.
Limping implies heaviness indeed.

Fields of meaning

Turn-away, *GUAI*: turn your back on something and focus on its opposite; contradict, resist; part ways, separate oneself from; cunning, crafty; perverse. **Necessarily**, *BI*: unavoidably, certainly. **Possess**, *YOU*: general term indicating possession; have, own, be endowed with. **Heaviness**, *NAN*: difficulty, hardship, distress; arduous, grievous; harass; contrasts with versatility, *YI*, deal lightly with. Ideogram: bird with clipped tail on drying sticky soil. To **anterior acquiescence belongs** the **use** of, *GU SHOU ZHI YI*: understanding and accepting the preceding statement allows the consultant to make proper use of this hexagram. **Limp**, *JIAN*: see *Image of the Situation*. **Imply**, *ZHE*: further signify; additional meaning. **Indeed**, *YE*: emphasizes and intensifies the previous statement.

Hexagrams in Pairs

Unraveling: **delay indeed**.
Limping: **heaviness indeed**.

Fields of meaning

Unravel, *XIE*: disjoin, untie, disperse, dissolve, release; analyze, explain, understand; dispel sorrow, eliminate effects, solve problems; solution, deliverance. **Delay**, *HUAN*: retard, put off; let things take their course; tie loosely; gradually, leisurely; lax, tardy, negligent. **Indeed**, *YE*: see *Preceding Situation*. **Limp**, *JIAN*: see *Image of the Situation*. **Heaviness**, *NAN*: see *Preceding Situation*.

Patterns of Wisdom

The **mountain possesses stream above**. **Limping**.
A **jun zi uses reversing individuality** to **renovate actualizing-dao**.

Fields of meaning

Mountain, *SHAN*: mountain; large, immense; limit, boundary; Symbol of the trigram Bound, *GEN*. Ideogram: three peaks, a mountain range. **Possess**, *YOU*: see *Preceding Situation*. **Stream**, *SHUI*: flowing water; river, tide, flood; fluid, dissolving; Symbol of the trigram Gorge, *KAN*. Ideogram: rippling water. **Above**, *SHANG*: anything above in all senses; higher, upper, outer; upper trigram. **Limp**, *JIAN*: see *Image of the Situation*. **Jun zi**: ideal of a person who orders his/her life in accordance with dao rather than willful intention, and uses divination in this spirit. **Use**, *YI*: by means of; owing to; make use of, employ. **Reverse**, *FAN*: turn and move in the opposite direction; turn around or upside down (180 degrees); change to the opposite position; contrary. **Individuality**, *SHEN*: total person: psyche, body and lifespan; character, virtue, duty, pregnancy; distinct from body, *GONG*, physical being. **Renovate**, *XIU*: repair, mend, improve, adjust, regulate; clean, adorn; practice, acquire skills. **Actualize-dao**, *DE*: realize dao in action; power, virtue; ability to follow the course traced by the ongoing process of the cosmos. Ideogram: go, straight, and heart. Linked with acquire, *DE*: acquiring that which makes a being become what it is meant to be.

Transforming Lines

INITIAL SIX

Going limping, coming praise.

Comments
Going limping, coming praise.
Proper to **await indeed**.

Fields of meaning

Go, *WANG*: move away in time or space, depart; become past; dead, gone; contrasts with come, *LAI*, approach in time or space. **Limp**, *JIAN*: see *Image of the Situation*. **Come**, *LAI*: approach in time or space; move toward, arrive at; future; contrasts with go, *WANG*, move away or become past. **Praise**, *YU*: magnify, eulogize; flatter; fame, reputation. Ideogram: offering words.

Proper, *YI*: reasonable, fit, right, harmonious; ought, should. **Await**, *DAI*: expect, wait for, prepare to meet (friendly or hostile); provide against. **Indeed**, *YE*: see *Preceding Situation*.

SIX AT SECOND

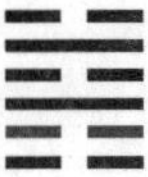

A **king**, a **servant**: **limping, limping**.
In-no-way to the **body belongs anteriority**.

Comments
A **king**, a **servant**: **limping, limping**.
Completing without surpassing indeed.

Fields of meaning

King, *WANG*: sovereign, effective ruler, emperor, seen as connecting heaven and earth; reign, govern. **Servant**, *CHEN*: attendant, minister, vassal; courtier who can speak to the sovereign; wait on, serve in office. Ideogram: person bowing low. **Limp**, *JIAN*: see *Image of the Situation*. **In-no-way**, *FEI*: strong negative; not so; bandit, rebel; unjust, immoral. Ideogram: a box filled with opposition. **Body**, *GONG*: physical being, power and self-expression; oneself; innate quality; distinct from individuality, *SHEN*, which includes the notion of lifespan. **Belong/it**, *ZHI*: establishes between two terms a connection similar to the Saxon genitive, in which the second term belongs to the first one; at the end of a sentence it refers to something previously mentioned or implied. **Anterior**, *GU*: come before as cause; former, ancient; reason, purpose, intention; grievance, dissatisfaction, sorrow, resulting from previous causes and intentions; situation leading to a divination.

Complete, *ZHONG*: completion of a cycle that begins the next; entire, whole, all. Ideogram: silk cocoons, follow and ice, winter linking one year with the next. **Without**, *WU*: devoid of; there is not. **Surpass**, *YOU*: exceed, transgress; beyond measure, extraordinary; blame. **Indeed**, *YE*: see *Preceding Situation*.

NINE AT THIRD

Going limping, coming reversal.

Comments

Going limping, coming reversal.
Inside rejoicing in **it indeed.**

Fields of meaning

Go, *WANG*: move away in time or space, depart; become past; dead, gone; contrasts with come, *LAI*, approach in time or space. **Limp**, *JIAN*: see *Image of the Situation*. **Come**, *LAI*: approach in time or space; move toward, arrive at; future; contrasts with go, *WANG*, move away or become past. **Reverse**, *FAN*: turn and move in the opposite direction; turn around or upside down (180 degrees); change to the opposite position; contrary.

Inside, *NEI*: within, inner, interior; inside of the house and those who work there, particularly women; inside of the body, inner organs; the lower trigram, as opposed to outside, *WAI*, the upper. Ideogram: border and enter. **Joy/rejoice**, *XI*: delight, exult; cheerful, merry. Ideogram: joy (music) and mouth, expressing joy. **It/belong**, *ZHI*: establishes between two terms a connection similar to the Saxon genitive, in which the second term belongs to the first one; at the end of a sentence it refers to something previously mentioned or implied. **Indeed**, *YE*: see *Preceding Situation*.

SIX AT FOURTH

Going limping, coming continuity.

Comments

Going limping, coming continuity.
Appropriate position: substance indeed.

Fields of meaning

Go, *WANG*: move away in time or space, depart; become past; dead, gone; contrasts with come, *LAI*, approach in time or space. **Limp**, *JIAN*: see *Image of the Situation*. **Come**, *LAI*: approach in time or space; move toward, arrive at; future; contrasts with go, *WANG*, move away or become past. **Continuity**, *LIAN*: connected, attached, annexed, consistent; follow, reach, stick to, join; series.

Appropriate, *DANG*: suitable, capable, worthy, adequate, competent, equal to; opportune, convenient; whole lines in odd places and opened lines in even places. **Position**, *WEI*: place, location; be at; social standing, rank; position of a line in a hexagram. Ideogram: person standing. **Substance**, *SHI*: fullness, richness; essence; real, solid, consistent; results, fruits, possessions; honest, sincere. Ideogram: string of coins under a roof, wealth in the house. **Indeed**, *YE*: see *Preceding Situation*.

Nine at Fifth

The **great**'s **limping**, **partners coming**.

Comments

The **great**'s **limping**, **partners coming**.
Using the **center articulating indeed**.

Fields of meaning

Great, *DA*: see *Image of the Situation*. **Limp**, *JIAN*: see *Image of the Situation*. **Partner**, *PENG*: companion, friend, peer; join, associate for mutual benefit; commercial venture; two equal or similar things. Ideogram: linked strings of cowries or coins. **Come**, *LAI*: approach in time or space; move toward, arrive at; future; contrasts with go, *WANG*, move away or become past.

Use, *YI*: see *Patterns of Wisdom*. **Center**, *ZHONG*: inner, central; put in the center; middle, stable point enabling you to face inner and outer changes; middle line of a trigram. Ideogram: field divided in two equal parts. **Articulate**, *JIE*: joint, articulation; a separation which simultaneously establishes the identity of the parts and their connection; express thought through speech; section, chapter, interval; temperance, virtue; rite, ceremony; lit.: nodes of bamboo stalks. **Indeed** *YE*: see *Preceding Situation*.

Six Above

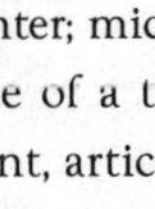

Going limping, **coming ripeness**. **Significant**.
Harvesting: **viewing** the **great** in the **person**.

Comments
Going limping, coming ripeness.
Purpose located inside indeed.
Harvesting: viewing the **great** in the **person.**
Using adhering to **value indeed.**

Fields of meaning

Go, *WANG*: move away in time or space, depart; become past; dead, gone; contrasts with come, *LAI*, approach in time or space. Limp, *JIAN*: see *Image of the Situation.* Come, *LAI*: approach in time or space; move toward, arrive at; future; contrasts with go, *WANG*, move away or become past. Ripe, *SHI*: mature, full-grown; great, eminent. Significant, *JI*: see *Image of the Situation.* Harvesting: viewing the great in the person, *LI JIAN DA REN*: see *Image of the Situation.*

Purpose, *ZHI*: focus of mind and heart; intention, will, inclination; continuity in the direction of life. Ideogram: heart and scholar, high inner resolve. Locate, *ZAI*: be at, be situated at, dwell, reside; in, within; involved with, in the process of. Ideogram: earth and persevere, a place on the earth. Inside, *NEI*: within, inner, interior; inside of the house and those who work there, particularly women; inside of the body, inner organs; the lower trigram, as opposed to outside, *WAI*, the upper. Ideogram: border and enter. Indeed, *YE*: see *Preceding Situation.* Use, *YI*: see *Patterns of Wisdom.* Adhere, *CONG*: follow, agree with, comply with, obey; join a doctrine, school, or person; servant, follower. Ideogram: two men walking, one following the other. Value, *GUI*: regard as valuable, give worth and dignity to; precious, honorable, exalted, illustrious. Ideogram: cowries (coins) and basket.

Image Tradition

Limping. Heaviness indeed.
Venturing located in **precedence indeed.**
Viewing venturing and-also able to **stop.**
Knowing actually in-fact.

Limping. Harvesting: Western South.
Going acquires the **center indeed.**
Not Harvesting: Eastern North.
One's dao exhausted indeed.

Harvesting: viewing the **great** in the **person.**
Going possesses achievement indeed.
Appropriate position. Trial, significant.

Using the **correct fiefdoms indeed.**
The **season belonging** to **limping avails** of the **great actually in-fact.**

Fields of meaning

Limp, *JIAN*: see *Image of the Situation.* Heaviness, *NAN*: see *Preceding Situation.* Indeed, *YE*: see *Preceding Situation.* Venture, *XIAN*: face a severe difficulty or obstruction; risk; precipice, cliff, abyss; key point, point of danger; Action of the trigram Gorge, *KAN*. Ideogram: mound and all, everything engaged at one point. Locate, *ZAI*: be at, be situated at, dwell, reside; in, within; involved with, in the process of. Ideogram: earth and persevere, a place on the earth. Precede, *QIAN*: before, earlier; anterior, former, ancient; ahead, in front. View, *JIAN*: see *Image of the Situation.* And-also, *ER*: joins and contrasts two terms. Able/enable, *NENG*: ability, power, skill, art; competent, talented; duty, function, capacity. Ideogram: an animal with strong hooves and bones, able to carry and defend. Stop, *ZHI*: bring or come to a standstill, cease, terminate; Action of the trigram Bound, *GEN*. Ideogram: a foot stops walking. Know, *ZHI*: have knowledge of, perceive, experience, remember; know intimately; informed, aware, wise. Ideogram: arrow and mouth, words focused and swift. Actually, *YI*: truly, really, at present. Ideogram: a dart and done, strong intention fully expressed. In-fact, *ZAI*: emphatic exclamation; truly, indeed.

Harvesting: Western South, *LI XI NAN*: see *Image of the Situation.* Go, *WANG*: move away in time or space, depart; become past; dead, gone; contrasts with come, *LAI*, approach in time or space. Acquire, *DE*: obtain the desired object; possession; satisfied, fulfilled; it is permitted; agree with; wish for, desire covetously. Ideogram: go and obstacle, going through obstacles to the goal. Center, *ZHONG*: inner, central; put in the center; middle, stable point enabling you to face inner and outer changes; middle line of a trigram. Ideogram: field divided in two equal parts. Indeed, *YE*: see *Preceding Situation.* Not Harvesting: Eastern North, *BU LI DONG BEI*: see *Image of the Situation.* One/one's, *QI*: general third person pronoun and possessive adjective; also: it/its, he/his, she/her, they/their. Dao, *DAO*: way or path; ongoing process of being and the course it traces for each person or thing; ultimate reality, intrinsic nature; origin. Ideogram: go and head, opening a path. Exhaust, *QIONG*: bring to an end; limit, extremity; investigate exhaustively; destitute, indigent; end without a new beginning; distinct from complete, *ZHONG*, end of a cycle that begins the next one. Ideogram: cave and naked person, bent with disease or old age.

Viewing the great in the person, *JIAN DA REN*: see *Image of the Situation.* Possess, *YOU*: see *Preceding Situation.* Achieve, *GONG*: work done, results, actual accomplishment; praise, worth, merit. Ideogram: workman's square and forearm, combining craft and strength. **Appropriate,** *DANG*: suitable, capable, worthy, adequate, competent, equal to; opportune, convenient; whole lines in odd places and opened lines in even places. **Position,** *WEI*: place, location; be at; social standing, rank; position of a line in a hexagram. Ideogram: person standing. **Trial, significant,** *ZHEN JI*: see *Image of the Situation*. **Use,** *YI*: see *Patterns of Wisdom*. **Correct,** *ZHENG*: rectify deviation or one-sidedness; proper, straight, exact, regular; constant, rule, model. Ideogram: stop and one, hold to one thing. **Fiefdom,** *BANG*: region governed by a feudatory. **Season,** *SHI*: quality of the time; the right time, opportune, in harmony; planning in accord with the time; season of the year. Ideogram: sun and temple, sacred time. **Belong/it,** *ZHI*: establishes between two terms a connection similar to the Saxon genitive, in which the second term belongs to the first one; at the end of a sentence it refers to something previously mentioned or implied. **Avail,** *YONG*: use, employ for a specific purpose; take advantage of; benefit from; capacity. Ideogram: to divine and center, applying divination to central concerns.

解

40 UNRAVELING | *Xie*

The situation described by this hexagram is characterized by analyzing, dissolving obstacles to understanding, freeing energy that was previously blocked.

Image of the Situation

> **Unraveling.**
> **Harvesting: Western South.**
> **Without** a **place** to **go:**
> **one's coming return, significant.**
> **Possessing directed going:**
> **daybreak, significant.**

Fields of meaning

Unravel, *XIE*: disjoin, untie, disperse, dissolve, release; analyze, explain, understand; dispel sorrow, eliminate effects, solve problems; solution, deliverance. **Harvest,** *LI*: benefit, advantage, profit; realization; sharp, acute, insightful; quality of autumn and West, third stage of the Time Cycle. Ideogram: ripe grain and blade. **Western South,** *XI NAN*: corresponds to the neutral Earthy Moment between the Yang and Yin hemicycles; bring forth concrete results, ripe fruits of late summer. **Without,** *WU*: devoid of; there is not. **Place,** *SUO*: position, location; residence, dwelling; where something belongs or comes from; habitual focus or object. **Go,** *WANG*: move away in time or space, depart; become past; dead, gone; contrasts with come, *LAI*, approach in time or space. **One/one's,** *QI*: general third person pronoun and possessive adjective; also: it/its, he/his, she/her, they/their. **Come,** *LAI*: approach in time or space; move toward, arrive at; future; contrasts with go, *WANG*, move away or become past. **Return,** *FU*: go back, turn or lead back; recur, reappear, come again; restore, renew, recover; return to an earlier time or place. Ideogram: step and retrace a path. **Significant,** *JI*: leads to the experience of meaning; favorable, propitious, appropriate. Ideogram: scholar and mouth, wise words of a sage. **Possessing directed going,** *YOU YOU WANG*: having a goal or purpose, moving in a specific direction. **Daybreak,** *SU*: first light, after dawn; early morning; early, careful attention.

Outer and Inner Trigram

The upper trigram, **Shake**, *ZHEN*, describes the outer aspects of the situation. It has the following associations: arouse, excite, inspire; awe, alarm, trembling; thunder rising from the depth of the earth; fertilizing intrusion. Ideogram: excite and rain. *Symbol*: thunder, *LEI*, arousing power emerging from the depth of the earth. *Action*: stir-up, *DONG*, excite, influence, move, affect; work, take action; come out of the egg or the bud. Ideogram: strength and heavy, move weighty things. In the family of trigrams *ZHEN* is the eldest son.

The lower trigram, **Gorge**, *KAN*, describes the inner aspects of the situation. It has the following associations: precipice, dangerous place; hole, cavity, pit, snare, trap, grave; critical time, test; risky. Ideogram: earth and cavity. *Symbol*: stream, *SHUI*, flowing water; river, tide, flood; fluid, dissolving. Ideogram: rippling water. *Actions*: venture and fall. Venture, *XIAN*: face a severe difficulty or obstruction; risk; precipice, cliff, abyss; key point, point of danger. Ideogram: mound and all, everything engaged at one point. Fall, *XIAN*: fall down or into, sink, drop, descend; pit, trap, fault; falling water. In the family of trigrams *KAN* is the middle son.

Counter Hexagram

The Counter Hexagram of **Unraveling** is hexagram 63, **Already Fording**, which switches the emphasis from the open-ended analysis and understanding of **Unraveling** to being engaged in a process which is already on its way to completion.

Preceding Situation

> **Beings not permitted** to **use completing heaviness**.
> To **anterior acquiescence belongs** the **use** of **unraveling**.
> **Unraveling implies delay indeed**.

Fields of meaning

Beings not permitted (to **use**), *WU BU KE (YI)*: it is not possible; no one is allowed; it is not in the nature of things. **Complete**, *ZHONG*: completion of a cycle that begins the next; entire, whole, all. Ideogram: silk cocoons, follow and ice, winter linking one year with the next. **Heaviness**, *NAN*: difficulty, hardship, distress; arduous, grievous; harass; contrasts with versatility, *YI*, deal lightly with. Ideogram: bird with clipped tail on drying sticky soil. To **anterior acquiescence belongs** the **use** of, *GU SHOU ZHI YI*: understanding and accepting the preceding statement allows the consultant to make proper use of this hexagram. **Unravel**, *XIE*: see *Image of the Situation*. **Imply**, *ZHE*: further signify; additional meaning.

Delay, *HUAN*: retard, put off; let things take their course; tie loosely; gradually, leisurely; lax, tardy, negligent. Indeed, *YE*: emphasizes and intensifies the previous statement.

Hexagrams in Pairs

> **Unraveling**: **delay indeed**.
> **Limping**: **heaviness indeed**.

Fields of meaning

Unravel, *XIE*: see *Image of the Situation*. **Delay**, *HUAN*: see *Preceding Situation*. **Indeed**, *YE*: see *Preceding Situation*. **Limp**, *JIAN*: proceed haltingly; lame, weak-legged, afflicted; slow, feeble, weak; unfortunate, difficult. Ideogram: foot and cold, impeded circulation in the feet. **Heaviness**, *NAN*: see *Preceding Situation*.

Patterns of Wisdom

> **Thunder** and **rain arousing**. **Unraveling**.
> A **jun zi uses forgiving excess** to **pardon offenses**.

Fields of meaning

Thunder, *LEI*: thunder; arousing power emerging from the depth of the earth; Symbol of the trigram Shake, *ZHEN*. **Rain**, *YU*: rain and all precipitations; sudden shower, fast and furious; abundant dispensation of benefits; associated with the trigram Gorge, *KAN*, and the Streaming Moment. **Arouse**, *ZUO*: stimulate, stir up from inactivity; arise, appear; generate; begin, invent, make. Ideogram: person and beginning. **Unravel**, *XIE*: see *Image of the Situation*. **Jun zi**: ideal of a person who orders his/her life in accordance with dao rather than willful intention, and uses divination in this spirit. **Use**, *YI*: by means of; owing to; make use of, employ. **Forgive**, *SHE*: pardon, excuse, absolve, pass over, reprieve. **Exceed**, *GUO*: go beyond, pass by, pass over; surpass, transgress; error, fault, calamity. **Pardon**, *YOU*: forgive, indulge, relax; lenient. **Offense**, *ZUI*: crime, sin, fault; violate laws or rules; punishment. Ideogram: net and wrong, entangled in guilt.

Transforming Lines

INITIAL SIX

Without fault.

Comments
To **solid** and **supple belongs** a **border**.
Righteous, **without fault indeed**.

Fields of meaning

Without fault, *WU JIU*: no error or harm in the situation.

Solid, *GANG*: quality of the whole lines; firm, strong, unyielding, persisting. Supple, *ROU*: quality of the opened lines; flexible, pliant, adaptable, tender. Belong/it, *ZHI*: establishes between two terms a connection similar to the Saxon genitive, in which the second term belongs to the first one; at the end of a sentence it refers to something previously mentioned or implied. Border, *JI*: boundary, frontier, line that joins and divides; meet, face to face. Ideogram: place and sacrifice, meeting point of the human and the spirit world. Righteous, *YI*: proper, just, virtuous, upright; the heart that rules itself; benevolent, loyal, devoted to public good. Indeed, *YE*: see *Preceding Situation*.

Nine at Second

The **fields**, **capturing three foxes**.
Acquiring a **yellow arrow**.
Trial, **significant**.

Comments
Nine at **second**: **Trial**, **significant**.
Acquiring the **center**: **dao indeed**.

Fields of meaning

Field, *TIAN*: cultivated land, farming land; preferred terrain for hunting, since game in the fields cannot escape the hunt. Ideogram: square divided into four sections, delineating fields. Capture, *HUO*: obtain, seize, reach; take in a hunt, catch a thief; hit the mark, opportune moment; prisoner, spoils, prey, slave, servant. Three/thrice, *SAN*: number three; third time or place; active phases of a cycle; superlative; beginning of repetition (since one and two are entities in themselves). Fox, *HU*: crafty, shape-changing animal; used by spirits, often female; ambivalent night-spirit that can create havoc and bestow abundance. Acquire, *DE*: obtain the desired object; possession; satisfied, fulfilled; it is permitted; agree with; wish for, desire covetously. Ideogram: go and obstacle, going through obstacles to the goal. Yellow, *HUANG*: color of the soil in central China, associated with the Earthy Moment leading from the Yang to the Yin hemicycle; emblematic and imperial color of China since the Yellow Emperor (2500 BC). Arrow, *SHI*: arrow, javelin, dart; swift, direct as an arrow. Trial, *ZHEN*: inquiry by divination and its result; righteous, firm; separating wheat from chaff; the kernel, the proven core; quality of winter and North, fourth stage of the Time Cycle. Ideogram: pearl and divination. Significant, *JI*: see *Image of the Situation*.

Nine, *JIU*: number nine; transforming whole line; superlative: best, perfect. Two/second, *ER*: number two; pair, even numbers, binary, duplicate. Center, *ZHONG*: inner, central; put in the center; middle, stable point enabling you to face inner and outer changes; middle line of a trigram. Ideogram: field divided in two equal parts. Dao, *DAO*: way or path; ongoing process of being and the course it traces for each person or thing; ultimate reality, intrinsic nature; origin. Ideogram: go and head, opening a path.

SIX AT THIRD

䷧

Bearing, **moreover riding**.
Involvement in **illegality culminating**.
Trial, **abashment**.

Comments
Bearing, **moreover riding**.
Truly permitting the **demoniac indeed**.
Originating from **my involvement** with **weapons**.
Furthermore whose fault indeed?

Fields of meaning
Bear, *FU*: carry on one's back; take on a responsibility; rely on, depend on; burden, duty; mathematical term for minus; defeated; guilty; betray, reject. Moreover, *QIE*: further, and also. Ride, *CHENG*: ride an animal or a chariot; have the upper hand, control a stronger power; an opened line above controlling a whole line below. Involve, *ZHI*: devote oneself to; induce, cause, implicate; approach; manifest, express; reach the highest degree of. Ideogram: reach and come up behind. Illegality, *KOU*: take by force, violate, invade, sack, break the laws; brutality; enemies, outcasts, bandits. Culminate, *ZHI*: bring to the highest degree; arrive at the end or summit; superlative; reaching one's goal. Trial, *ZHEN*: inquiry by divination and its result; righteous, firm; separating wheat from chaff; the kernel, the proven core; quality of winter and North, fourth stage of the Time Cycle. Ideogram: pearl and divination. Abashment, *LIN*: distress, shame, regret, humiliation; aware of having lost the right track; leads to repenting, *HUI*, correcting the direction of mind and life.

Truly, *YI*: in fact; also; nevertheless. Permit, *KE*: possible because in harmony with an inherent principle; capable of; approve, authorize. Ideogram: mouth and breath, silent consent. Demon, *CHOU*: malignant genius; horror; ugly, vile, disgraceful, shameful; drunken; detest, hate; strange, ominous; class, group, crowd; similar. Ideogram: fermented liquor and soul. Demon and tiger are opposed on the North–South axis of the Universal Compass; the tiger (Extreme Yang) protects against the demons of Extreme Yin. Indeed, *YE*: see *Preceding Situation*. Origin, *ZI*: source, beginning, ground; cause, reason, motive; tracing back to the source; oneself, by oneself; spontaneous, intrinsic. I/me/my, *WO*: first person pronoun; the use of a specific personal pronoun, as opposed to the generic one's, *QI*, indicates an unusually strong emphasis on personal involvement. Weapons, *RONG*: arms; armed people, soldiers; military, violent. Ideogram: spear and armor, offensive and defensive weapons. Furthermore, *YOU*: moreover; in addition to; again. Whose, *SHUI*: relative and interrogative pronoun, often introducing a rhetorical question; anybody. Fault, *JIU*: unworthy conduct that leads to harm, illness, misfortune; guilt, crime, punishment. Ideogram: person and differ, differ from what you should be.

NINE AT FOURTH

Unraveling and-also the **thumbs**.
Partnering culminating, **splitting-off conforming**.

Comments
Unraveling and-also the **thumbs**.
Not-yet an **appropriate position indeed**.

Fields of meaning

Unravel, *XIE*: see *Image of the Situation*. And-also, *ER*: joins and contrasts two terms. Thumb/big-toe, *MU*: in the lower trigram, big-toe; in the upper trigram, thumb; the big-toe enables the foot to walk as the thumb enables the hand to grasp. Partner, *PENG*: companion, friend, peer; join, associate for mutual benefit; commercial venture; two equal or similar things. Ideogram: linked strings of cowries or coins. Culminate, *ZHI*: bring to the highest degree; arrive at the end or summit; superlative; reaching one's goal. Split-off, *SI*: lop off, split with an ax, rive; white (color eliminated). Ideogram: ax and possessive, splitting what belongs together. Conform, *FU*: accord between inner and outer; sincere, truthful, verified, reliable; capture; prisoners, spoils. Ideogram: claws over child, a bird brooding on the nest.

Not-yet, *WEI*: temporal negative indicating that something is expected to happen but has not yet occurred. Appropriate, *DANG*: suitable, capable, worthy, adequate, competent, equal to; opportune, convenient; whole lines in odd places and opened lines in even places. Position, *WEI*: place, location; be at; social standing, rank; position of a line in a hexagram. Ideogram: person standing. Indeed, *YE*: see *Preceding Situation*.

SIX AT FIFTH

A **jun zi holding-fast possesses unraveling**.
Significant.
Possessing conformity tending-towards the **small** in the **person**.

Comments
A **jun zi possesses unraveling**.
The **small** in the **person withdraws indeed**.

Fields of meaning

Jun zi: see *Patterns of Wisdom*. Hold-fast, *WEI*: tie, connect, hold together; rope, reins, net. Possess, *YOU*: general term indicating possession; have, own, be endowed with. Unravel, *XIE*: see *Image of the Situation*. Significant, *JI*: see *Image of the Situation*. Conform, *FU*: accord between inner and outer; sincere, truthful, verified, reliable; capture; prisoners, spoils. Ideogram: claws over child, a bird brooding on the nest. Tend-towards, *YU*: move toward without necessarily reaching, in the direction of. Small, *XIAO*: little, common, unimportant; adapting to what crosses your path; ability to move in harmony with the vicissitudes of life; contrasts with great, *DA*, self-imposed theme or goal. Person/people, *REN*: humans individually and collectively; an individual; humankind.

Withdraw, *TUI*: draw back, retreat, recede; decline, refuse. Indeed, *YE*: see *Preceding Situation*.

SIX ABOVE

A **prince avails** of **shooting** a **hawk tending-towards** the **above belonging** to the **high rampart**.
Capturing it, without not Harvesting.

Comments
A **prince avails** of **shooting** a **hawk**.
Using unraveling rebellion indeed.

Fields of meaning

Prince, *GONG*: highest title of nobility; noble acting as minister of state in the capital; contrasts with feudatory, *HOU*, governor of a province. Avail, *YONG*: use, employ for a specific purpose; take advantage of; benefit from; capacity. Ideogram: to divine and center, applying divination to central concerns. Shoot, *SHE*: shoot an arrow; archer; project, eject, spurt, issue forth; glance at; scheme for. Ideogram: arrow and body. Hawk, *SHUN*: falcon, kestrel, bird of prey used in hunting. Tend-towards, *YU*: move toward without necessarily reaching, in the direction of. Above, *SHANG*: anything above in all senses; higher, upper, outer; upper trigram. Belong/it, *ZHI*: establishes between two terms a connection similar to the Saxon genitive, in which the second term belongs to the first one; at the end of a sentence it refers to something previously mentioned or implied. High, *GAO*: high, elevated, lofty, eminent; honor, respect. Ideogram: high tower. Rampart, *YONG*: defensive wall; bulwark, redoubt. Capture, *HUO*: obtain, seize, reach; take in a hunt, catch a thief; hit the mark, opportune moment; prisoner, spoils, prey, slave, servant. It/belong, *ZHI*: establishes between two terms a connection similar to the Saxon genitive, in which the second term belongs to the first one; at the end of a sentence it refers to something previously mentioned or implied. Without not Harvesting, *WU BU LI*: turning point where the balance is swinging from not Harvesting to actually Harvesting.

Use, *YI*: see *Patterns of Wisdom*. Unravel, *XIE*: see *Image of the Situation*. Rebel, *BEI*: oppose, resist; go against nature or usage; insubordinate; perverse, unreasonable. Indeed, *YE*: see *Preceding Situation*.

Image Tradition

Unraveling. Venturing uses stirring-up.
Stirring-up and-also evading reaching venturing.
Unraveling.

Unraveling. Harvesting: Western South.
Going acquires crowds indeed.
One's coming return, significant.
Thereupon acquiring the **center indeed.**
Possessing directed going: daybreak, significant.
Going possesses achievement indeed.

Heaven and **earth unraveling and-also thunder** and **rain arousing.**
Thunder and **rain arousing and-also** the **hundred**

fruits, **grasses**, **trees**, **altogether seedburst**'s **boundary**.
The **season belonging** to **unraveling great actually in-fact**.

Fields of meaning

Unravel, *XIE*: see *Image of the Situation*. Venture, *XIAN*: face a severe difficulty or obstruction; risk; precipice, cliff, abyss; key point, point of danger; Action of the trigram Gorge, *KAN*. Ideogram: mound and all, everything engaged at one point. Use, *YI*: see *Patterns of Wisdom*. Stir-up, *DONG*: excite, influence, move, affect; work, take action; come out of the egg or the bud; Action of the trigram Shake, *ZHEN*. Ideogram: strength and heavy, move weighty things. And-also, *ER*: joins and contrasts two terms. Evade, *MIAN*: avoid, escape from, get away; be free of, dispense with; remove from office. Ideogram: a hare, known for its evasive skill. Reach, *HU*: arrive at a goal; move toward and achieve; to, at, in; distinct from tend-towards, *YOU*.

Harvesting: Western South, *LI XI NAN*: see *Image of the Situation*. Go, *WANG*: see *Image of the Situation*. Acquire, *DE*: obtain the desired object; possession; satisfied, fulfilled; it is permitted; agree with; wish for, desire covetously. Ideogram: go and obstacle, going through obstacles to the goal. Crowds, *ZHONG*: many people, large group, masses; all, all beings. Indeed, *YE*: see *Preceding Situation*. One's coming return, significant, *QI LAI FU JI*: see *Image of the Situation*. Thereupon, *NAI*: on that ground, then, only then; finally; in spite of that. Center, *ZHONG*: inner, central; put in the center; middle, stable point enabling you to face inner and outer changes; middle line of a trigram. Ideogram: field divided in two equal parts. Possessing directed going, *YOU YOU WANG*: see *Image of the Situation*. Daybreak, *SU*: see *Image of the Situation*. Possess, *YOU*: general term indicating possession; have, own, be endowed with. Achieve, *GONG*: work done, results, actual accomplishment; praise, worth, merit. Ideogram: workman's square and forearm, combining craft and strength.

Heaven, *TIAN*: sky, firmament, heavens; the highest realm, situated above the human world, as opposed to the earth, *DI*, located below; Symbol of the trigram Energy, *QIAN*. Ideogram: great and the one above. Earth, *DI*: the earth, ground on which the human world rests; basis of all things, nourishes all things; essential Yin; Symbol of the trigram Space, *KUN*. Thunder, *LEI*: see *Patterns of Wisdom*. Rain, *YU*: see *Patterns of Wisdom*. Arouse, *ZUO*: see *Patterns of Wisdom*. Hundred, *BO*: numerous, many, all; a whole class or type. Fruit, *GUO*: tree fruit; fruition, fruit of action; result, effect, product, conclusion; reliable, decisive. Ideogram: tree topped by a round fruit. Grass, *CAO*: all grassy plants and herbs; young, tender plants; rough draft; hastily. Tree/wood, *MU*: trees and all things woody or wooden; associated with the Wooden Moment; wood and wind are the Symbols of the trigram Ground, *SUN*. Ideogram: a tree with roots and branches. Altogether, *JIE*: all, the whole; the same sort, alike; entirely. Seedburst, *JIA*: seeds bursting forth in spring; first month of springtime; beginning, number one; associated with the Wooden Moment. Boundary, *JI*: border, limit, frontier. Season, *SHI*: quality of the time; the right time, opportune, in harmony; planning in accord with the time; season of the year. Ideogram: sun and temple, sacred time. Belong/it, *ZHI*: establishes between two terms a connection similar to the Saxon genitive, in which the second term belongs to the first one; at the end of a sentence it refers to something previously mentioned or implied. Great, *DA*: big, noble, important, very; orient the will toward a self-imposed goal, impose direction; ability to lead or guide one's life; contrasts with small, *XIAO*, flexible adaptation to what crosses one's path. Actually, *YI*: truly, really, at present. Ideogram: a dart and done, strong intention fully expressed. In-fact, *ZAI*: emphatic exclamation; truly, indeed.

損 ䷨

41 DIMINISHING | *Sun*

The situation described by this hexagram is characterized by decrease, reducing one's involvement, withdrawing energy from the matter at hand.

Image of the Situation

> **Diminishing.**
> **Possessing conformity.**
> **Spring, significant.**
> **Without fault, permitting Trial.**
> **Harvesting: possessing directed going.**
> To **what belongs availing?**
> **Two platters permit availing** of **presenting.**

Fields of meaning

Diminish, *SUN*: lessen, make smaller, take away from; lose, damage, spoil, wound; blame, criticize; offer up, give away. Ideogram: hand and ceremonial vessel, offering sacrifice. **Possess,** *YOU*: general term indicating possession; have, own, be endowed with. **Conform,** *FU*: accord between inner and outer; sincere, truthful, verified, reliable; capture; prisoners, spoils. Ideogram: claws over child, a bird brooding on the nest. **Spring,** *YUAN*: source, origin, head; arise, begin; first generating impulse; great, excellent; quality of springtime and East, first stage of the Time Cycle. **Significant,** *JI*: leads to the experience of meaning; favorable, propitious, appropriate. Ideogram: scholar and mouth, wise words of a sage. **Without fault,** *WU JIU*: no error or harm in the situation. **Permit,** *KE*: possible because in harmony with an inherent principle; capable of; approve, authorize. Ideogram: mouth and breath, silent consent. **Trial,** *ZHEN*: inquiry by divination and its result; righteous, firm; separating wheat from chaff; the kernel, the proven core; quality of winter and North, fourth stage of the Time Cycle. Ideogram: pearl and divination. **Harvest,** *LI*: benefit, advantage, profit; realization; sharp, acute, insightful; quality of autumn and West, third stage of the Time Cycle. Ideogram: ripe grain and blade. **Possessing directed going,** *YOU YOU WANG*: having a goal or purpose, moving in a specific direction. **What?,** *HE*: interjection: what? which? where?

why? how? how can it be! **Belong/it**, *ZHI*: establishes between two terms a connection similar to the Saxon genitive, in which the second term belongs to the first one; at the end of a sentence it refers to something previously mentioned or implied. **Avail**, *YONG*: use, employ for a specific purpose; take advantage of; benefit from; capacity. Ideogram: to divine and center, applying divination to central concerns. **Two/second**, *ER*: number two; pair, even numbers, binary, duplicate. **Present**, *XIANG*: offer in sacrifice, give to the gods or a superior; give a banquet; accept an offering; enjoy, receive.

Outer and Inner Trigram

The upper trigram, **Bound**, *GEN*, describes the outer aspects of the situation. It has the following associations: limit, frontier; obstacle that prevents from seeing further; stop; still, quiet, motionless; confine, enclose; mountain, sunset, beginning of winter; solid, steady, unshakable; straight, hard, adamant, obstinate. *Symbol*: mountain, *SHAN*, large, immense; limit, boundary. Ideogram: three peaks, a mountain range. *Action*: stop, *ZHI*, bring or come to a standstill, cease, terminate. Ideogram: a foot stops walking. In the family of trigrams *GEN* is the youngest son.

The lower trigram, **Open**, *DUI*, describes the inner aspects of the situation. It has the following associations: an open surface, promoting interaction and interpenetration; pleasant, easy, responsive, free, unhindered; opening, passage; the mouth; exchange, barter; straight, direct; meet, gather; place where water accumulates. Ideogram: mouth and vapor, communication through speech. *Symbol*: marsh, *ZE*, open surface of a flat body of water and the vapors rising from it; fertilize, enrich; kindness, favor. *Action*: stimulate, *SHUO*, rouse to action and good feeling; stir up, urge on; exhort, persuade; say, tell, relate; cheer, delight; joyous, peaceful, restful. Ideogram: words and exchange. In the family of trigrams *DUI* is the youngest daughter.

Counter Hexagram

The Counter Hexagram of **Diminishing** is hexagram 24, **Return**, which switches the emphasis from leaving something behind by diminishing one's involvement to a re-emergence of the past.

Preceding Situation

> **Delaying necessarily possesses** a **place** to **let-go**.
> To **anterior acquiescence belongs** the **use** of **diminishing**.

Fields of meaning
Delay, *HUAN*: retard, put off; let things take their course; tie loosely; gradually, leisurely; lax, tardy, negligent. **Necessarily**, *BI*: unavoidably, certainly. **Possess**, *YOU*: see *Image of the Situation*. **Place**, *SUO*: position, location; residence, dwelling; where something belongs or comes from; habitual focus or object. **Let-go**, *SHI*: lose, let slip; omit, miss, fail; lose control of. Ideogram: drop from the hand. **To anterior acquiescence belongs the use of**, *GU SHOU ZHI YI*: understanding and accepting the preceding statement allows the consultant to make proper use of this hexagram. **Diminish**, *SUN*: see *Image of the Situation*.

Hexagrams in Pairs

> **Diminishing**, **augmenting**.
> **Increasing**: the **beginning belonging** to **decreasing indeed**.

Fields of meaning
Diminish, *SUN*: see *Image of the Situation*. **Augment**, *YI*: increase, advance, promote, enrich, benefit, strengthen; pour in more; superabundant; excessive. Ideogram: water and vessel, pouring in more. **Increase**, *SHENG*: fill up; abundant, copious; vigorous, flourishing, exuberant; peak, culmination; exalt. **Begin**, *SHI*: commence, start, open; earliest, first; generate. Ideogram: woman and eminent, eminent feminine function of giving birth. **Belong/it**, *ZHI*: see *Image of the Situation*. **Decrease**, *SHUAI*: weaken, fade, decline, decay, diminish, cut off; grow old; adversity, misfortune. **Indeed**, *YE*: emphasizes and intensifies the previous statement.

Additional Texts

> **Diminishing**: **adjustment belonging** to **actualizing-dao indeed**.
> **Diminishing**: **beforehand heaviness and-also afterwards versatility**.
> **Diminishing**: **using distancing harm**.

Fields of meaning
Diminish, *SUN*: see *Image of the Situation*. **Adjust**, *XIU*: regulate, repair, clean up, renovate. **Belong/it**, *ZHI*: see *Image of the Situation*. **Actualize-dao**, *DE*: realize dao in action; power, virtue; ability to follow the course traced by the ongoing process of the cosmos. Ideogram: go, straight, and heart. Linked with acquire, *DE*:

acquiring that which makes a being become what it is meant to be. **Indeed**, *YE*: see *Hexagrams in Pairs*. **Before(hand)/earlier**, *XIAN*: anterior, preceding in time; former, past, previous; first, at first. **Heaviness**, *NAN*: difficulty, hardship, distress; arduous, grievous; harass; contrasts with versatility, *YI*, deal lightly with. Ideogram: bird with clipped tail on drying sticky soil. **And-also**, *ER*: joins and contrasts two terms. **After(wards)/later**, *HOU*: come after in time, subsequent; put oneself after; behind, back, draw back; the second; attendants, heirs, successors, posterity. **Versatility**, *YI*: sudden and unpredictable change, and the mental mobility and openness required in order to face it; easy, light, simple; occurs in the name of the *Yi Jing*. **Use**, *YI*: by means of; owing to; make use of, employ. **Distance**, *YUAN*: far off, remote; keep at a distance; a long time, far away in time. Ideogram: go and a long way. **Harm**, *HAI*: damage, injure, offend; suffer, become ill; obstacle, hindrance; fearful, anxious.

Patterns of Wisdom

The **mountain possesses pond below**. **Diminishing**.
A **jun zi uses curbing anger** and **blocking appetites**.

Fields of meaning

Mountain, *SHAN*: mountain; large, immense; limit, boundary; Symbol of the trigram Bound, *GEN*. Ideogram: three peaks, a mountain range. **Possess**, *YOU*: see *Image of the Situation*. **Pond**, *ZE*: open surface of a flat body of water and the vapors rising from it; fertilize, enrich; kindness, favor; Symbol of the trigram Open, *DUI*. **Below**, *XIA*: anything below, in all senses; lower, inner; lower trigram. **Diminish**, *SUN*: see *Image of the Situation*. **Jun zi**: ideal of a person who orders his/her life in accordance with dao rather than willful intention, and uses divination in this spirit. **Use**, *YI*: see *Additional Texts*. **Curb**, *CHENG*: reject, contain, abstain, correct, punish; reprimand, reprove; warn, caution. The heart and action, the heart acting on itself. **Anger**, *FEN*: resentment; cross, wrathful; irritated at, indignant. Ideogram: heart and divide, the heart dividing people. **Block**, *ZHI*: obstruct, close, restrain, fill up. **Appetites**, *YU*: drives, instinctive cravings; wishes, passions, desires, aspirations; long for, seek ardently, covet.

Transforming Lines

INITIAL NINE

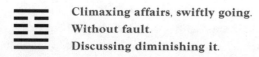

Climaxing affairs, **swiftly going**.
Without fault.
Discussing diminishing it.

Comments
Climaxing affairs, swiftly going.
Honoring uniting purposes indeed.

Fields of meaning
Climax, *YI*: come to a high point and stop; bring to an end, complete; renounce, desist, decline, reject; that is all; already; excessive. **Affairs**, *SHI*: all kinds of personal activity; matters at hand; business; function, occupation; manage; perform a task; incident, event; case in court. **Swiftly**, *CHUAN*: quickly; hurry, hasten. Go, *WANG*: move away in time or space, depart; become past; dead, gone; contrasts with come, *LAI*, approach in time or space. **Without fault**, *WU JIU*: see *Image of the Situation*. **Discuss**, *ZHUO*: deliberate; hear opinions, consult; banquet, feast. Ideogram: wine and ladle, pouring out wine to open discussion. **Diminish**, *SUN*: see *Image of the Situation*. **It/belong**, *ZHI*: establishes between two terms a connection similar to the Saxon genitive, in which the second term belongs to the first one; at the end of a sentence it refers to something previously mentioned or implied.

Honor, *SHANG*: esteem, give high rank to, exalt, celebrate; rise, elevate; put one thing on top of another. **Unite**, *HE*: join, match, correspond; unison, harmony; together; close the jaws, shut the mouth. Ideogram: mouths speaking in unison. **Purpose**, *ZHI*: focus of mind and heart; intention, will, inclination; continuity in the direction of life. Ideogram: heart and scholar, high inner resolve. **Indeed** YE: see *Hexagrams in Pairs*.

NINE AT SECOND

Harvesting, Trial.
Disciplining, pitfall.
Nowhere diminishing, augmenting it.

Comments
Nine at **second: Harvesting, Trial.**
In the **center using activating purpose indeed.**

Fields of meaning
Harvest, *LI*: see *Image of the Situation*. **Trial**, *ZHEN*: see *Image of the Situation*. **Discipline**, *ZHENG*: subjugate vassals, reduce to order; punishing expedition. Ideogram: step and correct, a rectifying move. **Pitfall**, *XIONG*: unfortunate situation, in which the flow of life and spirit is blocked and the experience of meaning is lost; stuck and exposed to danger; inappropriate attitude. Ideogram:

person in a pit. **Nowhere/nothing**, *FU*: strong negative; not a single thing/place; deny, disapprove; impossible, incorrect. **Diminish**, *SUN*: see *Image of the Situation*. **Augment**, *YI*: see *Hexagrams in Pairs*. **It/belong**, *ZHI*: establishes between two terms a connection similar to the Saxon genitive, in which the second term belongs to the first one; at the end of a sentence it refers to something previously mentioned or implied.

Nine, *JIU*: number nine; transforming whole line; superlative: best, perfect. **Two/second**, *ER*: see *Image of the Situation*. **Center**, *ZHONG*: inner, central; put in the center; middle, stable point enabling you to face inner and outer changes; middle line of a trigram. Ideogram: field divided in two equal parts. **Use**, *YI*: see *Additional Texts*. **Activate**, *WEI*: act or cause to act; do, make, manage, make active; be, become; attend to, help; because of. **Purpose**, *ZHI*: focus of mind and heart; intention, will, inclination; continuity in the direction of life. Ideogram: heart and scholar, high inner resolve. **Indeed**, *YE*: see *Hexagrams in Pairs*.

SIX AT THIRD

Three people moving.
By **consequence diminishing** by **one person**.
One person moving.
By **consequence acquiring one's friend**.

Comments
One person moving.
Three by **consequence doubtful indeed**.

Fields of meaning

Three/thrice, *SAN*: number three; third time or place; active phases of a cycle; superlative; beginning of repetition (since one and two are entities in themselves). **People/person**, *REN*: humans individually and collectively; an individual; humankind. **Move**, *XING*: move or move something; motivate; emotionally moving; walk, act, do. Ideogram: successive steps. **Consequence**, *ZE*: reason, cause, result; rule, law, pattern, standard; therefore; very strong connection. **Diminish**, *SUN*: see *Image of the Situation*. **One**, *YI*: a single unit; number one; undivided, simple, whole; unique; first. **Acquire**, *DE*: obtain the desired object; possession; satisfied, fulfilled; it is permitted; agree with; wish for, desire covetously. Ideogram: go and obstacle, going through obstacles to the goal. **One/one's**, *QI*: general third person pronoun and possessive adjective; also: it/its, he/his, she/her, they/their. **Friend**, *YOU*: companion, associate; of the same mind; attached, in pairs. Ideogram: two hands joined.

Doubt, *YI*: suspect, distrust, wonder; uncertain, dubious; surmise, conjecture, fear. Indeed, *YE*: see *Hexagrams in Pairs*.

SIX AT FOURTH

Diminishing one's affliction.
Commissioning swiftly possesses joy.
Without fault.

Comments
Diminishing one's affliction.
Truly permitting joy indeed.

Fields of meaning

Diminish, *SUN*: see *Image of the Situation*. One/one's, *QI*: general third person pronoun and possessive adjective; also: it/its, he/his, she/her, they/their. Affliction, *JI*: sickness, disorder, defect, calamity, injury; poison, hate, dislike; cruel, jealous, envious. Ideogram: sickness and dart, a sudden affliction. Commission, *SHI*: charge somebody with a task; command, order; messenger, agent; obey, follow. Ideogram: person and office. Swiftly, *CHUAN*: quickly; hurry, hasten. Possess, *YOU*: see *Image of the Situation*. Joy/rejoice, *XI*: delight, exult; cheerful, merry. Ideogram: joy (music) and mouth, expressing joy. Without fault, *WU JIU*: see *Image of the Situation*.

Truly, *YI*: in fact; also; nevertheless. Permit, *KE*: see *Image of the Situation*. Indeed, *YE*: see *Hexagrams in Pairs*.

SIX AT FIFTH

Maybe to **augmenting belongs ten.**
To **partnering belongs** a **tortoise.**
Nowhere controlling contradiction.
Spring, significant.

Comments
Six at **fifth: Spring, significant.**
The **origin above shielding indeed.**

Fields of meaning

Maybe, *HUO*: possible but not certain, perhaps. Augment, *YI*: see *Hexagrams in Pairs*. Belong/it, *ZHI*: see *Image of the Situation*. Ten, *SHI*: number ten; goal and end of reckoning; whole, complete, all; entire, perfected. Ideogram: East–West line crosses North–South line, a grid that contains all. **Partner**, *PENG*: companion, friend, peer; join, associate for mutual benefit; commercial venture; two equal or similar things. Ideogram: linked strings of cowries or coins. **Tortoise**, *GUI*: turtles; armored animals, shells and shields; long-living; practice divination; image of the macrocosm: heaven, earth and between them the soft flesh of humans. **Nowhere/nothing**, *FU*: strong negative; not a single thing/place; deny, disapprove; impossible, incorrect. **Control**, *KE*: be in charge; capable of, able to, adequate; check, obstruct, repress. Ideogram: roof beams supporting a house. **Contradict**, *WEI*: oppose, disregard, disobey; seditious, perverse. **Spring**, *YUAN*: see *Image of the Situation*. **Significant**, *JI*: see *Image of the Situation*.

Six, *LIU*: number six; transforming opened line; six lines of a hexagram. **Five**, *WU*: number five; fivefold articulation of the Universal Compass; the Five Moments and all related qualities: directions, colors, smells, tastes, tones, feelings. **Origin**, *ZI*: source, beginning, ground; cause, reason, motive; tracing back to the source; oneself, by oneself; spontaneous, intrinsic. **Above**, *SHANG*: anything above in all senses; higher, upper, outer; upper trigram. **Shield**, *YOU*: heavenly kindness and protection. Ideogram: numinous and right hand, spirit power. **Indeed**, *YE*: see *Hexagrams in Pairs*.

NINE ABOVE

Nowhere diminishing, augmenting it.
Without fault.
Trial, significant.
Harvesting: possesing directed going.
Acquiring a **servant without** a **household.**

Comments
Nowhere diminishing, augmenting it.
The **great acquires purpose indeed.**

Fields of meaning

Nowhere/nothing, *FU*: strong negative; not a single thing/place; deny, disapprove; impossible, incorrect. **Diminish**, *SUN*: see *Image of the Situation*. **Augment**, *YI*: see *Hexagrams in Pairs*. **It/belong**, *ZHI*: establishes between two terms a connection similar to the Saxon genitive, in which the second term belongs to the first one; at the end of a sentence it refers to something previously mentioned or implied. **Without fault**, *WU JIU*: see *Image of the Situation*. **Trial**, *ZHEN*: see *Image of the Situation*. **Significant**, *JI*: see *Image of the Situation*. **Harvest**,

LI: see *Image of the Situation*. **Possessing directed going**, *YOU YOU WANG*: see *Image of the Situation*. **Acquire**, *DE*: obtain the desired object; possession; satisfied, fulfilled; it is permitted; agree with; wish for, desire covetously. Ideogram: go and obstacle, going through obstacles to the goal. **Servant**, *CHEN*: attendant, minister, vassal; courtier who can speak to the sovereign; wait on, serve in office. Ideogram: person bowing low. **Without**, *WU*: devoid of; there is not. **Household**, *JIA*: home, house; family; dwell, reside; domestic, within doors; shop, school, doctrine. Ideogram: roof and pig or dog, the most valued domestic animals, living under the same roof with the family.

Great, *DA*: big, noble, important, very; orient the will toward a self-imposed goal, impose direction; ability to lead or guide one's life; contrasts with small, *XIAO*, flexible adaptation to what crosses one's path. **Purpose**, *ZHI*: focus of mind and heart; intention, will, inclination; continuity in the direction of life. Ideogram: heart and scholar, high inner resolve. **Indeed**, *YE*: see *Hexagrams in Pairs*.

Image Tradition

Diminishing.
Diminishing below, augmenting above.
One's dao moving above.
Diminishing and-also possessing conformity.

Spring, significant.
Without fault, permitting Trial.
Harvesting: possessing directed going.
To **what belongs availing?**
Two platters permit availing of **presenting**.

Two platters corresponding possess the **season**.
Diminishing the **solid**, **augmenting** the **supple**
possesses the **season**.
Diminishing, augmenting: overfilling emptiness.
Associating with the **season**, **accompanying** the
movement.

Fields of meaning

Diminish, *SUN*: see *Image of the Situation*. **Below**, *XIA*: see *Patterns of Wisdom*. **Augment**, *YI*: see *Hexagrams in Pairs*. **Above**, *SHANG*: anything above in all senses; higher, upper, outer; upper trigram. **One/one's**, *QI*: general third person pronoun and possessive adjective; also: it/its, he/his, she/her, they/their. **Dao**, *DAO*: way or path; ongoing process of being and the course it traces for each person or thing; ultimate reality, intrinsic nature; origin. Ideogram: go and head, opening a path. **Move**, *XING*: move or move something; motivate; emotionally moving; walk, act, do. Ideogram: successive steps. **And-also**, *ER*: see *Additional Texts*. **Possessing conformity**, *YOU FU*: see *Image of the Situation*.

Spring, significant, *YUAN JI*: see *Image of the Situation*. **Without fault, permitting Trial**, *WU JIU KE ZHEN*: see *Image of the Situation*. **Harvesting: possessing directed going**, *LI YOU YOU WANG*: see *Image of the Situation*. **To what belongs availing?**, *HE ZHI YONG*: see *Image of the Situation*. **Two platters permit availing** of **presenting**, *ER GUI KE YONG XIANG*: see *Image of the Situation*.

Correspond, *YING*: be in agreement or harmony; proper, suitable; resonate together, answer to; relation between the lines (1 and 4, 2 and 5, 3 and 6) when they form the pair opened and whole, supple and solid. Ideogram: heart and obey. **Season**, *SHI*: quality of the time; the right time, opportune, in harmony; planning in accord with the time; season of the year. Ideogram: sun and temple, sacred time. **Solid**, *GANG*: quality of the whole lines; firm, strong, unyielding, persisting. **Supple**, *ROU*: quality of the opened lines; flexible, pliant, adaptable, tender. **Overfill**, *YING*: fill completely; full, at the point of overflowing; excess, arrogance. Ideogram: vessel and overflow. **Empty**, *XU*: void; absence of images and concepts; vacant, insubstantial; empty yet fertile space. **Associate**, *YU*: consort with, combine; companions; group, band, company; agree with, comply, help; in favor of. Ideogram: a pair of hands reaching downward meets a pair of hands reaching upward, helpful association. **Accompany**, *XIE*: take or go along with; together; harmonize; totally, everywhere.

益

42 AUGMENTING | *Yi*

The situation described by this hexagram is characterized by increase, expanding one's involvement, pouring more energy into the matter at hand.

Image of the Situation

> **Augmenting**.
> **Harvesting**: **possessing directed going**.
> **Harvesting**: **wading** the **great river**.

Fields of meaning

Augment, *YI*: increase, advance, promote, enrich, benefit, strengthen; pour in more; superabundant; excessive. Ideogram: water and vessel, pouring in more. **Harvest**, *LI*: benefit, advantage, profit; realization; sharp, acute, insightful; quality of autumn and West, third stage of the Time Cycle. Ideogram: ripe grain and blade. **Possessing directed going**, *YOU YOU WANG*: having a goal or purpose, moving in a specific direction. **Wading the Great River**, *SHE DA CHUAN*: enter the stream of life with a goal or purpose; embark on a significant enterprise.

Outer and Inner Trigram

The upper trigram, **Root**, *SUN*, describes the outer aspects of the situation. It has the following associations: base on which things rest, ground, foundation; mild, subtly penetrating; nourishing. *Symbols*: tree/wood and wind. Tree/wood, *MU*: trees and all things woody or wooden; associated with the Wooden Moment. Ideogram: a tree with roots and branches. Wind, *FENG*: wind, breeze, gust; weather and its influence on mood and humor; fashion, usage. *Action*: enter, *RU*, penetrate, go into, enter on, encroach on; progress; put into. In the family of trigrams *SUN* is the eldest daughter.

The lower trigram, **Shake**, *ZHEN*, describes the inner aspects of the situation. It has the following associations: arouse, excite, inspire; awe, alarm, trembling; thunder rising from the depth of the earth; fertilizing intrusion. Ideogram: excite and rain. *Symbol*: thunder, *LEI*, arousing power emerging from the depth of the earth. *Action*: stir-up, *DONG*, excite, influence, move, affect; work, take action; come out of the egg or the bud. Ideogram: strength and heavy, move weighty things. In the family of trigrams *ZHEN* is the eldest son.

Counter Hexagram

The Counter Hexagram of **Augmenting** is hexagram 23, **Stripping**, which switches the emphasis from augmenting one's involvement to getting rid of something that has become obsolete.

Preceding Situation

> **Diminishing and-also not climaxing necessarily augments.**
> To **anterior acquiescence belongs** the **use** of **augmenting**.

Fields of meaning

Diminish, *SUN*: lessen, make smaller, take away from; lose, damage, spoil, wound; blame, criticize; offer up, give away. Ideogram: hand and ceremonial vessel, offering sacrifice. **And-also**, *ER*: joins and contrasts two terms. **Not**, *BU*: common term of negation. **Climax**, *YI*: come to a high point and stop; bring to an end, complete; renounce, desist, decline, reject; that is all; already; excessive. **Necessarily**, *BI*: unavoidably, certainly. **Augment**, *YI*: see *Image of the Situation*. To **anterior acquiescence belongs** the **use** of, *GU SHOU ZHI YI*: understanding and accepting the preceding statement allows the consultant to make proper use of this hexagram.

Hexagrams in Pairs

> **Diminishing**, **augmenting**.
> **Decreasing**: the **beginning belonging** to **increasing indeed**.

Fields of meaning

Diminish, *SUN*: see *Preceding Situation*. **Augment**, *YI*: see *Image of the Situation*. **Decrease**, *SHUAI*: weaken, fade, decline, decay, diminish, cut off; grow old; adversity, misfortune. **Begin**, *SHI*: commence, start, open; earliest, first; generate. Ideogram: woman and eminent, eminent feminine function of giving birth. **Belong/it**, *ZHI*: establishes between two terms a connection similar to the Saxon genitive, in which the second term belongs to the first one; at the end of a sentence it refers to something previously mentioned or implied. **Increase**, *SHENG*:

fill up; abundant, copious; vigorous, flourishing, exuberant; peak, culmination; exalt. **Indeed**, *YE*: emphasizes and intensifies the previous statement.

Additional Texts

> **Augmenting**: **enriching belonging** to **actualizing-dao indeed**.
> **Augmenting**: **long-living enriching and-also not setting-up**.
> **Augmenting**: **using** the **rising Harvest**.

Fields of meaning

Augment, *YI*: see *Image of the Situation*. **Enrich**, *YU*: make richer; material, mental or spiritual wealth; bequeath; generous, abundant. Ideogram: garments, portable riches. **Belong/it**, *ZHI*: see *Hexagrams in Pairs*. **Actualize-dao**, *DE*: realize dao in action; power, virtue; ability to follow the course traced by the ongoing process of the cosmos. Ideogram: go, straight, and heart. Linked with acquire, *DE*: acquiring that which makes a being become what it is meant to be. **Indeed**, *YE*: see *Hexagrams in Pairs*. **Long-living**, *ZHANG*: enduring, lasting, constant; extended, long, large; senior, superior, greater; increase, prosper; respect, elevate. **And-also**, *ER*: see *Preceding Situation*. **Not**, *BU*: common term of negation. **Set-up**, *SHE*: establish, institute; arrange, set in order. Ideogram: words and impel, establish with words. **Use**, *YI*: by means of; owing to; make use of, employ. **Rise**, *XING*: get up, grow, lift; stimulate, promote; enjoy. Ideogram: lift, two hands and unite, lift with both hands. **Harvest**, *LI*: see *Image of the Situation*.

Patterns of Wisdom

> **Wind** and **thunder**. **Augmenting**.
> A **jun zi uses viewing improvement**, by **consequence shifting**.
> And **possessing excess**, by **consequence amending**.

Fields of meaning

Wind, *FENG*: wind, breeze, gust; weather and its influence on mood and humor; fashion, usage; wind and wood are the Symbols of the trigram Root, *SUN*. **Thunder**, *LEI*: thunder; arousing power emerging from the depth of the earth; Symbol of the trigram Shake, *ZHEN*. **Augment**, *YI*: see *Image of the Situation*. **Jun zi**: ideal of a person who orders his/her life in accordance with dao rather than willful intention, and uses divination in this spirit. **Use**, *YI*: see *Additional Texts*.

View, *JIAN*: vision in all its aspects: seeing, being visible, forming mental images; visit, call on, consult. Ideogram: eye above person, active and receptive sight. **Improve**, *SHAN*: make better, reform, perfect; virtuous, wise; mild, docile; clever, skillful. Ideogram: mouth and sheep, gentle speech. **Consequence**, *ZE*: reason, cause, result; rule, law, pattern, standard; therefore; very strong connection. **Shift**, *QIAN*: move, change, transpose; improve, ascend, be promoted; deport, dismiss, remove. **Possess**, *YOU*: general term indicating possession; have, own, be endowed with. **Exceed**, *GUO*: go beyond, pass by, pass over; surpass, transgress; error, fault, calamity. **Amend**, *GAI*: correct, reform, renew, alter, mend. Ideogram: self and strike, fighting one's own errors.

Transforming Lines

Initial Nine

Harvesting: **availing** of **activating** the **great**, **arousing**.
Spring, **significant**.
Without fault.

Comments
Spring, **significant**, **without fault**.
Below not munificent affairs indeed.

Fields of meaning
Harvest, *LI*: see *Image of the Situation*. **Avail**, *YONG*: use, employ for a specific purpose; take advantage of; benefit from; capacity. Ideogram: to divine and center, applying divination to central concerns. **Activate**, *WEI*: act or cause to act; do, make, manage, make active; be, become; attend to, help; because of. **Great**, *DA*: big, noble, important, very; orient the will toward a self-imposed goal, impose direction; ability to lead or guide one's life; contrasts with small, *XIAO*, flexible adaptation to what crosses one's path. **Arouse**, *ZUO*: stimulate, stir up from inactivity; arise, appear; generate; begin, invent, make. Ideogram: person and beginning. **Spring**, *YUAN*: source, origin, head; arise, begin; first generating impulse; great, excellent; quality of springtime and East, first stage of the Time Cycle. **Significant**, *JI*: leads to the experience of meaning; favorable, propitious, appropriate. Ideogram: scholar and mouth, wise words of a sage. **Without fault**, *WU JIU*: no error or harm in the situation.

Below, *XIA*: anything below, in all senses; lower, inner; lower trigram. **Not**, *BU*: common term of negation. **Munificent**, *HOU*: liberal, kind, generous; create abundance; thick, large. Ideogram: gift of a superior to an inferior. **Affairs**, *SHI*: all kinds of personal activity; matters at hand; business; function, occupation;

manage; perform a task; incident, event; case in court. **Indeed**, *YE*: see *Hexagrams in Pairs.*

SIX AT SECOND

Maybe to **augmenting belongs ten**.
To **partnering belongs** a **tortoise**.
Nowhere controlling contradiction.
Perpetual Trial, **significant**.
The **king avails** of **presenting tending-towards** the **supreme**, **significant**.

Comments
Maybe augmenting it.
Origin outside, **coming indeed**.

Fields of meaning

Maybe, *HUO*: possible but not certain, perhaps. **Augment**, *YI*: see *Image of the Situation*. **Belong/it**, *ZHI*: see *Hexagrams in Pairs*. **Ten**, *SHI*: number ten; goal and end of reckoning; whole, complete, all; entire, perfected. Ideogram: East–West line crosses North–South line, a grid that contains all. **Partner**, *PENG*: companion, friend, peer; join, associate for mutual benefit; commercial venture; two equal or similar things. Ideogram: linked strings of cowries or coins. **Tortoise**, *GUI*: turtles; armored animals, shells and shields; long-living; practice divination; image of the macrocosm: heaven, earth and between them the soft flesh of humans. **Nowhere/nothing**, *FU*: strong negative; not a single thing/place; deny, disapprove; impossible, incorrect. **Control**, *KE*: be in charge; capable of, able to, adequate; check, obstruct, repress. Ideogram: roof beams supporting a house. **Contradict**, *WEI*: oppose, disregard, disobey; seditious, perverse. **Perpetual**, *YONG*: continual, everlasting, eternal. Ideogram: flowing water. **Trial**, *ZHEN*: inquiry by divination and its result; righteous, firm; separating wheat from chaff; the kernel, the proven core; quality of winter and North, fourth stage of the Time Cycle. Ideogram: pearl and divination. **Significant**, *JI*: leads to the experience of meaning; favorable, propitious, appropriate. Ideogram: scholar and mouth, wise words of a sage. **King**, *WANG*: sovereign, effective ruler, emperor, seen as connecting heaven and earth; reign, govern. **Avail**, *YONG*: use, employ for a specific purpose; take advantage of; benefit from; capacity. Ideogram: to divine and center, applying divination to central concerns. **Present**, *XIANG*: offer in sacrifice, give to the gods or a superior; give a banquet; accept an offering; enjoy, receive. **Tend-towards**, *YU*: move toward without necessarily reaching, in the direction of.

Supreme, *DI*: highest, above all on earth; sovereign, lord, emperor.

Origin, *ZI*: source, beginning, ground; cause, reason, motive; tracing back to the source; oneself, by oneself; spontaneous, intrinsic. **Outside**, *WAI*: outer, external; unfamiliar, foreign; ignore, reject; work done outside the home; the upper trigram as indication of the outer aspects of the situation. **Come**, *LAI*: approach in time or space; move toward, arrive at; future; contrasts with go, *WANG*, move away or become past. **Indeed**, *YE*: see *Hexagrams in Pairs*.

SIX AT THIRD

☴☳

To **augmenting belongs availing** of **pitfall affairs**.
Without fault.
Possessing conformity, the **center moving**.
Notifying the **prince**, **availing** of the **scepter**.

Comments
Augmenting: **availing** of **pitfall affairs**.
Firmly possessing it indeed.

Fields of meaning

Augment, *YI*: see *Image of the Situation*. **Belong/it**, *ZHI*: see *Hexagrams in Pairs*. **Avail**, *YONG*: use, employ for a specific purpose; take advantage of; benefit from; capacity. Ideogram: to divine and center, applying divination to central concerns. **Pitfall**, *XIONG*: unfortunate situation, in which the flow of life and spirit is blocked and the experience of meaning is lost; stuck and exposed to danger; inappropriate attitude. Ideogram: person in a pit. **Affairs**, *SHI*: all kinds of personal activity; matters at hand; business; function, occupation; manage; perform a task; incident, event; case in court. **Without fault**, *WU JIU*: no error or harm in the situation. **Possess**, *YOU*: see *Patterns of Wisdom*. **Conform**, *FU*: accord between inner and outer; sincere, truthful, verified, reliable; capture; prisoners, spoils. Ideogram: claws over child, a bird brooding on the nest. **Center**, *ZHONG*: inner, central; put in the center; middle, stable point enabling you to face inner and outer changes; middle line of a trigram. Ideogram: field divided in two equal parts. **Move**, *XING*: move or move something; motivate; emotionally moving; walk, act, do. Ideogram: successive steps. **Notify**, *GAO*: proclaim, order, decree; advise, inform; accuse, denounce. Ideogram: mouth and ox head, impressive speech. **Prince**, *GONG*: highest title of nobility; noble acting as minister of state in the capital; contrasts with feudatory, *HOU*, governor of a province. **Scepter**, *GUI*: small stone scepter given to nobles as sign of rank.

Firm, *GU*: steady, solid, strong, secure; constant, fixed. Ideogram: old and enclosure, long preserved. **Indeed**, *YE*: see *Hexagrams in Pairs.*

Six at Fourth

The **center moving**.
Notifying the **prince**, **adhering**.
Harvesting: **availing** of **activating depends** on **shifting** the **city**.

Comments
Notifying the **prince**, **adhering**.
Using augmenting's **purpose**.

Fields of meaning

Center, *ZHONG*: inner, central; put in the center; middle, stable point enabling you to face inner and outer changes; middle line of a trigram. Ideogram: field divided in two equal parts. **Move**, *XING*: move or move something; motivate; emotionally moving; walk, act, do. Ideogram: successive steps. **Notify**, *GAO*: proclaim, order, decree; advise, inform; accuse, denounce. Ideogram: mouth and ox head, impressive speech. **Prince**, *GONG*: highest title of nobility; noble acting as minister of state in the capital; contrasts with feudatory, *HOU*, governor of a province. **Adhere**, *CONG*: follow, agree with, comply with, obey; join a doctrine, school, or person; servant, follower. Ideogram: two men walking, one following the other. **Harvest**, *LI*: see *Image of the Situation*. **Avail**, *YONG*: use, employ for a specific purpose; take advantage of; benefit from; capacity. Ideogram: to divine and center, applying divination to central concerns. **Activate**, *WEI*: act or cause to act; do, make, manage, make active; be, become; attend to, help; because of. **Depend**, *YI*: rely on, trust; conform to; image, illustration; acquiesce, obey. **Shift**, *QIAN*: see *Patterns of Wisdom*. **City**, *GUO*: city, state, country, nation; area of only human constructions; first of the territorial zones: city, suburbs, countryside, forest.

Use, *YI*: see *Additional Texts*. **Augment**, *YI*: see *Image of the Situation*. **Purpose**, *ZHI*: focus of mind and heart; intention, will, inclination; continuity in the direction of life. Ideogram: heart and scholar, high inner resolve.

Nine at Fifth

Possessing conformity, a **benevolent heart**.
No question, **Spring significant**.
Possessing conformity, **benevolence**: **my actualizing-dao**.

Comments
Possessing conformity, a **benevolent heart**.
No questioning it actually.
Benevolence: **my actualizing-dao**.
The **great acquires purpose indeed**.

Fields of meaning

Possess, *YOU*: see *Patterns of Wisdom*. Conform, *FU*: accord between inner and outer; sincere, truthful, verified, reliable; capture; prisoners, spoils. Ideogram: claws over child, a bird brooding on the nest. Benevolence, *HUI*: regard for others, humanity; fulfill social duties; unselfish, kind, merciful. Heart, *XIN*: the heart as center of being; seat of mind, imagination and affect; moral nature; source of desires, intentions, will. No, *WU*: common term of negation. Question, *WEN*: ask, inquire about, examine; clear up doubts. Spring, *YUAN*: source, origin, head; arise, begin; first generating impulse; great, excellent; quality of springtime and East, first stage of the Time Cycle. Significant, *JI*: leads to the experience of meaning; favorable, propitious, appropriate. Ideogram: scholar and mouth, wise words of a sage. I/me/my, *WO*: first person pronoun; the use of a specific personal pronoun, as opposed to the generic one's, *QI*, indicates an unusually strong emphasis on personal involvement. Actualize-dao, *DE*: see *Additional Texts*.

It/belong, *ZHI*: establishes between two terms a connection similar to the Saxon genitive, in which the second term belongs to the first one; at the end of a sentence it refers to something previously mentioned or implied. Actually, *YI*: truly, really, at present. Ideogram: a dart and done, strong intention fully expressed. Great, *DA*: big, noble, important, very; orient the will toward a self-imposed goal, impose direction; ability to lead or guide one's life; contrasts with small, *XIAO*, flexible adaptation to what crosses one's path. Acquire, *DE*: obtain the desired object; possession; satisfied, fulfilled; it is permitted; agree with; wish for, desire covetously. Ideogram: go and obstacle, going through obstacles to the goal. Purpose, *ZHI*: focus of mind and heart; intention, will, inclination; continuity in the direction of life. Ideogram: heart and scholar, high inner resolve. Indeed, *YE*: see *Hexagrams in Pairs*.

NINE ABOVE

Abstaining from **augmenting it**.
Maybe smiting it.
Establishing the **heart**, **no persevering**.
Pitfall.

Comments
Abstaining from **augmenting it**.
One-sided evidence indeed.
Maybe smiting it.
Origin outside, coming indeed.

Fields of meaning
Abstain/absolutely-nothing, *MO*: complete elimination; do not, not any, by no means. Augment, *YI*: see *Image of the Situation*. It/belong, *ZHI*: establishes between two terms a connection similar to the Saxon genitive, in which the second term belongs to the first one; at the end of a sentence it refers to something previously mentioned or implied. Maybe, *HUO*: possible but not certain, perhaps. Smite, *JI*: hit, beat, attack; hurl against, rush a position; rouse to action. Ideogram: hand and hit, fist punching. Establish, *LI*: set up, institute, order, arrange; stand erect; settled principles. Heart, *XIN*: the heart as center of being; seat of mind, imagination and affect; moral nature; source of desires, intentions, will. No, *WU*: common term of negation. Persevere, *HENG*: continue in the same way or spirit; constant, habitual, regular; self-renewing. Pitfall, *XIONG*: unfortunate situation, in which the flow of life and spirit is blocked and the experience of meaning is lost; stuck and exposed to danger; inappropriate attitude. Ideogram: person in a pit.

One-sided, *PIAN*: slanted, inclined to one side; excessive, partial, selfish. Evidence, *CI*: word, expression; verbal explanation; excuse; instruction, order, argument; apology. Indeed, *YE*: emphasizes and intensifies the previous statement. Origin, *ZI*: source, beginning, ground; cause, reason, motive; tracing back to the source; oneself, by oneself; spontaneous, intrinsic. Outside, *WAI*: outer, external; unfamiliar, foreign; ignore, reject; work done outside the home; the upper trigram as indication of the outer aspects of the situation. Come, *LAI*: approach in time or space; move toward, arrive at; future; contrasts with go, *WANG*, move away or become past.

Image Tradition

Diminishing above, augmenting below.
The **commoners stimulated without delimiting**.
The **origin above**, the **below below**.
One's dao: the **great shining**.

Harvesting: **possessing directed going**.
The **center**'s **correctness possesses reward**.
Harvesting: **wading** the **great river**.
Woody dao, **thereupon movement**.

Augmenting: **stirring-up and-also** the **root**.
The **sun advances without delimiting**.
Heaven spreads, **earth generates**.
One's augmenting without sides.
Dao belonging to **total augmenting**.
Associating with the **season**, **accompanying** the **movement**.

Fields of meaning

Diminish, *SUN*: see *Preceding Situation*. Above, *SHANG*: anything above in all senses; higher, upper, outer; upper trigram. Augment, *YI*: see *Image of the Situation*. Below, *XIA*: anything below, in all senses; lower, inner; lower trigram. Commoners, *MIN*: common people, masses; working class supporting the social hierarchy; undeveloped potential in the individual. Stimulate, *SHUO*: rouse to action and good feeling; stir up, urge on; exhort, persuade; say, tell, relate; cheer, delight; joyous, peaceful, restful; Action of the trigram Open, *DUI*. Ideogram: words and exchange. Without, *WU*: devoid of; there is not. Delimit, *JIANG*: define frontiers, boundaries, draw limits. Origin, *ZI*: source, beginning, ground; cause, reason, motive; tracing back to the source; oneself, by oneself; spontaneous, intrinsic. One/one's, *QI*: general third person pronoun and possessive adjective; also: it/its, he/his, she/her, they/their. Dao, *DAO*: way or path; ongoing process of being and the course it traces for each person or thing; ultimate reality, intrinsic nature; origin. Ideogram: go and head, opening a path. Great, *DA*: big, noble, important, very; orient the will toward a self-imposed goal, impose direction; ability to lead or guide one's life; contrasts with small, *XIAO*, flexible adaptation to what crosses one's path. Shine, *GUANG*: illuminate, emit light; brilliant, splendid; honor, glory, éclat; distinct from brightness, *MING*, light of heavenly bodies. Ideogram: fire above person.

Harvesting: possessing directed going, *LI YOU YOU WANG*: see *Image of the Situation*. Center, *ZHONG*: inner, central; put in the center; middle, stable point enabling you to face inner and outer changes; middle line of a trigram. Ideogram: field divided in two equal parts. Correct, *ZHENG*: rectify deviation or one-sidedness; proper, straight, exact, regular; constant, rule, model. Ideogram: stop and one, hold to one thing. Possess, *YOU*: see *Patterns of Wisdom*. Reward, *QING*: gift given out of gratitude or benevolence; favor from heaven. Ideogram: heart, follow and deer, the heart expressed through the gift of a deer's skin. **Wading the Great River**, *SHE DA CHUAN*: see *Image of the Situation*. **Wood/tree**, *MU*: trees and all things woody or wooden; associated with the Wooden Moment; wood and wind are the Symbols of the trigram Ground, *SUN*. Ideogram: a tree with roots and branches. **Thereupon**, *NAI*: on that ground, then, only then; finally; in spite of that. **Move**, *XING*: move or move something; motivate; emotionally moving; walk, act, do. Ideogram: successive steps.

Stir-up, *DONG*: excite, influence, move, affect; work, take action; come out of the egg or the bud; Action of the trigram Shake, *ZHEN*. Ideogram: strength and heavy, move weighty things. **And-also**, *ER*: see *Preceding Situation*. **Root**, *SUN*: base on which things rest, ground, foundation; mild, subtly penetrating; nourishing. **Sun/day**, *RI*: actual sun and the time of a sun-cycle, a day. **Advance**, *JIN*: move forward, progress, climb; promote or be promoted; further the development of, augment; offer, introduce. **Heaven**, *TIAN*: sky, firmament, heavens; the highest realm, situated above the human world, as opposed to the earth, *DI*, located below; Symbol of the trigram Energy, *QIAN*. Ideogram: great and the one above. **Spread**, *SHI*: expand, diffuse, distribute, arrange, exhibit; add to; aid. Ideogram: flag and indeed, claiming new country. **Earth**, *DI*: the earth, ground on which the human world rests; basis of all things, nourishes all things; essential Yin; Symbol of the trigram Space, *KUN*. **Generate**, *SHENG*: give birth; be born, arise, grow; beget; life, vitality. Ideogram: earth and sprout. **Sides**, *FANG*: cardinal directions; surface of the earth extending to the four cardinal points; everywhere; limits, boundaries. **Belong/it**, *ZHI*: see *Hexagrams in Pairs*. **Total**, *FAN*: all, everything; the world. **Associate**, *YU*: consort with, combine; companions; group, band, company; agree with, comply, help; in favor of. Ideogram: a pair of hands reaching downward meets a pair of hands reaching upward, helpful association. **Season**, *SHI*: quality of the time; the right time, opportune, in harmony; planning in accord with the time; season of the year. Ideogram: sun and temple, sacred time. **Accompany**, *XIE*: take or go along with; together; harmonize; totally, everywhere.

夬

43 PARTING | *Guai*

The situation described by this hexagram is characterized by a breakthrough or resolution after a long accumulated tension, like a flooding river overflowing its banks and parting into different streams.

Image of the Situation

> **Parting**.
> **Displaying tending-towards** the **king**'s **chambers**.
> **Conformity crying-out possesses adversity**.
> **Notifying originates** from the **capital**.
> **Not Harvesting**: **approaching weapons**.
> **Harvesting**: **possessing directed going**.

Fields of meaning

Part, *GUAI*: separate, fork, cut off, flow in different directions; decide, resolve; prompt, certain, settled. **Display**, *YANG*: spread, extend, scatter, divulge, promote. Ideogram: hand and expand, spreading a message. **Tend-towards**, *YU*: move toward without necessarily reaching, in the direction of. **King**, *WANG*: sovereign, effective ruler, emperor, seen as connecting heaven and earth; reign, govern. **Chambers**, *TING*: family rooms; courtyard, hall; domestic. Ideogram: shelter and hall, a secure place. **Conform**, *FU*: accord between inner and outer; sincere, truthful, verified, reliable; capture; prisoners, spoils. Ideogram: claws over child, a bird brooding on the nest. **Cry-out/outcry**, *HAO*: call out, proclaim; order, command; mark, label, sign; designate, name. **Possess**, *YOU*: general term indicating possession; have, own, be endowed with. **Adversity**, *LI*: danger, hardship, severe; threat or difficulty that must be encountered, rather than avoided; grinding stone; polish, sharpen; a challenge that strengthens and perfects the character; stimulate, excite; cruel demon. **Notify**, *GAO*: proclaim, order, decree; advise, inform; accuse, denounce. Ideogram: mouth and ox head, impressive speech. **Origin**, *ZI*: source, beginning, ground; cause, reason, motive; tracing back to the source; oneself, by oneself; spontaneous, intrinsic. **Capital**, *YI*: populous fortified city, center and symbol of the region it rules. Ideogram: enclosure and official seal. **Not**, *BU*: common term of negation. **Harvest**, *LI*: benefit, advantage, profit; realization; sharp, acute, insightful; quality of autumn and West, third stage of the Time Cycle. Ideogram: ripe grain and blade. **Approach**, *JI*: come near to, advance toward, reach; nearby; soon, immediately. **Weapons**, *RONG*: arms; armed people, soldiers; military, violent. Ideogram: spear and armor, offensive and defensive weapons. **Possessing directed going**, *YOU YOU WANG*: having a goal or purpose, moving in a specific direction.

Outer and Inner Trigram

The upper trigram, **Open**, *DUI*, describes the outer aspects of the situation. It has the following associations: an open surface, promoting interaction and interpenetration; pleasant, easy, responsive, free, unhindered; opening, passage; the mouth; exchange, barter; straight, direct; meet, gather; place where water accumulates. Ideogram: mouth and vapor, communication through speech. *Symbol*: marsh, *ZE*, open surface of a flat body of water and the vapors rising from it; fertilize, enrich; kindness, favor. *Action*: stimulate, *SHUO*, rouse to action and good feeling; stir up, urge on; exhort, persuade; say, tell, relate; cheer, delight; joyous, peaceful, restful. Ideogram: words and exchange. In the family of trigrams *DUI* is the youngest daughter.

The lower trigram, **Energy/parch**, *QIAN/GAN*, describes the inner aspects of the situation. It has the following associations: unceasing forward movement, dynamic, enduring, untiring; spirit power, manifestation of Yang, that activates all creation and destruction in Space; heaven, sovereign, father. With the pronunciation *GAN*: parch, dry up, burn, exhaust. Ideogram: sprouts or vapors rising from the ground and sunlight, both fecundating moisture and scorching drought. *Symbol*: heaven, *TIAN*; sky, firmament, heavens; the highest realm, situated above the human world, as opposed to the earth, *DI*, located below. Ideogram: great and the one above. *Action*: persist, *JIAN*; tenacious, persevering; strong, robust, dynamic; constant as the motion of heavenly bodies in their orbits. In the family of trigrams *QIAN* is the father.

Counter Hexagram

The Counter Hexagram of **Parting** is hexagram 1, **Energy**, which switches the emphasis from a flood parting into different streams to the persistent drive of **Energy**, unceasingly moving forward and ever renewing itself.

Preceding Situation

> **Augmenting and-also not climaxing necessarily breaks-up.**

> To **anterior acquiescence belongs** the **use** of **parting**.
> **Parting implies breaking-up indeed**.

Fields of meaning

Augment, *YI*: increase, advance, promote, enrich, benefit, strengthen; pour in more; superabundant; excessive. Ideogram: water and vessel, pouring in more. **And-also**, *ER*: joins and contrasts two terms. **Not**, *BU*: common term of negation. **Climax**, *YI*: come to a high point and stop; bring to an end, complete; renounce, desist, decline, reject; that is all; already; excessive. **Necessarily**, *BI*: unavoidably, certainly. **Break-up**, *JUE*: streams diverging; open a passage for water; break through a dam; separate, break into parts; cut through; decide, pass sentence; absolutely, certainly. Ideogram: water and parting. To **anterior acquiescence belongs** the **use** of, *GU SHOU ZHI YI*: understanding and accepting the preceding statement allows the consultant to make proper use of this hexagram. **Part**, *GUAI*: see *Image of the Situation*. **Imply**, *ZHE*: further signify; additional meaning. **Indeed**, *YE*: emphasizes and intensifies the previous statement.

Hexagrams in Pairs

> **Coupling**: **meeting indeed**.
> The **supple meets** the **solid indeed**.
> **Parting**: **breaking-up indeed**.
> The **solid breaks-up** the **supple indeed**.

Fields of meaning

Couple, *GOU*: driven encounter, compelled by primal instinctual forces, fusion of Yin and Yang; meet, encounter, associate with; copulate, mating animals; magnetism, gravity; be gripped by impersonal forces. **Meet**, *YU*: come on unexpectedly, encounter; occur, happen; pleasant meeting, lucky coincidence; agree. **Indeed**, *YE*: see *Preceding Situation*. **Supple**, *ROU*: quality of the opened lines; flexible, pliant, adaptable, tender. **Solid**, *GANG*: quality of the whole lines; firm, strong, unyielding, persisting. **Part**, *GUAI*: see *Image of the Situation*. **Break-up**, *JUE*: see *Preceding Situation*.

Patterns of Wisdom

> **Pond above with-respect-to heaven**. **Parting**.
> A **jun zi uses spreading benefits extending** to the **below**.
> And **residing** in **actualizing-dao**, by **consequence keeping-aloof**.

Fields of meaning

Pond, *ZE*: open surface of a flat body of water and the vapors rising from it; fertilize, enrich; kindness, favor; Symbol of the trigram Open, *DUI*. **Above**, *SHANG*: anything above in all senses; higher, upper, outer; upper trigram. **With-respect-to**, *YU*: in relation to, referring to, according to; in, at, until. **Heaven**, *TIAN*: sky, firmament, heavens; the highest realm, situated above the human world, as opposed to the earth, *DI*, located below; Symbol of the trigram Energy, *QIAN*. Ideogram: great and the one above. **Part**, *GUAI*: see *Image of the Situation*. **Jun zi**: ideal of a person who orders his/her life in accordance with dao rather than willful intention, and uses divination in this spirit. **Use**, *YI*: by means of; owing to; make use of, employ. **Spread**, *SHI*: expand, diffuse, distribute, arrange, exhibit; add to; aid. Ideogram: flag and indeed, claiming new country. **Benefits**, *LU*: pay, salary, income; have the use of; goods received, revenues; official function. **Extend**, *JI*: reach to; draw out, prolong; continuous, enduring. **Below**, *XIA*: anything below, in all senses; lower, inner; lower trigram. **Reside**, *JU*: dwell, live in, stay; sit down; fill an office; well-being, rest. Ideogram: body and seat. **Actualize-dao**, *DE*: realize dao in action; power, virtue; ability to follow the course traced by the ongoing process of the cosmos. Ideogram: go, straight, and heart. Linked with acquire, *DE*: acquiring that which makes a being become what it is meant to be. **Consequence**, *ZE*: reason, cause, result; rule, law, pattern, standard; therefore; very strong connection. **Keep-aloof**, *JI*: keep at a distance; avoid, fear, shun, abstain from; prohibition. Ideogram: heart and self, keeping to oneself.

Transforming Lines

INITIAL NINE

The **vigor tends-towards** the **preceding foot**.
Going, not mastering: **activating fault**.

Comments
Not mastering and-also going.
Fault indeed.

Fields of meaning

Vigor, *ZHUANG*: power, strength; energetic, robust, fully grown, flourishing, abundant; at the peak of age and form; inspirit, animate; damage through unrestrained strength. Ideogram: strength and scholar, intellectual impact. **Tend-towards**, *YU*: see *Image of the Situation*. **Precede**, *QIAN*: before, earlier; anterior, former, ancient; ahead, in front. **Foot**, *ZHI*: foot, footprint; foundation, base; walk; stop where the foot rests. **Go**, *WANG*: move away in time or space, depart; become past; dead, gone; contrasts with come, *LAI*, approach in time or space. Not, *BU*: common term of negation. Master, *SHENG*: have the upper hand; control, command, win, conquer, check (as in the cycle of the Five Transformative Moments); worthy of, able to. Activate, *WEI*: act or cause to act; do, make, manage, make active; be, become; attend to, help; because of. Fault, *JIU*: unworthy conduct that leads to harm, illness, misfortune; guilt, crime, punishment. Ideogram: person and differ, differ from what you should be.

And-also, *ER*: see *Preceding Situation*. Indeed, *YE*: see *Preceding Situation*.

NINE AT SECOND

Awe: an **outcry**, **absolutely-nothing**.
At **night possessing weapons**.
No cares.

Comments
Possessing weapons, **no cares**.
Acquiring the **center**, **dao indeed**.

Fields of meaning

Awe, *TI*: respect, regard, fear; alarmed and cautious, worried; on guard. Ideogram: heart and versatility, the heart expecting change. Cry-out/outcry, *HAO*: see *Image of the Situation*. Absolutely-nothing/abstain, *MO*: complete elimination; do not, not any, by no means. Night, *YE*: dark half of the 24-hour cycle. Possess, *YOU*: see *Image of the Situation*. Weapons, *RONG*: see *Image of the Situation*. No, *WU*: common term of negation. Care, *XU*: fear, doubt, concern; heartfelt attachment; relieve, soothe, aid; sympathy, compassion, consolation. Ideogram: heart and blood, the heart's blood affected.

Acquire, *DE*: obtain the desired object; possession; satisfied, fulfilled; it is permitted; agree with; wish for, desire covetously. Ideogram: go and obstacle, going through obstacles to the goal. Center, *ZHONG*: inner, central; put in the center; middle, stable point enabling you to face inner and outer changes; middle line of a trigram. Ideogram: field divided in two equal parts. Dao, *DAO*: way or path; ongoing process of being and the course it traces for each person or thing; ultimate reality, intrinsic nature; origin. Ideogram: go and head, opening a path. Indeed, *YE*: see *Preceding Situation*.

NINE AT THIRD

The **vigor tends-towards** the **cheek-bones**.
Possessing pitfall.
A **jun zi**: **parting**, **parting**.
Solitary going, **meeting rain**.
Like soaked, **possessing indignation**.
Without fault.

Comments
A **jun zi**: **parting**, **parting**.
Completing without fault indeed.

Fields of meaning

Vigor, *ZHUANG*: power, strength; energetic, robust, fully grown, flourishing, abundant; at the peak of age and form; inspirit, animate; damage through unrestrained strength. Ideogram: strength and scholar, intellectual impact. Tend-towards, *YU*: see *Image of the Situation*. Cheek-bones, *CHUAN*: facial feature denoting character. Possess, *YOU*: see *Image of the Situation*. Pitfall, *XIONG*: unfortunate situation, in which the flow of life and spirit is blocked and the experience of meaning is lost; stuck and exposed to danger; inappropriate attitude. Ideogram: person in a pit. Jun zi: see *Patterns of Wisdom*. Part, *GUAI*: see *Image of the Situation*. Solitary, *DI*: alone, single; isolated, abandoned. Go, *WANG*: move away in time or space, depart; become past; dead, gone; contrasts with come, *LAI*, approach in time or space. Meet, *YU*: see *Hexagrams in Pairs*. Rain, *YU*: rain and all precipitations; sudden shower, fast and furious; abundant dispensation of benefits; associated with the trigram Gorge, *KAN*, and the Streaming Moment. Like, *RUO*: same as, just as; conform, imitate; adverbial suffix indicating similarity. Soak, *RU*: immerse, steep; damp, wet; stain, pollute, blemish; urinate on. Indignation, *WEN*: irritation, wrath, rage, hate; feeling of injustice. Without fault, *WU JIU*: no error or harm in the situation.

Complete, *ZHONG*: completion of a cycle that begins the next; entire, whole, all. Ideogram: silk cocoons, follow and ice, winter linking one year with the next. Without, *WU*: devoid of; there is not. Fault, *JIU*: unworthy conduct that leads to harm, illness, misfortune; guilt, crime, punishment. Ideogram: person and differ, differ from what you should be. Indeed, *YE*: see *Preceding Situation*.

NINE AT FOURTH

☱
☰

The **sacrum without flesh**.
One's moving the **camp moreover**.
Hauling-along the **goat**, **repenting extinguished**.
Hearing words not trustworthy.

Comments
One's moving the **camp moreover**.
Position not appropriate indeed.
Hearing words not trustworthy.
Understanding not bright indeed.

Fields of meaning

Sacrum, *TUN*: lower back, buttocks, lower spine; bottom. Without, *WU*: devoid of; there is not. Flesh, *FU*: skin, muscles and organs as different from bones. One/one's, *QI*: general third person pronoun and possessive adjective; also: it/its, he/his, she/her, they/their. Move, *XING*: move or move something; motivate; emotionally moving; walk, act, do. Ideogram: successive steps. Camp, *CI*: resting place, inn, shed; halt, breathing-spell. Ideogram: two and breath, pausing to breathe. Moreover, *QIE*: further, and also. Haul-along, *QIAN*: haul or pull, drag behind; pull an animal on a rope. Ideogram: ox and halter. Goat, *YANG*: sheep and goats; associated with stubborn, determined thought and action. Repenting extinguished, *HUI WANG*: previous errors are corrected, all causes for repenting disappear. Hear, *WEN*: perceive sound; learn by report; news, fame. Ideogram: ear and door. Word, *YAN*: spoken word, speech, saying; talk, discuss, address; name, signify. Ideogram: mouth and rising vapor. Not, *BU*: common term of negation. Trustworthy, *XIN*: truthful, faithful, consistent over time; count on, confide in; examine, verify, prove; loyalty, integrity. Ideogram: person and word, true speech.

Position, *WEI*: place, location; be at; social standing, rank; position of a line in a hexagram. Ideogram: person standing. Appropriate, *DANG*: suitable, capable, worthy, adequate, competent, equal to; opportune, convenient; whole lines in odd places and opened lines in even places. Indeed, *YE*: see *Preceding Situation*. Understand, *CONG*: perceive quickly, astute, sharp; discriminate intelligently. Ideogram: ear and quick. Brightness, *MING*: light, radiance, clarity; distinguish, discern, understand; light-giving aspect of fire, of heavenly bodies and of consciousness; brightness and fire are the Symbols of the trigram Radiance, *LI*.

NINE AT FIFTH

The **reeds**, the **highlands**: **parting**, **parting**.
The **center moves**, **without fault**.

Comments
The **center moves**, **without fault**.
The **center not-yet shining indeed**.

Fields of meaning

Reeds, *GUAN*: marsh and swamp plants, rushes. Highlands, *LU*: high, dry land as distinct from swamps; mountain, plateau. Part, *GUAI*: see *Image of the Situation*. Center, *ZHONG*: inner, central; put in the center; middle, stable point enabling you to face inner and outer changes; middle line of a trigram. Ideogram: field divided in two equal parts. Move, *XING*: move or move something; motivate; emotionally moving; walk, act, do. Ideogram: successive steps. Without fault, *WU JIU*: no error or harm in the situation.

Not-yet, *WEI*: temporal negative indicating that something is expected to happen but has not yet occurred. Shine, *GUANG*: illuminate, emit light; brilliant, splendid; honor, glory, éclat; distinct from brightness, *MING*, light of heavenly bodies. Ideogram: fire above person. Indeed, *YE*: see *Preceding Situation*.

SIX ABOVE

Without crying-out.
Completing possesses pitfall.

Comments
To **without crying-out belongs pitfall**.
Completing not permitting long-living indeed.

Fields of meaning

Without, *WU*: devoid of; there is not. Cry-out/outcry, *HAO*: see *Image of the Situation*. Complete, *ZHONG*: completion of a cycle that begins the next; entire, whole, all. Ideogram: silk cocoons, follow and ice, winter linking one year with the next. Possess, *YOU*: see *Image of the Situation*. Pitfall, *XIONG*: unfortunate situation, in which the flow of life and spirit is blocked and the experience of meaning is lost; stuck and exposed to danger; inappropriate attitude. Ideogram: person in a pit.

Belong/it, *ZHI*: establishes between two terms a connection similar to the Saxon genitive, in which the second term belongs to the first one; at the end of a sentence it refers to something previously mentioned or implied. **Not**, *BU*: common term of negation. **Permit**, *KE*: possible because in harmony with an inherent principle; capable of; approve, authorize. Ideogram: mouth and breath, silent consent. **Long-living**, *ZHANG*: enduring, lasting, constant; extended, long, large; senior, superior, greater; increase, prosper; respect, elevate. **Indeed**, *YE*: see *Preceding Situation*.

Image Tradition

Parting. **Breaking-up indeed**.
The **solid breaks-up** the **supple indeed**.
Persisting and-also stimulating.
Breaking-up and-also harmonizing.

Displaying tending-towards the **king**'s **chambers**.
The **supple rides five solids indeed**.
Conformity crying-out possesses adversity.
One's exposure thereupon shining indeed.

Notifying originates from the **capital**.
Not Harvesting: **approaching weapons**.
The **place** to **honor thereupon exhausted indeed**.
Harvesting: **possessing directed going**.
The **solid long-living**, **thereupon completion indeed**.

Fields of meaning

Part, *GUAI*: see *Image of the Situation*. **Break-up**, *JUE*: see *Preceding Situation*. **Indeed**, *YE*: see *Preceding Situation*. **Solid**, *GANG*: see *Hexagrams in Pairs*. **Supple**, *ROU*: see *Hexagrams in Pairs*. **Persist**, *JIAN*: tenacious, persevering; strong, robust, dynamic; constant as the motion of heavenly bodies in their orbits; Action of the trigram Force, *QIAN*. **And-also**, *ER*: see *Preceding Situation*. **Stimulate**, *SHUO*: rouse to action and good feeling; stir up, urge on; exhort, persuade; say, tell, relate; cheer, delight; joyous, peaceful, restful; Action of the trigram Open, *DUI*. Ideogram: words and exchange. **Harmony**, *HE*: concord, union; conciliate; at peace, mild; fit, tune, adjust.

Displaying tending-towards the **king**'s **chambers**, *YANG YU WANG TING*: see *Image of the Situation*. **Ride**, *CHENG*: ride an animal or a chariot; have the upper hand, control a stronger power; an opened line above controlling a whole line below. **Five**, *WU*: number five; fivefold articulation of the Universal Compass; the Five Moments and all related qualities: directions, colors, smells, tastes, tones, feelings. **Conformity crying-out possesses adversity,** *FU HAO YOU LI*: see *Image of the Situation*. **One/one's,** *QI*: general third person pronoun and possessive adjective; also: it/its, he/his, she/her, they/their. **Exposure,** *WEI*: being exposed to danger; precipitous, unsteady, too high, dangerously leaning. Ideogram: overhanging rock, person and limit, exposure in an extreme position. **Thereupon,** *NAI*: on that ground, then, only then; finally; in spite of that. **Shine,** *GUANG*: illuminate, emit light; brilliant, splendid; honor, glory, éclat; distinct from brightness, *MING*, light of heavenly bodies. Ideogram: fire above person.

Notifying originates from the **capital,** *GAO ZI YI*: see *Image of the Situation*. **Not Harvesting: approaching weapons,** *BU LI JI RONG*: see *Image of the Situation*. **Place,** *SUO*: position, location; residence, dwelling; where something belongs or comes from; habitual focus or object. **Honor,** *SHANG*: esteem, give high rank to, exalt, celebrate; rise, elevate; put one thing on top of another. **Exhaust,** *QIONG*: bring to an end; limit, extremity; investigate exhaustively; destitute, indigent; end without a new beginning; distinct from complete, *ZHONG*, end of a cycle that begins the next one. Ideogram: cave and naked person, bent with disease or old age. **Possessing directed going,** *YOU YOU WANG*: see *Image of the Situation*. **Long-living,** *ZHANG*: enduring, lasting, constant; extended, long, large; senior, superior, greater; increase, prosper; respect, elevate. **Complete,** *ZHONG*: completion of a cycle that begins the next; entire, whole, all. Ideogram: silk cocoons, follow and ice, winter linking one year with the next.

姤

䷫

44 COUPLING | *Gou*

The situation described by this hexagram is characterized by the magnetic attraction of primal Yin and Yang, a meeting driven by powerful instinctual forces, beyond the control of social or personal considerations.

Image of the Situation

> **Coupling**.
> **Woman**'s **vigor**.
> **No availing** of **grasping womanhood**.

Fields of meaning

Couple, *GOU*: driven encounter, compelled by primal instinctual forces, fusion of Yin and Yang; meet, encounter, associate with; copulate, mating animals; magnetism, gravity; be gripped by impersonal forces. Woman(hood), *NÜ*: woman and what is inherently female. Vigor, *ZHUANG*: power, strength; energetic, robust, fully grown, flourishing, abundant; at the peak of age and form; inspirit, animate; damage through unrestrained strength. Ideogram: strength and scholar, intellectual impact. No, *WU*: common term of negation. Avail, *YONG*: use, employ for a specific purpose; take advantage of; benefit from; capacity. Ideogram: to divine and center, applying divination to central concerns. Grasp, *QU*: seize with effort, take and use, appropriate; take as a wife; grasp the meaning, understand. Ideogram: ear and hand, hear and grasp.

Outer and Inner Trigram

The upper trigram, **Energy/parch**, *QIAN/GAN*, describes the outer aspects of the situation. It has the following associations: unceasing forward movement, dynamic, enduring, untiring; spirit power, manifestation of Yang, that activates all creation and destruction in Space; heaven, sovereign, father. With the pronunciation *GAN*: parch, dry up, burn, exhaust. Ideogram: sprouts or vapors rising from the ground and sunlight, both fecundating moisture and scorching drought. *Symbol*: heaven, *TIAN*; sky, firmament, heavens; the highest realm, situated above the human world, as opposed to the earth, *DI*, located below. Ideogram: great and

the one above. *Action*: persist, *JIAN*; tenacious, persevering; strong, robust, dynamic; constant as the motion of heavenly bodies in their orbits. In the family of trigrams *QIAN* is the father.

The lower trigram, **Root**, *SUN*, describes the inner aspects of the situation. It has the following associations: base on which things rest, ground, foundation; mild, subtly penetrating; nourishing. *Symbols*: tree/wood and wind. Tree/wood, *MU*: trees and all things woody or wooden; associated with the Wooden Moment. Ideogram: a tree with roots and branches. Wind, *FENG*: wind, breeze, gust; weather and its influence on mood and humor; fashion, usage. *Action*: enter, *RU*, penetrate, go into, enter on, encroach on; progress; put into. In the family of trigrams *SUN* is the eldest daughter.

Counter Hexagram

The Counter Hexagram of **Coupling** is hexagram 1, **Energy**, which switches the emphasis from an energetic but temporary meeting spurred by powerful instinctual forces to the persistent drive of **Energy**, unceasingly moving forward and ever renewing itself.

Preceding Situation

Breaking-up necessarily possesses meeting.
To **anterior acquiescence belongs** the **use** of **coupling**.
Coupling implies meeting indeed.

Fields of meaning

Break-up, *JUE*: streams diverging; open a passage for water; break through a dam; separate, break into parts; cut through; decide, pass sentence; absolutely, certainly. Ideogram: water and parting. Necessarily, *BI*: unavoidably, certainly. Possess, *YOU*: general term indicating possession; have, own, be endowed with. Meet, *YU*: come on unexpectedly, encounter; occur, happen; pleasant meeting, lucky coincidence; agree. To anterior acquiescence belongs the use of, *GU SHOU ZHI YI*: understanding and accepting the preceding statement allows the consultant to make proper use of this hexagram. Couple, *GOU*: see *Image of the Situation*. Imply, *ZHE*: further signify; additional meaning. Indeed, *YE*: emphasizes and intensifies the previous statement.

Hexagrams in Pairs

Coupling: **meeting indeed**.
The **supple meets** the **solid indeed**.
Parting: **breaking-up indeed**.
The **solid breaks-up** the **supple indeed**.

Fields of meaning

Couple, *GOU*: see *Image of the Situation*. Meet, *YU*: see *Preceding Situation*. Indeed, *YE*: see *Preceding Situation*. Supple, *ROU*: quality of the opened lines; flexible, pliant, adaptable, tender. Solid, *GANG*: quality of the whole lines; firm, strong, unyielding, persisting. Part, *GUAI*: separate, fork, cut off, flow in different directions; decide, resolve; prompt, certain, settled. Break-up, *JUE*: see *Preceding Situation*.

Patterns of Wisdom

Heaven possessing wind below. **Coupling**.
The **crown prince uses spreading fate** to **command**
the **four sides**.

Fields of meaning

Heaven, *TIAN*: sky, firmament, heavens; the highest realm, situated above the human world, as opposed to the earth, *DI*, located below; Symbol of the trigram Energy, *QIAN*. Ideogram: great and the one above. Possess, *YOU*: see *Preceding Situation*. Wind, *FENG*: wind, breeze, gust; weather and its influence on mood and humor; fashion, usage; wind and wood are the Symbols of the trigram Root, *SUN*. Below, *XIA*: anything below, in all senses; lower, inner; lower trigram. Couple, *GOU*: see *Image of the Situation*. Crown prince, *HOU*: sovereign; prince; empress, mother of an imperial prince. Ideogram: one, mouth and shelter, one with the sovereign's orders. Use, *YI*: by means of; owing to; make use of, employ. Spread, *SHI*: expand, diffuse, distribute, arrange, exhibit; add to; aid. Ideogram: flag and indeed, claiming new country. Fate, *MING*: individual destiny; birth and death as limits of life; issue orders with authority; consult the gods. Ideogram: mouth and order, words with heavenly authority. Command, *GAO*: give orders; inform, notify, instruct; official seal. Ideogram: words and announce, verbal commands. Four, *SI*: number four; number of the cardinal directions and of the seasons; everywhere, on all sides; fourfold articulation of the Universal Compass. Sides, *FANG*: cardinal directions; surface of the earth extending to the four cardinal points; everywhere; limits, boundaries.

Transforming Lines

Initial Six

Attachment tending-towards a **metallic chock**.
Trial, **significant**.
Possessing directed going.
Viewing pitfall.
Ruined the **pig**'s **conformity**: **hoof dragging**.

Comments
Attachment tending-towards a **metallic chock**.
The **supple**'s **dao hauling-along indeed**.

Fields of meaning
Attach, *XI*: fasten to, bind, tie; retain, continue; keep in mind; emotional bond. Tend-towards, *YU*: move toward without necessarily reaching, in the direction of. Metal, *JIN*: all metals, particularly gold; smelting and casting; perfection, richness; autumn, West, sunset; one of the Five Transformative Moments. Chock, *NI*: block used to stop a cart wheel; terminate; inquire, investigate. Trial, *ZHEN*: inquiry by divination and its result; righteous, firm; separating wheat from chaff; the kernel, the proven core; quality of winter and North, fourth stage of the Time Cycle. Ideogram: pearl and divination. Significant, *JI*: leads to the experience of meaning; favorable, propitious, appropriate. Ideogram: scholar and mouth, wise words of a sage. Possessing directed going, *YOU YOU WANG*: having a goal or purpose, moving in a specific direction. View, *JIAN*: vision in all its aspects: seeing, being visible, forming mental images; visit, call on, consult. Ideogram: eye above person, active and receptive sight. Pitfall, *XIONG*: unfortunate situation, in which the flow of life and spirit is blocked and the experience of meaning is lost; stuck and exposed to danger; inappropriate attitude. Ideogram: person in a pit. Ruin, *LEI*: destroy, break, overturn; debilitated, meager, emaciated; entangled. Pig, *SHI*: all swine, symbol of wealth and good fortune, associated with the Streaming Moment. Conform, *FU*: accord between inner and outer; sincere, truthful, verified, reliable; capture; prisoners, spoils. Ideogram: claws over child, a bird brooding on the nest. Hoof, *DI*: horse's hooves and pig's trotters. Drag, *ZHU*: pull along a hurt or malfunctioning foot; limping, lame. Ideogram: foot and worm, an infected foot.

Supple, *ROU*: see *Hexagrams in Pairs*. Dao, *DAO*: way or path; ongoing process of being and the course it traces for each person or thing; ultimate reality, intrinsic nature; origin. Ideogram: go and head, opening a path. Haul-along, *QIAN*: haul or pull, drag behind; pull an animal on a rope. Ideogram: ox and halter. Indeed, *YE*: see *Preceding Situation*.

NINE AT SECOND

Enwrapping possesses fish.
Without fault.
Not Harvesting: hospitality.

Comments
Enwrapping possesses fish.
Righteously not extending hospitality indeed.

Fields of meaning

Enwrap, *BAO*: envelop, hold, contain; patient, engaged. Ideogram: enfold and self, a fetus in the womb. Possess, *YOU*: see *Preceding Situation*. Fish, *YU*: all scaly aquatic beings hidden in the water; symbol of abundance; connected with the Streaming Moment. Without fault, *WU JIU*: no error or harm in the situation. Not, *BU*: common term of negation. Harvest, *LI*: benefit, advantage, profit; realization; sharp, acute, insightful; quality of autumn and West, third stage of the Time Cycle. Ideogram: ripe grain and blade. Hospitality, *BIN*: both entertain a guest, receive a stranger, and visit someone, enjoy hospitality.

Righteous, *YI*: proper, just, virtuous, upright; the heart that rules itself; benevolent, loyal, devoted to public good. Extend, *JI*: reach to; draw out, prolong; continuous, enduring. Indeed, *YE*: see *Preceding Situation*.

NINE AT THIRD

The **sacrum without flesh.**
One's moving the **camp moreover.**
Adversity.
Without the **great: faulty.**

Comments
One's moving the **camp moreover.**
Moving, not-yet hauling-along indeed.

Fields of meaning

Sacrum, *TUN*: lower back, buttocks, lower spine; bottom. Without, *WU*: devoid of; there is not. Flesh, *FU*: skin, muscles and organs as different from bones. One/one's, *QI*: general third person pronoun and possessive adjective; also: it/its, he/his, she/her, they/their. Move, *XING*: move or move something; motivate; emotionally moving; walk, act, do. Ideogram: successive steps. Camp, *CI*: resting place, inn, shed; halt, breathing-spell. Ideogram: two and breath, pausing to breathe. **Moreover**, *QIE*: further, and also. **Adversity**, *LI*: danger, hardship, severe; threat or difficulty that must be encountered, rather than avoided; grinding stone; polish, sharpen; a challenge that strengthens and perfects the character; stimulate, excite; cruel demon. **Without**, *WU*: devoid of; there is not. **Great**, *DA*: big, noble, important, very; orient the will toward a self-imposed goal, impose direction; ability to lead or guide one's life; contrasts with small, *XIAO*, flexible adaptation to what crosses one's path. **Fault**, *JIU*: unworthy conduct that leads to harm, illness, misfortune; guilt, crime, punishment. Ideogram: person and differ, differ from what you should be.

Not-yet, *WEI*: temporal negative indicating that something is expected to happen but has not yet occurred. **Haul-along**, *QIAN*: haul or pull, drag behind; pull an animal on a rope. Ideogram: ox and halter. **Indeed**, *YE*: see *Preceding Situation*.

NINE AT FOURTH

Enwrapping without fish.
Rising-up, pitfall.

Comments
To **without fish belongs** a **pitfall**.
Distancing the **commoners indeed**.

Fields of meaning

Enwrap, *BAO*: envelop, hold, contain; patient, engaged. Ideogram: enfold and self, a fetus in the womb. **Without**, *WU*: devoid of; there is not. **Fish**, *YU*: all scaly aquatic beings hidden in the water; symbol of abundance; connected with the Streaming Moment. **Rise-up**, *QI*: stand up, erect; stimulate, excite; undertake, begin, develop. **Pitfall**, *XIONG*: unfortunate situation, in which the flow of life and spirit is blocked and the experience of meaning is lost; stuck and exposed to danger; inappropriate attitude. Ideogram: person in a pit.

Belong/it, *ZHI*: establishes between two terms a connection similar to the Saxon genitive, in which the second term belongs to the first one; at the end of a sentence it refers to something previously mentioned or implied. **Distance**, *YUAN*: far off, remote; keep at a distance; a long time, far away in time. Ideogram: go and a long way. **Commoners**, *MIN*: common people, masses; working class supporting the social hierarchy; undeveloped potential in the individual. **Indeed**, *YE*: see *Preceding Situation*.

NINE AT FIFTH

Using osier to **enwrap melons**.
Containing composition.
Possessing tumbling originating from **heaven**.

Comments
Nine at **fifth**: **containing composition**.
The **center correct indeed**.
Possessing tumbling originating from **heaven**.
Purpose: **not stowing** away **fate indeed**.

Fields of meaning

Use, *YI*: see *Patterns of Wisdom*. Osier, *QI*: willow branches used to make baskets. Enwrap, *BAO*: envelop, hold, contain; patient, engaged. Ideogram: enfold and self, a fetus in the womb. Melon, *GUA*: general term for melon, gourd, squash, cucumber; symbol of heaven and earth, the cosmos. Contain, *HAN*: retain, embody, cherish; withhold, tolerate; contain in the mouth, put a coin in a corpse's mouth. Composition, *ZHANG*: a well-composed whole and its structure; beautiful creation; elegant, clear, brilliant; chapter, strophe; distinct from pattern, *WEN*, beauty of intrinsic design. Possess, *YOU*: see *Preceding Situation*. Tumble, *YUN*: fall with a crash, fall from the sky; roll down. Origin, *ZI*: source, beginning, ground; cause, reason, motive; tracing back to the source; oneself, by oneself; spontaneous, intrinsic. Heaven, *TIAN*: see *Patterns of Wisdom*.

Nine, *JIU*: number nine; transforming whole line; superlative: best, perfect. Five, *WU*: number five; fivefold articulation of the Universal Compass; the Five Moments and all related qualities: directions, colors, smells, tastes, tones, feelings. Center, *ZHONG*: inner, central; put in the center; middle, stable point enabling you to face inner and outer changes; middle line of a trigram. Ideogram: field divided in two equal parts. Correct, *ZHENG*: rectify deviation or one-sidedness; proper, straight, exact, regular; constant, rule, model. Ideogram: stop and one, hold to one thing. Indeed, *YE*: see *Preceding Situation*. Purpose, *ZHI*: focus of mind and heart; intention, will, inclination; continuity in the direction of life. Ideogram: heart and scholar, high inner resolve. Not, *BU*: common term of negation. Stow, *SHE*: set aside, put away, store, keep; halt, rest in; lodge, hut. Fate, *MING*: see *Patterns of Wisdom*.

NINE ABOVE

Coupling: one's horns.
Abashment.
Without fault.

Comments
Coupling: one's horns.
Above exhausting abashment indeed.

Fields of meaning

Couple, *GOU*: see *Image of the Situation*. One/one's, *QI*: general third person pronoun and possessive adjective; also: it/its, he/his, she/her, they/their. Horns, *JIAO*: physical horns; butt, attack, gore; dispute, test one's strength; headland. Abashment, *LIN*: distress, shame, regret, humiliation; aware of having lost the right track; leads to repenting, *HUI*, correcting the direction of mind and life. Without fault, *WU JIU*: no error or harm in the situation.

Above, *SHANG*: anything above in all senses; higher, upper, outer; upper trigram. Exhaust, *QIONG*: bring to an end; limit, extremity; investigate exhaustively; destitute, indigent; end without a new beginning; distinct from complete, *ZHONG*, end of a cycle that begins the next one. Ideogram: cave and naked person, bent with disease or old age. Indeed, *YE*: see *Preceding Situation*.

Image Tradition

Coupling. Meeting indeed.
The **supple meets** the **solid indeed.**
No availing of **grasping womanhood.**
Not permitted association long-living indeed.

Heaven and **earth reciprocally meeting.**
The **kinds** of **beings conjoin** in **composition indeed.**

The **solid meets** the **center**'s **correctness.**
Below heaven the **great moves indeed.**
The **season belonging** to **coupling righteously great actually in-fact.**

Fields of meaning

Couple, *GOU*: see *Image of the Situation*. Meet, *YU*: see *Preceding Situation*. Indeed, *YE*: see *Preceding Situation*. Supple, *ROU*: see *Hexagrams in Pairs*. Solid, *GANG*: see

Hexagrams in Pairs. **No availing** of **grasping womanhood**, *WU YONG QU NÜ*: see *Image of the Situation*. **Not**, *BU*: common term of negation. **Permit**, *KE*: possible because in harmony with an inherent principle; capable of; approve, authorize. Ideogram: mouth and breath, silent consent. **Associate**, *YU*: consort with, combine; companions; group, band, company; agree with, comply, help; in favor of. Ideogram: a pair of hands reaching downward meets a pair of hands reaching upward, helpful association. **Long-living**, *ZHANG*: enduring, lasting, constant; extended, long, large; senior, superior, greater; increase, prosper; respect, elevate.

Heaven, *TIAN*: see *Patterns of Wisdom*. **Earth**, *DI*: the earth, ground on which the human world rests; basis of all things, nourishes all things; essential Yin; Symbol of the trigram Space, *KUN*. **Reciprocal**, *XIANG*: mutual; assist, encourage, help; bring together, blend with; examine, inspect; by turns. **Kinds**, *PIN*: species and their essential qualities; sort, class, degree; numerous, innumerable. **Being**, *WU*: creature, thing, any single being; matter, substance, essence; nature of things. **Conjoin**, *XIAN*: come in contact with, join; put together as parts of a previously separated whole; conjunction of celestial bodies; totally, completely; accord, harmony, mutual influence; lit.: broken piece of pottery, the halves of which join to identify partners. **Composition**, *ZHANG*: a well-composed whole and its structure; beautiful creation; elegant, clear, brilliant; chapter, strophe; distinct from pattern, *WEN*, beauty of intrinsic design.

Center, *ZHONG*: inner, central; put in the center; middle, stable point enabling you to face inner and outer changes; middle line of a trigram. Ideogram: field divided in two equal parts. **Correct**, *ZHENG*: rectify deviation or one-sidedness; proper, straight, exact, regular; constant, rule, model. Ideogram: stop and one, hold to one thing. **Below heaven**, *TIAN XIA*: human world, between heaven and earth. **Great**, *DA*: big, noble, important, very; orient the will toward a self-imposed goal, impose direction; ability to lead or guide one's life; contrasts with small, *XIAO*, flexible adaptation to what crosses one's path. **Move**, *XING*: move or move something; motivate; emotionally moving; walk, act, do. Ideogram: successive steps. **Season**, *SHI*: quality of the time; the right time, opportune, in harmony; planning in accord with the time; season of the year. Ideogram: sun and temple, sacred time. **Belong/it**, *ZHI*: establishes between two terms a connection similar to the Saxon genitive, in which the second term belongs to the first one; at the end of a sentence it refers to something previously mentioned or implied. **Righteous**, *YI*: proper, just, virtuous, upright; the heart that rules itself; benevolent, loyal, devoted to public good. **Actually**, *YI*: truly, really, at present. Ideogram: a dart and done, strong intention fully expressed. **In-fact**, *ZAI*: emphatic exclamation; truly, indeed.

45 CLUSTERING | *Cui*

The situation described by this hexagram is characterized by people or things assembling and forming compact clusters, like grass densely intertwined.

Image of the Situation

> **Clustering**.
> **Growing**.
> The **king imagines possessing** a **temple**.
> **Harvesting**: **viewing** the **great** in the **person**.
> **Growing**, **Harvesting**, **Trial**.
> **Availing** of the **great**'s **sacrificial-victims**, **significant**.
> **Harvesting**: **possessing directed going**.

Fields of meaning

Cluster, *CUI*: dense, thick; tight groups of people, animals, things; collect, gather, assemble, concentrate; bunch, crowd; lit.: dense, tussocky grass. Grow, *HENG*: heavenly influence pervading and nourishing all things; prosper, succeed, expand, develop; effective, favorable; quality of summer and South, second stage of the Time Cycle. With the pronunciation *XIANG*: offer a sacrifice; offer a gift to a superior; accept, enjoy. King, *WANG*: sovereign, effective ruler, emperor, seen as connecting heaven and earth; reign, govern. Imagine, *JIA*: create in the mind; fantasize, suppose; pretend, imitate; fiction, illusion; costume. Ideogram: person and borrow. Possess, *YOU*: general term indicating possession; have, own, be endowed with. Temple, *MIAO*: building used to honor gods and ancestors. Harvest, *LI*: benefit, advantage, profit; realization; sharp, acute, insightful; quality of autumn and West, third stage of the Time Cycle. Ideogram: ripe grain and blade. View, *JIAN*: vision in all its aspects: seeing, being visible, forming mental images; visit, call on, consult. Ideogram: eye above person, active and receptive sight. Great, *DA*: big, noble, important, very; orient the will toward a self-imposed goal, impose direction; ability to lead or guide one's life; contrasts with small, *XIAO*, flexible adaptation to what crosses one's path. Person/people, *REN*:

humans individually and collectively; an individual; humankind. **Trial**, *ZHEN*: inquiry by divination and its result; righteous, firm; separating wheat from chaff; the kernel, the proven core; quality of winter and North, fourth stage of the Time Cycle. Ideogram: pearl and divination. **Avail**, *YONG*: use, employ for a specific purpose; take advantage of; benefit from; capacity. Ideogram: to divine and center, applying divination to central concerns. **Sacrificial-victims**, *SHENG*: the six sacrificial animals: horse, ox, lamb, cock, dog and pig. **Significant**, *JI*: leads to the experience of meaning; favorable, propitious, appropriate. Ideogram: scholar and mouth, wise words of a sage. **Possessing directed going**, *YOU YOU WANG*: having a goal or purpose, moving in a specific direction.

Outer and Inner Trigram

The upper trigram, **Open**, *DUI*, describes the outer aspects of the situation. It has the following associations: an open surface, promoting interaction and interpenetration; pleasant, easy, responsive, free, unhindered; opening, passage; the mouth; exchange, barter; straight, direct; meet, gather; place where water accumulates. Ideogram: mouth and vapor, communication through speech. *Symbol*: marsh, *ZE*, open surface of a flat body of water and the vapors rising from it; fertilize, enrich; kindness, favor. *Action*: stimulate, *SHUO*, rouse to action and good feeling; stir up, urge on; exhort, persuade; say, tell, relate; cheer, delight; joyous, peaceful, restful. Ideogram: words and exchange. In the family of trigrams *DUI* is the youngest daughter.

The lower trigram, **Space**, *KUN*, describes the inner aspects of the situation. It has the following associations: surface of the world; support of all existence, manifestation of Yin, where Energy or Yang activates all creation and destruction; all-involving service; earth; moon, wife, mother; rest, receptivity, docile obedience. Ideogram: terrestrial globe and stretch out. *Symbol*: earth, *DI*; the earth, ground on which the human world rests; basis of all things, nourishes all things; essential Yin. *Action*: yield, *SHUN*: give way, comply, agree, follow, obey; docile, flexible; bear produce, nourish, provide. In the family of trigrams *KUN* is the mother.

Counter Hexagram

The Counter Hexagram of **Clustering** is hexagram 53, **Infiltrating**, which switches the emphasis from the intricate holding together of **Clustering** to a gradual and steady penetration.

Preceding Situation

> **Beings reciprocally meeting and-also afterwards assembling.**

> To **anterior acquiescence belongs** the **use** of **clustering**.
> **Clustering implies assembling indeed**.

Fields of meaning

Being, *WU*: creature, thing, any single being; matter, substance, essence; nature of things. **Reciprocal**, *XIANG*: mutual; assist, encourage, help; bring together, blend with; examine, inspect; by turns. **Meet**, *YU*: come on unexpectedly, encounter; occur, happen; pleasant meeting, lucky coincidence; agree. **And-also**, *ER*: joins and contrasts two terms. **After(wards)/later**, *HOU*: come after in time, subsequent; put oneself after; behind, back, draw back; the second; attendants, heirs, successors, posterity. **Assemble**, *JU*: gather, bring together, collect, amass; call to assembly; dwell together, converge; meeting place, dwelling place. Ideogram: three (meaning many) people. To **anterior acquiescence belongs** the **use** of, *GU SHOU ZHI YI*: understanding and accepting the preceding statement allows the consultant to make proper use of this hexagram. **Cluster**, *CUI*: see *Image of the Situation*. **Imply**, *ZHE*: further signify; additional meaning. **Indeed**, *YE*: emphasizes and intensifies the previous statement.

Hexagrams in Pairs

> **Clustering**: **assembling**, **and-also**
> **ascending**: **not coming indeed**.

Fields of meaning

Cluster, *CUI*: see *Image of the Situation*. **Assemble**, *JU*: see *Preceding Situation*. **And-also**, *ER*: see *Preceding Situation*. **Ascend**, *SHENG*: rise, augment, grow; climb step by step; rise in office; advance through effort; offer a sacrifice; lit.: a measure for fermented liquor, ascension as distillation. **Not**, *BU*: common term of negation. **Come**, *LAI*: approach in time or space; move toward, arrive at; future; contrasts with go, *WANG*, move away or become past. **Indeed**, *YE*: see *Preceding Situation*.

Patterns of Wisdom

> **Pond above with-respect-to earth**. **Clustering**.
> A **jun zi uses eliminating weapons** for **implements**.
> And **warning**, **not precautions**.

Fields of meaning

Pond, *ZE*: open surface of a flat body of water and the vapors rising from it;

fertilize, enrich; kindness, favor; Symbol of the trigram Open, *DUI*. **Above**, *SHANG*: anything above in all senses; higher, upper, outer; upper trigram. **With-respect-to**, *YU*: in relation to, referring to, according to; in, at, until. **Earth**, *DI*: the earth, ground on which the human world rests; basis of all things, nourishes all things; essential Yin; Symbol of the trigram Space, *KUN*. **Cluster**, *CUI*: see *Image of the Situation*. **Jun zi**: ideal of a person who orders his/her life in accordance with dao rather than willful intention, and uses divination in this spirit. **Use**, *YI*: by means of; owing to; make use of, employ. **Eliminate**, *CHU*: root out, remove, do away with, take off; keep out; vacate, exchange. **Weapons**, *RONG*: arms; armed people, soldiers; military, violent. Ideogram: spear and armor, offensive and defensive weapons. **Implements**, *QI*: utensils, tools; molded or carved objects; use a person or thing suitably; capacity, talent, intelligence. **Warn**, *JIE*: alarm, alert, put on guard; caution, inform; guard against, refrain from. Ideogram: spear held in both hands, warning enemies. **Not**, *BU*: common term of negation. **Precaution**, *YU*: provide against, preventive measures; anxious, vigilant, ready; think about, expect; mishap, accident.

Transforming Lines

INITIAL SIX

Possessing conformity, not completing.
Thereupon disarraying, thereupon clustering.
Like an **outcry, one handful activates laughter.**
No cares.
Going, without fault.

Comments
Thereupon disarraying, thereupon clustering.
One's purpose disarrayed indeed.

Fields of meaning

Possess, *YOU*: see *Image of the Situation*. **Conform**, *FU*: accord between inner and outer; sincere, truthful, verified, reliable; capture; prisoners, spoils. Ideogram: claws over child, a bird brooding on the nest. **Not**, *BU*: common term of negation. **Complete**, *ZHONG*: completion of a cycle that begins the next; entire, whole, all. Ideogram: silk cocoons, follow and ice, winter linking one year with the next. **Thereupon**, *NAI*: on that ground, then, only then; finally; in spite of that. **Disarray**, *LUAN*: throw into disorder, mislay, confuse; out of place; discord, insurrection, anarchy. **Cluster**, *CUI*: see *Image of the Situation*. **Like**, *RUO*: same as, just as; conform, imitate; adverbial suffix indicating similarity. **Cry-out/outcry**, *HAO*:

call out, proclaim; order, command; mark, label, sign; designate, name. **One**, *YI*: a single unit; number one; undivided, simple, whole; unique; first. **Handful**, *WU*: as much as the hand can hold; a little; grasp, hold. **Activate**, *WEI*: act or cause to act; do, make, manage, make active; be, become; attend to, help; because of. **Laugh**, *XIAO*: manifest joy or mirth; giggle, joke, laugh at, tease; desire; open (of a flower); associated with the Fiery Moment. **No**, *WU*: common term of negation. **Care**, *XU*: fear, doubt, concern; heartfelt attachment; relieve, soothe, aid; sympathy, compassion, consolation. Ideogram: heart and blood, the heart's blood affected. **Go**, *WANG*: move away in time or space, depart; become past; dead, gone; contrasts with come, *LAI*, approach in time or space. **Without fault**, *WU JIU*: no error or harm in the situation.

One/one's, *QI*: general third person pronoun and possessive adjective; also: it/its, he/his, she/her, they/their. **Purpose**, *ZHI*: focus of mind and heart; intention, will, inclination; continuity in the direction of life. Ideogram: heart and scholar, high inner resolve. **Indeed**, *YE*: see *Preceding Situation*.

SIX AT SECOND

Protracting: **significant**, **without fault**.
Conforming, **thereupon Harvesting**: **availing** of **dedicating**.

Comments
Protracting: **significant**, **without fault**.
The **center not-yet transformed indeed**.

Fields of meaning
Protract, *YIN*: draw out, prolong; pull, stretch; lasting, perennial. Ideogram: draw a bow. **Significant**, *JI*: see *Image of the Situation*. **Without fault**, *WU JIU*: no error or harm in the situation. **Conform**, *FU*: accord between inner and outer; sincere, truthful, verified, reliable; capture; prisoners, spoils. Ideogram: claws over child, a bird brooding on the nest. **Thereupon**, *NAI*: on that ground, then, only then; finally; in spite of that. **Harvest**, *LI*: see *Image of the Situation*. **Avail**, *YONG*: see *Image of the Situation*. **Dedicate**, *YUE*: imperial offering at the spring equinox, when stores are low; offer a sacrifice with limited resources. Ideogram: spring and thin.

Center, *ZHONG*: inner, central; put in the center; middle, stable point enabling you to face inner and outer changes; middle line of a trigram. Ideogram: field divided in two equal parts. **Not-yet**, *WEI*: temporal negative indicating that something is expected to happen but has not yet occurred. **Transform**, *BIAN*:

abrupt, radical passage from one state to another; transformation of opened and whole lines into each other in hexagrams; contrasts with change, *HUA*, gradual mutation. **Indeed**, *YE*: see *Preceding Situation*.

Six at Third

Clustering thus, **lamenting thus**.
Without direction Harvesting.
Going, **without fault**.
The **small abashed**.

Comments
Going, **without fault**.
Above the **root indeed**.

Fields of meaning

Cluster, *CUI*: see *Image of the Situation*. **Thus**, *RU*: as, in this way; comparable, similar. **Lament**, *JUE*: sigh, express intense regret or sorrow, mourn over; painful recollections. **Without direction Harvesting**, *WU YOU LI*: in order to take advantage of the situation, do not impose a direction on events. **Go**, *WANG*: move away in time or space, depart; become past; dead, gone; contrasts with come, *LAI*, approach in time or space. **Without fault**, *WU JIU*: no error or harm in the situation. **Small**, *XIAO*: little, common, unimportant; adapting to what crosses your path; ability to move in harmony with the vicissitudes of life; contrasts with great, *DA*, self-imposed theme or goal. **Abashment**, *LIN*: distress, shame, regret, humiliation; aware of having lost the right track; leads to repenting, *HUI*, correcting the direction of mind and life.

Above, *SHANG*: see *Patterns of Wisdom*. **Root**, *SUN*: base on which things rest, ground, foundation; mild, subtly penetrating; nourishing. **Indeed**, *YE*: see *Preceding Situation*.

Nine at Fourth

The **great**: **significant**, **without fault**.

Comments
The **great**: **significant**, **without fault**.
Position not appropriate indeed.

Fields of meaning

Great, *DA*: see *Image of the Situation.* **Significant**, *JI*: see *Image of the Situation.* **Without fault**, *WU JIU*: no error or harm in the situation.

Position, *WEI*: place, location; be at; social standing, rank; position of a line in a hexagram. Ideogram: person standing. **Not**, *BU*: common term of negation. **Appropriate**, *DANG*: suitable, capable, worthy, adequate, competent, equal to; opportune, convenient; whole lines in odd places and opened lines in even places. **Indeed**, *YE*: see *Preceding Situation.*

NINE AT FIFTH

Clustering possesses the **position**.
Without fault.
In-no-way conforming.
Spring, **perpetual Trial**.
Repenting extinguished.

Comments
Clustering possesses the **position**.
Purpose not-yet shining indeed.

Fields of meaning

Cluster, *CUI*: see *Image of the Situation.* **Possess**, *YOU*: see *Image of the Situation.* **Position**, *WEI*: place, location; be at; social standing, rank; position of a line in a hexagram. Ideogram: person standing. **Without fault**, *WU JIU*: no error or harm in the situation. **In-no-way**, *FEI*: strong negative; not so; bandit, rebel; unjust, immoral. Ideogram: a box filled with opposition. **Conform**, *FU*: accord between inner and outer; sincere, truthful, verified, reliable; capture; prisoners, spoils. Ideogram: claws over child, a bird brooding on the nest. **Spring**, *YUAN*: source, origin, head; arise, begin; first generating impulse; great, excellent; quality of springtime and East, first stage of the Time Cycle. **Perpetual**, *YONG*: continual, everlasting, eternal. Ideogram: flowing water. **Trial**, *ZHEN*: see *Image of the Situation.* **Repenting extinguished**, *HUI WANG*: previous errors are corrected, all causes for repenting disappear.

Purpose, *ZHI*: focus of mind and heart; intention, will, inclination; continuity in the direction of life. Ideogram: heart and scholar, high inner resolve. **Not-yet**, *WEI*: temporal negative indicating that something is expected to happen but has not yet occurred. **Shine**, *GUANG*: illuminate, emit light; brilliant, splendid; honor, glory, éclat; distinct from brightness, *MING*, light of heavenly bodies. Ideogram: fire above person. **Indeed**, *YE*: see *Preceding Situation.*

SIX ABOVE

Paying-tribute: sighs, tears, snot.
Without fault.

Comments
Paying-tribute: sighs, tears, snot.
Not-yet peaceful above indeed.

Fields of meaning
Pay-tribute, *JI*: compulsory payments; present property to a superior. **Sigh**, *ZI*: lament, express grief, sorrow or yearning. **Tears**, *TI*: tears; weep, cry. **Snot**, *YI*: mucus from the nose; snivel, whine. **Without fault**, *WU JIU*: no error or harm in the situation.

Not-yet, *WEI*: temporal negative indicating that something is expected to happen but has not yet occurred. Peace, *AN*: quiet, still, settled, secure, contented; calm, tranquilize, console. Ideogram: woman under a roof, a tranquil home. Above, *SHANG*: see *Patterns of Wisdom*. Indeed, *YE*: see *Preceding Situation*.

Image Tradition

Clustering. Assembling indeed.
Yielding uses stimulating.
The **solid** in the **center and-also corresponding.**
Anterior assembling indeed.

The **king imagines possessing** a **temple.**
Involving reverent presenting indeed.
Harvesting: viewing the **great** in the **person. Growing.**
Assembling uses correctness indeed.

Availing of the **great**'s **sacrificial-victims, significant.**
Harvesting: possessing directed going.
Yielding to **heaven**'s **fate indeed.**
Overseeing one's place to **assemble.**
And-also the **motives belonging** to **heaven** and **earth**'s
myriad beings permit viewing actually.

Fields of meaning
Cluster, *CUI*: see *Image of the Situation*. **Assemble**, *JU*: see *Preceding Situation*. **Indeed**, *YE*: see *Preceding Situation*. **Yield**, *SHUN*: give way, comply, agree, follow,

obey; docile, flexible; bear produce, nourish, provide; Action of the trigram Field, *KUN*. **Use**, *YI*: see *Patterns of Wisdom*. **Stimulate**, *SHUO*: rouse to action and good feeling; stir up, urge on; exhort, persuade; say, tell, relate; cheer, delight; joyous, peaceful, restful; Action of the trigram Open, *DUI*. Ideogram: words and exchange. **Solid**, *GANG*: quality of the whole lines; firm, strong, unyielding, persisting. **Center**, *ZHONG*: inner, central; put in the center; middle, stable point enabling you to face inner and outer changes; middle line of a trigram. Ideogram: field divided in two equal parts. **And-also**, *ER*: see *Preceding Situation*. **Correspond**, *YING*: be in agreement or harmony; proper, suitable; resonate together, answer to; relation between the lines (1 and 4, 2 and 5, 3 and 6) when they form the pair opened and whole, supple and solid. Ideogram: heart and obey. **Anterior**, *GU*: come before as cause; former, ancient; reason, purpose, intention; grievance, dissatisfaction, sorrow, resulting from previous causes and intentions; situation leading to a divination.

The **king imagines possessing** a **temple**, *WANG JIA YOU MIAO*: see *Image of the Situation*. **Involve**, *ZHI*: devote oneself to; induce, cause, implicate; approach; manifest, express; reach the highest degree of. Ideogram: reach and come up behind. **Reverent**, *XIAO*: filial duty, respect and obedience owed to parents and elders; loyally accomplishing the ancestors' will; period of mourning for deceased parents; virtuous son. **Present**, *XIANG*: offer in sacrifice, give to the gods or a superior; give a banquet; accept an offering; enjoy, receive. **Harvesting**: **viewing** the **great** in the **person**, *LI JIAN DA REN*: see *Image of the Situation*. **Grow**, *HENG*: see *Image of the Situation*. **Correct**, *ZHENG*: rectify deviation or one-sidedness; proper, straight, exact, regular; constant, rule, model. Ideogram: stop and one, hold to one thing.

Availing of the **great**'s **sacrificial-victims**, **significant**, *YONG DA SHENG JI*: see *Image of the Situation*. **Possessing directed going**, *YOU YOU WANG*: see *Image of the Situation*. **Yield**, *SHUN*: give way, comply, agree, follow, obey; docile, flexible; bear produce, nourish, provide; Action of the trigram Field, *KUN*. **Heaven**, *TIAN*: sky, firmament, heavens; the highest realm, situated above the human world, as opposed to the earth, *DI*, located below; Symbol of the trigram Energy, *QIAN*. Ideogram: great and the one above. **Fate**, *MING*: individual destiny; birth and death as limits of life; issue orders with authority; consult the gods. Ideogram: mouth and order, words with heavenly authority. **Oversee**, *GUAN*: contemplate, observe from a distance; look at carefully, gaze at; a high place from where one sees far, monastery, observatory; intelligence, clairvoyance; scry, divine through liquid in a cup. Ideogram: sight and waterbird, aerial view. **One/one's**, *QI*: general third person pronoun and possessive adjective; also: it/its, he/his, she/her, they/their. **Place**, *SUO*: position, location; residence, dwelling; where something belongs or comes from; habitual focus or object. **Motive**, *QING*: true nature;

feelings, desires, passions; sincere, true, real; state of affairs, circumstances. Ideogram: heart and green, germinated in the heart. **Belong/it**, *ZHI*: establishes between two terms a connection similar to the Saxon genitive, in which the second term belongs to the first one; at the end of a sentence it refers to something previously mentioned or implied. **Earth**, *DI*: see *Patterns of Wisdom*. **Myriad**, *WAN*: ten thousand; countless, many, everyone. Ideogram: swarm of insects. **Being**, *WU*: creature, thing, any single being; matter, substance, essence; nature of things. **Permit**, *KE*: possible because in harmony with an inherent principle; capable of; approve, authorize. Ideogram: mouth and breath, silent consent. **View**, *JIAN*: see *Image of the Situation*. **Actually**, *YI*: truly, really, at present. Ideogram: a dart and done, strong intention fully expressed.

升

46 ASCENDING
Sheng

The situation described by this hexagram is characterized by ascending, being promoted, climbing step by step, moving towards a higher or finer goal.

Image of the Situation

Ascending.
Spring, **Growing**.
Availing of **viewing** the **great** in the **person**.
No cares.
The **South**: **disciplining**, **significant**.

Fields of meaning

Ascend, *SHENG*: rise, augment, grow; climb step by step; rise in office; advance through effort; offer a sacrifice; lit.: a measure for fermented liquor, ascension as distillation. Spring, *YUAN*: source, origin, head; arise, begin; first generating impulse; great, excellent; quality of springtime and East, first stage of the Time Cycle. Grow, *HENG*: heavenly influence pervading and nourishing all things; prosper, succeed, expand, develop; effective, favorable; quality of summer and South, second stage of the Time Cycle. With the pronunciation *XIANG*: offer a sacrifice; offer a gift to a superior; accept, enjoy. Avail, *YONG*: use, employ for a specific purpose; take advantage of; benefit from; capacity. Ideogram: to divine and center, applying divination to central concerns. View, *JIAN*: vision in all its aspects: seeing, being visible, forming mental images; visit, call on, consult. Ideogram: eye above person, active and receptive sight. Great, *DA*: big, noble, important, very; orient the will toward a self-imposed goal, impose direction; ability to lead or guide one's life; contrasts with small, *XIAO*, flexible adaptation to what crosses one's path. Person/people, *REN*: humans individually and collectively; an individual; humankind. No, *WU*: common term of negation. Care, *XU*: fear, doubt, concern; heartfelt attachment; relieve, soothe, aid; sympathy, compassion, consolation. Ideogram: heart and blood, the heart's blood affected. South, *NAN*: southern direction, corresponds to noon, summer and the Fiery

Moment in the Universal Compass; culmination of the Yang hemicycle; reference point of compass; true principles and correct decisions; rulers face South when in their governing function. **Discipline**, *ZHENG*: subjugate vassals, reduce to order; punishing expedition. Ideogram: step and correct, a rectifying move. **Significant**, *JI*: leads to the experience of meaning; favorable, propitious, appropriate. Ideogram: scholar and mouth, wise words of a sage.

Outer and Inner Trigram

The upper trigram, **Space**, *KUN*, describes the outer aspects of the situation. It has the following associations: surface of the world; support of all existence, manifestation of Yin, where Energy or Yang activates all creation and destruction; all-involving service; earth; moon, wife, mother; rest, receptivity, docile obedience. Ideogram: terrestrial globe and stretch out. *Symbol*: earth, *DI*; the earth, ground on which the human world rests; basis of all things, nourishes all things; essential Yin. *Action*: yield, *SHUN*: give way, comply, agree, follow, obey; docile, flexible; bear produce, nourish, provide. In the family of trigrams *KUN* is the mother.

The lower trigram, **Root**, *SUN*, describes the inner aspects of the situation. It has the following associations: base on which things rest, ground, foundation; mild, subtly penetrating; nourishing. *Symbols*: tree/wood and wind. Tree/wood, *MU*: trees and all things woody or wooden; associated with the Wooden Moment. Ideogram: a tree with roots and branches. Wind, *FENG*: wind, breeze, gust; weather and its influence on mood and humor; fashion, usage. *Action*: enter, *RU*, penetrate, go into, enter on, encroach on; progress; put into. In the family of trigrams *SUN* is the eldest daughter.

Counter Hexagram

The Counter Hexagram of **Ascending** is hexagram 54, **Converting Maidenhood**, which switches the emphasis from ascending to a higher level to realizing one's nature by simply accepting one's allotted destiny.

Preceding Situation

> **Assembling and-also** the **above implies** the
> **designation belonging** to **ascending**.
> To **anterior acquiescence belongs** the **use** of
> **ascending**.

Fields of meaning

Assemble, *JU*: gather, bring together, collect, amass; call to assembly; dwell together, converge; meeting place, dwelling place. Ideogram: three (meaning many) people. **And-also**, *ER*: joins and contrasts two terms. **Above**, *SHANG*: anything above in all senses; higher, upper, outer; upper trigram. **Imply**, *ZHE*: further signify; additional meaning. **Designate**, *WEI*: say, express in words, give a name; mean, signify; consider as; talk about. Ideogram: words and belly, describing the essential. **Belong/it**, *ZHI*: establishes between two terms a connection similar to the Saxon genitive, in which the second term belongs to the first one; at the end of a sentence it refers to something previously mentioned or implied. **Ascend**, *SHENG*: see *Image of the Situation*. To **anterior acquiescence belongs** the **use** of, *GU SHOU ZHI YI*: understanding and accepting the preceding statement allows the consultant to make proper use of this hexagram.

Hexagrams in Pairs

> **Clustering**: **assembling**, **and-also**
> **ascending**: **not coming indeed**.

Fields of meaning

Cluster, *CUI*: dense, thick; tight groups of people, animals, things; collect, gather, assemble, concentrate; bunch, crowd; lit.: dense, tussocky grass. **Assemble**, *JU*: see *Preceding Situation*. **And-also**, *ER*: see *Preceding Situation*. **Ascend**, *SHENG*: see *Image of the Situation*. **Not**, *BU*: common term of negation. **Come**, *LAI*: approach in time or space; move toward, arrive at; future; contrasts with go, *WANG*, move away or become past. **Indeed**, *YE*: emphasizes and intensifies the previous statement.

Patterns of Wisdom

> The **earth**'s **center generates wood**. **Ascending**.
> A **jun zi uses yielding** to **actualizing-dao**.
> And **amassing** the **small** to **use** the **high great**.

Fields of meaning

Earth, *DI*: the earth, ground on which the human world rests; basis of all things, nourishes all things; essential Yin; Symbol of the trigram Space, *KUN*. **Center**, *ZHONG*: inner, central; put in the center; middle, stable point enabling you to face inner and outer changes; middle line of a trigram. Ideogram: field divided in two equal parts. **Generate**, *SHENG*: give birth; be born, arise, grow; beget; life, vitality. Ideogram: earth and sprout. **Wood/tree**, *MU*: trees and all things woody or wooden; associated with the Wooden Moment; wood and wind are the Symbols of the trigram Ground, *SUN*. Ideogram: a tree with roots and branches. **Ascend**,

SHENG: see *Image of the Situation*. Jun zi: ideal of a person who orders his/her life in accordance with dao rather than willful intention, and uses divination in this spirit. Use, *YI*: by means of; owing to; make use of, employ. Yield, *SHUN*: give way, comply, agree, follow, obey; docile, flexible; bear produce, nourish, provide; Action of the trigram Field, *KUN*. Actualize-dao, *DE*: realize dao in action; power, virtue; ability to follow the course traced by the ongoing process of the cosmos. Ideogram: go, straight, and heart. Linked with acquire, *DE*: acquiring that which makes a being become what it is meant to be. Amass, *JI*: hoard, accumulate, pile up, add up, increase; repeated action, habit; follow, pursue. Small, *XIAO*: little, common, unimportant; adapting to what crosses your path; ability to move in harmony with the vicissitudes of life; contrasts with great, *DA*, self-imposed theme or goal. High, *GAO*: high, elevated, lofty, eminent; honor, respect. Ideogram: high tower. Great, *DA*: see *Image of the Situation*.

Transforming Lines

INITIAL SIX

Sincere ascending: the **great**, **significant**.

Comments

Sincere ascending: the **great**, **significant**.
Above uniting purposes indeed.

Fields of meaning

Sincere, *YUN*: true, honest, loyal; according to the facts; have confidence in, permit, assent. Ideogram: vapor rising, words directed upward. Ascend, *SHENG*: see *Image of the Situation*. Great, *DA*: see *Image of the Situation*. Significant, *JI*: see *Image of the Situation*.

Above, *SHANG*: see *Preceding Situation*. Unite, *HE*: join, match, correspond; unison, harmony; together; close the jaws, shut the mouth. Ideogram: mouths speaking in unison. Purpose, *ZHI*: focus of mind and heart; intention, will, inclination; continuity in the direction of life. Ideogram: heart and scholar, high inner resolve. Indeed, *YE*: see *Hexagrams in Pairs*.

NINE AT SECOND

Conforming, thereupon Harvesting: **availing** of **dedicating**.
Without fault.

Comments
To **nine** at **second belongs conforming**.
Possessing joy indeed.

Fields of meaning
Conform, *FU*: accord between inner and outer; sincere, truthful, verified, reliable; capture; prisoners, spoils. Ideogram: claws over child, a bird brooding on the nest. **Thereupon**, *NAI*: on that ground, then, only then; finally; in spite of that. **Harvest**, *LI*: benefit, advantage, profit; realization; sharp, acute, insightful; quality of autumn and West, third stage of the Time Cycle. Ideogram: ripe grain and blade. **Avail**, *YONG*: see *Image of the Situation*. **Dedicate**, *YUE*: imperial offering at the spring equinox, when stores are low; offer a sacrifice with limited resources. Ideogram: spring and thin. **Without fault**, *WU JIU*: no error or harm in the situation.

Nine, *JIU*: number nine; transforming whole line; superlative: best, perfect. **Two/second**, *ER*: number two; pair, even numbers, binary, duplicate. **Belong/it**, *ZHI*: see *Preceding Situation*. **Possess**, *YOU*: general term indicating possession; have, own, be endowed with. **Joy/rejoice**, *XI*: delight, exult; cheerful, merry. Ideogram: joy (music) and mouth, expressing joy. **Indeed**, *YE*: see *Hexagrams in Pairs*.

NINE AT THIRD

Ascending an **empty capital**.

Comments
Ascending an **empty capital**.
Without a **place** to **doubt indeed**.

Fields of meaning
Ascend, *SHENG*: see *Image of the Situation*. **Empty**, *XU*: void; absence of images and concepts; vacant, insubstantial; empty yet fertile space. **Capital**, *YI*: populous fortified city, center and symbol of the region it rules. Ideogram: enclosure and official seal.

Without, *WU*: devoid of; there is not. **Place**, *SUO*: position, location; residence, dwelling; where something belongs or comes from; habitual focus or object. **Doubt**, *YI*: suspect, distrust, wonder; uncertain, dubious; surmise, conjecture, fear. **Indeed**, *YE*: see *Hexagrams in Pairs*.

Six at Fourth

The **king avails** of **Growing tending-towards** the **twin-peaked mountain**.
Significant, without fault.

Comments
The **king avails** of **Growing tending-towards** the **twin-peaked mountain**.
Yielding affairs indeed.

Fields of meaning

King, *WANG*: sovereign, effective ruler, emperor, seen as connecting heaven and earth; reign, govern. **Avail**, *YONG*: see *Image of the Situation*. **Grow**, *HENG*: see *Image of the Situation*. **Tend-towards**, *YU*: move toward without necessarily reaching, in the direction of. **Twin-peaked**, *QI*: mountain with two peaks; forked road; diverge, ambiguous. Ideogram: mountain and branched. Twin-peaked Mountain, *QI SHAN*, is the ancestral shrine of the Zhou Dynasty. **Mountain**, *SHAN*: mountain; large, immense; limit, boundary; Symbol of the trigram Bound, *GEN*. Ideogram: three peaks, a mountain range. **Significant**, *JI*: see *Image of the Situation*. **Without fault**, *WU JIU*: no error or harm in the situation.

Yield, *SHUN*: see *Patterns of Wisdom*. **Affairs**, *SHI*: all kinds of personal activity; matters at hand; business; function, occupation; manage; perform a task; incident, event; case in court. **Indeed**, *YE*: see *Hexagrams in Pairs*.

Six at Fifth

Trial, **significant**: **ascending steps**.

Comments
Trial, **significant**: **ascending steps**.
The **great acquires purpose indeed**.

Fields of meaning

Trial, *ZHEN*: inquiry by divination and its result; righteous, firm; separating wheat from chaff; the kernel, the proven core; quality of winter and North, fourth stage of the Time Cycle. Ideogram: pearl and divination. **Significant**, *JI*: see *Image of the Situation*. **Ascend**, *SHENG*: see *Image of the Situation*. **Steps**, *JIE*: steps of stairs leading to a gate or hall; grade, degree, rank; ascend, rise.

Great, *DA*: see *Image of the Situation*. **Acquire**, *DE*: obtain the desired object;

possession; satisfied, fulfilled; it is permitted; agree with; wish for, desire covetously. Ideogram: go and obstacle, going through obstacles to the goal. **Purpose**, *ZHI*: focus of mind and heart; intention, will, inclination; continuity in the direction of life. Ideogram: heart and scholar, high inner resolve. **Indeed**, *YE*: see *Hexagrams in Pairs.*

SIX ABOVE

Dim ascending.
Harvesting: to **tending-towards not pausing belongs**
Trial.

Comments
Dim ascending located above.
Dissolving, **not affluence indeed**.

Fields of meaning

Dim, *MING*: dark, obscure; obtuse, immature; cavern, the underworld. Ideogram: 16th day of the lunar month, when the moon begins to dim. **Ascend**, *SHENG*: see *Image of the Situation*. **Harvest**, *LI*: benefit, advantage, profit; realization; sharp, acute, insightful; quality of autumn and West, third stage of the Time Cycle. Ideogram: ripe grain and blade. **Tend-towards**, *YU*: move toward without necessarily reaching, in the direction of. **Not**, *BU*: common term of negation. **Pause**, *XI*: breathe; rest, repose, a breathing-spell; suspended. **Belong/it**, *ZHI*: see *Preceding Situation*. **Trial**, *ZHEN*: inquiry by divination and its result; righteous, firm; separating wheat from chaff; the kernel, the proven core; quality of winter and North, fourth stage of the Time Cycle. Ideogram: pearl and divination.

Locate, *ZAI*: be at, be situated at, dwell, reside; in, within; involved with, in the process of. Ideogram: earth and persevere, a place on the earth. **Above**, *SHANG*: see *Preceding Situation*. **Dissolve**, *XIAO*: liquefy, melt, thaw; diminish, disperse; eliminate, exhaust. Ideogram: water dissolving differences. **Affluence**, *FU*: rich, abundant; wealth; enrich, provide for; flow toward, accrue. **Indeed**, *YE*: see *Hexagrams in Pairs.*

Image Tradition

The **supple uses** the **season**. **Ascending**.
The **root and-also yielding**.
The **solid** in the **center and-also corresponding**.
That uses the **great**, **Growing**.

Availing of **viewing** the **great** in the **person**.
No cares.
Possessing reward indeed.
The **South**: **disciplining**, **significant**.
Purpose moves indeed.

Fields of meaning

Supple, *ROU*: quality of the opened lines; flexible, pliant, adaptable, tender. Use, *YI*: see *Patterns of Wisdom*. Season, *SHI*: quality of the time; the right time, opportune, in harmony; planning in accord with the time; season of the year. Ideogram: sun and temple, sacred time. Ascend, *SHENG*: see *Image of the Situation*. Root, *SUN*: base on which things rest, ground, foundation; mild, subtly penetrating; nourishing. And-also, *ER*: see *Preceding Situation*. Yield, *SHUN*: see *Patterns of Wisdom*. Solid, *GANG*: quality of the whole lines; firm, strong, unyielding, persisting. Center, *ZHONG*: see *Patterns of Wisdom*. Correspond, *YING*: be in agreement or harmony; proper, suitable; resonate together, answer to; relation between the lines (1 and 4, 2 and 5, 3 and 6) when they form the pair opened and whole, supple and solid. Ideogram: heart and obey. That, *SHI*: refers to the preceding statement. Use, *YI*: see *Patterns of Wisdom*. Great, *DA*: see *Image of the Situation*. Grow, *HENG*: see *Image of the Situation*.

Availing of viewing the great in the person, *YONG JIAN DA REN*: see *Image of the Situation*. No cares, *WU XU*: see *Image of the Situation*. Possess, *YOU*: general term indicating possession; have, own, be endowed with. Reward, *QING*: gift given out of gratitude or benevolence; favor from heaven. Ideogram: heart, follow and deer, the heart expressed through the gift of a deer's skin. Indeed, *YE*: see *Hexagrams in Pairs*. The South: disciplining, significant, *NAN ZHENG JI*: see *Image of the Situation*. Purpose, *ZHI*: focus of mind and heart; intention, will, inclination; continuity in the direction of life. Ideogram: heart and scholar, high inner resolve. Move, *XING*: move or move something; motivate; emotionally moving; walk, act, do. Ideogram: successive steps.

困

47 CONFINEMENT
Kun

The situation described by this hexagram is characterized by an enclosure or restriction that causes the life energy to contract and forces one to find a way to grow within the limitations imposed by the circumstances.

Image of the Situation

> **Confinement**.
> **Growing**.
> **Trial**: the **great** in the **person**, **significant**.
> **Without fault**.
> **Possessing words not trustworthy**.

Fields of meaning

Confine, *KUN*: enclose, restrict, limit, oppress; impoverished, distressed, afflicted, exhausted, disheartened, weary. Ideogram: tree in a narrow enclosure. **Grow**, *HENG*: heavenly influence pervading and nourishing all things; prosper, succeed, expand, develop; effective, favorable; quality of summer and South, second stage of the Time Cycle. With the pronunciation *XIANG*: offer a sacrifice; offer a gift to a superior; accept, enjoy. **Trial**, *ZHEN*: inquiry by divination and its result; righteous, firm; separating wheat from chaff; the kernel, the proven core; quality of winter and North, fourth stage of the Time Cycle. Ideogram: pearl and divination. **Great**, *DA*: big, noble, important, very; orient the will toward a self-imposed goal, impose direction; ability to lead or guide one's life; contrasts with small, *XIAO*, flexible adaptation to what crosses one's path. **Person/people**, *REN*: humans individually and collectively; an individual; humankind. **Significant**, *JI*: leads to the experience of meaning; favorable, propitious, appropriate. Ideogram: scholar and mouth, wise words of a sage. **Without fault**, *WU JIU*: no error or harm in the situation. **Possess**, *YOU*: general term indicating possession; have, own, be endowed with. **Word**, *YAN*: spoken word, speech, saying; talk, discuss, address; name, signify. Ideogram: mouth and rising vapor. **Not**, *BU*: common term of negation. **Trustworthy**, *XIN*: truthful, faithful, consistent over time; count on, confide in; examine, verify, prove; loyalty, integrity. Ideogram: person and word, true speech.

Outer and Inner Trigram

The upper trigram, **Open**, *DUI*, describes the outer aspects of the situation. It has the following associations: an open surface, promoting interaction and interpenetration; pleasant, easy, responsive, free, unhindered; opening, passage; the mouth; exchange, barter; straight, direct; meet, gather; place where water accumulates. Ideogram: mouth and vapor, communication through speech. *Symbol:* marsh, *ZE*, open surface of a flat body of water and the vapors rising from it; fertilize, enrich; kindness, favor. *Action*: stimulate, *SHUO*, rouse to action and good feeling; stir up, urge on; exhort, persuade; say, tell, relate; cheer, delight; joyous, peaceful, restful. Ideogram: words and exchange. In the family of trigrams *DUI* is the youngest daughter.

The lower trigram, **Gorge**, *KAN*, describes the inner aspects of the situation. It has the following associations: precipice, dangerous place; hole, cavity, pit, snare, trap, grave; critical time, test; risky. Ideogram: earth and cavity. *Symbol:* stream, *SHUI*, flowing water; river, tide, flood; fluid, dissolving. Ideogram: rippling water. *Actions*: venture and fall. Venture, *XIAN*: face a severe difficulty or obstruction; risk; precipice, cliff, abyss; key point, point of danger. Ideogram: mound and all, everything engaged at one point. Fall, *XIAN*: fall down or into, sink, drop, descend; pit, trap, fault; falling water. In the family of trigrams *KAN* is the middle son.

Counter Hexagram

The Counter Hexagram of **Confinement** is hexagram 37, **Household People**, which switches the emphasis from the stifling enclosure of **Confinement** to the supportive enclosure of a household.

Preceding Situation

> **Ascending and-also not climaxing necessarily confines.**
> To **anterior acquiescence belongs** the **use** of **confinement**.

Fields of meaning

Ascend, *SHENG*: rise, augment, grow; climb step by step; rise in office; advance through effort; offer a sacrifice; lit.: a measure for fermented liquor, ascension as distillation. And-also, *ER*: joins and contrasts two terms. Not, *BU*: common term of negation. Climax, *YI*: come to a high point and stop; bring to an end, complete; renounce, desist, decline, reject; that is all; already; excessive. Necessarily, *BI*: unavoidably, certainly. Confine, *KUN*: see *Image of the Situation*. To anterior acquiescence belongs the use of, *GU SHOU ZHI YI*: understanding and accepting the preceding statement allows the consultant to make proper use of this hexagram.

Hexagrams in Pairs

> The **well**: **interpenetrating**, **and-also**
> **confinement**: **reciprocal meeting indeed**.

Fields of meaning

Well, *JING*: water well at the center of the fields; rise and flow of water in a well; life-water surging from the depths; found a capital city. Ideogram: two vertical lines crossing two horizontal ones, eight fields with equal access to a well at the center. Interpenetrate, *TONG*: penetrate freely and reciprocally, permeate, flow through, open a way; see clearly, understand deeply; communicate with; together. And-also, *ER*: see *Preceding Situation*. Confine, *KUN*: see *Image of the Situation*. Reciprocal, *XIANG*: mutual; assist, encourage, help; bring together, blend with; examine, inspect; by turns. Meet, *YU*: come on unexpectedly, encounter; occur, happen; pleasant meeting, lucky coincidence; agree. Indeed, *YE*: emphasizes and intensifies the previous statement.

Additional Texts

> **Confinement**: **marking-off belonging** to **actualizing-dao indeed**.
> **Confinement**: **exhausting and-also interpenetrating**.
> **Confinement**: **using few grudges**.

Fields of meaning

Confine, *KUN*: see *Image of the Situation*. Mark-off, *BIAN*: distinguish by dividing; mark off a plot of land; discern, discriminate, differentiate; discuss and dispute; frame which divides a bed from its stand. Ideogram: knife and acrid, sharp division. Belong/it, *ZHI*: establishes between two terms a connection similar to the Saxon genitive, in which the second term belongs to the first one; at the end of a sentence it refers to something previously mentioned or implied. Actualize-dao, *DE*: realize dao in action; power, virtue; ability to follow the course traced by the ongoing process of the cosmos. Ideogram: go, straight, and heart. Linked with acquire, *DE*: acquiring that which makes a being become what it is meant to be. Indeed, *YE*: see *Hexagrams in Pairs*. Exhaust, *QIONG*: bring to an end; limit, extremity; investigate exhaustively; destitute, indigent; end without a new beginning; distinct from complete, *ZHONG*, end of a cycle that begins the next one. Ideogram: cave and naked person, bent with disease or old age. And-also, *ER*: see *Preceding Situation*. Interpenetrate, *TONG*: see *Hexagrams in Pairs*. Use, *YI*: by means of; owing to; make use of, employ. Few, *GUA*: small number; seldom; reduce, diminish; unsupported, solitary. Grudges, *YUAN*: bitter feelings, ill-will; hate, abhor; murmur against. Ideogram: heart and overturn, upset emotion.

Patterns of Wisdom

Pond without stream. Confinement.
A **jun zi uses involving** in **fate** to **release purpose**.

Fields of meaning
Pond, *ZE*: open surface of a flat body of water and the vapors rising from it; fertilize, enrich; kindness, favor; Symbol of the trigram Open, *DUI*. Without, *WU*: devoid of; there is not. Stream, *SHUI*: flowing water; river, tide, flood; fluid, dissolving; Symbol of the trigram Gorge, *KAN*. Ideogram: rippling water. Confine, *KUN*: see *Image of the Situation*. Jun zi: ideal of a person who orders his/her life in accordance with dao rather than willful intention, and uses divination in this spirit. Use, *YI*: see *Additional Texts*. Involve, *ZHI*: devote oneself to; induce, cause, implicate; approach; manifest, express; reach the highest degree of. Ideogram: reach and come up behind. Fate, *MING*: individual destiny; birth and death as limits of life; issue orders with authority; consult the gods. Ideogram: mouth and order, words with heavenly authority. Release, *SUI*: let go, free; unhindered; advance, progress; promote, further; reach, succeed; in accord with, conforming to. Ideogram: go and follow one's wishes, unimpeded movement. Purpose, *ZHI*: focus of mind and heart; intention, will, inclination; continuity in the direction of life. Ideogram: heart and scholar, high inner resolve.

Transforming Lines

INITIAL SIX

The **sacrum confined tending-towards** a **wooden stump**.
Entering tending-towards a **shady gully**.
Three year's-time not encountering.

Comments
Entering tending-towards a **shady gully**.
Shady, not bright indeed.

Fields of meaning

Sacrum, *TUN*: lower back, buttocks, lower spine; bottom. **Confine**, *KUN*: see *Image of the Situation*. **Tend-towards**, *YU*: move toward without necessarily reaching, in the direction of. **Wood/tree**, *MU*: trees and all things woody or wooden; associated with the Wooden Moment; wood and wind are the Symbols of the trigram Ground, *SUN*. Ideogram: a tree with roots and branches. **Stump**, *ZHU*: trunk, bole, stalk; wooden post; keep down, degrade. **Enter**, *RU*: penetrate, go into, enter on, encroach on; progress; put into; Action of the trigram Root, *SUN*. **Shady**, *YOU*: retired, solitary, secret, hidden from view; dark, obscure, occult, mysterious; ignorant. Ideogram: small within hill, a cave or grotto. **Gully**, *GU*: valley, ravine, river bed, gap. Ideogram: divide and river, a river bed separating hills. **Three/thrice**, *SAN*: number three; third time or place; active phases of a cycle; superlative; beginning of repetition (since one and two are entities in themselves). **Year's-time**, *SUI*: duration of a year; beginning of a year. **Not**, *BU*: common term of negation. **Encounter**, *DI*: see face to face; visit, interview.

Brightness, *MING*: light, radiance, clarity; distinguish, discern, understand; light-giving aspect of fire, of heavenly bodies and of consciousness; brightness and fire are the Symbols of the trigram Radiance, *LI*. **Indeed**, *YE*: see *Hexagrams in Pairs*.

Nine at Second

Confinement tending-towards liquor taking-in.
Scarlet sashes on all **sides coming**.
Harvesting: **availing** of **presenting oblations**.
Disciplining, **pitfall**.
Without fault.

Comments
Confinement tending-towards liquor taking-in.
The **center possesses reward indeed**.

Fields of meaning

Confine, *KUN*: see *Image of the Situation*. **Tend-towards**, *YU*: move toward without necessarily reaching, in the direction of. **Liquor**, *JIU*: alcoholic beverages, distilled spirits; spirit which perfects the good and evil in human nature. Ideogram: liquid above fermenting must, separating the spirits. **Take-in**, *SHI*: eat, drink, ingest, absorb, incorporate; food, nourishment. **Scarlet**, *ZHU*: vivid red signifying honor, luck, marriage, riches, literary accomplishment; culmination of the Wooden Moment. **Sash**, *FU*: ceremonial belt of official which holds seal of office. **Sides**, *FANG*: cardinal directions; surface of the earth extending to the four cardinal points; everywhere; limits, boundaries. **Come**, *LAI*: approach in time or space; move toward, arrive at; future; contrasts with go, *WANG*, move away or become past. **Harvest**, *LI*: benefit, advantage, profit; realization; sharp, acute, insightful; quality of autumn and West, third stage of the Time Cycle. Ideogram: ripe grain and blade. **Avail**, *YONG*: use, employ for a specific purpose; take advantage of; benefit from; capacity. Ideogram: to divine and center, applying divination to central concerns. **Present**, *XIANG*: offer in sacrifice, give to the gods or a superior; give a banquet; accept an offering; enjoy, receive. **Oblations**, *SI*: sacrifices offered to the gods and the dead. **Discipline**, *ZHENG*: subjugate vassals, reduce to order; punishing expedition. Ideogram: step and correct, a rectifying move. **Pitfall**, *XIONG*: unfortunate situation, in which the flow of life and spirit is blocked and the experience of meaning is lost; stuck and exposed to danger; inappropriate attitude. Ideogram: person in a pit. **Without fault**, *WU JIU*: see *Image of the Situation*.

Center, *ZHONG*: inner, central; put in the center; middle, stable point enabling you to face inner and outer changes; middle line of a trigram. Ideogram: field divided in two equal parts. **Possess**, *YOU*: see *Image of the Situation*. **Reward**, *QING*: gift given out of gratitude or benevolence; favor from heaven. Ideogram: heart, follow and deer, the heart expressed through the gift of a deer's skin. **Indeed**, *YE*: see *Hexagrams in Pairs*.

SIX AT THIRD

Confinement tending-towards petrification.
Seizing tending-towards star thistles.
Entering tending-towards one's house.
Not viewing one's consort.
Pitfall.

Comments
Seizing tending-towards star thistles.
Riding a **solid indeed.**
Entering tending-towards one's house.
Not viewing one's consort.
Not auspicious indeed.

Fields of meaning

Confine, *KUN*: see *Image of the Situation*. **Tend-towards**, *YU*: move toward without necessarily reaching, in the direction of. **Petrify**, *SHI*: become stone or stony; rocks, stones; firm, decided; barren, sterile. Seize, *JU*: lay hands on, lean on, rely on; maintain, become concrete; testimony, evidence. Star thistles, *JI LI*: spiny weeds; caltrops, metal snares. Enter, *RU*: penetrate, go into, enter on, encroach on; progress; put into; Action of the trigram Root, *SUN*. One/one's, *QI*: general third person pronoun and possessive adjective; also: it/its, he/his, she/her, they/their. House, *GONG*: residence, mansion; surround; fence, walls, roof. Not, *BU*: common term of negation. View, *JIAN*: vision in all its aspects: seeing, being visible, forming mental images; visit, call on, consult. Ideogram: eye above person, active and receptive sight. Consort, *QI*: official partner; legal status of married woman (first wife); distinct from wife, *FU*, which indicates her role as head of the household, and from concubine, *QIE*, secondary wife. Pitfall, *XIONG*: unfortunate situation, in which the flow of life and spirit is blocked and the experience of meaning is lost; stuck and exposed to danger; inappropriate attitude. Ideogram: person in a pit.

Ride, *CHENG*: ride an animal or a chariot; have the upper hand, control a stronger power; an opened line above controlling a whole line below. Solid, *GANG*: quality of the whole lines; firm, strong, unyielding, persisting. Indeed, *YE*: see *Hexagrams in Pairs*. Auspicious, *XIANG*: auspices of good luck and prosperity; sign, omen (good or bad).

NINE AT FOURTH

Coming: ambling, ambling.
Confinement tending-towards a **metallic chariot.**
Abashment.
Possessing completion.

Comments
Coming: ambling, ambling.
Purpose located below indeed.
Although not an **appropriate position, possessing associates indeed.**

Fields of meaning

Come, *LAI*: approach in time or space; move toward, arrive at; future; contrasts with go, *WANG*, move away or become past. Amble, *XU*: walk quietly and carefully, leisurely, tardy, slow; composed, dignified. Confine, *KUN*: see *Image of the Situation*. Tend-towards, *YU*: move toward without necessarily reaching, in the direction of. Metal, *JIN*: all metals, particularly gold; smelting and casting; perfection, richness; autumn, West, sunset; one of the Five Transformative

Moments. **Chariot**, *CHE*: cart, wheeled traveling vehicle. **Abashment**, *LIN*: distress, shame, regret, humiliation; aware of having lost the right track; leads to repenting, *HUI*, correcting the direction of mind and life. **Possess**, *YOU*: see *Image of the Situation*. **Complete**, *ZHONG*: completion of a cycle that begins the next; entire, whole, all. Ideogram: silk cocoons, follow and ice, winter linking one year with the next.

Purpose, *ZHI*: see *Patterns of Wisdom*. **Locate**, *ZAI*: be at, be situated at, dwell, reside; in, within; involved with, in the process of. Ideogram: earth and persevere, a place on the earth. **Below**, *XIA*: anything below, in all senses; lower, inner; lower trigram. **Indeed**, *YE*: see *Hexagrams in Pairs*. **Although**, *SUI*: even though, supposing that, if, even if. **Not**, *BU*: common term of negation. **Appropriate**, *DANG*: suitable, capable, worthy, adequate, competent, equal to; opportune, convenient; whole lines in odd places and opened lines in even places. **Position**, *WEI*: place, location; be at; social standing, rank; position of a line in a hexagram. Ideogram: person standing. **Associate**, *YU*: consort with, combine; companions; group, band, company; agree with, comply, help; in favor of. Ideogram: a pair of hands reaching downward meets a pair of hands reaching upward, helpful association.

NINE AT FIFTH

Nose-cut, foot-cut.
Confinement tending-towards a **crimson sash.**
Thereupon ambling possesses stimulating.
Harvesting: availing of **offering oblations.**

Comments
Nose-cut, foot-cut.
Purpose not-yet acquired indeed.
Thereupon ambling possesses stimulating.
Using the **center: straightening indeed.**
Harvesting: availing of **offering oblations.**
Acquiescing in **blessing indeed.**

Fields of meaning

Nose-cutting, *YI*: punishment through loss of public face or honor; distinct from foot-cutting, *YE*, crippling punishment for serious crime. **Foot-cutting**, *YUEH*: crippling punishment for serious crimes. **Confine**, *KUN*: see *Image of the Situation*. **Tend-towards**, *YU*: move toward without necessarily reaching, in the direction of. **Crimson**, *CHI*: color associated with the Fiery Moment, the South and the bursting phase of Yang; ardent, burning; naked, barren; color of new-born child, of drunkenness and of anger; also: sign of official rank. **Sash**, *FU*: ceremonial belt of official which holds seal of office. **Thereupon**, *NAI*: on that ground, then, only then; finally; in spite of that. **Amble**, *XU*: walk quietly and carefully, leisurely, tardy, slow; composed, dignified. **Possess**, *YOU*: see *Image of the Situation*. **Stimulate**, *SHUO*: rouse to action and good feeling; stir up, urge on; exhort, persuade; say, tell, relate; cheer, delight; joyous, peaceful, restful; Action of the trigram Open, *DUI*. Ideogram: words and exchange. **Harvest**, *LI*: benefit, advantage, profit; realization; sharp, acute, insightful; quality of autumn and West, third stage of the Time Cycle. Ideogram: ripe grain and blade. **Avail**, *YONG*: use, employ for a specific purpose; take advantage of; benefit from; capacity. Ideogram: to divine and center, applying divination to central concerns. **Offer**, *JI*: offer a sacrifice. Ideogram: hand, meat and worship. **Oblations**, *SI*: sacrifices offered to the gods and the dead.

Purpose, *ZHI*: see *Patterns of Wisdom*. **Not-yet**, *WEI*: temporal negative indicating that something is expected to happen but has not yet occurred. **Acquire**, *DE*: obtain the desired object; possession; satisfied, fulfilled; it is permitted; agree with; wish for, desire covetously. Ideogram: go and obstacle, going through obstacles to the goal. **Indeed**, *YE*: see *Hexagrams in Pairs*. **Acquiesce**, *SHOU*: accept, make peace with, agree to, receive; at rest, satisfied; patient. **Bless**, *FU*: heavenly gifts and favor; happiness, prosperity; spiritual power and goodwill. Ideogram: spirit and plenty.

SIX ABOVE

䷮

Confinement tending-towards trailing creepers.
Tending-towards the **unsteady** and **unsettled.**
Named: stirring-up repenting possesses repenting.
Disciplining, significant.

Comments
Confinement tending-towards trailing creepers.
Not-yet appropriate indeed.
Stirring-up repenting possesses repenting.
Significant, moving indeed.

Fields of meaning

Confine, *KUN*: see *Image of the Situation*. **Tend-towards**, *YU*: move toward without necessarily reaching, in the direction of. **Trailing creeper**, *GE LEI*: lush, fast-growing plants; spread rapidly and widely; numerous progeny. **Unsteady** and

unsettled, *NIE WU*: unstable; uncertain; agitated. **Name**, *YUE*: speak, declare, call. Ideogram: open mouth and tongue. **Stir-up**, *DONG*: excite, influence, move, affect; work, take action; come out of the egg or the bud; Action of the trigram Shake, *ZHEN*. Ideogram: strength and heavy, move weighty things. **Repent**, *HUI*: regret, dissatisfaction with past conduct inducing a change of heart; proceeds from abashment, *LIN*, shame and confusion at having lost the right way. **Possess**, *YOU*: see *Image of the Situation*. **Discipline**, *ZHENG*: subjugate vassals, reduce to order; punishing expedition. Ideogram: step and correct, a rectifying move. **Significant**, *JI*: see *Image of the Situation*.

Not-yet, *WEI*: temporal negative indicating that something is expected to happen but has not yet occurred. **Appropriate**, *DANG*: suitable, capable, worthy, adequate, competent, equal to; opportune, convenient; whole lines in odd places and opened lines in even places. **Indeed**, *YE*: see *Hexagrams in Pairs*. **Move**, *XING*: move or move something; motivate; emotionally moving; walk, act, do. Ideogram: successive steps.

Image Tradition

Confinement.
The **solid enshrouded indeed**.
Venturing uses stimulating.
Confinement and-also not letting-go one's place:
Growing.

One's very jun zi reached.
Trial: the **great** in the **person**, **significant**.
Using the **solid** in the **center indeed**.
Possessing words not trustworthy.
Honoring the **mouth thereupon exhausted indeed**.

Fields of meaning

Confine, *KUN*: see *Image of the Situation*. **Solid**, *GANG*: quality of the whole lines; firm, strong, unyielding, persisting. **Enshroud**, *YAN*: screen, shade from view, hide, cover. Ideogram: hand and cover. **Indeed**, *YE*: see *Hexagrams in Pairs*. **Venture**, *XIAN*: face a severe difficulty or obstruction; risk; precipice, cliff, abyss; key point, point of danger; Action of the trigram Gorge, *KAN*. Ideogram: mound and all, everything engaged at one point. **Use**, *YI*: see *Additional Texts*. **Stimulate**, *SHUO*: rouse to action and good feeling; stir up, urge on; exhort, persuade; say, tell, relate; cheer, delight; joyous, peaceful, restful; Action of the trigram Open, *DUI*. Ideogram: words and exchange. **And-also**, *ER*: see *Preceding Situation*. **Not**, *BU*:

common term of negation. **Let-go**, *SHI*: lose, let slip; omit, miss, fail; lose control of. Ideogram: drop from the hand. **One/one's**, *QI*: general third person pronoun and possessive adjective; also: it/its, he/his, she/her, they/their. **Place**, *SUO*: position, location; residence, dwelling; where something belongs or comes from; habitual focus or object. **Grow**, *HENG*: see *Image of the Situation*.

Very/verily, *WEI*: the only; in truth; answer; acquiesce; yes. **Jun zi**: see *Patterns of Wisdom*. **Reach**, *HU*: arrive at a goal; move toward and achieve; to, at, in; distinct from tend-towards, *YOU*. **Trial**: the **great** in the **person**, **significant**, *ZHEN DA REN JI*: see *Image of the Situation*. **Center**, *ZHONG*: inner, central; put in the center; middle, stable point enabling you to face inner and outer changes; middle line of a trigram. Ideogram: field divided in two equal parts. **Possessing words not trustworthy**, *YOU YAN BU XIN*: see *Image of the Situation*. **Honor**, *SHANG*: esteem, give high rank to, exalt, celebrate; rise, elevate; put one thing on top of another. **Mouth**, *KOU*: mouth, mouthful; words going out and food coming into the mouth; entrance, hole, passageway. **Thereupon**, *NAI*: on that ground, then, only then; finally; in spite of that. **Exhaust**, *QIONG*: see *Additional Texts*.

48 THE WELL | *Jing*

The situation described by this hexagram is characterized by the waters of life welling up from the depth. Maintaining a clear access to this central life source is crucial for one's well-being and nourishment.

Image of the Situation

> The **well**.
> **Amending** the **capital**, **not amending** the **well**.
> **Without losing**, **without acquiring**.
> **Going**, **coming**: **welling**, **welling**.
> **Muddy culmination**: **truly not-yet** the **well-rope** in the **well**.
> **Ruining one's pitcher**: **pitfall**.

Fields of meaning

Well, *JING*: water well at the center of the fields; rise and flow of water in a well; life-water surging from the depths; found a capital city. Ideogram: two vertical lines crossing two horizontal ones, eight fields with equal access to a well at the center. **Amend**, *GAI*: correct, reform, renew, alter, mend. Ideogram: self and strike, fighting one's own errors. **Capital**, *YI*: populous fortified city, center and symbol of the region it rules. Ideogram: enclosure and official seal. **Not**, *BU*: common term of negation. **Without**, *WU*: devoid of; there is not. **Lose**, *SANG*: be deprived of, forget; destruction, ruin, death; corpse; lament, mourn; funeral. Ideogram: weep and dead. **Acquire**, *DE*: obtain the desired object; possession; satisfied, fulfilled; it is permitted; agree with; wish for, desire covetously. Ideogram: go and obstacle, going through obstacles to the goal. **Go**, *WANG*: move away in time or space, depart; become past; dead, gone; contrasts with come, *LAI*, approach in time or space. **Come**, *LAI*: approach in time or space; move toward, arrive at; future; contrasts with go, *WANG*, move away or become past. **Mud**, *XI*: ground left wet by water, muddy shores; danger; shed tears; nearly. **Culminate**, *ZHI*: bring to the highest degree; arrive at the end or summit; superlative; reaching one's goal. **Truly**, *YI*: in fact; also; nevertheless. **Not-yet**, *WEI*: temporal negative indicating that something is expected to happen but has not yet occurred. **Well-rope**, *YU*: rope used to draw water. **Ruin**, *LEI*: destroy, break, overturn; debilitated, meager, emaciated; entangled. **One/one's**, *QI*: general third person pronoun and possessive adjective; also: it/its, he/his, she/her, they/their. **Pitcher**, *PING*: clay jug or vase. **Pitfall**, *XIONG*: unfortunate situation, in which the flow of life and spirit is blocked and the experience of meaning is lost; stuck and exposed to danger; inappropriate attitude. Ideogram: person in a pit.

Outer and Inner Trigram

The upper trigram, **Gorge**, *KAN*, describes the outer aspects of the situation. It has the following associations: precipice, dangerous place; hole, cavity, pit, snare, trap, grave; critical time, test; risky. Ideogram: earth and cavity. *Symbol*: stream, *SHUI*, flowing water; river, tide, flood; fluid, dissolving. Ideogram: rippling water. *Actions*: venture and fall. Venture, *XIAN*: face a severe difficulty or obstruction; risk; precipice, cliff, abyss; key point, point of danger. Ideogram: mound and all, everything engaged at one point. Fall, *XIAN*: fall down or into, sink, drop, descend; pit, trap, fault; falling water. In the family of trigrams *KAN* is the middle son.

The lower trigram, **Root**, *SUN*, describes the inner aspects of the situation. It has the following associations: base on which things rest, ground, foundation; mild, subtly penetrating; nourishing. *Symbols*: tree/wood and wind. Tree/wood, *MU*: trees and all things woody or wooden; associated with the Wooden Moment. Ideogram: a tree with roots and branches. Wind, *FENG*: wind, breeze, gust; weather and its influence on mood and humor; fashion, usage. *Action*: enter, *RU*, penetrate, go into, enter on, encroach on; progress; put into. In the family of trigrams *SUN* is the eldest daughter.

Counter Hexagram

The Counter Hexagram of **The Well** is hexagram 38, **Polarizing**, which switches the emphasis from the centrality and general availability of **The Well** to a polar opposition.

Preceding Situation

> **Confinement reaching above implies necessarily reversing** to the **below**.
> To **anterior acquiescence belongs** the **use** of the **well**.

Fields of meaning

Confine, *KUN*: enclose, restrict, limit, oppress; impoverished, distressed, afflicted, exhausted, disheartened, weary. Ideogram: tree in a narrow enclosure. **Reach**, *HU*:

arrive at a goal; move toward and achieve; to, at, in; distinct from tend-towards, *YOU*. **Above**, *SHANG*: anything above in all senses; higher, upper, outer; upper trigram. **Imply**, *ZHE*: further signify; additional meaning. **Necessarily**, *BI*: unavoidably, certainly. **Reverse**, *FAN*: turn and move in the opposite direction; turn around or upside down (180 degrees); change to the opposite position; contrary. **Below**, *XIA*: anything below, in all senses; lower, inner; lower trigram. To **anterior acquiescence belongs** the **use** of, *GU SHOU ZHI YI*: understanding and accepting the preceding statement allows the consultant to make proper use of this hexagram. **Well**, *JING*: see *Image of the Situation*.

Hexagrams in Pairs

The **well**: **interpenetrating**, **and-also**
confinement: **reciprocal meeting indeed**.

Fields of meaning
Well, *JING*: see *Image of the Situation*. **Interpenetrate**, *TONG*: penetrate freely and reciprocally, permeate, flow through, open a way; see clearly, understand deeply; communicate with; together. **And-also**, *ER*: joins and contrasts two terms. **Confine**, *KUN*: see *Preceding Situation*. **Reciprocal**, *XIANG*: mutual; assist, encourage, help; bring together, blend with; examine, inspect; by turns. **Meet**, *YU*: come on unexpectedly, encounter; occur, happen; pleasant meeting, lucky coincidence; agree. **Indeed**, *YE*: emphasizes and intensifies the previous statement.

Additional Texts

The **well**: **actualizing-dao belonging** to **earth indeed**.
The **well**: **residing** in **one's place and-also shifting**.
The **well**: **using differentiating righteously**.

Fields of meaning
Well, *JING*: see *Image of the Situation*. **Actualize-dao**, *DE*: realize dao in action; power, virtue; ability to follow the course traced by the ongoing process of the cosmos. Ideogram: go, straight, and heart. Linked with acquire, *DE*: acquiring that which makes a being become what it is meant to be. **Belong/it**, *ZHI*: establishes between two terms a connection similar to the Saxon genitive, in which the second term belongs to the first one; at the end of a sentence it refers to something previously mentioned or implied. **Earth**, *DI*: the earth, ground on which the human world rests; basis of all things, nourishes all things; essential Yin; Symbol of the trigram Space, *KUN*. **Indeed**, *YE*: see *Hexagrams in Pairs*.

Reside, *JU*: dwell, live in, stay; sit down; fill an office; well-being, rest. Ideogram: body and seat. **One/one's**, *QI*: see *Image of the Situation*. **Place**, *SUO*: position, location; residence, dwelling; where something belongs or comes from; habitual focus or object. **And-also**, *ER*: see *Hexagrams in Pairs*. **Shift**, *QIAN*: move, change, transpose; improve, ascend, be promoted; deport, dismiss, remove. **Use**, *YI*: by means of; owing to; make use of, employ. **Differentiate**, *BIAN*: argue, dispute, criticize; sophisticated, artful. Ideogram: words and sharp or pungent. **Righteous**, *YI*: proper, just, virtuous, upright; the heart that rules itself; benevolent, loyal, devoted to public good.

Patterns of Wisdom

Wood possesses stream above. The **well**.
A **jun zi uses** the **toiling commoners** to **encourage reciprocity**.

Fields of meaning

Wood/tree, *MU*: trees and all things woody or wooden; associated with the Wooden Moment; wood and wind are the Symbols of the trigram Ground, *SUN*. Ideogram: a tree with roots and branches. **Possess**, *YOU*: general term indicating possession; have, own, be endowed with. **Stream**, *SHUI*: flowing water; river, tide, flood; fluid, dissolving; Symbol of the trigram Gorge, *KAN*. Ideogram: rippling water. **Above**, *SHANG*: see *Preceding Situation*. **Well**, *JING*: see *Image of the Situation*. **Jun zi**: ideal of a person who orders his/her life in accordance with dao rather than willful intention, and uses divination in this spirit. **Use**, *YI*: see *Additional Texts*. **Toil**, *LAO*: hardship, labor; exert oneself, exhaust oneself; burdened, careworn; worthy actions. Ideogram: strength and fire. **Commoners**, *MIN*: common people, masses; working class supporting the social hierarchy; undeveloped potential in the individual. **Encourage**, *CHUAN*: exhort, stimulate; advise, persuade; admonish. **Reciprocal**, *XIANG*: see *Hexagrams in Pairs*.

Transforming Lines

Initial Six

The **well**: a **bog**, **not taking-in**.
The **ancient well without wildfowl**.

Comments
The **well**: a **bog**, **not taking-in**.
Below indeed.

The **ancient well without wildfowl**.
The **season stowed** away **indeed**.

Fields of meaning

Well, *JING*: see *Image of the Situation*. **Bog**, *NI*: wet spongy soil; mire, slush, quicksand; unable to move. **Not**, *BU*: common term of negation. **Take-in**, *SHI*: eat, drink, ingest, absorb, incorporate; food, nourishment. **Ancient**, *JIU*: of old, long before; worn out, spoiled; defunct. **Without**, *WU*: see *Image of the Situation*. **Wildfowl**, *QIN*: birds; four-legged animals; hunt, shoot with an arrow; capture; prisoner.

Below, *XIA*: see *Preceding Situation*. **Indeed**, *YE*: see *Hexagrams in Pairs*. **Season**, *SHI*: quality of the time; the right time, opportune, in harmony; planning in accord with the time; season of the year. Ideogram: sun and temple, sacred time. **Stow**, *SHE*: set aside, put away, store, keep; halt, rest in; lodge, hut.

Nine at Second

The **well**: a **gully**, **shooting bass**.
The **jug cracked**, **leaking**.

Comments
The **well**: a **gully**, **shooting bass**.
Without associates indeed.

Fields of meaning

Well, *JING*: see *Image of the Situation*. **Gully**, *GU*: valley, ravine, river bed, gap. Ideogram: divide and river, a river bed separating hills. **Shoot**, *SHE*: shoot an arrow; archer; project, eject, spurt, issue forth; glance at; scheme for. Ideogram: arrow and body. **Bass**, *FU*: freshwater fish moving in pairs, mutually faithful. **Jug**, *WENG*: earthen jar; jug used to draw water. **Cracked**, *BI*: broken, ruined, tattered; unfit, unworthy. Ideogram: strike and break. **Leak**, *LOU*: seep, drip, ooze out; reveal; forget, let slip.

Without, *WU*: see *Image of the Situation*. **Associate**, *YU*: consort with, combine; companions; group, band, company; agree with, comply, help; in favor of. Ideogram: a pair of hands reaching downward meets a pair of hands reaching upward, helpful association. **Indeed**, *YE*: see *Hexagrams in Pairs*.

NINE AT THIRD

The well: oozing, not taking-in.
Activating my heart's ache.
Permitting availing of **drawing-water**.
Kingly brightness.
Together acquiescing in **one's blessing**.

Comments
The **well**: **oozing**, **not taking-in**.
Moving, **aching indeed**.
Seeking kingly brightness.
Acquiescing in **blessing indeed**.

Fields of meaning
Well, *JING*: see *Image of the Situation*. **Ooze**, *DIE*: exude moisture; mud, slime; turbid, tainted. **Not**, *BU*: common term of negation. **Take-in**, *SHI*: eat, drink, ingest, absorb, incorporate; food, nourishment. **Activate**, *WEI*: act or cause to act; do, make, manage, make active; be, become; attend to, help; because of. **I/me/my**, *WO*: first person pronoun; the use of a specific personal pronoun, as opposed to the generic one's, *QI*, indicates an unusually strong emphasis on personal involvement. **Heart**, *XIN*: the heart as center of being; seat of mind, imagination and affect; moral nature; source of desires, intentions, will. **Ache**, *CE*: acute pain or grief; pity, sympathy, sorrow, grief. **Permit**, *KE*: possible because in harmony with an inherent principle; capable of; approve, authorize. Ideogram: mouth and breath, silent consent. **Avail**, *YONG*: use, employ for a specific purpose; take advantage of; benefit from; capacity. Ideogram: to divine and center, applying divination to central concerns. **Draw-water**, *JI*: draw water from a well; draw forth, lead; assimilate a doctrine or an example. Ideogram: water and reach to. **King**, *WANG*: sovereign, effective ruler, emperor, seen as connecting heaven and earth; reign, govern. **Brightness**, *MING*: light, radiance, clarity; distinguish, discern, understand; light-giving aspect of fire, of heavenly bodies and of consciousness; brightness and fire are the Symbols of the trigram Radiance, *LI*. **Together**, *BING*: both at the same time, jointly, side to side. Ideogram: two people standing together. **Acquiesce**, *SHOU*: accept, make peace with, agree to, receive; at rest, satisfied; patient. **One/one's**, *QI*: see *Image of the Situation*. **Bless**, *FU*: heavenly gifts and favor; happiness, prosperity; spiritual power and goodwill. Ideogram: spirit and plenty.

Move, *XING*: move or move something; motivate; emotionally moving; walk, act, do. Ideogram: successive steps. **Indeed**, *YE*: see *Hexagrams in Pairs*. **Seek**, *QIU*: search for, aim at, wish for, desire; implore, supplicate; covetous.

Six at Fourth

The **well**: **lining**, **without fault**.

Comments

The **well**: **lining**, **without fault**.
Adjusting the **well indeed**.

Fields of meaning

Well, *JING*: see *Image of the Situation*. **Line**, *COU*: line or repair a well; masonry lining the inside of a well. **Without fault**, *WU JIU*: no error or harm in the situation.

Adjust, *XIU*: regulate, repair, clean up, renovate. **Indeed**, *YE*: see *Hexagrams in Pairs*.

Nine at Fifth

The **well**: **limpid**.
Cold springwater taken-in.

Comments

To **cold springwater belongs taking-in**.
The **center correct indeed**.

Fields of meaning

Well, *JING*: see *Image of the Situation*. **Limpid**, *LIE*: pure, clear, clean liquid; wash clean. **Cold**, *HAN*: chilled, wintry; destitute, poor; shiver; fear; associated with the Streaming Moment. Ideogram: person huddled in straw under a roof. **Springwater**, *QUAN*: source, spring, fountain, headwaters of a river. Ideogram: water and white, pure water at the source. **Take-in**, *SHI*: eat, drink, ingest, absorb, incorporate; food, nourishment.

Belong/it, *ZHI*: see *Additional Texts*. **Center**, *ZHONG*: inner, central; put in the center; middle, stable point enabling you to face inner and outer changes; middle line of a trigram. Ideogram: field divided in two equal parts. **Correct**, *ZHENG*: rectify deviation or one-sidedness; proper, straight, exact, regular; constant, rule, model. Ideogram: stop and one, hold to one thing. **Indeed**, *YE*: see *Hexagrams in Pairs*.

SIX ABOVE

The **well**: **collecting**, **no cover**.
Possessing conformity: **Spring**, **significant**.

Comments
Spring, **significance located above**.
The **great accomplishes indeed**.

Fields of meaning
Well, *JING*: see *Image of the Situation*. **Collect**, *SHOU*: gather, harvest; receive what is due; involve, snare, bind, restrain. **No**, *WU*: common term of negation. **Cover**, *MU*: canvas covering; tent, screen, tarpaulin. **Possess**, *YOU*: see *Patterns of Wisdom*. **Conform**, *FU*: accord between inner and outer; sincere, truthful, verified, reliable; capture; prisoners, spoils. Ideogram: claws over child, a bird brooding on the nest. **Spring**, *YUAN*: source, origin, head; arise, begin; first generating impulse; great, excellent; quality of springtime and East, first stage of the Time Cycle. **Significant**, *JI*: leads to the experience of meaning; favorable, propitious, appropriate. Ideogram: scholar and mouth, wise words of a sage.

Locate, *ZAI*: be at, be situated at, dwell, reside; in, within; involved with, in the process of. Ideogram: earth and persevere, a place on the earth. **Above**, *SHANG*: see *Preceding Situation*. **Great**, *DA*: big, noble, important, very; orient the will toward a self-imposed goal, impose direction; ability to lead or guide one's life; contrasts with small, *XIAO*, flexible adaptation to what crosses one's path. **Accomplish**, *CHENG*: complete, finish, bring about; perfect, full, whole; play one's part, do one's duty; mature. Ideogram: weapon and man, able to bear arms, thus fully developed. **Indeed**, *YE*: see *Hexagrams in Pairs*.

Image Tradition

Root reaching stream and-also stream above. The **well**.
The **well**: **nourishing and-also not exhausted indeed**.

Amending the **capital**, **not amending** the **well**.
Thereupon using the **solid** in the **center indeed**.

Muddy culmination: **truly not-yet** the **well-rope** in the **well**.
Not-yet possessing achievement indeed.
Ruining one's pitcher: **that uses** a **pitfall indeed**.

Fields of meaning

Root, *SUN*: base on which things rest, ground, foundation; mild, subtly penetrating; nourishing. **Reach**, *HU*: see *Preceding Situation*. **Stream**, *SHUI*: see *Patterns of Wisdom*. **And-also**, *ER*: see *Hexagrams in Pairs*. **Above**, *SHANG*: see *Preceding Situation*. **Well**, *JING*: see *Image of the Situation*. **Nourish**, *YANG*: feed, sustain, support, provide, care for; generate; raise, grow. **Not**, *BU*: common term of negation. **Exhaust**, *QIONG*: bring to an end; limit, extremity; investigate exhaustively; destitute, indigent; end without a new beginning; distinct from complete, *ZHONG*, end of a cycle that begins the next one. Ideogram: cave and naked person, bent with disease or old age. **Indeed**, *YE*: see *Hexagrams in Pairs*.

Amending the **capital**, *GAI YI*: see *Image of the Situation*. **Thereupon**, *NAI*: on that ground, then, only then; finally; in spite of that. **Use**, *YI*: see *Additional Texts*. **Solid**, *GANG*: quality of the whole lines; firm, strong, unyielding, persisting. **Center**, *ZHONG*: inner, central; put in the center; middle, stable point enabling you to face inner and outer changes; middle line of a trigram. Ideogram: field divided in two equal parts.

Muddy culmination: **truly not-yet** the **well-rope** in the **well**, *XI ZHI YI WEI YU JING*: see *Image of the Situation*. **Possess**, *YOU*: see *Patterns of Wisdom*. **Achieve**, *GONG*: work done, results, actual accomplishment; praise, worth, merit. Ideogram: workman's square and forearm, combining craft and strength. **Ruining one's pitcher**, *LEI QI PING*: see *Image of the Situation*. **That**, *SHI*: refers to the preceding statement. **Pitfall**, *XIONG*: see *Image of the Situation*.

革

49 SKINNING | *Ge*

The situation described by this hexagram is characterized by radically renewing one's presentation, peeling away an old skin which is no longer adequate.

Image of the Situation

Skinning.
Before-zenith sun, thereupon conforming.
Spring, Growing, Harvesting, Trial.
Repenting extinguished.

Fields of meaning

Skin, *GE*: human or animal skin; hide, leather; armor, protection; peel off, remove the covering, skin or hide; change, renew, molt; overthrow, degrade from office. **Before-zenith sun**, *SSU RI*: double hour from 9 to 11 a.m. and month of June, both symbolized by the serpent; about to, on the point of. **Sun/day**, *RI*: actual sun and the time of a sun-cycle, a day. **Thereupon**, *NAI*: on that ground, then, only then; finally; in spite of that. **Conform**, *FU*: accord between inner and outer; sincere, truthful, verified, reliable; capture; prisoners, spoils. Ideogram: claws over child, a bird brooding on the nest. **Spring, Growing, Harvesting, Trial**, *YUAN HENG LI ZHEN*: Spring, Growing, Harvesting and Trial are the four stages of the Time Cycle, the model for all dynamic processes. They indicate that your question is connected to the cycle as a whole rather than a part of it. **Repenting extinguished**, *HUI WANG*: previous errors are corrected, all causes for repenting disappear.

Outer and Inner Trigram

The upper trigram, **Open**, *DUI*, describes the outer aspects of the situation. It has the following associations: an open surface, promoting interaction and interpenetration; pleasant, easy, responsive, free, unhindered; opening, passage; the mouth; exchange, barter; straight, direct; meet, gather; place where water accumulates. Ideogram: mouth and vapor, communication through speech. *Symbol:*

marsh, *ZE*, open surface of a flat body of water and the vapors rising from it; fertilize, enrich; kindness, favor. *Action*: stimulate, *SHUO*, rouse to action and good feeling; stir up, urge on; exhort, persuade; say, tell, relate; cheer, delight; joyous, peaceful, restful. Ideogram: words and exchange. In the family of trigrams *DUI* is the youngest daughter.

The lower trigram, **Radiance**, *LI*, describes the inner aspects of the situation. It has the following associations: glowing light, spreading in all directions; the power of consciousness; discriminate, articulate, divide and arrange in order; assemble, attract. Ideogram: bird and weird, magical fire-bird with brilliant plumage. *Symbols*: fire and brightness. Fire, *HUO*: flame, burn; warming and consuming aspect of burning. Brightness, *MING*: light, radiance, clarity; distinguish, discern, understand; light-giving aspect of fire, of heavenly bodies and of consciousness. *Action*: congregate, *LI*, cling together, adhere to, rely on; couple, pair, herd; beautiful, elegant. Ideogram: deer flocking together. In the family of trigrams *LI* is the middle daughter.

Counter Hexagram

The Counter Hexagram of **Skinning** is hexagram 44, **Coupling**, which switches the emphasis from the renewal impulse of **Skinning** to the reproductive drive powered by the attraction of primal Yin and Yang.

Preceding Situation

The **well**'s **dao not permitting not skinning**.
To **anterior acquiescence belongs** the **use** of **skinning**.

Fields of meaning

Well, *JING*: water well at the center of the fields; rise and flow of water in a well; life-water surging from the depths; found a capital city. Ideogram: two vertical lines crossing two horizontal ones, eight fields with equal access to a well at the center. Dao, *DAO*: way or path; ongoing process of being and the course it traces for each person or thing; ultimate reality, intrinsic nature; origin. Ideogram: go and head, opening a path. **Not**, *BU*: common term of negation. **Permit**, *KE*: possible because in harmony with an inherent principle; capable of; approve, authorize. Ideogram: mouth and breath, silent consent. **Skin**, *GE*: see *Image of the Situation*. To **anterior acquiescence belongs** the **use** of, *GU SHOU ZHI YI*: understanding and accepting the preceding statement allows the consultant to make proper use of this hexagram.

Hexagrams in Pairs

> **Skinning**: **departing anteriority indeed**.
> The **vessel**: **grasping renewal indeed**.

Fields of meaning

Skin, *GE*: see *Image of the Situation*. **Depart**, *QU*: leave, quit, go; far away, far from; remove, reject, dismiss; lost, gone. **Anterior**, *GU*: come before as cause; former, ancient; reason, purpose, intention; grievance, dissatisfaction, sorrow, resulting from previous causes and intentions; situation leading to a divination. **Indeed**, *YE*: emphasizes and intensifies the previous statement. **Vessel**, *DING*: bronze cauldron with three feet and two ears, sacred vessel used to cook food for sacrifice to gods and ancestors; founding symbol of family or dynasty; hold, contain, transform; establish, secure; precious, noble. **Grasp**, *QU*: seize with effort, take and use, appropriate; take as a wife; grasp the meaning, understand. Ideogram: ear and hand, hear and grasp. **Renew**, *XIN*: new, novel, fresh, recent; restore, improve, correct.

Patterns of Wisdom

> The **pond** in the **center possesses fire**. **Skinning**.
> A **jun zi uses regulating** the **calendar** to **brighten** the **seasons**.

Fields of meaning

Pond, *ZE*: open surface of a flat body of water and the vapors rising from it; fertilize, enrich; kindness, favor; Symbol of the trigram Open, *DUI*. **Center**, *ZHONG*: inner, central; put in the center; middle, stable point enabling you to face inner and outer changes; middle line of a trigram. Ideogram: field divided in two equal parts. **Possess**, *YOU*: general term indicating possession; have, own, be endowed with. **Fire**, *HUO*: fire, flame, burn; warming and consuming aspect of burning; fire and brightness are the Symbols of the trigram Radiance, *LI*. **Skin**, *GE*: see *Image of the Situation*. **Jun zi**: ideal of a person who orders his/her life in accordance with dao rather than willful intention, and uses divination in this spirit. **Use**, *YI*: by means of; owing to; make use of, employ. **Regulate**, *ZHI*: govern well, ensure prosperity; arrange, remedy disorder, heal; fit to govern. **Calendar**, *LI*: reckon the course of heavenly bodies, astronomical events; establish the calendar. **Brightness**, *MING*: light, radiance, clarity; distinguish, discern, understand; light-giving aspect of fire, of heavenly bodies and of consciousness; brightness and fire are the Symbols of the trigram Radiance, *LI*. **Season**, *SHI*:

quality of the time; the right time, opportune, in harmony; planning in accord with the time; season of the year. Ideogram: sun and temple, sacred time.

Transforming Lines

Initial Nine

Thonging avails of **skin belonging** to **yellow cattle**.

Comments

Thonging avails of **yellow cattle**.

Not permitted to **use possessing activity indeed**.

Fields of meaning

Thong, *GONG*: bind with thongs, secure; solid, firm; well-guarded. **Avail**, *YONG*: use, employ for a specific purpose; take advantage of; benefit from; capacity. Ideogram: to divine and center, applying divination to central concerns. **Skin**, *GE*: see *Image of the Situation*. **Belong/it**, *ZHI*: establishes between two terms a connection similar to the Saxon genitive, in which the second term belongs to the first one; at the end of a sentence it refers to something previously mentioned or implied. **Yellow**, *HUANG*: color of the soil in central China, associated with the Earthy Moment leading from the Yang to the Yin hemicycle; emblematic and imperial color of China since the Yellow Emperor (2500 BC). **Cattle**, *NIU*: ox, bull, cow, calf; power and strength of work animals; stubborn.

Not, *BU*: common term of negation. **Permit**, *KE*: see *Preceding Situation*. **Possess**, *YOU*: see *Patterns of Wisdom*. **Activate**, *WEI*: act or cause to act; do, make, manage, make active; be, become; attend to, help; because of. **Indeed**, *YE*: see *Hexagrams in Pairs*.

Six at second

Before-zenith sun, **thereupon skinning it**.
Disciplining significant, **without fault**.

Comments

Before-zenith sun skinning it.

Moving possesses excellence indeed.

Fields of meaning

Before-zenith sun, *SSU RI*: see *Image of the Situation*. **Sun/day**, *RI*: see *Image of the Situation*. **Thereupon**, *NAI*: see *Image of the Situation*. **Skin**, *GE*: see *Image of* *the Situation*. **It/belong**, *ZHI*: establishes between two terms a connection similar to the Saxon genitive, in which the second term belongs to the first one; at the end of a sentence it refers to something previously mentioned or implied. **Discipline**, *ZHENG*: subjugate vassals, reduce to order; punishing expedition. Ideogram: step and correct, a rectifying move. **Significant**, *JI*: leads to the experience of meaning; favorable, propitious, appropriate. Ideogram: scholar and mouth, wise words of a sage. **Without fault**, *WU JIU*: no error or harm in the situation.

Move, *XING*: move or move something; motivate; emotionally moving; walk, act, do. Ideogram: successive steps. **Possess**, *YOU*: see *Patterns of Wisdom*. **Excellence**, *JIA*: superior quality; fine, beautiful, glorious; happy, pleased; rejoice in, praise. **Indeed**, *YE*: see *Hexagrams in Pairs*.

NINE AT THIRD

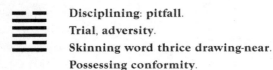

Disciplining: pitfall.
Trial, adversity.
Skinning word thrice drawing-near.
Possessing conformity.

Comments
Skinning word thrice drawing-near.
Furthermore is it actually?

Fields of meaning

Discipline, *ZHENG*: subjugate vassals, reduce to order; punishing expedition. Ideogram: step and correct, a rectifying move. **Pitfall**, *XIONG*: unfortunate situation, in which the flow of life and spirit is blocked and the experience of meaning is lost; stuck and exposed to danger; inappropriate attitude. Ideogram: person in a pit. **Trial**, *ZHEN*: inquiry by divination and its result; righteous, firm; separating wheat from chaff; the kernel, the proven core; quality of winter and North, fourth stage of the Time Cycle. Ideogram: pearl and divination. **Adversity**, *LI*: danger, hardship, severe; threat or difficulty that must be encountered, rather than avoided; grinding stone; polish, sharpen; a challenge that strengthens and perfects the character; stimulate, excite; cruel demon. **Skin**, *GE*: see *Image of the Situation*. **Word**, *YAN*: spoken word, speech, saying; talk, discuss, address; name, signify. Ideogram: mouth and rising vapor. **Three/thrice**, *SAN*: number three; third time or place; active phases of a cycle; superlative; beginning of repetition (since one and two are entities in themselves). **Draw-near**, *JIU*: approach; near completion; composed, finished; able, willing; shortly. **Possess**, *YOU*: see *Patterns* *of Wisdom.* **Conform,** *FU*: see *Image of the Situation.*

Furthermore, *YOU*: moreover; in addition to; again. **Is?,** *HE*: ask, inquire; what? which? who? how? why? where? an interrogative particle, often introducing a rhetorical question: is it? is it not? **It/belong,** *ZHI*: establishes between two terms a connection similar to the Saxon genitive, in which the second term belongs to the first one; at the end of a sentence it refers to something previously mentioned or implied. **Actually,** *YI*: truly, really, at present. Ideogram: a dart and done, strong intention fully expressed.

NINE AT FOURTH

Repenting extinguished, possessing conformity.
Amending fate, significant.

Comments
To **amending fate belongs significance.**
Trustworthy purpose indeed.

Fields of meaning

Repenting extinguished, *HUI WANG*: see *Image of the Situation.* **Possess,** *YOU*: see *Patterns of Wisdom.* **Conform,** *FU*: see *Image of the Situation.* **Amend,** *GAI*: correct, reform, renew, alter, mend. Ideogram: self and strike, fighting one's own errors. **Fate,** *MING*: individual destiny; birth and death as limits of life; issue orders with authority; consult the gods. Ideogram: mouth and order, words with heavenly authority. **Significant,** *JI*: leads to the experience of meaning; favorable, propitious, appropriate. Ideogram: scholar and mouth, wise words of a sage.

Belong/it, *ZHI*: establishes between two terms a connection similar to the Saxon genitive, in which the second term belongs to the first one; at the end of a sentence it refers to something previously mentioned or implied. **Trustworthy,** *XIN*: truthful, faithful, consistent over time; count on, confide in; examine, verify, prove; loyalty, integrity. Ideogram: person and word, true speech. **Purpose,** *ZHI*: focus of mind and heart; intention, will, inclination; continuity in the direction of life. Ideogram: heart and scholar, high inner resolve. **Indeed,** *YE*: see *Hexagrams in Pairs.*

NINE AT FIFTH

The **great** in the **person**: a **tiger transforming**.
Not-yet an **augury**, **possessing conformity**.

Comments
The **great** in the **person**: a **tiger transforming**.
One's pattern luminous indeed.

Fields of meaning
Great, *DA*: big, noble, important, very; orient the will toward a self-imposed goal, impose direction; ability to lead or guide one's life; contrasts with small, *XIAO*, flexible adaptation to what crosses one's path. **Person/people**, *REN*: humans individually and collectively; an individual; humankind. **Tiger**, *HU*: fierce king of animals; extreme Yang; opposed to and protecting against the demons of extreme Yin on the North–South axis of the Universal Compass. **Transform**, *BIAN*: abrupt, radical passage from one state to another; transformation of opened and whole lines into each other in hexagrams; contrasts with change, *HUA*, gradual mutation. **Not-yet**, *WEI*: temporal negative indicating that something is expected to happen but has not yet occurred. **Augury**, *ZHAN*: sign, omen; divine by casting lots; look at as a sign or augury. **Possess**, *YOU*: see *Patterns of Wisdom*. **Conform**, *FU*: see *Image of the Situation*.

One/one's, *QI*: general third person pronoun and possessive adjective; also: it/its, he/his, she/her, they/their. **Pattern**, *WEN*: intrinsic or natural design, pattern of wood, stone or animal fur; ideograms, the symbols of writing as revelation of the intrinsic nature of things; language, civilization, culture; harmonious, beautiful, elegant, polite. **Luminous**, *BING*: bright, fiery, light-giving; clear, evident; alert, intelligent. **Indeed**, *YE*: see *Hexagrams in Pairs*.

SIX ABOVE

A **jun zi**: a **leopard transforming**.
The **small** in the **person skins** the **face**.
Disciplining, **pitfall**.
Residing in **Trial**, **significant**.

Comments
A **jun zi**: a **leopard transforming**.
One's pattern beautiful indeed.
The **small** in the **person skins** the **face**.
Yielding uses adhering to a **chief indeed**.

Fields of meaning

Jun zi: see *Patterns of Wisdom*. **Leopard**, *BAO*: spotted wild cats, beautiful and independent; mark of high-ranking officers. **Transform**, *BIAN*: abrupt, radical passage from one state to another; transformation of opened and whole lines into each other in hexagrams; contrasts with change, *HUA*, gradual mutation. **Small**, *XIAO*: little, common, unimportant; adapting to what crosses your path; ability to move in harmony with the vicissitudes of life; contrasts with great, *DA*, self-imposed theme or goal. **Person/people**, *REN*: humans individually and collectively; an individual; humankind. **Skin**, *GE*: see *Image of the Situation*. **Face**, *MIAN*: visage, countenance, outer expression of the heart; honor, character, reputation; front, surface; face to face. **Discipline**, *ZHENG*: subjugate vassals, reduce to order; punishing expedition. Ideogram: step and correct, a rectifying move. **Pitfall**, *XIONG*: unfortunate situation, in which the flow of life and spirit is blocked and the experience of meaning is lost; stuck and exposed to danger; inappropriate attitude. Ideogram: person in a pit. **Reside**, *JU*: dwell, live in, stay; sit down; fill an office; well-being, rest. Ideogram: body and seat. **Trial**, *ZHEN*: inquiry by divination and its result; righteous, firm; separating wheat from chaff; the kernel, the proven core; quality of winter and North, fourth stage of the Time Cycle. Ideogram: pearl and divination. **Significant**, *JI*: leads to the experience of meaning; favorable, propitious, appropriate. Ideogram: scholar and mouth, wise words of a sage.

One/one's, *QI*: general third person pronoun and possessive adjective; also: it/its, he/his, she/her, they/their. **Pattern**, *WEN*: intrinsic or natural design, pattern of wood, stone or animal fur; ideograms, the symbols of writing as revelation of the intrinsic nature of things; language, civilization, culture; harmonious, beautiful, elegant, polite. **Beautiful**, *WEI*: elegant, classic, fine; luxuriant, lush. **Indeed**, *YE*: emphasizes and intensifies the previous statement. **Yield**, *SHUN*: give way, comply, agree, follow, obey; docile, flexible; bear produce, nourish, provide; Action of the trigram Field, *KUN*. **Use**, *YI*: see *Patterns of Wisdom*. **Adhere**, *CONG*: follow, agree with, comply with, obey; join a doctrine, school, or person; servant, follower. Ideogram: two men walking, one following the other. **Chief**, *JUN*: prince, ruler; lead, direct; wise person. Ideogram: mouth and direct, giving orders.

Image Tradition

> **Skinning**. **Stream** and **fire reciprocally** giving **pause**.
> **Two women concording**, **residing**.
> **Their purposes not reciprocally acquired**: **named skinning**.

Before-zenith sun, thereupon conforming.
Skinning and-also trusting it.

Pattern brightening uses stimulating.
The **great**'s **Growing uses correctness.**
Skinning and-also appropriate.
One's repenting thereupon extinguished.

Heaven and **earth skinning and-also** the **four seasons accomplishing.**
Redressing martially, skinning fate.
Yielding reaches heaven and-also the **correspondence reaches people.**
The **season belonging** to **skinning great actually in-fact.**

Fields of meaning

Skin, *GE*: see *Image of the Situation*. **Stream**, *SHUI*: flowing water; river, tide, flood; fluid, dissolving; Symbol of the trigram Gorge, *KAN*. Ideogram: rippling water. **Fire**, *HUO*: see *Patterns of Wisdom*. **Reciprocal**, *XIANG*: mutual; assist, encourage, help; bring together, blend with; examine, inspect; by turns. **Pause**, *XI*: breathe; rest, repose, a breathing-spell; suspended. **Two/second**, *ER*: number two; pair, even numbers, binary, duplicate. **Woman(hood)**, *NÜ*: woman and what is inherently female. **Concord**, *TONG*: harmonize, unite, equalize, assemble; agree, share in; together, at once, same time and place. Ideogram: cover and mouth, silent understanding and perfect fit. **Reside**, *JU*: dwell, live in, stay; sit down; fill an office; well-being, rest. Ideogram: body and seat. **They/their**, *QI*: general third person pronoun and possessive adjective; also: one/one's, it/its, he/his, she/her. **Purpose**, *ZHI*: focus of mind and heart; intention, will, inclination; continuity in the direction of life. Ideogram: heart and scholar, high inner resolve. **Not**, *BU*: common term of negation. **Acquire**, *DE*: obtain the desired object; possession; satisfied, fulfilled; it is permitted; agree with; wish for, desire covetously. Ideogram: go and obstacle, going through obstacles to the goal. **Name**, *YUE*: speak, declare, call. Ideogram: open mouth and tongue.

Before-zenith sun, thereupon conforming, *SSU RI NAI FU*: see *Image of the Situation*. **And-also**, *ER*: joins and contrasts two terms. **Trustworthy**, *XIN*: truthful, faithful, consistent over time; count on, confide in; examine, verify, prove; loyalty, integrity. Ideogram: person and word, true speech.

Pattern, *WEN*: intrinsic or natural design, pattern of wood, stone or animal fur; ideograms, the symbols of writing as revelation of the intrinsic nature of things; language, civilization, culture; harmonious, beautiful, elegant, polite. **Brightness**, *MING*: light, radiance, clarity; distinguish, discern, understand; light-giving aspect of fire, of heavenly bodies and of consciousness; brightness and fire are the Symbols of the trigram Radiance, *LI*. **Use**, *YI*: see *Patterns of Wisdom*. **Stimulate**, *SHUO*: rouse to action and good feeling; stir up, urge on; exhort, persuade; say, tell, relate; cheer, delight; joyous, peaceful, restful; Action of the trigram Open, *DUI*. Ideogram: words and exchange. **Great**, *DA*: big, noble, important, very; orient the will toward a self-imposed goal, impose direction; ability to lead or guide one's life; contrasts with small, *XIAO*, flexible adaptation to what crosses one's path. **Grow**, *HENG*: heavenly influence pervading and nourishing all things; prosper, succeed, expand, develop; effective, favorable; quality of summer and South, second stage of the Time Cycle. With the pronunciation *XIANG*: offer a sacrifice; offer a gift to a superior; accept, enjoy. **Correct**, *ZHENG*: rectify deviation or one-sidedness; proper, straight, exact, regular; constant, rule, model. Ideogram: stop and one, hold to one thing. **Appropriate**, *DANG*: suitable, capable, worthy, adequate, competent, equal to; opportune, convenient; whole lines in odd places and opened lines in even places. **One/one's**, *QI*: general third person pronoun and possessive adjective; also: it/its, he/his, she/her, they/their. **Repenting extinguished**, *HUI WANG*: see *Image of the Situation*.

Heaven, *TIAN*: sky, firmament, heavens; the highest realm, situated above the human world, as opposed to the earth, *DI*, located below; Symbol of the trigram Energy, *QIAN*. Ideogram: great and the one above. **Earth**, *DI*: the earth, ground on which the human world rests; basis of all things, nourishes all things; essential Yin; Symbol of the trigram Space, *KUN*. **Four**, *SI*: number four; number of the cardinal directions and of the seasons; everywhere, on all sides; fourfold articulation of the Universal Compass. **Season**, *SHI*: see *Patterns of Wisdom*. **Accomplish**, *CHENG*: complete, finish, bring about; perfect, full, whole; play one's part, do one's duty; mature. Ideogram: weapon and man, able to bear arms, thus fully developed. **Redress**, *TANG*: repel injustice, correct grievances; grand, awesome; hot water, hot spring; soup, broth; Tang is the name of the founder of the Shang dynasty. Ideogram: water and expand, a large river and its periodic floods. **Martial**, *WU*: warrior, military, warlike; valiant, powerful; strong, stern; Wu is the name of the son of King Wen, who defeated the last Shang emperor and founded the Zhou dynasty. Ideogram: fight and stop, force deterring aggression. **Fate**, *MING*: individual destiny; birth and death as limits of life; issue orders with authority; consult the gods. Ideogram: mouth and order, words with heavenly authority. **Yield**, *SHUN*: give way, comply, agree, follow, obey; docile, flexible; bear produce, nourish, provide; Action of the trigram Field, *KUN*. **Reach**, *HU*: arrive at a goal; move toward and achieve; to, at, in; distinct from tend-towards, *YOU*. **Correspond**, *YING*: be in agreement or harmony; proper, suitable; resonate together, answer to; relation between the lines (1 and 4, 2 and 5, 3 and 6) when they form the pair opened and whole, supple and solid. Ideogram: heart and obey. **People/person**, *REN*: humans individually and collectively; an individual; humankind. **Belong/it**, *ZHI*: establishes between two terms a connection similar to the Saxon genitive, in which the second term belongs to the first one; at the end of a sentence it refers to something previously mentioned or implied. **Actually**, *YI*: truly, really, at present. Ideogram: a dart and done, strong intention fully expressed. **In-fact**, *ZAI*: emphatic exclamation; truly, indeed.

50 THE VESSEL | *Ding*

The situation described by this hexagram is characterized by the alchemical image of a sacred vessel which transforms its content into spiritual nourishment, an offering to higher powers.

Image of the Situation

> The **vessel**.
> **Spring, significant**.
> **Growing**.

Fields of meaning

Vessel, *DING*: bronze cauldron with three feet and two ears, sacred vessel used to cook food for sacrifice to gods and ancestors; founding symbol of family or dynasty; hold, contain, transform; establish, secure; precious, noble. **Spring**, *YUAN*: source, origin, head; arise, begin; first generating impulse; great, excellent; quality of springtime and East, first stage of the Time Cycle. **Significant**, *JI*: leads to the experience of meaning; favorable, propitious, appropriate. Ideogram: scholar and mouth, wise words of a sage. **Grow**, *HENG*: heavenly influence pervading and nourishing all things; prosper, succeed, expand, develop; effective, favorable; quality of summer and South, second stage of the Time Cycle. With the pronunciation *XIANG*: offer a sacrifice; offer a gift to a superior; accept, enjoy.

Outer and Inner Trigram

The upper trigram, **Radiance**, *LI*, describes the outer aspects of the situation. It has the following associations: glowing light, spreading in all directions; the power of consciousness; discriminate, articulate, divide and arrange in order; assemble, attract. Ideogram: bird and weird, magical fire-bird with brilliant plumage. *Symbols*: fire and brightness. Fire, *HUO*: flame, burn; warming and consuming aspect of burning. Brightness, *MING*: light, radiance, clarity; distinguish, discern, understand; light-giving aspect of fire, of heavenly bodies and of consciousness. *Action*: congregate, *LI*, cling together, adhere to, rely on; couple, pair, herd; beautiful, elegant. Ideogram: deer flocking together. In the family of trigrams *LI* is the middle daughter.

The lower trigram, **Root**, *SUN*, describes the inner aspects of the situation. It has the following associations: base on which things rest, ground, foundation; mild, subtly penetrating; nourishing. *Symbols*: tree/wood and wind. Tree/wood, *MU*: trees and all things woody or wooden; associated with the Wooden Moment. Ideogram: a tree with roots and branches. Wind, *FENG*: wind, breeze, gust; weather and its influence on mood and humor; fashion, usage. *Action*: enter, *RU*, penetrate, go into, enter on, encroach on; progress; put into. In the family of trigrams *SUN* is the eldest daughter.

Counter Hexagram

The Counter Hexagram of **The Vessel** is hexagram 43, **Parting**, which switches the emphasis from the containing and transforming capacity of **The Vessel** to a river overflowing its banks and parting into different streams.

Preceding Situation

> **Skinning beings implies absolutely-nothing like** a **vessel**.
> To **anterior acquiescence belongs** the **use** of the **vessel**.

Fields of meaning

Skin, *GE*: human or animal skin; hide, leather; armor, protection; peel off, remove the covering, skin or hide; change, renew, molt; overthrow, degrade from office. **Being**, *WU*: creature, thing, any single being; matter, substance, essence; nature of things. **Imply**, *ZHE*: further signify; additional meaning. **Absolutely-nothing like**, *MO RUO*: nothing is comparable to; the best for this specific purpose is. **Vessel**, *DING*: see *Image of the Situation*. To **anterior acquiescence belongs** the **use** of, *GU SHOU ZHI YI*: understanding and accepting the preceding statement allows the consultant to make proper use of this hexagram.

Hexagrams in Pairs

> **Skinning**: **departing anteriority indeed**.
> The **vessel**: **grasping renewal indeed**.

Fields of meaning

Skin, *GE*: see *Preceding Situation*. **Depart**, *QU*: leave, quit, go; far away, far from; remove, reject, dismiss; lost, gone. **Anterior**, *GU*: come before as cause; former, ancient; reason, purpose, intention; grievance, dissatisfaction, sorrow, resulting from previous causes and intentions; situation leading to a divination. **Indeed,** *YE*: emphasizes and intensifies the previous statement. **Vessel,** *DING*: see *Image of the Situation*. **Grasp,** *QU*: seize with effort, take and use, appropriate; take as a wife; grasp the meaning, understand. Ideogram: ear and hand, hear and grasp. **Renew,** *XIN*: new, novel, fresh, recent; restore, improve, correct.

Patterns of Wisdom

Wood possesses fire above. The **vessel**.
A **jun zi uses correcting** the **position** to **solidify fate**.

Fields of meaning

Wood/tree, *MU*: trees and all things woody or wooden; associated with the Wooden Moment; wood and wind are the Symbols of the trigram Ground, *SUN*. Ideogram: a tree with roots and branches. **Possess,** *YOU*: general term indicating possession; have, own, be endowed with. **Fire,** *HUO*: fire, flame, burn; warming and consuming aspect of burning; fire and brightness are the Symbols of the trigram Radiance, *LI*. **Above,** *SHANG*: anything above in all senses; higher, upper, outer; upper trigram. **Vessel,** *DING*: see *Image of the Situation*. **Jun zi**: ideal of a person who orders his/her life in accordance with dao rather than willful intention, and uses divination in this spirit. **Use,** *YI*: by means of; owing to; make use of, employ. **Correct,** *ZHENG*: rectify deviation or one-sidedness; proper, straight, exact, regular; constant, rule, model. Ideogram: stop and one, hold to one thing. **Position,** *WEI*: place, location; be at; social standing, rank; position of a line in a hexagram. Ideogram: person standing. **Solidify,** *NING*: congeal, freeze, curdle, stiffen; coagulate, make solid or firm. **Fate,** *MING*: individual destiny; birth and death as limits of life; issue orders with authority; consult the gods. Ideogram: mouth and order, words with heavenly authority.

Transforming Lines

Initial Six

The **vessel**: **toppling** the **foot**.
Harvesting: **emerging** from **obstruction**.
Acquiring a **concubine**, **using one's son**.
Without fault.

Comments

The **vessel**: **toppling** the **foot**.
Not-yet rebelling indeed.
Harvesting: **emerging** from **obstruction**.
Using adhering to **value indeed**.

Fields of meaning

Vessel, *DING*: see *Image of the Situation*. **Topple**, *DIAN*: fall over because top-heavy; top, summit. **Foot**, *ZHI*: foot, footprint; foundation, base; walk; stop where the foot rests. **Harvest**, *LI*: benefit, advantage, profit; realization; sharp, acute, insightful; quality of autumn and West, third stage of the Time Cycle. Ideogram: ripe grain and blade. **Emerge**, *CHU*: come out of, proceed from, spring from, issue forth; appear, be born; bear, generate; leave, flee; Action of the trigram Shake, *ZHEN*. Ideogram: stem with branches and leaves emerging. **Obstruct**, *PI*: closed, stopped; bar the way; obstacle; unfortunate, wicked; refuse, disapprove, deny. Ideogram: mouth and not, blocked communication. **Acquire**, *DE*: obtain the desired object; possession; satisfied, fulfilled; it is permitted; agree with; wish for, desire covetously. Ideogram: go and obstacle, going through obstacles to the goal. **Concubine**, *QIE*: secondary wife taken without ceremony to ensure a male descendant; handmaid. **Use**, *YI*: see *Patterns of Wisdom*. **One/one's**, *QI*: general third person pronoun and possessive adjective; also: it/its, he/his, she/her, they/their. **Son(hood)**, *ZI*: son, male child; heirs, offspring, posterity; living up to the ideal of the ancestors as highest human aspiration; seed, kernel, egg; sage, teacher; nadir, deepest point, midnight, mid-winter. **Without fault**, *WU JIU*: no error or harm in the situation.

Not-yet, *WEI*: temporal negative indicating that something is expected to happen but has not yet occurred. **Rebel**, *BEI*: oppose, resist; go against nature or usage; insubordinate; perverse, unreasonable. **Indeed**, *YE*: see *Hexagrams in Pairs*. **Use**, *YI*: see *Patterns of Wisdom*. **Adhere**, *CONG*: follow, agree with, comply with, obey; join a doctrine, school, or person; servant, follower. Ideogram: two men walking, one following the other. **Value**, *GUI*: regard as valuable, give worth and dignity to; precious, honorable, exalted, illustrious. Ideogram: cowries (coins) and basket.

NINE AT SECOND

The **vessel possesses substance**.
My companion possesses affliction.
Not me able to **approach**.
Significant.

Comments
The **vessel possesses substance**.
Considering the **place** of **it indeed**.
My companion possesses affliction.
Completing without surpassing indeed.

Fields of meaning

Vessel, *DING*: see *Image of the Situation*. **Possess**, *YOU*: see *Patterns of Wisdom*. **Substance**, *SHI*: fullness, richness; essence; real, solid, consistent; results, fruits, possessions; honest, sincere. Ideogram: string of coins under a roof, wealth in the house. **I/me/my**, *WO*: first person pronoun; the use of a specific personal pronoun, as opposed to the generic one's, *QI*, indicates an unusually strong emphasis on personal involvement. **Companion**, *QIU*: close personal relation; partner, spouse; unite, join in marriage. With the pronunciation *CHOU*: opponent, rival, enemy; contradict, hate. **Affliction**, *JI*: sickness, disorder, defect, calamity, injury; poison, hate, dislike; cruel, jealous, envious. Ideogram: sickness and dart, a sudden affliction. **Not**, *BU*: common term of negation. **I/me/my**, *WO*: first person pronoun; the use of a specific personal pronoun, as opposed to the generic one's, *QI*, indicates an unusually strong emphasis on personal involvement. **Able/enable**, *NENG*: ability, power, skill, art; competent, talented; duty, function, capacity. Ideogram: an animal with strong hooves and bones, able to carry and defend. **Approach**, *JI*: come near to, advance toward, reach; nearby; soon, immediately. **Significant**, *JI*: see *Image of the Situation*.

Consider, *SHEN*: act carefully, seriously; cautious, attentive, circumspect; still, quiet, sincere. Ideogram: heart and true. **Place**, *SUO*: position, location; residence, dwelling; where something belongs or comes from; habitual focus or object. **It/belong**, *ZHI*: establishes between two terms a connection similar to the Saxon genitive, in which the second term belongs to the first one; at the end of a sentence it refers to something previously mentioned or implied. **Indeed**, *YE*: see *Hexagrams in Pairs*. **Complete**, *ZHONG*: completion of a cycle that begins the next; entire, whole, all. Ideogram: silk cocoons, follow and ice, winter linking one year with the next. **Without**, *WU*: devoid of; there is not. **Surpass**, *YOU*: exceed, transgress; beyond measure, extraordinary; blame.

NINE AT THIRD

The **vessel**'s **ears skinned**.
Its movement impeded.
The **pheasant**'s **juice not taken-in**.
On all **sides rain lessens repenting**.
Completing significant.

Comments
The **vessel**'s **ears skinned**.
Letting-go one's righteousness indeed.

Fields of meaning

Vessel, *DING*: see *Image of the Situation*. **Ear**, *ER*: ear; handle; side. **Skin**, *GE*: see *Preceding Situation*. **It/its**, *QI*: general third person pronoun and possessive adjective; also: one/one's, he/his, she/her, they/their. **Move**, *XING*: move or move something; motivate; emotionally moving; walk, act, do. Ideogram: successive steps. **Impede**, *SAI*: clog, fill up, close, obstruct; hinder, prevent; hide; unintelligent, dull. **Pheasant**, *ZHI*: beautiful bird associated with the trigram Radiance, *LI*; embrasures on ramparts and forts; arrange, put in order. **Juice**, *GAO*: active essence; oil, grease, ointment; fertilizing, rich; genius. **Not**, *BU*: common term of negation. **Take-in**, *SHI*: eat, drink, ingest, absorb, incorporate; food, nourishment. **Sides**, *FANG*: cardinal directions; surface of the earth extending to the four cardinal points; everywhere; limits, boundaries. **Rain**, *YU*: rain and all precipitations; sudden shower, fast and furious; abundant dispensation of benefits; associated with the trigram Gorge, *KAN*, and the Streaming Moment. **Lessen**, *KUI*: diminish, injure, wane; lack, defect. **Repent**, *HUI*: regret, dissatisfaction with past conduct inducing a change of heart; proceeds from abashment, *LIN*, shame and confusion at having lost the right way. **Complete**, *ZHONG*: completion of a cycle that begins the next; entire, whole, all. Ideogram: silk cocoons, follow and ice, winter linking one year with the next. **Significant**, *JI*: see *Image of the Situation*.

Let-go, *SHI*: lose, let slip; omit, miss, fail; lose control of. Ideogram: drop from the hand. **One/one's**, *QI*: general third person pronoun and possessive adjective; also: it/its, he/his, she/her, they/their. **Righteous**, *YI*: proper, just, virtuous, upright; the heart that rules itself; benevolent, loyal, devoted to public good. **Indeed**, *YE*: see *Hexagrams in Pairs*.

NINE AT FOURTH

The **vessel**'s **severed stand**.
Overthrowing a **princely stew**.
One's form soiled, **pitfall**.

Comments
Overthrowing a **princely stew**.
Is it **trustworthy thus indeed?**

Fields of meaning
Vessel, *DING*: see *Image of the Situation*. **Sever**, *ZHE*: break off, separate, sunder, cut in two; discriminate, pass judgment on. **Stand**, *ZU*: base, foot, leg; rest on, support; stance; sufficient, capable, worth. Ideogram: foot and calf resting. **Overthrow**, *FU*: subvert, upset, defeat, throw down. **Prince**, *GONG*: highest title of nobility; noble acting as minister of state in the capital; contrasts with feudatory, *HOU*, governor of a province. **Stew**, *SU*: cooked or boiled rice and meat; mixed contents of a pot. **One/one's**, *QI*: general third person pronoun and possessive adjective; also: it/its, he/his, she/her, they/their. **Form**, *XING*: shape, bodily or material appearance; aspect, configuration, circumstance. **Soil**, *WU*: moisten, soak; dirty, stain. **Pitfall**, *XIONG*: unfortunate situation, in which the flow of life and spirit is blocked and the experience of meaning is lost; stuck and exposed to danger; inappropriate attitude. Ideogram: person in a pit.

Is?, *HE*: ask, inquire; what? which? who? how? why? where? an interrogative particle, often introducing a rhetorical question: is it? is it not? **Trustworthy**, *XIN*: truthful, faithful, consistent over time; count on, confide in; examine, verify, prove; loyalty, integrity. Ideogram: person and word, true speech. **Thus**, *RU*: as, in this way; comparable, similar. **Indeed**, *YE*: see *Hexagrams in Pairs*.

SIX AT FIFTH

The **vessel**'s **yellow ears**, **metallic rings**.
Harvesting, **Trial**.

Comments
The **vessel**'s **yellow ears**.
The **center uses activating substance indeed**.

Fields of meaning
Vessel, *DING*: see *Image of the Situation*. **Yellow**, *HUANG*: color of the soil in central China, associated with the Earthy Moment leading from the Yang to the

Yin hemicycle; emblematic and imperial color of China since the Yellow Emperor (2500 BC). **Ear**, *ER*: ear; handle; side. **Metal**, *JIN*: all metals, particularly gold; smelting and casting; perfection, richness; autumn, West, sunset; one of the Five Transformative Moments. **Rings**, *XUAN*: handles or ears for carrying a tripod. **Harvest**, *LI*: benefit, advantage, profit; realization; sharp, acute, insightful; quality of autumn and West, third stage of the Time Cycle. Ideogram: ripe grain and blade. **Trial**, *ZHEN*: inquiry by divination and its result; righteous, firm; separating wheat from chaff; the kernel, the proven core; quality of winter and North, fourth stage of the Time Cycle. Ideogram: pearl and divination.

Center, *ZHONG*: inner, central; put in the center; middle, stable point enabling you to face inner and outer changes; middle line of a trigram. Ideogram: field divided in two equal parts. **Use**, *YI*: see *Patterns of Wisdom*. **Activate**, *WEI*: act or cause to act; do, make, manage, make active; be, become; attend to, help; because of. **Substance**, *SHI*: fullness, richness; essence; real, solid, consistent; results, fruits, possessions; honest, sincere. Ideogram: string of coins under a roof, wealth in the house. **Indeed**, *YE*: see *Hexagrams in Pairs*.

NINE ABOVE

The **vessel**'s **jade rings**.
The **great**, **significant**.
Without not Harvesting.

Comments
Jade rings located above.
Solid and **supple articulated indeed**.

Fields of meaning

Vessel, *DING*: see *Image of the Situation*. **Jade**, *YU*: jade and all gemstones; precious, beautiful; delightful, happy, perfect, clear. **Rings**, *XUAN*: handles or ears for carrying a tripod. **Great**, *DA*: big, noble, important, very; orient the will toward a self-imposed goal, impose direction; ability to lead or guide one's life; contrasts with small, *XIAO*, flexible adaptation to what crosses one's path. **Significant**, *JI*: see *Image of the Situation*. **Without not Harvesting**, *WU BU LI*: turning point where the balance is swinging from not Harvesting to actually Harvesting.

Locate, *ZAI*: be at, be situated at, dwell, reside; in, within; involved with, in the process of. Ideogram: earth and persevere, a place on the earth. **Above**, *SHANG*: see *Patterns of Wisdom*. **Solid**, *GANG*: quality of the whole lines; firm, strong, unyielding, persisting. **Supple**, *ROU*: quality of the opened lines; flexible, pliant, adaptable, tender. **Articulate**, *JIE*: joint, articulation; a separation which simultaneously establishes the identity of the parts and their connection; express thought through speech; section, chapter, interval; temperance, virtue; rite, ceremony; lit.: nodes of bamboo stalks. **Indeed,** *YE*: see *Hexagrams in Pairs.*

Image Tradition

The **vessel**. A **symbol indeed**.
Using wood, the **root**, **fire**.
Growing: **cooking indeed**.

The **wise person**'s **Growing uses presenting** to the **supreme above**.
And-also the **great**'s **Growing uses nourishing** the **wise** and the **eminent**.
The **root and-also** the **ear** and the **eye**: **understanding bright**.

The **supple advances and-also moves above**.
Acquires the **center and-also** the **correspondence reaches** the **solid**.
That uses Spring, **Growing**.

Fields of meaning

Vessel, *DING*: see *Image of the Situation.* **Symbol,** *XIANG*: image invested with magic connecting visible and invisible; figure, form, shape, likeness; pattern, model; act, play, write. Ideogram: elephant (in ancient times the bones of a dead elephant used to be assembled to look like the living animal). **Indeed,** *YE*: see *Hexagrams in Pairs.* **Use,** *YI*: see *Patterns of Wisdom.* **Wood/tree,** *MU*: see *Patterns of Wisdom.* **Root,** *SUN*: base on which things rest, ground, foundation; mild, subtly penetrating; nourishing. **Fire,** *HUO*: see *Patterns of Wisdom.* **Grow,** *HENG*: see *Image of the Situation.* **Cook,** *REN*: cook very thoroughly; transform completely. Ideogram: food and full or complete.

Wise, *SHENG*: intuitive universal wisdom; profound understanding; mythical sages of old; holy, sacred, mark of highest distinction. Ideogram: ear and inform, one who knows all from a single sound. **Person/people,** *REN*: humans individually and collectively; an individual; humankind. **Present,** *XIANG*: offer in sacrifice, give to the gods or a superior; give a banquet; accept an offering; enjoy, receive. **Supreme above,** *SHANG DI*: highest power in universe. **And-also,** *ER*: joins and contrasts two terms. **Great,** *DA*: big, noble, important, very; orient the will toward a self-imposed goal, impose direction; ability to lead or guide one's life;

contrasts with small, *XIAO*, flexible adaptation to what crosses one's path. **Nourish**, *YANG*: feed, sustain, support, provide, care for; generate; raise, grow. **Wise**, *SHENG*: intuitive universal wisdom; profound understanding; mythical sages of old; holy, sacred, mark of highest distinction. Ideogram: ear and inform, one who knows all from a single sound. **Eminent**, *XIAN*: worthy, excellent, virtuous; endowed with moral and intellectual power; second only to the wise, *SHENG*. **Ear**, *ER*: ear; handle; side. **Eye**, *MU*: eye and vision; look, see, glance, observe. **Understand**, *CONG*: perceive quickly, astute, sharp; discriminate intelligently. Ideogram: ear and quick. **Brightness**, *MING*: light, radiance, clarity; distinguish, discern, understand; light-giving aspect of fire, of heavenly bodies and of consciousness; brightness and fire are the Symbols of the trigram Radiance, *LI*.

Supple, *ROU*: quality of the opened lines; flexible, pliant, adaptable, tender. **Advance**, *JIN*: move forward, progress, climb; promote or be promoted; further the development of, augment; offer, introduce. **Move**, *XING*: move or move something; motivate; emotionally moving; walk, act, do. Ideogram: successive steps. **Above**, *SHANG*: see *Patterns of Wisdom*. **Acquire**, *DE*: obtain the desired object; possession; satisfied, fulfilled; it is permitted; agree with; wish for, desire covetously. Ideogram: go and obstacle, going through obstacles to the goal. **Center**, *ZHONG*: inner, central; put in the center; middle, stable point enabling you to face inner and outer changes; middle line of a trigram. Ideogram: field divided in two equal parts. **Correspond**, *YING*: be in agreement or harmony; proper, suitable; resonate together, answer to; relation between the lines (1 and 4, 2 and 5, 3 and 6) when they form the pair opened and whole, supple and solid. Ideogram: heart and obey. **Reach**, *HU*: arrive at a goal; move toward and achieve; to, at, in; distinct from tend-towards, *YOU*. **Solid**, *GANG*: quality of the whole lines; firm, strong, unyielding, persisting. **That**, *SHI*: refers to the preceding statement. **Spring**, *YUAN*: see *Image of the Situation*.

震

䷲

51 THE SHAKE | *Zhen*

The situation described by this hexagram is characterized by a powerful energy rising from the depth, a sudden frightening, awakening and inspiring shock. The hexagram The Shake is the doubling of the corresponding trigram, and partakes of its attributes.

Image of the Situation

> The **shake**.
> **Growing**.
> The **shake coming**: **frightening**, **frightening**.
> **Laughing words**, **shrieking**, **shrieking**.
> The **shake scares** a **hundred miles**.
> **Not losing** the **ladle** and the **libation**.

Fields of meaning

Shake, *ZHEN*: arouse, excite, inspire; awe, alarm, trembling; thunder rising from the depth of the earth; fertilizing intrusion. Ideogram: excite and rain. *Symbol*: thunder, *LEI*, arousing power emerging from the depth of the earth. *Action*: stir-up, *DONG*, excite, influence, move, affect; work, take action; come out of the egg or the bud. Ideogram: strength and heavy, move weighty things. In the family of trigrams *ZHEN* is the eldest son. Grow, *HENG*: heavenly influence pervading and nourishing all things; prosper, succeed, expand, develop; effective, favorable; quality of summer and South, second stage of the Time Cycle. With the pronunciation *XIANG*: offer a sacrifice; offer a gift to a superior; accept, enjoy. Come, *LAI*: approach in time or space; move toward, arrive at; future; contrasts with go, *WANG*, move away or become past. **Frighten**, *XI*: feel or provoke fear, alarm, terror, awe. **Laugh**, *XIAO*: manifest joy or mirth; giggle, joke, laugh at, tease; desire; open (of a flower); associated with the Fiery Moment. **Word**, *YAN*: spoken word, speech, saying; talk, discuss, address; name, signify. Ideogram: mouth and rising vapor. **Shriek**, *YA*: confused noise, like the clamor of a school-room; cries of birds; sounds of a child learning to speak; exclamations; hoarse, dumb. **Scare**, *JING*: fear, alarm; cause fear, terrify; apprehensive, surprised. Ideogram: horse and strike, havoc created by a terrified horse. **Hundred**, *BO*: numerous, many, all; a whole class or type. **Mile**, *LI*: measure of distance, about 600 meters; street, native village, community. **Not**, *BU*: common term of negation. **Lose**, *SANG*: be deprived of, forget; destruction, ruin, death; corpse; lament, mourn; funeral. Ideogram: weep and dead. **Ladle**, *BI*: ceremonial spoon used to pour libations. **Libation**, *CHANG*: fermented millet liquor, offered to ancestors or poured out to draw the gods near.

Outer and Inner Trigram

In this hexagram the outer and inner aspects of the situation are identical, and they are described by the trigram **Shake**. Its associations are listed in the corresponding *Field of meaning* above.

Counter Hexagram

The Counter Hexagram of **The Shake** is hexagram 39, **Limping**, which switches the emphasis from a powerful burst of energy rising from the depth to a slow, halting progress.

Preceding Situation

> A **lord**'s **implements imply absolutely-nothing like** the **long-living son**.
> To **anterior acquiescence belongs** the **use** of the **shake**.
> The **shake implies stirring-up indeed**.

Fields of meaning

Lord, *ZHU*: ruler, master, chief, authority; host; domination in the cycle of the Five Transformative Moments. Ideogram: lamp and flame, giving light. **Implements**, *QI*: utensils, tools; molded or carved objects; use a person or thing suitably; capacity, talent, intelligence. **Imply**, *ZHE*: further signify; additional meaning. **Absolutely-nothing like**, *MO RUO*: nothing is comparable to; the best for this specific purpose is. **Long-living**, *ZHANG*: enduring, lasting, constant; extended, long, large; senior, superior, greater; increase, prosper; respect, elevate. **Son(hood)**, *ZI*: son, male child; heirs, offspring, posterity; living up to the ideal of the ancestors as highest human aspiration; seed, kernel, egg; sage, teacher; nadir, deepest point, midnight, mid-winter. To **anterior acquiescence belongs** the **use** of, *GU SHOU ZHI YI*: understanding and accepting the preceding statement allows the consultant to make proper use of this hexagram. **Shake**, *ZHEN*: see *Image of the Situation*. **Stir-up**, *DONG*: excite, influence, move, affect; work, take action; come out of the egg or the bud; Action of the trigram Shake, *ZHEN*. Ideogram: strength and heavy, move weighty things. **Indeed**, *YE*: emphasizes and intensifies the previous statement.

Hexagrams in Pairs

The **shake**: **rising-up indeed**.
The **bound**: **stopping indeed**.

Fields of meaning

Shake, *ZHEN*: see *Image of the Situation*. **Rise-up**, *QI*: stand up, erect; stimulate, excite; undertake, begin, develop. **Indeed**, *YE*: see *Preceding Situation*. **Bound**, *GEN*: limit, frontier; obstacle that prevents from seeing further; stop; still, quiet, motionless; confine , enclose; mountain, sunset, beginning of winter; solid, steady, unshakable; straight, hard, adamant, obstinate. **Stop**, *ZHI*: bring or come to a standstill, cease, terminate; Action of the trigram Bound, *GEN*. Ideogram: a foot stops walking.

Patterns of Wisdom

Reiterated thunder. The **shake**.
A **jun zi uses anxiety** and **fear** to **adjust inspections**.

Fields of meaning

Reiterate, *JIAN*: repeat, duplicate; recurrent. **Thunder**, *LEI*: thunder; arousing power emerging from the depth of the earth; Symbol of the trigram Shake, *ZHEN*. **Shake**, *ZHEN*: see *Image of the Situation*. **Jun zi**: ideal of a person who orders his/her life in accordance with dao rather than willful intention, and uses divination in this spirit. **Use**, *YI*: by means of; owing to; make use of, employ. **Anxiety**, *KONG*: apprehensive, alarmed, agitated; suspicious of. Ideogram: heart and sick, agitated within. **Fear**, *JU*: afraid, apprehensive; stand in awe of; intimidate. **Adjust**, *XIU*: regulate, repair, clean up, renovate. **Inspect**, *XING*: examine, inquire, reflect, consider; visit.

Transforming Lines

INITIAL NINE

The **shake coming**: **frightening**, **frightening**.
After laughing words, **shrieking**, **shrieking**.
Significant.

Comments

The **shake coming**: **frightening**, **frightening**.
Anxiety involves blessing indeed.
Laughing words, **shrieking**, **shrieking**.
Afterwards possessing by **consequence indeed**.

Fields of meaning

The **shake coming**: **frightening**, **frightening**, *ZHEN LAI XI XI*: see *Image of the Situation*. **After(wards)/later**, *HOU*: come after in time, subsequent; put oneself after; behind, back, draw back; the second; attendants, heirs, successors, posterity. **Laughing words**, **shrieking**, **shrieking**, *XIAO YAN YA YA*: see *Image of the Situation*. **Significant**, *JI*: leads to the experience of meaning; favorable, propitious, appropriate. Ideogram: scholar and mouth, wise words of a sage.

Anxiety, *KONG*: see *Hexagrams in Pairs*. **Involve**, *ZHI*: devote oneself to; induce, cause, implicate; approach; manifest, express; reach the highest degree of. Ideogram: reach and come up behind. **Bless**, *FU*: heavenly gifts and favor; happiness, prosperity; spiritual power and goodwill. Ideogram: spirit and plenty. **Indeed**, *YE*: see *Preceding Situation*. **Possess**, *YOU*: general term indicating possession; have, own, be endowed with. **Consequence**, *ZE*: reason, cause, result; rule, law, pattern, standard; therefore; very strong connection.

Six at Second

The **shake coming**, **adversity**.
A **hundred-thousand coins lost**.
Climbing tending-towards the **ninth mound**.
No pursuit.
The **seventh day acquiring**.

Comments

The **shake coming**, **adversity**.
Riding a **solid indeed**.

Fields of meaning

Shake, *ZHEN*: see *Image of the Situation*. **Come**, *LAI*: see *Image of the Situation*. **Adversity**, *LI*: danger, hardship, severe; threat or difficulty that must be encountered, rather than avoided; grinding stone; polish, sharpen; a challenge that strengthens and perfects the character; stimulate, excite; cruel demon. **Hundred-thousand**, *YI*: a huge quantity. Ideogram: man and thought, a number that can only be imagined. **Coins**, *BEI*: cowry shells used for money; adorned with shell;

money, riches; precious, valuable. **Lose**, *SANG*: see *Image of the Situation*. **Climb**, *JI*: ascend, scale; climb steep cliffs; rise as clouds. **Tend-towards**, *YU*: move toward without necessarily reaching, in the direction of. **Nine**, *JIU*: number nine; transforming whole line; superlative: best, perfect. **Mound**, *LING*: grave-mound, barrow; small hill. **No**, *WU*: common term of negation. **Pursue**, *ZHU*: chase, follow closely, press hard; expel, drive out. Ideogram: pig (wealth) and go, chasing fortune. **Seven**, *QI*: number seven; seven planets; seventh day when moon changes from crescent to waxing; the Tangram game analyzes all forms in terms of seven basic shapes. **Day/sun**, *RI*: the sun and the time of a sun-cycle, a day. **Acquire**, *DE*: obtain the desired object; possession; satisfied, fulfilled; it is permitted; agree with; wish for, desire covetously. Ideogram: go and obstacle, going through obstacles to the goal.

Ride, *CHENG*: ride an animal or a chariot; have the upper hand, control a stronger power; an opened line above controlling a whole line below. **Solid**, *GANG*: quality of the whole lines; firm, strong, unyielding, persisting. **Indeed**, *YE*: see *Preceding Situation*.

Six at Third

The **shake reviving, reviving**.
The **shake moving**: **without blunder**.

Comments
The **shake reviving, reviving**.
Position not appropriate indeed.

Fields of meaning

Shake, *ZHEN*: see *Image of the Situation*. **Revive**, *SU*: regain vital energy, courage or strength; bring back to life, cheer up, relieve. Ideogram: herb whose smell revives weary spirits. **Move**, *XING*: move or move something; motivate; emotionally moving; walk, act, do. Ideogram: successive steps. **Without**, *WU*: devoid of; there is not. **Blunder**, *SHENG*: mistake due to ignorance or fault; contrasts with calamity, *ZAI*, disaster from without. Ideogram: eye and growth, a film clouding sight.

Position, *WEI*: place, location; be at; social standing, rank; position of a line in a hexagram. Ideogram: person standing. **Not**, *BU*: common term of negation. **Appropriate**, *DANG*: suitable, capable, worthy, adequate, competent, equal to; opportune, convenient; whole lines in odd places and opened lines in even places. **Indeed**, *YE*: see *Preceding Situation*.

Nine at Fourth

The **shake releases** the **bog**.

Comments

The **shake releases** the **bog**.
Not-yet shining indeed.

Fields of meaning

Shake, *ZHEN*: see *Image of the Situation*. **Release**, *SUI*: let go, free; unhindered; advance, progress; promote, further; reach, succeed; in accord with, conforming to. Ideogram: go and follow one's wishes, unimpeded movement. **Bog**, *NI*: wet spongy soil; mire, slush, quicksand; unable to move.

Not-yet, *WEI*: temporal negative indicating that something is expected to happen but has not yet occurred. **Shine**, *GUANG*: illuminate, emit light; brilliant, splendid; honor, glory, éclat; distinct from brightness, *MING*, light of heavenly bodies. Ideogram: fire above person. **Indeed**, *YE*: see *Preceding Situation*.

Six at Fifth

The **shake going** and **coming**, **adversity**.
Hundred-thousand without loss, **possessing affairs**.

Comments

The **shake going** and **coming**, **adversity**.
Exposing movement indeed.
One's affairs located in the **center**.
The **great without loss indeed**.

Fields of meaning

Shake, *ZHEN*: see *Image of the Situation*. **Go**, *WANG*: move away in time or space, depart; become past; dead, gone; contrasts with come, *LAI*, approach in time or space. **Come**, *LAI*: see *Image of the Situation*. **Adversity**, *LI*: danger, hardship, severe; threat or difficulty that must be encountered, rather than avoided; grinding stone; polish, sharpen; a challenge that strengthens and perfects the character; stimulate, excite; cruel demon. **Hundred-thousand**, *YI*: a huge quantity. Ideogram: man and thought, a number that can only be imagined. **Without**, *WU*: devoid of; there is not. **Lose**, *SANG*: see *Image of the Situation*. **Possess**, *YOU*: general term indicating possession; have, own, be endowed with. **Affairs**, *SHI*: all kinds of personal activity; matters at hand; business; function, occupation; manage; perform a task; incident, event; case in court.

Exposure, *WEI*: being exposed to danger; precipitous, unsteady, too high, dangerously leaning. Ideogram: overhanging rock, person and limit, exposure in an extreme position. **Move**, *XING*: move or move something; motivate; emotionally moving; walk, act, do. Ideogram: successive steps. **Indeed**, *YE*: see *Preceding Situation*. **One/one's**, *QI*: general third person pronoun and possessive adjective; also: it/its, he/his, she/her, they/their. **Locate**, *ZAI*: be at, be situated at, dwell, reside; in, within; involved with, in the process of. Ideogram: earth and persevere, a place on the earth. **Center**, *ZHONG*: inner, central; put in the center; middle, stable point enabling you to face inner and outer changes; middle line of a trigram. Ideogram: field divided in two equal parts. **Great**, *DA*: big, noble, important, very; orient the will toward a self-imposed goal, impose direction; ability to lead or guide one's life; contrasts with small, *XIAO*, flexible adaptation to what crosses one's path.

Six Above

The **shake twining, twining**.
Observing: **terror, terror**.
Disciplining: **pitfall**.
The **shake not tending-towards one's body**.
Tending-towards one's neighbor.
Without fault.
Matrimonial alliance possesses words.

Comments
The **shake twining, twining**.
The **center not-yet acquired indeed**.
Although a **pitfall, without fault**.
The **dreading neighbor**, a **warning indeed**.

Fields of meaning
Shake, *ZHEN*: see *Image of the Situation*. **Twine**, *SUO*: string or rope of many strands twisted together; tie up, bind together; ruling ideas, obligations; anxiety (twisted bowels). **Observe**, *SHI*: see, examine, inspect; consider as; compare, imitate. Ideogram: see and omen, taking what you see into account. **Terror**, *QIAO*: look around in great alarm. Ideogram: eyes of bird trapped by a hand. **Discipline**, *ZHENG*: subjugate vassals, reduce to order; punishing expedition. Ideogram: step and correct, a rectifying move. **Pitfall**, *XIONG*: unfortunate situation, in which the flow of life and spirit is blocked and the experience of meaning is lost; stuck and exposed to danger; inappropriate attitude. Ideogram: person in a pit. **Not**, *BU*:

common term of negation. **Tend-towards**, *YU*: move toward without necessarily reaching, in the direction of. **One/one's**, *QI*: general third person pronoun and possessive adjective; also: it/its, he/his, she/her, they/their. **Body**, *GONG*: physical being, power and self-expression; oneself; innate quality; distinct from individuality, *SHEN*, which includes the notion of lifespan. **Neighbor**, *LIN*: person living nearby; extended family; assist, support. **Without fault**, *WU JIU*: no error or harm in the situation. **Matrimonial alliance**, *HUN GOU*: legal institution of marriage; union of two families by marriage. **Possess**, *YOU*: general term indicating possession; have, own, be endowed with. **Word**, *YAN*: see *Image of the Situation*.

Center, *ZHONG*: inner, central; put in the center; middle, stable point enabling you to face inner and outer changes; middle line of a trigram. Ideogram: field divided in two equal parts. **Not-yet**, *WEI*: temporal negative indicating that something is expected to happen but has not yet occurred. **Acquire**, *DE*: obtain the desired object; possession; satisfied, fulfilled; it is permitted; agree with; wish for, desire covetously. Ideogram: go and obstacle, going through obstacles to the goal. **Indeed**, *YE*: see *Preceding Situation*. **Although**, *SUI*: even though, supposing that, if, even if. **Dread**, *WEI*: fear, respect, stand in awe of; apprehensive; envious. **Warn**, *JIE*: alarm, alert, put on guard; caution, inform; guard against, refrain from. Ideogram: spear held in both hands, warning enemies.

Image Tradition

The **shake**. **Growing**.
The **shake coming**: **frightening**, **frightening**.
Anxiety involves blessing indeed.

Laughing words, **shrieking**, **shrieking**.
Afterwards possessing by **consequence indeed**.

The **shake scares** a **hundred miles**.
Scaring the **distant and-also fearing** the **nearby indeed**.

Not losing the **ladle** and the **libation**.
Emerging permits using guarding the **ancestral temple**, the **field-altar**, the **offertory-millet**.
Using activating the **offering lord indeed**.

Fields of meaning

The **shake. Growing**, *ZHEN HENG*: see *Image of the Situation*. The **shake coming: frightening, frightening**, *ZHEN LAI XI XI*: see *Image of the Situation*. **Anxiety**,

KONG: see *Hexagrams in Pairs.* **Involve**, *ZHI*: devote oneself to; induce, cause, implicate; approach; manifest, express; reach the highest degree of. Ideogram: reach and come up behind. **Bless**, *FU*: heavenly gifts and favor; happiness, prosperity; spiritual power and goodwill. Ideogram: spirit and plenty. **Indeed**, *YE*: see *Preceding Situation.*

Laughing words, shrieking, shrieking, *XIAO YAN YA YA*: see *Image of the Situation.* **After(wards)/later**, *HOU*: come after in time, subsequent; put oneself after; behind, back, draw back; the second; attendants, heirs, successors, posterity. **Possess**, *YOU*: general term indicating possession; have, own, be endowed with. **Consequence**, *ZE*: reason, cause, result; rule, law, pattern, standard; therefore; very strong connection.

The **shake scares** a **hundred miles**, *ZHEN JING BO LI*: see *Image of the Situation.* **Distance**, *YUAN*: far off, remote; keep at a distance; a long time, far away in time. Ideogram: go and a long way. **And-also**, *ER*: joins and contrasts two terms. **Fear**, *JU*: see *Hexagrams in Pairs.* **Nearby**, *ER*: near, close in space; approach.

Not losing the **ladle** and the **libation**, *BU SANG BI CHANG*: see *Image of the Situation.* **Emerge**, *CHU*: come out of, proceed from, spring from, issue forth; appear, be born; bear, generate; leave, flee; Action of the trigram Shake, *ZHEN*. Ideogram: stem with branches and leaves emerging. **Permit**, *KE*: possible because in harmony with an inherent principle; capable of; approve, authorize. Ideogram: mouth and breath, silent consent. **Use**, *YI*: see *Hexagrams in Pairs.* **Guard**, *SHOU*: keep in custody; protect, ward off harm, attend to, supervise. **Ancestry**, *ZONG*: clan, kin, origin; those who bear the same surname; ancestral hall and tablets; honor, revere. **Temple**, *MIAO*: building used to honor gods and ancestors. **Field-altar**, *SHE*: altar; sacrifices to spirits of place; village, with a common god and field-altar. **Offertory-millet**, *JI*: grain presented to the god of agriculture; presence of the god in the grain. **Activate**, *WEI*: act or cause to act; do, make, manage, make active; be, become; attend to, help; because of. **Offer**, *JI*: offer a sacrifice. Ideogram: hand, meat and worship. **Lord**, *ZHU*: see *Preceding Situation.*

52 THE BOUND | *Gen*

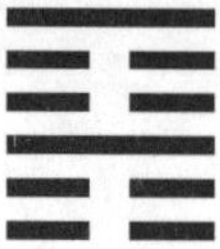

The situation described by this hexagram is characterized by a limit or boundary which marks the end of a cycle, a time to stop, reflect and prepare for the transition to a new phase. The hexagram The Bound is the doubling of the corresponding trigram, and partakes of its attributes.

Image of the Situation

> The **bound**: **one's back**.
> **Not capturing one's individuality**.
> **Moving one's chambers**.
> **Not viewing one's people**.
> **Without fault**.

Fields of meaning

Bound, *GEN*: limit, frontier; obstacle that prevents from seeing further; stop; still, quiet, motionless; confine, enclose; mountain, sunset, beginning of winter; solid, steady, unshakable; straight, hard, adamant, obstinate. *Symbol*: mountain, *SHAN*, large, immense; limit, boundary. Ideogram: three peaks, a mountain range. *Action*: stop, *ZHI*, bring or come to a standstill, cease, terminate. Ideogram: a foot stops walking. In the family of trigrams *GEN* is the youngest son. **One/one's**, *QI*: general third person pronoun and possessive adjective; also: it/its, he/his, she/her, they/their. **Back**, *BEI*: spine; behind, rear, hidden; turn the back on; North side; oppose, disobey, reject. Ideogram: North and body (facing South). **Not**, *BU*: common term of negation. **Capture**, *HUO*: obtain, seize, reach; take in a hunt, catch a thief; hit the mark, opportune moment; prisoner, spoils, prey, slave, servant. **Individuality**, *SHEN*: total person: psyche, body and lifespan; character, virtue, duty, pregnancy; distinct from body, *GONG*, physical being. **Move**, *XING*: move or move something; motivate; emotionally moving; walk, act, do. Ideogram: successive steps. **Chambers**, *TING*: family rooms; courtyard, hall; domestic. Ideogram: shelter and hall, a secure place. **View**, *JIAN*: vision in all its aspects: seeing, being visible, forming mental images; visit, call on, consult. Ideogram: eye above person, active and receptive sight. **People/person**, *REN*: humans individually and collectively; an individual; humankind. **Without fault**, *WU JIU*: no error or harm in the situation.

Outer and Inner Trigram

In this hexagram the outer and inner aspects of the situation are identical, and they are described by the trigram **Bound**. Its associations are listed in the corresponding *Field of meaning* above.

Counter Hexagram

The Counter Hexagram of **The Bound** is hexagram 40, **Unraveling**, which switches the emphasis from a limit or boundary which marks the end of a cycle to focusing on analysis and understanding.

Preceding Situation

> **Beings not permitted** to **use completing stirring-up**.
> **Stopping it**.
> To **anterior acquiescence belongs** the **use** of the **bound**.
> The **bound implies stopping indeed**.

Fields of meaning

Beings not permitted (to **use**), *WU BU KE (YI)*: it is not possible; no one is allowed; it is not in the nature of things. **Complete**, *ZHONG*: completion of a cycle that begins the next; entire, whole, all. Ideogram: silk cocoons, follow and ice, winter linking one year with the next. **Stir-up**, *DONG*: excite, influence, move, affect; work, take action; come out of the egg or the bud; Action of the trigram Shake, *ZHEN*. Ideogram: strength and heavy, move weighty things. **Stop**, *ZHI*: bring or come to a standstill, cease, terminate; Action of the trigram Bound, *GEN*. Ideogram: a foot stops walking. **It/belong**, *ZHI*: establishes between two terms a connection similar to the Saxon genitive, in which the second term belongs to the first one; at the end of a sentence it refers to something previously mentioned or implied. To **anterior acquiescence belongs** the **use** of, *GU SHOU ZHI YI*: understanding and accepting the preceding statement allows the consultant to make proper use of this hexagram. **Bound**, *GEN*: see *Image of the Situation*. **Imply**, *ZHE*: further signify; additional meaning. **Indeed**, *YE*: emphasizes and intensifies the previous statement.

Hexagrams in Pairs

The **shake**: **rising-up indeed**.
The **bound**: **stopping indeed**.

Fields of meaning

Shake, *ZHEN*: arouse, excite, inspire; awe, alarm, trembling; thunder rising from the depth of the earth; fertilizing intrusion. Ideogram: excite and rain. **Rise-up**, *QI*: stand up, erect; stimulate, excite; undertake, begin, develop. **Indeed**, *YE*: see *Preceding Situation*. **Bound**, *GEN*: see *Image of the Situation*. **Stop**, *ZHI*: see *Preceding Situation*.

Patterns of Wisdom

Joined mountains. The **bound**.
A **jun zi uses pondering not** to **emerge** from **one's position**.

Fields of meaning

Join, *JIAN*: add or bring together, unite; absorb, assimilate; simultaneously, also. Ideogram: hand grasping two grain stalks, two things at once. **Mountain**, *SHAN*: mountain; large, immense; limit, boundary; Symbol of the trigram Bound, *GEN*. Ideogram: three peaks, a mountain range. **Bound**, *GEN*: see *Image of the Situation*. **Jun zi**: ideal of a person who orders his/her life in accordance with dao rather than willful intention, and uses divination in this spirit. **Use**, *YI*: by means of; owing to; make use of, employ. **Ponder**, *SI*: reflect, consider, remember; deep thought; desire, wish. Ideogram: heart and field, the heart's concerns. **Not**, *BU*: common term of negation. **Emerge**, *CHU*: come out of, proceed from, spring from, issue forth; appear, be born; bear, generate; leave, flee; Action of the trigram Shake, *ZHEN*. Ideogram: stem with branches and leaves emerging. **One/one's**, *QI*: see *Image of the Situation*. **Position**, *WEI*: place, location; be at; social standing, rank; position of a line in a hexagram. Ideogram: person standing.

Transforming Lines

INITIAL SIX

The **bound**: **one's feet**.
Without fault.
Harvesting: **perpetual Trial**.

Comments
The **bound**: **one's feet**.
Not-yet letting-go correcting indeed.

Fields of meaning
Bound, *GEN*: see *Image of the Situation*. **One/one's**, *QI*: see *Image of the Situation*. **Foot**, *ZHI*: foot, footprint; foundation, base; walk; stop where the foot rests. **Without fault**, *WU JIU*: see *Image of the Situation*. **Harvest**, *LI*: benefit, advantage, profit; realization; sharp, acute, insightful; quality of autumn and West, third stage of the Time Cycle. Ideogram: ripe grain and blade. **Perpetual**, *YONG*: continual, everlasting, eternal. Ideogram: flowing water. **Trial**, *ZHEN*: inquiry by divination and its result; righteous, firm; separating wheat from chaff; the kernel, the proven core; quality of winter and North, fourth stage of the Time Cycle. Ideogram: pearl and divination.

Not-yet, *WEI*: temporal negative indicating that something is expected to happen but has not yet occurred. **Let-go**, *SHI*: lose, let slip; omit, miss, fail; lose control of. Ideogram: drop from the hand. **Correct**, *ZHENG*: rectify deviation or one-sidedness; proper, straight, exact, regular; constant, rule, model. Ideogram: stop and one, hold to one thing. **Indeed**, *YE*: see *Preceding Situation*.

Six at Second

The **bound**: **one's calves**.
Not rescuing one's following.
One's heart not keen.

Comments
Not rescuing one's following.
Not-yet withdrawing from **hearkening indeed**.

Fields of meaning
Bound, *GEN*: see *Image of the Situation*. **One/one's**, *QI*: see *Image of the Situation*. **Calf**, *FEI*: calf; rely on; prop, rest; sick, weak. **Not**, *BU*: common term of negation. **Rescue**, *ZHENG*: aid, deliver from trouble; pull out, raise up, lift. Ideogram: hand and aid, a helping hand. **Follow**, *SUI*: step behind, come after, move in the same direction; comply with what is ahead; pursue; follow a way or religion; conform to; next, subsequent. Ideogram: go and fall, unavoidable movement. **Heart**, *XIN*: the heart as center of being; seat of mind, imagination and affect; moral nature; source of desires, intentions, will. **Keen**, *KUAI*: joyous, cheerful, lively, spirited; eager, prompt, ready; capable of.

Not-yet, *WEI*: temporal negative indicating that something is expected to happen but has not yet occurred. **Withdraw**, *TUI*: draw back, retreat, recede; decline, refuse. **Hearken**, *TING*: listen attentively, obey, accept, acknowledge; examine, judge, decide. Ideogram: ear and actualizing-dao. **Indeed**, *YE*: see *Preceding Situation*.

NINE AT THIRD

The **bound**: **one's limit**.
Attributed to **one's loins**.
Adversity smothers the **heart**.

Comments
The **bound**: **one's limit**.
Exposure smothers the **heart indeed**.

Fields of meaning

Bound, *GEN*: see *Image of the Situation*. **One/one's**, *QI*: see *Image of the Situation*. **Limit**, *XIAN*: boundary, frontier, threshold; restriction, impediment; set a limit, distinguish, separate. **Attribute**, *LIE*: align, arrange in order; assign, place according to rank; distinguish, separate; obstacle, block. **Loins**, *YIN*: hips, pelvis, lumbar region, kidneys; respect, honor; money belt. **Adversity**, *LI*: danger, hardship, severe; threat or difficulty that must be encountered, rather than avoided; grinding stone; polish, sharpen; a challenge that strengthens and perfects the character; stimulate, excite; cruel demon. **Smother**, *XUN*: suffocate, smoke out; fog, steam, miasma, vapor; broil, parch; offend; evening mists. **Heart**, *XIN*: the heart as center of being; seat of mind, imagination and affect; moral nature; source of desires, intentions, will.

Exposure, *WEI*: being exposed to danger; precipitous, unsteady, too high, dangerously leaning. Ideogram: overhanging rock, person and limit, exposure in an extreme position. **Indeed**, *YE*: see *Preceding Situation*.

SIX AT FOURTH

The **bound**: **one's individuality**.
Without fault.

Comments
The **bound**: **one's individuality**.
Stopping relates to the **body indeed**.

Fields of meaning

Bound, *GEN*: see *Image of the Situation*. **One/one's**, *QI*: see *Image of the Situation*. **Individuality**, *SHEN*: see *Image of the Situation*. **Without fault**, *WU JIU*: see *Image of the Situation*.

Stop, *ZHI*: see *Preceding Situation*. **Relate**, *ZHU*: in regard to; all, every, several. Ideogram: words and imply. **Body**, *GONG*: physical being, power and self-expression; oneself; innate quality; distinct from individuality, *SHEN*, which includes the notion of lifespan. **Indeed**, *YE*: see *Preceding Situation*.

SIX AT FIFTH

The **bound**: **one's jawbones**.
Words possess sequence.
Repenting extinguished.

Comments
The **bound**: **one's jawbones**.
Using the **center**, **correcting indeed**.

Fields of meaning

Bound, *GEN*: see *Image of the Situation*. **One/one's**, *QI*: see *Image of the Situation*. **Jawbones/brace**, *FU*: braces of a cart; cheeks, maxillary bones; support, consolidate, strengthen, prop up; steady, firm, rigid; help, rescue. **Word**, *YAN*: spoken word, speech, saying; talk, discuss, address; name, signify. Ideogram: mouth and rising vapor. **Possess**, *YOU*: general term indicating possession; have, own, be endowed with. **Sequence**, *XU*: order, precedence, series; follow in order. **Repenting extinguished**, *HUI WANG*: previous errors are corrected, all causes for repenting disappear.

Use, *YI*: see *Patterns of Wisdom*. **Center**, *ZHONG*: inner, central; put in the center; middle, stable point enabling you to face inner and outer changes; middle line of a trigram. Ideogram: field divided in two equal parts. **Correct**, *ZHENG*: rectify deviation or one-sidedness; proper, straight, exact, regular; constant, rule, model. Ideogram: stop and one, hold to one thing. **Indeed**, *YE*: see *Preceding Situation*.

NINE ABOVE

Magnanimous bound, significant.

Comments

To **magnanimous bound belongs significance**.
Using munificence to **complete indeed**.

Fields of meaning

Magnanimous, *DUN*: generous, honest, sincere; important, wealthy; honor, increase; firm, solid. Ideogram: strike and accept, warrior magnanimous in giving and receiving blows. **Bound**, *GEN*: see *Image of the Situation*. **Significant**, *JI*: leads to the experience of meaning; favorable, propitious, appropriate. Ideogram: scholar and mouth, wise words of a sage.

Belong/it, *ZHI*: establishes between two terms a connection similar to the Saxon genitive, in which the second term belongs to the first one; at the end of a sentence it refers to something previously mentioned or implied. **Use**, *YI*: see *Patterns of Wisdom*. **Munificent**, *HOU*: liberal, kind, generous; create abundance; thick, large. Ideogram: gift of a superior to an inferior. **Complete**, *ZHONG*: see *Preceding Situation*. **Indeed**, *YE*: see *Preceding Situation*.

Image Tradition

The **bound**: **stopping indeed**.
The **season stopping**, by **consequence stopping**.
The **season moving**, by **consequence moving**.
Stirring-up, **stilling**, **not letting-go one's season**.
One's dao: **shining brightness**.
The **bound**: **one's stopping**.
Stopping at **one's place indeed**.

Above and **below**: **antagonistic correspondence**.
Not reciprocally associating indeed.
That uses not capturing one's individuality.
Moving one's chambers, **not viewing one's people**.
Without fault indeed.

Fields of meaning

Bound, *GEN*: see *Image of the Situation*. **Stop**, *ZHI*: see *Preceding Situation*. **Indeed**, *YE*: see *Preceding Situation*. **Season**, *SHI*: quality of the time; the right time, opportune, in harmony; planning in accord with the time; season of the year. Ideogram: sun and temple, sacred time. **Consequence**, *ZE*: reason, cause, result; rule, law, pattern, standard; therefore; very strong connection. **Move**, *XING*: see *Image of the Situation*. **Stir-up**, *DONG*: see *Preceding Situation*. **Still**, *JING*: peaceful, quiet, at rest, silent, imperturbable. **Not**, *BU*: common term of negation. **Let-go**, *SHI*: lose, let slip; omit, miss, fail; lose control of. Ideogram: drop from the hand. **One/one's**, *QI*: see *Image of the Situation*. **Dao**, *DAO*: way or path; ongoing process of being and the course it traces for each person or thing; ultimate reality, intrinsic nature; origin. Ideogram: go and head, opening a path. **Shine**, *GUANG*: see *Hexagrams in Pairs*. **Brightness**, *MING*: light, radiance, clarity; distinguish, discern, understand; light-giving aspect of fire, of heavenly bodies and of consciousness; brightness and fire are the Symbols of the trigram Radiance, *LI*. **Place**, *SUO*: position, location; residence, dwelling; where something belongs or comes from; habitual focus or object.

Above, *SHANG*: anything above in all senses; higher, upper, outer; upper trigram. **Below**, *XIA*: anything below, in all senses; lower, inner; lower trigram. **Antagonistic**, *DI*: opposed and equal; competitor, enemy; a contest between equals. **Correspond**, *YING*: be in agreement or harmony; proper, suitable; resonate together, answer to; relation between the lines (1 and 4, 2 and 5, 3 and 6) when they form the pair opened and whole, supple and solid. Ideogram: heart and obey. **Reciprocal**, *XIANG*: mutual; assist, encourage, help; bring together, blend with; examine, inspect; by turns. **Associate**, *YU*: consort with, combine; companions; group, band, company; agree with, comply, help; in favor of. Ideogram: a pair of hands reaching downward meets a pair of hands reaching upward, helpful association. **That**, *SHI*: refers to the preceding statement. **Use**, *YI*: see *Patterns of Wisdom*. **Not capturing one's individuality**, *BU HUO QI SHEN*: see *Image of the Situation*. **Moving one's chambers**, *XING QI TING*: see *Image of the Situation*. **Not viewing one's people**, *BU JIAN QI REN*: see *Image of the Situation*. **Without fault**, *WU JIU*: see *Image of the Situation*.

漸

䷴

53 INFILTRATING
Jian

The situation described by this hexagram is characterized by a gradual and steady penetration extending its influence by degrees, like water seeping into cracks.

Image of the Situation

> **Infiltrating.**
> **Womanhood converting, significant.**
> **Harvesting, Trial.**

Fields of meaning

Infiltrate, *JIAN*: penetrate slowly and surely, as water; diffuse throughout; advance by degrees; gradual process; influence, affect. Ideogram: water and cut into. **Woman(hood)**, *NÜ*: woman and what is inherently female. **Convert**, *GUI*: accomplish one's destiny; revert to the original place or state; restore, revert; turn into; goal, destination, intention; a girl getting married. Ideogram: arrive and wife, become mistress of a household. **Significant**, *JI*: leads to the experience of meaning; favorable, propitious, appropriate. Ideogram: scholar and mouth, wise words of a sage. **Harvest**, *LI*: benefit, advantage, profit; realization; sharp, acute, insightful; quality of autumn and West, third stage of the Time Cycle. Ideogram: ripe grain and blade. **Trial**, *ZHEN*: inquiry by divination and its result; righteous, firm; separating wheat from chaff; the kernel, the proven core; quality of winter and North, fourth stage of the Time Cycle. Ideogram: pearl and divination.

Outer and Inner Trigram

The upper trigram, **Root**, *SUN*, describes the outer aspects of the situation. It has the following associations: base on which things rest, ground, foundation; mild, subtly penetrating; nourishing. *Symbols*: tree/wood and wind. Tree/wood, *MU*: trees and all things woody or wooden; associated with the Wooden Moment. Ideogram: a tree with roots and branches. Wind, *FENG*: wind, breeze, gust; weather and its influence on mood and humor; fashion, usage. *Action*: enter, *RU*, penetrate, go into, enter on, encroach on; progress; put into. In the family of trigrams *SUN* is the eldest daughter.

The lower trigram, **Bound**, *GEN*, describes the inner aspects of the situation. It has the following associations: limit, frontier; obstacle that prevents from seeing further; stop; still, quiet, motionless; confine, enclose; mountain, sunset, beginning of winter; solid, steady, unshakable; straight, hard, adamant, obstinate. *Symbol*: mountain, *SHAN*, large, immense; limit, boundary. Ideogram: three peaks, a mountain range. *Action*: stop, *ZHI*, bring or come to a standstill, cease, terminate. Ideogram: a foot stops walking. In the family of trigrams *GEN* is the youngest son.

Counter Hexagram

The Counter Hexagram of **Infiltrating** is hexagram 64, **Not Yet Fording**, which switches the emphasis from infiltrating by a gradual and steady penetration to being still on the brink of a move whose outcome cannot yet be discerned.

Preceding Situation

> **Beings not permitted** to **use completing stopping**.
> To **anterior acquiescence belongs** the **use** of **infiltrating**.
> **Infiltrating implies advancing indeed**.

Fields of meaning

Beings not permitted (to **use**), *WU BU KE (YI)*: it is not possible; no one is allowed; it is not in the nature of things. **Complete**, *ZHONG*: completion of a cycle that begins the next; entire, whole, all. Ideogram: silk cocoons, follow and ice, winter linking one year with the next. **Stop**, *ZHI*: bring or come to a standstill, cease, terminate; Action of the trigram Bound, *GEN*. Ideogram: a foot stops walking. To **anterior acquiescence belongs** the **use** of, *GU SHOU ZHI YI*: understanding and accepting the preceding statement allows the consultant to make proper use of this hexagram. **Infiltrate**, *JIAN*: see *Image of the Situation*. **Imply**, *ZHE*: further signify; additional meaning. **Advance**, *JIN*: move forward, progress, climb; promote or be promoted; further the development of, augment; offer, introduce. **Indeed**, *YE*: emphasizes and intensifies the previous statement.

Hexagrams in Pairs

> **Infiltrating**: **womanhood converting awaits manhood moving indeed**.
> **Converting maidenhood**: the **completion belonging** to **womanhood indeed**.

Fields of meaning

Infiltrate, *JIAN*: see *Image of the Situation*. **Woman(hood),** *NÜ*: see *Image of the Situation*. **Convert,** *GUI*: see *Image of the Situation*. **Await,** *DAI*: expect, wait for, prepare to meet (friendly or hostile); provide against. **Man(hood),** *NAN*: a man; what is inherently male; husband, son. Ideogram: field and strength, men's hard work in the fields. **Move,** *XING*: move or move something; motivate; emotionally moving; walk, act, do. Ideogram: successive steps. **Indeed,** *YE*: see *Preceding Situation*. **Maidenhood,** *MEI*: girl not yet nubile, virgin; younger sister; daughter of a secondary wife. Ideogram: woman and not-yet. **Complete,** *ZHONG*: see *Preceding Situation*. **Belong/it,** *ZHI*: establishes between two terms a connection similar to the Saxon genitive, in which the second term belongs to the first one; at the end of a sentence it refers to something previously mentioned or implied.

Patterns of Wisdom

> The **mountain possesses wood above**. **Infiltrating**.
> A **jun zi uses residing** in **eminent actualizing-dao** to
> **improve** the **customs**.

Fields of meaning

Mountain, *SHAN*: mountain; large, immense; limit, boundary; Symbol of the trigram Bound, *GEN*. Ideogram: three peaks, a mountain range. **Possess,** *YOU*: general term indicating possession; have, own, be endowed with. **Wood/tree,** *MU*: trees and all things woody or wooden; associated with the Wooden Moment; wood and wind are the Symbols of the trigram Ground, *SUN*. Ideogram: a tree with roots and branches. **Above,** *SHANG*: anything above in all senses; higher, upper, outer; upper trigram. **Infiltrate,** *JIAN*: see *Image of the Situation*. **Jun zi**: ideal of a person who orders his/her life in accordance with dao rather than willful intention, and uses divination in this spirit. **Use,** *YI*: by means of; owing to; make use of, employ. **Reside,** *JU*: dwell, live in, stay; sit down; fill an office; well-being, rest. Ideogram: body and seat. **Eminent,** *XIAN*: worthy, excellent, virtuous; endowed with moral and intellectual power; second only to the wise, *SHENG*. **Actualize-dao,** *DE*: realize dao in action; power, virtue; ability to follow the course traced by the ongoing process of the cosmos. Ideogram: go, straight, and heart. Linked with acquire, *DE*: acquiring that which makes a being become what it is meant to be. **Improve,** *SHAN*: make better, reform, perfect; virtuous, wise; mild, docile; clever, skillful. Ideogram: mouth and sheep, gentle speech. **Customs,** *SU*: habit, usage, tradition; common people; ordinary, vulgar, trivial; worldly, secular.

Transforming Lines

Initial Six

The **swan infiltrating tending-towards** the **barrier**.
The **small son, adversity**.
Possessing words.
Lacking fault.

Comments
To the **small son belongs adversity**.
Righteous, without fault indeed.

Fields of meaning

Swan, *HONG*: large white water bird, wild swan, wild goose; symbol of the soul and its spiritual aspirations; emblem of conjugal fidelity; messenger; strong, vast, profound, far-reaching. **Infiltrate**, *JIAN*: see *Image of the Situation*. **Tend-towards**, *YU*: move toward without necessarily reaching, in the direction of. **Barrier**, *GAN*: boundary, limit; fend off, protect; river bank; shield, defensive armor; the Ten Heavenly Barriers articulate the year in the Chinese calendar. **Small**, *XIAO*: little, common, unimportant; adapting to what crosses your path; ability to move in harmony with the vicissitudes of life; contrasts with great, *DA*, self-imposed theme or goal. **Son(hood)**, *ZI*: son, male child; heirs, offspring, posterity; living up to the ideal of the ancestors as highest human aspiration; seed, kernel, egg; sage, teacher; nadir, deepest point, midnight, mid-winter. **Adversity**, *LI*: danger, hardship, severe; threat or difficulty that must be encountered, rather than avoided; grinding stone; polish, sharpen; a challenge that strengthens and perfects the character; stimulate, excite; cruel demon. **Possess**, *YOU*: see *Patterns of Wisdom*. **Word**, *YAN*: spoken word, speech, saying; talk, discuss, address; name, signify. Ideogram: mouth and rising vapor. **Lack**, *WU*: strong negative; there is no, without, empty of, absence. **Fault**, *JIU*: unworthy conduct that leads to harm, illness, misfortune; guilt, crime, punishment. Ideogram: person and differ, differ from what you should be.

Belong/it, *ZHI*: see *Hexagrams in Pairs*. **Righteous**, *YI*: proper, just, virtuous, upright; the heart that rules itself; benevolent, loyal, devoted to public good. **Without fault**, *WU JIU*: no error or harm in the situation. **Indeed**, *YE*: see *Preceding Situation*.

Six at Second

䷴

The **swan infiltrating tending-towards** the **stone**.
Drinking and **taking-in**: **feasting**, **feasting**.
Significant.

Comments
Drinking and **taking-in**: **feasting**, **feasting**.
Not sheer satiation indeed.

Fields of meaning

Swan, *HONG*: large white water bird, wild swan, wild goose; symbol of the soul and its spiritual aspirations; emblem of conjugal fidelity; messenger; strong, vast, profound, far-reaching. **Infiltrate**, *JIAN*: see *Image of the Situation*. **Tend-towards**, *YU*: move toward without necessarily reaching, in the direction of. **Stone**, *PAN*: large conspicuous rock, foundation stone; stable, immovable. **Drink**, *YIN*: drink, swallow, ingest liquid or food; inhale, suck in. **Take-in**, *SHI*: eat, drink, ingest, absorb, incorporate; food, nourishment. **Feast**, *KAN*: take part in or give a feast; rejoice, give pleasure; contented, at ease. **Significant**, *JI*: see *Image of the Situation*.

Not, *BU*: common term of negation. **Sheer**, *SU*: plain, unadorned; original color or state; clean, pure, natural. Ideogram: white silk. **Satiation**, *BAO*: full, replete, satisfied; swollen, sated; gratified, flattered. **Indeed**, *YE*: see *Preceding Situation*.

Nine at Third

䷴

The **swan infiltrating tending-towards** the **highlands**.
The **husband disciplined**, **not returning**.
The **wife pregnant**, **not nurturing**.
Pitfall.
Harvesting: **resisting illegality**.

Comments
The **husband disciplined**, **not returning**.
Radiating a **flock** of **demons indeed**.
The **wife pregnant**, **not nurturing**.
Letting-go one's dao indeed.
Harvesting: **availing** of **resisting illegality**.
Yielding: **reciprocal protection indeed**.

Fields of meaning

Swan, *HONG*: large white water bird, wild swan, wild goose; symbol of the soul and its spiritual aspirations; emblem of conjugal fidelity; messenger; strong, vast, profound, far-reaching. **Infiltrate**, *JIAN*: see *Image of the Situation*. **Tend-towards**, *YU*: move toward without necessarily reaching, in the direction of. **Highlands**, *LU*: high, dry land as distinct from swamps; mountain, plateau. **Husband**, *FU*: adult, man, male spouse; scholar, distinguished man; one who can help; manage a household. Ideogram: man with a pin in his hair to show that he is of age. **Discipline**, *ZHENG*: subjugate vassals, reduce to order; punishing expedition. Ideogram: step and correct, a rectifying move. **Not**, *BU*: common term of negation. **Return**, *FU*: go back, turn or lead back; recur, reappear, come again; restore, renew, recover; return to an earlier time or place. Ideogram: step and retrace a path. **Wife**, *FU*: position of married woman as head of the household; distinct from consort, *QI*, which denotes her legal status, and from concubine, *QIE*, secondary wife. Ideogram: woman, hand and broom, household duties. **Pregnant**, *REN*: conceive and carry a child; give birth. **Nurture**, *YU*: give birth; bring up, rear, raise. **Pitfall**, *XIONG*: unfortunate situation, in which the flow of life and spirit is blocked and the experience of meaning is lost; stuck and exposed to danger; inappropriate attitude. Ideogram: person in a pit. **Harvest**, *LI*: see *Image of the Situation*. **Resist**, *YU*: withstand, oppose; bring to an end; prevent. Ideogram: rule and worship, imposing ethical or religious limits. **Illegality**, *KOU*: take by force, violate, invade, sack, break the laws; brutality; enemies, outcasts, bandits.

Radiance, *LI*: glowing light, spreading in all directions; the power of consciousness; discriminate, articulate, divide and arrange in order; assemble, attract. Ideogram: bird and weird, magical fire-bird with brilliant plumage. **Flock**, *QUN*: herd, group; people of the same kind, friends, equals; crowd, multitude; move in unison, flock together. Ideogram: chief and sheep, flock around a leader. **Demon**, *CHOU*: malignant genius; horror; ugly, vile, disgraceful, shameful; drunken; detest, hate; strange, ominous; class, group, crowd; similar. Ideogram: fermented liquor and soul. Demon and tiger are opposed on the North–South axis of the Universal Compass; the tiger (Extreme Yang) protects against the demons of Extreme Yin. **Indeed**, *YE*: see *Preceding Situation*. **Let-go**, *SHI*: lose, let slip; omit, miss, fail; lose control of. Ideogram: drop from the hand. **One/one's**, *QI*: general third person pronoun and possessive adjective; also: it/its, he/his, she/her, they/their. **Dao**, *DAO*: way or path; ongoing process of being and the course it traces for each person or thing; ultimate reality, intrinsic nature; origin. Ideogram: go and head, opening a path. **Avail**, *YONG*: use, employ for a specific purpose; take advantage of; benefit from; capacity. Ideogram: to divine and center, applying divination to central concerns. **Yield**, *SHUN*: give way, comply, agree, follow, obey; docile, flexible; bear produce, nourish, provide; Action of the trigram Field, *KUN*.

Reciprocal, *XIANG*: mutual; assist, encourage, help; bring together, blend with; examine, inspect; by turns. **Protect**, *BAO*: guard, defend, keep safe; nourish, support.

SIX AT FOURTH

The **swan infiltrating tending-towards** the **trees**.
Maybe acquiring one's rafter.
Without fault.

Comments
Maybe acquiring one's rafter.
Yielding uses the **root indeed**.

Fields of meaning

Swan, *HONG*: large white water bird, wild swan, wild goose; symbol of the soul and its spiritual aspirations; emblem of conjugal fidelity; messenger; strong, vast, profound, far-reaching. **Infiltrate**, *JIAN*: see *Image of the Situation*. **Tend-towards**, *YU*: move toward without necessarily reaching, in the direction of. **Tree/wood**, *MU*: trees and all things woody or wooden; associated with the Wooden Moment; wood and wind are the Symbols of the trigram Ground, *SUN*. Ideogram: a tree with roots and branches. **Maybe**, *HUO*: possible but not certain, perhaps. **Acquire**, *DE*: obtain the desired object; possession; satisfied, fulfilled; it is permitted; agree with; wish for, desire covetously. Ideogram: go and obstacle, going through obstacles to the goal. **One/one's**, *QI*: general third person pronoun and possessive adjective; also: it/its, he/his, she/her, they/their. **Rafter**, *JUE*: roof beam; flat branch. **Without fault**, *WU JIU*: no error or harm in the situation.

Yield, *SHUN*: give way, comply, agree, follow, obey; docile, flexible; bear produce, nourish, provide; Action of the trigram Field, *KUN*. **Use**, *YI*: see *Patterns of Wisdom*. **Root**, *SUN*: base on which things rest, ground, foundation; mild, subtly penetrating; nourishing. **Indeed**, *YE*: see *Preceding Situation*.

NINE AT FIFTH

The **swan infiltrating tending-towards** the **mound**.
The **wife**, **three year's-time not pregnant**.
To **completing abstention belongs mastering**.
Significant.

Comments

To **completing abstention belongs mastering, significant.**
Acquiring the **place desired indeed.**

Fields of meaning

Swan, *HONG*: large white water bird, wild swan, wild goose; symbol of the soul and its spiritual aspirations; emblem of conjugal fidelity; messenger; strong, vast, profound, far-reaching. **Infiltrate,** *JIAN*: see *Image of the Situation*. **Tend-towards,** *YU*: move toward without necessarily reaching, in the direction of. **Mound,** *LING*: grave-mound, barrow; small hill. **Wife,** *FU*: position of married woman as head of the household; distinct from consort, *QI*, which denotes her legal status, and from concubine, *QIE*, secondary wife. Ideogram: woman, hand and broom, household duties. **Three/thrice,** *SAN*: number three; third time or place; active phases of a cycle; superlative; beginning of repetition (since one and two are entities in themselves). **Year's-time,** *SUI*: duration of a year; beginning of a year. **Not,** *BU*: common term of negation. **Pregnant,** *REN*: conceive and carry a child; give birth. **Complete,** *ZHONG*: see *Preceding Situation*. **Abstain/absolutely-nothing,** *MO*: complete elimination; do not, not any, by no means. **Belong/it,** *ZHI*: see *Hexagrams in Pairs*. **Master,** *SHENG*: have the upper hand; control, command, win, conquer, check (as in the cycle of the Five Transformative Moments); worthy of, able to. **Significant,** *JI*: see *Image of the Situation*.

Acquire, *DE*: obtain the desired object; possession; satisfied, fulfilled; it is permitted; agree with; wish for, desire covetously. Ideogram: go and obstacle, going through obstacles to the goal. **Place,** *SUO*: position, location; residence, dwelling; where something belongs or comes from; habitual focus or object. **Desire,** *YUAN*: wish, hope or long for; covet; desired object. **Indeed,** *YE*: see *Preceding Situation*.

NINE ABOVE

The **swan infiltrating tending-towards** the **highlands.**
Its feathers permit availing of **activating** the **fundamentals.**
Significant.

Comments

Its feathers permit availing of **activating** the **fundamentals, significant.**
Not permitting disarray indeed.

Fields of meaning

Swan, *HONG*: large white water bird, wild swan, wild goose; symbol of the soul and its spiritual aspirations; emblem of conjugal fidelity; messenger; strong, vast, profound, far-reaching. **Infiltrate**, *JIAN*: see *Image of the Situation*. **Tend-towards**, *YU*: move toward without necessarily reaching, in the direction of. **Highlands**, *LU*: high, dry land as distinct from swamps; mountain, plateau. **It/its**, *QI*: general third person pronoun and possessive adjective; also: one/one's, he/his, she/her, they/their. **Feathers**, *YOU*: plumes, wings; feathered; flying. **Permit**, *KE*: possible because in harmony with an inherent principle; capable of; approve, authorize. Ideogram: mouth and breath, silent consent. **Avail**, *YONG*: use, employ for a specific purpose; take advantage of; benefit from; capacity. Ideogram: to divine and center, applying divination to central concerns. **Activate**, *WEI*: act or cause to act; do, make, manage, make active; be, become; attend to, help; because of. **Fundamentals**, *YI*: basic components, essentials; correct, proper, just; rule, rite, etiquette; paired, matched. Ideogram: person and righteous. **Significant**, *JI*: see *Image of the Situation*.

Not, *BU*: common term of negation. **Disarray**, *LUAN*: throw into disorder, mislay, confuse; out of place; discord, insurrection, anarchy. **Indeed**, *YE*: see *Preceding Situation*.

Image Tradition

To **infiltrating belongs advancing indeed**.
Womanhood converting, significant indeed.
Advancing acquires the **position**.
Going possesses achievement indeed.

Advancing uses correcting.
Permitted to **use correcting** the **fiefdoms indeed**.
One's position: the **solid acquires** the **center indeed**.

Stopping and-also the **root**.
Stirring-up not exhausted indeed.

Fields of meaning

Infiltrate, *JIAN*: see *Image of the Situation*. **Belong/it**, *ZHI*: see *Hexagrams in Pairs*. **Advance**, *JIN*: see *Preceding Situation*. **Indeed**, *YE*: see *Preceding Situation*. **Womanhood converting, significant**, *NÜ GUI JI*: see *Image of the Situation*. **Advance**, *JIN*: see *Preceding Situation*. **Acquire**, *DE*: obtain the desired object; possession; satisfied, fulfilled; it is permitted; agree with; wish for, desire covetously.

Ideogram: go and obstacle, going through obstacles to the goal. **Position**, *WEI*: place, location; be at; social standing, rank; position of a line in a hexagram. Ideogram: person standing. **Go**, *WANG*: move away in time or space, depart; become past; dead, gone; contrasts with come, *LAI*, approach in time or space. **Possess**, *YOU*: see *Patterns of Wisdom*. **Achieve**, *GONG*: work done, results, actual accomplishment; praise, worth, merit. Ideogram: workman's square and forearm, combining craft and strength.

Use, *YI*: see *Patterns of Wisdom*. **Correct**, *ZHENG*: rectify deviation or one-sidedness; proper, straight, exact, regular; constant, rule, model. Ideogram: stop and one, hold to one thing. **Permit**, *KE*: possible because in harmony with an inherent principle; capable of; approve, authorize. Ideogram: mouth and breath, silent consent. **Fiefdom**, *BANG*: region governed by a feudatory. **One/one's**, *QI*: general third person pronoun and possessive adjective; also: it/its, he/his, she/her, they/their. **Solid**, *GANG*: quality of the whole lines; firm, strong, unyielding, persisting. **Center**, *ZHONG*: inner, central; put in the center; middle, stable point enabling you to face inner and outer changes; middle line of a trigram. Ideogram: field divided in two equal parts.

Stop, *ZHI*: see *Preceding Situation*. **And-also**, *ER*: joins and contrasts two terms. **Root**, *SUN*: base on which things rest, ground, foundation; mild, subtly penetrating; nourishing. **Stir-up**, *DONG*: excite, influence, move, affect; work, take action; come out of the egg or the bud; Action of the trigram Shake, *ZHEN*. Ideogram: strength and heavy, move weighty things. **Not**, *BU*: common term of negation. **Exhaust**, *QIONG*: bring to an end; limit, extremity; investigate exhaustively; destitute, indigent; end without a new beginning; distinct from complete, *ZHONG*, end of a cycle that begins the next one. Ideogram: cave and naked person, bent with disease or old age.

歸妹

54 CONVERTING MAIDENHOOD | *Gui Mei*

The situation described by this hexagram is characterized by realizing one's nature by accepting one's allotted destiny, as in the traditional image of a maiden finding her social maturity by entering the house of her husband.

Image of the Situation

> **Converting maidenhood.**
> **Disciplining, pitfall.**
> **Without direction Harvesting.**

Fields of meaning

Convert, *GUI*: accomplish one's destiny; revert to the original place or state; restore, revert; turn into; goal, destination, intention; a girl getting married. Ideogram: arrive and wife, become mistress of a household. **Maidenhood**, *MEI*: girl not yet nubile, virgin; younger sister; daughter of a secondary wife. Ideogram: woman and not-yet. **Discipline**, *ZHENG*: subjugate vassals, reduce to order; punishing expedition. Ideogram: step and correct, a rectifying move. **Pitfall**, *XIONG*: unfortunate situation, in which the flow of life and spirit is blocked and the experience of meaning is lost; stuck and exposed to danger; inappropriate attitude. Ideogram: person in a pit. **Without direction Harvesting**, *WU YOU LI*: in order to take advantage of the situation, do not impose a direction on events.

Outer and Inner Trigram

The upper trigram, **Shake**, *ZHEN*, describes the outer aspects of the situation. It has the following associations: arouse, excite, inspire; awe, alarm, trembling; thunder rising from the depth of the earth; fertilizing intrusion. Ideogram: excite and rain. *Symbol*: thunder, *LEI*, arousing power emerging from the depth of the earth. *Action*: stir-up, *DONG*, excite, influence, move, affect; work, take action;

come out of the egg or the bud. Ideogram: strength and heavy, move weighty things. In the family of trigrams *ZHEN* is the eldest son.

The lower trigram, **Open**, *DUI*, describes the inner aspects of the situation. It has the following associations: an open surface, promoting interaction and interpenetration; pleasant, easy, responsive, free, unhindered; opening, passage; the mouth; exchange, barter; straight, direct; meet, gather; place where water accumulates. Ideogram: mouth and vapor, communication through speech. *Symbol*: marsh, *ZE*, open surface of a flat body of water and the vapors rising from it; fertilize, enrich; kindness, favor. *Action*: stimulate, *SHUO*, rouse to action and good feeling; stir up, urge on; exhort, persuade; say, tell, relate; cheer, delight; joyous, peaceful, restful. Ideogram: words and exchange. In the family of trigrams *DUI* is the youngest daughter.

Counter Hexagram

The Counter Hexagram of **Converting Maidenhood** is hexagram 63, **Already Fording**, which switches the emphasis from standing on the threshold of a new life to being engaged in a process which is already on its way to completion.

Preceding Situation

> **Advancing necessarily possesses** a **place** for **converting**.
> To **anterior acquiescence belongs** the **use** of **converting maidenhood**.

Fields of meaning

Advance, *JIN*: move forward, progress, climb; promote or be promoted; further the development of, augment; offer, introduce. **Necessarily**, *BI*: unavoidably, certainly. **Possess**, *YOU*: general term indicating possession; have, own, be endowed with. **Place**, *SUO*: position, location; residence, dwelling; where something belongs or comes from; habitual focus or object. **Convert**, *GUI*: see *Image of the Situation*. **To anterior acquiescence belongs** the **use** of, *GU SHOU ZHI YI*: understanding and accepting the preceding statement allows the consultant to make proper use of this hexagram. **Maidenhood**, *MEI*: see *Image of the Situation*.

Hexagrams in Pairs

> **Infiltrating**: **womanhood converting awaits manhood moving indeed**.
> **Converting maidenhood**: the **completion belonging** to **womanhood indeed**.

Fields of meaning

Infiltrate, *JIAN*: penetrate slowly and surely, as water; diffuse throughout; advance by degrees; gradual process; influence, affect. Ideogram: water and cut into. **Woman(hood)**, *NÜ*: woman and what is inherently female. **Convert**, *GUI*: see *Image of the Situation*. **Await**, *DAI*: expect, wait for, prepare to meet (friendly or hostile); provide against. **Man(hood)**, *NAN*: a man; what is inherently male; husband, son. Ideogram: field and strength, men's hard work in the fields. **Move**, *XING*: move or move something; motivate; emotionally moving; walk, act, do. Ideogram: successive steps. **Indeed**, *YE*: emphasizes and intensifies the previous statement. **Maidenhood**, *MEI*: see *Image of the Situation*. **Complete**, *ZHONG*: completion of a cycle that begins the next; entire, whole, all. Ideogram: silk cocoons, follow and ice, winter linking one year with the next. **Belong/it**, *ZHI*: establishes between two terms a connection similar to the Saxon genitive, in which the second term belongs to the first one; at the end of a sentence it refers to something previously mentioned or implied.

Patterns of Wisdom

> The **pond possesses thunder above**. **Converting maidenhood**.
> A **jun zi uses perpetually completing** to **know** the **cracked**.

Fields of meaning

Pond, *ZE*: open surface of a flat body of water and the vapors rising from it; fertilize, enrich; kindness, favor; Symbol of the trigram Open, *DUI*. **Possess**, *YOU*: see *Preceding Situation*. **Thunder**, *LEI*: thunder; arousing power emerging from the depth of the earth; Symbol of the trigram Shake, *ZHEN*. **Above**, *SHANG*: anything above in all senses; higher, upper, outer; upper trigram. **Convert**, *GUI*: see *Image of the Situation*. **Maidenhood**, *MEI*: see *Image of the Situation*. **Jun zi**: ideal of a person who orders his/her life in accordance with dao rather than willful intention, and uses divination in this spirit. **Use**, *YI*: by means of; owing to; make use of, employ. **Perpetual**, *YONG*: continual, everlasting, eternal. Ideogram: flowing water. **Complete**, *ZHONG*: see *Hexagrams in Pairs*. **Know**, *ZHI*: have knowledge of, perceive, experience, remember; know intimately; informed, aware, wise. Ideogram: arrow and mouth, words focused and swift. **Cracked**, *BI*: broken, ruined, tattered; unfit, unworthy. Ideogram: strike and break.

Transforming Lines

Initial Nine

Converting maidenhood uses the **junior-sister.**
Halting enables treading.
Disciplining, significant.

Comments
Converting maidenhood uses the **junior-sister.**
Using perseverance indeed.
Halting enables treading, significant.
Reciprocal receiving indeed.

Fields of meaning

Convert, *GUI*: see *Image of the Situation.* **Maidenhood**, *MEI*: see *Image of the Situation.* **Use**, *YI*: see *Patterns of Wisdom.* **Junior-sister**, *DI*: younger woman in family or clan; younger sister married to the same man as the elder sister; young concubine, servant. **Halt**, *PO*: limp; lame, crippled. **Able/enable**, *NENG*: ability, power, skill, art; competent, talented; duty, function, capacity. Ideogram: an animal with strong hooves and bones, able to carry and defend. **Tread**, *LÜ*: walk a path or way; step, path, track; footsteps; course of the stars; appropriate action; virtue; salary, means of subsistence. Ideogram: body and repeating steps. **Discipline**, *ZHENG*: see *Image of the Situation.* **Significant**, *JI*: leads to the experience of meaning; favorable, propitious, appropriate. Ideogram: scholar and mouth, wise words of a sage.

Persevere, *HENG*: continue in the same way or spirit; constant, habitual, regular; self-renewing. **Indeed**, *YE*: see *Hexagrams in Pairs.* **Reciprocal**, *XIANG*: mutual; assist, encourage, help; bring together, blend with; examine, inspect; by turns. **Receive**, *CHENG*: receive gifts or commands from superiors or customers; take in hand; give, offer respectfully; help, support. Ideogram: accepting a seal of office.

Nine at Second

Squinting enables observing.
Harvesting: Trial belonging to **shady people.**

Comments
Harvesting: Trial belonging to **shady people.**
Not-yet transforming constancy indeed.

Fields of meaning

Squint, *MIAO*: look at with one eye; one-eyed; obstructed vision; glance at. **Able/enable**, *NENG*: ability, power, skill, art; competent, talented; duty, function, capacity. Ideogram: an animal with strong hooves and bones, able to carry and defend. **Observe**, *SHI*: see, examine, inspect; consider as; compare, imitate. Ideogram: see and omen, taking what you see into account. **Harvest**, *LI*: benefit, advantage, profit; realization; sharp, acute, insightful; quality of autumn and West, third stage of the Time Cycle. Ideogram: ripe grain and blade. **Trial**, *ZHEN*: inquiry by divination and its result; righteous, firm; separating wheat from chaff; the kernel, the proven core; quality of winter and North, fourth stage of the Time Cycle. Ideogram: pearl and divination. **Belong/it**, *ZHI*: see *Hexagrams in Pairs*. **Shady**, *YOU*: retired, solitary, secret, hidden from view; dark, obscure, occult, mysterious; ignorant. Ideogram: small within hill, a cave or grotto. **People/person**, *REN*: humans individually and collectively; an individual; humankind.

Not-yet, *WEI*: temporal negative indicating that something is expected to happen but has not yet occurred. **Transform**, *BIAN*: abrupt, radical passage from one state to another; transformation of opened and whole lines into each other in hexagrams; contrasts with change, *HUA*, gradual mutation. **Constancy**, *CHANG*: immutable order; permanent, unchanging, habitual; always; law, rule, custom. **Indeed**, *YE*: see *Hexagrams in Pairs*.

Six at Third

Converting maidenhood uses hair-growing.
Reversed converting uses the **junior-sister**.

Comments
Converting maidenhood uses hair-growing.
Not-yet appropriate indeed.

Fields of meaning

Convert, *GUI*: see *Image of the Situation*. **Maidenhood**, *MEI*: see *Image of the Situation*. **Use**, *YI*: see *Patterns of Wisdom*. **Hair-growing**, *XU*: beard, hair; patience symbolized as waiting for hair to grow; hold back, wait for; slow; necessary. **Reverse**, *FAN*: turn and move in the opposite direction; turn around or upside down (180 degrees); change to the opposite position; contrary. **Junior-sister**, *DI*: younger woman in family or clan; younger sister married to the same man as the elder sister; young concubine, servant.

Not-yet, *WEI*: temporal negative indicating that something is expected to happen but has not yet occurred. **Appropriate**, *DANG*: suitable, capable, worthy, adequate, competent, equal to; opportune, convenient; whole lines in odd places and opened lines in even places. **Indeed**, *YE*: see *Hexagrams in Pairs.*

NINE AT FOURTH

Converting maidenhood overruns the **term**.
Procrastinating converting possesses the **season**.

Comments
To **overrunning** the **term belongs purpose**.
Possessing awaiting and-also moving indeed.

Fields of meaning

Convert, *GUI*: see *Image of the Situation*. **Maidenhood**, *MEI*: see *Image of the Situation*. **Overrun**, *QIAN*: pass the limit; mistake, transgression, disease. **Term**, *QI*: set time, fixed period, agreed date; limit, deadline; hope, ardent desire. **Procrastinate**, *CHI*: delay, retard; leisurely, slow, late. **Possess**, *YOU*: see *Preceding Situation*. **Season**, *SHI*: quality of the time; the right time, opportune, in harmony; planning in accord with the time; season of the year. Ideogram: sun and temple, sacred time.

Belong/it, *ZHI*: see *Hexagrams in Pairs*. **Purpose**, *ZHI*: focus of mind and heart; intention, will, inclination; continuity in the direction of life. Ideogram: heart and scholar, high inner resolve. **Await**, *DAI*: see *Hexagrams in Pairs*. **And-also**, *ER*: joins and contrasts two terms. **Move**, *XING*: see *Hexagrams in Pairs*. **Indeed**, *YE*: see *Hexagrams in Pairs*.

SIX AT FIFTH

The **supreme burgeoning converting maidenhood**.
The **sleeves belonging** to **one's chief**,
not thus fine the **sleeves belonging** to **one's junior-sister**.
The **moon almost full**, **significant**.

Comments
The **supreme burgeoning converting maidenhood**.
Not thus fine the **sleeves belonging** to **one's junior-sister**.
One's position located in the **center**.
Using valuing movement indeed.

Fields of meaning

Supreme, *DI*: highest, above all on earth; sovereign, lord, emperor. **Burgeon**, *YI*: beginning of growth after seedburst, CHIA; early spring; associated with the Wooden Moment. **Convert**, *GUI*: see *Image of the Situation*. **Maidenhood**, *MEI*: see *Image of the Situation*. **Sleeve**, *MEI*: sleeve of a garment, on which signs indicating the rank of the wearer are displayed. **Belong/it**, *ZHI*: see *Hexagrams in Pairs*. **One/one's**, *QI*: general third person pronoun and possessive adjective; also: it/its, he/his, she/her, they/their. **Chief**, *JUN*: prince, ruler; lead, direct; wise person. Ideogram: mouth and direct, giving orders. **Not**, *BU*: common term of negation. **Thus**, *RU*: as, in this way; comparable, similar. **Fine**, *LIANG*: excellent, refined, valuable; gentle, considerate, kind; natural. **Junior-sister**, *DI*: younger woman in family or clan; younger sister married to the same man as the elder sister; young concubine, servant. **Moon**, *YUE*: moon and moon-cycle, month; menstruation; Yin. **Almost/hint**, *JI*: nearly, about to; subtle; barely perceptible first sign. **Full**, *WANG*: moon directly facing the sun; 15th day of the lunar month; hopes, expectations, desires. **Significant**, *JI*: leads to the experience of meaning; favorable, propitious, appropriate. Ideogram: scholar and mouth, wise words of a sage.

Position, *WEI*: place, location; be at; social standing, rank; position of a line in a hexagram. Ideogram: person standing. **Locate**, *ZAI*: be at, be situated at, dwell, reside; in, within; involved with, in the process of. Ideogram: earth and persevere, a place on the earth. **Center**, *ZHONG*: inner, central; put in the center; middle, stable point enabling you to face inner and outer changes; middle line of a trigram. Ideogram: field divided in two equal parts. **Use**, *YI*: see *Patterns of Wisdom*. **Value**, *GUI*: regard as valuable, give worth and dignity to; precious, honorable, exalted, illustrious. Ideogram: cowries (coins) and basket. **Move**, *XING*: see *Hexagrams in Pairs*. **Indeed**, *YE*: see *Hexagrams in Pairs*.

SIX ABOVE

A **woman receives** a **basket without substance**.
A **scholar disembowels** a **goat without blood**.
Without direction Harvesting.

Comments

Six above: **without substance**.
Receiving an **empty basket indeed**.

Fields of meaning

Woman(hood), *NÜ*: see *Hexagrams in Pairs*. **Receive**, *CHENG*: receive gifts or commands from superiors or customers; take in hand; give, offer respectfully;

help, support. Ideogram: accepting a seal of office. **Basket**, *KUANG*: open basket; put in a basket. **Without**, *WU*: devoid of; there is not. **Substance**, *SHI*: fullness, richness; essence; real, solid, consistent; results, fruits, possessions; honest, sincere. Ideogram: string of coins under a roof, wealth in the house. **Scholar**, *SHI*: cultured, learned, upright; gentleman, man of distinction, officer. **Disembowel**, *KUI*: butcher and bleed an animal; cut open and clean a fish; prepare for sacrifice. **Goat**, *YANG*: sheep and goats; associated with stubborn, determined thought and action. **Blood**, *XUE*: blood, the Yin fluid that maintains life; money, property. **Without direction Harvesting**, *WU YOU LI*: see *Image of the Situation*.

Six, *LIU*: number six; transforming opened line; six lines of a hexagram. **Above**, *SHANG*: see *Patterns of Wisdom*. **Empty**, *XU*: void; absence of images and concepts; vacant, insubstantial; empty yet fertile space. **Indeed**, *YE*: see *Hexagrams in Pairs*.

Image Tradition

Converting maidenhood.
The **great**'s **righteousness belonging** to **heaven** and **earth**.
Heaven and **earth not mingling**.
And-also the **myriad beings not rising**.
Converting maidenhood.

The **beginning** of **completion belonging** to a **person**.
Stimulating uses stirring-up.
A **place** for **converting maidenhood indeed**.
Disciplining, **pitfall**.
Position not appropriate indeed.

Without direction Harvesting.
The **supple rides** the **solid indeed**.

Fields of meaning

Convert, *GUI*: see *Image of the Situation*. **Maidenhood**, *MEI*: see *Image of the Situation*. **Great**, *DA*: big, noble, important, very; orient the will toward a self-imposed goal, impose direction; ability to lead or guide one's life; contrasts with small, *XIAO*, flexible adaptation to what crosses one's path. **Righteous**, *YI*: proper, just, virtuous, upright; the heart that rules itself; benevolent, loyal, devoted to public good. **Belong/it**, *ZHI*: see *Hexagrams in Pairs*. **Heaven**, *TIAN*: sky, firmament, heavens; the highest realm, situated above the human world, as opposed to the earth, *DI*, located below; Symbol of the trigram Energy, *QIAN*. Ideogram: great and the one above. **Earth**, *DI*: the earth, ground on which the human world rests; basis of all things, nourishes all things; essential Yin; Symbol of the trigram Space, *KUN*. **Not**, *BU*: common term of negation. **Mingle**, *JIAO*: blend with, communicate, join, exchange; trade; copulation; friendship. Ideogram: legs crossed. **And-also**, *ER*: joins and contrasts two terms. **Myriad**, *WAN*: ten thousand; countless, many, everyone. Ideogram: swarm of insects. **Being**, *WU*: creature, thing, any single being; matter, substance, essence; nature of things. **Rise**, *XING*: get up, grow, lift; stimulate, promote; enjoy. Ideogram: lift, two hands and unite, lift with both hands.

Begin, *SHI*: commence, start, open; earliest, first; generate. Ideogram: woman and eminent, eminent feminine function of giving birth. **Complete**, *ZHONG*: see *Hexagrams in Pairs*. **Person/people**, *REN*: humans individually and collectively; an individual; humankind. **Stimulate**, *SHUO*: rouse to action and good feeling; stir up, urge on; exhort, persuade; say, tell, relate; cheer, delight; joyous, peaceful, restful; Action of the trigram Open, *DUI*. Ideogram: words and exchange. **Use**, *YI*: see *Patterns of Wisdom*. **Stir-up**, *DONG*: excite, influence, move, affect; work, take action; come out of the egg or the bud; Action of the trigram Shake, *ZHEN*. Ideogram: strength and heavy, move weighty things. **Place**, *SUO*: see *Preceding Situation*. **Indeed**, *YE*: see *Hexagrams in Pairs*. **Disciplining, pitfall**, *ZHENG XIONG*: see *Image of the Situation*. **Position**, *WEI*: place, location; be at; social standing, rank; position of a line in a hexagram. Ideogram: person standing. **Appropriate**, *DANG*: suitable, capable, worthy, adequate, competent, equal to; opportune, convenient; whole lines in odd places and opened lines in even places.

Without direction Harvesting, *WU YOU LI*: see *Image of the Situation*. **Supple**, *ROU*: quality of the opened lines; flexible, pliant, adaptable, tender. **Ride**, *CHENG*: ride an animal or a chariot; have the upper hand, control a stronger power; an opened line above controlling a whole line below. **Solid**, *GANG*: quality of the whole lines; firm, strong, unyielding, persisting.

豐

55 ABOUNDING | *Feng* ䷶

The situation described by this hexagram is characterized by a peak of development, a culmination that can be fully expressed and enjoyed, even with the awareness that it will be inevitably followed by a decline.

Image of the Situation

> **Abounding**.
> **Growing**.
> The **king imagines it**.
> **No grief**. **Properly** the **sun** in the **center**.

Fields of meaning

Abound, *FENG*: abundant, plentiful, copious; grow wealthy; at the point of overflowing; exuberant, fertile, prolific, rich in talents, property, friends; fullness, culmination; ripe, sumptuous, fat. **Grow**, *HENG*: heavenly influence pervading and nourishing all things; prosper, succeed, expand, develop; effective, favorable; quality of summer and South, second stage of the Time Cycle. With the pronunciation *XIANG*: offer a sacrifice; offer a gift to a superior; accept, enjoy. **King**, *WANG*: sovereign, effective ruler, emperor, seen as connecting heaven and earth; reign, govern. **Imagine**, *JIA*: create in the mind; fantasize, suppose; pretend, imitate; fiction, illusion; costume. Ideogram: person and borrow. **It/belong**, *ZHI*: establishes between two terms a connection similar to the Saxon genitive, in which the second term belongs to the first one; at the end of a sentence it refers to something previously mentioned or implied. **No**, *WU*: common term of negation. **Grieve**, *YOU*: mourn; sorrow, melancholy, anxiety, care, hidden sorrow. Ideogram: heart, head, and limp, heart-sick and anxious. **Proper**, *YI*: reasonable, fit, right, harmonious; ought, should. **Sun/day**, *RI*: actual sun and the time of a sun-cycle, a day. **Center**, *ZHONG*: inner, central; put in the center; middle, stable point enabling you to face inner and outer changes; middle line of a trigram. Ideogram: field divided in two equal parts.

Outer and Inner Trigram

The upper trigram, **Shake**, *ZHEN*, describes the outer aspects of the situation. It has the following associations: arouse, excite, inspire; awe, alarm, trembling; thunder rising from the depth of the earth; fertilizing intrusion. Ideogram: excite and rain. *Symbol*: thunder, *LEI*, arousing power emerging from the depth of the earth. *Action*: stir-up, *DONG*, excite, influence, move, affect; work, take action; come out of the egg or the bud. Ideogram: strength and heavy, move weighty things. In the family of trigrams *ZHEN* is the eldest son.

The lower trigram, **Radiance**, *LI*, describes the inner aspects of the situation. It has the following associations: glowing light, spreading in all directions; the power of consciousness; discriminate, articulate, divide and arrange in order; assemble, attract. Ideogram: bird and weird, magical fire-bird with brilliant plumage. *Symbols*: fire and brightness. Fire, *HUO*: flame, burn; warming and consuming aspect of burning. Brightness, *MING*: light, radiance, clarity; distinguish, discern, understand; light-giving aspect of fire, of heavenly bodies and of consciousness. *Action*: congregate, *LI*, cling together, adhere to, rely on; couple, pair, herd; beautiful, elegant. Ideogram: deer flocking together. In the family of trigrams *LI* is the middle daughter.

Counter Hexagram

The Counter Hexagram of **Abounding** is hexagram 28, **The Great Exceeding**, which switches the emphasis from a culmination that can be fully enjoyed to the excessive predominance of a central idea or goal, which may become too heavy to bear.

Preceding Situation

> **Acquiring one's place** for **converting implies necessarily** the **great**.
> To **anterior acquiescence belongs** the **use** of **abounding**.
> **Abounding implies** the **great indeed**.

Fields of meaning

Acquire, *DE*: obtain the desired object; possession; satisfied, fulfilled; it is permitted; agree with; wish for, desire covetously. Ideogram: go and obstacle, going through obstacles to the goal. **One/one's**, *QI*: general third person pronoun and possessive adjective; also: it/its, he/his, she/her, they/their. **Place**, *SUO*: position, location; residence, dwelling; where something belongs or comes from; habitual focus or object. **Convert**, *GUI*: accomplish one's destiny; revert to the original place or state; restore, revert; turn into; goal, destination, intention; a girl getting married. Ideogram: arrive and wife, become mistress of a household. **Imply**, *ZHE*: further signify; additional meaning. **Necessarily**, *BI*: unavoidably, certainly. **Great**, *DA*: big, noble, important, very; orient the will toward a self-imposed goal, impose direction; ability to lead or guide one's life; contrasts with small, *XIAO*, flexible adaptation to what crosses one's path. To **anterior acquiescence belongs** the **use** of, *GU SHOU ZHI YI*: understanding and accepting the preceding statement allows the consultant to make proper use of this hexagram. **Abound**, *FENG*: see *Image of the Situation*. **Indeed**, *YE*: emphasizes and intensifies the previous statement.

Hexagrams in Pairs

Abounding: **numerous anteriority indeed**.
Connecting with **few**: **sojourning indeed**.

Fields of meaning

Abound, *FENG*: see *Image of the Situation*. **Numerous**, *DUO*: great number, many; often. **Anterior**, *GU*: come before as cause; former, ancient; reason, purpose, intention; grievance, dissatisfaction, sorrow, resulting from previous causes and intentions; situation leading to a divination. **Indeed**, *YE*: see *Preceding Situation*. **Connect**, *QIN*: be close, approach, come near; cherish, help, favor; intimate; relatives, kin. **Few**, *GUA*: small number; seldom; reduce, diminish; unsupported, solitary. **Sojourn**, *LÜ*: travel, stay in places other than your home; itinerant troops, temporary residents; visitor, guest, lodger. Ideogram: banner and people around it.

Patterns of Wisdom

Thunder and **lightning altogether culminating**.
Abounding.
A **jun zi uses severing litigations involving punishment**.

Fields of meaning

Thunder, *LEI*: thunder; arousing power emerging from the depth of the earth; Symbol of the trigram Shake, *ZHEN*. **Lightning**, *DIAN*: lighting flash, electric discharge; sudden clarity; look attentively. **Altogether**, *JIE*: all, the whole; the same sort, alike; entirely. **Culminate**, *ZHI*: bring to the highest degree; arrive at the end or summit; superlative; reaching one's goal. **Abound**, *FENG*: see *Image of the Situation*. **Jun zi**: ideal of a person who orders his/her life in accordance with dao rather than willful intention, and uses divination in this spirit. **Use**, *YI*: by means of; owing to; make use of, employ. **Sever**, *ZHE*: break off, separate, sunder, cut in two; discriminate, pass judgment on. **Litigate**, *YU*: legal proceedings, trial, sentence; dispute; take a case to court. Ideogram: two dogs and words, barking arguments at each other. **Involve**, *ZHI*: devote oneself to; induce, cause, implicate; approach; manifest, express; reach the highest degree of. Ideogram: reach and come up behind. **Punish**, *XING*: legal punishment; physical penalty for a severe criminal offense; whip, torture, behead.

Transforming Lines

INITIAL NINE

Meeting one's equal lord.
Although a **decade**, **without fault**.
Going possesses honor.

Comments
Although a **decade**, **without fault**.
Exceeding a **decade**: **calamity indeed**.

Fields of meaning

Meet, *YU*: come on unexpectedly, encounter; occur, happen; pleasant meeting, lucky coincidence; agree. **One/one's**, *QI*: see *Preceding Situation*. **Equal**, *PEI*: on the same level; compete with; accord with; pair; husband or wife; together. **Lord**, *ZHU*: ruler, master, chief, authority; host; domination in the cycle of the Five Transformative Moments. Ideogram: lamp and flame, giving light. **Although**, *SUI*: even though, supposing that, if, even if. **Decade**, *XUN*: ten days or years; complete time period. **Without fault**, *WU JIU*: no error or harm in the situation. **Go**, *WANG*: move away in time or space, depart; become past; dead, gone; contrasts with come, *LAI*, approach in time or space. **Possess**, *YOU*: general term indicating possession; have, own, be endowed with. **Honor**, *SHANG*: esteem, give high rank to, exalt, celebrate; rise, elevate; put one thing on top of another.

Exceed, *GUO*: go beyond, pass by, pass over; surpass, transgress; error, fault, calamity. **Calamity**, *ZAI*: disaster from outside; fire, flood, plague, drought, blight, ruin; contrasts with blunder, *SHENG*, indicating personal fault. Ideogram: water and fire, elemental powers. **Indeed**, *YE*: see *Preceding Situation*.

SIX AT SECOND

Abounding: **one's screen**.
The **sun** in the **center**: **viewing** a **bin**.
Going acquires doubt, **affliction**.
Possessing conformity, **like shooting-forth**.
Significant.

Comments
Possessing conformity, **like shooting-forth**.
Trustworthiness uses shooting-forth purpose indeed.

Fields of meaning

Abound, *FENG*: see *Image of the Situation*. **One/one's**, *QI*: see *Preceding Situation*. **Screen**, *PU*: curtain, veil, awning, hanging mat; hide, protect; luxuriant plant growth. **Sun/day**, *RI*: see *Image of the Situation*. **Center**, *ZHONG*: see *Image of the Situation*. **View**, *JIAN*: vision in all its aspects: seeing, being visible, forming mental images; visit, call on, consult. Ideogram: eye above person, active and receptive sight. **Bin**, *DOU*: measure and container for grain; wine cup; hold, contain. **Go**, *WANG*: move away in time or space, depart; become past; dead, gone; contrasts with come, *LAI*, approach in time or space. **Acquire**, *DE*: see *Preceding Situation*. **Doubt**, *YI*: suspect, distrust, wonder; uncertain, dubious; surmise, conjecture, fear. **Affliction**, *JI*: sickness, disorder, defect, calamity, injury; poison, hate, dislike; cruel, jealous, envious. Ideogram: sickness and dart, a sudden affliction. **Possess**, *YOU*: general term indicating possession; have, own, be endowed with. **Conform**, *FU*: accord between inner and outer; sincere, truthful, verified, reliable; capture; prisoners, spoils. Ideogram: claws over child, a bird brooding on the nest. **Like**, *RUO*: same as, just as; conform, imitate; adverbial suffix indicating similarity. **Shoot-forth**, *FA*: emit, send out, shoot an arrow; ferment, rise; express, raise one's voice. Ideogram: stance, bow and arrow, shooting from a solid base. **Significant**, *JI*: leads to the experience of meaning; favorable, propitious, appropriate. Ideogram: scholar and mouth, wise words of a sage.

Trustworthy, *XIN*: truthful, faithful, consistent over time; count on, confide in; examine, verify, prove; loyalty, integrity. Ideogram: person and word, true speech. **Use**, *YI*: see *Patterns of Wisdom*. **Purpose**, *ZHI*: focus of mind and heart; intention, will, inclination; continuity in the direction of life. Ideogram: heart and scholar, high inner resolve. **Indeed**, *YE*: see *Preceding Situation*.

NINE AT THIRD

Abounding: **one's overflowing**.
The **sun** in the **center**: **viewing froth**.
Severing one's right arm.
Without fault.

Comments
Abounding: **one's overflowing**.
Not permitted the **great** in **affairs indeed**.
Severing one's right arm.
Completing, **not permitted availing** of **indeed**.

Fields of meaning

Abound, *FENG*: see *Image of the Situation*. **One/one's**, *QI*: see *Preceding Situation*. **Overflow**, *PEI*: spread and flow in many directions, like rain or rivers; enlarge; irrigate; luxuriant water plants. The **sun** in the **center**, *RI ZHONG*: see *Image of the Situation*. **View**, *JIAN*: vision in all its aspects: seeing, being visible, forming mental images; visit, call on, consult. Ideogram: eye above person, active and receptive sight. **Froth**, *MO*: spume, foam, bubbles; perspire, drool. **Sever**, *ZHE*: see *Patterns of Wisdom*. **Right**, *YOU*: right side, right hand; West, situated at the right of South, which is the reference direction; place of honor. **Arm**, *GONG*: the arm as body's instrument; staunch supporter; officer, minister of state. **Without fault**, *WU JIU*: no error or harm in the situation.

Not, *BU*: common term of negation. **Permit**, *KE*: possible because in harmony with an inherent principle; capable of; approve, authorize. Ideogram: mouth and breath, silent consent. **Great**, *DA*: see *Preceding Situation*. **Affairs**, *SHI*: all kinds of personal activity; matters at hand; business; function, occupation; manage; perform a task; incident, event; case in court. **Indeed**, *YE*: see *Preceding Situation*. **Complete**, *ZHONG*: completion of a cycle that begins the next; entire, whole, all. Ideogram: silk cocoons, follow and ice, winter linking one year with the next. **Avail**, *YONG*: use, employ for a specific purpose; take advantage of; benefit from; capacity. Ideogram: to divine and center, applying divination to central concerns.

NINE AT FOURTH

Abounding: **one's screen**.
The **sun** in the **center**: **viewing** a **bin**.
Meeting one's hidden lord.
Significant.

Comments

Abounding: **one's screen**.
Position not appropriate indeed.
The **sun** in the **center**: **viewing** a **bin**.
Shade, **not brightness indeed**.
Meeting one's hidden lord.
Significant movement indeed.

Fields of meaning

Abound, *FENG*: see *Image of the Situation*. **One/one's**, *QI*: see *Preceding Situation*. **Screen**, *PU*: curtain, veil, awning, hanging mat; hide, protect; luxuriant plant growth. **Sun/day**, *RI*: see *Image of the Situation*. **Center**, *ZHONG*: see *Image of the Situation*. **View**, *JIAN*: vision in all its aspects: seeing, being visible, forming mental images; visit, call on, consult. Ideogram: eye above person, active and receptive sight. **Bin**, *DOU*: measure and container for grain; wine cup; hold, contain. **Meet**, *YU*: come on unexpectedly, encounter; occur, happen; pleasant meeting, lucky coincidence; agree. **Hide**, *YI*: squat, even, level, equalize; cut, wound, destroy, exterminate; pacified; colorless; distant, remote, barbarian. **Lord**, *ZHU*: ruler, master, chief, authority; host; domination in the cycle of the Five Transformative Moments. Ideogram: lamp and flame, giving light. **Significant**, *JI*: leads to the experience of meaning; favorable, propitious, appropriate. Ideogram: scholar and mouth, wise words of a sage.

Position, *WEI*: place, location; be at; social standing, rank; position of a line in a hexagram. Ideogram: person standing. **Not**, *BU*: common term of negation. **Appropriate**, *DANG*: suitable, capable, worthy, adequate, competent, equal to; opportune, convenient; whole lines in odd places and opened lines in even places. **Indeed**, *YE*: see *Preceding Situation*. **Shady**, *YOU*: retired, solitary, secret, hidden from view; dark, obscure, occult, mysterious; ignorant. Ideogram: small within hill, a cave or grotto. **Brightness**, *MING*: light, radiance, clarity; distinguish, discern, understand; light-giving aspect of fire, of heavenly bodies and of consciousness; brightness and fire are the Symbols of the trigram Radiance, *LI*. **Move**, *XING*: move or move something; motivate; emotionally moving; walk, act, do. Ideogram: successive steps.

SIX AT FIFTH

Coming composition.
Possessing reward and **praise**, **significant**.

Comments
To **six** at **fifth belongs significance**.
Possessing reward indeed.

Fields of meaning

Come, *LAI*: approach in time or space; move toward, arrive at; future; contrasts with go, *WANG*, move away or become past. **Composition**, *ZHANG*: a well-composed whole and its structure; beautiful creation; elegant, clear, brilliant; chapter, strophe; distinct from pattern, *WEN*, beauty of intrinsic design. **Possess**, *YOU*: general term indicating possession; have, own, be endowed with. **Reward**, *QING*: gift given out of gratitude or benevolence; favor from heaven. Ideogram: heart, follow and deer, the heart expressed through the gift of a deer's skin. **Praise**, *YU*: magnify, eulogize; flatter; fame, reputation. Ideogram: offering words. **Significant**, *JI*: leads to the experience of meaning; favorable, propitious, appropriate. Ideogram: scholar and mouth, wise words of a sage.

Six, *LIU*: number six; transforming opened line; six lines of a hexagram. **Five**, *WU*: number five; fivefold articulation of the Universal Compass; the Five Moments and all related qualities: directions, colors, smells, tastes, tones, feelings. **Belong/it**, *ZHI*: establishes between two terms a connection similar to the Saxon genitive, in which the second term belongs to the first one; at the end of a sentence it refers to something previously mentioned or implied. **Indeed**, *YE*: see *Preceding Situation*.

SIX ABOVE

Abounding: **one's roof**.
Screening one's household.
Peeping through **one's door**.
Living-alone, **one without people**.
Three year's-time not encountering.
Pitfall.

Comments
Abounding: **one's roof**.
The **heavenly border**, **hovering indeed**.
Peeping through **one's door**.
Living-alone, **one without people**.
Originating from **concealment indeed**.

Fields of meaning

Abound, *FENG*: see *Image of the Situation*. **One/one's**, *QI*: see *Preceding Situation*. **Roof**, *WU*: cover, shelter; house, room, cabin, tent; stop or remain at. **Screen**, *PU*: curtain, veil, awning, hanging mat; hide, protect; luxuriant plant growth. **Household**, *JIA*: home, house; family; dwell, reside; domestic, within doors; shop, school, doctrine. Ideogram: roof and pig or dog, the most valued domestic animals, living under the same roof with the family. **Peep**, *KUI*: observe from hiding; stealthy, furtive. **Door**, *HU*: inner door, chamber door; a household; distinct from gate, *MEN*, outer door. **Live-alone**, *QU*: lonely, solitary; quiet, still, deserted. **One**, *YI*: a single unit; number one; undivided, simple, whole; unique; first. **Without**, *WU*: devoid of; there is not. **People/person**, *REN*: humans individually and collectively; an individual; humankind. **Three/thrice**, *SAN*: number three; third time or place; active phases of a cycle; superlative; beginning of repetition (since one and two are entities in themselves). **Year's-time**, *SUI*: duration of a year; beginning of a year. **Not**, *BU*: common term of negation. **Encounter**, *DI*: see face to face; visit, interview. **Pitfall**, *XIONG*: unfortunate situation, in which the flow of life and spirit is blocked and the experience of meaning is lost; stuck and exposed to danger; inappropriate attitude. Ideogram: person in a pit.

Heaven, *TIAN*: sky, firmament, heavens; the highest realm, situated above the human world, as opposed to the earth, *DI*, located below; Symbol of the trigram Energy, *QIAN*. Ideogram: great and the one above. **Border**, *JI*: boundary, frontier, line that joins and divides; meet, face to face. Ideogram: place and sacrifice, meeting point of the human and the spirit world. **Hover**, *XIANG*: rise, soar, glide, fly above, roam. **Indeed**, *YE*: see *Preceding Situation*. **Origin**, *ZI*: source, beginning, ground; cause, reason, motive; tracing back to the source; oneself, by oneself; spontaneous, intrinsic. **Conceal**, *CANG*: hide from view; store, put aside, accumulate; keep in one's heart; internal organs.

Image Tradition

Abounding, the **great indeed**.
Brightness uses stirring-up. **Anterior abounding**.

The **king imagines it**.
Honoring the **great indeed**.
No grief, **properly** the **sun** in the **center**.
Properly illuminating below heaven indeed.

The **sun** in the **center**, by **consequence setting**.
The **moon overfilling**, by **consequence taken-in**.

Heaven and **earth overfilling emptiness**.
Associating with the **season**'s **dissolving pause**.
And-also even-more with-respect-to reaching people.
Even-more with-respect-to reaching soul and **spirit**.

Fields of meaning

Abound, *FENG*: see *Image of the Situation*. **Great**, *DA*: see *Preceding Situation*. **Indeed**, *YE*: see *Preceding Situation*. **Brightness**, *MING*: light, radiance, clarity; distinguish, discern, understand; light-giving aspect of fire, of heavenly bodies and of consciousness; brightness and fire are the Symbols of the trigram Radiance, *LI*. **Use**, *YI*: see *Patterns of Wisdom*. **Stir-up**, *DONG*: excite, influence, move, affect; work, take action; come out of the egg or the bud; Action of the trigram Shake, *ZHEN*. Ideogram: strength and heavy, move weighty things. **Anterior**, *GU*: see *Hexagrams in Pairs*.

The **king imagines it**, *WANG JIA ZHI*: see *Image of the Situation*. **Honor**, *SHANG*: esteem, give high rank to, exalt, celebrate; rise, elevate; put one thing on top of another. **Indeed**, *YE*: see *Preceding Situation*. **No**, *WU*: common term of negation. **Grieve**, *YOU*: see *Image of the Situation*. **Properly** the **sun** in the **center**, *YI RI ZHONG*: see *Image of the Situation*. **Illuminate**, *ZHAO*: shine light on, enlighten; care for, supervise. Ideogram: fire and brightness. **Below heaven**, *TIAN XIA*: human world, between heaven and earth.

Consequence, *ZE*: reason, cause, result; rule, law, pattern, standard; therefore; very strong connection. **Set**, *ZE*: sunset, afternoon; waning moon; decline. **Moon**, *YUE*: moon and moon-cycle, month; menstruation; Yin. **Overfill**, *YING*: fill completely; full, at the point of overflowing; excess, arrogance. Ideogram: vessel and overflow. **Take-in**, *SHI*: eat, drink, ingest, absorb, incorporate; food, nourishment. **Heaven**, *TIAN*: sky, firmament, heavens; the highest realm, situated above the human world, as opposed to the earth, *DI*, located below; Symbol of the trigram Energy, *QIAN*. Ideogram: great and the one above. **Earth**, *DI*: the earth, ground on which the human world rests; basis of all things, nourishes all things; essential Yin; Symbol of the trigram Space, *KUN*. **Empty**, *XU*: void; absence of images and concepts; vacant, insubstantial; empty yet fertile space. **Associate**, *YU*: consort with, combine; companions; group, band, company; agree with, comply, help; in favor of. Ideogram: a pair of hands reaching downward meets a pair of hands reaching upward, helpful association. **Season**, *SHI*: quality of the time; the right time, opportune, in harmony; planning in accord with the time; season of the year. Ideogram: sun and temple, sacred time. **Dissolving pause**, *XIAO XI*: transitional phase of the Universal Compass in which Yin or structure dissolves so that Yang or action may again emerge. **And-also**, *ER*: joins and contrasts two terms. **Even-more**, *KUANG*: even more so, all the more. **With-respect-to**, *YU*: in relation to, referring to, according to; in, at, until. **Reach**, *HU*: arrive at a goal; move toward and achieve; to, at, in; distinct from tend-towards, *YOU*. **People/person**, *REN*: humans individually and collectively; an individual; humankind. **Soul**, *GUI*: power that creates individual existence; union of volatile-soul, *HUN*, spiritual and intellectual power, and dense-soul, *PO*, bodily strength and movement. *HUN* rises after death, *PO* remains with the body and may communicate with the living. **Spirit**, *SHEN*: spiritual power that confers intensity on heart and mind by acting on the soul, *GUI*; vitality, energy; spirits, ancestors, gods.

旅

56 SOJOURNING | *Lü* ䷷

The situation described by this hexagram is characterized by traveling, being away from home, living abroad, residing in a foreign context.

Image of the Situation

> **Sojourning**.
> The **small, growing**.
> **Sojourning**: **Trial**, **significant**.

Fields of meaning

Sojourn, *LÜ*: travel, stay in places other than your home; itinerant troops, temporary residents; visitor, guest, lodger. Ideogram: banner and people around it. **Small**, *XIAO*: little, common, unimportant; adapting to what crosses your path; ability to move in harmony with the vicissitudes of life; contrasts with great, *DA*, self-imposed theme or goal. **Grow**, *HENG*: heavenly influence pervading and nourishing all things; prosper, succeed, expand, develop; effective, favorable; quality of summer and South, second stage of the Time Cycle. With the pronunciation *XIANG*: offer a sacrifice; offer a gift to a superior; accept, enjoy. **Trial**, *ZHEN*: inquiry by divination and its result; righteous, firm; separating wheat from chaff; the kernel, the proven core; quality of winter and North, fourth stage of the Time Cycle. Ideogram: pearl and divination. **Significant**, *JI*: leads to the experience of meaning; favorable, propitious, appropriate. Ideogram: scholar and mouth, wise words of a sage.

Outer and Inner Trigram

The upper trigram, **Radiance**, *LI*, describes the outer aspects of the situation. It has the following associations: glowing light, spreading in all directions; the power of consciousness; discriminate, articulate, divide and arrange in order; assemble, attract. Ideogram: bird and weird, magical fire-bird with brilliant plumage. *Symbols*: fire and brightness. Fire, *HUO*: flame, burn; warming and consuming aspect of burning. Brightness, *MING*: light, radiance, clarity; distinguish, discern, understand; light-giving aspect of fire, of heavenly bodies and of consciousness. *Action*: congregate, *LI*, cling together, adhere to, rely on; couple, pair, herd;

beautiful, elegant. Ideogram: deer flocking together. In the family of trigrams *LI* is the middle daughter.

The lower trigram, **Bound**, *GEN*, describes the inner aspects of the situation. It has the following associations: limit, frontier; obstacle that prevents from seeing further; stop; still, quiet, motionless; confine, enclose; mountain, sunset, beginning of winter; solid, steady, unshakable; straight, hard, adamant, obstinate. *Symbol*: mountain, *SHAN*, large, immense; limit, boundary. Ideogram: three peaks, a mountain range. *Action*: stop, *ZHI*, bring or come to a standstill, cease, terminate. Ideogram: a foot stops walking. In the family of trigrams *GEN* is the youngest son.

Counter Hexagram

The Counter Hexagram of **Sojourning** is hexagram 28, **The Great Exceeding**, which switches the emphasis from the flexible adaptation of **Sojourning** to the excessive predominance of a central idea or goal.

Preceding Situation

> **Exhausting** the **great implies necessarily letting-go one's residing**.
> To **anterior acquiescence belongs** the **use** of **sojourning**.

Fields of meaning

Exhaust, *QIONG*: bring to an end; limit, extremity; investigate exhaustively; destitute, indigent; end without a new beginning; distinct from complete, *ZHONG*, end of a cycle that begins the next one. Ideogram: cave and naked person, bent with disease or old age. **Great**, *DA*: big, noble, important, very; orient the will toward a self-imposed goal, impose direction; ability to lead or guide one's life; contrasts with small, *XIAO*, flexible adaptation to what crosses one's path. **Imply**, *ZHE*: further signify; additional meaning. **Necessarily**, *BI*: unavoidably, certainly. **Let-go**, *SHI*: lose, let slip; omit, miss, fail; lose control of. Ideogram: drop from the hand. **One/one's**, *QI*: general third person pronoun and possessive adjective; also: it/its, he/his, she/her, they/their. **Reside**, *JU*: dwell, live in, stay; sit down; fill an office; well-being, rest. Ideogram: body and seat. To **anterior acquiescence belongs** the **use** of, *GU SHOU ZHI YI*: understanding and accepting the preceding statement allows the consultant to make proper use of this hexagram. **Sojourn**, *LÜ*: see *Image of the Situation*.

Hexagrams in Pairs

Abounding: **numerous anteriority indeed**.
Connecting with **few**: **sojourning indeed**.

Fields of meaning

Abound, *FENG*: abundant, plentiful, copious; grow wealthy; at the point of overflowing; exuberant, fertile, prolific, rich in talents, property, friends; fullness, culmination; ripe, sumptuous, fat. **Numerous**, *DUO*: great number, many; often. **Anterior**, *GU*: come before as cause; former, ancient; reason, purpose, intention; grievance, dissatisfaction, sorrow, resulting from previous causes and intentions; situation leading to a divination. **Indeed**, *YE*: emphasizes and intensifies the previous statement. **Connect**, *QIN*: be close, approach, come near; cherish, help, favor; intimate; relatives, kin. **Few**, *GUA*: small number; seldom; reduce, diminish; unsupported, solitary. **Sojourn**, *LÜ*: see *Image of the Situation*.

Patterns of Wisdom

The **mountain possesses fire above**. **Sojourning**.
A **jun zi uses bright consideration availing** of
punishment and-also not detaining litigations.

Fields of meaning

Mountain, *SHAN*: mountain; large, immense; limit, boundary; Symbol of the trigram Bound, *GEN*. Ideogram: three peaks, a mountain range. **Possess**, *YOU*: general term indicating possession; have, own, be endowed with. **Fire**, *HUO*: fire, flame, burn; warming and consuming aspect of burning; fire and brightness are the Symbols of the trigram Radiance, *LI*. **Above**, *SHANG*: anything above in all senses; higher, upper, outer; upper trigram. **Sojourn**, *LÜ*: see *Image of the Situation*. **Jun zi**: ideal of a person who orders his/her life in accordance with dao rather than willful intention, and uses divination in this spirit. **Use**, *YI*: by means of; owing to; make use of, employ. **Brightness**, *MING*: light, radiance, clarity; distinguish, discern, understand; light-giving aspect of fire, of heavenly bodies and of consciousness; brightness and fire are the Symbols of the trigram Radiance, *LI*. **Consider**, *SHEN*: act carefully, seriously; cautious, attentive, circumspect; still, quiet, sincere. Ideogram: heart and true. **Avail**, *YONG*: use, employ for a specific purpose; take advantage of; benefit from; capacity. Ideogram: to divine and center, applying divination to central concerns. **Punish**, *XING*: legal punishment; physical penalty for a severe criminal offense; whip, torture, behead. **And-also**, *ER*: joins and contrasts two terms. **Not**, *BU*: common term of negation. **Detain**, *LIU*:

delay, postpone, protract; keep, retain (a guest); a long time, always. **Litigate**, *YU*: legal proceedings, trial, sentence; dispute; take a case to court. Ideogram: two dogs and words, barking arguments at each other.

Transforming Lines

Initial Six

Sojourning: **fragmenting**, **fragmenting**.
Splitting-off one's place: **grasping calamity**.

Comments
Sojourning: **fragmenting**, **fragmenting**.
Purpose exhausted: **calamity indeed**.

Fields of meaning
Sojourn, *LÜ*: see *Image of the Situation*. **Fragment**, *SUO*: break into small pieces; broken parts; minute, fine, petty, trivial. Ideogram: small and cowry shells, the tinkling of small coins. **Split-off**, *SI*: lop off, split with an ax, rive; white (color eliminated). Ideogram: ax and possessive, splitting what belongs together. **One/one's**, *QI*: see *Preceding Situation*. **Place**, *SUO*: position, location; residence, dwelling; where something belongs or comes from; habitual focus or object. **Grasp**, *QU*: seize with effort, take and use, appropriate; take as a wife; grasp the meaning, understand. Ideogram: ear and hand, hear and grasp. **Calamity**, *ZAI*: disaster from outside; fire, flood, plague, drought, blight, ruin; contrasts with blunder, *SHENG*, indicating personal fault. Ideogram: water and fire, elemental powers.

Purpose, *ZHI*: focus of mind and heart; intention, will, inclination; continuity in the direction of life. Ideogram: heart and scholar, high inner resolve. **Exhaust**, *QIONG*: see *Preceding Situation*. **Indeed**, *YE*: see *Hexagrams in Pairs*.

Six at Second

Sojourning: **approaching** a **camp**.
Cherishing one's own.
Acquiring a **youthful vassal**, **Trial**.

Comments
Acquiring a **youthful vassal**, **Trial**.
Completing without surpassing indeed.

Fields of meaning

Sojourn, *LÜ*: see *Image of the Situation*. **Approach**, *JI*: come near to, advance toward, reach; nearby; soon, immediately. **Camp**, *CI*: resting place, inn, shed; halt, breathing-spell. Ideogram: two and breath, pausing to breathe. **Cherish**, *HUAI*: carry in the heart or womb; dwell on, think fondly of; cling to; heart, breast. Ideogram: heart and hide, cherish in the heart. **One/one's**, *QI*: see *Preceding Situation*. **Own**, *ZI*: possession and the things possessed; avail of, depend on; property, riches. **Acquire**, *DE*: obtain the desired object; possession; satisfied, fulfilled; it is permitted; agree with; wish for, desire covetously. Ideogram: go and obstacle, going through obstacles to the goal. **Youthful**, *TONG*: young person (between eight and fifteen); childish, immature; servant, slave. **Vassal**, *PU*: servant, menial, retainer; helper in heavy work; palace officers, chamberlains; follow, serve, belong to. **Trial**, *ZHEN*: see *Image of the Situation*.

Complete, *ZHONG*: completion of a cycle that begins the next; entire, whole, all. Ideogram: silk cocoons, follow and ice, winter linking one year with the next. **Without**, *WU*: devoid of; there is not. **Surpass**, *YOU*: exceed, transgress; beyond measure, extraordinary; blame. **Indeed**, *YE*: see *Hexagrams in Pairs*.

NINE AT THIRD

Sojourning: **burning one's camp**.
Losing one's youthful vassal.
Trial, **adversity**.

Comments
Sojourning: **burning one's camp**.
Truly using injury actually.
Using sojourning to **associate below**.
One's righteousness lost indeed.

Fields of meaning

Sojourn, *LÜ*: see *Image of the Situation*. **Burn**, *FEN*: set fire to, destroy, die. **One/one's**, *QI*: see *Preceding Situation*. **Camp**, *CI*: resting place, inn, shed; halt, breathing-spell. Ideogram: two and breath, pausing to breathe. **Lose**, *SANG*: be deprived of, forget; destruction, ruin, death; corpse; lament, mourn; funeral. Ideogram: weep and dead. **Youthful**, *TONG*: young person (between eight and fifteen); childish, immature; servant, slave. **Vassal**, *PU*: servant, menial, retainer; helper in heavy work; palace officers, chamberlains; follow, serve, belong to. **Trial**, *ZHEN*: see *Image of the Situation*. **Adversity**, *LI*: danger, hardship, severe; threat or difficulty that must be encountered, rather than avoided; grinding stone; polish, sharpen; a challenge that strengthens and perfects the character; stimulate, excite; cruel demon.

Truly, *YI*: in fact; also; nevertheless. **Use**, *YI*: see *Patterns of Wisdom*. **Injure**, *SHANG*: hurt, wound, damage; grief, distress, mourning; sad at heart, afflicted. **Actually**, *YI*: truly, really, at present. Ideogram: a dart and done, strong intention fully expressed. **Associate**, *YU*: consort with, combine; companions; group, band, company; agree with, comply, help; in favor of. Ideogram: a pair of hands reaching downward meets a pair of hands reaching upward, helpful association. **Below**, *XIA*: anything below, in all senses; lower, inner; lower trigram. **Righteous**, *YI*: proper, just, virtuous, upright; the heart that rules itself; benevolent, loyal, devoted to public good. **Indeed**, *YE*: see *Hexagrams in Pairs*.

Nine at Fourth

Sojourning: **tending-towards abiding**.
Acquiring one's own emblem-ax.
My heart not keen.

Comments
Sojourning: **tending-towards abiding**.
Not-yet acquiring the **position indeed**.
Acquiring one's own emblem-ax.
The **heart not-yet keen indeed**.

Fields of meaning

Sojourn, *LÜ*: see *Image of the Situation*. **Tend-towards**, *YU*: move toward without necessarily reaching, in the direction of. **Abide**, *CHU*: rest in, dwell; stop oneself; arrive at a place or condition; distinguish, decide; do what is proper. Ideogram: tiger, stop and seat, powerful movement coming to rest. **Acquire**, *DE*: obtain the desired object; possession; satisfied, fulfilled; it is permitted; agree with; wish for, desire covetously. Ideogram: go and obstacle, going through obstacles to the goal. **One/one's**, *QI*: see *Preceding Situation*. **Own**, *ZI*: possession and the things possessed; avail of, depend on; property, riches. **Emblem-ax**, *FU*: moon-shaped ax, symbol of governmental power. **I/me/my**, *WO*: first person pronoun; the use of a specific personal pronoun, as opposed to the generic one's, *QI*, indicates an unusually strong emphasis on personal involvement. **Heart**, *XIN*: the heart as center of being; seat of mind, imagination and affect; moral nature; source of desires, intentions, will. **Not**, *BU*: common term of negation. **Keen**, *KUAI*: joyous, cheerful, lively, spirited; eager, prompt, ready; capable of.

Not-yet, *WEI*: temporal negative indicating that something is expected to happen but has not yet occurred. **Position**, *WEI*: place, location; be at; social standing, rank; position of a line in a hexagram. Ideogram: person standing. **Indeed**, *YE*: see *Hexagrams in Pairs*.

SIX AT FIFTH

Shooting a **pheasant**.
One arrow extinguishing.
Completion uses praising fate.

Comments
Completion uses praising fate.
Reaching-up to the **above indeed**.

Fields of meaning
Shoot, *SHE*: shoot an arrow; archer; project, eject, spurt, issue forth; glance at; scheme for. Ideogram: arrow and body. **Pheasant**, *ZHI*: beautiful bird associated with the trigram Radiance, *LI*; embrasures on ramparts and forts; arrange, put in order. **One**, *YI*: a single unit; number one; undivided, simple, whole; unique; first. **Arrow**, *SHI*: arrow, javelin, dart; swift, direct as an arrow. **Extinguish**, *WANG*: ruin, destroy; cease, go, die; lost without trace; forget, out of mind; absence, exile. Ideogram: person concealed by a wall, out of sight. **Complete**, *ZHONG*: completion of a cycle that begins the next; entire, whole, all. Ideogram: silk cocoons, follow and ice, winter linking one year with the next. **Use**, *YI*: see *Patterns of Wisdom*. **Praise**, *YU*: magnify, eulogize; flatter; fame, reputation. Ideogram: offering words. **Fate**, *MING*: individual destiny; birth and death as limits of life; issue orders with authority; consult the gods. Ideogram: mouth and order, words with heavenly authority.

Reach-up, *DI*: reach to, come up to; till, until, when. Ideogram: go, hand and reach. **Above**, *SHANG*: see *Patterns of Wisdom*. **Indeed**, *YE*: see *Hexagrams in Pairs*.

NINE ABOVE

A **bird burns its nest**.
Sojourning people beforehand laugh, **afterwards cry-out sobbing**.
Losing the **cattle**, **tending-towards versatility**.
Pitfall.

Comments
Using sojourning located above.
One's righteousness burnt indeed.
Losing the **cattle, tending-towards versatility.**
To **completing absolutely-nothing belongs hearing indeed.**

Fields of meaning

Bird, *NIAO*: all feathered animals; associated with the Fiery Moment. **Burn**, *FEN*: set fire to, destroy, die. **It/its**, *QI*: general third person pronoun and possessive adjective; also: one/one's, he/his, she/her, they/their. **Nest**, *CHAO*: nest; haunt, retreat. **Sojourn**, *LÜ*: see *Image of the Situation*. **People/person**, *REN*: humans individually and collectively; an individual; humankind. **Before(hand)/earlier**, *XIAN*: anterior, preceding in time; former, past, previous; first, at first. **Laugh**, *XIAO*: manifest joy or mirth; giggle, joke, laugh at, tease; desire; open (of a flower); associated with the Fiery Moment. **After(wards)/later**, *HOU*: come after in time, subsequent; put oneself after; behind, back, draw back; the second; attendants, heirs, successors, posterity. **Cry-out/outcry**, *HAO*: call out, proclaim; order, command; mark, label, sign; designate, name. **Sob**, *TAO*: cry, weep aloud; wailing children. Ideogram: mouth and omen, ominous sounds. **Lose**, *SANG*: be deprived of, forget; destruction, ruin, death; corpse; lament, mourn; funeral. Ideogram: weep and dead. **Cattle**, *NIU*: ox, bull, cow, calf; power and strength of work animals; stubborn. **Tend-towards**, *YU*: move toward without necessarily reaching, in the direction of. **Versatility**, *YI*: sudden and unpredictable change, and the mental mobility and openness required in order to face it; easy, light, simple; occurs in the name of the *Yi Jing*. **Pitfall**, *XIONG*: unfortunate situation, in which the flow of life and spirit is blocked and the experience of meaning is lost; stuck and exposed to danger; inappropriate attitude. Ideogram: person in a pit.

Use, *YI*: see *Patterns of Wisdom*. **Locate**, *ZAI*: be at, be situated at, dwell, reside; in, within; involved with, in the process of. Ideogram: earth and persevere, a place on the earth. **Above**, *SHANG*: see *Patterns of Wisdom*. **One/one's**, *QI*: see *Preceding Situation*. **Righteous**, *YI*: proper, just, virtuous, upright; the heart that rules itself; benevolent, loyal, devoted to public good. **Indeed**, *YE*: see *Hexagrams in Pairs*. **Complete**, *ZHONG*: completion of a cycle that begins the next; entire, whole, all. Ideogram: silk cocoons, follow and ice, winter linking one year with the next. **Absolutely-nothing/abstain**, *MO*: complete elimination; do not, not any, by no means. **Belong/it**, *ZHI*: establishes between two terms a connection similar to the Saxon genitive, in which the second term belongs to the first one; at the end of a sentence it refers to something previously mentioned or implied. **Hear**, *WEN*: perceive sound; learn by report; news, fame. Ideogram: ear and door.

Image Tradition

Sojourning. The **small**, **Growing**.
The **supple acquires** the **center reaching outside and-also yielding reaches** the **solid**.

Stopping and-also congregating reaches brightness.
That uses the **small**, **Growing**.

Sojourning: **Trial**, **significant indeed**.
The **season belonging** to **sojourning righteously great actually in-fact**.

Fields of meaning

Sojourning. The **small**, **growing**, *LÜ XIAO HENG*: see *Image of the Situation*. **Supple**, *ROU*: quality of the opened lines; flexible, pliant, adaptable, tender. **Acquire**, *DE*: obtain the desired object; possession; satisfied, fulfilled; it is permitted; agree with; wish for, desire covetously. Ideogram: go and obstacle, going through obstacles to the goal. **Center**, *ZHONG*: inner, central; put in the center; middle, stable point enabling you to face inner and outer changes; middle line of a trigram. Ideogram: field divided in two equal parts. **Reach**, *HU*: arrive at a goal; move toward and achieve; to, at, in; distinct from tend-towards, *YOU*. **Outside**, *WAI*: outer, external; unfamiliar, foreign; ignore, reject; work done outside the home; the upper trigram as indication of the outer aspects of the situation. **And-also**, *ER*: see *Patterns of Wisdom*. **Yield**, *SHUN*: give way, comply, agree, follow, obey; docile, flexible; bear produce, nourish, provide; Action of the trigram Field, *KUN*. **Solid**, *GANG*: quality of the whole lines; firm, strong, unyielding, persisting.

Stop, *ZHI*: bring or come to a standstill, cease, terminate; Action of the trigram Bound, *GEN*. Ideogram: a foot stops walking. **Congregate**, *LI*: cling together, adhere to, rely on; couple, pair, herd; beautiful, elegant; Action of the trigram Radiance, *LI*. Ideogram: deer flocking together. **Brightness**, *MING*: see *Patterns of Wisdom*. **That**, *SHI*: refers to the preceding statement. **Use**, *YI*: see *Patterns of Wisdom*.

Trial, **significant**, *ZHEN JI*: see *Image of the Situation*. **Indeed**, *YE*: see *Hexagrams in Pairs*. **Season**, *SHI*: quality of the time; the right time, opportune, in harmony; planning in accord with the time; season of the year. Ideogram: sun and temple, sacred time. **Belong/it**, *ZHI*: establishes between two terms a connection similar to the Saxon genitive, in which the second term belongs to the first one; at the end of a sentence it refers to something previously mentioned or implied. **Righteous**, *YI*: proper, just, virtuous, upright; the heart that rules itself; benevolent, loyal, devoted to public good. **Great**, *DA*: see *Preceding Situation*. **Actually**, *YI*: truly, really, at present. Ideogram: a dart and done, strong intention fully expressed. **In-fact**, *ZAI*: emphatic exclamation; truly, indeed.

巽 ䷸

57 THE ROOT | *Sun*

The situation described by this hexagram is characterized by grounding, gently supporting and nourishing things from below. The hexagram The Root is the doubling of the corresponding trigram, and partakes of its attributes.

Image of the Situation

> The **root**.
> The **small**, **Growing**.
> **Harvesting**: **possessing directed going**.
> **Harvesting**: **viewing** the **great** in the **person**.

Fields of meaning

Root, *SUN*: base on which things rest, ground, foundation; mild, subtly penetrating; nourishing. *Symbols*; tree/wood and wind. Tree/wood, *MU*; trees and all things woody or wooden; associated with the Wooden Moment. Ideogram: a tree with roots and branches. Wind, *FENG*: wind, breeze, gust; weather and its influence on mood and humor; fashion, usage. *Action*: enter, *RU*, penetrate, go into, enter on, encroach on; progress; put into. In the family of trigrams *SUN* is the eldest daughter. **Small**, *XIAO*: little, common, unimportant; adapting to what crosses your path; ability to move in harmony with the vicissitudes of life; contrasts with great, *DA*, self-imposed theme or goal. **Grow**, *HENG*: heavenly influence pervading and nourishing all things; prosper, succeed, expand, develop; effective, favorable; quality of summer and South, second stage of the Time Cycle. With the pronunciation *XIANG*: offer a sacrifice; offer a gift to a superior; accept, enjoy. **Harvest**, *LI*: benefit, advantage, profit; realization; sharp, acute, insightful; quality of autumn and West, third stage of the Time Cycle. Ideogram: ripe grain and blade. **Possessing directed going**, *YOU YOU WANG*: having a goal or purpose, moving in a specific direction. **View**, *JIAN*: vision in all its aspects: seeing, being visible, forming mental images; visit, call on, consult. Ideogram: eye above person, active and receptive sight. **Great**, *DA*: big, noble, important, very; orient the will toward a self-imposed goal, impose direction; ability to lead or guide one's life; contrasts with small, *XIAO*, flexible adaptation to what crosses one's path. **Person/people**, *REN*: humans individually and collectively; an individual; humankind.

Outer and Inner Trigram

In this hexagram the outer and inner aspects of the situation are identical, and they are described by the trigram **Root**. Its associations are listed in the corresponding *Field of meaning* above.

Counter Hexagram

The Counter Hexagram of **The Root** is hexagram 38, **Polarizing**, which switches the emphasis from gently supporting and nourishing things from below to focusing on a polar opposition.

Preceding Situation

> **Sojourning and-also lacking** a **place** for **tolerance**.
> To **anterior acquiescence belongs** the **use** of the **root**.
> The **root implies entering indeed**.

Fields of meaning

Sojourn, *LÜ*: travel, stay in places other than your home; itinerant troops, temporary residents; visitor, guest, lodger. Ideogram: banner and people around it. **And-also**, *ER*: joins and contrasts two terms. **Lack**, *WU*: strong negative; there is no, without, empty of, absence. **Place**, *SUO*: position, location; residence, dwelling; where something belongs or comes from; habitual focus or object. **Tolerate**, *RONG*: allow, contain, endure, bear; accept graciously. Ideogram: full stream bed, tolerating and containing. To **anterior acquiescence belongs** the **use** of, *GU SHOU ZHI YI*: understanding and accepting the preceding statement allows the consultant to make proper use of this hexagram. **Root**, *SUN*: see *Image of the Situation*. **Imply**, *ZHE*: further signify; additional meaning. **Enter**, *RU*: penetrate, go into, enter on, encroach on; progress; put into; Action of the trigram Root, *SUN*. **Indeed**, *YE*: emphasizes and intensifies the previous statement.

Hexagrams in Pairs

> The **open**: **viewing**, **and-also**
> the **root**: **hidden-away indeed**.

Fields of meaning

Open, *DUI*: an open surface, promoting interaction and interpenetration; pleasant, easy, responsive, free, unhindered; opening, passage; the mouth; exchange, barter;

straight, direct; meet, gather; place where water accumulates. Ideogram: mouth and vapor, communication through speech. **View**, *JIAN*: see *Image of the Situation.* **And-also**, *ER*: see *Preceding Situation.* **Root**, *SUN*: see *Image of the Situation.* **Hide-away**, *FU*: hide, conceal; ambush; secret, silent; prostrate, submit. Ideogram: man and crouching dog. **Indeed**, *YE*: see *Preceding Situation.*

Additional Texts

> The **root**: **paring belonging** to **actualizing-dao indeed**.
> The **root**: **evaluating and-also occulting**.
> The **root**: **using** the **movement** of the **counterpoise**.

Fields of meaning

Root, *SUN*: see *Image of the Situation.* **Pare**, *ZHI*: cut away, tailor, carve; form, invent; institution, rule; limit, prevent. Ideogram: knife and incomplete. **Belong/it**, *ZHI*: establishes between two terms a connection similar to the Saxon genitive, in which the second term belongs to the first one; at the end of a sentence it refers to something previously mentioned or implied. **Actualize-dao**, *DE*: realize dao in action; power, virtue; ability to follow the course traced by the ongoing process of the cosmos. Ideogram: go, straight, and heart. Linked with acquire, *DE*: acquiring that which makes a being become what it is meant to be. **Indeed**, *YE*: see *Preceding Situation.* **Evaluate**, *CHENG*: assess, appraise; weigh, estimate, reckon; designate, name. Ideogram: weigh and grain, attributing value. **And-also**, *ER*: see *Preceding Situation.* **Occult**, *YIN*: hide, obscure; hidden from view; mysterious, subtle; retired. **Use**, *YI*: by means of; owing to; make use of, employ. **Move**, *XING*: move or move something; motivate; emotionally moving; walk, act, do. Ideogram: successive steps. **Counterpoise**, *QUAN*: weight of a scale; weigh, examine, compare; balance, equalize; act as the position demands; influential; lit.: balance on a sliding scale.

Patterns of Wisdom

> **Following winds**. The **root**.
> A **jun zi uses assigning fate** to **move affairs**.

Fields of meaning

Follow, *SUI*: step behind, come after, move in the same direction; comply with what is ahead; pursue; follow a way or religion; conform to; next, subsequent. Ideogram: go and fall, unavoidable movement. **Wind**, *FENG*: wind, breeze, gust; weather and its influence on mood and humor; fashion, usage; wind and wood are the Symbols of the trigram Root, *SUN*. **Root**, *SUN*: see *Image of the Situation*. **Jun zi**: ideal of a person who orders his/her life in accordance with dao rather than willful intention, and uses divination in this spirit. **Use**, *YI*: see *Additional Texts*. **Assign**, *SHEN*: give out, allot, distribute; spread, scatter, diffuse. **Fate**, *MING*: individual destiny; birth and death as limits of life; issue orders with authority; consult the gods. Ideogram: mouth and order, words with heavenly authority. **Move**, *XING*: see *Additional Texts*. **Affairs**, *SHI*: all kinds of personal activity; matters at hand; business; function, occupation; manage; perform a task; incident, event; case in court.

Transforming Lines

Initial Six

Advancing, **withdrawing**.
Harvesting: to **martial people belongs Trial**.

Comments
Advancing, **withdrawing**.
Purpose doubtful indeed.
Harvesting: to **martial people belongs Trial**.
Purpose regulating indeed.

Fields of meaning

Advance, *JIN*: move forward, progress, climb; promote or be promoted; further the development of, augment; offer, introduce. **Withdraw**, *TUI*: draw back, retreat, recede; decline, refuse. **Harvest**, *LI*: see *Image of the Situation*. **Martial**, *WU*: warrior, military, warlike; valiant, powerful; strong, stern; Wu is the name of the son of King Wen, who defeated the last Shang emperor and founded the Zhou dynasty. Ideogram: fight and stop, force deterring aggression. **People/person**, *REN*: humans individually and collectively; an individual; humankind. **Trial**, *ZHEN*: inquiry by divination and its result; righteous, firm; separating wheat from chaff; the kernel, the proven core; quality of winter and North, fourth stage of the Time Cycle. Ideogram: pearl and divination.

Purpose, *ZHI*: focus of mind and heart; intention, will, inclination; continuity in the direction of life. Ideogram: heart and scholar, high inner resolve. **Doubt**, *YI*: suspect, distrust, wonder; uncertain, dubious; surmise, conjecture, fear. **Indeed**, *YE*: see *Preceding Situation*. **Belong/it**, *ZHI*: see *Additional Texts*. **Regulate**, *ZHI*: govern well, ensure prosperity; arrange, remedy disorder, heal; fit to govern.

Nine at Second

The **root located below** the **bed**.
Availing of **chroniclers** and **shamans**.
Disorder like, **significant**.
Without fault.

Comments
To the **disorder like belongs significance**.
Acquiring the **center indeed**.

Fields of meaning

Root, *SUN*: see *Image of the Situation*. **Locate**, *ZAI*: be at, be situated at, dwell, reside; in, within; involved with, in the process of. Ideogram: earth and persevere, a place on the earth. **Below**, *XIA*: anything below, in all senses; lower, inner; lower trigram. **Bed**, *CHUANG*: sleeping place; couch, sofa, lounge; bench around a well. **Avail**, *YONG*: use, employ for a specific purpose; take advantage of; benefit from; capacity. Ideogram: to divine and center, applying divination to central concerns. **Chroniclers**, *SHI*: administrative officer; record-keeper, narrator, annalist; histories, authoritative records, annals. **Shaman**, *WU*: magician, sorcerer, healer, wizard, witch; perform magic. **Disorder**, *FEN*: trouble, doubt; affairs, multiple occupations; mixed, assorted; confused, perplexed; variegated, spotted. **Like**, *RUO*: same as, just as; conform, imitate; adverbial suffix indicating similarity. **Significant**, *JI*: leads to the experience of meaning; favorable, propitious, appropriate. Ideogram: scholar and mouth, wise words of a sage. **Without fault**, *WU JIU*: no error or harm in the situation.

Belong/it, *ZHI*: see *Additional Texts*. **Acquire**, *DE*: obtain the desired object; possession; satisfied, fulfilled; it is permitted; agree with; wish for, desire covetously. Ideogram: go and obstacle, going through obstacles to the goal. **Center**, *ZHONG*: inner, central; put in the center; middle, stable point enabling you to face inner and outer changes; middle line of a trigram. Ideogram: field divided in two equal parts. **Indeed**, *YE*: see *Preceding Situation*.

Nine at Third

Imminent root, **abashment**.

Comments
To **imminent root belongs abashment**.
Purpose exhausted indeed.

Fields of meaning

Imminent, *PIN*: on the brink of; pressing, urgent; often, repeatedly. **Root**, *SUN*: see *Image of the Situation*. **Abashment**, *LIN*: distress, shame, regret, humiliation; aware of having lost the right track; leads to repenting, *HUI*, correcting the direction of mind and life.

Belong/it, *ZHI*: see *Additional Texts*. **Purpose**, *ZHI*: focus of mind and heart; intention, will, inclination; continuity in the direction of life. Ideogram: heart and scholar, high inner resolve. **Exhaust**, *QIONG*: bring to an end; limit, extremity; investigate exhaustively; destitute, indigent; end without a new beginning; distinct from complete, *ZHONG*, end of a cycle that begins the next one. Ideogram: cave and naked person, bent with disease or old age. **Indeed**, *YE*: see *Preceding Situation*.

Six at Fourth

Repenting extinguished.
The **fields**: **capturing three kinds**.

Comments
The **fields**: **capturing three kinds**.
Possessing achievement indeed.

Fields of meaning

Repenting extinguished, *HUI WANG*: previous errors are corrected, all causes for repenting disappear. **Field**, *TIAN*: cultivated land, farming land; preferred terrain for hunting, since game in the fields cannot escape the hunt. Ideogram: square divided into four sections, delineating fields. **Capture**, *HUO*: obtain, seize, reach; take in a hunt, catch a thief; hit the mark, opportune moment; prisoner, spoils, prey, slave, servant. **Three/thrice**, *SAN*: number three; third time or place; active phases of a cycle; superlative; beginning of repetition (since one and two are entities in themselves). **Kinds**, *PIN*: species and their essential qualities; sort, class, degree; numerous, innumerable.

Possess, *YOU*: general term indicating possession; have, own, be endowed with. **Achieve**, *GONG*: work done, results, actual accomplishment; praise, worth, merit. Ideogram: workman's square and forearm, combining craft and strength. **Indeed**, *YE*: see *Preceding Situation*.

NINE AT FIFTH

Trial, significant.
Repenting extinguished.
Without not harvesting.
Without initially possessing completion.
Before husking, three days.
After husking, three days.
Significant.

Comments
To **nine** at **fifth belongs significance.**
Position correct in the **center indeed.**

Fields of meaning
Trial, *ZHEN*: inquiry by divination and its result; righteous, firm; separating wheat from chaff; the kernel, the proven core; quality of winter and North, fourth stage of the Time Cycle. Ideogram: pearl and divination. **Significant**, *JI*: leads to the experience of meaning; favorable, propitious, appropriate. Ideogram: scholar and mouth, wise words of a sage. **Repenting extinguished**, *HUI WANG*: previous errors are corrected, all causes for repenting disappear. **Without not Harvesting**, *WU BU LI*: turning point where the balance is swinging from not Harvesting to actually Harvesting. **Without**, *WU*: devoid of; there is not. **Initial**, *CHU*: beginning, incipient, first step or part; bottom line of a hexagram. Ideogram: knife and garment, cutting out the pattern. **Possess**, *YOU*: general term indicating possession; have, own, be endowed with. **Complete**, *ZHONG*: completion of a cycle that begins the next; entire, whole, all. Ideogram: silk cocoons, follow and ice, winter linking one year with the next. **Before(hand)/earlier**, *XIAN*: anterior, preceding in time; former, past, previous; first, at first. **Husking**, *GENG*: fruit and grain husks bursting in autumn; seventh of the Ten Heavenly Barriers in calendar system; bestow, reward; blade or sword; associated with the Metallic Moment. Ideogram: two hands threshing grain. **Three/thrice**, *SAN*: number three; third time or place; active phases of a cycle; superlative; beginning of repetition (since one and two are entities in themselves). **Day/sun**, *RI*: the sun and the time of a sun-cycle, a day. **After(wards)/later**, *HOU*: come after in time, subsequent; put oneself after; behind, back, draw back; the second; attendants, heirs, successors, posterity. **Significant**, *JI*: leads to the experience of meaning; favorable, propitious, appropriate. Ideogram: scholar and mouth, wise words of a sage.

Nine, *JIU*: number nine; transforming whole line; superlative: best, perfect. **Five**, *WU*: number five; fivefold articulation of the Universal Compass; the Five Moments and all related qualities: directions, colors, smells, tastes, tones, feelings.

Belong/it, *ZHI*: see *Additional Texts*. **Position**, *WEI*: place, location; be at; social standing, rank; position of a line in a hexagram. Ideogram: person standing. **Correct**, *ZHENG*: rectify deviation or one-sidedness; proper, straight, exact, regular; constant, rule, model. Ideogram: stop and one, hold to one thing. **Center**, *ZHONG*: inner, central; put in the center; middle, stable point enabling you to face inner and outer changes; middle line of a trigram. Ideogram: field divided in two equal parts. **Indeed**, *YE*: see *Preceding Situation*.

NINE ABOVE

The **root located below** the **bed**.
Losing one's own emblem-ax.
Trial, **pitfall**.

Comments
The **root located below** the **bed**.
Above exhaustion indeed.
Losing one's own emblem-ax.
Correcting reaches a **pitfall indeed**.

Fields of meaning
Root, *SUN*: see *Image of the Situation*. **Locate**, *ZAI*: be at, be situated at, dwell, reside; in, within; involved with, in the process of. Ideogram: earth and persevere, a place on the earth. **Below**, *XIA*: anything below, in all senses; lower, inner; lower trigram. **Bed**, *CHUANG*: sleeping place; couch, sofa, lounge; bench around a well. **Lose**, *SANG*: be deprived of, forget; destruction, ruin, death; corpse; lament, mourn; funeral. Ideogram: weep and dead. **One/one's**, *QI*: general third person pronoun and possessive adjective; also: it/its, he/his, she/her, they/their. **Emblem-ax**, *FU*: moon-shaped ax, symbol of governmental power. **Trial**, *ZHEN*: inquiry by divination and its result; righteous, firm; separating wheat from chaff; the kernel, the proven core; quality of winter and North, fourth stage of the Time Cycle. Ideogram: pearl and divination. **Pitfall**, *XIONG*: unfortunate situation, in which the flow of life and spirit is blocked and the experience of meaning is lost; stuck and exposed to danger; inappropriate attitude. Ideogram: person in a pit.

Above, *SHANG*: anything above in all senses; higher, upper, outer; upper trigram. **Exhaust**, *QIONG*: bring to an end; limit, extremity; investigate exhaustively; destitute, indigent; end without a new beginning; distinct from complete, *ZHONG*, end of a cycle that begins the next one. Ideogram: cave and naked person, bent with disease or old age. **Indeed**, *YE*: see *Preceding Situation*. **Correct**, *ZHENG*: rectify deviation or one-sidedness; proper, straight, exact, regular; constant, rule, model. Ideogram: stop and one, hold to one thing. **Reach**, *HU*: arrive at a goal; move toward and achieve; to, at, in; distinct from tend-towards, *YOU*.

Image Tradition

> **Redoubled root uses assigning fate**.
> **Solid root reaches** the **center correctly and-also** the **purpose moves**.
> The **supple altogether yielding reaches** the **solid**.
> **That uses** the **small**, **Growing**.
> **Harvesting**: **possessing directed going**.
> **Harvesting**: **viewing** the **great** in the **person**.

Fields of meaning

Redouble, *CHONG*: repeat, reiterate, add to; weight, heaviness; important, difficult. **Root**, *SUN*: see *Image of the Situation*. **Use**, *YI*: see *Additional Texts*. **Assign**, *SHEN*: see *Patterns of Wisdom*. **Fate**, *MING*: see *Patterns of Wisdom*. **Solid**, *GANG*: quality of the whole lines; firm, strong, unyielding, persisting. **Reach**, *HU*: arrive at a goal; move toward and achieve; to, at, in; distinct from tend-towards, *YOU*. **Center**, *ZHONG*: inner, central; put in the center; middle, stable point enabling you to face inner and outer changes; middle line of a trigram. Ideogram: field divided in two equal parts. **Correct**, *ZHENG*: rectify deviation or one-sidedness; proper, straight, exact, regular; constant, rule, model. Ideogram: stop and one, hold to one thing. **And-also**, *ER*: see *Preceding Situation*. **Purpose**, *ZHI*: focus of mind and heart; intention, will, inclination; continuity in the direction of life. Ideogram: heart and scholar, high inner resolve. **Move**, *XING*: see *Additional Texts*. **Supple**, *ROU*: quality of the opened lines; flexible, pliant, adaptable, tender. **Altogether**, *JIE*: all, the whole; the same sort, alike; entirely. **Yield**, *SHUN*: give way, comply, agree, follow, obey; docile, flexible; bear produce, nourish, provide; Action of the trigram Field, *KUN*. **That**, *SHI*: refers to the preceding statement. **Use**, *YI*: see *Additional Texts*. The **small**, **Growing**, *XIAO HENG*: see *Image of the Situation*. **Harvesting**: **possessing directed going**, *LI YOU YOU WANG*: see *Image of the Situation*. **Viewing** the **great** in the **person**, *JIAN DA REN*: see *Image of the Situation*.

58 THE OPEN | *Dui*

The situation described by this hexagram is characterized by an openness to interaction, communication and exchange, which brings joyous stimulation. The hexagram The Open is the doubling of the corresponding trigram, and partakes of its attributes.

Image of the Situation

> The **open**.
> **Growing**, **Harvesting**, **Trial**.

Fields of meaning

Open, *DUI*: an open surface, promoting interaction and interpenetration; pleasant, easy, responsive, free, unhindered; opening, passage; the mouth; exchange, barter; straight, direct; meet, gather; place where water accumulates. Ideogram: mouth and vapor, communication through speech. *Symbol*: marsh, *ZE*, open surface of a flat body of water and the vapors rising from it; fertilize, enrich; kindness, favor. *Action*: stimulate, *SHUO*, rouse to action and good feeling; stir up, urge on; exhort, persuade; say, tell, relate; cheer, delight; joyous, peaceful, restful. Ideogram: words and exchange. In the family of trigrams *DUI* is the youngest daughter. **Grow**, *HENG*: heavenly influence pervading and nourishing all things; prosper, succeed, expand, develop; effective, favorable; quality of summer and South, second stage of the Time Cycle. With the pronunciation *XIANG*: offer a sacrifice; offer a gift to a superior; accept, enjoy. **Harvest**, *LI*: benefit, advantage, profit; realization; sharp, acute, insightful; quality of autumn and West, third stage of the Time Cycle. Ideogram: ripe grain and blade. **Trial**, *ZHEN*: inquiry by divination and its result; righteous, firm; separating wheat from chaff; the kernel, the proven core; quality of winter and North, fourth stage of the Time Cycle. Ideogram: pearl and divination.

Outer and Inner Trigram

In this hexagram the outer and inner aspects of the situation are identical, and they are described by the trigram **Open**. Its associations are listed in the corresponding *Field of meaning* above.

Counter Hexagram

The Counter Hexagram of **The Open** is hexagram 37, **Household People**, which switches the emphasis from the openness to general interaction, communication and exchange characterizing **The Open** to the intimate community of a household.

Preceding Situation

> **Entering and-also afterwards stimulating it**.
> To **anterior acquiescence belongs** the **use** of the **open**.
> The **open implies stimulating indeed**.

Fields of meaning

Enter, *RU*: penetrate, go into, enter on, encroach on; progress; put into; Action of the trigram Root, *SUN*. **And-also**, *ER*: joins and contrasts two terms. **After(wards)/later**, *HOU*: come after in time, subsequent; put oneself after; behind, back, draw back; the second; attendants, heirs, successors, posterity. **Stimulate**, *SHUO*: rouse to action and good feeling; stir up, urge on; exhort, persuade; say, tell, relate; cheer, delight; joyous, peaceful, restful; Action of the trigram Open, *DUI*. Ideogram: words and exchange. **It/belong**, *ZHI*: establishes between two terms a connection similar to the Saxon genitive, in which the second term belongs to the first one; at the end of a sentence it refers to something previously mentioned or implied. To **anterior acquiescence belongs** the **use** of, *GU SHOU ZHI YI*: understanding and accepting the preceding statement allows the consultant to make proper use of this hexagram. **Open**, *DUI*: see *Image of the Situation*. **Imply**, *ZHE*: further signify; additional meaning. **Indeed**, *YE*: emphasizes and intensifies the previous statement.

Hexagrams in Pairs

> The **open**: **viewing**, **and-also**
> the **root**: **hidden-away indeed**.

Fields of meaning

Open, *DUI*: see *Image of the Situation*. **View**, *JIAN*: vision in all its aspects: seeing, being visible, forming mental images; visit, call on, consult. Ideogram: eye above person, active and receptive sight. **And-also**, *ER*: see *Preceding Situation*. **Root**, *SUN*: base on which things rest, ground, foundation; mild, subtly penetrating; nourishing. **Hide-away**, *FU*: hide, conceal; ambush; secret, silent; prostrate, submit. Ideogram: man and crouching dog. **Indeed**, *YE*: see *Preceding Situation*.

Patterns of Wisdom

Congregating ponds. The **open**.
A **jun zi uses partnering** with **friends** to **explicate repeatedly**.

Fields of meaning
Congregate, *LI*: cling together, adhere to, rely on; couple, pair, herd; beautiful, elegant; Action of the trigram Radiance, *LI*. Ideogram: deer flocking together. **Pond**, *ZE*: open surface of a flat body of water and the vapors rising from it; fertilize, enrich; kindness, favor; Symbol of the trigram Open, *DUI*. **Open**, *DUI*: see *Image of the Situation*. **Jun zi**: ideal of a person who orders his/her life in accordance with dao rather than willful intention, and uses divination in this spirit. **Use**, *YI*: by means of; owing to; make use of, employ. **Partner**, *PENG*: companion, friend, peer; join, associate for mutual benefit; commercial venture; two equal or similar things. Ideogram: linked strings of cowries or coins. **Friend**, *YOU*: companion, associate; of the same mind; attached, in pairs. Ideogram: two hands joined. **Explicate**, *JIANG*: explain, unfold, narrate; converse, speak; plan, discuss. Ideogram: speech and crossing beams, speech blending harmoniously. **Repeat**, *XI*: perform a series of similar acts, practice, rehearse; habit, custom; familiar with, skilled. Ideogram: little bird practicing flight.

Transforming Lines

INITIAL NINE

Harmonious opening, **significant**.

Comments
To the **harmonious opening belongs significance**.
Moving, **not-yet doubting indeed**.

Fields of meaning
Harmony, *HE*: concord, union; conciliate; at peace, mild; fit, tune, adjust. **Open**, *DUI*: see *Image of the Situation*. **Significant**, *JI*: leads to the experience of meaning; favorable, propitious, appropriate. Ideogram: scholar and mouth, wise words of a sage.

Belong/it, *ZHI*: establishes between two terms a connection similar to the Saxon genitive, in which the second term belongs to the first one; at the end of a sentence it refers to something previously mentioned or implied. **Move**, *XING*: move or move something; motivate; emotionally moving; walk, act, do. Ideogram:

successive steps. **Not-yet**, *WEI*: temporal negative indicating that something is expected to happen but has not yet occurred. **Doubt**, *YI*: suspect, distrust, wonder; uncertain, dubious; surmise, conjecture, fear. **Indeed**, *YE*: see *Preceding Situation*.

Nine at Second

Conforming opening, **significant**.
Repenting extinguished.

Comments
To **conforming opening belongs significance**.
Trustworthy purpose indeed.

Fields of meaning
Conform, *FU*: accord between inner and outer; sincere, truthful, verified, reliable; capture; prisoners, spoils. Ideogram: claws over child, a bird brooding on the nest. **Open**, *DUI*: see *Image of the Situation*. **Significant**, *JI*: leads to the experience of meaning; favorable, propitious, appropriate. Ideogram: scholar and mouth, wise words of a sage. **Repenting extinguished**, *HUI WANG*: previous errors are corrected, all causes for repenting disappear.

Belong/it, *ZHI*: establishes between two terms a connection similar to the Saxon genitive, in which the second term belongs to the first one; at the end of a sentence it refers to something previously mentioned or implied. **Trustworthy**, *XIN*: truthful, faithful, consistent over time; count on, confide in; examine, verify, prove; loyalty, integrity. Ideogram: person and word, true speech. **Purpose**, *ZHI*: focus of mind and heart; intention, will, inclination; continuity in the direction of life. Ideogram: heart and scholar, high inner resolve. **Indeed**, *YE*: see *Preceding Situation*.

Six at Third

Coming opening, **pitfall**.

Comments
To **coming opening belongs** a **pitfall**.
Position not appropriate indeed.

Fields of meaning
Come, *LAI*: approach in time or space; move toward, arrive at; future; contrasts with go, *WANG*, move away or become past. **Open**, *DUI*: see *Image of the Situation*.

Pitfall, *XIONG*: unfortunate situation, in which the flow of life and spirit is blocked and the experience of meaning is lost; stuck and exposed to danger; inappropriate attitude. Ideogram: person in a pit.

Belong/it, *ZHI*: establishes between two terms a connection similar to the Saxon genitive, in which the second term belongs to the first one; at the end of a sentence it refers to something previously mentioned or implied. **Position**, *WEI*: place, location; be at; social standing, rank; position of a line in a hexagram. Ideogram: person standing. **Not**, *BU*: common term of negation. **Appropriate**, *DANG*: suitable, capable, worthy, adequate, competent, equal to; opportune, convenient; whole lines in odd places and opened lines in even places. **Indeed**, *YE*: see *Preceding Situation*.

NINE AT FOURTH

Bargaining opening, not-yet soothing.
The **cuirass' affliction possesses joy**.

Comments
To **nine** at **fourth belongs joy**.
Possessing reward indeed.

Fields of meaning
Bargain, *SHANG*: argue over prices; consult, deliberate, do business; traveling merchants; hour before sunrise and sunset. Ideogram: stutter and sentences, repetitive speaking. **Open**, *DUI*: see *Image of the Situation*. **Not-yet**, *WEI*: temporal negative indicating that something is expected to happen but has not yet occurred. **Soothe**, *NING*: calm, pacify; create peace of mind; tranquil, quiet. Ideogram: shelter above heart, dish and breath, physical and spiritual comfort. **Cuirass**, *JIE*: armor; tortoise or crab shell; protective covering; border, limit, interval; protection, support; steady, rigid, solid. **Affliction**, *JI*: sickness, disorder, defect, calamity, injury; poison, hate, dislike; cruel, jealous, envious. Ideogram: sickness and dart, a sudden affliction. **Possess**, *YOU*: general term indicating possession; have, own, be endowed with. **Joy/rejoice**, *XI*: delight, exult; cheerful, merry. Ideogram: joy (music) and mouth, expressing joy.

Nine, *JIU*: number nine; transforming whole line; superlative: best, perfect. **Four**, *SI*: number four; number of the cardinal directions and of the seasons; everywhere, on all sides; fourfold articulation of the Universal Compass. **Belong/it**, *ZHI*: establishes between two terms a connection similar to the Saxon genitive, in which the second term belongs to the first one; at the end of a sentence it refers to something previously mentioned or implied. **Reward**, *QING*:

gift given out of gratitude or benevolence; favor from heaven. Ideogram: heart, follow and deer, the heart expressed through the gift of a deer's skin. **Indeed**, *YE*: see *Preceding Situation*.

Nine at Fifth

Conformity tending-towards stripping.
Possessing adversity.

Comments
Conformity tending-towards stripping.
Position correct and **appropriate indeed**.

Fields of meaning

Conform, *FU*: accord between inner and outer; sincere, truthful, verified, reliable; capture; prisoners, spoils. Ideogram: claws over child, a bird brooding on the nest. **Tend-towards**, *YU*: move toward without necessarily reaching, in the direction of. **Strip**, *BO*: flay, peel, skin; remove, uncover; split, slice; reduce to essentials; degrade, decay; slaughter an animal. Ideogram: knife and carve, trenchant action. **Possess**, *YOU*: general term indicating possession; have, own, be endowed with. **Adversity**, *LI*: danger, hardship, severe; threat or difficulty that must be encountered, rather than avoided; grinding stone; polish, sharpen; a challenge that strengthens and perfects the character; stimulate, excite; cruel demon.

Position, *WEI*: place, location; be at; social standing, rank; position of a line in a hexagram. Ideogram: person standing. **Correct**, *ZHENG*: rectify deviation or one-sidedness; proper, straight, exact, regular; constant, rule, model. Ideogram: stop and one, hold to one thing. **Appropriate**, *DANG*: suitable, capable, worthy, adequate, competent, equal to; opportune, convenient; whole lines in odd places and opened lines in even places. **Indeed**, *YE*: see *Preceding Situation*.

Six Above

Protracted opening.

Comments
Six above: **protracted opening**.
Not-yet shining indeed.

Fields of meaning

Protract, *YIN*: draw out, prolong; pull, stretch; lasting, perennial. Ideogram: draw a bow. **Open**, *DUI*: see *Image of the Situation*.

Six, *LIU*: number six; transforming opened line; six lines of a hexagram. **Above**, *SHANG*: anything above in all senses; higher, upper, outer; upper trigram. **Not-yet**, *WEI*: temporal negative indicating that something is expected to happen but has not yet occurred. **Shine**, *GUANG*: illuminate, emit light; brilliant, splendid; honor, glory, éclat; distinct from brightness, *MING*, light of heavenly bodies. Ideogram: fire above person. **Indeed**, *YE*: see *Preceding Situation*.

Image Tradition

The **open**: **stimulating indeed**.
The **solid** in the **center and-also** the **supple outside**.
Stimulating uses Harvesting, **Trial**.
That uses yielding reaching heaven and-also correspondence reaching people.

Stimulating uses beforehand the **commoners**.
The **commoners forget their toil**.
Stimulating uses opposing heaviness.
The **commoners forget their death**.
To **stimulating belongs** the **great**.
The **commoners encouraged actually in-fact**.

Fields of meaning

Open, *DUI*: see *Image of the Situation*. **Stimulate**, *SHUO*: see *Preceding Situation*. **Indeed**, *YE*: see *Preceding Situation*. **Solid**, *GANG*: quality of the whole lines; firm, strong, unyielding, persisting. **Center**, *ZHONG*: inner, central; put in the center; middle, stable point enabling you to face inner and outer changes; middle line of a trigram. Ideogram: field divided in two equal parts. **And-also**, *ER*: see *Preceding Situation*. **Supple**, *ROU*: quality of the opened lines; flexible, pliant, adaptable, tender. **Outside**, *WAI*: outer, external; unfamiliar, foreign; ignore, reject; work done outside the home; the upper trigram as indication of the outer aspects of the situation. **Use**, *YI*: see *Patterns of Wisdom*. **Harvest**, *LI*: see *Image of the Situation*. **Trial**, *ZHEN*: inquiry by divination and its result; righteous, firm; separating wheat from chaff; the kernel, the proven core; quality of winter and North, fourth stage of the Time Cycle. Ideogram: pearl and divination. **That**, *SHI*: refers to the preceding statement. **Yield**, *SHUN*: give way, comply, agree, follow, obey; docile, flexible; bear produce, nourish, provide; Action of the trigram Field, *KUN*. **Reach**,

HU: arrive at a goal; move toward and achieve; to, at, in; distinct from tend-towards, *YOU*. **Heaven**, *TIAN*: sky, firmament, heavens; the highest realm, situated above the human world, as opposed to the earth, *DI*, located below; Symbol of the trigram Energy, *QIAN*. Ideogram: great and the one above. **Correspond**, *YING*: be in agreement or harmony; proper, suitable; resonate together, answer to; relation between the lines (1 and 4, 2 and 5, 3 and 6) when they form the pair opened and whole, supple and solid. Ideogram: heart and obey. **People/person**, *REN*: humans individually and collectively; an individual; humankind.

Before(hand)/earlier, *XIAN*: anterior, preceding in time; former, past, previous; first, at first. **Commoners**, *MIN*: common people, masses; working class supporting the social hierarchy; undeveloped potential in the individual. **Forget**, *WANG*: escape the mind; leave undone, disregard, neglect. Ideogram: heart and lost. **They/their**, *QI*: general third person pronoun and possessive adjective; also: one/one's, it/its, he/his, she/her. **Toil**, *LAO*: hardship, labor; exert oneself, exhaust oneself; burdened, careworn; worthy actions. Ideogram: strength and fire. **Oppose**, *FAN*: resist; violate, offend, attack; possessed by an evil spirit; criminal. Ideogram: violate and dog, brutal offense. **Heaviness**, *NAN*: difficulty, hardship, distress; arduous, grievous; harass; contrasts with versatility, *YI*, deal lightly with. Ideogram: bird with clipped tail on drying sticky soil. **Die**, *SI*: sudden or untimely death; death penalty; run out of energy; inert, stagnant, fixed. **Belong/it**, *ZHI*: establishes between two terms a connection similar to the Saxon genitive, in which the second term belongs to the first one; at the end of a sentence it refers to something previously mentioned or implied. **Great**, *DA*: big, noble, important, very; orient the will toward a self-imposed goal, impose direction; ability to lead or guide one's life; contrasts with small, *XIAO*, flexible adaptation to what crosses one's path. **Encourage**, *CHUAN*: exhort, stimulate; advise, persuade; admonish. **Actually**, *YI*: truly, really, at present. Ideogram: a dart and done, strong intention fully expressed. **In-fact**, *ZAI*: emphatic exclamation; truly, indeed.

渙

59 DISPERSING | *Huan*

The situation described by this hexagram is characterized by dissolving obstacles, illusions or misunderstandings, like clouds clearing away.

Image of the Situation

> **Dispersing**.
> **Growing**.
> The **king imagines possessing** a **temple**.
> **Harvesting**: **wading** the **great river**.
> **Harvesting**, **Trial**.

Fields of meaning

Disperse, *HUAN*: spread, disperse, distribute; scatter clouds or crowds; dispel illusions, fears and suspicions; dissolve, evaporate, vanish; fog lifting or clearing away. **Grow**, *HENG*: heavenly influence pervading and nourishing all things; prosper, succeed, expand, develop; effective, favorable; quality of summer and South, second stage of the Time Cycle. With the pronunciation *XIANG*: offer a sacrifice; offer a gift to a superior; accept, enjoy. **King**, *WANG*: sovereign, effective ruler, emperor, seen as connecting heaven and earth; reign, govern. **Imagine**, *JIA*: create in the mind; fantasize, suppose; pretend, imitate; fiction, illusion; costume. Ideogram: person and borrow. **Possess**, *YOU*: general term indicating possession; have, own, be endowed with. **Temple**, *MIAO*: building used to honor gods and ancestors. **Harvest**, *LI*: benefit, advantage, profit; realization; sharp, acute, insightful; quality of autumn and West, third stage of the Time Cycle. Ideogram: ripe grain and blade. **Wading the Great River**, *SHE DA CHUAN*: enter the stream of life with a goal or purpose; embark on a significant enterprise. **Trial**, *ZHEN*: inquiry by divination and its result; righteous, firm; separating wheat from chaff; the kernel, the proven core; quality of winter and North, fourth stage of the Time Cycle. Ideogram: pearl and divination.

Outer and Inner Trigram

The upper trigram, **Root**, *SUN*, describes the outer aspects of the situation. It has the following associations: base on which things rest, ground, foundation; mild, subtly penetrating; nourishing. *Symbols*: tree/wood and wind. Tree/wood, *MU*: trees and all things woody or wooden; associated with the Wooden Moment. Ideogram: a tree with roots and branches. Wind, *FENG*: wind, breeze, gust; weather and its influence on mood and humor; fashion, usage. *Action*: enter, *RU*, penetrate, go into, enter on, encroach on; progress; put into. In the family of trigrams *SUN* is the eldest daughter.

The lower trigram, **Gorge**, *KAN*, describes the inner aspects of the situation. It has the following associations: precipice, dangerous place; hole, cavity, pit, snare, trap, grave; critical time, test; risky. Ideogram: earth and cavity. *Symbol*: stream, *SHUI*, flowing water; river, tide, flood; fluid, dissolving. Ideogram: rippling water. *Actions*: venture and fall. Venture, *XIAN*: face a severe difficulty or obstruction; risk; precipice, cliff, abyss; key point, point of danger. Ideogram: mound and all, everything engaged at one point. Fall, *XIAN*: fall down or into, sink, drop, descend; pit, trap, fault; falling water. In the family of trigrams *KAN* is the middle son.

Counter Hexagram

The Counter Hexagram of **Dispersing** is hexagram 27, **The Jaws**, which switches the emphasis from dissolving illusions and misunderstandings to focusing on seeking nourishment.

Preceding Situation

> **Stimulating and-also afterwards scattering it**.
> To **anterior acquiescence belongs** the **use** of **dispersing**.
> **Dispersing implies radiance indeed**.

Fields of meaning

Stimulate, *SHUO*: rouse to action and good feeling; stir up, urge on; exhort, persuade; say, tell, relate; cheer, delight; joyous, peaceful, restful; Action of the trigram Open, *DUI*. Ideogram: words and exchange. **And-also**, *ER*: joins and contrasts two terms. **After(wards)/later**, *HOU*: come after in time, subsequent; put oneself after; behind, back, draw back; the second; attendants, heirs, successors, posterity. **Scatter**, *SAN*: disperse in small pieces; separate, divide, distribute. Ideogram: strike and crumble. **It/belong**, *ZHI*: establishes between two terms a connection similar to the Saxon genitive, in which the second term belongs to the first one; at the end of a sentence it refers to something previously mentioned or implied. To **anterior acquiescence belongs** the **use** of, *GU SHOU ZHI YI*: understanding and accepting the preceding statement allows the consultant to make proper use of this hexagram. **Disperse**, *HUAN*: see *Image of the Situation*. **Imply**, *ZHE*: further signify; additional meaning. **Radiance**, *LI*: glowing light, spreading in all directions; the power of consciousness; discriminate, articulate, divide and arrange in order; assemble, attract. Ideogram: bird and weird, magical fire-bird with brilliant plumage. **Indeed**, *YE*: emphasizes and intensifies the previous statement.

Hexagrams in Pairs

> **Dispersing**: **radiance indeed**.
> **Articulating**: **stopping indeed**.

Fields of meaning

Disperse, *HUAN*: see *Image of the Situation*. **Radiance**, *LI*: see *Preceding Situation*. **Indeed**, *YE*: see *Preceding Situation*. **Articulate**, *JIE*: joint, articulation; a separation which simultaneously establishes the identity of the parts and their connection; express thought through speech; section, chapter, interval; temperance, virtue; rite, ceremony; lit.: nodes of bamboo stalks. **Stop**, *ZHI*: bring or come to a standstill, cease, terminate; Action of the trigram Bound, *GEN*. Ideogram: a foot stops walking.

Patterns of Wisdom

> **Wind moves above stream**. **Dispersing**.
> The **earlier kings used presenting tending-towards** the **supreme** to **establish** the **temples**.

Fields of meaning

Wind, *FENG*: wind, breeze, gust; weather and its influence on mood and humor; fashion, usage; wind and wood are the Symbols of the trigram Root, *SUN*. **Move**, *XING*: move or move something; motivate; emotionally moving; walk, act, do. Ideogram: successive steps. **Above**, *SHANG*: anything above in all senses; higher, upper, outer; upper trigram. **Stream**, *SHUI*: flowing water; river, tide, flood; fluid, dissolving; Symbol of the trigram Gorge, *KAN*. Ideogram: rippling water. **Disperse**, *HUAN*: see *Image of the Situation*. **Earlier Kings**, *XIAN WANG*: ideal rulers of old; the golden age, primal time; mythical sages in harmony with nature. **Use**, *YI*: by means of; owing to; make use of, employ. **Present**, *XIANG*: offer in sacrifice, give to the gods or a superior; give a banquet; accept an offering; enjoy, receive. **Tend-towards**, *YU*: move toward without necessarily reaching, in the direction of. **Supreme**, *DI*: highest, above all on earth; sovereign, lord, emperor. **Establish**, *LI*: set up, institute, order, arrange; stand erect; settled principles. **Temple**, *MIAO*: see *Image of the Situation*.

Transforming Lines

Initial Six

Availing of a **rescuing horse**'s **vigor**, **significant**.

Comments
To **initial six belongs significance**.
Yielding indeed.

Fields of meaning
Avail, *YONG*: use, employ for a specific purpose; take advantage of; benefit from; capacity. Ideogram: to divine and center, applying divination to central concerns. **Rescue**, *ZHENG*: aid, deliver from trouble; pull out, raise up, lift. Ideogram: hand and aid, a helping hand. **Horse**, *MA*: symbol of spirited strength in the natural world, earthly counterpart of the dragon; associated with the trigram Energy, *QIAN*, heaven, and high noon. **Vigor**, *ZHUANG*: power, strength; energetic, robust, fully grown, flourishing, abundant; at the peak of age and form; inspirit, animate; damage through unrestrained strength. Ideogram: strength and scholar, intellectual impact. **Significant**, *JI*: leads to the experience of meaning; favorable, propitious, appropriate. Ideogram: scholar and mouth, wise words of a sage.

Initial, *CHU*: beginning, incipient, first step or part; bottom line of a hexagram. Ideogram: knife and garment, cutting out the pattern. **Six**, *LIU*: number six; transforming opened line; six lines of a hexagram. **Belong/it**, *ZHI*: establishes between two terms a connection similar to the Saxon genitive, in which the second term belongs to the first one; at the end of a sentence it refers to something previously mentioned or implied. **Yield**, *SHUN*: give way, comply, agree, follow, obey; docile, flexible; bear produce, nourish, provide; Action of the trigram Field, *KUN*. **Indeed**, *YE*: see *Preceding Situation*.

Nine at Second

Dispersing: **fleeing one's bench**.
Repenting extinguished.

Comments
Dispersing: **fleeing one's bench**.
Acquiring the **desired indeed**.

Fields of meaning
Disperse, *HUAN*: see *Image of the Situation*. **Flee**, *BEN*: run away; urgent, hurried;

bustle, confusion; marry without rites. Ideogram: three oxen and fright, a stampede. **One/one's**, *QI*: general third person pronoun and possessive adjective; also: it/its, he/his, she/her, they/their. **Bench**, *JI*: low table used to lean on; side-table; stool or support. **Repenting extinguished**, *HUI WANG*: previous errors are corrected, all causes for repenting disappear.

Acquire, *DE*: obtain the desired object; possession; satisfied, fulfilled; it is permitted; agree with; wish for, desire covetously. Ideogram: go and obstacle, going through obstacles to the goal. **Desire**, *YUAN*: wish, hope or long for; covet; desired object. **Indeed**, *YE*: see *Preceding Situation*.

SIX AT THIRD

Dispersing one's body.
Without repenting.

Comments
Dispersing one's body.
Purpose located outside indeed.

Fields of meaning
Disperse, *HUAN*: see *Image of the Situation*. **One/one's**, *QI*: general third person pronoun and possessive adjective; also: it/its, he/his, she/her, they/their. **Body**, *GONG*: physical being, power and self-expression; oneself; innate quality; distinct from individuality, *SHEN*, which includes the notion of lifespan. **Without**, *WU*: devoid of; there is not. **Repent**, *HUI*: regret, dissatisfaction with past conduct inducing a change of heart; proceeds from abashment, *LIN*, shame and confusion at having lost the right way.

Purpose, *ZHI*: focus of mind and heart; intention, will, inclination; continuity in the direction of life. Ideogram: heart and scholar, high inner resolve. **Locate**, *ZAI*: be at, be situated at, dwell, reside; in, within; involved with, in the process of. Ideogram: earth and persevere, a place on the earth. **Outside**, *WAI*: outer, external; unfamiliar, foreign; ignore, reject; work done outside the home; the upper trigram as indication of the outer aspects of the situation. **Indeed**, *YE*: see *Preceding Situation*.

SIX AT FOURTH

Dispersing one's flock: **Spring, significant.**
Dispersing possesses the **hill-top.**
In-no-way hidden, a **place** to **ponder.**

Comments

Dispersing one's flock: Spring, significant.
The **shining great indeed.**

Fields of meaning

Disperse, *HUAN*: see *Image of the Situation.* **One/one's,** *QI*: general third person pronoun and possessive adjective; also: it/its, he/his, she/her, they/their. **Flock,** *QUN*: herd, group; people of the same kind, friends, equals; crowd, multitude; move in unison, flock together. Ideogram: chief and sheep, flock around a leader. **Spring,** *YUAN*: source, origin, head; arise, begin; first generating impulse; great, excellent; quality of springtime and East, first stage of the Time Cycle. **Significant,** *JI*: leads to the experience of meaning; favorable, propitious, appropriate. Ideogram: scholar and mouth, wise words of a sage. **Possess,** *YOU*: see *Image of the Situation.* **Hill-top,** *QIU*: hill with hollow top used for worship and as grave-site; knoll, hillock. **In-no-way,** *FEI*: strong negative; not so; bandit, rebel; unjust, immoral. Ideogram: a box filled with opposition. **Hide,** *YI*: squat, even, level, equalize; cut, wound, destroy, exterminate; pacified; colorless; distant, remote, barbarian. **Place,** *SUO*: position, location; residence, dwelling; where something belongs or comes from; habitual focus or object. **Ponder,** *SI*: reflect, consider, remember; deep thought; desire, wish. Ideogram: heart and field, the heart's concerns.

Shine, *GUANG*: illuminate, emit light; brilliant, splendid; honor, glory, éclat; distinct from brightness, *MING*, light of heavenly bodies. Ideogram: fire above person. **Great,** *DA*: big, noble, important, very; orient the will toward a self-imposed goal, impose direction; ability to lead or guide one's life; contrasts with small, *XIAO*, flexible adaptation to what crosses one's path. **Indeed,** *YE*: see *Preceding Situation.*

NINE AT FIFTH

Dispersing sweat: one's great cries-out.
Dispersing.
The **king**'s **residing, without fault.**

Comments

The **king**'s **residing, without fault.**
Correct position indeed.

Fields of meaning

Disperse, *HUAN*: see *Image of the Situation.* **Sweat,** *HAN*: perspiration; labor, trouble. Dispersing sweat, *HUAN HAN*, denotes an irrevocable decision (just as sweat cannot be reabsorbed). **One/one's**, *QI*: general third person pronoun and possessive adjective; also: it/its, he/his, she/her, they/their. **Great**, *DA*: big, noble, important, very; orient the will toward a self-imposed goal, impose direction; ability to lead or guide one's life; contrasts with small, *XIAO*, flexible adaptation to what crosses one's path. **Cry-out/outcry**, *HAO*: call out, proclaim; order, command; mark, label, sign; designate, name. **King**, *WANG*: see *Image of the Situation*. **Reside**, *JU*: dwell, live in, stay; sit down; fill an office; well-being, rest. Ideogram: body and seat. **Without fault**, *WU JIU*: no error or harm in the situation.

Correct, *ZHENG*: rectify deviation or one-sidedness; proper, straight, exact, regular; constant, rule, model. Ideogram: stop and one, hold to one thing. **Position**, *WEI*: place, location; be at; social standing, rank; position of a line in a hexagram. Ideogram: person standing. **Indeed**, *YE*: see *Preceding Situation*.

Nine Above

Dispersing one's blood.
Departing far-away.
Emerging, without fault.

Comments
Dispersing one's blood.
Distancing harm indeed.

Fields of meaning

Disperse, *HUAN*: see *Image of the Situation*. **One/one's**, *QI*: general third person pronoun and possessive adjective; also: it/its, he/his, she/her, they/their. **Blood**, *XUE*: blood, the Yin fluid that maintains life; money, property. **Depart**, *QU*: leave, quit, go; far away, far from; remove, reject, dismiss; lost, gone. **Far-away**, *DI*: far, remote; send away, exile. **Emerge**, *CHU*: come out of, proceed from, spring from, issue forth; appear, be born; bear, generate; leave, flee; Action of the trigram Shake, *ZHEN*. Ideogram: stem with branches and leaves emerging. **Without fault**, *WU JIU*: no error or harm in the situation.

Distance, *YUAN*: far off, remote; keep at a distance; a long time, far away in time. Ideogram: go and a long way. **Harm**, *HAI*: damage, injure, offend; suffer, become ill; obstacle, hindrance; fearful, anxious. **Indeed**, *YE*: see *Preceding Situation*.

Image Tradition

Dispersing. Growing.
The **solid comes and-also not exhausted.**
The **supple acquires** the **position reaching outside and-also above concording.**

The **king imagines possessing** a **temple.**
The **king thereupon located** in the **center indeed.**

Harvesting: wading the **great river.**
Riding wood possesses achievement indeed.

Fields of meaning

Dispersing. Growing, *HUAN HENG*: see *Image of the Situation*. **Solid,** *GANG*: quality of the whole lines; firm, strong, unyielding, persisting. **Come,** *LAI*: approach in time or space; move toward, arrive at; future; contrasts with go, *WANG*, move away or become past. **And-also,** *ER*: see *Preceding Situation*. **Not,** *BU*: common term of negation. **Exhaust,** *QIONG*: bring to an end; limit, extremity; investigate exhaustively; destitute, indigent; end without a new beginning; distinct from complete, *ZHONG*, end of a cycle that begins the next one. Ideogram: cave and naked person, bent with disease or old age. **Supple,** *ROU*: quality of the opened lines; flexible, pliant, adaptable, tender. **Acquire,** *DE*: obtain the desired object; possession; satisfied, fulfilled; it is permitted; agree with; wish for, desire covetously. Ideogram: go and obstacle, going through obstacles to the goal. **Position,** *WEI*: place, location; be at; social standing, rank; position of a line in a hexagram. Ideogram: person standing. **Reach,** *HU*: arrive at a goal; move toward and achieve; to, at, in; distinct from tend-towards, *YOU*. **Outside,** *WAI*: outer, external; unfamiliar, foreign; ignore, reject; work done outside the home; the upper trigram as indication of the outer aspects of the situation. **Above,** *SHANG*: see *Patterns of Wisdom*. **Concord,** *TONG*: harmonize, unite, equalize, assemble; agree, share in; together, at once, same time and place. Ideogram: cover and mouth, silent understanding and perfect fit.

The **king imagines possessing** a **temple,** *WANG JIA YOU MIAO*: see *Image of the Situation*. **Thereupon,** *NAI*: on that ground, then, only then; finally; in spite of that. **Locate,** *ZAI*: be at, be situated at, dwell, reside; in, within; involved with, in the process of. Ideogram: earth and persevere, a place on the earth. **Center,** *ZHONG*: inner, central; put in the center; middle, stable point enabling you to face inner and outer changes; middle line of a trigram. Ideogram: field divided in two equal parts. **Indeed,** *YE*: see *Preceding Situation*.

Harvesting: **wading** the **great river**, *LI SHE DA CHUAN*: see *Image of the Situation*. **Ride**, *CHENG*: ride an animal or a chariot; have the upper hand, control a stronger power; an opened line above controlling a whole line below. **Wood/tree**, *MU*: trees and all things woody or wooden; associated with the Wooden Moment; wood and wind are the Symbols of the trigram Ground, *SUN*. Ideogram: a tree with roots and branches. **Possess**, *YOU*: see *Image of the Situation*. **Achieve**, *GONG*: work done, results, actual accomplishment; praise, worth, merit. Ideogram: workman's square and forearm, combining craft and strength.

節

䷻

60 ARTICULATING

Jie

The situation described by this hexagram is characterized by clearly expressing boundaries and connections, correctly partitioning a whole while acknowledging its essential unity.

Image of the Situation

Articulating.
Growing.
Bitter articulating not permitting Trial.

Fields of meaning

Articulate, *JIE*: joint, articulation; a separation which simultaneously establishes the identity of the parts and their connection; express thought through speech; section, chapter, interval; temperance, virtue; rite, ceremony; lit.: nodes of bamboo stalks. **Grow**, *HENG*: heavenly influence pervading and nourishing all things; prosper, succeed, expand, develop; effective, favorable; quality of summer and South, second stage of the Time Cycle. With the pronunciation *XIANG*: offer a sacrifice; offer a gift to a superior; accept, enjoy. **Bitter**, *KU*: one of the five tastes: sour, bitter, sweet, acrid and salty; unpleasant, troublesome; hardship, affliction; suffer, bear; take pains; urgent, pressing; dislike, hate; corresponding to the Fiery Moment. **Not**, *BU*: common term of negation. **Permit**, *KE*: possible because in harmony with an inherent principle; capable of; approve, authorize. Ideogram: mouth and breath, silent consent. **Trial**, *ZHEN*: inquiry by divination and its result; righteous, firm; separating wheat from chaff; the kernel, the proven core; quality of winter and North, fourth stage of the Time Cycle. Ideogram: pearl and divination.

Outer and Inner Trigram

The upper trigram, **Gorge**, *KAN*, describes the outer aspects of the situation. It has the following associations: precipice, dangerous place; hole, cavity, pit, snare, trap, grave; critical time, test; risky. Ideogram: earth and cavity. *Symbol*: stream,

SHUI, flowing water; river, tide, flood; fluid, dissolving. Ideogram: rippling water. *Actions*: venture and fall. Venture, *XIAN*: face a severe difficulty or obstruction; risk; precipice, cliff, abyss; key point, point of danger. Ideogram: mound and all, everything engaged at one point. Fall, *XIAN*: fall down or into, sink, drop, descend; pit, trap, fault; falling water. In the family of trigrams *KAN* is the middle son.

The lower trigram, **Open**, *DUI*, describes the inner aspects of the situation. It has the following associations: an open surface, promoting interaction and interpenetration; pleasant, easy, responsive, free, unhindered; opening, passage; the mouth; exchange, barter; straight, direct; meet, gather; place where water accumulates. Ideogram: mouth and vapor, communication through speech. *Symbol*: marsh, *ZE*, open surface of a flat body of water and the vapors rising from it; fertilize, enrich; kindness, favor. *Action*: stimulate, *SHUO*, rouse to action and good feeling; stir up, urge on; exhort, persuade; say, tell, relate; cheer, delight; joyous, peaceful, restful. Ideogram: words and exchange. In the family of trigrams *DUI* is the youngest daughter.

Counter Hexagram

The Counter Hexagram of **Articulating** is hexagram 27, **The Jaws**, which switches the emphasis from clearly expressing connections and boundaries to focusing on seeking nourishment.

Preceding Situation

> **Beings not permitted** to **use completing radiance**.
> To **anterior acquiescence belongs** the **use** of
> **articulating**.

Fields of meaning

Beings not permitted (to **use**), *WU BU KE (YI)*: it is not possible; no one is allowed; it is not in the nature of things. **Complete**, *ZHONG*: completion of a cycle that begins the next; entire, whole, all. Ideogram: silk cocoons, follow and ice, winter linking one year with the next. **Radiance**, *LI*: glowing light, spreading in all directions; the power of consciousness; discriminate, articulate, divide and arrange in order; assemble, attract. Ideogram: bird and weird, magical fire-bird with brilliant plumage. To **anterior acquiescence belongs** the **use** of, *GU SHOU ZHI YI*: understanding and accepting the preceding statement allows the consultant to make proper use of this hexagram. **Articulate**, *JIE*: see *Image of the Situation*.

Hexagrams in Pairs

> **Dispersing**: **radiance indeed**.
> **Articulating**: **stopping indeed**.

Fields of meaning

Disperse, *HUAN*: spread, disperse, distribute; scatter clouds or crowds; dispel illusions, fears and suspicions; dissolve, evaporate, vanish; fog lifting or clearing away. **Radiance**, *LI*: see *Preceding Situation*. **Indeed**, *YE*: emphasizes and intensifies the previous statement. **Articulate**, *JIE*: see *Image of the Situation*. **Stop**, *ZHI*: bring or come to a standstill, cease, terminate; Action of the trigram Bound, *GEN*. Ideogram: a foot stops walking.

Patterns of Wisdom

> The **pond possesses stream above**. **Articulating**.
> A **jun zi uses paring** and **reckoning** the **measures**.
> And **deliberating actualizing-dao** in **movement**.

Fields of meaning

Pond, *ZE*: open surface of a flat body of water and the vapors rising from it; fertilize, enrich; kindness, favor; Symbol of the trigram Open, *DUI*. **Possess**, *YOU*: general term indicating possession; have, own, be endowed with. **Stream**, *SHUI*: flowing water; river, tide, flood; fluid, dissolving; Symbol of the trigram Gorge, *KAN*. Ideogram: rippling water. **Above**, *SHANG*: anything above in all senses; higher, upper, outer; upper trigram. **Articulate**, *JIE*: see *Image of the Situation*. **Jun zi**: ideal of a person who orders his/her life in accordance with dao rather than willful intention, and uses divination in this spirit. **Use**, *YI*: by means of; owing to; make use of, employ. **Pare**, *ZHI*: cut away, tailor, carve; form, invent; institution, rule; limit, prevent. Ideogram: knife and incomplete. **Reckon**, *SHU*: count, enumerate, evaluate; number, quantity; natural law, rule, reason. **Measures**, *DU*: rules, regulations, norms; measuring instrument; limit, test; capacity, endurance; interval in music, punctuation in a sentence. **Deliberate**, *YI*: consult, discuss, weigh the options and find the best course; arrange, select; criticize. Ideogram: words and right. **Actualize-dao**, *DE*: realize dao in action; power, virtue; ability to follow the course traced by the ongoing process of the cosmos. Ideogram: go, straight, and heart. Linked with acquire, *DE*: acquiring that which makes a being become what it is meant to be. **Move**, *XING*: move or move something; motivate; emotionally moving; walk, act, do. Ideogram: successive steps.

Transforming Lines

INITIAL NINE

Not emerging from the **door chambers**.
Without fault.

Comments
Not emerging from the **door chambers**.
Knowing interpenetration impeded indeed.

Fields of meaning

Not, *BU*: common term of negation. **Emerge**, *CHU*: come out of, proceed from, spring from, issue forth; appear, be born; bear, generate; leave, flee; Action of the trigram Shake, *ZHEN*. Ideogram: stem with branches and leaves emerging. **Door**, *HU*: inner door, chamber door; a household; distinct from gate, *MEN*, outer door. **Chambers**, *TING*: family rooms; courtyard, hall; domestic. Ideogram: shelter and hall, a secure place. **Without fault**, *WU JIU*: no error or harm in the situation.

Know, *ZHI*: have knowledge of, perceive, experience, remember; know intimately; informed, aware, wise. Ideogram: arrow and mouth, words focused and swift. **Interpenetrate**, *TONG*: penetrate freely and reciprocally, permeate, flow through, open a way; see clearly, understand deeply; communicate with; together. **Impede**, *SAI*: clog, fill up, close, obstruct; hinder, prevent; hide; unintelligent, dull. **Indeed**, *YE*: see *Hexagrams in Pairs*.

NINE AT SECOND

Not emerging from the **gate chambers**.
Pitfall.

Comments
Not emerging from the **gate chambers**, **pitfall**.
Letting-go the **season**: **end indeed**.

Fields of meaning

Not, *BU*: common term of negation. **Emerge**, *CHU*: come out of, proceed from, spring from, issue forth; appear, be born; bear, generate; leave, flee; Action of the trigram Shake, *ZHEN*. Ideogram: stem with branches and leaves emerging. **Gate**, *MEN*: outer door, between courtyard and street; family, sect; a text or master as gate to a school of thought. **Chambers**, *TING*: family rooms; courtyard, hall; domestic. Ideogram: shelter and hall, a secure place. **Pitfall**, *XIONG*: unfortunate situation, in which the flow of life and spirit is blocked and the experience of meaning is lost; stuck and exposed to danger; inappropriate attitude. Ideogram: person in a pit.

Let-go, *SHI*: lose, let slip; omit, miss, fail; lose control of. Ideogram: drop from the hand. **Season**, *SHI*: quality of the time; the right time, opportune, in harmony; planning in accord with the time; season of the year. Ideogram: sun and temple, sacred time. **End**, *JI*: last or highest point; final, extreme; ridgepole of a house. **Indeed**, *YE*: see *Hexagrams in Pairs*.

Six at Third

Not like articulating, by **consequence like lamenting**.
Without fault.

Comments
To **not articulating belongs lamenting**.
Furthermore whose fault indeed?

Fields of meaning
Not, *BU*: common term of negation. **Like**, *RUO*: same as, just as; conform, imitate; adverbial suffix indicating similarity. **Articulate**, *JIE*: see *Image of the Situation*. **Consequence**, *ZE*: reason, cause, result; rule, law, pattern, standard; therefore; very strong connection. **Lament**, *JUE*: sigh, express intense regret or sorrow, mourn over; painful recollections. **Without fault**, *WU JIU*: no error or harm in the situation.

Belong/it, *ZHI*: establishes between two terms a connection similar to the Saxon genitive, in which the second term belongs to the first one; at the end of a sentence it refers to something previously mentioned or implied. **Furthermore**, *YOU*: moreover; in addition to; again. **Whose**, *SHUI*: relative and interrogative pronoun, often introducing a rhetorical question; anybody. **Fault**, *JIU*: unworthy conduct that leads to harm, illness, misfortune; guilt, crime, punishment. Ideogram: person and differ, differ from what you should be. **Indeed**, *YE*: see *Hexagrams in Pairs*.

Six at Fourth

Peaceful articulating, **Growing**.

Comments
To **peaceful articulating belongs Growing**.
Receiving dao above indeed.

Fields of meaning

Peace, *AN*: quiet, still, settled, secure, contented; calm, tranquilize, console. Ideogram: woman under a roof, a tranquil home. **Articulate**, *JIE*: see *Image of the Situation*. **Grow**, *HENG*: see *Image of the Situation*.

Belong/it, *ZHI*: establishes between two terms a connection similar to the Saxon genitive, in which the second term belongs to the first one; at the end of a sentence it refers to something previously mentioned or implied. **Receive**, *CHENG*: receive gifts or commands from superiors or customers; take in hand; give, offer respectfully; help, support. Ideogram: accepting a seal of office. **Dao**, *DAO*: way or path; ongoing process of being and the course it traces for each person or thing; ultimate reality, intrinsic nature; origin. Ideogram: go and head, opening a path. **Above**, *SHANG*: see *Patterns of Wisdom*. **Indeed**, *YE*: see *Hexagrams in Pairs*.

NINE AT FIFTH

Sweet articulating, significant.
Going possesses honor.

Comments

To **sweet articulating belongs significance**.
Residing in the **position** at the **center indeed**.

Fields of meaning

Sweet, *GAN*: one of the five tastes: sour, bitter, sweet, acrid and salty; agreeable, pleasant, delightful, refreshing; corresponding to the Earthy Moment. **Articulate**, *JIE*: see *Image of the Situation*. **Significant**, *JI*: leads to the experience of meaning; favorable, propitious, appropriate. Ideogram: scholar and mouth, wise words of a sage. **Go**, *WANG*: move away in time or space, depart; become past; dead, gone; contrasts with come, *LAI*, approach in time or space. **Possess**, *YOU*: see *Patterns of Wisdom*. **Honor**, *SHANG*: esteem, give high rank to, exalt, celebrate; rise, elevate; put one thing on top of another.

Belong/it, *ZHI*: establishes between two terms a connection similar to the Saxon genitive, in which the second term belongs to the first one; at the end of a sentence it refers to something previously mentioned or implied. **Reside**, *JU*: dwell, live in, stay; sit down; fill an office; well-being, rest. Ideogram: body and seat. **Position**, *WEI*: place, location; be at; social standing, rank; position of a line in a hexagram. Ideogram: person standing. **Center**, *ZHONG*: inner, central; put in the center; middle, stable point enabling you to face inner and outer changes; middle line of a trigram. Ideogram: field divided in two equal parts. **Indeed**, *YE*: see *Hexagrams in Pairs*.

SIX ABOVE

Bitter articulating: Trial, pitfall.
Repenting extinguished.

Comments
Bitter articulating: Trial, pitfall.
One's dao exhausted indeed.

Fields of meaning

Bitter, *KU*: see *Image of the Situation.* **Articulate**, *JIE*: see *Image of the Situation.* **Trial**, *ZHEN*: see *Image of the Situation.* **Pitfall**, *XIONG*: unfortunate situation, in which the flow of life and spirit is blocked and the experience of meaning is lost; stuck and exposed to danger; inappropriate attitude. Ideogram: person in a pit. **Repenting extinguished**, *HUI WANG*: previous errors are corrected, all causes for repenting disappear.

One/one's, *QI*: general third person pronoun and possessive adjective; also: it/its, he/his, she/her, they/their. **Dao**, *DAO*: way or path; ongoing process of being and the course it traces for each person or thing; ultimate reality, intrinsic nature; origin. Ideogram: go and head, opening a path. **Exhaust**, *QIONG*: bring to an end; limit, extremity; investigate exhaustively; destitute, indigent; end without a new beginning; distinct from complete, *ZHONG*, end of a cycle that begins the next one. Ideogram: cave and naked person, bent with disease or old age. **Indeed**, *YE*: see *Hexagrams in Pairs.*

Image Tradition

Articulating. Growing.
Solid and **supple apportioned and-also** the **solid acquiring** the **center.**
Bitter articulating not permitting Trial.

Stimulating uses moving and **venturing.**
The **appropriate position uses articulating.**
The **center**'s **correctness uses interpenetrating.**
Heaven and **earth articulating and-also** the **four seasons accomplishing.**

Articulating uses paring the **measures.**
Not injuring property.
Not harming the **commoners.**

Fields of meaning

Articulating. Growing, *JIE HENG*: see *Image of the Situation*. **Solid**, *GANG*: quality of the whole lines; firm, strong, unyielding, persisting. **Supple**, *ROU*: quality of the opened lines; flexible, pliant, adaptable, tender. **Apportion**, *FEN*: divide, distribute, distinguish, sort out; part, element. **And-also**, *ER*: joins and contrasts two terms. **Acquire**, *DE*: obtain the desired object; possession; satisfied, fulfilled; it is permitted; agree with; wish for, desire covetously. Ideogram: go and obstacle, going through obstacles to the goal. **Center**, *ZHONG*: inner, central; put in the center; middle, stable point enabling you to face inner and outer changes; middle line of a trigram. Ideogram: field divided in two equal parts. **Bitter articulating not permitting Trial**, *KU JIE BU KE ZHEN*: see *Image of the Situation*.

Stimulate, *SHUO*: rouse to action and good feeling; stir up, urge on; exhort, persuade; say, tell, relate; cheer, delight; joyous, peaceful, restful; Action of the trigram Open, *DUI*. Ideogram: words and exchange. **Use**, *YI*: see *Patterns of Wisdom*. **Move**, *XING*: see *Patterns of Wisdom*. **Venture**, *XIAN*: face a severe difficulty or obstruction; risk; precipice, cliff, abyss; key point, point of danger; Action of the trigram Gorge, *KAN*. Ideogram: mound and all, everything engaged at one point. **Appropriate**, *DANG*: suitable, capable, worthy, adequate, competent, equal to; opportune, convenient; whole lines in odd places and opened lines in even places. **Position**, *WEI*: place, location; be at; social standing, rank; position of a line in a hexagram. Ideogram: person standing. **Center**, *ZHONG*: inner, central; put in the center; middle, stable point enabling you to face inner and outer changes; middle line of a trigram. Ideogram: field divided in two equal parts. **Correct**, *ZHENG*: rectify deviation or one-sidedness; proper, straight, exact, regular; constant, rule, model. Ideogram: stop and one, hold to one thing. **Interpenetrate**, *TONG*: penetrate freely and reciprocally, permeate, flow through, open a way; see clearly, understand deeply; communicate with; together. **Heaven**, *TIAN*: sky, firmament, heavens; the highest realm, situated above the human world, as opposed to the earth, *DI*, located below; Symbol of the trigram Energy, *QIAN*. Ideogram: great and the one above. **Earth**, *DI*: the earth, ground on which the human world rests; basis of all things, nourishes all things; essential Yin; Symbol of the trigram Space, *KUN*. **Four**, *SI*: number four; number of the cardinal directions and of the seasons; everywhere, on all sides; fourfold articulation of the Universal Compass. **Season**, *SHI*: quality of the time; the right time, opportune, in harmony; planning in accord with the time; season of the year. Ideogram: sun and temple, sacred time. **Accomplish**, *CHENG*: complete, finish, bring about; perfect, full, whole; play one's part, do one's duty; mature. Ideogram: weapon and man, able to bear arms, thus fully developed.

Pare, *ZHI*: see *Patterns of Wisdom*. **Measures**, *DU*: see *Patterns of Wisdom*. **Injure**, *SHANG*: hurt, wound, damage; grief, distress, mourning; sad at heart, afflicted. **Property**, *CAI*: possessions, goods, substance, wealth. Ideogram: pearl and value. **Harm**, *HAI*: damage, injure, offend; suffer, become ill; obstacle, hindrance; fearful, anxious. **Commoners**, *MIN*: common people, masses; working class supporting the social hierarchy; undeveloped potential in the individual.

中孚 ䷼

61 THE CENTER CONFORMING | *Zhong Fu*

The situation described by this hexagram is characterized by bringing one's inner being and outer circumstances into a sincere and reliable accord.

Image of the Situation

> The **center conforming**: **hog fish**, **significant**.
> **Harvesting**: **wading** the **great river**.
> **Harvesting**, **Trial**.

Fields of meaning

Center, *ZHONG*: inner, central; put in the center; middle, stable point enabling you to face inner and outer changes; middle line of a trigram. Ideogram: field divided in two equal parts. **Conform**, *FU*: accord between inner and outer; sincere, truthful, verified, reliable; capture; prisoners, spoils. Ideogram: claws over child, a bird brooding on the nest. **Hog fish**, *TUN YU*: aquatic mammals; porpoise, dolphin; sign of abundance and good luck. **Significant**, *JI*: leads to the experience of meaning; favorable, propitious, appropriate. Ideogram: scholar and mouth, wise words of a sage. **Harvest**, *LI*: benefit, advantage, profit; realization; sharp, acute, insightful; quality of autumn and West, third stage of the Time Cycle. Ideogram: ripe grain and blade. **Wading the Great River**, *SHE DA CHUAN*: enter the stream of life with a goal or purpose; embark on a significant enterprise. **Trial**, *ZHEN*: inquiry by divination and its result; righteous, firm; separating wheat from chaff; the kernel, the proven core; quality of winter and North, fourth stage of the Time Cycle. Ideogram: pearl and divination.

Outer and Inner Trigram

The upper trigram, **Root**, *SUN*, describes the outer aspects of the situation. It has the following associations: base on which things rest, ground, foundation; mild, subtly penetrating; nourishing. *Symbols*: tree/wood and wind. Tree/wood, *MU*: trees and all things woody or wooden; associated with the Wooden Moment. Ideogram: a tree with roots and branches. Wind, *FENG*: wind, breeze, gust; weather and its influence on mood and humor; fashion, usage. *Action*: enter, *RU*, penetrate, go into, enter on, encroach on; progress; put into. In the family of trigrams *SUN* is the eldest daughter.

The lower trigram, **Open**, *DUI*, describes the inner aspects of the situation. It has the following associations: an open surface, promoting interaction and interpenetration; pleasant, easy, responsive, free, unhindered; opening, passage; the mouth; exchange, barter; straight, direct; meet, gather; place where water accumulates. Ideogram: mouth and vapor, communication through speech. *Symbol*: marsh, *ZE*, open surface of a flat body of water and the vapors rising from it; fertilize, enrich; kindness, favor. *Action*: stimulate, *SHUO*, rouse to action and good feeling; stir up, urge on; exhort, persuade; say, tell, relate; cheer, delight; joyous, peaceful, restful. Ideogram: words and exchange. In the family of trigrams *DUI* is the youngest daughter.

Counter Hexagram

The Counter Hexagram of **The Center Conforming** is hexagram 27, **The Jaws**, which switches the emphasis from bringing one's inner being and outer manifestation into accord to focusing on seeking nourishment.

Preceding Situation

> **Articulating and-also trusting it**.
> To **anterior acquiescence belongs** the **use** of the **center conforming**.

Fields of meaning

Articulate, *JIE*: joint, articulation; a separation which simultaneously establishes the identity of the parts and their connection; express thought through speech; section, chapter, interval; temperance, virtue; rite, ceremony; lit.: nodes of bamboo stalks. **And-also**, *ER*: joins and contrasts two terms. **Trustworthy**, *XIN*: truthful, faithful, consistent over time; count on, confide in; examine, verify, prove; loyalty, integrity. Ideogram: person and word, true speech. **It/belong**, *ZHI*: establishes between two terms a connection similar to the Saxon genitive, in which the second term belongs to the first one; at the end of a sentence it refers to something previously mentioned or implied. To **anterior acquiescence belongs** the **use** of, *GU SHOU ZHI YI*: understanding and accepting the preceding statement allows the consultant to make proper use of this hexagram. The **center conforming**, *ZHONG FU*: see *Image of the Situation*.

Hexagrams in Pairs

> The **small exceeding**: **excess indeed**.
> The **center conforming**: **trustworthiness indeed**.

Fields of meaning

Small, *XIAO*: little, common, unimportant; adapting to what crosses your path; ability to move in harmony with the vicissitudes of life; contrasts with great, *DA*, self-imposed theme or goal. **Exceed**, *GUO*: go beyond, pass by, pass over; surpass, transgress; error, fault, calamity. **Indeed**, *YE*: emphasizes and intensifies the previous statement. The **center conforming**, *ZHONG FU*: see *Image of the Situation*. **Trustworthy**, *XIN*: see *Preceding Situation*.

Patterns of Wisdom

> The **pond possesses wind above**. The **center conforming**.
> A **jun zi uses deliberating litigations** to **delay death**.

Fields of meaning

Pond, *ZE*: open surface of a flat body of water and the vapors rising from it; fertilize, enrich; kindness, favor; Symbol of the trigram Open, *DUI*. **Possess**, *YOU*: general term indicating possession; have, own, be endowed with. **Wind**, *FENG*: wind, breeze, gust; weather and its influence on mood and humor; fashion, usage; wind and wood are the Symbols of the trigram Root, *SUN*. **Above**, *SHANG*: anything above in all senses; higher, upper, outer; upper trigram. The **center conforming**, *ZHONG FU*: see *Image of the Situation*. **Jun zi**: ideal of a person who orders his/her life in accordance with dao rather than willful intention, and uses divination in this spirit. **Use**, *YI*: by means of; owing to; make use of, employ. **Deliberate**, *YI*: consult, discuss, weigh the options and find the best course; arrange, select; criticize. Ideogram: words and right. **Litigate**, *YU*: legal proceedings, trial, sentence; dispute; take a case to court. Ideogram: two dogs and words, barking arguments at each other. **Delay**, *HUAN*: retard, put off; let things take their course; tie loosely; gradually, leisurely; lax, tardy, negligent. **Die**, *SI*: sudden or untimely death; death penalty; run out of energy; inert, stagnant, fixed.

Transforming Lines

Initial Nine

Precaution significant.
Possessing a **burden**, **not** a **swallow**.

Comments
Initial nine: **precaution significant**.
Purpose not-yet transformed indeed.

Fields of meaning

Precaution, *YU*: provide against, preventive measures; anxious, vigilant, ready; think about, expect; mishap, accident. **Significant**, *JI*: see *Image of the Situation*. **Possess**, *YOU*: see *Patterns of Wisdom*. **Burden**, *DUO*: load of an animal. With the pronunciation *TA*: he, she, it; other, stranger, having a different intention. Ideogram: person and also. **Not**, *BU*: common term of negation. **Swallow**, *YAN*: house swallow, martin, swift; retired from official life; ease, peace; feast; relation between elder and younger brother.

Initial, *CHU*: beginning, incipient, first step or part; bottom line of a hexagram. Ideogram: knife and garment, cutting out the pattern. **Nine**, *JIU*: number nine; transforming whole line; superlative: best, perfect. **Purpose**, *ZHI*: focus of mind and heart; intention, will, inclination; continuity in the direction of life. Ideogram: heart and scholar, high inner resolve. **Not-yet**, *WEI*: temporal negative indicating that something is expected to happen but has not yet occurred. **Transform**, *BIAN*: abrupt, radical passage from one state to another; transformation of opened and whole lines into each other in hexagrams; contrasts with change, *HUA*, gradual mutation. **Indeed**, *YE*: see *Hexagrams in Pairs*.

Nine at Second

Calling crane located in **Yin**.
One's sonhood harmonizing with **it**.
I possess a **loved wine-cup**.
Myself associating: **simply spilling it**.

Comments
One's sonhood harmonizing with **it**.
In the **center** the **heart**'s **desire indeed**.

Fields of meaning

Call, *MING*: bird and animal cries, through which they recognize each other; distinctive sound, song, statement. Ideogram: bird and mouth, a distinguishing call. **Crane**, *HAO*: large wading bird, sign of long life, wisdom and bliss; relation between father and son; messenger to the immortals. **Locate**, *ZAI*: be at, be situated at, dwell, reside; in, within; involved with, in the process of. Ideogram: earth and persevere, a place on the earth. **Yin**, *YIN*: shady slope of a hill or bank of a river; consolidating, dark aspect of the basic duality (Yin and Yang) manifesting in all phenomena; Yin creates and conserves structure; spatial extension; build, make things concrete; quality of an opened line. **One/one's**, *QI*: general third person pronoun and possessive adjective; also: it/its, he/his, she/her, they/their. **Son(hood)**, *ZI*: son, male child; heirs, offspring, posterity; living up to the ideal of the ancestors as highest human aspiration; seed, kernel, egg; sage, teacher; nadir, deepest point, midnight, mid-winter. **Harmony**, *HE*: concord, union; conciliate; at peace, mild; fit, tune, adjust. **It/belong**, *ZHI*: see *Preceding Situation*. **I/me/my**, *WO*: first person pronoun; the use of a specific personal pronoun, as opposed to the generic one's, *QI*, indicates an unusually strong emphasis on personal involvement. **Possess**, *YOU*: see *Patterns of Wisdom*. **Love**, *HAO*: affection; fond of, take pleasure in; fine, graceful. **Wine-cup**, *JIAO*: libation cup originally in the form of a bird. **Myself**, *WU*: first person intensifier; the particular person I am; I, my, we, our. **Associate**, *YU*: consort with, combine; companions; group, band, company; agree with, comply, help; in favor of. Ideogram: a pair of hands reaching downward meets a pair of hands reaching upward, helpful association. **Simply**, *ER*: just so, only. **Spill**, *MI*: pour out; disperse, spread; waste, overturn; showy, extravagant.

Center, *ZHONG*: see *Image of the Situation*. **Heart**, *XIN*: the heart as center of being; seat of mind, imagination and affect; moral nature; source of desires, intentions, will. **Desire**, *YUAN*: wish, hope or long for; covet; desired object. **Indeed**, *YE*: see *Hexagrams in Pairs*.

Six at Third

Acquiring antagonist.
Maybe drumbeating, maybe desisting.
Maybe weeping, maybe singing.

Comments
Maybe drumbeating, maybe desisting.
Position not appropriate indeed.

Fields of meaning

Acquire, *DE*: obtain the desired object; possession; satisfied, fulfilled; it is permitted; agree with; wish for, desire covetously. Ideogram: go and obstacle, going through obstacles to the goal. **Antagonistic**, *DI*: opposed and equal; competitor, enemy; a contest between equals. **Maybe**, *HUO*: possible but not certain, perhaps. **Drumbeating**, *GU*: beat a skin or earthenware drum; excite, arouse, encourage; joyous, happy. **Desist**, *BA*: cease, leave off, discontinue, finish; enough. **Weep**, *QI*: lament wordlessly; grieved, heartbroken. **Sing**, *GE*: chant, sing elegies; associated with the Earthy Moment, turning point from Yang to Yin.

Position, *WEI*: place, location; be at; social standing, rank; position of a line in a hexagram. Ideogram: person standing. **Not**, *BU*: common term of negation. **Appropriate**, *DANG*: suitable, capable, worthy, adequate, competent, equal to; opportune, convenient; whole lines in odd places and opened lines in even places. **Indeed**, *YE*: see *Hexagrams in Pairs.*

SIX AT FOURTH

The **moon almost full**.
The **horse team extinguished**.
Without fault.

Comments
The **horse team extinguished**.
Cutting-off, sorting above indeed.

Fields of meaning

Moon, *YUE*: moon and moon-cycle, month; menstruation; Yin. **Almost/hint**, *JI*: nearly, about to; subtle; barely perceptible first sign. **Full**, *WANG*: moon directly facing the sun; 15th day of the lunar month; hopes, expectations, desires. **Horse**, *MA*: symbol of spirited strength in the natural world, earthly counterpart of the dragon; associated with the trigram Energy, *QIAN*, heaven, and high noon. **Team**, *PI*: pair, couple; fellow, mate; connect, associate; matched horses. **Extinguish**, *WANG*: ruin, destroy; cease, go, die; lost without trace; forget, out of mind; absence, exile. Ideogram: person concealed by a wall, out of sight. **Without fault**, *WU JIU*: no error or harm in the situation.

Cut-off, *JUE*: cut, interrupt, disconnect, break off, separate; destroy; renounce; difficult access; worn out, alone, indigent. Ideogram: silk, knife and knot, cutting through. **Sort**, *LEI*: group according to kind, compare; species, class, genus; resemble; analog, like nature or purpose; norm, model. **Above**, *SHANG*: see *Patterns of Wisdom*. **Indeed**, *YE*: see *Hexagrams in Pairs.*

NINE AT FIFTH

Possessing conformity, binding thus.
Without fault.

Comments
Possessing conformity, binding thus.
Position correct and **appropriate indeed.**

Fields of meaning

Possess, *YOU*: see *Patterns of Wisdom*. **Conform**, *FU*: see *Image of the Situation*. **Bind**, *LÜAN*: tie, connect; bent, contracted; interdependent, inseparable. Ideogram: hand and connect. **Thus**, *RU*: as, in this way; comparable, similar. **Without fault**, *WU JIU*: no error or harm in the situation.

Position, *WEI*: place, location; be at; social standing, rank; position of a line in a hexagram. Ideogram: person standing. **Correct**, *ZHENG*: rectify deviation or one-sidedness; proper, straight, exact, regular; constant, rule, model. Ideogram: stop and one, hold to one thing. **Appropriate**, *DANG*: suitable, capable, worthy, adequate, competent, equal to; opportune, convenient; whole lines in odd places and opened lines in even places. **Indeed**, *YE*: see *Hexagrams in Pairs*.

NINE ABOVE

A **soaring sound mounts tending-towards heaven.**
Trial, pitfall.

Comments
A **soaring sound mounts tending-towards heaven.**
Is it **permitted long-living indeed?**

Fields of meaning

Soar, *HAN*: fly high; rising sun; firebird with red plumage; white horse; long and hard feather; drawing brush. Ideogram: feathers and dawn. **Sound**, *YIN*: any sound; tone, resonance; pronunciation of words. Ideogram: words and hold in the mouth, vocal sound. **Mount**, *DENG*: ascend, rise; ripen, complete. **Tend-towards**, *YU*: move toward without necessarily reaching, in the direction of. **Heaven**, *TIAN*: sky, firmament, heavens; the highest realm, situated above the human world, as opposed to the earth, *DI*, located below; Symbol of the trigram Energy, *QIAN*. Ideogram: great and the one above. **Trial**, *ZHEN*: see *Image of the Situation*. **Pitfall**,

XIONG: unfortunate situation, in which the flow of life and spirit is blocked and the experience of meaning is lost; stuck and exposed to danger; inappropriate attitude. Ideogram: person in a pit.

Is?, *HE*: ask, inquire; what? which? who? how? why? where? an interrogative particle, often introducing a rhetorical question: is it? is it not? **Permit**, *KE*: possible because in harmony with an inherent principle; capable of; approve, authorize. Ideogram: mouth and breath, silent consent. **Long-living**, *ZHANG*: enduring, lasting, constant; extended, long, large; senior, superior, greater; increase, prosper; respect, elevate. **Indeed**, *YE*: see *Hexagrams in Pairs*.

Image Tradition

The **center conforming**.
The **supple located inside and-also** the **solid acquires** the **center**.
Stimulating and-also the **root**: **conforming**.
Thereupon changing the **fiefdoms indeed**.

Hog fish, **significant**.
Trustworthiness extends to **hog fish indeed**.
Harvesting: **wading** the **great river**.
Riding a **wooden dugout**: **emptiness indeed**.

The **center conforming uses Harvesting**, **Trial**.
Thereupon the **correspondence reaches heaven indeed**.

Fields of meaning

The **center conforming**, *ZHONG FU*: see *Image of the Situation*. **Supple**, *ROU*: quality of the opened lines; flexible, pliant, adaptable, tender. **Locate**, *ZAI*: be at, be situated at, dwell, reside; in, within; involved with, in the process of. Ideogram: earth and persevere, a place on the earth. **Inside**, *NEI*: within, inner, interior; inside of the house and those who work there, particularly women; inside of the body, inner organs; the lower trigram, as opposed to outside, *WAI*, the upper. Ideogram: border and enter. **And-also**, *ER*: see *Preceding Situation*. **Solid**, *GANG*: quality of the whole lines; firm, strong, unyielding, persisting. **Acquire**, *DE*: obtain the desired object; possession; satisfied, fulfilled; it is permitted; agree with; wish for, desire covetously. Ideogram: go and obstacle, going through obstacles to the goal. **Center**, *ZHONG*: see *Image of the Situation*. **Stimulate**, *SHUO*: rouse to action and good feeling; stir up, urge on; exhort, persuade; say, tell, relate; cheer, delight; joyous, peaceful, restful; Action of the trigram Open, *DUI*. Ideogram: words and exchange. **Root**, *SUN*: base on which things rest, ground, foundation; mild, subtly penetrating; nourishing. **Thereupon**, *NAI*: on that ground, then, only then; finally; in spite of that. **Change**, *HUA*: gradual, continuous change; melt, dissolve; be born, die; influence; contrasts with transform, *BIAN*, sudden mutation. Ideogram: person alive and dead, the life process. **Fiefdom**, *BANG*: region governed by a feudatory. **Indeed**, *YE*: see *Hexagrams in Pairs.*

Hog fish, **significant**, *TUN YU JI*: see *Image of the Situation*. **Trustworthy**, *XIN*: see *Preceding Situation*. **Extend**, *JI*: reach to; draw out, prolong; continuous, enduring. **Harvesting**: **wading** the **great river**, *LI SHE DA CHUAN*: see *Image of the Situation*. **Ride**, *CHENG*: ride an animal or a chariot; have the upper hand, control a stronger power; an opened line above controlling a whole line below. **Wood/tree**, *MU*: trees and all things woody or wooden; associated with the Wooden Moment; wood and wind are the Symbols of the trigram Ground, *SUN*. Ideogram: a tree with roots and branches. **Dugout**, *ZHOU*: hollowed log, canoe; boat, ride or transport by boat. **Empty**, *XU*: void; absence of images and concepts; vacant, insubstantial; empty yet fertile space.

Use, *YI*: see *Patterns of Wisdom*. **Harvesting**, **Trial**, *LI ZHEN*: see *Image of the Situation*. **Correspond**, *YING*: be in agreement or harmony; proper, suitable; resonate together, answer to; relation between the lines (1 and 4, 2 and 5, 3 and 6) when they form the pair opened and whole, supple and solid. Ideogram: heart and obey. **Reach**, *HU*: arrive at a goal; move toward and achieve; to, at, in; distinct from tend-towards, *YOU*. **Heaven**, *TIAN*: sky, firmament, heavens; the highest realm, situated above the human world, as opposed to the earth, *DI*, located below; Symbol of the trigram Energy, *QIAN*. Ideogram: great and the one above.

小過

62 THE SMALL EXCEEDING | *Xiao Guo*

The situation described by this hexagram is characterized by the excessive predominance of a variety of small concerns, which might obscure the overall significance.

Image of the Situation

> The **small exceeding**.
> **Growing**.
> **Harvesting**, **Trial**.
> **Permitted** the **small** in **affairs**.
> **Not permitted** the **great** in **affairs**.
> To the **flying bird abandoning belongs** a **sound**.
> **Not proper above**, **proper below**.
> The **great**, **significant**.

Fields of meaning

Small, *XIAO*: little, common, unimportant; adapting to what crosses your path; ability to move in harmony with the vicissitudes of life; contrasts with great, *DA*, self-imposed theme or goal. **Exceed**, *GUO*: go beyond, pass by, pass over; surpass, transgress; error, fault, calamity. **Grow**, *HENG*: heavenly influence pervading and nourishing all things; prosper, succeed, expand, develop; effective, favorable; quality of summer and South, second stage of the Time Cycle. With the pronunciation *XIANG*: offer a sacrifice; offer a gift to a superior; accept, enjoy. **Harvest**, *LI*: benefit, advantage, profit; realization; sharp, acute, insightful; quality of autumn and West, third stage of the Time Cycle. Ideogram: ripe grain and blade. **Trial**, *ZHEN*: inquiry by divination and its result; righteous, firm; separating wheat from chaff; the kernel, the proven core; quality of winter and North, fourth stage of the Time Cycle. Ideogram: pearl and divination. **Permit**, *KE*: possible because in harmony with an inherent principle; capable of; approve, authorize. Ideogram: mouth and breath, silent consent. **Affairs**, *SHI*: all kinds of personal activity; matters at hand; business; function, occupation; manage; perform a task; incident, event; case in court. **Not**, *BU*: common term of negation. **Great**, *DA*: big, noble, important, very; orient the will toward a self-imposed goal, impose direction; ability to lead or guide one's life; contrasts with small, *XIAO*, flexible adaptation to what crosses one's path. **Fly**, *FEI*: rise in the air, spread one's wings, fly away; let fly; swift. **Bird**, *NIAO*: all feathered animals; associated with the Fiery Moment. **Abandon**, *YI*: leave behind, forget; die; lose through unawareness. Ideogram: go and value, value is gone. **Belong/it**, *ZHI*: establishes between two terms a connection similar to the Saxon genitive, in which the second term belongs to the first one; at the end of a sentence it refers to something previously mentioned or implied. **Sound**, *YIN*: any sound; tone, resonance; pronunciation of words. Ideogram: words and hold in the mouth, vocal sound. **Proper**, *YI*: reasonable, fit, right, harmonious; ought, should. **Above**, *SHANG*: anything above in all senses; higher, upper, outer; upper trigram. **Below**, *XIA*: anything below, in all senses; lower, inner; lower trigram. **Significant**, *JI*: leads to the experience of meaning; favorable, propitious, appropriate. Ideogram: scholar and mouth, wise words of a sage.

Outer and Inner Trigram

The upper trigram, **Shake**, *ZHEN*, describes the outer aspects of the situation. It has the following associations: arouse, excite, inspire; awe, alarm, trembling; thunder rising from the depth of the earth; fertilizing intrusion. Ideogram: excite and rain. *Symbol*: thunder, *LEI*, arousing power emerging from the depth of the earth. *Action*: stir-up, *DONG*, excite, influence, move, affect; work, take action; come out of the egg or the bud. Ideogram: strength and heavy, move weighty things. In the family of trigrams *ZHEN* is the eldest son.

The lower trigram, **Bound**, *GEN*, describes the inner aspects of the situation. It has the following associations: limit, frontier; obstacle that prevents from seeing further; stop; still, quiet, motionless; confine, enclose; mountain, sunset, beginning of winter; solid, steady, unshakable; straight, hard, adamant, obstinate. *Symbol*: mountain, *SHAN*, large, immense; limit, boundary. Ideogram: three peaks, a mountain range. *Action*: stop, *ZHI*, bring or come to a standstill, cease, terminate. Ideogram: a foot stops walking. In the family of trigrams *GEN* is the youngest son.

Counter Hexagram

The Counter Hexagram of **The Small Exceeding** is hexagram 28, **The Great Exceeding**, which switches the emphasis from the excessive predominance of a variety of small concerns to the excessive predominance of a single overriding theme or long-term goal.

Preceding Situation

> **Possessing one's trustworthiness implies necessarily moving it.**
> To **anterior acquiescence belongs** the **use** of the **small exceeding**.

Fields of meaning

Possess, *YOU*: general term indicating possession; have, own, be endowed with. **One/one's**, *QI*: general third person pronoun and possessive adjective; also: it/its, he/his, she/her, they/their. **Trustworthy**, *XIN*: truthful, faithful, consistent over time; count on, confide in; examine, verify, prove; loyalty, integrity. Ideogram: person and word, true speech. **Imply**, *ZHE*: further signify; additional meaning. **Necessarily**, *BI*: unavoidably, certainly. **Move**, *XING*: move or move something; motivate; emotionally moving; walk, act, do. Ideogram: successive steps. **It/belong**, *ZHI*: establishes between two terms a connection similar to the Saxon genitive, in which the second term belongs to the first one; at the end of a sentence it refers to something previously mentioned or implied. To **anterior acquiescence belongs** the **use** of, *GU SHOU ZHI YI*: understanding and accepting the preceding statement allows the consultant to make proper use of this hexagram. The **small exceeding**, *XIAO GUO*: see *Image of the Situation*.

Hexagrams in Pairs

> The **small exceeding**: **excess indeed**.
> The **center conforming**: **trustworthiness indeed**.

Fields of meaning

The **small exceeding**, *XIAO GUO*: see *Image of the Situation*. **Indeed**, *YE*: emphasizes and intensifies the previous statement. **Center**, *ZHONG*: inner, central; put in the center; middle, stable point enabling you to face inner and outer changes; middle line of a trigram. Ideogram: field divided in two equal parts. **Conform**, *FU*: accord between inner and outer; sincere, truthful, verified, reliable; capture; prisoners, spoils. Ideogram: claws over child, a bird brooding on the nest. **Trustworthy**, *XIN*: see *Preceding Situation*.

Patterns of Wisdom

The **mountain possesses thunder above**. The **small exceeding**.
A **jun zi uses moving** in **excess** to **reach courtesy**.
And **losing** in **excess** to **reach mourning**.
And **avails** of **excess** to **reach parsimony**.

Fields of meaning

Mountain, *SHAN*: mountain; large, immense; limit, boundary; Symbol of the trigram Bound, *GEN*. Ideogram: three peaks, a mountain range. **Possess**, *YOU*: see *Preceding Situation*. **Thunder**, *LEI*: thunder; arousing power emerging from the depth of the earth; Symbol of the trigram Shake, *ZHEN*. **Above**, *SHANG*: see *Image of the Situation*. The **small exceeding**, *XIAO GUO*: see *Image of the Situation*. **Jun zi**: ideal of a person who orders his/her life in accordance with dao rather than willful intention, and uses divination in this spirit. **Use**, *YI*: by means of; owing to; make use of, employ. **Move**, *XING*: see *Preceding Situation*. **Reach**, *HU*: arrive at a goal; move toward and achieve; to, at, in; distinct from tend-towards, *YOU*. **Courtesy**, *GONG*: display respect, show reverence; affable, decorous, modest, polite; obsequious. **Lose**, *SANG*: be deprived of, forget; destruction, ruin, death; corpse; lament, mourn; funeral. Ideogram: weep and dead. **Mourn**, *AI*: grieve, lament over something gone; distress, sorrow; compassion. Ideogram: mouth and clothes, display of feelings. **Avail**, *YONG*: use, employ for a specific purpose; take advantage of; benefit from; capacity. Ideogram: to divine and center, applying divination to central concerns. **Parsimonious**, *JIAN*: thrifty; moderate, temperate; stingy, scanty.

Transforming Lines

INITIAL SIX

The **flying bird**: **using** a **pitfall**.

Comments
The **flying bird**: **using** a **pitfall**.
Not permitted thus, **is** it **indeed?**

Fields of meaning

Fly, *FEI*: see *Image of the Situation*. **Bird**, *NIAO*: see *Image of the Situation*. **Use**, *YI*: see *Patterns of Wisdom*. **Pitfall**, *XIONG*: see *Image of the Situation*.

Not, *BU*: common term of negation. **Permit**, *KE*: see *Image of the Situation*.

Thus, *RU*: as, in this way; comparable, similar. **Is?**, *HE*: ask, inquire; what? which? who? how? why? where? an interrogative particle, often introducing a rhetorical question: is it? is it not? **Indeed**, *YE*: see *Hexagrams in Pairs*.

SIX AT SECOND

Exceeding one's grandfather.
Meeting one's grandmother.
Not extending to **one's chief.**
Meeting one's servant.
Without fault.

Comments
Not extending to **one's chief.**
A **servant not permitted exceeding indeed.**

Fields of meaning
Exceed, *GUO*: see *Image of the Situation*. **One/one's**, *QI*: see *Preceding Situation*. **Grandfather**, *ZU*: second ancestor generation; deceased grandfather, honored more than actual father. **Meet**, *YU*: come on unexpectedly, encounter; occur, happen; pleasant meeting, lucky coincidence; agree. **Grandmother**, *BI*: second ancestor generation; deceased grandmother, venerated as source of her many descendants. **Not**, *BU*: common term of negation. **Extend**, *JI*: reach to; draw out, prolong; continuous, enduring. **Chief**, *JUN*: prince, ruler; lead, direct; wise person. Ideogram: mouth and direct, giving orders. **Servant**, *CHEN*: attendant, minister, vassal; courtier who can speak to the sovereign; wait on, serve in office. Ideogram: person bowing low. **Without fault**, *WU JIU*: no error or harm in the situation.

Permit, *KE*: see *Image of the Situation*. **Indeed**, *YE*: see *Hexagrams in Pairs*.

NINE AT THIRD

Nowhere exceeding, defending-against it.
Adhering maybe kills it.
Pitfall.

Comments
Adhering maybe kills it.
Pitfall thus, is it not **indeed?**

Fields of meaning

Nowhere/nothing, *FU*: strong negative; not a single thing/place; deny, disapprove; impossible, incorrect. **Exceed**, *GUO*: see *Image of the Situation*. **Defend-against**, *FANG*: keep off, protect from, guard against; rampart, dam; erect a protective barrier. Ideogram: open space and earthen ramparts. **It/belong**, *ZHI*: see *Preceding Situation*. **Adhere**, *CONG*: follow, agree with, comply with, obey; join a doctrine, school, or person; servant, follower. Ideogram: two men walking, one following the other. **Maybe**, *HUO*: possible but not certain, perhaps. **Kill**, *QIANG*: murder, put to death, particularly a sovereign or a chief; assault, wound, maltreat, misuse. **Pitfall**, *XIONG*: see *Image of the Situation*.

Thus, *RU*: as, in this way; comparable, similar. **Is?**, *HE*: ask, inquire; what? which? who? how? why? where? an interrogative particle, often introducing a rhetorical question: is it? is it not? **Indeed**, *YE*: see *Hexagrams in Pairs*.

NINE AT FOURTH

Without fault.
Nowhere exceeding, **meeting it**.
Going: **adversity necessarily** a **warning**.
No availing of **perpetual Trial**.

Comments
Nowhere exceeding, **meeting it**.
Position not appropriate indeed.
Going: **adversity necessarily** a **warning**.
Completion not permitted long-living indeed.

Fields of meaning

Without fault, *WU JIU*: no error or harm in the situation. **Nowhere/nothing**, *FU*: strong negative; not a single thing/place; deny, disapprove; impossible, incorrect. **Exceed**, *GUO*: see *Image of the Situation*. **Meet**, *YU*: come on unexpectedly, encounter; occur, happen; pleasant meeting, lucky coincidence; agree. **It/belong**, *ZHI*: see *Preceding Situation*. **Go**, *WANG*: move away in time or space, depart; become past; dead, gone; contrasts with come, *LAI*, approach in time or space. **Adversity**, *LI*: danger, hardship, severe; threat or difficulty that must be encountered, rather than avoided; grinding stone; polish, sharpen; a challenge that strengthens and perfects the character; stimulate, excite; cruel demon. **Necessarily**, *BI*: see *Preceding Situation*. **Warn**, *JIE*: alarm, alert, put on guard; caution, inform; guard against, refrain from. Ideogram: spear held in both hands, warning enemies. **No**, *WU*: common term of negation. **Avail**, *YONG*: see *Patterns* *of Wisdom*. **Perpetual**, *YONG*: see *Image of the Situation*. **Trial**, *ZHEN*: see *Image of the Situation*.

Position, *WEI*: place, location; be at; social standing, rank; position of a line in a hexagram. Ideogram: person standing. **Not**, *BU*: common term of negation. **Appropriate**, *DANG*: suitable, capable, worthy, adequate, competent, equal to; opportune, convenient; whole lines in odd places and opened lines in even places. **Indeed**, *YE*: see *Hexagrams in Pairs*. **Complete**, *ZHONG*: completion of a cycle that begins the next; entire, whole, all. Ideogram: silk cocoons, follow and ice, winter linking one year with the next. **Permit**, *KE*: see *Image of the Situation*. **Long-living**, *ZHANG*: enduring, lasting, constant; extended, long, large; senior, superior, greater; increase, prosper; respect, elevate.

SIX AT FIFTH

Shrouding clouds, not raining.
Originating from **my Western suburbs**.
A **prince**'s **string-arrow grasps someone located** in a **cave**.

Comments
Shrouding clouds, not raining.
Climaxing above indeed.

Fields of meaning

Shroud, *MI*: dense, close together, thick, tight; hidden, secret. **Clouds**, *YUN*: fog, mist, water vapor; connected with the Streaming Moment. **Not**, *BU*: common term of negation. **Rain**, *YU*: rain and all precipitations; sudden shower, fast and furious; abundant dispensation of benefits; associated with the trigram Gorge, *KAN*, and the Streaming Moment. **Origin**, *ZI*: source, beginning, ground; cause, reason, motive; tracing back to the source; oneself, by oneself; spontaneous, intrinsic. **I/me/my**, *WO*: first person pronoun; the use of a specific personal pronoun, as opposed to the generic one's, *QI*, indicates an unusually strong emphasis on personal involvement. **West**, *XI*: western direction, corresponding to autumn, Harvest, the Metallic Moment and the first phase of the Yin hemicycle of the Universal Compass. **Suburbs**, *JIAO*: area adjoining a city where human constructions and nature interpenetrate; second of the territorial zones: city, suburbs, countryside, forest. **Prince**, *GONG*: highest title of nobility; noble acting as minister of state in the capital; contrasts with feudatory, *HOU*, governor of a province. **String-arrow**, *YI*: arrow with string attached used to retrieve what is shot; seize, appropriate; arrest a criminal. **Grasp**, *QU*: seize with effort, take and use, appropriate; take as a wife; grasp the meaning, understand. Ideogram: ear and hand, hear and grasp. **Someone**, *BI*: that, those, there; he, she, it, they; the other; exclude, leave out. **Locate**, *ZAI*: be at, be situated at, dwell, reside; in, within; involved with, in the process of. Ideogram: earth and persevere, a place on the earth. **Cave**, *XUE*: cavern, den, pit; hole used for dwelling; open grave; pierce through.

Climax, *YI*: come to a high point and stop; bring to an end, complete; renounce, desist, decline, reject; that is all; already; excessive. **Above**, *SHANG*: see *Image of the Situation*. **Indeed**, *YE*: see *Hexagrams in Pairs*.

SIX ABOVE

Nowhere meeting, **exceeding it**.
To the **flying bird**'s **radiance belongs** a **pitfall**.
That designates calamity and **blunder**.

Comments
Nowhere meeting, **exceeding it**.
Climaxing overbearing indeed.

Fields of meaning

Nowhere/nothing, *FU*: strong negative; not a single thing/place; deny, disapprove; impossible, incorrect. **Meet**, *YU*: come on unexpectedly, encounter; occur, happen; pleasant meeting, lucky coincidence; agree. **Exceed**, *GUO*: see *Image of the Situation*. **It/belong**, *ZHI*: see *Preceding Situation*. **Fly**, *FEI*: see *Image of the Situation*. **Bird**, *NIAO*: see *Image of the Situation*. **Radiance**, *LI*: glowing light, spreading in all directions; the power of consciousness; discriminate, articulate, divide and arrange in order; assemble, attract. Ideogram: bird and weird, magical fire-bird with brilliant plumage. **Belong/it**, *ZHI*: see *Image of the Situation*. **Pitfall**, *XIONG*: see *Image of the Situation*. **That**, *SHI*: refers to the preceding statement. **Designate**, *WEI*: say, express in words, give a name; mean, signify; consider as; talk about. Ideogram: words and belly, describing the essential. **Calamity**, *ZAI*: disaster from outside; fire, flood, plague, drought, blight, ruin; contrasts with blunder, *SHENG*, indicating personal fault. Ideogram: water and fire, elemental powers. **Blunder**, *SHENG*: mistake due to ignorance or fault; contrasts with calamity, *ZAI*, disaster from without. Ideogram: eye and growth, a film clouding sight.

Climax, *YI*: come to a high point and stop; bring to an end, complete; renounce, desist, decline, reject; that is all; already; excessive. **Overbearing**, *KANG*: haughty, fierce, overpowering, rigid, unbending; excessive display of force. **Indeed**, *YE*: see *Hexagrams in Pairs*.

Image Tradition

The **small exceeding**.
The **small implies exceeding and-also Growing indeed**.
Exceeding uses Harvesting, **Trial**.
Associating with the **season**'s **movement indeed**.

The **supple acquires** the **center**.
That uses the **small** in **affairs**, **significant indeed**.
The **solid letting-go** the **position and-also not** in the **center**.
That uses not permitting the **great** in **affairs indeed**.

Possessing the **symbol belonging** to the **flying bird in-truth**.
To the **flying bird abandoning belongs** a **sound**.
Not **proper above**, **proper below**.
The **great**, **significant**.
Above revolting and-also below yielding indeed.

Fields of meaning

The **small exceeding**, *XIAO GUO*: see *Image of the Situation*. **Imply**, *ZHE*: see *Preceding Situation*. **And-also**, *ER*: joins and contrasts two terms. **Grow**, *HENG*: see *Image of the Situation*. **Use**, *YI*: see *Patterns of Wisdom*. **Harvesting**, **Trial**, *LI ZHEN*: see *Image of the Situation*. **Associate**, *YU*: consort with, combine; companions; group, band, company; agree with, comply, help; in favor of. Ideogram: a pair of hands reaching downward meets a pair of hands reaching upward, helpful association. **Season**, *SHI*: quality of the time; the right time, opportune, in harmony; planning in accord with the time; season of the year. Ideogram: sun and temple, sacred time. **Move**, *XING*: see *Preceding Situation*. **Indeed**, *YE*: see *Hexagrams in Pairs*.

Supple, *ROU*: quality of the opened lines; flexible, pliant, adaptable, tender. **Acquire**, *DE*: obtain the desired object; possession; satisfied, fulfilled; it is permitted; agree with; wish for, desire covetously. Ideogram: go and obstacle, going through obstacles to the goal. **Center**, *ZHONG*: see *Hexagrams in Pairs*. **That**, *SHI*: refers to the preceding statement. **Affairs**, *SHI*: see *Image of the Situation*. **Significant**, *JI*: see *Image of the Situation*. **Solid**, *GANG*: quality of the whole lines; firm, strong, unyielding, persisting. **Let-go**, *SHI*: lose, let slip; omit, miss, fail; lose control of. Ideogram: drop from the hand. **Position**, *WEI*: place, location; be at; social standing, rank; position of a line in a hexagram. Ideogram: person standing.

Not, *BU*: common term of negation. **Permit**, *KE*: see *Image of the Situation*. **Great**, *DA*: see *Image of the Situation*.

Possess, *YOU*: see *Preceding Situation*. **Symbol**, *XIANG*: image invested with magic connecting visible and invisible; figure, form, shape, likeness; pattern, model; act, play, write. Ideogram: elephant (in ancient times the bones of a dead elephant used to be assembled to look like the living animal). **Belong/it**, *ZHI*: see *Image of the Situation*. **Flying bird**, *FEI NIAO*: see *Image of the Situation*. **In-truth**, *YAN*: a final affirmative particle; the preceding statement is complete and correct. **Abandon**, *YI*: see *Image of the Situation*. **Sound**, *YIN*: see *Image of the Situation*. **Not proper above, proper below**, *BU YI SHANG YI XIA*: see *Image of the Situation*. **Revolt**, *NI*: oppose, resist, seek out; contrary, rebellious, refractory. Ideogram: go and rise against, active revolt. **Yield**, *SHUN*: give way, comply, agree, follow, obey; docile, flexible; bear produce, nourish, provide; Action of the trigram Field, *KUN*.

既濟

63 ALREADY FORDING | *Ji Ji*

The situation described by this hexagram is characterized by involvement in a process which is already on its way to completion, being already engaged in a course of action.

Image of the Situation

> **Already fording**.
> **Growing**, the **small**.
> **Harvesting**, **Trial**.
> **Initially**: **significant**.
> **Completing**: **disarray**.

Fields of meaning

Already, *JI*: completed, done, occurred, finished; past tense; shortly after. **Ford**, *JI*: cross a river at a ford or shallow place; embark on a course of action; complete, finish, succeed; help, relieve. Ideogram: water and level, running smooth over a flat bottom. **Grow**, *HENG*: heavenly influence pervading and nourishing all things; prosper, succeed, expand, develop; effective, favorable; quality of summer and South, second stage of the Time Cycle. With the pronunciation *XIANG*: offer a sacrifice; offer a gift to a superior; accept, enjoy. **Small**, *XIAO*: little, common, unimportant; adapting to what crosses your path; ability to move in harmony with the vicissitudes of life; contrasts with great, *DA*, self-imposed theme or goal. **Harvest**, *LI*: benefit, advantage, profit; realization; sharp, acute, insightful; quality of autumn and West, third stage of the Time Cycle. Ideogram: ripe grain and blade. **Trial**, *ZHEN*: inquiry by divination and its result; righteous, firm; separating wheat from chaff; the kernel, the proven core; quality of winter and North, fourth stage of the Time Cycle. Ideogram: pearl and divination. **Initial**, *CHU*: beginning, incipient, first step or part; bottom line of a hexagram. Ideogram: knife and garment, cutting out the pattern. **Significant**, *JI*: leads to the experience of meaning; favorable, propitious, appropriate. Ideogram: scholar and mouth, wise words of a sage. **Complete**, *ZHONG*: completion of a cycle that begins the next; entire, whole, all. Ideogram: silk cocoons, follow and ice, winter linking one year with the next. **Disarray**, *LUAN*: throw into disorder, mislay, confuse; out of place; discord, insurrection, anarchy.

Outer and Inner Trigram

The upper trigram, **Gorge**, *KAN*, describes the outer aspects of the situation. It has the following associations: precipice, dangerous place; hole, cavity, pit, snare, trap, grave; critical time, test; risky. Ideogram: earth and cavity. *Symbol*: stream, *SHUI*, flowing water; river, tide, flood; fluid, dissolving. Ideogram: rippling water. *Actions*: venture and fall. Venture, *XIAN*: face a severe difficulty or obstruction; risk; precipice, cliff, abyss; key point, point of danger. Ideogram: mound and all, everything engaged at one point. Fall, *XIAN*: fall down or into, sink, drop, descend; pit, trap, fault; falling water. In the family of trigrams *KAN* is the middle son.

The lower trigram, **Radiance**, *LI*, describes the inner aspects of the situation. It has the following associations: glowing light, spreading in all directions; the power of consciousness; discriminate, articulate, divide and arrange in order; assemble, attract. Ideogram: bird and weird, magical fire-bird with brilliant plumage. *Symbols*: fire and brightness. Fire, *HUO*: flame, burn; warming and consuming aspect of burning. Brightness, *MING*: light, radiance, clarity; distinguish, discern, understand; light-giving aspect of fire, of heavenly bodies and of consciousness. *Action*: congregate, *LI*, cling together, adhere to, rely on; couple, pair, herd; beautiful, elegant. Ideogram: deer flocking together. In the family of trigrams *LI* is the middle daughter.

Counter Hexagram

The Counter Hexagram of **Already Fording** is hexagram 64, **Not Yet Fording**, which switches the emphasis from being engaged in a process which is already on its way to completion to being still on the brink of a move whose outcome cannot yet be discerned.

Preceding Situation

> **Beings possessing excess implies necessarily fording**.
> To **anterior acquiescence belongs** the **use** of **already fording**.

Fields of meaning

Being, *WU*: creature, thing, any single being; matter, substance, essence; nature of things. **Possess**, *YOU*: general term indicating possession; have, own, be endowed with. **Exceed**, *GUO*: go beyond, pass by, pass over; surpass, transgress; error, fault, calamity. **Imply**, *ZHE*: further signify; additional meaning. **Necessarily**, *BI*: unavoidably, certainly. **Ford**, *JI*: see *Image of the Situation*. To **anterior acquiescence belongs** the **use** of, *GU SHOU ZHI YI*: understanding and accepting the preceding statement allows the consultant to make proper use of this hexagram. **Already**, *JI*: see *Image of the Situation*.

Hexagrams in Pairs

Already fording: **rectifying indeed**.
Not-yet fording: to **manhood belongs exhaustion indeed**.

Fields of meaning
Already fording, *JI JI*: see *Image of the Situation*. **Rectify**, *DING*: correct, settle, fix; peaceful, tranquil, stable; certain, invariable. **Indeed**, *YE*: emphasizes and intensifies the previous statement. **Not-yet**, *WEI*: temporal negative indicating that something is expected to happen but has not yet occurred. **Man(hood)**, *NAN*: a man; what is inherently male; husband, son. Ideogram: field and strength, men's hard work in the fields. **Belong/it**, *ZHI*: establishes between two terms a connection similar to the Saxon genitive, in which the second term belongs to the first one; at the end of a sentence it refers to something previously mentioned or implied. **Exhaust**, *QIONG*: bring to an end; limit, extremity; investigate exhaustively; destitute, indigent; end without a new beginning; distinct from complete, *ZHONG*, end of a cycle that begins the next one. Ideogram: cave and naked person, bent with disease or old age.

Patterns of Wisdom

Stream located above fire. **Already fording**.
A **jun zi uses pondering** on **distress and-also providing**
for **defending-against it**.

Fields of meaning
Stream, *SHUI*: flowing water; river, tide, flood; fluid, dissolving; Symbol of the trigram Gorge, *KAN*. Ideogram: rippling water. **Locate**, *ZAI*: be at, be situated at, dwell, reside; in, within; involved with, in the process of. Ideogram: earth and persevere, a place on the earth. **Above**, *SHANG*: anything above in all senses; higher, upper, outer; upper trigram. **Fire**, *HUO*: fire, flame, burn; warming and consuming aspect of burning; fire and brightness are the Symbols of the trigram

Radiance, *LI*. **Already fording**, *JI JI*: see *Image of the Situation*. **Jun zi**: ideal of a person who orders his/her life in accordance with dao rather than willful intention, and uses divination in this spirit. **Use**, *YI*: by means of; owing to; make use of, employ. **Ponder**, *SI*: reflect, consider, remember; deep thought; desire, wish. Ideogram: heart and field, the heart's concerns. **Distress**, *HUAN*: tribulation, grief, affliction, illness. Ideogram: heart and clamor, the heart distressed. **And-also**, *ER*: joins and contrasts two terms. **Provide**, *YU*: prepare for, pre-arrange, think beforehand; ready, satisfied, contented, at ease, relaxed; enthusiasm, joy, pleasure. Ideogram: sonhood and elephant, careful, reverent and strong. **Defend-against**, *FANG*: keep off, protect from, guard against; rampart, dam; erect a protective barrier. Ideogram: open space and earthen ramparts. **It/belong**, *ZHI*: establishes between two terms a connection similar to the Saxon genitive, in which the second term belongs to the first one; at the end of a sentence it refers to something previously mentioned or implied.

Transforming Lines

INITIAL NINE

Pulling-back one's wheels.
Soaking one's tail.
Without fault.

Comments
Pulling-back one's wheels.
Righteous, without fault indeed.

Fields of meaning
Pull-back, *YI*: pull or drag something towards you; drag behind; leave traces. **One/one's**, *QI*: general third person pronoun and possessive adjective; also: it/its, he/his, she/her, they/their. **Wheel**, *LUN*: disk, circle, round; revolution, circuit; rotate, roll; by turns. **Soak**, *RU*: immerse, steep; damp, wet; stain, pollute, blemish; urinate on. **Tail**, *WEI*: animal's tail; end, last, extreme, remnant. **Without fault**, *WU JIU*: no error or harm in the situation.

Righteous, *YI*: proper, just, virtuous, upright; the heart that rules itself; benevolent, loyal, devoted to public good. **Indeed**, *YE*: see *Hexagrams in Pairs*.

Six at Second

A **wife loses her veil**.
No pursuing.
The **seventh day acquiring**.

Comments
The **seventh day acquiring**.
Using the **center**'s **dao indeed**.

Fields of meaning

Wife, *FU*: position of married woman as head of the household; distinct from consort, *QI*, which denotes her legal status, and from concubine, *QIE*, secondary wife. Ideogram: woman, hand and broom, household duties. **Lose**, *SANG*: be deprived of, forget; destruction, ruin, death; corpse; lament, mourn; funeral. Ideogram: weep and dead. **She/her**, *QI*: general third person pronoun and possessive adjective; also: one/one's, it/its, he/his, they/their. **Veil**, *FU*: screen on person or carriage; hair ornament; luxuriant, tangled vegetation that conceals the path. **No**, *WU*: common term of negation. **Pursue**, *ZHU*: chase, follow closely, press hard; expel, drive out. Ideogram: pig (wealth) and go, chasing fortune. **Seven**, *QI*: number seven; seven planets; seventh day when moon changes from crescent to waxing; the Tangram game analyzes all forms in terms of seven basic shapes. **Day/sun**, *RI*: the sun and the time of a sun-cycle, a day. **Acquire**, *DE*: obtain the desired object; possession; satisfied, fulfilled; it is permitted; agree with; wish for, desire covetously. Ideogram: go and obstacle, going through obstacles to the goal.

Use, *YI*: see *Patterns of Wisdom*. **Center**, *ZHONG*: inner, central; put in the center; middle, stable point enabling you to face inner and outer changes; middle line of a trigram. Ideogram: field divided in two equal parts. **Dao**, *DAO*: way or path; ongoing process of being and the course it traces for each person or thing; ultimate reality, intrinsic nature; origin. Ideogram: go and head, opening a path. **Indeed**, *YE*: see *Hexagrams in Pairs*.

Nine at Third

The **High Ancestor subjugates souls** on all **sides**.
Three years controlling it.
The **small** in the **person**, **no availing** of.

Comments
Three years controlling it.
Weariness indeed.

Fields of meaning

High, *GAO*: high, elevated, lofty, eminent; honor, respect. Ideogram: high tower. **Ancestry**, *ZONG*: clan, kin, origin; those who bear the same surname; ancestral hall and tablets; honor, revere. **Subjugate**, *FA*: hit, cut; submit, make dependent; chastise rebels, subject to rule. Ideogram: man and lance, armed soldiers. **Soul**, *GUI*: power that creates individual existence; union of volatile-soul, *HUN*, spiritual and intellectual power, and dense-soul, *PO*, bodily strength and movement. *HUN* rises after death, *PO* remains with the body and may communicate with the living. **Sides**, *FANG*: cardinal directions; surface of the earth extending to the four cardinal points; everywhere; limits, boundaries. **Three/thrice**, *SAN*: number three; third time or place; active phases of a cycle; superlative; beginning of repetition (since one and two are entities in themselves). **Year**, *NIAN*: year, annual; harvest; years revolved, years of age. **Control**, *KE*: be in charge; capable of, able to, adequate; check, obstruct, repress. Ideogram: roof beams supporting a house. **Small**, *XIAO*: see *Image of the Situation*. **Person/people**, *REN*: humans individually and collectively; an individual; humankind. **No**, *WU*: common term of negation. **Avail**, *YONG*: use, employ for a specific purpose; take advantage of; benefit from; capacity. Ideogram: to divine and center, applying divination to central concerns.

Weariness, *BAI*: fatigue; debilitated, exhausted, distressed; weak. **Indeed**, *YE*: see *Hexagrams in Pairs*.

Six at Fourth

A **token**: **possessing clothes** in **tatters**.
Completing the **day**: a **warning**.

Comments
Completing the **day**: a **warning**.
Possessing a **place** to **doubt indeed**.

Fields of meaning

Token, *XU*: halves of a torn piece of silk which identify the bearers when joined. **Possess**, *YOU*: see *Preceding Situation*. **Clothes**, *YI*: upper body garments and clothes in general; dress; cover, husk. **Tatters**, *RU*: worn-out garments, used for padding or stopping leaks. **Complete**, *ZHONG*: see *Image of the Situation*. **Day/sun**, *RI*: the sun and the time of a sun-cycle, a day. **Warn**, *JIE*: alarm, alert, put on guard; caution, inform; guard against, refrain from. Ideogram: spear held in both hands, warning enemies.

Place, *SUO*: position, location; residence, dwelling; where something belongs or comes from; habitual focus or object. **Doubt**, *YI*: suspect, distrust, wonder; uncertain, dubious; surmise, conjecture, fear. **Indeed**, *YE*: see *Hexagrams in Pairs.*

NINE AT FIFTH

The **Eastern neighbor slaughters cattle**.
Not thus the **dedicated offering belonging** to the **Western neighbor**.
Substance: **acquiescing** in **one's blessing**.

Comments
The **Eastern neighbor slaughters cattle**.
Not thus the **season belonging** to the **Western neighbor**.
Substance: **acquiescing** in **one's blessing**.
Significant. The **great coming indeed**.

Fields of meaning
East, *DONG*: eastern direction, corresponding to morning, spring and to the Wooden Moment in the Universal Compass; stirring up and germination of a new life-cycle; place of honor and the person occupying it. **Neighbor**, *LIN*: person living nearby; extended family; assist, support. **Slaughter**, *SHA*: kill, murder, execute; hunt game. **Cattle**, *NIU*: ox, bull, cow, calf; power and strength of work animals; stubborn. **Not**, *BU*: common term of negation. **Thus**, *RU*: as, in this way; comparable, similar. **Dedicate**, *YUE*: imperial offering at the spring equinox, when stores are low; offer a sacrifice with limited resources. Ideogram: spring and thin. **Offer**, *JI*: offer a sacrifice. Ideogram: hand, meat and worship. **Belong/it**, *ZHI*: see *Hexagrams in Pairs*. **West**, *XI*: western direction, corresponding to autumn, Harvest, the Metallic Moment and the first phase of the Yin hemicycle of the Universal Compass. **Substance**, *SHI*: fullness, richness; essence; real, solid, consistent; results, fruits, possessions; honest, sincere. Ideogram: string of coins under a roof, wealth in the house. **Acquiesce**, *SHOU*: accept, make peace with, agree to, receive; at rest, satisfied; patient. **One/one's**, *QI*: general third person pronoun and possessive adjective; also: it/its, he/his, she/her, they/their. **Bless**, *FU*: heavenly gifts and favor; happiness, prosperity; spiritual power and goodwill. Ideogram: spirit and plenty.

Season, *SHI*: quality of the time; the right time, opportune, in harmony; planning in accord with the time; season of the year. Ideogram: sun and temple, sacred time. **Significant**, *JI*: see *Image of the Situation*. **Great**, *DA*: big, noble, important, very; orient the will toward a self-imposed goal, impose direction; ability to lead or guide one's life; contrasts with small, *XIAO*, flexible adaptation to what crosses one's path. **Come**, *LAI*: approach in time or space; move toward, arrive at; future; contrasts with go, *WANG*, move away or become past. **Indeed**, YE: see *Hexagrams in Pairs*.

SIX ABOVE

Soaking one's head.
Adversity.

Comments
Soaking one's head, adversity.
Is it **permitted** to **last indeed?**

Fields of meaning

Soak, *RU*: immerse, steep; damp, wet; stain, pollute, blemish; urinate on. **One/one's**, *QI*: general third person pronoun and possessive adjective; also: it/its, he/his, she/her, they/their. **Head**, *SHOU*: physical head; leader, sovereign; beginning, origin, model; foremost, superior, upper, front. **Adversity**, *LI*: danger, hardship, severe; threat or difficulty that must be encountered, rather than avoided; grinding stone; polish, sharpen; a challenge that strengthens and perfects the character; stimulate, excite; cruel demon.

Is?, *HE*: ask, inquire; what? which? who? how? why? where? an interrogative particle, often introducing a rhetorical question: is it? is it not? **Permit**, *KE*: possible because in harmony with an inherent principle; capable of; approve, authorize. Ideogram: mouth and breath, silent consent. **Last**, *JIU*: endure; long, protracted, permanent, eternal; old, ancient. **Indeed**, *YE*: see *Hexagrams in Pairs*.

Image Tradition

Already fording. Growing.
The **small implies Growing indeed.**
Harvesting, Trial.
Solid and **supple correct and-also position appropriate indeed.**

Initially: significant.
The **supple acquires** the **center indeed.**
Completing: stopping, by **consequence disarray.**
One's dao exhausted indeed.

Fields of meaning

Already fording, *JI JI*: see *Image of the Situation*. **Growing**, the **small**, *HENG XIAO*: see *Image of the Situation*. **Imply**, *ZHE*: see *Preceding Situation*. **Indeed**, *YE*: see *Hexagrams in Pairs*. **Harvesting**, **Trial**, *LI ZHEN*: see *Image of the Situation*. **Solid**, *GANG*: quality of the whole lines; firm, strong, unyielding, persisting. **Supple**, *ROU*: quality of the opened lines; flexible, pliant, adaptable, tender. **Correct**, *ZHENG*: rectify deviation or one-sidedness; proper, straight, exact, regular; constant, rule, model. Ideogram: stop and one, hold to one thing. **And-also**, *ER*: see *Patterns of Wisdom*. **Position**, *WEI*: place, location; be at; social standing, rank; position of a line in a hexagram. Ideogram: person standing. **Appropriate**, *DANG*: suitable, capable, worthy, adequate, competent, equal to; opportune, convenient; whole lines in odd places and opened lines in even places.

Initially: **significant**, *CHU JI*: see *Image of the Situation*. **Acquire**, *DE*: obtain the desired object; possession; satisfied, fulfilled; it is permitted; agree with; wish for, desire covetously. Ideogram: go and obstacle, going through obstacles to the goal. **Center**, *ZHONG*: inner, central; put in the center; middle, stable point enabling you to face inner and outer changes; middle line of a trigram. Ideogram: field divided in two equal parts. **Complete**, *ZHONG*: see *Image of the Situation*. **Stop**, *ZHI*: bring or come to a standstill, cease, terminate; Action of the trigram Bound, *GEN*. Ideogram: a foot stops walking. **Consequence**, *ZE*: reason, cause, result; rule, law, pattern, standard; therefore; very strong connection. **Disarray**, *LUAN*: see *Image of the Situation*. **One/one's**, *QI*: general third person pronoun and possessive adjective; also: it/its, he/his, she/her, they/their. **Dao**, *DAO*: way or path; ongoing process of being and the course it traces for each person or thing; ultimate reality, intrinsic nature; origin. Ideogram: go and head, opening a path. **Exhaust**, *QIONG*: see *Hexagrams in Pairs*.

未濟

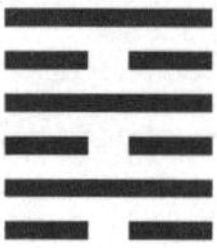

64 NOT YET FORDING | *Wei Ji*

The situation described by this hexagram is characterized by involvement in a process which is still far from completion, being on the brink of a move whose outcome cannot yet be discerned.

Image of the Situation

> **Not-yet fording**.
> **Growing**.
> The **small fox** in a **muddy ford**.
> **Soaking its tail**.
> **Without direction Harvesting**.

Fields of meaning

Not-yet, *WEI*: temporal negative indicating that something is expected to happen but has not yet occurred. **Ford**, *JI*: cross a river at a ford or shallow place; embark on a course of action; complete, finish, succeed; help, relieve. Ideogram: water and level, running smooth over a flat bottom. **Grow**, *HENG*: heavenly influence pervading and nourishing all things; prosper, succeed, expand, develop; effective, favorable; quality of summer and South, second stage of the Time Cycle. With the pronunciation *XIANG*: offer a sacrifice; offer a gift to a superior; accept, enjoy. **Small**, *XIAO*: little, common, unimportant; adapting to what crosses your path; ability to move in harmony with the vicissitudes of life; contrasts with great, *DA*, self-imposed theme or goal. **Fox**, *HU*: crafty, shape-changing animal; used by spirits, often female; ambivalent night-spirit that can create havoc and bestow abundance. **Mud**, *XI*: ground left wet by water, muddy shores; danger; shed tears; nearly. **Soak**, *RU*: immerse, steep; damp, wet; stain, pollute, blemish; urinate on. **It/its**, *QI*: general third person pronoun and possessive adjective; also: one/one's, he/his, she/her, they/their. **Tail**, *WEI*: animal's tail; end, last, extreme, remnant. **Without direction Harvesting**, *WU YOU LI*: in order to take advantage of the situation, do not impose a direction on events.

Outer and Inner Trigram

The upper trigram, **Radiance**, *LI*, describes the outer aspects of the situation. It has the following associations: glowing light, spreading in all directions; the power of consciousness; discriminate, articulate, divide and arrange in order; assemble, attract. Ideogram: bird and weird, magical fire-bird with brilliant plumage. *Symbols*: fire and brightness. Fire, *HUO*: flame, burn; warming and consuming aspect of burning. Brightness, *MING*: light, radiance, clarity; distinguish, discern, understand; light-giving aspect of fire, of heavenly bodies and of consciousness. *Action*: congregate, *LI*, cling together, adhere to, rely on; couple, pair, herd; beautiful, elegant. Ideogram: deer flocking together. In the family of trigrams *LI* is the middle daughter.

The lower trigram, **Gorge**, *KAN*, describes the inner aspects of the situation. It has the following associations: precipice, dangerous place; hole, cavity, pit, snare, trap, grave; critical time, test; risky. Ideogram: earth and cavity. *Symbol*: stream, *SHUI*, flowing water; river, tide, flood; fluid, dissolving. Ideogram: rippling water. *Actions*: venture and fall. Venture, *XIAN*: face a severe difficulty or obstruction; risk; precipice, cliff, abyss; key point, point of danger. Ideogram: mound and all, everything engaged at one point. Fall, *XIAN*: fall down or into, sink, drop, descend; pit, trap, fault; falling water. In the family of trigrams *KAN* is the middle son.

Counter Hexagram

The Counter Hexagram of **Not Yet Fording** is hexagram 63, **Already Fording**, which switches the emphasis from being still on the brink of a move whose outcome cannot yet be discerned to being engaged in a process which is already on its way to completion.

Preceding Situation

> **Beings not permitted exhausting indeed**.
> To **anterior acquiescence belongs** the **use** of **not-yet fording**'s **completion in-truth**.

Fields of meaning

Beings not permitted (to **use**), *WU BU KE (YI)*: it is not possible; no one is allowed; it is not in the nature of things. **Exhaust**, *QIONG*: bring to an end; limit, extremity; investigate exhaustively; destitute, indigent; end without a new beginning; distinct from complete, *ZHONG*, end of a cycle that begins the next one. Ideogram: cave and naked person, bent with disease or old age. **Indeed**, *YE*: emphasizes and intensifies the previous statement. To **anterior acquiescence**

belongs the **use** of, *GU SHOU ZHI YI*: understanding and accepting the preceding statement allows the consultant to make proper use of this hexagram. **Not-yet fording**, *WEI JI*: see *Image of the Situation*. **Complete**, *ZHONG*: completion of a cycle that begins the next; entire, whole, all. Ideogram: silk cocoons, follow and ice, winter linking one year with the next. **In-truth**, *YAN*: a final affirmative particle; the preceding statement is complete and correct.

Hexagrams in Pairs

> **Already fording**: **rectifying indeed**.
> **Not-yet fording**: to **manhood belongs exhaustion indeed**.

Fields of meaning

Already, *JI*: completed, done, occurred, finished; past tense; shortly after. **Ford**, *JI*: see *Image of the Situation*. **Rectify**, *DING*: correct, settle, fix; peaceful, tranquil, stable; certain, invariable. **Indeed**, *YE*: see *Preceding Situation*. **Not-yet**, *WEI*: see *Image of the Situation*. **Man(hood)**, *NAN*: a man; what is inherently male; husband, son. Ideogram: field and strength, men's hard work in the fields. **Belong/it**, *ZHI*: establishes between two terms a connection similar to the Saxon genitive, in which the second term belongs to the first one; at the end of a sentence it refers to something previously mentioned or implied. **Exhaust**, *QIONG*: see *Preceding Situation*.

Patterns of Wisdom

> **Fire located above stream**. **Not-yet fording**.
> A **jun zi uses considerately marking-off** the **beings residing** on all **sides**.

Fields of meaning

Fire, *HUO*: fire, flame, burn; warming and consuming aspect of burning; fire and brightness are the Symbols of the trigram Radiance, *LI*. **Locate**, *ZAI*: be at, be situated at, dwell, reside; in, within; involved with, in the process of. Ideogram: earth and persevere, a place on the earth. **Above**, *SHANG*: anything above in all senses; higher, upper, outer; upper trigram. **Stream**, *SHUI*: flowing water; river, tide, flood; fluid, dissolving; Symbol of the trigram Gorge, *KAN*. Ideogram: rippling water. **Not-yet fording**, *WEI JI*: see *Image of the Situation*. **Jun zi**: ideal of a person who orders his/her life in accordance with dao rather than willful intention, and uses divination in this spirit. **Use**, *YI*: by means of; owing to; make use of, employ. **Consider**, *SHEN*: act carefully, seriously; cautious, attentive, circumspect; still, quiet, sincere. Ideogram: heart and true. **Mark-off**, *BIAN*: distinguish by dividing; mark off a plot of land; discern, discriminate, differentiate; discuss and dispute; frame which divides a bed from its stand. Ideogram: knife and acrid, sharp division. **Being**, *WU*: creature, thing, any single being; matter, substance, essence; nature of things. **Reside**, *JU*: dwell, live in, stay; sit down; fill an office; well-being, rest. Ideogram: body and seat. **Sides**, *FANG*: cardinal directions; surface of the earth extending to the four cardinal points; everywhere; limits, boundaries.

Transforming Lines

INITIAL SIX

Soaking one's tail.
Abashment.

Comments
Soaking one's tail.
Truly not knowing the **end indeed**.

Fields of meaning

Soak, *RU*: see *Image of the Situation*. **One/one's**, *QI*: general third person pronoun and possessive adjective; also: it/its, he/his, she/her, they/their. **Tail**, *WEI*: see *Image of the Situation*. **Abashment**, *LIN*: distress, shame, regret, humiliation; aware of having lost the right track; leads to repenting, *HUI*, correcting the direction of mind and life.

Truly, *YI*: in fact; also; nevertheless. **Not**, *BU*: common term of negation. **Know**, *ZHI*: have knowledge of, perceive, experience, remember; know intimately; informed, aware, wise. Ideogram: arrow and mouth, words focused and swift. **End**, *JI*: last or highest point; final, extreme; ridgepole of a house. **Indeed**, *YE*: see *Preceding Situation*.

NINE AT SECOND

Pulling-back one's wheels.
Trial, significant.

Comments
Nine at **second**: **Trial, significant**.
In the **center using movement** to **correct indeed**.

Fields of meaning

Pull-back, *YI*: pull or drag something towards you; drag behind; leave traces. **One/one's**, *QI*: general third person pronoun and possessive adjective; also: it/its, he/his, she/her, they/their. **Wheel**, *LUN*: disk, circle, round; revolution, circuit; rotate, roll; by turns. **Trial**, *ZHEN*: inquiry by divination and its result; righteous, firm; separating wheat from chaff; the kernel, the proven core; quality of winter and North, fourth stage of the Time Cycle. Ideogram: pearl and divination. **Significant**, *JI*: leads to the experience of meaning; favorable, propitious, appropriate. Ideogram: scholar and mouth, wise words of a sage.

Nine, *JIU*: number nine; transforming whole line; superlative: best, perfect. **Two/second**, *ER*: number two; pair, even numbers, binary, duplicate. **Center**, *ZHONG*: inner, central; put in the center; middle, stable point enabling you to face inner and outer changes; middle line of a trigram. Ideogram: field divided in two equal parts. **Use**, *YI*: see *Patterns of Wisdom*. **Move**, *XING*: move or move something; motivate; emotionally moving; walk, act, do. Ideogram: successive steps. **Correct**, *ZHENG*: rectify deviation or one-sidedness; proper, straight, exact, regular; constant, rule, model. Ideogram: stop and one, hold to one thing. **Indeed**, *YE*: see *Preceding Situation*.

SIX AT THIRD

Not-yet fording: **disciplining**, **pitfall**.
Harvesting: **wading** the **great river**.

Comments

Not-yet fording: **disciplining**, **pitfall**.
Position not appropriate indeed.

Fields of meaning

Not-yet fording, *WEI JI*: see *Image of the Situation*. **Discipline**, *ZHENG*: subjugate vassals, reduce to order; punishing expedition. Ideogram: step and correct, a rectifying move. **Pitfall**, *XIONG*: unfortunate situation, in which the flow of life and spirit is blocked and the experience of meaning is lost; stuck and exposed to danger; inappropriate attitude. Ideogram: person in a pit. **Harvest**, *LI*: benefit, advantage, profit; realization; sharp, acute, insightful; quality of autumn and West, third stage of the Time Cycle. Ideogram: ripe grain and blade. **Wading the Great River**, *SHE DA CHUAN*: enter the stream of life with a goal or purpose; embark on a significant enterprise.

Position, *WEI*: place, location; be at; social standing, rank; position of a line in a hexagram. Ideogram: person standing. **Not**, *BU*: common term of negation.

Appropriate, *DANG*: suitable, capable, worthy, adequate, competent, equal to; opportune, convenient; whole lines in odd places and opened lines in even places. **Indeed**, *YE*: see *Preceding Situation*.

NINE AT FOURTH

Trial, **significant**, **repenting extinguished**.
The **shake avails** of **subjugating souls** on all **sides**.
Three years, **possessing** a **donation tending-towards** the **great city**.

Comments

Trial, **significant**, **repenting extinguished**.
Purpose moving indeed.

Fields of meaning

Trial, *ZHEN*: inquiry by divination and its result; righteous, firm; separating wheat from chaff; the kernel, the proven core; quality of winter and North, fourth stage of the Time Cycle. Ideogram: pearl and divination. **Significant**, *JI*: leads to the experience of meaning; favorable, propitious, appropriate. Ideogram: scholar and mouth, wise words of a sage. **Repenting extinguished**, *HUI WANG*: previous errors are corrected, all causes for repenting disappear. **Shake**, *ZHEN*: arouse, excite, inspire; awe, alarm, trembling; thunder rising from the depth of the earth; fertilizing intrusion. Ideogram: excite and rain. **Avail**, *YONG*: use, employ for a specific purpose; take advantage of; benefit from; capacity. Ideogram: to divine and center, applying divination to central concerns. **Subjugate**, *FA*: hit, cut; submit, make dependent; chastise rebels, subject to rule. Ideogram: man and lance, armed soldiers. **Soul**, *GUI*: power that creates individual existence; union of volatile-soul, *HUN*, spiritual and intellectual power, and dense-soul, *PO*, bodily strength and movement. *HUN* rises after death, *PO* remains with the body and may communicate with the living. **Sides**, *FANG*: see *Patterns of Wisdom*. **Three/thrice**, *SAN*: number three; third time or place; active phases of a cycle; superlative; beginning of repetition (since one and two are entities in themselves). **Year**, *NIAN*: year, annual; harvest; years revolved, years of age. **Possess**, *YOU*: general term indicating possession; have, own, be endowed with. **Donate**, *SHANG*: bestow, confer, grant; rewards, gifts; celebrate, take pleasure in. **Tend-towards**, *YU*: move toward without necessarily reaching, in the direction of. **Great**, *DA*: big, noble, important, very; orient the will toward a self-imposed goal, impose direction; ability to lead or guide one's life; contrasts with small, *XIAO*, flexible adaptation to what crosses one's path. **City**, *GUO*: city, state, country, nation; area of only human constructions; first of the territorial zones: city, suburbs, countryside, forest.

Purpose, *ZHI*: focus of mind and heart; intention, will, inclination; continuity in the direction of life. Ideogram: heart and scholar, high inner resolve. **Move**, *XING*: move or move something; motivate; emotionally moving; walk, act, do. Ideogram: successive steps. **Indeed**, *YE*: see *Preceding Situation*.

SIX AT FIFTH

Trial, significant, without repenting.
To a **jun zi belongs shining**.
Possessing conformity, significant.

Comments
To a **jun zi belongs shining**.
One's brilliance significant indeed.

Fields of meaning

Trial, *ZHEN*: inquiry by divination and its result; righteous, firm; separating wheat from chaff; the kernel, the proven core; quality of winter and North, fourth stage of the Time Cycle. Ideogram: pearl and divination. **Significant**, *JI*: leads to the experience of meaning; favorable, propitious, appropriate. Ideogram: scholar and mouth, wise words of a sage. **Without**, *WU*: devoid of; there is not. **Repent**, *HUI*: regret, dissatisfaction with past conduct inducing a change of heart; proceeds from abashment, *LIN*, shame and confusion at having lost the right way. **Jun zi**: see *Patterns of Wisdom*. **Belong/it**, *ZHI*: see *Hexagrams in Pairs*. **Shine**, *GUANG*: illuminate, emit light; brilliant, splendid; honor, glory, éclat; distinct from brightness, *MING*, light of heavenly bodies. Ideogram: fire above person. **Possess**, *YOU*: general term indicating possession; have, own, be endowed with. **Conform**, *FU*: accord between inner and outer; sincere, truthful, verified, reliable; capture; prisoners, spoils. Ideogram: claws over child, a bird brooding on the nest.

One/one's, *QI*: general third person pronoun and possessive adjective; also: it/its, he/his, she/her, they/their. **Brilliance**, *HUI*: sunlight, sunbeam; bright, splendid. **Indeed**, *YE*: see *Preceding Situation*.

NINE ABOVE

Possessing conformity tending-towards drinking liquor.
Without fault.

Soaking one's head.
Possessing conformity: **letting-go that**.

Comments
Drinking liquor, **soaking** the **head**.
Truly not knowing articulation indeed.

Fields of meaning
Possess, *YOU*: general term indicating possession; have, own, be endowed with. **Conform**, *FU*: accord between inner and outer; sincere, truthful, verified, reliable; capture; prisoners, spoils. Ideogram: claws over child, a bird brooding on the nest. **Tend-towards**, *YU*: move toward without necessarily reaching, in the direction of. **Drink**, *YIN*: drink, swallow, ingest liquid or food; inhale, suck in. **Liquor**, *JIU*: alcoholic beverages, distilled spirits; spirit which perfects the good and evil in human nature. Ideogram: liquid above fermenting must, separating the spirits. **Without fault**, *WU JIU*: no error or harm in the situation. **Soak**, *RU*: see *Image of the Situation*. **One/one's**, *QI*: general third person pronoun and possessive adjective; also: it/its, he/his, she/her, they/their. **Head**, *SHOU*: physical head; leader, sovereign; beginning, origin, model; foremost, superior, upper, front. **Let-go**, *SHI*: lose, let slip; omit, miss, fail; lose control of. Ideogram: drop from the hand. **That**, *SHI*: refers to the preceding statement.

Truly, *YI*: in fact; also; nevertheless. **Not**, *BU*: common term of negation. **Know**, *ZHI*: have knowledge of, perceive, experience, remember; know intimately; informed, aware, wise. Ideogram: arrow and mouth, words focused and swift. **Articulate**, *JIE*: joint, articulation; a separation which simultaneously establishes the identity of the parts and their connection; express thought through speech; section, chapter, interval; temperance, virtue; rite, ceremony; lit.: nodes of bamboo stalks. **Indeed**, *YE*: see *Preceding Situation*.

Image Tradition

Not-yet fording. **Growing**.
The **supple acquires** the **center indeed**.

The **small fox** in a **muddy ford**.
Not-yet emerging from the **center indeed**.
Soaking its tail.
Without direction Harvesting.
Not continuing to **completion indeed**.

Although not in **appropriate positions**, **solid** and **supple correspond indeed**.

Fields of meaning

Not-yet fording. **Growing**, *WEI JI HENG*: see *Image of the Situation*. **Supple**, *ROU*: quality of the opened lines; flexible, pliant, adaptable, tender. **Acquire**, *DE*: obtain the desired object; possession; satisfied, fulfilled; it is permitted; agree with; wish for, desire covetously. Ideogram: go and obstacle, going through obstacles to the goal. **Center**, *ZHONG*: inner, central; put in the center; middle, stable point enabling you to face inner and outer changes; middle line of a trigram. Ideogram: field divided in two equal parts. **Indeed**, *YE*: see *Preceding Situation*.

The **small fox** in a **muddy ford**, *XIAO HU XI JI*: see *Image of the Situation*. **Emerge**, *CHU*: come out of, proceed from, spring from, issue forth; appear, be born; bear, generate; leave, flee; Action of the trigram Shake, *ZHEN*. Ideogram: stem with branches and leaves emerging. **Soaking its tail**, *RU QI WEI*: see *Image of the Situation*. **Without direction Harvesting**, *WU YOU LI*: see *Image of the Situation*. **Not**, *BU*: common term of negation. **Continue**, *XU*: carry on what another began; succeed to, inherit, transmit; keep up, follow. **Complete**, *ZHONG*: see *Preceding Situation*.

Although, *SUI*: even though, supposing that, if, even if. **Appropriate**, *DANG*: suitable, capable, worthy, adequate, competent, equal to; opportune, convenient; whole lines in odd places and opened lines in even places. **Position**, *WEI*: place, location; be at; social standing, rank; position of a line in a hexagram. Ideogram: person standing. **Solid**, *GANG*: quality of the whole lines; firm, strong, unyielding, persisting. **Correspond**, *YING*: be in agreement or harmony; proper, suitable; resonate together, answer to; relation between the lines (1 and 4, 2 and 5, 3 and 6) when they form the pair opened and whole, supple and solid. Ideogram: heart and obey.

Part Three

The Concordance

CONCORDANCE TO THE ORACULAR TEXTS

This concordance lists all the occurrences of each term appearing in the oracular texts of the *Yi Jing*. In the Eranos *Yi Jing* each Chinese ideogram is always consistently translated by the same English word (core-word), and the imaginal content of the ideogram is further illustrated by the associated Field of meaning. This concordance lists core-words in alphabetical order, with their Pinyin transcription and associated Field of meaning, followed by a list of all the sentences where the ideogram occurs in the oracular texts.

Listings for terms frequently recurring in all hexagrams have been omitted, as not particularly revealing. Likewise, when a term is part of the name of a hexagram and therefore recurs throughout its texts, only the occurrences in other hexagrams have been listed. About composite entries, special cases and idiomatic phrases see the Introduction, p. 29–31.

Each sentence is accompanied by the indication of the hexagram and section where it occurs. Hexagrams are indicated by their number and sections are abbreviated according to the following code:

IM *Image of the Situation*
PS *Preceding Situation*
HP *Hexagrams in Pairs*
AT *Additional Texts*
PW *Patterns of Wisdom*
a *Transforming Lines* – main text
b *Transforming Lines* – *Comments*
IT *Image Tradition*

E.g., the sentence

42.6a/6b Abstaining from augmenting it.

occurs both in the main text and in the *Comments* of the sixth line (*Nine above*) of hexagram 42, Augmenting.

Hexagrams 1 and 2 have special texts for the case in which all the lines are transforming, here indicated by the number 7. E.g., the sentence

1.7a Viewing a flock of dragons without head.

occurs in the main text of "all the lines transforming" (*Availing of nines*) of hexagram 1, Energy.

Abandon, *YI*: leave behind, forget; die; lose through unawareness. Ideogram: go and value, value is gone.

11.2a **Not putting-off abandoning.**
62.IM/IT To the **flying bird abandoning belongs** a **sound.**

Abashment, *LIN*: distress, shame, regret, humiliation; aware of having lost the right track; leads to repenting, *HUI*, correcting the direction of mind and life.

3.3a **Going, abashment.**
3.3b A **jun zi stowing it: going, abashment, exhaustion indeed.**
4.1a **Using going: abashment.**
4.4a **Confining enveloping. Abashment.**
4.4b To **confining enveloping belongs abashment.**
11.6a **Trial, abashment.**
13.2a **Abashment.**
13.2b **Abashment: dao indeed.**
18.4a **Going, viewing abashment.**
20.1a A **jun zi: abashment.**
21.3a The **small: abashment.**
22.5a **Abashment.**
28.4a **Possessing more: abashment.**
31.3a **Going, abashment.**
32.3a **Trial, abashment.**
35.6a **Trial, abashment.**
37.3a **Completing, abashment.**
40.3a **Trial, abashment.**
44.6a **Abashment.**
44.6b **Above exhausting abashment indeed.**
45.3a The **small abashed.**
47.4a **Abashment.**
57.3a **Imminent root, abashment.**
57.3b To **imminent root belongs abashment.**
64.1a **Abashment.**

Abide, *CHU*: rest in, dwell; stop oneself; arrive at a place or condition; distinguish, decide; do what is proper. Ideogram: tiger, stop and seat, powerful movement coming to rest.

9/10.HP **Treading: not abiding indeed.**
9.6a/6b **Already rain, already abiding.**
31.3b **Truly not abiding indeed.**
56.4a/4b **Sojourning: tending-towards abiding.**

Able/enable, *NENG*: ability, power, skill, art; competent, talented; duty, function, capacity. Ideogram: an animal with strong hooves and bones, able to carry and defend.

7.IT **Able** to **use crowds** for **correcting.**
9.3b **Not able** to **correct** the **home indeed.**
10.3a/3b **Squinting enables observing.**
10.3a/3b **Halting enables treading.**
13.IT **Verily** a **jun zi activating enables interpenetration** of **purposes belonging** to **below heaven.**
16.PS **Possessing** the **great and-also enabling humbleness necessarily provides.**
26.IT **Able** to **stop** and **persist.**
32.2b **Able** to **last** in the **center indeed.**
32.IT **Sun** and **moon: acquiring heaven and-also enabling lasting** and **illuminating.**
32.IT The **four seasons: transforming changes and-also enabling lasting** and **accomplishing.**
34.6a/6b **Not able** to **withdraw, not able** to **release.**
36.IT **Inside heaviness and-also able** to **correct one's purpose.**
39.IT **Viewing venturing and-also able** to **stop.**
50.2a **Not me able** to **approach.**
54.1a **Halting enables treading.**
54.1b **Halting enables treading, significant.**
54.2a **Squinting enables observing.**

Abound, *FENG*: abundant, plentiful, copious; grow wealthy; at the point of overflowing; exuberant, fertile, prolific, rich in talents, property, friends; fullness, culmination; ripe, sumptuous, fat.

This term is the name of hexagram 55 and recurs throughout its texts. It also occurs in:

56.HP **Abounding: numerous**

anteriority indeed.

Above, *SHANG*: anything above in all senses; higher, upper, outer; upper trigram.

This term frequently occurs in the Patterns of Wisdon and Image Tradition sections, referring to the upper trigram and lines. It also occurs at:

4.6b **Above** and **below yielding indeed.**

6.2b **Origin below, arguing above.**

6.3b **Adhering** to the **above, significant indeed.**

8.4b **Using adhering** to the **above indeed.**

8.5b **Above commissioning** in the **center indeed.**

9.4b **Above uniting purposes indeed.**

10.6b **Spring: significance located above.**

14.6b **Great possessing, above: significant.**

16.6b **Dim providing located above.**

17.6b **Above exhausted indeed.**

22.2b **Associating above, rising indeed.**

22.6b **Above acquiring purpose indeed.**

23.3b **Letting-go above** and **below indeed.**

24.PS **Stripping exhausted above, reversing below.**

26.3b **Above uniting purposes indeed.**

27.4b **Above spreading shine indeed.**

27.5b **Yielding uses adhering** to the **above indeed.**

29/30.HP The **radiance above and-also** the **gorge below indeed.**

29.6b **Six above, letting-go dao.**

31.PS **Therefore afterwards possessing above** and **below.**

31.PS **Possessing above** and **below.**

32.6b **Rousing persevering located above.**

35.3b **Above moving indeed.**

40.6a A **prince avails** of **shooting** a **hawk tending-towards** the **above belonging** to the **high rampart.**

41.5b The **origin above shielding indeed.**

44.6b **Above exhausting abashment indeed.**

45.3b **Above** the **root indeed.**

45.6b **Not-yet peaceful above indeed.**

46.PS **Assembling and-also** the **above implies** the **designation belonging** to **ascending.**

46.1b **Above uniting purposes indeed.**

46.6b **Dim ascending located above.**

48.PS **Confining reaching above implies necessarily reversing** to the **below.**

48.6b **Spring, significance located above.**

50.6b **Jade rings located above.**

54.6b **Six above: without substance.**

56.5b **Reaching-up** to the **above indeed.**

56.6b **Using sojourning located above.**

57.6b **Above exhaustion indeed.**

58.6b **Six above: protracted open.**

60.4b **Receiving dao above indeed.**

61.4b **Cutting-off, sorting above indeed.**

62.IM **Not proper above, proper below.**

62.5b **Climaxing above indeed.**

Absence, WANG: emptiness, vacancy; lit.: a net, open spaces between threads; used as a negative. Ideogram: net and lost, empty spaces divide what is kept from what is lost.

34.3a A **jun zi avails** of **absence.**

34.3b A **jun zi** of **absence indeed.**

35.1a **Absence: conforming.**

Abstain/absolutely-nothing, MO: complete elimination; do not, not any, by no means.

22.3b To **completing abstention belongs** a **mound indeed.**

33.2a To **abstaining belongs mastering stimulation.**

42.6a/6b **Abstaining** from **augmenting it.**

43.2a **Awe**: an **outcry**, **absolutely-nothing**.
50.PS **Skinning beings implies absolutely-nothing like** a **vessel**.
51.PS A **lord**'s **implements imply absolutely-nothing like** the **long-living son**.
53.5a To **completing abstention belongs mastering**.
53.5b To **completing abstention belongs mastering**, **significant**.
56.6b To **completing abstention belongs hearing indeed**.

Abyss, *YUAN*: deep hole or gulf, where backwaters eddy and accumulate; whirlpool, deep water; unfathomable; depth of feelings, deep sincerity.
1.4a/4b **Maybe capering located** at the **abyss**.
6.IT **Entering tending-towards** the **abyss indeed**.

Accompany, *XIE*: take or go along with; together; harmonize; totally, everywhere.
41.IT **Associating** with the **season**, **accompanying** the **movement**.
42.IT **Associating** with the **season**, **accompanying** the **movement**.

Accomplish, *CHENG*: complete, finish, bring about; perfect, full, whole; play one's part, do one's duty; mature. Ideogram: weapon and man, able to bear arms, thus fully developed.
1.IT In the **six positions** the **season accomplishes**.
2.3a **Without accomplishing**, **possessing completion**.
6.3a **Without accomplishment**.
6.IT **Arguing not permitting accomplishment indeed**.
11.PW The **crown prince uses property** to **accomplish** the **dao belonging** to **heaven** and **earth**.
16.6a **Accomplishment possesses retraction**.
22.IT **Using changes** to **accomplish below heaven**.
30.IT **Thereupon changes accomplished below heaven**.
32.IT The **four seasons**: **transforming changes and-also enabling lasting** and **accomplishing**.
32.IT The **wise person**: **lasting with-respect-to one's dao and-also below heaven changing** and **accomplishing**.
48.6b The **great accomplishes indeed**.
49.IT **Heaven** and **earth skinning and-also** the **four seasons accomplishing**.
60.IT **Heaven** and **earth articulating and-also** the **four seasons accomplishing**.

Accumulate, *CHU*: retain, hoard, gather, herd together; control, restrain; domesticate, tame, train; raise, feed, sustain, bring up. Ideogram: field and black, fertile black soil, accumulated through retaining silt.
This term occurs in the names of of hexagrams 9 and 26 and recurs throughout their texts. It also occurs in:
7.PW A **jun zi uses tolerating** the **commoners** to **accumulate crowds**.
10.PS **Beings accumulate**, **therefore afterwards possess codes**.
10.HP The **small accumulating**: **few indeed**.
25.HP The **great accumulating**: **season indeed**.
27.PS **Beings accumulate**, **therefore afterwards permitted** to **nourish**.
30.IM **Growing**. **Accumulating female cattle**.
30.IT **That uses accumulating female cattle**, **significant indeed**.
33.3a/3b **Accumulating servants**, **concubines**, **significant**.

Ache, *CE*: acute pain or grief; pity, sympathy, sorrow, grief.
48.3a **Activating my heart**'s **ache**.
48.3b **Moving**, **aching indeed**.

Achieve, *GONG*: work done, results, actual accomplishment; praise, worth, merit. Ideogram: workman's square and forearm, combining craft and strength.
4.IT **Wise achievement indeed**.
5.IT **Going possesses achievement**

indeed.
7.3b The **great without achievement indeed.**
7.6b **Using correct achievement indeed.**
17.1a/1b **Emerging** from the **gate, mingling possesses achievement.**
17.4b **Brightness achieving indeed.**
29.3b **Completing without achieving indeed.**
29.IT **Movement possesses honor. Going possesses achievement indeed.**
32.6b The **great without achievement indeed.**
39.IT **Going possesses achievement indeed.**
40.IT **Going possesses achievement indeed.**
48.IT **Not-yet possessing achievement indeed.**
53.IT **Going possesses achievement indeed.**
57.4b **Possessing achievement indeed.**
59.IT **Riding wood possesses achievement indeed.**

Acquiesce, *SHOU*: accept, make peace with, agree to, receive; at rest, satisfied; patient.
See also: **To anterior acquiescence belongs the use of**
6.6b **Using arguing acquiesces** in **submitting.**
31.PW A **jun zi uses emptiness** to **acquiesce** the **people.**
35.1b **Not-yet acquiescing** in **fate indeed.**
35.2a/2b **Acquiescing** in a **compact cuirass: blessing.**
47.5b **Acquiescing** in **blessing indeed.**
48.3a **Together acquiescing** in **one's blessing.**
48.3b **Acquiescing** in **blessing indeed.**
63.5a/5b **Substance: acquiescing** in **one's blessing.**

Acquire, *DE*: obtain the desired object; possession; satisfied, fulfilled; it is permitted; agree with; wish for, desire covetously. Ideogram: go and obstacle, going through obstacles to the goal.
2.IM **Beforehand delusion, afterwards acquiring.**
2.IM/IT **Western South: acquiring partnering.**
2.IT **Afterwards yielding: acquiring constancy.**
3.1b The **great acquires** the **commoners indeed.**
6.IT The **solid comes and-also acquires** the **center indeed.**
9.IT The **supple acquires** the **position and-also above** and **below correspond** to **it.**
11.2a **Acquiring honor tending-towards** the **center: movement.**
11.2b **Enwrapped** in **wasteland, acquiring honor tending-towards** the **center: movement.**
13.6b **Purpose not-yet acquired indeed.**
13.IT The **supple acquires** the **position, acquires** the **center and-also** the **correspondence reaches energy.**
14.IT The **supple acquires** the **noble position:** the **great** in the **center.**
15.2b In the **center** the **heart acquiring indeed.**
15.6b **Purpose not-yet acquired indeed.**
16.4a The **great possesses acquiring.**
16.4b **Antecedent providing,** the **great possesses acquiring.**
17.3a **Following possesses seeking** and **acquiring.**
18.2b **Acquiring** the **center: dao indeed.**
18.4b **Going, not-yet acquiring indeed.**
21.4a **Acquiring** a **metallic arrow.**
21.5a **Acquiring yellow metal.**
21.5b **Acquiring: appropriate indeed.**
21.IT The **supple acquires** the **center and-also above moves.**
22.6b **Above acquiring purpose indeed.**
23.6a/6b A **jun zi acquires** a **cart.**
25.1b **Acquiring purpose indeed.**
25.3a To **moving people belongs acquiring.**

25.3b Moving people acquire cattle.
28.2a A venerable husband acquires his woman consort.
28.5a A venerable wife acquires her scholarly husband.
29.2a/2b Seeking the small: acquiring.
29.6a Three year's-time, not acquiring.
30.2b Acquiring the center: dao indeed.
32.4b Peacefully acquiring wildfowl indeed.
32.IT Sun and moon: acquiring heaven and-also enabling lasting and illuminating.
35.5a/5b Letting-go, acquiring: no cares.
36.3a Acquiring one's great's head.
36.3b Thereupon acquiring the great indeed.
38.IT Acquiring the center and-also correspondence reaching the solid.
39.IT Going acquires the center indeed.
40.2a Acquiring a yellow arrow.
40.2b Acquiring the center: dao indeed.
40.IT Going acquires crowds indeed.
40.IT Thereupon acquiring the center indeed.
41.3a By consequence acquiring one's friend.
41.6a Acquiring a servant without a household.
41.6b The great acquires purpose indeed.
42.5b The great acquires purpose indeed.
43.2b Acquiring the center, dao indeed.
46.5b The great acquires purpose indeed.
47.5b Purpose not-yet acquired indeed.
48.IM Without losing, without acquiring.
49.IT Their purposes not reciprocally acquired: named skinning.
50.1a Acquiring a concubine, using one's son.
50.IT Acquires the center and-also the correspondence reaches the solid.
51.2a The seventh day acquiring.
51.6b The center not-yet acquired indeed.
53.4a/4b Maybe acquiring one's rafter.
53.5b Acquiring the place desired indeed.
53.IT Advancing acquires the position.
53.IT One's position: the solid acquires the center indeed.
55.PS Acquiring one's place for converting implies necessarily the great.
55.2a Going acquires doubt, affliction.
56.2a/2b Acquiring a youthful vassal, Trial.
56.4a Acquiring one's own emblem-ax.
56.4b Not-yet acquiring the position indeed.
56.4b Acquiring one's own emblem-ax.
56.IT The supple acquires the center reaching outside and-also yielding reaches the solid.
57.2b Acquiring the center indeed.
59.2b Acquiring the desired indeed.
59.IT The supple acquires the position reaching outside and-also above concording.
60.IT Solid and supple apportioned and-also the solid acquiring the center.
61.3a Acquiring antagonist.
61.IT The supple located inside and-also the solid acquires the center.
62.IT The supple acquires the center.
63.2a/2b The seventh day acquiring.
63.IT The supple acquires the center indeed.
64.IT The supple acquires the center indeed.

Activate, *WEI*: act or cause to act; do, make, manage, make active; be, become; attend to, help; because of.

1.7b **Heavenly actualizing-dao not permitting activating** the **head indeed**.
4.6a **Not Harvesting: activating illegality**.
10.3a/3b **Martial people activate tending-towards** a **great chief**.
13.IT **Verily** a **jun zi activating enables interpenetration** of **purposes belonging** to **below heaven**.
25.IT **And-also activates** a **lord with-respect-to** the **inside**.
41.2b In the **center using activating purpose indeed**.
42.1a **Harvesting: availing** of **activating** the **great, arousing**.
42.4a **Harvesting: availing** of **activating depends** on **shifting** the **city**.
43.1a **Going, not mastering: activating fault**.
45.1a **Like** an **outcry, one handful activates laughter**.
48.3a **Activating my heart**'s **ache**.
49.1b **Not permitted** to **use possessing activity indeed**.
50.5b The **center uses activating substance indeed**.
51.IT **Using activating** the **offering lord indeed**.
53.6a **Its feathers permit availing** of **activating** the **fundamentals**.
53.6b **Its feathers permit availing** of **activating** the **fundamentals, significant**.

Actualize-dao, *DE*: realize dao in action; power, virtue; ability to follow the course traced by the ongoing process of the cosmos. Ideogram: go, straight, and heart. Linked with acquire, *DE*: acquiring that which makes a being become what it is meant to be.

1.2b **Actualizing-dao spreading throughout indeed**.
1.7b **Heavenly actualizing-dao not permitting activating** the **head indeed**.
2.PW A **jun zi uses munificent actualizing-dao** to **carry** the **beings**.
2.IT **Actualizing-dao unites without delimiting**.
4.PW A **jun zi uses** the **fruits** of **movement** to **nurture actualizing-dao**.
6.3a/3b **Taking-in** the **ancients' actualizing-dao**.
9.PW A **jun zi uses highlighting** the **pattern** to **actualize-dao**.
9.6a **Honoring actualizing-dao: carrying**.
9.6b **Actualizing-dao amassing: carrying indeed**.
10.AT **Treading: foundation belonging** to **actualizing-dao indeed**.
12.PW A **jun zi uses parsimonious actualizing-dao** to **expel heaviness**.
14.IT **One's actualizing-dao: solid persisting and-also pattern brightening**.
15.AT **Humbling**: the **handle belonging** to **actualizing-dao indeed**.
16.PW The **earlier kings used arousing delight** to **extol actualizing-dao**.
18.PW A **jun zi uses rousing** the **commoners** to **nurture actualizing-dao**.
18.5b **Receiving uses actualizing-dao indeed**.
24.AT **Return**: the **base belonging** to **actualizing-dao indeed**.
26.PW And **uses accumulating one's actualizing-dao**.
26.IT The **day renewing one's actualizing-dao**.
29.PW A **jun zi uses constancy** in **actualizing-dao** to **move**.
32.AT **Persevering: firmness belonging** to **actualizing-dao indeed**.
32.AT **Persevering: using** the **one actualizing-dao**.
32.3a/3b **Not persevering** in **one's actualizing-dao**.
32.5a **Persevering** in **one's actualizing-dao, Trial**.
35.PW A **jun zi uses originating**

enlightening to brighten actualizing-dao.

39.PW A jun zi uses reversing individuality to renovate actualizing-dao.

41.AT Diminishing: adjustment belonging to actualizing-dao indeed.

42.AT Augmenting: enriching belonging to actualizing-dao indeed.

42.5a Possessing conformity, benevolence: my actualizing-dao.

42.5b Benevolence: my actualizing-dao.

43.PW And residing in actualizing-dao, by consequence keeping-aloof.

46.PW A jun zi uses yielding to actualizing-dao.

47.AT Confining: marking-off belonging to actualizing-dao indeed.

48.AT The well: actualizing-dao belonging to earth indeed.

53.PW A jun zi uses residing in eminent actualizing-dao to improve the customs.

57.AT The root: paring belonging to actualizing-dao indeed.

60.PW And deliberating actualizing-dao in movement.

Actually, YI: truly, really, at present. Ideogram: a dart and done, strong intention fully expressed.

5.IT One's righteousness not confined nor exhausted actually.

7.IT Actually permitted using kinghood.

7.IT Significant, furthermore is it actually faulty?

16.IT The season belonging to providing righteously great actually in-fact.

17.IT To following's season belongs the righteously great actually in-fact.

20.IT And-also below heaven submits actually.

23.PS Involved in embellishing, therefore afterwards Growing, by consequence used-up actually.

25.PS Returning, by consequence not entangled actually.

25.IT Is it actually?

25.IT Moving actually in-fact.

27.IT The season belonging to the jaws great actually in-fact.

28.IT The season belonging to the great exceeding great actually in-fact.

29.IT The season belonging to venturing avails of the great actually in-fact.

31.IT And-also the motives belonging to heaven and earth's myriad beings permit viewing actually.

32.IT And-also the motives belonging to heaven and earth's myriad beings permit viewing actually.

33.IT The season belonging to retiring righteously great actually in-fact.

34.IT The correct great and-also the motives belonging to heaven and earth permit viewing actually.

38.IT The season belonging to polarizing avails of the great actually in-fact.

39.IT Knowing actually in-fact.

39.IT The season belonging to limping avails of the great actually in-fact.

40.IT The season belonging to loosening great actually in-fact.

42.5b No questioning it actually.

44.IT The season belonging to coupling righteously great actually in-fact.

45.IT And-also the motives belonging to heaven and earth's myriad beings permit viewing actually.

49.3b Furthermore is it actually?

49.IT The season belonging to skinning great actually in-fact.

56.3b Truly using injury actually.

56.IT The season belonging to sojourning righteously great actually in-fact.

58.IT The commoners encouraged actually in-fact.

Add, *ER*: join to something previous; reiterate, repeat; second, double; assistant.

29.4a/4b A **cup** of **liquor**, a **platter added**.

Adhere, *CONG*: follow, agree with, comply with, obey; join a doctrine, school, or person; servant, follower. Ideogram: two men walking, one following the other.

2.3a/3b **Maybe adhering** to **kingly affairs**.

3.3b **Using adhering** to **wildfowl indeed**.

6.3a **Maybe adhering** to **kingly affairs**.

6.3b **Adhering** to the **above**, **significant indeed**.

7.IT **And-also** the **commoners adhere** to **it**.

8.4b **Using adhering** to the **above indeed**.

8.IT **Below yielding**, **adhering indeed**.

17.1b **Adhering** to **correctness**, **significant indeed**.

17.6a **Thereupon adhering**: **holding-fast** to **it**.

24.4b **Using adhering** to **dao indeed**.

27.5b **Yielding uses adhering** to the **above indeed**.

31.4a **Partners adhere** to **simply pondering**.

32.5b **Adhering** to the **one and-also completing indeed**.

32.5b **Adhering** to the **wife**, **pitfall indeed**.

39.6b **Using adhering** to **value indeed**.

42.4a/4b **Notifying** the **prince**, **adhering**.

49.6b **Yielding uses adhering** to a **chief indeed**.

50.1b **Using adhering** to **value indeed**.

62.3a/3b **Adhering maybe kills it**.

Adjoin, *FU*: next to, lean on; join; near, approaching.

23.PW **Mountain adjoining with-respect-to earth**. **Stripping**.

Adjust, *XIU*: regulate, repair, clean up, renovate.

24.1b **Using adjusting individuality indeed**.

41.AT **Diminishing**: **adjustment belonging** to **actualizing-dao indeed**.

48.4b **Adjusting** the **well indeed**.

51.PW A **jun zi uses anxiety** and **fear** to **adjust inspections**.

Admonish, *JIE*: warn, scold; precept, order, prohibition. Ideogram: words and warning.

8.5a/5b The **capital's people not admonished**.

Adorn, *BI*: embellish, ornament, deck out, beautify; variegated (flowers); magnificent, elegant, brilliant; also: energetic, passionate, eager, capable of great effort; brave. Ideogram: cowry shells (money) and flowers, linking ornaments and value.

This term is the name of hexagram 22 and recurs throughout its texts. It also occurs in:

21.HP **Adorning**: **without complexion indeed**.

Advance, *JIN*: move forward, progress, climb; promote or be promoted; further the development of, augment; offer, introduce.

1.4b **Advancing**: **without fault indeed**.

5/6.HP **Attending**: **not advancing indeed**.

20.3a/3b **Overseeing my generation**: **advancing**, **withdrawing**.

35.PS **Prospering implies advancing indeed**.

35.IT **Prospering**. **Advancing indeed**.

35.IT The **supple advances and-also moves above**.

36.PS **Advancing necessarily possesses** a **place** for **injury**.

38.IT The **supple advances and-also moves above**.

42.IT The **sun advances without delimiting**.

50.IT The **supple advances and-also moves above**.

53.PS **Infiltrating implies advancing indeed.**
53.IT To **infiltrating belongs advancing indeed.**
53.IT **Advancing acquires** the **position.**
53.IT **Advancing uses correcting.**
54.PS **Advancing necessarily possesses** a **place** for **converting.**
57.1a/1b **Advancing, withdrawing.**

Adversity, *LI*: danger, hardship, severe; threat or difficulty that must be encountered, rather than avoided; grinding stone; polish, sharpen; a challenge that strengthens and perfects the character; stimulate, excite; cruel demon.
1.3a At **nightfall awe like** in **adversity.**
6.3a **Adversity: completing, significant.**
9.6a The **wife's Trial: adversity.**
10.5a/5b **Parting, treading. Trial, adversity.**
18.1a **Adversity's completion, significant.**
21.5a **Trial, adversity.**
21.5b **Trial, adversity without fault.**
24.3a **Imminent return. Adversity.**
24.3b To **imminent return belongs adversity.**
26.1a **Possessing adversity.**
26.1b **Possessing adversity, Harvesting, climaxing.**
27.6a **Adversity, significant.**
27.6b **Antecedent jaws, adversity, significant.**
33.1a **Retiring's tail, adversity.**
33.1b To **retiring's tail belongs adversity.**
33.3a **Tied retiring. Possessing affliction, adversity.**
33.3b To **tied retiring belongs adversity.**
34.3a **Trial, adversity.**
35.4a **Trial, adversity.**
35.4b **Bushy-tailed rodents: Trial, adversity.**
35.6a **Adversity, significant.**
37.3a **Repenting, adversity, significant.**
38.4a **Adversity, without fault.**
43.IM/ IT **Conformity crying-out possesses adversity.**
44.3a **Adversity.**
49.3a **Trial, adversity.**
51.2a/2b The **shake comes, adversity.**
51.5a/5b The **shake going** and **coming, adversity.**
52.3a **Adversity smothers** the **heart.**
53.1a The **small son, adversity.**
53.1b To the **small son belongs adversity.**
56.3a **Trial, adversity.**
58.5a **Possessing adversity.**
62.4a/4b **Going: adversity necessarily** a **warning.**
63.6a **Adversity.**
63.6b **Soaking one's head, adversity.**

Affairs, *SHI*: all kinds of personal activity; matters at hand; business; function, occupation; manage; perform a task; incident, event; case in court.
2.3a/3b **Maybe adhering** to **kingly affairs.**
6.PW A **jun zi uses arousing affairs** to **plan beginnings.**
6.1a/1b **Not** a **perpetual place, affairs.**
6.3a **Maybe adhering** to **kingly affairs.**
18.PS **Using joy** in **following people implies necessarily possessing affairs.**
18.PS **Decay implies affairs indeed.**
18.6a/6b **Not affairs,** a **king's feudatory.**
18.IT **Going possesses affairs indeed.**
19.PS **Possessing affairs and-also afterwards permitted** the **great.**
29.PW And **repetition** to **teach affairs.**
33.3b **Not permitted** the **great** in **affairs indeed.**
38.IM **Polarizing.** The **small's affairs, significant.**
38.IT **That uses** the **small's affairs, significant.**
38.IT **Heaven** and **earth: polarizing and-also their affairs concording indeed.**

38.IT The **myriad beings: polarizing and-also their affairs sorted indeed.**
41.1a/1b **Climaxing affairs, swiftly going.**
42.1b **Below not munificent affairs indeed.**
42.3a To **augmenting belongs availing** of **pitfall affairs.**
42.3b **Augmenting: availing** of **pitfall affairs.**
46.4b **Yielding affairs indeed.**
51.5a **Hundred-thousand without loss, possessing affairs.**
51.5b **One's affairs located** in the **center.**
55.3b **Not permitted** the **great** in **affairs indeed.**
57.PW A **jun zi uses assigning fate** to **move affairs.**
62.IM **Permitted** the **small** in **affairs.**
62.IM **Not permitted** the **great** in **affairs.**
62.IT **That uses** the **small** in **affairs, significant indeed.**
62.IT **That uses not permitting** the **great** in **affairs indeed.**

Affection, *AI*: love, show affection; benevolent feelings; kindness, regard.
37.5b **Mingling: reciprocal affection indeed.**

Affliction, *JI*: sickness, disorder, defect, calamity, injury; poison, hate, dislike; cruel, jealous, envious. Ideogram: sickness and dart, a sudden affliction.
16.5a **Trial, affliction.**
16.5b **Six** at **fifth: Trial, affliction.**
24.IM **Emerging, entering, without affliction.**
24.IT **That uses emerging, entering, without affliction.**
25.5a To **without entanglement belongs affliction.**
33.3a **Tied retiring. Possessing affliction, adversity.**
33.3b **Possessing affliction, weariness indeed.**
36.3a **Not permitted affliction, Trial.**
41.4a/4b **Diminishing one's affliction.**
50.2a/2b **My companion possesses affliction.**
55.2a **Going acquires doubt, affliction.**
58.4a The **cuirass' affliction possesses joy.**

Affluence, *FU*: rich, abundant; wealth; enrich, provide for; flow toward, accrue.
9.5a **Affluence: using one's neighbor.**
9.5b **Not solitary affluence indeed.**
11.4a **Not affluence: using one's neighbor.**
11.4b **Fluttering, fluttering, not affluence.**
15.5a **Not affluence: using one's neighbor.**
25.2b **Not tilling** the **crop. Not-yet affluence indeed.**
37.4a/4b **Affluent household:** the **great, significant.**
46.6b **Dissolving, not affluence indeed.**

Afoot, *TU*: travel on foot; footman, foot-soldier; follower, disciple; ruffian, bond-servant; empty, alone.
22.1a/1b **Stowing** the **chariot and-also afoot.**

After(wards)/later, *HOU*: come after in time, subsequent; put oneself after; behind, back, draw back; the second; attendants, heirs, successors, posterity.
This term occurs throughout the hexagram texts.

Age, *SHI*: an age, an epoch, a generation; the world, mankind; time as 'in the time of'.
28.PW And **retiring** from the **age without melancholy.**

Agencies, *QI*: fluid energy, breath, air; configurative power, vital force; interacts with essence, *JING*, to produce things and beings. Ideogram: vapor and rice, heat and moisture producing substance.
31.IT The **two agencies' influences correspond using reciprocal association.**

Aggression, *GONG*: assault, attack; apply to; criticize; stimulate the vital power; urgent desire. Ideogram: toil and strike.

13.4a **Nowhere controlling aggression.**

Alliance, see **Matrimonial alliance**

Almost/hint, *JI*: nearly, about to; subtle; barely perceptible first sign.

3.3a A **jun zi: hint not thus stowed** away.

9.6a The **moon almost full.**

54.5a The **moon almost full, significant.**

61.4a The **moon almost full.**

Alone, *GU*: solitary; without a protector; fatherless, orphan-like; unique, exceptional.

See also: **Live-alone**

38.4a/6a **Polarizing alone.**

Aloof, see **Keep-aloof**

Already, *JI*: completed, done, occurred, finished; past tense; shortly after.

This term occurs in the name of hexagram 63 and recurs throughout its texts. It also occurs in:

9.6a/6b **Already rain, already abiding.**

19.3a/3b **Already grieving** over **it.**

29.5a **Merely already evened.**

Altar, see **Field-altar**

Although, *SUI*: even though, supposing that, if, even if.

3.1b **Although** a **stone pillar, purpose moving correctly indeed.**

5.2b **Although** the **small possesses words, using completing significant indeed.**

5.6b **Although not** an **appropriate position, not-yet** the **great letting-go indeed.**

6.1b **Although** the **small possesses words, one's differentiation brightening indeed.**

21.IT **Although not** an **appropriate position, Harvesting avails** of **litigating indeed.**

31.2b **Although** a **pitfall, residing significant.**

47.4b **Although not** an **appropriate position, possessing associates indeed.**

51.6b **Although** a **pitfall, without fault.**

55.1a/1b **Although** a **decade, without fault.**

64.IT **Although not** in **appropriate positions, solid** and **supple correspond indeed.**

Altogether, *JIE*: all, the whole; the same sort, alike; entirely.

11.4b **Altogether letting-go** the **substance indeed.**

32.IT **Solid** and **supple altogether corresponding. Persevering.**

40.IT **Thunder** and **rain arousing and-also** the **hundred fruits, grasses, trees, altogether seedburst**'s **boundary.**

55.PW **Thunder** and **lightning altogether culminating. Abounding.**

57.IT The **supple altogether yielding reaches** the **solid.**

Amass, *JI*: hoard, accumulate, pile up, add up, increase; repeated action, habit; follow, pursue.

9.6b **Actualizing-dao amassing: carrying indeed.**

14.2b **Amassing** in the **center, not destroying indeed.**

46.PW And **amassing** the **small** to **use** the **high great.**

Amble, *XU*: walk quietly and carefully, leisurely, tardy, slow; composed, dignified.

47.4a/4b **Coming: ambling, ambling.**

47.5a/5b **Thereupon ambling possesses stimulating.**

Amend, *GAI*: correct, reform, renew, alter, mend. Ideogram: self and strike, fighting one's own errors.

42.PW And **possessing excess**, by **consequence amending.**

48.IM The **well. Amending** the **capital, not amending** the **well.**

48.IT **Amending** the **capital, not amending** the **well.**

49.4a **Amending fate, significant.**

49.4b To **amending fate belongs significance.**

Ancestry, *ZONG*: clan, kin, origin; those who bear the same surname; ancestral hall and tablets; honor, revere.

13.2a/2b **Concording people tend-towards** the **ancestors**.
38.5a/5b **Your ancestor gnawing flesh**.
51.IT **Emerging permits using guarding** the **ancestral temple**, the **field-altar**, the **offertory-millet**.
63.3a The **High Ancestor subjugates souls** on all **sides**.

Ancient, *JIU*: of old, long before; worn out, spoiled; defunct.
6.3a/3b **Taking-in** the **ancients' actualizing-dao**.
48.1a/1b The **ancient well without wildfowl**.

And-also, *ER*: joins and contrasts two terms.
This term occurs throughout the hexagram texts.

Anger, *FEN*: resentment; cross, wrathful; irritated at, indignant. Ideogram: heart and divide, the heart dividing people.
41.PW A **jun zi uses curbing anger** and **blocking appetites**.

Antagonistic, *DI*: opposed and equal; competitor, enemy; a contest between equals.
13.3b **Antagonistic solid indeed**.
52.IT **Above** and **below**: **antagonistic correspondence**.
61.3a **Acquiring antagonist**.

Antecedent, *YOU*: come before as origin and cause; through, by, from; depend on; enter by way of.
16.4a **Antecedent providing**.
16.4b **Antecedent providing**, the **great possesses acquiring**.
27.6a **Antecedent jaws**.
27.6b **Antecedent jaws, adversity, significant**.

Anterior, *GU*: come before as cause; former, ancient; reason, purpose, intention; grievance, dissatisfaction, sorrow, resulting from previous causes and intentions; situation leading to a divination.
16.IT To **anterior heaven** and **earth** it **thus belongs**.
16.IT **Anterior sun** and **moon not exceeding**.
17/18.HP **Following: without anteriority indeed**.
22.IT **Anterior Growing**.
22.IT The **anterior small**.
30.IT **Anterior Growing**.
34.IT The **solid uses stirring-up. Anterior vigor**.
39.2a **In-no-way** to the **body belongs anteriority**.
45.IT **Anterior assembling indeed**.
49/50.HP **Skinning: departing anteriority indeed**.
55/56.HP **Abounding: numerous anteriority indeed**.
55.IT **Brightness uses stirring-up. Anterior abounding**.

To anterior acquiescence belongs the use of, *GU SHOU ZHI YI*: understanding and accepting the preceding statement allows the consultant to make proper use of this hexagram.
This sentence occurs in the Preceding Situation section of hexagrams 3-64.

Anxiety, *KONG*: apprehensive, alarmed, agitated; suspicious of. Ideogram: heart and sick, agitated within.
51.PW A **jun zi uses anxiety** and **fear** to **adjust inspections**.
51.1b/ IT **Anxiety involves blessing indeed**.

Appetites, *YU*: drives, instinctive cravings; wishes, passions, desires, aspirations; long for, seek ardently, covet.
27.4a **Its appetites: pursuing, pursuing**.
41.PW A **jun zi uses curbing anger** and **blocking appetites**.

Apportion, *FEN*: divide, distribute, distinguish, sort out; part, element.
21.IT **Solid** and **supple apportioned**.
22.IT **Apportioning** the **solid above and-also patterning** the **supple**.
60.IT **Solid** and **supple apportioned and-also** the **solid acquiring** the **center**.

Apprehensive, *CHOU*: worried, anxious, anticipating adversity, afraid of what approaches; sadness, melancholy. Ideogram: heart and autumn, dreading

the coming winter.
35.2a **Prospering thus, apprehensive thus.**

Approach, *JI*: come near to, advance toward, reach; nearby; soon, immediately.
3.3a/3b **Approaching** a **stag: lacking precaution.**
6.4a/4b **Returning, approaching fate.**
43.IM/ IT **Not Harvesting: approaching weapons.**
50.2a **Not me able** to **approach.**
56.2a **Sojourning: approaching** a **camp.**

Appropriate, *DANG*: suitable, capable, worthy, adequate, competent, equal to; opportune, convenient; whole lines in odd places and opened lines in even places.
This term occurs throughout the hexagram texts.

Apron, *SHANG*: ceremonial garment; skirt, clothes; curtains of a carriage. Ideogram: garment and manifest, clothing as display.
2.5a/5b A **yellow apron. Spring, significant.**

Argue, *SONG*: dispute, plead in court, contend before a ruler, demand justice; wrangle, quarrel, litigation. Ideogram: words and public, public disputation.
This term is the name of hexagram 6 and recurs throughout its texts. It also occurs in:
5.HP **Arguing: not connecting indeed.**

Arm, *GONG*: the arm as body's instrument; staunch supporter; officer, minister of state.
55.3a/3b **Severing one's right arm.**

Arouse, *ZUO*: stimulate, stir up from inactivity; arise, appear; generate; begin, invent, make. Ideogram: person and beginning.
See also: **Rouse**
6.PW A **jun zi uses arousing affairs** to **plan beginnings.**
16.PW The **earlier kings used arousing delight** to **extol actualizing-dao.**
30.PW **Brightness doubled arouses** the **radiance.**
40.PW **Thunder** and **rain arousing. Unraveling.**
40.IT **Heaven** and **earth unraveling and-also thunder** and **rain arousing.**
40.IT **Thunder** and **rain arousing and-also** the **hundred fruits, grasses, trees, altogether seedburst**'s **boundary.**
42.1a **Harvesting: availing** of **activating** the **great, arousing.**

Array, *BAN*: classify and display; arrange according to rank; assign to a group, as soldiers to their units. Ideogram: knife between two gems, separating values.
3.2a/4a/6a **Riding** a **horse, arraying thus.**

Arrest, *CUI*: stop, drive back, repress; break, destroy, humiliate; force obedience, overpower.
35.1a/1b **Prospering thus, arresting thus.**

Arrow, *SHI*: arrow, javelin, dart; swift, direct as an arrow.
See also: **String-arrow**
21.4a **Acquiring** a **metallic arrow.**
40.2a **Acquiring** a **yellow arrow.**
56.5a **One arrow extinguishing.**

Articulate, *JIE*: joint, articulation; a separation which simultaneously establishes the identity of the parts and their connection; express thought through speech; section, chapter, interval; temperance, virtue; rite, ceremony; lit.: nodes of bamboo stalks.
This term is the name of hexagram 60 and recurs throughout its texts. It also occurs in:
4.2b **Solid** and **supple articulated indeed.**
27.PW And **articulation** in **drinking** and **taking-in.**
37.3b **Letting-go** the **household**'s **articulation indeed.**
39.5b **Using** the **center articulating indeed.**
50.6b **Solid** and **supple articulated indeed.**
59.HP **Articulating: stopping indeed.**

61.PS **Articulating and-also trusting it.**

64.6b **Truly not knowing articulation indeed.**

Ascend, *SHENG*: rise, augment, grow; climb step by step; rise in office; advance through effort; offer a sacrifice; lit.: a measure for fermented liquor, ascension as distillation.

This term is the name of hexagram 46 and recurs throughout its texts. It also occurs in:

13.3a **Ascending one's high mound.**

29.IT **Heaven's venture: not permitting ascending indeed.**

45.HP **ascending: not coming indeed.**

47.PS **Ascending and-also not climaxing necessarily confines.**

Assail, *TU*: rush against; abrupt attack, suddenly stricken; insolent, offensive.

30.4a/4b **Assailing thus, its coming thus.**

Assemble, *JU*: gather, bring together, collect, amass; call to assembly; dwell together, converge; meeting place, dwelling place. Ideogram: three (meaning many) people.

45.PS **Beings reciprocally meeting and-also afterwards assembling.**

45.PS **Clustering implies assembling indeed.**

45/46.HP **Clustering: assembling, and-also**

45.IT **Clustering. Assembling indeed.**

45.IT **Anterior assembling indeed.**

45.IT **Assembling uses correctness indeed.**

45.IT **Overseeing one's place** to **assemble.**

46.PS **Assembling and-also** the **above implies** the **designation belonging** to **ascending.**

Assign, *SHEN*: give out, allot, distribute; spread, scatter, diffuse.

57.PW A **jun zi uses assigning fate** to **move affairs.**

57.IT **Redoubled root uses assigning fate.**

Associate, *YU*: consort with, combine; companions; group, band, company; agree with, comply, help; in favor of. Ideogram: a pair of hands reaching downward meets a pair of hands reaching upward, helpful association.

2.IT **Thereupon associating: sorting movement.**

6.PW **Heaven associated** with **stream: contradicting movements. Arguing.**

10.3b **Not** the **stand** to **use associating** with **movement indeed.**

13.PW **Heaven associated** with **fire. Concording people.**

14.PS **Associating** with **people concording implies beings necessarily converting in-truth.**

17.2b **Nowhere joining** in **association indeed.**

19/20.HP **Maybe associating, maybe seeking.**

22.2b **Associating above, rising indeed.**

23.2b **Not-yet possessing association indeed.**

25.PW **Below heaven thunder moves. Beings associate without entanglement.**

28.2b **Exceeding uses reciprocal association indeed.**

31.IT The **two agencies' influences correspond using reciprocal association.**

32.IT **Thunder** and **wind reciprocally associating.**

33.IT **Associating** with the **season's movement indeed.**

41.IT **Associating** with the **season, accompanying** the **movement.**

42.IT **Associating** with the **season, accompanying** the **movement.**

44.IT **Not permitted association long-living indeed.**

47.4b **Although not** an **appropriate position, possessing associates indeed.**

48.2b **Without associates indeed.**

52.IT **Not reciprocally associating indeed.**

55.IT **Associating** with the **season's**

dissolving pause.

56.3b **Using sojourning** to **associate below.**

61.2a **Myself associating: simply spilling it.**

62.IT **Associating** with the **season**'s **movement indeed.**

Attach, *XI*: fasten to, bind, tie; retain, continue; keep in mind; emotional bond.

12.5a **Attachment tending-towards** a **grove** of **mulberry-trees.**

25.3a **Maybe** to **attaching belongs cattle.**

44.1a/1b **Attachment tending-towards** a **metallic chock.**

Attend, *XU*: wait, await, wait on; hesitation, delay, doubt; take care of, turn one's mind to; need, require, necessity; obstinate, fixed on. Ideogram: rain and stopped, compelled to wait, or rain and origin, providing what is needed.

This term is the name of hexagram 5 and recurs throughout its texts. It also occurs in:

6.HP **Attending: not advancing indeed.**

Attribute, *LIE*: align, arrange in order; assign, place according to rank; distinguish, separate; obstacle, block.

52.3a **Attributed** to **one's loins.**

Augment, *YI*: increase, advance, promote, enrich, benefit, strengthen; pour in more; superabundant; excessive. Ideogram: water and vessel, pouring in more.

This term is the name of hexagram 42 and recurs throughout its texts. It also occurs in:

15.PW A **jun zi uses reducing** the **numerous** to **augment** the **few.**

15.IT **Heavenly dao lessens overfilling and-also augments humbling.**

41.HP **Diminishing, augmenting.**

41.2a **Nowhere diminishing, augmenting it.**

41.5a **Maybe** to **augmenting belongs ten.**

41.6a/6b **Nowhere diminishing, augmenting it.**

41.IT **Diminishing below, augmenting above.**

41.IT **Diminishing** the **solid, augmenting** the **supple possesses** the **season.**

41.IT **Diminishing, augmenting: overfilling emptiness.**

43.PS **Augmenting and-also not climaxing necessarily breaks-up.**

Augury, *ZHAN*: sign, omen; divine by casting lots; look at as a sign or augury.

49.5a **Not-yet** an **augury, possessing conformity.**

Auspicious, *XIANG*: auspices of good luck and prosperity; sign, omen (good or bad).

10.6a **Observing treading: predecessors auspicious.**

47.3b **Not auspicious indeed.**

Avail, *YONG*: use, employ for a specific purpose; take advantage of; benefit from; capacity. Ideogram: to divine and center, applying divination to central concerns.

This term occurs throughout the hexagram texts.

Await, *DAI*: expect, wait for, prepare to meet (friendly or hostile); provide against.

16.AT **Used** to **await violent visitors.**

39.1b **Proper** to **await indeed.**

53/54.HP **Infiltrating: womanhood converting awaits manhood moving indeed.**

54.4b **Possessing awaiting and-also moving indeed.**

Awe, *TI*: respect, regard, fear; alarmed and cautious, worried; on guard. Ideogram: heart and versatility, the heart expecting change.

1.3a At **nightfall awe like** in **adversity.**

6.IM **Blocking awe.**

6.IT **Blocking awe**: the **center, significant.**

9.4a **Blood departing, awe emerging.**

9.4b **Possessing conformity, awe emerging.**

43.2a **Awe**: an **outcry, absolutely-nothing**.

Ax, see **Emblem-ax**

Axle-bearing, *FU*: device that fastens the body of a cart to axle and wheels.

26.2a/2b **Carting**: **stimulating** the **axle-bearing**.

34.4a **Vigor tends-towards** the **great**: to a **cart belong axle-bearings**.

Back, *BEI*: spine; behind, rear, hidden; turn the back on; North side; oppose, disobey, reject. Ideogram: North and body (facing South).

52.IM The **bound**: **one's back**.

Bag, *NANG*: sack, purse, put in a bag; property, salary.

2.4a **Bundled** in the **bag**.

2.4b **Bundled** in the **bag, without fault**.

Bar, *BI*: close a door, stop up a hole; obstruct, exclude, screen. Ideogram: door and hand, closing the door.

24.PW The **earlier kings used culminating sun** to **bar** the **passages**.

Bargain, *SHANG*: argue over prices; consult, deliberate, do business; traveling merchants; hour before sunrise and sunset. Ideogram: stutter and sentences, repetitive speaking.

24.PW **Bargaining sojourners** used culminating sun **not** to **move**.

58.4a **Bargaining open, not-yet soothing**.

Barrier, GAN: boundary, limit; fend off, protect; river bank; shield, defensive armor; the Ten Heavenly Barriers articulate the year in the Chinese calendar.

53.1a The **swan infiltrating tending-towards** the **barrier**.

Base, *BEN*: root, trunk; origin, cause, foundation. Ideogram: tree with roots in the earth.

24.AT **Return**: the **base belonging** to **actualizing-dao indeed**.

28.IT **Base** and **tip fading indeed**.

Basket, *KUANG*: open basket; put in a basket.

54.6a A **woman receives** a **basket without substance**.

54.6b **Receiving** an **empty basket indeed**.

Bass, *FU*: freshwater fish moving in pairs, mutually faithful.

48.2a/2b The **well**: a **gully, shooting bass**.

Bear, *FU*: carry on one's back; take on a responsibility; rely on, depend on; burden, duty; mathematical term for minus; defeated; guilty; betray, reject.

38.6a **Viewing** a **pig bearing mire**.

40.3a/3b **Bearing, moreover riding**.

Beater, *CHU*: servant who drives animals toward hunters; order people to their places; drive on, whip up, animate, exhort.

8.5a The **king avails** of **three beaters**.

Beautiful, *WEI*: elegant, classic, fine; luxuriant, lush.

49.6b **One's pattern beautiful indeed**.

Bed, *CHUANG*: sleeping place; couch, sofa, lounge; bench around a well.

23.1a/1b **Stripping** the **bed, using** the **stand**.

23.2a/2b **Stripping** the **bed, using marking-off**.

23.4a/4b **Stripping** the **bed, using** the **flesh**.

57.2a/6a/6b The **root located below** the **bed**.

Before(hand)/earlier, *XIAN*: anterior, preceding in time; former, past, previous; first, at first.

This term occurs throughout the hexagram texts.

Before-zenith sun, *SSU RI*: double hour from 9 to 11 a.m. and month of June, both symbolized by the serpent; about to, on the point of.

49.IM **Skinning. Before-zenith sun, thereupon conformity**.

49.2a **Before-zenith sun, thereupon skinning it**.

49.2b **Before-zenith sun skinning it**.

49.IT **Before-zenith sun, thereupon conformity.**

Begin, *SHI*: commence, start, open; earliest, first; generate. Ideogram: woman and eminent, eminent feminine function of giving birth.

1.IT The **myriad beings' own beginning.**
1.IT The **great brightening completes** the **beginning.**
2.1b **Yin beginning solidification indeed.**
3.PS **Sprouting implies** a **beginning belonging** to **beings' generation indeed.**
3.IT **Solid** and **supple begin** to **mingle and-also** in **heaviness generate.**
6.PW A **jun zi uses arousing affairs** to **plan beginnings.**
18.IT **Completing**, by **consequence possessing** a **beginning.**
32.1b **Beginning seeking depth indeed.**
32.IT **Completing**, by **consequence possessing beginning indeed.**
41.HP **Increasing**: the **beginning belonging** to **decreasing indeed.**
42.HP **Decreasing**: the **beginning belonging** to **increasing indeed.**
54.IT The **beginning** of **completion belonging** to a **person.**

Being, *WU*: creature, thing, any single being; matter, substance, essence; nature of things.

See also: **Beings not permitted (to use)**

1.IT The **myriad beings' own beginning.**
1.IT The **kinds** of **beings diffuse** in **forms.**
1.IT **Heads emerging** from the **multitude** of **beings.**
2.PW A **jun zi uses munificent actualizing-dao** to **carry** the **beings.**
2.IT The **myriad beings' own generation.**
2.IT **Space: munificent carrying** the **beings.**
2.IT The **kinds** of the **beings conjoining, Growing.**
3.PS **Therefore afterwards** the **myriad beings' generation in-truth.**
3.PS **Overfilling** the **interspace belonging** to **heaven** and **earth implies verily** the **myriad beings.**
3.PS **Sprouting implies** a **beginning belonging** to **beings' generation indeed.**
4.PS **Beings' generation necessarily enveloped.**
4.PS To **beings belongs immaturity indeed.**
5.PS **Being's immaturity not permitted not nourishing indeed.**
10.PS **Beings accumulate, therefore afterwards possess codes.**
11.IT By **consequence** of **that heaven** and **earth mingling and-also** the **myriad beings interpenetrating indeed.**
12.IT By **consequence** of **that heaven** and **earth not mingling and-also** the **myriad beings not interpenetrating indeed.**
13.PW A **jun zi uses sorting** the **clans** to **mark-off** the **beings.**
14.PS **Associating** with **people concording implies beings necessarily converting in-truth.**
15.PW And **evaluating** the **beings** to **even spreading.**
20.PS The **beings' great, therefore afterwards permitted overseeing.**
21.IT **Jaws' center possesses being.**
24.AT **Return**: the **small and-also marking-off with-respect-to beings.**
25.PW **Below heaven thunder moves. Beings associate without entanglement.**
25.PW The **earlier kings used** the **luxuriance suiting** the **season** to **nurture** the **myriad beings.**
27.PS **Beings accumulate, therefore afterwards permitted** to **nourish.**
27.IT **Heaven** and **earth nourish** the **myriad beings.**
31.PS **Therefore afterwards possessing** the **myriad beings.**
31.PS **Possessing** the **myriad beings.**
31.IT **Heaven** and **earth influence and-also** the **myriad beings**

change and **generate**.

31.IT **And-also** the **motives belonging** to **heaven** and **earth**'s **myriad beings permit viewing actually**.

32.IT **And-also** the **motives belonging** to **heaven** and **earth**'s **myriad beings permit viewing actually**.

37.PW A **jun zi uses words** to **possess beings and-also movement** to **possess perseverance**.

37.5a **Beings' care**, **significant**.

38.IT The **myriad beings**: **polarizing and-also their affairs sorted indeed**.

44.IT The **kinds** of **beings conjoin** in **composition indeed**.

45.PS **Beings reciprocally meeting and-also afterwards assembling**.

45.IT **And-also** the **motives belonging** to **heaven** and **earth**'s **myriad beings permit viewing actually**.

50.PS **Skinning beings implies absolutely-nothing like** a **vessel**.

54.IT **And-also** the **myriad beings not rising**.

63.PS **Beings possessing excess implies necessarily fording**.

64.PW A **jun zi uses considerately marking-off** the **beings residing** on all **sides**.

Beings not permitted (to use), *WU BU KE (YI)*: it is not possible; no one is allowed; it is not in the nature of things.

12.PS **Beings not permitted** to **use completing interpenetration**.

13.PS **Beings not permitted** to **use completing obstruction**.

22.PS **Beings not permitted** to **use unconsidered uniting and-also climaxing**.

24.PS **Beings not permitted** to **use completing using-up**.

29.PS **Beings not permitted** to **use completing exceeding**.

33.PS **Beings not permitted** to **use lasting residing** in **their place**.

34.PS **Beings not permitted** to **use completing retiring**.

35.PS **Beings not permitted** to **use completing vigor**.

40.PS **Beings not permitted** to **use completing heaviness**.

52.PS **Beings not permitted** to **use completing stirring-up**.

53.PS **Beings not permitted** to **use completing stopping**.

60.PS **Beings not permitted** to **use completing radiance**.

64.PS **Beings not permitted exhausting indeed**.

Belly, *FU*: abdomen, receptacle of vital breath; interior; carry on the breast; the left part of the belly is considered to be the seat of emotion.

36.4a/4b **Entering tending-towards** the **left** of the **belly**.

Belong/it, *ZHI*: establishes between two terms a connection similar to the Saxon genitive, in which the second term belongs to the first one; at the end of a sentence it refers to something previously mentioned or implied.

This term occurs throughout the hexagram texts.

Below, *XIA*: anything below, in all senses; lower, inner; lower trigram.

See also: **Below heaven**

This term frequently occurs in the Patterns of Wisdon and Image Tradition sections, referring to the upper trigram and lines. It also occurs at:

1.1b **Yang located below indeed**.

3.1b **Using valuing** the **below** and the **mean**.

4.6b **Above** and **below yielding indeed**.

6.2b **Origin below**, **arguing above**.

17.3b **Purpose**: **stowing** away the **below indeed**.

23.1b **Using submerging below indeed**.

23.3b **Letting-go above** and **below indeed**.

24.PS **Stripping exhausted above**, **reversing below**.

24.2b **Below using humanity indeed**.

28.1b The **supple located below indeed**.

28.4b **Not sagging, reaching** the **below indeed.**
29/30.HP The **radiance above and-also** the **gorge below indeed.**
31.PS **Therefore afterwards possessing above** and **below.**
31.PS **Possessing above** and **below.**
31.3b A **place** for **holding-on** to the **below indeed.**
42.1b **Below not munificent affairs indeed.**
47.4b **Purpose located below indeed.**
48.PS **Confining reaching above implies necessarily reversing** to the **below.**
48.1b **Below indeed.**
56.3b **Using sojourning** to **associate below.**
57.2a/6a/6b The **root located below** the **bed.**
62.IM **Not proper above, proper below.**

Below heaven, *TIAN XIA*: human world, between heaven and earth.
7.IT **Using** the **latter rules below heaven.**
12.IT **Above** and **below not mingling and-also below heaven without fiefdoms indeed.**
13.IT **Verily** a **jun zi activating enables interpenetration** of **purposes belonging** to **below heaven.**
17.IT **And-also below heaven following** the **season.**
18.IT **Decay: Spring, Growing, and-also below heaven regulated indeed.**
20.IT The **center's correctness uses overseeing below heaven.**
20.IT **And-also below heaven submits actually.**
22.IT **Using changes** to **accomplish below heaven.**
25.PW **Below heaven thunder moves. Beings associate without entanglement.**
30.IT **Thereupon changes accomplished below heaven.**
31.IT The **wise person influences people's heart and-also below heaven harmonizes evenness.**
32.IT The **wise person: lasting with-respect-to one's dao and-also below heaven changing** and **accomplishing.**
37.IT **Correct household and-also below heaven rectified.**
44.IT **Below heaven** the **great moves indeed.**
55.IT **Properly illuminating below heaven indeed.**

Belt, see **Pouched belt**

Bench, *JI*: low table used to lean on; side-table; stool or support.
59.2a/2b **Dispersing: fleeing one's bench.**

Benefits, *LU*: pay, salary, income; have the use of; goods received, revenues; official function.
12.PW And **not permitting splendor** in **using benefits.**
43.PW A **jun zi uses spreading benefits extending** to the **below.**

Benevolence, *HUI*: regard for others, humanity; fulfill social duties; unselfish, kind, merciful.
42.5a/5b **Possessing conformity**, a **benevolent heart.**
42.5a **Possessing conformity, benevolence: my actualizing-dao.**
42.5b **Benevolence: my actualizing-dao.**

Bestow, *XI*: grant, confer upon; reward, gift; tin, pewter. Ideogram: metal and change.
6.6a **Maybe** to **bestowing belongs** a **pouched belt.**
7.2a/2b The **king thrice bestows fate.**
35.IM **Prospering.** A **content feudatory avails** of **bestowing horses** to **enhance** the **multitudes.**
35.IT **That uses** a **content feudatory availing** of **bestowing horses** to **enhance** the **multitudes.**

Big-toe/thumb, *MU*: in the lower trigram, big-toe; in the upper trigram, thumb; the big-toe enables the foot to walk as the thumb enables the hand to grasp.

31.1a/1b **Conjunction** of **one's big-toes.**

40.4a/4b **Unraveling and-also** the **thumbs.**

Bin, *DOU*: measure and container for grain; wine cup; hold, contain.

55.2a/4a/4b The **sun** in the **center**: **viewing** a **bin**.

Bind, *LÜAN*: tie, connect; bent, contracted; interdependent, inseparable. Ideogram: hand and connect.

9.5a/5b **Possessing conformity, binding thus.**

61.5a/5b **Possessing conformity, binding thus.**

Bird, *NIAO*: all feathered animals; associated with the Fiery Moment.

56.6a A **bird burns its nest.**

62.IM To the **flying bird abandoning belongs** a **sound.**

62.1a/1b The **flying bird: using** a **pitfall.**

62.6a To the **flying bird**'s **radiance belongs** a **pitfall.**

62.IT **Possessing** the **symbol belonging** to the **flying bird in-truth.**

62.IT To the **flying bird abandoning belongs** a **sound.**

Bite, *HE*: close the jaws, bite through, crush between the teeth; unite, close. Ideogram: mouth and cover.

This term occurs in the name of hexagram 21 and recurs throughout its texts. It also occurs in:

22.HP **Gnawing** and **biting: taking-in indeed.**

Bitter, *KU*: one of the five tastes: sour, bitter, sweet, acrid and salty; unpleasant, troublesome; hardship, affliction; suffer, bear; take pains; urgent, pressing; dislike, hate; corresponding to the Fiery Moment.

60.IM/IT **Bitter articulating not permitting Trial.**

60.6a/6b **Bitter articulating: Trial, pitfall.**

Bless, *FU*: heavenly gifts and favor; happiness, prosperity; spiritual power and goodwill. Ideogram: spirit and plenty.

11.3a **Tending-towards taking-in possesses blessing.**

15.IT **Soul** and **spirit harm overfilling and-also bless humbling.**

35.2a/2b **Acquiescing** in a **compact cuirass: blessing.**

47.5b **Acquiescing** in **blessing indeed.**

48.3a **Together acquiescing** in **one's blessing.**

48.3b **Acquiescing** in **blessing indeed.**

51.1b/ IT **Anxiety involves blessing indeed.**

63.5a/5b **Substance: acquiescing** in **one's blessing.**

Block, *ZHI*: obstruct, close, restrain, fill up.

6.IM **Blocking awe.**

6.IT **Blocking awe**: the **center, significant.**

41.PW A **jun zi uses curbing anger** and **blocking appetites.**

Blood, *XUE*: blood, the Yin fluid that maintains life; money, property.

2.6a **Their blood indigo** and **yellow.**

3.6a/6b **Weeping, blood flowing thus.**

5.4a/4b **Attending tending-towards blood.**

9.4a **Blood departing, awe emerging.**

54.6a A **scholar disembowels** a **goat without blood.**

59.6a/6b **Dispersing one's blood.**

Blunder, *SHENG*: mistake due to ignorance or fault; contrasts with calamity, *ZAI*, disaster from without. Ideogram: eye and growth, a film clouding sight.

6.2a **Without blunder.**

24.6a **Possessing calamity** and **blunder.**

25.IM/IT **One's in-no-way correcting possesses blunder.**

25.6a **Moving possesses blunder.**

51.3a The **shake moving: without blunder.**

62.6a **That designates calamity** and **blunder.**

Body, *GONG*: physical being, power and self-expression; oneself; innate quality; distinct from individuality, *SHEN*, which includes the notion of lifespan.
4.3a **Not possessing body.**
39.2a **In-no-way** to the **body belongs anteriority.**
51.6a The **shake not tending-towards one's body.**
52.4b **Stopping relates** to the **body indeed.**
59.3a/3b **Dispersing one's body.**

Bog, *NI*: wet spongy soil; mire, slush, quicksand; unable to move.
5.3a/3b **Attending tending-towards** the **bogs.**
48.1a/1b The **well**: a **bog, not taking-in.**
51.4a/4b The **shake releases** the **bog.**

Bonds, *YUE*: tie; cords, ropes; contracts, treaties, legal and moral obligations; moderate, restrain; poor.
29.4a **Letting-in bonds originating** from the **window.**

Border, *JI*: boundary, frontier, line that joins and divides; meet, face to face. Ideogram: place and sacrifice, meeting point of the human and the spirit world.
11.3b **Heaven** and **earth**'s **border indeed.**
29.4b **Solid** and **supple**'s **border indeed.**
40.1b To **solid** and **supple belongs** a **border.**
55.6b The **heavenly border, hovering indeed.**

Bound, *GEN*: limit, frontier; obstacle that prevents from seeing further; stop; still, quiet, motionless; confine, enclose; mountain, sunset, beginning of winter; solid, steady, unshakable; straight, hard, adamant, obstinate.
This term is the name of hexagram 52 and recurs throughout its texts. It also occurs in:
51.HP The **bound**: **stopping indeed.**

Boundary, *JI*: border, limit, frontier.
40.IT **Thunder** and **rain arousing and-also** the **hundred fruits, grasses, trees, altogether seedburst**'s **boundary.**

Bow, *HU*: wooden bow; curved flag pole; curved, arched.
38.6a **Beforehand** to the **bow belongs stretching.**
38.6a **Afterwards** to the **bow belongs stimulating.**

Brace/jawbones, *FU*: braces of a cart; cheeks, maxillary bones; support, consolidate, strengthen, prop up; steady, firm, rigid; help, rescue.
8.IT **Grouping. Bracing indeed.**
11.PW And **braces** the **reciprocity properly belonging** to **heaven** and **earth.**
28.3b **Not permitted** to **use** the **possession** of **bracing indeed.**
31.6a/6b **Conjunction** of **one's jawbones, cheeks** and **tongue.**
52.5a/5b The **bound: one's jawbones.**

Break-up, *JUE*: streams diverging; open a passage for water; break through a dam; separate, break into parts; cut through; decide, pass sentence; absolutely, certainly. Ideogram: water and parting.
34.4a/4b The **hedge broken-up, not ruined.**
43.PS **Augmenting and-also not climaxing necessarily breaks-up.**
43.PS **Parting implies breaking-up indeed.**
43/44.HP **Parting: breaking-up indeed.**
43/44.HP The **solid breaks-up** the **supple indeed.**
43.IT **Parting. Breaking-up indeed.**
43.IT The **solid breaks-up** the **supple indeed.**
43.IT **Breaking-up and-also harmonizing.**
44.PS **Breaking-up necessarily possesses meeting.**

Brightness, *MING*: light, radiance, clarity; distinguish, discern, understand; light-giving aspect of fire, of heavenly bodies and of consciousness; brightness and fire are the Symbols of the trigram Radiance, LI.

This term occurs in the name of hexagram 36 and recurs throughout its texts. It also occurs in:

1.IT The **great brightening completes** the **beginning**.

3.4b **Brightness indeed**.

6.1b **Although** the **small possesses words, one's differentiation brightening indeed**.

10.3b **Not** the **stand** to **use possessing brightness indeed**.

10.IT **Shining brightness indeed**.

13.IT **Pattern**'s **brightness uses persistence**.

14.4b **Brightness differentiates clearly indeed**.

14.IT **One's actualizing-dao: solid persisting and-also pattern brightening**.

15.IT **Heavenly dao**: **below fording and-also shining brightness**.

17.4a **Possessing conformity, locating** in **dao, using brightness**.

17.4b **Brightness achieving indeed**.

21.PW The **earlier kings used brightness** in **flogging** to **enforce** the **laws**.

21.6b **Understanding not bright indeed**.

21.IT **Stirring-up and-also brightening**.

22.PW A **jun zi uses brightening** the **multitude** of **standards without daring** to **sever litigations**.

22.IT **Pattern**'s **brightness uses stopping**.

30.PW **Brightness doubled arouses** the **radiance**.

30.PW The **great** in the **person uses consecutive brightening** to **illuminate tending-towards** the **four sides**.

30.IT **Redoubled brightness uses congregating** to **reach correcting**.

35.HP **Brightness hidden: proscribed indeed**.

35.PW **Brightness emerging above** the **earth. Prospering**.

35.PW A **jun zi uses originating enlightening** to **brighten actualizing-dao**.

35.IT **Brightness emerging above** the **earth**.

35.IT **Yielding and-also congregating reaching** the **great**'s **brightness**.

38.IT **Stimulating and-also congregating reaching brightness**.

43.4b **Understanding not bright indeed**.

47.1b **Shady, not bright indeed**.

48.3a **Kingly brightness**.

48.3b **Seeking kingly brightness**.

49.PW A **jun zi uses regulating** the **calendar** to **brighten** the **seasons**.

49.IT **Pattern brightening uses stimulating**.

50.IT The **root and-also** the **ear** and the **eye**: **understanding bright**.

52.IT **One's dao**: **shining brightness**.

55.4b **Shade, not brightness indeed**.

55.IT **Brightness uses stirring-up. Anterior abounding**.

56.PW A **jun zi uses bright consideration availing** of **punishment and-also not detaining litigations**.

56.IT **Stopping and-also congregating reaches brightness**.

Brilliance, *HUI*: sunlight, sunbeam; bright, splendid.

64.5b **One's brilliance significant indeed**.

Buckle, *RAO*: bend, twist; distort, wrench out of shape; weak, fragile; flexible.

28.3a The **ridgepole buckling. Pitfall**.

28.3b To the **ridgepole buckling belongs** a **pitfall**.

Bulwark, *CHENG*: rampart, city wall; citadel, place walled for defense.

11.6a/6b The **bulwark returns tending-towards** the **moat**.

Bundle, *GUA*: enclose, envelop, tie up; embrace, include.

2.4a **Bundled** in the **bag**.

2.4b **Bundled** in the **bag, without fault**.

Burden, *DUO*: load of an animal. With the pronunciation *TA*: he, she, it; other, stranger, having a different intention. Ideogram: person and also.

61.1a **Possessing** a **burden, not** a **swallow.**

Burgeon, *YI*: beginning of growth after seedburst, CHIA; early spring; associated with the Wooden Moment.

11.5a **Supreme Burgeoning converting maidenhood.**

54.5a/5b The **supreme burgeoning converting maidenhood.**

Burn, *FEN*: set fire to, destroy, die.

30.4a **Burning thus. Dying thus. Thrown-out thus.**

56.3a/3b **Sojourning: burning one's camp.**

56.6a A **bird burns its nest.**

56.6b **One's righteousness burnt indeed.**

Bushy-tailed rodent, *SHI SHU*: squirrels and other animals who destroy stored grain; mean, thieving people; timid, skulking, mournful, brooding.

35.4a **Prospering, thus bushy-tailed rodents.**

35.4b **Bushy-tailed rodents: Trial, adversity.**

Butt, *ZHU*: push or strike with the horns; attack, oppose, offend; stir up, excite; associated with the Wooden Moment.

34.3a/6a The **he goat butts** a **hedge.**

Calamity, *ZAI*: disaster from outside; fire, flood, plague, drought, blight, ruin; contrasts with blunder, *SHENG*, indicating personal fault. Ideogram: water and fire, elemental powers.

5.3b **Calamity located outside indeed.**

23.4b **Slicing close** to **calamity indeed.**

24.6a **Possessing calamity** and **blunder.**

25/26.HP **Without entanglement: calamity indeed.**

25.3a To **without entanglement belongs calamity.**

25.3a To **capital's people belongs calamity.**

25.3b **Capital's people, calamity indeed.**

25.6b To **exhaustion belongs calamity indeed.**

26.1b **Not opposing calamity indeed.**

33.1b **Not going, is** it a **calamity indeed?**

55.1b **Exceeding** a **decade: calamity indeed.**

56.1a **Splitting-off one's place: grasping calamity.**

56.1b **Purpose exhausted: calamity indeed.**

62.6a **That designates calamity** and **blunder.**

Calendar, *LI*: reckon the course of heavenly bodies, astronomical events; establish the calendar.

49.PW A **jun zi uses regulating** the **calendar** to **brighten** the **seasons.**

Calf, *FEI*: calf; rely on; prop, rest; sick, weak.

31.2a **Conjunction** of **one's calves.**

52.2a The **bound: one's calves.**

Call, *MING*: bird and animal cries, through which they recognize each other; distinctive sound, song, statement. Ideogram: bird and mouth, a distinguishing call.

15.2a/2b/6a/6b The **call** of **humbling.**

16.1a The **call** of **providing.**

16.1b **Initial six**: the **call** of **providing.**

61.2a **Calling crane located** in **Yin.**

Camp, *CI*: resting place, inn, shed; halt, breathing-spell. Ideogram: two and breath, pausing to breathe.

7.4a The **legions' left camp.**

7.4b The **left camp, without fault.**

43.4a/4b **One's moving** the **camp moreover.**

44.3a/3b **One's moving** the **camp moreover.**

56.2a **Sojourning: approaching** a **camp.**

56.3a/3b **Sojourning: burning one's camp.**

Canons, *JING*: standards, laws; regular, regulate; the Five Classics. Ideogram: warp-threads in a loom.

3.PW A **jun zi uses** the **canons** to **coordinate**.

27.2a **Rejecting** the **canons**, **tending-towards** the **hill-top**.

27.5a **Rejecting** the **canons**.

Caper, *YUE*: play, frolic, dance and leap for joy, frisk, gambol. Ideogram: foot and feather, light-footed.

1.4a/4b **Maybe capering located** at the **abyss**.

Capital, *YI*: populous fortified city, center and symbol of the region it rules. Ideogram: enclosure and official seal.

6.2a **Converting and-also escaping** from **one's capital**.

8.5a/5b The **capital**'s **people not admonished**.

11.6a **Originating** from the **capital**, **notifying fate**.

15.6a **Disciplining** the **capital city**.

15.6b **Disciplining** the **capital city indeed**.

25.3a To **capital**'s **people belongs calamity**.

25.3b **Capital**'s **people**, **calamity indeed**.

35.6a/6b **Holding-fast avails** of **subjugating** the **capital**.

43.IM/ IT **Notifying originates** from the **capital**.

46.3a/3b **Ascending** an **empty capital**.

48.IM The **well**. **Amending** the **capital**, **not amending** the **well**.

48.IT **Amending** the **capital**, **not amending** the **well**.

Capture, *HUO*: obtain, seize, reach; take in a hunt, catch a thief; hit the mark, opportune moment; prisoner, spoils, prey, slave, servant.

17.4a/4b **Following possesses capture**.

30.6a **Severing** the **head**. **Capturing in-no-way its demons**.

36.4a **Capturing** the **heart belonging** to **brightness hidden**.

36.4b **Capturing** the **heart**: **intention indeed**.

40.2a The **fields**, **capturing three foxes**.

40.6a **Capturing it**, **without not Harvesting**.

52.IM **Not capturing one's individuality**.

52.IT **That uses not capturing one's individuality**.

57.4a/4b The **fields**: **capturing three kinds**.

Care, *XU*: fear, doubt, concern; heartfelt attachment; relieve, soothe, aid; sympathy, compassion, consolation. Ideogram: heart and blood, the heart's blood affected.

11.3a **No cares**: **one's conformity**.

35.5a/5b **Letting-go**, **acquiring**: **no cares**.

37.5a **Beings**' **care**, **significant**.

43.2a **No cares**.

43.2b **Possessing weapons**, **no cares**.

45.1a **No cares**.

46.IM/ IT **No cares**.

Carry, *ZAI*: bear, carry with you; contain, sustain, support; load a ship or cart, cargo; fill in.

2.PW A **jun zi uses munificent actualizing-dao** to **carry** the **beings**.

2.IT **Space**: **munificent carrying** the **beings**.

9.6a **Honoring actualizing-dao**: **carrying**.

9.6b **Actualizing-dao amassing**: **carrying indeed**.

14.2a/2b The **great chariot used** to **carry**.

23.6b **Commoners** acquire a **place** to **carry indeed**.

38.6a **Carrying souls**: the **one chariot**.

Cart, *YU*: a vehicle and its carrying capacity; contain, hold, sustain.

7.3a/3b The **legions maybe carting corpses**.

7.5a/5b The **junior son carts corpses**.

9.3a **Carting**: **stimulating** the **spokes**.

23.6a/6b A **jun zi acquires** a **cart**.

26.2a/2b **Carting**: **stimulating** the **axle-bearing**.

26.3a **Named: enclosing** the **cart, escorting.**
34.4a **Vigor tends-towards** the **great:** to a **cart belong axle-bearings.**
38.3a/3b **Viewing** the **cart pulled-back.**

Cattle, *NIU*: ox, bull, cow, calf; power and strength of work animals; stubborn.
25.3a **Maybe** to **attaching belongs cattle.**
25.3b **Moving people acquire cattle.**
26.4a To **youthful cattle belongs** a **stable.**
30.IM **Growing. Accumulating female cattle.**
30.IT **That uses accumulating female cattle, significant indeed.**
33.2a To **holding-on belongs availing** of **skin belonging** to **yellow cattle.**
33.2b **Holding-on avails** of **yellow cattle.**
38.3a **One's cattle hampered.**
49.1a **Thonging avails** of **skin belonging** to **yellow cattle.**
49.1b **Thonging avails** of **yellow cattle.**
56.6a/6b **Losing** the **cattle, tending-towards versatility.**
63.5a/5b The **Eastern neighbor slaughters cattle.**

Cave, *XUE*: cavern, den, pit; hole used for dwelling; open grave; pierce through.
5.4a **Emerging originating** from the **cave.**
5.6a **Entering tending-towards** the **cave.**
62.5a A **prince's string-arrow grasps someone located** in a **cave.**

Center, *ZHONG*: inner, central; put in the center; middle, stable point enabling you to face inner and outer changes; middle line of a trigram. Ideogram: field divided in two equal parts.
This term occurs in the name of hexagram 61 and recurs throughout its texts. It also occurs in:
2.5b **Pattern located** in the **center indeed.**
3.3a **Thinking** of **entering tending-towards** the **forest's center.**
3.IT **Stirring-up reaches** to **venturing's center.**
4.IT The **season's center indeed.**
4.IT **Using** a **solid** in the **center indeed.**
5.2b **Inundation located** in the **center indeed.**
5.5b/ IT **Using** the **center's correctness indeed.**
6.IM The **center, significant. Completing, pitfall.**
6.5b **Using** the **center's correctness indeed.**
6.IT **Blocking awe**: the **center, significant.**
6.IT The **solid comes and-also acquires** the **center indeed.**
6.IT **Honoring** the **center's correctness indeed.**
7.PW The **earth's center possesses stream.** The **legions.**
7.2a/2b **Locating** the **legions** in the **center, significant.**
7.5b **Using** the **center moving indeed.**
7.IT The **solid** in the **center and-also** in **correspondence.**
8.5b **Position correct** in the **center indeed.**
8.5b **Above commissioning** in the **center indeed.**
8.IT **Using** a **solid** in the **center indeed.**
9.2b **Hauling-along returning located** in the **center.**
9.IT The **solid** in the **center and-also** the **purpose moving.**
10.2b The **center not** the **origin** of **disarray indeed.**
10.IT The **solid** in the **center** and **correct.**
11.2a **Acquiring honor tending-towards** the **center: movement.**
11.2b **Enwrapped** in **wasteland, acquiring honor tending-towards** the **center: movement.**
11.4b In the **center** the **heart's desire indeed.**
11.5b In the **center using** the **movement** of **desire indeed.**
13.5b **Using** the **center: straightening indeed.**
13.IT The **supple acquires** the

position, acquires the center and-also the correspondence reaches energy.

13.IT The center correct and-also corresponding.

14.2b Amassing in the center, not destroying indeed.

14.IT The supple acquires the noble position: the great in the center.

15.PW The earth's center possesses mountain. Humbling.

15.2b In the center the heart acquiring indeed.

16.2b Using the center's correctness indeed.

16.5b The center not-yet extinguished indeed.

17.PW The pond in the center possesses thunder. Following.

17.5b Position correct in the center indeed.

18.2b Acquiring the center: dao indeed.

19.5b To moving the center belongs designating indeed.

19.IT The solid in the center and-also corresponding.

20.IT The center's correctness uses overseeing below heaven.

21.IT Jaws' center possesses being.

21.IT The supple acquires the center and-also above moves.

24.PW Thunder located in the earth's center. Return.

24.4a/4b The center moving, solitary return.

24.5b The center uses the origin from the predecessors indeed.

25.IT The solid in the center and-also corresponding.

26.PW Heaven located in the mountain's center. The great accumulating.

26.2b The center, without surpassing indeed.

28.IT The solid exceeding and-also in the center.

29.2b Not-yet emerging from the center indeed.

29.5b In the center not-yet the great indeed.

29.IT Thereupon using the solid in the center indeed.

30.2b Acquiring the center: dao indeed.

30.IT The supple congregating reaches the center's correctness.

32.2b Able to last in the center indeed.

34.2b Using the center indeed.

35.2b Using the center's correctness indeed.

36.PW/ IT Brightness entering the earth's center. Brightness hidden.

37.2a Located in the center, feeding.

38.IT Acquiring the center and-also correspondence reaching the solid.

39.5b Using the center articulating indeed.

39.IT Going acquires the center indeed.

40.2b Acquiring the center: dao indeed.

40.IT Thereupon acquiring the center indeed.

41.2b In the center using activating purpose indeed.

42.3a Possessing conformity, the center moving.

42.4a The center moving.

42.IT The center's correctness possesses reward.

43.2b Acquiring the center, dao indeed.

43.5a/5b The center moves, without fault.

43.5b The center not-yet shining indeed.

44.5b The center correct indeed.

44.IT The solid meets the center's correctness.

45.2b The center not-yet transformed indeed.

45.IT The solid in the center and-also corresponding.

46.PW The earth's center generates wood. Ascending.

46.IT The solid in the center and-also corresponding.

47.2b The center possesses reward indeed.

47.5b Using the center: straightening indeed.

47.IT Using the solid in the center indeed.

48.5b The **center correct indeed.**
48.IT **Thereupon using** the **solid** in the **center indeed.**
49.PW The **pond** in the **center possesses fire. Skinning.**
50.5b The **center uses activating substance indeed.**
50.IT **Acquires** the **center and-also** the **correspondence reaches** the **solid.**
51.5b **One's affairs located** in the **center.**
51.6b The **center not-yet acquired indeed.**
52.5b **Using** the **center, correcting indeed.**
53.IT **One's position**: the **solid acquires** the **center indeed.**
54.5b **One's position located** in the **center.**
55.IM **No grief. Properly** the **sun** in the **center.**
55.2a/4a/4b The **sun** in the **center: viewing** a **bin.**
55.3a The **sun** in the **center: viewing froth.**
55.IT **No grief, properly** the **sun** in the **center.**
55.IT The **sun** in the **center,** by **consequence setting.**
56.IT The **supple acquires** the **center reaching outside and-also yielding reaches** the **solid.**
57.2b **Acquiring** the **center indeed.**
57.5b **Position correct** in the **center indeed.**
57.IT **Solid root reaches** the **center correctly and-also** the **purpose moves.**
58.IT The **solid** in the **center and-also** the **supple outside.**
59.IT The **king thereupon located** in the **center indeed.**
60.5b **Residing** in the **position** in the **center indeed.**
60.IT **Solid** and **supple apportioned and-also** the **solid acquiring** the **center.**
60.IT The **center's correctness uses interpenetrating.**
62.HP The **center conforming: trustworthiness indeed.**
62.IT The **supple acquires** the **center.**
62.IT The **solid letting-go** the **position and-also not** in the **center.**
63.2b **Using** the **center's dao indeed.**
63.IT The **supple acquires** the **center indeed.**
64.2b In the **center using movement** to **correct indeed.**
64.IT The **supple acquires** the **center indeed.**
64.IT **Not-yet emerging** from the **center indeed.**

Chambers, *TING*: family rooms; courtyard, hall; domestic. Ideogram: shelter and hall, a secure place.
36.4a **Tending-towards emerging** from the **gate chambers.**
43.IM **Parting. Displaying tending-towards** the **king's chambers.**
43.IT **Displaying tending-towards** the **king's chambers.**
52.IM **Moving one's chambers.**
52.IT **Moving one's chambers, not viewing one's people.**
60.1a/1b **Not emerging** from the **door chambers.**
60.2a **Not emerging** from the **gate chambers.**
60.2b **Not emerging** from the **gate chambers, pitfall.**

Change, *HUA*: gradual, continuous change; melt, dissolve; be born, die; influence; contrasts with transform, *BIAN*, sudden mutation. Ideogram: person alive and dead, the life process.
1.IT **Energy's dao transforming** and **changing.**
20.IT **Overseeing below and-also changing indeed.**
22.IT **Using changes** to **accomplish below heaven.**
30.IT **Thereupon changes accomplished below heaven.**
31.IT **Heaven** and **earth influence and-also** the **myriad beings change** and **generate.**
32.IT The **four seasons: transforming changes and-also enabling lasting** and **accomplishing.**

32.IT The **wise person: lasting with-respect-to one's dao and-also below heaven changing** and **accomplishing.**

61.IT **Thereupon changing** the **fiefdoms indeed.**

Chariot, *CHE*: cart, wheeled traveling vehicle.

14.2a/2b The **great chariot used** to **carry.**

22.1a/1b **Stowing** the **chariot and-also afoot.**

38.6a **Carrying souls**: the **one chariot.**

47.4a **Confinement tending-towards** a **metallic chariot.**

Cheek-bones, *CHUAN*: facial feature denoting character.

43.3a The **vigor tends-towards** the **cheek-bones.**

Cheeks, *JIA*: cheeks, jaws; speak, articulate.

31.6a/6b **Conjunction** of **one's jawbones, cheeks** and **tongue.**

Cherish, *HUAI*: carry in the heart or womb; dwell on, think fondly of; cling to; heart, breast. Ideogram: heart and hide, cherish in the heart.

7.2b **Cherishing** the **myriad fiefdoms indeed.**

56.2a **Cherishing one's own.**

Chief, *JUN*: prince, ruler; lead, direct; wise person. Ideogram: mouth and direct, giving orders.

7.6a/6b The **great** in the **chief possesses fate.**

10.3a/3b **Martial people activate tending-towards** a **great chief.**

12.1b **Purpose located** in a **chief indeed.**

19.5a/5b To the **great** in the **chief belongs propriety.**

24.6a **Using one's city**'s **chief: pitfall.**

24.6b **Reversing** the **chief**'s **dao indeed.**

31.PS **Therefore afterwards possessing chief** and **servant.**

31.PS **Possessing chief** and **servant.**

37.IT **Household people possess** an **intimidating chief in-truth.**

49.6b **Yielding uses adhering** to a **chief indeed.**

54.5a The **sleeves belonging** to **one's chief,**

62.2a/2b **Not extending** to **one's chief.**

Chock, *NI*: block used to stop a cart wheel; terminate; inquire, investigate.

44.1a/1b **Attachment tending-towards** a **metallic chock.**

Chroniclers, *SHI*: administrative officer; record-keeper, narrator, annalist; histories, authoritative records, annals.

57.2a **Availing** of **chroniclers** and **shamans.**

City, *GUO*: city, state, country, nation; area of only human constructions; first of the territorial zones: city, suburbs, countryside, forest.

1.IT The **myriad cities conjoining** to **soothe.**

7.6a **Disclosing** the **city, receiving** a **household.**

8.PW The **earlier kings used installing** a **myriad cities** to **connect** the **related feudatories.**

15.6a **Disciplining** the **capital city.**

15.6b **Disciplining** the **capital city indeed.**

20.4a/4b **Overseeing** the **shine belonging** to the **city.**

24.6a **Using one's city**'s **chief: pitfall.**

29.IT The **king** and the **princes set-up venturing used** to **guard their city.**

36.6b **Illuminating** the **four cities indeed.**

42.4a **Harvesting: availing** of **activating depends** on **shifting** the **city.**

64.4a **Three years, possessing** a **donation tending-towards** the **great city.**

Clan, *ZU*: extended family with the same ancestor and surname; kin, relatives; tribe, class, kind. Ideogram: flag and spear, a rallying point.

13.PW A **jun zi uses sorting** the **clans** to **mark-off** the **beings.**

Clapper, *TUO*: board used by

watchmen to strike the hours.
16.AT **Redoubling gates, smiting clappers.**

Classification, *HUI*: class, collection, series; same kind; put or group together.
11.1a **Using one's classification.**
12.1a **Using one's classification.**

Clear, *ZI*: cultivate wild or overgrown land; reclaim.
25.2a **Not tilling** the **crop. Not clearing** the **plow-land.**

Clearly, *ZHE*: brilliant, luminous, shining; perceptive; intuitive knowledge.
14.4b **Brightness differentiates clearly indeed.**

Climax, *YI*: come to a high point and stop; bring to an end, complete; renounce, desist, decline, reject; that is all; already; excessive.
22.PS **Beings not permitted** to **use unconsidered uniting and-also climaxing.**
26.1a **Harvesting: climaxing.**
26.1b **Possessing adversity, Harvesting, climaxing.**
32.IT **Persevering lasting and-also not climaxing indeed.**
41.1a/1b **Climaxing affairs, swiftly going.**
42.PS **Diminishing and-also not climaxing necessarily augments.**
43.PS **Augmenting and-also not climaxing necessarily breaks-up.**
47.PS **Ascending and-also not climaxing necessarily confines.**
62.5b **Climaxing above indeed.**
62.6b **Climaxing overbearing indeed.**

Climb, *JI*: ascend, scale; climb steep cliffs; rise as clouds.
51.2a **Climbing tending-towards** the **ninth mound.**

Close, *JIN*: near in time or place, next to; approach; recently, lately; familiar.
23.4b **Slicing close** to **calamity indeed.**

Clothes, *YI*: upper body garments and clothes in general; dress; cover, husk.
63.4a A **token: possessing clothes in tatters.**

Clouds, *YUN*: fog, mist, water vapor; connected with the Streaming Moment.
1.IT **Clouds moving, rain spreading.**
3.PW **Clouds** and **thunder: sprouting.**
5.PW **Clouds above with-respect-to heaven. Attending.**
9.IM/ IT **Shrouding clouds, not raining.**
62.5a/5b **Shrouding clouds, not raining.**

Cluster, *CUI*: dense, thick; tight groups of people, animals, things; collect, gather, assemble, concentrate; bunch, crowd; lit.: dense, tussocky grass.
This term is the name of hexagram 45 and recurs throughout its texts. It also occurs in:
46.HP **Clustering: assembling, and-also**

Codes, *LI*: rites, rules, ritual, etiquette; usage, manners; honor, worship. Ideogram: worship and sacrificial vase, handling a sacred vessel.
10.PS **Beings accumulate, therefore afterwards possess codes.**
15.AT **Humbling: using paring** the **codes.**
31.PS **Therefore afterwards** the **codes' righteousness possesses** a **polishing place.**
34.PW A **jun zi uses no codes whatever, nowhere treading.**

Coins, *BEI*: cowry shells used for money; adorned with shell; money, riches; precious, valuable.
51.2a A **hundred-thousand coins lost.**

Cold, *HAN*: chilled, wintry; destitute, poor; shiver; fear; associated with the Streaming Moment. Ideogram: person huddled in straw under a roof.
48.5a **Cold springwater taken-in.**
48.5b To **cold springwater belongs taking-in.**

Collect, *SHOU*: gather, harvest; receive what is due; involve, snare, bind, restrain.
48.6a The **well: collecting, no cover.**

Come, *LAI*: approach in time or space; move toward, arrive at; future; contrasts with go, *WANG*, move away or become past.

5.6a **Possessing visitors belonging** to **not inviting**: **three people coming**.
5.6b **Visitors belonging** to **not inviting come**.
6.IT The **solid comes and-also acquires** the **center indeed**.
8.IM/IT **Not soothing**, on all **sides coming**.
8.1a **Completion coming**, **possessing more**, **significant**.
11.IM The **small going**, the **great coming**.
11.IT The **small going**, the **great coming**: **significance Growing**.
12.IM/ IT The **great going**, the **small coming**.
17.IT **Following**. The **solid comes and-also below** the **supple**.
22.IT The **supple comes and-also patterns** the **solid**.
24.IM/IT **Partners come**, **without fault**.
24.IM/IT The **seventh day comes return**.
25.IT A **solid originating** from the **outside comes**.
29.3a/3b To **coming belongs gorge**, **gorge**.
30.4a/4b **Assailing thus**, **its coming thus**.
31.4a/4b **Wavering**, **wavering**: **going**, **coming**.
39.1a/1b **Going limping**, **coming praise**.
39.3a/3b **Going limping**, **coming reversal**.
39.4a/4b **Going limping**, **coming continuity**.
39.5a/5b The **great**'s **limping**, **partners coming**.
39.6a **Going limping**, **coming ripeness**. **Significant**.
39.6b **Going limping**, **coming ripeness**.
40.IM/IT **One's coming return**, **significant**.
42.2b/6b **Origin outside**, **coming indeed**.
45/46.HP **ascending**: **not coming indeed**.
47.2a **Scarlet sashes** on all **sides coming**.
47.4a/4b **Coming**: **ambling**, **ambling**.
48.IM **Going**, **coming**: **welling**, **welling**.
51.IM/1a/1b/IT The **shake coming**: **frightening**, **frightening**.
51.2a/2b The **shake coming**, **adversity**.
51.5a/5b The **shake going** and **coming**, **adversity**.
55.5a **Coming composition**.
58.3a **Coming open**, **pitfall**.
58.3b To the **coming open belongs** a **pitfall**.
59.IT The **solid comes and-also not exhausted**.
63.5b **Significant**. The **great coming indeed**.

Command, *GAO*: give orders; inform, notify, instruct; official seal. Ideogram: words and announce, verbal commands.

44.PW The **crown prince uses spreading fate** to **command** the **four sides**.

Commission, *SHI*: charge somebody with a task; command, order; messenger, agent; obey, follow. Ideogram: person and office.

7.5b **Commissioning not appropriate indeed**.
8.5b **Above commissioning** in the **center indeed**.
41.4a **Commissioning swiftly possesses joy**.

Commoners, *MIN*: common people, masses; working class supporting the social hierarchy; undeveloped potential in the individual.

3.1b The **great acquires** the **commoners indeed**.
7.PW A **jun zi uses tolerating** the **commoners** to **accumulate crowds**.
7.IT **And-also** the **commoners adhere** to **it**.
10.PW And **rectifying** the **commoners' purpose**.
11.PW And **uses** at **left** and **right** the

commoners.

15.3b The **myriad commoners submit indeed.**

16.IT By **consequence punishing flogging purifies and-also** the **commoners submit.**

18.PW A **jun zi uses rousing** the **commoners** to **nurture actualizing-dao.**

19.PW And **tolerating** to **protect** the **commoners without delimiting.**

20.PW The **earlier kings used inspecting** on all **sides** and **overseeing** the **commoners** to **set-up teaching.**

20.5b **Overseeing** the **commoners indeed.**

23.6b **Commoners** acquire a **place** to **carry indeed.**

27.IT The **wise person nourishes eminence used** to **extend** to the **myriad commoners.**

42.IT The **commoners stimulated without delimiting.**

44.4b **Distancing** the **commoners indeed.**

48.PW A **jun zi uses** the **toiling commoners** to **encourage reciprocity.**

58.IT **Stimulating uses beforehand** the **commoners.**

58.IT The **commoners forget their toil.**

58.IT The **commoners forget their death.**

58.IT The **commoners encouraged actually in-fact.**

60.IT **Not harming** the **commoners.**

Compact, *ZI*: close textured, dense, solid, impenetrable. Ideogram: herb and silk, dense fabric or foliage.

35.2a/2b **Acquiescing** in a **compact cuirass: blessing.**

Companion, *QIU*: close personal relation; partner, spouse; unite, join in marriage. With the pronunciation *CHOU*: opponent, rival, enemy; contradict, hate.

50.2a/2b **My companion possesses affliction.**

Compenetrate, *TAI*: communicate, permeate, diffuse; excellent, eminent, supreme; abundant, prosperous; smooth, slippery; extreme, extravagant, prodigal. Ideogram: person in water, connected to the universal medium.

This term is the name of hexagram 11 and recurs throughout its texts. It also occurs in:

12.HP **Obstruction** and **compenetration: reversing one's sorting indeed.**

Complete, *ZHONG*: completion of a cycle that begins the next; entire, whole, all. Ideogram: silk cocoons, follow and ice, winter linking one year with the next.

1.3a A **jun zi completing** the **day: energy parching.**

1.3b **Completing** the **day: energy parching.**

1.IT The **great brightening completes** the **beginning.**

2.3a **Without accomplishing, possessing completion.**

2.7b **Using** the **great** for **completion indeed.**

2.IT **Thereupon completing possesses reward.**

5.2a **Completing, significant.**

5.2b **Although** the **small possesses words, using completing significant indeed.**

5.6a/6b To **respecting belongs completion, significant.**

6.IM The **center, significant. Completing, pitfall.**

6.1a **Completing significant.**

6.3a **Adversity: completing, significant.**

6.6a **Completing dawn thrice depriving** of **it.**

6.IT **Completing, pitfall.**

8.1a **Completion coming, possessing more, significant.**

8.6b **Without** a **place** to **complete indeed.**

10.4a/4b **Watch-out! Watch-out! Completing significant.**

12.PS **Beings not permitted** to **use completing interpenetration.**

12.6b **Obstruction completed**, by **consequence subverting.**

13.PS **Beings not permitted** to **use**

completing obstruction.
15.IM A **jun zi possesses completing.**
15.3a **Possessing completion, significant.**
15.IT The **completion belonging** to a **jun zi indeed.**
16.2a **Not completing** the **day.**
16.2b **Not completing** the **day, Trial, significant.**
18.1a **Adversity's completion, significant.**
18.3b **Completing without fault indeed.**
18.IT **Completing,** by **consequence possessing** a **beginning.**
22.3b To **completing abstention belongs** a **mound indeed.**
22.4b **Completing without surpassing indeed.**
22.5a **Completing significant.**
23.5b **Completing without surpassing indeed.**
23.6b **Completing not permitted availing** of **indeed.**
24.PS **Beings not permitted** to **use completing using-up.**
24.6a **Completing possesses great destruction.**
29.PS **Beings not permitted** to **use completing exceeding.**
29.3b **Completing without achieving indeed.**
29.4a **Completing, without fault.**
32.5b **Adhering** to the **one and-also completing indeed.**
32.IT **Completing,** by **consequence possessing beginning indeed.**
34.PS **Beings not permitted** to **use completing retiring.**
35.PS **Beings not permitted** to **use completing vigor.**
37.3a **Completing, abashment.**
37.6a **Completing, significant.**
38.3a/3b **Without initially possessing completion.**
39.2b **Completing without surpassing indeed.**
40.PS **Beings not permitted** to **use completing heaviness.**
43.3b **Completing without fault indeed.**
43.6a **Completing possesses pitfall.**
43.6b **Completing not permitting long-living indeed.**
43.IT The **solid long-living, thereupon completion indeed.**
45.1a **Possessing conformity, not completing.**
47.4a **Possessing completion.**
50.2b **Completing without surpassing indeed.**
50.3a **Completing significant.**
52.PS **Beings not permitted** to **use completing stirring-up.**
52.6b **Using munificence** to **complete indeed.**
53.PS **Beings not permitted** to **use completing stopping.**
53/54.HP **Converting maidenhood:** the **completion belonging** to **womanhood indeed.**
53.5a To **completing abstention belongs mastering.**
53.5b To **completing abstention belongs mastering, significant.**
54.PW A **jun zi uses perpetually completing** to **know** the **cracked.**
54.IT The **beginning** of **completion belonging** to a **person.**
55.3b **Completing, not permitted availing** of **indeed.**
56.2b **Completing without surpassing indeed.**
56.5a/5b **Completion uses praising fate.**
56.6b To **completing abstention belongs hearing indeed.**
57.5a **Without initially possessing completion.**
60.PS **Beings not permitted** to **use completing radiance.**
62.4b **Completion not permitted long-living indeed.**
63.IM **Completing: disarray.**
63.4a/4b **Completing** the **day:** a **warning.**
63.IT **Completing: stopping,** by **consequence disarray.**
64.PS To **anterior acquiescence belongs** the **use** of **not-yet fording's completion in-truth.**
64.IT **Not continuing** to **completion indeed.**

Complexion, *SE*: color, hue; physical appearance, expression; beauty.

21/22.HP **Adorning: without complexion indeed.**

Composition, *ZHANG*: a well-composed whole and its structure; beautiful creation; elegant, clear, brilliant; chapter, strophe; distinct from pattern, *WEN*, beauty of intrinsic design.

2.3a/3b **Containing composition permits Trial.**

21.IT **Thunder** and **lightning uniting and-also composing.**

44.5a **Containing composition.**

44.5b **Nine** at **fifth: containing composition.**

44.IT The **kinds** of **beings conjoin** in **composition indeed.**

55.5a **Coming composition.**

Conceal, *CANG*: hide from view; store, put aside, accumulate; keep in one's heart; internal organs.

55.6b **Originating** from **concealment indeed.**

Concord, *TONG*: harmonize, unite, equalize, assemble; agree, share in; together, at once, same time and place. Ideogram: cover and mouth, silent understanding and perfect fit.

This term occurs in the name of hexagram 13 and recurs throughout its texts. It also occurs in:

11.IT **Above** and **below mingling and-also their purposes concording indeed.**

14.PS **Associating** with **people concording implies beings necessarily converting in-truth.**

14.HP **Concording people: connecting indeed.**

38.PW A **jun zi uses concording and-also dividing.**

38.IT **Two women concording: residing.**

38.IT **Their purposes not concording: moving.**

38.IT **Heaven** and **earth: polarizing and-also their affairs concording indeed.**

49.IT **Two women concording, residing.**

59.IT The **supple acquires** the **position reaching outside and-also above concording.**

Concubine, *QIE*: secondary wife taken without ceremony to ensure a male descendant; handmaid.

33.3a/3b **Accumulating servants, concubines, significant.**

50.1a **Acquiring** a **concubine, using one's son.**

Conduct, *SHUAI*: lead; leader, chief, commander; follow, follower.

7.5a/5b The **long-living son conducts** the **legions.**

Confine, *KUN*: enclose, restrict, limit, oppress; impoverished, distressed, afflicted, exhausted, disheartened, weary. Ideogram: tree in a narrow enclosure.

This term is the name of hexagram 47 and recurs throughout its texts. It also occurs in:

4.4a **Confining enveloping. Abashment.**

4.4b To **confining enveloping belongs abashment.**

5.IT **One's righteousness not confined** nor **exhausted actually.**

13.4b By **consequence confinement and-also reversal** by **consequence indeed.**

48.PS **Confining reaching above implies necessarily reversing** to the **below.**

48.HP **confining: reciprocal meeting indeed.**

Conform, *FU*: accord between inner and outer; sincere, truthful, verified, reliable; capture; prisoners, spoils. Ideogram: claws over child, a bird brooding on the nest.

This term occurs in the name of hexagram 61 and recurs throughout its texts. It also occurs in:

5.IM/ IT **Attending. Possessing conformity.**

6.IM/ IT **Arguing. Possessing conformity.**

8.1a **Possessing conformity: grouping it.**

8.1a **Possessing conformity: overfilling** the **jar.**

9.4a **Possessing conformity.**

9.4b **Possessing conformity, awe emerging.**

9.5a/5b **Possessing conformity binds thus.**
11.3a **No cares: one's conformity.**
11.4a/4b **Not warning: using conformity.**
14.5a/5b **Your conforming: mingling thus.**
17.4a **Possessing conformity, locating in dao, using brightness.**
17.4b **Possessing conformity, locating** in **dao.**
17.5a/5b **Conformity tends-towards excellence. Significant.**
20.IM/ IT **Possessing conformity like** a **presence.**
29.IM **Possessing conformity.**
34.1a **Possessing conformity.**
34.1b **One's conformity exhausted indeed.**
35.1a **Absence: conforming.**
37.6a **Possessing conformity, impressing thus.**
38.4a **Mingling, conforming.**
38.4b **Mingling, conforming, without fault.**
40.4a **Partnering culminating, splitting-off conforming.**
40.5a **Possessing conformity tending-towards** the **small** in the **person.**
41.IM **Diminishing. Possessing conformity.**
41.IT **Diminishing and-also possessing conformity.**
42.3a **Possessing conformity**, the **center moving.**
42.5a **Possessing conformity**, a **benevolent heart.**
42.5a **Possessing conformity, benevolence: my actualizing-dao.**
42.5b **Possessing conformity**, a **benevolent heart.**
43.IM/ IT **Conformity crying-out possesses adversity.**
44.1a **Ruined** the **pig**'s **conformity: hoof dragging.**
45.1a **Possessing conformity, not completing.**
45.2a **Conforming, thereupon Harvesting: availing** of **dedicating.**
45.5a **In-no-way conforming.**
46.2a **Conforming, thereupon Harvesting: availing** of **dedicating.**
46.2b To **nine** at **second belongs conforming.**
48.6a **Possessing conformity: Spring, significant.**
49.IM **Skinning. Before-zenith sun, thereupon conformity.**
49.3a **Possessing conformity.**
49.4a **Repenting extinguished, possessing conformity.**
49.5a **Not-yet** an **augury, possessing conformity.**
49.IT **Before-zenith sun, thereupon conformity.**
55.2a/2b **Possessing conformity, like shooting-forth.**
58.2a **Conforming open, significant.**
58.2b To the **conforming open belongs significance.**
58.5a/5b **Conformity tending-towards stripping.**
61.5a/5b **Possessing conformity, binding thus.**
62.HP **The center conforming: trustworthiness indeed.**
64.5a **Possessing conformity, significant.**
64.6a **Possessing conformity tending-towards drinking liquor.**
64.6a **Possessing conformity: letting-go that.**

Congregate, *LI*: cling together, adhere to, rely on; couple, pair, herd; beautiful, elegant; Action of the trigram Radiance, *LI*. Ideogram: deer flocking together.
30.PS **Falling necessarily possesses** a **place** to **congregate.**
30.PS **Radiance implies congregating indeed.**
30.IT **Radiance. Congregating indeed.**
30.IT **Sun** and **moon congregating reaching heaven.**
30.IT The **hundred grains, grasses, trees congregating reaching** the **earth.**
30.IT **Redoubled brightness uses congregating** to **reach correcting.**
30.IT The **supple congregating reaches** the **center's correctness.**
35.IT **Yielding and-also congregating reaching** the **great**'s **brightness.**

38.IT **Stimulating and-also congregating reaching brightness.**
56.IT **Stopping and-also congregating reaches brightness.**
58.PW **Congregating ponds.** The **open.**

Conjoin, *XIAN*: come in contact with, join; put together as parts of a previously separated whole; conjunction of celestial bodies; totally, completely; accord, harmony, mutual influence; lit.: broken piece of pottery, the halves of which join to identify partners.

This term is the name of hexagram 31 and recurs throughout its texts. It also occurs in:
1.IT The **myriad cities conjoining** to **soothe.**
2.IT The **kinds** of the **beings conjoining, Growing.**
19.1a/1b **Conjunction nearing: Trial, significant.**
19.2a/2b **Conjunction nearing, significant.**
32.HP **Conjunction: inviting indeed.**
44.IT The **kinds** of **beings conjoin** in **composition indeed.**

Connect, *QIN*: be close, approach, come near; cherish, help, favor; intimate; relatives, kin.
5/6.HP **Arguing: not connecting indeed.**
8.PW The **earlier kings used installing** a **myriad cities** to **connect** the **related feudatories.**
13/14.HP **Concording people: connecting indeed.**
55/56.HP **Connecting** with **few: sojourning indeed.**

Consecutive, *JI*: connect, join; continue; line of succession, adoption. Ideogram: continuity of silk thread connecting cocoons.
30.PW The **great** in the **person uses consecutive brightening** to **illuminate tending-towards** the **four sides.**

Consequence, *ZE*: reason, cause, result; rule, law, pattern, standard; therefore; very strong connection.

This term occurs throughout the hexagram texts.

Consider, *SHEN*: act carefully, seriously; cautious, attentive, circumspect; still, quiet, sincere. Ideogram: heart and true.
2.4b **Considering not harmful indeed.**
5.3b **Respectful consideration, not destroying indeed.**
27.PW A **jun zi uses considerate words** to **inform.**
50.2b **Considering** the **place** of **it indeed.**
56.PW A **jun zi uses bright consideration availing** of **punishment and-also not detaining litigations.**
64.PW A **jun zi uses considerately marking-off** the **beings residing** on all **sides.**

Consort, *QI*: official partner; legal status of married woman (first wife); distinct from wife, *FU*, which indicates her role as head of the household, and from concubine, *QIE*, secondary wife.
9.3a/3b **Husband** and **consort reversing** the **eyes.**
28.2a A **venerable husband acquires his woman consort.**
28.2b A **venerable husband** and a **woman consort.**
47.3a/3b **Not viewing one's consort.**

Conspicuous, *ZHU*: manifest, obvious, clear; publish.
3/4.HP **Enveloping: motley and-also conspicuous.**

Constancy, *CHANG*: immutable order; permanent, unchanging, habitual; always; law, rule, custom.
2.IT **Afterwards yielding: acquiring constancy.**
3.2b **Reversing constancy indeed.**
5.1b **Not-yet letting-go constancy indeed.**
7.4b **Not-yet letting-go constancy indeed.**
29.PW A **jun zi uses constancy** in **actualizing-dao** to **move.**
54.2b **Not-yet transforming constancy indeed.**

Contain, *HAN*: retain, embody, cherish; withhold, tolerate; contain in the mouth, put a coin in a corpse's mouth.

2.3a/3b **Containing composition permits Trial.**

2.IT **Containing generosity**: the **shine** of the **great.**

44.5a **Containing composition.**

44.5b **Nine** at **fifth**: **containing composition.**

Content, *KANG*: peaceful, prosper, at ease; confident strength and poise; joy, delight.

35.IM **Prospering.** A **content feudatory avails** of **bestowing horses** to **enhance** the **multitudes.**

35.IT **That uses** a **content feudatory availing** of **bestowing horses** to **enhance** the **multitudes.**

Continue, *XU*: carry on what another began; succeed to, inherit, transmit; keep up, follow.

64.IT **Not continuing** to **completion indeed.**

Continuity, *LIAN*: connected, attached, annexed, consistent; follow, reach, stick to, join; series.

39.4a/4b **Going limping, coming continuity.**

Contradict, *WEI*: oppose, disregard, disobey; seditious, perverse.

6.PW **Heaven associated** with **stream: contradicting movements. Arguing.**

15.4b **Not contradicting** by **consequence indeed.**

41.5a **Nowhere controlling contradiction.**

42.2a **Nowhere controlling contradiction.**

Control, *KE*: be in charge; capable of, able to, adequate; check, obstruct, repress. Ideogram: roof beams supporting a house.

4.2a/2b The **son controls** the **household.**

6.2a/2b/4a **Not controlling arguing.**

13.4a **Nowhere controlling aggression.**

13.4b **Righteousness nowhere controlling indeed.**

13.5a/5b **Great legions control** the **reciprocal meeting.**

13.5b **Words reciprocally controlling indeed.**

14.3a The **small** in the **person nowhere controlling.**

24.6a **Culminating tending-towards ten years not controlling disciplining.**

41.5a **Nowhere controlling contradiction.**

42.2a **Nowhere controlling contradiction.**

63.3a/3b **Three years controlling it.**

Convert, *GUI*: accomplish one's destiny; revert to the original place or state; restore, revert; turn into; goal, destination, intention; a girl getting married. Ideogram: arrive and wife, become mistress of a household.

This term occurs in the name of hexagram 54 and recurs throughout its texts. It also occurs in:

6.2a **Converting and-also escaping** from **one's capital.**

6.2b **Converting, escaping: skulking indeed.**

11.5a **Supreme Burgeoning converting maidenhood.**

14.PS **Associating** with **people concording implies beings necessarily converting in-truth.**

53.IM **Infiltrating. Womanhood converting, significant.**

53.HP **Infiltrating: womanhood converting awaits manhood moving indeed.**

53.HP **Converting maidenhood**: the **completion belonging** to **womanhood indeed.**

53.IT **Womanhood converting, significant indeed.**

55.PS **Acquiring one's place** for **converting implies necessarily** the **great.**

Cook, *REN*: cook very thoroughly; transform completely. Ideogram: food and full or complete.

50.IT **Growing: cooking indeed.**

Coordinate, *LUN*: twist fibers to make a rope; bind, weave together; adjust, order; lit.: twist silk together into threads.

3.PW A **jun zi uses** the **canons** to **coordinate**.

Corpse, *SHI*: dead human body, effigy, statue; inefficient, useless; impersonate.

7.3a/3b The **legions maybe carting corpses**.

7.5a/5b The **junior son carts corpses**.

Correct, *ZHENG*: rectify deviation or one-sidedness; proper, straight, exact, regular; constant, rule, model. Ideogram: stop and one, hold to one thing.

1.IT **Each correcting innate fate**.

3.1b **Although** a **stone pillar, purpose moving correctly indeed**.

4.1b **Using correcting** by **law indeed**.

4.IT **Enveloping uses nourishing correctness**.

5.5b/ IT **Using** the **center**'s **correctness indeed**.

6.5b **Using** the **center**'s **correctness indeed**.

6.IT **Honoring** the **center**'s **correctness indeed**.

7.6b **Using correct achievement indeed**.

7.IT **Trial. Correcting indeed**.

7.IT **Able** to **use crowds** for **correcting**.

8.5b **Position correct** in the **center indeed**.

9.3b **Not able** to **correct** the **home indeed**.

10.5b **Position correct** and **appropriate indeed**.

10.IT The **solid** in the **center** and **correct**.

12.5b **Position correct** and **appropriate indeed**.

13.IT The **center correct and-also corresponding**.

13.IT A **jun zi correct indeed**.

16.2b **Using** the **center**'s **correctness indeed**.

17.1b **Adhering** to **correctness, significant indeed**.

17.5b **Position correct** in the **center indeed**.

19.1b **Purpose moving correctly indeed**.

19.IT **Great Growing uses correcting**.

20.IT The **center**'s **correctness uses overseeing below heaven**.

25.IM **One's in-no-way correcting possesses blunder**.

25.IT The **great**'s **Growing uses correcting**.

25.IT **One's in-no-way correcting possesses blunder**.

26.IT The **great correcting indeed**.

27/28.HP The **jaws: nourishing correctly indeed**.

27.IT **Nourishing correctly**, by **consequence significance indeed**.

30.6b **Using correcting** the **fiefdoms indeed**.

30.IT **Redoubled brightness uses congregating** to **reach correcting**.

30.IT The **supple congregating reaches** the **center**'s **correctness**.

33.5b **Using** the **correct purpose indeed**.

34.IT The **great implies correcting indeed**.

34.IT The **correct great and-also** the **motives belonging** to **heaven** and **earth permit viewing actually**.

35.1b **Solitary movement: correcting indeed**.

35.2b **Using** the **center**'s **correctness indeed**.

36.IT **Inside heaviness and-also able** to **correct one's purpose**.

37.IT The **woman** in the **correct position reaching** the **inside**.

37.IT The **man** in the **correct position reaching** the **outside**.

37.IT **Man** and **woman correct**.

37.IT **And-also household**'s **dao correct**.

37.IT **Correct household and-also below heaven rectified**.

39.IT **Using** the **correct fiefdoms indeed**.

42.IT The **center**'s **correctness possesses reward**.

44.5b The **center correct indeed**.

44.IT The **solid meets** the **center**'s **correctness**.

45.IT **Assembling uses correctness indeed.**
48.5b The **center correct indeed.**
49.IT The **great's Growing uses correctness.**
50.PW A **jun zi uses correcting** the **position** to **solidify fate.**
52.1b **Not-yet letting-go correcting indeed.**
52.5b **Using** the **center, correcting indeed.**
53.IT **Advancing uses correcting.**
53.IT **Permitted** to **use correcting** the **fiefdoms indeed.**
57.5b **Position correct** in the **center indeed.**
57.6b **Correcting reaches** a **pitfall indeed.**
57.IT **Solid root reaches** the **center correctly and-also** the **purpose moves.**
58.5b **Position correct** and **appropriate indeed.**
59.5b **Correct position indeed.**
60.IT The **center's correctness uses interpenetrating.**
61.5b **Position correct** and **appropriate indeed.**
63.IT **Solid** and **supple correct and-also position appropriate indeed.**
64.2b In the **center using movement** to **correct indeed.**

Correspond, *YING*: be in agreement or harmony; proper, suitable; resonate together, answer to; relation between the lines (1:4, 2:5, 3:6) when they form the pair opened and whole, supple and solid. Ideogram: heart and obey.
This term occurs in the Image Tradition of most hexagrams.

Counterpoise, *QUAN*: weight of a scale; weigh, examine, compare; balance, equalize; act as the position demands; influential; lit.: balance on a sliding scale.
57.AT The **root: using** the **movement** of the **counterpoise.**

Countryside, *YE*: cultivated fields and grassland, where nature and human construction interact; third of the territorial zones: city, suburbs, countryside, forest.
2.6a/6b **Dragons struggle tending-towards** the **countryside.**
13.IM/ IT **Concording people tend-towards** the **countryside.**

Couple, *GOU*: driven encounter, compelled by primal instinctual forces, fusion of Yin and Yang; meet, encounter, associate with; copulate, mating animals; magnetism, gravity; be gripped by impersonal forces.
This term is the name of hexagram 44 and recurs throughout its texts. It also occurs in:
43.HP **Coupling: meeting indeed.**

Courtesy, *GONG*: display respect, show reverence; affable, decorous, modest, polite; obsequious.
62.PW A **jun zi uses moving** in **excess** to **reach courtesy.**

Cover, *MU*: canvas covering; tent, screen, tarpaulin.
48.6a The **well: collecting, no cover.**

Cracked, *BI*: broken, ruined, tattered; unfit, unworthy. Ideogram: strike and break.
48.2a The **jug cracked, leaking.**
54.PW A **jun zi uses perpetually completing** to **know** the **cracked.**

Crane, *HE*: large wading bird, sign of long life, wisdom and bliss; relation between father and son; messenger to the immortals.
61.2a **Calling crane located** in **Yin.**

Create, *ZAO*: make, construct, build, form, establish.
1.5b The **great** in the **person creative indeed.**
3.IT **Heaven creates grasses' duskiness.**

Creeper, see **Trailing creeper**

Crimson, *CHI*: color associated with the Fiery Moment, the South and the bursting phase of Yang; ardent, burning; naked, barren; color of new-born child, of drunkenness and of anger; also: sign of official rank.
47.5a **Confinement tending-towards** a **crimson sash.**

Crop, *HUO*: grain gathered in autumn; reap, harvest.

25.2a **Not tilling** the **crop. Not clearing** the **plow-land.**
25.2b **Not tilling** the **crop. Not-yet affluence indeed.**

Cross, *PING*: cross a dry or frozen river. Ideogram: horse and ice.
11.2a **Availing** of **crossing** the **watercourse.**

Crowds, *ZHONG*: many people, large group, masses; all, all beings.
7.PS **Arguing necessarily possesses crowds rising-up.**
7.PS The **legions imply crowds indeed.**
7.PW A **jun zi uses tolerating** the **commoners** to **accumulate crowds.**
7.IT The **legions. Crowds indeed.**
7.IT **Able** to **use crowds** for **correcting.**
8.PS **Crowds necessarily possess** a **place** to **group.**
13/14.HP **Great possessing: crowds indeed.**
35.3a **Crowds: sincerity, repenting extinguished.**
35.3b **Crowds:** to **sincerity belongs purpose.**
36.PW A **jun zi uses supervising** the **crowds availing** of **darkening and-also brightening.**
40.IT **Going acquires crowds indeed.**

Crown, *LONG*: high, above all others; peak; grandiose, majestic, eminent, venerable.
28.4a The **ridgepole crowning. Significant.**
28.4b To the **ridgepole crowning belongs significance.**

Crown prince, *HOU*: sovereign; prince; empress, mother of an imperial prince. Ideogram: one, mouth and shelter, one with the sovereign's orders.
11.PW The **crown prince uses property** to **accomplish** the **dao belonging** to **heaven** and **earth.**
24.PW The **crown prince** used culminating sun **not** to **inspect** on all **sides.**
44.PW The **crown prince uses spreading fate** to **command** the **four sides.**

Cry-out/outcry, *HAO*: call out, proclaim; order, command; mark, label, sign; designate, name.
13.5a **Concording people beforehand cry-out** and **sob and-also afterwards laugh.**
43.IM/IT **Conformity crying-out possesses adversity.**
43.2a **Awe:** an **outcry, absolutely-nothing.**
43.6a **Without crying-out.**
43.6b To **without crying-out belongs pitfall.**
45.1a **Like** an **outcry, one handful activates laughter.**
56.6a **Sojourning people beforehand laugh, afterwards cry-out sobbing.**
59.5a **Dispersing sweat: one's great cries-out.**

Cuirass, *JIE*: armor; tortoise or crab shell; protective covering; border, limit, interval; protection, support; steady, rigid, solid.
16.2a The **cuirass tends-towards petrification.**
35.2a/2b **Acquiescing** in a **compact cuirass: blessing.**
58.4a The **cuirass' affliction possesses joy.**

Culminate, *ZHI*: bring to the highest degree; arrive at the end or summit; superlative; reaching one's goal.
2.1a **Treading frost, hard ice** as **culmination.**
2.1b **Culmination: hard ice indeed.**
2.IT **Culminating in-fact: space's Spring.**
5.3a **Involvement** in **illegality culminating.**
6.2b **Distress culminating reaping indeed.**
10.AT **Treading: harmony and-also culmination.**
19.IM/IT **Culminating tending-towards** the **eighth moon possesses pifall.**
19.4a **Culmination nearing.**
19.4b **Culmination nearing, without fault.**

24.6a **Culminating tending-towards ten years not controlling disciplining.**
29.PW **Streams reiterated culminate. Repeated gorge.**
40.3a **Involvement** in **illegality culminating.**
40.4a **Partnering culminating, splitting-off conforming.**
48.IM/ IT **Muddy culmination: truly not-yet** the **well-rope** in the **well.**
55.PW **Thunder** and **lightning altogether culminating. Abounding.**

Culminating sun, *ZHI RI*: acme of any time period; midday, summer solstice; midpoint of life.
24.PW The **earlier kings used culminating sun** to **bar** the **passages.**

Cultivate, *CHOU*: till fields or gardens; repeat continually, like annual plowing. Ideogram: fields and long life.
12.4a **Cultivating radiant satisfaction.**

Cup, *ZUN*: quantity a libation vessel contains; wine cup, glass, bottle.
29.4a/4b A **cup** of **liquor**, a **platter added.**

Curb, *CHENG*: reject, contain, abstain, correct, punish; reprimand, reprove; warn, caution. The heart and action, the heart acting on itself.
41.PW A **jun zi uses curbing anger** and **blocking appetites.**

Customs, *SU*: habit, usage, tradition; common people; ordinary, vulgar, trivial; worldly, secular.
53.PW A **jun zi uses residing** in **eminent actualizing-dao** to **improve** the **customs.**

Cut-off, *JUE*: cut, interrupt, disconnect, break off, separate; destroy; renounce; difficult access; worn out, alone, indigent. Ideogram: silk, knife and knot, cutting through.
61.4b **Cutting-off, sorting above indeed.**

Dao, *DAO*: way or path; ongoing process of being and the course it traces for each person or thing; ultimate reality, intrinsic nature; origin. Ideogram: go and head, opening a path.
1.3b **Reversing: returning** to **dao indeed.**
1.IT **Energy**'s **dao transforming** and **changing.**
2.1b **Docile involvement** in **one's dao.**
2.2b **Earth**'s **dao shines indeed.**
2.6b **Their dao exhausted indeed.**
2.IT **Beforehand delusion: letting-go dao.**
5.PS **Attending implies** the **dao belonging** to **drinking** and **taking-in.**
8.IT **One's dao exhausted indeed.**
9.1a/1b **Returning** to the **origin**'s **dao.**
10.2a **Treading** in **dao: smoothing, smoothing.**
11.PW The **crown prince uses property** to **accomplish** the **dao belonging** to **heaven** and **earth.**
11.IT A **jun zi**'s **dao long-living.**
11.IT The **small** in the **person**'s **dao dissolving indeed.**
12.IT The **small** in the **person**'s **dao long-living.**
12.IT A **jun zi**'s **dao dissoving indeed.**
13.2b **Abashment: dao indeed.**
15.IT **Heavenly dao: below fording and-also shining brightness.**
15.IT **Earthly dao: lowly and-also above moving.**
15.IT **Heavenly dao lessens overfilling and-also augments humbling.**
15.IT **Earthly dao transforms overfilling and-also diffuses humbling.**
15.IT **People**'s **dao hates overfilling and-also loves humbling.**
17.4a **Possessing conformity, locating in dao, using brightness.**
17.4b **Possessing conformity, locating** in **dao.**
18.2b **Acquiring** the **center: dao**

indeed.
19.IT **Dao belonging** to **heaven indeed.**
20.1b The **small** in the **person**'s **dao indeed.**
20.3b **Not-yet letting-go dao indeed.**
20.IT **Overseeing** the **spirit dao belonging** to **heaven.**
20.IT The **wise person uses spirit dao** to **set-up teaching.**
24.IM/IT **Reversing: returning** to **one's dao.**
24.4b **Using adhering** to **dao indeed.**
24.6b **Reversing** the **chief**'s **dao indeed.**
26.6b **Dao:** the **great moving indeed.**
27.3b **Dao:** the **great rebels indeed.**
29.1b **Letting-go dao: pitfall indeed.**
29.6b **Six above, letting-go dao.**
30.2b **Acquiring** the **center: dao indeed.**
32.PS **Dao belonging** to **husband** and **wife.**
32.IT **Lasting with-respect-to one's dao indeed.**
32.IT **Dao belonging** to **heaven** and **earth.**
32.IT The **wise person: lasting with-respect-to one's dao and-also below heaven changing** and **accomplishing.**
35.6b **Dao not-yet shining indeed.**
37.IT **And-also household's dao correct.**
38.PS **Household**'s **dao exhausted, necessarily turning-away.**
38.2b **Not-yet letting-go dao indeed.**
39.IT **One's dao exhausted indeed.**
40.2b **Acquiring** the **center: dao indeed.**
41.IT **One's dao moving above.**
42.IT **One's dao:** the **great shining.**
42.IT **Woody dao, thereupon movement.**
42.IT **Dao belonging** to **total augmenting.**
43.2b **Acquiring** the **center, dao indeed.**
44.1b The **supple**'s **dao hauling-along indeed.**
49.PS The **well**'s **dao not permitting not skinning.**
52.IT **One's dao: shining brightness.**
53.3b **Letting-go one's dao indeed.**
60.4b **Receiving dao above indeed.**
60.6b **One's dao exhausted indeed.**
63.2b **Using** the **center**'s **dao indeed.**
63.IT **One's dao exhausted indeed.**

Dare, *GAN*: have the courage to, try, permit oneself; bold, intrepid; rash, offensive.
22.PW A **jun zi uses brightening** the **multitude** of **standards without daring** to **sever litigations.**

Darkness, *HUI*: obscurity, night, mist; make or become dark; last day of the lunar month.
17.PW A **jun zi uses turning** to **darkness** to **enter** a **reposing pause.**
36.PW A **jun zi uses supervising** the **crowds availing** of **darkening and-also brightening.**
36.6a **Not brightness, darkness.**
36.IT **Darkening one's brightness indeed.**

Dawn, *ZHAO*: early morning, before daybreak.
6.6a **Completing dawn thrice depriving** of **it.**

Day/sun, *RI*: the sun and the time of a sun-cycle, a day.
See also **Before-zenith sun, Culminating sun, Daybreak, Day-time**
1.3a A **jun zi completing** the **day: energy parching.**
1.3b **Completing** the **day: energy parching.**
16.2a **Not completing** the **day.**
16.2b **Not completing** the **day, Trial, significant.**
16.IT **Anterior sun** and **moon not exceeding.**
18.IM/IT **Before seedburst three days.**
18.IM/IT **After seedburst three days.**

24.IM/ IT The **seventh day comes return**.
24.PW The **earlier kings used culminating sun** to **bar** the **passages**.
26.IT The **day renewing one's actualizing-dao**.
30.3a/3b **Radiance belonging** to the **sun setting**.
30.IT **Sun** and **moon congregating reaching heaven**.
32.IT **Sun** and **moon**: **acquiring heaven and-also enabling lasting** and **illuminating**.
35.IM **Day time sun thrice reflected**.
35.IT **Day-time sun thrice reflected indeed**.
36.1a **Three days not taking-in**.
42.IT The **sun advances without delimiting**.
51.2a The **seventh day acquiring**.
55.IM **No grief. Properly** the **sun** in the **center**.
55.2a/4a/4b The **sun** in the **center**: **viewing** a **bin**.
55.3a The **sun** in the **center**: **viewing froth**.
55.IT **No grief, properly** the **sun** in the **center**.
55.IT The **sun** in the **center**, by **consequence setting**.
57.5a **Before husking, three days**.
57.5a **After husking, three days**.
63.2a/2b The **seventh day acquiring**.
63.4a/4b **Completing** the **day**: a **warning**.

Daybreak, *SU*: first light, after dawn; early morning; early, careful attention.
40.IM **daybreak, significant**.
40.IT **Possessing directed going**: **daybreak, significant**.

Day-time, *ZHOU*: daylight half of the 24-hour cycle.
35.IM **Day-time sun thrice reflected**.
35/36.HP **Prospering**: **day-time indeed**.
35.IT **Day-time sun thrice reflected indeed**.

Decade, *XUN*: ten days or years; complete time period.
55.1a/1b **Although** a **decade**, **without fault**.
55.1b **Exceeding** a **decade**: **calamity indeed**.

Decay, *GU*: rotting, poisonous; intestinal worms, venomous insects; evil magic; disorder, error; pervert by seduction or flattery; unquiet ghost. Ideogram: dish and worms, putrefaction and poisonous decay.
This term is the name of hexagram 18 and recurs throughout its texts. It also occurs in:
17.HP **Decay**: by **consequence stability indeed**.

Decrease, *SHUAI*: weaken, fade, decline, decay, diminish, cut off; grow old; adversity, misfortune.
41.HP **Increasing**: the **beginning belonging** to **decreasing indeed**.
42.HP **Decreasing**: the **beginning belonging** to **increasing indeed**.

Dedicate, *YUE*: imperial offering at the spring equinox, when stores are low; offer a sacrifice with limited resources. Ideogram: spring and thin.
45.2a **Conforming, thereupon Harvesting**: **availing** of **dedicating**.
46.2a **Conforming, thereupon Harvesting**: **availing** of **dedicating**.
63.5a **Not thus** the **dedicated offering belonging** to the **Western neighbor**.

Defend-against, *FANG*: keep off, protect from, guard against; rampart, dam; erect a protective barrier. Ideogram: open space and earthen ramparts.
62.3a **Nowhere exceeding, defending-against it**.
63.PW A **jun zi uses pondering** on **distress and-also providing** for **defending-against it**.

Delay, *HUAN*: retard, put off; let things take their course; tie loosely; gradually, leisurely; lax, tardy, negligent.
39/40.HP **Unraveling**: **delay indeed**.
40.PS **Unraveling implies delay indeed**.
41.PS **Delaying necessarily possesses** a **place** to **let-go**.

61.PW A **jun zi uses deliberating litigations** to **delay death**.

Deliberate, *YI*: consult, discuss, weigh the options and find the best course; arrange, select; criticize. Ideogram: words and right.

60.PW And **deliberating actualizing-dao** in **movement**.

61.PW A **jun zi uses deliberating litigations** to **delay death**.

Delight, *LUO*: take joy or pleasure in; pleasant, relaxed; music as harmony, elegance and pleasure.

5.PW A **jun zi uses drinking** and **taking-in** to **repose delightfully**.

7/8.HP **Grouping**: **delight**.

16.PW The **earlier kings used arousing delight** to **extol actualizing-dao**.

Delimit, *JIANG*: define frontiers, boundaries, draw limits.

2.IT **Actualizing-dao unites without delimiting**.

2.IT **Moving** on the **earth without delimiting**.

2.IT **Corresponding** to the **earth without delimiting**.

19.PW And **tolerating** to **protect** the **commoners without delimiting**.

42.IT The **commoners stimulated without delimiting**.

42.IT The **sun advances without delimiting**.

Delude, *MI*: bewitch, fascinate, deceive; confused, stupefied, infatuated; blinded by vice.

2.IM **Beforehand delusion**, **afterwards acquiring**.

2.IT **Beforehand delusion**: **letting-go dao**.

24.6a **Deluding return**. **Pitfall**.

24.6b To the **deluding return belongs pifall**.

Demon, *CHOU*: malignant genius; horror; ugly, vile, disgraceful, shameful; drunken; detest, hate; strange, ominous; class, group, crowd; similar. Ideogram: fermented liquor and soul. Demon and tiger are opposed on the North–South axis of the Universal Compass; the tiger (Extreme Yang) protects against the demons of Extreme Yin.

20.2b **Truly permitting** the **demoniac indeed**.

28.5b **Truly permitting** the **demoniac indeed**.

30.6a **Severing** the **head**. **Capturing in-no-way its demons**.

40.3b **Truly permitting** the **demoniac indeed**.

53.3b **Radiating** a **flock** of **demons indeed**.

Dense, *CONG*: close-set, bushy, crowded; a grove.

29.6a **Dismissing tending-towards dense jujube-trees**.

Depart, *QU*: leave, quit, go; far away, far from; remove, reject, dismiss; lost, gone.

9.4a **Blood departing**, **awe emerging**.

49/50.HP **Skinning**: **departing anteriority indeed**.

59.6a **Departing far-away**.

Depend, *YI*: rely on, trust; conform to; image, illustration; acquiesce, obey.

42.4a **Harvesting**: **availing** of **activating depends** on **shifting** the **city**.

Deprive, *CHI*: strip of rank, take away a ceremonial garment; lose authority or enthusiasm.

6.6a **Completing dawn thrice depriving** of **it**.

Depth, *SHEN*: deep water; profound, abstruse; ardent, strong, intense, inner; sound the depths.

32.1b **Beginning seeking depth indeed**.

Designate, *WEI*: say, express in words, give a name; mean, signify; consider as; talk about. Ideogram: words and belly, describing the essential.

19.5b To **moving** the **center belongs designating indeed**.

37.6b **Reversing designation belonging** to **individuality indeed**.

37.IT To **father** and **mother belongs designation**.

46.PS **Assembling and-also** the **above implies** the **designation belonging** to **ascending**.

62.6a **That designates calamity** and **blunder**.

Desire, *YUAN*: wish, hope or long for; covet; desired object.

10.1b **Solitarily moving desire indeed**.

11.4b In the **center** the **heart**'s **desire indeed**.

11.5b In the **center using** the **movement** of **desire indeed**.

53.5b **Acquiring** the **place desired indeed**.

59.2b **Acquiring** the **desired indeed**.

61.2b In the **center** the **heart**'s **desire indeed**.

Desist, *BA*: cease, leave off, discontinue, finish; enough.

61.3a/3b **Maybe drumbeating, maybe desisting**.

Destroy, *BAI*: ruin, defeat, failure; violate, subvert, decompose.

5.3b **Respectful consideration, not destroying indeed**.

14.2b **Amassing** in the **center, not destroying indeed**.

24.6a **Completing possesses great destruction**.

Detain, *LIU*: delay, postpone, protract; keep, retain (a guest); a long time, always.

56.PW **A jun zi uses bright consideration availing** of **punishment and-also not detaining litigations**.

Die, *SI*: sudden or untimely death; death penalty; run out of energy; inert, stagnant, fixed.

16.5a/5b **Persevering, not dying**.

30.4a **Burning thus. Dying thus. Thrown-out thus**.

58.IT The **commoners forget their death**.

61.PW A **jun zi uses deliberating litigations** to **delay death**.

Differentiate, *BIAN*: argue, dispute, criticize; sophisticated, artful. Ideogram: words and sharp or pungent.

6.1b **Although** the **small possesses words, one's differentiation brightening indeed**.

10.PW A **jun zi uses differentiating above** and **below**.

14.4b **Brightness differentiates clearly indeed**.

48.AT The **well**: **using differentiating righteously**.

Diffuse, *LIU*: flow out, spread, permeate.

1.IT The **kinds** of **beings diffuse** in **forms**.

15.IT **Earthly dao transforms overfilling and-also diffuses humbling**.

29.IT **Stream diffusing and-also not overfilling**.

Dim, *MING*: dark, obscure; obtuse, immature; cavern, the underworld. Ideogram: 16th day of the lunar month, when the moon begins to dim.

16.6a **Dim providing**.

16.6b **Dim providing located above**.

46.6a **Dim ascending**.

46.6b **Dim ascending located above**.

Diminish, *SUN*: lessen, make smaller, take away from; lose, damage, spoil, wound; blame, criticize; offer up, give away. Ideogram: hand and ceremonial vessel, offering sacrifice.

This term is the name of hexagram 41 and recurs throughout its texts. It also occurs in:

42.PS **Diminishing and-also not climaxing necessarily augments**.

42.HP **Diminishing, augmenting**.

42.IT **Diminishing above, augmenting below**.

Direct, *YOU*: move on or through water; place, residence, focus; that which. Ideogram: pole to sound the depth of water.

See also: **Possessing directed going, Without direction Harvesting**

2.IT A **jun zi**: **directed moving**.

37.2a **Without direction releasing**.

Disarray, *LUAN*: throw into disorder, mislay, confuse; out of place; discord, insurrection, anarchy.

7.6b **Necessarily disarraying** the **fiefdoms indeed**.

10.2b The **center not** the **origin** of **disarray indeed**.
11.6b **One's fate disarrayed indeed**.
12.2b **Not disarraying** the **flock indeed**.
45.1a/1b **Thereupon disarraying, thereupon clustering**.
45.1b **One's purpose disarrayed indeed**.
53.6b **Not permitting disarray indeed**.
63.IM **Completing: disarray**.
63.IT **Completing: stopping**, by **consequence disarray**.

Discard, *MIE*: disregard, ignore; petty, worthless, insignificant, trash.
23.1a/2a **Discarding Trial, pitfall**.

Discipline, *ZHENG*: subjugate vassals, reduce to order; punishing expedition. Ideogram: step and correct, a rectifying move.
9.6a/6b A **jun zi disciplining, pitfall**.
11.1a **Disciplining, significant**.
11.1b **Eradicating thatch-grass: disciplining, significant**.
15.5b **Disciplining, not submitting indeed**.
15.6a **Disciplining** the **capital city**.
15.6b **Disciplining** the **capital city indeed**.
24.6a **Culminating tending-towards ten years not controlling disciplining**.
27.2a The **jaws disciplined, pitfall**.
27.2b **Six** at **second: disciplining, pitfall**.
30.6a/6b The **king avails** of **emerging** to **discipline**.
34.1a **Disciplining, pitfall**.
41.2a **Disciplining, pitfall**.
46.IM/IT The **South**: **disciplining, significant**.
47.2a **Disciplining, pitfall**.
47.6a **Disciplining, significant**.
49.2a **Disciplining significant, without fault**.
49.3a/6a **Disciplining: pitfall**.
51.6a **Disciplining: pitfall**.
53.3a/3b The **husband disciplined, not returning**.
54.IM **Converting maidenhood. Disciplining, pitfall**.
54.1a **Disciplining, significant**.
54.IT **Disciplining, pitfall**.
64.3a/3b **Not-yet fording: disciplining, pitfall**.

Disclose, *KAI*: open, reveal, unfold, display; enact rites, clear land; final phase of both hemicycles in the Universal Compass. Ideogram: house doors bursting open.
7.6a **Disclosing** the **city, receiving** a **household**.

Discuss, *ZHUO*: deliberate; hear opinions, consult; banquet, feast. Ideogram: wine and ladle, pouring out wine to open discussion.
41.1a **Discussing diminishing it**.

Disembowel, *KUI*: butcher and bleed an animal; cut open and clean a fish; prepare for sacrifice.
54.6a A **scholar disembowels** a **goat without blood**.

Disheartened, *JIU*: chronic disease; sadness, distress; poverty; mourning.
10.IT **Treading** on the **supreme position and-also not disheartened**.

Dismiss, *ZHI*: put aside, reject; judge and find wanting.
29.6a **Dismissing tending-towards dense jujube-trees**.

Disorder, *FEN*: trouble, doubt; affairs, multiple occupations; mixed, assorted; confused, perplexed; variegated, spotted.
57.2a **Disorder like, significant**.
57.2b To the **disorder like belongs significance**.

Disperse, *HUAN*: spread, disperse, distribute; scatter clouds or crowds; dispel illusions, fears and suspicions; dissolve, evaporate, vanish; fog lifting or clearing away.
This term is the name of hexagram 59 and recurs throughout its texts. It also occurs in:
60.HP **Dispersing: radiance indeed**.

Display, *YANG*: spread, extend, scatter, divulge, promote. Ideogram: hand and expand, spreading a message.
14.PW A **jun zi uses terminating**

hatred to **display improvement.**
43.IM **Parting. Displaying tending-towards** the **king's chambers.**
43.IT **Displaying tending-towards** the **king's chambers.**

Dissolve, *XIAO*: liquefy, melt, thaw; diminish, disperse; eliminate, exhaust. Ideogram: water dissolving differences.
See also: **Dissolving pause**
11.IT The **small** in the **person's dao dissolving indeed.**
12.IT A **jun zi's dao dissolving indeed.**
19.IT **Dissolving not lasting indeed.**
46.6b **Dissolving, not affluence indeed.**

Dissolving pause, *XIAO XI*: transitional phase of the Universal Compass in which Yin or structure dissolves so that Yang or action may again emerge.
23.IT A **jun zi honors** the **dissolving pause** to **overfill emptiness.**
55.IT **Associating** with the **season's dissolving pause.**

Distance, *YUAN*: far off, remote; keep at a distance; a long time, far away in time. Ideogram: go and a long way.
4.4b **Solitude distancing substance indeed.**
24.1a **Not distancing return.**
24.1b To **not distancing belongs return.**
33.PW A **jun zi uses distancing** the **small** in the **person.**
41.AT **Diminishing: using distancing harm.**
44.4b **Distancing** the **commoners indeed.**
59.6b **Distancing harm indeed.**

Distress, *HUAN*: tribulation, grief, affliction, illness. Ideogram: heart and clamor, the heart distressed.
6.2b **Distress culminating reaping indeed.**
63.PW A **jun zi uses pondering** on **distress and-also providing** for **defending-against it.**

Dive, *JUN*: deep water; dig; profound, abstruse.
32.1a **Diving persevering: Trial, pitfall.**
32.1b To **diving persevering belongs pitfall.**

Divide, *YI*: separate, break apart, sever; oppose; different, foreign, strange, rare.
38.PW A **jun zi uses concording and-also dividing.**

Docile, *XUN*: amiable, mild, yielding, tame; gradual; a docile horse.
2.1b **Docile involvement** in **one's dao.**

Donate, *SHANG*: bestow, confer, grant; rewards, gifts; celebrate, take pleasure in.
64.4a **Three years, possessing** a **donation tending-towards** the **great city.**

Door, *HU*: inner door, chamber door; a household; distinct from gate, *MEN*, outer door.
6.2a **People, three hundred doors.**
55.6a/6b **Peeping** through **one's door.**
60.1a/1b **Not emerging** from the **door chambers.**

Doubled, *LIANG*: twice, both; again; dual, a pair.
See also: **Redouble**
30.PW **Brightness doubled arouses** the **radiance.**

Doubt, *YI*: suspect, distrust, wonder; uncertain, dubious; surmise, conjecture, fear.
9.6b **Possessing** a **place** to **doubt indeed.**
16.4a **No doubt.**
22.4b **Six** at **fourth.** An **appropriate position** to **doubt indeed.**
33.6b **Without** a **place** to **doubt indeed.**
38.6b The **flock, doubt extinguished indeed.**
41.3b **Three** by **consequence doubtful indeed.**
46.3b **Without** a **place** to **doubt indeed.**
55.2a **Going acquires doubt, affliction.**
57.1b **Purpose doubtful indeed.**
58.1b **Moving, not-yet doubting indeed.**

63.4b **Possessing** a **place** to **doubt indeed**.

Drag, *ZHU*: pull along a hurt or malfunctioning foot; limping, lame. Ideogram: foot and worm, an infected foot.

44.1a **Ruined** the **pig**'s **conformity**: **hoof dragging**.

Dragon, *LONG*: mythical spirit-being endowed with supreme power, associated with the energy of heaven; can change its shape at will; sleeps under the earth or at the bottom of the waters, wherefrom it emerges in the springtime and rises up to heaven. In the Universal Compass it is associated to the East and to the beginning of the Yang hemicycle.

1.1a/1b **Immersed dragon, no availing** of.

1.2a/2b **Viewing** a **dragon located** in the **fields**.

1.5a/5b **Flying dragon located** in **heaven**.

1.6a/6b **Overbearing dragon possesses repenting**.

1.7a **Viewing** a **flock** of **dragons without head**.

1.IT The **season rides six dragons used** to **drive** up to **heaven**.

2.6a/6b **Dragons struggle tending-towards** the **countryside**.

Draw-near, *JIU*: approach; near completion; composed, finished; able, willing; shortly.

49.3a/3b **Skinning word thrice drawing-near**.

Draw-water, *JI*: draw water from a well; draw forth, lead; assimilate a doctrine or an example. Ideogram: water and reach to.

48.3a **Permitting availing** of **drawing-water**.

Dread, *WEI*: fear, respect, stand in awe of; apprehensive; envious.

51.6b The **dreading neighbor**, a **warning indeed**.

Drench, *JIN*: soak, penetrate, immerse, steep in; infiltrate gradually; progressive accumulation.

19.IT The **solid drenched and-also long-living**.

33.IT **Drenched and-also long-living**.

Drink, *YIN*: drink, swallow, ingest liquid or food; inhale, suck in.

5.PS **Attending implies** the **dao belonging** to **drinking** and **taking-in**.

5.PW A **jun zi uses drinking** and **taking-in** to **repose delightfully**.

6.PS **Drinking** and **taking-in necessarily possess arguing**.

27.PW And **articulation** in **drinking** and **taking-in**.

53.2a/2b **Drinking** and **taking-in**: **feasting, feasting**.

64.6a **Possessing conformity tending-towards drinking liquor**.

64.6b **Drinking liquor, soaking** the **head**.

Drive, *YU*: drive a cart, ride or tame a horse; govern, rule. With the pronunciation *YA*: go to meet, encounter.

1.IT The **season rides six dragons used** to **drive** up to **heaven**.

Droop, *CHUI*: hang down, let fall; bow; condescend to inferiors; almost, near; suspended; hand down to posterity.

36.1a **Drooping one's wings**.

Drudgery, *JIAN*: difficult, hard, repetitive work; distressing, sorrowful. Ideogram: perverse and sticky earth, soil difficult to cultivate.

11.3a **Drudgery**: **Trial, without fault**.

14.1a **Drudgery** by **consequence without fault**.

21.4a **Harvesting drudgery, Trial**.

21.4b **Harvesting drudgery, Trial**: **significant**.

26.3a **Harvesting drudgery, Trial**.

34.6a/6b **Drudgery**, by **consequence significant**.

36.IM/ IT **Harvesting**: **drudgery, Trial**.

Drumbeating, *GU*: beat a skin or earthenware drum; excite, arouse, encourage; joyous, happy.

30.3a **Not drumbeating** a **jar and-also singing**.

61.3a/3b **Maybe drumbeating, maybe desisting**.

Dugout, *ZHOU*: hollowed log, canoe; boat, ride or transport by boat.
61.IT **Riding** a **wooden dugout**: **emptiness indeed**.

Duskiness, *MEI*: obscure, indistinct; insufficient light; times of day when it is not fully light. Ideogram: day and not-yet.
3.IT **Heaven creates grasses' duskiness**.

Each, *GE*: each separate person or thing; particular, distinct; every, all.
1.IT **Each correcting innate fate**.

Ear, *ER*: ear; handle; side.
21.6a/6b **Is** not **locking-up submerging** the **ears**?
50.3a/3b The **vessel's ears skinned**.
50.5a The **vessel's yellow ears, metallic rings**.
50.5b The **vessel's yellow ears**.
50.IT The **root and-also** the **ear** and the **eye**: **understanding bright**.

Earlier Kings, *XIAN WANG*: ideal rulers of old; the golden age, primal time; mythical sages in harmony with nature.
This expression occurs in the Patterns of Wisdom section of Hexagrams 8, 16, 20, 21, 24, 25, 59.

Earth, *DI*: the earth, ground on which the human world rests; basis of all things, nourishes all things; essential Yin; Symbol of the trigram Space, *KUN*.
2.PW **Earth's potency**: **space**.
2.2b **Earth's dao shines indeed**.
2.IT The **female horse**: to the **earth sorted**.
2.IT **Moving** on the **earth without delimiting**.
2.IT **Corresponding** to the **earth without delimiting**.
3.PS **Possessing heaven** and **earth**.
3.PS **Overfilling** the **interspace belonging** to **heaven** and **earth implies verily** the **myriad beings**.
7.PW The **earth's center possesses stream**. The **legions**.
8.PW The **earth possesses stream above**. **Grouping**.
11.PW **Heaven** and **earth mingling**. **Compenetration**.
11.PW The **crown prince uses property** to **accomplish** the **dao belonging** to **heaven** and **earth**.
11.PW And **braces** the **reciprocity properly belonging** to **heaven** and **earth**.
11.3b **Heaven** and **earth's border indeed**.
11.IT By **consequence** of **that heaven** and **earth mingling and-also** the **myriad beings interpenetrating indeed**.
12.PW **Heaven** and **earth not mingling**. **Obstruction**.
12.IT By **consequence** of **that heaven** and **earth not mingling and-also** the **myriad beings not interpenetrating indeed**.
15.PW The **earth's center possesses mountain**. **Humbling**.
15.IT **Earthly dao**: **lowly and-also above moving**.
15.IT **Earthly dao transforms overfilling and-also diffuses humbling**.
16.PW **Thunder emerges** from the **earth impetuously**. **Providing**.
16.IT To **anterior heaven** and **earth** it **thus belongs**.
16.IT **Heaven** and **earth use yielding** and **stirring-up**.
19.PW The **pond possesses earth above**. **Nearing**.
20.PW **Wind moves above** the **earth**. **Overseeing**.
23.PW **Mountain adjoining with-respect-to earth**. **Stripping**.
24.PW **Thunder located** in the **earth's center**. **Return**.
24.IT **Return** to **one's viewing** the **heart belonging** to **heaven** and **earth reached**.
27.IT **Heaven** and **earth nourish** the **myriad beings**.
29.IT **Earth's venture**: **mountains, rivers, hill-tops, mounds indeed**.
30.IT The **hundred grains, grasses, trees congregating reaching** the **earth**.
31.PS **Possessing heaven** and **earth**.
31.IT **Heaven** and **earth influence**

and-also the **myriad beings change** and **generate**.
31.IT **And-also** the **motives belonging** to **heaven** and **earth**'s **myriad beings permit viewing actually**.
32.IT **Dao belonging** to **heaven** and **earth**.
32.IT **And-also** the **motives belonging** to **heaven** and **earth**'s **myriad beings permit viewing actually**.
34.IT The **correct great and-also** the **motives belonging** to **heaven** and **earth permit viewing actually**.
35.PW **Brightness emerging above** the **earth**. **Prospering**.
35.IT **Brightness emerging above** the **earth**.
36.PW/IT **Brightness entering** the **earth**'s **center**. **Brightness hidden**.
36.6a/6b **Afterwards entering tending-towards earth**.
37.IT The **great belonging** to **heaven** and **earth righteous indeed**.
38.IT **Heaven** and **earth**: **polarizing and-also their affairs concording indeed**.
40.IT **Heaven** and **earth unraveling and-also thunder** and **rain arousing**.
42.IT **Heaven spreads**, **earth generates**.
44.IT **Heaven** and **earth reciprocally meeting**.
45.PW **Pond above with-respect-to earth**. **Clustering**.
45.IT **And-also** the **motives belonging** to **heaven** and **earth**'s **myriad beings permit viewing actually**.
46.PW The **earth**'s **center generates wood**. **Ascending**.
48.AT The **well**: **actualizing-dao belonging** to **earth indeed**.
49.IT **Heaven** and **earth skinning and-also** the **four seasons accomplishing**.
54.IT The **great**'s **righteousness belonging** to **heaven** and **earth**.
54.IT **Heaven** and **earth not mingling**.
55.IT **Heaven** and **earth overfilling emptiness**.
60.IT **Heaven** and **earth articulating and-also** the **four seasons accomplishing**.

East, *DONG*: eastern direction, corresponding to morning, spring and to the Wooden Moment in the Universal Compass; stirring up and germination of a new life-cycle; place of honor and the person occupying it.
See also: **Eastern North**
63.5a/5b The **Eastern neighbor slaughters cattle**.

Eastern North, *DONG BEI*: the Eastern side of North, direction corresponding to the completion of a cycle; border, limit, boundary; mountain; accomplishing words, summing up previous experience; dark, cold winter night.
2.IM/ IT **Eastern North**: **losing partnering**.
39.IM/ IT **Not Harvesting**: **Eastern North**.

Eight, *BA*: number eight; number of highly valued essentials: eight trigrams, eight immortals, eight compass points.
19.IM/ IT **Culminating tending-towards** the **eighth moon possesses pifall**.

Eliminate, *CHU*: root out, remove, do away with, take off; keep out; vacate, exchange.
45.PW A **jun zi uses eliminating weapons** for **implements**.

Embarrassment, *XIU*: shame, confusion; conscious of guilt or fault; shy, blushing; humble offering. Ideogram: sheep, sheepish feeling.
12.3a/3b **Enwrapped** in **embarrassment**.
32.3a **Maybe** to **receiving belongs embarrassment**.

Embellish, *SHI*: ornament, paint, brighten, clean; apply cosmetics; patch up the appearance; pretend, make believe.
22.PS **Adorning implies embellishing indeed**.
23.PS **Involved** in **embellishing**, **therefore afterwards Growing**, by

consequence used-up actually.

Emblem-ax, *FU*: moon-shaped ax, symbol of governmental power.

56.4a/4b **Acquiring one's own emblem-ax.**

57.6a/6b **Losing one's own emblem-ax.**

Emerge, *CHU*: come out of, proceed from, spring from, issue forth; appear, be born; bear, generate; leave, flee; Action of the trigram Shake, *ZHEN*. Ideogram: stem with branches and leaves emerging.

1.IT **Heads emerging** from the **multitude** of **beings.**

4.PW **Below** the **mountain emerges springwater. Enveloping.**

5.4a **Emerging originating** from the **cave.**

7.1a/1b The **legions emerging using ordinance.**

9.4a **Blood departing, awe emerging.**

9.4b **Possessing conformity, awe emerging.**

13.1b **Emerging** from the **gate concording people.**

16.PW **Thunder emerges** from the **earth impetuously. Providing.**

17.1a/1b **Emerging** from the **gate, mingling possesses achievement.**

24.IM **Emerging, entering, without affliction.**

24.IT **That uses emerging, entering, without affliction.**

29.2b **Not-yet emerging** from the **center indeed.**

30.5a **Emerging tears like gushing.**

30.6a/6b The **king avails** of **emerging** to **discipline.**

35.PW **Brightness emerging above** the **earth. Prospering.**

35.IT **Brightness emerging above** the **earth.**

36.4a **Tending-towards emerging** from the **gate chambers.**

37.PW **Wind originating** from **fire emerging. Household people.**

50.1a/1b **Harvesting: emerging** from **obstruction.**

51.IT **Emerging permits using guarding** the **ancestral temple,** the **field-altar,** the **offertory-millet.**

52.PW A **jun zi uses pondering not** to **emerge** from **one's position.**

59.6a **Emerging, without fault.**

60.1a/1b **Not emerging** from the **door chambers.**

60.2a **Not emerging** from the **gate chambers.**

60.2b **Not emerging** from the **gate chambers, pitfall.**

64.IT **Not-yet emerging** from the **center indeed.**

Eminent, *XIAN*: worthy, excellent, virtuous; endowed with moral and intellectual power; second only to the wise, *SHENG*.

8.4b **Outside grouping with-respect-to eminence.**

26.IT The **solid above and-also honoring eminence.**

26.IT **Nourishing eminence indeed.**

27.IT The **wise person nourishes eminence used** to **extend** to the **myriad commoners.**

50.IT **And-also** the **great**'s **Growing uses nourishing** the **wise** and the **eminent.**

53.PW A **jun zi uses residing** in **eminent actualizing-dao** to **improve** the **customs.**

Empty, *XU*: void; absence of images and concepts; vacant, insubstantial; empty yet fertile space.

23.IT A **jun zi honors** the **dissolving pause** to **overfill emptiness.**

31.PW A **jun zi uses emptiness** to **acquiesce** the **people.**

41.IT **Diminishing, augmenting: overfilling emptiness.**

46.3a/3b **Ascending** an **empty capital.**

54.6b **Receiving** an **empty basket indeed.**

55.IT **Heaven** and **earth overfilling emptiness.**

61.IT **Riding** a **wooden dugout: emptiness indeed.**

Enable, see **Able/enable**

Enclose, *XIAN*: put inside a fence or barrier; pen, corral; protect; restrain, obstruct; rule, model.

26.3a **Named: enclosing** the **cart, escorting.**
37.1a/1b **Enclosure: possessing household.**

Encounter, *DI*: see face to face; visit, interview.
47.1a **Three year's-time not encountering.**
55.6a **Three year's-time not encountering.**

Encourage, *CHUAN*: exhort, stimulate; advise, persuade; admonish.
48.PW A **jun zi uses** the **toiling commoners** to **encourage reciprocity.**
58.IT The **commoners encouraged actually in-fact.**

Encroach, *QIN*: invade, usurp, appropriate; advance stealthily, enter secretly.
15.5a/5b **Harvesting: availing** of **encroaching** and **subjugating.**

End, *JI*: last or highest point; final, extreme; ridgepole of a house.
60.2b **Letting-go** the **season: end indeed.**
64.1b **Truly not knowing** the **end indeed.**

Energy/parch, *QIAN/GAN*: unceasing forward movement, dynamic, enduring, untiring; spirit power, manifestation of yang, that activates all creation and destruction in Space; heaven, sovereign, father. With the pronunciation GAN: parch, dry up, burn, exhaust. Ideogram: sprouts or vapors rising from the ground and sunlight, both fecundating moisture and scorching drought.
This term is the name of hexagram 1 and recurs throughout its texts. It also occurs in:
2.HP **Energy: solid.**
10.IT **Stimulating and-also corresponding reaches energy.**
13.IT The **supple acquires** the **position, acquires** the **center and-also** the **correspondence reaches energy.**
13.IT **Energy moving indeed.**
21.4a **Gnawing parched meat-bones.**
21.5a **Gnawing parched meat.**

Enforce, *LAI*: compel obedience; imposed by highest authority; arrest, deliver for punishment.
21.PW The **earlier kings used brightness** in **flogging** to **enforce** the **laws.**

Enhance, *FAN*: augment, enhance, increase; thriving, plentiful.
35.IM **Prospering.** A **content feudatory avails** of **bestowing horses** to **enhance** the **multitudes.**
35.IT **That uses** a **content feudatory availing** of **bestowing horses** to **enhance** the **multitudes.**

Enlighten, *ZHAO*: cast light on, display, show; instruct, give knowledge; manifest, bright, splendid. Ideogram: sun and call, bring into the light.
35.PW A **jun zi uses originating enlightening** to **brighten actualizing-dao.**

Enrich, *YU*: make richer; material, mental or spiritual wealth; bequeath; generous, abundant. Ideogram: garments, portable riches.
See also: **Rich**
18.4a/4b **Enriching** the **decay belonging** to the **father.**
35.1a/1b **Enriching, without fault.**
42.AT **Augmenting: enriching belonging** to **actualizing-dao indeed.**
42.AT **Augmenting: long-living enriching and-also not setting-up.**

Enshroud, *YAN*: screen, shade from view, hide, cover. Ideogram: hand and cover.
See also: **Shroud**
47.IT The **solid enshrouded indeed.**

Entangle, *WANG*: embroil; caught up, involved; disorder, incoherence; foolish, wild, reckless; false, brutish behavior; vain, idle, futile.
This term occurs in the name of hexagram 25 and recurs throughout its texts. It also occurs in:
26.PS **Possessing without entanglement, therefore afterwards permitted accumulating.**

26.HP **Without entanglement: calamity indeed.**

Enter, *RU*: penetrate, go into, enter on, encroach on; progress; put into; Action of the trigram Root, *SUN*.

3.3a **Thinking** of **entering tending-towards** the **forest's center.**

5.6a **Entering tending-towards** the **cave.**

6.IT **Entering tending-towards** the **abyss indeed.**

17.PW A **jun zi uses turning** to **darkness** to **enter** a **reposing pause.**

24.IM **Emerging, entering, without affliction.**

24.IT **That uses emerging, entering, without affliction.**

29.1a **Entering tending-towards** the **gorge's recess.**

29.1b **Repeated gorge: entering** the **gorge.**

29.3a **Entering tending-towards** the **gorge's recess.**

36.PW/IT **Brightness entering** the **earth's center. Brightness hidden.**

36.4a/4b **Entering tending-towards** the **left** of the **belly.**

36.6a/6b **Afterwards entering tending-towards earth.**

47.1a/1b **Entering tending-towards** a **shady gully.**

47.3a/3b **Entering tending-towards one's house.**

57.PS The **root implies entering indeed.**

58.PS **Entering and-also afterwards stimulating it.**

Envelop, *MENG*: cover, pull over, hide, conceal; lid or cover; clouded awareness, dull; ignorance, immaturity; unseen beginnings. Ideogram: plant and covered, hidden growth.

This term is the name of hexagram 4 and recurs throughout its texts. It also occurs in:

3.HP **Enveloping: motley and-also conspicuous.**

36.IT **Using enveloping** the **great: heaviness.**

Enwrap, *BAO*: envelop, hold, contain; patient, engaged. Ideogram: enfold and self, a fetus in the womb.

4.2a **Enwrapping enveloping, significant.**

11.2a **Enwrapped** in **wasteland.**

11.2b **Enwrapped** in **wasteland, acquiring honor tending-towards** the **center: movement.**

12.2a **Enwrapped** in **receiving.**

12.3a/3b **Enwrapped** in **embarrassment.**

44.2a/2b **Enwrapping possesses fish.**

44.4a **Enwrapping without fish.**

44.5a **Using osier** to **enwrap melons.**

Equal, *PEI*: on the same level; compete with; accord with; pair; husband or wife; together.

16.PW **Using equaling grandfathers** and **predecessors.**

55.1a **Meeting one's equal lord.**

Eradicate, *BA*: pull up, root out, extirpate; extricate from difficulties; elevate, promote.

11.1a **Eradicating thatch-grass intertwisted.**

11.1b **Eradicating thatch-grass: disciplining, significant.**

12.1a **Eradicating thatch-grass intertwisted.**

12.1b **Eradicating thatch-grass: Trial, significant.**

Escape, *PU*: flee, run away, turn tail; deserter, fugitive. Ideogram: go and first, precipitous flight.

6.2a **Converting and-also escaping** from **one's capital.**

6.2b **Converting, escaping: skulking indeed.**

Escort, *WEI*: accompany, protect, defend, restrain; guard of honor; military outpost.

26.3a **Named: enclosing** the **cart, escorting.**

Establish, *LI*: set up, institute, order, arrange; stand erect; settled principles.

28.PW A **jun zi uses solitary establishing not** to **fear.**

32.PW A **jun zi uses establishing, not versatility** on all **sides.**

42.6a **Establishing** the **heart, no**

persevering.

59.PW The **earlier kings used presenting tending-towards** the **supreme** to **establish** the **temples.**

Evade, *MIAN*: avoid, escape from, get away; be free of, dispense with; remove from office. Ideogram: a hare, known for its evasive skill.

40.IT **Stirring-up and-also evading reaching venturing. Unraveling.**

Evaluate, *CHENG*: assess, appraise; weigh, estimate, reckon; designate, name. Ideogram: weigh and grain, attributing value.

15.PW And **evaluating** the **beings** to **even spreading.**

57.AT The **root: evaluating and-also occulting.**

Even, *PING*: level, flatten, equalize; balanced, regular; uniform, peaceful, tranquil; restore quiet, harmonize.

11.3a **Without evening, not unevening.**

15.PW And **evaluating** the **beings** to **even spreading.**

20.6b **Purpose not-yet evened indeed.**

29.5a **Merely already evened.**

31.IT The **wise person influences people**'s **heart and-also below heaven harmonizes evenness.**

Even-more, *KUANG*: even more so, all the more.

16.IT **And-also even-more installing feudatories** to **move legions reached.**

55.IT **And-also even-more with-respect-to reaching people.**

55.IT **Even-more with-respect-to reaching soul** and **spirit.**

Evidence, *CI*: word, expression; verbal explanation; excuse; instruction, order, argument; apology.

42.6b **One-sided evidence indeed.**

Exalting worship, *YIN JIAN*: superlative of worship; glorify; intensify feelings of praise and awe.

16.PW To **exalting worship belongs** the **supreme above.**

Exceed, *GUO*: go beyond, pass by, pass over; surpass, transgress; error, fault, calamity.

This term occurs in the name of hexagrams 28 and 62 and recurs throughout their texts. It also occurs in:

16.IT **Anterior sun** and **moon not exceeding.**

27.HP The **great exceeding: toppling indeed.**

29.PS **Beings not permitted** to **use completing exceeding.**

40.PW A **jun zi uses forgiving excess** to **pardon offenses.**

42.PW And **possessing excess**, by **consequence amending.**

55.1b **Exceeding** a **decade: calamity indeed.**

61.HP The **small exceeding: excess indeed.**

63.PS **Beings possessing excess implies necessarily fording.**

Excellence, *JIA*: superior quality; fine, beautiful, glorious; happy, pleased; rejoice in, praise.

17.5a/5b **Conformity tends-towards excellence. Significant.**

30.6a **Possessing excellence.**

33.5a/5b **Excellent retiring, Trial, significant.**

49.2b **Moving possesses excellence indeed.**

Exhaust, *QIONG*: bring to an end; limit, extremity; investigate exhaustively; destitute, indigent; end without a new beginning; distinct from complete, *ZHONG*, end of a cycle that begins the next one. Ideogram: cave and naked person, bent with disease or old age.

2.6b **Their dao exhausted indeed.**

3.3b A **jun zi stowing it: going, abashment, exhaustion indeed.**

5.IT **One's righteousness not confined** nor **exhausted actually.**

8.IT **One's dao exhausted indeed.**

16.1b **Purpose exhausted, pitfall indeed.**

17.6b **Above exhausted indeed.**

19.PW A **jun zi uses teaching** to **ponder without exhausting.**

24.PS **Stripping exhausted above, reversing below.**

25.6b To **exhaustion belongs calamity indeed.**
34.1b **One's conformity exhausted indeed.**
38.PS **Household's dao exhausted, necessarily turning-away.**
39.IT **One's dao exhausted indeed.**
43.IT The **place** to **honor thereupon exhausted indeed.**
44.6b **Above exhausting abashment indeed.**
47.AT **Confining: exhausting and-also interpenetrating.**
47.IT **Honoring** the **mouth thereupon exhausted indeed.**
48.IT The **well: nourishing and-also not exhausted indeed.**
53.IT **Stirring-up not exhausted indeed.**
56.PS **Exhausting** the **great implies necessarily letting-go one's residing.**
56.1b **Purpose exhausted: calamity indeed.**
57.3b **Purpose exhausted indeed.**
57.6b **Above exhaustion indeed.**
59.IT The **solid comes and-also not exhausted.**
60.6b **One's dao exhausted indeed.**
63/64.HP **Not-yet fording:** to **manhood belongs exhaustion indeed.**
63.IT **One's dao exhausted indeed.**
64.PS **Beings not permitted exhausting indeed.**

Expel, *PI*: cast out, repress, exclude, punish; exclusionary laws and their enforcement. Ideogram: punish, authority and mouth, giving order to expel.
12.PW A **jun zi uses parsimonious actualizing-dao** to **expel heaviness.**
30.1b/1b **Using expelling fault indeed.**

Explicate, *JIANG*: explain, unfold, narrate; converse, speak; plan, discuss. Ideogram: speech and crossing beams, speech blending harmoniously.
58.PW A **jun zi uses partnering** with **friends** to **explicate repeatedly.**

Exposure, *WEI*: being exposed to danger; precipitous, unsteady, too high, dangerously leaning. Ideogram: overhanging rock, person and limit, exposure in an extreme position.
43.IT **One's exposure thereupon shining indeed.**
51.5b **Exposing movement indeed.**
52.3b **Exposure smothers** the **heart indeed.**

Extend, *JI*: reach to; draw out, prolong; continuous, enduring.
27.IT The **wise person nourishes eminence used** to **extend** to the **myriad commoners.**
43.PW A **jun zi uses spreading benefits extending** to the **below.**
44.2b **Righteously not extending hospitality indeed.**
61.IT **Trustworthiness extends** to **hog fish indeed.**
62.2a/2b **Not extending** to **one's chief.**

Extinguish, *WANG*: ruin, destroy; cease, go, die; lost without trace; forget, out of mind; absence, exile. Ideogram: person concealed by a wall, out of sight.
See also: **Repenting extinguished**
11.2a **Partnering extinguished.**
12.5a **Its extinction, its extinction.**
16.5b The **center not-yet extinguished indeed.**
38.6b The **flock, doubt extinguished indeed.**
56.5a **One arrow extinguishing.**
61.4a/4b The **horse team extinguished.**

Extol, *CHONG*: praise, honor, magnify, revere, worship; eminent, lofty.
16.PW The **earlier kings used arousing delight** to **extol actualizing-dao.**

Eye, *MU*: eye and vision; look, see, glance, observe.
9.3a/3b **Husband** and **consort reversing** the **eyes.**
50.IT The **root and-also** the **ear** and the **eye: understanding bright.**

Face, *MIAN*: visage, countenance, outer expression of the heart; honor, character, reputation; front, surface; face to face.
49.6a/6b The **small** in the **person skins** the **face**.

Fade, *RUO*: lose strength or freshness, wither, wane: fragile, feeble, weak.
28.IT **Base** and **tip fading indeed**.

Fall, *XIAN*: fall down or into, sink, drop, descend; pit, trap, fault; falling water; Action of the trigram Gorge, *KAN*.
5.IT **Solid persisting and-also not falling**.
29.PS **Gorge implies falling indeed**.
30.PS **Falling necessarily possesses** a **place** to **congregate**.

Far-away, *DI*: far, remote; send away, exile.
59.6a **Departing far-away**.

Fate, *MING*: individual destiny; birth and death as limits of life; issue orders with authority; consult the gods. Ideogram: mouth and order, words with heavenly authority.
1.IT **Each correcting innate fate**.
6.4a/4b **Returning, approaching fate**.
7.2a/2b The **king thrice bestows fate**.
7.6a/6b The **great** in the **chief possesses fate**.
11.6a **Originating** from the **capital, notifying fate**.
11.6b **One's fate disarrayed indeed**.
12.4a/4b **Possessing fate, without fault**.
14.PW And **yielding** to **heaven** to **relax** into **fate**.
19.2b **Not-yet yielding** to **fate indeed**.
25.IT **Fate belonging** to **heaven indeed**.
25.IT **Heavenly fate not shielding**.
35.1b **Not-yet acquiescing** in **fate indeed**.
44.PW The **crown prince uses spreading fate** to **command** the **four sides**.
44.5b **Purpose**: **not stowing** away **fate indeed**.
45.IT **Yielding** to **heaven's fate indeed**.
47.PW A **jun zi uses involving** in **fate** to **release purpose**.
49.4a **Amending fate, significant**.
49.4b To **amending fate belongs significance**.
49.IT **Redressing martially, skinning fate**.
50.PW A **jun zi uses correcting** the **position** to **solidify fate**.
56.5a/5b **Completion uses praising fate**.
57.PW A **jun zi uses assigning fate** to **move affairs**.
57.IT **Redoubled root uses assigning fate**.

Father, *FU*: father, act as a father, paternal, patriarchal; authoritative rule. Ideogram: hand and rod, the chastising father.
18.1a/1b/3a/3b/5a **Managing** the **decay belonging** to the **father**.
18.4a/4b **Enriching** the **decay belonging** to the **father**.
18.5b **Managing** the **father avails** of **praise**.
31.PS **Therefore afterwards possessing father** and **son**.
31.PS **Possessing father** and **son**.
37.IT To **father** and **mother belongs designation**.
37.IT The **father**, a **father**. The **son**, a **son**.

Fault, *JIU*: unworthy conduct that leads to harm, illness, misfortune; guilt, crime, punishment. Ideogram: person and differ, differ from what you should be.
See also: **Without fault**
7.IT **Significant, furthermore is** it **actually faulty?**
9.1a **Is** it **one's fault?**
13.1b **Furthermore whose fault indeed?**
14.1a **In-no-way faulty**.
17.4a **Is** it **faulty?**
18.3a **Without** the **great, faulty**.
19.3b **Fault not long-living indeed**.
28.6b **Not permitted fault indeed**.
30.1b **Using expelling fault indeed**.
34.6b **Fault not long-living indeed**.
38.1b **Using expelling fault indeed**.
38.5a **Going, is** it **faulty?**

40.3b Furthermore whose fault indeed?
43.1a Going, not mastering: activating fault.
43.1b Fault indeed.
44.3a Without the great: faulty.
53.1a Lacking fault.
60.3b Furthermore whose fault indeed?

Favor, *CHONG*: receive or confer gifts; obtain grace, win favor; dote on a woman; affection, benevolence towards a subordinate.

7.2b Receiving heavenly favor indeed.
23.5a/5b Using house people's favor.

Fear, *JU*: afraid, apprehensive; stand in awe of; intimidate.

28.PW A jun zi uses solitary establishing not to fear.
51.PW A jun zi uses anxiety and fear to adjust inspections.
51.IT Scaring the distant and-also fearing the nearby indeed.

Feast, *KAN*: take part in or give a feast; rejoice, give pleasure; contented, at ease.

53.2a/2b Drinking and taking-in: feasting, feasting.

Feathers, *YOU*: plumes, wings; feathered; flying.

53.6a Its feathers permit availing of activating the fundamentals.
53.6b Its feathers permit availing of activating the fundamentals, significant.

Feed, *KUI*: nourish, prepare and present food; provisions.

37.2a Located in the center, feeding.

Female, *PIN*: female animal; female sexual organs, particularly of farm animals; concave, hollow. Ideogram: cattle and ladle, a hollow, reproductive organ.

2.IM Space. Spring, Growing, Harvesting, Trial belonging to the female horse.
2.IT The female horse: to the earth sorted.
30.IM Growing. Accumulating female cattle.
30.IT That uses accumulating female cattle, significant indeed.

Fetter, *ZHI*: tie, manacle; restrain and hinder movement, clog wheels; impede.

4.1a Availing of stimulating shackles to fetter.

Feudatory, *HOU*: noble entrusted with governing a province; in charge of executive tasks; distinct from prince, GONG, representative of the central decisional power at the court.

3.IM/1a Harvesting: installing feudatories.
3.IT Proper installing feudatories and-also not soothing.
8.PW The earlier kings used installing a myriad cities to connect the related feudatories.
16.IM Harvesting: installing feudatories, moving legions.
16.IT And-also even-more installing feudatories to move legions reached.
18.6a/6b Not affairs, a king's feudatory.
35.IM Prospering. A content feudatory avails of bestowing horses to enhance the multitudes.
35.IT That uses a content feudatory availing of bestowing horses to enhance the multitudes.

Few, *GUA*: small number; seldom; reduce, diminish; unsupported, solitary.

9/10.HP The small accumulating: few indeed.
15.PW A jun zi uses reducing the numerous to augment the few.
47.AT Confining: using few grudges.
55/56.HP Connecting with few: sojourning indeed.

Fiefdom, *BANG*: region governed by a feudatory.

7.2b Cherishing the myriad fiefdoms indeed.
7.6b Necessarily disarraying the fiefdoms indeed.
12.IT Above and below not mingling and-also below heaven without fiefdoms indeed.

30.6b **Using correcting** the **fiefdoms indeed.**
39.IT **Using** the **correct fiefdoms indeed.**
53.IT **Permitted** to **use correcting** the **fiefdoms indeed.**
61.IT **Thereupon changing** the **fiefdoms indeed.**

Field, *TIAN*: cultivated land, farming land; preferred terrain for hunting, since game in the fields cannot escape the hunt. Ideogram: square divided into four sections, delineating fields.
1.2a/2b **Viewing** a **dragon located** in the **fields.**
7.5a The **fields possess wildfowl.**
32.4a The **fields without wildfowl.**
40.2a The **fields, capturing three foxes.**
57.4a/4b The **fields: capturing three kinds.**

Field-altar, *SHE*: altar; sacrifices to spirits of place; village, with a common god and field-altar.
51.IT **Emerging permits using guarding** the **ancestral temple**, the **field-altar**, the **offertory-millet**.

Fine, *LIANG*: excellent, refined, valuable; gentle, considerate, kind; natural.
26.3a A **fine horse, pursuing.**
54.5a/5b **Not thus fine** the **sleeves belonging** to **one's junior-sister.**

Fire, *HUO*: fire, flame, burn; warming and consuming aspect of burning; fire and brightness are the Symbols of the trigram Radiance, *LI*.
13.PW **Heaven associated** with **fire. Concording people.**
14.PW **Fire located above heaven. Great possessing.**
22.PW The **mountain possesses fire below. Adorning.**
37.PW **Wind originating** from **fire emerging. Household people.**
38.PW **Fire above, pond below. Polarizing.**
38.IT **Fire stirring-up and-also above.**
49.PW The **pond** in the **center possesses fire. Skinning.**
49.IT **Skinning. Stream** and **fire reciprocally** giving **pause.**
50.PW **Wood possesses fire above.** The **vessel.**
50.IT **Using wood**, the **root, fire.**
56.PW The **mountain possesses fire above. Sojourning.**
63.PW **Stream located above fire. Already fording.**
64.PW **Fire located above stream. Not-yet fording.**

Firm, *GU*: steady, solid, strong, secure; constant, fixed. Ideogram: old and enclosure, long preserved.
25.4b **Firmly possessing it indeed.**
32.AT **Persevering: firmness belonging** to **actualizing-dao indeed.**
33.2b **Firm purpose indeed.**
42.3b **Firmly possessing it indeed.**

Fish, *YU*: all scaly aquatic beings hidden in the water; symbol of abundance; connected with the Streaming Moment.
See also: **Hog fish**
23.5a **Threading fish.**
44.2a/2b **Enwrapping possesses fish.**
44.4a **Enwrapping without fish.**
44.4b To **without fish belongs** a **pitfall.**

Five, *WU*: number five; fivefold articulation of the Universal Compass; the Five Moments and all related qualities: directions, colors, smells, tastes, tones, feelings.
16.5b **Six** at **fifth: Trial, affliction.**
22.5b To **six** at **fifth belongs significance.**
26.5b To **six** at **fifth belongs significance.**
30.5b To **six** at **fifth belongs significance.**
41.5b **Six** at **fifth: Spring, significant.**
43.IT The **supple rides five solids indeed.**
44.5b **Nine** at **fifth: containing composition.**
55.5b To **six** at **fifth belongs significance.**
57.5b To **nine** at **fifth belongs**

significance.

Flee, *BEN*: run away; urgent, hurried; bustle, confusion; marry without rites. Ideogram: three oxen and fright, a stampede.

59.2a/2b **Dispersing**: **fleeing one's bench.**

Flesh, *FU*: skin, muscles and organs as different from bones.

21.2a/2b **Gnawing flesh, submerging** the **nose**.

23.4a/4b **Stripping** the **bed**, **using** the **flesh**.

38.5a/5b **Your ancestor gnawing flesh.**

43.4a The **sacrum without flesh**.

44.3a The **sacrum without flesh**.

Flock, *QUN*: herd, group; people of the same kind, friends, equals; crowd, multitude; move in unison, flock together. Ideogram: chief and sheep, flock around a leader.

1.7a **Viewing** a **flock** of **dragons without head.**

12.2b **Not disarraying** the **flock indeed.**

38.6b The **flock**, **doubt extinguished indeed.**

53.3b **Radiating** a **flock** of **demons indeed.**

59.4a/4b **Dispersing one's flock**: **Spring**, **significant**.

Flog, *FA*: punish with blows, beat, whip; used to find out the truth in judicial proceedings.

16.IT By **consequence punishing flogging purifies and-also** the **commoners submit.**

21.PW The **earlier kings used brightness** in **flogging** to **enforce** the **laws**.

Flow, *LIAN*: move like ripples spreading on water; running tears.

3.6a/6b **Weeping**, **blood flowing thus.**

Flower, *HUA*: symbol of beauty, elegance, abundance, culture and literature as blooming of the human mind; splendid, noble.

28.5a/5b A **withered willow generates flowers.**

Flutter, *PIAN*: fly or run about; bustle, fussy. Ideogram: young bird leaving the nest.

11.4a **Fluttering, fluttering.**

11.4b **Fluttering, fluttering, not affluence.**

Fly, *FEI*: rise in the air, spread one's wings, fly away; let fly; swift.

1.5a/5b **Flying dragon located** in **heaven.**

36.1a **Brightness hidden tends-towards flying.**

62.IM To the **flying bird abandoning belongs** a **sound.**

62.1a/1b The **flying bird**: **using** a **pitfall.**

62.6a To the **flying bird**'s **radiance belongs** a **pitfall.**

62.IT **Possessing** the **symbol belonging** to the **flying bird in-truth.**

62.IT To the **flying bird abandoning belongs** a **sound.**

Follow, *SUI*: step behind, come after, move in the same direction; comply with what is ahead; pursue; follow a way or religion; conform to; next, subsequent. Ideogram: go and fall, unavoidable movement.

This term is the name of hexagram 17 and recurs throughout its texts. It also occurs in:

18.PS **Using joy** in **following people implies necessarily possessing affairs.**

18.HP **Following**: **without anteriority indeed.**

31.3a **Holding-on** to **one's following.**

31.3b **Purpose located** in **following people.**

52.2a/2b **Not rescuing one's following.**

57.PW **Following winds**. The **root**.

Foot, *ZHI*: foot, footprint; foundation, base; walk; stop where the foot rests.

See also: **Afoot, Foot-cutting**

21.1a/1b **Shoes locked-up, submerged feet.**

22.1a **Adorning one's feet.**

34.1a/1b **Vigor tends-towards** the **feet.**

43.1a The **vigor tends-towards** the

preceding foot.

50.1a/1b The **vessel: toppling** the **foot.**

52.1a/1b The **bound: one's feet.**

Foot-cutting, *YUEH*: crippling punishment for serious crimes.

47.5a/5b **Nose-cut, foot-cut.**

Ford, *JI*: cross a river at a ford or shallow place; embark on a course of action; complete, finish, succeed; help, relieve. Ideogram: water and level, running smooth over a flat bottom.

This term occurs in the name of hexagrams 63 and 64 and recurs throughout their texts. It also occurs in:

15.IT **Heavenly dao: below fording and-also shining brightness.**

Forest, *LIN*: woods, wilderness; area with no mark of human civilization; fourth of the territorial zones: city, suburbs, countryside, forest.

3.3a **Thinking** of **entering tending-towards** the **forest's center.**

Forget, *WANG*: escape the mind; leave undone, disregard, neglect. Ideogram: heart and lost.

58.IT The **commoners forget their toil.**

58.IT The **commoners forget their death.**

Forgive, *SHE*: pardon, excuse, absolve, pass over, reprieve.

40.PW A **jun zi uses forgiving excess** to **pardon offenses.**

Form, *XING*: shape, bodily or material appearance; aspect, configuration, circumstance.

1.IT The **kinds** of **beings diffuse** in **forms.**

50.4a **One's form soiled, pitfall.**

Foundation, *JI*: base of wall or building; ground, root, basis, starting point; establish.

10.AT **Treading: foundation belonging** to **actualizing-dao indeed.**

Four, *SI*: number four; number of the cardinal directions and of the seasons; everywhere, on all sides; fourfold articulation of the Universal Compass.

16.IT **And-also** the **four seasons not straying.**

20.IT **And-also** the **four seasons not straying.**

22.4b **Six** at **fourth.** An **appropriate position** to **doubt indeed.**

26.4b **Six** at **fourth: Spring, significant.**

30.PW The **great** in the **person uses consecutive brightening** to **illuminate tending-towards** the **four sides.**

32.IT The **four seasons: transforming changes and-also enabling lasting** and **accomplishing.**

36.6b **Illuminating** the **four cities indeed.**

44.PW The **crown prince uses spreading fate** to **command** the **four sides.**

49.IT **Heaven** and **earth skinning and-also** the **four seasons accomplishing.**

58.4b To **nine** at **fourth belongs joy.**

60.IT **Heaven** and **earth articulating and-also** the **four seasons accomplishing.**

Fox, *HU*: crafty, shape-changing animal; used by spirits, often female; ambivalent night-spirit that can create havoc and bestow abundance.

40.2a The **fields, capturing three foxes.**

64.IM/ IT The **small fox** in a **muddy ford.**

Fragment, *SUO*: break into small pieces; broken parts; minute, fine, petty, trivial. Ideogram: small and cowry shells, the tinkling of small coins.

56.1a/1b **Sojourning: fragmenting, fragmenting.**

Friend, *YOU*: companion, associate; of the same mind; attached, in pairs. Ideogram: two hands joined.

41.3a By **consequence acquiring one's friend.**

58.PW A **jun zi uses partnering** with **friends** to **explicate repeatedly.**

Frighten, *XI*: feel or provoke fear, alarm, terror, awe.

51.IM/1a/1b/ IT The **shake comes: frightening, frightening.**

Frost, *SHUANG*: frozen dew, hoar-frost; severe, frigid.

2.1a **Treading frost, hard ice** as **culmination.**

2.1b **Treading frost, hard ice.**

Froth, *MO*: spume, foam, bubbles; perspire, drool.

55.3a The **sun** in the **center: viewing froth.**

Fruit, *GUO*: tree fruit; fruition, fruit of action; result, effect, product, conclusion; reliable, decisive. Ideogram: tree topped by a round fruit.

4.PW A **jun zi uses** the **fruits** of **movement** to **nurture actualizing-dao.**

23.6a The **ripe fruit not taken-in.**

40.IT **Thunder** and **rain arousing and-also** the **hundred fruits, grasses, trees, altogether seedburst's boundary.**

Full, *WANG*: moon directly facing the sun; 15th day of the lunar month; hopes, expectations, desires.

9.6a The **moon almost full.**

54.5a The **moon almost full, significant.**

61.4a The **moon almost full.**

Fundamentals, *YI*: basic components, essentials; correct, proper, just; rule, rite, etiquette; paired, matched. Ideogram: person and righteous.

53.6a **Its feathers permit availing** of **activating** the **fundamentals.**

53.6b **Its feathers permit availing** of **activating** the **fundamentals, significant.**

Furthermore, *YOU*: moreover; in addition to; again.

7.IT **Significant, furthermore is** it **actually faulty?**

13.1b **Furthermore whose fault indeed?**

40.3b **Furthermore whose fault indeed?**

49.3b **Furthermore is it actually?**

60.3b **Furthermore whose fault indeed?**

Garden, *YUAN*: enclosed garden; park, yard; imperial tombs.

22.5a **Adorning tends-towards** a **hill-top garden.**

Gate, *MEN*: outer door, between courtyard and street; family, sect; a text or master as gate to a school of thought.

13.1a **Concording people tend-towards** the **gate.**

13.1b **Emerging** from the **gate concording people.**

16.AT **Redoubling gates, smiting clappers.**

17.1a/1b **Emerging** from the **gate, mingling possesses achievement.**

36.4a **Tending-towards emerging** from the **gate chambers.**

60.2a **Not emerging** from the **gate chambers.**

60.2b **Not emerging** from the **gate chambers, pitfall.**

Geld, *FEN*: castrate a male pig; deprive, take out.

26.5a To a **gelded pig belong tusks.**

Generate, *SHENG*: give birth; be born, arise, grow; beget; life, vitality. Ideogram: earth and sprout.

2.IT The **myriad beings' own generation.**

3.PS **Therefore afterwards** the **myriad beings' generation in-truth.**

3.PS **Sprouting implies** a **beginning belonging** to **beings' generation indeed.**

3.IT **Solid** and **supple begin** to **mingle and-also** in **heaviness generate.**

4.PS **Beings' generation necessarily enveloped.**

20.3a/3b **Overseeing my generation: advancing, withdrawing.**

20.5a/5b **Overseeing my generation.**

20.6a/6b **Overseeing one's generation.**

28.2a A **withered willow generates** a **sprig.**

28.5a/5b A **withered willow generates flowers.**

31.IT **Heaven** and **earth influence**

and-also the **myriad beings change** and **generate**.
42.IT **Heaven spreads, earth generates.**
46.PW The **earth's center generates wood. Ascending.**

Generous, *HONG*: liberal, munificent; large, vast, expanded; give or share willingly; develop fully.
2.IT **Containing generosity**: the **shine** of the **great**.

Giggle, *XI*: laugh or titter uncontrollably; merriment, delight, surprise; foolish.
37.3a/3b The **wife**, the **son, giggling, giggling**.

Glare, *DAN*: stare intensely; obstruct, prevent. Ideogram: look and hesitate, staring without acting.
27.4a A **tiger observing: glaring, glaring**.

Gnaw, *SHI*: chew, bite persistently, bite away; snap at, nibble; reach the essential by removing the unnecessary. Ideogram: mouth and divination, revealing the essential.
This term occurs in the name of hexagram 21 and recurs throughout its texts. It also occurs in:
22.HP **Gnawing** and **biting: taking-in indeed.**
38.5a/5b **Your ancestor gnawing flesh.**

Go, *WANG*: move away in time or space, depart; become past; dead, gone; contrasts with come, *LAI*, approach in time or space.
See also: **Possessing directed going**
3.3a **Going, abashment.**
3.3b A **jun zi stowing it: going, abashment, exhaustion indeed.**
3.4a **Going, significant.**
3.4b **Seeking and-also going.**
4.1a **Using going: abashment.**
5.IT **Going possesses achievement indeed.**
9.IT **Honoring going indeed.**
10.1a **Sheer treading: going.**
10.1b To **sheer treading belongs going.**
11.IM The **small going**, the **great coming.**
11.3a/3b **Without going, not returning.**
11.IT The **small going**, the **great coming: significance Growing.**
12.IM/ IT The **great going**, the **small coming.**
18.4a **Going, viewing abashment.**
18.4b **Going, not-yet acquiring indeed.**
18.IT **Going possesses affairs indeed.**
25.1a **Going, significant.**
25.1b/ IT To **without entanglement belongs going.**
26.PW A **jun zi uses** the **numerous recorded preceding words** to **go** and **move.**
29.IT **Movement possesses honor. Going possesses achievement indeed.**
31.3a **Going, abashment.**
31.4a/4b **Wavering, wavering: going, coming.**
33.1b **Not going, is** it a **calamity indeed?**
34.4b **Honoring going indeed.**
35.5a **Going significant, without not Harvesting.**
35.5b **Going possesses reward indeed.**
38.5a **Going, is** it **faulty?**
38.5b **Going possesses reward indeed.**
38.6a **Going meets rain**, by **consequence significant.**
39.1a/1b **Going limping, coming praise.**
39.3a/3b **Going limping, coming reversal.**
39.4a/4b **Going limping, coming continuity.**
39.6a **Going limping, coming ripeness. Significant.**
39.6b **Going limping, coming ripeness.**
39.IT **Going acquires** the **center indeed.**
39.IT **Going possesses achievement indeed.**
40.IM **Without** a **place** to **go**:
40.IT **Going acquires crowds**

indeed.

40.IT **Going possesses achievement indeed.**

41.1a/1b **Climaxing affairs, swiftly going.**

43.1a **Going, not mastering: activating fault.**

43.1b **Not mastering and-also going.**

43.3a **Solitary going, meeting rain.**

45.1a/3a/3b **Going, without fault.**

48.IM **Going, coming: welling, welling.**

51.5a/5b The **shake going** and **coming, adversity.**

53.IT **Going possesses achievement indeed.**

55.1a **Going possesses honor.**

55.2a **Going acquires doubt, affliction.**

60.5a **Going possesses honor.**

62.4a/4b **Going: adversity necessarily** a **warning.**

Goat, *YANG*: sheep and goats; associated with stubborn, determined thought and action.

See also: **He-goat**

34.5a/5b **Losing** the **goat, tending-towards versatility.**

43.4a **Hauling-along** the **goat, repenting extinguished.**

54.6a A **scholar disembowels** a **goat without blood.**

Gorge, *KAN*: precipice, dangerous place; hole, cavity, pit, snare, trap, grave; critical time, test; risky. Ideogram: earth and cavity.

This term is the name of hexagram 29 and recurs throughout its texts. It also occurs in:

30.HP The **radiance above and-also** the **gorge below indeed.**

Grains, *GU*: cereal crops, corn; income; substantial, prosperous, bless with plenty.

30.IT The **hundred grains, grasses, trees congregating reaching** the **earth.**

Grandfather, *ZU*: second ancestor generation; deceased grandfather, honored more than actual father.

16.PW **Using equaling grandfathers** and **predecessors.**

62.2a **Exceeding one's grandfather.**

Grandmother, *BI*: second ancestor generation; deceased grandmother, venerated as source of her many descendants.

62.2a **Meeting one's grandmother.**

Grapple, *JU*: grasp and detain; restrain, attach to, hook; stubborn, firm.

17.6a/6b **Grappling ties** to **it.**

Grasp, *QU*: seize with effort, take and use, appropriate; take as a wife; grasp the meaning, understand. Ideogram: ear and hand, hear and grasp.

4.3a/3b **No availing** of **grasping womanhood.**

8.5b **Stowing** away **revolt, grasping yielding.**

16.AT **Surely grasping relates** to **providing.**

31.IM **Grasping womanhood, significant.**

31.IT **Grasping womanhood, significant indeed.**

44.IM/ IT **No availing** of **grasping womanhood.**

49/50.HP The **vessel: grasping renewal indeed.**

56.1a **Splitting-off one's place: grasping calamity.**

62.5a A **prince's string-arrow grasps someone located** in a **cave.**

Grass, *CAO*: all grassy plants and herbs; young, tender plants; rough draft; hastily.

See also: **Thatch-grass**

3.IT **Heaven creates grasses' duskiness.**

30.IT The **hundred grains, grasses, trees congregating reaching** the **earth.**

40.IT **Thunder** and **rain arousing and-also** the **hundred fruits, grasses, trees, altogether seedburst's boundary.**

Great, *DA*: big, noble, important, very; orient the will toward a self-imposed goal, impose direction; ability to lead or guide one's life; contrasts with small, *XIAO*, flexible adaptation to what crosses one's path.

See also: **Wading the great river**

This term occurs in the names of hexagrams 14, 26, 28 and 34 and recurs throughout their texts. It also occurs in:

1.2a/5a **Harvesting**: **viewing** the **great** in the **person**.

1.5b The **great** in the **person creative indeed**.

1.IT The **great**: **in-fact energy's Spring**.

1.IT The **great brightening completes** the **beginning**.

1.IT **Protection**: **uniting** with the **great's harmony**.

2.2a **Straightening** on all **sides**: the **great**.

2.3b **Knowing** the **shine** of the **great indeed**.

2.7b **Using** the **great** for **completion indeed**.

2.IT **Containing generosity**: the **shine** of the **great**.

3.1b The **great acquires** the **commoners indeed**.

3.5a The **great**: **Trial**, **pitfall**.

3.IT The **great**: **Growing**, **Trial**.

5.6b **Although not** an **appropriate position**, **not-yet** the **great letting-go indeed**.

6.IM/ IT **Harvesting**: **viewing** the **great** in the **person**.

7.3b The **great without achievement indeed**.

7.6a/6b The **great** in the **chief possesses fate**.

10.3a/3b **Martial people activate tending-towards** the **great** in the **chief**.

10.6b The **great possesses reward indeed**.

11.IM The **small going**, the **great coming**.

11.2b **Using** the **shining great indeed**.

11.IT The **small going**, the **great coming**: **significance Growing**.

12.IM/IT The **great going**, the **small coming**.

12.2a/2b The **great** in the **person obstructed**.

12.5a The **great** in the **person**, **significant**.

12.5b To the **great** in the **person belongs significance**.

13.HP **Great possessing**: **crowds indeed**.

13.5a/5b **Great legions control** the **reciprocal meeting**.

15.PS **Possessing** the **great implies**: **not permitted using overfilling**.

16.PS **Possessing** the **great and-also enabling humbleness necessarily provides**.

16.4a The **great possesses acquiring**.

16.4b **Antecedent providing**, the **great possesses acquiring**.

16.4b **Purpose**: the **great moving indeed**.

16.IT The **season belonging** to **providing righteously great actually in-fact**.

17.IT The **great Growing**, **Trial**, **without fault**.

17.IT To **following's season belongs** the **righteously great actually in-fact**.

18.3a **Without** the **great**, **faulty**.

19.PS **Possessing affairs and-also afterwards permitted** the **great**.

19.PS **Nearing implies** the **great indeed**.

19.5a/5b To the **great** in the **chief belongs propriety**.

19.IT **Great Growing uses correcting**.

20.PS The **beings' great**, **therefore afterwards permitted overseeing**.

20.IT The **great**: **overseeing located above**.

24.6a **Completing possesses great destruction**.

25.HP The **great accumulating**: **season indeed**.

25.IT The **great's Growing uses correcting**.

27.HP The **great exceeding**: **toppling indeed**.

27.3b **Dao**: the **great rebels indeed**.

27.6b The **great possesses reward indeed**.

27.IT The **season belonging** to the **jaws great actually in-fact**.

29.5b In the **center not-yet** the **great indeed**.

29.IT The **season belonging** to

venturing avails of the **great actually in-fact.**

30.PW The **great** in the **person uses consecutive brightening** to **illuminate tending-towards** the **four sides.**

30.3a By **consequence** to the **great** in **old-age belongs lamenting.**

31.4b **Not-yet** the **shining great indeed.**

32.6b The **great without achievement indeed.**

33.HP The **great**'s **vigor**: by **consequence stopping.**

33.3b **Not permitted** the **great** in **affairs indeed.**

33.IT The **season belonging** to **retiring righteously great actually in-fact.**

35.IT **Yielding and-also congregating reaching** the **great**'s **brightness.**

36.3a **Acquiring one's great**'s **head.**

36.3b **Thereupon acquiring** the **great indeed.**

36.IT **Using enveloping** the **great**: **heaviness.**

37.4a/4b **Affluent household**: the **great, significant.**

37.IT The **great belonging** to **heaven** and **earth righteous indeed.**

38.IT The **season belonging** to **polarizing avails** of the **great actually in-fact.**

39.IM/6a/6b/ IT **Harvesting: viewing** the **great** in the **person.**

39.5a/5b **The great**'s **limping, partners coming.**

39.IT The **season belonging** to **limping avails** of the **great actually in-fact.**

40.IT The **season belonging** to **unraveling great actually in-fact.**

41.6b The **great acquires purpose indeed.**

42.1a **Harvesting: availing** of **activating** the **great, arousing.**

42.5b The **great acquires purpose indeed.**

42.IT **One's dao**: the **great shining.**

44.3a **Without** the **great: faulty.**

44.IT **Below heaven** the **great moves indeed.**

44.IT The **season belonging** to **coupling righteously great actually in-fact.**

45.IM **Harvesting: viewing** the **great** in the **person.**

45.IM/IT **Availing** of the **great**'s **sacrificial-victims, significant.**

45.4a/4b The **great: significant, without fault.**

45.IT **Harvesting: viewing** the **great** in the **person. Growing.**

46.IM **Availing** of **viewing** the **great** in the **person.**

46.PW And **amassing** the **small** to **use** the **high great.**

46.1a/1b **Sincere ascending**: the **great, significant.**

46.5b The **great acquires purpose indeed.**

46.IT **That uses** the **great, Growing.**

46.IT **Availing** of **viewing** the **great** in the **person.**

47.IM/ IT **Trial**: the **great** in the **person, significant.**

48.6b The **great accomplishes indeed.**

49.5a/5b The **great** in the **person**: a **tiger transforming.**

49.IT The **great**'s **Growing uses correctness.**

49.IT The **season belonging** to **skinning great actually in-fact.**

50.6a The **great, significant.**

50.IT **And-also** the **great**'s **Growing uses nourishing** the **wise** and the **eminent.**

51.5b The **great without loss indeed.**

54.IT The **great**'s **righteousness belonging** to **heaven** and **earth.**

55.PS **Acquiring one's place** for **converting implies necessarily** the **great.**

55.PS **Abounding implies** the **great indeed.**

55.3b **Not permitted** the **great** in **affairs indeed.**

55.IT **Abounding**, the **great indeed.**

55.IT **Honoring** the **great indeed.**

56.PS **Exhausting** the **great implies necessarily letting-go one's residing.**

56.IT The **season belonging** to

sojourning righteously great actually in-fact.
57.IM/ IT **Harvesting: viewing** the **great** in the **person.**
58.IT To **stimulating belongs** the **great.**
59.4b The **shining great indeed.**
59.5a **Dispersing sweat: one's great cries-out.**
62.IM **Not permitted** the **great** in **affairs.**
62.IM/IT The **great, significant.**
62.IT **That uses not permitting** the **great** in **affairs indeed.**
63.5b **Significant.** The **great coming indeed.**
64.4a **Three years, possessing** a **donation tending-towards** the **great city.**

Grieve, *YOU*: mourn; sorrow, melancholy, anxiety, care, hidden sorrow. Ideogram: heart, head, and limp, heart-sick and anxious.
7/8.HP The **legions: grief.**
19.3a/3b **Already grieving** over **it.**
55.IM/ IT **No grief. Properly** the **sun** in the **center.**

Group, *BI*: compare and select, order things and put them in classes; find what you belong with; associate with, unite, join, harmonize; neighbor, near. Ideogram: two men following each other.
This term is the name of hexagram 8 and recurs throughout its texts. It also occurs in:
7.HP **Grouping: delight.**
9.PS **Grouping necessarily possesses** a **place** to **accumulate.**

Grove, *BAO*: luxuriant growth, dense thicket; conceal, screen; sleeping mats; wrapping for food gifts. Ideogram: wrap and bushes.
12.5a **Attachment tending-towards** a **grove** of **mulberry-trees.**

Grow, *HENG*: heavenly influence pervading and nourishing all things; prosper, succeed, expand, develop; effective, favorable; quality of summer and South, second stage of the Time Cycle. With the pronunciation *XIANG*: offer a sacrifice; offer a gift to a superior; accept, enjoy.
See also: **Hair-growing, Spring, Growing, Harvesting, Trial**
2.IT The **kinds** of the **beings conjoining, Growing.**
3.IT The **great: Growing, Trial.**
4.IM/ IT **Enveloping. Growing.**
4.IT **Using Growing** to **move.**
5.IM/ IT **Shining Growing, Trial, significant.**
9.IM The **small accumulating. Growing.**
9.IT **Thereupon Growing.**
10.IM **Growing.**
10.IT **Not snapping** at **people. Growing.**
11.IM **Significance Growing.**
11.IT The **small going,** the **great coming: significance Growing.**
12.1a/2a/2b **Growing.**
13.IM/ IT **Growing.**
14.IM **Spring, Growing.**
14.3a/3b A **prince avails** of **Growing tending-towards heavenly sonhood.**
14.IT **That uses Spring, Growing.**
15.IM/ IT **Humbling. Growing.**
17.6a The **king avails** of **Growing tending-towards** the **Western mountain.**
17.IT The **great Growing, Trial, without fault.**
18.IM **Decay. Spring, Growing.**
18.IT **Decay: Spring, Growing, and-also below heaven regulated indeed.**
19.IT **Great Growing uses correcting.**
21.IM **Gnawing** and **biting. Growing.**
21.IT **Gnawing** and **biting and-also Growing.**
22.IM/ IT **Adorning, Growing.**
22.IT **Anterior Growing.**
23.PS **Involved** in **embellishing, therefore afterwards Growing,** by **consequence used-up actually.**
24.IM/ IT **Return. Growing.**
25.IT The **great's Growing uses correcting.**
26.6a **Growing.**
28.IM **Growing.**
28.IT **Thereupon Growing.**

29.IM/ IT **Holding-fast** the **heart**, **Growing**.
30.IM **Growing**. **Accumulating female cattle**.
30.IT **Anterior Growing**.
31.IM **Growing**, **Harvesting**, **Trial**.
31.IT **That uses Growing**, **Harvesting**, **Trial**.
32.IM **Persevering**. **Growing**.
32.IT **Persevering Growing**, **without fault**.
33.IM/ IT **Retiring**. **Growing**.
33.IT **Retiring and-also Growing indeed**.
45.IM **Clustering**. **Growing**.
45.IM **Growing**, **Harvesting**, **Trial**.
45.IT **Harvesting**: **viewing** the **great** in the **person**. **Growing**.
46.IM **Ascending**. **Spring**, **Growing**.
46.4a/4b The **king avails** of **Growing tending-towards** the **twin-peaked mountain**.
46.IT **That uses** the **great**, **Growing**.
47.IM **Confining**. **Growing**.
47.IT **Confining and-also not letting-go one's place**: **Growing**.
49.IT The **great's Growing uses correctness**.
50.IM **Growing**.
50.IT **Growing**: **cooking indeed**.
50.IT The **wise person's Growing uses presenting** to the **supreme above**.
50.IT **And-also** the **great's Growing uses nourishing** the **wise** and the **eminent**.
50.IT **That uses Spring**, **Growing**.
51.IM/ IT The **shake**. **Growing**.
55.IM **Abounding**. **Growing**.
56.IM/ IT **Sojourning**. The **small**, **growing**.
56.IT **That uses** the **small**, **Growing**.
57.IM The **root**. The **small**, **Growing**.
57.IT **That uses** the **small**, **Growing**.
58.IM **Growing**, **Harvesting**, **Trial**.
59.IM/ IT **Dispersing**. **Growing**.
60.IM/IT **Articulating**. **Growing**.
60.4a **Peaceful articulating**, **Growing**.
60.4b To **peaceful articulating belongs Growing**.
62.IM The **small exceeding**. **Growing**.
62.IT The **small implies exceeding and-also Growing indeed**.
63.IM **Already fording**. **Growing**, the **small**.
63.IT **Already fording**. **Growing**.
63.IT The **small implies Growing indeed**.
64.IM/ IT **Not-yet fording**. **Growing**.

Grudges, *YUAN*: bitter feelings, ill-will; hate, abhor; murmur against. Ideogram: heart and overturn, upset emotion.
47.AT **Confining**: **using few grudges**.

Guard, *SHOU*: keep in custody; protect, ward off harm, attend to, supervise.
29.IT The **king** and the **princes set-up venturing used** to **guard their city**.
51.IT **Emerging permits using guarding** the **ancestral temple**, the **field-altar**, the **offertory-millet**.

Gully, *GU*: valley, ravine, river bed, gap. Ideogram: divide and river, a river bed separating hills.
47.1a/1b **Entering tending-towards** a **shady gully**.
48.2a/2b The **well**: a **gully**, **shooting bass**.

Gush, *TUO*: water surging in streams; falling tears; heavy rain.
30.5a **Emerging tears like gushing**.

Hair-growing, *XU*: beard, hair; patience symbolized as waiting for hair to grow; hold back, wait for; slow; necessary.
5.IT **Attending**. **Hair-growing indeed**.
22.2a/2b **Adorning**: **one's hair-growing**.
54.3a/3b **Converting maidenhood uses hair-growing**.

Halt, *PO*: limp; lame, crippled.
10.3a/3b **Halting enables treading**.
54.1a **Halting enables treading**.
54.1b **Halting enables treading**, **significant**.

Hamper, *CHE*: hinder, obstruct, hold or pull back; embarrass. Ideogram: hand

and limit.
38.3a **One's cattle hampered.**

Handful, *WU*: as much as the hand can hold; a little; grasp, hold.
45.1a **Like** an **outcry, one handful activates laughter.**

Handle, *BING*: haft; control of, power to.
15.AT **Humbling**: the **handle belonging** to **actualizing-dao indeed.**

Hand-washing, *GUAN*: wash the hands before a sacramental act; ablutions, basin.
20.IM/ IT **Overseeing. Hand-washing and-also not worshipping.**

Hard, *JIAN*: solid, strong, rigid; harden, fortify, consolidate; resolute, fearless.
2.1a **Treading frost, hard ice** as **culmination.**
2.1b **Treading frost, hard ice.**
2.1b **Culmination: hard ice indeed.**

Harm, *HAI*: damage, injure, offend; suffer, become ill; obstacle, hindrance; fearful, anxious.
2.4b **Considering not harmful indeed.**
14.1a **Without mingling** with **harm.**
14.1b **Without mingling** with **harm indeed.**
14.3b The **small** in the **person harmful indeed.**
15.IT **Soul** and **spirit harm overfilling and-also bless humbling.**
31.2b **Yielding not harmful indeed.**
31.4b **Not-yet influencing harmful indeed.**
41.AT **Diminishing: using distancing harm.**
59.6b **Distancing harm indeed.**
60.IT **Not harming** the **commoners.**

Harmony, *HE*: concord, union; conciliate; at peace, mild; fit, tune, adjust.
1.IT **Protection: uniting** with the **great**'s **harmony.**
10.AT **Treading: harmony and-also culmination.**
10.AT **Treading: using harmonious movement.**
31.IT The **wise person influences people**'s **heart and-also below heaven harmonizes evenness.**
43.IT **Breaking-up and-also harmonizing.**
58.1a **Harmonious open, significant.**
58.1b To the **harmonious open belongs significance.**
61.2a/2b **One's sonhood harmonizing** with **it.**

Harvest, *LI*: benefit, advantage, profit; realization; sharp, acute, insightful; quality of autumn and West, third stage of the Time Cycle. Ideogram: ripe grain and blade.
See also: **Spring, Growing, Harvesting, Trial, Without direction Harvesting, Without not Harvesting**
1.2a/5a **Harvesting: viewing** the **great** in the **person.**
1.IT **Thereupon Harvesting, Trial.**
2.IM A **lord Harvesting.**
2.7a **Harvesting perpetual Trial.**
2.IT The **supple yielding, Harvesting, Trial.**
3.IM **Harvesting: installing feudatories.**
3.1a **Harvesting: residing** in **Trial.**
3.1a **Harvesting: installing feudatories.**
4.IM **Harvesting, Trial.**
4.1a/1b **Harvesting: availing** of **punishing people.**
4.6a **Not Harvesting: activating illegality.**
4.6a **Harvesting: resisting illegality.**
4.6b **Harvesting: availing** of **resisting illegality.**
5.IM/IT **Harvesting: wading** the **great river.**
5.1a **Harvesting: availing** of **perseverance.**
5.1b **Harvesting: availing** of **perseverance, without fault.**
6.IM/IT **Harvesting: viewing** the **great** in the **person.**
6.IM/ IT **Not harvesting: wading** the **great river.**
7.5a **Harvesting: holding-on** to **words.**

12.IM/ IT **Not harvesting**: a **jun zi's Trial.**
13.IM/IT **Harvesting**: **wading** the **great river.**
13.IM **Harvesting**: a **jun zi's Trial.**
15.5a/5b **Harvesting**: **availing** of **encroaching** and **subjugating.**
15.6a **Harvesting**: **availing** of **moving legions.**
16.IM **Harvesting**: **installing feudatories, moving legions.**
17.3a **Harvesting**: **residing** in **Trial.**
18.IM/ IT **Harvesting**: **wading** the **great river.**
20.2a **Harvesting**: **woman's Trial.**
20.4a **Harvesting**: **availing** of **hospitality tending-towards** the **king.**
21.IM **Harvesting**: **availing** of **litigating.**
21.4a **Harvesting drudgery, Trial.**
21.4b **Harvesting drudgery, Trial**: **significant.**
21.IT **Although not** an **appropriate position, Harvesting avails** of **litigating indeed.**
22.IM/ IT **Harvesting**: **possessing directed going.**
23.IM/ IT **Not Harvesting**: **possessing directed going.**
24.IM/ IT **Harvesting**: **possessing directed going.**
25.IM/IT **Not Harvesting**: **possessing directed going.**
25.2a By **consequence, Harvesting**: **possessing directed going.**
26.IM **Harvesting, Trial.**
26.IM/IT **Harvesting**: **wading** the **great river.**
26.1a **Harvesting**: **climaxing.**
26.1b **Possessing adversity, Harvesting, climaxing.**
26.3a **Harvesting drudgery, Trial.**
26.3a/3b **Harvesting**: **possessing directed going.**
27.6a **Harvesting**: **wading** the **great river.**
28.IM/ IT **Harvesting**: **possessing directed going.**
30.IM **Harvesting, Trial.**
31.IM **Growing, Harvesting, Trial.**
31.IT **That uses Growing, Harvesting, Trial.**
32.IM/IT **Harvesting, Trial.**
32.IM/ IT **Harvesting**: **possessing directed going.**
33.IM/ IT The **small, Harvesting, Trial.**
34.IM/ IT The **great's vigor. Harvesting, Trial.**
36.IM/IT **Harvesting**: **drudgery, Trial.**
36.5a **Harvesting, Trial.**
37.IM **Household people. Harvesting**: **woman's Trial.**
39.IM/IT **Limping. Harvesting**: **Western South.**
39.IM/IT **Not Harvesting**: **Eastern North.**
39.IM/6a/6b/ IT **Harvesting**: **viewing** the **great** in the **person.**
40.IM/ IT **Unraveling. Harvesting**: **Western South.**
41.IM/IT/6a **Harvesting**: **possessing directed going.**
41.2a **Harvesting, Trial.**
41.2b **Nine** at **second**: **Harvesting, Trial.**
42.IM/ IT **Harvesting**: **possessing directed going.**
42.IM/ IT **Harvesting**: **wading** the **great river.**
42.AT **Augmenting**: **using** the **rising Harvest.**
42.1a **Harvesting**: **availing** of **activating** the **great, arousing.**
42.4a **Harvesting**: **availing** of **activating depends** on **shifting** the **city.**
43.IM/ IT **Not Harvesting**: **approaching weapons.**
43.IM/ IT **Harvesting**: **possessing directed going.**
44.2a **Not Harvesting**: **hospitality.**
45.IM **Harvesting**: **viewing** the **great** in the **person.**
45.IM **Growing, Harvesting, Trial.**
45.IM/ IT **Harvesting**: **possessing directed going.**
45.2a **Conforming, thereupon Harvesting**: **availing** of **dedicating.**
45.IT **Harvesting**: **viewing** the **great** in the **person. Growing.**
46.2a **Conforming, thereupon Harvesting**: **availing** of **dedicating.**
46.6a **Harvesting**: to **tending-**

towards not pausing belongs Trial.
47.2a **Harvesting: availing** of **presenting oblations.**
47.5a/5b **Harvesting: availing** of **offering oblations.**
50.1a/1b **Harvesting: emerging** from **obstruction.**
50.5a **Harvesting, Trial.**
52.1a **Harvesting: perpetual Trial.**
53.IM **Harvesting, Trial.**
53.3a **Harvesting: resisting illegality.**
53.3b **Harvesting: availing** of **resisting illegality.**
54.2a/2b **Harvesting: Trial belonging** to **shady people.**
57.IM/ IT **Harvesting: possessing directed going.**
57.IM/ IT **Harvesting: viewing** the **great** in the **person.**
57.1a/1b **Harvesting:** to **martial people belongs Trial.**
58.IM **Growing, Harvesting, Trial.**
58.IT **Stimulating uses Harvesting, Trial.**
59.IM/ IT **Harvesting: wading** the **great river.**
59.IM **Harvesting, Trial.**
61.IM/ IT **Harvesting: wading** the **great river.**
61.IM **Harvesting, Trial.**
61.IT The **center conforming uses Harvesting, Trial.**
62.IM **Harvesting, Trial.**
62.IT **Exceeding uses Harvesting, Trial.**
63.IM/ IT **Harvesting, Trial.**
64.3a **Harvesting: wading** the **great river.**

Hate, *WU*: detest, dread, dislike; averse to, ashamed of; repulsive, vicious, vile, ugly, wicked. Ideogram: twisted bowels and heart.
14.PW A **jun zi uses terminating hatred** to **display improvement.**
15.IT **People**'s **dao hates overfilling and-also loves humbling.**
33.PW And **not hating and-also intimidating.**
38.1a/1b **Viewing hatred** in the **person.**

Haul-along, *QIAN*: haul or pull, drag behind; pull an animal on a rope. Ideogram: ox and halter.
9.2a **Hauling-along returning.**
9.2b **Hauling-along returning located** in the **center.**
43.4a **Hauling-along** the **goat, repenting extinguished.**
44.1b The **supple**'s **dao hauling-along indeed.**
44.3b **Moving, not-yet hauling-along indeed.**

Hawk, *SHUN*: falcon, kestrel, bird of prey used in hunting.
40.6a A **prince avails** of **shooting** a **hawk tending-towards** the **above belonging** to the **high rampart.**
40.6b A **prince avails** of **shooting** a **hawk.**

He/his, *QI*: general third person pronoun and possessive adjective; also: one/one's, it/its, she/her, they/their.
This term occurs throughout the hexagram texts.

He-goat, *DI YANG*: ram or buck, particularly a three-year-old male at the peak of strength.
See also: **Goat**
34.3a/6a The **he-goat butts** a **hedge.**

Head, *SHOU*: physical head; leader, sovereign; beginning, origin, model; foremost, superior, upper, front.
1.7a **Viewing** a **flock** of **dragons without head.**
1.7b **Heavenly actualizing-dao not permitting activating** the **head indeed.**
1.IT **Heads emerging** from the **multitude** of **beings.**
8.6a/6b To **grouping belongs without** a **head.**
30.6a **Severing** the **head. Capturing in-no-way its demons.**
36.3a **Acquiring one's great**'s **head.**
63.6a **Soaking one's head.**
63.6b **Soaking one's head, adversity.**
64.6a **Soaking one's head.**
64.6b **Drinking liquor, soaking** the **head.**

Hear, *WEN*: perceive sound; learn by report; news, fame. Ideogram: ear and door.

43.4a/4b **Hearing words not trustworthy.**

56.6b To **completing abstention belongs hearing indeed.**

Hearken, *TING*: listen attentively, obey, accept, acknowledge; examine, judge, decide. Ideogram: ear and actualizing-dao.

5.4b **Yielding uses hearkening indeed.**

52.2b **Not-yet withdrawing** from **hearkening indeed.**

Heart, *XIN*: the heart as center of being; seat of mind, imagination and affect; moral nature; source of desires, intentions, will.

11.4b In the **center** the **heart**'s **desire indeed.**

15.2b In the **center** the **heart acquiring indeed.**

24.IT **Return** to **one's viewing** the **heart belonging** to **heaven** and **earth reached.**

29.IM/ IT **Holding-fast** the **heart**, **Growing.**

31.IT The **wise person influences people**'s **heart and-also below heaven harmonizes evenness.**

36.4a **Capturing** the **heart belonging** to **brightness hidden.**

36.4b **Capturing** the **heart**: **intention indeed.**

42.5a/5b **Possessing conformity**, a **benevolent heart.**

42.6a **Establishing** the **heart**, **no persevering.**

48.3a **Activating my heart**'s **ache.**

52.2a **One's heart not keen.**

52.3a **Adversity smothers** the **heart.**

52.3b **Exposure smothers** the **heart indeed.**

56.4a **My heart not keen.**

56.4b The **heart not-yet keen indeed.**

61.2b In the **center** the **heart**'s **desire indeed.**

Heaven, *TIAN*: sky, firmament, heavens; the highest realm, situated above the human world, as opposed to the earth, *DI*, located below; Symbol of the trigram Energy, *QIAN*. Ideogram: great and the one above.

See also: **Below heaven**

1.PW **Heaven moves persistently.**

1.5a/5b **Flying dragon located** in **heaven.**

1.7b **Heavenly actualizing-dao not permitting activating** the **head indeed.**

1.IT **Thereupon primordial heaven.**

1.IT The **season rides six dragons used** to **drive** up to **heaven.**

2.IT **Thereupon yielding receives heaven.**

3.PS **Possessing heaven** and **earth.**

3.PS **Overfilling** the **interspace belonging** to **heaven** and **earth implies verily** the **myriad beings.**

3.IT **Heaven creates grasses' duskiness.**

5.PW **Clouds above with-respect-to heaven. Attending.**

5.IT The **position reaching** the **heavenly position.**

6.PW **Heaven associated** with **stream**: **contradicting movements. Arguing.**

7.2b **Receiving heavenly favor indeed.**

9.PW **Wind moves above heaven.** The **small accumulating.**

10.PW **Heaven above, pond below. Treading.**

11.PW **Heaven** and **earth mingling. Compenetration.**

11.PW The **crown prince uses property** to **accomplish** the **dao belonging** to **heaven** and **earth.**

11.PW And **braces** the **reciprocity properly belonging** to **heaven** and **earth.**

11.3b **Heaven** and **earth**'s **border indeed.**

11.IT By **consequence** of **that heaven** and **earth mingling and-also** the **myriad beings interpenetrating indeed.**

12.PW **Heaven** and **earth not mingling. Obstruction.**

12.IT By **consequence** of **that heaven** and **earth not mingling and-also** the **myriad beings not**

interpenetrating indeed.
13.PW Heaven associated with fire. Concording people.
14.PW Fire located above heaven. Great possessing.
14.PW And yielding to heaven to relax into fate.
14.3a/3b A prince avails of Growing tending-towards heavenly sonhood.
14.6a The origin in heaven shields it.
14.6b The origin in heaven shields indeed.
14.IT The correspondence reaches heaven and-also the season moves.
15.IT Heavenly dao: below fording and-also shining brightness.
15.IT Heavenly dao lessens overfilling and-also augments humbling.
16.IT To anterior heaven and earth it thus belongs.
16.IT Heaven and earth use yielding and stirring-up.
18.IT Heaven moving indeed.
19.IT Dao belonging to heaven indeed.
20.IT Overseeing the spirit dao belonging to heaven.
22.IT Heavenly pattern indeed.
22.IT Overseeing reaches the heavenly pattern.
23.IT Heaven moves indeed.
24.IT Heaven moves indeed.
24.IT Return to one's viewing the heart belonging to heaven and earth reached.
25.IT Fate belonging to heaven indeed.
25.IT Heavenly fate not shielding.
26.PW Heaven located in the mountain's center. The great accumulating.
26.6a/6b Is it not the highway belonging to heaven?
26.IT Correspondence reaching heaven indeed.
27.IT Heaven and earth nourish the myriad beings.
29.IT Heaven's venture: not permitting ascending indeed.
30.IT Sun and moon congregating reaching heaven.
31.PS Possessing heaven and earth.
31.IT Heaven and earth influence and-also the myriad beings change and generate.
31.IT And-also the motives belonging to heaven and earth's myriad beings permit viewing actually.
32.IT Dao belonging to heaven and earth.
32.IT Sun and moon: acquiring heaven and-also enabling lasting and illuminating.
32.IT And-also the motives belonging to heaven and earth's myriad beings permit viewing actually.
33.PW Heaven possesses mountain below. Retiring.
34.PW Thunder located above heaven. The great's vigor.
34.IT The correct great and-also the motives belonging to heaven and earth permit viewing actually.
36.6a/6b Initially mounting tending-towards heaven.
37.IT The great belonging to heaven and earth righteous indeed.
38.IT Heaven and earth: polarizing and-also their affairs concording indeed.
40.IT Heaven and earth unraveling and-also thunder and rain arousing.
42.IT Heaven spreads, earth generates.
43.PW Pond above with-respect-to heaven. Parting.
44.PW Heaven possessing wind below. Coupling.
44.5a/5b Possessing tumbling originating from heaven.
44.IT Heaven and earth reciprocally meeting.
45.IT Yielding to heaven's fate indeed.
45.IT And-also the motives belonging to heaven and earth's myriad beings permit viewing actually.
49.IT Heaven and earth skinning and-also the four seasons

accomplishing.

49.IT **Yielding reaches heaven and-also** the **correspondence reaches people.**

54.IT The **great**'s **righteousness belonging** to **heaven** and **earth.**

54.IT **Heaven** and **earth not mingling.**

55.6b The **heavenly border, hovering indeed.**

55.IT **Heaven** and **earth overfilling emptiness.**

58.IT **That uses yielding reaching heaven and-also correspondence reaching people.**

60.IT **Heaven** and **earth articulating and-also** the **four seasons accomplishing.**

61.6a/6b A **soaring sound mounts tending-towards heaven.**

61.IT **Thereupon** the **correspondence reaches heaven indeed.**

Heaviness, *NAN*: difficulty, hardship, distress; arduous, grievous; harass; contrasts with versatility, *YI*, deal lightly with. Ideogram: bird with clipped tail on drying sticky soil.

3.2b To **six** at **second belongs heaviness.**

3.IT **Solid** and **supple begin** to **mingle and-also** in **heaviness generate.**

5.1b **Not opposing heaviness** in **movement.**

12.PW A **jun zi uses parsimonious actualizing-dao** to **expel heaviness.**

36.IT **Using enveloping** the **great: heaviness.**

36.IT **Inside heaviness and-also able** to **correct one's purpose.**

39.PS **Turning-away necessarily possesses heaviness.**

39.PS **Limping implies heaviness indeed.**

39/40.HP **Limping: heaviness indeed.**

39.IT **Limping. Heaviness indeed.**

40.PS **Beings not permitted** to **use completing heaviness.**

41.AT **Diminishing: beforehand heaviness and-also afterwards versatility.**

58.IT **Stimulating uses opposing heaviness.**

Hedge, *FAN*: row of bushes, fence, boundary; enclose, protect, fend off.

34.3a/6a The **he-goat butts** a **hedge.**

34.4a/4b The **hedge broken-up, not ruined.**

Herd, *MU*: tend cattle; watch over, superintend; ruler, teacher.

15.1b **Lowliness uses originating herding indeed.**

Hide, *YI*: squat, even, level, equalize; cut, wound, destroy, exterminate; pacified; colorless; distant, remote, barbarian.

This term occurs in the name of hexagram 36 and recurs throughout its texts. It also occurs in:

35.HP **Brightness hidden: proscribed indeed.**

55.4a/4b **Meeting one's hidden lord.**

59.4a **In-no-way hidden**, a **place** to **ponder.**

Hide-away, *FU*: hide, conceal; ambush; secret, silent; prostrate, submit. Ideogram: man and crouching dog.

13.3a/3b **Hiding-away weapons tending-towards** the **thickets.**

57/58.HP the **root: hidden-away indeed.**

High, *GAO*: high, elevated, lofty, eminent; honor, respect. Ideogram: high tower.

13.3a **Ascending one's high mound.**

18.6a **Honoring highness: one's affair.**

40.6a A **prince avails** of **shooting** a **hawk tending-towards** the **above belonging** to the **high rampart.**

46.PW And **amassing** the **small** to **use** the **high great.**

63.3a The **High Ancestor subjugates souls** on all **sides.**

Highlands, *LU*: high, dry land as distinct from swamps; mountain, plateau.

43.5a The **reeds**, the **highlands: parting, parting.**

53.3a/6a The **swan infiltrating tending-towards** the **highlands**.

Highlight, *YI*: praise something worthy; inherent goodness, excellence, beauty, perfect virtue, modesty.

9.PW A **jun zi uses highlighting** the **pattern** to **actualize-dao**.

Highway, *CHU*: main road, thoroughfare; crossing, intersection.

26.6a/6b **Is** it not the **highway belonging** to **heaven**?

Hill-top, *QIU*: hill with hollow top used for worship and as grave-site; knoll, hillock.

22.5a **Adorning tends-towards** a **hill-top garden**.

27.2a **Rejecting** the **canons**, **tending-towards** the **hill-top**.

29.IT **Earth**'s **venture**: **mountains**, **rivers**, **hill-tops**, **mounds indeed**.

59.4a **Dispersing possesses** the **hill-top**.

Hinder, *ZHAN*: obstacle, difficulty; advance hesitantly; detour.

3.2a **Sprouting thus**, **hindered thus**.

Hoary, *BO*: silvery grey hair; old and venerable.

22.4a **Adorned thus**, **hoary thus**.

Hog fish, *TUN YU*: aquatic mammals; porpoise, dolphin; sign of abundance and good luck.

61.IM The **center conforming**: **hog fish**, **significant**.

61.IT **Hog fish**, **significant**.

61.IT **Trustworthiness extends** to **hog fish indeed**.

Hold-fast, *WEI*: tie, connect, hold together; rope, reins, net.

17.6a **Thereupon adhering**: **holding-fast** to **it**.

29.IM/ IT **Holding-fast** the **heart**, **Growing**.

35.6a/6b **Holding-fast avails** of **subjugating** the **capital**.

40.5a A **jun zi holding-fast possesses unraveling**. **Significant**.

Hold-on, *ZHI*: lay hold of, seize, take in hand; keep, maintain, look after; manage, control. Ideogram: criminal and seize.

7.5a **Harvesting**: **holding-on** to **words**.

31.3a **Holding-on** to **one's following**.

31.3b A **place** for **holding-on** to the **below indeed**.

33.2a To **holding-on belongs availing** of **skin belonging** to **yellow cattle**.

33.2b **Holding-on avails** of **yellow cattle**.

Home, *SHI*: room, house, dwelling; family; the grave.

9.3b **Not able** to **correct** the **home indeed**.

Honor, *SHANG*: esteem, give high rank to, exalt, celebrate; rise, elevate; put one thing on top of another.

6.IT **Honoring** the **center**'s **correctness indeed**.

9.6a **Honoring actualizing-dao**: **carrying**.

9.IT **Honoring going indeed**.

11.2a **Acquiring honor tending-towards** the **center**: **movement**.

11.2b **Enwrapped** in **wasteland**, **acquiring honor tending-towards** the **center**: **movement**.

18.6a **Honoring highness**: **one's affair**.

20.4b **Honoring hospitality indeed**.

23.IT A **jun zi honors** the **dissolving pause** to **overfill emptiness**.

26.IT The **solid above and-also honoring eminence**.

29.IM **Movement possesses honor**.

29.IT **Movement possesses honor**. **Going possesses achievement indeed**.

34.4b **Honoring going indeed**.

41.1b **Honoring uniting purposes indeed**.

43.IT The **place** to **honor thereupon exhausted indeed**.

47.IT **Honoring** the **mouth thereupon exhausted indeed**.

55.1a **Going possesses honor**.

55.IT **Honoring** the **great indeed**.

60.5a **Going possesses honor**.

Hoof, *DI*: horse's hooves and pig's trotters.

44.1a **Ruined** the **pig's conformity**: **hoof dragging**.

Horns, *JIAO*: physical horns; butt, attack, gore; dispute, test one's strength; headland.

34.3a **Ruins its horns.**
35.6a **Prospering: one's horns.**
44.6a/6b **Coupling: one's horns.**

Horse, *MA*: symbol of spirited strength in the natural world, earthly counterpart of the dragon; associated with the trigram Energy, *QIAN*, heaven, and high noon.

2.IM **Space. Spring, Growing, Harvesting, Trial belonging** to the **female horse.**
2.IT The **female horse**: to the **earth sorted.**
3.2a/4a/6a **Riding** a **horse, arraying thus.**
22.4a A **white horse soaring thus.**
26.3a A **fine horse, pursuing.**
35.IM **Prospering.** A **content feudatory avails** of **bestowing horses** to **enhance** the **multitudes.**
35.IT **That uses** a **content feudatory availing** of **bestowing horses** to **enhance** the **multitudes.**
36.2a **Availing** of a **rescuing horse**'s **vigor, significant.**
38.1a **Losing** the **horse, no pursuing: originating** from **returning.**
59.1a **Availing** of a **rescuing horse**'s **vigor, significant.**
61.4a/4b The **horse team extinguished.**

Hospitality, *BIN*: both entertain a guest, receive a stranger, and visit someone, enjoy hospitality.

20.4a **Harvesting: availing** of **hospitality tending-towards** the **king.**
20.4b **Honoring hospitality indeed.**
44.2a **Not Harvesting: hospitality.**
44.2b **Righteously not extending hospitality indeed.**

Hound, *SHOU*: hunt with dogs; annual winter hunt; pursue closely, press hard; burn dry fields to drive game; military expedition.

36.3a **Brightness hidden tends-towards** the **Southern hounding.**
36.3b To the **Southern hounding belongs purpose.**

House, *GONG*: residence, mansion; surround; fence, walls, roof.

23.5a/5b **Using house people**'s **favor.**
47.3a/3b **Entering tending-towards one's house.**

Household, *JIA*: home, house; family; dwell, reside; domestic, within doors; shop, school, doctrine. Ideogram: roof and pig or dog, the most valued domestic animals, living under the same roof with the family.

This term occurs in the name of hexagram 37 and recurs throughout its texts. It also occurs in:

4.2a/2b The **son controls** the **household.**
7.6a **Disclosing** the **city, receiving** a **household.**
26.IM/ IT **Not** in the **household taking-in. Significant.**
38.PS **Household**'s **dao exhausted, necessarily turning-away.**
38.HP **Household people: inside indeed.**
41.6a **Acquiring** a **servant without** a **household.**
55.6a **Screening one's household.**

Hover, *XIANG*: rise, soar, glide, fly above, roam.

55.6b The **heavenly border, hovering indeed.**

Humanity, *REN*: fellow-feeling, regard for others; benevolence, kindness, compassion; fulfill social duties.

24.2b **Below using humanity indeed.**

Humble, *QIAN*: think and speak of oneself in a modest way; respectful, unassuming, retiring, unobtrusive; yielding, compliant, reverent, lowly. Ideogram: words and unite, keeping words close to underlying facts.

This term is the name of hexagram 15 and recurs throughout its texts. It also occurs in:

16.PS **Possessing** the **great and-also enabling humbleness necessarily provides.**
16.HP **Humbling: levity.**

Hundred, *BO*: numerous, many, all; a whole class or type.

6.2a **People, three hundred doors.**

30.IT The **hundred grains, grasses, trees congregating reaching** the **earth**.

40.IT **Thunder** and **rain arousing and-also** the **hundred fruits, grasses, trees, altogether seedburst's boundary**.

51.IM/ IT The **shake scares** a **hundred miles**.

Hundred-thousand, *YI*: a huge quantity. Ideogram: man and thought, a number that can only be imagined.

51.2a A **hundred-thousand coins lost**.

51.5a **Hundred-thousand without loss, possessing affairs**.

Husband, *FU*: adult, man, male spouse; scholar, distinguished man; one who can help; manage a household. Ideogram: man with a pin in his hair to show that he is of age.

4.3a **Viewing** a **metallic husband**.

8.IM/ IT **Afterwards husbanding: pitfall**.

9.3a/3b **Husband** and **consort reversing** the **eyes**.

17.2a **Letting-go** the **respectable husband**.

17.3a/3b **Tied** to the **respectable husband**.

28.2a A **venerable husband acquires his woman consort**.

28.2b A **venerable husband** and a **woman consort**.

28.5a A **venerable wife acquires her scholarly husband**.

28.5b A **venerable wife** and a **scholarly husband**.

31.PS **Therefore afterwards possessing husband** and **wife**.

31.PS **Possessing husband** and **wife**.

32.PS **Dao belonging** to **husband** and **wife**.

32.5a The **husband** and the **son, pitfall**.

32.5b The **husband** and the **son, paring righteously**.

37.IT The **husband**, a **husband**. The **wife**, a **wife**.

38.4a **Meeting Spring, husbanding**.

53.3a/3b The **husband disciplined, not returning**.

Husking, *GENG*: fruit and grain husks bursting in autumn; seventh of the Ten Heavenly Barriers in calendar system; bestow, reward; blade or sword; associated with the Metallic Moment. Ideogram: two hands threshing grain.

57.5a **Before husking, three days**.

57.5a **After husking, three days**.

Hut, *LU*: thatched hut, cottage, roadside lodge, hovel.

23.6a/6b The **small** in the **person strips** the **hut**.

I/me/my, *WO*: first person pronoun; the use of a specific personal pronoun, as opposed to the generic one's, *QI*, indicates an unusually strong emphasis on personal involvement.

4.IM/ IT **In-no-way I seek** the **youthful enveloping**.

4.IM/ IT The **youthful enveloping seeks me**.

5.3b **Originating** from **my involvement** in **illegality**.

9.IM/ IT **Originating** from **my Western suburbs**.

20.3a/3b **Overseeing my generation: advancing, withdrawing**.

20.5a/5b **Overseeing my generation**.

27.1a/1b **Overseeing my pendent jaw**.

40.3b **Originating** from **my involvement** with **weapons**.

42.5a **Possessing conformity, benevolence: my actualizing-dao**.

42.5b **Benevolence: my actualizing-dao**.

48.3a **Activating my heart's ache**.

50.2a/2b **My companion possesses affliction**.

50.2a **Not me able** to **approach**.

56.4a **My heart not keen**.

61.2a **I possess** a **loved wine-cup**.

62.5a **Originating** from **my Western suburbs**.

I Ice

Ice, *BING*: frozen water; icy, freezing; clear, pure.

2.1a **Treading frost, hard ice** as **culmination**.
2.1b **Treading frost, hard ice**.
2.1b **Culmination: hard ice indeed**.

Illegality, *KOU*: take by force, violate, invade, sack, break the laws; brutality; enemies, outcasts, bandits.

3.2a **In-no-way illegality, matrimonial alliance**.
4.6a **Not Harvesting: activating illegality**.
4.6a **Harvesting: resisting illegality**.
4.6b **Harvesting: availing** of **resisting illegality**.
5.3a **Involvement** in **illegality culminating**.
5.3b **Originating** from **my involvement** in **illegality**.
22.4a/4b **In-no-way illegality, matrimonial alliance**.
38.6a **In-no-way illegality, matrimonial alliance**.
40.3a **Involvement** in **illegality culminating**.
53.3a **Harvesting: resisting illegality**.
53.3b **Harvesting: availing** of **resisting illegality**.

Illuminate, *ZHAO*: shine light on, enlighten; care for, supervise. Ideogram: fire and brightness.

30.PW The **great** in the **person uses consecutive brightening** to **illuminate tending-towards** the **four sides**.
32.IT **Sun** and **moon: acquiring heaven and-also enabling lasting** and **illuminating**.
36.6b **Illuminating** the **four cities indeed**.
55.IT **Properly illuminating below heaven indeed**.

Imagine, *JIA*: create in the mind; fantasize, suppose; pretend, imitate; fiction, illusion; costume. Ideogram: person and borrow.

37.5a/5b The **king imagines possessing** a **household**.
45.IM/ IT The **king imagines possessing** a **temple**.
55.IM/ IT The **king imagines it**.
59.IM/ IT The **king imagines possessing** a **temple**.

Immature, *ZHI*: small, tender, young, delicate; undeveloped; conceited, haughty; late grain.

4.PS To **beings belongs immaturity indeed**.
5.PS **Being**'s **immaturity not permitted not nourishing indeed**.

Immerse, *QIAN*: submerge, hide in water; deep, secret, reserved; retire, withdraw.

1.1a/1b **Immersed dragon, no availing** of.

Imminent, *PIN*: on the brink of; pressing, urgent; often, repeatedly.

24.3a **Imminent return. Adversity**.
24.3b To **imminent return belongs adversity**.
57.3a **Imminent root, abashment**.
57.3b To **imminent root belongs abashment**.

Impede, *SAI*: clog, fill up, close, obstruct; hinder, prevent; hide; unintelligent, dull.

50.3a **Its movement impeded**.
60.1b **Knowing interpenetration impeded indeed**.

Impetuous, *FEN*: sudden energy; lively, spirited, impulsive; excite, arouse.

16.PW **Thunder emerges** from the **earth impetuously. Providing**.

Implements, *QI*: utensils, tools; molded or carved objects; use a person or thing suitably; capacity, talent, intelligence.

45.PW A **jun zi uses eliminating weapons** for **implements**.
51.PS A **lord**'s **implements imply absolutely-nothing like** the **long-living son**.

Imply, *ZHE*: further signify; additional meaning.

This term occurs in the Preceding Situation of most hexagrams. It also occurs in:
28.IT The **great implies exceeding indeed**.
34.IT The **great implies vigor**

indeed.
34.IT The **great implies correcting indeed.**
62.IT The **small implies exceeding and-also Growing indeed.**
63.IT The **small implies Growing indeed.**

Impress, *WEI*: impose on, intimidate; august, solemn; pomp, majesty.
14.5a **Impressing thus. Significant.**
14.5b To **impressing thus belongs significance.**
37.6a **Possessing conformity, impressing thus.**
37.6b To **impressing thus belongs significance.**

Improve, *SHAN*: make better, reform, perfect; virtuous, wise; mild, docile; clever, skillful. Ideogram: mouth and sheep, gentle speech.
14.PW A **jun zi uses terminating hatred** to **display improvement.**
42.PW A **jun zi uses viewing improvement**, by **consequence shifting.**
53.PW A **jun zi uses residing** in **eminent actualizing-dao** to **improve** the **customs.**

Increase, *SHENG* : fill up; abundant, copious; vigorous, flourishing, exuberant; peak, culmination; exalt.
41.HP **Increasing**: the **beginning belonging** to **decreasing indeed.**
42.HP **Decreasing**: the **beginning belonging** to **increasing indeed.**

Indeed, *YE*: emphasizes and intensifies the previous statement.
This term occurs throughout the hexagram texts.

Indignation, *WEN*: irritation, wrath, rage, hate; feeling of injustice.
43.3a **Like soaked, possessing indignation.**

Indigo, *XUAN*: color associated with the Metallic Moment; deep blue-black, color of the sky's depths; profound, subtle, deep.
2.6a **Their blood indigo** and **yellow.**

Individuality, *SHEN*: total person: psyche, body and lifespan; character, virtue, duty, pregnancy; distinct from body, *GONG*, physical being.
24.1b **Using adjusting individuality indeed.**
37.6b **Reversing designation belonging** to **individuality indeed.**
39.PW A **jun zi uses reversing individuality** to **renovate actualizing-dao.**
52.IM **Not capturing one's individuality.**
52.4a/4b The **bound: one's individuality.**
52.IT **That uses not capturing one's individuality.**

Indolence, *DAI*: lazy, idle, inattentive, careless; self-indulgent; disdainful, contemptuous.
15/16.HP **And-also providing: indolence indeed.**

In-fact, *ZAI*: emphatic exclamation; truly, indeed.
1.IT The **great: in-fact energy**'s **Spring.**
2.IT **Culminating in-fact: space**'s **Spring.**
16.IT The **season belonging** to **providing righteously great actually in-fact.**
17.IT To **following**'s **season belongs** the **righteously great actually in-fact.**
25.IT **Moving actually in-fact.**
27.IT The **season belonging** to the **jaws great actually in-fact.**
28.IT The **season belonging** to the **great exceeding great actually in-fact.**
29.IT The **season belonging** to **venturing avails** of the **great actually in-fact.**
33.IT The **season belonging** to **retiring righteously great actually in-fact.**
38.IT The **season belonging** to **polarizing avails** of the **great actually in-fact.**
39.IT **Knowing actually in-fact.**
39.IT The **season belonging** to **limping avails** of the **great**

actually in-fact.
40.IT The **season belonging** to **unraveling great actually in-fact.**
44.IT The **season belonging** to **coupling righteously great actually in-fact.**
49.IT The **season belonging** to **skinning great actually in-fact.**
56.IT The **season belonging** to **sojourning righteously great actually in-fact.**
58.IT The **commoners encouraged actually in-fact.**

Infiltrate, *JIAN*: penetrate slowly and surely, as water; diffuse throughout; advance by degrees; gradual process; influence, affect. Ideogram: water and cut into.
This term occurs in the name of hexagram 53 and recurs throughout its texts. It also occurs in:
54.HP **Infiltrating: womanhood converting awaits manhood moving indeed.**

Influence, *GAN*: excite, act on, touch; affect someone's feelings, move the heart; emotion, feeling. Ideogram: heart and all, pervasive influence.
31.4b **Not-yet influencing harmful indeed.**
31.IT **Conjunction. Influencing indeed.**
31.IT The **two agencies' influences correspond using reciprocal association.**
31.IT **Heaven** and **earth influence and-also** the **myriad beings change** and **generate**.
31.IT The **wise person influences people's heart and-also below heaven harmonizes evenness.**
31.IT **Overseeing one's place** to **influence.**

Inform, *YU*: tell; warn; converse, exchange ideas.
27.PW A **jun zi uses considerate words** to **inform.**

Initial, *CHU*: beginning, incipient, first step or part; bottom line of a hexagram. Ideogram: knife and garment, cutting out the pattern.
4.IM/ IT The **initial oracle-consulting notifies.**
8.1b **Initial six belonging** to **grouping.**
14.1b **Great possessing, initial nine.**
16.1b **Initial six**: the **call** of **providing.**
20.1b **Initial six, youthful overseeing.**
36.6a/6b **Initially mounting tending-towards heaven.**
38.3a/3b **Without initially possessing completion.**
57.5a **Without initially possessing completion.**
59.1b To **initial six belongs significance.**
61.1b **Initial nine: precaution significant.**
63.IM/ IT **Initially: significant.**

Injure, *SHANG*: hurt, wound, damage; grief, distress, mourning; sad at heart, afflicted.
8.3b **Not truly injuring reached.**
36.PS **Advancing necessarily possesses** a **place** for **injury.**
36.PS **Hiding implies injury indeed.**
37.PS **Injury with-respect-to** the **outside implies necessarily reversing with-respect-to** the **household.**
56.3b **Truly using injury actually.**
60.IT **Not injuring property.**

Innate, *XING*: inborn character; spirit, quality, ability; natural, without constraint. Ideogram: heart and produce, spontaneous feeling.
1.IT **Each correcting innate fate.**

In-no-way, *FEI*: strong negative; not so; bandit, rebel; unjust, immoral. Ideogram: a box filled with opposition.
3.2a **In-no-way illegality, matrimonial alliance.**
4.IM/ IT **In-no-way I seek** the **youthful enveloping.**
8.3a/3b To **grouping belongs in-no-way people.**
12.IM/ IT To **obstruction belongs in-no-way people.**
14.1a **In-no-way faulty.**
14.4a/4b **In-no-way one's**

preponderance.
22.4a/4b **In-no-way illegality, matrimonial alliance.**
25.IM/ IT **One's in-no-way correcting possesses blunder.**
30.6a **Severing** the **head. Capturing in-no-way its demons.**
38.6a **In-no-way illegality, matrimonial alliance.**
39.2a **In-no-way** to the **body belongs anteriority.**
45.5a **In-no-way conforming.**
59.4a **In-no-way hidden,** a **place** to **ponder.**

Inside, *NEI*: within, inner, interior; inside of the house and those who work there, particularly women; inside of the body, inner organs; the lower trigram, as opposed to outside, *WAI*, the upper. Ideogram: border and enter.
8.2a/2b To **grouping belongs** an **origin inside.**
11.IT **Inside** Yang **and-also outside Yin.**
11.IT **Inside persisting and-also outside yielding.**
11.IT **Inside jun zi and-also outside** the **small** in the **person.**
12.IT **Inside** Yin **and-also outside Yang.**
12.IT **Inside supple and-also outside solid.**
12.IT **Inside** the **small** in the **person and-also outside jun zi.**
19.6b **Purpose located inside indeed.**
25.IT **And-also activates** a **lord with-respect-to** the **inside.**
36.IT **Inside pattern bright and-also outside supple yielding.**
36.IT **Inside heaviness and-also able** to **correct one's purpose.**
37/38.HP **Household people: inside indeed.**
37.IT The **woman** in the **correct position reaching** the **inside.**
39.3b **Inside rejoicing** in **it indeed.**
39.6b **Purpose located inside indeed.**
61.IT The **supple located inside and-also** the **solid acquires** the **center.**

Inspect, *XING*: examine, inquire, reflect, consider; visit.
20.PW The **earlier kings used inspecting** on all **sides** and **overseeing** the **commoners** to **set-up teaching.**
24.PW The **crown prince** used culminating sun **not** to **inspect** on all **sides.**
51.PW A **jun zi uses anxiety** and **fear** to **adjust inspections.**

Install, *JIAN*: set up, establish, erect, nominate; robust, solid; confirm a law or an institution.
3.IM/1a **Harvesting: installing feudatories.**
3.IT **Proper installing feudatories and-also not soothing.**
8.PW The **earlier kings used installing** a **myriad cities** to **connect** the **related feudatories.**
16.IM **Harvesting: installing feudatories, moving legions.**
16.IT **And-also even-more installing feudatories** to **move legions reached.**

Intention, *YI*: thought, idea, opinion; project, expectation; meaning, connotation. Ideogram: heart and sound, the heart behind the words.
18.1b **Intention received** from the **predecessors indeed.**
36.4b **Capturing** the **heart: intention indeed.**

Interpenetrate, *TONG*: penetrate freely and reciprocally, permeate, flow through, open a way; see clearly, understand deeply; communicate with; together.
11.PS **Compenetration implies interpenetrating indeed.**
11.IT By **consequence** of **that heaven** and **earth mingling and-also** the **myriad beings interpenetrating indeed.**
12.PS **Beings not permitted** to **use completing interpenetration.**
12.IT By **consequence** of **that heaven** and **earth not mingling and-also** the **myriad beings not interpenetrating indeed.**
13.IT **Verily** a **jun zi activating**

enables interpenetration of **purposes belonging** to **below heaven.**

38.IT **Man** and **woman: polarizing and-also their purposes interpenetrating indeed.**

47/48.HP The **well: interpenetrating, and-also**

47.AT **Confining: exhausting and-also interpenetrating.**

60.1b **Knowing interpenetration impeded indeed.**

60.IT The **center's correctness uses interpenetrating.**

Interspace, *XIAN*: space between, interval; vacant, empty. Ideogram: moonlight coming in through a door ajar.

3.PS **Overfilling** the **interspace belonging** to **heaven** and **earth implies verily** the **myriad beings.**

Intertwist, *RU*: interlaced, entangled, as roots; forage, straw.

11.1a **Eradicating thatch-grass intertwisted.**

12.1a **Eradicating thatch-grass intertwisted.**

Intimidate, *YAN*: inspire with fear or awe; severe, rigid, strict, austere, demanding; a severe father; tight, a closed door.

33.PW And **not hating and-also intimidating.**

37.IT **Household people possess** an **intimidating chief in-truth.**

In-truth, *YAN*: a final affirmative particle; the preceding statement is complete and correct.

3.PS **Therefore afterwards** the **myriad beings' generation in-truth.**

14.PS **Associating** with **people concording implies beings necessarily converting in-truth.**

37.IT **Household people possess** an **intimidating chief in-truth.**

62.IT **Possessing** the **symbol belonging** to the **flying bird in-truth.**

64.PS To **anterior acquiescence belongs** the **use** of **not-yet fording's completion in-truth.**

Inundation, *YAN*: overflowing; propagate, multiply, spread out; abundance, opulence; superfluous.

5.2b **Inundation located** in the **center indeed.**

Invite, *SU*: call; urge, exert pressure upon; quick, hurried.

5.6a **Possessing visitors belonging** to **not inviting: three people coming.**

5.6b **Visitors belonging** to **not inviting come.**

31/32.HP **Conjunction: inviting indeed.**

Involve, *ZHI*: devote oneself to; induce, cause, implicate; approach; manifest, express; reach the highest degree of. Ideogram: reach and come up behind.

2.1b **Docile involvement** in **one's dao.**

5.3a **Involvement** in **illegality culminating.**

5.3b **Originating** from **my involvement** in **illegality.**

23.PS **Involved** in **embellishing, therefore afterwards Growing**, by **consequence used-up actually.**

40.3a **Involvement** in **illegality culminating.**

40.3b **Originating** from **my involvement** with **weapons.**

45.IT **Involving reverent presenting indeed.**

47.PW A **jun zi uses involving** in **fate** to **release purpose.**

51.1b/ IT **Anxiety involves blessing indeed.**

55.PW A **jun zi uses severing litigations involving punishment.**

Is?, *HE*: ask, inquire; what? which? who? how? why? where? an interrogative particle, often introducing a rhetorical question: is it? is it not?

3.6b **Is** it **permitted long-living indeed?**

7.IT **Significant, furthermore is** it **actually faulty?**

9.1a **Is** it **one's fault?**

12.6b **Is** it **permitted long-living indeed?**

16.6b **Is** it **permitted long-living indeed?**
17.4a **Is** it **faulty**?
21.6a/6b **Is** not **locking-up submerging** the **ears**?
25.IT **Is it actually**?
26.6a/6b **Is** it not the **highway belonging** to **heaven**?
28.5b **Is** it **permitted** to **last indeed**?
30.3b **Is** it **permitted** to **last indeed**?
33.1b **Not going, is** it a **calamity indeed?**
38.5a **Going, is it faulty?**
49.3b **Furthermore is it actually?**
50.4b **Is** it **trustworthy thus indeed?**
61.6b **Is** it **permitted long-living indeed?**
62.1b **Not permitted thus, is** it **indeed?**
62.3b **Pitfall thus**, it **is indeed!**
63.6b **Is** it **permitted** to **last indeed?**

It/its, *QI*: general third person pronoun and possessive adjective; also: one/one's, he/his, she/her, they/their.
This term occurs throughout the hexagram texts.

Jade, *YU*: jade and all gemstones; precious, beautiful; delightful, happy, perfect, clear.
50.6a The **vessel's jade rings**.
50.6b **Jade rings located above**.

Jar, *FOU*: earthenware vessels; wine-jars and drums. Ideogram: jar containing liquor.
8.1a **Possessing conformity**: **overfilling** the **jar**.
29.4a **Availing** of a **jar**.
30.3a **Not drumbeating** a **jar and-also singing**.

Jawbones, see **Brace/jawbones**

Jaws, *YI*: mouth, jaws, cheeks, chin; swallow, take in, ingest; feed, nourish, sustain, rear. Ideogram: open jaws.
This term is the name of hexagram 27 and recurs throughout its texts. It also occurs in:
21.IT **Jaws' center possesses being**.
28.HP The **jaws**: **nourishing correctly indeed**.

Join, *JIAN*: add or bring together, unite; absorb, assimilate; simultaneously, also. Ideogram: hand grasping two grain stalks, two things at once.
17.2b **Nowhere joining** in **association indeed**.
52.PW **Joined mountains**. The **bound**.

Join-together, *HE*: unite for a purpose. Ideogram: a vase and its lid.
16.4a **Partners join-together suddenly**.

Joy/rejoice, *XI*: delight, exult; cheerful, merry. Ideogram: joy (music) and mouth, expressing joy.
12.6a **Beforehand obstruction, afterwards joy**.
18.PS **Using joy** in **following people implies necessarily possessing affairs**.
22.5b **Possessing joy indeed**.
25.5a **No simple possesses joy**.
26.4b **Possessing joy indeed**.
39.3b **Inside rejoicing** in **it indeed**.
41.4a **Commissioning swiftly possesses joy**.
41.4b **Truly permitting joy indeed**.
46.2b **Possessing joy indeed**.
58.4a The **cuirass' affliction possesses joy**.
58.4b To **nine** at **fourth belongs joy**.

Jug, *WENG*: earthen jar; jug used to draw water.
48.2a The **jug cracked, leaking**.

Juice, *GAO*: active essence; oil, grease, ointment; fertilizing, rich; genius.
3.5a/5b **Sprouting**: **one's juice**.
50.3a The **pheasant's juice not taken-in**.

Jujube-tree, *JI*: thorny bush or tree; sign of a court of justice or site of official literary examinations; difficulties, pains; firm, correct, strict.
29.6a **Dismissing tending-towards dense jujube-trees**.

J Jun zi

Jun zi: ideal of a person who orders his/her life in accordance with dao rather than willful intention, and uses divination in this spirit.

1.PW A **jun zi uses originating strength not** to **pause**.
1.3a A **jun zi completing** the **day**: **energy parching**.
2.IM A **jun zi possesses directed going**.
2.PW A **jun zi uses munificent actualizing-dao** to **carry** the **beings**.
2.IT A **jun zi**: **directed moving**.
3.PW A **jun zi uses** the **canons** to **coordinate**.
3.3a A **jun zi**: **hint not thus stowed** away.
3.3b A **jun zi stowing it**: **going, abashment, exhaustion indeed**.
4.PW A **jun zi uses** the **fruits** of **movement** to **nurture actualizing-dao**.
5.PW A **jun zi uses drinking** and **taking-in** to **repose delightfully**.
6.PW A **jun zi uses arousing affairs** to **plan beginnings**.
7.PW A **jun zi uses tolerating** the **commoners** to **accumulate crowds**.
9.PW A **jun zi uses highlighting** the **pattern** to **actualize-dao**.
9.6a/6b A **jun zi disciplining, pitfall**.
10.PW A **jun zi uses differentiating above** and **below**.
11.IT **Inside jun zi and-also outside** the **small** in the **person**.
11.IT A **jun zi's dao long-living**.
12.IM/IT **Not harvesting**: a **jun zi's Trial**.
12.PW A **jun zi uses parsimonious actualizing-dao** to **expel heaviness**.
12.IT **Inside** the **small** in the **person and-also outside jun zi**.
12.IT A **jun zi's dao dissolving indeed**.
13.IM **Harvesting**: a **jun zi's Trial**.
13.PW A **jun zi uses sorting** the **clans** to **mark-off** the **beings**.
13.IT A **jun zi correct indeed**.
13.IT **Verily** a **jun zi activating enables interpenetration** of **purposes belonging** to **below heaven**.
14.PW A **jun zi uses terminating hatred** to **display improvement**.
15.IM A **jun zi possesses completing**.
15.PW A **jun zi uses reducing** the **numerous** to **augment** the **few**.
15.1a/1b **Humbling, humbling**: **jun zi**.
15.3a/3b The **toil** of **humbling**: **jun zi**.
15.IT The **completion belonging** to a **jun zi indeed**.
17.PW A **jun zi uses turning** to **darkness** to **enter** a **reposing pause**.
18.PW A **jun zi uses rousing** the **commoners** to **nurture actualizing-dao**.
19.PW A **jun zi uses teaching** to **ponder without exhausting**.
20.1a A **jun zi**: **abashment**.
20.5a/6a A **jun zi**: **without fault**.
22.PW A **jun zi uses brightening** the **multitude** of **standards without daring** to **sever litigations**.
23.6a/6b A **jun zi acquires** a **cart**.
23.IT A **jun zi honors** the **dissolving pause** to **overfill emptiness**.
26.PW A **jun zi uses** the **numerous recorded preceding words** to **go** and **move**.
27.PW A **jun zi uses considerate words** to **inform**.
28.PW A **jun zi uses solitary establishing not** to **fear**.
29.PW A **jun zi uses constancy** in **actualizing-dao** to **move**.
31.PW A **jun zi uses emptiness** to **acquiesce** the **people**.
32.PW A **jun zi uses establishing, not versatility** on all **sides**.
33.PW A **jun zi uses distancing** the **small** in the **person**.
33.4a A **jun zi, significant**.
33.4b A **jun zi lovingly retiring**.
34.PW A **jun zi uses no codes whatever, nowhere treading**.
34.3a A **jun zi avails** of **absence**.

34.3b A **jun zi** of **absence indeed**.
35.PW A **jun zi uses originating enlightening** to **brighten actualizing-dao**.
36.PW A **jun zi uses supervising** the **crowds availing** of **darkening and-also brightening**.
36.1a/1b A **jun zi tends-towards moving**.
37.PW A **jun zi uses words** to **possess beings and-also movement** to **possess perseverance**.
38.PW A **jun zi uses concording and-also dividing**.
39.PW A **jun zi uses reversing individuality** to **renovate actualizing-dao**.
40.PW A **jun zi uses forgiving excess** to **pardon offenses**.
40.5a A **jun zi holding-fast possesses unraveling. Significant**.
40.5b A **jun zi possesses unraveling**.
41.PW A **jun zi uses curbing anger** and **blocking appetites**.
42.PW A **jun zi uses viewing improvement**, by **consequence shifting**.
43.PW A **jun zi uses spreading benefits extending** to the **below**.
43.3a/3b A **jun zi**: **parting, parting**.
45.PW A **jun zi uses eliminating weapons** for **implements**.
46.PW A **jun zi uses yielding** to **actualizing-dao**.
47.PW A **jun zi uses involving** in **fate** to **release purpose**.
47.IT **One's very jun zi reached**.
48.PW A **jun zi uses** the **toiling commoners** to **encourage reciprocity**.
49.PW A **jun zi uses regulating** the **calendar** to **brighten** the **seasons**.
49.6a/6b A **jun zi**: a **leopard transforming**.
50.PW A **jun zi uses correcting** the **position** to **solidify fate**.
51.PW A **jun zi uses anxiety** and **fear** to **adjust inspections**.
52.PW A **jun zi uses pondering not** to **emerge** from **one's position**.
53.PW A **jun zi uses residing** in **eminent actualizing-dao** to **improve** the **customs**.
54.PW A **jun zi uses perpetually completing** to **know** the **cracked**.
55.PW A **jun zi uses severing litigations involving punishment**.
56.PW A **jun zi uses bright consideration availing** of **punishment and-also not detaining litigations**.
57.PW A **jun zi uses assigning fate** to **move affairs**.
58.PW A **jun zi uses partnering** with **friends** to **explicate repeatedly**.
60.PW A **jun zi uses paring** and **reckoning** the **measures**.
61.PW A **jun zi uses deliberating litigations** to **delay death**.
62.PW A **jun zi uses moving** in **excess** to **reach courtesy**.
63.PW A **jun zi uses pondering** on **distress and-also providing** for **defending-against it**.
64.PW A **jun zi uses considerately marking-off** the **beings residing** on all **sides**.
64.5a/5b To a **jun zi belongs shining**.

Junior, *DI*: younger relatives who owe respect to their elders.
7.5a/5b The **junior son carts corpses**.
37.IT The **senior**, a **senior**. The **junior**, a **junior**.

Junior-sister, *DI*: younger woman in family or clan; younger sister married to the same man as the elder sister; young concubine, servant.
54.1a/1b **Converting maidenhood uses** the **junior-sister**.
54.3a **Reversed converting uses** the **junior-sister**.
54.5a/5b **Not thus fine** the **sleeves belonging** to **one's junior-sister**.

Keen, *KUAI*: joyous, cheerful, lively, spirited; eager, prompt, ready; capable of.
52.2a **One's heart not keen**.
56.4a **My heart not keen**.

56.4b The **heart not-yet keen indeed.**

Keep-aloof, *JI*: keep at a distance; avoid, fear, shun, abstain from; prohibition. Ideogram: heart and self, keeping to oneself.

43.PW And **residing** in **actualizing-dao**, by **consequence keeping-aloof.**

Kill, *QIANG*: murder, put to death, particularly a sovereign or a chief; assault, wound, maltreat, misuse.

62.3a/3b **Adhering maybe kills it.**

Kinds, *PIN*: species and their essential qualities; sort, class, degree; numerous, innumerable.

1.IT The **kinds** of **beings diffuse** in **forms.**

2.IT The **kinds** of the **beings conjoining, Growing.**

44.IT The **kinds** of **beings conjoin** in **composition indeed.**

57.4a/4b The **fields: capturing three kinds.**

King, *WANG*: sovereign, effective ruler, emperor, seen as connecting heaven and earth; reign, govern.

See also: **Earlier kings**

2.3a/3b **Maybe adhering** to **kingly affairs.**

6.3a **Maybe adhering** to **kingly affairs.**

7.2a/2b The **king thrice bestows fate.**

7.IT **Actually permitted using kinghood.**

8.5a The **king avails** of **three beaters.**

17.6a The **king avails** of **Growing tending-towards** the **Western mountain.**

18.6a/6b **Not affairs**, a **king's feudatory.**

20.4a **Harvesting: availing** of **hospitality tending-towards** the **king.**

29.IT The **king** and the **princes set-up venturing used** to **guard their city.**

30.5b **Radiance: king** and **princes indeed.**

30.6a/6b The **king avails** of **emerging** to **discipline.**

35.2a **Tending-towards one's kingly mother.**

36.IT The **Pattern King uses it.**

37.5a/5b The **king imagines possessing** a **household.**

39.2a/2b A **king**, a **servant: limping, limping.**

42.2a The **king avails** of **presenting tending-towards** the **supreme, significant.**

43.IM **Parting. Displaying tending-towards** the **king's chambers.**

43.IT **Displaying tending-towards** the **king's chambers.**

45.IM/ IT The **king imagines possessing** a **temple.**

46.4a/4b The **king avails** of **Growing tending-towards** the **twin-peaked mountain.**

48.3a **Kingly brightness.**

48.3b **Seeking kingly brightness.**

55.IM/ IT The **king imagines it.**

59.IM/IT The **king imagines possessing** a **temple.**

59.5a/5b The **king's residing, without fault.**

59.IT The **king thereupon located** in the **center indeed.**

Know, *ZHI*: have knowledge of, perceive, experience, remember; know intimately; informed, aware, wise. Ideogram: arrow and mouth, words focused and swift.

2.3b **Knowing** the **shine** of the **great indeed.**

19.5a **Knowledge nearing.**

24.AT **Return: using** the **origin's knowledge.**

39.IT **Knowing actually in-fact.**

54.PW A **jun zi uses perpetually completing** to **know** the **cracked.**

60.1b **Knowing interpenetration impeded indeed.**

64.1b **Truly not knowing** the **end indeed.**

64.6b **Truly not knowing articulation indeed.**

Lack, *WU*: strong negative; there is no, without, empty of, absence.
- 3.3a **Approaching** a **stag**: **lacking precaution.**
- 53.1a **Lacking fault.**
- 57.PS **Sojourning and-also lacking** a **place** for **tolerance.**

Ladle, *BI*: ceremonial spoon used to pour libations.
- 51.IM/ IT **Not losing** the **ladle** and the **libation.**

Lament, *JUE*: sigh, express intense regret or sorrow, mourn over; painful recollections.
- 30.3a By **consequence** to the **great** in **old-age belongs lamenting.**
- 30.5a **Sadness like lamenting.**
- 45.3a **Clustering thus, lamenting thus.**
- 60.3a **Not like articulating,** by **consequence like lamenting.**
- 60.3b To **not articulating belongs lamenting.**

Last, *JIU*: endure; long, protracted, permanent, eternal; old, ancient.
- 1.6b **Overfilling not permitting** to **last indeed.**
- 19.IT **Dissolving not lasting indeed.**
- 28.5b **Is** it **permitted** to **last indeed?**
- 30.3b **Is** it **permitted** to **last indeed?**
- 31.HP **Persevering: lasting indeed.**
- 32.PS **Not permitted** to **use not lasting indeed.**
- 32.PS **Persevering implies lasting indeed.**
- 32.HP **Persevering: lasting indeed.**
- 32.2b **Able** to **last** in the **center indeed.**
- 32.4b **No lasting whatever** in **one's position.**
- 32.IT **Persevering. Lasting indeed.**
- 32.IT **Lasting with-respect-to one's dao indeed.**
- 32.IT **Persevering lasting and-also not climaxing indeed.**
- 32.IT **Sun** and **moon: acquiring heaven and-also enabling lasting** and **illuminating.**
- 32.IT The **four seasons: transforming changes and-also enabling lasting** and **accomplishing.**
- 32.IT The **wise person: lasting with-respect-to one's dao and-also below heaven changing** and **accomplishing.**
- 33.PS **Beings not permitted** to **use lasting residing** in **their place.**
- 63.6b **Is** it **permitted** to **last indeed?**

Latter, *CI*: this, that, what was last spoken of.
- 7.IT **Using** the **latter rules below heaven.**

Laugh, *XIAO*: manifest joy or mirth; giggle, joke, laugh at, tease; desire; open (of a flower); associated with the Fiery Moment.
- 13.5a **Concording people beforehand cry-out** and **sob and-also afterwards laugh.**
- 45.1a **Like** an **outcry, one handful activates laughter.**
- 51.IM/1b/IT **Laughing words, shrieking, shrieking.**
- 51.1a **After laughing words, shrieking, shrieking.**
- 56.6a **Sojourning people beforehand laugh, afterwards cry-out sobbing.**

Laws, *FA*: rules, norms, statutes; model; obey the law.
- 4.1b **Using correcting** by **law indeed.**
- 21.PW The **earlier kings used brightness** in **flogging** to **enforce** the **laws.**

Leak, *LOU*: seep, drip, ooze out; reveal; forget, let slip.
- 48.2a The **jug cracked, leaking.**

Left, *ZUO*: left side, left hand; East; secondary, assistant, inferior; defective, unfavorable.
- 7.4a The **legions' left camp.**
- 7.4b The **left camp, without fault.**
- 11.PW And **uses** at **left** and **right** the **commoners.**
- 36.2a **Hiding tending-towards** the **left thigh.**
- 36.4a/4b **Entering tending-towards** the **left** of the **belly.**

Legions, *SHI*: army, troops; leader, general, model, master; organize, make functional; take as a model, imitate, follow. Ideogram: heap and whole, turn confusion into a functional unit.

This term is the name of hexagram 7 and recurs throughout its texts. It also occurs in:

8.HP The **legions: grief.**

11.6a **No availing** of **legions.**

13.5a/5b **Great legions control** the **reciprocal meeting.**

15.6a **Harvesting: availing** of **moving legions.**

15.6b **Permitted availing** of **moving legions.**

16.IM **Harvesting: installing feudatories, moving legions.**

16.IT **And-also even-more installing feudatories** to **move legions reached.**

24.6a **Availing** of **moving legions.**

Leopard, *BAO*: spotted wild cats, beautiful and independent; mark of high-ranking officers.

49.6a/6b A **jun zi**: a **leopard transforming.**

Lessen, *KUI*: diminish, injure, wane; lack, defect.

15.IT **Heavenly dao lessens overfilling and-also augments humbling.**

50.3a On all **sides rain lessens repenting.**

Let-go, *SHI*: lose, let slip; omit, miss, fail; lose control of. Ideogram: drop from the hand.

2.IT **Beforehand delusion: letting-go dao.**

3/4.HP **Sprouting: viewing and-also not letting-go one's residing.**

5.1b **Not-yet letting-go constancy indeed.**

5.6b **Although not** an **appropriate position, not-yet** the **great letting-go indeed.**

6.4b **Not letting-go indeed.**

7.1b **Letting-go** the **ordinance: pitfall indeed.**

7.4b **Not-yet letting-go constancy indeed.**

8.2b **Not** the **origin letting-go indeed.**

8.5a **Letting-go** the **preceding wildfowl.**

8.5b **Letting-go** the **preceding wildfowl.**

9.2b **Truly not** the **origin letting-go indeed.**

11.4b **Altogether letting-go** the **substance indeed.**

17.1b **Not letting-go indeed.**

17.2a **Letting-go** the **respectable husband.**

17.3a **Letting-go** the **small son.**

20.3b **Not-yet letting-go dao indeed.**

23.3b **Letting-go above** and **below indeed.**

27.2b **Movement letting-go sorting indeed.**

29.1b **Letting-go dao: pitfall indeed.**

29.6b **Six above, letting-go dao.**

29.IT **Movement: venturing and-also not letting-go one's trustworthiness.**

35.5a/5b **Letting-go, acquiring: no cares.**

36.6b **Letting-go** by **consequence indeed.**

37.3b **Not-yet letting-go indeed.**

37.3b **Letting-go** the **household**'s **articulation indeed.**

38.2b **Not-yet letting-go dao indeed.**

41.PS **Delaying necessarily possesses** a **place** to **let-go.**

47.IT **Confining and-also not letting-go one's place: Growing.**

50.3b **Letting-go one's righteousness indeed.**

52.1b **Not-yet letting-go correcting indeed.**

52.IT **Stirring-up, stilling, not letting-go one's season.**

53.3b **Letting-go one's dao indeed.**

56.PS **Exhausting** the **great implies necessarily letting-go one's residing.**

60.2b **Letting-go** the **season: end indeed.**

62.IT The **solid letting-go** the **position and-also not** in the **center.**

64.6a **Possessing conformity:**

letting-go that.

Let-in, *NA*: allow to enter; include, receive, accept, welcome; marry.

4.2a **Letting-in** the **wife, significant.**

29.4a **Letting-in bonds originating** from the **window.**

Levity, *QING*: light, soft; gentle, easy; alert, agile; frivolous, unimportant, superficial. Ideogram: cart and stream, empty cart floating downstream.

15/16.HP **Humbling: levity.**

Libation, *CHANG*: fermented millet liquor, offered to ancestors or poured out to draw the gods near.

51.IM/ IT **Not losing** the **ladle** and the **libation.**

Lightning, *DIAN*: lighting flash, electric discharge; sudden clarity; look attentively.

21.PW **Thunder** and **lightning: gnawing** and **biting.**

21.IT **Thunder** and **lightning uniting and-also composing.**

55.PW **Thunder** and **lightning altogether culminating. Abounding.**

Like, *RUO*: same as, just as; conform, imitate; adverbial suffix indicating similarity.

1.3a At **nightfall awe like** in **adversity.**

20.IM/ IT **Possessing conformity like** a **presence.**

30.5a **Emerging tears like gushing.**

30.5a **Sadness like lamenting.**

43.3a **Like soaked, possessing indignation.**

45.1a **Like** an **outcry, one handful activates laughter.**

50.PS **Skinning beings implies absolutely-nothing like** a **vessel.**

51.PS A **lord's implements imply absolutely-nothing like** the **long-living son.**

55.2a/2b **Possessing conformity, like shooting-forth.**

57.2a **Disorder like, significant.**

57.2b To the **disorder like belongs significance.**

60.3a **Not like articulating,** by **consequence like lamenting.**

Limit, *XIAN*: boundary, frontier, threshold; restriction, impediment; set a limit, distinguish, separate.

52.3a/3b The **bound: one's limit.**

Limp, *JIAN*: proceed haltingly; lame, weak-legged, afflicted; slow, feeble, weak; unfortunate, difficult. Ideogram: foot and cold, impeded circulation in the feet.

This term is the name of hexagram 39 and recurs throughout its texts. It also occurs in:

40.HP **Limping: heaviness indeed.**

Limpid, *LIE*: pure, clear, clean liquid; wash clean.

48.5a The **well: limpid.**

Line, *COU*: line or repair a well; masonry lining the inside of a well.

48.4a/4b The **well: lining, without fault.**

Liquor, *JIU*: alcoholic beverages, distilled spirits; spirit which perfects the good and evil in human nature. Ideogram: liquid above fermenting must, separating the spirits.

5.5a **Attending tending-towards taking-in liquor.**

5.5b **Taking-in liquor: Trial, significant.**

29.4a/4b A **cup** of **liquor**, a **platter added.**

47.2a/2b **Confinement tending-towards liquor taking-in.**

64.6a **Possessing conformity tending-towards drinking liquor.**

64.6b **Drinking liquor, soaking** the **head.**

Litigate, *YU*: legal proceedings, trial, sentence; dispute; take a case to court. Ideogram: two dogs and words, barking arguments at each other.

21.IM **Harvesting: availing** of **litigating.**

21.IT **Although not** an **appropriate position, Harvesting avails** of **litigating indeed.**

22.PW A **jun zi uses brightening** the **multitude** of **standards without daring** to **sever litigations.**

55.PW A **jun zi uses severing litigations involving punishment.**

56.PW **A jun zi uses bright consideration availing** of **punishment and-also not detaining litigations.**

61.PW A **jun zi uses deliberating litigations** to **delay death.**

Live-alone, *QU*: lonely, solitary; quiet, still, deserted.

55.6a/6b **Living-alone, one without people.**

Locate, *ZAI*: be at, be situated at, dwell, reside; in, within; involved with, in the process of. Ideogram: earth and persevere, a place on the earth.

1.1b **Yang located below indeed.**

1.2a/2b **Viewing** a **dragon located** in the **fields.**

1.4a/4b **Maybe capering located** at the **abyss.**

1.5a/5b **Flying dragon located** in **heaven.**

2.5b **Pattern located** in the **center indeed.**

5.2b **Inundation located** in the **center indeed.**

5.3b **Calamity located outside indeed.**

5.IT **Venturing located** in **precedence indeed.**

7.2a/2b **Locating** the **legions** in the **center, significant.**

9.2b **Hauling-along returning located** in the **center.**

10.6b **Spring: significance located above.**

11.1b **Purpose located outside indeed.**

12.1b **Purpose located** in a **chief indeed.**

14.PW **Fire located above heaven. Great possessing.**

16.6b **Dim providing located above.**

17.4a **Possessing conformity, locating** in **dao, using brightness.**

17.4b **Possessing conformity, locating** in **dao.**

19.6b **Purpose located inside indeed.**

20.IT The **great: overseeing located above.**

24.PW **Thunder located** in the **earth's center. Return.**

26.PW **Heaven located** in the **mountain's center.** The **great accumulating.**

28.1b The **supple located below indeed.**

31.1b **Purpose located outside indeed.**

31.3b **Purpose located** in **following people.**

32.6b **Rousing persevering located above.**

34.PW **Thunder located above heaven.** The **great's vigor.**

37.2a **Located** in the **center, feeding.**

37.4b **Yielding located** in the **position indeed.**

39.6b **Purpose located inside indeed.**

39.IT **Venturing located** in **precedence indeed.**

46.6b **Dim ascending located above.**

47.4b **Purpose located below indeed.**

48.6b **Spring, significance located above.**

50.6b **Jade rings located above.**

51.5b **One's affairs located** in the **center.**

54.5b **One's position located** in the **center.**

56.6b **Using sojourning located above.**

57.2a/6a/6b The **root located below** the **bed.**

59.3b **Purpose located outside indeed.**

59.IT The **king thereupon located** in the **center indeed.**

61.2a **Calling crane located** in **Yin.**

61.IT The **supple located inside and-also** the **solid acquires** the **center.**

62.5a A **prince's string-arrow grasps someone located** in a **cave.**

63.PW **Stream located above fire. Already fording.**

64.PW **Fire located above stream. Not-yet fording.**

Lock-up, *JIAO*: imprison, lock up the

feet; prison, pen.
21.1a/1b **Shoes locked-up, submerged feet.**
21.6a/6b **Is** not **locking-up submerging** the **ears**?

Loins, *YIN*: hips, pelvis, lumbar region, kidneys; respect, honor; money belt.
52.3a **Attributed** to **one's loins**.

Long-living, *ZHANG*: enduring, lasting, constant; extended, long, large; senior, superior, greater; increase, prosper; respect, elevate.
3.6b **Is** it **permitted long-living indeed?**
6.1b **Arguing not permitting long-living indeed.**
7.5a/5b The **long-living son conducts** the **legions**.
11.IT A **jun zi**'s **dao long-living**.
12.6b **Is** it **permitted long-living indeed?**
12.IT The **small** in the **person**'s **dao long-living**.
16.6b **Is** it **permitted long-living indeed?**
19.3b **Fault not long-living indeed.**
19.IT The **solid drenched and-also long-living**.
23.IT The **small** in the **person long-living indeed.**
24.IT The **solid**: **long-living indeed.**
33.IT **Drenched and-also long-living.**
34.6b **Fault not long-living indeed.**
42.AT **Augmenting**: **long-living enriching and-also not setting-up.**
43.6b **Completing not permitting long-living indeed.**
43.IT The **solid long-living, thereupon completion indeed.**
44.IT **Not permitted association long-living indeed.**
51.PS A **lord**'s **implements imply absolutely-nothing like** the **long-living son**.
61.6b **Is** it **permitted long-living indeed?**
62.4b **Completion not permitted long-living indeed.**

Lord, *ZHU*: ruler, master, chief, authority; host; domination in the cycle of the Five Transformative Moments. Ideogram: lamp and flame, giving light.
2.IM A **lord Harvesting**.
25.IT **And-also activates** a **lord with-respect-to** the **inside**.
36.1a A **lordly person possesses words**.
38.2a/2b **Meeting** a **lord tending-towards** the **street**.
51.PS A **lord**'s **implements imply absolutely-nothing like** the **long-living son**.
51.IT **Using activating** the **offering lord indeed.**
55.1a **Meeting one's equal lord.**
55.4a/4b **Meeting one's hidden lord.**

Lose, *SANG*: be deprived of, forget; destruction, ruin, death; corpse; lament, mourn; funeral. Ideogram: weep and dead people.
2.IM/ IT **Eastern North**: **losing partnering**.
34.5a/5b **Losing** the **goat**, **tending-towards versatility**.
38.1a **Losing** the **horse**, **no pursuing**: **originating** from **returning**.
48.IM **Without losing, without acquiring.**
51.IM **Not losing** the **ladle** and the **libation**.
51.2a A **hundred-thousand coins lost.**
51.5a **Hundred-thousand without loss, possessing affairs.**
51.5b The **great without loss indeed.**
51.IT **Not losing** the **ladle** and the **libation**.
56.3a/3b **Losing one's youthful vassal.**
56.6a/6b **Losing** the **cattle**, **tending-towards versatility**.
57.6a/6b **Losing one's own emblem-ax.**
62.PW And **losing** in **excess** to **reach mourning**.
63.2a A **wife loses her veil.**

Love, *HAO*: affection; fond of, take pleasure in; fine, graceful.
15.IT **People**'s **dao hates overfilling and-also loves humbling.**

33.4a **Loving retiring.**
33.4b A **jun zi lovingly retiring.**
61.2a **I possess** a **loved wine-cup.**

Lowly, *BEI*: speak and think of oneself humbly; modest, yielding, respectful; decline, decrease; base, mean, contemptible.
15.1b **Lowliness uses originating herding indeed.**
15.IT **Earthly dao: lowly and-also above moving.**
15.IT **Lowliness and-also not permitted** to **pass-beyond.**

Luminous, *BING*: bright, fiery, light-giving; clear, evident; alert, intelligent.
49.5b **One's pattern luminous indeed.**

Luxuriance, *MAO*: thriving, flourishing, exuberant; highly developed, elegant. Ideogram: plants and flourish.
25.PW The **earlier kings used** the **luxuriance suiting** the **season** to **nurture** the **myriad beings.**

Magic, *LING*: wonderful, subtle; effectiveness, power, intelligence; life force, vital energy; spirit of a being; wizard, diviner.
27.1a **Stowing simply** the **magic tortoise.**

Magnanimous, *DUN*: generous, honest, sincere; important, wealthy; honor, increase; firm, solid. Ideogram: strike and accept, warrior magnanimous in giving and receiving blows.
19.6a **Magnanimity nearing.**
19.6b To **magnanimity nearing belongs significance.**
24.5a **Magnanimous return.**
24.5b **Magnanimous return, without repenting.**
52.6a **Magnanimous bound, significant.**
52.6b To **magnanimous bound belongs significance.**

Maidenhood, *MEI*: girl not yet nubile, virgin; younger sister; daughter of a secondary wife. Ideogram: woman and not-yet.
This term occurs in the name of hexagram 54 and recurs throughout its texts. It also occurs in:
11.5a **Supreme Burgeoning converting maidenhood.**
53.HP **Converting maidenhood**: the **completion belonging** to **womanhood indeed.**

Manage, *GAN*: cope with, deal with; attend to the essential; trunk, stem, spine, skeleton.
18.1a/1b **Managing** the **decay belonging** to the **father.**
18.2a/2b **Managing** the **decay belonging** to the **mother.**
18.3a/3b **Managing** the **decay belonging** to the **father.**
18.5a **Managing** the **decay belonging** to the **father.**
18.5b **Managing** the **father avails** of **praise.**

Man(hood), *NAN*: a man; what is inherently male; husband, son. Ideogram: field and strength, men's hard work in the fields.
31.PS **Therefore afterwards possessing man** and **woman.**
31.PS **Possessing man** and **woman.**
31.IT **Manhood below womanhood.**
37.IT The **man** in the **correct position reaching** the **outside.**
37.IT **Man** and **woman correct.**
38.IT **Man** and **woman: polarizing and-also their purposes interpenetrating indeed.**
53/54.HP **Infiltrating: womanhood converting awaits manhood moving indeed.**
63/64.HP **Not-yet fording**: to **manhood belongs exhaustion indeed.**

Manifest, *XIAN*: apparent, conspicuous; illustrious; make clear.
8.5a **Manifest grouping.**
8.5b To **manifest grouping belongs significance.**

Mark-off, *BIAN*: distinguish by dividing; mark off a plot of land; discern, discriminate, differentiate; discuss and dispute; frame which divides a bed from its stand. Ideogram: knife

and acrid, sharp division.
13.PW A **jun zi uses sorting** the **clans** to **mark-off** the **beings**.
23.2a/2b **Stripping** the **bed, using marking-off**.
24.AT **Return**: the **small and-also marking-off with-respect-to beings**.
47.AT **Confining**: **marking-off belonging** to **actualizing-dao indeed**.
64.PW A **jun zi uses considerately marking-off** the **beings residing** on all **sides**.

Martial, *WU*: warrior, military, warlike; valiant, powerful; strong, stern; Wu is the name of the son of King Wen, who defeated the last Shang emperor and founded the Zhou dynasty. Ideogram: fight and stop, force deterring aggression.
10.3a/3b **Martial people activate tending-towards** the **great** in the **chief**.
49.IT **Redressing martially, skinning fate**.
57.1a/1b **Harvesting**: to **martial people belongs Trial**.

Master, *SHENG*: have the upper hand; control, command, win, conquer, check (as in the cycle of the Five Transformative Moments); worthy of, able to.
33.2a To **abstaining belongs mastering stimulation**.
43.1a **Going, not mastering**: **activating fault**.
43.1b **Not mastering and-also going**.
53.5a To **completing abstention belongs mastering**.
53.5b To **completing abstention belongs mastering, significant**.

Matrimonial alliance, *HUN GOU*: legal institution of marriage; union of two families by marriage.
3.2a **In-no-way illegality, matrimonial alliance**.
3.4a **Seeking matrimonial alliance**.
22.4a/4b **In-no-way illegality, matrimonial alliance**.
38.6a **In-no-way illegality, matrimonial alliance**.
51.6a **Matrimonial alliance possesses words**.

Maybe, *HUO*: possible but not certain, perhaps.
1.4a/4b **Maybe capering located** at the **abyss**.
2.3a/3b **Maybe adhering** to **kingly affairs**.
6.3a **Maybe adhering** to **kingly affairs**.
6.6a **Maybe** to **bestowing belongs** a **pouched belt**.
7.3a/3b The **legions maybe carting corpses**.
19/20.HP **Maybe associating, maybe seeking**.
25.3a **Maybe** to **attaching belongs cattle**.
32.3a **Maybe** to **receiving belongs embarrassment**.
41.5a **Maybe** to **augmenting belongs ten**.
42.2a **Maybe** to **augmenting belongs ten**.
42.2b **Maybe augmenting it**.
42.6a/6b **Maybe smiting it**.
53.4a/4b **Maybe acquiring one's rafter**.
61.3a/3b **Maybe drumbeating, maybe desisting**.
61.3a **Maybe weeping, maybe singing**.
62.3a/3b **Adhering maybe kills it**.

Mean, *JIAN*: low, poor, cheap; depreciate, undervalue; opposite of value, *GUI*.
3.1b **Using valuing** the **below** and the **mean**.

Measures, *DU*: rules, regulations, norms; measuring instrument; limit, test; capacity, endurance; interval in music, punctuation in a sentence.
60.PW A **jun zi uses paring** and **reckoning** the **measures**.
60.IT **Articulating uses paring** the **measures**.

Meat, *RU*: flesh of animals; pulp of fruit.
21.3a/5a **Gnawing seasoned meat**.

Meat-bones, *ZI*: dried meat with bones; bones left after a meal.

21.4a **Gnawing parched meat-bones.**

Meet, *YU*: come on unexpectedly, encounter; occur, happen; pleasant meeting, lucky coincidence; agree.

13.5a/5b **Great legions control** the **reciprocal meeting.**
21.3a/3b **Meeting poison.**
38.2a/2b **Meeting** a **lord tending-towards** the **street.**
38.3b **Meeting** a **solid indeed.**
38.4a **Meeting Spring, husbanding.**
38.6a **Going meets rain**, by **consequence significant.**
38.6b To **meeting rain belongs significance.**
43/44.HP **Coupling: meeting indeed.**
43/44.HP The **supple meets** the **solid indeed.**
43.3a **Solitary going, meeting rain.**
44.PS **Breaking-up necessarily possesses meeting.**
44.PS **Coupling implies meeting indeed.**
44.IT **Coupling. Meeting indeed.**
44.IT The **supple meets** the **solid indeed.**
44.IT **Heaven** and **earth reciprocally meeting.**
44.IT The **solid meets** the **center**'s **correctness.**
45.PS **Beings reciprocally meeting and-also afterwards assembling.**
47/48.HP **confining: reciprocal meeting indeed.**
55.1a **Meeting one's equal lord.**
55.4a/4b **Meeting one's hidden lord.**
62.2a **Meeting one's grandmother.**
62.2a **Meeting one's servant.**
62.4a/4b **Nowhere exceeding, meeting it.**
62.6a/6b **Nowhere meeting, exceeding it.**

Melancholy, *MEN*: sad, unhappy, chagrined, heavy-hearted. Ideogram: gate and heart, the heart confined or melancholy as gate to the heart.

28.PW And **retiring** from the **age without melancholy.**

Melon, *GUA*: general term for melon, gourd, squash, cucumber; symbol of heaven and earth, the cosmos.

44.5a **Using osier** to **enwrap melons.**

Merely, *ZHI*: only, just, simply; respect, venerate.

24.1a **Without merely repenting.**
29.5a **Merely already evened.**

Metallic, *JIN*: all things pertaining to metal, particularly gold; smelting and casting; perfection, richness; autumn, West, sunset; one of the Five Transformative Moments.

4.3a **Viewing** a **metallic husband.**
21.4a **Acquiring** a **metallic arrow.**
21.5a **Acquiring yellow metal.**
44.1a/1b **Attachment tending-towards** a **metallic chock.**
47.4a **Confinement tending-towards** a **metallic chariot.**
50.5a The **vessel**'s **yellow ears, metallic rings.**

Mile, *LI*: measure of distance, about 600 meters; street, native village, community.

51.IM/ IT The **shake scares** a **hundred miles.**

Mingle, *JIAO*: blend with, communicate, join, exchange; trade; copulation; friendship. Ideogram: legs crossed.

3.IT **Solid** and **supple begin** to **mingle and-also** in **heaviness generate.**
11.PW **Heaven** and **earth mingling. Compenetration.**
11.IT By **consequence** of **that heaven** and **earth mingling and-also** the **myriad beings interpenetrating indeed.**
11.IT **Above** and **below mingling and-also their purposes concording indeed.**
12.PW **Heaven** and **earth not mingling. Obstruction.**
12.IT By **consequence** of **that heaven** and **earth not mingling and-also** the **myriad beings not interpenetrating indeed.**
12.IT **Above** and **below not mingling and-also below heaven without fiefdoms indeed.**

14.1a **Without mingling** with **harm.**
14.1b **Without mingling** with **harm indeed.**
14.5a/5b **Your conforming: mingling thus.**
17.1a/1b **Emerging** from the **gate, mingling possesses achievement.**
37.5b **Mingling: reciprocal affection indeed.**
38.4a **Mingling, conforming.**
38.4b **Mingling, conforming, without fault.**
54.IT **Heaven** and **earth not mingling.**

Mire, *TU*: mud, dirt, filth; besmear, blot out. Ideogram: earth and water.
38.6a **Viewing** a **pig bearing mire.**

Moat, *HUANG*: ditch around a city or a fort.
11.6a/6b The **bulwark returns tending-towards** the **moat.**

Moon, *YUE*: moon and moon-cycle, month; menstruation; Yin.
9.6a The **moon almost full.**
16.IT **Anterior sun** and **moon not exceeding.**
19.IM/ IT **Culminating tending-towards** the **eighth moon possesses pifall.**
30.IT **Sun** and **moon congregating reaching heaven.**
32.IT **Sun** and **moon: acquiring heaven and-also enabling lasting** and **illuminating.**
54.5a The **moon almost full, significant.**
55.IT The **moon overfilling,** by **consequence taken-in.**
61.4a The **moon almost full.**

More, *TUO*: another, something else; add to.
8.1a **Completion coming, possessing more, significant.**
8.1b **Possessing more, significant indeed.**
28.4a **Possessing more: abashment.**

Moreover, *QIE*: further, and also.
29.3a **Venturing, moreover reclining.**
38.3a **One's person stricken, moreover nose-cut.**
40.3a/3b **Bearing, moreover riding.**
43.4a/4b **One's moving** the **camp moreover.**
44.3a/3b **One's moving** the **camp moreover.**

Mother, *MU*: mother, maternal, feminine; child-bearing and nourishing. Ideogram: two breasts.
18.2a/2b **Managing** the **decay belonging** to the **mother.**
35.2a **Tending-towards one's kingly mother.**
37.IT To **father** and **mother belongs designation.**

Motive, *QING*: true nature; feelings, desires, passions; sincere, true, real; state of affairs, circumstances. Ideogram: heart and green, germinated in the heart.
31.IT **And-also** the **motives belonging** to **heaven** and **earth**'s **myriad beings permit viewing actually.**
32.IT **And-also** the **motives belonging** to **heaven** and **earth**'s **myriad beings permit viewing actually.**
34.IT The **correct great and-also** the **motives belonging** to **heaven** and **earth permit viewing actually.**
45.IT **And-also** the **motives belonging** to **heaven** and **earth**'s **myriad beings permit viewing actually.**

Motley, *ZA*: mingled, variegated, mixed; disorder.
3/4.HP **Enveloping: motley and-also conspicuous.**
32.AT **Persevering: motley and-also not restricting.**

Mound, *LING*: grave-mound, barrow; small hill.
13.3a **Ascending one's high mound.**
22.3b To **completing abstention belongs** a **mound indeed.**
29.IT **Earth**'s **venture: mountains, rivers, hill-tops, mounds indeed.**
51.2a **Climbing tending-towards** the **ninth mound.**
53.5a The **swan infiltrating tending-towards** the **mound.**

Mount, *DENG*: ascend, rise; ripen, complete.
36.6a/6b **Initially mounting tending-towards heaven.**
61.6a/6b A **soaring sound mounts tending-towards heaven.**

Mountain, *SHAN*: mountain; large, immense; limit, boundary; Symbol of the trigram Bound, *GEN*. Ideogram: three peaks, a mountain range.
4.PW **Below** the **mountain emerges springwater. Enveloping.**
4.IT **Enveloping. Below mountain possesses venturing.**
15.PW The **earth's center possesses mountain. Humbling.**
17.6a The **king avails** of **Growing tending-towards** the **Western mountain.**
18.PW The **mountain possesses wind below. Decay.**
22.PW The **mountain possesses fire below. Adorning.**
23.PW **Mountain adjoining with-respect-to earth. Stripping.**
26.PW **Heaven located** in the **mountain's center.** The **great accumulating.**
27.PW The **mountain possesses thunder below.** The **jaws.**
29.IT **Earth's venture: mountains, rivers, hill-tops, mounds indeed.**
31.PW The **mountain possesses pond above. Conjunction.**
33.PW **Heaven possesses mountain below. Retiring.**
39.PW The **mountain possesses stream above. Limping.**
41.PW The **mountain possesses pond below. Diminishing.**
46.4a/4b The **king avails** of **Growing tending-towards** the **twin-peaked mountain.**
52.PW **Joined mountains.** The **bound.**
53.PW The **mountain possesses wood above. Infiltrating.**
56.PW The **mountain possesses fire above. Sojourning.**
62.PW The **mountain possesses thunder above.** The **small exceeding.**

Mourn, *AI*: grieve, lament over something gone; distress, sorrow; compassion. Ideogram: mouth and clothes, display of feelings.
62.PW And **losing** in **excess** to **reach mourning.**

Mouth, *KOU*: mouth, mouthful; words going out and food coming into the mouth; entrance, hole, passageway.
27.IM/ IT The **origin** of **seeking mouth's substance.**
31.6b The **spouting mouth stimulating indeed.**
47.IT **Honoring** the **mouth thereupon exhausted indeed.**

Move, *XING*: move or move something; motivate; emotionally moving; walk, act, do. Ideogram: successive steps.
This term occurs throughout the hexagram texts.

Mud, *XI*: ground left wet by water, muddy shores; danger; shed tears; nearly.
48.IM/ IT **Muddy culmination: truly not-yet** the **well-rope** in the **well.**
64.IM/ IT The **small fox** in a **muddy ford.**

Mulberry-tree, *SANG*: the tree on which silkworms live; rural place, tranquillity, retirement.
12.5a **Attachment tending-towards** a **grove** of **mulberry-trees.**

Multitude, *SHU*: crowd, many people; mass, herd; all, the whole.
1.IT **Heads emerging** from the **multitude** of **beings.**
22.PW A **jun zi uses brightening** the **multitude** of **standards without daring** to **sever litigations.**
35.IM **Prospering.** A **content feudatory avails** of **bestowing horses** to **enhance** the **multitudes.**
35.IT **That uses** a **content feudatory availing** of **bestowing horses** to **enhance** the **multitudes.**

Munificence, *HOU*: liberal, kind, generous; create abundance; thick, large. Ideogram: gift of a superior to an inferior.

2.PW A **jun zi uses munificent actualizing-dao** to **carry** the **beings**.
2.IT **Space**: **munificent carrying** the **beings**.
23.PW **Above using munificence**, **below pacifying** the **situation**.
42.1b **Below not munificent affairs indeed**.
52.6b **Using munificence** to **complete indeed**.

Myriad, *WAN*: ten thousand; countless, many, everyone. Ideogram: swarm of insects.
1.IT The **myriad beings' own beginning**.
1.IT The **myriad cities conjoining** to **soothe**.
2.IT The **myriad beings' own generation**.
3.PS **Therefore afterwards** the **myriad beings' generation in-truth**.
3.PS **Overfilling** the **interspace belonging** to **heaven** and **earth implies verily** the **myriad beings**.
7.2b **Cherishing** the **myriad fiefdoms indeed**.
8.PW The **earlier kings used installing** a **myriad cities** to **connect** the **related feudatories**.
11.IT By **consequence** of **that heaven** and **earth mingling and-also** the **myriad beings interpenetrating indeed**.
12.IT By **consequence** of **that heaven** and **earth not mingling and-also** the **myriad beings not interpenetrating indeed**.
15.3b The **myriad commoners submit indeed**.
25.PW The **earlier kings used** the **luxuriance suiting** the **season** to **nurture** the **myriad beings**.
27.IT **Heaven** and **earth nourish** the **myriad beings**.
27.IT The **wise person nourishes eminence used** to **extend** to the **myriad commoners**.
31.PS **Therefore afterwards possessing** the **myriad beings**.
31.PS **Possessing** the **myriad beings**.
31.IT **Heaven** and **earth influence and-also** the **myriad beings change** and **generate**.
31.IT **And-also** the **motives belonging** to **heaven** and **earth**'s **myriad beings permit viewing actually**.
32.IT **And-also** the **motives belonging** to **heaven** and **earth**'s **myriad beings permit viewing actually**.
38.IT The **myriad beings**: **polarizing and-also their affairs sorted indeed**.
45.IT **And-also** the **motives belonging** to **heaven** and **earth**'s **myriad beings permit viewing actually**.
54.IT **And-also** the **myriad beings not rising**.

Myself, *WU*: first person intensifier; the particular person I am; I, my, we, our.
61.2a **Myself associating**: **simply spilling it**.

Name, *YUE*: speak, declare, call. Ideogram: open mouth and tongue.
9.IT **Named**: the **small accumulating**.
13.IT **Named**: **concording people**.
13.IT **Concording people**: **thus named**.
14.IT **Named**: the **great possessing**.
21.IT **Named**: **gnawing** and **biting**.
26.3a **Named**: **enclosing** the **cart**, **escorting**.
47.6a **Named**: **stirring-up repenting possesses repenting**.
49.IT **Their purposes not reciprocally acquired**: **named skinning**.

Near, *LIN*: approach or be approached: behold with care, look on sympathetically; condescend; bless or curse by coming nearer; a superior visits an inferior.
This term is the name of hexagram 19 and recurs throughout its texts. It also occurs in:
See also: **Draw-near**

20.HP To **nearing** and **overseeing belongs righteousness**.

Nearby, *ER*: near, close in space; approach.

51.IT **Scaring** the **distant and-also fearing** the **nearby indeed**.

Necessarily, *BI*: unavoidably, certainly.

4.PS **Beings' generation necessarily enveloped**.

6.PS **Drinking** and **taking-in necessarily possess arguing**.

7.PS **Arguing necessarily possesses crowds rising-up**.

7.6b **Necessarily disarraying** the **fiefdoms indeed**.

8.PS **Crowds necessarily possess** a **place** to **group**.

9.PS **Grouping necessarily possesses** a **place** to **accumulate**.

14.PS **Associating** with **people concording implies beings necessarily converting in-truth**.

16.PS **Possessing** the **great and-also enabling humbleness necessarily provides**.

17.PS **Providing necessarily possesses following**.

18.PS **Using joy** in **following people implies necessarily possessing affairs**.

30.PS **Falling necessarily possesses** a **place** to **congregate**.

36.PS **Advancing necessarily possesses** a **place** for **injury**.

37.PS **Injury with-respect-to** the **outside implies necessarily reversing with-respect-to** the **household**.

38.PS **Household's dao exhausted, necessarily turning-away**.

39.PS **Turning-away necessarily possesses heaviness**.

41.PS **Delaying necessarily possesses** a **place** to **let-go**.

42.PS **Diminishing and-also not climaxing necessarily augments**.

43.PS **Augmenting and-also not climaxing necessarily breaks-up**.

44.PS **Breaking-up necessarily possesses meeting**.

47.PS **Ascending and-also not climaxing necessarily confines**.

48.PS **Confining reaching above implies necessarily reversing** to the **below**.

54.PS **Advancing necessarily possesses** a **place** for **converting**.

55.PS **Acquiring one's place** for **converting implies necessarily** the **great**.

56.PS **Exhausting** the **great implies necessarily letting-go one's residing**.

62.PS **Possessing one's trustworthiness implies necessarily moving it**.

62.4a/4b **Going: adversity necessarily** a **warning**.

63.PS **Beings possessing excess implies necessarily fording**.

Neck, *MEI*: muscular base of neck, shoulders and arms; source of strength in arms and shoulders; persist.

31.5a/5b **Conjunction** of **one's neck**.

Neighbor, *LIN*: person living nearby; extended family; assist, support.

9.5a **Affluence: using one's neighbor**.

11.4a **Not affluence: using one's neighbor**.

15.5a **Not affluence: using one's neighbor**.

51.6a **Tending-towards one's neighbor**.

51.6b The **dreading neighbor**, a **warning indeed**.

63.5a/5b The **Eastern neighbor slaughters cattle**.

63.5a **Not thus** the **dedicated offering belonging** to the **Western neighbor**.

63.5b **Not thus** the **season belonging** to the **Western neighbor**.

Nest, *CHAO*: nest; haunt, retreat.

56.6a A **bird burns its nest**.

Nightfall, *XI*: day's end, dusk; late; last day of month or year.

1.3a At **nightfall awe like** in **adversity**.

Night, *YE*: dark half of the 24-hour cycle.

43.2a At **night possessing weapons.**

Nine, *JIU*: number nine; transforming whole line; superlative: best, perfect.

1.7b **Availing** of **nines.**
14.1b **Great possessing, initial nine.**
32.2b **Nine** at **second, repenting extinguished.**
34.2b **Nine** at **second: Trial, significant.**
40.2b **Nine** at **second: Trial, significant.**
41.2b **Nine** at **second: Harvesting, Trial.**
44.5b **Nine** at **fifth: containing composition.**
46.2b To **nine** at **second belongs conforming.**
51.2a **Climbing tending-towards** the **ninth mound.**
57.5b To **nine** at **fifth belongs significance.**
58.4b To **nine** at **fourth belongs joy.**
61.1b **Initial nine: precaution significant.**
64.2b **Nine** at **second: Trial, significant.**

No, *WU*: common term of negation.
This term occurs throughout the hexagram texts.

Noble, *ZUN*: honorable, worthy of respect, eminent. Ideogram: presenting wine to a guest.

14.IT The **supple acquires** the **noble position:** the **great** in the **center.**
15.AT/ IT **Humbling: noble and-also shining.**

North, see **Eastern North**

Nose, *BI*: nose; handle.

21.2a/2b **Gnawing flesh, submerging** the **nose.**

Nose-cutting, *YI*: punishment through loss of public face or honor; distinct from foot-cutting, *YE*, crippling punishment for serious crime.

38.3a **One's person stricken, moreover nose-cut.**
47.5a/5b **Nose-cut, foot-cut.**

Not, *BU*: common term of negation.
This term occurs throughout the hexagram texts.

Nothing/nowhere, *FU*: strong negative; not a single thing/place; deny, disapprove; impossible, incorrect.

See also: **Absolutely-nothing**

13.4a **Nowhere controlling aggression.**
13.4b **Righteousness nowhere controlling indeed.**
14.3a The **small** in the **person nowhere controlling.**
17.2b **Nowhere joining** in **association indeed.**
22.1b **Righteously nothing** to **ride indeed.**
34.PW A **jun zi uses no codes whatever, nowhere treading.**
41.2a **Nowhere diminishing, augmenting it.**
41.5a **Nowhere controlling contradiction.**
41.6a/6b **Nowhere diminishing, augmenting it.**
42.2a **Nowhere controlling contradiction.**
62.3a **Nowhere exceeding, defending-against it.**
62.4a/4b **Nowhere exceeding, meeting it.**
62.6a/6b **Nowhere meeting, exceeding it.**

Notify, *GAO*: proclaim, order, decree; advise, inform; accuse, denounce. Ideogram: mouth and ox head, impressive speech.

4.IM/IT The **initial oracle-consulting notifies.**
4.IM/ IT **Obscuring**, by **consequence not notifying.**
11.6a **Originating** from the **capital, notifying fate.**
42.3a **Notifying** the **prince, availing** of the **scepter.**
42.4a/4b **Notifying** the **prince, adhering.**
43.IM/ IT **Notifying originates** from the **capital.**

Not-yet, *WEI*: temporal negative indicating that something is expected to happen but has not yet occurred.
This term occurs in the name of hexagram 64 and recurs throughout its texts. It also occurs in:

3.5b **Spreading, not-yet shining indeed.**
5.1b **Not-yet letting-go constancy indeed.**
5.6b **Although not** an **appropriate position, not-yet** the **great letting-go indeed.**
7.4b **Not-yet letting-go constancy indeed.**
9.IT **Spreading, not-yet moving indeed.**
13.6b **Purpose not-yet acquired indeed.**
15.6b **Purpose not-yet acquired indeed.**
16.5b The **center not-yet extinguished indeed.**
18.4b **Going, not-yet acquiring indeed.**
19.2b **Not-yet yielding** to **fate indeed.**
20.3b **Not-yet letting-go dao indeed.**
20.6b **Purpose not-yet evened indeed.**
21.4b **Not-yet shining indeed.**
23.2b **Not-yet possessing association indeed.**
25.2b **Not tilling** the **crop. Not-yet affluence indeed.**
29.2b **Not-yet emerging** from the **center indeed.**
29.5b In the **center not-yet** the **great indeed.**
31.4b **Not-yet influencing harmful indeed.**
31.4b **Not-yet** the **shining great indeed.**
35.1b **Not-yet acquiescing** in **fate indeed.**
35.6b **Dao not-yet shining indeed.**
37.1b **Purpose not-yet transformed indeed.**
37.3b **Not-yet letting-go indeed.**
38.2b **Not-yet letting-go dao indeed.**
40.4b **Not-yet** an **appropriate position indeed.**
43.5b The **center not-yet shining indeed.**
44.3b **Moving, not-yet hauling-along indeed.**
45.2b The **center not-yet transformed indeed.**
45.5b **Purpose not-yet shining indeed.**
45.6b **Not-yet peaceful above indeed.**
47.5b **Purpose not-yet acquired indeed.**
47.6b **Not-yet appropriate indeed.**
48.IM/ IT **Muddy culmination: truly not-yet** the **well-rope** in the **well.**
48.IT **Not-yet possessing achievement indeed.**
49.5a **Not-yet** an **augury, possessing conformity.**
50.1b **Not-yet rebelling indeed.**
51.4b **Not-yet shining indeed.**
51.6b The **center not-yet acquired indeed.**
52.1b **Not-yet letting-go correcting indeed.**
52.2b **Not-yet withdrawing** from **hearkening indeed.**
54.2b **Not-yet transforming constancy indeed.**
54.3b **Not-yet appropriate indeed.**
56.4b **Not-yet acquiring** the **position indeed.**
56.4b The **heart not-yet keen indeed.**
58.1b **Moving, not-yet doubting indeed.**
58.4a **Bargaining open, not-yet soothing.**
58.6b **Not-yet shining indeed.**
61.1b **Purpose not-yet transformed indeed.**
63.HP **Not-yet fording:** to **manhood belongs exhaustion indeed.**

Nourish, YANG: feed, sustain, support, provide, care for; generate; raise, grow.
4.IT **Enveloping uses nourishing correctness.**
5.PS **Being's immaturity not permitted not nourishing indeed.**
26.IT **Nourishing eminence indeed.**
27.PS **Beings accumulate, therefore afterwards permitted** to **nourish.**
27.PS The **jaws imply nourishing indeed.**
27/28.HP The **jaws: nourishing correctly indeed.**

27.IT **Nourishing correctly**, by **consequence significance indeed.**
27.IT **Overseeing one's place** of **nourishment indeed.**
27.IT **Overseeing one's origin**: **nourishment indeed.**
27.IT **Heaven** and **earth nourish** the **myriad beings.**
27.IT The **wise person nourishes eminence used** to **extend** to the **myriad commoners.**
28.PS **Not nourished**, by **consequence not permitted stirring-up.**
48.IT The **well**: **nourishing and-also not exhausted indeed.**
50.IT **And-also** the **great's Growing uses nourishing** the **wise** and the **eminent.**

No ... whatever, *FEI*: strongest negative; not at all!
32.4b **No lasting whatever** in **one's position.**
34.PW A **jun zi uses no codes whatever, nowhere treading.**

Nowhere, see **Nothing/nowhere**

Numerous, *DUO*: great number, many; often.
15.PW A **jun zi uses reducing** the **numerous** to **augment** the **few.**
26.PW A **jun zi uses** the **numerous recorded preceding words** to **go** and **move.**
55/56.HP **Abounding**: **numerous anteriority indeed.**

Nurse, *ZI*: care for and protect, act as a mother, love; give birth, raise. Ideogram: child and shelter.
3.2a **Woman** and **son's Trial**: **not nursing.**
3.2a/2b **Ten years, thereupon nursing.**

Nurture, *YU*: give birth; bring up, rear, raise.
4.PW A **jun zi uses** the **fruits** of **movement** to **nurture actualizing-dao.**
18.PW A **jun zi uses rousing** the **commoners** to **nurture actualizing-dao.**
25.PW The **earlier kings used** the **luxuriance suiting** the **season** to **nurture** the **myriad beings.**
53.3a/3b The **wife pregnant, not nurturing.**

Oblations, *SI*: sacrifices offered to the gods and the dead.
47.2a **Harvesting**: **availing** of **presenting oblations.**
47.5a/5b **Harvesting**: **availing** of **offering oblations.**

Obscure, *DU*: confuse, muddle; cloudy, turbid; agitated water; annoy through repetition; disrespectful, corrupted.
4.IM/IT **Twice, thrice**: **obscuring.**
4.IM/IT **Obscuring**, by **consequence not notifying.**
4.IT **Obscuring enveloping indeed.**

Observe, *SHI*: see, examine, inspect; consider as; compare, imitate. Ideogram: see and omen, taking what you see into account.
10.3a/3b **Squinting enables observing.**
10.6a **Observing treading**: **predecessors auspicious.**
27.4a A **tiger observing**: **glaring, glaring.**
51.6a **Observing**: **terror, terror.**
54.2a **Squinting enables observing.**

Obstruct, *PI*: closed, stopped; bar the way; obstacle; unfortunate, wicked; refuse, disapprove, deny. Ideogram: mouth and not, blocked communication.
This term is the name of hexagram 12 and recurs throughout its texts. It also occurs in:
7.1a **Obstructing virtue**: **pitfall.**
11.HP **Obstruction** and **compenetration**: **reversing one's sorting indeed.**
13.PS **Beings not permitted** to **use completing obstruction.**
33.4a The **small** in the **person obstructing.**
33.4b The **small** in the **person obstructing indeed.**
50.1a/1b **Harvesting**: **emerging** from **obstruction.**

Occult, *YIN*: hide, obscure; hidden from view; mysterious, subtle; retired.

57.AT The **root: evaluating and-also occulting.**

Offense, *ZUI*: crime, sin, fault; violate laws or rules; punishment. Ideogram: net and wrong, entangled in guilt.

40.PW A **jun zi uses forgiving excess** to **pardon offenses.**

Offer, *JI*: offer a sacrifice. Ideogram: hand, meat and worship.

47.5a/5b **Harvesting: availing** of **offering oblations.**

51.IT **Using activating** the **offering lord indeed.**

63.5a **Not thus** the **dedicated offering belonging** to the **Western neighbor.**

Offertory-millet, *JI*: grain presented to the god of agriculture; presence of the god in the grain.

51.IT **Emerging permits using guarding** the **ancestral temple**, the **field-altar**, the **offertory-millet.**

Official, *GUAN*: government official, magistrate, dignitary.

17.1a/1b An **official possesses retraction.**

Old-age, *DIE*: seventy or older; aged, no longer active.

30.3a By **consequence** to the **great** in **old-age belongs lamenting.**

One, *YI*: a single unit; number one; undivided, simple, whole; unique; first.

32.AT **Persevering: using** the **one actualizing-dao.**

32.5b **Adhering** to the **one and-also completing indeed.**

38.6a **Carrying souls:** the **one chariot.**

41.3a By **consequence diminishing** by **one person.**

41.3a/3b **One person moving.**

45.1a **Like** an **outcry, one handful activates laughter.**

56.5a **One arrow extinguishing.**

One/one's, *QI*: general third person pronoun and possessive adjective; also: it/its, he/his, she/her, they/their.

This term occurs throughout the hexagram texts.

One-sided, *PIAN*: slanted, inclined to one side; excessive, partial, selfish.

42.6b **One-sided evidence indeed.**

Ooze, *DIE*: exude moisture; mud, slime; turbid, tainted.

48.3a/3b The **well: oozing, not taking-in.**

Open, *DUI*: an open surface, promoting interaction and interpenetration; pleasant, easy, responsive, free, unhindered; opening, passage; the mouth; exchange, barter; straight, direct; meet, gather; place where water accumulates. Ideogram: person, mouth and vapor, communication through speech.

This term is the name of hexagram 58 and recurs throughout its texts. It also occurs in:

57.HP The **open: viewing, and-also**

Oppose, *FAN*: resist; violate, offend, attack; possessed by an evil spirit; criminal. Ideogram: violate and dog, brutal offense.

5.1b **Not opposing heaviness** in **movement.**

26.1b **Not opposing calamity indeed.**

58.IT **Stimulating uses opposing heaviness.**

Oracle-consulting, *SHI*: yarrow stalks and their use in divination.

4.IM/ IT The **initial oracle-consulting notifies.**

8.IM/ IT **Retracing** the **oracle-consulting: Spring, perpetual Trial.**

Ordinance, *LÜ*: law, regulation; discipline, self-mastery. Ideogram: writing and move, codes that govern action.

7.1a/1b The **legions emerging using ordinance.**

7.1b **Letting-go** the **ordinance: pitfall indeed.**

Origin, *ZI*: source, beginning, ground; cause, reason, motive; tracing back to the source; oneself, by oneself; spontaneous, intrinsic.

1.PW A **jun zi uses originating strength not** to **pause.**

5.3b **Originating** from **my**

involvement in **illegality**.
5.4a **Emerging originating** from the **cave**.
6.2b **Origin below, arguing above**.
8.2a/2b To **grouping belongs** an **origin inside**.
8.2b **Not** the **origin letting-go indeed**.
9.IM/IT **Originating** from **my Western suburbs**.
9.1a/1b **Returning** to the **origin**'s **dao**.
9.2b **Truly not** the **origin letting-go indeed**.
10.2b The **center not** the **origin** of **disarray indeed**.
11.6a **Originating** from the **capital**, **notifying fate**.
14.6a The **origin** in **heaven shields it**.
14.6b The **origin** in **heaven shields indeed**.
15.1b **Lowliness uses originating herding indeed**.
24.AT **Return**: **using** the **origin**'s **knowledge**.
24.5b The **center uses** the **origin** from the **predecessors indeed**.
25.IT A **solid originating** from the **outside comes**.
27.IM/ IT The **origin** of **seeking mouth**'s **substance**.
27.IT **Overseeing one's origin**: **nourishment indeed**.
29.4a **Letting-in bonds originating** from the **window**.
35.PW A **jun zi uses originating enlightening** to **brighten actualizing-dao**.
37.PW **Wind originating** from **fire emerging. Household people**.
38.1a **Losing** the **horse**, **no pursuing**: **originating** from **returning**.
40.3b **Originating** from **my involvement** with **weapons**.
41.5b The **origin above shielding indeed**.
42.2b/6b **Origin outside, coming indeed**.
42.IT The **origin above**, the **below below**.
43.IM/ IT **Notifying originates** from the **capital**.
44.5a/5b **Possessing tumbling originating** from **heaven**.
55.6b **Originating** from **concealment indeed**.
62.5a **Originating** from **my Western suburbs**.

Osier, *QI*: willow branches used to make baskets.
44.5a **Using osier** to **enwrap melons**.

Outcry, see **Cry-out/outcry**

Outside, *WAI*: outer, external; unfamiliar, foreign; ignore, reject; work done outside the home; the upper trigram as indication of the outer aspects of the situation.
5.3b **Calamity located outside indeed**.
8.4a **Outside grouping it**.
8.4b **Outside grouping with-respect-to eminence**.
11.1b **Purpose located outside indeed**.
11.IT **Inside Yang and-also outside Yin**.
11.IT **Inside persisting and-also outside yielding**.
11.IT **Inside jun zi and-also outside** the **small** in the **person**.
12.IT **Inside Yin and-also outside Yang**.
12.IT **Inside supple and-also outside solid**.
12.IT **Inside** the **small** in the **person and-also outside jun zi**.
25.IT A **solid originating** from the **outside comes**.
31.1b **Purpose located outside indeed**.
36.IT **Inside pattern bright and-also outside supple yielding**.
37.PS **Injury with-respect-to** the **outside implies necessarily reversing with-respect-to** the **household**.
37/38.HP **Polarizing**: **outside indeed**.
37.IT The **man** in the **correct position reaching** the **outside**.
42.2b/6b **Origin outside, coming indeed**.

56.IT The **supple acquires** the **center reaching outside and-also yielding reaches** the **solid**.
58.IT The **solid** in the **center and-also** the **supple outside**.
59.3b **Purpose located outside indeed**.
59.IT The **supple acquires** the **position reaching outside and-also above concording**.

Overbearing, *KANG*: haughty, fierce, overpowering, rigid, unbending; excessive display of force.
1.6a/6b **Overbearing dragon possesses repenting**.
62.6b **Climaxing overbearing indeed**.

Overfill, *YING*: fill completely; full, at the point of overflowing; excess, arrogance. Ideogram: vessel and overflow.
1.6b **Overfilling not permitting** to **last indeed**.
3.PS **Overfilling** the **interspace belonging** to **heaven** and **earth implies verily** the **myriad beings**.
3.PS **Sprouting implies overfilling indeed**.
3.IT To **thunder** and **rain belongs stirring-up**: **plenitude overfilled**.
8.1a **Possessing conformity**: **overfilling** the **jar**.
15.PS **Possessing** the **great implies**: **not permitted using overfilling**.
15.IT **Heavenly dao lessens overfilling and-also augments humbling**.
15.IT **Earthly dao transforms overfilling and-also diffuses humbling**.
15.IT **Soul** and **spirit harm overfilling and-also bless humbling**.
15.IT **People's dao hates overfilling and-also loves humbling**.
23.IT A **jun zi honors** the **dissolving pause** to **overfill emptiness**.
29.5a/5b The **gorge not overfilled**.
29.IT **Stream diffusing and-also not overfilling**.
41.IT **Diminishing, augmenting**: **overfilling emptiness**.
55.IT The **moon overfilling**, by **consequence taken-in**.
55.IT **Heaven** and **earth overfilling emptiness**.

Overflow, *PEI*: spread and flow in many directions, like rain or rivers; enlarge; irrigate; luxuriant water plants.
55.3a/3b **Abounding: one's overflowing**.

Overrun, *QIAN*: pass the limit; mistake, transgression, disease.
54.4a **Converting maidenhood overruns** the **term**.
54.4b To **overrunning** the **term belongs purpose**.

Oversee, *GUAN*: contemplate, observe from a distance; look at carefully, gaze at; a high place from where one sees far, monastery, observatory; intelligence, clairvoyance; scry, divine through liquid in a cup. Ideogram: sight and waterbird, aerial view.
This term is the name of hexagram 20 and recurs throughout its texts. It also occurs in:
19.HP To **nearing** and **overseeing belongs righteousness**.
21.PS **Permitted overseeing and-also afterwards possessing** a **place** to **unite**.
22.IT **Overseeing reaches** the **heavenly pattern**.
22.IT **Overseeing reaches** the **personal pattern**.
23.IT **Overseeing symbols indeed**.
27.IM/IT **Overseeing** the **jaws**.
27.1a/1b **Overseeing my pendent jaw**.
27.IT **Overseeing one's place** of **nourishment indeed**.
27.IT **Overseeing one's origin**: **nourishment indeed**.
31.IT **Overseeing one's place** to **influence**.
32.IT **Overseeing one's place** to **persevere**.
45.IT **Overseeing one's place** to **assemble**.

Overthrow, *FU*: subvert, upset, defeat, throw down.
50.4a/4b **Overthrowing** a **princely stew**.

Own, *ZI*: possession and the things possessed; avail of, depend on; property, riches.

1.IT The **myriad beings' own beginning**.

2.IT The **myriad beings' own generation**.

56.2a **Cherishing one's own**.

56.4a/4b **Acquiring one's own emblem-ax**.

57.6a/6b **Losing one's own emblem-ax**.

Parch, see **Energy/parch**

Pardon, *YOU*: forgive, indulge, relax; lenient.

40.PW A **jun zi uses forgiving excess** to **pardon offenses**.

Pare, *ZHI*: cut away, tailor, carve; form, invent; institution, rule; limit, prevent. Ideogram: knife and incomplete.

15.AT **Humbling**: **using paring** the **codes**.

32.5b The **husband** and the **son, paring righteously**.

57.AT The **root**: **paring belonging** to **actualizing-dao indeed**.

60.PW A **jun zi uses paring** and **reckoning** the **measures**.

60.IT **Articulating uses paring** the **measures**.

Parsimonious, *JIAN*: thrifty; moderate, temperate; stingy, scanty.

12.PW A **jun zi uses parsimonious actualizing-dao** to **expel heaviness**.

62.PW And **avails** of **excess** to **reach parsimony**.

Part, *GUAI*: separate, fork, cut off, flow in different directions; decide, resolve; prompt, certain, settled.

This term is the name of hexagram 43 and recurs throughout its texts. It also occurs in:

10.5a/5b **Parting, treading. Trial, adversity**.

44.HP **Parting: breaking-up indeed**.

Partner, *PENG*: companion, friend, peer; join, associate for mutual benefit; commercial venture; two equal or similar things. Ideogram: linked strings of cowries or coins.

2.IM/IT **Western South: acquiring partnering**.

2.IM/IT **Eastern North: losing partnering**.

11.2a **Partnering extinguished**.

16.4a **Partners join-together suddenly**.

24.IM/ IT **Partners come, without fault**.

31.4a **Partners adhere** to **simply pondering**.

39.5a/5b **The great**'s **limping, partners coming**.

40.4a **Partnering culminating, splitting-off conforming**.

41.5a To **partnering belongs** a **tortoise**.

42.2a To **partnering belongs** a **tortoise**.

58.PW A **jun zi uses partnering** with **friends** to **explicate repeatedly**.

Passage, *GUAN*: market gate, customs house, frontier post; limit, crisis, important point.

24.PW The **earlier kings used culminating sun** to **bar** the **passages**.

Pass-beyond, *YU*: go beyond set time or limits; get over a wall or obstacle.

15.IT **Lowliness and-also not permitted** to **pass-beyond**.

Pattern, *WEN*: intrinsic or natural design, pattern of wood, stone or animal fur; ideograms, the symbols of writing as revelation of the intrinsic nature of things; language, civilization, culture; harmonious, beautiful, elegant, polite.

2.5b **Pattern located** in the **center indeed**.

9.PW A **jun zi uses highlighting** the **pattern** to **actualize-dao**.

13.IT **Pattern**'s **brightness uses persistence**.

14.IT **One's actualizing-dao: solid persisting and-also pattern brightening**.

22.IT The **supple comes and-also patterns** the **solid**.

22.IT **Apportioning** the **solid above and-also patterning** the **supple.**
22.IT **Heavenly pattern indeed.**
22.IT **Pattern**'s **brightness uses stopping.**
22.IT **Personal pattern indeed.**
22.IT **Overseeing reaches** the **heavenly pattern.**
22.IT **Overseeing reaches** the **personal pattern.**
36.IT **Inside pattern bright and-also outside supple yielding.**
49.5b **One's pattern luminous indeed.**
49.6b **One's pattern beautiful indeed.**
49.IT **Pattern brightening uses stimulating.**

Pattern King, *WEN WANG*, is the name of the founder of the Zhou dynasty and mythical author of the *Yi Jing*.
36.IT The **Pattern King uses it.**

Pause, *XI*: breathe; rest, repose, a breathing-spell; suspended.

See also: **Dissolving pause**
1.PW A **jun zi uses originating strength not** to **pause.**
17.PW A **jun zi uses turning** to **darkness** to **enter** a **reposing pause.**
36.5b **Brightness not permitted** to **pause indeed.**
46.6a **Harvesting**: to **tending-towards not pausing belongs Trial.**
49.IT **Skinning. Stream** and **fire reciprocally** giving **pause.**

Pay-tribute, *JI*: compulsory payments; present property to a superior.
45.6a/6b **Paying-tribute: sighs, tears, snot.**

Peace, *AN*: quiet, still, settled, secure, contented; calm, tranquilize, console. Ideogram: woman under a roof, a tranquil home.
2.IM **Peaceful Trial, significant.**
2.IT To **peaceful Trial belongs significance.**
6.4a/4b **Retracting, peaceful Trial.**
11.PS **Therefore afterwards peace.**
13.3b **Peaceful movement indeed.**
23.PW **Above using munificence, below pacifying** the **situation.**
32.4b **Peacefully acquiring wildfowl indeed.**
45.6b **Not-yet peaceful above indeed.**
60.4a **Peaceful articulating, Growing.**
60.4b To **peaceful articulating belongs Growing.**

Peak, *DING*: top of the head, summit, crown; carry on the head; superior.
28.6a **Exceeding wading, submerging** the **peak. Pitfall.**

Peep, *KUI*: observe from hiding; stealthy, furtive.
20.2a **Peeping overseeing.**
20.2b **Peeping overseeing: woman**'s **Trial.**
55.6a/6b **Peeping** through **one's door.**

Pendent, *DUO*: hanging; flowering branch, date or grape cluster.
27.1a/1b **Overseeing my pendent jaw.**

People/person, *REN*: humans individually and collectively; an individual; humankind.
This term occurs in the name of hexagrams 13 and 37 and recurs throughout their texts. It also occurs in:
1.2a/5a **Harvesting: viewing** the **great** in the **person.**
1.5b The **great** in the **person creative indeed.**
4.1a/1b **Harvesting: availing** of **punishing people.**
5.6a **Possessing visitors belonging** to **not inviting: three people coming.**
6.IM/ IT **Harvesting: viewing** the **great** in the **person.**
6.2a **People, three hundred doors.**
7.IM The **respectable person, significant.**
7.6a/6b The **small** in the **person**, no **availing** of.
8.3a/3b To **grouping belongs in-no-way people.**

8.5a/5b The **capital's people not admonished.**
10.IM **Not snapping** at **people.**
10.2a/2b **Shady people: Trial, significant.**
10.3a **Snapping** at **people: pitfall.**
10.3a/3b **Martial people activate tending-towards** the **great** in the **chief.**
10.3b To **snapping** at **people belongs** a **pitfall.**
10.IT **Not snapping** at **people. Growing.**
11.IT **Inside jun zi and-also outside** the **small** in the **person.**
11.IT The **small** in the **person**'s **dao dissolving indeed.**
12.IM/ IT To **obstruction belongs in-no-way people.**
12.2a The **small** in the **person significant.**
12.2a/2b The **great** in the **person obstructed.**
12.5a The **great** in the **person, significant.**
12.5b To the **great** in the **person belongs significance.**
12.IT **Inside** the **small** in the **person and-also outside jun zi.**
12.IT The **small** in the **person**'s **dao long-living.**
14.PS **Associating** with **people concording implies beings necessarily converting in-truth.**
14.HP **Concording people: connecting indeed.**
14.3a The **small** in the **person nowhere controlling.**
14.3b The **small** in the **person harmful indeed.**
15.IT **People's dao hates overfilling and-also loves humbling.**
16.IT The **wise person uses yielding** and **stirring-up.**
18.PS **Using joy** in **following people implies necessarily possessing affairs.**
20.1a The **small** in the **person: without fault.**
20.1b The **small** in the **person**'s **dao indeed.**
20.IT The **wise person uses spirit dao** to **set-up teaching.**
22.IT **Personal pattern indeed.**
22.IT **Overseeing reaches** the **personal pattern.**
23.5a/5b **Using house people**'s **favor.**
23.6a/6b The **small** in the **person strips** the **hut.**
23.IT The **small** in the **person long-living indeed.**
25.3a To **moving people belongs acquiring.**
25.3a To **capital**'s **people belongs calamity.**
25.3b **Moving people acquire cattle.**
25.3b **Capital**'s **people, calamity indeed.**
27.IT The **wise person nourishes eminence used** to **extend** to the **myriad commoners.**
30.PW The **great** in the **person uses consecutive brightening** to **illuminate tending-towards** the **four sides.**
31.PW A **jun zi uses emptiness** to **acquiesce** the **people.**
31.3b **Purpose located** in **following people.**
31.IT The **wise person influences people**'s **heart and-also below heaven harmonizes evenness.**
32.5a The **wife**'s **people, significant.**
32.5b The **wife**'s **people: Trial, significant.**
32.IT The **wise person: lasting with-respect-to one's dao and-also below heaven changing** and **accomplishing.**
33.PW A **jun zi uses distancing** the **small** in the **person.**
33.4a The **small** in the **person obstructing.**
33.4b The **small** in the **person obstructing indeed.**
34.3a/3b The **small** in the **person avails of vigor.**
36.1a A **lordly person possesses words.**
38.HP **Household people: inside indeed.**
38.1a/1b **Viewing hatred** in the **person.**
38.3a **One's person stricken,**

moreover nose-cut.
39.IM/6a/6b/ IT Harvesting: viewing the great in the person.
40.5a Possessing conformity tending-towards the small in the person.
40.5b The small in the person withdraws indeed.
41.3a Three people moving.
41.3a By consequence diminishing by one person.
41.3a/3b One person moving.
45.IM Harvesting: viewing the great in the person.
45.IT Harvesting: viewing the great in the person. Growing.
46.IM/ IT Availing of viewing the great in the person.
47.IM/ IT Trial: the great in the person, significant.
49.5a/5b The great in the person: a tiger transforming.
49.6a/6b The small in the person skins the face.
49.IT Yielding reaches heaven and-also the correspondence reaches people.
50.IT The wise person's Growing uses presenting to the supreme above.
52.IM Not viewing one's people.
52.IT Moving one's chambers, not viewing one's people.
54.2a/2b Harvesting: Trial belonging to shady people.
54.IT The beginning of completion belonging to a person.
55.6a/6b Living-alone, one without people.
55.IT And-also even-more with-respect-to reaching people.
56.6a Sojourning people beforehand laugh, afterwards cry-out sobbing.
57.IM/ IT Harvesting: viewing the great in the person.
57.1a/1b Harvesting: to martial people belongs Trial.
58.IT That uses yielding reaching heaven and-also correspondence reaching people.
63.3a The small in the person, no availing of.

Permit, *KE*: possible because in harmony with an inherent principle; capable of; approve, authorize. Ideogram: mouth and breath, silent consent.

See also: **Beings not permitted (to use)**

1.6b Overfilling not permitting to last indeed.
1.7b Heavenly actualizing-dao not permitting activating the head indeed.
2.3a/3b Containing composition permits Trial.
3.6b Is it permitted long-living indeed?
5.PS Being's immaturity not permitted not nourishing indeed.
6.1b Arguing not permitting long-living indeed.
6.IT Arguing not permitting accomplishment indeed.
7.IT Actually permitted using kinghood.
12.PW And not permitting splendor in using benefits.
12.6b Is it permitted long-living indeed?
15.PS Possessing the great implies: not permitted using overfilling.
15.6b Permitted availing of moving legions.
15.IT Lowliness and-also not permitted to pass-beyond.
16.6b Is it permitted long-living indeed?
18.2a Not permitting Trial.
18.6b Purpose permitted by consequence indeed.
19.PS Possessing affairs and-also afterwards permitted the great.
20.PS The beings' great, therefore afterwards permitted overseeing.
20.2b Truly permitting the demoniac indeed.
21.PS Permitted overseeing and-also afterwards possessing a place to unite.
23.6b Completing not permitted availing of indeed.
25.4a Permitting Trial.
25.4b Permitting Trial, without fault.
25.5b Not permitted testing

indeed.
26.PS Possessing without entanglement, therefore afterwards permitted accumulating.
27.PS Beings accumulate, therefore afterwards permitted to nourish.
27.5a Not permitted to wade the great river.
28.PS Not nourished, by consequence not permitted stirring-up.
28.3b Not permitted to use the possession of bracing indeed.
28.5b Is it permitted to last indeed?
28.5b Truly permitting the demoniac indeed.
28.6b Not permitted fault indeed.
29.IT Heaven's venture: not permitting ascending indeed.
30.3b Is it permitted to last indeed?
31.IT And-also the motives belonging to heaven and earth's myriad beings permit viewing actually.
32.PS Not permitted to use not lasting indeed.
32.IT And-also the motives belonging to heaven and earth's myriad beings permit viewing actually.
33.3b Not permitted the great in affairs indeed.
34.IT The correct great and-also the motives belonging to heaven and earth permit viewing actually.
36.3a Not permitted affliction, Trial.
36.5b Brightness not permitted to pause indeed.
40.3b Truly permitting the demoniac indeed.
41.IM/IT Without fault, permitting Trial.
41.IM/IT Two platters permit availing of presenting.
41.4b Truly permitting joy indeed.
43.6b Completing not permitting long-living indeed.
44.IT Not permitted association long-living indeed.
45.IT And-also the motives belonging to heaven and earth's myriad beings permit viewing actually.
48.3a Permitting availing of drawing-water.
49.PS The well's dao not permitting not skinning.
49.1b Not permitted to use possessing activity indeed.
51.IT Emerging permits using guarding the ancestral temple, the field-altar, the offertory-millet.
53.6a Its feathers permit availing of activating the fundamentals.
53.6b Its feathers permit availing of activating the fundamentals, significant.
53.6b Not permitting disarray indeed.
53.IT Permitted to use correcting the fiefdoms indeed.
55.3b Not permitted the great in affairs indeed.
55.3b Completing, not permitted availing of indeed.
60.IM/ IT Bitter articulating not permitting Trial.
61.6b Is it permitted long-living indeed?
62.IM Permitted the small in affairs.
62.IM Not permitted the great in affairs.
62.1b Not permitted thus, is it indeed?
62.2b A servant not permitted exceeding indeed.
62.4b Completion not permitted long-living indeed.
62.IT That uses not permitting the great in affairs indeed.
63.6b Is it permitted to last indeed?
64.PS Beings not permitted exhausting indeed.

Perpetual, YONG: continual, everlasting, eternal. Ideogram: flowing water.

2.7a Harvesting perpetual Trial.
2.7b Availing of sixes: perpetual Trial.

6.1a/1b **Not** a **perpetual place, affairs.**
8.IM/ IT **Retracing** the **oracle-consulting: Spring, perpetual Trial.**
22.3a **Perpetual Trial, significant.**
22.3b To **perpetual Trial belongs significance.**
42.2a **Perpetual Trial, significant.**
45.5a **Spring, perpetual Trial.**
52.1a **Harvesting: perpetual Trial.**
54.PW A **jun zi uses perpetually completing** to **know** the **cracked.**
62.4a **No availing** of **perpetual Trial.**

Persevere, *HENG*: continue in the same way or spirit; constant, habitual, regular; self-renewing.

This term is the name of hexagram 32 and recurs throughout its texts. It also occurs in:

5.1a **Harvesting: availing** of **perseverance.**
5.1b **Harvesting: availing** of **perseverance, without fault.**
16.5a/5b **Persevering, not dying.**
31.HP **Persevering: lasting indeed.**
37.PW A **jun zi uses words** to **possess beings and-also movement** to **possess perseverance.**
42.6a **Establishing** the **heart, no persevering.**
54.1b **Using perseverance indeed.**

Persist, *JIAN*: tenacious, persevering; strong, robust, dynamic; constant as the motion of heavenly bodies in their orbits; Action of the trigram Force, *QIAN*.

1.PW **Heaven moves persistently.**
5.IT **Solid persisting and-also not falling.**
6.IT **Venturing and-also persisting. Arguing.**
9.IT **Persistence and-also root.**
11.IT **Inside persisting and-also outside yielding.**
13.IT **Pattern's brightness uses persistence.**
14.IT **One's actualizing-dao: solid persisting and-also pattern brightening.**
25.IT **Stirring-up and-also persisting.**
26.IT **Solid persisting: staunch substance, resplendent shining.**
26.IT **Ability** to **stop** and **persist.**
43.IT **Persisting and-also stimulating.**

Person, see **People/person**

Petrify, *SHI*: become stone or stony; rocks, stones; firm, decided; barren, sterile.

16.2a The **cuirass tends-towards petrification.**
47.3a **Confinement tending-towards petrification.**

Petty, *JIAN*: little, small, insignificant.

22.5a A **roll** of **plain-silk: petty, petty.**

Pheasant, *ZHI*: beautiful bird associated with the trigram Radiance, *LI*; embrasures on ramparts and forts; arrange, put in order.

50.3a The **pheasant**'s **juice not taken-in.**
56.5a **Shooting** a **pheasant.**

Pig, *SHI*: all swine, symbol of wealth and good fortune, associated with the Streaming Moment.

26.5a To a **gelded pig belong tusks.**
38.6a **Viewing** a **pig bearing mire.**
44.1a **Ruined** the **pig**'s **conformity: hoof dragging.**

Pillar, *HUAN*: post or tablet marking a grave.

3.1a A **stone pillar.**
3.1b **Although** a **stone pillar, purpose moving correctly indeed.**

Pitcher, *PING*: clay jug or vase.

48.IM **Ruining one's pitcher: pitfall.**
48.IT **Ruining one's pitcher: that uses** a **pitfall indeed.**

Pitfall, *XIONG*: unfortunate situation, in which the flow of life and spirit is blocked and the experience of meaning is lost; stuck and exposed to danger; inappropriate attitude. Ideogram: person in a pit.

3.5a The **great: Trial, pitfall.**
6.IM The **center, significant. Completing, pitfall.**

6.IT Completing, pitfall.
7.1a Obstructing virtue: pitfall.
7.1b Letting-go the ordinance: pitfall indeed.
7.3a Pitfall.
7.5a Trial, pitfall.
8.IM/IT Afterwards husbanding: pitfall.
8.6a Pitfall.
9.6a/6b A jun zi disciplining, pitfall.
10.3a Snapping at people: pitfall.
10.3b To snapping at people belongs a pitfall.
16.1a Pitfall.
16.1b Purpose exhausted, pitfall indeed.
17.4a Trial, pitfall.
17.4b One's righteousness: pitfall indeed.
19.IM/IT Culminating tending-towards the eighth moon possesses a pitfall.
21.6a Pitfall.
23.1a/2a Discarding Trial, pitfall.
23.4a Pitfall.
24.6a Deluding return. Pitfall.
24.6a Using one's city's chief: pitfall.
24.6b To the deluding return belongs a pitfall.
27.1a Pitfall.
27.2a The jaws disciplined, pitfall.
27.2b Six at second: disciplining, pitfall.
27.3a Rejecting the jaws. Trial, pitfall.
28.3a The ridgepole buckling. Pitfall.
28.3b To the ridgepole buckling belongs a pitfall.
28.6a Exceeding wading, submerging the peak. Pitfall.
28.6b To exceeding wading belongs a pitfall.
29.1a Pitfall.
29.1b Letting-go dao: pitfall indeed.
29.6a Pitfall.
29.6b Pitfall, three year's-time indeed.
30.3a Pitfall.
31.2a Pitfall.
31.2b Although a pitfall, residing significant.
32.1a Diving persevering: Trial, pitfall.
32.1b To diving persevering belongs pitfall.
32.5a The husband and the son, pitfall.
32.5b Adhering to the wife, pitfall indeed.
32.6a Rousing persevering, pitfall.
34.1a Disciplining, pitfall.
41.2a Disciplining, pitfall.
42.3a To augmenting belongs availing of pitfall affairs.
42.3b Augmenting: availing of pitfall affairs.
42.6a Pitfall.
43.3a Possessing pitfall.
43.6a Completing possesses pitfall.
43.6b To without crying-out belongs pitfall.
44.1a Viewing pitfall.
44.4a Rising-up, pitfall.
44.4b To without fish belongs a pitfall.
47.2a Disciplining, pitfall.
47.3a Pitfall.
48.IM Ruining one's pitcher: pitfall.
48.IT Ruining one's pitcher: that uses a pitfall indeed.
49.3a/6a Disciplining: pitfall.
50.4a One's form soiled, pitfall.
51.6a Disciplining: pitfall.
51.6b Although a pitfall, without fault.
53.3a Pitfall.
54.IM Converting maidenhood. Disciplining, pitfall.
54.IT Disciplining, pitfall.
55.6a Pitfall.
56.6a Pitfall.
57.6a Trial, pitfall.
57.6b Correcting reaches a pitfall indeed.
58.3a Coming open, pitfall.
58.3b To the coming open belongs a pitfall.
60.2a Pitfall.
60.2b Not emerging from the gate chambers, pitfall.
60.6a/6b Bitter articulating: Trial, pitfall.
61.6a Trial, pitfall.

62.1a/1b The **flying bird**: **using** a **pitfall**.
62.3a **Pitfall**.
62.3b **Pitfall thus**, it **is indeed!**
62.6a To the **flying bird**'s **radiance belongs** a **pitfall**.
64.3a/3b **Not-yet fording**: **disciplining**, **pitfall**.

Place, *SUO*: position, location; residence, dwelling; where something belongs or comes from; habitual focus or object.
6.1a/1b **Not** a **perpetual place**, **affairs**.
8.PS **Crowds necessarily possess** a **place** to **group**.
8.6b **Without** a **place** to **complete indeed**.
9.PS **Grouping necessarily possesses** a **place** to **accumulate**.
9.6b **Possessing** a **place** to **doubt indeed**.
21.PS **Permitted overseeing and-also afterwards possessing** a **place** to **unite**.
23.6b **Commoners** acquire a **place** to **carry indeed**.
27.IT **Overseeing one's place** of **nourishment indeed**.
30.PS **Falling necessarily possesses** a **place** to **congregate**.
30.4b **Without** a **place** of **tolerance indeed**.
31.PS **Therefore afterwards** the **codes' righteousness possesses** a **polishing place**.
31.3b A **place** for **holding-on** to the **below indeed**.
31.IT **Overseeing one's place** to **influence**.
32.3b **Without** a **place** to **tolerate indeed**.
32.IT **Overseeing one's place** to **persevere**.
33.PS **Beings not permitted** to **use lasting residing** in **their place**.
33.6b **Without** a **place** to **doubt indeed**.
36.PS **Advancing necessarily possesses** a **place** for **injury**.
40.IM **Without** a **place** to **go**:
41.PS **Delaying necessarily possesses** a **place** to **let-go**.
43.IT The **place** to **honor thereupon exhausted indeed**.
45.IT **Overseeing one's place** to **assemble**.
46.3b **Without** a **place** to **doubt indeed**.
47.IT **Confining and-also not letting-go one's place**: **Growing**.
48.AT The **well**: **residing** in **one's place and-also shifting**.
50.2b **Considering** the **place** of **it indeed**.
52.IT **Stopping** at **one's place indeed**.
53.5b **Acquiring** the **place desired indeed**.
54.PS **Advancing necessarily possesses** a **place** for **converting**.
54.IT A **place** for **converting maidenhood indeed**.
55.PS **Acquiring one's place** for **converting implies necessarily** the **great**.
56.1a **Splitting-off one's place**: **grasping calamity**.
57.PS **Sojourning and-also lacking** a **place** for **tolerance**.
59.4a **In-no-way hidden**, a **place** to **ponder**.
63.4b **Possessing** a **place** to **doubt indeed**.

Plain-silk, *BAI*: unbleached, undyed silk, used as a gift or as a support for writing.
22.5a A **roll** of **plain-silk**: **petty**, **petty**.

Plan, *MOU*: plot, ponder, deliberate; project, device, stratagem.
6.PW A **jun zi uses arousing affairs** to **plan beginnings**.

Platter, *GUI*: wood or bamboo plate; bronze vessel for food; sacrificial utensil.
29.4a/4b A **cup** of **liquor**, a **platter added**.
41.IM/ IT **Two platters permit availing** of **presenting**.
41.IT **Two platters corresponding possess** the **season**.

Plenitude, *MAN*: fullness; replete, complete, bulging, abundant; proud.

3.IT To **thunder** and **rain belongs stirring-up: plenitude overfilled.**

Plow-land, *YU*: newly opened fields, after two or three years plowing.

25.2a **Not tilling** the **crop. Not clearing** the **plow-land.**

Poison/rule, *DU*: noxious, malignant, hurtful, destructive; despise, hate; sickness, affliction; govern, direct educate.

7.IT **Using** the **latter rules below heaven.**

21.3a/3b **Meeting poison.**

Polarize, *KUI*: separate, oppose; contrary, mutually exclusive; distant, absent, remote; conflict, discord, animosity; astronomical or polar opposition.

This term is the name of hexagram 38 and recurs throughout its texts. It also occurs in:

37.HP **Polarizing: outside indeed.**

Polish, *CUO*: file away imperfections; wash or plate with gold; confused, in disorder, mixed. Ideogram: metal and old, clearing away accumulated disorder.

30.1a **Treading, polishing therefore. Respecting it.**

30.1b To **treading** and **polishing belongs respect.**

31.PS **Therefore afterwards** the **codes' righteousness possesses** a **polishing place.**

Pond, *ZE*: open surface of a flat body of water and the vapors rising from it; fertilize, enrich; kindness, favor; Symbol of the trigram Open, *DUI*.

10.PW **Heaven above, pond below. Treading.**

17.PW The **pond** in the **center possesses thunder. Following.**

19.PW The **pond possesses earth above. Nearing.**

28.PW The **pond submerges wood.** The **great exceeding.**

31.PW The **mountain possesses pond above. Conjunction.**

38.PW **Fire above, pond below. Polarizing.**

38.IT **Pond stirring-up and-also below.**

41.PW The **mountain possesses pond below. Diminishing.**

43.PW **Pond above with-respect-to heaven. Parting.**

45.PW **Pond above with-respect-to earth. Clustering.**

47.PW **Pond without stream. Confining.**

49.PW The **pond** in the **center possesses fire. Skinning.**

54.PW The **pond possesses thunder above. Converting maidenhood.**

58.PW **Congregating ponds.** The **open.**

60.PW The **pond possesses stream above. Articulating.**

61.PW The **pond possesses wind above.** The **center conforming.**

Ponder, *SI*: reflect, consider, remember; deep thought; desire, wish. Ideogram: heart and field, the heart's concerns.

19.PW A **jun zi uses teaching** to **ponder without exhausting.**

31.4a **Partners adhere** to **simply pondering.**

52.PW A **jun zi uses pondering not** to **emerge** from **one's position.**

59.4a **In-no-way hidden**, a **place** to **ponder.**

63.PW A **jun zi uses pondering** on **distress and-also providing** for **defending-against it.**

Position, *WEI*: place, location; be at; social standing, rank; position of a line in a hexagram. Ideogram: person standing.

1.IT In the **six positions** the **season accomplishes.**

5.6b **Although not** an **appropriate position, not-yet** the **great letting-go indeed.**

5.IT The **position reaching** the **heavenly position.**

8.5b **Position correct** in the **center indeed.**

9.IT The **supple acquires** the **position and-also above** and **below correspond** to **it.**

10.3b **Position not appropriate indeed.**

10.5b **Position correct** and **appropriate indeed.**

P Position

10.IT **Treading** on the **supreme position and-also not disheartened.**

12.3b **Position not appropriate indeed.**

12.5b **Position correct** and **appropriate indeed.**

13.IT The **supple acquires** the **position, acquires** the **center and-also** the **correspondence reaches energy.**

14.IT The **supple acquires** the **noble position:** the **great** in the **center.**

16.3b **Position not appropriate indeed.**

17.5b **Position correct** in the **center indeed.**

19.3b **Position not appropriate indeed.**

19.4b **Position appropriate indeed.**

21.3b **Position not appropriate indeed.**

21.IT **Although not** an **appropriate position, Harvesting avails** of **litigating indeed.**

22.4b **Six** at **fourth.** An **appropriate position** to **doubt indeed.**

32.4b **No lasting whatever** in **one's position.**

33.IT The **solid** in the **appropriate position and-also corresponding.**

34.5b **Position not appropriate indeed.**

35.4b **Position not appropriate indeed.**

37.4b **Yielding located** in the **position indeed.**

37.IT The **woman** in the **correct position reaching** the **inside.**

37.IT The **man** in the **correct position reaching** the **outside.**

38.3b **Position not appropriate indeed.**

39.4b **Appropriate position: substance indeed.**

39.IT **Appropriate position. Trial, significant.**

40.4b **Not-yet** an **appropriate position indeed.**

43.4b **Position not appropriate indeed.**

45.4b **Position not appropriate indeed.**

45.5a/5b **Clustering possesses** the **position.**

47.4b **Although not** an **appropriate position, possessing associates indeed.**

50.PW A **jun zi uses correcting** the **position** to **solidify fate.**

51.3b **Position not appropriate indeed.**

52.PW A **jun zi uses pondering not** to **emerge** from **one's position.**

53.IT **Advancing acquires** the **position.**

53.IT **One's position:** the **solid acquires** the **center indeed.**

54.5b **One's position located** in the **center.**

54.IT **Position not appropriate indeed.**

55.4b **Position not appropriate indeed.**

56.4b **Not-yet acquiring** the **position indeed.**

57.5b **Position correct** in the **center indeed.**

58.3b **Position not appropriate indeed.**

58.5b **Position correct** and **appropriate indeed.**

59.5b **Correct position indeed.**

59.IT The **supple acquires** the **position reaching outside and-also above concording.**

60.5b **Residing** in the **position** in the **center indeed.**

60.IT The **appropriate position uses articulating.**

61.3b **Position not appropriate indeed.**

61.5b **Position correct** and **appropriate indeed.**

62.4b **Position not appropriate indeed.**

62.IT The **solid letting-go** the **position and-also not** in the **center.**

63.IT **Solid** and **supple correct and-also position appropriate indeed.**

64.3b **Position not appropriate indeed.**

64.IT **Although not** in **appropriate positions, solid** and **supple correspond indeed.**

Possess, *YOU*: general term indicating possession; have, own, be endowed with.
This term occurs throughout the hexagram texts.

Possessing directed going, *YOU YOU WANG*: having a goal or purpose, moving in a specific direction.
2.IM A **jun zi possesses directed going**.
3.IM **No availing** of **possessing directed going**.
14.2a **Possessing directed going**.
22.IM **Harvesting**: **possessing directed going**.
22.IT **Harvesting**: **possessing directed going**.
23.IM **Not Harvesting**: **possessing directed going**.
23.IT **Not Harvesting**: **possessing directed going**.
24.IM/ IT **Harvesting**: **possessing directed going**.
25.IM/IT **Not Harvesting**: **possessing directed going**.
25.2a By **consequence**, **Harvesting**: **possessing directed going**.
26.3a/3b **Harvesting**: **possessing directed going**.
28.IM/ IT **Harvesting**: **possessing directed going**.
32.IM/ IT **Harvesting**: **possessing directed going**.
33.1a **No availing** of **possessing directed going**.
36.1a **Possessing directed going**.
40.IM **Possessing directed going**:
40.IT **Possessing directed going**: **daybreak**, **significant**.
41.IM/6a/ IT **Harvesting**: **possessing directed going**.
42.IM/ IT **Harvesting**: **possessing directed going**.
43.IM/ IT **Harvesting**: **possessing directed going**.
44.1a **Possessing directed going**.
45.IM/ IT **Harvesting**: **possessing directed going**.
57.IM/ IT **Harvesting**: **possessing directed going**.

Potency, *SHI*: power, influence, strength; authority, dignity. Ideogram: strength and skill.
2.PW **Earth's potency**: **space**.

Pouched belt, *PAN DAI*: sash that serves as a purse; money-belt.
6.6a **Maybe** to **bestowing belongs** a **pouched belt**.

Praise, *YU*: magnify, eulogize; flatter; fame, reputation. Ideogram: offering words.
2.4a **Without fault**, **without praise**.
18.5a **Availing** of **praise**.
18.5b **Managing** the **father avails** of **praise**.
28.5a **Without fault**, **without praise**.
39.1a/1b **Going limping**, **coming praise**.
55.5a **Possessing reward** and **praise**, **significant**.
56.5a/5b **Completion uses praising fate**.

Precaution, *YU*: provide against, preventive measures; anxious, vigilant, ready; think about, expect; mishap, accident.
3.3a **Approaching** a **stag**: **lacking precaution**.
3.3b **Approaching** a **stag without precaution**.
45.PW And **warning**, **not precautions**.
61.1a **Precaution significant**.
61.1b **Initial nine**: **precaution significant**.

Precede, *QIAN*: before, earlier; anterior, former, ancient; ahead, in front.
5.IT **Venturing located** in **precedence indeed**.
8.5a **Letting-go** the **preceding wildfowl**.
8.5b **Letting-go** the **preceding wildfowl**.
26.PW A **jun zi uses** the **numerous recorded preceding words** to **go** and **move**.
39.IT **Venturing located** in **precedence indeed**.
43.1a The **vigor tends-towards** the **preceding foot**.

Predecessor, *KAO*: deceased father or grandfather; ancestors, the ancients; aged, long-lived; interrogate, test, verify.

Ideogram: old and ingenious, wise old man.

10.6a **Observing treading: predecessors auspicious.**

16.PW **Using equaling grandfathers** and **predecessors.**

18.1a **Predecessors without fault.**

18.1b **Intention received** from the **predecessors indeed.**

24.5b The **center uses** the **origin** from the **predecessors indeed.**

Pregnant, *REN*: conceive and carry a child; give birth.

53.3a/3b The **wife pregnant, not nurturing.**

53.5a The **wife, three year's-time not pregnant.**

Prepare, *BEI*: make ready, provide for; available; complete, sufficient.

14.5b **Versatility and-also without preparing indeed.**

Preponderance, *PENG*: forceful, dominant; overbearing, encroaching. Ideogram: drum beats, dominating sound.

14.4a/4b **In-no-way one's preponderance.**

Presence, *YONG*: a large head; noble bearing; prestige, dignity; imposing; haughty, conceited.

20.IM/ IT **Possessing conformity like** a **presence.**

Present, *XIANG*: offer in sacrifice, give to the gods or a superior; give a banquet; accept an offering; enjoy, receive.

41.IM/ IT **Two platters permit availing** of **presenting.**

42.2a The **king avails** of **presenting tending-towards** the **supreme, significant.**

45.IT **Involving reverent presenting indeed.**

47.2a **Harvesting: availing** of **presenting oblations.**

50.IT The **wise person**'s **Growing uses presenting** to the **supreme above.**

59.PW The **earlier kings used presenting tending-towards** the **supreme** to **establish** the **temples.**

Primordial, *TONG*: original; beginning of a series or lineage; clue, hint; whole, general.

1.IT **Thereupon primordial heaven.**

Prince, *GONG*: highest title of nobility; noble acting as minister of state in the capital; contrasts with feudatory, *HOU*, governor of a province.

See also: **Crown prince**

14.3a/3b A **prince avails** of **Growing tending-towards heavenly sonhood.**

29.IT The **king** and the **princes set-up venturing used** to **guard their city.**

30.5b **Radiance: king** and **princes indeed.**

40.6a A **prince avails** of **shooting** a **hawk tending-towards** the **above belonging** to the **high rampart.**

40.6b A **prince avails** of **shooting** a **hawk.**

42.3a **Notifying** the **prince, availing** of the **scepter.**

42.4a/4b **Notifying** the **prince, adhering.**

50.4a/4b **Overthrowing** a **princely stew.**

62.5a A **prince**'s **string-arrow grasps someone located** in a **cave.**

Procrastinate, *CHI*: delay, retard; leisurely, slow, late.

16.3a **Procrastinating possesses repenting.**

54.4a **Procrastinating converting possesses** the **season.**

Proper, *YI*: reasonable, fit, right, harmonious; ought, should.

3.IT **Proper installing feudatories and-also not soothing.**

11.PW And **braces** the **reciprocity properly belonging** to **heaven** and **earth.**

19.5a/5b To the **great** in the **chief belongs propriety.**

39.1b **Proper** to **await indeed.**

55.IM/ IT **No grief. Properly** the **sun** in the **center.**

55.IT **Properly illuminating below heaven indeed.**

62.IM/ IT **Not proper above, proper below.**

Property, *CAI*: possessions, goods, substance, wealth. Ideogram: pearl and value.

11.PW The **crown prince uses property** to **accomplish** the **dao belonging** to **heaven** and **earth**.

60.IT **Not injuring property**.

Proscribe, *ZHU*: exclude, reject by proclamation; denounce, forbid; reprove, seek as a criminal; condemn to death; clear away.

35/36.HP **Brightness hidden**: **proscribed indeed**.

Prosper, *JIN*: grow and flourish as young plants in the sun; increase, progress, permeate, impregnate; attached to. Ideogram: sun and reaching, the daylight world.

This term is the name of hexagram 35 and recurs throughout its texts. It also occurs in:

36.HP **Prospering**: **day-time indeed**.

Protect, *BAO*: guard, defend, keep safe; nourish, support.

1.IT **Protection**: **uniting** with the **great**'s **harmony**.

19.PW And **tolerating** to **protect** the **commoners without delimiting**.

53.3b **Yielding**: **reciprocal protection indeed**.

Protract, *YIN*: draw out, prolong; pull, stretch; lasting, perennial. Ideogram: draw a bow.

45.2a/2b **Protracting**: **significant**, **without fault**.

58.6a **Protracted open**.

58.6b **Six above**: **protracted open**.

Provide, *YU*: prepare for, pre-arrange, think beforehand; ready, satisfied, contented, at ease, relaxed; enthusiasm, joy, pleasure. Ideogram: sonhood and elephant, careful, reverent and strong.

This term is the name of hexagram 16 and recurs throughout its texts. It also occurs in:

15.HP **And-also providing**: **indolence indeed**.

17.PS **Providing necessarily possesses following**.

63.PW A **jun zi uses pondering** on **distress and-also providing** for **defending-against it**.

Pull-back, *YI*: pull or drag something towards you; drag behind; leave traces.

38.3a/3b **Viewing** the **cart pulled-back**.

63.1a/1b **Pulling-back one's wheels**.

64.2a **Pulling-back one's wheels**.

Punish, *XING*: legal punishment; physical penalty for a severe criminal offense; whip, torture, behead.

4.1a/1b **Harvesting**: **availing** of **punishing people**.

16.IT By **consequence punishing flogging purifies and-also** the **commoners submit**.

55.PW A **jun zi uses severing litigations involving punishment**.

56.PW A **jun zi uses bright consideration availing** of **punishment and-also not detaining litigations**.

Purify, *QING*: clean a water course; limpid, unsullied; right principles.

16.IT By **consequence punishing flogging purifies and-also** the **commoners submit**.

Purpose, *ZHI*: focus of mind and heart; intention, will, inclination; continuity in the direction of life. Ideogram: heart and scholar, high inner resolve.

3.1b **Although** a **stone pillar**, **purpose moving correctly indeed**.

4.IT **Purposes** in **correspondence indeed**.

9.4b **Above uniting purposes indeed**.

9.IT The **solid** in the **center and-also** the **purpose moving**.

10.PW And **rectifying** the **commoners' purpose**.

10.3b **Purpose solid indeed**.

10.4b **Purpose moving indeed**.

11.1b **Purpose located outside indeed**.

11.IT **Above** and **below mingling and-also their purposes concording indeed**.

12.1b **Purpose located** in a **chief indeed**.

12.4b **Purpose moving indeed**.

13.6b **Purpose not-yet acquired indeed**.

13.IT **Verily a jun zi activating enables interpenetration** of **purposes belonging** to **below heaven.**
14.5b **Trustworthiness uses shooting-forth purpose indeed.**
15.6b **Purpose not-yet acquired indeed.**
16.1b **Purpose exhausted, pitfall indeed.**
16.4b **Purpose**: the **great moving indeed.**
16.IT **Providing.** The **solid corresponding and-also** the **purpose moving.**
17.3b **Purpose**: **stowing** away the **below indeed.**
18.6b **Purpose permitted** by **consequence indeed.**
19.1b **Purpose moving correctly indeed.**
19.6b **Purpose located inside indeed.**
20.6b **Purpose not-yet evened indeed.**
22.6b **Above acquiring purpose indeed.**
25.1b **Acquiring purpose indeed.**
26.3b **Above uniting purposes indeed.**
31.1b **Purpose located outside indeed.**
31.3b **Purpose located** in **following people.**
31.5b The **purpose**: **tip indeed.**
33.2b **Firm purpose indeed.**
33.5b **Using** the **correct purpose indeed.**
35.3b **Crowds**: to **sincerity belongs purpose.**
36.3b To the **Southern hounding belongs purpose.**
36.IT **Inside heaviness and-also able** to **correct one's purpose.**
37.1b **Purpose not-yet transformed indeed.**
38.4b **Purpose moving indeed.**
38.IT **Their purposes not concording: moving.**
38.IT **Man** and **woman**: **polarizing and-also their purposes interpenetrating indeed.**
39.6b **Purpose located inside indeed.**
41.1b **Honoring uniting purposes indeed.**
41.2b In the **center using activating purpose indeed.**
41.6b The **great acquires purpose indeed.**
42.4b **Using augmenting**'s **purpose.**
42.5b The **great acquires purpose indeed.**
44.5b **Purpose**: **not stowing** away **fate indeed.**
45.1b **One's purpose disarrayed indeed.**
45.5b **Purpose not-yet shining indeed.**
46.1b **Above uniting purposes indeed.**
46.5b The **great acquires purpose indeed.**
46.IT **Purpose moves indeed.**
47.PW A **jun zi uses involving** in **fate** to **release purpose.**
47.4b **Purpose located below indeed.**
47.5b **Purpose not-yet acquired indeed.**
49.4b **Trustworthy purpose indeed.**
49.IT **Their purposes not reciprocally acquired: named skinning.**
54.4b To **overrunning** the **term belongs purpose.**
55.2b **Trustworthiness uses shooting-forth purpose indeed.**
56.1b **Purpose exhausted: calamity indeed.**
57.1b **Purpose doubtful indeed.**
57.1b **Purpose regulating indeed.**
57.3b **Purpose exhausted indeed.**
57.IT **Solid root reaches** the **center correctly and-also** the **purpose moves.**
58.2b **Trustworthy purpose indeed.**
59.3b **Purpose located outside indeed.**
61.1b **Purpose not-yet transformed indeed.**
64.4b **Purpose moving indeed.**

Pursue, *ZHU*: chase, follow closely, press hard; expel, drive out. Ideogram:

pig (wealth) and go, chasing fortune.
26.3a A **fine horse**, **pursuing**.
27.4a **Its appetites**: **pursuing**, **pursuing**.
38.1a **Losing** the **horse**, **no pursuing**: **originating** from **returning**.
51.2a **No pursuit**.
63.2a **No pursuing**.

Put-off, *XIA*: delay; put at a distance; far away, remote in time.
11.2a **Not putting-off abandoning**.

Question, *WEN*: ask, inquire about, examine; clear up doubts.
42.5a **No question**, **Spring significant**.
42.5b **No questioning it actually**.

Radiance, *LI*: glowing light, spreading in all directions; the power of consciousness; discriminate, articulate, divide and arrange in order; assemble, attract. Ideogram: bird and weird, magical fire-bird with brilliant plumage.
This term is the name of hexagram 30 and recurs throughout its texts. It also occurs in:
29.HP The **radiance above and-also** the **gorge below indeed**.
53.3b **Radiating** a **flock** of **demons indeed**.
59.PS **Dispersing implies radiance indeed**.
59/60.HP **Dispersing**: **radiance indeed**.
60.PS **Beings not permitted** to **use completing radiance**.
62.6a To the **flying bird**'s **radiance belongs** a **pitfall**.

Rafter, *JUE*: roof beam; flat branch.
53.4a/4b **Maybe acquiring one's rafter**.

Rain, *YU*: rain and all precipitations; sudden shower, fast and furious; abundant dispensation of benefits; associated with the trigram Gorge, *KAN*, and the Streaming Moment.
1.IT **Clouds moving**, **rain spreading**.
3.IT To **thunder** and **rain belongs stirring-up**: **plenitude overfilled**.
9.IM/IT **Shrouding clouds**, **not raining**.
9.6a/6b **Already rain**, **already abiding**.
38.6a **Going meets rain**, by **consequence significant**.
38.6b To **meeting rain belongs significance**.
40.PW **Thunder** and **rain arousing**. **Unraveling**.
40.IT **Heaven** and **earth unraveling and-also thunder** and **rain arousing**.
40.IT **Thunder** and **rain arousing and-also** the **hundred fruits**, **grasses**, **trees**, **altogether seedburst**'s **boundary**.
43.3a **Solitary going**, **meeting rain**.
50.3a On all **sides rain lessens repenting**.
62.5a/5b **Shrouding clouds**, **not raining**.

Rampart, *YONG*: defensive wall; bulwark, redoubt.
13.4a/4b **Riding one's rampart**.
40.6a A **prince avails** of **shooting** a **hawk tending-towards** the **above belonging** to the **high rampart**.

Reach, *HU*: arrive at a goal; move toward and achieve; to, at, in; distinct from tend-towards, *YOU*.
This term occurs throughout the hexagram texts.

Reach-up, *DI*: reach to, come up to; till, until, when. Ideogram: go, hand and reach.
56.5b **Reaching-up** to the **above indeed**.

Reap, *DUO*: harvest, collect, gather, pick. Ideogram: hand and join, taking in both hands.
6.2b **Distress culminating reaping indeed**.

Rebel, *BEI*: oppose, resist; go against nature or usage; insubordinate; perverse, unreasonable.
27.3b **Dao**: the **great rebels indeed**.

40.6b **Using unraveling rebellion indeed.**
50.1b **Not-yet rebelling indeed.**

Receive, *CHENG*: receive gifts or commands from superiors or customers; take in hand; give, offer respectfully; help, support. Ideogram: accepting a seal of office.
2.IT **Thereupon yielding receives heaven.**
7.2b **Receiving heavenly favor indeed.**
7.6a **Disclosing** the **city**, **receiving** a **household.**
12.2a **Enwrapped** in **receiving.**
18.1b **Intention received** from the **predecessors indeed.**
18.5b **Receiving uses actualizing-dao indeed.**
32.3a **Maybe** to **receiving belongs embarrassment.**
54.1b **Reciprocal receiving indeed.**
54.6a A **woman receives** a **basket without substance.**
54.6b **Receiving** an **empty basket indeed.**
60.4b **Receiving dao above indeed.**

Recess, *DAN*: pit within a large cave; trap.
29.1a/3a **Entering tending-towards** the **gorge's recess.**

Reciprocal, *XIANG*: mutual; assist, encourage, help; bring together, blend with; examine, inspect; by turns.
11.PW And **braces** the **reciprocity properly belonging** to **heaven** and **earth.**
13.5a/5b **Great legions control** the **reciprocal meeting.**
13.5b **Words reciprocally controlling indeed.**
28.2b **Exceeding uses reciprocal association indeed.**
31.IT The **two agencies' influences correspond using reciprocal association.**
32.IT **Thunder** and **wind reciprocally associating.**
37.5b **Mingling: reciprocal affection indeed.**
44.IT **Heaven** and **earth reciprocally meeting.**
45.PS **Beings reciprocally meeting and-also afterwards assembling.**
47/48.HP **confining: reciprocal meeting indeed.**
48.PW A **jun zi uses** the **toiling commoners** to **encourage reciprocity.**
49.IT **Skinning. Stream** and **fire reciprocally** giving **pause.**
49.IT **Their purposes not reciprocally acquired: named skinning.**
52.IT **Not reciprocally associating indeed.**
53.3b **Yielding: reciprocal protection indeed.**
54.1b **Reciprocal receiving indeed.**

Reckon, *SHU*: count, enumerate, evaluate; number, quantity; natural law, rule, reason.
60.PW A **jun zi uses paring** and **reckoning** the **measures.**

Recline, *ZHEN*: lean back or on; soften, relax; head rest, back support.
29.3a **Venturing, moreover reclining.**

Record, *SHI*: write down, inscribe; learn, memorize, know; annals, monuments.
26.PW A **jun zi uses** the **numerous recorded preceding words** to **go** and **move.**

Rectify, *DING*: correct, settle, fix; peaceful, tranquil, stable; certain, invariable.
10.PW And **rectifying** the **commoners' purpose.**
37.IT **Correct household and-also below heaven rectified.**
63/64.HP **Already fording: rectifying indeed.**

Recur, *XUAN*: return to the same point; turn, pivot, orbit, revolve, spiral.
10.6a **One's recurring Spring, significant.**

Redouble, *CHONG*: repeat, reiterate, add to; weight, heaviness; important, difficult.
16.AT **Redoubling gates, smiting clappers.**
29.IT **Redoubled venturing indeed.**

30.IT **Redoubled brightness uses congregating** to **reach correcting**.
57.IT **Redoubled root uses assigning fate**.

Redress, *TANG*: repel injustice, correct grievances; grand, awesome; hot water, hot spring; soup, broth; Tang is the name of the founder of the Shang dynasty. Ideogram: water and expand, a large river and its periodic floods.
49.IT **Redressing martially, skinning fate**.

Reduce, *POU*: diminish in number; assemble, collect in fewer, larger groups.
15.PW A **jun zi uses reducing** the **numerous** to **augment** the **few**.

Reeds, *GUAN*: marsh and swamp plants, rushes.
43.5a The **reeds**, the **highlands**: **parting, parting**.

Reflect, *JIE*: receive and pass on; follow in office; inherit; face, respond.
35.IM **Day-time sun thrice reflected**.
35.IT **Day-time sun thrice reflected indeed**.

Regulate, *ZHI*: govern well, ensure prosperity; arrange, remedy disorder, heal; fit to govern.
18.IT **Decay: Spring, Growing, and-also below heaven regulated indeed**.
49.PW A **jun zi uses regulating** the **calendar** to **brighten** the **seasons**.
57.1b **Purpose regulating indeed**.

Reiterate, *JIAN*: repeat, duplicate; recurrent.
29.PW **Streams reiterated culminate. Repeated gorge**.
51.PW **Reiterated thunder**. The **shake**.

Reject, *FU*: push away, brush off; oppose, contradict, resist; perverse, proud. Ideogram: hand and not, pushing something away.
27.2a **Rejecting** the **canons, tending-towards** the **hill-top**.
27.3a **Rejecting** the **jaws. Trial, pitfall**.
27.5a **Rejecting** the **canons**.

Rejoice, see **Joy/rejoice**

Relate, *ZHU*: in regard to; all, every, several. Ideogram: words and imply.
8.PW The **earlier kings used installing** a **myriad cities** to **connect** the **related feudatories**.
16.AT **Surely grasping relates** to **providing**.
52.4b **Stopping relates** to the **body indeed**.

Relax, *XIU*: rest, stop temporarily; resign, retire; advantage, prosperity. Ideogram: person leaning on a tree.
12.5a **Relaxing** the **obstruction**.
14.PW And **yielding** to **heaven** to **relax** into **fate**.
24.2a **Relaxing return**.
24.2b To **relaxing return belongs significance**.

Release, *SUI*: let go, free; unhindered; advance, progress; promote, further; reach, succeed; in accord with, conforming to. Ideogram: go and follow one's wishes, unimpeded movement.
34.6a/6b **Not able** to **withdraw, not able** to **release**.
37.2a **Without direction releasing**.
47.PW A **jun zi uses involving** in **fate** to **release purpose**.
51.4a/4b The **shake releases** the **bog**.

Renew, *XIN*: new, novel, fresh, recent; restore, improve, correct.
26.IT The **day renewing one's actualizing-dao**.
49/50.HP The **vessel: grasping renewal indeed**.

Renovate, *XIU*: repair, mend, improve, adjust, regulate; clean, adorn; practice, acquire skills.
39.PW A **jun zi uses reversing individuality** to **renovate actualizing-dao**.

Repeat, *XI*: perform a series of similar acts, practice, rehearse; habit, custom; familiar with, skilled. Ideogram: little bird practicing flight.
2.2a/2b **Not repeating: without not Harvesting**.
29.IM **Repeated gorge**.
29.PW **Streams reiterated**

culminate. Repeated gorge.
29.PW And **repetition** to **teach affairs.**
29.1a **Repeated gorge.**
29.1b **Repeated gorge: entering** the **gorge.**
29.IT **Repeated gorge.**
58.PW A **jun zi uses partnering** with **friends** to **explicate repeatedly.**

Repent, *HUI*: regret, dissatisfaction with past conduct inducing a change of heart; proceeds from abashment, *LIN*, shame and confusion at having lost the right way.
1.6a/6b **Overbearing dragon possesses repenting.**
13.6a **Without repenting.**
16.3a **Skeptical providing: repenting.**
16.3a **Procrastinating possesses repenting.**
16.3b **Skeptical providing possesses repenting.**
18.3a The **small possesses repenting.**
24.1a **Without merely repenting.**
24.5a **Without repenting.**
24.5b **Magnanimous return, without repenting.**
31.5a **Without repenting.**
34.5a **Without repenting.**
37.3a **Repenting, adversity, significant.**
47.6a **Named: stirring-up repenting possesses repenting.**
47.6b **Stirring-up repenting possesses repenting.**
50.3a On all **sides rain lessens repenting.**
59.3a **Without repenting.**
64.5a **Trial, significant, without repenting.**

Repenting extinguished, *HUI WANG*: previous errors are corrected, all causes for repenting disappear.
31.4a/4b **Trial, significant. Repenting extinguished.**
32.2a **Repenting extinguished.**
32.2b **Nine** at **second, repenting extinguished.**
34.4a **Repenting extinguished.**
35.3a **Crowds: sincerity, repenting extinguished.**
35.5a **Repenting extinguished.**
37.1a **Repenting extinguished.**
38.1a/5a **Repenting extinguished.**
43.4a **Hauling-along** the **goat, repenting extinguished.**
45.5a **Repenting extinguished.**
49.IM **Repenting extinguished.**
49.4a **Repenting extinguished, possessing conformity.**
49.IT **One's repenting thereupon extinguished.**
52.5a **Repenting extinguished.**
57.4a/5a **Repenting extinguished.**
58.2a **Repenting extinguished.**
59.2a **Repenting extinguished.**
60.6a **Repenting extinguished.**
64.4a/4b **Trial, significant, repenting extinguished.**

Repose, *YAN*: rest, leisure, tranquillity; banquet, feast; pleasure, joy. Ideogram: shelter and rest, a wayside inn.
5.PW A **jun zi uses drinking** and **taking-in** to **repose delightfully.**
17.PW A **jun zi uses turning** to **darkness** to **enter** a **reposing pause.**

Rescue, *ZHENG*: aid, deliver from trouble; pull out, raise up, lift. Ideogram: hand and aid, a helping hand.
36.2a **Availing** of a **rescuing horse**'s **vigor, significant.**
52.2a/2b **Not rescuing one's following.**
59.1a **Availing** of a **rescuing horse**'s **vigor, significant.**

Reside, *JU*: dwell, live in, stay; sit down; fill an office; well-being, rest. Ideogram: body and seat.
3/4.HP **Sprouting: viewing and-also not letting-go one's residing.**
3.1a **Harvesting: residing** in **Trial.**
17.3a **Harvesting: residing** in **Trial.**
27.5a **Residing** in **Trial, significant.**
27.5b To **residing** in **Trial belongs significance.**
31.2a **Residing, significant.**
31.2b **Although** a **pitfall, residing significant.**
33.PS **Beings not permitted** to **use lasting residing** in **their place.**

38.IT **Two women concording: residing.**
43.PW And **residing** in **actualizing-dao**, by **consequence keeping-aloof.**
48.AT The **well: residing** in **one's place and-also shifting.**
49.6a **Residing** in **Trial, significant.**
49.IT **Two women concording, residing.**
53.PW A **jun zi uses residing** in **eminent actualizing-dao** to **improve** the **customs.**
56.PS **Exhausting** the **great implies necessarily letting-go one's residing.**
59.5a/5b The **king's residing, without fault.**
60.5b **Residing** in the **position** in the **center indeed.**
64.PW A **jun zi uses considerately marking-off** the **beings residing** on all **sides.**

Resist, *YU*: withstand, oppose; bring to an end; prevent. Ideogram: rule and worship, imposing ethical or religious limits.
4.6a **Harvesting: resisting illegality.**
4.6b **Harvesting: availing** of **resisting illegality.**
53.3a **Harvesting: resisting illegality.**
53.3b **Harvesting: availing** of **resisting illegality.**

Respect, *JING*: stand in awe of, honor; reverent, attentive; warn; inner vigilance. Ideogram: teacher's rod taming speech and attitude.
5.3b **Respectful consideration, not destroying indeed.**
5.6a/6b To **respecting belongs completion, significant.**
6.6b **Truly not standing respectfully indeed.**
30.1a **Treading, polishing therefore. Respecting it.**
30.1b To **treading** and **polishing belongs respect.**

Respectable, *ZHANG*: exemplary person, worthy of respect, elder.
7.IM The **respectable person, significant.**
17.2a **Letting-go** the **respectable husband.**
17.3a/3b **Tied** to the **respectable husband.**

Resplendent, *HUI*: refulgent, splendid, glorious.
26.IT **Solid persisting: staunch substance, resplendent shining.**

Restrict, *YA*: repress, oppress, contain, subjugate; narrow, obedient.
32.AT **Persevering: motley and-also not restricting.**

Retire, *DUN*: withdraw; run away, flee; conceal yourself, become obscure, invisible; secluded, non-social. Ideogram: walk and swine (wealth through walking away).
This term is the name of hexagram 33 and recurs throughout its texts. It also occurs in:
28.PW And **retiring** from the **age without melancholy.**
34.PS **Beings not permitted** to **use completing retiring.**
34.HP **Retiring:** by **consequence withdrawing indeed.**

Retrace, *YUAN*: source, origin, beginning; going back to the source; repeat; a second time. Ideogram: pure water at its source.
8.IM/ IT **Retracing** the **oracle-consulting: Spring, perpetual Trial.**

Retract, *YU*: turn around; change one's attitude; denounce an agreement, repudiate.
6.4a/4b **Retracting, peaceful Trial.**
16.6a **Accomplishment possesses retraction.**
17.1a/1b An **official possesses retraction.**

Return, *FU*: go back, turn or lead back; recur, reappear, come again; restore, renew, recover; return to an earlier time or place. Ideogram: step and retrace a path.
This term is the name of hexagram 24 and recurs throughout its texts. It also occurs in:
1.3b **Reversing: returning** to **dao indeed.**

6.4a/4b **Returning, approaching fate.**
9.1a/1b **Returning** to the **origin**'s **dao.**
9.2a **Hauling-along returning.**
9.2b **Hauling-along returning located** in the **center.**
11.3a/3b **Without going, not returning.**
11.6a/6b The **bulwark returns tending-towards** the **moat.**
23.HP **Return: reversing indeed.**
25.PS **Returning,** by **consequence not entangled actually.**
38.1a **Losing** the **horse, no pursuing: originating** from **returning.**
40.IM/ IT **One's coming return, significant.**
53.3a/3b The **husband disciplined, not returning.**

Reverent, *XIAO*: filial duty, respect and obedience owed to parents and elders; loyally accomplishing the ancestors' will; period of mourning for deceased parents; virtuous son.
45.IT **Involving reverent presenting indeed.**

Reverse, *FAN*: turn and move in the opposite direction; turn around or upside down (180 degrees); change to the opposite position; contrary.
1.3b **Reversing: returning** to **dao indeed.**
3.2b **Reversing constancy indeed.**
9.3a/3b **Husband** and **consort reversing** the **eyes.**
11/12.HP **Obstruction** and **compenetration: reversing one's sorting indeed.**
13.4b By **consequence confinement and-also reversal** by **consequence indeed.**
23/24.HP **Return: reversing indeed.**
24.IM **Reversing: returning** to **one's dao.**
24.PS **Stripping exhausted above, reversing below.**
24.6b **Reversing** the **chief's dao indeed.**
24.IT **Solid reversing.**
24.IT **Reversing: returning** to **one's dao.**
37.PS **Injury with-respect-to** the **outside implies necessarily reversing with-respect-to** the **household.**
37.6b **Reversing designation belonging** to **individuality indeed.**
39.PW A **jun zi uses reversing individuality** to **renovate actualizing-dao.**
39.3a/3b **Going limping, coming reversal.**
48.PS **Confining reaching above implies necessarily reversing** to the **below.**
54.3a **Reversed converting uses** the **junior-sister.**

Revive, *SU*: regain vital energy, courage or strength; bring back to life, cheer up, relieve. Ideogram: herb whose smell revives weary spirits.
51.3a/3b The **shake reviving, reviving.**

Revolt, *NI*: oppose, resist, seek out; contrary, rebellious, refractory. Ideogram: go and rise against, active revolt.
8.5b **Stowing** away **revolt, grasping yielding.**
62.IT **Above revolting and-also below yielding indeed.**

Reward, *QING*: gift given out of gratitude or benevolence; favor from heaven. Ideogram: heart, follow and deer, the heart expressed through the gift of a deer's skin.
2.IT **Thereupon completing possesses reward.**
10.6b The **great possesses reward indeed.**
26.5b **Possessing reward indeed.**
27.6b The **great possesses reward indeed.**
35.5b **Going possesses reward indeed.**
38.5b **Going possesses reward indeed.**
42.IT The **center's correctness possesses reward.**
46.IT **Possessing reward indeed.**
47.2b The **center possesses reward indeed.**

55.5a **Possessing reward** and **praise, significant.**
55.5b **Possessing reward indeed.**
58.4b **Possessing reward indeed.**

Rich, *FEI*: fertile, abundant, fat; manure, fertilizer.
See also: **Enrich**
33.6a/6b **Rich retiring, without not Harvesting.**

Ride, *CHENG*: ride an animal or a chariot; have the upper hand, control a stronger power; an opened line above controlling a whole line below.
1.IT The **season rides six dragons used** to **drive** up to **heaven.**
3.2a/4a/6a **Riding** a **horse, arraying thus.**
3.2b **Riding** a **solid indeed.**
13.4a/4b **Riding one's rampart.**
16.5b **Riding** a **solid indeed.**
21.2b **Riding** a **solid indeed.**
22.1b **Righteously nothing** to **ride indeed.**
40.3a/3b **Bearing, moreover riding.**
43.IT The **supple rides five solids indeed.**
47.3b **Riding** a **solid indeed.**
51.2b **Riding** a **solid indeed.**
54.IT The **supple rides** the **solid indeed.**
59.IT **Riding wood possesses achievement indeed.**
61.IT **Riding** a **wooden dugout: emptiness indeed.**

Ridgepole, *DONG*: highest and key beam in a house; summit, crest.
28.IM The **great exceeding.** The **ridgepole sagging.**
28.3a The **ridgepole buckling. Pitfall.**
28.3b To the **ridgepole buckling belongs** a **pitfall.**
28.4a The **ridgepole crowning. Significant.**
28.4b To the **ridgepole crowning belongs significance.**
28.IT The **ridgepole sagging.**

Right, *YOU*: right side, right hand; West, situated at the right of South, which is the reference direction; place of honor.
11.PW And **uses** at **left** and **right** the **commoners.**
55.3a/3b **Severing one's right arm.**

Righteous, *YI*: proper, just, virtuous, upright; the heart that rules itself; benevolent, loyal, devoted to public good.
5.IT **One's righteousness not confined** nor **exhausted actually.**
9.1b **One's righteousness, significant indeed.**
13.4b **Righteousness nowhere controlling indeed.**
16.IT The **season belonging** to **providing righteously great actually in-fact.**
17.4b **One's righteousness: pitfall indeed.**
17.IT To **following's season belongs** the **righteously great actually in-fact.**
19/20.HP To **nearing** and **overseeing belongs righteousness.**
22.1b **Righteously nothing** to **ride indeed.**
24.3b **Righteous, without fault indeed.**
31.PS **Therefore afterwards** the **codes' righteousness possesses** a **polishing place.**
32.5b The **husband** and the **son, paring righteously.**
33.IT The **season belonging** to **retiring righteously great actually in-fact.**
36.1b **Righteously not taking-in indeed.**
37.IT The **great belonging** to **heaven** and **earth righteous indeed.**
40.1b **Righteous, without fault indeed.**
44.2b **Righteously not extending hospitality indeed.**
44.IT The **season belonging** to **coupling righteously great actually in-fact.**
48.AT The **well: using differentiating righteously.**
50.3b **Letting-go one's righteousness indeed.**
53.1b **Righteous, without fault indeed.**

54.IT The **great's righteousness belonging** to **heaven** and **earth**.
56.3b **One's righteousness lost indeed.**
56.6b **One's righteousness burnt indeed.**
56.IT The **season belonging** to **sojourning righteously great actually in-fact.**
63.1b **Righteous, without fault indeed.**

Rings, *XUAN*: handles or ears for carrying a tripod.
50.5a The **vessel**'s **yellow ears, metallic rings.**
50.6a The **vessel**'s **jade rings.**
50.6b **Jade rings located above.**

Ripe, *SHI*: mature, full-grown; great, eminent.
23.6a The **ripe fruit not taken-in.**
39.6a **Going limping, coming ripeness. Significant.**
39.6b **Going limping, coming ripeness.**

Rise, *XING*: get up, grow, lift; stimulate, promote; enjoy. Ideogram: lift, two hands and unite, lift with both hands.
13.3a/3b **Three year's-time not rising.**
22.2b **Associating above, rising indeed.**
42.AT **Augmenting**: **using** the **rising Harvest.**
54.IT **And-also** the **myriad beings not rising.**

Rise-up, *QI*: stand up, erect; stimulate, excite; undertake, begin, develop.
7.PS **Arguing necessarily possesses crowds rising-up.**
44.4a **Rising-up, pitfall.**
51.HP The **shake**: **rising-up indeed.**

River, *CHUAN*: watercourse, large river, stream; flow; continuous, unceasing; associated with the Streaming Moment and the trigram Gorge, *KAN*.
See also: **Wading the great river**
29.IT **Earth's venture: mountains, rivers, hill-tops, mounds indeed.**

Rodent, see **Bushy-tailed rodent**

Roll, *SHU*: gather into a bundle, bind together; restrain.
22.5a A **roll** of **plain-silk: petty, petty.**

Roof, *WU*: cover, shelter; house, room, cabin, tent; stop or remain at.
55.6a/6b **Abounding: one's roof.**

Root, *SUN*: base on which things rest, ground, foundation; mild, subtly penetrating; nourishing.
This term is the name of hexagram 57 and recurs throughout its texts. It also occurs in:
4.5b **Yielding uses** the **root indeed.**
9.IT **Persistence and-also root.**
18.IT **Root and-also stopping. Decay.**
20.IT **Yielding and-also** the **root.**
28.IT **Root and-also stimulating movement.**
32.IT **Root and-also stirring-up.**
37.2b **Yielding uses** the **root indeed.**
42.IT **Augmenting: stirring-up and-also** the **root.**
45.3b **Above** the **root indeed.**
46.IT The **root and-also yielding.**
48.IT **Root reaching stream and-also stream above.** The **well.**
50.IT **Using wood**, the **root, fire.**
50.IT The **root and-also** the **ear** and the **eye: understanding bright.**
53.4b **Yielding uses** the **root indeed.**
53.IT **Stopping and-also** the **root.**
58.HP the **root: hidden-away indeed.**
61.IT **Stimulating and-also** the **root: conforming.**

Rope, see **Stranded ropes**

Rotten, *LAN*: corrupt, putrid, dirty, worn out; softened, crumbling.
23/24.HP **Stripping: rotten indeed.**

Rouse, *ZHEN*: stir up, excite, stimulate; issue forth; put in order. Ideogram: hand and shake, shaking things up.
See also: **Arouse**
18.PW A **jun zi uses rousing** the **commoners** to **nurture actualizing-dao.**
32.6a **Rousing persevering, pitfall.**
32.6b **Rousing persevering located above.**

Ruin, *LEI*: destroy, break, overturn; debilitated, meager, emaciated; entangled.

34.3a **Ruins its horns.**

34.4a/4b The **hedge broken-up, not ruined.**

44.1a **Ruined** the **pig's conformity: hoof dragging.**

48.IM **Ruining one's pitcher: pitfall.**

48.IT **Ruining one's pitcher: that uses** a **pitfall indeed.**

Rule, see **Poison/rule**

Ruminate, *XIANG*: ponder and discuss; examine minutely, pay attention to; explain thoroughly. Ideogram: word and sheep, ruminating on words.

34.6b **Not ruminating indeed.**

Sacrifice, *JIE*: straw mat used to hold offerings; make offerings to gods and the dead; depend on, call on, borrow.

28.1a/1b **Sacrificing avails** of **white thatch-grass.**

Sacrificial-victims, *SHENG*: the six sacrificial animals: horse, ox, lamb, cock, dog and pig.

45.IM/ IT **Availing** of the **great**'s **sacrificial-victims, significant.**

Sacrum, *TUN*: lower back, buttocks, lower spine; bottom.

43.4a The **sacrum without flesh.**

44.3a The **sacrum without flesh.**

47.1a The **sacrum confined tending-towards** a **wooden stump.**

Sad, *QI*: unhappy, low in spirits, distressed; mourn, sorrow over; commiserate with.

30.5a **Sadness like lamenting.**

Sag, *NAO*: yield, bend, distort, twist; disturbed, confused.

28.IM The **great exceeding.** The **ridgepole sagging.**

28.4b **Not sagging, reaching** the **below indeed.**

28.IT The **ridgepole sagging.**

Sands, *SHA*: beach, sandbanks, shingle; gravel, pebbles; granulated. Ideogram: water and few, areas laid bare by receding water.

5.2a/2b **Attending tending-towards** the **sands.**

Sash, *FU*: ceremonial belt of official which holds seal of office.

47.2a **Scarlet sashes** on all **sides coming.**

47.5a **Confinement tending-towards** a **crimson sash.**

Satiation, *BAO*: full, replete, satisfied; swollen, sated; gratified, flattered.

53.2b **Not sheer satiation indeed.**

Satisfaction, *ZHI*: fulfillment, gratification, happiness; take pleasure in, fulfill a need.

11.5a/5b **Using satisfaction: Spring, significant.**

12.4a **Cultivating radiant satisfaction.**

Scare, *JING*: fear, alarm; cause fear, terrify; apprehensive, surprised. Ideogram: horse and strike, havoc created by a terrified horse.

51.IM/ IT The **shake scares** a **hundred miles.**

51.IT **Scaring** the **distant and-also fearing** the **nearby indeed.**

Scarlet, *ZHU*: vivid red signifying honor, luck, marriage, riches, literary accomplishment; culmination of the Wooden Moment.

47.2a **Scarlet sashes** on all **sides coming.**

Scatter, *SAN*: disperse in small pieces; separate, divide, distribute. Ideogram: strike and crumble.

59.PS **Stimulating and-also afterwards scattering it.**

Scepter, *GUI*: small stone scepter given to nobles as sign of rank.

42.3a **Notifying** the **prince, availing** of the **scepter.**

Scholar, *SHI*: cultured, learned, upright; gentleman, man of distinction, officer.

28.5a A **venerable wife acquires her scholarly husband.**

28.5b A **venerable wife** and a **scholarly husband.**

54.6a A **scholar disembowels** a **goat without blood.**

Scold, *HE*: rebuke, blame, enforce obedience; severe, stern.
37.3a/3b **Household people, scolding, scolding.**

Screen, *PU*: curtain, veil, awning, hanging mat; hide, protect; luxuriant plant growth.
55.2a/4a/4b **Abounding: one's screen.**
55.6a **Screening one's household.**

Scrutinize, *CHA*: investigate, observe carefully, get at the truth. Ideogram: sacrifice as central to understanding.
22.IT **Using scrutinizing** the **seasons' transformation.**

Season, *SHI*: quality of the time; the right time, opportune, in harmony; planning in accord with the time; season of the year. Ideogram: sun and temple, sacred time.
1.IT In the **six positions** the **season accomplishes.**
1.IT The **season rides six dragons used** to **drive** up to **heaven.**
2.3b **Using** the **season** to **shoot-forth indeed.**
4.IT The **season**'s **center indeed.**
14.IT The **correspondence reaches heaven and-also** the **season moves.**
16.IT **And-also** the **four seasons not straying.**
16.IT The **season belonging** to **providing righteously great actually in-fact.**
17.IT **And-also below heaven following** the **season.**
17.IT To **following**'s **season belongs** the **righteously great actually in-fact.**
20.IT **And-also** the **four seasons not straying.**
22.IT **Using scrutinizing** the **seasons' transformation.**
25/26.HP The **great accumulating: season indeed.**
25.PW The **earlier kings used** the **luxuriance suiting** the **season** to **nurture** the **myriad beings.**
27.IT The **season belonging** to the **jaws great actually in-fact.**
28.IT The **season belonging** to the **great exceeding great actually in-fact.**
29.IT The **season belonging** to **venturing avails** of the **great actually in-fact.**
32.IT The **four seasons: transforming changes and-also enabling lasting** and **accomplishing.**
33.IT **Associating** with the **season**'s **movement indeed.**
33.IT The **season belonging** to **retiring righteously great actually in-fact.**
38.IT The **season belonging** to **polarizing avails** of the **great actually in-fact.**
39.IT The **season belonging** to **limping avails** of the **great actually in-fact.**
40.IT The **season belonging** to **unraveling great actually in-fact.**
41.IT **Two platters corresponding possess** the **season.**
41.IT **Diminishing** the **solid, augmenting** the **supple possesses** the **season.**
41.IT **Associating** with the **season, accompanying** the **movement.**
42.IT **Associating** with the **season, accompanying** the **movement.**
44.IT The **season belonging** to **coupling righteously great actually in-fact.**
46.IT The **supple uses** the **season. Ascending.**
48.1b The **season stowed** away **indeed.**
49.PW A **jun zi uses regulating** the **calendar** to **brighten** the **seasons.**
49.IT **Heaven** and **earth skinning and-also** the **four seasons accomplishing.**
49.IT The **season belonging** to **skinning great actually in-fact.**
52.IT The **season stopping**, by **consequence stopping.**
52.IT The **season moving**, by **consequence moving.**
52.IT **Stirring-up, stilling, not letting-go one's season.**
54.4a **Procrastinating converting possesses** the **season.**
55.IT **Associating** with the **season**'s

dissolving pause.
56.IT The **season belonging** to **sojourning righteously great actually in-fact.**
60.2b **Letting-go** the **season**: **end indeed.**
60.IT **Heaven** and **earth articulating and-also** the **four seasons accomplishing.**
62.IT **Associating** with the **season**'s **movement indeed.**
63.5b **Not thus** the **season belonging** to the **Western neighbor.**

Seasoned, *XI*: dried meat, prepared for a journey.
21.3a **Gnawing seasoned meat.**

Second, see **Two/second**

Seedburst, *JIA*: seeds bursting forth in spring; first month of springtime; beginning, number one; associated with the Wooden Moment.
18.IM/ IT **Before seedburst three days.**
18.IM/ IT **After seedburst three days.**
40.IT **Thunder** and **rain arousing and-also** the **hundred fruits, grasses, trees, altogether seedburst**'s **boundary.**

Seek, *QIU*: search for, aim at, wish for, desire; implore, supplicate; covetous.
3.4a **Seeking matrimonial alliance.**
3.4b **Seeking and-also going.**
4.IM/IT **In-no-way I seek** the **youthful enveloping.**
4.IM/IT The **youthful enveloping seeks me.**
17.3a **Following possesses seeking** and **acquiring.**
19/20.HP **Maybe associating, maybe seeking.**
27.IM/ IT The **origin** of **seeking mouth**'s **substance.**
29.2a/2b **Seeking** the **small**: **acquiring.**
32.1b **Beginning seeking depth indeed.**
48.3b **Seeking kingly brightness.**

Seize, *JU*: lay hands on, lean on, rely on; maintain, become concrete; testimony, evidence.
47.3a/3b **Seizing tending-towards star thistles.**

Senior, *XIONG*: elder brother; elder, one to whom respect is due.
37.IT The **senior**, a **senior**. The **junior**, a **junior.**

Sequence, *XU*: order, precedence, series; follow in order.
52.5a **Words possess sequence.**

Servant, *CHEN*: attendant, minister, vassal; courtier who can speak to the sovereign; wait on, serve in office. Ideogram: person bowing low.
31.PS **Therefore afterwards possessing chief** and **servant.**
31.PS **Possessing chief** and **servant.**
33.3a/3b **Accumulating servants, concubines, significant.**
39.2a/2b A **king**, a **servant**: **limping, limping.**
41.6a **Acquiring** a **servant without** a **household.**
62.2a **Meeting one's servant.**
62.2b A **servant not permitted exceeding indeed.**

Set, *ZE*: sunset, afternoon; waning moon; decline.
30.3a/3b **Radiance belonging** to the **sun setting.**
55.IT The **sun** in the **center**, by **consequence setting.**

Set-up, *SHE*: establish, institute; arrange, set in order. Ideogram: words and impel, establish with words.
20.PW The **earlier kings used inspecting** on all **sides** and **overseeing** the **commoners** to **set-up teaching.**
20.IT The **wise person uses spirit dao** to **set-up teaching.**
29.IT The **king** and the **princes set-up venturing used** to **guard their city.**
42.AT **Augmenting**: **long-living enriching and-also not setting-up.**

Seven, *QI*: number seven; seven planets; seventh day when moon changes from crescent to waxing; the Tangram game analyzes all forms in terms of seven basic shapes.

24.IM/ IT The **seventh day comes return.**
51.2a The **seventh day acquiring.**
63.2a/2b The **seventh day acquiring.**

Sever, *ZHE*: break off, separate, sunder, cut in two; discriminate, pass judgment on.
22.PW A **jun zi uses brightening** the **multitude** of **standards without daring** to **sever litigations.**
30.6a **Severing** the **head. Capturing in-no-way its demons.**
50.4a The **vessel's severed stand.**
55.PW A **jun zi uses severing litigations involving punishment.**
55.3a/3b **Severing one's right arm.**

Shackles, *GU*: chains used to secure prisoners; restrain freedom; self-restraint.
4.1a **Availing** of **stimulating shackles** to **fetter.**

Shady, *YOU*: retired, solitary, secret, hidden from view; dark, obscure, occult, mysterious; ignorant. Ideogram: small within hill, a cave or grotto.
10.2a/2b **Shady people: Trial, significant.**
47.1a/1b **Entering tending-towards** a **shady gully.**
47.1b **Shady, not bright indeed.**
54.2a/2b **Harvesting: Trial belonging** to **shady people.**
55.4b **Shade, not brightness indeed.**

Shake, *ZHEN*: arouse, excite, inspire; awe, alarm, trembling; thunder rising from the depth of the earth; fertilizing intrusion. Ideogram: excite and rain.
This term is the name of hexagram 51 and recurs throughout its texts. It also occurs in:
52.HP The **shake: rising-up indeed.**
64.4a The **shake avails** of **subjugating souls** on all **sides.**

Shaman, *WU*: magician, sorcerer, healer, wizard, witch; perform magic.
57.2a **Availing** of **chroniclers** and **shamans.**

She/her, *QI*: general third person pronoun and possessive adjective; also: one/one's, it/its, he/his, they/their.
This term occurs throughout the hexagram texts.

Sheer, *SU*: plain, unadorned; original color or state; clean, pure, natural. Ideogram: white silk.
10.1a **Sheer treading: going.**
10.1b To **sheer treading belongs going.**
53.2b **Not sheer satiation indeed.**

Shield, *YOU*: heavenly kindness and protection. Ideogram: numinous and right hand, spirit power.
14.6a The **origin** in **heaven shields it.**
14.6b The **origin** in **heaven shields indeed.**
25.IT **Heavenly fate not shielding.**
41.5b The **origin above shielding indeed.**

Shift, *QIAN*: move, change, transpose; improve, ascend, be promoted; deport, dismiss, remove.
42.PW A **jun zi uses viewing improvement**, by **consequence shifting.**
42.4a **Harvesting: availing** of **activating depends** on **shifting** the **city.**
48.AT The **well: residing** in **one's place and-also shifting.**

Shine, *GUANG*: illuminate, emit light; brilliant, splendid; honor, glory, éclat; distinct from brightness, *MING*, light of heavenly bodies. Ideogram: fire above person.
2.2b **Earth's dao shines indeed.**
2.3b **Knowing** the **shine** of the **great indeed.**
2.IT **Containing generosity**: the **shine** of the **great.**
3.5b **Spreading, not-yet shining indeed.**
5.IM/ IT **Shining Growing, Trial, significant.**
10.IT **Shining brightness indeed.**
11.2b **Using** the **shining great indeed.**
15.AT **Humbling: noble and-also shining.**
15.IT **Heavenly dao: below fording**

and-also **shining brightness.**
15.IT **Humbling: noble and-also shining.**
20.4a/4b **Overseeing** the **shine belonging** to the **city.**
21.4b **Not-yet shining indeed.**
26.IT **Solid persisting: staunch substance, resplendent shining.**
27.4b **Above spreading shine indeed.**
31.4b **Not-yet** the **shining great indeed.**
35.6b **Dao not-yet shining indeed.**
42.IT **One's dao:** the **great shining.**
43.5b The **center not-yet shining indeed.**
43.IT **One's exposure thereupon shining indeed.**
45.5b **Purpose not-yet shining indeed.**
51.4b **Not-yet shining indeed.**
52.IT **One's dao: shining brightness.**
58.6b **Not-yet shining indeed.**
59.4b The **shining great indeed.**
64.5a/5b To a **jun zi belongs shining.**

Shoes, *JU*: footwear, sandals.
21.1a/1b **Shoes locked-up, submerged feet.**

Shoot, *SHE*: shoot an arrow; archer; project, eject, spurt, issue forth; glance at; scheme for. Ideogram: arrow and body.
40.6a A **prince avails** of **shooting** a **hawk tending-towards** the **above belonging** to the **high rampart.**
40.6b A **prince avails** of **shooting** a **hawk.**
48.2a/2b The **well:** a **gully, shooting bass.**
56.5a **Shooting** a **pheasant.**

Shoot-forth, *FA*: emit, send out, shoot an arrow; ferment, rise; express, raise one's voice. Ideogram: stance, bow and arrow, shooting from a solid base.
2.3b **Using** the **season** to **shoot-forth indeed.**
4.1a **Shooting-forth enveloping.**
14.5b **Trustworthiness uses shooting-forth purpose indeed.**
55.2a/2b **Possessing conformity, like shooting-forth.**
55.2b **Trustworthiness uses shooting-forth purpose indeed.**

Show, *HUI*: show, signal, point out. Ideogram: hand and act, giving signals.
15.4a/4b **Without not harvesting: showing humbleness.**

Shriek, *YA*: confused noise, like the clamor of a school-room; cries of birds; sounds of a child learning to speak; exclamations; hoarse, dumb.
51.IM/IT **Laughing words, shrieking, shrieking.**
51.1a **After laughing words, shrieking, shrieking.**
51.1b **Laughing words, shrieking, shrieking.**

Shroud, *MI*: dense, close together, thick, tight; hidden, secret.
See also: **Enshroud**
9.IM/ IT **Shrouding clouds, not raining.**
62.5a/5b **Shrouding clouds, not raining.**

Sides, *FANG*: cardinal directions; surface of the earth extending to the four cardinal points; everywhere; limits, boundaries.
2.2a **Straightening** on all **sides:** the **great.**
2.2b **Straightening used** on all **sides indeed.**
8.IM/ IT **Not soothing,** on all **sides coming.**
20.PW The **earlier kings used inspecting** on all **sides** and **overseeing** the **commoners** to **set-up teaching.**
24.PW The **crown prince** used culminating sun **not** to **inspect** on all **sides.**
30.PW The **great** in the **person uses consecutive brightening** to **illuminate tending-towards** the **four sides.**
32.PW A **jun zi uses establishing, not versatility** on all **sides.**
42.IT **One's augmenting without sides.**
44.PW The **crown prince uses spreading fate** to **command** the **four sides.**

47.2a **Scarlet sashes** on all **sides coming.**
50.3a On all **sides rain lessens repenting.**
63.3a The **High Ancestor subjugates souls** on all **sides.**
64.PW A **jun zi uses considerately marking-off** the **beings residing** on all **sides.**
64.4a The **shake avails** of **subjugating souls** on all **sides.**

Sigh, *ZI*: lament, express grief, sorrow or yearning.
45.6a/6b **Paying-tribute: sighs, tears, snot.**

Significant, *JI*: leads to the experience of meaning; favorable, propitious, appropriate. Ideogram: scholar and mouth, wise words of a sage.
1.7a **Significant.**
2.IM **Peaceful Trial, significant.**
2.5a/5b A **yellow apron. Spring, significant.**
2.IT To **peaceful Trial belongs significance.**
3.4a **Going, significant.**
3.5a The **small: Trial, significant.**
4.2a **Enwrapping enveloping, significant.**
4.2a **Letting-in** the **wife, significant.**
4.5a **Youthful enveloping. Significant.**
4.5b To a **youthful enveloping belongs significance.**
5.IM/IT **Shining Growing, Trial, significant.**
5.2a **Completing, significant.**
5.2b **Although** the **small possesses words, using completing significant indeed.**
5.5a **Trial, significant.**
5.5b **Taking-in liquor: Trial, significant.**
5.6a/6b To **respecting belongs completion, significant.**
6.IM The **center, significant. Completing, pitfall.**
6.1a **Completing significant.**
6.3a **Adversity: completing, significant.**
6.3b **Adhering** to the **above, significant indeed.**
6.4a **Significant.**
6.5a/5b **Arguing. Spring significant.**
6.IT **Blocking awe:** the **center, significant.**
7.IM The **respectable person, significant.**
7.2a/2b **Locating** the **legions** in the **center, significant.**
7.IT **Significant, furthermore is** it **actually faulty?**
8.IM **Grouping. Significant.**
8.1a **Completion coming, possessing more, significant.**
8.1b **Possessing more, significant indeed.**
8.2a/4a **Trial, significant.**
8.5a **Significant.**
8.5b To **manifest grouping belongs significance.**
8.IT **Grouping. Significant indeed.**
9.1a **Significant.**
9.1b **One's righteousness, significant indeed.**
9.2a **Significant.**
10.2a/2b **Shady people: Trial, significant.**
10.4a/4b **Watch-out! Watch-out! Completing significant.**
10.6a **One's recurring Spring, significant.**
10.6b **Spring: significance located above.**
11.IM **Significance Growing.**
11.1a **Disciplining, significant.**
11.1b **Eradicating thatch-grass: disciplining, significant.**
11.5a/5b **Using satisfaction: Spring, significant.**
11.IT The **small going,** the **great coming: significance Growing.**
12.1a **Trial, significant.**
12.1b **Eradicating thatch-grass: Trial, significant.**
12.2a The **small** in the **person significant.**
12.5a The **great** in the **person, significant.**
12.5b To the **great** in the **person belongs significance.**
13.4a **Significant.**
13.4b **One's significance.**
14.5a **Impressing thus. Significant.**

14.5b To impressing thus belongs significance.
14.6a Significant, without not Harvesting.
14.6b Great possessing, above: significant.
15.1a Significant.
15.2a/2b Trial, significant.
15.3a Possessing completion, significant.
16.2a Trial, significant.
16.2b Not completing the day, Trial, significant.
17.1a Trial, significant.
17.1b Adhering to correctness, significant indeed.
17.5a/5b Conformity tends-towards excellence. Significant.
18.1a Adversity's completion, significant.
19.1a Conjunction nearing: Trial, significant.
19.1b/2a Conjunction nearing: Trial, significant.
19.2b Conjunction nearing, significant.
19.5a/6a Significant.
19.6b To magnanimity nearing belongs significance.
21.4a Significant.
21.4b Harvesting drudgery, Trial: significant.
22.3a Perpetual Trial, significant.
22.3b To perpetual Trial belongs significance.
22.5a Completing significant.
22.5b To six at fifth belongs significance.
24.1a Spring, significant.
24.2a Significant.
24.2b To relaxing return belongs significance.
25.1a Going, significant.
26.IM/IT Not in the household taking-in. Significant.
26.4a Spring, significant.
26.4b Six at fourth: Spring, significant.
26.5a Significant.
26.5b To six at fifth belongs significance.
27.IM/IT The jaws. Trial, significant.
27.4a Toppling jaws. Significant.
27.4b To toppling jaws belongs significance.
27.5a Residing in Trial, significant.
27.5b To residing in Trial belongs significance.
27.6a Adversity, significant.
27.6b Antecedent jaws, adversity, significant.
27.IT Nourishing correctly, by consequence significance indeed.
28.4a The ridgepole crowning. Significant.
28.4b To the ridgepole crowning belongs significance.
30.IM Significant.
30.2a/2b Yellow radiance. Spring, significant.
30.5a Significant.
30.5b To six at fifth belongs significance.
30.IT That uses accumulating female cattle, significant indeed.
31.IM Grasping womanhood, significant.
31.2a Residing, significant.
31.2b Although a pitfall, residing significant.
31.4a/4b Trial, significant. Repenting extinguished.
31.IT Grasping womanhood, significant indeed.
32.5a The wife's people, significant.
32.5b The wife's people: Trial, significant.
33.3a/3b Accumulating servants, concubines, significant.
33.4a A jun zi, significant.
33.5a/5b Excellent retiring, Trial, significant.
34.2a Trial, significant.
34.2b Nine at second: Trial, significant.
34.4a Trial, significant.
34.6a/6b Drudgery, by consequence significant.
35.1a/2a Trial, significant.
35.5a Going significant, without not Harvesting.
35.6a Adversity, significant.
36.2a Availing of a rescuing horse's vigor, significant.
36.2b To six at second belongs significance.

S Significant

37.2a **Trial, significant.**
37.2b To **six** at **second belongs significance.**
37.3a **Repenting, adversity, significant.**
37.4a/4b **Affluent household**: the **great, significant.**
37.5a **Beings' care, significant.**
37.6a **Completing, significant.**
37.6b To **impressing thus belongs significance.**
38.IM **Polarizing.** The **small's affairs, significant.**
38.6a **Going meets rain**, by **consequence significant.**
38.6b To **meeting rain belongs significance.**
38.IT **That uses** the **small's affairs, significant.**
39.IM **Trial, significant.**
39.6a **Going limping, coming ripeness. Significant.**
39.IT **Appropriate position. Trial, significant.**
40.IM/IT **one's coming return, significant.**
40.IM **daybreak, significant.**
40.2a **Trial, significant.**
40.2b **Nine** at **second: Trial, significant.**
40.5a A **jun zi holding-fast possesses unraveling. Significant.**
40.IT **Possessing directed going: daybreak, significant.**
41.IM/5a/IT **Spring, significant.**
41.5b **Six** at **fifth: Spring, significant.**
41.6a **Trial, significant.**
42.1a **Spring, significant.**
42.1b **Spring, significant, without fault.**
42.2a **Perpetual Trial, significant.**
42.2a The **king avails** of **presenting tending-towards** the **supreme, significant.**
42.5a **No question, Spring significant.**
44.1a **Trial, significant.**
45.IM/IT **Availing** of the **great's sacrificial-victims, significant.**
45.2a/2b **Protracting: significant, without fault.**
45.4a/4b The **great: significant, without fault.**
46.IM/IT The **South: disciplining, significant.**
46.1a/1b **Sincere ascending**: the **great, significant.**
46.4a **Significant, without fault.**
46.5a/5b **Trial, significant: ascending steps.**
47.IM/IT **Trial**: the **great** in the **person, significant.**
47.6a **Disciplining, significant.**
47.6b **Significant, moving indeed.**
48.6a **Possessing conformity: Spring, significant.**
48.6b **Spring, significance located above.**
49.2a **Disciplining significant, without fault.**
49.4a **Amending fate, significant.**
49.4b To **amending fate belongs significance.**
49.6a **Residing** in **Trial, significant.**
50.IM The **vessel. Spring, significant.**
50.2a **Significant.**
50.3a **Completing significant.**
50.6a The **great, significant.**
51.1a **Significant.**
52.6a **Magnanimous bound, significant.**
52.6b To **magnanimous bound belongs significance.**
53.IM **Infiltrating. Womanhood converting, significant.**
53.2a/5a **Significant.**
53.5b To **completing abstention belongs mastering, significant.**
53.6a **Significant.**
53.6b **Its feathers permit availing** of **activating** the **fundamentals, significant.**
53.IT **Womanhood converting, significant indeed.**
54.1a **Disciplining, significant.**
54.1b **Halting enables treading, significant.**
54.5a The **moon almost full, significant.**
55.2a/4a **Significant.**
55.4b **Significant movement indeed.**
55.5a **Possessing reward** and **praise, significant.**

55.5b To **six** at **fifth belongs significance**.
56.IM **Sojourning**: **Trial, significant**.
56.IT **Sojourning**: **Trial, significant indeed**.
57.2a **Disorder like, significant**.
57.2b To the **disorder like belongs significance**.
57.5a **Trial, significant**.
57.5a **Significant**.
57.5b To **nine** at **fifth belongs significance**.
58.1a/1b **Harmonious open, significant**.
58.2a **Conforming open, significant**.
58.2b To the **conforming open belongs significance**.
59.1a **Availing** of a **rescuing horse**'s **vigor, significant**.
59.1b To **initial six belongs significance**.
59.4a/4b **Dispersing one's flock**: **Spring, significant**.
60.5a **Sweet articulating, significant**.
60.5b To **sweet articulating belongs significance**.
61.IM The **center conforming**: **hog fish, significant**.
61.1a **Precaution significant**.
61.1b **Initial nine**: **precaution significant**.
61.IT **Hog fish, significant**.
62.IM The **great, significant**.
62.IT **That uses** the **small** in **affairs, significant indeed**.
62.IT The **great, significant**.
63.IM/IT **Initially**: **significant**.
63.5b **Significant**. The **great coming indeed**.
64.2a **Trial, significant**.
64.2b **Nine** at **second**: **Trial, significant**.
64.4a/4b **Trial, significant, repenting extinguished**.
64.5a **Trial, significant, without repenting**.
64.5a **Possessing conformity, significant**.
64.5b **One's brilliance significant indeed**.

Silk, see **Plain-silk**

Simples, *YAO*: medicinal herbs, plants used as remedies; herbal healing; medicine; poison.
25.5a **No simple possesses joy**.
25.5b To **without entanglement belong simples**.

Simply, *ER*: just so, only.
27.1a **Stowing simply** the **magic tortoise**.
31.4a **Partners adhere** to **simply pondering**.
61.2a **Myself associating**: **simply spilling it**.

Sincere, *YUN*: true, honest, loyal; according to the facts; have confidence in, permit, assent. Ideogram: vapor rising, words directed upward.
35.3a **Crowds**: **sincerity, repenting extinguished**.
35.3b **Crowds**: to **sincerity belongs purpose**.
46.1a/1b **Sincere ascending**: the **great, significant**.

Sing, *GE*: chant, sing elegies; associated with the Earthy Moment, turning point from Yang to Yin.
30.3a **Not drumbeating** a **jar and-also singing**.
61.3a **Maybe weeping, maybe singing**.

Situation, *ZHAI*: office, function, place in a hierarchy; dwelling, residence.
23.PW **Above using munificence, below pacifying** the **situation**.

Six, *LIU*: number six; transforming opened line; six lines of a hexagram.
This term frequently occurs in the text of transforming opened lines. It also occurs in:
1.IT In the **six positions** the **season accomplishes**.
1.IT The **season rides six dragons used** to **drive** up to **heaven**.

Skeptical, *YU*: wonder at, wide-eyed surprise; doubtful; hopeful.
16.3a **Skeptical providing**: **repenting**.
16.3b **Skeptical providing possesses repenting**.

Skin, *GE*: human or animal skin; hide, leather; armor, protection; peel off, remove the covering, skin or hide; change, renew, molt; overthrow, degrade from office.

This term is the name of hexagram 49 and recurs throughout its texts. It also occurs in:

33.2a To **holding-on belongs availing** of **skin belonging** to **yellow cattle**.

50.PS **Skinning beings implies absolutely-nothing like** a **vessel**.

50.HP **Skinning: departing anteriority indeed**.

50.3a/3b The **vessel**'s **ears skinned**.

Skulk, *CUAN*: sneak away and hide; furtive, stealthy; seduce into evil. Ideogram: cave and rat, rat lurking in its hole.

6.2b **Converting, escaping: skulking indeed**.

Slaughter, *SHA*: kill, murder, execute; hunt game.

63.5a/5b The **Eastern neighbor slaughters cattle**.

Sleeve, *MEI*: sleeve of a garment, on which signs indicating the rank of the wearer are displayed.

54.5a The **sleeves belonging** to **one's chief**,

54.5a/5b **not thus fine** the **sleeves belonging** to **one's junior-sister**.

Slice, *QIE*: cut, carve, mince; urge, press; come close, approach, touch; tangent.

23.4b **Slicing close** to **calamity indeed**.

Small, *XIAO*: little, common, unimportant; adapting to what crosses your path; ability to move in harmony with the vicissitudes of life; contrasts with great, *DA*, self-imposed theme or goal.

This term occurs in the name of hexagrams 9 and 62 and recurs throughout their texts. It also occurs in:

3.5a The **small: Trial, significant**.

5.2a The **small possesses words**.

5.2b **Although** the **small possesses words, using completing significant indeed**.

6.1a The **small possesses words**.

6.1b **Although** the **small possesses words, one's differentiation brightening indeed**.

7.6a/6b The **small** in the **person**, no **availing** of.

10.HP The **small accumulating: few indeed**.

11.IM The **small going**, the **great coming**.

11.IT The **small going**, the **great coming: significance Growing**.

11.IT **Inside jun zi and-also outside** the **small** in the **person**.

11.IT The **small** in the **person**'s **dao dissolving indeed**.

12.IM/IT The **great going**, the **small coming**.

12.2a The **small** in the **person significant**.

12.IT **Inside** the **small** in the **person and-also outside jun zi**.

12.IT The **small** in the **person**'s **dao long-living**.

14.3a The **small** in the **person nowhere controlling**.

14.3b The **small** in the **person harmful indeed**.

17.2a/2b **Tied** to the **small son**.

17.3a **Letting-go** the **small son**.

18.3a The **small possesses repenting**.

20.1a The **small** in the **person**: **without fault**.

20.1b The **small** in the **person**'s **dao indeed**.

21.3a The **small: abashment**.

22.IM The **small**.

22.IT The **anterior small**.

23.6a/6b The **small** in the **person strips** the **hut**.

23.IT The **small** in the **person long-living indeed**.

24.AT **Return**: the **small and-also marking-off with-respect-to beings**.

29.2a/2b **Seeking** the **small: acquiring**.

33.IM/IT The **small, Harvesting, Trial**.

33.PW A **jun zi uses distancing** the **small** in the **person**.

33.4a The **small** in the **person obstructing**.
33.4b The **small** in the **person obstructing indeed**.
34.3a/3b The **small** in the **person avails** of **vigor**.
38.IM **Polarizing**. The **small's affairs, significant**.
38.IT **That uses** the **small's affairs, significant**.
40.5a **Possessing conformity tending-towards** the **small** in the **person**.
40.5b The **small** in the **person withdraws indeed**.
45.3a The **small abashed**.
46.PW And **amassing** the **small** to **use** the **high great**.
49.6a/6b The **small** in the **person skins** the **face**.
53.1a The **small son, adversity**.
53.1b To the **small son belongs adversity**.
56.IM **Sojourning**. The **small, growing**.
56.IT **Sojourning**. The **small, Growing**.
56.IT **That uses** the **small, Growing**.
57.IM The **root**. The **small, Growing**.
57.IT **That uses** the **small, Growing**.
61.HP The **small exceeding: excess indeed**.
63.IM **Already fording. Growing**, the **small**.
63.3a The **small** in the **person, no availing** of.
63.IT The **small implies Growing indeed**.
64.IM/ IT The **small fox** in a **muddy ford**.

Smite, *JI*: hit, beat, attack; hurl against, rush a position; rouse to action. Ideogram: hand and hit, fist punching.
4.6a **Smiting enveloping**.
16.AT **Redoubling gates, smiting clappers**.
42.6a/6b **Maybe smiting it**.

Smooth, *TAN*: level, even, flat; extended, vast; tranquil, composed, at ease.
10.2a **Treading** in **dao: smoothing, smoothing**.

Smother, *XUN*: suffocate, smoke out; fog, steam, miasma, vapor; broil, parch; offend; evening mists.
52.3a **Adversity smothers** the **heart**.
52.3b **Exposure smothers** the **heart indeed**.

Snap, *DIE*: bite, seize with the teeth. Ideogram: mouth and reach.
10.IM **Not snapping** at **people**.
10.3a **Snapping** at **people: pitfall**.
10.3b To **snapping** at **people belongs** a **pitfall**.
10.IT **Not snapping** at **people. Growing**.

Snot, *YI*: mucus from the nose; snivel, whine.
45.6a/6b **Paying-tribute: sighs, tears, snot**.

Soak, *RU*: immerse, steep; damp, wet; stain, pollute, blemish; urinate on.
22.3a **Adorned thus, soaked thus**.
43.3a **Like soaked, possessing indignation**.
63.1a **Soaking one's tail**.
63.6a **Soaking one's head**.
63.6b **Soaking one's head, adversity**.
64.IM/IT **Soaking its tail**.
64.1a/1b **Soaking one's tail**.
64.6a **Soaking one's head**.
64.6b **Drinking liquor, soaking** the **head**.

Soar, *HAN*: fly high; rising sun; firebird with red plumage; white horse; long and hard feather; drawing brush. Ideogram: feathers and dawn.
22.4a A **white horse soaring thus**.
61.6a/6b A **soaring sound mounts tending-towards heaven**.

Sob, *TAO*: cry, weep aloud; wailing children. Ideogram: mouth and omen, ominous sounds.
13.5a **Concording people beforehand cry-out** and **sob and-also afterwards laugh**.
56.6a **Sojourning people beforehand laugh, afterwards cry-out sobbing**.

Soil, *WU*: moisten, soak; dirty, stain.
50.4a **One's form soiled, pitfall**.

Sojourn, *LÜ*: travel, stay in places other than your home; itinerant troops, temporary residents; visitor, guest, lodger. Ideogram: banner and people around it.

This term is the name of hexagram 56 and recurs throughout its texts. It also occurs in:

24.PW **Bargaining sojourners** used culminating sun **not** to **move**.

55.HP **Connecting** with **few**: **sojourning indeed**.

57.PS **Sojourning and-also lacking** a **place** for **tolerance**.

Solid, *GANG*: quality of the whole lines; firm, strong, unyielding, persisting.

This term frequently occurs in the Comments of the Transforming Lines and in the Image Tradition. It also occurs in:

1/2.HP **Energy**: **solid**.

43/44.HP The **supple meets** the **solid indeed**.

43/44.HP The **solid breaks-up** the **supple indeed**.

Solidify, *NING*: congeal, freeze, curdle, stiffen; coagulate, make solid or firm.

2.1b **Yin beginning solidification indeed**.

50.PW A **jun zi uses correcting** the **position** to **solidify fate**.

Solitary, *DI*: alone, single; isolated, abandoned.

4.4b **Solitude distancing substance indeed**.

9.5b **Not solitary affluence indeed**.

10.1b **Solitarily moving desire indeed**.

24.4a/4b The **center moving**, **solitary return**.

28.PW A **jun zi uses solitary establishing not** to **fear**.

35.1b **Solitary movement**: **correcting indeed**.

43.3a **Solitary going**, **meeting rain**.

Someone, *BI*: that, those, there; he, she, it, they; the other; exclude, leave out.

62.5a A **prince**'s **string-arrow grasps someone located** in a **cave**.

Son(hood), *ZI*: son, male child; heirs, offspring, posterity; living up to the ideal of the ancestors as highest human aspiration; seed, kernel, egg; sage, teacher; nadir, deepest point, midnight, midwinter.

3.2a **Woman** and **son**'s **Trial**: **not nursing**.

4.2a/2b The **son controls** the **household**.

7.5a/5b The **long-living son conducts** the **legions**.

7.5a/5b The **junior son carts corpses**.

14.3a/3b A **prince avails** of **Growing tending-towards heavenly sonhood**.

17.2a/2b **Tied** to the **small son**.

17.3a **Letting-go** the **small son**.

18.1a **Possessing sonhood**.

31.PS **Therefore afterwards possessing father** and **son**.

31.PS **Possessing father** and **son**.

32.5a The **husband** and the **son**, **pitfall**.

32.5b The **husband** and the **son**, **paring righteously**.

36.5a To the **Winnowing Son belongs brightness hidden**.

36.5b To the **Winnowing Son belongs Trial**.

36.IT The **Winnowing Son uses it**.

37.3a/3b The **wife**, the **son**, **giggling**, **giggling**.

37.IT The **father**, a **father**. The **son**, a **son**.

50.1a **Acquiring** a **concubine**, **using one's son**.

51.PS A **lord**'s **implements imply absolutely-nothing like** the **long-living son**.

53.1a The **small son**, **adversity**.

53.1b To the **small son belongs adversity**.

61.2a/2b **One's sonhood harmonizing** with **it**.

Soothe, *NINÇ*: calm, pacify; create peace of mind; tranquil, quiet. Ideogram: shelter above heart, dish and breath, physical and spiritual comfort.

1.IT The **myriad cities conjoining** to **soothe**.

3.IT **Proper installing feudatories and-also not soothing**.

8.IM/ IT **Not soothing**, on all **sides**

coming.
58.4a **Bargaining open, not-yet soothing.**

Sort, *LEI*: group according to kind, compare; species, class, genus; resemble; analog, like nature or purpose; norm, model.
2.IT The **female horse**: to the **earth sorted.**
2.IT **Thereupon associating: sorting movement.**
11/12.HP **Obstruction** and **compenetration: reversing one's sorting indeed.**
13.PW A **jun zi uses sorting** the **clans** to **mark-off** the **beings.**
27.2b **Movement letting-go sorting indeed.**
38.IT The **myriad beings: polarizing and-also their affairs sorted indeed.**
61.4b **Cutting-off, sorting above indeed.**

Soul, *GUI*: power that creates individual existence; union of volatile-soul, *HUN*, spiritual and intellectual power, and dense-soul, *PO*, bodily strength and movement. *HUN* rises after death, *PO* remains with the body and may communicate with the living.
15.IT **Soul** and **spirit harm overfilling and-also bless humbling.**
38.6a **Carrying souls**: the **one chariot.**
55.IT **Even-more with-respect-to reaching soul** and **spirit.**
63.3a The **High Ancestor subjugates souls** on all **sides.**
64.4a The **shake avails** of **subjugating souls** on all **sides.**

Sound, *YIN*: any sound; tone, resonance; pronunciation of words. Ideogram: words and hold in the mouth, vocal sound.
61.6a/6b A **soaring sound mounts tending-towards heaven.**
62.IM/ IT To the **flying bird abandoning belongs** a **sound.**

South, *NAN*: southern direction, corresponds to noon, summer and the Fiery Moment in the Universal Compass; culmination of the Yang hemicycle; reference point of compass; true principles and correct decisions; rulers face South when in their governing function.
See also: **Western South**
36.3a **Brightness hidden tends-towards** the **Southern hounding.**
36.3b To the **Southern hounding belongs purpose.**
46.IM/ IT The **South: disciplining, significant.**

Space, *KUN*: surface of the world; support of all existence, manifestation of Yin, where Energy or Yang activates all creation and destruction; all-involving service; earth; moon, wife, mother; rest, receptivity, docile obedience. Ideogram: terrestrial globe and stretch out. *Symbol*: earth, *DI*; the earth, ground on which the human world rests; basis of all things, nourishes all things; essential Yin. *Action*: yield, *SHUN*: give way, comply, agree, follow, obey; docile, flexible; bear produce, nourish, provide.
This term is the name of hexagram 2 and recurs throughout its texts. It also occurs in:
1.HP **Space: supple.**

Spill, *MI*: pour out; disperse, spread; waste, overturn; showy, extravagant.
61.2a **Myself associating: simply spilling it.**

Spirit, *SHEN*: spiritual power that confers intensity on heart and mind by acting on the soul, *GUI*; vitality, energy; spirits, ancestors, gods.
15.IT **Soul** and **spirit harm overfilling and-also bless humbling.**
20.IT **Overseeing** the **spirit dao belonging** to **heaven.**
20.IT The **wise person uses spirit dao** to **set-up teaching.**
55.IT **Even-more with-respect-to reaching soul** and **spirit.**

Splendor, *RONG*: flowering, luxuriant; glory, elegance, honor, beauty; elaborately carved corners of a temple roof.

12.PW And **not permitting splendor** in **using benefits**.

Split-off, *SI*: lop off, split with an ax, rive; white (color eliminated). Ideogram: ax and possessive, splitting what belongs together.

40.4a **Partnering culminating, splitting-off conforming**.

56.1a **Splitting-off one's place**: **grasping calamity**.

Spokes, *FU*: braces that connect hub and rim of wheel.

9.3a **Carting**: **stimulating** the **spokes**.

Spout, *TENG*: spurt, burst forth; open mouth, loud talk.

31.6b The **spouting mouth stimulating indeed**.

Spread, *SHI*: expand, diffuse, distribute, arrange, exhibit; add to; aid. Ideogram: flag and indeed, claiming new country.

1.2b **Actualizing-dao spreading throughout indeed**.

1.IT **Clouds moving, rain spreading**.

3.5b **Spreading, not-yet shining indeed**.

9.IT **Spreading, not-yet moving indeed**.

15.PW And **evaluating** the **beings** to **even spreading**.

27.4b **Above spreading shine indeed**.

42.IT **Heaven spreads, earth generates**.

43.PW A **jun zi uses spreading benefits extending** to the **below**.

44.PW The **crown prince uses spreading fate** to **command** the **four sides**.

Sprig, *TI*: tender new shoot of a tree, twig, new branch.

28.2a A **withered willow generates** a **sprig**.

Spring, *YUAN*: source, origin, head; arise, begin; first generating impulse; great, excellent; quality of springtime and East, first stage of the Time Cycle.

1.IT The **great**: **in-fact energy**'s **Spring**.

2.5a/5b A **yellow apron**. **Spring, significant**.

2.IT **Culminating in-fact**: **space**'s **Spring**.

6.5a/5b **Arguing**. **Spring significant**.

8.IM/ IT **Retracing** the **oracle-consulting**: **Spring, perpetual Trial**.

10.6a **One's recurring Spring, significant**.

10.6b **Spring**: **significance located above**.

11.5a/5b **Using satisfaction**: **Spring, significant**.

14.IM **Spring, Growing**.

14.IT **That uses Spring, Growing**.

18.IM **Decay**. **Spring, Growing**.

18.IT **Decay**: **Spring, Growing, and-also below heaven regulated indeed**.

24.1a **Spring, significant**.

26.4a **Spring, significant**.

26.4b **Six** at **fourth**: **Spring, significant**.

30.2a/2b **Yellow radiance**. **Spring, significant**.

38.4a **Meeting Spring, husbanding**.

41.IM/5a/ IT **Spring, significant**.

41.5b **Six** at **fifth**: **Spring, significant**.

42.1a **Spring, significant**.

42.1b **Spring, significant, without fault**.

42.5a **No question, Spring significant**.

45.5a **Spring, perpetual Trial**.

46.IM **Ascending**. **Spring, Growing**.

48.6a **Possessing conformity**: **Spring, significant**.

48.6b **Spring, significance located above**.

50.IM The **vessel**. **Spring, significant**.

50.IT **That uses Spring, Growing**.

59.4a/4b **Dispersing one's flock**: **Spring, significant**.

Spring, Growing, Harvesting, Trial, *YUAN HENG LI ZHEN*: Spring, Growing, Harvesting and Trial are the four stages of the Time Cycle, the model for all dynamic processes. They indicate that your question is connected to the

cycle as a whole rather than a part of it.
1.IM **Energy. Spring, Growing, Harvesting, Trial.**
2.IM **Space. Spring, Growing, Harvesting, Trial belonging** to the **female horse.**
3.IM **Sprouting. Spring, Growing, Harvesting, Trial.**
17.IM **Spring, Growing, Harvesting, Trial.**
19.IM **Nearing. Spring, Growing, Harvesting, Trial.**
25.IM **Spring, Growing, Harvesting, Trial.**
49.IM **Spring, Growing, Harvesting, Trial.**

Springwater, *QUAN*: source, spring, fountain, headwaters of a river. Ideogram: water and white, pure water at the source.
4.PW **Below** the **mountain emerges springwater. Enveloping.**
48.5a **Cold springwater taken-in.**
48.5b To **cold springwater belongs taking-in.**

Sprout, *ZHUN*: beginning of growth; collect, assemble, accumulate; difficulty, hardship. Ideogram: sprout piercing hard soil.
This term is the name of hexagram 3 and recurs throughout its texts. It also occurs in:
4.HP **Sprouting: viewing and-also not letting-go one's residing.**

Squint, *MIAO*: look at with one eye; one-eyed; obstructed vision; glance at.
10.3a/3b **Squinting enables observing.**
54.2a **Squinting enables observing.**

Stability, *CHI*: firmness, solidity; prepare, arrange; careful, respectful.
17/18.HP **Decay:** by **consequence stability indeed.**

Stable, *GU*: shed or pen for cattle and horses.
26.4a To **youthful cattle belongs** a **stable.**

Stag, *LU*: mature male deer with horns.
3.3a/3b **Approaching** a **stag: lacking precaution.**

Stand, *ZU*: base, foot, leg; rest on, support; stance; sufficient, capable, worth. Ideogram: foot and calf resting.
6.6b **Truly not standing respectfully indeed.**
10.3b **Not** the **stand** to **use possessing brightness indeed.**
10.3b **Not** the **stand** to **use associating** with **movement indeed.**
23.1a/1b **Stripping** the **bed, using** the **stand.**
27.1b **Truly not** a **stand** for **valuing indeed.**
50.4a The **vessel's severed stand.**

Standard, *ZHENG*: rule, principle; adjust, correct; measure, limit; musical interval.
22.PW A **jun zi uses brightening** the **multitude** of **standards without daring** to **sever litigations.**

Star thistles, *JI LI*: spiny weeds; caltrops, metal snares.
47.3a/3b **Seizing tending-towards star thistles.**

Staunch, *DU*: firm, solid, reliable; pure, sincere, honest; consolidate, establish.
26.IT **Solid persisting: staunch substance, resplendent shining.**

Steps, *JIE*: steps of stairs leading to a gate or hall; grade, degree, rank; ascend, rise.
46.5a/5b **Trial, significant: ascending steps.**

Stew, *SU*: cooked or boiled rice and meat; mixed contents of a pot.
50.4a/4b **Overthrowing** a **princely stew.**

Still, *JING*: peaceful, quiet, at rest, silent, imperturbable.
52.IT **Stirring-up, stilling, not letting-go one's season.**

Stimulate, *SHUO*: rouse to action and good feeling; stir up, urge on; exhort, persuade; say, tell, relate; cheer, delight; joyous, peaceful, restful; Action of the trigram Open, *DUI*. Ideogram: words and exchange.
4.1a **Availing** of **stimulating**

shackles to **fetter.**
9.3a **Carting: stimulating** the **spokes.**
10.IT **Stimulating and-also corresponding reaches energy.**
17.IT **Stirring-up and-also stimulating. Following.**
19.IT **Stimulating and-also yielding.**
26.2a/2b **Carting: stimulating** the **axle-bearing.**
28.IT **Root and-also stimulating movement.**
31.6b The **spouting mouth stimulating indeed.**
31.IT **Stopping and-also stimulating.**
33.2a To **abstaining belongs mastering stimulation.**
38.6a **Afterwards** to the **bow belongs stimulating.**
38.IT **Stimulating and-also congregating reaching brightness.**
42.IT The **commoners stimulated without delimiting.**
43.IT **Persisting and-also stimulating.**
45.IT **Yielding uses stimulating.**
47.5a/5b **Thereupon ambling possesses stimulating.**
47.IT **Venturing uses stimulating.**
49.IT **Pattern brightening uses stimulating.**
54.IT **Stimulating uses stirring-up.**
58.PS **Entering and-also afterwards stimulating it.**
58.PS The **open implies stimulating indeed.**
58.IT The **open: stimulating indeed.**
58.IT **Stimulating uses Harvesting, Trial.**
58.IT **Stimulating uses beforehand** the **commoners.**
58.IT **Stimulating uses opposing heaviness.**
58.IT To **stimulating belongs** the **great.**
59.PS **Stimulating and-also afterwards scattering it.**
60.IT **Stimulating uses moving** and **venturing.**
61.IT **Stimulating and-also** the **root: conforming.**

Stir-up, *DONG*: excite, influence, move, affect; work, take action; come out of the egg or the bud; Action of the trigram Shake, *ZHEN*. Ideogram: strength and heavy, move weighty things.
2.2b To **six** at **second belongs stirring-up.**
3.IT **Stirring-up reaches** to **venturing's center.**
3.IT To **thunder** and **rain belongs stirring-up: plenitude overfilled.**
16.IT **Providing uses stirring-up. Providing.**
16.IT **Providing: yielding uses stirring-up.**
16.IT **Heaven** and **earth use yielding** and **stirring-up.**
16.IT The **wise person uses yielding** and **stirring-up.**
17.IT **Stirring-up and-also stimulating. Following.**
21.IT **Stirring-up and-also brightening.**
24.IT **Stirring-up and-also using yielding movement.**
25.IT **Stirring-up and-also persisting.**
28.PS **Not nourished**, by **consequence not permitted stirring-up.**
32.IT **Root and-also stirring-up.**
34.IT The **solid uses stirring-up. Anterior vigor.**
38.IT **Fire stirring-up and-also above.**
38.IT **Pond stirring-up and-also below.**
40.IT **Unraveling. Venturing uses stirring-up.**
40.IT **Stirring-up and-also evading reaching venturing. Unraveling.**
42.IT **Augmenting: stirring-up and-also** the **root.**
47.6a **Named: stirring-up repenting possesses repenting.**
47.6b **Stirring-up repenting possesses repenting.**
51.PS The **shake implies stirring-up indeed.**
52.PS **Beings not permitted** to **use completing stirring-up.**
52.IT **Stirring-up, stilling, not letting-go one's season.**

53.IT **Stirring-up not exhausted indeed.**
54.IT **Stimulating uses stirring-up.**
55.IT **Brightness uses stirring-up. Anterior abounding.**

Stone, *PAN*: large conspicuous rock, foundation stone; stable, immovable.
3.1a A **stone pillar.**
3.1b **Although** a **stone pillar, purpose moving correctly indeed.**
53.2a The **swan infiltrating tending-towards** the **stone.**

Stop, *ZHI*: bring or come to a standstill, cease, terminate; Action of the trigram Bound, *GEN*. Ideogram: a foot stops walking.
4.IT **Venturing and-also stopping. Enveloping.**
18.IT **Root and-also stopping. Decay.**
22.IT **Pattern**'s **brightness uses stopping.**
23.IT **Yielding and-also stopping it.**
26.IT **Able** to **stop** and **persist.**
31.IT **Stopping and-also stimulating.**
33/34.HP The **great**'s **vigor**: by **consequence stopping.**
39.IT **Viewing venturing and-also able** to **stop.**
51/52.HP The **bound: stopping indeed.**
52.PS **Stopping it.**
52.PS The **bound implies stopping indeed.**
52.4b **Stopping relates** to the **body indeed.**
52.IT The **bound: stopping indeed.**
52.IT The **season stopping**, by **consequence stopping.**
52.IT The **bound: one's stopping.**
52.IT **Stopping** at **one's place indeed.**
53.PS **Beings not permitted** to **use completing stopping.**
53.IT **Stopping and-also** the **root.**
56.IT **Stopping and-also congregating reaches brightness.**
59/60.HP **Articulating: stopping indeed.**
63.IT **Completing: stopping**, by **consequence disarray.**

Stow, *SHE*: set aside, put away, store, keep; halt, rest in; lodge, hut.
3.3a A **jun zi: hint not thus stowed** away.
3.3b A **jun zi stowing it: going, abashment, exhaustion indeed.**
8.5b **Stowing** away **revolt, grasping yielding.**
17.3b **Purpose: stowing** away the **below indeed.**
22.1a/1b **Stowing** the **chariot and-also afoot.**
27.1a **Stowing simply** the **magic tortoise.**
44.5b **Purpose: not stowing** away **fate indeed.**
48.1b The **season stowed** away **indeed.**

Straighten, *ZHI*: rectify; upright; correct the crooked; proceed directly; sincere, just; blunt, outspoken.
2.2a **Straightening** on all **sides**: the **great.**
2.2b **Straightening used** on all **sides indeed.**
13.5b **Using** the **center: straightening indeed.**
47.5b **Using** the **center: straightening indeed.**

Stranded ropes, *HUI MO*: three-stranded ropes; royal garments; beautiful, honorable.
29.6a **Tied availing** of **stranded ropes.**

Stray, *TE*: wander, deviate, err; alter; doubt; excess.
16.IT **And-also** the **four seasons not straying.**
20.IT **And-also** the **four seasons not straying.**

Stream, *SHUI*: flowing water; river, tide, flood; fluid, dissolving; Symbol of the trigram Gorge, *KAN*. Ideogram: rippling water.
6.PW **Heaven associated** with **stream: contradicting movements. Arguing.**
7.PW The **earth**'s **center possesses stream.** The **legions.**
8.PW The **earth possesses stream above. Grouping.**

29.PW **Streams reiterated culminate. Repeated gorge.**
29.IT **Stream diffusing and-also not overfilling.**
39.PW The **mountain possesses stream above. Limping.**
47.PW **Pond without stream. Confining.**
48.PW **Wood possesses stream above.** The **well.**
48.IT **Root reaching stream and-also stream above.** The **well.**
49.IT **Skinning. Stream** and **fire reciprocally** giving **pause.**
59.PW **Wind moves above stream. Dispersing.**
60.PW The **pond possesses stream above. Articulating.**
63.PW **Stream located above fire. Already fording.**
64.PW **Fire located above stream. Not-yet fording.**

Street, *XIANG*: public space between dwellings, public square; side-street, alley, lane. Ideogram: place and public.
38.2a/2b **Meeting** a **lord tending-towards** the **street.**

Strength, *QIANG*: force, vigor; fortify, invigorate; compel, rely on force; overcome; effort, labor; determined, stubborn.
1.PW A **jun zi uses originating strength not** to **pause.**

Stretch, *ZHANG*: draw a bow taut; open, extend, spread, display.
38.6a **Beforehand** to the **bow belongs stretching.**

Stricken, *YAO*: afflicted by fate; untimely, premature death; bend, break; suffer a wrong. Ideogram: great with a broken point, interrupted growth.
38.3a **One's person stricken, moreover nose-cut.**

String-arrow, *YI*: arrow with string attached used to retrieve what is shot; seize, appropriate; arrest a criminal.
62.5a A **prince's string-arrow grasps someone located** in a **cave.**

Strip, *BO*: flay, peel, skin; remove, uncover; split, slice; reduce to essentials; degrade, decay; slaughter an animal. Ideogram: knife and carve, trenchant action.
This term is the name of hexagram 23 and recurs throughout its texts. It also occurs in:
24.PS **Stripping exhausted above, reversing below.**
24.HP **Stripping: rotten indeed.**
58.5a/5b **Conformity tending-towards stripping.**

Struggle, *ZHAN*: battle, fight, combat; hostilities; alarmed, terrified.
2.6a/6b **Dragons struggle tending-towards** the **countryside.**

Stump, *ZHU*: trunk, bole, stalk; wooden post; keep down, degrade.
47.1a The **sacrum confined tending-towards** a **wooden stump.**

Subjugate, *FA*: hit, cut; submit, make dependent; chastise rebels, subject to rule. Ideogram: man and lance, armed soldiers.
15.5a/5b **Harvesting: availing** of **encroaching** and **subjugating.**
35.6a/6b **Holding-fast avails** of **subjugating** the **capital.**
63.3a The **High Ancestor subjugates souls** on all **sides.**
64.4a The **shake avails** of **subjugating souls** on all **sides.**

Submerge, *MIE*: put out a fire, exterminate; plunge under water, sink, perish. Ideogram: water and destroy.
21.1a/1b **Shoes locked-up, submerged feet.**
21.2a/2b **Gnawing flesh, submerging** the **nose.**
21.6a/6b **Is** not **locking-up submerging** the **ears?**
23.1b **Using submerging below indeed.**
28.PW The **pond submerges wood.** The **great exceeding.**
28.6a **Exceeding wading, submerging** the **peak. Pitfall.**

Submit, *FU*: yield, obey, acquiesce; enforce obedience.
6.6b **Using arguing acquiesces** in **submitting.**
15.3b The **myriad commoners submit indeed.**

15.5b **Disciplining, not submitting indeed.**
16.IT By **consequence punishing flogging purifies and-also** the **commoners submit.**
20.IT **And-also below heaven submits actually.**

Substance, *SHI*: fullness, richness; essence; real, solid, consistent; results, fruits, possessions; honest, sincere. Ideogram: string of coins under a roof, wealth in the house.
4.4b **Solitude distancing substance indeed.**
11.4b **Altogether letting-go** the **substance indeed.**
26.IT **Solid persisting: staunch substance, resplendent shining.**
27.IM/ IT The **origin** of **seeking mouth's substance.**
39.4b **Appropriate position: substance indeed.**
50.2a/2b The **vessel possesses substance.**
50.5b The **center uses activating substance indeed.**
54.6a A **woman receives** a **basket without substance.**
54.6b **Six above: without substance.**
63.5a/5b **Substance: acquiescing** in **one's blessing.**

Suburbs, *JIAO*: area adjoining a city where human constructions and nature interpenetrate; second of the territorial zones: city, suburbs, countryside, forest.
5.1a/1b **Attending tending-towards** the **suburbs.**
9.IM/ IT **Originating** from **my Western suburbs.**
13.6a/6b **Concording people tend-towards** the **suburbs.**
62.5a **Originating** from **my Western suburbs.**

Subvert, *JING*: overturn, overthrow; leaning, falling; pour out, empty. Ideogram: man, head and ladle, emptying out old ideas.
12.6a **Subverting** the **obstruction.**
12.6b **Obstruction completed**, by **consequence subverting.**

Suddenly, *ZAN*: quick, prompt, abrupt; collect together. Ideogram: clasp used to gather the hair.
16.4a **Partners join-together suddenly.**

Suit, *DUI*: correspond to, agree with; consistent; pair; parallel sentences in poetic language.
25.PW The **earlier kings used** the **luxuriance suiting** the **season** to **nurture** the **myriad beings.**

Sun/day, see **Day/sun**

Supervise, *LI*: oversee, inspect, administer; visit subordinates.
36.PW A **jun zi uses supervising** the **crowds availing** of **darkening and-also brightening.**

Supple, *ROU*: quality of the opened lines; flexible, pliant, adaptable, tender.
This term frequently occurs in the Comments of the Transforming Lines and in the Image Tradition. It also occurs in:
1/2.HP **Space: supple.**
43/44.HP The **supple meets** the **solid indeed.**

Supreme, *DI*: highest, above all on earth; sovereign, lord, emperor.
10.IT **Treading** on the **supreme position and-also not disheartened.**
11.5a **Supreme Burgeoning converting maidenhood.**
42.2a The **king avails** of **presenting tending-towards** the **supreme, significant.**
54.5a/5b The **supreme burgeoning converting maidenhood.**
59.PW The **earlier kings used presenting tending-towards** the **supreme** to **establish** the **temples.**

Supreme Above, *SHANG DI*: highest power in universe.
16.PW To **exalting worship belongs** the **supreme above.**
50.IT The **wise person's Growing uses presenting** to the **supreme above.**

Surely, *GAI*: the preceding statement is undoubtedly true.

16.AT **Surely grasping relates** to **providing.**

Surpass, *YOU*: exceed, transgress; beyond measure, extraordinary; blame.

22.4b **Completing without surpassing indeed.**

23.5b **Completing without surpassing indeed.**

26.2b The **center, without surpassing indeed.**

39.2b **Completing without surpassing indeed.**

50.2b **Completing without surpassing indeed.**

56.2b **Completing without surpassing indeed.**

Swallow, *YAN*: house swallow, martin, swift; retired from official life; ease, peace; feast; relation between elder and younger brother.

61.1a **Possessing** a **burden, not** a **swallow.**

Swan, *HONG*: large white water bird, wild swan, wild goose; symbol of the soul and its spiritual aspirations; emblem of conjugal fidelity; messenger; strong, vast, profound, far-reaching.

53.1a The **swan infiltrating tending-towards** the **barrier.**

53.2a The **swan infiltrating tending-towards** the **stone.**

53.3a/6a The **swan infiltrating tending-towards** the **highlands.**

53.4a The **swan infiltrating tending-towards** the **trees.**

53.5a The **swan infiltrating tending-towards** the **mound.**

Sweat, *HAN*: perspiration; labor, trouble. Dispersing sweat, *HUAN HAN*, denotes an irrevocable decision (just as sweat cannot be reabsorbed).

59.5a **Dispersing sweat: one's great cries-out.**

Sweet, *GAN*: one of the five tastes: sour, bitter, sweet, acrid and salty; agreeable, pleasant, delightful, refreshing; corresponding to the Earthy Moment.

19.3a/3b **Sweetness nearing.**

60.5a **Sweet articulating, significant.**

60.5b To **sweet articulating belongs significance.**

Swiftly, *CHUAN*: quickly; hurry, hasten.

41.1a/1b **Climaxing affairs, swiftly going.**

41.4a **Commissioning swiftly possesses joy.**

Symbol, *XIANG*: image invested with magic connecting visible and invisible; figure, form, shape, likeness; pattern, model; act, play, write. Ideogram: elephant (in ancient times the bones of a dead elephant used to be assembled to look like the living animal).

23.IT **Overseeing symbols indeed.**

50.IT The **vessel.** A **symbol indeed.**

62.IT **Possessing** the **symbol belonging** to the **flying bird in-truth.**

Tail, *WEI*: animal's tail; end, last, extreme, remnant.

See also: **Bushy-tailed rodent**

10.IM/3a/4a **Treading** on a **tiger**'s **tail.**

10.IT **That uses treading** on a **tiger**'s **tail.**

33.1a **Retiring**'s **tail, adversity.**

33.1b To **retiring**'s **tail belongs adversity.**

63.1a **Soaking one's tail.**

64.IM/IT **Soaking its tail.**

64.1a/1b **Soaking one's tail.**

Take-in, *SHI*: eat, drink, ingest, absorb, incorporate; food, nourishment.

5.PS **Attending implies** the **dao belonging** to **drinking** and **taking-in.**

5.PW A **jun zi uses drinking** and **taking-in** to **repose delightfully.**

5.5a **Attending tending-towards taking-in liquor.**

5.5b **Taking-in liquor: Trial, significant.**

6.PS **Drinking** and **taking-in necessarily possess arguing.**

6.3a/3b **Taking-in** the **ancients' actualizing-dao.**

11.3a **Tending-towards taking-in possesses blessing.**

21/22.HP **Gnawing** and **biting:**

taking-in indeed.
23.6a The **ripe fruit not taken-in.**
26.IM/ IT **Not** in the **household taking-in. Significant.**
27.PW And **articulation** in **drinking** and **taking-in.**
36.1a **Three days not taking-in.**
36.1b **Righteously not taking-in indeed.**
47.2a/2b **Confinement tending-towards liquor taking-in.**
48.1a/1b The **well**: a **bog, not taking-in.**
48.3a/3b The **well**: **oozing, not taking-in.**
48.5a **Cold springwater taken-in.**
48.5b To **cold springwater belongs taking-in.**
50.3a The **pheasant's juice not taken-in.**
53.2a/2b **Drinking** and **taking-in**: **feasting, feasting.**
55.IT The **moon overfilling**, by **consequence taken-in.**

Tatters, *RU*: worn-out garments, used for padding or stopping leaks.
63.4a A **token**: **possessing clothes** in **tatters.**

Teach, *JIAO*: instruct, educate, direct, guide; school, doctrine.
19.PW A **jun zi uses teaching** to **ponder without exhausting.**
20.PW The **earlier kings used inspecting** on all **sides** and **overseeing** the **commoners** to **set-up teaching.**
20.IT The **wise person uses spirit dao** to **set-up teaching.**
29.PW And **repetition** to **teach affairs.**

Team, *PI*: pair, couple; fellow, mate; connect, associate; matched horses.
61.4a/4b The **horse team extinguished.**

Tears, *TI*: tears; weep, cry.
30.5a **Emerging tears like gushing.**
45.6a/6b **Paying-tribute**: **sighs, tears, snot.**

Temple, *MIAO*: building used to honor gods and ancestors.
45.IM/ IT The **king imagines possessing** a **temple.**
51.IT **Emerging permits using guarding** the **ancestral temple**, the **field-altar**, the **offertory-millet.**
59.IM/IT The **king imagines possessing** a **temple.**
59.PW The **earlier kings used presenting tending-towards** the **supreme** to **establish** the **temples.**

Ten, *SHI*: number ten; goal and end of reckoning; whole, complete, all; entire, perfected. Ideogram: East–West line crosses North–South line, a grid that contains all.
3.2a/2b **Ten years, thereupon nursing.**
24.6a **Culminating tending-towards ten years not controlling disciplining.**
27.3a/3b **Ten years, no availing** of.
41.5a **Maybe** to **augmenting belongs ten.**
42.2a **Maybe** to **augmenting belongs ten.**

Tend-towards, *YU*: move toward without necessarily reaching, in the direction of.
This term occurs throughout the hexagram texts.

Term, *QI*: set time, fixed period, agreed date; limit, deadline; hope, ardent desire.
54.4a **Converting maidenhood overruns** the **term.**
54.4b To **overrunning** the **term belongs purpose.**

Terminate, *O*: stop, put an end to, bring to a standstill. Ideogram: go and why, no reason to move.
14.PW A **jun zi uses terminating hatred** to **display improvement.**

Terror, *QIAO*: look around in great alarm. Ideogram: eyes of bird trapped by a hand.
51.6a **Observing**: **terror, terror.**

Test, *SHI*: try, experiment; compare; use, employ.
25.5b **Not permitted testing indeed.**

That, *SHI*: refers to the preceding statement.

10.IT **That uses treading** on a **tiger**'s **tail.**
11.IT By **consequence** of **that heaven** and **earth mingling and-also** the **myriad beings interpenetrating indeed.**
12.IT By **consequence** of **that heaven** and **earth not mingling and-also** the **myriad beings not interpenetrating indeed.**
14.IT **That uses Spring, Growing.**
24.IT **That uses emerging, entering, without affliction.**
30.IT **That uses accumulating female cattle, significant indeed.**
31.IT **That uses Growing, Harvesting, Trial.**
35.IT **That uses** a **content feudatory availing** of **bestowing horses** to **enhance** the **multitudes.**
38.IT **That uses** the **small's affairs, significant.**
46.IT **That uses** the **great, Growing.**
48.IT **Ruining one's pitcher: that uses** a **pitfall indeed.**
50.IT **That uses Spring, Growing.**
52.IT **That uses not capturing one's individuality.**
56.IT **That uses** the **small, Growing.**
57.IT **That uses** the **small, Growing.**
58.IT **That uses yielding reaching heaven and-also correspondence reaching people.**
62.6a **That designates calamity** and **blunder.**
62.IT **That uses** the **small** in **affairs, significant indeed.**
62.IT **That uses not permitting** the **great** in **affairs indeed.**
64.6a **Possessing conformity: letting-go that.**

Thatch-grass, MAO: thick grass used for roofs of humble houses.
11.1a **Eradicating thatch-grass intertwisted.**
11.1b **Eradicating thatch-grass: disciplining, significant.**
12.1a **Eradicating thatch-grass intertwisted.**
12.1b **Eradicating thatch-grass: Trial, significant.**
28.1a/1b **Sacrificing avails** of **white thatch-grass.**

Therefore, *RAN*: thus, so it is; truly, certainly.
3.PS **Therefore afterwards** the **myriad beings' generation in-truth.**
10.PS **Beings accumulate, therefore afterwards possess codes.**
11.PS **Therefore afterwards peace.**
20.PS The **beings' great, therefore afterwards permitted overseeing.**
23.PS **Involved** in **embellishing, therefore afterwards Growing,** by **consequence used-up actually.**
26.PS **Possessing without entanglement, therefore afterwards permitted accumulating.**
27.PS **Beings accumulate, therefore afterwards permitted** to **nourish.**
30.1a **Treading, polishing therefore. Respecting it.**
31.PS **Therefore afterwards possessing** the **myriad beings.**
31.PS **Therefore afterwards possessing man** and **woman.**
31.PS **Therefore afterwards possessing husband** and **wife.**
31.PS **Therefore afterwards possessing father** and **son.**
31.PS **Therefore afterwards possessing chief** and **servant.**
31.PS **Therefore afterwards possessing above** and **below.**
31.PS **Therefore afterwards** the **codes' righteousness possesses** a **polishing place.**

Thereupon, *NAI*: on that ground, then, only then; finally; in spite of that.
1.IT **Thereupon primordial heaven.**
1.IT **Thereupon Harvesting, Trial.**
2.IT **Thereupon yielding receives heaven.**
2.IT **Thereupon associating: sorting movement.**
2.IT **Thereupon completing possesses reward.**
3.2a/2b **Ten years, thereupon nursing.**
9.IT **Thereupon Growing.**
17.6a **Thereupon adhering: holding-fast** to **it.**

28.IT **Thereupon Growing.**
29.IT **Thereupon using** the **solid** in the **center indeed.**
30.IT **Thereupon changes accomplished below heaven.**
36.3b **Thereupon acquiring** the **great indeed.**
40.IT **Thereupon acquiring** the **center indeed.**
42.IT **Woody dao, thereupon movement.**
43.IT **One's exposure thereupon shining indeed.**
43.IT The **place** to **honor thereupon exhausted indeed.**
43.IT The **solid long-living, thereupon completion indeed.**
45.1a/1b **Thereupon disarraying, thereupon clustering.**
45.2a **Conforming, thereupon Harvesting: availing** of **dedicating.**
46.2a **Conforming, thereupon Harvesting: availing** of **dedicating.**
47.5a/5b **Thereupon ambling possesses stimulating.**
47.IT **Honoring** the **mouth thereupon exhausted indeed.**
48.IT **Thereupon using** the **solid** in the **center indeed.**
49.IM **Skinning. Before-zenith sun, thereupon conformity.**
49.2a **Before-zenith sun, thereupon skinning it.**
49.IT **Before-zenith sun, thereupon conformity.**
49.IT **One's repenting thereupon extinguished.**
59.IT The **king thereupon located** in the **center indeed.**
61.IT **Thereupon changing** the **fiefdoms indeed.**
61.IT **Thereupon** the **correspondence reaches heaven indeed.**

They/their, *QI*: general third person pronoun and possessive adjective; also: one/one's, it/its, he/his, she/her.
This term occurs throughout the hexagram texts.

Thicket, *MANG*: high grass, underbrush, tangled vegetation; rustic, rude, socially inept.
13.3a/3b **Hiding-away weapons tending-towards** the **thickets.**

Thigh, *GU*: thigh; strand of a rope; part, section.
31.3a/3b **Conjunction** of **one's thighs.**
36.2a **Hiding tending-towards** the **left thigh.**

Think, *WEI*: consider, plan; consist in; and, also; just so, precisely.
3.3a **Thinking** of **entering tending-towards** the **forest's center.**

Thistle, see **Star thistles**

Thong, *GONG*: bind with thongs, secure; solid, firm; well-guarded.
49.1a **Thonging avails** of **skin belonging** to **yellow cattle.**
49.1b **Thonging avails** of **yellow cattle.**

Thread, *GUAN*: string together; string of a thousand coins; series, sequence.
23.5a **Threading fish.**

Three/thrice, *SAN*: number three; third time or place; active phases of a cycle; superlative; beginning of repetition (since one and two are entities in themselves).
4.IM/ IT **Twice, thrice: obscuring.**
5.6a **Possessing visitors belonging** to **not inviting: three people coming.**
6.2a **People, three hundred doors.**
6.6a **Completing dawn thrice depriving** of **it.**
7.2a/2b The **king thrice bestows fate.**
8.5a The **king avails** of **three beaters.**
13.3a/3b **Three year's-time not rising.**
18.IM/IT **Before seedburst three days.**
18.IM/IT **After seedburst three days.**
29.6a **Three year's-time, not acquiring.**
29.6b **Pitfall, three year's-time indeed.**
35.IM **Day-time sun thrice reflected.**
35.IT **Day-time sun thrice reflected**

indeed.
36.1a **Three days not taking-in.**
40.2a The **fields, capturing three foxes.**
41.3a **Three people moving.**
41.3b **Three** by **consequence doubtful indeed.**
47.1a **Three year's-time not encountering.**
49.3a/3b **Skinning word thrice drawing-near.**
53.5a The **wife, three year's-time not pregnant.**
55.6a **Three year's-time not encountering.**
57.4a/4b The **fields: capturing three kinds.**
57.5a **Before husking, three days.**
57.5a **After husking, three days.**
63.3a/3b **Three years controlling it.**
64.4a **Three years, possessing** a **donation tending-towards** the **great city.**

Throughout, *PU*: everywhere; universal, general; great, vast. Ideogram: sun and equal, equal to sunlight.
1.2b **Actualizing-dao spreading throughout indeed.**

Throw-out, *QI*: reject, discard, abandon, push aside; renounce, forget.
30.4a **Burning thus. Dying thus. Thrown-out thus.**

Thumb, see **Big-toe/thumb**

Thunder, *LEI*: thunder; arousing power emerging from the depth of the earth; Symbol of the trigram Shake, *ZHEN*.
3.PW **Clouds** and **thunder: sprouting.**
3.IT To **thunder** and **rain belongs stirring-up: plenitude overfilled.**
16.PW **Thunder emerges** from the **earth impetuously. Providing.**
17.PW The **pond** in the **center possesses thunder. Following.**
21.PW **Thunder** and **lightning: gnawing** and **biting.**
21.IT **Thunder** and **lightning uniting and-also composing.**
24.PW **Thunder located** in the **earth's center. Return.**
25.PW **Below heaven thunder moves. Beings associate without entanglement.**
27.PW The **mountain possesses thunder below.** The **jaws.**
32.PW **Thunder** and **wind. Persevering.**
32.IT **Thunder** and **wind reciprocally associating.**
34.PW **Thunder located above heaven.** The **great's vigor.**
40.PW **Thunder** and **rain arousing. Unraveling.**
40.IT **Heaven** and **earth unraveling and-also thunder** and **rain arousing.**
40.IT **Thunder** and **rain arousing and-also** the **hundred fruits, grasses, trees, altogether seedburst's boundary.**
42.PW **Wind** and **thunder. Augmenting.**
51.PW **Reiterated thunder.** The **shake.**
54.PW The **pond possesses thunder above. Converting maidenhood.**
55.PW **Thunder** and **lightning altogether culminating. Abounding.**
62.PW The **mountain possesses thunder above.** The **small exceeding.**

Thus, *RU*: as, in this way; comparable, similar.
3.2a **Sprouting thus, hindered thus.**
3.2a/4a/6a **Riding** a **horse, arraying thus.**
3.3a A **jun zi: hint not thus stowed** away.
3.6a/6b **Weeping, blood flowing thus.**
9.5a/5b **Possessing conformity, binding thus.**
14.5a **Your conforming: mingling thus.**
14.5a **Impressing thus. Significant.**
14.5b **Your conforming: mingling thus.**
14.5b To **impressing thus belongs significance.**
16.IT To **anterior heaven** and **earth** it **thus belongs.**
22.3a **Adorned thus, soaked thus.**

22.4a **Adorned thus, hoary thus.**
22.4a A **white horse soaring thus.**
30.4a **Assailing thus, its coming thus.**
30.4a **Burning thus. Dying thus. Thrown-out thus.**
30.4b **Assailing thus, its coming thus.**
35.1a/1b **Prospering thus, arresting thus.**
35.2a **Prospering thus, apprehensive thus.**
35.4a **Prospering, thus bushy-tailed rodents.**
37.6a **Possessing conformity, impressing thus.**
37.6b To **impressing thus belongs significance.**
45.3a **Clustering thus, lamenting thus.**
50.4b **Is** it **trustworthy thus indeed?**
54.5a/5b **not thus fine** the **sleeves belonging** to **one's junior-sister.**
61.5a/5b **Possessing conformity, binding thus.**
62.1b **Not permitted thus, is** it **indeed?**
62.3b **Pitfall thus,** it **is indeed!**
63.5a **Not thus** the **dedicated offering belonging** to the **Western neighbor.**
63.5b **Not thus** the **season belonging** to the **Western neighbor.**

Tie, *XI*: connect, attach, bind; devoted to; relatives. Ideogram: person and connect, ties between humans.
17.2a/2b **Tied** to the **small son.**
17.3a/3b **Tied** to the **respectable husband.**
17.6a/6b **Grappling ties** to **it.**
29.6a **Tied availing** of **stranded ropes.**
33.3a **Tied retiring. Possessing affliction, adversity.**
33.3b To **tied retiring belongs adversity.**

Tiger, *HU*: fierce king of animals; extreme Yang; opposed to and protecting against the demons of extreme Yin on the North–South axis of the Universal Compass.
10.IM/3a/4a **Treading** on a **tiger**'s **tail.**
10.IT **That uses treading** on a **tiger**'s **tail.**
27.4a A **tiger observing: glaring, glaring.**
49.5a/5b The **great** in the **person:** a **tiger transforming.**

Till, *GENG*: plow, cultivate; labor.
25.2a/2b **Not tilling** the **crop. Not clearing** the **plow-land.**

Tip, *MO*: outermost twig, growing end of a branch; last, most distant; secondary, insignificant.
28.IT **Base** and **tip fading indeed.**
31.5b The **purpose**'s **tip indeed.**

Together, *BING*: both at the same time, jointly, side to side. Ideogram: two people standing together.

See also: **Altogether, Join-together**
48.3a **Together acquiescing** in **one's blessing.**

Toil, *LAO*: hardship, labor; exert oneself, exhaust oneself; burdened, careworn; worthy actions. Ideogram: strength and fire.
15.3a/3b The **toil** of **humbling: jun zi.**
48.PW A **jun zi uses** the **toiling commoners** to **encourage reciprocity.**
58.IT The **commoners forget their toil.**

Token, *XU*: halves of a torn piece of silk which identify the bearers when joined.
63.4a A **token: possessing clothes** in **tatters.**

Tolerate, *RONG*: allow, contain, endure, bear; accept graciously. Ideogram: full stream bed, tolerating and containing.
7.PW A **jun zi uses tolerating** the **commoners** to **accumulate crowds.**
19.PW And **tolerating** to **protect** the **commoners without delimiting.**
30.4b **Without** a **place** of **tolerance indeed.**
32.3b **Without** a **place** to **tolerate indeed.**

57.PS **Sojourning and-also lacking** a **place** for **tolerance**.

Tongue, *SHE*: tongue; clapper in a bell; talkative, wordy.

31.6a/6b **Conjunction** of **one's jawbones, cheeks** and **tongue**.

Topple, *DIAN*: fall over because top-heavy; top, summit.

27/28.HP The **great exceeding**: **toppling indeed**.

27.2a **Toppling jaws**.

27.4a **Toppling jaws. Significant**.

27.4b To **toppling jaws belongs significance**.

50.1a/1b The **vessel**: **toppling** the **foot**.

Tortoise, *GUI*: turtles; armored animals, shells and shields; long-living; practice divination; image of the macrocosm: heaven, earth and between them the soft flesh of humans.

27.1a **Stowing simply** the **magic tortoise**.

41.5a To **partnering belongs** a **tortoise**.

42.2a To **partnering belongs** a **tortoise**.

Total, *FAN*: all, everything; the world.

42.IT **Dao belonging** to **total augmenting**.

Trailing creeper, *GE LEI*: lush, fast-growing plants; spread rapidly and widely; numerous progeny.

47.6a/6b **Confinement tending-towards trailing creepers**.

Transform, *BIAN*: abrupt, radical passage from one state to another; transformation of opened and whole lines into each other in hexagrams; contrasts with change, *HUA*, gradual mutation.

1.IT **Energy**'s **dao transforming** and **changing**.

15.IT **Earthly dao transforms overfilling and-also diffuses humbling**.

22.IT **Using scrutinizing** the **seasons' transformation**.

23.IT The **supple transforms** the **solid indeed**.

32.IT The **four seasons**: **transforming changes and-also enabling lasting** and **accomplishing**.

37.1b **Purpose not-yet transformed indeed**.

45.2b The **center not-yet transformed indeed**.

49.5a/5b The **great** in the **person**: a **tiger transforming**.

49.6a/6b A **jun zi**: a **leopard transforming**.

54.2b **Not-yet transforming constancy indeed**.

61.1b **Purpose not-yet transformed indeed**.

Tread, *LÜ*: walk a path or way; step, path, track; footsteps; course of the stars; appropriate action; virtue; salary, means of subsistence. Ideogram: body and repeating steps.

This term occurs in the name of hexagram 10 and recurs throughout its texts. It also occurs in:

2.1a **Treading frost, hard ice** as **culmination**.

2.1b **Treading frost, hard ice**.

9.HP **Treading**: **not abiding indeed**.

11.PS **Treading and-also compenetrating**.

30.1a **Treading, polishing therefore. Respecting it**.

30.1b To **treading** and **polishing belongs respect**.

34.PW A **jun zi uses no codes whatever, nowhere treading**.

54.1a **Halting enables treading**.

54.1b **Halting enables treading, significant**.

Tree, see **Wood/tree**

Trial, *ZHEN*: inquiry by divination and its result; righteous, firm; separating wheat from chaff; the kernel, the proven core; quality of winter and North, fourth stage of the Time Cycle. Ideogram: pearl and divin/ation.

1.IT **Thereupon Harvesting, Trial**.

2.IM **Peaceful Trial, significant**.

2.3a/3b **Containing composition permits Trial**.

2.7a **Harvesting perpetual Trial**.

2.7b **Availing** of **sixes**: **perpetual Trial**.

2.IT The supple yielding, Harvesting, Trial.
2.IT To peaceful Trial belongs significance.
3.1a Harvesting: residing in Trial.
3.2a Woman and son's Trial: not nursing.
3.5a The small: Trial, significant.
3.5a The great: Trial, pitfall.
3.IT The great: Growing, Trial.
4.IM Harvesting, Trial.
5.IM/IT Shining Growing, Trial, significant.
5.5a Trial, significant.
5.5b Taking-in liquor: Trial, significant.
6.3a Trial.
6.4a Retracting, peaceful Trial.
6.4b Retracting, peaceful Trial.
7.IM The legions. Trial.
7.5a Trial, pitfall.
7.IT Trial. Correcting indeed.
8.IM/IT Retracing the oracle-consulting: Spring, perpetual Trial.
8.2a/4a Trial, significant.
9.6a The wife's Trial: adversity.
10.2a/2b Shady people: Trial, significant.
10.5a/5b Parting, treading. Trial, adversity.
11.3a Drudgery: Trial, without fault.
11.6a Trial, abashment.
12.IM/IT Not harvesting: a jun zi's Trial.
12.1a Trial, significant.
12.1b Eradicating thatch-grass: Trial, significant.
13.IM Harvesting: a jun zi's Trial.
15.2a/2b Trial, significant.
16.2a Trial, significant.
16.2b Not completing the day, Trial, significant.
16.5a Trial, affliction.
16.5b Six at fifth: Trial, affliction.
17.1a Trial, significant.
17.3a Harvesting: residing in Trial.
17.4a Trial, pitfall.
17.IT The great Growing, Trial, without fault.
18.2a Not permitting Trial.
19.1a/1b Conjunction nearing: Trial, significant.
20.2a Harvesting: woman's Trial.
20.2b Peeping overseeing: woman's Trial.
21.4a Harvesting drudgery, Trial.
21.4b Harvesting drudgery, Trial: significant.
21.5a Trial, adversity.
21.5b Trial, adversity without fault.
22.3a Perpetual Trial, significant.
22.3b To perpetual Trial belongs significance.
23.1a/2a Discarding Trial, pitfall.
25.4a Permitting Trial.
25.4b Permitting Trial, without fault.
26.IM Harvesting, Trial.
26.3a Harvesting drudgery, Trial.
27.IM/IT The jaws. Trial, significant.
27.3a Rejecting the jaws. Trial, pitfall.
27.5a Residing in Trial, significant.
27.5b To residing in Trial belongs significance.
30.IM Harvesting, Trial.
31.IM Growing, Harvesting, Trial.
31.4a/4b Trial, significant. Repenting extinguished.
31.IT That uses Growing, Harvesting, Trial.
32.IM/IT Harvesting, Trial.
32.1a Diving persevering: Trial, pitfall.
32.3a Trial, abashment.
32.5a Persevering in one's actualizing-dao, Trial.
32.5b The wife's people: Trial, significant.
33.IM/IT The small, Harvesting, Trial.
33.5a/5b Excellent retiring, Trial, significant.
34.IM/IT The great's vigor. Harvesting, Trial.
34.2a Trial, significant.
34.2b Nine at second: Trial, significant.
34.3a Trial, adversity.
34.4a Trial, significant.
35.1a/2a Trial, significant.
35.4a Trial, adversity.
35.4b Bushy-tailed rodents: Trial, adversity.

35.6a **Trial, abashment.**
36.IM/IT **Harvesting: drudgery, Trial.**
36.3a **Not permitted affliction, Trial.**
36.5a **Harvesting, Trial.**
36.5b To the **Winnowing Son belongs Trial.**
37.IM **Household people. Harvesting: woman's Trial.**
37.2a **Trial, significant.**
39.IM **Trial, significant.**
39.IT **Appropriate position. Trial, significant.**
40.2a **Trial, significant.**
40.2b **Nine** at **second: Trial, significant.**
40.3a **Trial, abashment.**
41.IM/IT **Without fault, permitting Trial.**
41.2a **Harvesting, Trial.**
41.2b **Nine** at **second: Harvesting, Trial.**
41.6a **Trial, significant.**
42.2a **Perpetual Trial, significant.**
44.1a **Trial, significant.**
45.IM **Growing, Harvesting, Trial.**
45.5a **Spring, perpetual Trial.**
46.5a/5b **Trial, significant: ascending steps.**
46.6a **Harvesting:** to **tending-towards not pausing belongs Trial.**
47.IM/ IT **Trial:** the **great** in the **person, significant.**
49.3a **Trial, adversity.**
49.6a **Residing** in **Trial, significant.**
50.5a **Harvesting, Trial.**
52.1a **Harvesting: perpetual Trial.**
53.IM **Harvesting, Trial.**
54.2a/2b **Harvesting: Trial belonging** to **shady people.**
56.IM **Sojourning: Trial, significant.**
56.2a/2b **Acquiring** a **youthful vassal, Trial.**
56.3a **Trial, adversity.**
56.IT **Sojourning: Trial, significant indeed.**
57.1a/1b **Harvesting:** to **martial people belongs Trial.**
57.5a **Trial, significant.**
57.6a **Trial, pitfall.**
58.IM **Growing, Harvesting, Trial.**
58.IT **Stimulating uses Harvesting, Trial.**
59.IM **Harvesting, Trial.**
60.IM/IT **Bitter articulating not permitting Trial.**
60.6a/6b **Bitter articulating: Trial, pitfall.**
61.IM **Harvesting, Trial.**
61.6a **Trial, pitfall.**
61.IT The **center conforming uses Harvesting, Trial.**
62.IM **Harvesting, Trial.**
62.4a **No availing** of **perpetual Trial.**
62.IT **Exceeding uses Harvesting, Trial.**
63.IM/ IT **Harvesting, Trial.**
64.2a **Trial, significant.**
64.2b **Nine** at **second: Trial, significant.**
64.4a/4b **Trial, significant, repenting extinguished.**
64.5a **Trial, significant, without repenting.**

Truly, *YI*: in fact; also; nevertheless.
6.6b **Truly not standing respectfully indeed.**
8.3b **Not truly injuring reached.**
9.2b **Truly not** the **origin letting-go indeed.**
20.2b **Truly permitting** the **demoniac indeed.**
27.1b **Truly not** a **stand** for **valuing indeed.**
28.5b **Truly permitting** the **demoniac indeed.**
31.3b **Truly not abiding indeed.**
40.3b **Truly permitting** the **demoniac indeed.**
41.4b **Truly permitting joy indeed.**
48.IM/ IT **Muddy culmination: truly not-yet** the **well-rope** in the **well.**
56.3b **Truly using injury actually.**
64.1b **Truly not knowing** the **end indeed.**
64.6b **Truly not knowing articulation indeed.**

Trustworthy, *XIN*: truthful, faithful, consistent over time; count on, confide in; examine, verify, prove; loyalty, integrity. Ideogram: person and word, true speech.

14.5b **Trustworthiness uses shooting-forth purpose indeed.**

29.IT **Movement: venturing and-also not letting-go one's trustworthiness.**

43.4a/4b **Hearing words not trustworthy.**

47.IM/ IT **Possessing words not trustworthy.**

49.4b **Trustworthy purpose indeed.**

49.IT **Skinning and-also trusting it.**

50.4b **Is** it **trustworthy thus indeed?**

55.2b **Trustworthiness uses shooting-forth purpose indeed.**

58.2b **Trustworthy purpose indeed.**

61.PS **Articulating and-also trusting it.**

61/62.HP The **center conforming: trustworthiness indeed.**

61.IT **Trustworthiness extends** to **hog fish indeed.**

62.PS **Possessing one's trustworthiness implies necessarily moving it.**

Tumble, *YUN*: fall with a crash, fall from the sky; roll down.

44.5a/5b **Possessing tumbling originating** from **heaven.**

Turn, *XIANG*: direct your mind towards, face.

17.PW A **jun zi uses turning** to **darkness** to **enter** a **reposing pause.**

Turn-away, *GUAI*: turn your back on something and focus on its opposite; contradict, resist; part ways, separate oneself from; cunning, crafty; perverse.

38.PS **Household's dao exhausted, necessarily turning-away.**

38.PS **Polarizing implies turning-away indeed.**

39.PS **Turning-away necessarily possesses heaviness.**

Tusk, *YA*: animal's tooth.

26.5a To a **gelded pig belong tusks.**

Twice, *ZAI*: a second time, again; more, even more.

4.IM/ IT **Twice, thrice: obscuring.**

Twine, *SUO*: string or rope of many strands twisted together; tie up, bind together; ruling ideas, obligations; anxiety (twisted bowels).

51.6a/6b The **shake twining, twining.**

Twin-peaked, *QI*: mountain with two peaks; forked road; diverge, ambiguous. Ideogram: mountain and branched. Twin-peaked Mountain, *QI SHAN*, is the ancestral shrine of the Zhou Dynasty.

46.4a/4b The **king avails** of **Growing tending-towards** the **twin-peaked mountain.**

Two, *ER*: number two; pair, even numbers, binary, duplicate.

2.2b To **six** at **second belongs stirring-up.**

3.2b To **six** at **second belongs heaviness.**

27.2b **Six** at **second: disciplining, pitfall.**

31.IT The **two agencies' influences correspond using reciprocal association.**

32.2b **Nine** at **second, repenting extinguished.**

34.2b **Nine** at **second: Trial, significant.**

36.2b To **six** at **second belongs significance.**

37.2b To **six** at **second belongs significance.**

38.IT **Two women concording: residing.**

40.2b **Nine** at **second: Trial, significant.**

41.IM/ IT **Two platters permit availing** of **presenting.**

41.2b **Nine** at **second: Harvesting, Trial.**

41.IT **Two platters corresponding possess** the **season.**

46.2b To **nine** at **second belongs conforming.**

49.IT **Two women concording, residing.**

64.2b **Nine** at **second: Trial, significant.**

Unconsidered, *GOU*: offhand, impromptu, improvised, careless; improper, illicit.

22.PS **Beings not permitted** to **use unconsidered uniting and-also climaxing**.

Understand, *CONG*: perceive quickly, astute, sharp; discriminate intelligently. Ideogram: ear and quick.

21.6b **Understanding not bright indeed**.

43.4b **Understanding not bright indeed**.

50.IT The **root and-also** the **ear** and the **eye: understanding bright**.

Uneven, *BEI*: any difference in level; bank, shore, dam, dike; inclined, tipped over; partial, unjust.

11.3a **Without evening, not unevening**.

Unite, *HE*: join, match, correspond; unison, harmony; together; close the jaws, shut the mouth. Ideogram: mouths speaking in unison.

1.IT **Protection: uniting** with the **great**'s **harmony**.

2.IT **Actualizing-dao unites without delimiting**.

9.4b **Above uniting purposes indeed**.

21.PS **Permitted overseeing and-also afterwards possessing** a **place** to **unite**.

21.PS **Gnawing** and **biting imply uniting indeed**.

21.IT **Thunder** and **lightning uniting and-also composing**.

22.PS **Beings not permitted** to **use unconsidered uniting and-also climaxing**.

26.3b **Above uniting purposes indeed**.

41.1b **Honoring uniting purposes indeed**.

46.1b **Above uniting purposes indeed**.

Unravel, *XIE*: disjoin, untie, disperse, dissolve, release; analyze, explain, understand; dispel sorrow, eliminate effects, solve problems; solution, deliverance.

This term is the name of hexagram 40 and recurs throughout its texts. It also occurs in:

39.HP **Unraveling: delay indeed**.

Unsteady and unsettled, *NIE WU*: unstable; uncertain; agitated.

47.6a **Tending-towards** the **unsteady** and **unsettled**.

Use, *YI*: by means of; owing to; make use of, employ.

This term occurs throughout the hexagram texts.

Use-up, *JIN*: exhaust, use all; an empty vessel; extremity, limit.

23.PS **Involved** in **embellishing, therefore afterwards Growing**, by **consequence used-up actually**.

24.PS **Beings not permitted** to **use completing using-up**.

Value, *GUI*: regard as valuable, give worth and dignity to; precious, honorable, exalted, illustrious. Ideogram: cowries (coins) and basket.

3.1b **Using valuing** the **below** and the **mean**.

27.1b **Truly not** a **stand** for **valuing indeed**.

39.6b **Using adhering** to **value indeed**.

50.1b **Using adhering** to **value indeed**.

54.5b **Using valuing movement indeed**.

Vassal, *PU*: servant, menial, retainer; helper in heavy work; palace officers, chamberlains; follow, serve, belong to.

56.2a/2b **Acquiring** a **youthful vassal, Trial**.

56.3a **Losing one's youthful vassal**.

Veil, *FU*: screen on person or carriage; hair ornament; luxuriant, tangled vegetation that conceals the path.

63.2a A **wife loses her veil**.

Venerable, *LAO*: old, ancient; term of respect due to old age.

28.2a A **venerable husband acquires his woman consort**.

28.2b A **venerable husband** and a

woman consort.

28.5a A **venerable wife acquires her scholarly husband.**

28.5b A **venerable wife** and a **scholarly husband.**

Venture, *XIAN*: face a severe difficulty or obstruction; risk; precipice, cliff, abyss; key point, point of danger; Action of the trigram Gorge, *KAN*. Ideogram: mound and all, everything engaged at one point.

3.IT **Stirring-up reaches** to **venturing**'s **center.**

4.IT **Enveloping. Below mountain possesses venturing.**

4.IT **Venturing and-also stopping. Enveloping.**

5.IT **Venturing located** in **precedence indeed.**

6.IT **Arguing. Solid above, venture below.**

6.IT **Venturing and-also persisting. Arguing.**

7.IT **Moving: venturing and-also yielding.**

29.2a The **gorge possesses venturing.**

29.3a **Venturing, moreover reclining.**

29.IT **Redoubled venturing indeed.**

29.IT **Movement: venturing and-also not letting-go one's trustworthiness.**

29.IT **Heaven**'s **venture: not permitting ascending indeed.**

29.IT **Earth**'s **venture: mountains, rivers, hill-tops, mounds indeed.**

29.IT The **king** and the **princes set-up venturing used** to **guard their city.**

29.IT The **season belonging** to **venturing avails** of the **great actually in-fact.**

39.IT **Venturing located** in **precedence indeed.**

39.IT **Viewing venturing and-also able** to **stop.**

40.IT **Unraveling. Venturing uses stirring-up.**

40.IT **Stirring-up and-also evading reaching venturing. Unraveling.**

47.IT **Venturing uses stimulating.**

60.IT **Stimulating uses moving** and **venturing.**

Verily/very, *WEI*: the only; in truth; answer; acquiesce; yes.

3.PS **Overfilling** the **interspace belonging** to **heaven** and **earth implies verily** the **myriad beings.**

13.IT **Verily** a **jun zi activating enables interpenetration** of **purposes belonging** to **below heaven.**

47.IT **One's very jun zi reached.**

Versatility, *YI*: sudden and unpredictable change, and the mental mobility and openness required in order to face it; easy, light, simple; occurs in the name of the *Yi Jing*.

14.5b **Versatility and-also without preparing indeed.**

32.PW A **jun zi uses establishing, not versatility** on all **sides.**

34.5a/5b **Losing** the **goat, tending-towards versatility.**

41.AT **Diminishing: beforehand heaviness and-also afterwards versatility.**

56.6a/6b **Losing** the **cattle, tending-towards versatility.**

Vessel, *DING*: bronze cauldron with three feet and two ears, sacred vessel used to cook food for sacrifice to gods and ancestors; founding symbol of family or dynasty; hold, contain, transform; establish, secure; precious, noble.

This term is the name of hexagram 50 and recurs throughout its texts. It also occurs in:

49.HP The **vessel: grasping renewal indeed.**

View, *JIAN*: vision in all its aspects: seeing, being visible, forming mental images; visit, call on, consult. Ideogram: eye above person, active and receptive sight.

1.2a/2b **Viewing** a **dragon located** in the **fields.**

1.2a/5a **Harvesting: viewing** the **great** in the **person.**

1.7a **Viewing** a **flock** of **dragons without head.**

3/4.HP **Sprouting: viewing and-also**

not letting-go one's residing.
4.3a **Viewing** a **metallic husband.**
6.IM/ IT **Harvesting: viewing** the **great** in the **person.**
18.4a **Going, viewing abashment.**
24.IT **Return** to **one's viewing** the **heart belonging** to **heaven** and **earth reached.**
31.IT **And-also** the **motives belonging** to **heaven** and **earth**'s **myriad beings permit viewing actually.**
32.IT **And-also** the **motives belonging** to **heaven** and **earth**'s **myriad beings permit viewing actually.**
34.IT The **correct great and-also** the **motives belonging** to **heaven** and **earth permit viewing actually.**
38.1a/1b **Viewing hatred** in the **person.**
38.3a/3b **Viewing** the **cart pulled-back.**
38.6a **Viewing** a **pig bearing mire.**
39.IM/6a/6b/IT **Harvesting: viewing** the **great** in the **person.**
39.IT **Viewing venturing and-also able** to **stop.**
42.PW A **jun zi uses viewing improvement**, by **consequence shifting.**
44.1a **Viewing pitfall.**
45.IM **Harvesting: viewing** the **great** in the **person.**
45.IT **Harvesting: viewing** the **great** in the **person. Growing.**
45.IT **And-also** the **motives belonging** to **heaven** and **earth**'s **myriad beings permit viewing actually.**
46.IM **Availing** of **viewing** the **great** in the **person.**
46.IT **Availing** of **viewing** the **great** in the **person.**
47.3a/3b **Not viewing one's consort.**
52.IM **Not viewing one's people.**
52.IT **Moving one's chambers, not viewing one's people.**
55.2a/4a/4b The **sun** in the **center: viewing** a **bin.**
55.3a The **sun** in the **center: viewing froth.**
57.IM/IT **Harvesting: viewing** the **great** in the **person.**
57/58.HP The **open: viewing, and-also**

Vigor, *ZHUANG*: power, strength; energetic, robust, fully grown, flourishing, abundant; at the peak of age and form; inspirit, animate; damage through unrestrained strength. Ideogram: strength and scholar, intellectual impact. This term occurs in the name of hexagram 34 and recurs throughout its texts. It also occurs in:
33.HP The **great**'s **vigor**: by **consequence stopping.**
35.PS **Beings not permitted** to **use completing vigor.**
36.2a **Availing** of a **rescuing horse**'s **vigor, significant.**
43.1a The **vigor tends-towards** the **preceding foot.**
43.3a The **vigor tends-towards** the **cheek-bones.**
44.IM **Coupling. Woman**'s **vigor.**
59.1a **Availing** of a **rescuing horse**'s **vigor, significant.**

Violent, *BAO*: fierce, brutal, cruel; strike hard.
16.AT **Used** to **await violent visitors.**

Virtue, *ZANG*: goodness, generosity.
7.1a **Obstructing virtue: pitfall.**

Visitor, *KE*: guest; stranger, foreign, from afar; squatter; parasite; invader.
5.6a **Possessing visitors belonging** to **not inviting: three people coming.**
5.6b **Visitors belonging** to **not inviting come.**
16.AT **Used** to **await violent visitors.**

Wade, *SHE*: walk in or through a body of water. Ideogram: step and water.
28.6a **Exceeding wading, submerging** the **peak. Pitfall.**
28.6b To **exceeding wading belongs** a **pitfall.**

Wading the great river, *SHE DA CHUAN*: enter the stream of life with a goal or purpose; embark on a significant enterprise.

5.IM/ IT **Harvesting**: **wading** the **great river**.
6.IM/ IT **Not harvesting**: **wading** the **great river**.
13.IM/ IT **Harvesting**: **wading** the **great river**.
15.1a **Availing** of **wading** the **great river**.
18.IM/ IT **Harvesting**: **wading** the **great river**.
26.IM/ IT **Harvesting**: **wading** the **great river**.
27.5a **Not permitted** to **wade** the **great river**.
27.6a **Harvesting**: **wading** the **great river**.
42.IM/ IT **Harvesting**: **wading** the **great river**.
59.IM/ IT **Harvesting**: **wading** the **great river**.
61.IM/ IT **Harvesting**: **wading** the **great river**.
64.3a **Harvesting**: **wading** the **great river**.

Warn, *JIE*: alarm, alert, put on guard; caution, inform; guard against, refrain from. Ideogram: spear held in both hands, warning enemies.

11.4a/4b **Not warning**: **using conformity**.
45.PW And **warning**, **not precautions**.
51.6b The **dreading neighbor**, a **warning indeed**.
62.4a/4b **Going**: **adversity necessarily** a **warning**.
63.4a/4b **Completing** the **day**: a **warning**.

Wasteland, *HUANG*: wild, barren, deserted, unproductive land; jungle, moor, heath; reckless, neglectful.

11.2a **Enwrapped** in **wasteland**.
11.2b **Enwrapped** in **wasteland**, **acquiring honor tending-towards** the **center**: **movement**.

Watch-out, *SU*: warning; inform, relate; accuse; defend or prosecute a case in court.

10.4a/4b **Watch-out**! **Watch-out**! **Completing significant**.

Watercourse, *HE*: river, stream, running water.

11.2a **Availing** of **crossing** the **watercourse**.

Waver, *CHONG*: irresolute, hesitating, unsettled; fluctuate, sway to and fro.

31.4a/4b **Wavering**, **wavering**: **going**, **coming**.

Weapons, *RONG*: arms; armed people, soldiers; military, violent. Ideogram: spear and armor, offensive and defensive weapons.

13.3a/3b **Hiding-away weapons tending-towards** the **thickets**.
40.3b **Originating** from **my involvement** with **weapons**.
43.IM/IT **Not Harvesting**: **approaching weapons**.
43.2a At **night possessing weapons**.
43.2b **Possessing weapons**, **no cares**.
45.PW A **jun zi uses eliminating weapons** for **implements**.

Weariness, *BAI*: fatigue; debilitated, exhausted, distressed; weak.

33.3b **Possessing affliction**, **weariness indeed**.
63.3b **Weariness indeed**.

Weep, *QI*: lament wordlessly; grieved, heartbroken.

3.6a/6b **Weeping**, **blood flowing thus**.
61.3a **Maybe weeping**, **maybe singing**.

Well, *JING*: water well in the center of the fields; rise and flow of water in a well; life-water surging from the depths; found a capital city. Ideogram: two vertical lines crossing two horizontal ones, eight fields with equal access to a well in the center.

This term is the name of hexagram 48 and recurs throughout its texts. It also occurs in:

47.HP The **well**: **interpenetrating**, **and-also**
49.PS The **well's dao not permitting not skinning**.

Well-rope, *YU*: rope used to draw water.

48.IM/ IT **Muddy culmination**: **truly not-yet** the **well-rope** in the **well**.

West, *XI*: western direction, corresponding to autumn, Harvest, the Metallic Moment and the first phase of the Yin hemicycle of the Universal Compass.

9.IM/ IT **Originating** from **my Western suburbs**.

17.6a The **king avails** of **Growing tending-towards** the **Western mountain**.

62.5a **Originating** from **my Western suburbs**.

63.5a **Not thus** the **dedicated offering belonging** to the **Western neighbor**.

63.5b **Not thus** the **season belonging** to the **Western neighbor**.

Western South, *XI NAN*: corresponds to the neutral Earthy Moment between the Yang and Yin hemicycles; bring forth concrete results, ripe fruits of late summer.

2.IM/ IT **Western South**: **acquiring partnering**.

39.IM/ IT **Limping**. **Harvesting**: **Western South**.

40.IM/ IT **Unraveling**. **Harvesting**: **Western South**.

What?, *HE*: interjection: what? which? where? why? how? how can it be!

41.IM/ IT To **what belongs availing?**

Wheel, *LUN*: disk, circle, round; revolution, circuit; rotate, roll; by turns.

63.1a/1b **Pulling-back one's wheels**.

64.2a **Pulling-back one's wheels**.

White, *BO*: color associated with autumn, Harvest and the Metallic Moment; white hair, old age; clear, immaculate, plain, essential; color of death and mourning.

22.4a A **white horse soaring thus**.

22.6a **White adorning**.

22.6b **White adorning**, **without fault**.

28.1a/1b **Sacrificing avails** of **white thatch-grass**.

Whose, *SHUI*: relative and interrogative pronoun, often introducing a rhetorical question; anybody.

13.1b **Furthermore whose fault indeed?**

40.3b **Furthermore whose fault indeed?**

60.3b **Furthermore whose fault indeed?**

Wife, *FU*: position of married woman as head of the household; distinct from consort, *QI*, which denotes her legal status, and from concubine, *QIE*, secondary wife. Ideogram: woman, hand and broom, household duties.

4.2a **Letting-in** the **wife**, **significant**.

9.6a The **wife's Trial**: **adversity**.

28.5a A **venerable wife acquires her scholarly husband**.

28.5b A **venerable wife** and a **scholarly husband**.

31.PS **Therefore afterwards possessing husband** and **wife**.

31.PS **Possessing husband** and **wife**.

32.PS **Dao belonging** to **husband** and **wife**.

32.5a The **wife's people**, **significant**.

32.5b The **wife's people**: **Trial**, **significant**.

32.5b **Adhering** to the **wife**, **pitfall indeed**.

37.3a/3b The **wife**, the **son**, **giggling**, **giggling**.

37.IT The **husband**, a **husband**. The **wife**, a **wife**.

53.3a/3b The **wife pregnant**, **not nurturing**.

53.5a The **wife**, **three year's-time not pregnant**.

63.2a A **wife loses her veil**.

Wildfowl, *QIN*: birds; four-legged animals; hunt, shoot with an arrow; capture; prisoner.

3.3b **Using adhering** to **wildfowl indeed**.

7.5a The **fields possess wildfowl**.

8.5a/5b **Letting-go** the **preceding wildfowl**.

32.4a The **fields without wildfowl**.

32.4b **Peacefully acquiring wildfowl indeed**.

48.1a/1b The **ancient well without wildfowl**.

Willow, *YANG*: all fast growing trees: willow, poplar, tamarisk, aspen. Ideogram: tree and versatility.

28.2a A **withered willow generates** a **sprig**.

28.5a/5b A **withered willow generates flowers**.

Wind, *FENG*: wind, breeze, gust; weather and its influence on mood and humor; fashion, usage; wind and wood are the Symbols of the trigram Root, *SUN*.

9.PW **Wind moves above heaven**. The **small accumulating**.

18.PW The **mountain possesses wind below**. **Decay**.

20.PW **Wind moves above** the **earth**. **Overseeing**.

32.PW **Thunder** and **wind**. **Persevering**.

32.IT **Thunder** and **wind reciprocally associating**.

37.PW **Wind originating** from **fire emerging**. **Household people**.

42.PW **Wind** and **thunder**. **Augmenting**.

44.PW **Heaven possessing wind below**. **Coupling**.

57.PW **Following winds**. The **root**.

59.PW **Wind moves above stream**. **Dispersing**.

61.PW The **pond possesses wind above**. The **center conforming**.

Window, *YOU*: window; open, instruct, enlighten.

29.4a **Letting-in bonds originating** from the **window**.

Wine-cup, *JIAO*: libation cup originally in the form of a bird.

61.2a **I possess** a **loved wine-cup**.

Wings, *YI*: birds' wings; sails, flanks, side-rooms; shelter and defend.

36.1a **Drooping one's wings**.

Winnow, *JI*: separate grain from chaff by tossing it in the wind; sieve, winnowing-basket; separate the valuable from the worthless, good from bad.

36.5a To the **Winnowing Son belongs brightness hidden**.

36.5b To the **Winnowing Son belongs Trial**.

36.IT The **Winnowing Son uses it**.

Wise, *SHENG*: intuitive universal wisdom; profound understanding; mythical sages of old; holy, sacred, mark of highest distinction. Ideogram: ear and inform, one who knows all from a single sound.

4.IT **Wise achievement indeed**.

16.IT The **wise person uses yielding** and **stirring-up**.

20.IT The **wise person uses spirit dao** to **set-up teaching**.

27.IT The **wise person nourishes eminence used** to **extend** to the **myriad commoners**.

31.IT The **wise person influences people**'s **heart and-also below heaven harmonizes evenness**.

32.IT The **wise person**: **lasting with-respect-to one's dao and-also below heaven changing** and **accomplishing**.

50.IT The **wise person**'s **Growing uses presenting** to the **supreme above**.

50.IT **And-also** the **great**'s **Growing uses nourishing** the **wise** and the **eminent**.

Withdraw, *TUI*: draw back, retreat, recede; decline, refuse.

20.3a/3b **Overseeing my generation**: **advancing**, **withdrawing**.

33.PS **Retiring implies withdrawing indeed**.

33/34.HP **Retiring**: by **consequence withdrawing indeed**.

34.6a/6b **Not able** to **withdraw**, **not able** to **release**.

40.5b The **small** in the **person withdraws indeed**.

52.2b **Not-yet withdrawing** from **hearkening indeed**.

57.1a/1b **Advancing**, **withdrawing**.

Withered, *KU*: dried up, decayed, rotten; dry wood. Ideogram: tree and old.

28.2a A **withered willow generates** a **sprig**.

28.5a/5b A **withered willow generates flowers**.

Without, *WU*: devoid of; there is not.
This term occurs in the name of hexagram 25 and recurs throughout its texts. It also occurs in:

1.7a **Viewing** a **flock** of **dragons without head**.
2.3a **Without accomplishing, possessing completion**.
2.4a **Without fault, without praise**.
2.IT **Actualizing-dao unites without delimiting**.
2.IT **Moving** on the **earth without delimiting**.
2.IT **Corresponding** to the **earth without delimiting**.
3.3b **Approaching** a **stag without precaution**.
6.2a **Without blunder**.
6.3a **Without accomplishment**.
7.3b The **great without achievement indeed**.
8.6a/6b To **grouping belongs without** a **head**.
8.6b **Without** a **place** to **complete indeed**.
11.3a **Without evening, not unevening**.
11.3a/3b **Without going, not returning**.
12.IT **Above** and **below not mingling and-also below heaven without fiefdoms indeed**.
14.1a **Without mingling** with **harm**.
14.1b **Without mingling** with **harm indeed**.
14.5b **Versatility and-also without preparing indeed**.
17/18.HP **Following: without anteriority indeed**.
18.3a **Without** the **great, faulty**.
19.PW A **jun zi uses teaching** to **ponder without exhausting**.
19.PW And **tolerating** to **protect** the **commoners without delimiting**.
21/22.HP **Adorning: without complexion indeed**.
22.PW A **jun zi uses brightening** the **multitude** of **standards without daring** to **sever litigations**.
22.4b **Completing without surpassing indeed**.
23.5b **Completing without surpassing indeed**.
24.IM **Emerging, entering, without affliction**.
24.1a **Without merely repenting**.
24.IT **That uses emerging, entering, without affliction**.
26.PS **Possessing without entanglement, therefore afterwards permitted accumulating**.
26.HP **Without entanglement: calamity indeed**.
26.2b The **center, without surpassing indeed**.
28.PW And **retiring** from the **age without melancholy**.
28.5a **Without fault, without praise**.
29.3b **Completing without achieving indeed**.
30.4b **Without** a **place** of **tolerance indeed**.
32.3b **Without** a **place** to **tolerate indeed**.
32.4a The **fields without wildfowl**.
32.6b The **great without achievement indeed**.
33.6b **Without** a **place** to **doubt indeed**.
37.2a **Without direction releasing**.
38.3a/3b **Without initially possessing completion**.
39.2b **Completing without surpassing indeed**.
40.IM **Without** a **place** to **go**:
41.6a **Acquiring** a **servant without** a **household**.
42.IT The **commoners stimulated without delimiting**.
42.IT The **sun advances without delimiting**.
42.IT **One's augmenting without sides**.
43.4a The **sacrum without flesh**.
43.6a **Without crying-out**.
43.6b To **without crying-out belongs pitfall**.
44.3a The **sacrum without flesh**.
44.3a **Without** the **great**: **faulty**.
44.4a **Enwrapping without fish**.
44.4b To **without fish belongs** a **pitfall**.
46.3b **Without** a **place** to **doubt**

indeed.
47.PW **Pond without stream. Confining.**
48.IM **Without losing, without acquiring.**
48.1a/1b The **ancient well without wildfowl.**
48.2b **Without associates indeed.**
50.2b **Completing without surpassing indeed.**
51.3a The **shake moving: without blunder.**
51.5a **Hundred-thousand without loss, possessing affairs.**
51.5b The **great without loss indeed.**
54.6a A **woman receives** a **basket without substance.**
54.6a A **scholar disembowels** a **goat without blood.**
54.6b **Six above: without substance.**
55.6a/6b **Living-alone, one without people.**
56.2b **Completing without surpassing indeed.**
57.5a **Without initially possessing completion.**

Without direction Harvesting, *WU YOU LI*: in order to take advantage of the situation, do not impose a direction on events.
4.3a **Without direction Harvesting.**
19.3a **Without direction Harvesting.**
25.6a **Without direction Harvesting.**
27.3a **Without direction Harvesting.**
32.1a **Without direction Harvesting.**
34.6a **Without direction Harvesting.**
45.3a **Without direction Harvesting.**
54.IM/6a/ IT **Without direction Harvesting.**
64.IM/ IT **Without direction Harvesting.**

Without fault, *WU JIU*: no error or harm in the situation.
1.3a/4a **Without fault.**
1.4b **Advancing: without fault indeed.**
2.4a **Without fault, without praise.**
2.4b **Bundled** in the **bag, without fault.**
5.1a **Without fault.**
5.1b **Harvesting: availing** of **perseverance, without fault.**
7.IM/2a/4a/5a **Without fault.**
7.4b The **left camp, without fault.**
8.IM/1a/ IT **Without fault.**
9.4a **Without fault.**
10.1a **Without fault.**
11.3a **Drudgery: Trial, without fault.**
12.4a/4b **Possessing fate, without fault.**
13.1a **Without fault.**
14.1a **Drudgery** by **consequence without fault.**
14.2a/4a/4b **Without fault.**
16.6a **Without fault.**
17.IM **Without fault.**
17.IT The **great Growing, Trial, without fault.**
18.1a **Predecessors without fault.**
18.3b **Completing without fault indeed.**
19.3a/4a/6a **Without fault.**
19.4b **Culmination nearing, without fault.**
20.1a The **small** in the **person: without fault.**
20.5a/6a A **jun zi: without fault.**
21.1a/2a/3a/5a **Without fault.**
21.5b **Trial, adversity without fault.**
22.6a **Without fault.**
22.6b **White adorning, without fault.**
23.3a/3b To **stripping belongs without fault.**
24.IM/IT **Partners come, without fault.**
24.3a **Without fault.**
24.3b **Righteous, without fault indeed.**
25.4a **Without fault.**
25.4b **Permitting Trial, without fault.**
27.4a **Without fault.**
28.1a/6a **Without fault.**
28.5a **Without fault, without praise.**

29.4a **Completing, without fault.**
29.5a **Without fault.**
30.1a/6a **Without fault.**
32.IM **Without fault.**
32.IT **Persevering Growing, without fault.**
35.1a/1b **Enriching, without fault.**
35.6a **Without fault.**
38.1a/2a **Without fault.**
38.4a **Adversity, without fault.**
38.4b **Mingling, conforming, without fault.**
40.1a **Without fault.**
40.1b **Righteous, without fault indeed.**
41.IM/IT **Without fault, permitting Trial.**
41.1a/4a/6a **Without fault.**
42.1a **Without fault.**
42.1b **Spring, significant, without fault.**
42.3a **Without fault.**
43.3a **Without fault.**
43.3b **Completing without fault indeed.**
43.5a/5b The **center moves, without fault.**
44.2a/6a **Without fault.**
45.1a/3a/3b **Going, without fault.**
45.2a/2b **Protracting: significant, without fault.**
45.4a/4b The **great: significant, without fault.**
45.5a/6a **Without fault.**
46.2a **Without fault.**
46.4a **Significant, without fault.**
47.IM **Without fault.**
47.2a **Without fault.**
59.6a/1a **Emerging, without fault.**
60.3a **Without fault.**
61.4a/5a **Without fault.**
62.2a/4a **Without fault.**
63.1a **Without fault.**
63.1b **Righteous, without fault indeed.**
64.6a **Without fault.**

Without not Harvesting, *WU BU LI*: turning point where the balance is swinging from not Harvesting to actually Harvesting.

2.2a/2b **Not repeating: without not Harvesting.**
3.4a **Without not Harvesting.**
14.6a **Significant, without not Harvesting.**
15.4a/4b **Without not harvesting: showing humbleness.**
15.5a **Without not harvesting.**
19.2a/2b **Without not Harvesting.**
23.5a **Without not Harvesting.**
28.2a **Without not Harvesting.**
33.6a/6b **Rich retiring, without not Harvesting.**
35.5a **Going significant, without not Harvesting.**
40.6a **Capturing it, without not Harvesting.**
50.6a **Without not Harvesting.**
57.5a **Without not harvesting.**

Without repenting, *WU HUI*: there is no cause for sorrow, regret or a change of attitude.

13.6a **Without repenting.**
24.5a **Without repenting.**
24.5b **Magnanimous return, without repenting.**
31.5a **Without repenting.**
34.5a **Without repenting.**
59.3a **Without repenting.**
64.5a **Trial, significant, without repenting.**

With-respect-to, *YU*: in relation to, referring to, according to; in, at, until.

5.PW **Clouds above with-respect-to heaven. Attending.**
8.4b **Outside grouping with-respect-to eminence.**
23.PW **Mountain adjoining with-respect-to earth. Stripping.**
24.AT **Return**: the **small and-also marking-off with-respect-to beings.**
25.IT **And-also activates** a **lord with-respect-to** the **inside.**
32.IT **Lasting with-respect-to one's dao indeed.**
32.IT The **wise person: lasting with-respect-to one's dao and-also below heaven changing** and **accomplishing.**
37.PS **Injury with-respect-to** the **outside implies necessarily reversing with-respect-to** the **household.**

43.PW **Pond above with-respect-to heaven. Parting.**
45.PW **Pond above with-respect-to earth. Clustering.**
55.IT **And-also even-more with-respect-to reaching people.**
55.IT **Even-more with-respect-to reaching soul** and **spirit.**

Woman(hood), *NÜ*: woman and what is inherently female.
3.2a **Woman** and **son's Trial: not nursing.**
4.3a/3b **No availing** of **grasping womanhood.**
20.2a **Harvesting: woman's Trial.**
20.2b **Peeping overseeing: woman's Trial.**
28.2a A **venerable husband acquires his woman consort.**
28.2b A **venerable husband** and a **woman consort.**
31.IM **Grasping womanhood, significant.**
31.PS **Therefore afterwards possessing man** and **woman.**
31.PS **Possessing man** and **woman.**
31.IT **Manhood below womanhood.**
31.IT **Grasping womanhood, significant indeed.**
37.IM **Household people. Harvesting: woman's Trial.**
37.IT The **woman** in the **correct position reaching** the **inside.**
37.IT **Man** and **woman correct.**
38.IT **Man** and **woman: polarizing and-also their purposes interpenetrating indeed.**
44.IM **Coupling. Woman's vigor.**
44.IM/ IT **No availing** of **grasping womanhood.**
53.IM **Infiltrating. Womanhood converting, significant.**
53/54.HP **Infiltrating: womanhood converting awaits manhood moving indeed.**
53/54.HP **Converting maidenhood:** the **completion belonging** to **womanhood indeed.**
53.IT **Womanhood converting, significant indeed.**
54.6a A **woman receives** a **basket without substance.**

Wood/tree, *MU*: trees and all things woody or wooden; associated with the Wooden Moment; wood and wind are the Symbols of the trigram Ground, *SUN*. Ideogram: a tree with roots and branches.
28.PW The **pond submerges wood.** The **great exceeding.**
30.IT The **hundred grains, grasses, trees congregating reaching** the **earth.**
40.IT **Thunder** and **rain arousing** and-also the **hundred fruits, grasses, trees, altogether seedburst's boundary.**
42.IT **Woody dao, thereupon movement.**
46.PW The **earth's center generates wood. Ascending.**
47.1a The **sacrum confined tending-towards** a **wooden stump.**
48.PW **Wood possesses stream above.** The **well.**
50.PW **Wood possesses fire above.** The **vessel.**
50.IT **Using wood,** the **root, fire.**
53.PW The **mountain possesses wood above. Infiltrating.**
53.4a The **swan infiltrating tending-towards** the **trees.**
59.IT **Riding wood possesses achievement indeed.**
61.IT **Riding** a **wooden dugout: emptiness indeed.**

Word, *YAN*: spoken word, speech, saying; talk, discuss, address; name, signify. Ideogram: mouth and rising vapor.
5.2a The **small possesses words.**
5.2b **Although** the **small possesses words, using completing significant indeed.**
6.1a The **small possesses words.**
6.1b **Although** the **small possesses words, one's differentiation brightening indeed.**
7.5a **Harvesting: holding-on** to **words.**
13.5b **Words reciprocally controlling indeed.**
26.PW A **jun zi** uses the **numerous recorded preceding words** to go

and **move**.

27.PW A **jun zi uses considerate words** to **inform**.

36.1a A **lordly person possesses words**.

37.PW A **jun zi uses words** to **possess beings and-also movement** to **possess perseverance**.

43.4a/4b **Hearing words not trustworthy**.

47.IM/ IT **Possessing words not trustworthy**.

49.3a/3b **Skinning word thrice drawing-near**.

51.IM/IT **Laughing words, shrieking, shrieking**.

51.1a **After laughing words, shrieking, shrieking**.

51.1b **Laughing words, shrieking, shrieking**.

51.6a **Matrimonial alliance possesses words**.

52.5a **Words possess sequence**.

53.1a **Possessing words**.

Worship, *JIAN*: honor the gods and ancestors; offer a sacrifice; recommend, introduce.

16.PW To **exalting worship belongs** the **supreme above**.

20.IM/ IT **Overseeing. Hand-washing and-also not worshipping**.

Yang, *YANG*: sunny slope of a hill, sunny bank of a river; dynamic and bright aspect of the basic duality (Yin and Yang) manifesting in all phenomena; Yang arouses, transforms and dissolves existing structures; linear thrust, stimulus, drive, focus; quality of a whole line.

1.1b **Yang located below indeed**.

11.IT **Inside Yang and-also outside Yin.**

12.IT **Inside Yin and-also outside Yang.**

Year, *NIAN*: year, annual; harvest; years revolved, years of age.

3.2a/2b **Ten years, thereupon nursing**.

24.6a **Culminating tending-towards ten years not controlling disciplining**.

27.3a/3b **Ten years, no availing** of.

63.3a/3b **Three years controlling it**.

64.4a **Three years, possessing** a **donation tending-towards** the **great city**.

Year's-time, *SUI*: duration of a year; beginning of a year.

13.3a/3b **Three year's-time not rising**.

29.6a **Three year's-time, not acquiring**.

29.6b **Pitfall, three year's-time indeed**.

47.1a **Three year's-time not encountering**.

53.5a The **wife, three year's-time not pregnant**.

55.6a **Three year's-time not encountering**.

Yellow, *HUANG*: color of the soil in central China, associated with the Earthy Moment leading from the Yang to the Yin hemicycle; emblematic and imperial color of China since the Yellow Emperor (2500 BC).

2.5a/5b A **yellow apron. Spring, significant**.

2.6a **Their blood indigo** and **yellow**.

21.5a **Acquiring yellow metal**.

30.2a/2b **Yellow radiance. Spring, significant**.

33.2a To **holding-on belongs availing** of **skin belonging** to **yellow cattle**.

33.2b **Holding-on avails** of **yellow cattle**.

40.2a **Acquiring** a **yellow arrow**.

49.1a **Thonging avails** of **skin belonging** to **yellow cattle**.

49.1b **Thonging avails** of **yellow cattle**.

50.5a The **vessel's yellow ears, metallic rings**.

50.5b The **vessel's yellow ears**.

Yield, *SHUN*: give way, comply, agree,

follow, obey; docile, flexible; bear produce, nourish, provide; Action of the trigram Field, *KUN*.

2.IT **Thereupon yielding receives heaven.**

2.IT The **supple yielding, Harvesting, Trial.**

2.IT **Afterwards yielding: acquiring constancy.**

4.3b **Moving, not yielding indeed.**

4.5b **Yielding uses** the **root indeed.**

4.6b **Above** and **below yielding indeed.**

5.4b **Yielding uses hearkening indeed.**

7.IT **Moving: venturing and-also yielding.**

8.5b **Stowing** away **revolt, grasping yielding.**

8.IT **Below yielding, adhering indeed.**

11.IT **Inside persisting and-also outside yielding.**

14.PW And **yielding** to **heaven** to **relax** into **fate.**

16.IT **Providing: yielding uses stirring-up.**

16.IT **Heaven** and **earth use yielding** and **stirring-up.**

16.IT The **wise person uses yielding** and **stirring-up.**

19.2b **Not-yet yielding** to **fate indeed.**

19.IT **Stimulating and-also yielding.**

20.IT **Yielding and-also** the **root.**

23.IT **Yielding and-also stopping it.**

24.IT **Stirring-up and-also using yielding movement.**

27.5b **Yielding uses adhering** to the **above indeed.**

31.2b **Yielding not harmful indeed.**

35.IT **Yielding and-also congregating reaching** the **great's brightness.**

36.2b **Yielding used** by **consequence indeed.**

36.IT **Inside pattern bright and-also outside supple yielding.**

37.2b **Yielding uses** the **root indeed.**

37.4b **Yielding located** in the **position indeed.**

45.IT **Yielding uses stimulating.**

45.IT **Yielding** to **heaven's fate indeed.**

46.PW A **jun zi uses yielding** to **actualizing-dao.**

46.4b **Yielding affairs indeed.**

46.IT The **root and-also yielding.**

49.6b **Yielding uses adhering** to a **chief indeed.**

49.IT **Yielding reaches heaven and-also** the **correspondence reaches people.**

53.3b **Yielding: reciprocal protection indeed.**

53.4b **Yielding uses** the **root indeed.**

56.IT The **supple acquires** the **center reaching outside and-also yielding reaches** the **solid.**

57.IT The **supple altogether yielding reaches** the **solid.**

58.IT **That uses yielding reaching heaven and-also correspondence reaching people.**

59.1b **Yielding indeed.**

62.IT **Above revolting and-also below yielding indeed.**

Yin, *YIN*: shady slope of a hill or bank of a river; consolidating, dark aspect of the basic duality (Yin and Yang) manifesting in all phenomena; Yin creates and conserves structure; spatial extension; build, make things concrete; quality of an opened line.

2.1b **Yin beginning solidification indeed.**

11.IT **Inside Yang and-also outside Yin.**

12.IT **Inside Yin and-also outside Yang.**

61.2a **Calling crane located** in **Yin.**

Your/contracted, *JUE*: intensifying possessive pronoun and adjective; concentrate, tense, contract; whooping cough.

14.5a/5b **Your conforming: mingling thus.**

38.5a/5b **Your ancestor gnawing flesh.**

Youthful, *TONG*: young person (between eight and fifteen); childish, immature; servant, slave.

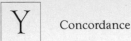

4.IM/IT **In-no-way I seek** the **youthful enveloping.**
4.IM/IT The **youthful enveloping seeks me.**
4.5a **Youthful enveloping. Significant.**
4.5b To a **youthful enveloping belongs significance.**
20.1a **Youthful overseeing.**
20.1b **Initial six, youthful overseeing.**
26.4a To **youthful cattle belongs** a **stable.**
56.2a/2b **Acquiring** a **youthful vassal, Trial.**
56.3a **Losing one's youthful vassal.**

Bibliography

With few exceptions, the following bibliography lists literature in the English language directly connected with the *Yi Jing*. Even though far from exhaustive, it is a significant sample of *Yi Jing*-related works at all levels, from the scholarly to the popular. A few works in other languages are included for their historical importance or because there is no equivalent in English. Finally a small selection of fundamental books about Chinese civilization and about the philosophy of divination is also included.

Albertson, Edward. *The Complete I Ching for the Millions*, Sherbourne Press, Los Angeles, 1969.

Allen, Sarah. *The Shape of the Turtle, Myth, Art and Cosmos in Early China*, State University of New York Press, New York, 1991.

Anagarika Govinda. *The Inner Structure of the I Ching*, Wheelwright Press, San Francisco, 1981.

Anthony, Carol K. *A Guide to the I Ching*, Anthony Publishing Company, Stow, MA, 1980.

- *The Philosophy of the I Ching*, Anthony Publishing Company, Stow, MA, 1981.

Bergeron, Marie-Ina. *Ciel/Terre/Homme, Le Yi Jing*, Guy Trédaniel, Paris, 1986.

- *Wang Pi, Philosophe du non-avoir*, Ricci Institute, Taipei, 1986.

Blofeld, John. *The Book of Change*, George Allen & Unwin, London, 1965, Mandala, London, 1984.

Cabot Reid, Jane. *Jung, My Mother and I, The Analytic Diaries of Catharine Rush Cabot*, Daimon Verlag, Einsiedeln, Switzerland, 2001.

Cheetham, Tom. *The World Turned Inside Out: Henry Corbin and Islamic Mysticism*, Spring Journal Books, Woodstock, CT, 2003.

Cheng, François. *L'écriture poétique chinoise*, Éditions du Seuil, Paris, 1977.

Cheng Yi, *I Ching, The Tao of Organization*, transl. Thomas Cleary, Shambala, Boston, 1988.

Chih-hsu Ou-i, *The Buddhist I Ching*, transl. Thomas Cleary, Shambala, Boston, 1987.

Chinese-English Bilingual Series of Chinese Classics, *Book of Changes*, Hunan Publishing House, 1992.

Cleary, Thomas. *The Taoist I Ching*, Shambala, Boston, 1986.

- *I Ching Mandalas*, Shambala, Boston, 1989.

Damian-Knight, Guy. *Karma and Destiny in the I Ching*, Arkana, London, 1987.

Dhiegh, Khigh Alx. *The Eleventh Wing*, Dell Publishing Co., New York, 1973.

Doeringer, F. M. "Oracle and symbol in the redaction of the I Ching", in *Philosophy East and West* 30, no. 2, April 1980.

- *Imaging the Imageless, Symbol and Perception in Early Chinese Thought*, presented at the International Society for Chinese Philosophy Meeting, Hilo, Hawaii, 1989.

Douglas, Alfred. *The Oracle of Change*, Penguin Books, Harmondsworth, Middlesex, Great Britain, 1972.

Ffarington Hook, Diana. *The I Ching and Mankind*, Routledge & Kegan Paul, London, 1975.

- *The I Ching and Its Associations*, Routledge & Kegan Paul, London, 1980.

Gia Fu Feng, Bailey, Sue, and Bink Kun Young. *Yi Jing, Book of Change*, Feng Books, Mullumbimby, NSW, Australia, 1985.

Granet, Marcel. *La civilization chinoise*, La Renaissance du Livre, Paris, 1929.

- *La pensée chinoise*, La Renaissance du Livre, Paris, 1934.

- *La religion des Chinois*, Presses Universitaires de France, Paris, 1951.

Hacker, Edward. *The I Ching Handbook*, Paradigm Publications, Brookline, MA, 1993.

Harvard-Yenching Institute, *A Concordance to the I Ching*, Sinological Index Series, Supplement No. 10, Peiping, 1935.

Henderson, John B. *The Development and Decline of Chinese Cosmology*, Columbia University Press, New York, 1984.

Hertzer, Dominique. *Das alte und das neue Yijing, Die Wandlungen des Buches der Wandlungen*, Eugen Diederichs Verlag, Munich, 1996.

- *Das Mawangdui-Yijing*, Eugen Diederichs Verlag, Munich, 1996.

Huang, Alfred. *The Complete I Ching*, Inner Traditions, Rochester, VT, 1998.

Huang, Kerson and Rosemary. *I Ching*, Workman Publishing, New York, 1985.

Javary, Cyrille, Zhu Xi, and Dautin, J.-P. "Dossier: Les hexagrammes nucléaires", in *Hexagrammes N° 1*, Centre Djohi, Paris, 1986.

Javary, Cyrille, and Faure, Pierre. *Yi Jing, Le Livre des Changements*, Albin Michel, Paris, 2002.

Jullien, François. *Figures del'immanence, Pour une lecture philosophique du Yi king*, Bernard Grasset, Paris, 1993.

Jung, Carl Gustav. Foreword to *The I Ching, or Book of Changes, Richard Wilhelm Translation*, Bollingen Series XIX, Princeton University Press, 1950.

- *Synchronicity, An Acausal Connecting Principle*, transl. R. F. C. Hull, Bollingen Series XX, Princeton University Press, 1960.

Karcher, Stephen. *How to Use the I Ching*, Element Books, Shaftesbury, Dorset, Great Britain, 1997.

- *Ta Chuan, The Great Treatise*, Carroll & Brown Publishers, London, 2000.

- *Total I Ching, Myths for Change*, Time Warner Books, London, 2003.

Jung Young Lee, *Understanding the I Ching*, University Books, New York, 1971.

- *The I Ching and Modern Man*, University Books, New York, 1975.

Legge, James. *I Ching, Book of Changes*, The Sacred Books of the East, vol. XVI, Clarendon Press, 1899, Bantam Books, New York, 1964.

Lynn, Richard John. *The Classic of Changes as Interpreted by Wang Bi*, Columbia University Press, New York, 1994.

Markert, Christopher. *I Ching, The No. 1 Success Formula*, Aquarian/Thorsons, London, 1986.

McClatchie, Canon. *A Translation of the Confucian Classic of Change*, American Presbyterian Mission Press, Shanghai, 1876.

McGuire, William. *Bollingen, An Adventure in Collecting the Past*, Bollingen Series, Princeton University Press, 1982.

Melyan, Gary G. and Wen-kuang Chu, *I-Ching, The Hexagrams Revealed*, Charles E. Tuttle Company, Rutland, VT, 1977.

Moore, Steve. *The Trigrams of Han, Inner Structures of the I Ching*, The Aquarian Press, Wellingborough, Northamptonshire, Great Britain, 1989.

Murphy, Joseph. *Secrets of the I Ching*, Parker Publishing Company, West Nyack, NY, 1970.

Needham, Joseph. *Science and Civilization in China*, Vol. 2, Cambridge University Press, 1956.

Palmer, Martin, Ramsay, Jay, and Zhao Xiaomin, *I Ching, The Shamanic Oracle of Change*, Thorsons, London, 1995.

Peterson, Willard J. "Making Connections: Commentary on the Attached Verbalizations", in *Harvard Journal of Asiatic Studies*, vol. 42, no. 1, June 1982, Harvard Yenching Institute.

Philastre, Paul-Louis-Félix. *Le Yi king*, 1881, Zulma, 1992.

Poncé, Charles. *The Nature of the I Ching*, Award Books, New York, 1970.

Porkert, Manfred. *The Theoretical Foundations of Chinese Medicine*, MIT Press, Cambridge, MA, 1974.

Reifler, Sam. *I Ching, A New Interpretation for Modern Times*, Bantam Books, New York, 1974.

Ritsema, Rudolf. "Notes for Differentiating Some Terms in the I Ching", in *Spring 1970, Spring 1971*, Zurich .

- "The Corrupted", in *Spring 1972*, Zurich.

- "The Pit and the Brilliance", in *Spring 1973*, Zurich .
- "The Quake and the Bound", in *Spring 1976, Spring 1977*, Zurich.
- "The Great's Vigour", in *Spring 1978*, Irving, TX.
- "The Hidden", in *Spring 1979*, Irving, TX.
- "Adorning", in *Spring 1982*, Dallas, TX.
- "Analyzing", in *Spring 1984*, Dallas, TX.

Ritsema, Rudolf, and Karcher, Stephen. *I Ching, The Classic Chinese Oracle of Change*, Element Books, Shaftesbury, Dorset, Great Britain, 1994.

Ritsema, Rudolf, and Sabbadini, Shantena. *Eranos I Ching, Il libro della versatilità*, Red Edizioni, Como, 1996.

Ritsema, Rudolf, and Sabbadini, Shantena. "Images of the Unknown, The Eranos I Ching Project 1989-1997", in *Gateways to Identity, Eranos Yearbook 66/1997*, Spring Journal, Woodstock, CT.

Ritsema, Rudolf, and Schneider, Hansjakob. *Eranos Yi Jing, Das Buch der Wandlungen*, O.W. Barth, Munich, 2000.

Rutt, Richard. *The Book of Changes (Zhouyi)*, Curzon, Richmond, Surrey, 1996.

Sabbadini, Shantena. *I Ching, Oracle and Divination*, CJP, Solna, Sweden, 1998.

Schulz, Larry J. *Lai Chih-te (1525-1604) and the Phenomenology of the Classic of Change*, University Microfilms, Ann Arbor, Michigan, 1982.

Schutskii, Iulian K. *Researches on the I Ching*, Bollingen Series LXII.2, Princeton University Press, 1979.

Secter, Mondo. *I Ching Clarified, A Practical Guide*, Charles E. Tuttle Company, Boston 1993.

Shaughnessy, Edward L. *I Ching, The Classic of Changes*, Ballantine Books, New York 1996.

Sherrill W.A., and Shu, W.K. *An Anthology of I Ching*, Routledge & Kegan Paul, London, 1977.

Shima, Miki. *The Medical I Ching*, Blue Poppy Press, Boulder, CO, 1992.

Schönberger, Martin. *The I Ching and the Genetic Code*, ASI Publishers, New York, 1979.

Siu, R. G. H. *The Man of Many Qualities, A Legacy of the I Ching*, MIT Press, Cambridge, MA, 1968.

Smith, Kidder Jr, Bol, Peter, Adler, Joseph, and Wyatt, Don. *Sung Dynasty Uses of the I Ching*, Princeton University Press, 1990.

Stein, Diane. *The Kwan Yin Book of Changes*, Llewellyn Publications, St. Paul, MN, 1993.

Sung, Z. D. *The Symbols of Yi King*, The China Modern Education Co., Shanghai, 1934.

- *The Text of the Yi King*, Shanghai, 1935, Paragon Book Reprint, New York, 1969.

Tjan Tjoe Som, *Po Hu T'ung, The Comprehensive Discussions in the White Tiger Hall*, E. J. Brill, Leiden, 1952.

van Over, Raymond, ed. *I Ching* (based on the translation by James Legge), The New American Library, New York, 1971.

Vandermeersch, Léon. "Origine de la divination par l'achillée et forme primitive du Yi Jing", in *Hexagrammes N° 4*, Centre Djohi, Paris, 1988.

von Franz, Marie-Louise. *On Divination and Synchronicity*, Inner City Books, Toronto, 1980.

Walker, Barbara G. *The I Ching of the Goddess*, Harper & Row, New York, 1986.

Wang Dongliang, *Les signes et les mutations*, L'Asiathèque, Paris, 1995.

Wei, Henry. *The Authentic I-Ching*, Newcastle Publishing Co., North Hollywood, CA, 1987.

Wei Tat, *An Exposition of the I Ching*, Institute of Cultural Studies, Taipei, 1970.

Whincup, Greg. *Rediscovering the I Ching*, Doubleday & Co., Garden City, NY, 1986.

Wilhelm, Hellmut. "The Interplay of Image and Concept in the Book of Changes", in *Eranos Jahrbuch XXXVI/1967*, Rhein Verlag, Zurich.

- *Heaven, Earth and Man in the Book of Changes*, Seven Eranos Lectures, University of Washington Press, Seattle, 1977.

- *Leibniz and the I Ching*, Collectanea Commissionis Synodalis, XVI, No. 3/4, Peking, 1943.

- *The Book of Changes in the Western Tradition, A Selective Bibliography*, Parerga 2, University of Washington, Seattle, 1975.

Wilhelm, Richard. *I Ging, Das Buch der Wandlungen*, Eugen Diederichs, Jena, 1923.

- *The I Ching, or Book of Changes*, Bollingen Series XIX, Princeton University Press, 1950.

- *Lectures on the I Ching, Constancy and Change*, Bollingen Series XIX.2, Princeton University Press, 1979.

Wilhelm, Richard and Hellmut. *Understanding the I Ching, The Wilhelm Lectures on the Book of Changes*, Princeton University Press, 1995.

Wu Jing-Nuan, *Yi Jing*, The Taoist Center, Washington, D.C., 1991.

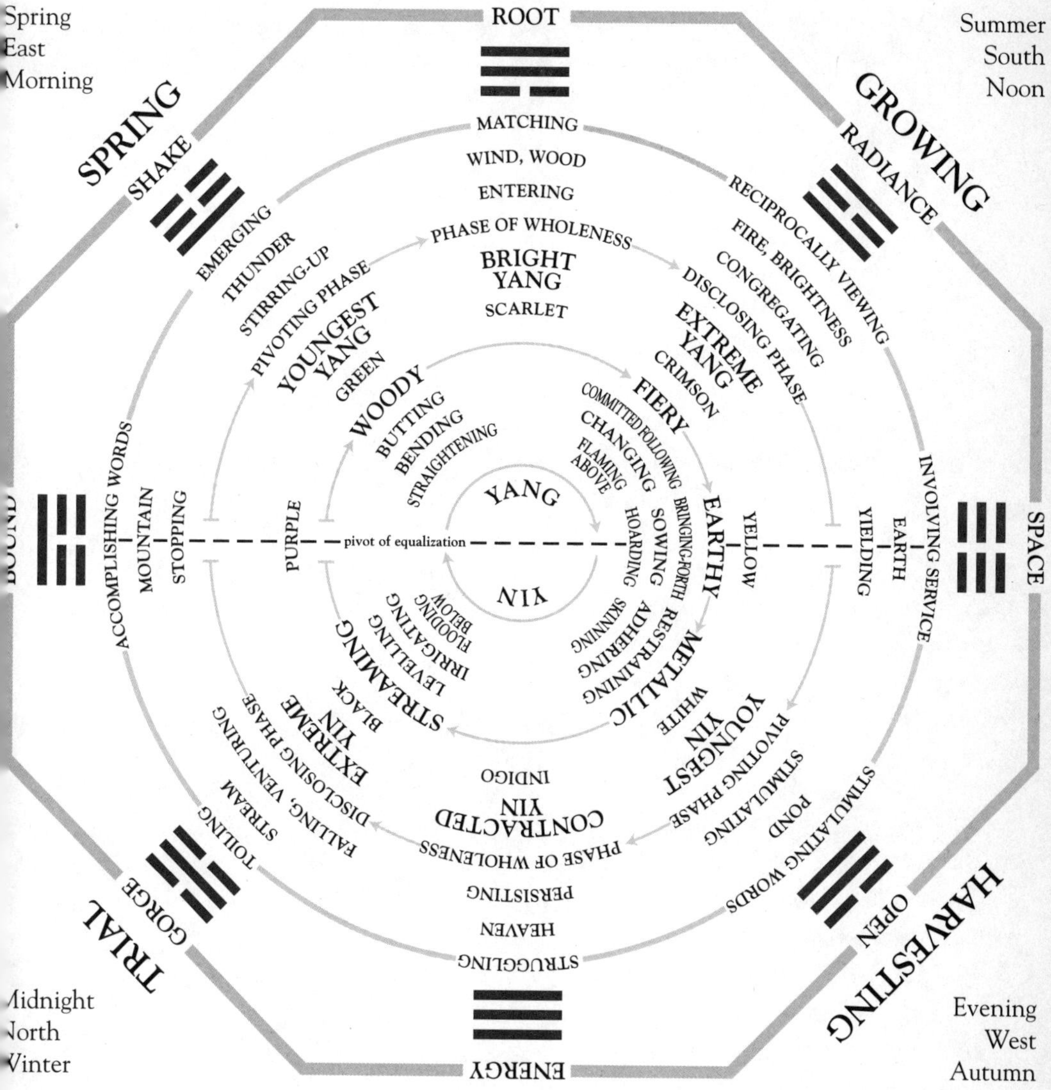

Spring
East
Morning
Summer
South
Noon
ROOT
MATCHING
WIND, WOOD
ENTERING
PHASE OF WHOLENESS
BRIGHT YANG
SCARLET
SPRING
SHAKE
EMERGING
THUNDER
STIRRING-UP
PIVOTING PHASE
YOUNGEST YANG
GREEN
WOODY
BUTTING
BENDING
STRAIGHTENING
GROWING
RADIANCE
RECIPROCALLY VIEWING
FIRE, BRIGHTNESS
CONGREGATING
DISCLOSING PHASE
EXTREME YANG
CRIMSON
FIERY
COMMITTED FOLLOWING
CHANGING
FLAMING ABOVE
YANG
YIN
pivot of equalization
ACCOMPLISHING WORDS
MOUNTAIN
STOPPING
PURPLE
EARTHY
BRINGING-FORTH
SOWING
HOARDING
YELLOW
INVOLVING SERVICE
EARTH
YIELDING
SPACE
METALLIC
RESTRAINING
ADHERING
SKINNING
WHITE
YOUNGEST YIN
PIVOTING PHASE
STIMULATING
POND
STIMULATING WORDS
HARVESTING
OPEN
STREAMING
LEVELLING
IRRIGATING
FLOODING BELOW
BLACK
EXTREME YIN
DISCLOSING PHASE
FALLING, VENTURING
STREAM
TOILING
TRIAL
GORGE
INDIGO
CONTRACTED YIN
PHASE OF WHOLENESS
PERSISTING
HEAVEN
STRUGGLING
ENERGY
Midnight
North
Winter
Evening
West
Autumn

The Universal Compass